Quantitative Methods

Quantitative Methods

[Mathematical, Statistical and Economic Techniques]

(For BBA, MBA, M.Com and Engineering Students)

Suranjan Saha MSc

Head, Department of Mathematics and Statistics
Heramba Chandra College
Formerly Part-time Lecturer in Mathematics and Statistics,
Sivnath Sastri College and Shri Shikshayatan College
Sometime Part-time Honarary Lecturer in
Business Mathematics and Statistics, *ICWAI (EIRC)*

Sampat Mukherjee MSc (London)

Ex-Chairman of the Board of Studies,
St. Xavier's College, Kolkata (Autonomous)

New Central Book Agency (P) Ltd

LONDON

HYDERABAD ERNAKULAM BHUBANESWAR
NEW DELHI KOLKATA PUNE GUWAHATI

NCBA

REGD OFFICE
8/1 Chintamoni Das Lane, Kolkata 700 009, India
email: ncbapvtltd@eth.net

OVERSEAS
NCBA (UK) Ltd, 149 Park Avenue North, Northampton, NN3 2HY, UK
email: ncbauk@yahoo.com

EXPORT
NCBA Exports Pvt. Ltd, 212 Shahpur Jat, New Delhi 110 049
email: ncbaexports@ncbapvtltd.com

BRANCHES

2/27 Ansari Road, 1st Floor
Daryaganj, **New Delhi** 110 002
email: ncbadel@ncbapvtltd.com

Shop Nos. 3 & 4, Vinayak Towers
681/B Budhwar Peth, Appa Balwant Chowk
Pune 411 002
email: ncbapune@ncbapvtltd.com

Shop No. 15, Bharati Towers, Ground Floor
Forest Park
Bhubaneswar 751 001
email: ncbabub@ncbapvtltd.com

House No. 3-1-315, 1st Floor
Nimboliadda, Kachiguda, **Hyderabad** 500 027
email: ncbahydb@ncbapvtltd.com

GSS Shopping Complex, 1st Floor
Opposite College Post Office, Convent Road
Ernakulam 682 035
0484-4021054/53

Radhamayee Complex (Second Floor)
Opp. SBI, Panbazar, Jaswanta Road
Guwahati 781 001
email: ncbaguwahati@ncbapvtltd.com

Quantitative Methods • Saha, Mukherjee

First Published: 1995, Second Edition: 1996, Third Edition: 1998, Fourth Edition: 2000
Fifth Edition : 2002, Reprinted: 2016

PUBLISHER AND TYPESETTER
New Central Book Agency (P) Ltd
8/1 Chintamoni Das Lane, Kolkata 700 009

PRINTER
New Central Book Agency (P) Ltd
Web-Offset Division, Dhulagarh, Sankrail, Howrah

COVER DESIGNER
Soumen Paul

PROJECT TEAM
Abhijit Sen, Subir Pal and Prabhat Jas

ISBN 978 81 7381 121 0

Price ₹ 485.00

PREFACE TO THE NEW REVISED FIFTH EDITION

(A) MATHEMATICAL AND STATISTICAL TECHNIQUES

Nowadays **a comprehensive grasp of Mathematics and Statistics is necessary for a meaningful study of business problems as well as profit-yielding decisions in the sphere of business.** This particular stress on Mathematical and Statistical Techniques is manifested in the revised curricula of the course in different Professional Institutes. **The present treatise is intended as a text book on *Quantitative Methods* for ICWAI Intermediate Examination. This book fully covers the NEW (REVISED) SYLLABUS of *Quantitative Methods* (Stage II : Part 8) which consists of *Mathematical, Statistical* and *Econonomic Techniques* for the Intermediate Examination of ICWAI (effective from December 2002).**

I have tried to write the book in a simple language so as to cater to the needs of all categories of students. In presenting the subject matter, I have tried my best to make the exposition very clear and concise, avoiding unnecessary details. **Theories and their applications run side by side and the book is full of illustrated problems.** In every exercise, **the problems have been graded with utmost care. In order to give the students an idea of the standard expected by the Professional Institutes a large number of typical problems set previously in different professional examinations (like ICWAI – Inter & Final, CA – Foundation & Inter, MBA, etc.) have been worked out at the appropriate places in each chapter of the book.** Every attempt has been made to create interest in the subject among the students.

I sincerely express my gratitude to *Dr. Anil Kumar Mukherjee,* Retired Head of the Department of Commerce, Calcutta University and *Prof. R. K. Ghosh,* Retired Head of the Department of Mathematics, St. Xavier's College, Kolkata, for encouraging me in writing books on Mathematics & Statistics for professional courses.

Finally, I thank the publishers for the patient cooperation they have extended to me in bringing out this treatise.

Any suggestions for improvement of the book will be most gratefully received and highly appreciated.

Kolkata
October 2002

SURANJAN SAHA

(B) ECONOMIC TECHNIQUES

Quantitative business economics is an interesting and functional part of what we broadly call quantitative techniques for business and management. **Mastering the subject requires a good understanding of how basic concepts of economics can be combined with tools of mathematics and statistics to analyse and make decisions involving scarce resources.** But, in the process of studying quantitative economics, students can get mired in the minutiae of data, graphs, equations and definitions. The obvious consequence is that they fail to appreciate fully the value of economic principles as a tool for decision-making.

This part of the book, **Economic Techniques,** is written with a two-fold objective. First, it is intended **that students will receive a complete and rigorous introduction to basic principles of quantitative microeconomics.** Albert Einstein once commented that things should be made as simple as possible but not more so. In this text peripheral points have been avoided in order to concentrate on fundamental concepts. **Only those concepts have been included which would provided important insights for decision-making.** Care has been taken to assure that the exposition of these concepts is as clear and uncomplicated as possible.

The second objective in writing this part is to **demonstrate how applications of economic theory can improve decision-making.** The approach followed here involves first introducing certain basic concepts of managerial economics and then using these principles to analyse decision problems faced by managers. In addition, **a few case examples and numerous solved problems have been included in each chapter to illustrate important principles and topics.** The use of concept/example format makes the title more readable and facilitates learning by allowing students to see how economic principles can be used in decision-making.

In short, **the object of this part of the book is to give the student an appreciation of the great value of economic techniques in solving business problems.** Few ICWAI students plan to become economists. They need an accessible but insightful analysis of problems they are likely to encounter. **Creative application of economic principles and theories is vital to successful use of economic tools in commerce on any level.** Information and technique can give no viable solution without real world application.

The author is thankful to Mr. Samir Kumar Chakraborty for preparing the first draft of certain portions of the title. He is also profoundly grateful to Mr. Amitabha Sen, Mrs. Ruba Sen, and, above all, to Mr. J. N. Sen for collaborating in the endeavour.

Kolkata
October 2002

SAMPAT MUKHERJEE

SYLLABUS

THE UNIVERSITY OF CALCUTTA

QUANTITATIVE METHODS

ONE PAPER : 3 HOURS : 100 MARKS

MATHEMATICAL TECHNIQUES (40 MARKS)

Algebra of vectors and matrices and determinants : Addition, subtraction, multiplication and inversion of vectors and matrices, solution of systems of linear equations with the help of matrix algebra.

Calculus : Variables, constants and functions – graphs of functions – limits of algebraic functions, simple differentiation of algebraic function – meaning of derivatives – evaluation of first and second order derivatives, partial differentiation; solution of problems involving maxima and minima of algebraic functions.

Integration (***by substitution and by parts***) : Determining indefinite and definite integrals for simple functions – application of integration to evaluate areas and volume of solids and revolution.

Optimisation of functions under constraints. Linear programming and simplex method of solution; **other operations research methods, e.g., games theory, simulation, transportation, queuing, etc.**

STATISTICAL TECHNIQUES (30 MARKS)

Probabilities : Meaning and definition of probability, mutually exclusive and collectively exhausting events, repeated trials, combinatorial analysis. Addition and multiplication rules. Bayes theorem and its application.

Population and samples : Sampling methods, uses of random numbers, simulated sampling, concept of sampling distribution and standard errors, concept of sampling distribution and standard errors, confidence intervals for means and percentages, testing hypothesis and uses of *z, t,* chi-square tests.

Decision-making under risks and uncertainty; decision tree analysis.

Simple regression and correlation.

ECONONIC TECHNIQUES (30 MARKS)

Demand analysis : The basis of demand, market demand function – industry demand versus firm's demand; the demand curve; relation between demand function and demand curve; change and shift in demand; demand relation and managerial decision; theory of consumer behaviour; substitution and income effects; price, income and cross-elasticities of demand, other demand elasticities; time impact on elasticity; price elasticity for derived products; revenue concepts; demand estimation.

Forecasting : Forecasting methodologies. Time series analysis, trend projection, barometric or leading indicator method; index number analysis – composite and diffusion indices. Econometric models, curve fitting and least square methods; correlation and regression analysis, multiple and partial correlation – input-output analysis; forecasting with input-output tables, criteria for forecasting demand for existing and new products.

Empirical production function analysis, empirical cost analysis, short and long run cost estimation, factor demand, joint product and multi-product firm, uncertainty in production function, profit planning under risk and uncertainty.

CONTENTS

PAGES

Part I
MATHEMATICAL TECHNIQUES

Part II
STATISTICAL TECHNIQUES

PAGES

Part III

ECONOMIC TECHNIQUES

APPENDIX

Part I

MATHEMATICAL TECHNIQUES

CHAPTER 1

ALGEBRA OF VECTORS

1.1. INTRODUCTION

We divide physical quantities into two classes: One class consists of those quantities which have magnitudes but no directions (**scalar quantities** or **Scalars**) and the other class contains those quantities which have both magnitude as well as direction (**Vector quantities** or **vectors**).

Scalars can be specified by numbers but vector quantities are specified by vectors (or **directed line segments**).

Thus, *a quantity which has only magnitude but no direction is called a* **scalar quantity** *or a* **scalar**. *And a quantity which has both magnitude and direction is called a* **vector quantity** *or a* **vector.**

Mass, temperature, time, length of a line are all *scalars* but displacement, velocity, force etc. are *vectors.* In this chapter, we shall identify a vector by a *directed line segment* (*which is a line segment with a sense associated with it*).

1.2. VECTORS

1. DEFINITION. *A Vector is a directed line segment.*

Thus, the segment $\overrightarrow{AB}$ (Fig. 1.1) is directed from A to B, i.e., A is the *initial point* and B the *terminal point.* The length AB gives the *magnitude* and the sense (i..e, from A to B) gives the direction.

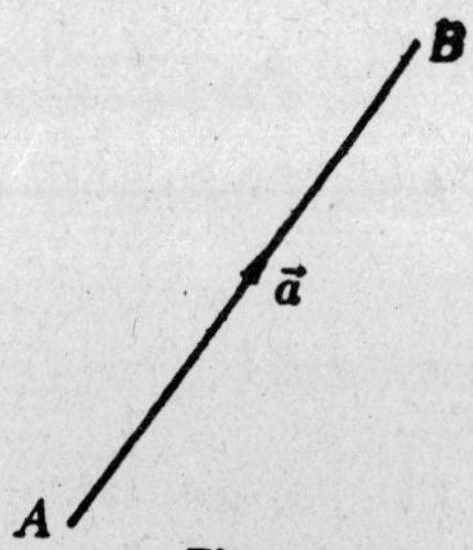

Fig 1.1

We denote this vector by $\overrightarrow{AB}$ or by a single letter **a** or $\vec{a}$.

2. NULL VECTOR. When the initial point and the terminal point *coincide*, we see that the *length is zero*. We call it a *null vector*. We denote such a vector by **0** or $\vec{0}$. It has magnitude *zero*, but no definite sense.

3. LENGTH OR MAGNITUDE OF A VECTOR. The length (or magnitude) of a vector $\overrightarrow{AB}$ is denoted by $|\overrightarrow{AB}|$. Thus, $|\overrightarrow{AB}| = AB$. Similarly, the length of $\vec{a}$ is $|\vec{a}|$, the length of $\vec{0}$ is $|\vec{0}| = 0$.

4. UNIT VECTOR. A vector whose length (or magnitude) is unity (i.e.,) is called a **unit vector**. It is a unit vector, then $|i| = 1$.

5. EQUAL VECTORS. Two vectors **a** and **b** are equal if they have the *same length and same direction*. They may lie on the same line or on parallel lines; (see Fig. 1.2.) A vector is not altered by shifting its position parallel to itself (i.e., keeping its magnitude and direction unaltered) in a plane or space.

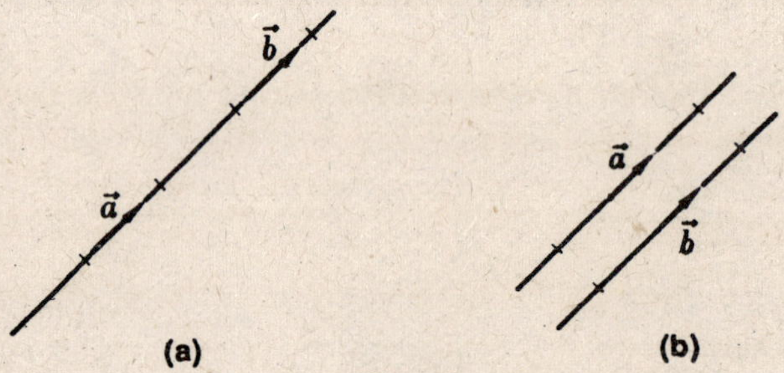

Fig 1.2

Like or Parallel Vectors

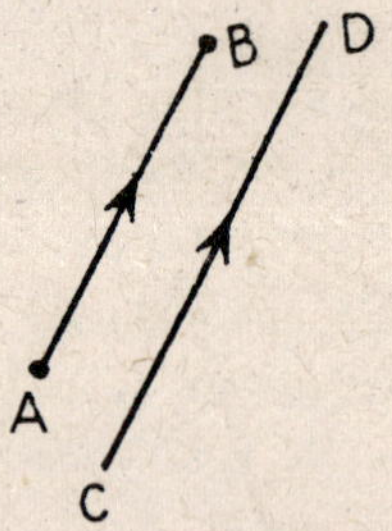

Fig 1.3

Two or more vectors are said to be *like* or *parallel* when they have the same direction; their magnitudes may or may not be the same. In the figure, $\overrightarrow{AB}$ and $\overrightarrow{CD}$ are like or parallel vectors. We can write

$$\overrightarrow{CD} = x \cdot \overrightarrow{AB} \quad \text{or,} \quad \overrightarrow{AB} = y \cdot \overrightarrow{CD},$$

where x, y scalars such that $CD = x \cdot AB$, or $AB = y \cdot CD$. Here $y = 1/x \cdot \overrightarrow{AB}$ and $\overrightarrow{CD}$ may lie on the same line or on parallel lines.

A unit vector in the direction of $\vec{a}$ **is** $\frac{\vec{a}}{|\vec{a}|}$, since $\left|\frac{\vec{a}}{|\vec{a}|}\right| = \frac{|\vec{a}|}{|\vec{a}|} = 1$.

Position Vectors

The position vector of a point, say P, in a plane or space is always defined with reference to an arbitrary point O as origin. The position vector of$P$ is the directed line segment $\overrightarrow{OP}$ and, in this case, we say that $\overrightarrow{OP}$ is the position vector of P with reference to O as origin. Similarly, $\overrightarrow{OQ}$ is the position vector of Q. Join PQ.

We can find $\overrightarrow{PQ}$ in terms of the position vectors of P and Q.

By *Triangle Rule,* we have

$$\overrightarrow{OP} + \overrightarrow{PQ} = \overrightarrow{OQ},$$

$$\text{or,} \quad \overrightarrow{PQ} = \overrightarrow{OQ} - \overrightarrow{OP}$$

$$= (P \cdot V \cdot \text{of } Q) - (P \cdot V \cdot \text{of} P).$$

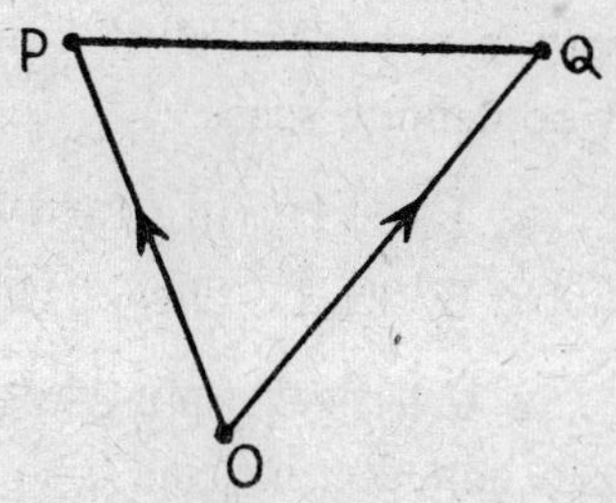

Fig 1.4

Co-initial and Co-terminous Vectors

Vectors drawn from the same initial point are called *co-initial vectors* and vectors having the same terminal point are called *co-terminous vector*. In Fig. $\overrightarrow{OP}$ and $\overrightarrow{OQ}$ are co-initial vectors.

COLLINEAR VECTORS. Two or more vectors are said to be collinear if they are along or parallel to the same line. Lengths of collinear vectors may or may not be the same, but they have the same or parallel support.

COPLANAR VECTORS. Two or more vectors are said to be *coplanar* if all of them lie on the same plane or they are all parallel to the same plane.

1.3. OPERATIONS ON VECTORS

I. Vector Addition (Triangle Rule)

Let $\vec{a}$ and $\vec{b}$ be two vectors. To find the sum $\vec{a}+\vec{b}$, first represent $\vec{a}$ by the directed line segment $\overrightarrow{AB}$ and then from the terminal point B draw $\overrightarrow{BC} = \vec{b}$. Now join AC. The sum $\vec{a}+\vec{b}$ is defined by the directed line segment $\overrightarrow{AC}$ i.e., $\vec{a}+\vec{b} = \overrightarrow{AC}$.

Thus, in $\Delta ABC, \overrightarrow{AB} + \overrightarrow{BC} = \overrightarrow{AC}$.

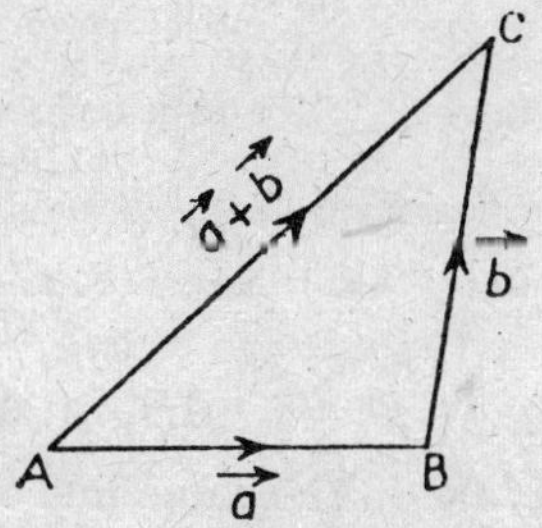

Fig 1.5

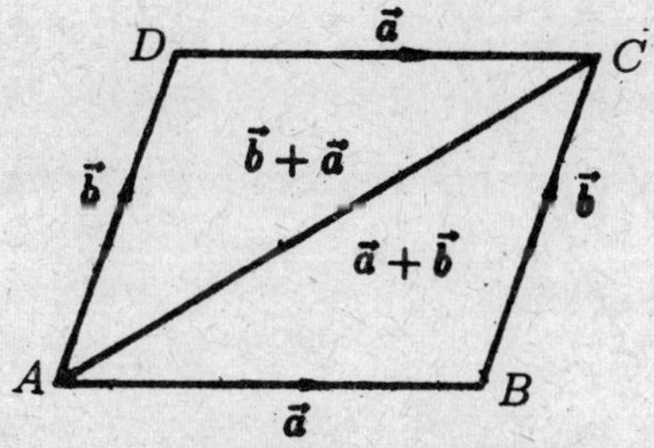

Fig 1.6

In parallelogram $ABCD$ with AB and BC as adjacent sides, the diagonal $\overrightarrow{AC}$ through A represents the sum i.e.,

$$\vec{a}+\vec{b} = \overrightarrow{AB} + \overrightarrow{BC} = \overrightarrow{AC}.$$

(a) COMMUTATIVE LAW. From Fig. 1.6 we can verify that $\vec{a}+\vec{b} = \vec{b}+\vec{a}$

Using Triangle Rule, from ΔABC

$$\overrightarrow{AB} + \overrightarrow{BC} = \overrightarrow{AC} \quad \text{i.e.,} \quad \vec{a}+\vec{b} = \overrightarrow{AC}.$$

Again, using the same triangle rule in the ΔADC, we have

$$\overrightarrow{AD} + \overrightarrow{DC} = \overrightarrow{AC} \quad \text{i.e.,} \quad \vec{b} + \vec{a} = \overrightarrow{AC}.$$

Hence, $\overrightarrow{AC} = \vec{a} + \vec{b} = \vec{b} + \vec{a}$.

NOTE. In case $\overrightarrow{AB}$ and $\overrightarrow{BC}$ are *parallel*, by *triangle law*, we can always write $\overrightarrow{AB} + \overrightarrow{BC} = \overrightarrow{AC}$.

(b) ASSOCIATIVE LAW. *For any three vectors $\vec{a}, \vec{b}$ and $\vec{c}$, we can prove that* $(\vec{a} + \vec{b}) + \vec{c} = \vec{a} + (\vec{b} + \vec{c})$.

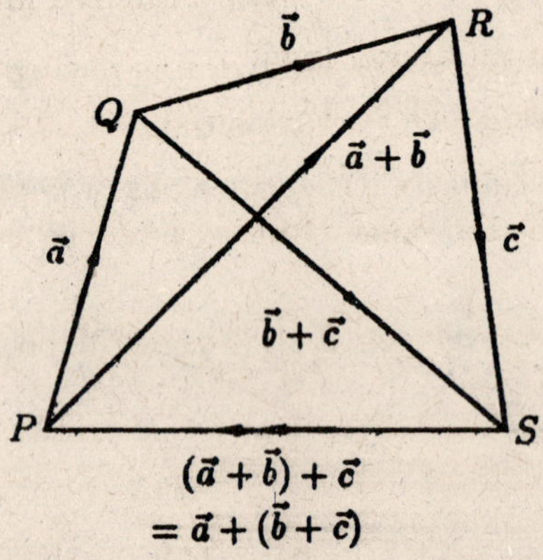

Fig 1.7

PROOF. In Fig. 1.7, we see that

$$\vec{a} = \overrightarrow{PQ}, \vec{b} = \overrightarrow{QR} \quad \text{and} \quad \vec{c} = \overrightarrow{RS}.$$

From $\Delta PQR, \overrightarrow{PQ} + \overrightarrow{QR} = \overrightarrow{PR}$,

i.e., $\vec{a} + \vec{b} = \overrightarrow{PR}$.

From $\Delta PRS, \overrightarrow{PR} + \overrightarrow{RS} = \overrightarrow{PS}$,

$$\text{i.e.,} \quad (\vec{a} + \vec{b}) + \vec{c} = \overrightarrow{PS} \qquad (1)$$

From $\Delta QRS, \overrightarrow{QR} + \overrightarrow{RS} = \overrightarrow{QS}$,

i.e., $\vec{b} + \vec{c} = \overrightarrow{QS}$.

From $\Delta PQS, \overrightarrow{PQ} + \overrightarrow{QS} = \overrightarrow{PS}$,

$$\text{i.e.,} \quad \vec{a} + (\vec{b} + \vec{c}) = \overrightarrow{PS}. \qquad (2)$$

$\therefore$ From (1) and (2), $\overrightarrow{PS} = (\vec{a} + \vec{b}) + \vec{c} = \vec{a} + (\vec{b} + \vec{c})$.

In addition of three vectors $\vec{a}, \vec{b}, \vec{c}$, we may simply write the sum $= \vec{a} + \vec{b} + \vec{c}$.

II. Subtraction of Vectors

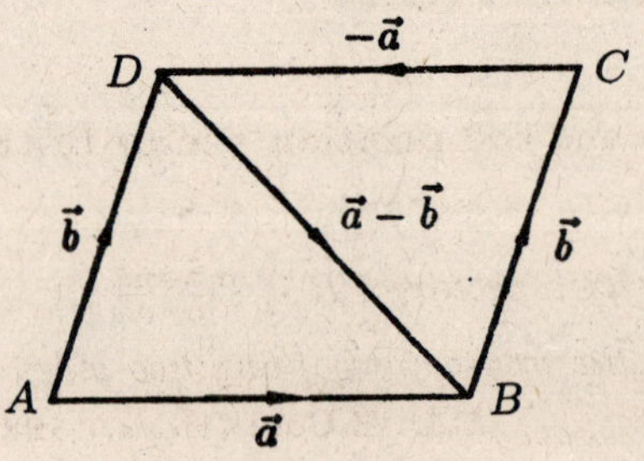

Fig 1.8

(i) If $\vec{a} = \overrightarrow{AB}$, we call $\overrightarrow{BA}$, **negative** of $\vec{a}$, denoted by $-\vec{a}$. Thus, whenever $\vec{a} = \overrightarrow{AB}$, we may write $-\vec{a} = \overrightarrow{BA}$, so that $\overrightarrow{BA} = -\overrightarrow{AB}$ and $\vec{a} + (-\vec{a}) = \overrightarrow{AB} + \overrightarrow{BA} = \overrightarrow{AA} = \vec{0}$.

(ii) The **difference** $\vec{a} - \vec{b}$ of two vectors $\vec{a}$ and $\vec{b}$ = sum of $\vec{a}$ and negative of $\vec{b} = \vec{a} + (-\vec{b})$.

In Fig. 1.8, $\vec{a} = \overrightarrow{AB}, \vec{b} = \overrightarrow{AD}$ and hence, $-\vec{b} = \overrightarrow{DA}$.

$\therefore$ $\vec{a} + (-\vec{b}) = \overrightarrow{AB} + \overrightarrow{DA} = \overrightarrow{DA} + \overrightarrow{AB} = \overrightarrow{DB}$, i.e., $\vec{a} - \vec{b} = \overrightarrow{DB}$.

Thus, the difference also can be represented by another **diagonal** of the parallelogram.

III. Multiplication of a Vector by a Scalar

DEFINITION. *If m is a scalar (a number $\neq 0$) and $\vec{a}$ is a vector then,*

(i) *$m\vec{a}$ = a vector whose direction is same as that of $\vec{a}$, if $m > 0$ and whose magnitude is m times the length of $\vec{a}$.*

(ii) *$m\vec{a}$ = a vector whose direction is opposite to that of $\vec{a}$, if $m < 0$ and whose magnitude is $|m|$ times the length of a.*

PROPERTIES. $m(n\vec{a}) = n(m\vec{a}) = nm\vec{a}$ **[Associative law]**; $(m+n)\vec{a} = m\vec{a} + n\vec{a}$ **[Distributive law]**;

$m(\vec{a}+\vec{b}) = m\vec{a} + m\vec{b}$ **[Distributive law]**; $m\vec{a} = \vec{a}m$ **[Commutative law]**.

These laws follow immediately from definitions given above.

1.3.1. DIVISION OF A SEGMENT IN A GIVEN RATIO

To find the position vector of the point which divides the segment joining two given points whose position vectors are $\vec{a}$ and $\vec{b}$ internally in the ratio $m : n$.

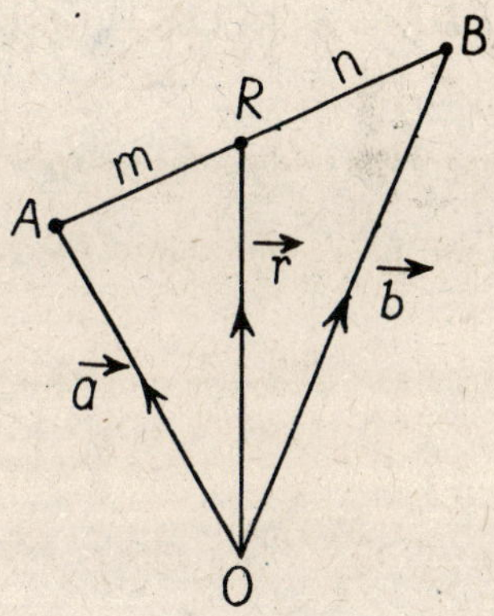

Fig 1.9

Let $\vec{a}$ and $\vec{b}$ be the position vectors of the two given points A and B with reference to O as origin and let R divide AB internally in the ratio $m : n$. Let $\vec{r}$ be the position vector of R, $\overrightarrow{OA} = \vec{a}$, $\overrightarrow{OB} = \vec{b}$ and $\overrightarrow{OR} = \vec{r}$.

From ΔOAR, by triangle rule

$$\overrightarrow{AR} = \overrightarrow{AO} + \overrightarrow{OR} = -\overrightarrow{OA} + \overrightarrow{OR} = -\vec{a} + \vec{r}.$$

Again, from ΔORB, we have,

$$\overrightarrow{RB} = \overrightarrow{RO} + \overrightarrow{OB} = -\overrightarrow{OR} + \overrightarrow{OB} = -\vec{r} + \vec{b}.$$

We have $AR : RB = m : n$, or, $n \cdot AR = m \cdot RB$.

$\therefore \quad m \cdot \overrightarrow{AR} = n \cdot \overrightarrow{RB}$. [$\because$ $\overrightarrow{AR}$ and $\overrightarrow{RB}$ are like vectors.]

or, $m(-\vec{a}+\vec{r}) = n(-\vec{r}+\vec{b})$, or, $-m\vec{a} + m\vec{r} = -n\vec{r} + n\vec{b}$,

or, $(m+n)\vec{r} = m\vec{a} + n\vec{b}$, or, $\vec{r} = \frac{\mathbf{m\vec{b}+n\vec{a}}}{\mathbf{m+n}}$, where $m+n \neq 0$.

CORROLLARY. (i) If R be the *mid-point* of AB, then $m = n$ and **the position vector of the mid-point of AB is** $\frac{\vec{\mathbf{a}}+\vec{\mathbf{b}}}{\mathbf{2}}$.

(ii) *If R divides AB externally in the ratio $m : n$, the position vector of R is* $\frac{\mathbf{m\vec{b}-n\vec{a}}}{\mathbf{m-n}}$.

EXAMPLE 1. *Prove, by vector method, that the line joining the mid-points of any two sides of a triangle is parallel to and half of the third side.* **[C.U. B.Com (Hons.) 1983]**

SOLUTION. Let $\vec{a}, \vec{b}, \vec{c}$ be the position vectors of the vertices A, B, C respectively of ΔABC with reference to O as origin. Let D and E be the mid-points of AB and AC respectively. Then, the position vectors of D and E are respectively $\frac{\vec{a}+\vec{b}}{2}$ and $\frac{\vec{a}+\vec{c}}{2}$.

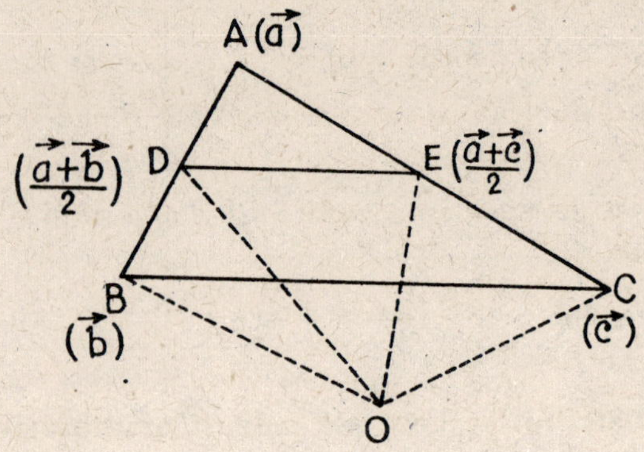

Fig 1.10

Then, $\overrightarrow{BC} = \overrightarrow{BO} + \overrightarrow{OC} = -\overrightarrow{OB} + \overrightarrow{OC} = -\vec{b} + \vec{c} = \vec{c} - \vec{b}$.

and $\overrightarrow{DE} = \overrightarrow{DO} + \overrightarrow{OE} = -\overrightarrow{OD} + \overrightarrow{OE} = -\frac{\vec{a}+\vec{b}}{2} + \frac{\vec{a}+\vec{c}}{2} = \frac{\vec{c}-\vec{b}}{2}. = \frac{1}{2}(\vec{c}-\vec{b}) = \frac{1}{2}\overrightarrow{BC}$. i.e., $\overrightarrow{DE} = \frac{1}{2}\overrightarrow{BC}$ and $|\overrightarrow{DE}| = \frac{1}{2}|\overrightarrow{BC}|$.

Thus, *DE is parallel to BC and is equal to* $\frac{1}{2}BC$. *Hence, the result follows.*

EXAMPLE 2. *Show that the medians of a triangle are concurrent at a point which trisects each of them.* **[C.U. B.Sc., 1987]**

SOLUTION. Let $\vec{a}, \vec{b}, \vec{c}$ be the position vectors of the vertices A, B, C of ΔABC referred to O as origin. Let AD be the median through A. Then, D is the mid-point of BC and the position vector of D is $\frac{\vec{b}+\vec{c}}{2}$.

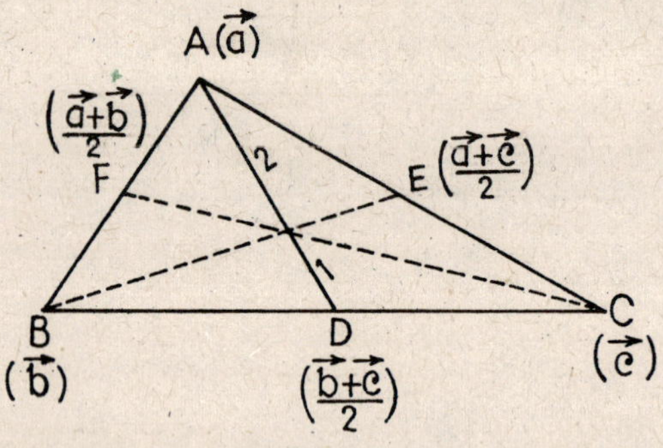

Fig 1.11

If G be the point on the median AD dividing it in the ratio 2 : 1, then the position vector of G is

$$\frac{2 \cdot \left(\frac{\vec{b}+\vec{c}}{2}\right) + 1 \cdot \vec{a}}{2+1} = \frac{\vec{a}+\vec{b}+\vec{c}}{3}. \tag{1}$$

From symmetry, we see that the point G whose position vector is given by (1) also lies on the other two medians BE and CF dividing each of them in the ratio 2 : 1.

Hence, the medians of a triangle are concurrent at a point which trisects each of them.

1.3.2. THEOREMS

THEOREM 1. *In a plane any vector* $\vec{a}$ *can be expressed as* $\vec{a} = x\mathbf{i} + y\mathbf{j}$ *where* $\mathbf{i}, \mathbf{j}$ *are two mutually perpendicular unit vectors and* $\vec{a}$ *is coplanar with* $\mathbf{i}$ *and* $\mathbf{j}$.

Let $\vec{a} = \overrightarrow{OP}$ and OX, OY be two rectangular axes through O. Let $\mathbf{i}, \mathbf{j}$ be two unit vectors along OX and OY respectively. Then, $|\mathbf{i}| = 1$ and $|\mathbf{j}| = 1$.

If (x, y) be the co-ordinates of P, then $ON = x$ and $NP = y = OM$.

From $\Delta OPN, \overrightarrow{OP} = \overrightarrow{ON} + \overrightarrow{NP} = \overrightarrow{ON} + \overrightarrow{OM}$

$$[\because \overrightarrow{OM} = \overrightarrow{NP}]$$

$$= x\mathbf{i} + y\mathbf{j}$$

$$[\because |\overrightarrow{ON}| = x \text{ and } |\overrightarrow{OM}| = y.]$$

i.e., $\vec{a} = x\mathbf{i} + y\mathbf{j}$. In this case, we may write $\vec{a} = (x, y)$.

Thus in a plane a vector may be written as an ordered pair.

Clearly, $|\vec{a}| = |\overrightarrow{OP}| = OP = \sqrt{ON^2 + NP^2}$
$= \sqrt{x^2 + y^2}$.

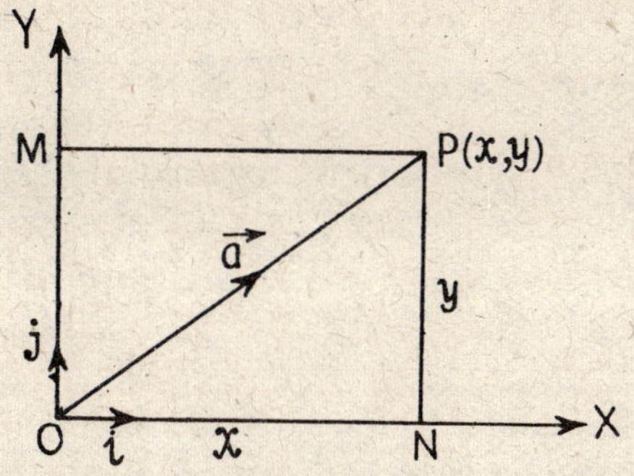

Fig 1.12

GENERAL CASE. *Any vector r, coplanar with two non-collinear vectors $\vec{a}$ and $\vec{b}$ can be expressed as $\vec{r} = x\vec{a} + y\vec{b}$, where x, y are scalars.*

THEOREM 2. *In three-dimensional space, any vector $\vec{r}$ can be expressed as $\vec{r} = x\mathbf{i} + y\mathbf{j} + z\mathbf{k}$, where $\mathbf{i}, \mathbf{j}, \mathbf{k}$ are three mutually perpendicular unit vectors.*

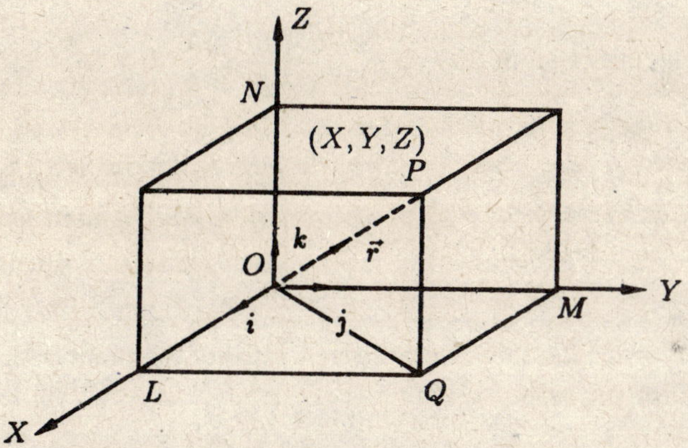

Fig 1.13

Let $\vec{r} = \overrightarrow{OP}$ be a vector and OX, OY, OZ be three mutually perpendicular axes through O. (See Fig. 1.13).

Complete the rectangular parallelopiped with OP as diagonal and with edges through O along the axes.

OL = scalar component of $\overrightarrow{OP}$ along OX (i.e., along $\mathbf{i}$) = x (say).

OM = scalar component of $\overrightarrow{OP}$ along OY (i.e., along $\mathbf{j}$) = y (say).

ON = scalar component of $\overrightarrow{OP}$ along OZ (i.e., along $\mathbf{k}$) = z (say).

Then the vector components $\overrightarrow{OL}, \overrightarrow{OM}, \overrightarrow{ON}$ are $x\mathbf{i}, y\mathbf{j}, z\mathbf{k}$ respectively.

By using "Triangle Rule of Addition" repeatedly, we get

$$\vec{r} = \overrightarrow{OP} = \overrightarrow{OQ} + \overrightarrow{QP} = (\overrightarrow{OL} + \overrightarrow{LQ}) + \overrightarrow{QP} = (\overrightarrow{OL} + \overrightarrow{OM}) + \overrightarrow{ON} = x\mathbf{i} + y\mathbf{j} + z\mathbf{k}.$$

x, y, z are also known as the coordinates of the vector $\vec{r}$.

We may write $\vec{r} = \overrightarrow{OP} = (x, y, z)$, which is an ordered triplet of real numbers.

Further,

$$OP^2 = OQ^2 + QP^2 = OL^2 + LQ^2 + QP^2 = OL^2 + OM^2 + ON^2 = x^2 + y^2 + z^2$$
$$= x^2 + y^2 + z^2$$
$$\therefore \quad |\overrightarrow{OP}| = \sqrt{x^2 + y^2 + z^2}.$$

EXAMPLE 3. *It α, β be two vectors given by $\alpha = 2i - 5j + 4k$ and $\beta = i - 4j + 6k$ where i, j, k are three unit vectors along three nuctually perpendicular directions, find the vector $2\alpha - \beta$. What is the unit vector in the direction of the vector $2\alpha - \beta$?* **[C.U. B.Com. (Hons.) 1982]**

SOLUTION.

$$2\alpha - \beta = 2(2i - 5j + 4k) - (i - 4j + 6k)$$
$$= 4i - 10j + 8k - i + 4j - 6k = \mathbf{3i} - \mathbf{6j} + \mathbf{2k}.$$
$$|2\alpha - \beta| = \sqrt{(3)^2 + (-6)^2 + (2)^2} = \sqrt{9 + 36 + 4} = \sqrt{49} = 7.$$

$$\therefore \quad \text{Unit vector in the direction of } 2\alpha - \beta = \frac{2\alpha - \beta}{|2\alpha - \beta|} = \frac{\mathbf{1}}{\mathbf{7}}(\mathbf{3i} - \mathbf{6j} + \mathbf{2k}).$$

EXAMPLE 4. (i) *Find the position vector of the point which divides the join of the points whose position vectors are respectively $3\vec{a} - \vec{b}$ and $\vec{a} - 2\vec{b}$ internally in the ratio 3 : 4.*

(ii) *Find the position vector of the point which divides the segment joining the points $\vec{a} + 2\vec{b}$ and $5\vec{a} - 3\vec{b}$ externally in the ratio 3 : 2.*

SOLUTION.

(i) If $\vec{\alpha} = 3\vec{a} - \vec{b}$ and $\vec{\beta} = \vec{a} - 2\vec{b}$, then the position vector of the point which divides the segment joining the points $\vec{\alpha}$ and $\vec{\beta}$ in the ratio 3 : 4 is

$$\frac{3\vec{\beta} + 4\vec{\alpha}}{3+4} = \frac{3(\vec{a} - 2\vec{b}) + 4(3\vec{a} - \vec{b})}{3+4} = \frac{3\vec{a} - 6\vec{b} + 12\vec{a} - 4\vec{b}}{7}$$
$$= \frac{15\vec{a} - 10\vec{b}}{7} = \frac{\mathbf{5}}{\mathbf{7}}(\mathbf{3\vec{a}} - \mathbf{2\vec{b}}).$$

(ii) Let $\alpha = \vec{a} + 2\vec{b}$ and $\vec{\beta} = 5\vec{a} - 3\vec{b}$. Then the position vector of the point which divides the join of $\vec{\alpha}$ and $\vec{\beta}$ externally in the ratio 3 : 2 is

$$\frac{3\vec{\beta} - 2\vec{\alpha}}{3-2} = \frac{3(5\vec{a} - 3\vec{b}) - 2(\vec{a} + 2\vec{b})}{3-2} = \frac{15\vec{a} - 9\vec{b} - 2\vec{a} - 4\vec{b}}{1}$$
$$= 13\vec{a} - 13\vec{b} = \mathbf{13}(\mathbf{\vec{a}} - \mathbf{\vec{b}}).$$

EXAMPLE 5. *If G be the centroid of the triangle ABC, prove by vector method that*

$$\overrightarrow{GA} + \overrightarrow{GB} + \overrightarrow{GC} = \vec{0}.$$

SOLUTION. Let $\vec{a}, \vec{b}, \vec{c}$ be the position vectors of the vertices A, B, C of the triangle ABC with reference to O as origin.

Let AD be the median through A. Then, D is the mid point of BC and the position vector of D is $\frac{\vec{b}+\vec{c}}{2}$.

If G be the centroid of ΔABC, then G divides AD in the ratio $2:1$.

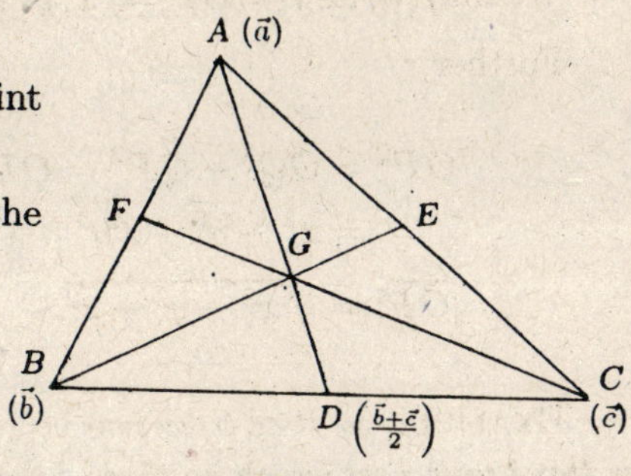

Fig 1.14

$\therefore$ The position vector of G is

$$\overrightarrow{OG} = \frac{2\cdot\left(\frac{\vec{b}+\vec{c}}{2}\right)+1\cdot\vec{a}}{2+1} = \frac{\vec{b}+\vec{c}+\vec{a}}{3} = \frac{\vec{a}+\vec{b}+\vec{c}}{3}.$$

$$\therefore\quad \overrightarrow{GA} = \overrightarrow{OA} - \overrightarrow{OG} = \vec{a} - \frac{\vec{a}+\vec{b}+\vec{c}}{3}.$$

Similarly, $\overrightarrow{GB} = \vec{b} - \frac{\vec{a}+\vec{b}+\vec{c}}{3}$ and $\overrightarrow{GC} = \vec{c} - \frac{\vec{a}+\vec{b}+\vec{c}}{3}$.

$$\therefore\quad \overrightarrow{GA}+\overrightarrow{GB}+\overrightarrow{GC} = \left(\vec{a}-\frac{\vec{a}+\vec{b}+\vec{c}}{3}\right)+\left(\vec{b}-\frac{\vec{a}+\vec{b}+\vec{c}}{3}\right)+\left(\vec{c}-\frac{\vec{a}+\vec{b}+\vec{c}}{3}\right)$$
$$= (\vec{a}+\vec{b}+\vec{c}) - (\vec{a}+\vec{b}+\vec{c}) = \vec{0}.$$

Hence, the result follows.

EXAMPLE 6. *Find the magnitude of the vectors $\vec{a}+\vec{b}, \vec{a}-\vec{b}$ and $3\vec{a}+2\vec{b}$ where $\vec{a} = 3\vec{i}+4\vec{j}+5\vec{k}$ and $\vec{b} = \vec{i}+2\vec{j}+3\vec{k}$.* **[C.U. 1985, 88]**

SOLUTION. We have

$$\vec{a}+\vec{b} = (3\vec{i}+4\vec{j}+5\vec{k}) + (\vec{i}+2\vec{j}+3\vec{k}) = 4\vec{i}+6\vec{j}+8\vec{k},$$
$$\vec{a}-\vec{b} = (3\vec{i}+4\vec{j}+5\vec{k}) - (\vec{i}+2\vec{j}+3\vec{k}) = 2\vec{i}+2\vec{j}+2\vec{k}$$

and
$$3\vec{a}+2\vec{b} = 3(3\vec{i}+4\vec{j}+5\vec{k}) + 2(\vec{i}+2\vec{j}+3\vec{k})$$
$$= 9\vec{i}+12\vec{j}+15\vec{k}+2\vec{i}+4\vec{j}+6\vec{k} = 11\vec{i}+16\vec{j}+21\vec{k}$$

$$\therefore\quad \text{Magnitude of } (\vec{a}+\vec{b}) = |\vec{a}+\vec{b}| = \sqrt{4^2+6^2+8^2} = \sqrt{116} = 2\sqrt{29}$$
$$\text{Magnitude of } (\vec{a}-\vec{b}) = |\vec{a}-\vec{b}| = \sqrt{2^2+2^2+2^2} = \sqrt{12} = 2\sqrt{3}$$
$$\text{and the magnitude of } (3\vec{a}+2\vec{b}) = \sqrt{(11)^2+(16)^2+(21)^2} = \sqrt{818}.$$

EXAMPLE 7. *If ABC be a triangle and AD, BE, CF be its three medians, then prove that $\overrightarrow{AD}+\overrightarrow{BE}+\overrightarrow{CF} = \vec{0}$.*

Let $\vec{a}, \vec{b}, \vec{c}$ be the position vectors of the vertices A, B, C with reference to O as origin.

Then, the position vectors of D, E, F are respectively

$$\frac{\vec{b}+\vec{c}}{2},\ \frac{\vec{c}+\vec{a}}{2},\ \frac{\vec{a}+\vec{b}}{2}.$$

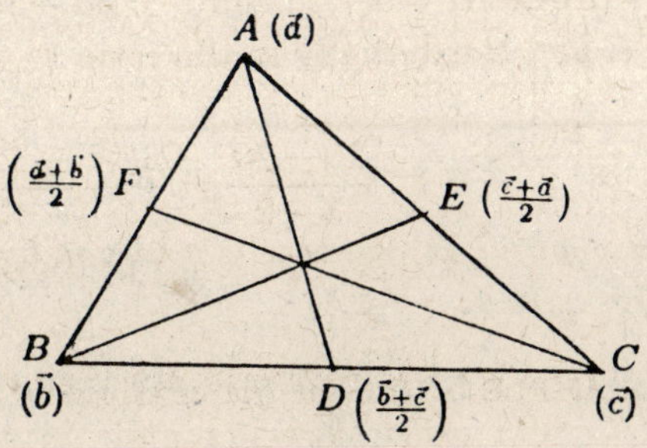

Fig 1.15

We have $\overrightarrow{OA} = \vec{a}, \overrightarrow{OB} = \vec{b}, \overrightarrow{OC} = \vec{c}$

$$\overrightarrow{OD} = \frac{\vec{b}+\vec{c}}{2},\ \overrightarrow{OE} = \frac{\vec{c}+\vec{a}}{2} \text{ and } \overrightarrow{OF} = \frac{\vec{a}+\vec{b}}{2}.$$

$$\therefore\quad \overrightarrow{AD} = \overrightarrow{OD} - \overrightarrow{OA} = \frac{\vec{b}+\vec{c}}{2} - \vec{a},$$

$\overrightarrow{BE} = \overrightarrow{OE} - \overrightarrow{OB} = \dfrac{\vec{c}+\vec{a}}{2} - \vec{b}$ and $\overrightarrow{CF} = \overrightarrow{OF} - \overrightarrow{OC} = \dfrac{\vec{a}+\vec{b}}{2} - \vec{c}$.

Hence,

$$\overrightarrow{AD} + \overrightarrow{BE} + \overrightarrow{CF} = \frac{\vec{b}+\vec{c}}{2} - \vec{a} + \frac{\vec{c}+\vec{a}}{2} - \vec{b} + \frac{\vec{a}+\vec{b}}{2} - \vec{c}$$
$$= (\vec{a}+\vec{b}+\vec{c}) - (\vec{a}+\vec{b}+\vec{c}) = \vec{0}.$$

IV. Dot Product or Scalar Product of two Vectors

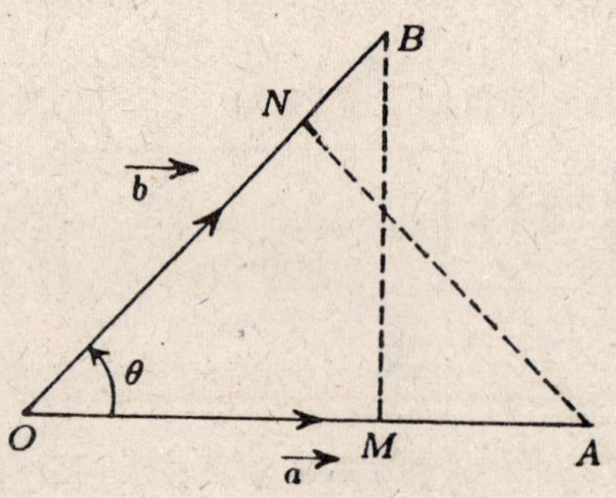

Fig 1.16

The dot or scalar product of two non-zero vectors $\vec{a}$ and $\vec{b}$, written as $\vec{a}\cdot\vec{b}$, is the **scalar** *defined by*

$$\vec{a}\cdot\vec{b} = |\vec{a}|\cdot|\vec{b}|\cos\theta \qquad (1)$$

where $|\vec{a}|, |\vec{b}|$ are the lengths of $\vec{a}, \vec{b}$ and θ is the angle between the vectors $\vec{a}$ and $\vec{b}$. If one or both of $\vec{a}, \vec{b}$ is $\vec{o}$, then $\vec{a}\cdot\vec{b} = 0$.

Clearly, $\vec{a}\cdot\vec{b} = \vec{b}\cdot\vec{a}$ i.e., dot product is *commutative.*

The scalar product $\vec{a}\cdot\vec{b}$ is positive or negative according as $\cos\theta$ is positive or negative as according as θ is acute or obtuse.

Geometrical meaning of $\mathbf{\vec{a}\cdot\vec{b}}$

We have

$$\vec{a}\cdot\vec{b} = |\vec{a}|\cdot|\vec{b}|\cos\theta = OA\cdot OB\cos\theta = OA\cdot OM$$

i.e., $\vec{a}\cdot\vec{b} =$ (Length of $\vec{a}$) · (Projection of $|\vec{b}|$ in the direction of $\vec{a}$)

Again, $\vec{b}\cdot\vec{a} = |\vec{b}|\cdot|\vec{a}|\cdot\cos\theta = OB\cdot OA\cos\theta = OB\cdot ON$

$=$ (length of $\vec{b}$) · (Projection of $|\vec{a}|$ in the direction of $\vec{b}$).

Some Important results

(i) The angle θ between the vectors $\vec{a}$ and $\vec{b}$ is given by $\cos\theta = \frac{\vec{a}\cdot\vec{b}}{|\vec{a}|\cdot|\vec{b}|}$.

(ii) If $\vec{a}$ is perpendicular to $\vec{b}$, then $\theta = 90°$ and $\cos\theta = \cos 90° = 0$.

$\therefore$ From (1), $\mathbf{\vec{a}\cdot\vec{b}} = 0$ *which is the condition for two vectors $\vec{a}$ and $\vec{b}$ to be* **perpendicular to each other.**

(iii) If $\mathbf{i}, \mathbf{j}, \mathbf{k}$ be three units vectors along three mutually perpendicular axes OX, OY and OZ, then $\mathbf{i}^2 = \mathbf{i}\cdot\mathbf{i} = |\mathbf{i}|\cdot|\mathbf{i}|\cos 0° = 1\cdot 1\cdot 1 = 1$; similarly $\mathbf{j}^2 = 1, \mathbf{k}^2 = 1$. Again, $\mathbf{i}\cdot\mathbf{j} = |\mathbf{i}|\cdot|\mathbf{j}|\cos 90° = 1\cdot 1\cdot 0 = 0$; similarly $\mathbf{j}\cdot\mathbf{k} = 0, \mathbf{k}\cdot\mathbf{i} = 0$.

Thus, $\mathbf{i}^2 = \mathbf{j}^2 = \mathbf{k}^2 = 1$ *and* $\mathbf{i}\cdot\mathbf{j} = \mathbf{j}\cdot\mathbf{i} = \mathbf{0}, \mathbf{j}\cdot\mathbf{k} = \mathbf{k}\cdot\mathbf{j} = \mathbf{0}, \mathbf{k}\cdot\mathbf{i} = \mathbf{i}\cdot\mathbf{k} = \mathbf{0}.$

(iv) *If* $\vec{a} = a_1 i + b_1 j + c_1 k$ *and* $\vec{b} = a_2 i + b_2 j + c_2 k$, *then* $\mathbf{\vec{a} \cdot \vec{b} = a_1 a_2 + b_1 b_2 + c_1 c_2}$.

$$\begin{aligned}\vec{a} \cdot \vec{b} &= (a_1 i + b_1 j + c_1 k) \cdot (a_2 i + b_2 j + c_2 k)\\ &= a_1 a_2 i^2 + a_1 b_2 i \cdot j + a_1 c_2 i \cdot k + b_1 a_2 j \cdot i + b_1 b_2 j^2 + b_1 c_2 j \cdot k + c_1 a_2 k \cdot i + c_1 b_2 k \cdot j + c_1 c_2 k^2\\ &= a_1 a_2 \cdot 1 + 0 + 0 + 0 + b_1 b_2 \cdot 1 + 0 + 0 + 0 + c_1 c_2 \cdot 1\\ &\qquad [\because \; i^2 = j^2 = k^2 = 1, i \cdot j = j \cdot i = 0, j \cdot k = k \cdot j = 0, k \cdot i = i \cdot k = 0]\\ &= a_1 a_2 + b_1 b_2 + c_1 c_2.\end{aligned}$$

In short, if $\vec{a} = a_1 \vec{i} + b_1 \vec{j} + c_1 \vec{k}$ and $\vec{b} = a_2 \vec{i} + b_2 \vec{j} + c_2 \vec{k}$, then $\vec{a} \cdot \vec{b} = a_1 a_2 + b_1 b_2 + c_1 c_2$.

V. Distributive Law

For three vectors $\vec{a}, \vec{b}, \vec{c}$, $\vec{a} \cdot (\vec{b} + \vec{c}) = \vec{a} \cdot \vec{b} + \vec{a} \cdot \vec{c}$.

PROOF. From Fig. 1.17, we see that

Scalar component of $\vec{b}$ along the direction of $\vec{a}$ is OL, that of $\vec{c}$ along the same direction is LM.

But $OL + LM = OM$

= scalar component of $\vec{b} + \vec{c}$ along $\vec{a}$.

Multiply both sides by the length $|\vec{a}|$ of the vector $\vec{a}$,

i.e., $|\vec{a}|OL + |\vec{a}|LM = |\vec{a}|OM$

$\therefore$ $|\vec{a}| \times$ scalar component of $\vec{b}$ along $\vec{a}$

$+|\vec{a}| \times$ scalar component of $\vec{c}$ along $\vec{a}$

$= |\vec{a}| \times$ scalar component of $\vec{b} + \vec{c}$ along $\vec{a}$.

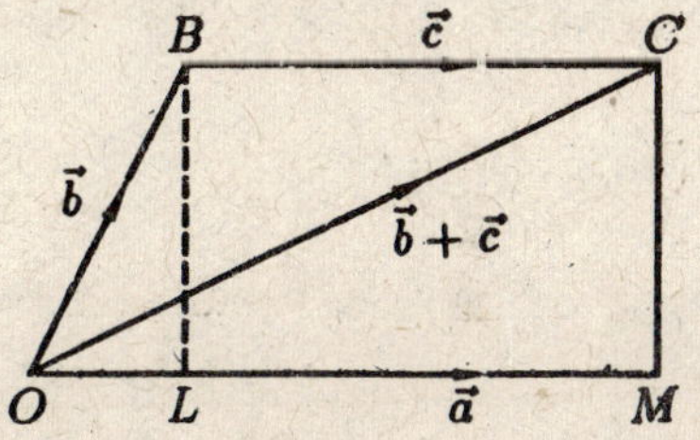

Fig 1.17

Hence, by definition, $\vec{a} \cdot \vec{b} + \vec{a} \cdot \vec{c} = \vec{a} \cdot (\vec{b} + \vec{c})$.

(vi) ***If m is a number, then, by definition, we have*** $m(\vec{a} \cdot \vec{b}) = (m\vec{a}) \cdot \vec{b} = \vec{a} \cdot (m\vec{b})$.

EXAMPLE 8. *If* $\vec{a} = 2\vec{j} + \vec{j} - \vec{k}$ *and* $\vec{b} = \vec{i} + \vec{j} + 3\vec{k}$, *show that* $\vec{a}$ *is perpendicular to* $\vec{b}$. *Find also the value of* $|\vec{a} + \vec{b}|$. **[C.U. B.Com. (Hons.) 1990]**

SOLUTION.

$$\begin{aligned}\vec{a} \cdot \vec{b} &= (2\vec{i} + \vec{j} - \vec{k}) \cdot (\vec{i} + \vec{j} + 3\vec{k}) = 2\vec{i}^2 + 2\vec{i} \cdot \vec{j} + 6\vec{i} \cdot \vec{k} + \vec{j} \cdot \vec{i} + \vec{j}^2 + 3\vec{j} \cdot \vec{k} - \vec{k} \cdot \vec{i} - \vec{k} \cdot \vec{j} - 3\vec{k}^2\\ &= 2 \cdot 1 + 2 \cdot 0 + 6 \cdot 0 + 0 + 1 + 3 \cdot 0 - 0 - 0 - 3 \cdot 1\\ &\qquad [\because \; \vec{i}^2 = 1 = \vec{j}^2 = \vec{k}^2, \vec{i} \cdot \vec{j} = \vec{j} \cdot \vec{i} = 0, \text{ etc.}]\\ &= 2 + 0 + 0 + 0 + 1 + 0 - 0 - 0 - 3 = 0.\end{aligned}$$

i.e., $\mathbf{\vec{a} \cdot \vec{b} = 0}$. *Hence* $\vec{a}$ *is perpendicular to* $\vec{b}$.

Again,

$$\vec{a} + \vec{b} = (2\vec{i} + \vec{j} - \vec{k}) + (\vec{i} + \vec{j} + 3\vec{k}) = 3\vec{i} + 2\vec{j} + 2\vec{k}$$

$$\therefore \; |\vec{a} + \vec{b}| = \sqrt{3^2 + 2^2 + 2^2} = \sqrt{9 + 4 + 4} = \sqrt{\mathbf{17}}.$$

EXAMPLE 9. *If* $\vec{a} = 3\vec{i} + 4\vec{j} + \vec{k}$ *and* $\vec{b} = 2\vec{i} - \vec{j} + 4\vec{k}$, *compute* $(2\vec{a} + 3\vec{b}) \cdot (\vec{a} - \vec{b})$.

[C.U. B.Com. (Hons.) 1992]

SOLUTION. We have

$$2\vec{a}+3\vec{b}=2(3\vec{i}+4\vec{j}+\vec{k})+3(2\vec{i}-\vec{j}+4\vec{k})$$
$$=6\vec{i}+8\vec{j}+2\vec{k}-6\vec{i}-3\vec{j}+12\vec{k}=5\vec{j}+14\vec{k}$$
$$\text{and}\quad \vec{a}-\vec{b}=(3\vec{i}+4\vec{j}+\vec{k})-(2\vec{i}-\vec{j}+4\vec{k})=\vec{i}+5\vec{j}-3\vec{k}$$
$$\therefore\quad (2\vec{a}+3\vec{b})\cdot(\vec{a}-\vec{b})=(5\vec{j}+14\vec{k})\cdot(\vec{i}+5\vec{j}-3\vec{k})$$
$$=5\vec{j}\cdot\vec{i}+25\vec{j}^{\,2}-15\vec{j}\cdot\vec{k}+14\vec{k}\cdot\vec{i}+70\vec{k}\cdot j-42\vec{k}^{\,2}$$
$$=5\cdot 0+25\cdot 1-15\cdot 0+14\cdot 0+70\cdot 0-42\cdot 1$$
$$[\because\ \vec{j}\cdot\vec{i}=0, \vec{j}^{\,2}=1, \vec{j}\cdot\vec{k}=\vec{k}\cdot\vec{j}=0, \text{ etc.}]$$
$$=25-42=\mathbf{-17}.$$

EXAMPLE 10. *Find the cosine of the angle between the vectors* $\vec{a}=3i+j+2k$ *and* $\vec{b}=2i-2j+4k$.

[C.U. B.Com. (Hons.) 1986]

SOLUTION.

$$\vec{a}\cdot\vec{b}=(3i+j+2k)\cdot(2i-2j+4k)$$
$$=6i^2-6i\cdot j+12i\cdot k+2j\cdot i-2j^2+4j\cdot k+4k\cdot i-4k\cdot j+8k^2$$
$$=6\cdot 1-6\cdot 0+12\cdot 0-2\cdot 0-2\cdot 1+4\cdot 0+4\cdot 0-4\cdot 0+8\cdot 1$$
$$=6-2+8=12,$$
$$|\vec{a}|=\sqrt{3^2+1^2+2^2}=\sqrt{14} \text{ and } |\vec{b}|=\sqrt{2^2+(-2)^2+4^2}=\sqrt{24}.$$
$$\therefore\quad \cos\theta=\frac{\vec{a}\cdot\vec{b}}{|\vec{a}|\cdot|\vec{b}|}=\frac{12}{\sqrt{14}\cdot\sqrt{24}}=\frac{12}{\sqrt{7\times 3\times 16}}=\frac{12}{4\sqrt{21}}=\frac{3}{\sqrt{21}}$$
$$=\frac{3\sqrt{21}}{\sqrt{21}\cdot\sqrt{21}}=\frac{3\sqrt{21}}{21}=\frac{1}{7}\sqrt{\mathbf{21}}.$$

EXAMPLE 11. *Given three vectors* $\vec{a},\vec{b},\vec{c}$, *such that* $\vec{a}=2i+3j+6k, \vec{b}=3i-6j+2k$, $\vec{c}=6i+2j-3k$; *prove that the vectors* $\vec{a},\vec{b},\vec{c}$ *are mutually perpendicular.*

[C.U. B.Com. (Hons.) 1987]

SOLUTION.

$$\vec{a}\cdot\vec{b}=(2i+3j+6k)\cdot(3i-6j+2k)$$
$$=6i^2-12i\cdot j+4i\cdot k+9j\cdot i+18j^2+6j\cdot k+18k\cdot i-36k\cdot j+12k^2$$
$$=6\cdot 1-12\cdot 0+4\cdot 0+9\cdot 0-18\cdot 1+6\cdot 0+18\cdot 0-36\cdot 0+12\cdot 1$$
$$=6-18+12=18-18=0.$$

$\therefore$ *$\vec{a}$ is perpendicular to $\vec{b}$.*

Similarly,

$$\vec{b}\cdot\vec{c}=(3i-6j+2k)\cdot(6i+2j-3k)=18-12-6=0$$
$$\text{and}\quad \vec{a}\cdot\vec{c}=(2i+3j+6k)\cdot(6i+2j-3k)=12+6-18=0.$$

∴ *$\vec{b}$ is perpendicular to $\vec{c}$ and $\vec{a}$ is perpendicular to $\vec{c}$. Hence, the result follows.*

EXAMPLE 12. *The dot product of a vector with the three vectors* $(2,0,0),(0,3,0)$ *and* $(0,0,4)$ *are respectively* $6, 18$ *and* 16. *Find the vector.* **[CA Inter November 1986]**

SOLUTION. We can write the three given vectors as follows:

$$\vec{a}=(2,0,0)=2\vec{i}+0\cdot\vec{j}+0\cdot\vec{k}=2\vec{i}$$
$$\vec{b}=(0,3,0)=0\vec{i}+3\vec{j}+0\vec{k}=3\vec{j}$$
$$\text{and}\quad \vec{c}=(0,0,4)=0\cdot\vec{i}+0\cdot\vec{j}+4\vec{k}=4\vec{k}.$$

If $\vec{r}=x\vec{i}+y\vec{j}+z\vec{k}$ be the required vector, then by the given conditions,

$$\vec{r}\cdot\vec{a}=6, \vec{r}\cdot\vec{b}=18 \text{ and } \vec{r}\cdot\vec{c}=16$$
$$\text{or,}\quad (x\vec{i}+y\vec{y}+z\vec{k})\cdot 2\vec{i}=6, (x\vec{i}+y\vec{j}+z\vec{k})\cdot 3\vec{j}=18$$
$$\text{and}\quad (x\vec{i}+y\vec{j}+z\vec{k})\cdot 4\vec{k}=16.$$
$$\text{or,}\quad 2x=6, 3y=18 \text{ and } 4z=16 \qquad \left[\because\ \vec{r}^{\,2}=\vec{j}^{\,2}=\vec{k}^{\,2}=1,\ \vec{j}\cdot\vec{i}=\vec{i}\cdot\vec{j}=0, \text{ etc.}\right]$$
$$\therefore\quad x=3, y=6 \text{ and } z=4.$$

Hence, the required vector is $\vec{r}=x\vec{i}+y\vec{j}+y\vec{j}+z\vec{k}=\mathbf{3i}+\mathbf{6j}+\mathbf{4k}$.

V. Vector Product or Cross Product of two Vectors

The vector or cross product of two vectors $\vec{a}$ and $\vec{b}$, written as $\vec{a}\times\vec{b}$, is a vector $\vec{V}$ which is perpendicular to both $\vec{a}$ and $\vec{b}$ and is defined by

$$\vec{V}=\vec{a}\times\vec{b}=|\vec{a}|\cdot|\vec{b}|\sin\theta\cdot\hat{n},$$

where $|\vec{a}|\cdot|\vec{b}|$ are the length of $\vec{a},\vec{b}$ and θ is the angle between the vectors $\vec{a}$ and $\vec{b}$ and $\hat{n}$ is a unit vector perpendicular to the plane of $\vec{a}$ and $\vec{b}$ and the direction (or sense) of $\hat{n}$ is such that $\vec{a},\vec{b},\hat{n}$ form a right handed triad of vectors.

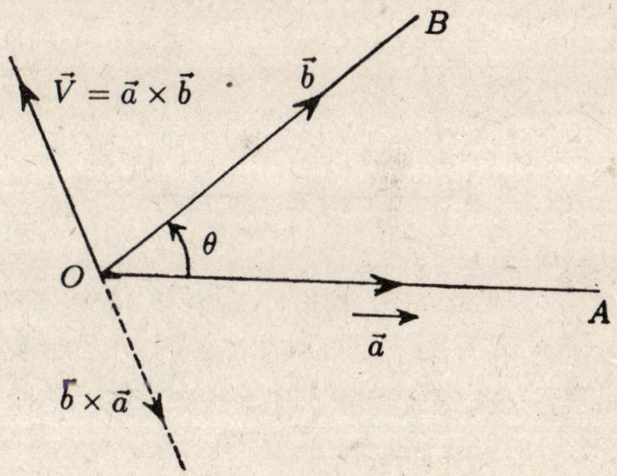

Fig 1.18

Some Important Results

(i) *The vector product is not commutative* i.e., $\vec{a}\times\vec{b}\neq\vec{b}\times\vec{a}$, but $\vec{a}\times\vec{b}=-\vec{b}\times\vec{a}$. [See Fig. 1.18.]

(ii) If $\vec{a}$ is parallel to $\vec{b}$, then $\theta=0$ so that $\sin\theta=0$ and $\vec{a}\times\vec{b}=0$. Clearly $\vec{a}\times\vec{a}=\vec{0}$.

(iii) If $\mathbf{i},\mathbf{j},\mathbf{k}$ be three unit vectors along three mutually perpendicular directions, then $\mathbf{i}\times\mathbf{i}=0$, $\mathbf{j}\times\mathbf{j}=0, \mathbf{k}\times\mathbf{k}=0$ and $\mathbf{i}\times\mathbf{j}=\mathbf{k}, \mathbf{j}\times\mathbf{i}=-\mathbf{k}, \mathbf{j}\times\mathbf{k}=\mathbf{i}, \mathbf{k}\times\mathbf{j}=-\mathbf{i}, \mathbf{k}\times\mathbf{i}=\mathbf{j}, \mathbf{i}\times\mathbf{k}=-\mathbf{j}$.

(iv) If $\vec{a}=a_1\mathbf{i}+b_1\mathbf{j}+c_1\mathbf{k}$ and $\vec{b}=a_2\mathbf{i}+b_2\mathbf{j}+c_2\mathbf{k}$, then $\vec{a}\times\vec{b}=\begin{vmatrix}\mathbf{i} & \mathbf{j} & \mathbf{k}\\ a_1 & b_1 & c_1\\ a_2 & b_2 & c_2\end{vmatrix}$.

PROOF.

$$\begin{aligned}\vec{a}\times\vec{b} &= (a_1\mathbf{i}+b_1\mathbf{j}+c_1\mathbf{k})\times(a_2\mathbf{i}+b_2\mathbf{j}+c_2\mathbf{k})\\
&= a_1a_2\mathbf{i}\times\mathbf{i}+a_1b_2\mathbf{i}\times\mathbf{j}+a_1c_2\mathbf{i}\times\mathbf{k}+b_1a_2\mathbf{j}\times\mathbf{i}+b_1b_2\mathbf{j}\times\mathbf{j}\\
&\quad+b_1c_2\mathbf{j}\times\mathbf{k}+c_1a_2\mathbf{k}\times\mathbf{i}+c_1b_2\mathbf{k}\times\mathbf{j}+c_1c_2\mathbf{k}\times\mathbf{k}\\
&= a_1a_2\cdot 0+a_1b_2\cdot\mathbf{k}+a_1c_2(-\mathbf{j})+a_2b_1(-\mathbf{k})+b_1b_2\cdot 0+b_1c_2\cdot\mathbf{i}\\
&\quad+a_2c_1\mathbf{j}+b_2c_1(-\mathbf{i})+c_1c_2\cdot 0.\\
&= (b_1c_2-b_2c_1)\mathbf{i}-(a_1c_2-a_2c_1)\mathbf{j}+(a_1b_2-a_2b_1)\mathbf{k}\\
&= \begin{vmatrix}\mathbf{i} & \mathbf{j} & \mathbf{k}\\ a_1 & b_1 & c_1\\ a_2 & b_2 & c_2\end{vmatrix}\quad \text{i.e.,}\quad \vec{\mathbf{a}}\times\vec{\mathbf{b}} = \begin{vmatrix}\mathbf{i} & \mathbf{j} & \mathbf{k}\\ \mathbf{a_1} & \mathbf{b_1} & \mathbf{c_1}\\ \mathbf{a_2} & \mathbf{b_2} & \mathbf{c_2}\end{vmatrix}\end{aligned}$$

[See definition of 3rd order determinant in the next chapter.]

This relation will be used as *formula to calculate* $\vec{a}\times\vec{b}$.

(v) **Distributive Law for Vector Products**

For three vectors $\vec{a}, \vec{b}$ *and* $\vec{c}$, *we have*

(i) $\vec{a}\times(\vec{b}+\vec{c}) = \vec{a}\times\vec{b}+\vec{a}\times\vec{c}$;

(ii) $(\vec{b}+\vec{c})\times\vec{a} = \vec{b}\times\vec{a}+\vec{c}\times\vec{a}$.

(vi) If m be a real number, then $m(\vec{a}\times\vec{b}) = (m\vec{a})\times\vec{b} = \vec{a}\times(m\vec{b})$.

(vii) *Geometrical meaning of* $\vec{a}\times\vec{b}$

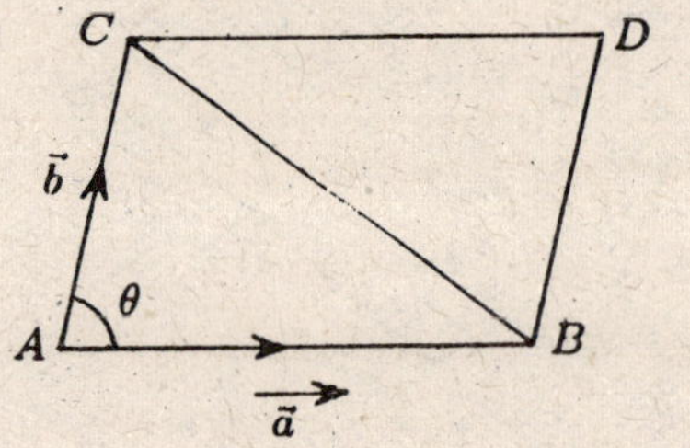

Fig 1.19

Let $ABDC$ be a parallelogram such that $\overrightarrow{AB} = \vec{a}$ and $\overrightarrow{AC} = \vec{b}$ and $\angle BAC = \theta$.

From Trigonometry, we have

$$\begin{aligned}\text{Area of } \Delta ABC &= \frac{1}{2}AB\cdot AC\sin\theta\\
&= \frac{1}{2}|\overrightarrow{AB}|\cdot|\overrightarrow{AC}|\cdot\sin\theta\\
&= \frac{1}{2}|\vec{a}|\cdot|\vec{b}|\cdot\sin\theta = \frac{1}{2}|\vec{a}\times\vec{b}|.\end{aligned}$$

$\therefore$ Area of the parallelogram $ABDC = 2\cdot(\text{Area of } \Delta ABC) = |\vec{a}|\cdot|\vec{b}|\sin\theta = |\vec{a}\times\vec{b}|$.

This shows that the *magnitude of the cross-product* $\vec{a}\times\vec{b}$ *geometrically represents the area of the parallelogram whose adjacent sides are of the lengths* $|\vec{a}|$ *and* $|\vec{b}|$.

In this case, we say that $\vec{a}\times\vec{b}$ *represents the vector area of the parallelogram* $ABDC$.

EXAMPLE 13. *Given* $\vec{a} = 2\vec{i}-5\vec{j}+11\vec{k}$ *and* $\vec{b} = 4\vec{i}+6\vec{j}+2\vec{k}$; *find* $\vec{a}\times\vec{b}$ *and* $|\vec{a}\times\vec{b}|$.

[C.U. B.Com. (Hons.) 1993]

SOLUTION. Given $\vec{a} = 2\vec{i}-5\vec{j}+11\vec{k}$ and $\vec{b} = 4\vec{i}+6\vec{j}+2\vec{k}$.

$$\therefore\quad \vec{a}\times\vec{b} = \begin{vmatrix}\vec{i} & \vec{j} & \vec{k}\\ 2 & -5 & 11\\ 4 & 6 & 2\end{vmatrix} = \vec{i}\begin{vmatrix}-5 & 11\\ 6 & 2\end{vmatrix} - \vec{j}\begin{vmatrix}2 & 11\\ 4 & 2\end{vmatrix} + \vec{k}\begin{vmatrix}2 & -5\\ 4 & 6\end{vmatrix}$$

$$= \vec{i}(-10-66)-\vec{j}(4-44)+\vec{k}(12+20) = -76\vec{i}+40j+32\vec{k}$$

$$\therefore\quad |\vec{a}\times\vec{b}| = \sqrt{(-76)^2+(40)^2+(32)^2} = \sqrt{5776+1600+1024} = \sqrt{8400} = \mathbf{20\sqrt{21}}.$$

EXAMPLE 14. *Find the unit vector perpendicular to each of* $\vec{\alpha} = 5\vec{i}+2\vec{j}+3\vec{k}$ *and* $\vec{\beta} = 3\vec{i}-6\vec{j}-2\vec{k}$. [C.U. 1987]

SOLUTION. By definition, $\vec{\alpha} \times \vec{\beta}$ is a vector perpendicular to both $\vec{\alpha}$ and $\vec{\beta}$, and

$$\vec{\alpha} \times \vec{\beta} = \begin{vmatrix} \vec{i} & \vec{j} & \vec{k} \\ 5 & 2 & 3 \\ 3 & -6 & -2 \end{vmatrix} = \vec{i}\begin{vmatrix} 2 & 3 \\ -6 & -2 \end{vmatrix} - \vec{j}\begin{vmatrix} 5 & 3 \\ 3 & -2 \end{vmatrix} + \vec{k}\begin{vmatrix} 5 & 2 \\ 3 & -6 \end{vmatrix}$$

$$= \vec{i}(-4+18) - \vec{j}(-10-9) + \vec{k}(-30-6) = 14\vec{i} + 19\vec{i} - 36\vec{k}.$$

$$\therefore \quad |\vec{\alpha} \times \vec{\beta}| = \sqrt{(14)^2 + (19)^2 + (-36)^2} = \sqrt{196 + 361 + 1296} = \sqrt{1853}.$$

$\therefore$ The required Unit vector is

$$\frac{\vec{\alpha} \times \vec{\beta}}{|\vec{\alpha} \times \vec{\beta}|} = \frac{14\vec{i} + 19\vec{j} - 36\vec{k}}{\sqrt{1853}} = \frac{1}{\sqrt{1853}}(14\vec{i} + 19\vec{j} - 36\vec{k}).$$

EXAMPLE 15. *For the vectors* $\vec{a}$ *and* $\vec{b}$ *where* $\vec{a} = 2\vec{i} + 3\vec{j} - 4\vec{k}$ *and* $\vec{b} = -\vec{i} + 2\vec{j} + \vec{k}$, *find the value* $|(\vec{a} + \vec{b}) \times (\vec{a} - \vec{b})|$, [C.U. B.Com. (Hons.) 1944]

SOLUTION. We have $\vec{a} + \vec{b} = (2\vec{i} + 3\vec{j} - 4\vec{k} + (-\vec{i} + 2\vec{j} + \vec{k}) = \vec{i} + 5\vec{j} - 3\vec{k}$ and
$\vec{a} - \vec{b} = 2\vec{i} + 3\vec{j} - 4\vec{k} - (-\vec{i} + 2\vec{j} + \vec{k}) = 3\vec{i} + \vec{j} - 5\vec{k}$

$$\therefore \quad (\vec{a} + \vec{b}) \times (\vec{a} - \vec{b}) = \begin{vmatrix} \vec{i} & \vec{j} & \vec{k} \\ 1 & 5 & -3 \\ 3 & 1 & -5 \end{vmatrix} = \vec{i}\begin{vmatrix} 5 & -3 \\ 1 & -5 \end{vmatrix} - \vec{j}\begin{vmatrix} 1 & -3 \\ 3 & -5 \end{vmatrix} + \vec{k}\begin{vmatrix} 1 & 5 \\ 3 & 1 \end{vmatrix}$$

$$= \vec{i}(-25+3) - \vec{j}(-5+9) + \vec{k}(1-15) = -22\vec{i} - 4\vec{j} - 14\vec{k}.$$

$$\therefore \quad |(\vec{a} + \vec{b}) \times (\vec{a} - \vec{b})| = \sqrt{(-22)^2 + (-4)^2 + (-14)^2} = \sqrt{484 + 16 + 196}$$

$$= \sqrt{696} = 2\sqrt{174}.$$

1.4. MISCELLANEOUS WORKED OUT EXAMPLES

EXAMPLE 1. *ABCD is a parallelogram. Let* $\overrightarrow{AB} = \vec{a}, \overrightarrow{AD} = \vec{d}$ (Fig. 1.20). *Express* $\overrightarrow{BC}, \overrightarrow{CD}, \overrightarrow{CA}$ *and* $\overrightarrow{BD}$ *in terms of* $\vec{a}$ *and* $\vec{d}$.

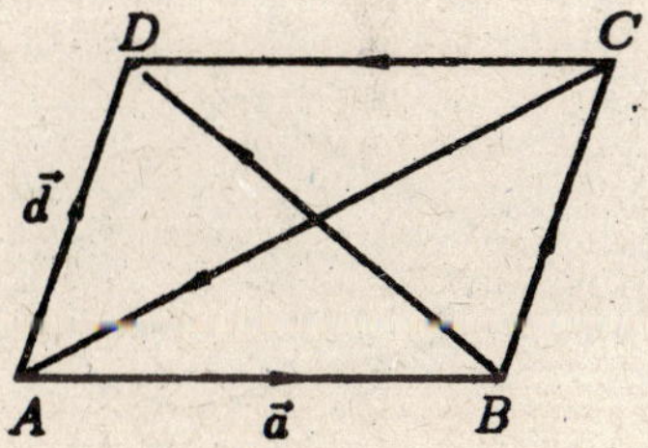

Fig 1.20

SOLUTION.

(i) BC is parallel and equal in length to AD and they are in the same sense;

$$\therefore \quad \overrightarrow{BC} = \overrightarrow{AD} = \vec{d}.$$

(ii) CD is parallel and equal in length to AB but they are in opposite sense;

$$\therefore \quad \overrightarrow{CD} = -\overrightarrow{AB} = -\vec{a}.$$

(iii) $\overrightarrow{AB} + \overrightarrow{BC} = \overrightarrow{AC}$ and $\overrightarrow{CA} = -\overrightarrow{AC}$

$$\therefore \quad \overrightarrow{CA} = -(\overrightarrow{AB} + \overrightarrow{BC}) = -(\vec{a} + \vec{d}) = -\vec{a} - \vec{d}.$$

(iv) $\overrightarrow{AB} + \overrightarrow{BD} = \overrightarrow{AD}$, and hence $\overrightarrow{BD} = \overrightarrow{AD} - \overrightarrow{AB} = \vec{d} - \vec{a}$.

EXAMPLE 2. *Show that* $|\vec{a}+\vec{b}| \le |\vec{a}| + |\vec{b}|$ *and* $|\vec{a}-\vec{b}| \ge ||\vec{a}| - |\vec{b}||$.

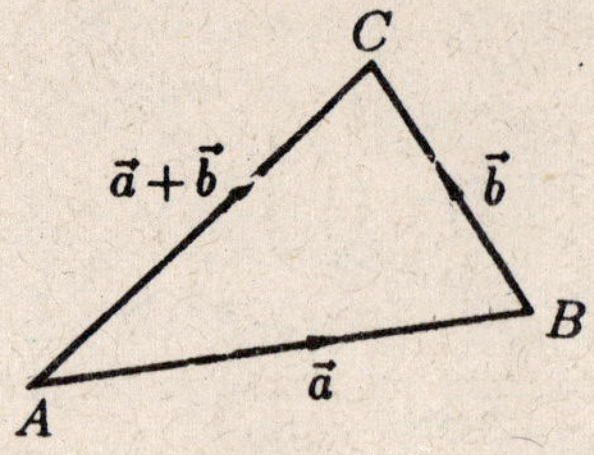

Fig 1.21

SOLUTION.

(i) In ΔABC (Fig. 1.20) let $\overrightarrow{AB} = \vec{a}, \overrightarrow{BC} = \vec{b}$.

Then $\overrightarrow{AC} = \vec{a} + \vec{b}$ (by triangle rule).

Now, from Geometry, the length of one side of a triangle $\le$ sum of the other two sides.

Hence, $|\overrightarrow{AC}| \le |\overrightarrow{AB}| + |\overrightarrow{BC}|$, or, $|\vec{a}+\vec{b}| \le |\vec{a}| + |\vec{b}|$.

(ii) We have, $|\vec{a}| = |(\vec{a}-\vec{b}) + \vec{b}| \le |\vec{a}-\vec{b}| + |\vec{b}|$, by (i)

$$\therefore \quad |\vec{a}| - |\vec{b}| \le |\vec{a}-\vec{b}|.$$

Now, if $|\vec{a}| > |\vec{b}|$, then $|\vec{a}| - |\vec{b}| = ||\vec{a}| - |\vec{b}||$ and the required result follows. If $|\vec{b}| > |\vec{a}|$ then the result can be proved by simply interchanging $\vec{a}$ and $\vec{b}$.

EXAMPLE 3. *If* $\lambda\vec{a} + \mu\vec{b} = \vec{0}$ *but not both* λ *and* μ *are zero, then* $\vec{a}$ *is parallel to* $\vec{b}$.

SOLUTION. Let us take at least $\lambda \neq 0$. Then $\vec{a} = -(\mu/\lambda)\vec{b} = m\vec{b}$ where $m = -\mu/\lambda$.

$\therefore$ $\vec{a}$ is a scalar multiple of $\vec{b}$ and, therefore, $\vec{a}$ *is parallel to* $\vec{b}$.

NOTE. If $\vec{a}$ and $\vec{b}$ are vectors and if there exist scalars λ and μ, not both zero, such that $\lambda\vec{a} + \mu\vec{b} = \vec{0}$, then we say that $\vec{a}$ and $\vec{b}$ are **linearly dependent.** On the other hand, if it so happens that whenever, a relation $\lambda\vec{a} + \mu\vec{b} = \vec{0}$ holds and λ and μ are both zero, then we say that $\vec{a}$ and $\vec{b}$ are **linearly independent.**

Thus, Example 3 can be stated as: "If $\vec{a}$ and $\vec{b}$ are linearly dependent, then $\vec{a}$ and $\vec{b}$ are parallel."

EXAMPLE 4. *If* P *is any point and* D, E, F *are the mid-points of the sides* BC, CA *and* AB *respectively of the triangle* ABC, *show that* $\overrightarrow{PA} + \overrightarrow{PB} + \overrightarrow{PC} = \overrightarrow{PD} + \overrightarrow{PE} + \overrightarrow{PF}$.

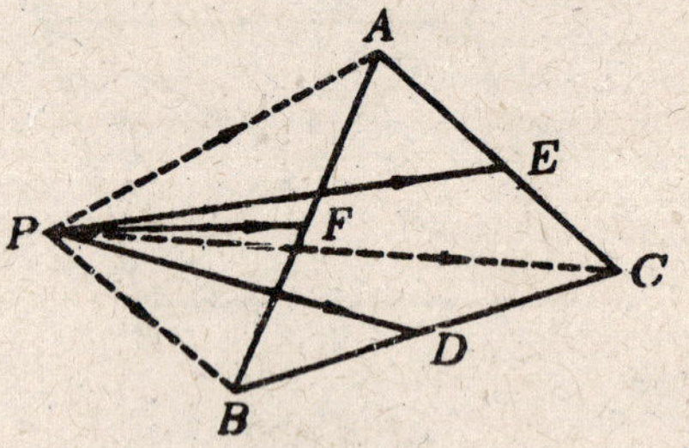

Fig 1.22

SOLUTION. $\overrightarrow{PA} = \overrightarrow{PF} + \overrightarrow{FA}, \overrightarrow{PB} = \overrightarrow{PF} + \overrightarrow{FB}$ (Fig. 1.22)

$$\therefore \quad \overrightarrow{PA} + \overrightarrow{PB} = 2\overrightarrow{PF} + (\overrightarrow{FA} + \overrightarrow{FB}) = 2\overrightarrow{PF}.$$

($\because$ $\overrightarrow{FA}$ and $\overrightarrow{FB}$ are equal and opposite vectors; hence their sum is zero).

Similarly, $\overrightarrow{PB} + \overrightarrow{PC} = 2\overrightarrow{PD}, \overrightarrow{PC} + \overrightarrow{PA} = 2\overrightarrow{PE}$.

On adding, $2(\overrightarrow{PA} + \overrightarrow{PB} + \overrightarrow{PC}) = 2(\overrightarrow{PD} + \overrightarrow{PE} + \overrightarrow{PF})$; hence the result follows.

EXAMPLE 5. *Prove that the necessary and sufficient condition that three distinct points* A, B, C, *whose position vectors are* $\vec{a}, \vec{b}$ *and* $\vec{c}$ *with reference to* O *as origin, are collinear is that there exist three scalars* α, β, γ *(not all zero) such that* $\alpha\vec{a} + \beta\vec{b} + \gamma\vec{c} = \vec{0}$ *when* $\alpha + \beta + \gamma = 0$.

SOLUTION. *To prove that the condition is necessary.*

Let A, B, C be *collinear* i.e., they lie on the same line.

We have to prove that there exist scalars α, β, γ, not all zero, such that

$$\alpha\vec{a} + \beta\vec{b} + \gamma\vec{c} = \vec{0}, \alpha + \beta + \gamma = 0.$$

Since A, B, C are three distinct points in the same line, one of them (say C) divides the join of A and B in some ratio, say $AC/CB = m/n$. Clearly, m/n is not 0 or -1.

Then, $\vec{c} = \frac{m\vec{b}+n\vec{a}}{m+n}$, or, $(m+n)\vec{c} - m\vec{b} - n\vec{a} = \vec{0}$.

Take $-n = \alpha, -m = \beta, m + n = \gamma$. Then, there exist three scalars α, β, γ, not all zero ($\because$ $m \neq 0, m + n \neq 0$), such that $\alpha\vec{a} + \beta\vec{b} + \gamma\vec{c} = \vec{0}$, where $\alpha + \beta + \gamma = (-n) + (-m) + (m + n) = 0$.

Thus, *the condition is necessary.*

Next, *to prove that the condition is sufficient.*

Let there exist three scalars α, β, γ not all zero, such that $\alpha\vec{a} + \beta\vec{b} + \gamma\vec{c} = \vec{0}$, where $\alpha + \beta + \gamma = 0$. Then, we have to prove that the three points whose position vectors are $\vec{a}, \vec{b}, \vec{c}$ are collinear i.e., lie on the same line.

Let $\gamma \neq 0$; then $\alpha + \beta = -\gamma \neq 0$.

From $\alpha\vec{a} + \beta\vec{b} + \gamma\vec{c} = \vec{0}$, we get

$$\gamma\vec{c} = -\alpha\vec{a} - \beta\vec{b}, \quad \text{or,} \quad \vec{c} = -\frac{\alpha}{\gamma}\vec{a} - \frac{\beta}{\gamma}\vec{b} = \frac{\alpha}{\alpha + \beta}\vec{a} + \frac{\beta}{\alpha + \beta}\vec{b} = \frac{\alpha\vec{a} + \beta\vec{b}}{\alpha + \beta}.$$

This shows that $\vec{c}$ divides the join of $\vec{a}$ and $\vec{b}$ in the ratio of $\beta : \alpha$, i.e., the points whose position vectors are $\vec{a}, \vec{b}, \vec{c}$ must be collinear.

Linear Combination of Vectors

A vector r is said to be a linear combination of the vectors $\vec{a}, \vec{b}, \vec{c}, \cdots$, if there exists scalars $x, y, z, \cdots$ such that

$$\vec{r} = x\vec{a} + y\vec{b} + z\vec{c} + \cdots.$$

Linear Dependent and Independent Vectors

A set of vectors $\vec{a}, \vec{b}, \vec{c}, \cdots$ is said to be linearly dependent if these exist scalars $x, y, z, \cdots$ not all zero, such that $x\vec{a} + y\vec{b} + z\vec{c} + \cdots = 0$.

A set of vectors $\vec{a}, \vec{b}, \vec{c}, \cdots$ is said to be linearly independent if $x\vec{a} + y\vec{b} + z\vec{c} + \cdots = 0$ implies that the scalars $x, y, z, \cdots$ are all zero i.e., $x = y = z = \cdots = 0$.

ILLUSTRATION. (i) We can write

$$\begin{aligned} \vec{a} &= 5\vec{i} - 2\vec{j} + 3\vec{k} = 2(\vec{i} + 2\vec{j} + 3\vec{k}) + 3(\vec{i} - 2\vec{j} - \vec{k}) \\ &= 2\vec{b} + 3\vec{c} \text{ (say)}. \end{aligned}$$

This shows that $\vec{a}$ is a linear combination of $\vec{b}$ and $\vec{c}$.

(ii) Two vectors $\vec{a} = (1, 2, 3)$ and $\vec{b} = (2, 4, 6)$ are *linearly dependent,* since $2\vec{a} - \vec{b} = \vec{0}$, where scalars 2 and -1 are *both non-zero.*

(iii) Two vectors $\vec{a} = (2,0,0), \vec{b} = (0,3,0), \vec{c} = (0,0,1)$ are *linearly independent,* because $x\vec{a} + y\vec{b} + z\vec{c} = \vec{0}$ implies $x(2,0,0) + y(0,3,0) + z(0,0,1) = \vec{0} = (0,0,0)$

or, $x = 0, y = 0$ and $z = 0$. $[\because \; 2x = 0, 3y = 0, z = 0]$.

(iv) The three vectors $\vec{\alpha} = (1,-1,1), \vec{\beta}(1,2,-1)$ and $\vec{\gamma} = (3,2,-5)$ are *linearly independent,* because $x\vec{\alpha} + y\vec{\beta} + z\vec{\gamma} = 0$ is satisfied only when $x = 0, y = 0, z = 0$ and for no other values of x, y, z.

EXAMPLE 6. *Show that the three vectors* $[1,0,0], [0,1,0]$ *and* $[0,0,1]$ *are linearly independent.*

[CA November 1992]

SOLUTION. Let $\vec{a} = [1,0,0], \vec{b} = [0,1,0]$ and $\vec{c} = [0,0,1]$.

Let x, y, z be three scalars. Then $x\vec{a} + y\vec{b} + z\vec{c} = \vec{0}$ implies that

$$x[1,0,0] + y[0,1,0] + z[0,0,1] = \vec{0} = [0,0,0]$$
$$\Rightarrow [x,y,z] = [0,0,0] \Rightarrow x = 0, y = 0, z = 0.$$

Thus $x\vec{a} + y\vec{b} + z\vec{c} = 0$ implies $x = y = z = 0$.

Hence *the three vectors* $\vec{a} = [1,0,0], \vec{b} = [0,1,0]$ *and* $\vec{c} = [0,0,1]$ *are* **linearly independent.**

EXAMPLE 7. *Prove that the three vectors* $\vec{\alpha} = (1,-2,3) \vec{\beta} = (-2,3,-4)$ *and* $\vec{r} = (0,-1,2)$ *form a linearly dependent system.* **[CA November 1991]**

SOLUTION. Let x, y, z be three scalars. Then $x\vec{\alpha} + y\vec{\beta} + z\vec{\gamma} = \vec{0}$ implies that

$$x(1,-2,3) + y(-2,3,-4) + z(0,-1,2) = \vec{0} \tag{1}$$

$$\text{or,} \quad (x - 2y, -2x + 3y - z, 3x - 4y + 2z) = (0,0,0)$$

$$\text{or,} \quad x - 2y = 0 \tag{1}$$

$$-2x + 3y - z = 0 \tag{2}$$

$$3x - 4y + 2z = 0 \tag{3}$$

From (1), $x = 2y$.

From (2), $-2 \cdot 2y + 3y - z = 0$, or, $z = -y$.

If $x = 2y, z = -y$, (3) is satisfied for any value of scalar y. If we take $y = 1$, then

$$x = 2.1 = 2, z = -1 \text{ and from (1), } 2\vec{\alpha} + 1 \cdot \vec{\beta} - 1 \cdot \vec{\gamma} = \vec{0}.$$

Thus, we can find *non-zero scalars* $x = 2, y = 1, z = -1$ such that $x\vec{\alpha} + y\vec{\beta} + z\vec{\gamma} = \vec{0}$.

Hence, $\vec{\alpha} = (1,-2,3), \vec{\beta} = (-2,3,-4)$ and $\vec{\gamma} = (0,-1,2)$ form a *linearly dependent system.*

EXAMPLE 8. *Find the angle between the two vectors* $\vec{\alpha}$ *and* $\vec{\beta}$, *where* $\vec{\alpha} = i + 2j + k$, *and* $\vec{\beta} = 7i - 4j + k$.

[ICWAI Final, December 1974]

SOLUTION. $\vec{\alpha} \cdot \vec{\beta} = (1,2,1) \cdot (7,-4,1) = 1 \times 7 + 2 \times (-4) + 1 \times 1 = 0$, i.e., $\vec{\alpha}$ and $\vec{\beta}$ are mutually at right angles; hence the angle between $\vec{\alpha}$ and $\vec{\beta}$ is $90°$.

EXAMPLE 9. *Find the cosine of the angle between* $\vec{a}$ *and* $\vec{b}$ *where* $\vec{a} = \mathbf{i} + 2\mathbf{j} - \mathbf{k}$ *and* $\vec{b} = -\mathbf{i} + \mathbf{j} - 2\mathbf{k}$.

SOLUTION.

$$\vec{a} \cdot \vec{b} = (1,2,-1) \cdot (-1,1,-2) = 1 \times (-1) + 2 \times 1 + (-1) \times (-2) = 3$$
$$|\vec{a}| = \sqrt{1^2 + 2^2 + (-1)^2} = \sqrt{6},$$
$$|\vec{b}| = \sqrt{(-1)^2 + 1^2 + (-2)^2} = \sqrt{6}.$$

We know that $\vec{a}\cdot\vec{b}=|\vec{a}||\vec{b}|\cos\theta$. $\therefore$ $\cos\theta=\dfrac{\vec{a}\cdot\vec{b}}{|\vec{a}||\vec{b}|}=\dfrac{3}{\sqrt{6}\cdot\sqrt{6}}=\dfrac{1}{2}$.

In fact, the angle between $\vec{a}$ and $\vec{b}$ is 60° $\left(\because \quad \cos 60^\circ=\frac{1}{2}\right)$.

EXAMPLE 10. *Under what condition we may write* $(\vec{a}\cdot\vec{b})^2=\vec{a}^{\,2}\vec{b}^{\,2}$?

SOLUTION. $(\vec{a}\cdot\vec{b})^2=\{|\vec{a}||\vec{b}|\cos\theta\}^2=|\vec{a}|^2|\vec{b}|^2\cos^2\theta=\vec{a}^{\,2}\vec{b}^{\,2}\cos^2\theta$

($\because$ square of a vector = square of its length)

$\therefore$ $(\vec{a}\cdot\vec{b})^2=\vec{a}^{\,2}\vec{b}^{\,2}$ is possible only when $\cos^2\theta=1$, i.e., when $\theta=0$, or, π

($\because$ $\cos 0=1, \cos\pi=-1$), i.e., *when* $\vec{a}$ *and* $\vec{b}$ *are parallel.*

EXAMPLE 11. *If* $\vec{a}\cdot\vec{e}_1=\vec{a}\cdot\vec{e}_2=\vec{a}\cdot\vec{e}_3=0$, *where* $\vec{e}_1,\vec{e}_2,\vec{e}_3$ *are three non-coplanar unit vectors, then* $\vec{a}=\vec{0}$.

SOLUTION. $\vec{a}\cdot\vec{e}_1=0\Rightarrow\vec{a}$ is perpendicular to $\vec{e}_1$; $\vec{a}\cdot\vec{e}_2=0\Rightarrow\vec{a}$ is perpendicular to $\vec{e}_2$.

$\therefore$ $\vec{a}$ is perpendicular to both $\vec{e}_1$ and $\vec{e}_2$, i.e., $\vec{a}$ is perpendicular to the plane in which $\vec{e}_1$ and $\vec{e}_2$ lie.

$\vec{e}_3$ does not lie in the plane of $\vec{e}_1$ and $\vec{e}_2$ (by hypothesis).

So $\vec{a}\cdot\vec{e}_3=0$ (which implies that $\vec{a}$ is perpendicular to $\vec{e}_3$, but here it is not possible) will lead to only one conclusion, viz., $\vec{a}=\vec{0}$.

EXAMPLE 12. *For the vectors* $\vec{a}=5\mathbf{i}-3\mathbf{j}+4\mathbf{k}$ *and* $\vec{b}=\mathbf{j}-\mathbf{k}$, *determine*

(i) $\vec{a}\times\vec{b}$; (ii) *the sine of the angle between* $\vec{a}$ *and* $\vec{b}$.

SOLUTION.

(i) We have $\vec{a}=5\vec{i}-3\vec{j}+4\vec{k}$ and $\vec{b}=\vec{j}-\vec{k}=0\cdot\vec{i}+1\cdot j-1k$

$$\therefore\quad \vec{a}\times\vec{b}=\begin{vmatrix} i & \mathbf{j} & \mathbf{k}\\ 5 & -3 & 4\\ 0 & 1 & -1\end{vmatrix}=\mathbf{i}\begin{vmatrix}-3 & 4\\ 1 & -1\end{vmatrix}+\mathbf{j}\begin{vmatrix}4 & 5\\ -1 & 0\end{vmatrix}+\mathbf{k}\begin{vmatrix}5 & -3\\ 0 & 1\end{vmatrix}=-\mathbf{i}+5\mathbf{j}+5\mathbf{k}.$$

(ii) We have $|\vec{a}\times\vec{b}|=|\vec{a}|\cdot|\vec{b}|\cdot\sin\theta$.

$$\text{Now}\quad |a\times\vec{b}|=\sqrt{(-1)^2+5^2+5^2}=\sqrt{51};$$

$$|\vec{a}|=\sqrt{5^2+(-3)^2+4^2}=\sqrt{50}; |\vec{b}|=\sqrt{0^2+(1)^2+(-1)^2}=\sqrt{2}.$$

$$\therefore\quad \sin\theta=\frac{|\vec{a}\times\vec{b}|}{|\vec{a}||\vec{b}|}=\frac{\sqrt{51}}{\sqrt{50}\cdot\sqrt{2}}=\frac{\mathbf{1}}{\mathbf{10}}\sqrt{\mathbf{51}}.$$

EXAMPLE 13. *Find the area of a triangle whose vertices are at* $A(0,0,0), B(1,1,1), C(0,2,3)$.

SOLUTION. Given:

position vector of $A=0\mathbf{i}+0\mathbf{j}+0\mathbf{k}=(0,0,0)$,

position vector of $B=1\mathbf{i}+1\mathbf{j}+1\mathbf{k}=(1,1,1)$,

and, position vector of $C=0\mathbf{i}+2\mathbf{j}+3\mathbf{k}=(0,2,3)$.

$\therefore$ $\overrightarrow{AB}$ = position vector of B-position vector of $A=(1,1,1)-(0,0,0)=(1,1,1)$.

$\overrightarrow{AC}$ = position vector of C-position vector of $A=(0,2,3)-(0,0,0)=(0,2,3)$.

Area of the triangle $ABC=\frac{1}{2}|\overrightarrow{AB}\times\overrightarrow{AC}|$.

But $\overrightarrow{AB} \times \overrightarrow{AC} = \begin{vmatrix} \mathbf{i} & \mathbf{j} & \mathbf{k} \\ 1 & 1 & 1 \\ 0 & 2 & 3 \end{vmatrix} = \mathbf{i} - 3\mathbf{j} + 2\mathbf{k}.$

$\therefore$ Area of the triangle $= \frac{1}{2}\sqrt{(1)^2 + (-3)^2 + 2^2} = \frac{1}{2}\sqrt{14}$ sq. units.

EXAMPLE 14. *Prove that* (i) $(\vec{a} \cdot \vec{b})^2 + (\vec{a} \times \vec{b})^2 = a^2b^2$; (ii) $(\vec{a} \cdot \vec{b})^2 - (\vec{a} \times \vec{b})^2 = a^2b^2 \cos 2\theta$, *here* $|\vec{a}| = a, |\vec{b}| = b$ *and* θ *is the angle between* $\vec{a}$ *and* $\vec{b}$.

SOLUTION. We have

$$(\vec{a} \cdot \vec{b})^2 = (|\vec{a}| \cdot |\vec{b}| \cos \theta)^2 = \vec{a}^{\,2} \vec{b}^{\,2} \cos^2 \theta = a^2b^2 \cos^2 \theta$$

and $$(\vec{a} \times \vec{b})^2 = |\vec{a} \times \vec{b}|^2 = (|\vec{a}| \cdot |\vec{b}| \sin \theta)^2 = \vec{a}^{\,2} \vec{b}^{\,2} \sin^2 \theta = a^2b^2 \sin^2 \theta.$$

(i) $(\vec{a} \cdot \vec{b})^2 + (\vec{a} \times \vec{b})^2 = a^2b^2 \cos^2 \theta + a^2b^2 \sin^2 \theta = a^2b^2.$

(ii) $(\vec{a} \cdot \vec{b})^2 - (\vec{a} \times \vec{b})^2 = a^2b^2 \cos^2 \theta - a^2b^2 \sin^2 \theta = a^2b^2 \cos 2\theta.$

(We know that $\cos^2 \theta - \sin^2 \theta = \cos 2\theta; \cos^2 \theta + \sin^2 \theta = 1$).

EXAMPLE 15. *Prove that an angle in a semicircle is a right angle.*

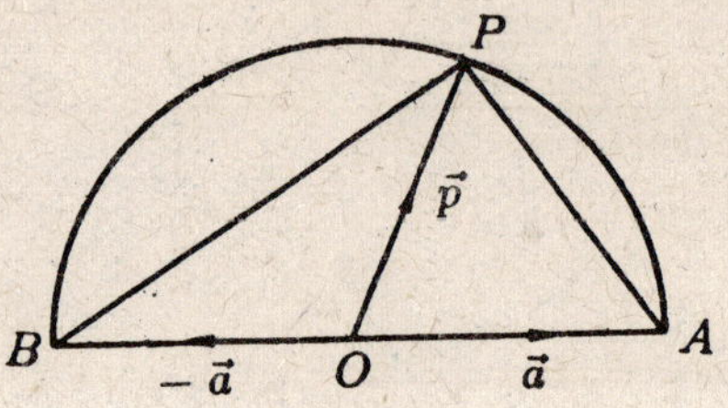

Fig 1.23

SOLUTION. Let us take the centre O of the circle as origin (Fig. 1.23). Let $\overrightarrow{OA} = \vec{a}$. Then $\overrightarrow{OB} = -\vec{a}$. AB is the diameter and P is any point on the semicircle. Let $\overrightarrow{OP} = \vec{p}$. Then

$|\vec{p}| = |\vec{a}| =$ radius of the circle $= r$ (say).

$\overrightarrow{AP} =$ position vector of $P-$position vector of A $= \vec{p} - \vec{a}$.

$\overrightarrow{BP} =$ position vector of $P-$position vector of B $= \vec{p} + \vec{a}$.

See that $\overrightarrow{AP} \cdot \overrightarrow{BP} = (\vec{p} - \vec{a}) \cdot (\vec{p} + \vec{a}) = \vec{p}^{\,2} - \vec{a}^{\,2} = |\vec{p}|^2 - |\vec{a}|^2 = r^2 - r^2 = 0.$

$\therefore$ $\overrightarrow{AP}$ is perpendicular to $\overrightarrow{BP}$, proving the desired result.

EXAMPLE 16. *Show, by vector method, that the three altitudes of a triangle are concurrent.*

SOLUTION. With reference to a origin O let the position vectors of the vertices A, B, C of the triangle ABC be $\vec{a}, \vec{b}, \vec{c}$ respectively (Fig. 1.24). Let Let the perpendicular BY from B to CA intersect the perpendicular AX from A to BC at the point H (position vector $\vec{h}$).

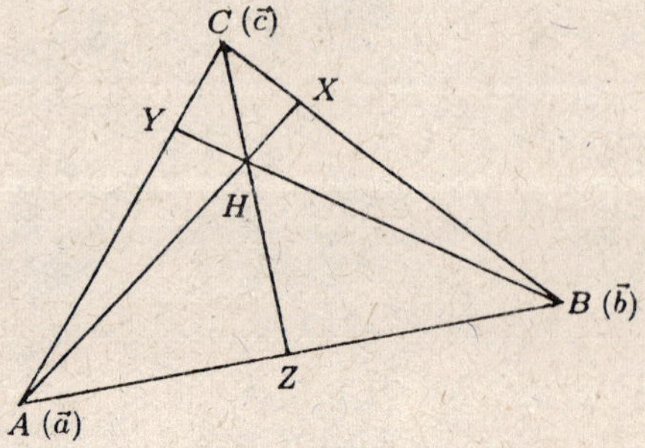

Fig 1.24

Then $\overrightarrow{AH} = \vec{h} - \vec{a}, \overrightarrow{BH} = \vec{h} - \vec{b}$ and $\overrightarrow{CH} = \vec{h} - \vec{c}$.

Since AX, i.e., AH is perpendicular to BC and BY is perpendicular to AC;

$$(\vec{b} - \vec{c}) \cdot (\vec{h} - \vec{a}) = 0$$

and $$(\vec{c} - a) \cdot (\vec{h} - \vec{b}) = 0$$

or, $$\vec{b} \cdot \vec{h} - \vec{b} \cdot \vec{a} - \vec{c} \cdot \vec{h} + \vec{c} \cdot \vec{a} = 0 \tag{1}$$

and $$\vec{c} \cdot \vec{h} - \vec{c} \cdot \vec{b} - \vec{a} \cdot \vec{h} + \vec{a} \cdot \vec{b} = 0 \tag{2}$$

Adding (1) and (2), we get, $\vec{b}\cdot\vec{h}+\vec{c}\cdot\vec{a}-\vec{c}\cdot\vec{b}-\vec{a}\cdot\vec{h}=0$.

or, $(\vec{b}-\vec{a})\cdot\vec{h}-(\vec{b}-\vec{a})\cdot\vec{c}=0$, or, $(\vec{b}-\vec{a})\cdot(\vec{h}-\vec{c})=0$, i.e., $\overrightarrow{CH}$ is perpendicular to $\overrightarrow{AB}$. Hence, *the three perpendiculars meet at H,* i.e., *they are concurrent at H.*

EXAMPLE 17. *Prove that* $(\vec{a}\times\vec{b})^2=\vec{a}^{\,2}\vec{b}^{\,2}-(\vec{a}\cdot\vec{b})^2$.

SOLUTION.

$$\begin{aligned}(\vec{a}\times\vec{b})^2 &= |\vec{a}\times\vec{b}|^2=|\vec{a}|^2|\vec{b}|^2\sin^2\theta\\ &= |\vec{a}|^2|\vec{b}|^2(1-\cos^2\theta),\ \text{where }\theta\text{ is the angle between }\vec{a}\text{ and }\vec{b}.\\ &= |\vec{a}|^2|\vec{b}|^2-|\vec{a}|^2|\vec{b}|^2\cos^2\theta=\vec{a}^{\,2}\vec{b}^{\,2}-(\vec{a}\cdot\vec{b})^2.\quad [\because\ |\vec{a}||\vec{b}|\cos\theta=\vec{a}\cdot\vec{b}.]\end{aligned}$$

EXAMPLE 18. *If* $\vec{a}=3\mathbf{i}+4\mathbf{j}+\mathbf{k}$ *and* $\vec{b}=2\mathbf{i}-\mathbf{j}+4\mathbf{k}$, *compute* $(2\vec{a}+3\vec{b})\cdot(\vec{a}-\vec{b})$.

[C.U. B.Com. (Hons.) 1992]

SOLUTION. We have

$$\begin{aligned}2\vec{a}+3\vec{b} &= 2(3\mathbf{i}+4\mathbf{j}+\mathbf{k})+3(2\mathbf{i}-\mathbf{j}+4\mathbf{k})=12\mathbf{i}+5\mathbf{j}+14\mathbf{k}\\ \text{and}\quad \vec{a}-\vec{b} &= (3\mathbf{i}+4\mathbf{j}+\mathbf{k})-(2\mathbf{i}-\mathbf{j}+4\mathbf{k})=\mathbf{i}+5\mathbf{j}-3\mathbf{k}\\ \therefore\quad (2\vec{a}+3\vec{b})\cdot(\vec{a}-\vec{b}) &= (12\mathbf{i}+5\mathbf{j}+14\mathbf{k})\cdot(\mathbf{i}+5\mathbf{j}-3k)\\ &= 12\times1+5\cdot(5)+14\cdot(-3)=-5.\end{aligned}$$

EXAMPLE 19. *Find a vector* α *which is perpendicular to both* $4\mathbf{i}+5\mathbf{j}-\mathbf{k}$ *and* $\mathbf{i}-4\mathbf{j}+5\mathbf{k}$ *and which satisfies the relation* $\alpha\cdot\beta=21$ *where* $\beta=3\mathbf{i}+\mathbf{j}-\mathbf{k}$. **[C.U. B.Com. (Hons.) 1991]**

SOLUTION. The required vector is perpendicular to both $\vec{a}=4\mathbf{i}+5\mathbf{j}-\mathbf{k}$ and $\vec{b}=\mathbf{i}-4\mathbf{j}+5\mathbf{k}$ and hence, parallel to their cross product $\vec{a}\times\vec{b}$.

$$\text{Now,}\quad \vec{a}\times\vec{b}=\begin{vmatrix}\mathbf{i}&\mathbf{j}&\mathbf{k}\\4&5&-1\\1&-4&5\end{vmatrix}=\mathbf{i}(25-4)-\mathbf{j}(20+1)+\mathbf{k}(-16-5)$$
$$=21\mathbf{i}-21\mathbf{j}-21\mathbf{k}=21(\mathbf{i}-\mathbf{j}-\mathbf{k}).$$

Since the required vector α is parallel to $21(i-j-k)$, we can take $\alpha=\lambda(21)(\mathbf{i}-\mathbf{j}-\mathbf{k})$, where λ is a scalar. But $\alpha\cdot\beta=21$ (given);

$$\begin{aligned}\therefore\quad & \lambda(21)(\mathbf{i}-\mathbf{j}-\mathbf{k})\cdot(3\mathbf{i}+\mathbf{j}-\mathbf{k})=21,\\ \text{or,}\quad & 21\lambda(3-1+1)=21,\quad [\because\ \mathbf{i}^2=\mathbf{j}^2=\mathbf{k}^2=1, \mathbf{i}\cdot\mathbf{j}=\mathbf{j}\cdot\mathbf{i}=0,\ \text{etc.}]\\ \text{or,}\quad & 3\lambda=1,\ \text{or, } \lambda=\frac{1}{3}\\ \text{Hence}\quad & \alpha=\frac{1}{3}\cdot21(\mathbf{i}-\mathbf{j}-\mathbf{k})=7(\mathbf{i}-\mathbf{j}-\mathbf{k})\end{aligned}$$

Exercise 1

[Vector Algebra]

THEORY

[A]

1. (a) Define a vector. What is the Triangle Law of addition of two vectors? Deduce the parallelogram Rule.

(b) Define a vector from the geometric concept. [C.U. B.Com. (Hons.) 1982]

2. Define a null vector and a unit vector. What do you mean by position vector of a point? Express the vector $\overrightarrow{AB}$ in terms of the position vectors $\vec{a}$ and $\vec{b}$ of the points A and B. What is the unit vector in the direction of $\vec{i}+\vec{j}$? Write down the value of $\overrightarrow{AB}+\overrightarrow{BA}$.

3. If the position vectors of three points be denoted by $\vec{\alpha}, \vec{\beta}, \vec{\gamma}$, show that the necessary and sufficient condition that the points be collinear is that there exists a linear relation $p\vec{\alpha}+q\vec{\beta}+r\vec{\gamma}=\vec{0}$ in which p, q, r are numbers, not all zero, which satisfy $p+q+r=0$.

4. Define dot product of two vectors and show that it satsifies the distributive law (i.e., $\vec{\alpha}\cdot(\vec{\beta}+\vec{\gamma})=\vec{\alpha}\cdot\vec{\beta}+\vec{\alpha}\cdot\vec{\gamma}$).

5. Show that a vector $\vec{a}$ in a plane can be expressed in the form $\vec{a}=x\vec{i}+y\vec{j}$ where $\vec{i},\vec{j}$ are unit vectors along two rectangular axes.

6. Express a vector $\vec{r}$ in three-dimensional space in the form $\vec{r}=x\vec{i}+y\vec{j}+z\vec{k}$ where $\vec{i},\vec{j},\vec{k}$ are unit vectors in three mutually perpendicular directions.

7. Define cross product of two vectors. How does the cross product behave regarding the commutative law? Give geometric interpretation of $\vec{\alpha}\times\vec{\beta}$.

8. With reference to an orthogonal system of axes, show that

$$\vec{\alpha}\times\vec{\beta}=(a_2b_3-a_3b_2)\vec{i}+(a_3b_1-a_1b_3)\vec{j}+(a_1b_2-a_2b_1)\vec{k}$$

where $\vec{i},\vec{j},\vec{k}$ are **unit vectors** in the positive directions of the axes, and $\vec{\alpha}=a_1\vec{i}+a_2\vec{j}+a_3\vec{k}$ and $\vec{\beta}=b_1\vec{i}+b_2\vec{j}+b_3\vec{k}$.

9. Define scalar and vector products of two vectors. State their geometric significance. State the distributive law for vector products.

Given: $\vec{a}=2\mathbf{i}-3\mathbf{j}+\mathbf{k}, \vec{b}=\mathbf{i}+2\mathbf{j}+3\mathbf{k}$ and $\vec{c}=-3\mathbf{i}+\mathbf{j}-2\mathbf{k}$. Verify that the distributive law holds good in this case.

[Verification:

$$\vec{b}+\vec{c}=-2\mathbf{i}+3\mathbf{j}+\mathbf{k}$$

$$\therefore\quad \vec{a}\times(\vec{b}+\vec{c})=\begin{vmatrix} i & \mathbf{j} & \mathbf{k} \\ 2 & -3 & 1 \\ -2 & 3 & 1 \end{vmatrix}=-6\mathbf{i}-4\mathbf{j}+0\mathbf{k}$$

$$\text{Again}\quad \vec{a}\times\vec{b}=\begin{vmatrix} \mathbf{i} & \mathbf{j} & \mathbf{k} \\ 2 & -3 & 1 \\ 1 & 2 & 3 \end{vmatrix}=-11\mathbf{i}-5\mathbf{j}+7\mathbf{k}$$

$$\text{and} \quad \vec{a} \times \vec{c} = \begin{vmatrix} i & \mathbf{j} & \mathbf{k} \\ 2 & -3 & 1 \\ -3 & 1 & -2 \end{vmatrix} = 5\mathbf{i} + \mathbf{j} - 7\mathbf{k}.$$

$$\therefore \quad \vec{a} \times \vec{b} + \vec{a} \times \vec{c} = (-11\mathbf{i} - 5\mathbf{j} + 7\mathbf{k}) + (5\mathbf{i} + \mathbf{j} - 7\mathbf{k}) = -6\mathbf{i} - 4\mathbf{j} + 0\mathbf{k} = \vec{a} \times (\vec{b} + \vec{c})$$

Hence $\vec{\mathbf{a}} \times (\vec{\mathbf{b}} + \vec{\mathbf{c}}) = \vec{\mathbf{a}} \times \vec{\mathbf{b}} + \vec{\mathbf{a}} \times \vec{\mathbf{c}}$.]

10. (i) Let $\vec{v}$ be any vector. How do you express unit vector along $\vec{v}$?

(ii) A vector of length 4 has the direction of a unit vector $\vec{u}$. Express the vector in terms of $\vec{u}$.

PROBLEMS

[B]

1. On a plain paper draw a vector $\vec{a}$. Then indicate the vectors: $-\vec{a}, 2\vec{a}, -\frac{1}{2}\vec{a}, \frac{1}{2}\vec{a}$.

2. If A, B, C are three points, not in the same straight line, express $\overrightarrow{BC}$ in terms of $\overrightarrow{AB}$ and $\overrightarrow{AC}$. Which vector is $\overrightarrow{BA} - \overrightarrow{BC}$?

3. If the position vectors of three points A, B, C are $\vec{a}, \vec{a} + \vec{b}, 3\vec{a} - \vec{b}$, express $\overrightarrow{AB}, \overrightarrow{BC}$ and $\overrightarrow{AC}$ in terms of $\vec{a}$ and $\vec{b}$.

4. A and B are two points. The position vector of the point A is $6\vec{a} - 2\vec{b}$. A point P divides the line AB in the ratio 1 : 2. If $\vec{a} - \vec{b}$ is the position vector of P, then find the position vector of B.

5. $ABCDEF$ is a regular hexagon (each side of length 5 units). Let $\overrightarrow{AB} = \vec{a}, \overrightarrow{BC} = \vec{b}$, find in terms of $\vec{a}$ and $\vec{b}$ the following:

(i) $\overrightarrow{AC}$, (ii) $\overrightarrow{AD}$, (iii) $\overrightarrow{CD}$,

(iv) $\overrightarrow{DE}$, (v) $\overrightarrow{EF}$, (vi) $\overrightarrow{FA}$,

(vii) $\overrightarrow{DA}$, (viii) $\overrightarrow{EB}$. (See Fig. 1.25)

[HINTS. $\overrightarrow{AB} + \overrightarrow{BC} + \overrightarrow{CD} = \overrightarrow{AD} = 2\vec{b}$]

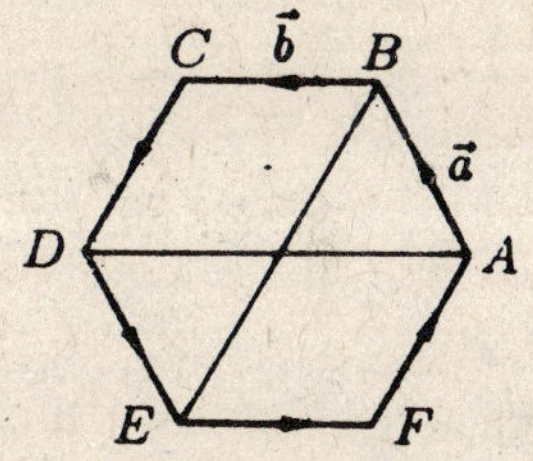

Fig 1.25

6. Show by vector method, that the medians of a triangle are concurrent at a point which trisects each of them.

7. Find the position vectors of the points which divide internally and externally in the ratio 2 : 3 the join of the points $2\vec{a} - 3\vec{b}$ and $3\vec{a} - 2\vec{b}$.

8. Show that the sum of the three vectors determined by the medians of a triangle, directed from the vertices is zero.

9. Show that the points, whose position vectors are $\vec{i} - 2\vec{j} + 3\vec{k}, 2\vec{i} - 3\vec{j} + 4\vec{k}$ and $-2\vec{i} + \vec{j}$ are collinear.

[HINTS. Referred to a origin O let A, B, C be the three points whose position vectors are given. Then $OA = \vec{i} - 2\vec{j} + 3\vec{k}, \overrightarrow{OB} = 2\vec{i} - 3\vec{j} + 4\vec{k}$ and $\overrightarrow{OC} = -2\vec{i} + \vec{j}$ and $\overrightarrow{AB} = \overrightarrow{OB} - \overrightarrow{OA} = \vec{i} - \vec{j} + \vec{k}, \overrightarrow{AC} = \overrightarrow{OC} - \overrightarrow{OA} = -3(i - j + \vec{k}) = -3\overrightarrow{AB}$. We see that AB is parallel to AC and A is the common point of AB and AC. Hence etc.]

10. Show that the vectors $2\vec{i} - \vec{j} + \vec{k}, \vec{i} - 3\vec{j} - 5\vec{k}$ and $3\vec{i} - 4\vec{j} - 4\vec{k}$ are coplanar.

[HINTS. For $\vec{a} = 2\vec{i} - \vec{j} + \vec{k}, \vec{b} = \vec{i} - 3\vec{j} - 5\vec{k}$ and $\vec{c} = 3\vec{i} - 4\vec{j} - 4\vec{k}$ to be *coplanar,* we have to find two scalars x and y such that $\vec{a} = x\vec{b} + y\vec{c} \cdots\cdots (1)$

From (1), $2\vec{i} - \vec{j} + \vec{k} = x(\vec{i} - 3\vec{j} - 5\vec{k}) + y(3\vec{i} - 4\vec{j} - 4\vec{k})$.

Equating coefficients of $\vec{i}, \vec{j}, \vec{k}$, we get

$$x + 3y = 2 \qquad (2)$$
$$-3x - 4y = -1$$
$$\text{or,} \quad 3x + 4y = 1 \qquad (3)$$
$$-5x - 4y = 1 \qquad (4)$$

Solving (3) and (4), $x = -1, y = 1$ which satisfy (2). Hence etc.]

11. Show that the middle points of the sides of a quadrilateral form the vertices of a parallelogram.

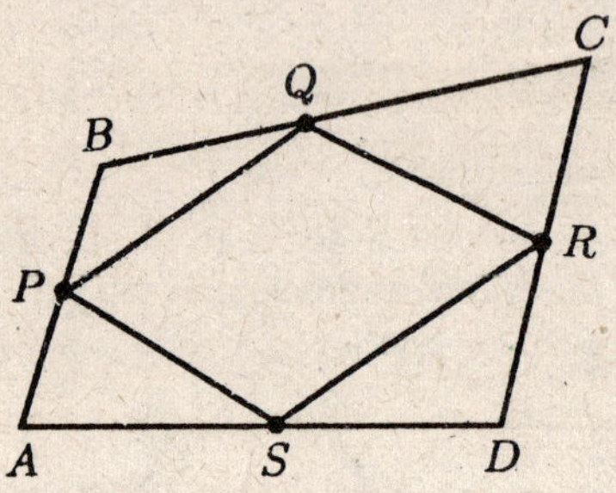

Fig 1.26

[SOLUTION. See Fig. 1.26

Let P, Q, R, S be the respective middle points of the sides AB, BC, CD, DA of the quadrilateral $ABCD$.

Let $\overrightarrow{AB} = \vec{a}, \overrightarrow{BC} = \vec{b}, \overrightarrow{CD} = \vec{c}$ and $\overrightarrow{DA} = \vec{d}$. Then $\overrightarrow{PB} = \frac{1}{2}\vec{a}$ and $\overrightarrow{BQ} = \frac{1}{2}\vec{b}$. Therefore, $\overrightarrow{PQ} = \frac{1}{2}(\vec{a} + \vec{b})$.

Similarly,

$$\overrightarrow{QR} = \tfrac{1}{2}(\vec{b} + \vec{c}), \overrightarrow{RS} = \tfrac{1}{2}(\vec{c} + \vec{d}), \overrightarrow{SP} = \tfrac{1}{2}(\vec{d} + \vec{a}).$$

But $\overrightarrow{AB} + \overrightarrow{BC} + \overrightarrow{CD} + \overrightarrow{DA} = \vec{0}$, i.e., $\vec{a} + \vec{b} + \vec{c} + \vec{d} = \vec{0}$.

Then, $\overrightarrow{PQ} = \frac{1}{2}(\vec{a}+\vec{b}) = -\frac{1}{2}(\vec{c}+\vec{d}) = -\overrightarrow{RS} = \overrightarrow{SR}$ and $\overrightarrow{QR} = \frac{1}{2}(\vec{b}+\vec{c}) = -\frac{1}{2}(\vec{a}+\vec{d}) = -\overrightarrow{SP} = \overrightarrow{PS}$

Thus, the opposite sides of the quadrilateral $PQRS$ are equal and parallel and hence it is a parallelogram.]

12. From the centre of a regular pentagon draw vectors to the vertices. Prove that the sum of these vectors is zero.

13. Show that three vectors α, β, γ given by $\alpha = \vec{b} + \vec{c} - 2\vec{a}, \beta = \vec{c} + \vec{a} - 2\vec{b}, \gamma = \vec{a} + \vec{b} - 2\vec{c}$ are linearly dependent.

[HINTS. See that $\alpha + \beta + \gamma = \vec{0}$; hence etc.]

14. If $ABCD$ is a parallelogram and P is the point of intersection of its diagonals. O is any point. Show that $\overrightarrow{OA} + \overrightarrow{OB} + \overrightarrow{OC} + \overrightarrow{OD} = 4\overrightarrow{OP}$.

15. Find the unit vector in the direction of the vector $\vec{a} - \vec{b}$ where $\vec{a} = \vec{i} + 3\vec{j} - \vec{k}$ and $\vec{b} = 3\vec{i} + 2\vec{j} + \vec{k}$.

16. Find the magnitudes of $\vec{a} + \vec{b}$ and $\vec{a} - \vec{b}$ where $\vec{a} = 3\vec{i} + 4\vec{j} + 5\vec{k}$ and $\vec{b} = \vec{i} + 2\vec{j} + 3\vec{k}$.

[C.U. B.Com. (Hons.) 1988]

[C]

1. Let $\vec{a} = 2\mathbf{i} - 3\mathbf{j} + 4\mathbf{k}, \vec{b} = \mathbf{i} + 2\mathbf{j} + \mathbf{k}$.

Find (i) $\vec{a} + 2\vec{b}$; (ii) $3\vec{a} - 2\vec{b}$; (iii) $|2\vec{a} + \vec{b}|$ (iv) Unit vector along $2\vec{a} + \vec{b}$.

2. For the vectors $\vec{a}$ and $\vec{b}$ where $\vec{a} = 2\vec{i} + 3\vec{j} - 4\vec{k}$ and $\vec{b} = -\vec{i} + 2\vec{j} + \vec{k}$, find $|\vec{a} + \vec{b}|$, $\vec{a} \cdot \vec{b}$ and the angle between $\vec{a}$ and $\vec{b}$. **[C.U. B.Com. (Hons.) 1984]**

3. If $\vec{a} = 2\mathbf{i} - 3\mathbf{j} + 4\mathbf{k}, \vec{b} = 2\mathbf{j} + 4\mathbf{k}$, find the scalar component of $\vec{a}$ along $\vec{b}$.

[HINTS. Scalar component of $\vec{a}$ along $\vec{b} = \vec{a}$. (unit vector along $\vec{b}$)

$$= (2\mathbf{i} - 3\mathbf{j} + 4\mathbf{k}) \cdot \frac{1}{\sqrt{20}}(2\mathbf{j} + 4\mathbf{k}) = \frac{10}{\sqrt{20}} = \frac{10\sqrt{20}}{20} = \sqrt{5}.]$$

4. Find the cosine of the angle between the vectors $\vec{a} = 2\mathbf{i} - 8\mathbf{j} + 3\mathbf{k}$ and $\vec{b} = 4\mathbf{j} + 3\mathbf{k}$.

5. If $\vec{a} = 3\vec{\mathbf{i}} + 4\vec{\mathbf{j}} + \vec{\mathbf{k}}$ and $\vec{b} = 2\vec{i} - \vec{j} + 4\vec{k}$, compute $(2\vec{a} + 3\vec{b}) \cdot (\vec{a} - \vec{b})$ **[C.U. B.Com. (Hons.) 1992]**

6. $\vec{a} = 2\mathbf{i} + 4\mathbf{j} - 7\mathbf{k}, \vec{b} = 2\mathbf{i} + 6\mathbf{j} + x\mathbf{k}$ (x is a scalar). Find x so that $\vec{a}$ and $\vec{b}$ are perpendicular.

[HINTS. $\vec{a} \cdot \vec{b} = 0$ gives $28 - 7x = 0$, whence $x = 4$]

7. When is $\vec{a} + \vec{b}$ perpendicular to $\vec{a} - \vec{b}$? When are they parallel?

8. Two vectors $\vec{a}$ and $\vec{b}$ are such that $(\vec{a} + \vec{b}) \cdot (\vec{a} - \vec{b}) = 0$. Show that $|\vec{a}| = |\vec{b}|$.

9. If $\vec{a}$ and $\vec{b}$ are two vectors such that $|\vec{a}| = 4, |\vec{b}| = 3$ and $\vec{a} \cdot \vec{b} = 6$, find the angle between $\vec{a}$ and $\vec{b}$.

10. If $\vec{a} \cdot \vec{b} = \vec{a} \cdot \vec{c}$, then prove that either $\vec{a} = \vec{0}$, or $\vec{b} = \vec{c}$, or $\vec{a}$ is perpendicular to $\vec{b} - \vec{c}$.

[HINTS. See that $\vec{a} \cdot \vec{b} = \vec{a} \cdot \vec{c} \Rightarrow \vec{a} \cdot (\vec{b} - \vec{c}) = 0$.]

11. If $\vec{a}$ and $\vec{b}$ be two vectors perpendicular to each other, prove that $(\vec{a} + \vec{b})^2 = (\vec{a} - \vec{b})^2$.

12. (i) For the vectors $\vec{a}$ and $\vec{b}$ where $\vec{a} = 2\mathbf{i} + 5\mathbf{j} + 3\mathbf{k}$ and $\vec{b} = \mathbf{i} - 2\mathbf{j} - 4\mathbf{k}$, find $\vec{a} \cdot \vec{b}$ and $|3\vec{a} + 2\vec{b}|$. **[C.U. B.Com. (Hons.) 1985]**

(ii) If $\vec{a} = 2i + j - k, \vec{b} = i + j + 3k$, show that $\vec{a}$ is perpendicular to $\vec{b}$. Find also the value of $|\vec{a} + \vec{b}|$. **[C.U. B.Com. (Hons.) 1990]**

13. Show by vector method that the diagonals of a rhombus intersect at right angles.

[HINTS. Let $ABCD$ be the *rhombus* such that $\overrightarrow{AB} = \vec{a}$ and $\overrightarrow{BC} = \vec{b}$. Then $\overrightarrow{DC} = \overrightarrow{AB} = \vec{a}, \overrightarrow{AD} = \overrightarrow{BC} = \vec{b}$. Also $AB = BC = CD = AD$.

$\therefore \quad |\vec{a}| = |\vec{b}|, \overrightarrow{AC} = \vec{a} + \vec{b}$ and $\overrightarrow{BD} = \vec{b} - \vec{a}$.

Now $\overrightarrow{AC} \cdot \overrightarrow{BD} = (\vec{a} + \vec{b}) \cdot (\vec{b} - \vec{a}) = \vec{b}^2 - \vec{a}^2 = |\vec{b}|^2 - |\vec{a}|^2 = 0$. Hence etc.]

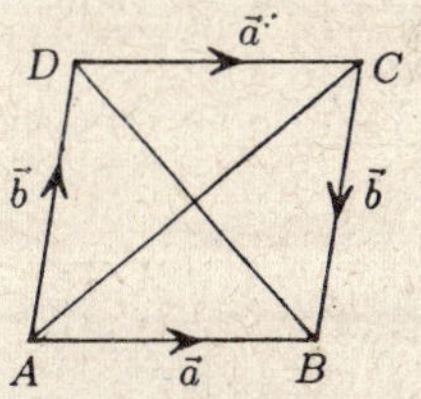

Fig 1.27

14. If $\vec{a} + 2\vec{b}$ and $5\vec{a} - 4\vec{b}$ are perpendicular where $\vec{a}$ and $\vec{b}$ are unit vectors, then find the angle between $\vec{a}$ and $\vec{b}$.

[HINTS. $(\vec{a} + 2\vec{b}) \cdot (5\vec{a} - 4\vec{b}) = 0, |\vec{a}| = 1, |\vec{b}| = 1$; find $\vec{a} \cdot \vec{b}$.]

15. A vector is a linear combination of the vectors $3\vec{i} + 4\vec{j} + 5\vec{k}$ and $6\vec{i} - 7\vec{j} - 3\vec{k}$ and is perpendicular to the vector $\vec{i} + \vec{j} - \vec{k}$. Find the vector. **[CA May 1986]**

[HINTS. A linear combination of the two given vectors is $(3\vec{i}+4\vec{j}+5\vec{k})+x(6\vec{i}-7\vec{j}-3\vec{k})$ where x is a scalar.

If this vector is perpendicular to $\vec{i}+\vec{j}-\vec{k}$, then

$$(3+6x)\cdot 1+(4-7x)\cdot 1+(5-3x)(-1)=0, \text{ or, } x=-1.]$$

[D]

[Use of Cross-product of two vectors]

1. If $\vec{a}=2\vec{i}-5\vec{j}+11\vec{k}$ and $\vec{b}=4\vec{i}+6\vec{j}+2\vec{k}$, find $\vec{a}\cdot\vec{b}$ and $|\vec{a}\times\vec{b}|$.**[C.U. B.Com. (Hons.) 1993]**

2. If $\vec{a}=2\mathbf{i}+5\mathbf{j}+3\mathbf{k}, \vec{b}=3\mathbf{i}+3\mathbf{j}+6\mathbf{k}, \vec{c}=2\mathbf{i}+7\mathbf{j}+4\mathbf{k}$, find (i) $(\vec{a}-\vec{b})\times(\vec{c}-\vec{a})$, (ii) $(\vec{a}-\vec{b})\times(\vec{c}-\vec{a})|$.

[HINTS. $(\vec{a}-\vec{b})=-\mathbf{i}+2\mathbf{j}-3\mathbf{k}$ and $(\vec{c}-\vec{a})=0\mathbf{i}+2\mathbf{j}+\mathbf{k}$

$$\therefore\quad (\vec{a}-\vec{b})\times(\vec{c}-\vec{a})=\begin{vmatrix}\mathbf{i} & \mathbf{j} & \mathbf{k}\\ -1 & 2 & -3\\ 0 & 2 & 1\end{vmatrix}=8\mathbf{i}+\mathbf{j}-2\mathbf{k}$$

whose length $=|(\vec{a}-\vec{b})\times(\vec{c}-\vec{a})|=\sqrt{8^2+1^2+(-2)^2}=\sqrt{69}]$

3. Find the vectors of unit length perpendicular to $\vec{a}=\mathbf{i}+\mathbf{j}+\mathbf{k}$ and $\vec{b}=2\mathbf{i}+3\mathbf{j}-\mathbf{k}$.

[HINTS. Obtain $\frac{\vec{a}\times\vec{b}}{|\vec{a}\times\vec{b}|}=\pm\frac{1}{\sqrt{26}}(-4\mathbf{i}+3\mathbf{j}+\mathbf{k})]$

4. Find $|\vec{a}\times\vec{b}|$ if $|\vec{a}|=10, |\vec{b}|-2$ and $\vec{a}\cdot\vec{b}=12$.

[HINTS. $|\vec{a}|\cdot|\vec{b}|\cdot\cos\theta=12$, or, $\cos\theta=\frac{3}{5}$; $\quad\therefore\quad \sin\theta=\frac{4}{5}]$.

5. Find $\vec{a}\cdot\vec{b}$ if $|\vec{a}|=2, |\vec{b}|=5$ and $|\vec{a}\times\vec{b}|=8$.

6. For any three vectors $\vec{a},\vec{b},\vec{c}$, prove that

(i) $\vec{a}\times(\vec{b}+\vec{c})+\vec{b}\times(\vec{c}+\vec{a})+\vec{c}\times(\vec{a}+\vec{b})=0$;

(ii) $(\vec{a}+\vec{b})\times(\vec{a}-\vec{b})=2(\vec{b}\times\vec{a})$.

[HINTS. Use Distributive Law.]

7. Find the area of the parallelogram formed by the vectors $3\vec{i}+2\vec{j}+\vec{k}$ and $\vec{i}+3\vec{j}+5\vec{k}$.

[HINTS. Area of the parallelogram formed by the vectors $\vec{a}$ and $\vec{b}=|\vec{a}\times\vec{b}|$.]

8. Find the area of a triangle whose vertices are $A(1,0,0), B(0,1,0)$ and $C(0,0,1)$.

[HINTS. Area of the triangle $ABC=\frac{1}{2}|\overrightarrow{BC}\times\overrightarrow{CA}|, \overrightarrow{BC}=(0,0,1)-(0,1,0)=(0,-1,1), \overrightarrow{CA}=(1,0,0)-(0,0,1)=(1,0,-1)$.

$$\therefore\quad \text{Reqd. area}=\frac{1}{2}\text{ of length of }\begin{vmatrix}\mathbf{i} & \mathbf{j} & \mathbf{k}\\ 0 & -1 & 1\\ 1 & 0 & -1\end{vmatrix}=\frac{1}{2}|\mathbf{i}+\mathbf{j}+\mathbf{k}|=\frac{\sqrt{3}}{2}\text{ sq. units}]$$

9. Given $\vec{a}=2\mathbf{i}-\mathbf{j}, \vec{b}=\mathbf{j}+\mathbf{k}$, If $|\vec{c}|=12$, and if $\vec{c}$ is perpendicular to both $\vec{a}$ and $\vec{b}$, write $\vec{c}$ in terms of $\mathbf{i},\mathbf{j},\mathbf{k}$.

[HINTS. $\vec{c}=12\cdot\frac{\vec{a}\times\vec{b}}{|\vec{a}\times\vec{b}|}=\pm(4\mathbf{i}+8\mathbf{j}-8\mathbf{k})$.]

10. Given $\vec{a} = 2\mathbf{i} - 3\mathbf{j} + \mathbf{k}, \vec{b} = -\mathbf{i} + \mathbf{k}$ and $\vec{c} = 2\mathbf{j} - \mathbf{k}$

(i) Calculate $\vec{a} \times \vec{b}, \vec{b} \times \vec{c}$ and $\vec{c} \times \vec{a}$.

(ii) Obtain a unit vector perpendicular to both $\vec{b}$ and $\vec{c}$.

(iii) Calculate the area of the parallelogram with the diagonals $\vec{a} + \vec{b}$ and $\vec{b} + \vec{c}$.

[HINTS. (iii) Let $ABCD$ be the parallelogram with diagonals AC and BD such that $\overrightarrow{AC} = \vec{a}+\vec{b} = \vec{i}-3\vec{j}+2\vec{k}$ and $\overrightarrow{BD} = \vec{b}+\vec{c} = 0\vec{i}+2\vec{j}$. If AC and BD meet at E, then $\overrightarrow{AE} = \frac{1}{2}\overrightarrow{AC}, \overrightarrow{BE} = \frac{1}{2}\overrightarrow{BD}$.

$\therefore \quad \overrightarrow{AB} = \overrightarrow{AE} + \overrightarrow{EB} = \frac{1}{2}(\overrightarrow{AC} - \overrightarrow{BD}) = \frac{1}{2}(2\vec{i} - 5\vec{j} + 2\vec{k})$. Similarly, find AD, etc.]

11. Let A, B, C be the vertices of a triangle ABC. Let $\vec{a}, \vec{b}$ and $\vec{c}$ represent $\overrightarrow{BC}, \overrightarrow{CA}$ and $\overrightarrow{AB}$ respectively. Show that $\vec{a} \times \vec{b} = \vec{b} \times \vec{c} = \vec{c} \times \vec{a}$.

Hence deduce that

$$\frac{\sin \hat{A}}{a} = \frac{\sin \hat{B}}{b} = \frac{\sin \hat{C}}{c}$$

where $\hat{A}, \hat{B}, \hat{C}$ are the angles and a, b, c are the lengths of their opposite sides of the triangle ABC.

[HINTS. $\overrightarrow{BC} + \overrightarrow{CA} + \overrightarrow{AB} = \vec{0}$, i.e., $\vec{a} + \vec{b} + \vec{c} = \vec{0}$, i.e., $\vec{b} + \vec{c} = -\vec{a}$, or, $(\vec{b} + \vec{c}) \times \vec{a} = (-a) \times \vec{a} = \vec{0}$, or, $\vec{b} \times \vec{a} = -\vec{c} \times \vec{a}$, or, $\vec{a} \times \vec{b} = \vec{c} \times \vec{a}$. Similarly, obtain $\vec{b} \times \vec{c} = \vec{c} \times \vec{a}$.

Now use $|\vec{a} \times \vec{b}| = \frac{1}{2}|\vec{a}||\vec{b}| \sin(\widehat{\vec{a}, \vec{b}}) = \frac{1}{2}ab \sin(\pi - C) = \frac{1}{2}ab \sin C$.]

12. Show, by vectors, that the perpendicular bisectors of the sides of a triangle are concurrent.

[HINTS. Let $\vec{a}, \vec{b}, \vec{c}$ be the position vectors of the three vertices of a triangle ABC. If D, E, F be the middle points of the sides BC, CA, AB respectively, then their position vectors are $\frac{\vec{b}+\vec{c}}{2}, \frac{\vec{c}+\vec{a}}{2}$ and $\frac{\vec{a}+\vec{b}}{2}$. Now suppose the perpendicular bisectors of the side BC and CA meet at a point L (position vector $\vec{l}$). Then we have LD is perpendicular to BC and LE is perpendicular to CA.

This gives $\left(\frac{\vec{b}+\vec{c}}{2} - \vec{l}\right) \cdot (\vec{b} - \vec{c}) = 0$ and $\left(\frac{\vec{c}+\vec{a}}{2} - \vec{l}\right) \cdot (\vec{c} - \vec{a}) = 0$, or, $\frac{\vec{b}^2 - \vec{c}^2}{2} - \vec{l} \cdot (\vec{b} - \vec{c}) = 0$ and $\frac{\vec{c}^2 - \vec{a}^2}{2} - \vec{l} \cdot (\vec{c} - \vec{a}) = 0$.

Adding we get $\frac{\vec{b}^2 - \vec{a}^2}{2} - \vec{l} \cdot (\vec{b} - \vec{a}) = 0$, or, $\left(\frac{\vec{b}+\vec{a}}{2} - \vec{l}\right) \cdot (\vec{b} - \vec{a}) = 0$, i.e; *LF is perpendicular to AB*.]

13. Given three vector $\vec{a}, \vec{b}, \vec{c}$ such that $\vec{a} = \frac{1}{7}(2\mathbf{i}+3\mathbf{j}+6\mathbf{k}), \vec{b} = \frac{1}{7}(3\mathbf{i}-6\mathbf{j}+2\mathbf{k}), \vec{c} = \frac{1}{7}(6\mathbf{i}+2\mathbf{j}-3\mathbf{k})$. Prove that $\vec{a}, \vec{b}, \vec{c}$ are mutually perpendicular unit vectors.

14. For two vectors $\vec{a}$ and $\vec{b}$, prove that $|\vec{a} \times \vec{b}|^2 = \vec{a}^2 \cdot \vec{b}^2 - (\vec{a} \cdot \vec{b})^2$.

15. Find the area of the triangle whose vertices are $A(1, -1, 2), B(2, 1, -1)$ and $C(3, -1, 2)$.

[E]

1. Three vectors $\vec{\alpha}, \vec{\beta}, \vec{\gamma}$ are given such that $\vec{\alpha} + \vec{\beta} + \vec{\gamma} = \vec{0}$ and $|\vec{\alpha}| = 3, |\vec{\beta}| = 5, |\vec{\gamma}| = 7$. Find the cosine of the least angle between $\vec{\alpha}$ and $\vec{\beta}$. **[ICWAI 1976]**

[HINTS. $-\vec{\gamma} = \vec{\alpha} + \vec{\beta}; (-\vec{\gamma}) \cdot (-\vec{\gamma}) = (\vec{\alpha} + \vec{\beta}) \cdot (\vec{\alpha} + \vec{\beta})$, or, $\vec{\gamma}^2 = \vec{\alpha}^2 + \vec{\beta}^2 + 2\vec{\alpha} \cdot \vec{\beta}$, or, $7^2 = 3^2 + 5^2 + 2|\vec{\alpha}||\vec{\beta}| \cos\theta$, or, $7^2 = 3^2 + 5^2 + 2(3)(5) \cos\theta$ and hence $\cos\theta = \frac{1}{2}$.]

2. Show that if the diagonals of a quadrilateral $ABCD$ bisect each other, the figure is a parallelogram.

3. $ABCD$ is a parallelogram. P, Q are the middle points of the sides AB and CD respectively. Show that DP and BQ trisect AC and are trisected by AC.

4. Find the area of the triangle OAB(O is the origin) with $A = (1, 2, 3), B = (-3, -2, 1)$.

5. Find a unit vector perpendicular to each of the vectors: $\vec{a} = 2\mathbf{i} - \mathbf{j} + \mathbf{k}, \vec{b} = 3\mathbf{i} + 4\mathbf{j} - \mathbf{k}$.

[ICWAI 1979]

6. Find a vector of magnitude 5 perpendicular to both $\vec{\alpha}$ and $\vec{\beta}$ where $\vec{\alpha} = 2\mathbf{i} + \mathbf{j} - 3\mathbf{k}$ and $\vec{\beta} = \mathbf{i} - 2\mathbf{j} + \mathbf{k}$.

[HINTS. The required vector = 5 (unit vector along $\alpha \times \beta$) $= 5\frac{\alpha \times \beta}{|\alpha \times \beta|} = \pm\frac{5\sqrt{3}}{3}(\mathbf{i} + \mathbf{j} + \mathbf{k})$]

7. Show that the vectors $\vec{a} = 2\mathbf{i} - \mathbf{j} + \mathbf{k}, \vec{b} = \mathbf{i} - 3\mathbf{j} - 5\mathbf{k}$ and $\vec{c} = 3\mathbf{i} - 4\mathbf{j} - 4\mathbf{k}$ form the sides of a right-angled triangle.

8. Show that the points $\mathbf{i} - 2\mathbf{j} + 3\mathbf{k}(A), 2\mathbf{i} - 3\mathbf{j} + 4\mathbf{k}(B)$ and $(-2\mathbf{i} + \mathbf{j})(C)$ are collinear.

9. Show that the three vectors $\vec{a} = (1, 0, 0), \vec{b} = (0, 1, 0)$ and $\vec{c} = (0, 0, 1)$ are linearly independent. **[CA November 1992]**

10. Show that the vectors $\vec{\alpha}_1 = (5, 7, 11), \vec{\alpha}_2 = (2, 1, 3)$ and $\vec{\alpha}_3 = (3, 6, 8)$ are linearly dependent.

[HINTS. Let there exist 3 scalars x, y, z such that $x\vec{\alpha}_1 + y\vec{\alpha}_2 + z\vec{\alpha}_3 = \vec{0}$.

Then $x(5, 7, 11) + y(2, 1, 3) + z(3, 6, 8) = (0, 0, 0)$

$\therefore \quad 5x + 2y + 3z = 0, 7x + y + 6z = 0, 11x + 3y + 8z = 0.$

Clearly, $x = -1, y = 1, z = 1$ satisfy this system of equations. [This solution is *not unique*, there exist *infinite number of solutions in this case.*]

Since a set of *non-zero values of* x, y, z *exists, the given vectors are linearly dependent.*]

11. Prove that the three vectors $(1, -2, 3), (-2, 3, -4)$ and $(0, -1, 2)$ form a linearly dependent system. **[[CA November 1991]**

12. Three persons made the following purchases:

A purchases 12 mangoes only, B purchases 6 oranges only and C purchases 8 guavas only. Represent the purchases of each of these individuals by means of a row vectors. Verify that these three row vectors are linearly independent. **[[CA May 1992]**

[HINTS. Let $\vec{a}, \vec{b}, \vec{c}$ be the three row vectors representing the purchases of A, B, C respectively. Then $\vec{a} = (12, 0, 0), \vec{b} = (0, 6, 0)$ and $\vec{c} = (0, 0, 8)$, where first element represents the no. of mangoes, second element the no. of oranges and the third element the no. of guavas.

Now, $x\vec{a} + y\vec{b} + z\vec{c} = \vec{0}$, where x, y, z are scalars, implies.

$$x(12, 0, 0) + y(0, 6, 0) + z(0, 0, 8) = (0, 0, 0)$$
$$\therefore \quad 12x = 0, 6y = 0, 8z = 0, \text{ or, } x = 0, y = 0, z = 0.$$

Thus, $x\vec{a} + y\vec{b} + z\vec{c} = \vec{0}$ implies $x = y = z = 0$. Hence, etc.]

Answers

[B]

2. $\overrightarrow{AC} - \overrightarrow{AB}; \overrightarrow{CA}$. **3.** $\vec{b}, 2(\vec{a} - \vec{b}), 2\vec{a} - \vec{b}$. **4.** $\vec{b} - 9\vec{a}$. **5.** (i) $\vec{a} + \vec{b}$; (ii) $2\vec{b}$; (iii) $\vec{b} - \vec{a}$; (iv) $-\vec{a}$; (v) $-\vec{b}$; (vi) $\vec{a} - \vec{b}$; (vii) $-2\vec{b}$; (viii) $2(\vec{a} - \vec{b})$. **7.** $\frac{1}{5}(12\vec{a} - 13\vec{b}); -5\vec{b}$. **15.** $\frac{1}{3}(-2\vec{i} + \vec{j} - 2\vec{k})$. **16.** $2\sqrt{29}; 2\sqrt{3}$.

[C]

1. (i) $4\vec{i} + \vec{j} + 6\vec{k}$; (ii) $4\vec{i} - 13\vec{j} + 10\vec{k}$; (iii) $3\sqrt{10}$; (iv) $\frac{1}{3\sqrt{10}}(5\vec{i} - 4\vec{j} + 7\vec{k})$. **2.** $\sqrt{35}; 0; 90°$. **3.** $\sqrt{5}$. **4.** $-\frac{23}{5\sqrt{77}}$. **5.** -5. **6.** 4. **7.** $\vec{a}^{\,2} = \vec{b}^{\,2}$; $\vec{a} \times \vec{b} = \vec{0}$. **9.** $60°$. **12.** (i) $-20; \sqrt{186}$; (ii) $\sqrt{17}$. **14.** $\frac{\pi}{3}$. **15.** $-3\vec{i} + 11\vec{j} + 8\vec{k}$.

[D]

1. $0; 20\sqrt{21}$. **2.** (i) $8\vec{i} + \vec{j} - 2\vec{k}$; (ii) $\sqrt{69}$. **3.** $\pm\frac{1}{\sqrt{26}}(-4\vec{i} + 3\vec{j} + \vec{k})$. **4.** 16. **5.** 6. **7.** $7\sqrt{6}$ sq. units. **8.** $\frac{\sqrt{3}}{2}$ sq. units. **9.** $\pm(4\vec{i} + 8\vec{j} - 5\vec{k})$. **10.** (i) $-3(i + j + k), -(2i + j + 2k), -(i + 2j + 4k)$; (ii) $\pm\frac{1}{3}(2i + j + 2k)$; (iii) $\frac{1}{2}\sqrt{21}$ sq. units. **15.** $\sqrt{13}$ sq. units.

[E]

1. $\frac{1}{2}$. **4.** $5\sqrt{2}$ sq. units. **5.** $\pm\frac{1}{\sqrt{155}}(-3\vec{i} + 5\vec{j} + 11\vec{k})$. **6.** $\pm\frac{5\sqrt{3}}{3}(i + j + k)$. **12.** $(12, 0, 0), (0, 6, 0), (0, 0, 8)$.

1.5. SCALAR AND VECTOR TRIPLE PRODUCTS

It $\vec{a}, \vec{b}, \vec{c}$ be three vectors, then we know that $\vec{a} \cdot \vec{b}$ and $\vec{b} \cdot \vec{c}$ are scalars, but $\vec{a} \times \vec{b}$ and $\vec{b} \times \vec{c}$ are vectors. Therefore, $\vec{a} \cdot (\vec{b} \cdot \vec{c})$ and $(\vec{a} \cdot \vec{b}) \times \vec{c}$ are not defined. But $\vec{a} \cdot (\vec{b} \times \vec{c})$ and $\vec{a} \times (\vec{b} \times \vec{c})$ are defined and we shall now consider, such products with the help of few worked out examples. We shall write $\vec{a} \cdot (\vec{b} \times \vec{c}) = [\vec{a}\vec{b}\vec{c}]$.

EXAMPLE 1. $\vec{a} = a_1\mathbf{i} + a_2\mathbf{j} + a_3\mathbf{k}, \vec{b} = b_1\mathbf{i} + b_2\mathbf{j} + b_3\mathbf{k}$ and $\vec{c} = c_1\mathbf{i} + c_2\mathbf{j} + c_3\mathbf{k}$.

Then

$$\vec{b} \times \vec{c} = \begin{vmatrix} \mathbf{i} & \mathbf{j} & \mathbf{k} \\ b_1 & b_2 & b_3 \\ c_1 & c_2 & c_3 \end{vmatrix} = \mathbf{i}(b_2c_3 - b_3c_2) + \mathbf{j}(b_3c_1 - b_1c_3) + \mathbf{k}(b_1c_2 - b_2c_1).$$

$$\therefore \quad [\vec{a}\vec{b}\vec{c}] = \vec{a} \cdot (\vec{b} \times \vec{c}) = a_1(b_2c_3 - b_3c_2) + a_2(b_3c_1 - b_1c_3) + a_3(b_1c_2 - b_2c_1) = \begin{vmatrix} a_1 & a_2 & a_3 \\ b_1 & b_2 & b_3 \\ c_1 & c_2 & c_3 \end{vmatrix}.$$

Geometrical significance. The scalar triple product $[\vec{a}\,\vec{b}\,\vec{c}]$ or $\vec{a} \cdot (\vec{b} \times \vec{c})$ is the volume of the parallelopiped formed by the three vectors when drawn from a common point O (see Fig. 1.28)

$$[\vec{b} \times \vec{c}] = |\vec{b}||\vec{c}| \sin\theta \vec{n}$$

($\vec{n}$ is the unit vector perpendicular to both $\vec{b}$ and $\vec{c}$).

$|\vec{b}||\vec{c}| \sin\theta$ is the area of the parallelogram at the base.

If α be the angle between $\vec{a}$ and $\vec{n}$, then

$$\vec{a} \cdot (\vec{b} \times \vec{c}) = |\vec{a}|\{|\vec{b}||\vec{c}| \sin\theta\} \cos\alpha$$
$$= \text{area of the base } \times \text{ height } = \text{volume}.$$

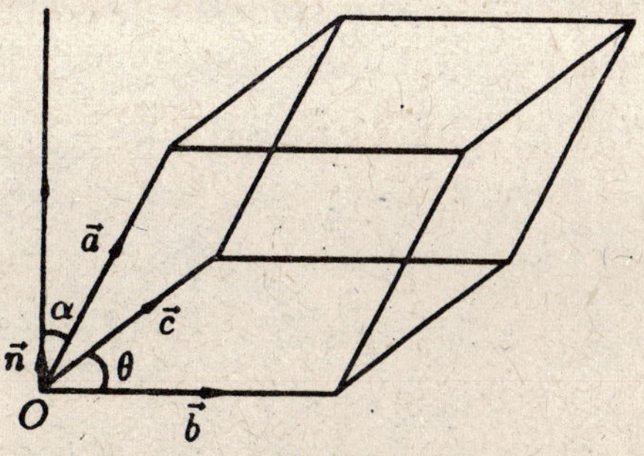

Fig 1.28

We can check that the volume is also given by $\vec{b}\cdot(\vec{c}\times\vec{a})$ or $\vec{c}\cdot(\vec{a}\times\vec{b})$.

Thus, $[\vec{a}\,\vec{b}\,\vec{c}] = [\vec{b}\,\vec{c}\,\vec{a}] = [\vec{c}\,\vec{a}\,\vec{b}]$, i.e., **the cyclic permutation of the vectors leaves the scalar triple product unchanged.**

Again, $\vec{a}\cdot(\vec{b}\times\vec{c}) = (\vec{a}\times\vec{b})\cdot\vec{c}$, i.e., **dot and cross operations are interchangeable.**

But see that for anticyclic order, $\vec{a}\cdot(\vec{b}\times\vec{c}) = -\vec{b}\cdot(\vec{a}\times\vec{c})$, i.e., $[\vec{a}\vec{b}\vec{c}] = -[\vec{b}\vec{a}\vec{c}]$.

EXAMPLE 2. *The three non-zero vectors are coplanar if and only if their scalar triple product is zero.*

SOLUTION. $\vec{a}\cdot(\vec{b}\times\vec{c}) = 0$, if any of the vectors be zero.

But if none is zero and if they are in the same plane, then the volume of the parallelopiped formed by them is zero, and consequently $\vec{a}\cdot(\vec{b}\times\vec{c}) = 0$.

Conversely, let three non-zero vectors $\vec{a},\vec{b}$ and $\vec{c}$ satisfy $\vec{a}\cdot(\vec{b}\times\vec{c}) = 0$. Then $\vec{a}$ is perpendicular to $\vec{b}\times\vec{c}$. But $\vec{b}\times\vec{c}$ is perpendicular to both $\vec{b}$ and $\vec{c}$. $\therefore$ $\vec{a},\vec{b}$ and $\vec{c}$ are all perpendicular to $\vec{b}\times\vec{c}$. Accordingly, $\vec{a},\vec{b}$ and $\vec{c}$ are coplanar.

EXAMPLE 3. *Find the value of* $\mathbf{i}\cdot(\mathbf{j}\times\mathbf{k}) = [\mathbf{i}\,\mathbf{j}\,\mathbf{k}]$.

$[i\,j\,k] = \mathbf{i}\cdot(\mathbf{j}\times\mathbf{k}) = \mathbf{i}\cdot\mathbf{i} = 1,$

$$\text{or, } [i\,j\,k] = \begin{vmatrix} 1 & 0 & 0 \\ 0 & 1 & 0 \\ 0 & 0 & 1 \end{vmatrix} = 1.$$

EXAMPLE 4. *Obtain the value of* λ *for which* $\mathbf{i}-\mathbf{j}+\mathbf{k}, 2\mathbf{i}+\mathbf{j}-\mathbf{k}$ *and* $\lambda\mathbf{i}-\mathbf{j}+\lambda\mathbf{k}$ *are coplanar.*

SOLUTION. The scalar triple product $(\mathbf{i}-\mathbf{j}+\mathbf{k})\cdot(2\mathbf{i}+\mathbf{j}-\mathbf{k})\times(\lambda\mathbf{i}-\mathbf{j}+\lambda\mathbf{k}) = \begin{vmatrix} 1 & -1 & 1 \\ 2 & 1 & -1 \\ \lambda & -1 & \lambda \end{vmatrix}$ should be zero,

$$\therefore\quad 1\cdot\begin{vmatrix} 1 & -1 \\ -1 & \lambda \end{vmatrix} + 1\cdot\begin{vmatrix} 2 & -1 \\ \lambda & \lambda \end{vmatrix} + 1\cdot\begin{vmatrix} 2 & 1 \\ \lambda & -1 \end{vmatrix} = 0$$

$$\text{or,}\quad (\lambda-1)+(2\lambda+\lambda)+(-2-\lambda) = 0,\quad 3\lambda-3=0,\quad \text{or,}\quad \lambda = \mathbf{1}.$$

EXAMPLE 5. *Prove that* $(\vec{a}+\vec{b})\cdot\{(\vec{b}+\vec{c})\times(\vec{c}+\vec{a})\} = 2[\vec{a}\vec{b}\vec{c}]$.

SOLUTION.

$$\begin{aligned}
(\vec{b}+\vec{c})\times(\vec{c}+\vec{a}) &= \vec{b}\times\vec{c}+\vec{c}\times\vec{c}+\vec{b}\times\vec{a}+\vec{c}\times\vec{a} \text{ (using Distributive Law)} \\
&= \vec{b}\times\vec{c}+\vec{b}\times\vec{a}+\vec{c}\times\vec{a} \quad (\because\ \vec{c}\times\vec{c}=0) \\
\therefore\quad (\vec{a}+\vec{b})\cdot(\vec{b}\times\vec{c}+\vec{b}\times\vec{a}+\vec{c}\times\vec{a}) &= \vec{a}\cdot(\vec{b}\times\vec{c})+\vec{a}\cdot(\vec{b}\times\vec{a})+\vec{a}\cdot(\vec{c}\times\vec{a}) \\
&\quad +\vec{b}\cdot(\vec{b}\times\vec{c})+\vec{b}\cdot(\vec{b}\times\vec{a})+\vec{b}\cdot(\vec{c}\times\vec{a}) \\
&= [\vec{a}\,\vec{b}\,\vec{c}]+[\vec{b}\,\vec{c}\,\vec{a}] = [\vec{a}\,\vec{b}\,\vec{c}]+[\vec{a}\,\vec{b}\,\vec{c}] = 2[\vec{a}\,\vec{b}\,\vec{c}]
\end{aligned}$$

$$[\because\ \ \vec{a}\cdot(\vec{b}\times\vec{a}) = -\vec{a}\cdot(\vec{a}\times\vec{b}) = -(\vec{a}\times\vec{b})\cdot\vec{b} = 0. \quad \text{Similarly, } \vec{a}\cdot(\vec{c}\times\vec{a}) = 0, \text{ etc.}]$$

EXAMPLE 6. $\vec{a} = 2\mathbf{i}-\mathbf{j}+3\mathbf{k}, \vec{b} = -\mathbf{i}+2\mathbf{j}+\mathbf{k}, \vec{c} = 3\mathbf{i}+\mathbf{j}-2\mathbf{k}$, *calculate* $\vec{a}\cdot(\vec{b}\times\vec{c})$ *and verify that* $\vec{a}\cdot(\vec{b}\times\vec{c}) = \vec{b}\cdot(\vec{c}\times\vec{a})$, *each being of magnitude* -32.

SOLUTION. We have

$$\vec{a}\cdot(\vec{b}\times\vec{c}) = \begin{vmatrix} 2 & -1 & 3 \\ -1 & 2 & 1 \\ 3 & 1 & -2 \end{vmatrix} = 2(-5)+1(-1)+3(-7) = -32$$

and $$\vec{b}\cdot(\vec{c}\times\vec{a}) = \begin{vmatrix} -1 & 2 & 1 \\ 3 & 1 & -2 \\ 2 & -1 & 3 \end{vmatrix} = -1(1)-2(13)+1(-5) = -32.$$

EXAMPLE 7. **Distributive Law of Cross products.** *An alternative Method of proof.*

$\vec{a}\times(\vec{b}+\vec{c}) = \vec{a}\times\vec{b}+\vec{a}\times\vec{c}$, where $\vec{a},\vec{b},\vec{c}$, are any three vectors.

SOLUTION. Let $\vec{r}$ be any vector whatsoever. We have

$$\vec{r}\cdot[\vec{a}\times(\vec{b}+\vec{c})-\vec{a}\times\vec{b}-\vec{a}\times\vec{c}] = \vec{r}\cdot\vec{a}\times(\vec{b}+\vec{c})-\vec{r}\cdot\vec{a}\times\vec{b}-\vec{r}\cdot\vec{a}\times\vec{c} \text{ (Distributive Law)}$$
$$= (\vec{r}\times\vec{a})\cdot(\vec{b}+\vec{c})-(\vec{r}\times\vec{a})\cdot\vec{b}-(\vec{r}\times\vec{a})\cdot\vec{c}$$
(since dot and cross interchangeable)
$$= (\vec{r}\times\vec{a})\cdot[(\vec{b}+\vec{c})-\vec{b}-\vec{c}] = (\vec{r}\times\vec{a})\cdot\vec{0} = 0.$$
$$\therefore\quad \vec{r}\cdot[\vec{a}\times(\vec{b}+\vec{c})-\vec{a}\times\vec{b}-\vec{a}\times\vec{c}] = 0$$

for every vector $\vec{r}$. This is only possible if and only if.

$$\vec{a}\times(\vec{b}+\vec{c})-\vec{a}\times\vec{b}-a\times\vec{c} = \vec{0}, \quad \text{i.e.,}\quad \vec{a}\times(\vec{b}+\vec{c}) = \vec{a}\times\vec{b}+\vec{a}\times\vec{c}.$$

Vector Triple Products. Cross product of two vectors one of which is a cross product; e.g., $\vec{a}\times(\vec{b}\times\vec{c})$ or $(\vec{a}\times\vec{b})\times\vec{c}$.

We have an important result: $\vec{a}\times(\vec{b}\times\vec{c}) = (\vec{a}\cdot\vec{c})\vec{b}-(\vec{a}\cdot\vec{b})\vec{c}$.

Using anticommutative property of cross products we obtain $(\vec{b}\times\vec{c})\times\vec{a} = (\vec{a}\cdot\vec{b})\vec{c}-(\vec{a}\cdot\vec{c})\vec{b}$.

EXAMPLE 8. *Prove that* $\vec{a}\times(\vec{b}\times\vec{c})+\vec{b}\times(\vec{c}\times\vec{a})+\vec{c}\times(\vec{a}\times\vec{b}) = \vec{0}$.

SOLUTION. We have

$$\vec{a}\times(\vec{b}\times\vec{c}) = (\vec{a}\cdot\vec{c})\vec{b}-(\vec{a}\cdot\vec{b})\vec{c},\quad \vec{b}\times(\vec{c}\times\vec{a}) = (\vec{b}\cdot\vec{a})\vec{c}-(\vec{b}\cdot\vec{c})\vec{a},$$
and $$\vec{c}\times(\vec{a}\times\vec{b}) = (\vec{c}\cdot\vec{b})\vec{a}-(\vec{c}\cdot\vec{a})\vec{b}.$$
$$\therefore\quad \text{L.H.S.} = (\vec{a}\cdot\vec{c})\vec{b}-(\vec{a}\cdot\vec{b})\vec{c}+(\vec{b}\cdot\vec{a})\vec{c}-(\vec{b}\cdot\vec{c})\vec{a}+(\vec{c}\cdot\vec{b})\vec{a}-(\vec{c}\cdot\vec{a})\vec{b}$$
$$= 0. \quad [\because\ \vec{a}\cdot\vec{c} = \vec{c}\cdot\vec{a}, \vec{a}\cdot\vec{b} = \vec{b}\cdot\vec{a} \text{ and } \vec{b}\cdot\vec{c} = \vec{c}\cdot\vec{b}.]$$

EXAMPLE 9. *Prove that* $\mathbf{i}\times(\mathbf{j}\times\mathbf{k}) = \vec{0}$.

SOLUTION. We have $\mathbf{j}\times\mathbf{k} = \mathbf{i}$, $\quad\therefore\quad \mathbf{i}\times(\mathbf{j}\times\mathbf{k}) = \mathbf{i}\times\mathbf{i} = \vec{0}$.

EXAMPLE 10. $\vec{a} = 2\mathbf{i}+3\mathbf{j}-\mathbf{k}, \vec{b} = \mathbf{i}-\mathbf{j}+\mathbf{k}$ *and* $\vec{c} = 3\mathbf{i}-\mathbf{j}-\mathbf{k}$, *find the vector* $\vec{a}\times(\vec{b}\times\vec{c})$.

[CA Inter November 1981]

SOLUTION. By the definition of *cross product*, we have

$$\vec{b}\times\vec{c}=\begin{vmatrix}\mathbf{i} & \mathbf{j} & \mathbf{k}\\ 1 & -1 & 1\\ 3 & -1 & -1\end{vmatrix}=\mathbf{i}(1+1)-\mathbf{j}(-1-3)+\mathbf{k}(-1+3)=2\mathbf{i}+4\mathbf{j}+2\mathbf{k}.$$

$$\therefore\quad \vec{a}\times(\vec{b}\times\vec{c})=\begin{vmatrix}\mathbf{i} & \mathbf{j} & \mathbf{k}\\ 2 & 3 & -1\\ 2 & 4 & 2\end{vmatrix}=i(6+4)-j(4+2)+k(8-6)=10\mathbf{i}-6\mathbf{j}+2\mathbf{k}.$$

Alternative Method

$$\begin{aligned}\vec{a}\times(\vec{b}\times\vec{c})&=(\vec{a}\cdot\vec{c})\vec{b}-(\vec{a}\cdot\vec{b})\vec{c}\\ &=\{(2\mathbf{i}+3\mathbf{j}-\mathbf{k})\cdot(3\mathbf{i}-\mathbf{j}-\mathbf{k})\}(\mathbf{i}-\mathbf{j}+\mathbf{k})-\{(2\mathbf{i}+3\mathbf{j}-\mathbf{k})\cdot(\mathbf{i}-\mathbf{j}+\mathbf{k})\}(3\mathbf{i}-\mathbf{j}-\mathbf{k})\\ &=(6-3+1)(\mathbf{i}-\mathbf{j}+\mathbf{k})-(2-3-1)(3\mathbf{i}-\mathbf{j}-\mathbf{k})=4\mathbf{i}-4\mathbf{j}+4\mathbf{k}+6\mathbf{i}-2\mathbf{j}-2\mathbf{k}\\ &=10\mathbf{i}-6\mathbf{j}+2\mathbf{k}.\end{aligned}$$

EXAMPLE 12. *If* $\vec{a}=3\mathbf{i}-\mathbf{j}+2\mathbf{k}, \vec{b}=2\mathbf{i}+\mathbf{j}-\mathbf{k}, \vec{c}=\mathbf{i}-2\mathbf{j}+2\mathbf{k}$, *find* $(\vec{a}\times\vec{b})\times\vec{c}$ *and* $\vec{a}\times(\vec{b}\times\vec{c})$ *and prove that they are not equal.* **[CA Inter May 1978]**

SOLUTION. We have

$$\vec{a}\times\vec{b}=\begin{vmatrix}i & \mathbf{j} & \mathbf{k}\\ 3 & -1 & 2\\ 2 & 1 & -1\end{vmatrix}=-\mathbf{i}+7\mathbf{j}+5\mathbf{k};\quad\therefore\quad(\vec{a}\times\vec{b})\times\vec{c}=\begin{vmatrix}i & \mathbf{j} & \mathbf{k}\\ -1 & 7 & 5\\ 1 & -2 & 2\end{vmatrix}=24\mathbf{i}-7\mathbf{i}-5\mathbf{k}$$

$$\vec{b}\times\vec{c}=\begin{vmatrix}i & \mathbf{j} & \mathbf{k}\\ 2 & 1 & -1\\ 1 & -2 & 2\end{vmatrix}=0\mathbf{i}+5\mathbf{j}-5\mathbf{k}\quad\therefore\quad\vec{a}\times(\vec{b}\times\vec{c})=\begin{vmatrix}i & \mathbf{j} & \mathbf{k}\\ 3 & -1 & 2\\ 0 & 5 & -5\end{vmatrix}=-5\mathbf{i}+15\mathbf{j}+15\mathbf{k}.$$

We see that $(\vec{a}\times\vec{b})\times\vec{c}\neq\vec{a}\times(\vec{b}\times\vec{c})$.

EXAMPLE 13. *Given* $\vec{a}=2\mathbf{i}-3\mathbf{j}+\mathbf{k}, \vec{b}=\mathbf{i}+2\mathbf{j}+5\mathbf{k}, \vec{c}=-3\mathbf{i}+\mathbf{j}-2\mathbf{k}$. *Find* $\vec{a}\cdot(\vec{b}\times\vec{c})$ *and* $\vec{a}\times(\vec{b}\times\vec{c})$. **[CA Inter November 1977]**

[**Ans.** 28 and $-(8\mathbf{i}+23\mathbf{j}+53\mathbf{k})$.]

This example is left as an exercise to the students.

EXAMPLE 14. *Prove that the box product of* $\vec{a}+\vec{b}, \vec{b}+\vec{c}, \vec{c}+\vec{a}=2$ {*box product of* $\vec{a},\vec{b},\vec{c}$}, *i.e.,* $[\vec{a}+\vec{b}, \vec{b}+\vec{c}, \vec{c}+\vec{a}]=2[\vec{a}\,\vec{b}\,\vec{c}]$. **[CA May 1983]**

[This problem is left as an exercise]

EXAMPLE 15. *Given four points whose position vectors with reference to an origin are* $4\mathbf{i}+5\mathbf{j}+\mathbf{k}, -\mathbf{j}-\mathbf{k}, 3\mathbf{i}+9\mathbf{j}+4\mathbf{k}$ *and* $-4\mathbf{i}+4\mathbf{j}+\mathbf{k}$. *Prove that they are coplanar.* **[CA November 1984]**

[HINTS. This problem is also left as an exercise.

Find $\overrightarrow{AB}\cdot(\overrightarrow{AC}\times\overrightarrow{AD})$, i.e., $[\overrightarrow{AB}\,\overrightarrow{AC}\,\overrightarrow{AD}]$ and show that $[\overrightarrow{AB}, \overrightarrow{AC}\,\overrightarrow{AD}]=0$, i.e., $\overrightarrow{AB}, \overrightarrow{AC}$ and $\overrightarrow{AD}$ are *coplanar*.

Also $\overrightarrow{AB}, \overrightarrow{AC}, \overrightarrow{AD}$ have a common point A. Hence etc.]

CHAPTER 2

MATRICES

2.1. INTRODUCTION

We often present a set of numbers (or elements) in the form of a rectangular array of rows and columns for keeping various records. Some illustrations are given below.

Illustrations

(i) If Arun secures 60 marks in English and 75 marks in Mathematics, we may express this as [60 75] or (60 75).

(ii) If Arun secures 60 marks in English, 75 in Mathematics and 80 in Statistics, then we may express this as

$$[60\ \ 75\ \ 80], \quad \text{or}, \quad (60\ \ 75\ \ 80). \tag{1}$$

(iii) Marks obtained by two students Arun and Barun in English, Mathematics and Statistics are as follows:

	English	Mathematics	Statistics
Arun	60	75	80
Barun	70	78	75

These marks may be represented by the following rectangular array enclosed by a pair of brackets [ ] or ( ):

$$\begin{bmatrix} 60 & 75 & 80 \\ 70 & 78 & 75 \end{bmatrix} \quad \text{or} \quad \begin{pmatrix} 60 & 75 & 80 \\ 70 & 78 & 75 \end{pmatrix}. \tag{2}$$

This rectangular array consists of two rows and three columns. The first row indicates the marks obtained by Arun in English, Mathematics and Statistics, respectively, second by Barun in the three respective subjects. The first column refers to the marks obtained by Arun and Barun in English, the second column in Mathematics and the third in Statistics.

Such a rectangular array, subject to certain rules of operation, is called a **matrix.** Thus, (2) is a matrix consisting of two rows and three columns i.e., it is a 2×3(2 by 3) matrix; (1) is a matrix consisting of one row only i.e., it is a 1×3 matrix and we call it a *row matrix.* Now we give below the proper definition of a matrix.

DEFINITION. *A matrix is a rectangular array of numbers enclosed by a pair of brackets* [ ] *or* ( ) *subject to certain rules of operation. A set of mn numbers* $a_{11}, a_{12}, \cdots, a_{mn}$ *arranged in a rectangular array of m rows and n columns like* $\begin{bmatrix} a_{11} & a_{12} & a_{13} & \cdots & a_{1n} \\ a_{21} & a_{22} & a_{23} & \cdots & a_{2n} \\ \cdots & \cdots & \cdots & \cdots & \cdots \\ a_{m1} & a_{m2} & a_{m3} & \cdots & a_{mn} \end{bmatrix}$ and subject to certain rules of operation is called an $m \times n$ (read "m by n") matrix.

The numbers $a_{11}, a_{12}, \cdots, a_{mn}$ *are called the elements* (or *entries*) *of the matrix.*

If $m = n$ *i.e., if the number of rows = the number of columns, then the matrix is called a* **square matrix** *of order n.*

Thus $\begin{bmatrix} a_{11} & a_{12} & \cdots & a_{1n} \\ a_{21} & a_{22} & \cdots & a_{2n} \\ \cdots & \cdots & \cdots & \cdots \\ a_{n1} & a_{n2} & \cdots & a_{nn} \end{bmatrix}$ is a square matrix of order n and the elements $a_{11}, a_{22}, \cdots, a_{nn}$ lying along the main (or leading) diagonal are called the diagonal elements of the matrix.

The matrix $\begin{bmatrix} 1 & 3 & 2 \\ 4 & -1 & 5 \end{bmatrix}$ has two rows and three columns and hence it is a 2×3 matrix.

Here element -1 occurs in the second row and second column, i.e., $a_{22} = -1$. Similarly, $a_{13} = 2, a_{21} = 4$.

$\begin{bmatrix} 2 & 1 \\ 3 & 4 \end{bmatrix}$ is a square matrix of order 2. $\begin{bmatrix} 3 \\ 2 \\ 5 \end{bmatrix}$ is a 3×1 matrix and $[1\ 3\ 7]$ is a 1×3 matrix.

An $m \times n$ matrix is shortly denoted by $[a_{ij}]_{m \times n}$ or $(a_{ij})_{m \times n}$ or simply by $[a_{ij}]$ or (a_{ij}). Here a_{ij} is the element in the ith row and the jth column of the matrix. Thus, a_{23} is the element in the 2nd row and the 3rd column.

We shall use capital letters $A, B, C, \cdots$ to denote matrices.

EXAMPLE 1. *A contractor builds three types of houses. Quantities of raw materials needed are given in the following table:*

	Cement (in tons)	Wood (in tons)	Steel (in tons)
Type 1	20	40	10
Type 2	40	60	12
Type 3	50	80	14

Represent the information by a matrix.

SOLUTION. *It can be represented by a square matrix of order three as shown below.*

$$\begin{bmatrix} 20 & 40 & 10 \\ 40 & 60 & 12 \\ 50 & 80 & 14 \end{bmatrix}_{3\times 3}$$

The rows refer to *"type of houses with raw materials needed" and the first column represents the "amount of cement needed";* similarly, we can interpret other columns.

2.2. FEW TYPES OF MATRICES

Row Matrix and Column Matrix

A matrix having only one row is called a **row matrix** (or a row vector). $[2\ 3\ 4]$ is a 1×3 *row matrix* and $[a_{11}, a_{12}, \cdots, a_{1n}]$ is a $1 \times n$ *row matrix.*

A matrix having only one column is called a **column matrix** (or a column vector). $\begin{bmatrix} 1 \\ 2 \\ 3 \end{bmatrix}$ is a 3×1 *column matrix* and $\begin{bmatrix} a_{11} \\ a_{21} \\ \vdots \\ a_{n1} \end{bmatrix}$ is an $n \times 1$ *column matrix.*

Null (or Zero) Matrix

A matrix of any order (rectangular or square) whose all elements are zero is called a **null matrix** (or a zero **matrix**) and is denoted by **O.**

ILLUSTRATION. $\begin{bmatrix} 0 & 0 \\ 0 & 0 \end{bmatrix}$, $\begin{bmatrix} 0 & 0 & 0 \\ 0 & 0 & 0 \end{bmatrix}$ are *null matrices* of order 2×2 and 2×3, respectively.

Diagonal Matrix

A **square matrix** *whose all elements except those in the main diagonal are zero* is called **a diagonal matrix.**

ILLUSTRATION. $\begin{bmatrix} 3 & 0 \\ 0 & 5 \end{bmatrix}$, $\begin{bmatrix} 2 & 0 & 0 \\ 0 & 3 & 0 \\ 0 & 0 & 6 \end{bmatrix}$ are *diagonal matrices* of orders 2 and 3, respectively.

Scalar Matrix

A *diagonal matrix* whose all the diagonal elements are *equal is a* **scalar matrix.**

ILLUSTRATION. $\begin{bmatrix} 3 & 0 \\ 0 & 3 \end{bmatrix}$, $\begin{bmatrix} 2 & 0 & 0 \\ 0 & 2 & 0 \\ 0 & 0 & 2 \end{bmatrix}$ are *scalar matrices* of order 2 and 3, respectively.

Unit (or Identity) Matrix

A square matrix whose main diagonal elements are all unity and the other elements are all zero is called a **Unit** (or **Identity**) **Matrix.** Thus, a diagonal matrix, each of whose diagonal elements is unity (or one), is called a *unit matrix.* A unit matrix of order n is denoted by I_n or simply by I.

ILLUSTRATION. $I_2 = \begin{bmatrix} 1 & 0 \\ 0 & 1 \end{bmatrix}$, $I_3 = \begin{bmatrix} 1 & 0 & 0 \\ 0 & 1 & 0 \\ 0 & 0 & 1 \end{bmatrix}$ are unit matrices of order 2 and 3, respectively.

Equality of Two Matrices

Two matrices A and B are said to be equal if and only if (i) A and B have the same order and (ii) each element of A is equal to the corresponding element of B.

ILLUSTRATION. $\begin{bmatrix} 1^2 & 2^2 & 3^2 \\ 2^2 & 3^2 & 1^2 \end{bmatrix}$ and $\begin{bmatrix} 1 & 4 & 9 \\ 4 & 9 & 1 \end{bmatrix}$ are equal matrices.

EXAMPLE 2. *Find x and y when* $\begin{bmatrix} 4 & x-1 \\ y & 6 \end{bmatrix} = \begin{bmatrix} x+1 & 2 \\ 4x-y & 6 \end{bmatrix}$.

SOLUTION. We have $\begin{bmatrix} 4 & x-1 \\ y & 6 \end{bmatrix} = \begin{bmatrix} x+1 & 2 \\ 4x-y & 6 \end{bmatrix}$.

Equating elements of the column from both sides, we get

$$4 = x + 1 \quad \text{and} \quad y = 4x - y$$

$$\therefore \quad x = 3 \quad \text{and} \quad 2y = 4x \quad \text{or,} \quad y = 2x = 2 \times 3 = 6.$$

Hence $\mathbf{x} = \mathbf{3}$ and $\mathbf{y} = \mathbf{6}$.

Transpose of a Matrix

The transpose of a matrix A is the matrix obtained from A by interchanging its rows and columns and it is denoted by A^T or A'. The order of the transpose of an $m \times n$ matrix is $n \times m$.

ILLUSTRATION. If $A = \begin{bmatrix} 3 & -1 & 2 \\ 0 & 4 & -7 \end{bmatrix}$, then $A^T = \begin{bmatrix} 3 & 0 \\ -1 & 4 \\ 2 & -7 \end{bmatrix}$. Note that A is a 2×3 matrix, but A^T is a 3×2 matrix.

2.3. RULES OF OPERATIONS ON MATRICES

I. Addition of Matrices

Two matrices A and B can be added only when they are of the *same order*, i.e., each of the two matrices must have the same number of rows and columns. When this condition is satisfied the process of addition consists of adding the corresponding elements of the two matrices.

EXAMPLE. $\begin{bmatrix} 2 & 3 & 4 \\ 5 & 2 & 3 \end{bmatrix} + \begin{bmatrix} 1 & 3 & 5 \\ 2 & 7 & 1 \end{bmatrix} = \begin{bmatrix} 3 & 6 & 9 \\ 7 & 9 & 4 \end{bmatrix}$.

General Rule

Let $A = (a_{ij})_{m\times n}$, $B = (b_{ij})_{m\times n}$, then their SUM $C = A + B = (c_{ij})_{m\times n}$, $c_{ij} = a_{ij} + b_{ij}$.

EXAMPLE. *Let* $A = (1\ 2\ 3)_{1\times 3}$ *be a row-vector showing that a man bought* 1 *dozen of mangoes,* 2 *dozen bananas and* 3 *dozen apples. Let* $B = (2\ 1\ 3)_{1\times 3}$ *be another row-vector showing that his wife purchased* 2 *dozen mangoes,* 1 *dozen bananas and* 3 *dozen apples. The sum* $A + B = (3\ 3\ 6)$ *shows that together they bought* 3 *dozen mangoes,* 3 *dozen bananas and* 6 *dozen apples.*

II. Scalar Multiplication of Matrices

Let A be a matrix and k be a scalar, (i.e., a real number) multiplication of A by k (denoted by kA) is effected by multiplying each element of A by k.

ILLUSTRATION. If $A = \underset{\text{Matrix}}{\begin{bmatrix} 2 & 3 & 4 \\ 5 & 2 & 3 \end{bmatrix}}$ Scalar $k=5$, then $5A = \begin{bmatrix} 10 & 15 & 20 \\ 25 & 10 & 15 \end{bmatrix}$.

ILLUSTRATION. *Let* $A = [5\ 1\ 4]$ *represent the cost of one mango* (Rs. 5) *one banana* (Rs. 1) *and one apple* (Rs. 4). *Then* $12A = [60\ 12\ 48]$ *represents the cost of* 1 *dozen of mangoes,* 1 dozen of bananas and 1 dozen of apples.

Negative of a Matrix

If A be a matrix and (-1) be a scalar, then $(-1)A = -A$ is called the *negative of A*.

EXAMPLE. *Let* $A = \begin{bmatrix} 2 & 4 & 6 & 9 \\ 1 & 2 & 3 & 0 \end{bmatrix}$.

Then negative of $A = -A = \begin{bmatrix} -2 & -4 & -6 & -9 \\ -1 & -2 & -3 & 0 \end{bmatrix}$.

III. Subtraction of Two Matrices

Let A and B be two matrices of **same order.**

Then $A - B$ is obtained by adding A to the negative of B; thus $A - B = A + (-B)$.

ILLUSTRATION. If $A = \begin{bmatrix} 2 & 5 & -3 \\ 4 & -6 & 7 \end{bmatrix}$ and $B = \begin{bmatrix} -1 & 3 & 2 \\ 6 & -4 & 8 \end{bmatrix}$, then

$$A - B = A + (-B) = \begin{bmatrix} 2 & 5 & -3 \\ 4 & -6 & 7 \end{bmatrix} + \begin{bmatrix} 1 & -3 & -2 \\ -6 & 4 & -8 \end{bmatrix}$$

$$= \begin{bmatrix} 2+1 & 5-3 & -3-2 \\ 4-6 & -6+4 & 7-8 \end{bmatrix} = \begin{bmatrix} 3 & 2 & -5 \\ -2 & -2 & -1 \end{bmatrix}.$$

Matrix Multiplication (Multiplication of a Matrix by a Matrix)

The product AB of two matrices A and B is defined only when **the number of columns in A is equal to the number of rows in B.** *If* A *be an* $m \times n$ *matrix and* B *be an* $n \times p$ *matrix, then the number of columns in* $A =$ *the number of rows in* B *and the product* $AB = C$ *is an* $m \times p$ *matrix whose* (i, j)*th element, say* c_{ij}*, is the sum of the products obtained by multiplying the elements of the* i*th row of* A *by the corresponding elements of the* j*th column of* B *i.e.,*

$$c_{i1} = a_{i1}b_{1j} + a_{i2}b_{2j} + \cdots + a_{in}b_{nj} = \sum_{k=1}^{n} a_{ik}b_{kj}.$$

When the number of columns in A = the number of rows in B, we say that A and B are *conformable for the product AB* i.e., the product AB is defined.

ILLUSTRATION 1. If $A = \begin{bmatrix} 1 & 2 \\ 3 & 4 \end{bmatrix}$ and $B = \begin{bmatrix} 2 & 3 \\ 5 & 1 \end{bmatrix}$, then A and B are two square matrices of the same order 2×2 and AB and BA are both defined.

$$AB = \begin{bmatrix} 1 & 2 \\ 3 & 4 \end{bmatrix} \times \begin{bmatrix} 2 & 3 \\ 5 & 1 \end{bmatrix} = \begin{bmatrix} 1 \times 2 + 2 \times 5 & 1 \times 3 + 2 \times 1 \\ 3 \times 2 + 4 \times 5 & 3 \times 3 + 4 \times 1 \end{bmatrix} = \begin{bmatrix} 12 & 5 \\ 26 & 13 \end{bmatrix}.$$

$$\text{and} \quad BA = \begin{bmatrix} 2 & 3 \\ 5 & 1 \end{bmatrix} \times \begin{bmatrix} 1 & 2 \\ 3 & 4 \end{bmatrix} = \begin{bmatrix} 2 \times 1 + 3 \times 3 & 2 \times 2 + 3 \times 4 \\ 5 \times 1 + 1 \times 3 & 5 \times 2 + 1 \times 4 \end{bmatrix} = \begin{bmatrix} 11 & 16 \\ 8 & 14 \end{bmatrix}.$$

Note that $AB \neq BA$.

ILLUSTRATION 2. *If* $A = \begin{bmatrix} 2 & -1 & 4 \\ 1 & 3 & -2 \end{bmatrix}$ *and* $B = \begin{bmatrix} 1 & 2 & 3 \\ -2 & 0 & 4 \\ 3 & -1 & 6 \end{bmatrix}$, *then* A *is* 2×3 *matrix and* B *is a* 3×3 *matrix.*

Since, the no. of columns in A = the no. of rows in B, the product AB is defined and it is a 2×3 matrix, but the product BA is not defined.

Now,

$$AB = \begin{bmatrix} 2 & -1 & 4 \\ 1 & 3 & -2 \end{bmatrix} \times \begin{bmatrix} 1 & 2 & 3 \\ -2 & 0 & 4 \\ 3 & -1 & 6 \end{bmatrix}$$

$$= \begin{bmatrix} 2 \times 1 + (-1) \times (-2) + 4 \times 3 & 2 \times 2 + (-1) \times 0 + 4 \times (-1) & 2 \times 3 + (-1) \times 4 + 4 \times 6 \\ 1 \times 1 + 3 \times (-2) + (-2) \times 3 & 1 \times 2 + 3 \times 0 + (-2) \times (-1) & 1 \times 3 + 3 \times 4 + (-2) \times 6 \end{bmatrix}$$

$$= \begin{bmatrix} 2 + 2 + 12 & 4 + 0 - 4 & 6 - 4 + 24 \\ 1 - 6 - 6 & 2 + 0 + 2 & 3 + 12 - 12 \end{bmatrix} = \begin{bmatrix} 16 & 0 & 26 \\ -11 & 4 & 3 \end{bmatrix}.$$

EXAMPLE 3. *A firm produces three different pump units, each of which requires some components, shown below in a tabular form:*

Pump	Housing	Impeller	Bolts	Couplings	Inlets	Armoured Hose
Type A	1	1	5	4	2	8 m
Type B	1	1	7	3	2	4 m
Type C	1	1	3	5	2	3 m

The firm receives an order for 8 *Type A pump units,* 4 *Type B units and* 2 *Type C units. Using the notion of Matrix multiplication obtain the matrix whose elements may represent the quantities of each item required to make up the order.* **[ICWAI December 1975]**

SOLUTION. Let X be the matrix representing the order for the three types of pumps and Y the matrix representing the different components with the three types of pumps. Then

$$X = [8 \ \ 4 \ \ 2] \quad \text{and} \quad Y = \begin{bmatrix} 1 & 1 & 5 & 4 & 2 & 8 \\ 1 & 1 & 7 & 3 & 2 & 4 \\ 1 & 1 & 3 & 5 & 2 & 3 \end{bmatrix}.$$

$\therefore$ The required matrix whose elements represent the quantities of each item required to make up the order

$$= X \cdot Y = \overrightarrow{[8\ 4\ 2]} \times \left\downarrow \begin{bmatrix} 1 & 1 & 5 & 4 & 2 & 8 \\ 1 & 1 & 7 & 3 & 2 & 4 \\ 1 & 1 & 3 & 5 & 2 & 3 \end{bmatrix} \right.$$

$$= \begin{matrix}[8\times1+4\times1+2\times1 & 8\times1+4\times1+2\times1 & 8\times5+4\times7+2\times3 \\ 8\times4+4\times3+2\times5 & 8\times2+4\times2+2\times2 & 8\times8+4\times4+2\times3]\end{matrix}$$

$$= [14\ \ 14\ \ 74\ \ 54\ \ 28\ \ 86].$$

2.4. LAWS OF MATRIX ALGEBRA

I. Properties of Addition of Matrices

(i) *If A and B be any two matrices of the same order $m \times n$, then $A + B = B + A$.*

[Commutative Law]

PROOF. If $A = (a_{ij})_{m\times n}$ and $B = (b_{ij})_{m\times n}$, then

$$A + B = (a_{ij})_{m\times n} + (b_{ij})_{m\times n} = (a_{ij} + b_{ij})_{m\times n}$$
$$\text{and} \quad B + A = (b_{ij})_{m\times n} + (a_{ij})_{m\times n} = (b_{ij} + a_{ij})_{m\times n} = (a_{ij} + b_{ij})_{m\times n}$$

Hence, $A + B = B + A$.

(ii) *If A, B, C be any three matrices of the same order $m\times n$, then $A+(B+C) = (A+B)+C$.*

[Associative Law]

PROOF. Let $A = (a_{ij})_{m\times n}, B = (b_{ij})_{m\times n}, C = (c_{ij})_{m\times n}$. Then

$$A + (B + C) = (a_{ij})_{m\times n} + (b_{ij} + c_{ij})_{m\times n} = (a_{ij} + b_{ij} + c_{ij})_{m\times n}$$
$$\text{and} \quad (A + B) + C = (a_{ij} + b_{ij})_{m\times n} + (c_{ij})_{m\times n} = (a_{ij} + b_{ij} + c_{ij})_{m\times n}.$$

Hence, $A + (B + C) = (A + B) + C$.

(iii) *If k be a scalar and A, B be two matrices of the same order $m \times n$, then*

$$k(A + B) = kA + kB.$$

Proof is left as an exercise to the students.

(iv) *If A be an $m \times n$ matrix and 0 be the null matrix of the same order, then*

(a) $A + 0 = 0 + A = A$ *and* (b) $A + (-A) = (-A) + A = 0.$

(v) *If A, B, C be any three matrices of the same order $m \times n$, then $A + C = B + C$ gives $A = B$.*

PROOF.

$$A + C = B + C, \text{ or, } (A + C) + (-C) = (B + C) + (-C),$$
$$\text{or, } \quad A + (C - C) = B + (C - C), \text{ or, } \quad A + 0 = B + 0, \text{ or, } A = B.$$

II. Properties of Matrix Multiplication

(i) *The product of matrices is not, in general,* **commutative** *i.e., if two matrices A, B are conformable for the products AB and BA, then, in general,* $\mathbf{AB} \neq \mathbf{BA}$.

(ii) *If A, B, C are three matrices such that* $AB = AC$, *then, in general,* $B \neq C$.

(iii) *If A, B, C be three matrices of order* $m \times n, n \times p, n \times p$, *respectively, then*

$$\mathbf{A} \cdot (\mathbf{B} + \mathbf{C}) = \mathbf{A} \cdot \mathbf{B} + \mathbf{A} \cdot \mathbf{C}.$$

[Distributive Law]

(iv) *If A, B, C be three matrices of order* $m \times n, n \times p, p \times q$, *respectively, then* $\mathbf{A}(\mathbf{BC}) = (\mathbf{AB})\mathbf{C}$.

[Associative Law]

(v) *If A is an* $m \times n$ *matrix and* 0 *an* $n \times m$ *null matrix, then* $\mathbf{A.0} = \mathbf{0.A} = \mathbf{0}$.

(vi) *If A be a square matrix of order n and I be the unit matrix of the same order, then* $\mathbf{AI} = \mathbf{IA} = \mathbf{A}$.

(vii) *If* $AB = 0$ *where A, B are two matrices, then, in general,* $A \neq 0$ *or* $B \neq 0$ *or* $A \neq 0$ *and* $B \neq 0$.

EXAMPLE 4. *If* $A = \begin{bmatrix} 1 & 2 & 4 \\ 3 & 0 & 5 \end{bmatrix}$ *and* $B = \begin{bmatrix} 2 & 4 & 1 \\ 0 & 3 & 2 \end{bmatrix}$. *Find the value of* $3A + 2B$.

SOLUTION. We have $3A = 3\begin{bmatrix} 1 & 2 & 4 \\ 3 & 0 & 5 \end{bmatrix} = \begin{bmatrix} 3 & 6 & 12 \\ 9 & 0 & 15 \end{bmatrix}$ and $2B = 2\begin{bmatrix} 2 & 4 & 1 \\ 0 & 3 & 2 \end{bmatrix} = \begin{bmatrix} 4 & 8 & 2 \\ 0 & 6 & 4 \end{bmatrix}$.

Hence, $3A + 2B = \begin{bmatrix} 3 & 6 & 12 \\ 9 & 0 & 15 \end{bmatrix} + \begin{bmatrix} 4 & 8 & 2 \\ 0 & 6 & 4 \end{bmatrix} = \begin{bmatrix} 3+4 & 6+8 & 12+2 \\ 9+0 & 0+6 & 15+4 \end{bmatrix} = \begin{bmatrix} 7 & 14 & 14 \\ 9 & 6 & 19 \end{bmatrix}$.

EXAMPLE 5. $A = \begin{bmatrix} 2 & 3 & 1 \\ 0 & -1 & 5 \end{bmatrix}$ *and* $B = \begin{bmatrix} 1 & 2 & -1 \\ 0 & -1 & 3 \end{bmatrix}$, *evaluate* $2A - 3B$. **[Magadh U. 1985]**

SOLUTION.

$$\begin{aligned} 2A - 3B &= 2\begin{bmatrix} 2 & 3 & 1 \\ 0 & -1 & 5 \end{bmatrix} - 3\begin{bmatrix} 1 & 2 & -1 \\ 0 & -1 & 3 \end{bmatrix} \\ &= \begin{bmatrix} 4 & 6 & 2 \\ 0 & -2 & 10 \end{bmatrix} - \begin{bmatrix} 3 & 6 & -3 \\ 0 & -3 & 9 \end{bmatrix} \\ &= \begin{bmatrix} 4-3 & 6-6 & 2+3 \\ 0-0 & -2+3 & 10-9 \end{bmatrix} = \begin{bmatrix} 1 & 0 & 5 \\ 0 & 1 & 1 \end{bmatrix}. \end{aligned}$$

EXAMPLE 6. *Determine the matrices A and B, when*

$$A + 2B = \begin{bmatrix} 1 & 2 & 0 \\ 6 & -3 & 3 \\ -5 & 3 & 1 \end{bmatrix} \quad \text{and} \quad 2A - B = \begin{bmatrix} 2 & -1 & 5 \\ 2 & -1 & 6 \\ 0 & 1 & 2 \end{bmatrix}.$$

[C.U. 1986]

SOLUTION. We have

$$A + 2B = \begin{bmatrix} 1 & 2 & 0 \\ 6 & -3 & 3 \\ -5 & 3 & 1 \end{bmatrix} \quad (1)$$

$$\text{and} \quad 2A - B = \begin{bmatrix} 2 & -1 & 5 \\ 2 & -1 & 6 \\ 0 & 1 & 2 \end{bmatrix}. \quad (2)$$

From (2),

$$2(2A-B)=2\begin{bmatrix}2 & -1 & 5\\ 2 & -1 & 6\\ 0 & 1 & 2\end{bmatrix}, \quad \text{or,} \quad 4A-2B=\begin{bmatrix}4 & -2 & 10\\ 4 & -2 & 12\\ 0 & 2 & 4\end{bmatrix} \tag{3}$$

Adding (1) and (3), we get

$$(A+2B)+(4A-2B)=\begin{bmatrix}1 & 2 & 0\\ 6 & -3 & 3\\ -5 & 3 & 1\end{bmatrix}+\begin{bmatrix}4 & -2 & 10\\ 4 & -2 & 12\\ 0 & 2 & 4\end{bmatrix}$$

$$\text{or,} \quad 5A=\begin{bmatrix}1+4 & 2-2 & 0+10\\ 6+4 & -3-2 & 3+12\\ -5+0 & 3+2 & 1+4\end{bmatrix}=\begin{bmatrix}5 & 0 & 10\\ 10 & -5 & 15\\ -5 & 5 & 5\end{bmatrix},$$

$$\text{or,} \quad \frac{1}{5}\times 5A=\frac{1}{5}\begin{bmatrix}5 & 0 & 10\\ 10 & -5 & 15\\ -5 & 5 & 5\end{bmatrix}, \quad \text{or,} \quad A=\begin{bmatrix}1 & 0 & 2\\ 2 & -1 & 3\\ -1 & 1 & 1\end{bmatrix}.$$

From (1),

$$2B=\begin{bmatrix}1 & 2 & 0\\ 6 & -3 & 3\\ -5 & 3 & 1\end{bmatrix}-\begin{bmatrix}1 & 0 & 2\\ 2 & -1 & 3\\ -1 & 1 & 1\end{bmatrix}=\begin{bmatrix}1-1 & 2-0 & 0-2\\ 6-2 & -3-(-1) & 3-3\\ -5-(-1) & 3-1 & 1-1\end{bmatrix},$$

$$\text{or,} \quad B=\frac{1}{2}\begin{bmatrix}0 & 2 & -2\\ 4 & -2 & 0\\ -4 & 2 & 0\end{bmatrix}=\begin{bmatrix}\mathbf{0} & \mathbf{1} & \mathbf{-1}\\ \mathbf{2} & \mathbf{-1} & \mathbf{0}\\ \mathbf{-2} & \mathbf{1} & \mathbf{0}\end{bmatrix}.$$

EXAMPLE 7. *Find the product AB of two matrices A and B where*

$$A=\begin{bmatrix}1\\ 0\\ 7\\ 8\end{bmatrix} \quad \text{and} \quad B=[2\ 4\ 9\ 6\ 5\ 0].$$ **[ICWAI June 1980]**

SOLUTION. $AB=\overrightarrow{\begin{bmatrix}1\\ 0\\ 7\\ 8\end{bmatrix}}\times\downarrow[2\ 4\ 9\ 6\ 5\ 0]=\begin{bmatrix}2 & 4 & 9 & 6 & 5 & 0\\ 0 & 0 & 0 & 0 & 0 & 0\\ 14 & 28 & 63 & 42 & 35 & 0\\ 16 & 32 & 72 & 48 & 40 & 0\end{bmatrix}.$

EXAMPLE 8. *A man buys* 8 *dozens of mangoes,* 10 *dozens of apples, and* 4 *dozens of bananas. Mangoes cost* Rs. 18 *per dozen, apples* Rs. 9 *per dozen, and bananas* Rs. 6 *per dozen. Represent the quantities bought by a row matrix and the prices by a column matrix and hence obtain the total cost.* **[ICWAI June 1979]**

SOLUTION. If A be the row matrix representing the quantities bought i.e., 8 dozens of mangoes, 10 dozens of apples, 4 dozens of bananas, then A is a 1×3 matrix given by $A=[8\ 10\ 4]$.

Similarly, the column matrix B representing the prices of mangoes, apples, bananas per dozen is a 3×1 matrix given by $B=\begin{bmatrix}18\\ 9\\ 6\end{bmatrix}$.

The total cost is given by the element of the product AB which is a 1×1 matrix and

$$AB = [8 \ \ 10 \ \ 4] \times \begin{bmatrix} 18 \\ 9 \\ 6 \end{bmatrix} = [8 \times 18 + 10 \times 9 + 4 \times 6] = [144 + 90 + 24] = [258].$$

Hence the required total cost is **Rs. 258.**

EXAMPLE 9. *If A and B are matrices and if $AB = \theta$ (0 being a zero matrix), give an example where neither A nor B is* 0.

SOLUTION. Let us consider the matrices A and B given by $A = \begin{bmatrix} 1 & -1 \\ -1 & 1 \end{bmatrix}$ and $B = \begin{bmatrix} 1 & 1 \\ 1 & 1 \end{bmatrix}$.

Then

$$AB = \overrightarrow{\begin{bmatrix} 1 & -1 \\ -1 & 1 \end{bmatrix}} \times \downarrow\begin{bmatrix} 1 & 1 \\ 1 & 1 \end{bmatrix} = \begin{bmatrix} 1 \times 1 - 1 \times 1 & 1 \times 1 - 1 \times 1 \\ -1 \times 1 + 1 \times 1 & -1 \times 1 + 1 \times 1 \end{bmatrix}.$$

$$= \begin{bmatrix} 0 & 0 \\ 0 & 0 \end{bmatrix} = \mathbf{0}, \quad \text{where } \mathbf{0} \text{ is the zero matrix of order 2.}$$

Thus, $AB = 0$ where neither A nor B is 0.

Hence, *the result follows.*

EXAMPLE 10. *If $A = \begin{pmatrix} 1 & 4 \\ 5 & 7 \end{pmatrix}$ and $B = \begin{pmatrix} 4 & 1 \\ 4 & 5 \end{pmatrix}$, verify by actual multiplication that*

$$AB \neq BA.$$

[CA May 1981]

SOLUTION. We have

$$AB = \overrightarrow{\begin{pmatrix} 1 & 4 \\ 5 & 7 \end{pmatrix}} \times \downarrow\begin{pmatrix} 4 & 1 \\ 4 & 5 \end{pmatrix} = \begin{pmatrix} 1 \times 4 + 4 \times 4 & 1 \times 1 + 4 \times 5 \\ 5 \times 4 + 7 \times 4 & 5 \times 1 + 7 \times 5 \end{pmatrix}$$

$$= \begin{pmatrix} 4 + 16 & 1 + 20 \\ 20 + 28 & 5 + 35 \end{pmatrix} = \begin{pmatrix} 20 & 21 \\ 48 & 40 \end{pmatrix} \quad (1)$$

$$\text{and } BA = \overrightarrow{\begin{pmatrix} 4 & 1 \\ 4 & 5 \end{pmatrix}} \times \downarrow\begin{pmatrix} 1 & 4 \\ 5 & 7 \end{pmatrix} = \begin{pmatrix} 4 \times 1 + 1 \times 5 & 4 \times 4 + 1 \times 7 \\ 4 \times 1 + 5 \times 5 & 4 \times 4 + 5 \times 7 \end{pmatrix}$$

$$= \begin{pmatrix} 4 + 5 & 16 + 7 \\ 4 + 25 & 16 + 35 \end{pmatrix} = \begin{pmatrix} 9 & 23 \\ 29 & 51 \end{pmatrix} \quad (2)$$

From (1) and (2), we see that $AB \neq BA$.

EXAMPLE 11. *If $A = \begin{bmatrix} 2 & 3 \\ 3 & 5 \end{bmatrix}$, show that $A^2 = 7A - I$ where $I = \begin{bmatrix} 1 & 0 \\ 0 & 1 \end{bmatrix}$.*

[ICWAI June 1982, '88]

SOLUTION. We have

$$A^2 = A \times A = \begin{bmatrix} 2 & 3 \\ 3 & 5 \end{bmatrix} \times \begin{bmatrix} 2 & 3 \\ 3 & 5 \end{bmatrix} = \begin{bmatrix} 2 \times 2 + 3 \times 3 & 2 \times 3 + 3 \times 5 \\ 3 \times 2 + 5 \times 3 & 3 \times 3 + 5 \times 5 \end{bmatrix} = \begin{bmatrix} 13 & 21 \\ 21 & 34 \end{bmatrix}, \quad (1)$$

$$7A = 7\begin{bmatrix} 2 & 3 \\ 3 & 5 \end{bmatrix} = \begin{bmatrix} 14 & 21 \\ 21 & 35 \end{bmatrix} \text{ and } I = \begin{bmatrix} 1 & 0 \\ 0 & 1 \end{bmatrix}.$$

$$\therefore \quad 7A - I = \begin{bmatrix} 14 & 21 \\ 21 & 35 \end{bmatrix} - \begin{bmatrix} 1 & 0 \\ 0 & 1 \end{bmatrix} = \begin{bmatrix} 13 & 21 \\ 21 & 34 \end{bmatrix} \quad (2)$$

From (1) and (2), we get $\mathbf{A^2 = 7A - I}$.

EXAMPLE 12. *If* $A = \begin{bmatrix} 1 & 0 & -2 \\ 2 & 2 & 4 \\ 0 & 0 & 2 \end{bmatrix}$, *verify* $A^2 - 3A + 2I = 0$. **[ICWAI December 1984, '85]**

SOLUTION. We have

$$A^2 = A \times A = \begin{bmatrix} 1 & 0 & -2 \\ 2 & 2 & 4 \\ 0 & 0 & 2 \end{bmatrix} \times \begin{bmatrix} 1 & 0 & -2 \\ 2 & 2 & 4 \\ 0 & 0 & 2 \end{bmatrix}$$

$$= \begin{bmatrix} 1+0+0 & 0+0+0 & -2+0-4 \\ 2+4+0 & 0+4+0 & -4+8+8 \\ 0+0+0 & 0+0+0 & 0+0+4 \end{bmatrix} = \begin{bmatrix} 1 & 0 & -6 \\ 6 & 4 & 12 \\ 0 & 0 & 4 \end{bmatrix}$$

$$3A = 3\begin{bmatrix} 1 & 0 & -2 \\ 2 & 2 & 4 \\ 0 & 0 & 2 \end{bmatrix} = \begin{bmatrix} 3 & 0 & -6 \\ 6 & 6 & 12 \\ 0 & 0 & 6 \end{bmatrix} \quad \text{and} \quad 2I = 2\begin{bmatrix} 1 & 0 & 0 \\ 0 & 1 & 0 \\ 0 & 0 & 1 \end{bmatrix} = \begin{bmatrix} 2 & 0 & 0 \\ 0 & 2 & 0 \\ 0 & 0 & 2 \end{bmatrix}$$

$$\therefore \quad A^2 - 3A + 2I = \begin{bmatrix} 1 & 0 & -6 \\ 6 & 4 & 12 \\ 0 & 0 & 4 \end{bmatrix} - \begin{bmatrix} 3 & 0 & -6 \\ 6 & 6 & 12 \\ 0 & 0 & 6 \end{bmatrix} + \begin{bmatrix} 2 & 0 & 0 \\ 0 & 2 & 0 \\ 0 & 0 & 2 \end{bmatrix}$$

$$= \begin{bmatrix} 1-3+2 & 0-0+0 & -6+6+0 \\ 6-6+0 & 4-6+2 & 12-12+0 \\ 0-0+0 & 0-0+0 & 4-6+2 \end{bmatrix} = \begin{bmatrix} 0 & 0 & 0 \\ 0 & 0 & 0 \\ 0 & 0 & 0 \end{bmatrix}$$

$= \mathbf{0}$, where $\mathbf{0}$ is the square null matrix of order 3.

Hence $\mathbf{A^2 - 3A + 2I = 0}$.

EXAMPLE 13. *If* $A = \begin{bmatrix} 2 & 1 \\ 3 & 4 \end{bmatrix}$ *and* $B = \begin{bmatrix} 1 & -2 \\ -1 & 1 \end{bmatrix}$, *verify that* $(AB)^T = B^T \cdot A^T$ *where* A^T *is the transpose matrix of A, etc.* **[C.U. B.Com. (Hons.) 1984, '89]**

SOLUTION. We have

$$AB = \overrightarrow{\begin{bmatrix} 2 & 1 \\ 3 & 4 \end{bmatrix}} \times \downarrow\begin{bmatrix} 1 & -2 \\ -1 & 1 \end{bmatrix} = \begin{bmatrix} 2 \times 1 + 1 \times (-1) & 2 \times (-2) + 1 \times 1 \\ 3 \times 1 + 4 \times (-1) & 3 \times (-2) + 4 \times 1 \end{bmatrix}$$

$$= \begin{bmatrix} 2-1 & -4+1 \\ 3-4 & -6+4 \end{bmatrix} = \begin{bmatrix} 1 & -3 \\ -1 & -2 \end{bmatrix}$$

$$\therefore \quad (AB)^T = \begin{bmatrix} 1 & -1 \\ -3 & -2 \end{bmatrix} \tag{1}$$

Now

$$A^T = \begin{bmatrix} 2 & 3 \\ 1 & 4 \end{bmatrix} \quad \text{and} \quad B^T = \begin{bmatrix} 1 & -1 \\ -2 & 1 \end{bmatrix}$$

$$\therefore \quad B^T \cdot A^T = \overrightarrow{\begin{bmatrix} 1 & -1 \\ -2 & 1 \end{bmatrix}} \times \downarrow\begin{bmatrix} 2 & 3 \\ 1 & 4 \end{bmatrix} = \begin{bmatrix} 1 \times 2 + (-1) \times 1 & 1 \times 3 + (-1) \times 4 \\ (-2) \times 2 + 1 \times 1 & (-2) \times 3 + 1 \times 4 \end{bmatrix}$$

$$= \begin{bmatrix} 2-1 & 3-4 \\ -4+1 & -6+4 \end{bmatrix} = \begin{bmatrix} 1 & -1 \\ -3 & -2 \end{bmatrix} \tag{2}$$

From (1) and (2), we get $\mathbf{(AB)^T = B^T \cdot A^T}$.

EXAMPLE 14. *Find ABC if* $A = [x \;\; y \;\; z]$, $B = \begin{bmatrix} a & h & g \\ h & b & f \\ g & f & c \end{bmatrix}$, $C = \begin{bmatrix} x \\ y \\ z \end{bmatrix}$.

[ICWAI June 1979]

SOLUTION.

$$BC = \begin{bmatrix} a & h & g \\ h & b & f \\ g & f & c \end{bmatrix} \times \begin{bmatrix} x \\ y \\ z \end{bmatrix} = \begin{bmatrix} ax+hy+gz \\ hx+by+fz \\ gx+fy+cz \end{bmatrix}$$

$$\therefore \quad ABC = [x \;\; y \;\; z] \times \begin{bmatrix} ax+hy+gz \\ hx+by+fz \\ gx+fy+cz \end{bmatrix}$$

$$= [\,ax^2 + hxy + gzx + hxy + by^2 + fyz + gzx + fyz + cz^2\,]$$

$$= [\,ax^2 + by^2 + cz^2 + 2hxy + 2fyz + 2gzx\,].$$

EXAMPLE 15. *Let two matrices A and B be given by*

$$A = \begin{bmatrix} 1 & -1 & 0 \\ 2 & 3 & 4 \\ 0 & 1 & 2 \end{bmatrix} \quad \text{and} \quad B = \begin{bmatrix} 2 & 2 & -4 \\ -4 & 2 & -4 \\ 2 & -1 & 5 \end{bmatrix},$$

verify that $BA = 6I$, where I is the unit matrix of order 3. **[ICWAI June 1974]**

SOLUTION.

$$BA = \begin{bmatrix} 2 & 2 & -4 \\ -4 & 2 & -4 \\ 2 & -1 & 5 \end{bmatrix} \times \begin{bmatrix} 1 & -1 & 0 \\ 2 & 3 & 4 \\ 0 & 1 & 2 \end{bmatrix}$$

$$= \begin{bmatrix} 2\times1+2\times2+(-4)\times0 & 2\times(-1)+2\times3+(-4)\times1 & 2\times0+2\times4+(-4)\times2 \\ (-4)\times1+2\times2+(-4)\times0 & (-4)\times(-1)+2\times3+(-4)\times1 & (-4)\times0+2\times4+(-4)\times2 \\ 2\times1+(-1)\times2+5\times0 & 2\times(-1)+(-1)\times3+5\times1 & 2\times0+(-1)\times4+5\times2 \end{bmatrix}$$

$$= \begin{bmatrix} 2+4+0 & -2+6-4 & 0+8-8 \\ -4+4+0 & 4+6-4 & 0+8-8 \\ 2-2+0 & -2-3+5 & 0-4+10 \end{bmatrix} = \begin{bmatrix} 6 & 0 & 0 \\ 0 & 6 & 0 \\ 0 & 0 & 6 \end{bmatrix} = 6\begin{bmatrix} 1 & 0 & 0 \\ 0 & 1 & 0 \\ 0 & 0 & 1 \end{bmatrix}$$

$$= 6I.$$

Hence, *the result follows.*

EXAMPLE 16. *Find the values of a, b, c if the matrix A given by*

$$A = \frac{1}{3}\begin{bmatrix} a & 2 & 2 \\ 2 & 1 & b \\ 2 & c & 1 \end{bmatrix}.$$

obeys the law $A \cdot A' = I$. (A' is the transpose of A and I is the unit matrix of order 3.)

[ICWAI December 1977]

SOLUTION. We have

$$A' = \frac{1}{3}\begin{bmatrix} a & 2 & 2 \\ 2 & 1 & c \\ 2 & b & 1 \end{bmatrix}$$

$$\therefore \quad A \cdot A' = \frac{1}{3}\begin{bmatrix} a & 2 & 2 \\ 2 & 1 & b \\ 2 & c & 1 \end{bmatrix} \times \frac{1}{3}\begin{bmatrix} a & 2 & 2 \\ 2 & 1 & c \\ 2 & b & 1 \end{bmatrix}$$

$$= \frac{1}{9}\begin{bmatrix} a \cdot a + 2 \cdot 2 + 2 \cdot 2 & a \cdot 2 + 2 \cdot 1 + 2 \cdot b & a \cdot 2 + 2 \cdot c + 2 \cdot 1 \\ 2 \cdot a + 1 \cdot 2 + b \cdot 2 & 2 \cdot 2 + 1 \cdot 1 + b \cdot b & 2 \cdot 2 + 1 \cdot c + b \cdot 1 \\ 2 \cdot a + c \cdot 2 + 1 \cdot 2 & 2 \cdot 2 + c \cdot 1 + 1 \cdot b & 2 \cdot 2 + c \cdot c + 1 \cdot 1 \end{bmatrix}$$

$$= \frac{1}{9}\begin{bmatrix} a^2 + 8 & 2a + 2b + 2 & 2a + 2c + 2 \\ 2a + 2b + 2 & b^2 + 5 & b + c + 4 \\ 2a + 2c + 2 & b + c + 4 & c^2 + 5 \end{bmatrix}$$

$$= \begin{bmatrix} 1 & 0 & 0 \\ 0 & 1 & 0 \\ 0 & 0 & 1 \end{bmatrix} \text{ (given)} \quad [\because \ AA' = 1]$$

Hence,

$$\frac{1}{9}(a^2 + 8) = 1, \quad \frac{1}{9}(b^2 + 5) = 1, \quad \frac{1}{9}(c^2 + 5) = 1, \qquad (1)$$

$$\text{and} \quad 2a + 2b + 2 = 0, \quad 2a + 2c + 2 = 0, \quad b + c + 4 = 0. \qquad (2)$$

From (1)

$$a^2 + 8 = 9, \qquad b^2 + 5 = 9, \qquad c^2 + 5 = 9$$

$$\text{or,} \quad a^2 = 1, \qquad b^2 = 4, \qquad c^2 = 4$$

$$\therefore \quad a = \pm 1, \qquad b = \pm 2, \qquad c = \pm 2.$$

Of these values of a, b, c, only $a = 1, b = -2, c = -2$ satisfy the relations (2).

Hence, $\mathbf{a = 1, b = -2, c = -2}$.

EXAMPLE 17. *Prove that the matrix A given by* $A = \begin{bmatrix} a & b \\ c & d \end{bmatrix}$ *satisfies the relation*

$A^2 - A(a + d) + (ad - bc)I = 0$, *where I is a unit matrix of order two.*

[ICWAI June 1975, '81; Lucknow U 1989]

SOLUTION.

$$A^2 = \begin{bmatrix} a & b \\ c & d \end{bmatrix} \times \begin{bmatrix} a & b \\ c & d \end{bmatrix} = \begin{bmatrix} a^2 + bc & ab + bd \\ ac + cd & bc + a^2 \end{bmatrix},$$

$$A(a + d) = \begin{bmatrix} a & b \\ c & d \end{bmatrix}(a + d) = \begin{bmatrix} a^2 + ad & ab + bd \\ ac + cd & ad + d^2 \end{bmatrix}$$

$$\text{and} \quad (ad - bc)I = (ad - bc)\begin{bmatrix} 1 & 0 \\ 0 & 1 \end{bmatrix} = \begin{bmatrix} ad - bc & 0 \\ 0 & ad - bc \end{bmatrix};$$

$$\therefore \quad A^2 - A(a+d) + (ad-bc)I = \begin{bmatrix} a^2+bc & ab+bd \\ ac+cd & bc+d^2 \end{bmatrix} - \begin{bmatrix} a^2+ad & ab+bd \\ ac+cd & ad+d^2 \end{bmatrix} + \begin{bmatrix} ad-bc & 0 \\ 0 & ad-bc \end{bmatrix}$$

$$= \begin{bmatrix} a^2+bc-a^2-ad+ad-bc & ab+bd-ab-bd+0 \\ ac+cd-ac-cd+0 & bc+d^2-ad-d^2+ad-bc \end{bmatrix}$$

$$= \begin{bmatrix} 0 & 0 \\ 0 & 0 \end{bmatrix} = 0.$$

Hence the matrix A satisfies the relation $A^2 - A(a+d) + (ad-bc)I = 0$.

EXAMPLE 18. *If* $A = \begin{pmatrix} 1 & -1 \\ 2 & -1 \end{pmatrix}$, $B = \begin{pmatrix} a & 1 \\ b & -1 \end{pmatrix}$ *and* $(A+B)^2 = A^2 + B^2$, *find a and b, using the values of a, b, verify whether* $AB = BA$. **[CA November 1987; ICWAI December 1987]**

SOLUTION.

$$A + B = \begin{pmatrix} 1 & -1 \\ 2 & -1 \end{pmatrix} + \begin{pmatrix} a & 1 \\ b & -1 \end{pmatrix} = \begin{pmatrix} 1+a & 0 \\ 2+b & -2 \end{pmatrix}$$

$$\therefore \quad (A+B)^2 = \begin{pmatrix} 1+a & 0 \\ 2+b & -2 \end{pmatrix} \times \begin{pmatrix} 1+a & 0 \\ 2+b & -2 \end{pmatrix} = \begin{pmatrix} (1+a)^2 & 0 \\ (2+b)(1+a) - 2(2+b) & 4 \end{pmatrix}$$

$$A^2 = \begin{pmatrix} 1 & -1 \\ 2 & -1 \end{pmatrix} \times \begin{pmatrix} 1 & -1 \\ 2 & -1 \end{pmatrix} = \begin{pmatrix} 1-2 & -1+1 \\ 2-2 & -2+1 \end{pmatrix} = \begin{pmatrix} -1 & 0 \\ 0 & -1 \end{pmatrix}$$

$$\text{and} \quad B^2 = \begin{pmatrix} a & 1 \\ b & -1 \end{pmatrix} \times \begin{pmatrix} a & 1 \\ b & -1 \end{pmatrix} = \begin{pmatrix} a^2+b & a-1 \\ ab-b & b+1 \end{pmatrix}$$

$$\therefore \quad A^2 + B^2 = \begin{pmatrix} -1 & 0 \\ 0 & -1 \end{pmatrix} + \begin{pmatrix} a^2+b & a-1 \\ ab-b & b+1 \end{pmatrix} = \begin{pmatrix} a^2+b-1 & a-1 \\ ab-b & b \end{pmatrix}.$$

Given, $(A+B)^2 = A^2 + B^2$, or, $\begin{pmatrix} (1+a)^2 & 0 \\ (2+b)(1+a) - 2(2+b) & 4 \end{pmatrix} = \begin{pmatrix} a^2+b-1 & a-1 \\ ab-b & b \end{pmatrix}$.

$$\therefore \quad (1+a)^2 = a^2 + b - 1 \qquad (1)$$

$$0 = a - 1 \qquad (2)$$

$$(2+b)(1+a) - 2(2+b) = ab - b \qquad (3)$$

$$\text{and} \quad 4 = b \qquad (4)$$

From (2) and (4), we get $a = 1$ and $b = 4$.

We see that $a = 1$ and $b = 4$ also satisfy (1) and (3).

Hence $\mathbf{a} = \mathbf{1}$ and $\mathbf{b} = \mathbf{4}$.

If $a = 1$ and $b = 4$, then $A = \begin{pmatrix} 1 & -1 \\ 2 & -1 \end{pmatrix}$ and $B = \begin{pmatrix} 1 & 1 \\ 4 & -1 \end{pmatrix}$.

$$\therefore \quad AB = \begin{pmatrix} 1 & -1 \\ 2 & -1 \end{pmatrix} \times \begin{pmatrix} 1 & 1 \\ 4 & -1 \end{pmatrix} = \begin{pmatrix} 1-4 & 1+1 \\ 2-4 & 2+1 \end{pmatrix} = \begin{pmatrix} -3 & 2 \\ -2 & 3 \end{pmatrix}$$

$$\text{and} \quad BA = \begin{pmatrix} 1 & 1 \\ 4 & -1 \end{pmatrix} \times \begin{pmatrix} 1 & -1 \\ 2 & -1 \end{pmatrix} = \begin{pmatrix} 1+2 & -1-1 \\ 4-2 & -4+1 \end{pmatrix} = \begin{pmatrix} 3 & -2 \\ 2 & -3 \end{pmatrix}.$$

$$\therefore \quad \mathbf{AB} \neq BA.$$

EXAMPLE 19. *If the matrix P is given by* $P = \begin{pmatrix} 3 & 4 \\ -1 & -1 \end{pmatrix}$, *then prove that* $P^n = \begin{pmatrix} 1+2n & 4n \\ -n & 1-2n \end{pmatrix}$ *for all positive integers* $n \geq 1$. **[ICWAI December 1981; CA May 1991]**

SOLUTION.

$$\begin{aligned} P^2 = P \cdot P &= \overrightarrow{\begin{pmatrix} 3 & 4 \\ -1 & -1 \end{pmatrix}} \times \downarrow\begin{pmatrix} 3 & 4 \\ -1 & -1 \end{pmatrix} = \begin{pmatrix} 9-4 & 12-4 \\ -3+1 & -4+1 \end{pmatrix} = \begin{pmatrix} 5 & 8 \\ -2 & -3 \end{pmatrix} \\ &= \begin{pmatrix} 1+2.2 & 4.2 \\ -2 & 1-2.2 \end{pmatrix}. \end{aligned}$$

This shows that the result is true for $n = 2$.

$$\begin{aligned} P^3 = P^2 \cdot P &= \overrightarrow{\begin{pmatrix} 5 & 8 \\ -2 & -3 \end{pmatrix}} \times \downarrow\begin{pmatrix} 3 & 4 \\ -1 & -1 \end{pmatrix} = \begin{pmatrix} 15-8 & 20-8 \\ -6+3 & -8+3 \end{pmatrix} = \begin{pmatrix} 7 & 12 \\ -3 & -5 \end{pmatrix} \\ &= \begin{pmatrix} 1+2.3 & 4.3 \\ -3 & 1-2.3 \end{pmatrix}. \end{aligned}$$

This shows that the result is true for $n = 3$.

Let us assume that the result is true for $n = m$, where m is a positive integer. Then

$$P^m = \begin{pmatrix} 1+2m & 4m \\ -m & 1-2m \end{pmatrix}.$$

$$\begin{aligned} \therefore \quad P^{m+1} = P^m \cdot P &= \overrightarrow{\begin{pmatrix} 1+2m & 4m \\ -m & 1-2m \end{pmatrix}} \times \downarrow\begin{pmatrix} 3 & 4 \\ -1 & -1 \end{pmatrix} \\ &= \begin{pmatrix} 3+6m-4m & 4+8m-4m \\ -3m-1+2m & -4m-1+2m \end{pmatrix} = \begin{pmatrix} 3+2m & 4+4m \\ -m-1 & -2m-1 \end{pmatrix}, \\ &= \begin{pmatrix} 1+2(m+1) & 4(m+1) \\ -(m+1) & 1-2(m+1) \end{pmatrix}. \end{aligned}$$

This shows that the result is true for $n = m+1$ if it is true for $n = m$. But it is seen to be true for $n = 2, 3$.

$\therefore$ The result is true for $n = 3+1$ i.e., 4 and so on.

Hence *the result is true for all positive integers* $n \geq 1$.

EXAMPLE 20. *Using matrices A, B and C, where* $A = \begin{bmatrix} 1 & -1 & 1 \\ 0 & 2 & 1 \end{bmatrix}$; $B = \begin{bmatrix} 1 & -1 & 0 \\ 0 & 1 & -1 \\ 1 & 1 & 1 \end{bmatrix}$; $C = \begin{bmatrix} 1 & 0 \\ 0 & 1 \\ 1. & 1 \end{bmatrix}$, *verify the rule:* $(AB)C = A(BC)$. **[ICWAI June 1976]**

SOLUTION.

$$AB = \begin{bmatrix} 1 & -1 & 1 \\ 0 & 2 & 1 \end{bmatrix} \times \begin{bmatrix} 1 & -1 & 0 \\ 0 & 1 & -1 \\ 1 & 1 & 1 \end{bmatrix}$$

$$= \begin{bmatrix} 1\times1+(-1)\times0+1\times1 & 1\times-1+(-1)\times1+1\times1 & 1\times0+(-1)\times(-1)+1\times1 \\ 0\times1+2\times0+1\times1 & 0\times-1+2\times1+1\times1 & 0\times0+2\times-1+1\times1 \end{bmatrix}$$

$$= \begin{bmatrix} 1+0+1 & -1-1+1 & 0+1+1 \\ 0+0+1 & 0+2+1 & 0-2+1 \end{bmatrix} = \begin{bmatrix} 2 & -1 & 2 \\ 1 & 3 & -1 \end{bmatrix};$$

$$\therefore\quad (AB)C = \begin{bmatrix} 2 & -1 & 2 \\ 1 & 3 & -1 \end{bmatrix} \times \begin{bmatrix} 1 & 0 \\ 0 & 1 \\ 1 & 1 \end{bmatrix} = \begin{bmatrix} 2+0+2 & 0-1+2 \\ 1+0-1 & 0+3-1 \end{bmatrix} = \begin{bmatrix} 4 & 1 \\ 0 & 2 \end{bmatrix}$$

Again, $$BC = \begin{bmatrix} 1 & -1 & 0 \\ 0 & 1 & -1 \\ 1 & 1 & 1 \end{bmatrix} \times \begin{bmatrix} 1 & 0 \\ 0 & 1 \\ 1 & 1 \end{bmatrix} = \begin{bmatrix} 1+0+0 & 0-1+0 \\ 0+0-1 & 0+1-1 \\ 1+0+1 & 0+1+1 \end{bmatrix} = \begin{bmatrix} 1 & -1 \\ -1 & 0 \\ 2 & 2 \end{bmatrix};$$

$$\therefore\quad A(BC) = \begin{bmatrix} 1 & -1 & 1 \\ 0 & 2 & 1 \end{bmatrix} \times \begin{bmatrix} 1 & -1 \\ -1 & 0 \\ 2 & 2 \end{bmatrix} = \begin{bmatrix} 1+1+2 & -1+0+2 \\ 0-2+2 & 0+0+2 \end{bmatrix} = \begin{bmatrix} 4 & 1 \\ 0 & 2 \end{bmatrix}.$$

Hence $(AB)C = A(BC)$.

EXAMPLE 21. *A, B, C and X are four matrices given by*

$$A = \begin{bmatrix} 1 & 2 & -3 \\ 0 & 1 & 2 \\ 0 & 0 & 1 \end{bmatrix};\ B = \begin{bmatrix} 1 & -2 & 7 \\ 0 & 1 & -2 \\ 0 & 0 & 1 \end{bmatrix};\ C = \begin{bmatrix} 0 \\ 11 \\ 5 \end{bmatrix} \text{ and } X = \begin{bmatrix} x_1 \\ x_2 \\ x_3 \end{bmatrix}$$

(i) *Verify : $AB = BA = I$(I is a unit matrix of order 3);*

(ii) *If $X = BC$, find x_1, x_2 and x_3.* **[ICWAI June 1975]**

SOLUTION.

$$\text{(i)}\quad AB = \begin{bmatrix} 1 & 2 & -3 \\ 0 & 1 & 2 \\ 0 & 0 & 1 \end{bmatrix} \times \begin{bmatrix} 1 & -2 & 7 \\ 0 & 1 & -2 \\ 0 & 0 & 1 \end{bmatrix}$$

$$= \begin{bmatrix} 1+0-0 & -2+2-0 & 7-4-3 \\ 0+0+0 & 0+1+0 & 0-2+2 \\ 0+0+0 & 0+0+0 & 0+0+1 \end{bmatrix} = \begin{bmatrix} 1 & 0 & 0 \\ 0 & 1 & 0 \\ 0 & 0 & 1 \end{bmatrix} = I,$$

$$\text{and}\quad BA = \begin{bmatrix} 1 & -2 & 7 \\ 0 & 1 & -2 \\ 0 & 0 & 1 \end{bmatrix} \times \begin{bmatrix} 1 & 2 & -3 \\ 0 & 1 & 2 \\ 0 & 0 & 1 \end{bmatrix} = \begin{bmatrix} 1 & 0 & 0 \\ 0 & 1 & 0 \\ 0 & 0 & 1 \end{bmatrix} = I.$$

Hence **AB = BA = 1.**

(ii) We have $X = BC$, or, $$\begin{bmatrix} x_1 \\ x_2 \\ x_3 \end{bmatrix} = \begin{bmatrix} 1 & -2 & 7 \\ 0 & 1 & -2 \\ 0 & 0 & 1 \end{bmatrix} \times \begin{bmatrix} 0 \\ 11 \\ 5 \end{bmatrix} = \begin{bmatrix} 0-22+35 \\ 0+11-10 \\ 0+0+5 \end{bmatrix} = \begin{bmatrix} 13 \\ 1 \\ 5 \end{bmatrix}.$$

Hence $x_1 = \mathbf{13}, x_2 = \mathbf{1}, x_3 = \mathbf{5}$.

EXAMPLE 22. *Three persons buy cold drinks of different brands A, B, C. The first person buys 12 bottles of A, 5 bottles of B and 3 bottles of C. The second person buys 4 bottles of A, 6 bottles* *of B and 10 bottles of C. The third person buys 6 bottles of A, 7 bottles of B and 9 bottles of C. Represent these information in the form of a matrix. If each bottle of A costs Rs. 4, each bottle of B costs Rs. 5 and each bottle of C costs Rs. 6, then using matrix operations find the total sum of money, spent individually by the three persons for the purchase of cold drinks.* **[CA November 1991]**

SOLUTION. Let S be the matrix representing the given information in which first, second and third column represent different brands A, B, C of cold drinks and the first, second, third row represent the no. of bottles bought by A, B, C, respectively. Let P be the matrix representing the prices (in Rs.) of brands A, B, C per bottle. Then,

$$S = \begin{bmatrix} 12 & 5 & 3 \\ 4 & 6 & 10 \\ 6 & 7 & 9 \end{bmatrix} \quad \text{and} \quad P = \begin{bmatrix} 4 \\ 5 \\ 6 \end{bmatrix}$$

[Here S is a 3×3 matrix and P is 3×1 matrix.]

Clearly, the product SP is a 3×1 column matrix whose elements represent the total sum of money spent individually by the three persons on cold drinks.

$$\therefore \quad SP = \begin{bmatrix} 12 & 5 & 3 \\ 4 & 6 & 10 \\ 6 & 7 & 9 \end{bmatrix} \times \begin{bmatrix} 4 \\ 5 \\ 6 \end{bmatrix} = \begin{bmatrix} 48 + 25 + 18 \\ 16 + 30 + 60 \\ 24 + 35 + 54 \end{bmatrix} = \begin{bmatrix} 91 \\ 106 \\ 113 \end{bmatrix}$$

Hence, *the total sum of money spent individually by the three persons for the purchase of cold drinks are, respectively,* Rs. 91, Rs. 106 *and* Rs. 113.

Exercise 2

Matrices

[A]

1. (i) If $A = \begin{bmatrix} 2 & -1 & 4 \\ 5 & 0 & 7 \end{bmatrix}$ and $B = \begin{bmatrix} 1 & 2 & -3 \\ 0 & 4 & 1 \end{bmatrix}$ find $A + B, A - B, 3A + 2B$ and $2A - 3B$.

(ii) Given $A = \begin{bmatrix} 4 & 2 & -1 \\ 3 & -7 & 1 \end{bmatrix}$ and $B = \begin{bmatrix} 2 & 3 \\ -3 & 0 \\ -1 & 5 \end{bmatrix}$, find where possible $A + B, A - B, AB$ and BA, stating the reason where the operations are not possible. **[C.U. B.Com. (Hons.) 1991]**

2. (i) Find X if $Y = \begin{bmatrix} 2 & 3 \\ -1 & 5 \end{bmatrix}$ and $2X + Y = \begin{bmatrix} 4 & -1 \\ 5 & 3 \end{bmatrix}$.

(ii) If $3A + 2B = \begin{bmatrix} 8 & 9 & 1 \\ 11 & 7 & 6 \end{bmatrix}$ and $2A - B = \begin{bmatrix} 3 & -1 & -4 \\ -2 & 7 & 4 \end{bmatrix}$, find the matrices A and B.

3. (i) Find the values of x and y when $\begin{bmatrix} 3 & x + 2 \\ y & 5 \end{bmatrix} = \begin{bmatrix} x - 1 & 6 \\ x - 3y & 5 \end{bmatrix}$.

(ii) Find the values of x, y and z when $2 \begin{bmatrix} 1 \\ 2 \\ 3 \end{bmatrix} + 3 \begin{bmatrix} x \\ y \\ z \end{bmatrix} = \begin{bmatrix} 8 \\ 7 \\ 15 \end{bmatrix}$.

4. (i) If $A = \begin{bmatrix} 2 & 5 \\ 1 & 3 \end{bmatrix}$ and $B = \begin{bmatrix} 1 & -1 \\ -3 & 2 \end{bmatrix}$, find, if possible, BA and AB. Is $AB = BA$?

[CA May 1976]

(ii) Find, if possible, the product of the two matrices $A = [1 \ 2 \ 3 \ 4]$ and $B = \begin{bmatrix} 1 \\ 2 \\ 3 \\ 4 \end{bmatrix}$.

[ICWAI June 1975]

5. If $A = \begin{pmatrix} 1 & i \\ -i & 1 \end{pmatrix}, B = \begin{pmatrix} i & -1 \\ -1 & -i \end{pmatrix}$ and $i = \sqrt{-1}$ and $i^2 = -1$, determine AB; compute also BA. **[CA November 1975]**

6. If $A = \begin{bmatrix} 1 & 2 \\ 2 & 1 \end{bmatrix}$, show that $A^2 - 3I = 2A$.

7. If $P = \begin{bmatrix} 9 & 1 \\ 4 & 3 \end{bmatrix}, Q = \begin{bmatrix} 1 & 5 \\ 7 & 12 \end{bmatrix}$, find the matrix R such that $5P + 3Q + 2R$ is a null matrix.

[ICWAI December 1986]

8. If $A = \begin{bmatrix} 1 & 0 \\ 0 & 1 \end{bmatrix}$ and $B = \begin{bmatrix} 0 & 1 \\ -1 & 0 \end{bmatrix}$, show that $(xA + yB)(xA - yB) = (x^2 + y^2)A$.

[CA May 1986; November 1989]

9. If $A = \begin{bmatrix} 2 & -1 \\ 4 & 3 \end{bmatrix}$ and $B = \begin{bmatrix} 2 \\ -3 \end{bmatrix}$, find the matrix X of a suitable order such that $AX = B$.

[CA November 1990]

[HINTS. Since A is a 2×2 matrix and AX i.e., B is a 2×1 matrix, X must be a 2×1 matrix. Let $X = \begin{bmatrix} x \\ y \end{bmatrix}$. Now, use the equation $AX = B$ to find x, y.]

10. Given three matrices defined by $X = \begin{pmatrix} 5 & 1 \\ 0 & 2 \end{pmatrix}, Y = \begin{pmatrix} -2 & 0 \\ 1 & -3 \end{pmatrix}, Z = \begin{pmatrix} 3 & 1 \\ 2 & 7 \end{pmatrix}$. Verify the Distributive Law: $X(Y + Z) = XY + XZ$. **[CA May 1992]**

11. Let the matrix $A = \begin{pmatrix} -1 & -1 \\ 2 & -2 \end{pmatrix}$, verify that $A^2 + 3A + 4I = 0$ (I is the unit matrix of order two; 0 is 2×2 null matrix). **[ICWAI June 1980]**

12. A man buys 8 dozen of mangoes, 10 dozen of apples and 4 dozen of bananas. Mangoes cost Rs. 18 per dozen, apples Rs. 9 per dozen and bananas Rs. 6 per dozen. Represent the quantities by a row matrix and prices by column matrix and hence obtain the total cost. **[ICWAI June 1979]**

13. An engineering product requires five kinds of materials, the quantities of which are given in the form of the vector (i.e., a row matrix) $q = [17 \ 4 \ 36 \ 18 \ 6]$. If $p = [5 \ 200 \ 4 \ 50 \ 3]$ represents a vector of the corresponding prices per unit in Rs., find the total expenses for the manufacture of the product. **[ICWAI June 1976]**

14. (i) The matrix A is given by $A = \begin{bmatrix} 1 & 2 \\ -3 & 0 \end{bmatrix}$. Find the matrix for the polynomial $A^2+3A+5I$ where I is the unit matrix of order 2. **[C.U. 1982; ICWAI December 1974]**

(ii) If $I = \begin{bmatrix} 1 & 0 \\ 0 & 1 \end{bmatrix}, E = \begin{bmatrix} 0 & 1 \\ 0 & 0 \end{bmatrix}$, prove that $(AI + bE)^3 = a^3I + 3a^2bE$.

[ICWAI December 1980]

15. Evaluate: $(2 \ 1 \ -1) \times \begin{pmatrix} 4 & -1 & 2 \\ -1 & 0 & 1 \\ 2 & 1 & 0 \end{pmatrix} \times \begin{pmatrix} 2 \\ 1 \\ -1 \end{pmatrix}$. **[ICWAI December, 1992]**

16. If $A = \begin{pmatrix} 1 & 2 & -1 \\ 2 & 3 & -1 \\ 3 & 4 & -1 \end{pmatrix}$ and $B = \begin{pmatrix} 1 & -3 & -5 \\ -1 & 3 & -5 \\ -1 & 3 & -5 \end{pmatrix}$, calculate AB.

17. A and B are two matrices where $A = \begin{bmatrix} 1 & 2 & 1 \\ 1 & -1 & 1 \\ 2 & 3 & -1 \end{bmatrix}$ and $B = \begin{bmatrix} 1 & 4 & 0 \\ -1 & 2 & 2 \\ 0 & 0 & 2 \end{bmatrix}$. Find the value of $AB - 2B$.

18. If $A = \begin{bmatrix} 0 & 1 & 2 \\ 1 & 2 & 3 \\ 3 & 1 & 1 \end{bmatrix}$ and $B = \begin{bmatrix} 2 & 1 & 3 \\ -1 & 0 & 1 \\ 3 & -1 & 4 \end{bmatrix}$, verify whether $AB = BA$.

[C.U. B.Com (Hons.) 1988]

19. For the matrix $P = \frac{1}{3}\begin{bmatrix} 1 & 2 & 2 \\ 2 & 1 & -2 \\ -2 & 2 & -1 \end{bmatrix}$, verify that $PP' = I = P'P$, where P' is the transpose of P and I is the unit matrix of order 3. **[ICWAI June 1989]**

20. If $A = \begin{bmatrix} 1 & 1 & 2 \\ 2 & 1 & 0 \end{bmatrix}$ and $B = \begin{bmatrix} 1 & 2 \\ 2 & 0 \\ -1 & 1 \end{bmatrix}$, verify that

(i) $B^T A^T = (AB)^T$ and (ii) $(A^T B^T)^T = BA$, where A^T, B^T are the transpose of A and B, respectively.

[B]

1. If $A = \begin{bmatrix} 0 & 2 & 3 \\ 2 & 1 & 4 \end{bmatrix}$ and $B = \begin{bmatrix} 7 & 6 & 3 \\ 1 & 4 & 5 \end{bmatrix}$, find the value of $2A + 3B$. **[CA November 1976]**

2. If $A = \begin{bmatrix} 2 & 3 & 1 \\ 0 & -1 & 5 \end{bmatrix}$ and $B = \begin{bmatrix} 1 & 2 & -1 \\ 0 & -1 & 3 \end{bmatrix}$, evaluate $3A - 4B$.

3. Find X and Y if $X + Y = \begin{bmatrix} 7 & 0 \\ 2 & 5 \end{bmatrix}$ and $X - Y = \begin{bmatrix} 3 & 0 \\ 0 & 3 \end{bmatrix}$.

4. If A and B be two matrices and if $AB = 0$ (0 being a zero matrix), give an example where neither A nor B is a null matrix.

5. If $A = \begin{bmatrix} 3 & 6 & 9 \\ 1 & 0 & 1 \\ 2 & 3 & 5 \end{bmatrix}$ and $B = \begin{bmatrix} 1 & 5 & 6 \\ 2 & 3 & 1 \\ 1 & 0 & 2 \end{bmatrix}$, find A^T, B^T and $(A+B)^T$ and hence, verify that $(A+B)^T = A^T + B^T$.

6. If $A = \begin{bmatrix} 1 & -1 & 2 \\ 2 & 1 & 0 \end{bmatrix}$ and $B = \begin{bmatrix} 1 & 3 \\ 2 & 0 \\ -1 & 1 \end{bmatrix}$, evaluate AB and then $(AB)^T$ Hence, verify that $(AB)^T = B^T A^T$.

7. (i) If $A = \begin{bmatrix} 1 & 2 & 0 \\ 1 & 1 & 0 \\ -1 & 4 & 0 \end{bmatrix}$ and $B = \begin{bmatrix} 0 & 0 & 0 \\ 0 & 0 & 0 \\ 1 & 4 & 9 \end{bmatrix}$, find AB. **[Kanpur 1985]**

(ii) If $A = \begin{bmatrix} 3 & 1 & 2 \\ 0 & 1 & 1 \\ 1 & 2 & 0 \end{bmatrix}$ and $B = \begin{bmatrix} 1 & 4 \\ 2 & 2 \\ 1 & 0 \end{bmatrix}$, then find AB.

Does BA exist? Give reason.

8. If $A = \begin{bmatrix} 2 & -1 & 1 \\ 0 & 1 & 2 \\ 1 & 0 & 1 \end{bmatrix}$, find A^3.

9. If $A = \begin{pmatrix} 3 & -4 \\ 1 & -1 \end{pmatrix}$, show that $A^n = \begin{pmatrix} 1+2n & -4n \\ n & 1-2n \end{pmatrix}$. **[Kanpur 1985, Merut 1990]**

10. Let $A = \begin{bmatrix} 1 & a \\ 0 & 1 \end{bmatrix}$, prove by mathematical induction that $A^n = \begin{bmatrix} 1 & na \\ 0 & 1 \end{bmatrix}$.

[CA May 1981, '86]

[**HINTS.** Show that the result is true for $n = 2, 3$ and then assuming the result to be true for $n = m$ where m is a positive integer, prove that the result is true for $n = m + 1$. See also worked out Example 18.]

11. If $P = \begin{bmatrix} 1 & -1 \\ 2 & -1 \end{bmatrix}$, $Q = \begin{bmatrix} p & 1 \\ q & -1 \end{bmatrix}$ and $(P+Q)^2 = P^2 + Q^2$, find p and q.

[ICWAI December 1987]

12. If $A = \begin{bmatrix} 1 & 2 & 3 \\ 1 & 3 & 3 \\ 1 & 2 & 4 \end{bmatrix}$ and $B = \begin{bmatrix} 6 & -2 & -3 \\ -1 & 1 & 0 \\ -1 & 0 & 1 \end{bmatrix}$, evaluate AB and also BA; check that $AB = BA$. Is it in general, true for matrix multiplication? Give an example to justify your assertion.

[C.U. 1983]

13. Show that $A = \begin{bmatrix} 1 & 0 & -2 \\ 2 & 2 & 4 \\ 0 & 0 & 2 \end{bmatrix}$ satisfies the equation $A^2 - 3A + 2I = 0$.

[ICWAI December 1984, '85]

14. (i) If $A = \begin{bmatrix} 1 & 2 & 3 \\ 3 & -2 & 1 \\ 4 & 2 & 1 \end{bmatrix}$, show that $A^3 - 23A - 40I = 0$, where I is the unit matrix of order 3 and 0 is the null matrix of order 3. **[ICWAI December 1982]**

(ii) If $A = \begin{bmatrix} 2 & 2 & 0 \\ 2 & 1 & 1 \\ -7 & 2 & -3 \end{bmatrix}$, verify that $A^3 - 13A + 12I = 0$, where 0 is a null matrix of order 3.

[CA May 1988]

15. (i) If $A = \begin{bmatrix} 1 & -1 & 0 \\ 0 & 1 & 2 \end{bmatrix}$, $B = \begin{bmatrix} 1 & -1 & 1 \\ 0 & -1 & 1 \\ 1 & 1 & 1 \end{bmatrix}$ and $C = \begin{bmatrix} 1 & 1 \\ 1 & 0 \\ 0 & 1 \end{bmatrix}$, verify that

$$A(BC) = (AB)C.$$

(ii) Find the values of x, y, z if the matrix $A = \begin{bmatrix} 0 & 2y & z \\ x & y & -z \\ x & -y & z \end{bmatrix}$ obeys the law $A^T \cdot A = I$.

[ICWAI December 1986]

16. If $A = \begin{bmatrix} 1 & -1 & 1 \\ 0 & 1 & 2 \\ 1 & 0 & 1 \end{bmatrix}$, $B = \begin{bmatrix} 2 & 0 & -1 \\ 0 & 2 & 1 \\ 1 & -1 & 0 \end{bmatrix}$ and $C = \begin{bmatrix} 1 & -1 & 0 \\ -1 & 0 & 2 \\ 0 & 1 & 1 \end{bmatrix}$, verify that

(i) $A \cdot (BC) = (AB) \cdot C$; (ii) $A \cdot (B + C) = A \cdot B + A \cdot C$ and $(A + B) \cdot C = A \cdot C + B \cdot C$.

17. A manufacturer produces three products A, B, C which are sold in Delhi and Calcutta. The annual sales of these products are given below:

	Products		
	A	B	C
Delhi	5,000	7,500	15,000
Calcutta	9,000	12,000	8,700

If the sale prices of the products A, B, C per unit be Rs. 2, Rs. 3, Rs. 4, respectively, Calculate the total revenue in each centre by using matrices. **[CA May 1990]**

18. There are two families A and B. There are 2 men, 3 women and 1 child in family A; 1 man, 1 woman and 2 children in family B. The recommended daily allowance for calories is: Men: 2,400; Women: 1,900 Children: 1,800 and for proteins is: Men: 55 gms; Women: 45 gms; Children: 33 gms.

Represent the above information by matrices. Using matrix multiplication, calculate the total requirements of calories and proteins for each of the two families. **[CA November 1980]**

19. A finance company has offices located in every division, every district and every taluka in a certain state in India. Assume that there are 5 divisions, 30 districts and 200 talukas in the state. Each office has 1 head clerk, 1 cashier, 1 clerk and 1 peon. A divisional office has, in addition, an office superintendent, 2 clerks, 1 typist and 1 peon. A district office has, in addition, 1 clerk and 1 peon. The basic monthly salaries are as follows: Office superintendent Rs. 500, Head clerk Rs. 200, Cashier Rs. 175, clerks and typists Rs. 150, and peons Rs. 100.

Using matrix notation find (i) the total no. of posts of each kind in all the offices taken together, (ii) the total basic monthly salary bill of each kind of office, and (iii) the total basic monthly salary bill of all the offices taken together. **[CA November 1974]**

Answers

[A]

1. (i) $\begin{bmatrix} 3 & 1 & 1 \\ 5 & 4 & 8 \end{bmatrix}$; $\begin{bmatrix} 1 & -3 & 7 \\ 5 & -4 & 6 \end{bmatrix}$; $\begin{bmatrix} 8 & 1 & 6 \\ 15 & 8 & 23 \end{bmatrix}$; $\begin{bmatrix} 1 & -8 & 17 \\ 10 & -12 & 11 \end{bmatrix}$; (ii) $A+B$ and $A-B$ are not possible, since A and B are not of the same order, $\begin{bmatrix} 3 & 7 \\ 26 & 14 \end{bmatrix}$ and $\begin{bmatrix} 17 & -17 & 1 \\ -12 & -6 & 3 \\ 11 & -37 & 6 \end{bmatrix}$.

2. (i) $\begin{bmatrix} 1 & -2 \\ 3 & -1 \end{bmatrix}$; (ii) $A = \begin{bmatrix} 2 & 1 & -1 \\ 1 & 3 & 2 \end{bmatrix}$ and $B = \begin{bmatrix} 1 & 3 & 2 \\ 4 & -1 & 0 \end{bmatrix}$.

3. (i) $x = 4, y = 1$; (ii) $x = 2, y = 1, z = 3$.

4. (i) $\begin{bmatrix} -13 & 8 \\ -8 & 5 \end{bmatrix}$; $\begin{bmatrix} 1 & 2 \\ -4 & -9 \end{bmatrix}$; No; (ii) [30].

5. $\begin{bmatrix} 0 & 0 \\ 0 & 0 \end{bmatrix}$; $\begin{bmatrix} 2i & -2 \\ -2 & -2i \end{bmatrix}$.

7. $\begin{bmatrix} -24 & -10 \\ -\frac{41}{2} & -\frac{51}{2} \end{bmatrix}$.

9. $\begin{bmatrix} \frac{3}{10} \\ \\ -\frac{7}{5} \end{bmatrix}$.

12. [8 10 4]; $\begin{bmatrix} 18 \\ 9 \\ 6 \end{bmatrix}$; Rs. 258.

13. Rs. 1,947. **14.** $\begin{bmatrix} 3 & 8 \\ -12 & -1 \end{bmatrix}$. **15.** [2].

16. $\begin{bmatrix} 0 & 0 & -10 \\ 0 & 0 & -20 \\ 0 & 0 & -30 \end{bmatrix}$.

17. $\begin{bmatrix} -3 & 0 & 6 \\ 4 & -2 & -4 \\ -1 & 14 & 0 \end{bmatrix}$.

[B]

1. $\begin{bmatrix} 21 & 22 & 15 \\ 7 & 14 & 23 \end{bmatrix}$. **2.** $\begin{bmatrix} 2 & 1 & 7 \\ 0 & 1 & 3 \end{bmatrix}$. **3.** $X = \begin{bmatrix} 5 & 0 \\ 1 & 4 \end{bmatrix}, Y = \begin{bmatrix} 2 & 0 \\ 1 & 1 \end{bmatrix}$.

4. $A = \begin{bmatrix} 1 & -1 \\ -1 & 1 \end{bmatrix}, B = \begin{bmatrix} 1 & 1 \\ 1 & 1 \end{bmatrix}$ or $A = \begin{bmatrix} 1 & -1 \\ -1 & 1 \end{bmatrix}, B = \begin{bmatrix} 0 & 1 \\ 0 & 1 \end{bmatrix}$ or $A = \begin{bmatrix} 1 & -1 \\ 0 & 0 \end{bmatrix}$, $B = \begin{bmatrix} 1 & 0 \\ 1 & 0 \end{bmatrix}$, etc.

5. $\begin{bmatrix} 3 & 1 & 2 \\ 6 & 0 & 3 \\ 9 & 1 & 5 \end{bmatrix}, \begin{bmatrix} 1 & 2 & 1 \\ 5 & 3 & 0 \\ 6 & 1 & 2 \end{bmatrix}; \begin{bmatrix} 4 & 3 & 3 \\ 11 & 3 & 3 \\ 15 & 2 & 7 \end{bmatrix}$.

6. $\begin{bmatrix} -3 & 5 \\ 3 & 6 \end{bmatrix}; \begin{bmatrix} -3 & 3 \\ 5 & 6 \end{bmatrix}$. **7.** (i) $\begin{bmatrix} 0 & 0 & 0 \\ 0 & 0 & 0 \\ 0 & 0 & 0 \end{bmatrix}$; (ii) $\begin{bmatrix} 7 & 14 \\ 3 & 2 \\ 5 & 8 \end{bmatrix}$, BA does not exist.

8. $\begin{bmatrix} 11 & -8 & 0 \\ 8 & -1 & 8 \\ 8 & -4 & 3 \end{bmatrix}$. **11.** $p = 1, q = 4$. **12.** $\begin{bmatrix} 1 & 0 & 0 \\ 0 & 1 & 0 \\ 0 & 0 & 1 \end{bmatrix} = AB = BA$.

15. (ii) $x = \pm\frac{1}{\sqrt{2}}, y = \pm\frac{1}{\sqrt{6}}, z = \pm\frac{1}{\sqrt{3}}$. **17.** Rs. 92,500; Rs. 88,800.

18. $\begin{bmatrix} 2 & 3 & 1 \\ 1 & 1 & 2 \end{bmatrix}$ and $\begin{bmatrix} 2,400 & 55 \\ 1,900 & 45 \\ 1,800 & 33 \end{bmatrix}$; A : 12,300 calories and 278 gms proteins, B : 7,900 calories and 166 gms proteins.

23. (i) $\begin{matrix} O & H & C & Cl & T & P \\ (5 & 235 & 235 & 275 & 5 & 270) \end{matrix}$, where O = office superintendent, H = head clerk, etc. (ii) Rs. 1,675; Rs. 875; Rs. 625; (iii) Rs. 1,59,625.

CHAPTER 3

DETERMINANTS

3.1. INTRODUCTION

With every *square matrix* A of certain order, we associate a number called the *determinant of* A and it is denoted by $|A|$ or det A. If a matrix is *not* a *square,* we cannot associate a *determinant* with it.

DEFINITION. For the square matrix $A = \begin{bmatrix} a_1 & b_1 \\ a_2 & b_2 \end{bmatrix}$ of second order, the symbol $|A| = \begin{vmatrix} a_1 & b_1 \\ a_2 & b_2 \end{vmatrix}$ is called a *determinant of second order* or *determinant of order* 2 and its value is defined by

$$\begin{vmatrix} a_1 & b_1 \\ a_2 & b_2 \end{vmatrix} = a_1 b_2 - a_2 b_1.$$

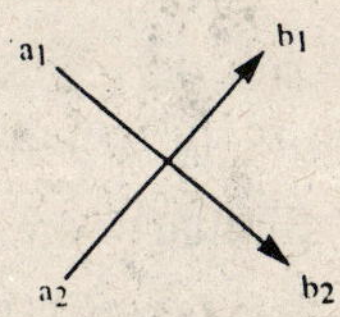

Fig 3.1

The four numbers a_1, b_1, a_2, b_2 are called *elements* of the determinant.

For the square matrix $A = \begin{bmatrix} a_1 & b_1 & c_1 \\ a_2 & b_2 & c_2 \\ a_3 & b_3 & c_3 \end{bmatrix}$ of order 3, the symbol $|A| = \begin{vmatrix} a_1 & b_1 & c_1 \\ a_2 & b_2 & c_2 \\ a_3 & b_3 & c_3 \end{vmatrix}$ consisting of nine numbers arranged in three rows and three columns is called a *determinant* of third order or *determinant of order* 3 and its value is defined by

$$|A| = a_1 \begin{vmatrix} b_2 & c_2 \\ b_3 & c_3 \end{vmatrix} - b_1 \begin{vmatrix} a_2 & c_2 \\ a_3 & c_3 \end{vmatrix} + c_1 \begin{vmatrix} a_2 & b_2 \\ a_3 & b_3 \end{vmatrix} \qquad (1)$$

RULE. Write down the elements of the first row (or first column) with alternately positive and negative sign, the first element having always positive sign before it. Multiply each signed element by a determinant of second order obtained after omitting the row and the column in which that element occurs.

ILLUSTRATIONS.

(i) $\begin{vmatrix} 2 & 3 \\ -4 & -5 \end{vmatrix} = 2 \times (-5) - 3 \times (-4) = -10 + 12 = \mathbf{2}.$

(ii) $\begin{vmatrix} 1 & -2 & 3 \\ 4 & -1 & -2 \\ -2 & 1 & 5 \end{vmatrix} = 1\begin{vmatrix} -1 & -2 \\ 1 & 5 \end{vmatrix} - (-2)\begin{vmatrix} 4 & -2 \\ -2 & 5 \end{vmatrix} + 3\begin{vmatrix} 4 & -1 \\ -2 & 1 \end{vmatrix}$

$= 1(-5+2) + 2(20-4) + 3(4-2) = -3 + 32 + 6 = 35.$

From (1), we have

$$\begin{aligned} |A| &= a_1(b_2c_3 - b_3c_2) - b_1(a_2c_3 - a_3c_2) + c_1(a_2b_3 - a_3b_2) \\ &= a_1b_2c_3 - a_1b_3c_2 - a_2b_1c_3 + a_3b_1c_2 + a_2b_3c_1 - a_3b_2c_1 \end{aligned} \quad (2)$$

In (1) we have expanded the determinant along the first row. If we expand it along the first column, we get

$$\begin{aligned} |A| &= a_1\begin{vmatrix} b_2 & c_2 \\ b_3 & c_3 \end{vmatrix} - a_2\begin{vmatrix} b_1 & c_1 \\ b_3 & c_3 \end{vmatrix} + a_3\begin{vmatrix} b_1 & c_1 \\ b_2 & c_2 \end{vmatrix} \\ &= a_1(b_2c_3 - b_3c_2) - a_2(b_1c_3 - b_3c_1) + a_3(b_1c_2 - b_2c_1) \\ &= a_1b_2c_3 - a_1b_3c_2 - a_2b_1c_3 + a_2b_3c_1 + a_3b_1c_2 - a_3b_2c_1 \end{aligned}$$

which is the same as (2).

Similarly, we can define determinants of fourth and higher orders.

REMARKS. Determinants are originally connected with the solution of linear equations.

Eliminating x and y from the two homogeneous equations

$$a_1x + b_1y = 0$$
$$a_2x + b_2y = 0$$

we obtain $a_1b_2 - a_2b_1 = 0$. The expression on the left side of this eliminant is symbolically written as $\begin{vmatrix} a_1 & b_1 \\ a_2 & b_2 \end{vmatrix}$ which is a *determinant of second order.*

Similarly, eliminating x, y, z from the three equations

$$a_1x + b_1y + c_1z = 0$$
$$a_2x + b_2y + c_2z = 0$$
$$a_3x + b_3y + c_3z = 0$$

we get $a_1(b_2c_3 - b_3c_2) + b_1(c_2a_3 - c_3a_2) + c_1(a_2b_3 - a_3b_2) = 0.$

The expression on the left side of this eliminant is symbolically written as $\begin{vmatrix} a_1 & b_1 & c_1 \\ a_2 & b_2 & c_2 \\ a_3 & b_3 & c_3 \end{vmatrix}$ which is a *determinant of third order.*

EXAMPLE 1. *Find the value of* $|A|$ *if matrix* A *is given by* $A = \begin{bmatrix} 2 & -3 \\ 4 & 9 \end{bmatrix}$.

SOLUTION. We have $A = \begin{bmatrix} 2 & -3 \\ 4 & 9 \end{bmatrix}$ $\quad\therefore\quad |A| = \begin{vmatrix} 2 & -3 \\ 4 & 9 \end{vmatrix} = 2 \times 9 - (-3) \times 4 = 18 + 12 = \mathbf{30}.$

3.2. MINORS AND COFACTORS OF THE ELEMENTS OF A DETERMINANT

Let us consider a determinant of third order given by

$$\Delta \equiv \begin{vmatrix} a_1 & b_1 & c_1 \\ a_2 & b_2 & c_2 \\ a_3 & b_3 & c_3 \end{vmatrix} \equiv \begin{vmatrix} a_{11} & a_{12} & a_{13} \\ a_{21} & a_{22} & a_{23} \\ a_{31} & a_{32} & a_{33} \end{vmatrix}.$$

The minor of any element in Δ *is a determinant of second order obtained by omitting from* Δ *the row and the column in which that element occurs.*

Thus, **minors** of a_1, b_1, c_1, a_2, b_2, etc. are respectively

$$\begin{vmatrix} b_2 & c_2 \\ b_3 & c_3 \end{vmatrix}, \begin{vmatrix} a_2 & c_2 \\ a_3 & c_3 \end{vmatrix}, \begin{vmatrix} a_2 & b_2 \\ a_3 & b_3 \end{vmatrix}, \begin{vmatrix} b_1 & c_1 \\ b_3 & c_3 \end{vmatrix}, \begin{vmatrix} a_1 & c_1 \\ a_3 & c_3 \end{vmatrix}, \text{ etc.}$$

Minors of $a_1, b_1, c_1, a_2, b_2, c_2, a_3, b_3, c_3$ are denoted by $M_{11}, M_{12}, M_{13}, M_{21}, M_{22}, M_{23}, M_{31}, M_{32}, M_{33}$, respectively.

The cofactors of any element in Δ *is the minor of that element in* Δ *with proper sign depending on the number of the row and the column in which the element occurs.* **If an element occurs in the ith row and jth column in Δ, then the cofactor of the element $= (-1)^{i+j} \times$ (minor of the element).**

Thus, **cofactors** of a_1, b_1, c_1, a_2, etc. in Δ are, respectively

$$(-1)^{1+1}\begin{vmatrix} b_2 & c_2 \\ b_3 & c_3 \end{vmatrix}, (-1)^{1+2}\begin{vmatrix} a_2 & c_2 \\ a_3 & c_3 \end{vmatrix}, (-1)^{1+3}\begin{vmatrix} a_2 & b_2 \\ a_3 & b_3 \end{vmatrix}, (-1)^{2+1}\begin{vmatrix} b_1 & c_1 \\ b_3 & c_3 \end{vmatrix}, \text{ etc.}$$

i.e., $\quad + \begin{vmatrix} b_2 & c_2 \\ b_3 & c_3 \end{vmatrix}, - \begin{vmatrix} a_2 & c_2 \\ a_3 & c_3 \end{vmatrix}, + \begin{vmatrix} a_2 & b_2 \\ a_3 & b_3 \end{vmatrix}, - \begin{vmatrix} b_1 & c_1 \\ b_3 & c_3 \end{vmatrix},$ etc.

We shall denote the cofactors of $a_1, b_1, c_1, a_2, b_2, c_2, a_3, b_3, c_3$ in Δ by $A_1, B_1, C_1, A_2, B_2, C_2, A_3, B_3, C_3$, respectively (or by $C_{11}, C_{12}, C_{13}, C_{21}, C_{22}, C_{23}, C_{31}, C_{32}, C_{33}$).

Thus, $A_1 = \begin{vmatrix} b_2 & c_2 \\ b_3 & c_3 \end{vmatrix}, \; B_1 = -\begin{vmatrix} a_2 & c_2 \\ a_3 & c_3 \end{vmatrix}, \; C_1 = \begin{vmatrix} a_2 & b_2 \\ a_3 & b_3 \end{vmatrix}, A_2 = -\begin{vmatrix} b_1 & c_1 \\ b_3 & c_3 \end{vmatrix}$, etc.

We have $\Delta = a_1 \begin{vmatrix} b_2 & c_2 \\ b_3 & c_3 \end{vmatrix} - b_1 \begin{vmatrix} a_2 & c_2 \\ a_3 & c_3 \end{vmatrix} + c_1 \begin{vmatrix} a_2 & b_2 \\ a_3 & b_3 \end{vmatrix} = a_1A_1 + b_1B_1 + c_1C_1.$

Similarly, we can prove that

$$a_2A_2 + b_2B_2 + c_2C_2 = \Delta, a_3A_3 + b_3B_3 + c_3C_3 = \Delta, a_1A_1 + a_2A_2 + a_3A_3 = \Delta, \text{ etc.}$$

From these results, it follows that we can find the value of the determinant Δ by expanding it along any row or any column.

For quick working, the signs of the different cofactors according to the positions of the corresponding elements in Δ are given by $\begin{vmatrix} + & - & + \\ - & + & - \\ + & - & + \end{vmatrix}$.

EXAMPLE 2. Write the cofactors of the elements of the second row of the following determinants and hence evaluate them: (i) $\begin{vmatrix} 1 & 2 & 3 \\ -4 & 3 & 6 \\ 2 & -7 & 9 \end{vmatrix}$; (ii) $\begin{vmatrix} 1 & a & bc \\ 1 & b & ca \\ 1 & c & ab \end{vmatrix}$.

SOLUTION. Let $\Delta \equiv \begin{vmatrix} 1 & 2 & 3 \\ -4 & 3 & 6 \\ 2 & -7 & 9 \end{vmatrix}$ and C_{21}, C_{22}, C_{23} be the cofactors of the elements of second row in Δ. Then

$$C_{21} = \text{cofactor of } (-4) = (-1)^{2+1} \begin{vmatrix} 2 & 3 \\ -7 & 9 \end{vmatrix} = -(18+21) = -39,$$

$$C_{22} = \text{cofactor of } 3 = (-1)^{2+2} \begin{vmatrix} 1 & 3 \\ 2 & 9 \end{vmatrix} = +(9-6) = 3,$$

$$C_{23} = \text{cofactor of } 6 = (-1)^{2+3} \begin{vmatrix} 1 & 2 \\ 2 & -7 \end{vmatrix} = -(-7-4) = 11.$$

$$\therefore \quad \Delta = -4C_{21} + 3C_{22} + 6C_{23} \quad \text{[along the 2nd row]}$$
$$= -4 \cdot (-39) + 3 \cdot 3 + 6 \cdot 11 = 156 + 9 + 66 = \mathbf{231}.$$

(ii) Let $\Delta \equiv \begin{vmatrix} 1 & a & bc \\ 1 & b & ca \\ 1 & c & ab \end{vmatrix}$; then

$$C_{21} = (-1)^{2+1} \begin{vmatrix} a & bc \\ c & ab \end{vmatrix} = -(a^2b - bc^2) = bc^2 - a^2b$$

$$C_{22} = (-1)^{2+2} \begin{vmatrix} 1 & bc \\ 1 & ab \end{vmatrix} = (ab - bc)$$

$$C_{23} = (-1)^{2+3} \begin{vmatrix} 1 & a \\ 1 & c \end{vmatrix} = -(c-a) = a - c.$$

$$\therefore \quad \Delta = 1 \cdot C_{21} + b \cdot C_{22} + ca \cdot C_{23} = bc^2 - a^2b + b(ab - bc) + ca(a-c)$$
$$= \mathbf{bc^2 - a^2b + ab^2 - b^2c + ca^2 - c^2a}.$$

Adjugate (or Adjoint) of a Determinant

The determinant $\Delta' = \begin{vmatrix} A_1 & B_1 & C_1 \\ A_2 & B_2 & C_2 \\ A_3 & B_3 & C_3 \end{vmatrix}$ *in which all the elements are the cofactors of the corresponding elements of the determinant* $\Delta = \begin{vmatrix} a_1 & b_1 & c_1 \\ a_2 & b_2 & c_2 \\ a_3 & b_3 & c_3 \end{vmatrix}$ *is called the* **adjugate** (or **adjoint**) *of* Δ.

EXAMPLE 3. *Find the cofactors of the elements of the determinant* $\begin{vmatrix} 2 & -3 & 7 \\ 4 & -9 & 1 \\ 6 & 5 & 0 \end{vmatrix}$ *and hence write down the adjugate of the determinant.*

SOLUTION.

$$A_1 = \text{Cofactor of } 2 = + \begin{vmatrix} -9 & 1 \\ 5 & 0 \end{vmatrix} = 0 - 5 = \mathbf{-5};$$

$$B_1 = \text{Cofactor of } -3 = - \begin{vmatrix} 4 & 1 \\ 6 & 0 \end{vmatrix} = -(0 - 6) = \mathbf{6};$$

$$C_1 = \text{Cofactor of } 7 = + \begin{vmatrix} 4 & -9 \\ 6 & 5 \end{vmatrix} = 20 + 54 = \mathbf{74};$$

$$A_2 = \text{Cofactor of } 4 = - \begin{vmatrix} -3 & 7 \\ 5 & 0 \end{vmatrix} = -(0 - 35) = \mathbf{35};$$

$$B_2 = \text{Cofactor of } -9 = + \begin{vmatrix} 2 & 7 \\ 6 & 0 \end{vmatrix} = 0 - 42 = \mathbf{-42};$$

$$C_2 = \text{Cofactor of } 1 = - \begin{vmatrix} 2 & -3 \\ 6 & 5 \end{vmatrix} = -(10 + 18) = \mathbf{-28};$$

$$A_3 = \text{Cofactor of } 6 = + \begin{vmatrix} -3 & 7 \\ -9 & 1 \end{vmatrix} = -3 + 63 = \mathbf{60};$$

$$B_3 = \text{Cofactor of } 5 = - \begin{vmatrix} 2 & 7 \\ 4 & 1 \end{vmatrix} = -(2 - 28) = \mathbf{26};$$

$$C_3 = \text{Cofactor of } 0 = + \begin{vmatrix} 2 & -3 \\ 4 & -9 \end{vmatrix} = -18 + 12 = \mathbf{-6}.$$

The Adjugate of the given determinant is $\begin{vmatrix} -5 & 6 & 74 \\ 35 & -42 & -28 \\ 60 & 26 & -6 \end{vmatrix}$

3.3. PROPERTIES OF DETERMINANTS

The following properties of determinants hold good for determinants of any order.

I. *The value of a determinant remains unaltered if the rows and columns are interchanged, i.e.,*

$$\begin{vmatrix} a_1 & b_1 & c_1 \\ a_2 & b_2 & c_2 \\ a_3 & b_3 & c_3 \end{vmatrix} = \begin{vmatrix} a_1 & a_2 & a_3 \\ b_1 & b_2 & b_3 \\ c_1 & c_2 & c_3 \end{vmatrix}.$$

PROOF. Left hand side

$$= a_1 \begin{vmatrix} b_2 & c_2 \\ b_3 & c_3 \end{vmatrix} - b_1 \begin{vmatrix} a_2 & c_2 \\ a_3 & c_3 \end{vmatrix} + c_1 \begin{vmatrix} a_2 & b_2 \\ a_3 & b_3 \end{vmatrix}$$

$$= a_1(b_2c_3 - b_3c_2) - b_1(a_2c_3 - a_3c_2) + c_1(a_2b_3 - a_3b_2)$$

$$= a_1(b_2c_3 - b_3c_2) - a_2b_1c_3 + a_3b_1c_2 + a_2b_3c_1 - a_3b_2c_1$$

$$= a_1(b_2c_3 - b_3c_2) - a_2(b_1c_3 - b_3c_1) + a_3(b_1c_2 - b_2c_1)$$

$$= \begin{vmatrix} a_1 & a_2 & a_3 \\ b_1 & b_2 & b_3 \\ c_1 & c_2 & c_3 \end{vmatrix} \quad \text{[By definition]}$$

= Right hand side.

II. *If two adjacent rows (or columns) of a determinant are interchanged, the numerical value remains the same, but the sign of the determinant is changed,* i.e.,

$$\begin{vmatrix} a_1 & b_1 & c_1 \\ a_2 & b_2 & c_2 \\ a_3 & b_3 & c_3 \end{vmatrix} = -\begin{vmatrix} a_2 & b_2 & c_2 \\ a_1 & b_1 & c_1 \\ a_3 & b_3 & c_3 \end{vmatrix}.$$

PROOF. Proceeding as in I, we can expand Left hand side and the Right hand side and then verify that L.H.S.=R.H.S.

Instead of the first two rows, we can interchange any two consecutive rows and verify the same result. The same result can also be verified by interchanging any two adjacent columns.

COROLLARY. *The sign of a determinant is either changed or is not changed according as the number of interchanges of two adjacent rows (or columns) is odd or even.*

This can be easily verified by using *Property* II.

III. *If two rows (or columns) of a determinant are identical, the value of the determinant is zero,* i.e.,

$$\begin{vmatrix} a_1 & b_1 & c_1 \\ a_1 & b_1 & c_1 \\ a_3 & b_3 & c_3 \end{vmatrix} = 0.$$

PROOF.

$$\begin{aligned} \text{L.H.S.} &= a_1\begin{vmatrix} b_1 & c_1 \\ b_3 & c_3 \end{vmatrix} - b_1\begin{vmatrix} a_1 & c_1 \\ a_3 & c_3 \end{vmatrix} + c_1\begin{vmatrix} a_1 & b_1 \\ a_3 & b_3 \end{vmatrix} \\ &= a_1((b_1c_3 - b_3c_1) - b_1(a_1c_3 - a_3c_1) + c_1(a_1b_3 - a_3b_1) \\ &= a_1b_1c_3 - a_1b_3c_1 - a_1b_1c_3 + a_3b_1c_1 + a_1b_3c_1 - a_3b_1c_1 \\ &= 0. \end{aligned}$$

Similarly, we can verify the result when two columns are identical.

IV. *If all the elements of any one row (or column) are multiplied by the same constant, then the original determinant is multiplied by that constant,* i.e.,

$$\begin{vmatrix} ka_1 & kb_1 & kc_1 \\ a_2 & b_2 & c_2 \\ a_3 & b_3 & c_3 \end{vmatrix} = k\begin{vmatrix} a_1 & b_1 & c_1 \\ a_2 & b_2 & c_2 \\ a_3 & b_3 & c_3 \end{vmatrix}.$$

PROOF.

$$\begin{aligned} \text{L.H.S.} &= ka_1\begin{vmatrix} b_2 & c_2 \\ b_3 & c_3 \end{vmatrix} - kb_1\begin{vmatrix} a_2 & c_2 \\ a_3 & c_3 \end{vmatrix} + kc_1\begin{vmatrix} a_2 & b_2 \\ a_3 & b_3 \end{vmatrix} \\ &= k\left\{a_1\begin{vmatrix} b_2 & c_2 \\ b_3 & c_3 \end{vmatrix} - b_1\begin{vmatrix} a_2 & c_2 \\ a_3 & c_3 \end{vmatrix} + c_1\begin{vmatrix} a_2 & b_2 \\ a_3 & b_3 \end{vmatrix}\right]\right\} \\ &= k\begin{vmatrix} a_1 & b_1 & c_1 \\ a_2 & b_2 & c_2 \\ a_3 & b_3 & c_3 \end{vmatrix} = \text{R.H.S.} \end{aligned}$$

Similarly, we can verify the result when all the elements of any one column are multiplied by the same constant k.

COROLLARY. By using Property IV, we have

$$\begin{vmatrix} ma_1 & mb_1 & mc_1 \\ na_2 & nb_2 & nc_2 \\ ka_3 & kb_3 & kc_3 \end{vmatrix} = mnk \begin{vmatrix} a_1 & b_1 & c_1 \\ a_2 & b_2 & c_2 \\ a_3 & b_3 & c_3 \end{vmatrix}.$$

V. *If the elements of any row (or column) of a determinant are multiplied in order by the cofactors of the corresponding elements of any other row (or column), then the sum of the products thus obtained is zero, i.e.,* $a_1A_2+b_1B_2+c_1C_2=0, a_2A_3+b_2B_3+c_2C_3=0$, *etc., and* $a_1B_1+a_2B_2+a_3B_3=0$, *etc.*

PROOF. Let $\Delta = \begin{vmatrix} a_1 & b_1 & c_1 \\ a_2 & b_2 & c_2 \\ a_3 & b_3 & c_3 \end{vmatrix}$ and $A_1, B_1, C_1, A_2, B_2, C_2$, etc. be the cofactors of a_1, b_1, c_1, a_2, b_2, c_2, etc., respectively in Δ.

$$\text{Then} \quad A_2 = -\begin{vmatrix} b_1 & c_1 \\ b_3 & c_3 \end{vmatrix} = -(b_1c_3 - b_3c_1) = -b_1c_3 + b_3c_1,$$

$$B_2 = +\begin{vmatrix} a_1 & c_1 \\ a_3 & c_3 \end{vmatrix} = a_1c_3 - a_3c_1,$$

$$C_2 = -\begin{vmatrix} a_1 & b_1 \\ a_3 & b_3 \end{vmatrix} = -(a_1b_3 - a_3b_1) = -a_1b_3 + a_3b_1$$

$$\begin{aligned} \therefore \quad a_1A_2 + b_1B_2 + c_1C_2 &= a_1(-b_1c_3 + b_3c_1) + b_1(a_1c_3 - a_3c_1) + c_1(-a_1b_3 + a_3b_1) \\ &= -a_1b_1c_3 + a_1b_3c_1 + a_1b_1c_3 - a_3b_1c_1 - a_1b_3c_1 + a_3b_1c_1 \\ &= 0. \end{aligned}$$

Similarly, we can prove the other similar results.

COROLLARY. *If the elements of any row (or column) are multiplied in order by the corresponding cofactors of the same elements, then the sum of these products thus obtained is the determinant itself.*

If $A_1, B_1, C_1, A_2, B_2, C_2, A_3, B_3, C_3$ be the cofactors of $a_1, b_1, c_1, a_2, b_2, c_2, a_3, b_3, c_3$, respectively in

$$\Delta = \begin{vmatrix} a_1 & b_1 & c_1 \\ a_2 & b_2 & c_2 \\ a_3 & b_3 & c_3 \end{vmatrix},$$

then we have already proved in **Art. 3.2** that $a_1A_1 + b_1B_1 + c_1C_1 = \Delta$.

We can similarly prove that $a_2A_2+b_2B_2+c_2C_2=\Delta, a_3A_3+b_3B_3+c_3C_3=\Delta, a_1A_1+a_2A_2+a_3A_3=\Delta$, etc.

VI. *If each element of any row (or column) is the sum of two numbers, then the determinant can be expressed as the sum of two determinants whose other rows (or columns) are not altered, i.e.,*

$$\begin{vmatrix} a_1+\alpha_1 & b_1+\beta_1 & c_1+\gamma_1 \\ a_2 & b_2 & c_2 \\ a_3 & b_3 & c_3 \end{vmatrix} = \begin{vmatrix} a_1 & b_1 & c_1 \\ a_2 & b_2 & c_2 \\ a_3 & b_3 & c_3 \end{vmatrix} + \begin{vmatrix} \alpha_1 & \beta_1 & \gamma_1 \\ a_2 & b_2 & c_2 \\ a_3 & b_3 & c_3 \end{vmatrix}.$$

PROOF. If A_1, B_1, C_1 be the cofactors of the elements $a_1+\alpha_1, b_1+\beta_1, c_+\gamma_1$ of the first row of the determinant on the left side, then

$$\begin{vmatrix} a_1+\alpha_1 & b_1+\beta_1 & c_1+\gamma_1 \\ a_2 & b_2 & c_2 \\ a_3 & b_3 & c_3 \end{vmatrix}$$
$$=(a_1+\alpha_1)A_1+(b_1+\beta_1)B_1+(c_1+\gamma_1)C_1$$
$$=(a_1A_1+b_1B_1+c_1C_1)+(\alpha_1A_1+\beta_1B_1+\gamma_1C_1)$$
$$=\begin{vmatrix} a_1 & b_1 & c_1 \\ a_2 & b_2 & c_2 \\ a_3 & b_3 & c_3 \end{vmatrix}+\begin{vmatrix} \alpha_1 & \beta_1 & \gamma_1 \\ a_2 & b_2 & c_2 \\ a_3 & b_3 & c_3 \end{vmatrix}=\text{R.H.S.}$$

Similarly, we can verify the property when each element of any column is the sum of two numbers.

VII. *The value of a determinant remains unaltered if to all the elements of any row (or column) are added the same multiples of the corresponding elements of any number of the other rows (or columns)* i.e.,

$$\begin{vmatrix} a_1+ma_2+na_3 & b_1+mb_2+nb_3 & c_1+mc_2+nc_3 \\ a_2 & b_2 & c_2 \\ a_3 & b_3 & c_3 \end{vmatrix}=\begin{vmatrix} a_1 & b_1 & c_1 \\ a_2 & b_2 & c_2 \\ a_3 & b_3 & c_3 \end{vmatrix}.$$

PROOF

$$\text{L.H.S.}=\begin{vmatrix} a_1 & b_1 & c_1 \\ a_2 & b_2 & c_2 \\ a_3 & b_3 & c_3 \end{vmatrix}+\begin{vmatrix} ma_2 & mb_2 & mc_2 \\ a_2 & b_2 & c_2 \\ a_3 & b_3 & c_3 \end{vmatrix}+\begin{vmatrix} na_3 & nb_3 & nc_3 \\ a_2 & b_2 & c_2 \\ a_3 & b_3 & c_3 \end{vmatrix}$$

[by **Property VI**]

$$=\begin{vmatrix} a_1 & b_1 & c_1 \\ a_2 & b_2 & c_2 \\ a_3 & b_3 & c_3 \end{vmatrix}+m\begin{vmatrix} a_2 & b_2 & c_2 \\ a_2 & b_2 & c_2 \\ a_3 & b_3 & c_3 \end{vmatrix}+n\begin{vmatrix} a_3 & b_3 & c_3 \\ a_2 & b_2 & c_2 \\ a_3 & b_3 & c_3 \end{vmatrix}$$

[$\because$ Two rows are identical]

$$=\text{R.H.S.}+m\times 0+n\times 0=\textbf{R.H.S.}$$

The same property can be verified by taking columns instead of rows.

VIII. *If the elements of a determinant are polynomials in x and two rows (or columns) of a determinant become identical when $x=a$, then $(x-a)$ is a factor of the determinant.*

[$a_\circ+a_1x, a_\circ+a_1x+a_2x^2, a_\circ+a_1x+a_2x^2+a_3x^3$, etc. are polynomials in x.]

PROOF. Let Δ be the determinant in which the elements are polynomials in x. Then after expansion, Δ will also be a polynomial in x. Let us denote it by $f(x)$.

When $x=a$ is substituted in Δ, two rows (or columns) become identical.

$\therefore$ When $x=a, \Delta=0$ and hence $f(a)=0$.

$\because$ $(x-a)$ is factor of $f(x)$ i.e., $(x-a)$ is a factor of Δ.

Hence, the property follows.

COROLLARY. *If r rows (or columns) of a determinant become identical when $x = a$, then $(x-a)^{r-1}$ is a factor of the determinant in which the elements are polynomials in x.*

This can be proved by using the **Property VIII.**

3.4. ILLUSTRATIVE EXAMPLES

EXAMPLE 4. *Find the value of the determinant* $\begin{vmatrix} 2 & 5 & 4 \\ 1 & 4 & 3 \\ 6 & 8 & 10 \end{vmatrix}$.

SOLUTION.

$$\begin{vmatrix} 2 & 5 & 4 \\ 1 & 4 & 3 \\ 6 & 8 & 10 \end{vmatrix} = \begin{vmatrix} 1 & 1 & 1 \\ 1 & 4 & 3 \\ 6 & 8 & 10 \end{vmatrix} \quad \text{[subtracting 2nd row from the first.]}$$

$$= \begin{vmatrix} 1 & 0 & 0 \\ 1 & 3 & 2 \\ 6 & 2 & 4 \end{vmatrix} \quad \text{[subtracting 1st column from the 2nd and 3rd.]}$$

$$= 1 \cdot \begin{vmatrix} 3 & 2 \\ 2 & 4 \end{vmatrix} = 12 - 4 = \mathbf{8}.$$

EXAMPLE 5. *Prove without expansion that*

$$\begin{vmatrix} a_1 + pb_1 + qc_1 & b_1 & c_1 \\ a_2 + pb_2 + qc_2 & b_2 & c_2 \\ a_3 + pb_3 + qc_3 & b_3 & c_3 \end{vmatrix} = \begin{vmatrix} a_1 & b_1 & c_1 \\ a_2 & b_2 & c_2 \\ a_3 & b_3 & c_3 \end{vmatrix}.$$

[ICWAI June 1974]

SOLUTION.

$$\begin{vmatrix} a_1 + pb_1 + qc_1 & b_1 & c_1 \\ a_2 + pb_2 + qc_2 & b_2 & c_2 \\ a_3 + pb_3 + qc_3 & b_3 & c_3 \end{vmatrix} = \begin{vmatrix} a_1 + qc_1 & b_1 & c_1 \\ a_2 + qc_2 & b_2 & c_2 \\ a_3 + qc_3 & b_3 & c_3 \end{vmatrix}$$

[subtracting p times the 2nd column from the first column]

$$= \begin{vmatrix} a_1 & b_1 & c_1 \\ a_2 & b_2 & c_2 \\ a_3 & b_3 & c_3 \end{vmatrix} \quad \text{[subtracting } q \text{ times the third column from the first.]}$$

=**R.H.S.**

EXAMPLE 6. *Without directly expanding the determinant, but using only the well-known properties, prove that*

$$\begin{vmatrix} a-b & 1 & a \\ b-c & 1 & b \\ c-a & 1 & c \end{vmatrix} = \begin{vmatrix} a & 1 & b \\ b & 1 & c \\ c & 1 & a \end{vmatrix}.$$

[ICWAI December 1979; June 1991]

SOLUTION.

$$\begin{vmatrix} a-b & 1 & a \\ b-c & 1 & b \\ c-a & 1 & c \end{vmatrix} = \begin{vmatrix} -b & 1 & a \\ -c & 1 & b \\ -a & 1 & c \end{vmatrix} \quad \text{[subtracting 3rd column from the first]}$$

$$= -\begin{vmatrix} b & 1 & a \\ c & 1 & b \\ a & 1 & c \end{vmatrix} = \begin{vmatrix} 1 & b & a \\ 1 & c & b \\ 1 & a & c \end{vmatrix} = -\begin{vmatrix} 1 & a & b \\ 1 & b & c \\ 1 & c & a \end{vmatrix} = \begin{vmatrix} \mathbf{a} & \mathbf{1} & \mathbf{b} \\ \mathbf{b} & \mathbf{1} & \mathbf{c} \\ \mathbf{c} & \mathbf{1} & \mathbf{a} \end{vmatrix}$$

[By Property II]

EXAMPLE 7. *Without directly expanding the determinant, show that*

$$\begin{vmatrix} x-y & y-z & z-x \\ y-z & z-x & x-y \\ z-x & x-y & y-z \end{vmatrix} = 0.$$ **[ICWAI June 1994]**

SOLUTION.

$$\text{Left side} = \begin{vmatrix} x-y & y-z & z-x \\ y-z & z-x & x-y \\ z-x & x-y & y-z \end{vmatrix}$$

$$= \begin{vmatrix} x-y+y-z+z-x & y-z & z-x \\ y-z+z-x+x-y & z-x & x-y \\ z-x+x-y+y-z & x-y & y-z \end{vmatrix}$$ [Adding 2nd and 3rd columns with the 1st]

$$= \begin{vmatrix} 0 & y-z & z-x \\ 0 & z-x & x-y \\ 0 & x-y & y-z \end{vmatrix} = 0.$$

EXAMPLE 8. Evaluate the following determinants:

(i) $\begin{vmatrix} a & a+b & a+b+c \\ 2a & 3a+2b & 4a+3b+2c \\ 3a & 6a+3b & 10a+6b+3c \end{vmatrix}$; (ii) $\begin{vmatrix} 1 & a & bc \\ 1 & b & ca \\ 1 & c & ab \end{vmatrix}$.

SOLUTION.

(i) We have

$$\begin{vmatrix} a & a+b & a+b+c \\ 2a & 3a+2b & 4a+3b+2c \\ 3a & 6a+3b & 10a+6b+3c \end{vmatrix} = \begin{vmatrix} a & a+b & a+b+c \\ 0 & a & 2a+b \\ 0 & 3a & 7a+3b \end{vmatrix}$$ [subtracting 2 times the first row from the second and 3 times the first row from the third]

$$= a\begin{vmatrix} a & 2a+b \\ 3a & 7a+3b \end{vmatrix}$$ [expanding along the first column]

$$= a(7a^2 + 3ab - 6a^2 - 3ab) = a \times a^2 = \mathbf{a^3}.$$

(ii) $$\begin{vmatrix} 1 & a & bc \\ 1 & b & ca \\ 1 & c & ab \end{vmatrix} = \begin{vmatrix} 1 & a & bc \\ 0 & b-a & ca-bc \\ 0 & c-a & ab-bc \end{vmatrix}$$ [subtracting first row from the second and third]

$$= 1\begin{vmatrix} b-a & ca-bc \\ c-a & ab-bc \end{vmatrix}$$ [expanding along the first column]

$$= \begin{vmatrix} b-a & -c(b-a) \\ c-a & -b(c-a) \end{vmatrix} = (b-a)(c-a)\begin{vmatrix} 1 & -c \\ 1 & -b \end{vmatrix}$$

$$= (b-a)(c-a)(-b+c) = \mathbf{(a-b)(b-c)(c-a)}.$$

EXAMPLE 9. Prove that $\begin{vmatrix} 1 & x & x^2-yz \\ 1 & y & y^2-zx \\ 1 & z & z^2-xy \end{vmatrix} = 0.$ **[ICWAI December 1986]**

SOLUTION.

$$\text{L.H.S.} = \begin{vmatrix} 1 & x & x^2 \\ 1 & y & y^2 \\ 1 & z & z^2 \end{vmatrix} - \begin{vmatrix} 1 & x & yz \\ 1 & y & zx \\ 1 & z & xy \end{vmatrix} \quad \text{[By **Property VI**]}$$

$$= \Delta_1 - \Delta_2 \quad \text{(say)}$$

$$\text{Now,} \quad \Delta_2 = \frac{1}{xyz}\begin{vmatrix} x & x^2 & xyz \\ y & y^2 & xyz \\ z & z^2 & xyz \end{vmatrix}$$

[multiplying 1st row by x, 2nd row by y, 3rd row by z and dividing the resulting determinant by xyz]

$$= \frac{1}{xyz}\cdot xyz\begin{vmatrix} x & x^2 & 1 \\ y & y^2 & 1 \\ z & z^2 & 1 \end{vmatrix} = -\begin{vmatrix} x & 1 & x^2 \\ y & 1 & y^2 \\ z & 1 & z^2 \end{vmatrix} = \begin{vmatrix} 1 & x & x^2 \\ 1 & y & y^2 \\ 1 & z & z^2 \end{vmatrix} = \Delta_1.$$

Hence L.H.S. $= \Delta_1 - \Delta_2 = \Delta_1 - \Delta_1 = \mathbf{0}$.

EXAMPLE 10. *Solve:*

$$\begin{vmatrix} x+a & b & c \\ c & x+b & a \\ a & b & x+c \end{vmatrix} = 0.$$

[C.U. 1982; ICWAI]

SOLUTION.

$$\begin{vmatrix} x+a & b & c \\ c & x+b & a \\ a & b & x+c \end{vmatrix} = 0, \quad \text{or,} \quad \begin{vmatrix} x+a+b+c & b & c \\ c+x+b+a & x+b & a \\ a+b+x+c & b & x+c \end{vmatrix} = 0;$$

$$\text{or,} \quad (x+a+b+c)\begin{vmatrix} 1 & b & c \\ 1 & x+b & a \\ 1 & b & x+c \end{vmatrix} = 0,$$

$$\text{or,} \quad (x+a+b+c)\begin{vmatrix} 1 & b & c \\ 0 & x & a-c \\ 0 & 0 & x \end{vmatrix} = 0,$$

[subtracting 1st row from the 2nd and 3rd]

$$\text{or,} \quad (x+a+b+c)\cdot 1\cdot\begin{vmatrix} x & a-c \\ 0 & x \end{vmatrix} = 0,$$

[expanding in terms of the elements of the first column.]

or, $(x+a+b+c)x^2 = 0$, $\therefore$ $\mathbf{x = 0}$, **or,** $\mathbf{x = -(a+b+c)}$.

EXAMPLE 11. *Show that* $\begin{vmatrix} b+c & a & a \\ b & c+a & b \\ c & c & a+b \end{vmatrix} = 4abc.$ **[ICWAI December 1992]**

SOLUTION.

$$\text{Left side} = \begin{vmatrix} 0 & -2c & -2b \\ b & c+a & b \\ c & c & a+b \end{vmatrix} = 2\begin{vmatrix} 0 & -c & -b \\ b & c+a & b \\ c & c & a+b \end{vmatrix}$$

[Applying $R_1 - (R_2 + R_3)$ where R_i represents ith row]

$$= 2\begin{vmatrix} 0 & -c & -b \\ b & a & 0 \\ c & 0 & a \end{vmatrix} = 2\{0 + c(ab-0) - b(0-ca)\}$$

[Applying $R_2 + R_1$ and $R_3 + R_1$]

$$= 2(abc + abc) = \mathbf{4abc}.$$

EXAMPLE 12. Prove that $\begin{vmatrix} a-b-c & 2b & 2c \\ 2a & b-c-a & 2c \\ 2a & 2b & c-a-b \end{vmatrix} = (a+b+c)^3.$ **[C.U. 1975]**

SOLUTION.

$$\text{L.H.S.} = \begin{vmatrix} a+b+c & 2b & 2c \\ a+b+c & b-c-a & 2c \\ a+b+c & 2b & c-a-b \end{vmatrix}$$ [adding 2nd and 3rd columns to the first.]

$$= (a+b+c)\begin{vmatrix} 1 & 2b & 2c \\ 1 & b-c-a & 2c \\ 1 & 2b & c-a-b \end{vmatrix}$$

$$= (a+b+c)\begin{vmatrix} 1 & 2b & 2c \\ 0 & -b-c-a & 0 \\ 0 & 0 & -c-a-b \end{vmatrix}$$ [subtracting 1st row from the 2nd and 3rd]

$$= (a+b+c)\cdot 1\cdot\begin{vmatrix} -b-c-a & 0 \\ 0 & -c-a-b \end{vmatrix}$$

$$= (a+b+c)(-b-c-a)(-c-a-b) = (a+b+c)(a+b+c)(a+b+c)$$

$$= \mathbf{(a+b+c)^3}.$$

EXAMPLE 13. *Prove that* $\begin{vmatrix} a^2 & 2ab & b^2 \\ b^2 & a^2 & 2ab \\ 2ab & b^2 & a^2 \end{vmatrix}$ *is a perfect square.*

[ICWAI June 1975, December 1990]

SOLUTION.

$$\begin{vmatrix} a^2 & 2ab & b^2 \\ b^2 & a^2 & 2ab \\ 2ab & b^2 & a^2 \end{vmatrix}$$

$$= \begin{vmatrix} a^2+2ab+b^2 & 2ab & b^2 \\ b^2+a^2+2ab & a^2 & 2ab \\ 2ab+b^2+a^2 & b^2 & a^2 \end{vmatrix}$$ [adding 2nd and 3rd columns to the first]

$$= \begin{vmatrix} (a+b)^2 & 2ab & b^2 \\ (a+b)^2 & a^2 & 2ab \\ (a+b)^2 & b^2 & a^2 \end{vmatrix} = (a+b)^2\begin{vmatrix} 1 & 2ab & b^2 \\ 1 & a^2 & 2ab \\ 1 & b^2 & a^2 \end{vmatrix}$$

$$=(a+b)^2\begin{vmatrix} 1 & 2ab & b^2 \\ 0 & a^2-2ab & 2ab-b^2 \\ 0 & b^2-2ab & a^2-b^2 \end{vmatrix}$$

$$=(a+b)^2\cdot 1\cdot\begin{vmatrix} a^2-2ab & 2ab-b^2 \\ b^2-2ab & a^2-b^2 \end{vmatrix}$$

$$=(a+b)^2\begin{vmatrix} a^2-b^2 & 2ab-b^2 \\ a^2-2ab & a^2-b^2 \end{vmatrix} = (a+b)^2\{(a^2-b^2)^2-(2ab-b^2)(\mathbf{a^2-2ab})\}$$ [adding 2nd column to the first]

$$=(a+b)^2(a^4+b^4-2a^2b^2-2a^3b+4a^2b^2+a^2b^2-2ab^3)$$

$$=(a+b)^2(a^4+b^4+a^2b^2-2a^3b-2ab^3+2a^2b^2)$$

$$=(a+b)^2(a^2-ab+b^2)^2 = \{(a+b)(a^2-ab+b^2)\}^2$$

$=\mathbf{(a^3+b^3)^2}$, **which is a perfect square.**

OTHERWISE:

$$\begin{vmatrix} a & b & 0 \\ 0 & a & b \\ b & 0 & a \end{vmatrix}^2 = \begin{vmatrix} a & b & 0 \\ 0 & a & b \\ b & 0 & a \end{vmatrix} \times \begin{vmatrix} a & b & 0 \\ 0 & a & b \\ b & 0 & a \end{vmatrix}$$

$$= -\begin{vmatrix} b & a & 0 \\ a & 0 & b \\ 0 & b & a \end{vmatrix} \times \begin{vmatrix} a & b & 0 \\ 0 & a & b \\ b & 0 & a \end{vmatrix} = -\begin{vmatrix} 2ab & a^2 & b^2 \\ a^2 & b^2 & 2ab \\ b^2 & 2ab & a^2 \end{vmatrix}$$

$$= \begin{vmatrix} a^2 & 2ab & b^2 \\ b^2 & a^2 & 2ab \\ 2ab & b^2 & a^2 \end{vmatrix} \text{ and } \begin{vmatrix} a & b & 0 \\ 0 & a & b \\ b & 0 & a \end{vmatrix} = a^3 + b^3.]$$

EXAMPLE 14. *Show that* $\begin{vmatrix} 1 & 1 & 1 \\ a & b & c \\ a^2 & b^2 & c^2 \end{vmatrix} = -(a-b)(b-c)(a-c)$

and hence deduce the linear factors of

$$\begin{vmatrix} 1 & 1 & 1 \\ a^2 & b^2 & c^2 \\ a^4 & b^4 & c^4 \end{vmatrix}.$$

[C.U. 1983; ICWAI December 1974]

SOLUTION.

$$\begin{vmatrix} 1 & 1 & 1 \\ a & b & c \\ a^2 & b^2 & c^2 \end{vmatrix} = \begin{vmatrix} 1 & 0 & 0 \\ a & b-a & c-a \\ a^2 & b^2-a^2 & c^2-a^2 \end{vmatrix}$$ [subtracting 1st column from the 2nd and the 3rd.]

$$= 1 \cdot \begin{vmatrix} b-a & c-a \\ b^2-a^2 & c^2-a^2 \end{vmatrix} = (b-a)(c-a) \begin{vmatrix} 1 & 1 \\ b+a & c+a \end{vmatrix}$$

$$= (a-b)(a-c) \cdot \{c+a-b-a\} = (a-b)(a-c)(c-b)$$

$$= -(\mathbf{a}-\mathbf{b})(\mathbf{b}-\mathbf{c})(\mathbf{a}-\mathbf{c}). \qquad (1)$$

2nd part:

$$\begin{vmatrix} 1 & 1 & 1 \\ a^2 & b^2 & c^2 \\ a^4 & b^4 & c^4 \end{vmatrix} = \begin{vmatrix} 1 & 1 & 1 \\ \alpha & \beta & \gamma \\ \alpha^2 & \beta^2 & \gamma^2 \end{vmatrix}, \text{ where } \alpha = a^2, \beta = b^2, \gamma = c^2.$$

$$= -(\alpha-\beta)(\beta-\gamma)(\alpha-\gamma) \quad \text{[by (1)]}$$

$$= -(a^2-b^2)(b^2-c^2)(a^2-c^2)$$

$$= -(\mathbf{a}+\mathbf{b})(\mathbf{a}-\mathbf{b})(\mathbf{b}+\mathbf{c})(\mathbf{b}-\mathbf{c})(\mathbf{a}+\mathbf{c})(\mathbf{a}-\mathbf{c}).$$

EXAMPLE 15. *If* $A_1, B_1, C_1, \cdots$ *are respectively the cofactors of the elements* $a_1, b_1, c_1, \cdots$ *of the determinant* D, *where*

$$D = \begin{vmatrix} a_1 & b_1 & c_1 \\ a_2 & b_2 & c_2 \\ a_3 & b_3 & c_3 \end{vmatrix}, \text{ prove that } \begin{vmatrix} B_2 & C_2 \\ B_3 & C_3 \end{vmatrix} = a_1 D.$$

[ICWAI June 1977]

SOLUTION.

$$
\begin{aligned}
D &= a_1\begin{vmatrix} b_2 & c_2 \\ b_3 & c_3 \end{vmatrix} - b_1\begin{vmatrix} a_2 & c_2 \\ a_3 & c_3 \end{vmatrix} + c_1\begin{vmatrix} a_2 & b_2 \\ a_3 & b_3 \end{vmatrix} \\
&= a_1(b_2c_3 - b_3c_2) - b_1(a_2c_3 - a_3c_2) + c_1(a_2b_3 - a_3b_2) \\
&= a_1b_2c_3 - a_1b_3c_2 - a_2b_1c_3 + a_3b_1c_2 + a_2b_3c_1 - a_3b_2c_1. \qquad (1)
\end{aligned}
$$

Now,

$$
\begin{aligned}
B_2 &= \text{ cofactor of } b_2 \text{ in } D = (-1)^{2+2}\begin{vmatrix} a_1 & c_1 \\ a_3 & c_3 \end{vmatrix} \\
&= +(a_1c_3 - a_3c_1) = a_1c_3 - a_3c_1; \\
C_2 &= \text{ cofactor of } c_2 \text{ in } D = (-1)^{2+3}\begin{vmatrix} a_1 & b_1 \\ a_3 & b_3 \end{vmatrix} \\
&= -(a_1b_3 - a_3b_1) = a_3b_1 - a_1b_3; \\
B_3 &= \text{ cofactor of } b_3 \text{ in } D = (-1)^{3+2}\begin{vmatrix} a_1 & c_1 \\ a_2 & c_2 \end{vmatrix} \\
&= -(a_1c_2 - a_2c_1) = a_2c_1 - a_1c_2; \\
C_3 &= \text{ cofactor of } c_3 \text{ in } D = (-1)^{3+3}\begin{vmatrix} a_1 & b_1 \\ a_2 & b_2 \end{vmatrix} \\
&= +(a_1b_2 - a_2b_1) = a_1b_2 - a_2b_1;
\end{aligned}
$$

$$
\begin{aligned}
\therefore \quad \begin{vmatrix} B_2 & C_2 \\ B_3 & C_3 \end{vmatrix} &= B_2C_3 - B_3C_2 \\
&= (a_1c_3 - a_3c_1)(a_1b_2 - a_2b_1) - (a_2c_1 - a_1c_2)(a_3b_1 - a_1b_3) \\
&= a_1^2b_2c_3 - a_1a_2b_1c_3 - a_1a_3b_2c_1 + a_2a_3b_1c_1 - (a_2a_3b_1c_1 - a_1a_2b_3c_1 - a_1a_3b_1c_2 + a_1^2b_3c_2) \\
&= a_1(a_1b_2c_3 - a_2b_1c_3 - a_3b_2c_1 + a_2b_3c_1 + a_3b_1c_2 - a_1b_3c_2) \\
&= \mathbf{a_1D}. \quad \text{[by (1)]}.
\end{aligned}
$$

EXAMPLE 16. *Prove that*

$$
\begin{vmatrix} (b+c)^2 & a^2 & a^2 \\ b^2 & (c+a)^2 & b^2 \\ c^2 & c^2 & (a+b)^2 \end{vmatrix} = 2abc(a+b+c)^3.
$$

SOLUTION.

$$
\text{L.H.S.} = \begin{vmatrix} (b+c)^2 & a^2-(b+c)^2 & a^2-(b+c)^2 \\ b^2 & (c+a)^2-b^2 & 0 \\ c^2 & 0 & (a+b)^2-c^2 \end{vmatrix} \quad \text{[subtracting 1st column from the 2nd and the third]}
$$

$$
= \begin{vmatrix} (b+c)^2 & (a+b+c)(a-b-c) & (a+b+c)(a-b-c) \\ b^2 & (c+a+b)(c+a-b) & 0 \\ c^2 & 0 & (a+b+c)(a+b-c) \end{vmatrix}
$$

$$
= (a+b+c)(a+b+c)\begin{vmatrix} (b+c)^2 & a-b-c & a-b-c \\ b^2 & c+a-b & 0 \\ c^2 & 0 & a+b-c \end{vmatrix}
$$

$$= (a+b+c)^2 \begin{vmatrix} 2bc & -2c & -2b \\ b^2 & c+a-b & 0 \\ c^2 & 0 & a+b-c \end{vmatrix}$$ [subtracting the sum of the 2nd and the 3rd row from the 1st.]

$$= 2(a+b+c)^2 \begin{vmatrix} bc & -c & -b \\ b^2 & c+a-b & 0 \\ c^2 & 0 & a+b-c \end{vmatrix}$$

$$= 2(a+b+c)^2 \begin{vmatrix} bc & 0 & 0 \\ b^2 & c+a & b^2/c \\ c^2 & c^2/b & a+b \end{vmatrix}$$ [adding $\frac{1}{b}$ times the first column to the 2nd and $\frac{1}{c}$ times the 1st column to the 3rd]

$$= 2(a+b+c)^2 \cdot bc \cdot \begin{vmatrix} c+a & \frac{b^2}{c} \\ \frac{c^2}{b} & a+b \end{vmatrix}$$

$$= 2bc(a+b+c)^2 \left\{ (c+a)(a+b) - \frac{c^2}{b} \times \frac{b^2}{c} \right\}$$

$$= 2bc(a+b+c)^2 \{ca + bc + a^2 + ab - bc\}$$

$$= 2bc(a+b+c)^2 \cdot a(c+a+b) = \mathbf{2abc(a+b+c)^3}.$$

Exercise 3(I)

[Determinants]

1. Find the value of each of the following determinants:

(i) $\begin{vmatrix} 1 & 2 & 0 \\ 0 & 1 & 2 \\ 1 & 0 & 2 \end{vmatrix}$; (ii) $\begin{vmatrix} 2 & 5 & 7 \\ 3 & 6 & 10 \\ 8 & 4 & 15 \end{vmatrix}$; (iii) $\begin{vmatrix} 46 & 32 & 15 \\ 27 & 21 & 9 \\ 17 & 16 & 7 \end{vmatrix}$;

(iv) $\begin{vmatrix} 1 & 1 & 1 \\ 1 & 1+a & 1 \\ 1 & 1 & 1+b \end{vmatrix}$; (v) $\begin{vmatrix} a & b & c \\ a & a+b & a+b+c \\ a & 2a+b & 3a+2b+c \end{vmatrix}$;

(vi) $\begin{vmatrix} 91 & 94 & 96 \\ 92 & 95 & 97 \\ 93 & 96 & 98 \end{vmatrix}$; (vii) $\begin{vmatrix} a & h & g \\ h & b & f \\ g & f & c \end{vmatrix}$.

2. Prove *without expansion* that

(i) $\begin{vmatrix} a_1+3b_1+5c_1 & b_1 & c_1 \\ a_2+3b_2+5c_2 & b_2 & c_2 \\ a_3+3b_3+5c_3 & b_3 & c_3 \end{vmatrix} = \begin{vmatrix} a_1 & b_1 & c_1 \\ a_2 & b_2 & c_2 \\ a_3 & b_3 & c_3 \end{vmatrix}$;

(ii) $\begin{vmatrix} a_1-pb_1-qc_1 & b_1 & c_1 \\ a_2-pb_2-qc_2 & b_2 & c_2 \\ a_3-pb_3-qc_3 & b_3 & c_3 \end{vmatrix} = \begin{vmatrix} a_1 & b_1 & c_1 \\ a_2 & b_2 & c_2 \\ a_3 & b_3 & c_3 \end{vmatrix}$;

(iii) $\begin{vmatrix} l & m & n \\ x & y & z \\ p & q & r \end{vmatrix} = \begin{vmatrix} y & m & q \\ x & l & p \\ z & n & r \end{vmatrix}$; (iv) $\begin{vmatrix} 0 & 99 & -998 \\ -99 & 0 & 997 \\ 998 & -997 & 0 \end{vmatrix} = 0$;

(v) $\begin{vmatrix} b+c & c+a & a+b \\ q+r & r+p & p+q \\ y+z & z+x & x+y \end{vmatrix} = 2\begin{vmatrix} a & b & c \\ p & q & r \\ x & y & z \end{vmatrix}$.

3. Evaluate each of the following determinants:

(i) $\begin{vmatrix} a-b & b-c & c-a \\ b-c & c-a & a-b \\ c-a & a-b & b-c \end{vmatrix}$; (ii) $\begin{vmatrix} 1 & x & y+z \\ 1 & y & z+x \\ 1 & z & x+y \end{vmatrix}$;

(iii) $\begin{vmatrix} 1 & bc & a(b+c) \\ 1 & ca & b(c+a) \\ 1 & ab & c(a+b) \end{vmatrix}$; (iv) $\begin{vmatrix} a & b & c \\ a-b & b-c & c-a \\ b+c & c+a & a+b \end{vmatrix}$. **[C.U. 1981]**

4. Prove without expansion that

(i) $\begin{vmatrix} 0 & a & b \\ -a & 0 & c \\ -b & -c & 0 \end{vmatrix} = 0$; (ii) $\begin{vmatrix} 1 & -a & b+c \\ 1 & -b & c+a \\ 1 & -c & a+b \end{vmatrix} = 0$.

5. Without actual expansion, but by using properties of determinants only, prove that

(i) $\begin{vmatrix} a^2 & a & bc \\ b^2 & b & ca \\ c^2 & c & ab \end{vmatrix} = \begin{vmatrix} a^3 & a^2 & 1 \\ b^3 & b^2 & 1 \\ c^3 & c^2 & 1 \end{vmatrix}$; **[ICWAI December 1975]**

(ii) $\begin{vmatrix} 1 & 1^2 & 2^2 \\ 2 & 2^2 & 4^2 \\ 3 & 3^2 & 6^2 \end{vmatrix} = 0$; (iii) $\begin{vmatrix} 1 & a & a^2-bc \\ 1 & b & b^2-ca \\ 1 & c & c^2-ab \end{vmatrix} = 0$. **[ICWAI December 1986, '93]**

6. Prove that

(i) $\begin{vmatrix} x+y & 2x+y & 3x+y \\ 2x+y & 3x+y & 4x+y \\ 5x+y & 6x+y & 7x+y \end{vmatrix} = 0$;

(ii) $\begin{vmatrix} 1+a & 1 & 1 \\ 1 & 1+a & 1 \\ 1 & 1 & 1+a \end{vmatrix} = a^2(a+3)$;

(iii) $\begin{vmatrix} 1+a_1 & a_2 & a_3 \\ a_1 & 1+a_2 & a_3 \\ a_1 & a_2 & 1+a_3 \end{vmatrix} = 1+a_1+a_2+a_3$.

7. Find the value of the determinant

$$\begin{vmatrix} x^2+y^2+1 & x^2+2y^2+3 & x^2+3y^2+4 \\ y^2+2 & 2y^2+6 & 3y^2+8 \\ y^2+1 & 2y^2+3 & 3y^2+4 \end{vmatrix}.$$

8. Prove that

(i) $\begin{vmatrix} a+b+2c & a & b \\ c & b+c+2a & b \\ c & a & c+a+2b \end{vmatrix} = 2(a+b+c)^3$; **[ICWAI June 1995]**

(ii) $\begin{vmatrix} 2a-b-c & 3b & 3c \\ 3a & 2b-c-a & 3c \\ 3a & 3b & 2c-a-b \end{vmatrix} = 2(a+b+c)^3$;

(iii) $\begin{vmatrix} a^2 & bc & c^2+ca \\ a^2+ab & b^2 & ca \\ ab & b^2+bc & c^2 \end{vmatrix} = 4a^2b^2c^2.$ **[B.U. 1970; N.B.U. 1975]**

[HINTS. Take a, b, c common from the 1st, 2nd and 3rd columns and then apply $c_1 + c_2 - c_3$,]

9. (a) Solve for x :

(i) $\begin{vmatrix} 1 & 1 & 1 \\ 1 & x & 1 \\ 1 & 1 & x \end{vmatrix} = 0$; (ii) $\begin{vmatrix} 1 & 1 & 1 \\ a & x & a \\ b & b & x \end{vmatrix} = 0$; **[ICWAI June 1983]**

(iii) $\begin{vmatrix} x & 1 & 1 \\ 1 & x & 1 \\ 1 & 1 & x \end{vmatrix} = 0.$ **[ICWAI June 1989]**

(b) Find the value (or values) of x from the following equations:

(i) $\begin{vmatrix} x+1 & 2 & 3 \\ 3 & x+2 & 1 \\ 1 & 2 & x+3 \end{vmatrix} = 0$; (ii) $\begin{vmatrix} x & a & b \\ a & x & b \\ a & b & x \end{vmatrix} = 0.$

10. (i) Show that $\begin{vmatrix} x^2 & 2x & 1 \\ 1 & x^2 & 2x \\ 2x & 1 & x^2 \end{vmatrix}$ is a perfect square.

(ii) Prove that $\begin{vmatrix} 1 & a & a^2 \\ a^2 & 1 & a \\ a & a^2 & 1 \end{vmatrix}$ is a perfect square.

(iii) Show that $\begin{vmatrix} -a^2 & ab & ac \\ ab & -b^2 & bc \\ ac & bc & -c^2 \end{vmatrix}$ is a perfect square. **[ICWAI June 1987; December 1991]**

[HINTS. Given determinant $= a \cdot b \cdot c \begin{vmatrix} -a & b & c \\ a & -b & c \\ a & b & -c \end{vmatrix}$

$= \begin{vmatrix} 0 & 0 & 2a \\ a & -b & c \\ 2a & 0 & 0 \end{vmatrix}$ [Adding 2nd row with the 1st and the 3rd row.]

$= 2c(0 + 2ab) = \mathbf{4abc}$.]

11. Show that $\begin{vmatrix} a^2 & a & 1 \\ b^2 & b & 1 \\ c^2 & c & 1 \end{vmatrix} = -(a-b)(b-c)(c-a).$ **[ICWAI June 1979]**

12. Show that $\begin{vmatrix} 1+a^2-b^2 & 2ab & -2b \\ 2ab & 1-a^2+b^2 & 2a \\ 2b & -2a & 1-a^2-b^2 \end{vmatrix} = (1+a^2+b^2)^3.$

13. Prove that

$\begin{vmatrix} 1+a_1 & 1 & 1 \\ 1 & 1+a_2 & 1 \end{vmatrix} = a_1a_2a_3\left(1 + \frac{1}{a_1} + \frac{1}{a_2} + \frac{1}{a_3}\right).$ **[C.U. B.Com. 1986; ICWAI June 1986]**

[HINTS. Take a_1, a_2, a_3 common from the 1st, 2nd and 3rd columns and then add 2nd and 3rd columns to the 1st.]

14. Prove that

(i) $\begin{vmatrix} 1 & x & x^2 \\ 1 & y & y^2 \\ 1 & z & z^2 \end{vmatrix} = (y-z)(z-x)(x-y);$ **[C.U. 1983; Bombay U.; ICWAI December 1994]**

(ii) $\begin{vmatrix} 1 & x & x^3 \\ 1 & y & y^3 \\ 1 & z & z^3 \end{vmatrix} = (x-y)(y-z)(z-x)(x+y+z).$

15. Prove that

$$\begin{vmatrix} (y+z)^2 & y^2 & z^2 \\ x^2 & (z+x)^2 & z^2 \\ x^2 & y^2 & (x+y)^2 \end{vmatrix} = 2xyz(x+y+z)^3.$$

16. If $A_1, B_1, C_1, A_2, B_2, \cdots$ are, respectively, the cofactors of $a_1, b_1, c_1, a_2, b_2, \cdots$ in the determinant Δ, where

$$\Delta \equiv \begin{vmatrix} a_1 & b_1 & c_1 \\ a_2 & b_2 & c_2 \\ a_3 & b_3 & c_3 \end{vmatrix},$$

prove that (i) $a_1A_2 + b_1B_2 + c_1C_2 = 0$,

(ii) $a_2A_2 + b_2B_2 + c_2C_2 = \Delta$, and (iii) $\begin{vmatrix} B_1 & C_1 \\ B_2 & C_2 \end{vmatrix} = a_3\Delta.$

17. Show that

$\begin{vmatrix} 0 & r & q \\ r & 0 & p \\ q & p & 0 \end{vmatrix}^2 = \begin{vmatrix} -p^2 & pq & pr \\ pq & -q^2 & qr \\ pr & qr & -r^2 \end{vmatrix} = (2pqr)^2.$ **[ICWAI December 1989]**

[HINTS.

Let $\Delta = \begin{vmatrix} 0 & r & q \\ r & 0 & p \\ q & p & 0 \end{vmatrix}$; then $\Delta' =$ adjugate of $\Delta = \begin{vmatrix} -p^2 & pq & pr \\ pq & -q^2 & qr \\ pr & qr & -r^2 \end{vmatrix}$;

$\therefore\ \ \Delta^2 = \Delta'.$

Also $\Delta = 2pqr$.

18. If $a \neq b \neq c$ and $\begin{vmatrix} a & a^2 & 1+a^3 \\ b & b^2 & 1+b^3 \\ c & c^2 & 1+c^3 \end{vmatrix} = 0,$ **[ICWAI December 1985]**

prove that $abc + 1 = 0$.

[HINTS.

$$\begin{vmatrix} a & a^2 & 1+a^3 \\ b & b^2 & 1+b^3 \\ c & c^2 & 1+c^3 \end{vmatrix} = \begin{vmatrix} a & a^2 & 1 \\ b & b^2 & 1 \\ c & c^2 & 1 \end{vmatrix} + \begin{vmatrix} a & a^2 & a^3 \\ b & b^2 & b^3 \\ c & c^2 & c^3 \end{vmatrix}$$

$$= \begin{vmatrix} 1 & a & a^2 \\ 1 & b & b^2 \\ 1 & c & c^2 \end{vmatrix} + abc \begin{vmatrix} 1 & a & a^2 \\ 1 & b & b^2 \\ 1 & c & c^2 \end{vmatrix} = \begin{vmatrix} 1 & a & a^2 \\ 1 & b & b^2 \\ 1 & c & c^2 \end{vmatrix} (1+abc)$$

$= (a-b)(b-c)(c-a)(1+abc)$. Hence etc.]

Answers

1. (i) 6; (ii) 23; (iii) 111; (iv) ab; (v) a^3; (vi) 0; (vii) $abc+2fgh-af^2-bg^2-ch^2$. **3.** (i) 0; (ii) 0; (iii) 0; (iv) $a^3+b^3+c^3-3abc$. **7.** x^2y^2. **9.** (a) (i) $x=1,1$; (ii) $x=a,b$; (b) (i) $x=0,-6$; (ii) $x=a,b,-(a+b)$. **10.** (i) $(x^2+1)^2$ which is a perfect square; (ii) $(1-a^3)^2$ which is a perfect square.

3.5. PRODUCT OF TWO DETERMINANTS

Let us consider the determinant

$$\Delta \equiv \begin{vmatrix} a_1\alpha_1+b_1\beta_1 & a_1\alpha_2+b_1\beta_2 \\ a_2\alpha_1+b_2\beta_1 & a_2\alpha_2+b_2\beta_2 \end{vmatrix} \qquad (1)$$

We can express this determinant as the sum of $2\times 2=4$ determinants i.e.

$$\Delta = \begin{vmatrix} a_1\alpha_1 & a_1\alpha_2 \\ a_2\alpha_1 & a_2\alpha_2 \end{vmatrix} + \begin{vmatrix} a_1\alpha_1 & b_1\beta_2 \\ a_2\alpha_1 & b_2\beta_2 \end{vmatrix} + \begin{vmatrix} b_1\beta_1 & a_1\alpha_2 \\ b_2\beta_1 & a_2\alpha_2 \end{vmatrix} + \begin{vmatrix} b_1\beta_1 & b_1\beta_2 \\ b_2\beta_1 & b_2\beta_2 \end{vmatrix}$$

$$= \alpha_1\alpha_2\begin{vmatrix} a_1 & a_1 \\ a_2 & a_2 \end{vmatrix} + \alpha_1\beta_2\begin{vmatrix} a_1 & b_1 \\ a_2 & b_2 \end{vmatrix} + \beta_1\alpha_2\begin{vmatrix} b_1 & a_1 \\ b_2 & a_2 \end{vmatrix} + \beta_1\beta_2\begin{vmatrix} b_1 & b_1 \\ b_2 & b_2 \end{vmatrix}$$

$$= \alpha_1\alpha_2\times 0 + \alpha_1\beta_2\begin{vmatrix} a_1 & b_1 \\ a_2 & b_2 \end{vmatrix} - \alpha_2\beta_1\begin{vmatrix} a_1 & b_1 \\ a_2 & b_2 \end{vmatrix} + \beta_1\beta_2\times 0$$

[∵ Two columns are identical]

$$= \begin{vmatrix} a_1 & b_1 \\ a_2 & b_2 \end{vmatrix}(\alpha_1\beta_2-\alpha_2\beta_1) = \begin{vmatrix} a_1 & b_1 \\ a_2 & b_2 \end{vmatrix} \times \begin{vmatrix} \alpha_1 & \beta_1 \\ \alpha_2 & \beta_2 \end{vmatrix}.$$

Thus, we have $\begin{vmatrix} a_1 & b_1 \\ a_2 & b_2 \end{vmatrix} \times \begin{vmatrix} \alpha_1 & \beta_1 \\ \alpha_2 & \beta_2 \end{vmatrix} = \begin{vmatrix} a_1\alpha_1+b_1\beta_1 & a_1\alpha_2+b_1\beta_2 \\ a_2\alpha_1+b_2\beta_1 & a_2\alpha_2+b_2\beta_2 \end{vmatrix}$

i.e., The product of two determinants of second order is also a determinant of second order.

Rule to find the product of two determinants

(*Row by row multiplication*)

Let us denote the two determinants in the above discussions by Δ_1 and Δ_2 and the product determinant by Δ. Then we can find the elements of Δ as follows:

Multiply the elements of the first row of Δ_1 by the corresponding elements of the first row of Δ_2 and add. This will give the first element of the first row of Δ. Again, multiply the elements of the first row of Δ_1 by the corresponding elements of the 2nd row of Δ_2 and add. This will give the second element of the first row of Δ.

Next multiply the elements of the second row of Δ_1 by the corresponding elements of the first row of Δ_2 and add. This will give the first element of the second row of Δ. Finally, multiply the elements of the second row of Δ_1 by the corresponding elements of the second row of Δ_2 and add to obtain the second element of the second row of Δ.

We are to apply exactly similar rule to find the product of two determinants of *third* and higher order.

EXAMPLE 1. *Find the square of the determinant* $\begin{vmatrix} a_1 & b_1 \\ a_2 & b_2 \end{vmatrix}$. What is the order of this new determinant?

SOLUTION.

$$\begin{vmatrix} a_1 & b_1 \\ a_2 & b_2 \end{vmatrix}^2 = \begin{vmatrix} a_1 & b_1 \\ a_2 & b_2 \end{vmatrix} \times \begin{vmatrix} a_1 & b_1 \\ a_2 & b_2 \end{vmatrix}$$

$$= \begin{vmatrix} a_1^2 + b_1^2 & a_1a_2 + b_1b_2 \\ a_1a_2 + b_1b_2 & a_2^2 + b_2^2 \end{vmatrix}$$

This new determinant is also of **order 2.**

EXAMPLE 2. *Express the square of the determinant* $\begin{vmatrix} a_1 & b_1 & 0 \\ a_2 & b_2 & 0 \\ a_3 & b_3 & 0 \end{vmatrix}$ *as a third order determinant. Now obtain the value of this third order determinant.*

[ICWAI June 1978; June 1990]

SOLUTION.

$$\begin{vmatrix} a_1 & b_1 & 0 \\ a_2 & b_2 & 0 \\ a_3 & b_3 & 0 \end{vmatrix}^2 = \begin{vmatrix} a_1 & b_1 & 0 \\ a_2 & b_2 & 0 \\ a_3 & b_3 & 0 \end{vmatrix} \times \begin{vmatrix} a_1 & b_1 & 0 \\ a_2 & b_2 & 0 \\ a_3 & b_3 & 0 \end{vmatrix}$$

$$= \begin{vmatrix} a_1.a_1 + b_1.b_1 + 0.0 & a_1.a_2 + b_1.b_2 + 0.0 & a_1.a_3 + b_1.b_3 + 0.0 \\ a_2.a_1 + b_2.b_1 + 0.0 & a_2.a_2 + b_2.b_2 + 0.0 & a_2.a_3 + b_2.b_3 + 0.0 \\ a_3.a_1 + b_3.b_1 + 0.0 & a_3.a_2 + b_3.b_2 + 0.0 & a_3.a_3 + b_3.b_3 + 0.0 \end{vmatrix}$$

$$= \begin{vmatrix} a_1^2 + b_1^2 & a_1a_2 + b_1b_2 & a_1a_3 + b_1b_3 \\ a_1a_2 + b_1b_2 & a_2^2 + b_2^2 & a_2a_3 + b_2b_3 \\ a_1a_3 + b_1b_3 & a_2a_3 + b_2b_3 & a_3^2 + b_3^2 \end{vmatrix} \quad (1)$$

This is a **third order determinant**

2nd part. $\begin{vmatrix} a_1 & b_1 & 0 \\ a_2 & b_2 & 0 \\ a_3 & b_3 & 0 \end{vmatrix} = 0; \quad \therefore \quad \begin{vmatrix} a_1 & b_1 & 0 \\ a_2 & b_2 & 0 \\ a_3 & b_3 & 0 \end{vmatrix}^2 = 0.$

∴ The value of the new determinant (1) is **zero.**

NOTE. Students may verify that if all the elements of any one column (or row) are zero, then the value of the determinant is also zero.

EXAMPLE 3. *Find the value of the determinant* $\begin{vmatrix} a & b & 0 \\ c & 0 & a \\ 0 & c & b \end{vmatrix}$ *and then express its square as a third order determinant. What is its value?* **[ICWAI December 1978, '80]**

SOLUTION. $\begin{vmatrix} a & b & 0 \\ c & 0 & a \\ 0 & c & b \end{vmatrix} = a\begin{vmatrix} 0 & a \\ c & b \end{vmatrix} - b\begin{vmatrix} c & a \\ 0 & b \end{vmatrix} + 0\begin{vmatrix} c & 0 \\ 0 & c \end{vmatrix}$

$$= a(0 - ac) - b(bc - 0) = -a^2c - b^2c = -c(a^2 + b^2).$$

$$\begin{vmatrix} a & b & 0 \\ c & 0 & a \\ 0 & c & b \end{vmatrix}^2 = \begin{vmatrix} a & b & 0 \\ c & 0 & a \\ 0 & c & b \end{vmatrix} \times \begin{vmatrix} a & b & 0 \\ c & 0 & a \\ 0 & c & b \end{vmatrix} = \begin{vmatrix} a^2 + b^2 & ac & bc \\ ac & c^2 + a^2 & ab \\ bc & ab & c^2 + b^2 \end{vmatrix}.$$

This is a **third order** determinant.

The value of this new determinant is $\{-c(a^2+b^2)\}^2 = c^2(a^2+b^2)^2$.

EXAMPLE 4. *If A_i, B_i, C_i are the cofactors of a_i, b_i, c_i, respectively, $(i = 1, 2, 3)$ in*

$$\Delta = \begin{vmatrix} a_1 & b_1 & c_1 \\ a_2 & b_2 & c_2 \\ a_3 & b_3 & c_3 \end{vmatrix},$$

prove that

$$\begin{vmatrix} A_1 & B_1 & C_1 \\ A_2 & B_2 & C_2 \\ A_3 & B_3 & C_3 \end{vmatrix} = \Delta^2$$

[C.U. 1971, '73, '78, '81; Delhi U.; Bombay U.]

SOLUTION. We have

$$\begin{vmatrix} a_1 & b_1 & c_1 \\ a_2 & b_2 & c_2 \\ a_3 & b_3 & c_3 \end{vmatrix} \times \begin{vmatrix} A_1 & B_1 & C_1 \\ A_2 & B_2 & C_2 \\ A_3 & B_3 & C_3 \end{vmatrix}$$

$$= \begin{vmatrix} a_1A_1+b_1B_1+c_1C_1 & a_1A_2+b_1B_2+c_1C_2 & a_1A_3+b_1B_3+c_1C_3 \\ a_2A_1+b_2B_1+c_2C_1 & a_2A_2+b_2B_2+c_2C_2 & a_2A_3+b_2B_3+c_2C_3 \\ a_3A_1+b_3B_1+c_3C_1 & a_3A_2+b_3B_2+c_3C_2 & a_3A_3+b_3B_3+c_3C_3 \end{vmatrix}$$

$$= \begin{vmatrix} \Delta & 0 & 0 \\ 0 & \Delta & 0 \\ 0 & 0 & \Delta \end{vmatrix} \quad \left[\because \begin{array}{l} a_1A_1+b_1B_1+c_1C_1 = \Delta \\ a_2A_2+b_2B_2+c_2C_2 = \Delta \\ a_3A_3+b_3B_3+c_3C_3 = \Delta \\ a_2A_1+b_2B_1+c_2C_1 = 0, \text{ etc.} \end{array}\right]$$

$$= \Delta \begin{vmatrix} \Delta & 0 \\ 0 & \Delta \end{vmatrix} = \Delta \cdot \Delta^2 = \Delta^3,$$

$$\text{i.e.,} \quad \Delta \times \begin{vmatrix} A_1 & B_1 & C_1 \\ A_2 & B_2 & C_2 \\ A_3 & B_3 & C_3 \end{vmatrix} = \Delta^3$$

$$\text{Hence} \quad \begin{vmatrix} A_1 & B_1 & C_1 \\ A_2 & B_2 & C_2 \\ A_3 & B_3 & C_3 \end{vmatrix} = \frac{\Delta^3}{\Delta} = \Delta^2. \quad [\text{where } \Delta \neq 0.]$$

Reciprocal Determinant

If $\Delta = \begin{vmatrix} a_1 & b_1 & c_1 \\ a_2 & b_2 & c_2 \\ a_3 & b_3 & c_3 \end{vmatrix} \neq 0$, then the adjugate Δ' of Δ is defined by $\Delta' = \begin{vmatrix} A_1 & B_1 & C_1 \\ A_2 & B_2 & C_2 \\ A_3 & B_3 & C_3 \end{vmatrix}$.

The determinant $\bar{\Delta}$ (or Δ^{-1}) obtained by dividing each element of the adjugate Δ' of Δ is called the **reciprocal** determinant of Δ. Thus

$$\bar{\Delta} = \begin{vmatrix} A_1/\Delta & B_1/\Delta & C_1/\Delta \\ A_2/\Delta & B_2/\Delta & C_2/\Delta \\ A_3/\Delta & B_3/\Delta & C_3/\Delta \end{vmatrix}.$$

We can write $\bar{\Delta} = \frac{1}{\Delta^3} \times \Delta^2 = \frac{1}{\Delta}$, or, $\Delta \times \bar{\Delta} = 1$.

EXAMPLE 5. *Using properties of determinants prove that*

$$\begin{vmatrix} a & b & c \\ b & c & a \\ c & a & b \end{vmatrix} = -(a^3 + b^3 + c^3 - abc),$$

and hence show that

$$\begin{vmatrix} 2bc - a^2 & c^2 & b^2 \\ c^2 & 2ac - b^2 & a^2 \\ b^2 & a^2 & 2ab - c^2 \end{vmatrix} = (a^3 + b^3 + c^3 - 3abc)^2.$$

[C.U. B.Com. (Hons.) 1983]

SOLUTION.

$$\begin{vmatrix} a & b & c \\ b & c & a \\ c & a & b \end{vmatrix} = \begin{vmatrix} a+b+c & b & c \\ b+c+a & c & a \\ c+a+b & a & b \end{vmatrix} = (a+b+c)\begin{vmatrix} 1 & b & c \\ 1 & c & a \\ 1 & a & b \end{vmatrix}$$

$$= (a+b+c)\begin{vmatrix} 1 & b & c \\ 0 & c-b & a-c \\ 0 & a-b & b-c \end{vmatrix} = (a+b+c)\cdot 1 \cdot \begin{vmatrix} c-b & a-c \\ a-b & b-c \end{vmatrix}$$

$$= (a+b+c)\{(c-b)(b-c) - (a-b)(a-c)\}$$

$$= (a+b+c)(bc - c^2 - b^2 + bc - a^2 + ac + ab - bc)$$

$$= -(a+b+c)(a^2 + b^2 + c^2 - ab - bc - ac)$$

$$= -(\mathbf{a^3 + b^3 + c^3 - 3abc}).$$

2nd part.

$$\begin{vmatrix} a & b & c \\ b & c & a \\ c & a & b \end{vmatrix}^2 = \begin{vmatrix} a & b & c \\ b & c & a \\ c & a & b \end{vmatrix} \times \begin{vmatrix} a & b & c \\ b & c & a \\ c & a & b \end{vmatrix} = \begin{vmatrix} a & b & c \\ b & c & a \\ c & a & b \end{vmatrix} \times \begin{vmatrix} -a & c & b \\ -b & a & c \\ -c & b & a \end{vmatrix}$$

[interchanging 2nd and 3rd columns.]

$$= \begin{vmatrix} -a^2 + bc + cb & -ab + ab + c^2 & -ac + b^2 + ac \\ -ab + c^2 + ab & -b^2 + ca + ac & -bc + bc + a^2 \\ -ac + ac + b^2 & -bc + a^2 + bc & -c^2 + ab + ab \end{vmatrix}$$

$$= \begin{vmatrix} 2bc - a^2 & c^2 & b^2 \\ c^2 & 2ac - b^2 & a^2 \\ b^2 & a^2 & 2ab - c^2 \end{vmatrix}.$$

Hence $\begin{vmatrix} 2bc - a^2 & c^2 & b^2 \\ c^2 & 2ac - b^2 & a^2 \\ b^2 & a^2 & 2ab - c^2 \end{vmatrix} = \begin{vmatrix} a & b & c \\ b & c & a \\ c & a & b \end{vmatrix}^2 = (\mathbf{a^3 + b^3 + c^3 - 3abc})^2.$

3.6. SOLUTIONS OF LINEAR EQUATIONS

Determinants can be usefully employed to solve simultaneous linear *equations* in two or mor unknowns.

1. Two linear equations in two unknowns

Let us consider *two linear equations* in two unknowns x and y:

$$a_1x + b_1y = c_1$$
$$a_2x + b_2y = c_2$$

Solving these two equations by ordinary rules, we get

$$x = \frac{c_1b_2 - c_2b_1}{a_1b_2 - a_2b_1} \quad \text{and} \quad y = \frac{a_1c_2 - a_2c_1}{a_1b_2 - a_2b_1}, \tag{1}$$

where $a_1b_2 - a_2b_1 \neq 0$.

Using determinants of second order, we can write the solutions (1) in the form:

$$x = \frac{\begin{vmatrix} c_1 & b_1 \\ c_2 & b_2 \end{vmatrix}}{\begin{vmatrix} a_1 & b_1 \\ a_2 & b_2 \end{vmatrix}} = \frac{\Delta_1}{\Delta} \quad \text{and} \quad y = \frac{\begin{vmatrix} a_1 & c_1 \\ a_2 & c_2 \end{vmatrix}}{\begin{vmatrix} a_1 & b_1 \\ a_2 & b_2 \end{vmatrix}} = \frac{\Delta_2}{\Delta} \tag{2}$$

or, in short, $x = \frac{|c \ \ b|}{|a \ \ b|}$ and $y = \frac{|a \ \ c|}{|a \ \ b|}$, where $|ab| \neq 0$.

This method of solving simultaneous linear equations by determinants is known as **Cramer's Rule.**

From (2), we see that the denominator in both the values of x and y is the determinant $\Delta \equiv \begin{vmatrix} a_1 & b_1 \\ a_2 & b_2 \end{vmatrix}$ which is formed by the coefficients of x and y as arranged in the given equations and the numerator is also a determinant which is obtained from Δ by replacing the 1st or the 2nd column by the column of numbers on the right side of the given equations (i.e., by the column of constants $[c_1, c_2]$) according as it is the value of x or y.

EXAMPLE 6. *Solve the following equations by Cramer's Rule:*

$$3x + 2y = 8$$
$$5x - 3y = 7.$$

SOLUTION. Here Δ = the determinant of the coefficients

$$= \begin{vmatrix} 3 & 2 \\ 5 & -3 \end{vmatrix} = -9 - 10 = -19 \neq 0.$$

By **Cramer's Rule,** we get

$$x = \frac{\Delta_1}{\Delta} = \frac{\begin{vmatrix} 8 & 2 \\ 7 & -3 \end{vmatrix}}{\begin{vmatrix} 3 & 2 \\ 5 & -3 \end{vmatrix}} = \frac{-24 - 14}{-19} = \frac{-38}{-19} = 2$$

$$\text{and} \quad y = \frac{\Delta_2}{\Delta} = \frac{\begin{vmatrix} 3 & 8 \\ 5 & 7 \end{vmatrix}}{\begin{vmatrix} 3 & 2 \\ 5 & -3 \end{vmatrix}} = \frac{21 - 40}{-19} = \frac{-19}{-19} = 1.$$

Hence the required solutions are $\mathbf{x = 2, y = 1}$.

II. Three linear equations in three unknowns

Let us consider the linear equations:

$$\left.\begin{aligned} a_1x + b_1y + c_1z &= d_1 \\ a_2x + b_2y + c_2z &= d_2 \\ a_3x + b_3y + c_3z &= d_3 \end{aligned}\right\}, \tag{1}$$

where

$$\Delta \equiv \begin{vmatrix} a_1 & b_1 & c_1 \\ a_2 & b_2 & c_2 \\ a_3 & b_3 & c_3 \end{vmatrix} \neq 0$$

Let A_i, B_i, C_i be the cofactors of a_i, b_i, c_i, respectively $(i = 1, 2, 3)$ in Δ. Multiplying the first, second and third equation of (1) by A_1, A_2, A_3, respectively, and then adding, we get

$$(a_1A_1 + a_2A_2 + a_3A_3)x + (b_1A_1 + b_2A_2 + b_3A_3)y$$
$$+ (c_1A_1 + c_2A_2 + c_3A_3)z = d_1A_1 + d_2A_2 + d_3A_3$$

$$\text{or,}\quad \Delta x + 0 \cdot y + 0 \cdot z = d_1 \begin{vmatrix} b_2 & c_2 \\ b_3 & c_3 \end{vmatrix} - d_2 \begin{vmatrix} b_1 & c_1 \\ b_3 & c_3 \end{vmatrix} + d_3 \begin{vmatrix} b_1 & c_1 \\ b_2 & c_2 \end{vmatrix},$$

$$\text{or,}\quad \begin{vmatrix} a_1 & b_1 & c_1 \\ a_2 & b_2 & c_2 \\ a_3 & b_3 & c_3 \end{vmatrix} x = \begin{vmatrix} d_1 & b_1 & c_1 \\ d_2 & b_2 & c_2 \\ d_3 & b_3 & c_3 \end{vmatrix}$$

$$\text{or,}\quad x = \frac{\begin{vmatrix} d_1 & b_1 & c_1 \\ d_2 & b_2 & c_2 \\ d_3 & b_3 & c_3 \end{vmatrix}}{\begin{vmatrix} a_1 & b_1 & c_1 \\ a_2 & b_2 & c_2 \\ a_3 & b_3 & c_3 \end{vmatrix}} = \frac{\Delta_1}{\Delta},\ \text{where } \Delta_1 = \begin{vmatrix} d_1 & b_1 & c_1 \\ d_2 & b_2 & c_2 \\ d_3 & b_3 & c_3 \end{vmatrix}$$

Similarly, we can find

$$y = \frac{\begin{vmatrix} a_1 & d_1 & c_1 \\ a_2 & d_2 & c_2 \\ a_3 & d_3 & c_3 \end{vmatrix}}{\begin{vmatrix} a_1 & b_1 & c_1 \\ a_2 & b_2 & c_2 \\ a_3 & b_3 & c_3 \end{vmatrix}} = \frac{\Delta_2}{\Delta} \quad \text{and} \quad z = \frac{\begin{vmatrix} a_1 & b_1 & d_1 \\ a_2 & b_2 & d_2 \\ a_3 & b_3 & d_3 \end{vmatrix}}{\begin{vmatrix} a_1 & b_1 & c_1 \\ a_2 & b_2 & c_2 \\ a_3 & b_3 & c_3 \end{vmatrix}} = \frac{\Delta_3}{\Delta}$$

Hence, we have $x = \frac{\Delta_1}{\Delta}, y = \frac{\Delta_2}{\Delta}, z = \frac{\Delta_3}{\Delta}$.

$$\text{i.e.,} x = \frac{\begin{vmatrix} d_1 & b_1 & c_1 \\ d_2 & b_2 & c_2 \\ d_3 & b_3 & c_3 \end{vmatrix}}{\begin{vmatrix} a_1 & b_1 & c_1 \\ a_2 & b_2 & c_2 \\ a_3 & b_3 & c_3 \end{vmatrix}}, y = \frac{\begin{vmatrix} a_1 & d_1 & c_1 \\ a_2 & d_2 & c_2 \\ a_3 & d_3 & c_3 \end{vmatrix}}{\begin{vmatrix} a_1 & b_1 & c_1 \\ a_2 & b_2 & c_2 \\ a_3 & b_3 & c_3 \end{vmatrix}} z = \frac{\begin{vmatrix} a_1 & b_1 & d_1 \\ a_2 & b_2 & d_2 \\ a_3 & b_3 & d_3 \end{vmatrix}}{\begin{vmatrix} a_1 & b_1 & c_1 \\ a_2 & b_2 & c_2 \\ a_3 & b_3 & c_3 \end{vmatrix}}$$

In short,

$$x = \frac{|d \quad b \quad c|}{|a \quad b \quad c|}, y = \frac{|a \quad d \quad c|}{|a \quad b \quad c|}, z = \frac{|a \quad b \quad d|}{|a \quad b \quad c|}.$$

This is known as **Cramer's Rule** for solving simultaneous linear equations by using determinants. *The rule cannot be applied if* $\Delta = 0$. The **Rule** runs as follows:

Write down the coefficient determinant Δ *as the denominator of each of the values of* x, y, z *and then write down the numerator as a determinant obtained from* Δ *by replacing the first, second or third column by the column* $[d_1, d_2, d_3]$ *of constants (i.e., the numbers on R.H.S. of the given equations) according as it is the value of* $x, y,$ *or* z.

EXAMPLE 7. *Solve the following equations by Cramer's Rule:*

$$\left.\begin{array}{ll} x+y+z & =3 \\ 2x+3y+4z & =9 \\ x+2y-4z & =-1 \end{array}\right\}.$$

[C.U. 1980; Delhi U.]

SOLUTION. Here $\Delta =$ coefficient determinant

$$= \begin{vmatrix} 1 & 1 & 1 \\ 2 & 3 & 4 \\ 1 & 2 & -4 \end{vmatrix} = \begin{vmatrix} 1 & 0 & 0 \\ 2 & 1 & 2 \\ 1 & 1 & -5 \end{vmatrix}$$

$$= \begin{vmatrix} 1 & 2 \\ 1 & -5 \end{vmatrix} = -5 - 2 = -7 \neq 0.$$

$\Delta_1 =$ determinant obtained frm Δ by replacing the first column by the column $[3 \;\; 9 \;\; -1]$

$$= \begin{vmatrix} 3 & 1 & 1 \\ 9 & 3 & 4 \\ -1 & 2 & -4 \end{vmatrix} = 3\begin{vmatrix} 3 & 4 \\ 2 & -4 \end{vmatrix} - 1\begin{vmatrix} 9 & 4 \\ -1 & -4 \end{vmatrix} + 1\begin{vmatrix} 9 & 3 \\ -1 & 2 \end{vmatrix}$$

$$= 3(-12-8) - 1(-36+4) + 1(18+3) = -60 + 32 + 21 = -7;$$

$\Delta_2 =$ determinant obtained from Δ by replacing the second column by $[3 \;\; 9 \;\; -1]$

$$= \begin{vmatrix} 1 & 3 & 1 \\ 2 & 9 & 4 \\ 1 & -1 & -4 \end{vmatrix} = 1(-36+4) - 3(-8-4) + 1(-2-9) = -7;$$

$\Delta_3 =$ determinant obtained from Δ by replacing the third column by $[3 \;\; 9 \;\; -1]$

$$= \begin{vmatrix} 1 & 1 & 3 \\ 2 & 3 & 9 \\ 1 & 2 & -1 \end{vmatrix} = 1(-3-18) - 1(-2-9) + 3(4-3) = -7.$$

By *Cramer's Rule,* we have

$$x = \frac{\Delta_1}{\Delta} = \frac{-7}{-7} = 1, y = \frac{\Delta_2}{\Delta} = \frac{-7}{-7} = 1 \text{ and } z = \frac{\Delta_3}{\Delta} = \frac{-7}{-7} = 1.$$

Hence the required solutions are $\mathbf{x = 1, y = 1, z = 1}$.

[Check: See that $x = 1, y = 1, z = 1$ satisfy all the three given equations.]

Exercise 3(II)

[Determinants]

1. Write down the determinant

$$\begin{vmatrix} ap+bq & ar+bs \\ cp+dq & cr+ds \end{vmatrix}$$

as the sum of four determinants and hence prove that it equals to the product of the two determinants, namely

$$\begin{vmatrix} a & b \\ c & d \end{vmatrix} \times \begin{vmatrix} p & q \\ r & s \end{vmatrix}$$

[ICWAI December, 1976]

2. Express the following as a second-order determinant:

(i) $\begin{vmatrix} a & b \\ c & d \end{vmatrix}^2$; (ii) $\begin{vmatrix} 1 & 2 \\ -1 & 1 \end{vmatrix} \times \begin{vmatrix} 2 & -1 \\ 1 & 2 \end{vmatrix}$; (iii) $\begin{vmatrix} 2 & -3 \\ -1 & 4 \end{vmatrix}^2$.

3. Express the square of the determinant $\begin{vmatrix} x & 0 & u \\ y & 0 & v \\ z & 0 & w \end{vmatrix}$ as a third order determinant and hence obtain the value of this new determinant.

4. Show that $\begin{vmatrix} 0 & z & y \\ z & 0 & x \\ y & x & 0 \end{vmatrix}^2 = \begin{vmatrix} y^2+z^2 & xy & zx \\ xy & x^2+z^2 & yz \\ zx & yz & x^2+y^2 \end{vmatrix} = 4x^2y^2z^2$.

5. Prove that

$$\begin{vmatrix} x & y & z \\ v & z & x \\ z & x & y \end{vmatrix}^2 = \begin{vmatrix} 2yz-x^2 & z^2 & y^2 \\ z^2 & 2zx-y^2 & x^2 \\ y^2 & x^2 & 2xy-z^2 \end{vmatrix} = (x^3+y^3+z^3-3xyz)^2.$$

6. Find the **adjugate** of

(i) $\begin{vmatrix} 1 & 2 & -1 \\ 3 & -2 & 4 \\ 0 & -3 & 5 \end{vmatrix}$; (ii) $\begin{vmatrix} x & c & -b \\ -c & x & a \\ b & -a & x \end{vmatrix}$.

7. Find the **reciprocal determinant** of $\begin{vmatrix} 1 & -2 & -3 \\ -1 & 1 & -2 \\ 2 & 1 & -1 \end{vmatrix}$

8. If A_i, B_i, C_i are the cofactors of a_i, b_i, c_i, respectively, $(i = 1, 2, 3)$ in the determinant

$$D = \begin{vmatrix} a_1 & a_2 & a_3 \\ b_1 & b_2 & b_3 \\ c_1 & c_2 & c_3 \end{vmatrix}, D \neq 0,$$

prove that

$$\begin{vmatrix} B_1+C_1 & C_1+A_1 & A_1+B_1 \\ B_2+C_2 & C_2+A_2 & A_2+B_2 \\ B_3+C_3 & C_3+A_3 & A_3+B_3 \end{vmatrix} = 2D^2.$$

[C.U. 1977, 1983; Madras U.; N.B.U.]

9. Multiply: $\begin{vmatrix} 0 & b & c \\ c & a & 0 \\ b & 0 & a \end{vmatrix} \times \begin{vmatrix} 0 & c & b \\ b & a & 0 \\ c & 0 & a \end{vmatrix}$

Express $\begin{vmatrix} b^2+c^2 & ab & ac \\ ba & c^2+a^2 & bc \\ ca & cb & a^2+b^2 \end{vmatrix}$ as the square of a determinant and hence find its value.

[HINTS. The last det. $= \begin{vmatrix} 0 & b & c \\ c & a & 0 \\ b & 0 & a \end{vmatrix} \times \begin{vmatrix} 0 & b & c \\ c & a & 0 \\ b & 0 & a \end{vmatrix} = \begin{vmatrix} 0 & b & c \\ c & a & 0 \\ b & 0 & a \end{vmatrix}^2 =$ etc.]

10. Prove that $\begin{vmatrix} a_1\alpha_1+b_1\beta_1 & a_2\alpha_1+b_2\beta_1 & a_3\alpha_1+b_3\beta_1 \\ a_1\alpha_2+b_1\beta_2 & a_2\alpha_2+b_2\beta_2 & a_3\alpha_2+b_3\beta_2 \\ a_1\alpha_3+b_1\beta_3 & a_2\alpha_3+b_2\beta_3 & a_3\alpha_3+b_3\beta_3 \end{vmatrix} = 0.$

11. Show that $\begin{vmatrix} a & b & 0 \\ 0 & a & b \\ b & 0 & a \end{vmatrix} = a^3+b^3$, and hence find the value of $\begin{vmatrix} 2ab & a^2 & b^2 \\ a^2 & b^2 & 2ab \\ b^2 & 2ab & a^2 \end{vmatrix}$.

12. Multiply: $\begin{vmatrix} a^2 & a & 1 \\ b^2 & b & 1 \\ c^2 & c & 1 \end{vmatrix} \times \begin{vmatrix} 1 & -2x & x^2 \\ 1 & -2y & y^2 \\ 1 & -2z & z^2 \end{vmatrix}$, and prove that

$$\begin{vmatrix} (a-x)^2 & (a-y)^2 & (a-z)^2 \\ (b-x)^2 & (b-y)^2 & (b-z)^2 \\ (c-x)^2 & (c-y)^2 & (c-z)^2 \end{vmatrix} = 2(b-c)(c-a)(a-b)(y-z)(z-x)(x-y).$$

13. Write down the product $\begin{vmatrix} a & b & c \\ b & c & a \\ c & a & b \end{vmatrix} \times \begin{vmatrix} x & y & z \\ z & x & y \\ y & z & x \end{vmatrix}$ as a determinant of third order. Hence show that the product of two expressions of the form $a^3+b^3+c^3-3abc$ is of the same form.

14. Prove that $\begin{vmatrix} yz-x^2 & zx-y^2 & xy-z^2 \\ zx-y^2 & xy-z^2 & yz-x^2 \\ xy-z^2 & yz-x^2 & zx-y^2 \end{vmatrix} = \begin{vmatrix} x & y & z \\ y & z & x \\ z & x & y \end{vmatrix}^2$

[HINTS. The determinant on the L.H.S. is the **adjugate** of the determinant on the R.H.S.]

15. Solve the following sets of equations by Cramer's Rule:

(i) $\left.\begin{matrix} 5x+3y=11 \\ 2x+y=4 \end{matrix}\right\}$; (ii) $\left.\begin{matrix} 2x-7y-13=0 \\ 5x+6y-9=0 \end{matrix}\right\}$; (iii) $\left.\begin{matrix} \frac{2}{x}+\frac{3}{y}=2 \\ \frac{5}{x}+\frac{8}{y}=\frac{31}{6} \end{matrix}\right\}$.

16. Solve the following system of equations by Cramer's Rule:

(i) $\left.\begin{array}{l} x+y+z=3 \\ 2x-3y+5z=4 \\ x+2y-4z=-1 \end{array}\right\}$; (ii) $\left.\begin{array}{l} 2x-3y+5z=11 \\ 3x+5y-2z=7 \\ x+2y-3z=-4 \end{array}\right\}$; **[Delhi U.]**

(iii) $\left.\begin{array}{l} x+2y-z=3 \\ 3x-y+z=8 \\ x+y+z=0 \end{array}\right\}$; **[C.U. 1978]** (iv) $\left.\begin{array}{l} 3x+y+z=10 \\ x+y-z=0 \\ 5x-9y=1 \end{array}\right\}$; **[C.U. 1975]**

(v) $\left.\begin{array}{ll} x+y-z & =-3 \\ 2x+3y+z & =2 \\ 8y+3z & =1 \end{array}\right\}$; **[C.U. B.Com. (Hons.) 1982]**

(vi) $\left.\begin{array}{ll} 2x+y+3z & =13 \\ 5x+2y+z & =12 \\ 3x+2y+4z & =19 \end{array}\right\}$; **[Bombay U.]**

(vii) $\left.\begin{array}{l} x+3y=4 \\ y+3z=7 \\ z+4x=6 \end{array}\right\}$; (viii) $\left.\begin{array}{ll} -x+3y+1 & =0 \\ 2x-y-4z-2 & =0 \\ y+2z-4 & =0 \end{array}\right\}$;

(ix) $\left.\begin{array}{ll} x-2y+z & =-1 \\ 3x+y-2z & =4 \\ y-z & =1 \end{array}\right\}$; **[C.U. 1984; ICWAI June 1992]**

(x) $\left.\begin{array}{ll} 2x+y+z & =7 \\ 3x-y-z & =-2 \\ x+2y-3z & =-4 \end{array}\right\}$; **[ICWAI December 1984]**

(xi) $\left.\begin{array}{ll} 3x-4y+5z & =25 \\ 2x+3y+z & =4 \\ x-y+2z & =9 \end{array}\right\}$; **[ICWAI June 1985]**

(xii) $\left.\begin{array}{ll} x+2y-z & =-3 \\ 3x+y+z & =4 \\ x-y+2z & =6 \end{array}\right\}$. **[ICWAI June 1993]**

Answers

2. (i) $\begin{vmatrix} a^2+b^2 & ac+bd \\ ac+bd & c^2+d^2 \end{vmatrix}$; (ii) $\begin{vmatrix} 0 & 5 \\ -3 & 1 \end{vmatrix}$; (iii) $\begin{vmatrix} 13 & -14 \\ -14 & 17 \end{vmatrix}$. **3.** $\begin{vmatrix} x^2+u^2 & xy+uv & xz+uw \\ xy+uv & y^2+v^2 & yz+vw \\ xz+uw & yz+vw & z^2+w^2 \end{vmatrix}$; 0.

6. (i) $\begin{vmatrix} 2 & -15 & -9 \\ -7 & 5 & 3 \\ 6 & -7 & -8 \end{vmatrix}$; (ii) $\begin{vmatrix} a^2+x^2 & ab+cx & ca-bx \\ ab-cx & b^2+x^2 & bc+ax \\ ca+bx & bc-ax & c^2+x^2 \end{vmatrix}$. **7.** $\begin{vmatrix} \frac{1}{20} & -\frac{1}{4} & \frac{7}{20} \\ -\frac{1}{4} & \frac{1}{4} & \frac{1}{4} \\ -\frac{3}{20} & -\frac{1}{4} & -\frac{1}{20} \end{vmatrix}$. **9.** $4a^2b^2c^2$.

11. $-(a^3+b^3)^2$. **15.** (i) $x=1, y=2$; (ii) $x=3, y=-1$; (iii) $x=2, y=3$. **16.** (i) $x=y=z=1$; (ii) $x=1, y=2, z=3$; (iii) $x=3, y=-1, z=-2$; (iv) $x=2, y=1, z=3$; (v) $x=1, y=-1, z=3$; (vi) $x=1, y=2, z=3$; (vii) $x=1, y=1, z=2$; (viii) $x=31/7, y=8/7, z=10/7$; (ix) $x=1, y=1, z=0$; (x) $x=1, y=2, z=3$; (xi) $x=2, y=-1, z=3$; (xii) $x=1, y=-1, z=2$.

CHAPTER 4

INVERSE AND RANK OF A MATRIX: SOLUTIONS OF EQUATIONS BY MATRIX METHOD

4.1. SINGULAR AND NON-SINGULAR MATRICES

A square matrix A is said to be **non-singular** if its determinant $|A| \neq 0$. If $|A| = 0$, then the matrix A is called a **singular matrix.**

ILLUSTRATION.

(i) If $A = \begin{bmatrix} 2 & 4 \\ -5 & -6 \end{bmatrix}$, then $|A| = \begin{vmatrix} 2 & 4 \\ -5 & -6 \end{vmatrix} = -12 + 20 = 8 \neq 0.$

$\therefore$ *A is a non-singular matrix* of order 2.

(ii) If $A = \begin{bmatrix} 3 & -6 \\ 1 & -2 \end{bmatrix}$, then $|A| = \begin{vmatrix} 3 & -6 \\ 1 & -2 \end{vmatrix} = -6 + 6 = 0.$

$\therefore$ A is a *singular matrix* of order 2.

Adjoint of a Square Matrix

Let $A = [a_{ij}]$ be a *square matrix* of order n. Then $|A|$ is the determinant of A of the same order n formed by the corresponding elements of A. If A_{ij} be the cofactors of a_{ij} in $|A|$, then the transpose of the matrix $[A_{ij}]$ obtained by replacing the elements of A by their corresponding cofactors in $|A|$ is called the **adjoint** (or *adjugate*) of the matrix A and it is denoted by **adj A**.

Thus, if $A = \begin{bmatrix} a_{11} & a_{12} & a_{13} \\ a_{21} & a_{22} & a_{23} \\ a_{31} & a_{32} & a_{33} \end{bmatrix}$, then $|A| = \begin{vmatrix} a_{11} & a_{12} & a_{13} \\ a_{21} & a_{22} & a_{23} \\ a_{31} & a_{32} & a_{33} \end{vmatrix}$ and the **adjoint of** A is given by

adj A $= \begin{bmatrix} A_{11} & A_{21} & A_{31} \\ A_{12} & A_{22} & A_{32} \\ A_{13} & A_{23} & A_{33} \end{bmatrix}$; where A_{ij} is the cofactors of a_{ij} in $|A|$, for all i, j in $1 \le i, j \le 3$.

EXAMPLE 1. *If* $A = \begin{bmatrix} 0 & 1 & 2 \\ 1 & 2 & 3 \\ 3 & 1 & 1 \end{bmatrix}$, *verify that* $A(\text{Adj}\, A) = |A|I$, *where* I *is the unit matrix of order* 3, $|A|$ *is the determinant of the matrix and* adj A *is the adjoint matrix of* A.

[ICWAI June 1987]

SOLUTION. Here $|A| = \begin{vmatrix} 0 & 1 & 2 \\ 1 & 2 & 3 \\ 3 & 1 & 1 \end{vmatrix} = 0 - 1\begin{vmatrix} 1 & 3 \\ 3 & 1 \end{vmatrix} + 2\begin{vmatrix} 1 & 2 \\ 3 & 1 \end{vmatrix} = -1(1-9)+2(1-6) = 8-10 = -2.$

$$\text{and adj}\, A = \begin{bmatrix} A_{11} & A_{21} & A_{31} \\ A_{12} & A_{22} & A_{32} \\ A_{13} & A_{23} & A_{33} \end{bmatrix} = \begin{bmatrix} +\begin{vmatrix} 2 & 3 \\ 1 & 1 \end{vmatrix} & -\begin{vmatrix} 1 & 2 \\ 1 & 1 \end{vmatrix} & +\begin{vmatrix} 1 & 2 \\ 2 & 3 \end{vmatrix} \\ -\begin{vmatrix} 1 & 3 \\ 3 & 1 \end{vmatrix} & +\begin{vmatrix} 0 & 2 \\ 3 & 1 \end{vmatrix} & -\begin{vmatrix} 0 & 2 \\ 1 & 3 \end{vmatrix} \\ +\begin{vmatrix} 1 & 2 \\ 3 & 1 \end{vmatrix} & -\begin{vmatrix} 0 & 1 \\ 3 & 1 \end{vmatrix} & +\begin{vmatrix} 0 & 1 \\ 1 & 2 \end{vmatrix} \end{bmatrix}$$

$$= \begin{bmatrix} -1 & 1 & -1 \\ 8 & -6 & 2 \\ -5 & 3 & -1 \end{bmatrix}$$

$$\therefore \quad A(\text{adj}\, A) = \begin{bmatrix} 0 & 1 & 2 \\ 1 & 2 & 3 \\ 3 & 1 & 1 \end{bmatrix} \times \begin{bmatrix} -1 & 1 & -1 \\ 8 & -6 & 2 \\ -5 & 3 & -1 \end{bmatrix}$$

$$= \begin{bmatrix} 0+8-10 & 0-6+6 & 0+2-2 \\ -1+16-15 & 1-12+9 & -1+4-3 \\ -3+8-5 & 3-6+3 & -3+2-1 \end{bmatrix} = \begin{bmatrix} -2 & 0 & 0 \\ 0 & -2 & 0 \\ 0 & 0 & -2 \end{bmatrix}$$

$$= -2\begin{bmatrix} 1 & 0 & 0 \\ 0 & 1 & 0 \\ 0 & 0 & 1 \end{bmatrix} = |A|I.$$

Reciprocal Matrix

If A be a non-singular matrix (i.e., if A be a square matrix such that $|A| \neq 0$), then the matrix $\frac{1}{|A|}$ adj A is called the **Reciprocal matrix** of A.

Thus, if $A = (a_{ij})_{3\times 3}$ such that $|A| \neq 0$,

then the Reciprocal matrix of $A = \frac{1}{|A|}$ adj $A = \frac{1}{|A|}\begin{bmatrix} A_{11} & A_{21} & A_{31} \\ A_{12} & A_{22} & A_{32} \\ A_{13} & A_{23} & A_{33} \end{bmatrix}$.

Inverse of a Square Matrix

If A *and* B *are two square matrices of the same order* n *such that* $AB = BA = I$, *where* I *is the unit matrix of order* n, *then either* A *is the inverse of* B *or* B *is the inverse of* A. *In the first case, we write* $A = B^{-1}$ *and in the second case,* $B = A^{-1}$.

Clearly, $AA^{-1} = A^{-1}A = 1$ and $BB^{-1} = B^{-1}B = I$.

THEOREM. *For a square matrix A of order 3, prove that*

$$\mathbf{A(adj\ A) = (adj\ A)A = |A|I}$$

where I is the unit matrix of order 3.

PROOF. Let $A = \begin{bmatrix} a_{11} & a_{12} & a_{13} \\ a_{21} & a_{22} & a_{23} \\ a_{31} & a_{32} & a_{33} \end{bmatrix}$; then $|A| = \begin{vmatrix} a_{11} & a_{12} & a_{13} \\ a_{21} & a_{22} & a_{23} \\ a_{31} & a_{32} & a_{33} \end{vmatrix}$; and adj $A = \begin{bmatrix} A_{11} & A_{21} & A_{31} \\ A_{12} & A_{22} & A_{32} \\ A_{13} & A_{23} & A_{33} \end{bmatrix}$,

where A_{ij} are the cofactors of a_{ij} in $|A|$ for $i = 1, 2, 3$ and $j = 1, 2, 3$. Then

$$A \operatorname{adj} A = \begin{bmatrix} a_{11}A_{11} + a_{12}A_{12} + a_{13}A_{13} & a_{11}A_{21} + a_{12}A_{22} + a_{13}A_{23} & a_{11}A_{31} + a_{12}A_{32} + a_{13}A_{33} \\ a_{21}A_{11} + a_{22}A_{12} + a_{23}A_{13} & a_{21}A_{21} + a_{22}A_{22} + a_{23}A_{23} & a_{21}A_{31} + a_{22}A_{32} - a_{23}A_{33} \\ a_{31}A_{11} + a_{32}A_{12} + a_{33}A_{13} & a_{31}A_{21} + a_{32}A_{22} + a_{33}A_{23} & a_{31}A_{31} + a_{32}A_{32} + a_{33}A_{33} \end{bmatrix}$$

$$= \begin{bmatrix} |A| & 0 & 0 \\ 0 & |A| & 0 \\ 0 & 0 & |A| \end{bmatrix} = |A| \begin{bmatrix} 1 & 0 & 0 \\ 0 & 1 & 0 \\ 0 & 0 & 1 \end{bmatrix} = |A|I.$$

Similarly, we can prove that $(\operatorname{adj} A)A = |A|I$.

Hence $A(\operatorname{adj} A) = (\operatorname{adj} A)A = |A|I$.

Similarly, we can prove this result when A is square matrix of order n.

Expression for the inverse of the matrix A

We have $A(\operatorname{adj} A) = (\operatorname{adj} A)A = |A|I$

or, $A\frac{\operatorname{adj} A}{|A|} = \frac{\operatorname{adj} A}{|A|}A = I$, provided $|A| \neq 0$.

This relation shows that $A^{-1} = \frac{\operatorname{adj} A}{|A|}$, where $|A| \neq 0$.

[$\because$ $AA^{-1} = A^{-1}A = I$ in this case.]

Hence A^{-1} = Inverse of the matrix $A = \frac{\operatorname{adj} A}{|A|}$, where $|A| \neq 0$.

$$= \frac{1}{|A|} \begin{bmatrix} A_{11} & A_{21} & A_{31} \\ A_{12} & A_{22} & A_{32} \\ A_{13} & A_{23} & A_{33} \end{bmatrix}.$$

EXAMPLE 2. *Verify that* $\frac{1}{6}\begin{bmatrix} 2 & 2 & -4 \\ -4 & 2 & -4 \\ 2 & -1 & 5 \end{bmatrix}$ *is the inverse of* $\begin{bmatrix} 1 & -1 & 0 \\ 2 & 3 & 4 \\ 0 & 1 & 2 \end{bmatrix}$.

[ICWAI December 1988]

SOLUTION. Let $A = \frac{1}{6}\begin{bmatrix} 2 & 2 & -4 \\ -4 & 2 & -4 \\ 2 & -1 & 5 \end{bmatrix}$ and $B = \begin{bmatrix} 1 & -1 & 0 \\ 2 & 3 & 4 \\ 0 & 1 & 2 \end{bmatrix}$.

Thus,

$$AB = \frac{1}{6}\begin{bmatrix} 2 & 2 & -4 \\ -4 & 2 & -4 \\ 2 & -1 & 5 \end{bmatrix} \times \begin{bmatrix} 1 & -1 & 0 \\ 2 & 3 & 4 \\ 0 & 1 & 2 \end{bmatrix}$$

$$= \frac{1}{6}\begin{bmatrix} 2\times 1+2\times 2-4\times 0 & 2\times -1+2\times 3-4\times 1 & 2\times 0+2\times 4-4\times 2 \\ -4\times 1+2\times 2-4\times 0 & -4\times -1+2\times 3-4\times 1 & -4\times 0+2\times 4-4\times 2 \\ 2\times 1-1\times 2+5\times 0 & 2\times(-1)-1\times 3+5\times 1 & 2\times 0-1\times 4+5\times 2 \end{bmatrix}$$

$$= \frac{1}{6}\begin{bmatrix} 2+4-0 & -2+6-4 & 0+8-8 \\ -4+4-0 & 4+6-4 & 0+8-8 \\ 2-2+0 & -2-3+5 & 0-4+10 \end{bmatrix} = \frac{1}{6}\begin{bmatrix} 6 & 0 & 0 \\ 0 & 6 & 0 \\ 0 & 0 & 6 \end{bmatrix}$$

$$= \frac{1}{6}\times 6\begin{bmatrix} 1 & 0 & 0 \\ 0 & 1 & 0 \\ 0 & 0 & 1 \end{bmatrix} = \begin{bmatrix} 1 & 0 & 0 \\ 0 & 1 & 0 \\ 0 & 0 & 1 \end{bmatrix} = I$$

Similarly, we can prove that $BA = I$.

Thus, $AB = BA = I$.

Hence $A = \frac{1}{6}\begin{bmatrix} 2 & 2 & -4 \\ -4 & 2 & -4 \\ 2 & -1 & 5 \end{bmatrix}$ is the inverse of $B = \begin{bmatrix} 1 & -1 & 0 \\ 2 & 3 & 4 \\ 0 & 1 & 2 \end{bmatrix}$.

EXAMPLE 3. *Find the inverse of the matrix* $A = \begin{bmatrix} 1 & 2 & 3 \\ 1 & 3 & 3 \\ 1 & 2 & 4 \end{bmatrix}$ *if it exists.*

SOLUTION.

$$|A| = \begin{vmatrix} a_{11} & a_{12} & a_{13} \\ a_{21} & a_{22} & a_{23} \\ a_{31} & a_{32} & a_{33} \end{vmatrix} = \begin{vmatrix} 1 & 2 & 3 \\ 1 & 3 & 3 \\ 1 & 2 & 4 \end{vmatrix} = \begin{vmatrix} 1 & 2 & 3 \\ 0 & 1 & 0 \\ 0 & 0 & 1 \end{vmatrix}$$

$$= 1 \neq 0.$$

$\therefore$ The inverse A^{-1} of the matrix A exists and

$$A^{-1} = \frac{1}{|A|}\begin{bmatrix} A_{11} & A_{21} & A_{31} \\ A_{12} & A_{22} & A_{32} \\ A_{13} & A_{23} & A_{33} \end{bmatrix}$$

$$\therefore \quad A^{-1} = \frac{1}{|A|}\begin{bmatrix} +\begin{vmatrix} 3 & 3 \\ 2 & 4 \end{vmatrix} & -\begin{vmatrix} 2 & 3 \\ 2 & 4 \end{vmatrix} & +\begin{vmatrix} 2 & 3 \\ 3 & 3 \end{vmatrix} \\ -\begin{vmatrix} 1 & 3 \\ 1 & 4 \end{vmatrix} & +\begin{vmatrix} 1 & 3 \\ 1 & 4 \end{vmatrix} & -\begin{vmatrix} 1 & 3 \\ 1 & 3 \end{vmatrix} \\ +\begin{vmatrix} 1 & 3 \\ 1 & 2 \end{vmatrix} & -\begin{vmatrix} 1 & 2 \\ 1 & 2 \end{vmatrix} & +\begin{vmatrix} 1 & 2 \\ 1 & 3 \end{vmatrix} \end{bmatrix}$$

(1st column consists of the cofactors of the elements of the 1st row in $|A|$; similarly, the 2nd and 3rd columns are cofactors of the elements of the 2nd and 3rd rows in $|A|$.)

$$= \frac{1}{1}\begin{bmatrix} 6 & -2 & -3 \\ -1 & 1 & 0 \\ -1 & 0 & 1 \end{bmatrix} = \begin{bmatrix} 6 & -2 & -3 \\ -1 & 1 & 0 \\ -1 & 0 & 1 \end{bmatrix}.$$

4.2. PROPERTIES OF THE INVERSE OF A MATRIX

I. *The inverse of a square matrix, if it exists, is unique, i.e., there cannot be two distinct inverses for the same matrix.*

PROOF. Let inverse of A exists and it is A^{-1}. Then

$$AA^{-1} = A^{-1}A = I \tag{1}$$

If possible, let there exist another inverse B of A.

Then,

$$AB = BA = I. \tag{2}$$

From (1) and (2), we have $AA^{-1} = AB$

$$\begin{aligned} \therefore \quad & A^{-1}(AA^{-1}) = A^{-1}(AB) \\ \text{(or,)} \quad & (A^{-1}A)A^{-1} = (A^{-1}A)B \quad \text{[By Associative Law]} \\ \textit{or}, \quad & IA^{-1} = IB \quad \text{or,} \quad A^{-1} = B. \end{aligned}$$

This shows that the matrix A cannot have two distinct inverses.

Hence the result follows.

II. *If A^{-1} exists, then* (i) $(A^{-1})^{-1} = A$ *and* (ii) $(A^T)^{-1} = (A^{-1})^T$.

PROOF. (i) Since A^{-1} of a square matrix A exists, we have

$$AA^{-1} = A^{-1}A = I.$$

This shows that the inverse of A^{-1} is A and it is unique.

Hence, $(A^{-1})^{-1} = A$.

(ii) We have $(AA^{-1})^T = (A^{-1})^T.A^T \quad [\because \quad (AB)^T = B^T \cdot A^T.]$

or, $(A^{-1})^T \cdot A^T = I^T = I. \quad [\because \quad AA^{-1} = I.]$

Similarly, $A^T \cdot (A^{-1})^T = (A^{-1}A)^T = I^T = I.$

Thus, $(A^{-1})^T \cdot A^T = A^T \cdot (A^{-1})^T = I.$

This shows that the inverse of A^T is $(A^{-1})^T$ i.e., $(A^T)^{-1} = (A^{-1})^T$.

III. *If A and B be two non-singular square matrices of the same order, then $(AB)^{-1} = B^{-1}A^{-1}$, where A^{-1}, B^{-1} are the inverses of A and B, respectively.*

PROOF. Since A^{-1} and B^{-1} are the inverses of A and B, respectively, we have

$$\begin{aligned} & AA^{-1} = A^{-1}A = I \quad \text{and} \quad BB^{-1} = B^{-1}B = I. \\ & (AB)(B^{-1}A^{-1}) = A(BB^{-1})A^{-1} = AIA^{-1} = (AI)A^{-1} = AA^{-1} = I \\ \text{and} \quad & (B^{-1}A^{-1})(AB) = B^{-1}(A^{-1}A)B = B^{-1}IB = (B^{-1}I)B = B^{-1}B = I. \end{aligned}$$

Thus, $(AB)(B^{-1}A^{-1}) = (B^{-1}A^{-1})(AB) = I.$

$\therefore$ By definition, $B^{-1}A^{-1}$ is the inverse of AB and it is unique.

Hence $(AB)^{-1} = B^{-1}A^{-1}$.

4.3. ORTHOGONAL MATRIX

If A be a square matrix of order n such that $AA^T = A^TA = I$ where A^T is the transpose of A and I is the unit matrix of order n, then A is called an **orthogonal matrix.**

If A be an *orthogonal matrix*, then A^T is the inverse of A, i.e.,

$$A^T = A^{-1}. \quad [\because \quad AA^T = A^TA = I].$$

For an orthogonal matrix A, $AA^T = I$.

$$\therefore \quad |AA^T| = |I| = 1, \quad \text{or,} \quad |A|\cdot|A^T| = 1,$$
$$\text{or,} \quad |A|^2 = 1 \quad [\because \quad |A| = |A^T|]; \quad \therefore \quad |A| = \pm 1.$$

If $|A| = 1$, A is called a **proper orthogonal matrix** and if $|A| = -1$, A is called an **improper orthogonal matrix.**

EXAMPLE 4. *Show that the matrix* $A = \begin{bmatrix} \frac{1}{\sqrt{2}} & \frac{1}{\sqrt{2}} \\ \frac{-1}{\sqrt{2}} & \frac{1}{\sqrt{2}} \end{bmatrix}$ *is orthogonal.* **[Delhi U.]**

SOLUTION. We have $A = \frac{1}{\sqrt{2}}\begin{bmatrix} 1 & 1 \\ -1 & 1 \end{bmatrix}$ and $A^T = \frac{1}{\sqrt{2}}\begin{bmatrix} 1 & -1 \\ 1 & 1 \end{bmatrix}$

$$\therefore \quad AA^T = \frac{1}{2}\begin{bmatrix} 1 & 1 \\ -1 & 1 \end{bmatrix} \times \begin{bmatrix} 1 & -1 \\ 1 & 1 \end{bmatrix} = \frac{1}{2}\begin{bmatrix} 2 & 0 \\ 0 & 2 \end{bmatrix} = \begin{bmatrix} 1 & 0 \\ 0 & 1 \end{bmatrix} = I,$$

$$\text{and } A^TA = \frac{1}{2}\begin{bmatrix} 1 & -1 \\ 1 & 1 \end{bmatrix} \times \begin{bmatrix} 1 & 1 \\ -1 & 1 \end{bmatrix} = \frac{1}{2}\begin{bmatrix} 2 & 0 \\ 0 & 2 \end{bmatrix} = \begin{bmatrix} 1 & 0 \\ 0 & 1 \end{bmatrix} = I.$$

Thus, $AA^T = A^TA = I$.

This shows that A is an **orthogonal matrix.**

NOTE. Here $|A| = \begin{vmatrix} \frac{1}{\sqrt{2}} & \frac{1}{\sqrt{2}} \\ -\frac{1}{\sqrt{2}} & \frac{1}{\sqrt{2}} \end{vmatrix} = \frac{1}{2} + \frac{1}{2} = 1.$

Hence, the matrix $A = \frac{1}{\sqrt{2}}\begin{bmatrix} 1 & 1 \\ -1 & 1 \end{bmatrix}$ is a **proper orthogonal matrix.**

4.4. SOLUTIONS OF LINEAR EQUATIONS BY MATRIX METHOD

(*Solutions by the method of Inversion of the coefficient matrix*).

I. Two linear equations in two unknowns

Let us consider two linear equations of x and y:

$$\left.\begin{aligned} a_{11}x + a_{12}y &= b_1 \\ a_{21}x + a_{22}y &= b_2 \end{aligned}\right\} \qquad (1)$$

Let $A = \begin{pmatrix} a_{11} & a_{12} \\ a_{21} & a_{22} \end{pmatrix}$, $X = \begin{pmatrix} x \\ y \end{pmatrix}$ and $B = \begin{pmatrix} b_1 \\ b_2 \end{pmatrix}$;

then the two equations in (1) can be written in the matrix form

$$AX = B \quad \left[\because \quad AX = \begin{pmatrix} a_{11}x + a_{12}y \\ a_{21}x + a_{22}y \end{pmatrix}.\right]$$

Suppose $|A| \neq 0$; then A^{-1} exists, and we have

$$A^{-1}(AX) = A^{-1}B, \quad \text{or,} \quad (A^{-1}A)X = A^{-1}B, \quad \text{or,} \quad IX = A^{-1}B,$$

or, $\mathbf{X} = \mathbf{A^{-1}B}$, which gives the **required solution.**

EXAMPLE 5. *Solve by matrix method:*

$$\left.\begin{array}{r} 2x - 3y = 1 \\ x + 5y = 7 \end{array}\right\}.$$

SOLUTION. Let $A = \begin{pmatrix} 2 & -3 \\ 1 & 5 \end{pmatrix}, X = \begin{pmatrix} x \\ y \end{pmatrix}$ and $B = \begin{pmatrix} 1 \\ 7 \end{pmatrix}$.

Then $|A| = \begin{vmatrix} 2 & -3 \\ 1 & 5 \end{vmatrix} = 10 + 3 = 13 \neq 0; \quad \therefore \quad A^{-1}$ exists.

The two equations can be written in the matrix form

$$AX = B \text{ which gives } X = A^{-1}B. \tag{1}$$

$$A^{-1} = \frac{1}{|A|}\begin{pmatrix} A_{11} & A_{21} \\ A_{12} & A_{22} \end{pmatrix} = \frac{1}{13}\begin{pmatrix} 5 & 3 \\ -1 & 2 \end{pmatrix}$$

[$\because$ A_{11} = cofactor of 2 in $|A| = +5, A_{12}$ = cofactor of -3 in $|A| = -1$, etc.]

$$A^{-1}B = \frac{1}{13}\begin{pmatrix} 5 & 3 \\ -1 & 2 \end{pmatrix} \times \begin{pmatrix} 1 \\ 7 \end{pmatrix} = \frac{1}{13}\begin{pmatrix} 5 \times 1 + 3 \times 7 \\ -1 \times 1 + 2 \times 7 \end{pmatrix}$$
$$= \frac{1}{13}\begin{pmatrix} 26 \\ 13 \end{pmatrix} = \begin{pmatrix} 2 \\ 1 \end{pmatrix}.$$

$\therefore$ From (1), we get $X = A^{-1}B$, or, $\begin{pmatrix} x \\ y \end{pmatrix} = \begin{pmatrix} 2 \\ 1 \end{pmatrix}$.

Hence, $\mathbf{x = 2, y = 1}$.

II. Three linear equations in three unknowns

Consider the three linear equations in x, y, z :

$$\begin{aligned} a_{11}x + a_{12}y + a_{13}z &= b_1 \\ a_{21}x + a_{22}y + a_{23}z &= b_2 \\ a_{31}x + a_{32}y + a_{33}z &= b_3. \end{aligned}$$

Let $A = \begin{pmatrix} a_{11} & a_{12} & a_{13} \\ a_{21} & a_{22} & a_{23} \\ a_{31} & a_{32} & a_{33} \end{pmatrix}, X = \begin{pmatrix} x \\ y \\ z \end{pmatrix}$ and $B = \begin{pmatrix} b_1 \\ b_2 \\ b_3 \end{pmatrix}$.

Then the three equations can be written in the matrix form

$$AX = B. \quad \left[\because \quad AX = \begin{pmatrix} a_{11}x + a_{12}y + a_{13}z \\ a_{21}x + a_{22}y + a_{23}z \\ a_{31}x + a_{32}y + a_{33}z \end{pmatrix}.\right]$$

Suppose $|A| \neq 0$, then A^{-1} exists and we have

$$A^{-1}(AX) = A^{-1}B, \quad \text{or,} \quad (A^{-1}A)X = A^{-1}B, \quad \text{or,} \quad IX = A^{-1}B,$$

or, $\mathbf{X} = \mathbf{A}^{-1}\mathbf{B}$, which gives the **required solutions.**

EXAMPLE 6. *Using matrices, solve the equations*

$$\begin{aligned} x + y + z &= 6 \\ x + 2y + 3z &= 14 \\ -x + y - z &= -2. \end{aligned}$$

[ICWAI June 1980; CA May 1978; November 1978]

SOLUTION. Let

$$A = \begin{pmatrix} 1 & 1 & 1 \\ 1 & 2 & 3 \\ -1 & 1 & -1 \end{pmatrix}, X = \begin{pmatrix} x \\ y \\ z \end{pmatrix} \quad \text{and} \quad B = \begin{pmatrix} 6 \\ 14 \\ -2 \end{pmatrix}.$$

Then the given equations can be written in the matrix form

$$AX = B, \tag{1}$$

$$\left[\because \quad AX = \begin{pmatrix} x + y + z \\ x + 2y + 3z \\ -x + y - z \end{pmatrix}. \right]$$

Now,

$$|A| = \begin{vmatrix} 1 & 1 & 1 \\ 1 & 2 & 3 \\ -1 & 1 & -1 \end{vmatrix} = \begin{vmatrix} a_{11} & a_{12} & a_{13} \\ a_{21} & a_{22} & a_{23} \\ a_{31} & a_{32} & a_{33} \end{vmatrix}.$$

$$= 1(-2-3) - 1(-1+3) + 1(1+2) = -5 - 2 + 3 = -4 \neq 0.$$

$\therefore$ A^{-1} exists and from (1), we get $\mathbf{X} = \mathbf{A}^{-1}\mathbf{B}$.

Now,

$$A^{-1} = \frac{1}{|A|} \begin{pmatrix} A_{11} & A_{21} & A_{31} \\ A_{12} & A_{22} & A_{32} \\ A_{13} & A_{23} & A_{33} \end{pmatrix} = \frac{1}{|A|} \begin{bmatrix} +\begin{vmatrix} 2 & 3 \\ 1 & -1 \end{vmatrix} & -\begin{vmatrix} 1 & 1 \\ 1 & -1 \end{vmatrix} & +\begin{vmatrix} 1 & 1 \\ 2 & 3 \end{vmatrix} \\ -\begin{vmatrix} 1 & 3 \\ -1 & -1 \end{vmatrix} & +\begin{vmatrix} 1 & 1 \\ -1 & -1 \end{vmatrix} & -\begin{vmatrix} 1 & 1 \\ 1 & 3 \end{vmatrix} \\ +\begin{vmatrix} 1 & 2 \\ -1 & 1 \end{vmatrix} & -\begin{vmatrix} 1 & 1 \\ -1 & 1 \end{vmatrix} & +\begin{vmatrix} 1 & 1 \\ 1 & 2 \end{vmatrix} \end{bmatrix}$$

$$= \frac{1}{-4} \begin{pmatrix} -5 & 2 & 1 \\ -2 & 0 & -2 \\ 3 & -2 & 1 \end{pmatrix}.$$

$$\therefore \quad A^{-1}B = -\frac{1}{4}\begin{pmatrix} -5 & 2 & 1 \\ -2 & 0 & -2 \\ 3 & -2 & 1 \end{pmatrix} \times \begin{pmatrix} 6 \\ 14 \\ -2 \end{pmatrix}$$

$$= -\frac{1}{4}\begin{pmatrix} -30+28-2 \\ -12+0+4 \\ 18-28-2 \end{pmatrix} = -\frac{1}{4}\begin{pmatrix} -4 \\ -8 \\ -12 \end{pmatrix} = \begin{pmatrix} 1 \\ 2 \\ 3 \end{pmatrix}$$

$$\therefore \quad X = A^{-1}B \text{ gives } \begin{pmatrix} x \\ y \\ z \end{pmatrix} = \begin{pmatrix} 1 \\ 2 \\ 3 \end{pmatrix}.$$

Hence, $\mathbf{x = 1, y = 2, z = 3}$.

4.5. FURTHER ILLUSTRATIVE EXAMPLES

EXAMPLE 1. *Two matrices A and B are given by* $A = \begin{bmatrix} 3 & 1 \\ 0 & 2 \end{bmatrix}$ *and* $B = \frac{1}{6}\begin{bmatrix} 2 & -1 \\ 0 & 3 \end{bmatrix}$. *Calculate AB and BA. Write down the inverse of the matrix A. Verify that* $(A')^{-1} = (A^{-1})'$ *where* A' *is the transpose of A and* A^{-1} *is the inverse of A.* **[ICWAI June 1981]**

SOLUTION.

$$AB = \begin{bmatrix} 3 & 1 \\ 0 & 2 \end{bmatrix} \times \frac{1}{6}\begin{bmatrix} 2 & -1 \\ 0 & 3 \end{bmatrix} = \frac{1}{6}\begin{bmatrix} 6 & 0 \\ 0 & 6 \end{bmatrix}$$

$$= \begin{bmatrix} 1 & 0 \\ 0 & 1 \end{bmatrix} = I$$

$$\text{and} \quad BA = \frac{1}{6}\begin{bmatrix} 2 & -1 \\ 0 & 3 \end{bmatrix} \times \begin{bmatrix} 3 & 1 \\ 0 & 2 \end{bmatrix} = \frac{1}{6}\begin{bmatrix} 6 & 0 \\ 0 & 6 \end{bmatrix}$$

$$= \begin{bmatrix} 1 & 0 \\ 0 & 1 \end{bmatrix} = I.$$

$$\therefore \quad AB = BA = I.$$

$\therefore$ B is the inverse of A i.e., $A^{-1} = B = \frac{1}{6}\begin{bmatrix} 2 & -1 \\ 0 & 3 \end{bmatrix}$.

$\therefore$ $(A^{-1})' =$ the transpose of $A^{-1} = \frac{1}{6}\begin{bmatrix} 2 & 0 \\ -1 & 3 \end{bmatrix}$.

$A' =$ the transpose of $A = \begin{bmatrix} 3 & 0 \\ 1 & 2 \end{bmatrix}$; $\therefore$ $|A'| = \begin{vmatrix} 3 & 0 \\ 1 & 2 \end{vmatrix} = 6 \neq 0$.

$$(A')^{-1} = \frac{1}{|A'|}\begin{bmatrix} A_{11} & A_{21} \\ A_{12} & A_{22} \end{bmatrix} = \frac{1}{6}\begin{bmatrix} 2 & 0 \\ -1 & 3 \end{bmatrix}.$$

Hence, $(A')^{-1} = (A^{-1})'$.

EXAMPLE 2. *Prove that the matrix* $A = \begin{bmatrix} 4 & 5 \\ 5 & 6 \end{bmatrix}$ *satisfies the relation* $A^2 - I = 10A$, *where I is the unit matrix of order* 2. *Hence (and not otherwise), find the inverse of A.* **[ICWAI June 1994]**

SOLUTION.

$$A^2 = \overrightarrow{\begin{bmatrix} 4 & 5 \\ 5 & 6 \end{bmatrix}} \times \downarrow \begin{bmatrix} 4 & 5 \\ 5 & 6 \end{bmatrix} = \begin{bmatrix} 16+25 & 20+30 \\ 20+30 & 25+36 \end{bmatrix} = \begin{bmatrix} 41 & 50 \\ 50 & 61 \end{bmatrix}$$

$$\therefore \quad A^2 - I = \begin{bmatrix} 41 & 50 \\ 50 & 61 \end{bmatrix} - \begin{bmatrix} 1 & 0 \\ 0 & 1 \end{bmatrix} = \begin{bmatrix} 40 & 50 \\ 50 & 60 \end{bmatrix} = 10 \begin{bmatrix} 4 & 5 \\ 5 & 6 \end{bmatrix} = \mathbf{10A}.$$

2nd part:

$$A^2 - I = 10A \tag{1}$$

$$\therefore \quad A^{-1}(A^2 - I) = A^{-1}(10A), \quad \text{or,} \quad A^{-1}(A^2) - A^{-1}I = 10(A^{-1}A)$$

$$\text{or,} \quad (A^{-1}A)A - A^{-1} = 10I \quad [\because \quad A^{-1}I = A^{-1} \text{ and } A^{-1}A = I]$$

$$\text{or,} \quad IA - A^{-1} = 10I \quad \text{or,} \quad A - A^{-1} = 10I.$$

$$\text{or,} \quad A^{-1} = A - 10I = \begin{bmatrix} 4 & 5 \\ 5 & 6 \end{bmatrix} - 10 \begin{bmatrix} 1 & 0 \\ 0 & 1 \end{bmatrix} = \begin{bmatrix} 4 & 5 \\ 5 & 6 \end{bmatrix} - \begin{bmatrix} 10 & 0 \\ 0 & 10 \end{bmatrix}$$

$$= \begin{bmatrix} 4-10 & 5-0 \\ 5-0 & 6-10 \end{bmatrix} = \begin{bmatrix} -6 & 5 \\ 5 & -4 \end{bmatrix}.$$

EXAMPLE 3. *Obtain the inverse of the matrix* $\begin{bmatrix} 1 & 3 \\ 2 & -2 \end{bmatrix}$ *and hence solve:*

$$x + 3y = 4, \quad 2x - 2y = 9.$$

[ICWAI June 1982]

SOLUTION. Let $A = \begin{bmatrix} 1 & 3 \\ 2 & -2 \end{bmatrix}$; then $|A| = \begin{vmatrix} 1 & 3 \\ 2 & -2 \end{vmatrix} = -2 - 6 = -8 \neq 0$.

$$A^{-1} = \frac{1}{|A|} \begin{bmatrix} A_{11} & A_{21} \\ A_{12} & A_{22} \end{bmatrix} = \frac{1}{-8} \begin{bmatrix} -2 & -3 \\ -2 & 1 \end{bmatrix} = \begin{bmatrix} 1/4 & 3/8 \\ 1/4 & -1/8 \end{bmatrix}$$

The given equations can be written in the matrix form

$$AX = B, \text{ where } A = \begin{bmatrix} 1 & 3 \\ 2 & -2 \end{bmatrix}, X = \begin{bmatrix} x \\ y \end{bmatrix}, B = \begin{bmatrix} 4 \\ 9 \end{bmatrix} \quad [\because \quad A^{-1} \text{ exists.}]$$

This equation gives $X = A^{-1}B$,

$$\text{or,} \quad \begin{bmatrix} x \\ y \end{bmatrix} = \begin{bmatrix} 1/4 & 3/8 \\ 1/4 & -1/8 \end{bmatrix} \times \begin{bmatrix} 4 \\ 9 \end{bmatrix} = \begin{bmatrix} 1 + 27/8 \\ 1 - 9/8 \end{bmatrix} = \begin{bmatrix} 35/8 \\ -1/8 \end{bmatrix}$$

Hence, $\mathbf{x = \frac{35}{8}}$ and $\mathbf{y = -\frac{1}{8}}$.

EXAMPLE 4. *If* $PQ = \begin{bmatrix} 22 & 6 \\ 11 & 3 \end{bmatrix}$ *and* $P = \begin{bmatrix} 4 & 1 \\ 7 & 4 \end{bmatrix}$, *find* Q. **[ICWAI December 1989]**

SOLUTION. We have $Q = IQ$, where $I = \begin{bmatrix} 1 & 0 \\ 0 & 1 \end{bmatrix}$

$$\therefore \quad Q = (P^{-1}P)Q = P^{-1}(PQ). \tag{1}$$

Now, $|P| = \begin{vmatrix} 4 & 1 \\ 7 & 2 \end{vmatrix} = 8 - 7 = 1 \neq 0.$

$$\therefore \quad P^{-1} = \frac{1}{|P|}\begin{bmatrix} A_{11} & A_{21} \\ A_{12} & A_{22} \end{bmatrix} = \frac{1}{1}\begin{bmatrix} 2 & -1 \\ -7 & 4 \end{bmatrix} = \begin{bmatrix} 2 & -1 \\ -7 & 4 \end{bmatrix}$$

$$\therefore \text{ From (1)}, \quad Q = \begin{bmatrix} 2 & -1 \\ -7 & 4 \end{bmatrix} \times \begin{bmatrix} 22 & 6 \\ 11 & 3 \end{bmatrix} = \begin{bmatrix} 44-11 & 12-3 \\ -154+44 & -42+12 \end{bmatrix} = \begin{bmatrix} \mathbf{33} & \mathbf{9} \\ \mathbf{-110} & \mathbf{-30} \end{bmatrix}.$$

EXAMPLE 5. *For a square matrix* $A = \begin{pmatrix} 1 & 1 & 1 \\ 1 & 2 & -3 \\ 2 & -1 & 3 \end{pmatrix}$, *prove that* $A(\text{adj}\,.A) = |A|\begin{pmatrix} 1 & 0 & 0 \\ 0 & 1 & 0 \\ 0 & 0 & 1 \end{pmatrix}$, *where* $|A|$ *is the determinant of the matrix* A. **[CA November 1981]**

SOLUTION.

$$|A| = \begin{vmatrix} 1 & 1 & 1 \\ 1 & 2 & -3 \\ 2 & -1 & 3 \end{vmatrix} = \begin{vmatrix} a_{11} & a_{12} & a_{13} \\ a_{21} & a_{22} & a_{23} \\ a_{31} & a_{32} & a_{33} \end{vmatrix}$$

$$= 1\begin{vmatrix} 2 & -3 \\ -1 & 3 \end{vmatrix} - 1\begin{vmatrix} 1 & -3 \\ 2 & 3 \end{vmatrix} + 1\begin{vmatrix} 1 & 2 \\ 2 & -1 \end{vmatrix}$$

$$= (6-3) - (3+6) + (-1-4) = -11.$$

$$\text{adj}\,A = \begin{pmatrix} A_{11} & A_{21} & A_{31} \\ A_{12} & A_{22} & A_{32} \\ A_{13} & A_{23} & A_{33} \end{pmatrix} = \begin{bmatrix} +\begin{vmatrix} 2 & -3 \\ -1 & 3 \end{vmatrix} & -\begin{vmatrix} 1 & 1 \\ -1 & 3 \end{vmatrix} & +\begin{vmatrix} 1 & 1 \\ 2 & -3 \end{vmatrix} \\ -\begin{vmatrix} 1 & -3 \\ 2 & 3 \end{vmatrix} & +\begin{vmatrix} 1 & 1 \\ 2 & 3 \end{vmatrix} & -\begin{vmatrix} 1 & 1 \\ 1 & -3 \end{vmatrix} \\ +\begin{vmatrix} 1 & 2 \\ 2 & -1 \end{vmatrix} & -\begin{vmatrix} 1 & 1 \\ 2 & -1 \end{vmatrix} & +\begin{vmatrix} 1 & 1 \\ 1 & 2 \end{vmatrix} \end{bmatrix}$$

$$= \begin{pmatrix} 3 & -4 & -5 \\ -9 & 1 & 4 \\ -5 & 3 & 1 \end{pmatrix}.$$

$$A(\text{adj}\,A) = \begin{bmatrix} 1 & 1 & 1 \\ 1 & 2 & -3 \\ 2 & -1 & 3 \end{bmatrix} \times \begin{bmatrix} 3 & -4 & -5 \\ -9 & 1 & 4 \\ -5 & 3 & 1 \end{bmatrix}$$

$$= \begin{bmatrix} 3-9-5 & -4+1+3 & -5+4+1 \\ 3-18+15 & -4+2-9 & -5+8-3 \\ 6+9-15 & -8-1+9 & -10-4+3 \end{bmatrix}$$

$$= \begin{pmatrix} -11 & 0 & 0 \\ 0 & -11 & 0 \\ 0 & 0 & -11 \end{pmatrix} = -11\begin{pmatrix} 1 & 0 & 0 \\ 0 & 1 & 0 \\ 0 & 0 & 1 \end{pmatrix}$$

$$= |A|\begin{pmatrix} 1 & 0 & 0 \\ 0 & 1 & 0 \\ 0 & 0 & 1 \end{pmatrix}.$$

Hence, the result follows.

EXAMPLE 6. *A square matrix A is called an* **orthogonal matrix** *if the transpose of A is equal to A^{-1} (i.e., the inverse of A). Using this definition verify that the following square matrix is orthogonal.* **[ICWAI December 1981]**

$$\begin{bmatrix} 1/3 & 2/3 & 2/3 \\ 2/3 & 1/3 & -2/3 \\ -2/3 & 2/3 & -1/3 \end{bmatrix}$$

SOLUTION. Let

$$A = \begin{bmatrix} 1/3 & 2/3 & 2/3 \\ 2/3 & 1/3 & -2/3 \\ -2/3 & 2/3 & -1/3 \end{bmatrix};$$

$$\text{then} \quad A^T = \begin{bmatrix} 1/3 & 2/3 & -2/3 \\ 2/3 & 1/3 & 2/3 \\ 2/3 & -2/3 & -1/3 \end{bmatrix}$$

$$|A| = \begin{vmatrix} 1/3 & 2/3 & 2/3 \\ 2/3 & 1/3 & -2/3 \\ -2/3 & 2/3 & -1/3 \end{vmatrix} = \frac{1}{3}\left(-\frac{1}{9}+\frac{4}{9}\right) - \frac{2}{3}\left(-\frac{2}{9}-\frac{4}{9}\right) + \frac{2}{3}\left(\frac{4}{9}+\frac{2}{9}\right)$$

$$= \frac{1}{9} + \frac{4}{9} + \frac{4}{9} = 1 \neq 0.$$

$$A^{-1} = \text{Inverse of } A = \frac{1}{|A|}\begin{bmatrix} A_{11} & A_{21} & A_{31} \\ A_{12} & A_{22} & A_{32} \\ A_{13} & A_{23} & A_{33} \end{bmatrix}$$

$$= \frac{1}{1}\begin{bmatrix} +\begin{vmatrix} 1/3 & -2/3 \\ 2/3 & -1/3 \end{vmatrix} & -\begin{vmatrix} 2/3 & 2/3 \\ 2/3 & -1/3 \end{vmatrix} & +\begin{vmatrix} 2/3 & 2/3 \\ 1/3 & -2/3 \end{vmatrix} \\ -\begin{vmatrix} 2/3 & -2/3 \\ -2/3 & -1/3 \end{vmatrix} & +\begin{vmatrix} 1/3 & 2/3 \\ -2/3 & -1/3 \end{vmatrix} & -\begin{vmatrix} 1/3 & 2/3 \\ 2/3 & -2/3 \end{vmatrix} \\ +\begin{vmatrix} 2/3 & 1/3 \\ -2/3 & 2/3 \end{vmatrix} & -\begin{vmatrix} 1/3 & 2/3 \\ -2/3 & 2/3 \end{vmatrix} & +\begin{vmatrix} 1/3 & 2/3 \\ 2/3 & 1/3 \end{vmatrix} \end{bmatrix}$$

$$= \begin{bmatrix} 1/3 & -2/3 & -2/3 \\ 2/3 & 1/3 & 2/3 \\ 2/3 & -2/3 & -1/3 \end{bmatrix} = A^T, \text{ i.e., } A^T = A^{-1}.$$

Hence, by the given definition, A is an **orthogonal matrix**.

EXAMPLE 7. *Show that the matrix* $A = \begin{bmatrix} 2 & -1 & 1 \\ -1 & 2 & -1 \\ 1 & -1 & 2 \end{bmatrix}$ *satisfies the equation*

$A^3 - 6A^2 + 9A - 4I = 0$ *and hence deduce* A^{-1}. **[CA May 1983]**

SOLUTION.

$$A^2 = \begin{bmatrix} 2 & -1 & 1 \\ -1 & 2 & -1 \\ 1 & -1 & 2 \end{bmatrix} \times \begin{bmatrix} 2 & -1 & 1 \\ -1 & 2 & -1 \\ 1 & -1 & 2 \end{bmatrix}$$

$$= \begin{bmatrix} 4+1+1 & -2-2-1 & 2+1+2 \\ -2-2-1 & 1+4+1 & -1-2-2 \\ 2+1+2 & -1-2-2 & 1+1+4 \end{bmatrix} = \begin{bmatrix} 6 & -5 & 5 \\ -5 & 6 & -5 \\ 5 & -5 & 6 \end{bmatrix}$$

$$A^3 = A \cdot A^2 = \begin{bmatrix} 2 & -1 & 1 \\ -1 & 2 & -1 \\ 1 & -1 & 2 \end{bmatrix} \times \begin{bmatrix} 6 & -5 & 5 \\ -5 & 6 & -5 \\ 5 & -5 & 6 \end{bmatrix}$$
$$= \begin{bmatrix} 22 & -21 & 21 \\ -21 & 22 & -21 \\ 21 & -21 & 22 \end{bmatrix}.$$

$$A^3 - 6A^2 + 9A - 4I = \begin{bmatrix} 22 & -21 & 21 \\ -21 & 22 & -21 \\ 21 & -21 & 22 \end{bmatrix} - 6\begin{bmatrix} 6 & -5 & 5 \\ -5 & 6 & -5 \\ 5 & -5 & 6 \end{bmatrix} + 9\begin{bmatrix} 2 & -1 & 1 \\ -1 & 2 & -1 \\ 1 & -1 & 2 \end{bmatrix} - 4\begin{bmatrix} 1 & 0 & 0 \\ 0 & 1 & 0 \\ 0 & 0 & 1 \end{bmatrix}$$
$$= \begin{bmatrix} 22 & -21 & 21 \\ -21 & 22 & -21 \\ 21 & -21 & 22 \end{bmatrix} - \begin{bmatrix} 36 & -30 & 30 \\ -30 & 36 & -30 \\ 30 & -30 & 36 \end{bmatrix} + \begin{bmatrix} 18 & -9 & 9 \\ -9 & 18 & -9 \\ 9 & -9 & 18 \end{bmatrix} - \begin{bmatrix} 4 & 0 & 0 \\ 0 & 4 & 0 \\ 0 & 0 & 4 \end{bmatrix}$$
$$= \begin{bmatrix} 22-36+18-4 & -21+30-9-0 & 21-30+9-0 \\ -21+30-9-0 & 22-36+18-4 & -21+30-9-0 \\ 21-30+9-0 & -21+30-9-0 & 22-36+18-4 \end{bmatrix}$$
$$= \begin{bmatrix} 0 & 0 & 0 \\ 0 & 0 & 0 \\ 0 & 0 & 0 \end{bmatrix} = 0, \text{ where } 0 \text{ is the zero matrix of order 3.}$$

Hence,

$$\mathbf{A^3 - 6A^2 + 9A - 4I = 0.} \tag{1}$$

2nd part. From (1), $A^3 - 6A^2 + 9A = 4I$,

$$\text{or,} \quad \frac{1}{4}A^3 - \frac{3}{2}A^2 + \frac{9}{4}A = I, \quad \text{or,} \quad A\left(\frac{1}{4}A^2 - \frac{3}{2}A + \frac{9}{4}I\right) = I,$$
$$\therefore \quad A^{-1}\left\{A\left(\frac{1}{4}A^2 - \frac{3}{2}A + \frac{9}{4}I\right) = A^{-1}I = A^{-1}\right.$$
$$\text{or,} \quad (A^{-1}A)\left(\frac{1}{4}A^2 - \frac{3}{2}A + \frac{9}{4}I\right) = A^{-1}, \text{ or, } I\left(\frac{1}{4}A^2 - \frac{3}{2}A + \frac{9}{4}I\right) = A^{-1}$$
$$\text{or,} \quad A^{-1} = \frac{1}{4}A^2 - \frac{3}{2}A + \frac{9}{4}I$$

$$= \frac{1}{4}\begin{bmatrix} 6 & -5 & 5 \\ -5 & 6 & -5 \\ 5 & -5 & 6 \end{bmatrix} - \frac{3}{2}\begin{bmatrix} 2 & -1 & 1 \\ -1 & 2 & -1 \\ 1 & -1 & 2 \end{bmatrix} + \frac{9}{4}\begin{bmatrix} 1 & 0 & 0 \\ 0 & 1 & 0 \\ 0 & 0 & 1 \end{bmatrix}$$
$$= \begin{bmatrix} \frac{6}{4} - \frac{6}{2} + \frac{9}{4} & -\frac{5}{4} + \frac{3}{2} + 0 & \frac{5}{4} - \frac{3}{2} + 0 \\ -\frac{5}{4} + \frac{3}{2} + 0 & \frac{6}{4} - \frac{6}{2} + \frac{9}{4} & -\frac{5}{4} + \frac{3}{2} + 0 \\ \frac{5}{4} - \frac{3}{2} + 0 & -\frac{5}{4} + \frac{3}{2} + 0 & \frac{6}{4} - \frac{6}{2} + \frac{9}{4} \end{bmatrix} = \begin{bmatrix} \frac{3}{4} & \frac{1}{4} & -\frac{1}{4} \\ \frac{1}{4} & \frac{3}{4} & \frac{1}{4} \\ -\frac{1}{4} & \frac{1}{4} & \frac{3}{4} \end{bmatrix}$$

EXAMPLE 8. *Find the adjoint and the inverse of the matrix* $\begin{bmatrix} 1 & -1 & 0 \\ 0 & 1 & -1 \\ 1 & 0 & 1 \end{bmatrix}$ *and hence solve:* $x - y = a, y - z = b, x + z = c.$

[ICWAI December 1982]

SOLUTION. Let $A = \begin{bmatrix} 1 & -1 & 0 \\ 0 & 1 & -1 \\ 1 & 0 & 1 \end{bmatrix} = \begin{bmatrix} a_{11} & a_{12} & a_{13} \\ a_{21} & a_{22} & a_{23} \\ a_{31} & a_{32} & a_{33} \end{bmatrix}$; then

$$|A| = \begin{vmatrix} 1 & -1 & 0 \\ 0 & 1 & -1 \\ 1 & 0 & 1 \end{vmatrix} = 1\begin{vmatrix} 1 & -1 \\ 0 & 1 \end{vmatrix} - (-1)\begin{vmatrix} 0 & -1 \\ 1 & 1 \end{vmatrix}$$
$$= 1(1-0) + 1(0+1)$$
$$= 1 + 1 = 2 \neq 0.$$

If A_{ij} be the cofactors of a_{ij} for $i = 1, 2, 3; j = 1, 2, 3$ in $|A|$, then

$$\text{Adj}\, A = \begin{bmatrix} A_{11} & A_{21} & A_{31} \\ A_{12} & A_{22} & A_{32} \\ A_{13} & A_{23} & A_{33} \end{bmatrix} = \begin{bmatrix} +\begin{vmatrix} 1 & -1 \\ 0 & 1 \end{vmatrix} & -\begin{vmatrix} -1 & 0 \\ 0 & 1 \end{vmatrix} & +\begin{vmatrix} -1 & 0 \\ 1 & -1 \end{vmatrix} \\ -\begin{vmatrix} 0 & -1 \\ 1 & 1 \end{vmatrix} & +\begin{vmatrix} 1 & 0 \\ 1 & 1 \end{vmatrix} & -\begin{vmatrix} 1 & 0 \\ 0 & -1 \end{vmatrix} \\ +\begin{vmatrix} 0 & 1 \\ 1 & 0 \end{vmatrix} & -\begin{vmatrix} 1 & -1 \\ 1 & 0 \end{vmatrix} & +\begin{vmatrix} 1 & -1 \\ 0 & 1 \end{vmatrix} \end{bmatrix} = \begin{bmatrix} 1 & 1 & 1 \\ -1 & 1 & 1 \\ -1 & -1 & 1 \end{bmatrix}.$$

$$A^{-1} = \frac{1}{|A|}\text{adj}.A = \frac{1}{|A|}\begin{bmatrix} A_{11} & A_{21} & A_{31} \\ A_{12} & A_{22} & A_{32} \\ A_{13} & A_{23} & A_{33} \end{bmatrix} = \frac{1}{2}\begin{bmatrix} 1 & 1 & 1 \\ -1 & 1 & 1 \\ -1 & -1 & 1 \end{bmatrix} = \begin{bmatrix} \frac{1}{2} & \frac{1}{2} & \frac{1}{2} \\ -\frac{1}{2} & \frac{1}{2} & \frac{1}{2} \\ -\frac{1}{2} & -\frac{1}{2} & \frac{1}{2} \end{bmatrix}$$

The given equations may be written in the matrix form $AX = B$, where $A = \begin{bmatrix} 1 & -1 & 0 \\ 0 & 1 & -1 \\ 1 & 0 & 1 \end{bmatrix}$.

$X = \begin{bmatrix} x \\ y \\ z \end{bmatrix}, B = \begin{bmatrix} a \\ b \\ c \end{bmatrix}$.

$\therefore\ X = A^{-1}B, \quad [\because\ A^{-1} \text{ exists.}]$

$$\text{or,} \quad \begin{bmatrix} x \\ y \\ z \end{bmatrix} = \begin{bmatrix} \frac{1}{2} & \frac{1}{2} & \frac{1}{2} \\ -\frac{1}{2} & \frac{1}{2} & \frac{1}{2} \\ -\frac{1}{2} & -\frac{1}{2} & \frac{1}{2} \end{bmatrix} \times \begin{bmatrix} a \\ b \\ c \end{bmatrix} = \begin{bmatrix} \frac{a}{2} + \frac{b}{2} + \frac{c}{2} \\ -\frac{a}{2} + \frac{b}{2} + \frac{c}{2} \\ -\frac{a}{2} - \frac{b}{2} + \frac{c}{2} \end{bmatrix} = \begin{bmatrix} \frac{1}{2}(a+b+c) \\ \frac{1}{2}(b+c-a) \\ \frac{1}{2}(c-a-b) \end{bmatrix}$$

Hence, $\mathbf{x = \frac{1}{2}(a+b+c), y = \frac{1}{2}(b+c-a), z = \frac{1}{2}(c-a-b)}$.

EXAMPLE 9. *Using matrix method, solve the equations (augmenting the coefficient matrix):*

$$x + y + z = 6, x - y + z = 2, 2x + y - z = 1$$ **[CA November 1982]**

SOLUTION.

[NOTE. By the method of reduction (or Pivotal Reduction method), we reduce the augmented matrix of the given equations into the form $\left[\begin{array}{ccc|c} 1 & 0 & 0 & d_1 \\ 0 & 1 & 0 & d_2 \\ 0 & 0 & 1 & d_3 \end{array}\right]$ by adding to all the elements of any row, the same multiples of the corresponding elements of any other row or by multiplying all the elements of any row by the same constant. After reduction of the augmented matrix into the above form, the given equations reduce to

$$\left.\begin{array}{l}1.x+0.y+0.z=d_1\\0.x+1.y+0.z=d_2\\0.x+0.y+1.z=d_3\end{array}\right\}\text{ which give }\left.\begin{array}{r}x=d_1,\\y=d_2,\\z=d_3.\end{array}\right\}.]$$

The augmented matrix of the three given equations is

$$\left(\begin{array}{ccc|c}1&1&1&6\\1&-1&1&2\\2&1&-1&1\end{array}\right)\xrightarrow[\& R_3-2R_1]{R_2-R_1}\left(\begin{array}{ccc|c}1&1&1&6\\0&-2&0&-4\\0&-1&-3&-11\end{array}\right)$$

[applying R_2-R_1 and R_3-2R_1 i.e. subtracting 1st row from the 2nd and twice the first row from the 3rd.]

$$\xrightarrow{-\frac{1}{2}R_2}\left(\begin{array}{ccc|c}1&1&1&6\\0&1&0&2\\0&-1&-3&-11\end{array}\right)$$

[multiplying the 2nd row by $-\frac{1}{2}$.]

$$\xrightarrow[\& R_3+R_2]{R_1-R_2}\left(\begin{array}{ccc|c}1&0&1&4\\0&1&0&2\\0&0&-3&-9\end{array}\right)$$

[subtracting 2nd row from the 1st and adding 2nd row with the 3rd.]

$$\xrightarrow{-\frac{1}{3}R_3}\left(\begin{array}{ccc|c}1&0&1&4\\0&1&0&2\\0&0&1&3\end{array}\right)$$

[multiplying the 3rd row by $-\frac{1}{3}$]

$$\xrightarrow{R_1-R_3}\left(\begin{array}{ccc|c}1&0&0&1\\0&1&0&2\\0&0&1&3\end{array}\right)$$

[subtracting 3rd row from the 1st].

This matrix is of the form $\left(\begin{array}{ccc|c}1&0&0&d_1\\0&1&0&d_2\\0&0&1&d_3\end{array}\right)$.

∴ The given equations reduce to

$$\left.\begin{array}{l}1.x+0.y+0.z=1\\0.x+1.y+0.z=2\\0.x+0.y+1.z=3\end{array}\right\}.\quad\text{Hence}\quad\left.\begin{array}{r}\mathbf{x=1}\\\mathbf{y=2}\\\mathbf{z=3}\end{array}\right\}.$$

EXAMPLE 10. *A manufacturer produces two types of products X and Y. Each product is first processed in a machine M_1 and then sent to another machine M_2 for finishing. Each unit of X requires* 20 *minutes' time in M_1 and* 10 *minutes' time in M_2 whereas each unit of Y requires* 10 *minutes' time in M_1 and* 20 *minutes' time in M_2. The total time available on each machine is* 600 *minutes. Calculate the number of units of two types of products produced by constructing a matrix equation of the form $AX = B$ and then solving it by the matrix inversion method.* **[CA May 1991]**

SOLUTION. We have

	Time required per unit in Machine M_1 (min.)	Time required per unit in Machine M_2 (min.)
Product X	20	10
Product Y	10	20
Total Time available	600	600

Let the number of units produced of two types X and Y be, respectively, x and y. Then we can write the above information as

$$\begin{pmatrix} 20 & 10 \\ 10 & 20 \end{pmatrix} \times \begin{pmatrix} x \\ y \end{pmatrix} = \begin{pmatrix} 600 \\ 600 \end{pmatrix}, \quad \text{or,} \quad AX = B \tag{1}$$

where $A = \begin{pmatrix} 20 & 10 \\ 10 & 20 \end{pmatrix}, X = \begin{pmatrix} x \\ y \end{pmatrix}$ and $B = \begin{pmatrix} 600 \\ 600 \end{pmatrix}$.

To find x and y, we have to solve the matrix equation (1).

Now $|A| = \begin{vmatrix} 20 & 10 \\ 10 & 20 \end{vmatrix} = 400 - 100 = 300 \neq 0.$

$\therefore \quad A^{-1}$ exists and $A^{-1} = \dfrac{1}{|A|} \begin{pmatrix} A_{11} & A_{21} \\ A_{12} & A_{22} \end{pmatrix}$, where $A \equiv \begin{pmatrix} a_{11} & a_{12} \\ a_{21} & a_{22} \end{pmatrix}$.

$\therefore \quad A^{-1} = \dfrac{1}{300} \begin{pmatrix} 20 & -10 \\ -10 & 20 \end{pmatrix} \quad \left[\because \begin{pmatrix} a_{11} & a_{12} \\ a_{21} & a_{22} \end{pmatrix} = A = \begin{pmatrix} 20 & 10 \\ 10 & 20 \end{pmatrix} \right]$.

Multiplying both sides of (1) by A^{-1}, we get

$$X = A^{-1}B = \frac{1}{300} \begin{pmatrix} 20 & -10 \\ -10 & 20 \end{pmatrix} \times \begin{pmatrix} 600 \\ 600 \end{pmatrix} = \frac{1}{300} \begin{pmatrix} 12000 - 6000 \\ -6000 + 12000 \end{pmatrix}$$

$$\text{or,} \quad \begin{pmatrix} x \\ y \end{pmatrix} = \frac{1}{300} \begin{pmatrix} 6000 \\ 6000 \end{pmatrix} = \begin{pmatrix} 20 \\ 20 \end{pmatrix}; \quad \therefore \quad x = 20 \quad \text{and} \quad y = 20.$$

Hence, the required no. of units of two types of products produced are **20 each.**

Exercise 4

[Inverse and Rank of a Matrix: Solution of Equations]

1. If $A = \begin{pmatrix} 2 & 1 \\ 4 & 2 \end{pmatrix}$ and $B = \begin{pmatrix} 1 & 2 & 3 \\ 3 & 2 & 1 \end{pmatrix}$, examine whether the following are defined or not

(i) AB, (ii) A^{-1}, (iii) $B + B'$.

2. Find the inverse of the matrix $A = \begin{pmatrix} 1 & 2 \\ 3 & 4 \end{pmatrix}$, and show that $AA^{-1} = A^{-1}A = I$.

3. (i) If $A = \begin{bmatrix} 1 & -2 \\ 2 & 1 \end{bmatrix}$, find the adjoint of A and show that $A(\operatorname{adj}.A) = |A| \begin{bmatrix} 1 & 0 \\ 0 & 1 \end{bmatrix}$, where $|A|$ is the determinant of the matrix A.

(ii) If $A = \begin{pmatrix} 1 & 0 & 2 \\ 0 & 2 & 3 \\ 1 & 3 & 4 \end{pmatrix}$, find Adj A. Prove that $A(\operatorname{Adj} A)$ is a scalar matrix.

4. If $A = \frac{1}{\sqrt{2}} \begin{bmatrix} 1 & -1 \\ 1 & 1 \end{bmatrix}$ show that A is a proper orthogonal.

5. (i) If $A = \begin{bmatrix} 4 & 2 \\ -1 & 1 \end{bmatrix}$ and I is a 2×2 unit matrix, calculate $(A - 2I)(A - 3I)$.

(ii) If $P = \begin{bmatrix} 1 & -1 \\ 2 & -1 \end{bmatrix}, Q = \begin{bmatrix} p & 1 \\ q & -1 \end{bmatrix}$ and $(P + Q)^2 = P^2 + Q^2$, find p and q.

[CA November 1987; ICWAI December 1987]

6. (i) If $A = \begin{bmatrix} 2 & 3 \\ 3 & 5 \end{bmatrix}$, then verify that $A^2 = 7A - I$ where $I = \begin{bmatrix} 1 & 0 \\ 0 & 1 \end{bmatrix}$ and hence obtain A^{-1} from this relationship. **[ICWAI June 1982]**

(ii) If $PQ = \begin{bmatrix} 22 & 6 \\ 11 & 3 \end{bmatrix}$ and $P = \begin{bmatrix} 4 & 1 \\ 7 & 2 \end{bmatrix}$, find Q.

7. (i) Let the matrix A be given by $A = \begin{bmatrix} 2 & 1 \\ 3 & 4 \end{bmatrix}$. Evaluate the polynomial $2A^2 + 3A + 5I$ (I is the unit matrix of order 2). Obtain a matrix B such that $AB = BA = I$. Using this matrix B, solve for x and y from the following two equations:

$$2x + y = 15; \quad 3x + 4y = 23.$$

[ICWAI December 1980]

(ii) If $A = \begin{bmatrix} 2 & -1 \\ -1 & 2 \end{bmatrix}$, show that $A^2 - 4A + 3I = 0$. Hence or otherwise obtain the inverse A^{-1} and solve by the matrix method the equations

$$2x - y = 3, -x + 2y = -3.$$

8. Let the matrix A be given by $A = \begin{bmatrix} -1 & -1 \\ 2 & -2 \end{bmatrix}$. Verify that $A^2 + 3A + 4I = 0$. [I is the unit matrix of order 2; 0 is the 2×2 zero matrix.] Hence obtain the inverse of A. **[ICWAI June 1980]**

9. Obtain a square matrix X of order 2, which satisfies the matrix equation $CX - AB = 0$, given that

$$A = \begin{bmatrix} 2 & 1 \\ 0 & 3 \end{bmatrix}, B = \begin{bmatrix} -1 & 1 \\ 2 & 1 \end{bmatrix}, C = \begin{bmatrix} 0 & 1 \\ -1 & 1 \end{bmatrix} \text{ and 0 is the null matrix of order 2.}$$

[ICWAI June 1978]

10. (i) Let the matrix B be given by $B = \begin{bmatrix} 1 & 1 & 2 \\ 2 & 1 & -1 \\ 3 & 1 & 1 \end{bmatrix}$. Find the adjugate of B and then verify: $\det(\text{Adj}.B) = (\det B)^2$. **[ICWAI June 1983]**

(ii) If $P = \begin{pmatrix} -1 & -2 & -2 \\ 2 & 1 & 2 \\ 2 & -2 & 1 \end{pmatrix}$, show that $\text{adj}\, P = 3P'$ (with usual notations).

[ICWAI June 1993]

11. Find the adjoint of the matrix $A = \begin{bmatrix} 1 & 4 & 0 \\ -1 & 2 & 2 \\ 0 & 0 & 2 \end{bmatrix}$. Hence obtain A^{-1}. Write down the adjoint of A^{-1} and now verify that $(\text{adj}\, A)^{-1} = \text{adj}\, A^{-1}$. **[ICWAI December 1979]**

12. (a) Find the inverse (if it exists) of the following matrices:

(i) $\begin{pmatrix} 3 & -1 \\ 1 & 2 \end{pmatrix}$; (ii) $\begin{pmatrix} 1 & -1 & 2 \\ -1 & 1 & -1 \\ 1 & -2 & 1 \end{pmatrix}$; (iii) $\begin{pmatrix} 0 & 1 & 2 \\ 1 & 2 & 3 \\ 3 & 1 & 1 \end{pmatrix}$; (iv) $\begin{pmatrix} 1 & 2 & 3 \\ 3 & -2 & 1 \\ 4 & 2 & 1 \end{pmatrix}$.

(b) Find the inverse of $\begin{bmatrix} 2 & -1 \\ -1 & 2 \end{bmatrix}$ and hence solve the equations $2x_1 - x_2 = 3, -x_1 + 2x_2 = -3$.

[ICWAI June 1987]

(c) If $A = \begin{bmatrix} 2 & -3 \\ 4 & -1 \end{bmatrix}$, obtain a matrix such that $AB = BA = I_2$. Hence solve the equations: $2x_1 - 3x_2 = 3, 4x_1 - x_2 = 11.$ **[ICWAI December 1993]**

13. If the matrix A is given by $A = \begin{pmatrix} 1 & 1 & 1 \\ 2 & -1 & 3 \\ 3 & 2 & -1 \end{pmatrix}$, obtain a matrix B such that

$AB = BA = I$, where I is a unit matrix of order 3. **[ICWAI December 1975]**

14. (i) Two square matrices of order 3 are given below:

$$A = \begin{bmatrix} -1 & 1 & 1 \\ 1 & -1 & 1 \\ 1 & 1 & -1 \end{bmatrix} \quad \text{and} \quad B = \begin{bmatrix} 0 & 1/2 & 1/2 \\ 1/2 & 0 & 1/2 \\ 1/2 & 1/2 & 0 \end{bmatrix}.$$

Verify that one is the inverse of the other. **[ICWAI December 1978]**

(ii) Evaluate the inverse of the matrix $\begin{bmatrix} 1 & 1 & 1 \\ 1 & 2 & 3 \\ 2 & 3 & 8 \end{bmatrix}$, if it exists. **[ICWAI June, 1983]**

15. Given two matrices A and B where

$$A = \begin{bmatrix} 1 & -1 & 0 \\ 2 & 3 & 4 \\ 0 & 1 & 2 \end{bmatrix} \quad \text{and} \quad B = \begin{bmatrix} 2 & 2 & -4 \\ -4 & 2 & -4 \\ 2 & -1 & 5 \end{bmatrix}$$

Verify that $BA = 6I$. Using this result solve the set of linear equations

$x - y = 3, 2x + 3y + 4z = 17, y + 2z = 7.$ **[ICWAI June 1974, '77]**

16. Find the matrix X from the equation $AX = B$ where

$$A = \begin{pmatrix} 1 & -1 & 0 \\ 0 & 1 & -1 \\ 1 & 1 & 1 \end{pmatrix} \quad \text{and} \quad B = \begin{pmatrix} 2 \\ 1 \\ 7 \end{pmatrix}.$$

17. (i) If $A = \begin{pmatrix} 0 & 1 & 2 \\ 1 & 2 & 3 \\ 3 & 1 & 1 \end{pmatrix}$, find A^{-1} and verify that $AA^{-1} = A^{-1}A = I$.

(ii) If $A = \begin{bmatrix} 0 & 1 & -1 \\ 2 & 0 & 0 \\ 1 & -1 & 0 \end{bmatrix}$ and $I = \begin{bmatrix} 1 & 0 & 0 \\ 0 & 1 & 0 \\ 0 & 0 & 1 \end{bmatrix}$, find $(A^2 + I)(A + 1)^{-1}$.

(iii) If $A = \begin{bmatrix} 1 & 0 & -1 \\ 1 & 0 & 0 \\ 0 & 1 & 0 \end{bmatrix}$ and $I = \begin{bmatrix} 1 & 0 & 0 \\ 0 & 1 & 0 \\ 0 & 0 & 1 \end{bmatrix}$, show that $(A^{-1})^2 + A = I$.

18. Verify that the matrix $\frac{1}{3}\begin{bmatrix} -1 & 2 & -2 \\ -2 & 1 & 2 \\ 2 & 2 & 1 \end{bmatrix}$ is orthogonal.

19. If $A = \begin{bmatrix} 1 & -1 & 1 \\ 2 & -1 & 0 \\ 1 & 0 & 0 \end{bmatrix}$, find A^2 and A^{-1} and show that $A^2 = A^{-1}$.

20. Show that the matrix $A = \begin{bmatrix} 1 & 2 & 2 \\ 2 & 1 & 2 \\ 2 & 2 & 1 \end{bmatrix}$ satisfies the equation $A^2 - 4A - 5I = 0$ where I is the 3×3 unit matrix and hence obtain A^{-1}.

21. Show that the matrix $A = \begin{bmatrix} 1 & 2 & 3 \\ 3 & -2 & 1 \\ 4 & 2 & 1 \end{bmatrix}$ satisfies the equation $A^3 - 23A - 40I = 0$, where I and 0 are the unit and zero matrices, each of order 3. Hence or otherwise, obtain the inverse matrix A^{-1} and solve by matrix method the equations:

$x + 2y + 3z = 6, 3x - 2y + z = 2, 4x + 2y + z = 7;$ **[ICWAI December 1982]**

22. Consider the matrix $A = \begin{pmatrix} 1 & 3 & 4 \\ 3 & -1 & 6 \\ -1 & 5 & 1 \end{pmatrix}$. Prove that $(A^T)^{-1} = (A^{-1})^T$.

[T represents transpose.] **[ICWAI June 1983]**

23. (i) Find the inverse of the matrix $\begin{pmatrix} 1 & 1 & 1 \\ 1 & 2 & 3 \\ 1 & 4 & 9 \end{pmatrix}$ and hence solve the equations:

$x + y + z = 6, x + 2y + 3z = 14, x + 4y + 9z = 36.$ **[ICWAI December 1981]**

(ii) Obtain the inverse of the matrix $\begin{pmatrix} 2 & 4 & -1 \\ 3 & 1 & 2 \\ 1 & 3 & -3 \end{pmatrix}$ and hence solve the following system of equations:

$2x + 4y - z = 9, 3x + y + 2z = 7, x + 3y - 3z = 4.$ **[ICWAI June 1979]**

24. (i) Find the inverse of the matrix $\begin{pmatrix} 2 & 5 & 3 \\ 3 & 1 & 2 \\ 1 & 2 & -1 \end{pmatrix}$ and apply the result to solve the equations:

$$2x + 5y + 3z = 9, 3x + y + 2z = 3, x + 2y - z = 6.$$

(ii) Find the inverse of the matrix $\begin{bmatrix} 7 & -1 & -1 \\ 10 & -2 & 1 \\ 6 & 3 & -2 \end{bmatrix}$ and hence solve the following system of equations:

$7x - y - z = 0, 10x - 2y + z = 8, 6x + 3y - 2z = 7.$ **[ICWAI June 1981]**

25. Solve by matrix method:

(i) $\left.\begin{array}{l} 3x - 2y = 4 \\ 4x - 3y = 5 \end{array}\right\}$;

(ii) $\left.\begin{array}{ll} 2x - y & = 13 \\ -x + 2y & = -11 \end{array}\right\}$;

(iii) $\left.\begin{array}{ll} 2x - 3y & = 3 \\ 4x - y & = 11 \end{array}\right\}$;

[CA November 1975]

(iv) $\left.\begin{array}{ll} x + y + z & = 6 \\ x - y + z & 2 \\ 2x + y - z & = 1 \end{array}\right\}$;

[ICWAI December 1979, CA November 1982]

(v) $\left.\begin{array}{ll} 2x + 4y + z & = 5 \\ x + y + z & = 6 \\ 2x + 3y + z & = 6 \end{array}\right\}$; [CA May 1980]

(vi) $\left.\begin{array}{ll} 2x + 3y - z & = 9 \\ x + y + z & = 9 \\ 3x - y - z & = -1 \end{array}\right\}$; [CA November 1979]

(vii) $\left.\begin{aligned} x+y+2z &= 4 \\ 2x-y+3z &= 9 \\ 3x-y-z &= 2 \end{aligned}\right\}$; **[CA May 1979]** (viii) $\left.\begin{aligned} 3x+2y+4z &= 19 \\ 2x-y+z &= 3 \\ 6x+7y-z &= 17 \end{aligned}\right\}$; **[ICWAI June 1978]**

(ix) $\left.\begin{aligned} 4x+3y+z &= 8 \\ 2x+y+4z &= -4 \\ 3x+z &= 1 \end{aligned}\right\}$; **[ICWAI December 1977]**

(x) $\left.\begin{aligned} x+2y-z &= 2 \\ 3x-4y+2z &= 1 \\ -x+3y-z &= 4 \end{aligned}\right\}$; **[ICWAI June 1986]**

(xi) $\left.\begin{aligned} x-y &= 3 \\ 2x+3y+4z &= 17 \\ y+2z &= 7 \end{aligned}\right\}$; **[ICWAI December 1988]**

Answers

1. (i) AB is defined and it is a 2×3 matrix ; (ii) A^{-1} is not defined, since $|A| = 0$; (iii) $B + B'$ is not defined since B is a 2×3 matrix and B' is a 3×2 matrix. **2.** $\frac{1}{-2}\begin{pmatrix} 4 & -2 \\ -3 & 1 \end{pmatrix}$. **3.** (i) $\begin{pmatrix} 1 & 2 \\ -2 & 1 \end{pmatrix}$; (ii) $\begin{pmatrix} -1 & 6 & -4 \\ 3 & 2 & -3 \\ -2 & -3 & 2 \end{pmatrix}$ and $A(\operatorname{Adj} A) = \begin{pmatrix} -5 & 0 & 0 \\ 0 & -5 & 0 \\ 0 & 0 & -5 \end{pmatrix}$ which is a scalar matrix. **5.** (i) $\begin{pmatrix} 0 & 0 \\ 0 & 0 \end{pmatrix}$; (ii) $p = 1, q = 4$. **6.** (i) $\begin{pmatrix} 5 & -3 \\ -3 & 2 \end{pmatrix}$; (ii) $\begin{bmatrix} 33 & 9 \\ -110 & -30 \end{bmatrix}$. **7.** (i) $\begin{pmatrix} 25 & 15 \\ 45 & 55 \end{pmatrix}$; $\begin{pmatrix} 4/5 & -1/5 \\ -3/5 & 2/5 \end{pmatrix}$; $\left.\begin{matrix} x & \frac{37}{5} \\ y & =\frac{1}{5} \end{matrix}\right\}$; (ii) $\frac{1}{3}\begin{pmatrix} 2 & 1 \\ 1 & 2 \end{pmatrix}$; $x = 1, y = -1$. **8.** $-\frac{1}{4}\begin{pmatrix} 2 & -1 \\ 2 & 1 \end{pmatrix}$. **9.** $\begin{bmatrix} -6 & 0 \\ 0 & 3 \end{bmatrix}$. **10.** $\begin{bmatrix} 2 & 1 & -3 \\ -5 & -5 & 5 \\ -1 & 2 & -1 \end{bmatrix}$. **11.** $\begin{bmatrix} 4 & -8 & 8 \\ 2 & 2 & -2 \\ 0 & 0 & 6 \end{bmatrix}$; $\frac{1}{12}\begin{bmatrix} 4 & -8 & 8 \\ 2 & 2 & -2 \\ 0 & 0 & 6 \end{bmatrix}$; $\begin{bmatrix} \frac{1}{12} & \frac{1}{3} & 0 \\ -\frac{1}{12} & \frac{1}{6} & \frac{1}{6} \\ 0 & 0 & \frac{1}{6} \end{bmatrix}$. **12.** (a) (i) $\frac{1}{7}\begin{pmatrix} 2 & 1 \\ -1 & 3 \end{pmatrix}$; (ii) $\begin{pmatrix} -1 & -3 & -1 \\ 0 & -1 & -1 \\ 1 & 1 & 0 \end{pmatrix}$; (iii) $-\frac{1}{2}\begin{pmatrix} -1 & 1 & -1 \\ 8 & -6 & 2 \\ -5 & 3 & -1 \end{pmatrix}$ (iv) $\frac{1}{40}\begin{pmatrix} -4 & 4 & 8 \\ 1 & -11 & 8 \\ 14 & 6 & -8 \end{pmatrix}$; (b) $\frac{1}{3}\begin{bmatrix} 2 & 1 \\ 1 & 2 \end{bmatrix}$; $(1, -1)$; (c) $\frac{1}{10}\begin{bmatrix} -1 & 3 \\ -4 & 2 \end{bmatrix}$; $\left.\begin{matrix} x_1 & =3 \\ x_2 & =1 \end{matrix}\right\}$. **13.** $\frac{1}{13}\begin{pmatrix} -5 & 3 & 4 \\ 11 & -4 & -1 \\ 7 & 1 & -3 \end{pmatrix}$. **14.** (ii) $\frac{1}{4}\begin{pmatrix} 7 & -5 & 1 \\ -2 & 6 & -2 \\ -1 & -1 & 1 \end{pmatrix}$. **15.** $x = 2, y = -1, z = 4$. **16.** $\begin{pmatrix} 4 \\ 2 \\ 1 \end{pmatrix}$. **17.** (i) $-\frac{1}{2}\begin{pmatrix} -1 & 1 & -1 \\ 8 & -6 & 2 \\ -5 & 3 & -1 \end{pmatrix}$; (ii) $\begin{pmatrix} 0 & 1 & 0 \\ 0 & 1 & -2 \\ -2 & 1 & -2 \end{pmatrix}$. **19.** $\begin{pmatrix} 0 & 0 & 1 \\ 0 & -1 & 2 \\ 1 & -1 & 1 \end{pmatrix}$; $\begin{pmatrix} 0 & 0 & 1 \\ 0 & -1 & 2 \\ 1 & -1 & 1 \end{pmatrix}$. **20.** $\frac{1}{5}\begin{bmatrix} -3 & 2 & 2 \\ 2 & -3 & 2 \\ ? & 2 & -3 \end{bmatrix}$. **21.** $\frac{1}{40}\begin{bmatrix} -4 & 4 & 8 \\ 1 & -11 & 8 \\ 14 & 6 & -8 \end{bmatrix}$; $x = y = z = 1$. **23.** (i) $\frac{1}{2}\begin{pmatrix} 6 & -5 & 1 \\ -6 & 8 & -2 \\ 2 & -3 & 1 \end{pmatrix}$; $\left.\begin{matrix} x=1 \\ y=2 \\ z=3 \end{matrix}\right\}$; (ii) $\frac{1}{18}\begin{pmatrix} -9 & 9 & 9 \\ 11 & -5 & -7 \\ 8 & -2 & -10 \end{pmatrix}$; $\left.\begin{matrix} x=1 \\ y=2 \\ z=1 \end{matrix}\right\}$. **24.** (i) $x = 1, y = 2, z = -1$; (ii) $\frac{1}{61}\begin{bmatrix} -1 & 5 & 3 \\ -26 & 8 & 17 \\ -42 & 27 & 4 \end{bmatrix}$; $\left.\begin{matrix} x=1 \\ y=3 \\ z=4 \end{matrix}\right\}$. **25.** (i) $\left.\begin{matrix} x=2 \\ y=1 \end{matrix}\right\}$; (ii) $\left.\begin{matrix} x=5 \\ y=-3 \end{matrix}\right\}$; (iii) $\left.\begin{matrix} x=3 \\ y=1 \end{matrix}\right\}$; (iv) $x = 1, y = 2, z = 3$; (v) $x = 2, y = -1, z = 5$; (vi) $x = 2, y = 3, z = 4$; (vii) $x = 1, y = -1, x = 2$; (viii) $x = 1, y = 2, z = 3$; (ix) $x = 1, y = 2, z = -2$. (x) $x = 1, y = 4, z = 7$; (xi) $x = 2, y = -1, z = 4$.

CHAPTER 5

REAL NUMBER SYSTEM: CONSTANTS, VARIABLES, FUNCTIONS AND GRAPHS OF FUNCTIONS

5.1. INTRODUCTION

The study of elementary calculus has its basis in the *real number system.* Our starting point is the set of **natural numbers** $1, 2, 3, \ldots$ etc. We then introduce negative integers $-1, -2, -3, \ldots$ etc. and zero. Next we consider the ratio of two integers (**rational numbers**). These rational numbers can be expressed either as a terminating decimal or as a recurring decimal. However, there are decimals which are neither terminating nor recurring—such decimals are not rational numbers; they are *irrational numbers.* The totality of rational and irrational numbers form the system of **real numbers**. Without going into very precise analysis we shall specify in this chapter some well-known properties of real number system.

Integers: Rational Numbers

1. We begin with symbols: $1, 2, 3, 4, \ldots$ etc.

This collection is called the set N of **natural numbers** or **whole numbers** or **positive integers.**

Any two members (or elements) of the set N can be *added* or *multiplied*—the results (*sum* or *product*) are also natural numbers (e.g., $2 + 8 = 10, 2.8 = 16$, both 10 and 16 are natural numbers).

We express this fact by stating **the set of natural numbers is closed under addition and multiplication.**

2. We have another operation, called *Subtraction*. To subtract a from b i.e., to find $(b - a)$ is to obtain a unique number c which when added to a gives b, i.e., $b - a = c$ if $c + a = b$ (e.g., $16 - 4 = 12$, because $12 + 4 = 16$).

Clearly subtraction of any two members of N may not be a member of N (e.g., $4 - 16$; there is no natural number c such that $c + 16 = 4$).

Thus, the set N of natural numbers is not closed under subtraction.

We, therefore, introduce the set of *negative integers* $-1, -2, -3, -4, \ldots$ etc. and the symbol 0 (zero). [$4 - 16 = -12$; we say -12 is the number which, when added to 16 gives 4.]

Zero has Two Properties

(i) $a - a = 0$ (i.e., $0 + a = a$); (ii) $a \cdot 0 = 0$ *where a is any number.*

We now consider the collection *of positive integers, negative integers* and *zero* and call the set I, **the set of integers:** $I = \{0, \pm 1, \pm 2, \pm 3, \ldots\}$.

The set I of integers is closed under Addition, Subtraction and Multiplication.

3. Our next fundamental operation is *Division* ($a \div b$ or a/b). To divide a by b is to obtain a unique number c such that $b.c = a$. See that $5/0$ does not give *any number* but $0/0$ can be taken to be equal to *any number* (i.e., $0/0$ is not a unique number). In view of this we state, once for all:

Division by Zero is not Defined

Whenever division by zero occurs, we shall say that the result *is undefined.* Clearly, the set I is not closed under division (e.g., $5/3 \rightarrow$ there is no integer which, when multiplied by 3, can give 5).

We, therefore, introduce **Rational numbers:**

DEFINITION. A number of the form p/q, where p and q are integers and $q \neq 0$, is called a **rational number.** It is the usual convention that we should take p and q prime to each other (i.e., there should be no common factor between p and q) and that we take q, always a positive integer.

Examples of rational numbers: $2/3, -2/3, 3/2, -3/2, 3/1 = 3, -2/1 = -2$. $0/1 = 0$, etc. For the rational number $3/27$ we shall write $1/9$.

To divide 4 by $3(4 \div 3$ or $4/3)$ we say that there is a rational number $4/3$ which, multiplied by 3, gives 4, (i.e., $4 \div 3 \Rightarrow \frac{4}{3} \times 3 = 4$).

Clearly, *The set of rational numbers* (denoted by Q) consists *of elements which are either positive integers or negative integers or zero or a fraction like* $a/b (b \neq 0)$, *where a and b are integers:* **Q = {Positive Integers, Negative Integers, Zero, Fractions}**.

5.1.1. A SHORT NOTE ON INEQUALITIES

Inequalities play an important role in all branches of mathematics including Calculus. We, therefore, give here the simplest rules concerning them:

DEFINITION 1. A number a is said to be *greater than* another number $b (a > b)$ if $a - b$ is *positive.*

DEFINITION 2. A number a is said to be *less than* another number $b (a < b)$ if $a - b$ is *negative.*

DEFINITION 3. A number a is said to be *equal* to another number $b (a = b)$ if $a - b$ is zero.

DEFINITION 4. Further see that every positive number is greater than zero and every negative number is less than zero. Hence

$$\begin{array}{ccc} a > b & & a-b > 0 \\ a = b & \text{according as} & a-b = 0 \\ a < b & & a-b < 0 \end{array}$$

e.g., if we are to see $\frac{2}{3} > \frac{3}{4}$ or $\frac{2}{3} < \frac{3}{4}$, we shall consider $\frac{2}{3} - \frac{3}{4}$. We see that $\frac{2}{3} - \frac{3}{4} = -\frac{1}{12}$ (negative); hence we shall conclude $\frac{2}{3} < \frac{3}{4}$.

Consequences of this Definition

(i) $a > b$ implies $b < a$ and $a < b$ implies $b > a$.

(ii) $a \geq b$ implies either $a > b$ or $a = b$. $a \gtrless b$ when $x \lesseqgtr y$ implies two statements—(1) $a > b$ when $x < y$; (2) $a < b$ when $x > y$.

(iii) If $a > b$, and $c > d$, then it is true that—(1) $a+c > b+d$; (2) $ac > bd$, if a, b, c, d are all positive

PROOF Since $a > b, c > d$, we have $a - b > 0, c - d > 0$.

Now $(a + c) - (b + d) = (a - b) + (c - d) > 0$; hence (1) follows.

Again $ac - bd = ac - ad + ad - bd = a(c - d) + d(a - b) > 0$; hence (2) follows.

(iv) If $a > b$, then $ac > bc$, if c is positive but $ac < bc$, if c is negative. In particular, if $a > b$, then $-a < -b$.

(v) If $a > b$ and a and b are positive, then $\frac{1}{a} < \frac{1}{b}$. [$\because$ $\frac{1}{a} - \frac{1}{b} = \frac{b-a}{ab} = -\frac{a-b}{ab}$ = negative; hence (v) follows]

5.1.2. Properties of Rational Numbers

I. Rational numbers are closed under addition, subtraction, multiplication and division (*except by zero*).

II. *Order property:*

(i) For any two rational numbers a and b, *either* $a > b$; or $a = b$; or $a < b$. (*Law of Trichotomy*)

(ii) $a < b$ *and* $b < c$ together imply $a < c$. (*Law of Transitivity*)

III. *Rational numbers form a dense set:*

By this we mean that between *any two rational numbers* a and b there exist *infinitely many* rational numbers.

[Clearly, $\frac{a+b}{2}$ lies between a and b; then $\frac{1}{2}\left(a + \frac{a+b}{2}\right)$ lies between a and $\frac{1}{2}(a+b)$; also $\frac{1}{2}\left(\frac{a+b}{2} + b\right)$ lies between $\frac{1}{2}(a + b)$ and b and so on.]

IV. *Decimal Representation:* A rational number can be expressed either as a *terminating decimal* or as a *recurring decimal.* e.g.,

$$\frac{1}{2} = 0.5, \quad \frac{3}{4} = 0.75, \quad \frac{3}{2} = 1.5, \quad \text{etc.}$$

$$\frac{1}{3} = 0.3333\ldots = 0.\dot{3}, \quad \frac{1}{7} = 0.\dot{1}4285\dot{7} \quad \text{etc.}$$

V. *Geometrical Representation:*

We take a *directed line,* a line in which we attribute one sense *positive* and the other sense *negative.* The positive sense will be indicated by an arrowhead. We take two points on the line $-O$, *the origin and* U, *the unit point* and take the length $OU = 1$ (Fig. 5.1); the point U is taken on the right of O (towards the arrowhead).

To represent any integer, say 3, we take a point A on the right of O such that $OA = 3OU$.

Take a *symmetric* point A' on the left of O (*by symmetric point we mean:* A, A' are symmetric, if O be the middle point of AA'). The point A' represents the integer -3.

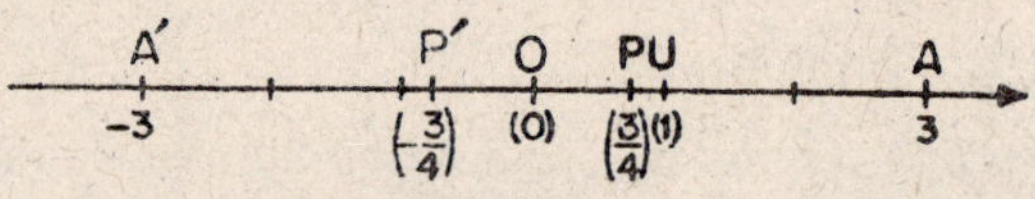

Fig 5.1

To represent a fraction, say 3/4. We first take the point A to represent the *numerator* 3 and then divide OA into 4 parts—the first part starting from O ends at P. The point P represents 3/4. The symmetric point P' on the left of O represents $-3/4$.

Thus, *given any rational number, we can represent it by a single point on a directed line where the origin and unit point are chosen arbitrarily, in advance.*

5.1.3. Irrational Numbers

Let us first prove that there exist numbers other than rational numbers.

EXAMPLE 1. *Prove that* $\sqrt{2}$ *is not a rational number.*

SOLUTION. If possible, let $\sqrt{2}$ be a rational number. Then we can write $\sqrt{2} = \frac{p}{q} \cdots (1)$ where p, q are integers prime to each other and $q \neq 0$.

Squaring both sides of (1), $2 = \frac{p^2}{q^2}$, or, $p^2 = 2q^2$. (2)

This shows that p^2 is even integer.

$\therefore$ p is an even integer. [$\because$ the square of an odd integer is always odd.]

Let $p = 2k$ where k is an integer.

$\therefore$ From (2), $(2k)^2 = 2q^2$, or, $q^2 = 2k^2$

$\therefore$ q^2 is an even integer and consequently q is an even integer.

Thus, p, q have a common factor 2. This contradicts the hypothesis that p and q are prime to each other.

$\therefore$ $\sqrt{2} = \frac{p}{q}$ is wrong. *Hence* $\sqrt{2}$ *is not a rational number.*

EXAMPLE 2. *Prove that* $\sqrt{3}$ *is not a rational number.*

SOLUTION. If possible, let $\sqrt{3} = \frac{p}{q}, \cdots\cdots (1)$ where p, q are integers prime to each other and $q \neq 0$.

From (1), $3 = \frac{p^2}{q^2}$, or, $p^2 = 3q^2$. (2)

Since $1^2 = 1, 2^2 = 4$ and $1^2 < 3 < 2^2$;

$$\because \quad 1^2 < \frac{p^2}{q^2} < 2^2, \text{ or, } 1 < \frac{p}{q} < 2, \text{ or, } q < p < 2q \quad \therefore \quad p - q < q$$

Now

$$\begin{aligned} 3(p-q)^2 &= 3p^2 + 3q^2 - 6pq = 3 \cdot 3q^2 + p^2 - 6pq \\ &= p^2 + 9q^2 - 6pq = (3q-p)^2 \\ \text{or,} \quad 3 &= \frac{(3q-p)^2}{(p-q)^2}; \quad \therefore \quad \sqrt{3} = \frac{3q-p}{p-q} = \frac{p}{q} \text{ where } p - q < q. \end{aligned}$$

Thus, $\sqrt{3}$ becomes equal to another rational number $(3q - p)/(p - q)$ where $p - q < q$.

This contradicts that p, q are prime to each other.

Hence $\sqrt{3}$ is *not rational.*

EXAMPLE 3. *Prove that $\sqrt{2} + \sqrt{3}$ is an irrational number.* **[CU B.Sc (Hons.) 1981]**

SOLUTION. If possible, let $(\sqrt{3} + \sqrt{2})$ be a rational number.

We have

$$\sqrt{3} - \sqrt{2} = \frac{(\sqrt{3}-\sqrt{2})(\sqrt{3}+\sqrt{2})}{(\sqrt{3}+\sqrt{2})} = \frac{3-2}{\sqrt{3}+\sqrt{2}} = \frac{1}{\sqrt{3}+\sqrt{2}} \tag{1}$$

$$\text{and} \quad (\sqrt{3}+\sqrt{2}) - (\sqrt{3}-\sqrt{2}) = 2\sqrt{2},$$

$$\text{or,} \quad \sqrt{2} = \frac{(\sqrt{3}+\sqrt{2}) - (\sqrt{3}-\sqrt{2})}{2} \tag{2}$$

Since $(\sqrt{3} + \sqrt{2})$ is a rational number, from (1) we see that $(\sqrt{3} - \sqrt{2})$, which is a quotient of two rational numbers, is a rational number.

$\therefore$ From (2), $\sqrt{2}$ is a rational number, since the difference and quotient (except denominator $= 0$) of two rational numbers are rational numbers.

But $\sqrt{2}$ is *not a rational number* [See **Ex. 1** (worked out)]. Thus, we arrive at a *contradiction.*

$\therefore$ Our assumption that $\sqrt{3} + \sqrt{2}$ is a rational number is wrong, i.e., $(\sqrt{3} + \sqrt{2})$ is *not a rational number.*

But $(\sqrt{3} + \sqrt{2})$ is a *real number.*

Hence $(\sqrt{3} + \sqrt{2})$ is an **irrational number.**

EXAMPLE 4. *If m is a positive integer which is not the square of another integer, show that $\sqrt{m}$ is not rational.* **[CU B.Sc (Hons.)]**

SOLUTION. If possible, let $\sqrt{m} = \frac{p}{q}, \cdots (1)$ where p, q are integers prime to each other and $q \neq 0$.

From (1), $m = \frac{p^2}{q^2}$ or $p^2 = mq^2$.

For the rational number $\frac{p}{q}$, we can always find two consecutive positive integers, say λ and $(\lambda + 1)$ such that

$$\lambda < \frac{p}{q} < \lambda + 1, \text{ or, } \lambda q < p < \lambda q + q; \quad \therefore \quad p - \lambda q < q.$$

Now,

$$m(p-\lambda q)^2 = m(p^2+\lambda^2q^2-2\lambda pq)$$
$$= mp^2+\lambda^2mq^2-2m\lambda pq = m\cdot mq^2+\lambda^2p^2-2m\lambda pq.$$
$$= m^2q^2+\lambda^2p^2-2mq\lambda p = (mq-\lambda p)^2$$

$$\text{or,}\quad m=\left(\frac{mq-\lambda p}{p-\lambda q}\right)^2; \quad \therefore \quad \sqrt{m}=\frac{mq-\lambda p}{p-\lambda q}=\frac{p}{q} \text{ where } p-\lambda q<q.$$

This contradicts that $\frac{p}{q}$ is in its lowest terms (i.e., p, q are prime to each other).

Hence $\sqrt{m}$ is *not rational.*

EXAMPLE 5. *Prove that* $\log_2 5$ *is no a rational number.*

SOLUTION. If possible, let $\log_2 5 = \frac{p}{q}, \cdots\cdots$ (1) where p, q are integers (prime to each other) and $q \neq 0$.

Then by definition of Logarithm, $2^{p/q}=5$, or, $2^p = 5^q$, which is *absurd,* since 2^p is an even integer and 5^q is not an even integer.

Hence $\log_2 5$ is not a rational number.

From the above examples, we see that there exist numbers other than rational numbers. These numbers are called **irrational numbers.**

DEFINITION. *A number, which* **cannot be expressed** *in the form p/q where p, q are integers (prime to each other) and $q \neq 0$, is called an* **irrational number.**

An *irrational number* can be expressed as a *non-terminating, non-recurring decimal.*

For example, $\sqrt{2} = 1{\cdot}4142134\cdots\cdots$, $\sqrt{3} = 1{\cdot}732050\cdots\cdots$, $\log_{10} 5$, etc. are *irrational numbers.* Also $\pi = 3\cdot14159265\cdots\cdots$ and $e = 2\cdot71828182\cdots\cdots$ are two important irrational numbers which are called transcendental numbers.

5.1.4. Real Numbers

The totality of the systems of rational and irrational numbers is said to form the system of real numbers.

In Fig. 5.1 we have represented rational numbers on a directed line (O, *origin* and U, *unit point*). Even when all rational points are represented on such a line there remain infinitely many gaps. These gaps correspond to irrational numbers. The existence of such an irrational point can be easily seen from Fig. 5.2 (B represents $\sqrt{2}$).

REMEMBER.

AXIOM. *There is a one-to-one correspondence between the points on a directed line and the system of real numbers.* [Cantor-Dedekind Axiom]

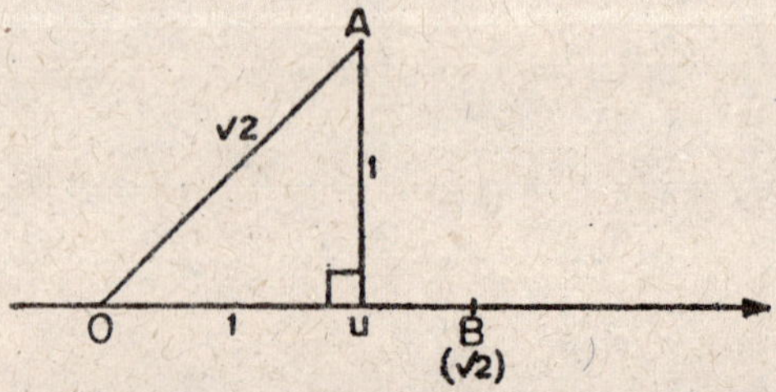

Fig 5.2

This line is called the axis of Reals.

The totality of points on the line is called the **straight-line Continuum** or **Geometric Continuum** or **Linear Continuum.**

The totality of real numbers form the *Arithmetic Continuum.* A theorem on *Arithmetic and Linear Continuum* is stated below.

There is a one-to-one correspondence between Arithmetic Continuum and Linear Continuum.

1. Properties of Real Numbers

(i) Real numbers are closed under addition, subtraction, multiplication and division (except divisor $= 0$) i.e., for any two real numbers $a, b (b \neq 0), a + b, a - b, a \cdot b$ and a/b are all real numbers;

(ii) Addition and multiplication are commutative and associative in R, i.e., for any $a, b, c \in R$;

(1) $a + b = b + a; a \cdot b = b \cdot a;$

(2) $a + (b + c) = (a + b) + c; a \cdot (b \cdot c) = (a \cdot b) \cdot c;$

(iii) Multiplication distributes over addition i.e., for any three real numbers $a, b, c \in R$,

$$a \cdot (b + c) = a \cdot b + a \cdot c \quad \text{and} \quad (b + c) \cdot a = b \cdot a + c \cdot a$$

2. Order Properties

(i) Given two real numbers a and b, we must have either $a > b$ or $a = b$ or $a < b$.

(ii) If $a > b$ and $b > c$, then $a > c$.

3. The system of real numbers is *dense* (i.e., between any two real numbers there exist infinitely many real numbers).

4. *Geometrically* every point on a directed line is a real number and conversely, given any real number there exists a unique point on the directed line.

5. Every real number is a decimal, either recurring or terminating or neither recurring nor terminating.

Complex Numbers

There exists no real number x such that $x^2 + 1 = 0$ or $x^2 + 4 = 0$ or $x^2 + 5 = 0$. Euler introduced the symbol i for the positive square root of -1 with $i^2 = -1$. The number $\sqrt{-1} = i$ is called an *imaginary number.*

Thus,

$$x^2 + 1 = 0 \quad \Rightarrow \quad x = \pm\sqrt{-1} = \pm i; x^2 + 4 = 0 \quad \Rightarrow x = \pm 2i$$

$$\text{and} \quad x^2 + 5 = 0 \quad \Rightarrow \quad x = \pm i\sqrt{5}, \quad \text{where } i = \sqrt{-1}.$$

A number of the form $a + ib$ where a and b are real numbers and $i = \sqrt{-1}$ is called a **complex number.**

In this book we shall deal with real numbers only. So the numbers other than real numbers are also undefined for the present purpose.

5.1.5. Variables and Constants

A **variable** *is a symbol x which can assume any value out of a given set of values.* The quantities like Profit, Sales, Revenue, National income, Exports, Imports, Heights, Weights, Time, Temperature etc. are examples of variables. The set of all possible values of x is called the domain of x. The variables are usually denoted by x, y, z, u, v, w, etc.

Continuous Variable

If a variable x can assume any real number between two given numbers, say a and $b\,(b > a)$ as its value, then x is called a **continuous real variable.** In this case, the **domain** or **interval** of x is **a < x < b** in which $x \neq a, b$. The interval $a < x < b$ is called an *open interval* and is denoted by] a, b [or (a, b). If x assumes any value in the range a to b including a and b, then the *domain* or *interval* of x is the **closed interval** $a \leq x \leq b$ which is denoted by $[a, b]$. If only 'a' is omitted, the domain becomes $a < x \leq b$ which is open at the left end. Similarly, $a \leq x < b$ is open at the right end.

Illustration: The expression $\sqrt{(x-2)(5-x)}$ is *real* only when $2 \leq x \leq 5$. Here x is a *continuous real variable.*

Constant

A **constant** is a, symbol, say a which does not change its value (i.e., retins the same value) throughout a set of mathematical operations. Constants are denoted by the letters a, b, c, α, β, etc. All numerical numbers are constants, *i.e.,* 2 is a constant, $\sqrt{3}$ is a constant, $\frac{2}{5}$ is a constant, etc.

Arbitrary Constants and Fixed Constants

We call specified numbers (e.g., $1, 2, 3, -3, \sqrt{5}$ etc.) as *fixed constants*—they do not change their values under any set of mathematical investigations. Sometimes we use symbols like a, b, c, d, l, m, n etc. to represent some real numbers which remain fixed for a particular investigation but may take up different values on different investigations. Such constants are called *arbitrary constants* (or *parameters*).

In co-ordinate geometry, we say "$y = mx$ represents a particular straight line passing through the origin *when m has a fixed numerical value*" but, it will represent a different straight line passing through the origin when *m has a different numerical value:* here m is a *parameter* or *an arbitrary constant.*

So when we are asked "What does $y = mx$ represent?" the correct answer should be:

"y = mx represents a family of lines passing through the origin".

Absolute Value (or Modulus)

The *absolute value* (or *modulus*) of a real number x, written as $|x|$, is its *numerical value which is always non-negative,* and is defined as follows:

$$\begin{aligned} |x| &= x, \text{ if } x \text{ is positive } (i.e., \text{ if } x > 0) \\ &= 0, \text{ if } x = 0 \\ &= -x, \text{ if } x \text{ is negative } (i.e., \text{ if } x < 0). \end{aligned}$$

Properties of Absolute Values

1. $|a| = |-a|$ [*Illustration:* $|2| = |-2| = 2$]

2. $|ab| = |a| \cdot |b|$ [*Illustration:* $|2 \times -3| = |2| \cdot ||-3| = 2 \cdot 3$.]

3. $\frac{|a|}{|b|} = \frac{|a|}{|b|}$ where $b \neq 0$. $\left[\textit{Illustration: } \left|\frac{-2}{3}\right| = \left|\frac{-2}{3}\right| = \frac{2}{3}\right]$.

4. $|a+b| \leq |a| + |b|$.

[*Illustration:* $|2+3| = |2|+|3|; |-2-3| = |-2|+|-3|; |2-3| < |2|+|-3|$ and $|-2+3| < |-2|+|3|$.]

5. $|a - b| \leq |a| + |b|$. [$\because$ $|a-b| = |a + (-b)| \leq |a| + |-b|$.]

6. $|a+b| \geq |a| - |b|$ if $|a| \geq |b|$
or, $\geq |b| - |a|$ if $|b| \geq |a|$.

7. *If* $|a| \leq b$, *then* $-b \leq a \leq b$.

PROOF. If $a > 0$, then $|a| = a$; $\therefore$ $a \leq b$. (1)

If $a < 0$, then $|a| = -a$; $\therefore$ $-a \leq b$, or, $a \geq -b$ (2)

From (1) and (2), we get $-b \leq a \leq b$.]

8. *If* $|a| > b > 0$, *then either* $a > b$ or $a < -b$.

[PROOF. If $a > 0$, then $|a| = a$; $\therefore$ $a > b$. But if $a < 0$, then $|a| = -a$;

$$\therefore \quad -a > b \text{ or, } \quad a < -b. \quad \text{Hence etc.]}$$

9. $0 < |x - a| \leq \delta$ *means* $a - \delta \leq x \leq a + \delta \ (x \neq a)$.

[PROOF. $|x - a| \leq \delta$ means $-\delta \leq x - a \leq \delta$, or, $a - \delta \leq x \leq a + \delta$; but $|x - a| > 0$ means $x \neq a$, for if $x = a$, then $|x - a| = 0$. Hence etc.]

EXAMPLE 6. *Prove that* $-7 \leq x \leq -3$ and $|x+5| \leq 2$ *are equivalent statements.*

SOLUTION. (i)

$$-7 \leq x \leq -3, \text{ or, } \quad -7-(-5) \leq x-(-5) \leq -3-(-5)$$
$$\text{or, } \quad -2 \leq x+5 \leq 2, \text{ or, } |x+5| \leq 2.$$

[See that the sum of the two ends $= -7 - 3 = -10$; half this sum $= -5$]

(ii) Again, if it is given $|x+5| \leq 2$, then we can write $-2 \leq x+5 \leq +2$,

or $-5 - 2 \leq x + 5 - 5 \leq 2 - 5$, or, $-7 \leq x \leq -3$.

$\therefore$ The two relations $-7 \leq x \leq -3$ and $|x+5| \leq 2$ are equivalent statements, i.e., one follows from the other.

5.2. FUNCTION

If there exists a relation between two real variables x and y such that for every value of x in a given set X, we get a definite value of y, then y is called a *function of* x and we write $y = f(x)$, x is called the *independent variable* and y the *dependent* variable. The set X in which x varies is called the **domain** of the function.

If for each value of x, we get two or more values of y, then y is called a *multiple-valued* function of x.

Illustration: (i) $y = 2x + 3,\ 1 \leq x \leq 3$, (ii) $y = 3x^2 + 4x + 5,\ 2 \leq x \leq 4$, (iii) $\begin{array}{c|c|c|c|} x & 1 & 3 & 4 \\ \hline y & 2 & 5 & 6 \end{array}$, etc. are single-valued functions of x. But $y^2 = 4x, 1 \leq x \leq 4$ and $y^3 = 8x, 2 \leq x \leq 3$, etc. are multiple-valued functions of x.

Definition of a Function as a Mapping

Let A and B be two non-empty sets (which may be equal) and x be a variable whose domain is A. Let there exist a rule f which associates with each element x of A a unique (one and only one) element y in B. Then f is called a **function** of x over the set A or the function f is defined over A or f maps A into B. A is called the *domain of definition* of the function f and B is the *co-domain.*

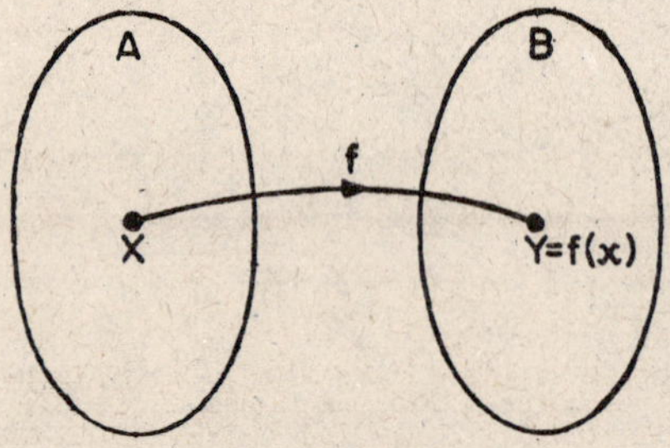

Fig 5.3

The element y which corresponds to a given x is written as $f(x)$ and is called the *image* of x under the rule f. $f(x)$ is also called the value of f at x.

Some important remarks

(1) All elements of B may not be images under f.

(2) For f to be a function over A, every element of A (without exception) must have a unique image in B.

(3) If an element x of the set A has *one and only one image* in B under f, then the function is called a **single-valued function** of x. But if for every $x \in A$, we get *two or more images* in B, then the function is called **multiple-valued function** of x. By *function* in this book we shall always mean *single-valued function.*

(4) The rule f which associates an element of A with a unique element of B may be given by a relation or by a set of pairwise values of A and B in the form of a table.

(5) If A is the set R of all real numbers (i.e., if $-\infty < x < \infty$) and B contains only one point c, then for every x of A, the image under f is the same real number c and the function f is called a *constant function* over R, and we write $f(x) = c$, for all $x \in R$.

(6) A function f is called an *even function* if for every $x \in A$, $f(-x) = f(x)$. If $f(x) = x^2$, then $f(-x) = (-x)^2 = x^2 = f(x)$ and hence $f(x)$ is an even function of x.

(7) A function f is called an *odd function* if for every $x \in A$, $f(-x) = -f(x)$. If $f(x) = x^3$, then $f(-x) = (-x)^3 = -x^3 = -f(x)$ and hence $f(x)$ is an odd function of x.

Explicit and Implicit functions

If a function is expressed directly in terms of the independent variable alone, then it is called an **explicit function.** Otherwise it is an **implicit function.** For example, $2x + 3y - 4 = 0$ is an implicit function, whereas $y = \frac{2(2-x)}{3}$ is an explicit function.

Parametric representation of a function

If both the independent and depedent variables are expressed as functions of a third variable, then the two relations define the parametric representation of the function. The third variable is called the *parameter.*

For example, $x = at^2$ and $y = 2at$ are the parametric representation of the function $y = 2\sqrt{ax}$.

Bounded functions

Let $f(x)$ be a function defined in the domain A. If two finite numbers k and K can be found such that $k \leq f(x) \leq K$ for every $x \in A$, then $f(x)$ is said to be bounded both below and above in the domain A and we say that $f(x)$ is bounded in A.

For example, the function $f(x) = x^2 + 2x + 3$ in the domain $1 \leq x \leq 3$ is bounded below by 6 and above by 18. Here 6 is the lower bound and 18 is the upper bound of the function in $1 \leq x \leq 3$.

Polynomial Function

Functions $a_\circ x + a_1, a_\circ x^2 + a_1 x + a_2, a_\circ x^3 + a_1 x^2 + a_2 x + a_3$, etc. are called *polynomials in x* of degrees, $1, 2, 3$, etc. respectively. Here $a_\circ, a_1, a_2, \cdots$ are all constants. Thus, $2x + 3, x^2 + 3x + 4, 2x^3 + 3x^2 + 5x + 6$, etc. are all *polynomial functions.*

Rational Function

It is the ratio of two polynomial functions, say $P(x)$ and $Q(x)$ of a variable x, i.e., $R(x) = \frac{P(x)}{Q(x)}$, where $Q(x) \neq 0$ for any value of x, is a *rational function of* x. For example, $\frac{2x+3}{3x-6}$ for $x \neq 2$,, $\frac{x^2+5x+3}{x^2-3x+2}$ for $x \neq 1, 2$, etc. are *rational functions.*

Algebraic Functions

A function which can be expressed as a polynomial, or as the ratio of two polynomials or as a root of a polynomial is called an *algebraic function.* Thus, $x, x^2, 2x + 3, x^2 + 3x + 2, \frac{3x+5}{2x+7} \left(x \neq -\frac{7}{2}\right)$, $\frac{x^2+3x+4}{x^2-5x+6}(x \neq 2, 3), \sqrt{3x+4}, \sqrt{x^2+5x+6}$, etc. are algebraic functions.

Irrational Functions

Functions like $\sqrt{x+5}, \sqrt{2x^2 - 3x + 4}, \frac{x}{\sqrt{2x+7}}$, etc. are *irrational functions.* Thus, algebraic functions which are not rational are irrational functions.

EXAMPLE 7. *A function f is completely defined by the following table:*

x	1	3	5	6
$y = f(x)$	0	2	4	5

Find the domain of definition of f. What is its range? If possible find $f(3), f(6), f(7)$.

SOLUTION. The set A of the values of x is $A = \{1, 3, 5, 6\}$. Here x is a discrete variable. This set A is the domain of definition of f. The set B of the corresponding values of y is $B = \{0, 2, 4, 5\}$ is the range of f.

$$\begin{aligned} f(3) &= \text{ image of 3 under } f = \text{ value of the function at } x = 3 \\ &= 2. \end{aligned}$$

Similarly, $f(6) = 5$. But 7 is not an element of A and therefore, $f(7)$ is not defined.

EXAMPLE 8. *Which of the following tables define y as a function f of x? Give reasons for your answer.*

(i) $\dfrac{x|1|2|3}{y|1|1|2}$; (ii) $\dfrac{x|1|2|2}{y|2|3|4}$; (iii) $\dfrac{x|2|3|5}{y|1|2|4}$

SOLUTION. By a function we shall mean a *single-valued function,* unless mentioned otherwise. Therefore, one value of x must associate with one and only one value of y.

In (i), two values of x associates with one value of y, in (ii) one value of x associates with two different values of y, and in (iii) again one value of x associates with one value of y.

Hence tables (i) and (iii) define y as a function f of x in each case. But Table (ii) does not define a function, since $x = 2$ cannot have two images 3 and 4.

NOTE. In (i), the same image 1 corresponds to two different values 1, 2 of x and this does not violate the definition of a function. Hence Table (i) represents y as a function of x. But in Table (ii); two different images 3 and 4 correspond to one value 2 of x. This violates the definition of function (i.e., single-valued function).

EXAMPLE 9. *The rule defining a function f is given below.*

(i) $f(x) = \frac{2}{x}$; (ii) $f(x) = \sqrt{x}$; (iii) $f(x) = \frac{x}{x-2}$.

Find the domain of definition of f in the above three cases.

SOLUTION. (i) $f(x) = \frac{2}{x}$.

$f(x)$ is not defined at $x = 0$, since division by zero is undefined in Mathematics. Hence the domain of definition of f is the set of all real numbers except 0.

(ii) $f(x) = \sqrt{x}$.

If x is negative (i.e., if $x < 0$), then $f(x)$ is not defined. Hence the domain of definition of f is $0 \le x < \infty$.

(iii) $f(x)$ is not defined at $x = 2$ only, since division by 0 is undefined. Hence the domain of definition of f is the set of all real numbers except 2.

EXAMPLE 10. *A function of x is given by the following relation:*

$$f(x) = \sqrt{21 - x - 2x^2}.$$

If x is real, find the domain of the definition of f. Obtain wherever possible, the values of $f(-3)$, $f(3)$ and $f(4)$.

SOLUTION. We have $f(x) = \sqrt{21 - x - 2x^2} = \sqrt{(3-x)(2x+7)}$ (1)

If x lies between $-\frac{7}{2}$ and 3, both $(3-x)$ and $(2x+7)$ are *positive* so that their product is also positive and $f(x)$ is real. But if $x < -\frac{7}{2}$, $(3-x)$ is positive and $2x+7$ is negative so that their product is negative and $f(x)$ becomes undefined (i.e., not real). If $x > 3$, then $3-x$ is negative and $2x+7$ is positive so that their product is negative and $f(x)$ becomes again undefined (i.e., not real). Therefore, $-\frac{7}{2} \le x \le 3$. Hence, the domain of the definition of f is $-\frac{7}{3} \le x \le 3$.

From (1),

$$\begin{aligned} f(-3) &= \sqrt{(3+3)(2\times -3+7)} = \sqrt{6\times 1} = \sqrt{\mathbf{6}}. \\ f(3) &= \sqrt{(3-3)(2\times 3+7)} = \sqrt{0\times 13} = \mathbf{0} \\ f(4) &= \sqrt{(3-4)(2\times 4+7)} = \sqrt{-1\times 15} \end{aligned}$$

which is *not real.*

Note that 4 does not lie in the domain of definition of $f(x)$.

EXAMPLE 11. *Find the domain of definition of the function f given by $f(x) = |x|$.*

SOLUTION. We know that

$$\begin{aligned} f(x) &= x \quad \text{if } x > 0 \\ &= 0 \quad \text{if } x = 0 \\ &= -x \quad \text{if } x < 0. \end{aligned}$$

We see that for every real number $x \in R$, we have unique value of $f(x)$.

Hence, the domain of definition of x is the set R of all real numbers.

EXAMPLE 12. *A function f over R is defined by $f(x) = 2x^2 + 5x - 7$; find the value of $\{f(3+h) - f(3)\}/h$.*

SOLUTION. We have $f(x) = 2x^2 + 5x - 7$;

$\therefore \quad f(3+h) = 2(3+h)^2 + 5(3+h) - 7$

and $f(3) = 2\cdot(3)^2 + 5.3 - 7 = 26.$

$$\begin{aligned} \therefore \quad \frac{f(3+h) - f(3)}{h} &= \frac{2(3+h)^2 + 5(3+h) - 7 - 26}{h} \\ &= \frac{2(9+6h+h^2) + 15 + 5h - 33}{h} \\ &= \frac{17h + 2h^2}{h} = \frac{h(17+2h)}{h} = \mathbf{17 + 2h}. \quad [h \neq 0] \end{aligned}$$

EXAMPLE 13. *If $f(x) = x^2 - x$, then prove that $f(h+1) = f(-h)$.* **[CU B.Com(Hons.) 1982]**

SOLUTION. We have $f(x) = x^2 - x$

$$\begin{aligned} \therefore \quad f(h+1) &= (h+1)^2 - (h+1) = h^2 + 2h + 1 - h - 1 \\ &= h^2 + h \\ \text{and} \quad f(-h) &= (-h)^2 - (-h) = h^2 + h. \end{aligned}$$

Hence, $f(h+1) = f(-h)$.

EXAMPLE 14. *If $f(x) = 2x^2 + 3x^4$ and $g(x) = 3x^3 + 5x$, show that $f(x)$ is an even function and $g(x)$ is an odd function of x.*

SOLUTION. We have $f(x) = 2x^2 + 3x^4$

$$\therefore \quad f(-x) = 2(-x)^2 + 3(-x)^4 = 2x^2 + 3x^4 = f(x).$$

Hence $f(x)$ is an *even function* of x

Again $g(x) = 3x^3 + 5x$

$$\therefore \quad g(-x) = 3(-x)^3 + 5(-x) = -3x^3 - 5x = -(3x^3 + 5x)$$
$$= -g(x).$$

Hence, $g(x)$ is an *odd function* of x.

EXAMPLE 15. *If $f(x) = x \cdot \frac{x-p}{q-p} + x \cdot \frac{x-q}{p-q}$ (where $p \neq q$), prove that $f(p) + f(q) = f(p+q)$.*

[CU B.Com(Hons.) 1981]

SOLUTION. We have $f(x) = x \cdot \frac{x-p}{q-p} + x \cdot \frac{x-q}{p-q}$

$$\therefore \quad f(p) = p \cdot \frac{p-p}{q-p} + p \cdot \frac{p-q}{p-q} = p \cdot 0 + p \cdot 1 = p,$$

$$f(q) = q \cdot \frac{q-p}{q-p} + q \cdot \frac{q-q}{p-q} = q \cdot 1 + q \cdot 0 = q,$$

$$\text{and} \quad f(p+q) = (p+q) \cdot \frac{p+q-p}{q-p} + (p+q) \cdot \frac{p+q-q}{p-q}$$

$$= \frac{(p+q)q}{q-p} + \frac{(p+q) \cdot p}{p-q} = \frac{pq+q^2}{q-p} - \frac{p^2+pq}{q-p}$$

$$= \frac{pq+q^2-p^2-pq}{q-p} = \frac{q^2-p^2}{q-p} = q+p = p+q.$$

$$\therefore \quad \text{L.H.S.} = f(p) + f(q) = p+q$$

$$\text{and} \quad \text{R.H.S.} = f(p+q) = p+q.$$

Hence **L.H.S. = R.H.S.**

5.3. BREAK-EVEN ANALYSIS

We shall denote

$C(x)$ = Cost function (x is the number of units produced)

$R(x)$ = Revenue function (revenue obtained by selling x units of commodity)

$P(x)$ = Profit function

We know that, Profit = Revenue − Cost, i.e., $P(x) = R(x) - C(x)$,

If $R(x) = C(x)$, then $P(x) = 0$, i.e., when the revenue equals cost, there is no profit or loss—this value is called the **break-even point.**

EXAMPLE 16. *The daily cost of production of x units of a commodity is* Rs. $C(x)$ *where* $C(x) = \text{Rs.}2.05x + \text{Rs.}550$.

(i) *If each unit is sold for* Rs. 3, *what is the minimum number that mut be produced and sold daily for ensuring no loss.*

(ii) *If this selling price is increased by* 30 *paise per unit, what would be the break-even point?*

(iii) *If it is given that at least* 500 *units can be sold daily, what price should be charged per unit to guarantee no loss?* **[CA May 1985]**

SOLUTION.

(i) $R(x)$ = Revenue from sales of x units = Rs. $3x$.

For the break-even point we have

$$C(x) = R(x), \quad \text{or,} \quad 2.05x + 550 = 3x$$

$$\text{or,} \quad 550 = 3x - 2.05x = 0.95x$$

$$\text{or,} \quad x = \frac{550}{0.95} = \frac{550 \times 100}{95} = \frac{11000}{19} = 578.95$$

Thus, at least 579 units are to be produced daily to ensure no loss.

(ii) In this case $R(x)$ = Rs. $3.30x$.

For the break-even point, we have $R(x) = C(x)$

$$3.30x = 2.05x + 550, \quad \text{or,} \quad (3.30 - 2.05)x = 550$$

$$\text{or,} \quad x = \frac{550}{1.25} = \frac{550}{125} \times 100 = \mathbf{440}.$$

$\therefore$ When the selling price is increased by 30 paise per unit, the break-even point is **440.**

(iii) If 500 units are sold daily, the price p per unit needed to ensure no loss is given by

$$500p = 2.05 \times 500 + 550 \Rightarrow p = \text{Rs.}3.15.$$

EXAMPLE 17. *A company decides to set up a small production plant for manufacturing electronic clocks. The total cost for initial set up (Fixed Cost) is Rs.* 9 *lakhs. The additional cost (Variable Cost) for producing each clock is Rs.* 300. *Each clock is sold at Rs.* 750. *During the first month* 1500 *clocks are produced and sold:*

(i) *Determine the cost function $C(x)$ for the total cost of producing x clocks.*

(ii) *Determine the Revenue function $R(x)$ for the total revenue from the sale of x clocks.*

(iii) *Determine the profit function $P(x)$ for the profit from the sale of x clocks.*

(iv) *What profit or loss the company incurs during the first month when all the* 1500 *clocks are sold?*

(v) *Determine the break-even point.* **[CA May 1992]**

SOLUTION.

(i) $C(x)$ = Fixed cost + Variable cost for x clocks = Rs. 9,00,000 + Rs. $300x$.

(ii) $R(x) = 750x$ = Revenue from the sale of x clocks.

(iii) Profit function $P(x) = R(x) - C(x) = 750x - (9,00,000 + 300x) = 450x - 9,00,000$.

(iv) $450 \times 1,500 - 9,00,000 = 6,75,000 - 9,00,000 = -2,25,000$. There is a loss of Rs. 2,25,000 on the first month.

(v) Break-even point is given by $P(x) = 0$, i.e., when $450x = 9,00,000$ i.e., when $x = \mathbf{2,000}$.

Exercise 5 (I)

A

[Number System, Functions]

1. What do you mean by a *rational number?* Which of the following are rational numbers?

$$0, -1, \frac{1}{2}, \frac{2}{0}, \frac{0}{1}, \frac{0}{0}, -\frac{2}{3}, \infty.$$

2. Prove that

(i) $\sqrt{2}$ is not a rational number;

(ii) $\sqrt{5}$ is not a rational number. **[C.U.]**

3. If $\sqrt{2}$ is not a rational number, prove that (i) $\sqrt{5}+\sqrt{2}$ cannot be a rational number;

(ii) $\sqrt{3}-\sqrt{2}$ cannot be a rational number.

4. Define an irrational number and show that $\sqrt{3}$ is not rational. **[C.U.]**

5. Assuming that the set of integers is closed under addition subtraction and multiplication, show that the sum, difference, product and quotient of two non-zero rational numbers are themselves rationals.

6. Which of the following are rationals and which are irrationals?

$$-\frac{1}{2}, \pi, \sqrt{2}, \frac{0}{\sqrt{3}}, e, \frac{2}{5}, \frac{-3}{5}, \sqrt{2}+\sqrt{3}, \frac{4}{0}, \sqrt{-7}.$$

7. Prove that $\log_{10} 5$ cannot be a rational number.

8. Prove that $a+b$ cannot be a rational number if a is rational and b is irrational.

[HINTS. If possible, let $a+b$ be a rational number c i.e., $a+b=c$ where c is a rational number. Then $b=c-a.\cdots\cdots$(i)

Now since a and c are rationals, $c-a$ is also rational. But b is irrational. $\therefore$ (i) is absurd. Hence, etc.]

9. If $y=2+|x|$, find the values of y when $x=-1,2,-3,5$.

10. Prove that ab and $a/b(b\neq 0)$ are not rational numbers if a is rational and b is irrational.

11. Express the following in modulus (or absolute value) notations:

(i) $-\frac{1}{2}<x<\frac{1}{2}$; (ii) $-5\leq x\leq 5$; (iii) $1\leq x\leq 5$;

(iv) $-12<x<2$; (v) $-15<x+3<7$.

12. Express the following in terms of equivalent inequality:

(i) $|x+1|\leq 2$; (ii) $0<|x-3|<\delta$; (iii) $0<|x-7|\leq 4$.

B

[Functions]

1. What do you mean by a *function?* Given $y = 3x + 2$. Is it a function? If so, what is its domain of definition?

2. A function f is completely defined by the following table. Find the domain of definition of f. What is its range?

(i) $\frac{x|1|2|4}{y|0|1|3}$; (ii) $\frac{x|2|3|4|5}{y|3|5|5|6}$.

[HINTS. See worked out **Ex. 6.**]

3. Which of the following tables define y as a function of x? Give reasons for your answer.

(i) $\frac{x|3|5|6}{y|2|4|7}$; (ii) $\frac{x|1|2|2}{y|3|4|5}$; (iii) $\frac{x|1|2|4}{y|0|3|3}$.

[HINTS. See worked out **Ex. 7.**]

4. Find the domain of definition of each of the following functions:

(i) $f(x) = x^2$; (ii) $f(x) = \frac{3}{x}$; (iii) $f(x) = \frac{1}{x-2}$.

5. Find the range of values of x for the following functions:

(i) $f(x) = \sqrt{x^2 - 4}$; (ii) $f(x) = \sqrt{8 + 2x - 3x^2}$.

6. If $f(x) = x^2 - 3x + 2$, find $f(0), f(1), f(-2)$ and $f(3)$.

7. If $f(x) = \sqrt{15 + x - 2x^2}$, find the domain of definition of $f(x)$. If possible, find the values of $f(0), f(4)$ and $f(-2)$.

8. (i) If $f(x) = 2x^2 - 5x + 2$, find the value of $\{f(4+h) - f(4)\}/h$.

(ii) If $f(x+3) = 2x^2 - 3x - 1$, find $f(x+1)$. **[ICWAI June 1998]**

9. If $f(x) = x + 3x^3$ and $g(x) = 3 - x^2$, show that $f(x)$ is an odd function and $g(x)$ is an even function of x.

10. If $f(x) = x^2 + x$, prove that $f(h+1) - f(h-2) = 6h$.

11. Given $f(x) = x$ and $g(x) = x^2/x$. Is $f(x) = g(x)$ always? Give reasons for your answer.

12. Show that the function $\frac{x^2+3x+5}{x^2-5x+4}$ is undefined at $x = 1$ and $x = 4$.

13. (i) If $f(x) = \log x (x > 0)$, show that $f(p) + f(q) + f(r) = f(pqr)$.

(ii) If $f(x) = e^x$, show that $f(a) \cdot f(b) = f(a+b)$.

14. If $f(x) = \frac{x}{1-x}$, show that $\frac{f(x+h)-f(x)}{h} = \frac{1}{(1-x)(1-x-h)}$.

15. If $y = g(x) = \frac{ax-b}{cx-a}$, then prove that $g(y) = x$.

16. If $f(x) = \frac{x-1}{x+1}$, prove that $\frac{f(x)-f(y)}{1+f(x)\cdot f(y)} = \frac{x-y}{1+xy}$.

17. If $f(x) = \frac{3x+2}{3x-2}$, prove that $\frac{f(x)+1}{f(x)-1} = \frac{3x}{2}$.

18. If $f(x) = e^{ax+b}$, prove that $f(l) \cdot f(m) \cdot f(n) = f(l+m+n) \cdot e^{2b}$.

19. If $f(x) = b \cdot \frac{x-a}{b-a} + a \cdot \frac{x-b}{a-b}$, prove that $f(a) + f(b) = f(a+b)$.

20. If $f(x) = ax^2 + bx + c$ and $f(1) = 6, f(2) = 11$ and $f(3) = 18$, find the values of a, b and c and hence find $f(-1)$.

21. If $f(x) = 2x^2 - 5x + 4$, for what values of x is $2f(x) = f(2x)$. **[CA May 1986]**

22. (i) If $f(x) = \frac{ax+b}{bx+a}$, prove that $f(x) \cdot f(\frac{1}{x}) = 1$. **[C.U. B.Com (Hons.) 1990]**

(ii) If $y = f(x) = \frac{x+1}{x+2}$, find $f(y)$ and $f\{f(\frac{1}{x})\}$. **[C.U. B.Com (Hons.) 1992]**

[HINTS.

$$f(y) = \frac{y+1}{y+2} = \frac{\frac{x+1}{x+2}+1}{\frac{x+1}{x+2}+2} = \frac{2x+3}{3x+5} \quad \left[\because \; f(x) = \frac{x+1}{x+2} = y\right]$$

$$\text{and} \quad f(\frac{1}{x}) = \frac{\frac{1}{x}+1}{\frac{1}{x}+2} = \frac{x+1}{2x+1}; \quad \therefore \; f\{f(\frac{1}{x})\} = \frac{\frac{x+1}{2x+1}+1}{\frac{x+1}{2x+1}+2} = \frac{3x+2}{5x+3}$$

Answers

A

1. $0, -1, \frac{1}{2}, \frac{0}{1}, \frac{-2}{3}$. **6.** Rational: $-\frac{1}{2}, \frac{0}{\sqrt{3}} = 0, \frac{2}{5}, \frac{-3}{5}$; irrationals: $\pi, \sqrt{2}, e, \sqrt{2}+\sqrt{3}$. **9.** $3, 4, 5, 7$. **11.** (i) $|x| < \frac{1}{2}$; (ii) $|x| \le 5$; (iii) $|x-3| \le 2$; (iv) $|x+5| < 7$; (v) $|x+7| < 11$. **12.** (i) $-3 \le x \le 1$; (ii) $3 - \delta < x < 3 + \delta (x \ne 3)$; (iii) $3 \le x \le 11 (x \ne 7)$.

B

1. Yes; the domain is R (the set of all real numbers). **2.** (i) The domain A is $A = \{1, 2, 4\}$ and the range $B = \{0, 1, 3\}$; (ii) $A = \{2, 3, 4, 5\}$ and $B = \{3, 5, 6\}$. **3.** (i) and (iii) define y as a function of x, since in (i) one value of x associates with one value of y and in (iii) two values of x associate with one value of y, but in (ii) one value of x associates with two values of y. **4.** (i) The set R of all real numbers; (ii) The set of all real numbers except 0; (iii) The set of all real numbers except 2. **5.** (i) $x \ge 2$ or $x \le -2$; (ii) $-\frac{4}{3} \le x \le 2$. **6.** $2, 0, 12, 2$. **7.** $\frac{-5}{2} \le x \le 3; f(0) = \sqrt{15}, f(4)$ is undefined and $f(-2) = \sqrt{5}$. **8.** $11 + 2h$. **11.** No. $f(x) = g(x)$ only when $x \ne 0$; at $x = 0, g(x)$ is undefined, but $f(x)$ is defined for all real values of x. **20.** $a = 1, b = 2, c = 3; 2$. **21.** ± 1. **22.** $\frac{2x+3}{3x+5}; \frac{3x+2}{5x+3}$.

5.4. GRAPHS OF FUNCTIONS

When y is a function of x, we get two sets of values, one of which is the *domain* of the independent variable x and the other is the *range* of the dependent variable y. Every value of x in the domain corresponds to a unique value of y in the *range*.

To draw the graph of a function, we take two rectangular axes $X'OX$ and $Y'OY, O$ being the origin, and then plot all the corresponding pairs of values of x and y as points on the plane of the axes. For example, if $y = y_1$, when $x = x_1$, we get an ordered pair (x_1, y_1) and plot this pair as a point. In this way we plot all the pairs of values of x and y as points. The totality of all such points forms the graph of the function.

In practical problems, we first tabulate a number of corresponding pairs of values of x and y for the given function and then plot them as points in the plane determined by the rectangular axes $X'OX$ and $Y'OY$. We illustrate the graphs of some functions in the following examples.

EXAMPLE 1. *Draw the graphs of the following functions:*

(i) $x = 3$; (ii) $y = 5$; (iii) $y = x$; (iv) $\frac{x}{5} + \frac{y}{4} = 1$.

The domain of definition in each case being the set of all real numbers.

SOLUTION. (i) Here $x = 2$ and y has any value in $-\infty < y < \infty$.

We have

x	3	3	3	3	3	⋯
y	0	1	2	−1	−2	⋯

When the corresponding pairs of values of x and y are plotted as points in the plane of OX and OY, we get an unbroken line parallel to y-axis at a distance of 2 units from it. This line is the required graph.

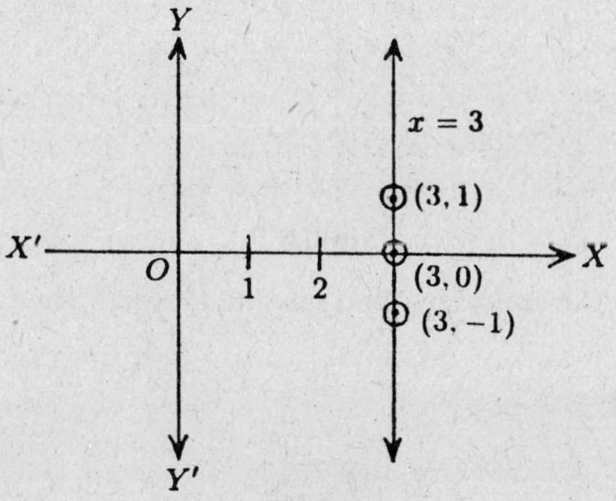

Fig 5.4

(ii) Here $y = 5$ and x has any value in $-\infty < x < \infty$.

We have

x	0	1	2	−1	−2	⋯
y	5	5	5	5	5	⋯

When the corresponding pairs of values of x and y are plotted as points in the plane of th rectangular axes, we get a straight line parallel to the x-axis at the height of 5 units from it.

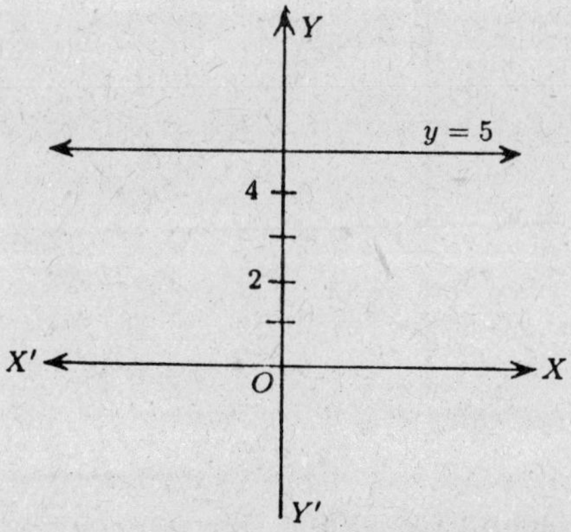

Fig 5.5

(iii) $y = x$. Here the domain of x is $-\infty < x < \infty$.

x	0	1	2	− 1	− 2	⋯
y	0	1	2	− 1	− 2	⋯

$(0,0), (1,1), (2,2), (-1,-1), (-2,-2)$, etc. are points on the graph.

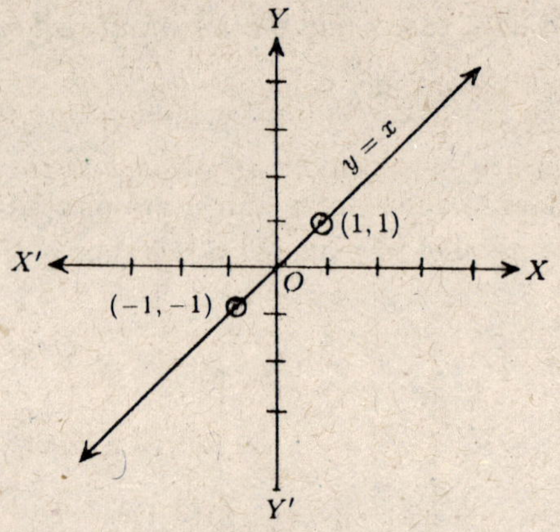

Fig 5.6

$\therefore$ $y = x$ gives a graph of an unbroken line passing through the origin and bisecting the angle between OX and OY.

(iv) The domain of x is $-\infty < x < \infty$.

$$\frac{x}{5} + \frac{y}{4} = 1 \tag{1}$$

If $x = 0, y = 4$ and if $y = 0, x = 5$.

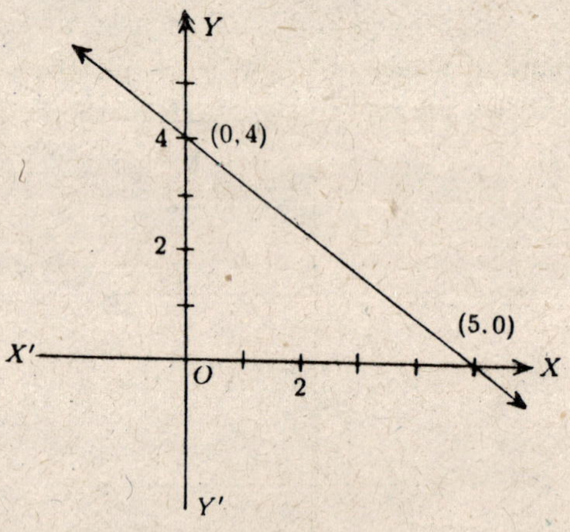

Fig 5.7

$\therefore$ $(5,0)$ and $(0,4)$ are points on the graph. We can tabulate other points from (1) and all these points lie on the line joining the two points $(5,0)$ and $(0,4)$. The graph is shown in the figure.

EXAMPLE 2. *Draw the graph of the following function*

$$\begin{aligned} y &= 1 \quad \text{when } x > 0, \\ &= 0 \quad \text{when } x = 0, \\ &= -1 \quad \text{when } x < 0. \end{aligned}$$

[C.U. B.Com(Hons.) 1988]

SOLUTION. $y = 1$ when $x > 0$ is the straight line in the first quadrant parallel to the x-axis at the height of 1 unit above it, $y = 0$ when $x = 0$ is the origin and $y = -1$ when $x < 0$ is the straight line in the third quadrant parallel to the x-axis at depth of 1 unit below it. The graph of the given function consisting of *one line in the first quadrant excluding the point* $(0, 1)$, *another line in the third quadrant excluding the point* $(0, -1)$, *and the origin is shown in the figure.*

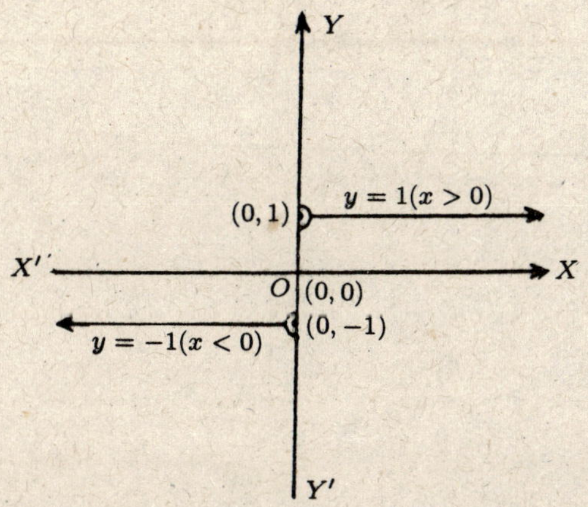

Fig 5.8

EXAMPLE 3. *Draw the graph of* $f(x) = |x|$, *i.e.*

$$\begin{aligned} f(x) &= x \quad \text{when } x > 0, \\ &= 0 \quad \text{when } x = 0, \\ &= -x \quad \text{when } x < 0. \end{aligned}$$

[C.U. B.Com (Hons.) 1982]

SOLUTION. $y = f(x) = x(x > 0)$ (1)

x	1	2	3	4	.5	1.5	$\cdots$
y	1	2	3	4	.5	1.5	$\cdots$

The graph of (1) is *the straight line in the first quadrant bisecting the angle* $\angle XOY$.

$$y = f(x) = 0 \text{ when } x = 0 \text{ is the origin } (0, 0).$$

$$y = f(x) = -x \text{ when } x < 0. \tag{2}$$

x	−1	−2	−3	−.5	−1.5	$\cdots$
y	1	2	3	.5	1.5	$\cdots$

The graph of (2) is *the straight line in the second quadrant bisecting the angle* $\angle X'OY$.

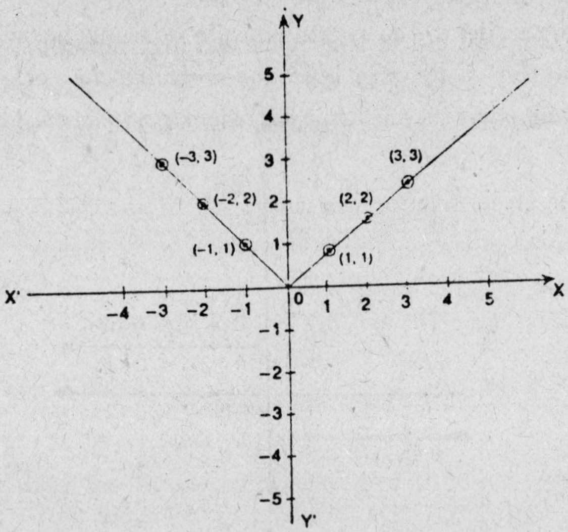

Fig 5.9

EXAMPLE 4. *Draw the graph of the functions:* $f(x) = \frac{x^2}{x}$ *and* $\phi(x) = x$*; point out the difference between the two graphs.*

SOLUTION. The function $f(x) = \frac{x^2}{x}$ is undefined at $x = 0$.

Thus, $f(x) = x$ if $x \neq 0$ and $f(0)$ is undefined. (1)

Some of the values of $y = \frac{x^2}{x}$ can be plotted as follows:

$x =$	0	1	2	3	−1	−2	−3
$y =$	Undefined	1	2	3	−1	−2	−3

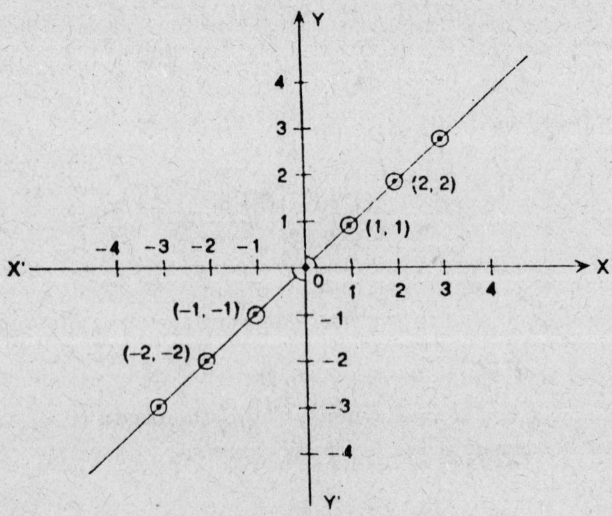

Fig 5.10

The graph of the function (1) is drawn in Fig. 5.10.

The graph has a break at the origin. We say that the function is not continuous at $(0, 0)$.

For the graph of the function $\phi(x) = x$ see Fig. 5.6.

From the graphs we see that $0(0, 0)$ is not included in the graph of Fig. 5.10 but it is included in the graph of Fig. 5.6.

EXAMPLE 5. *Draw the graph of the function:* $y = f(x) = [x]$, *where* $[x]$ *denotes the greatest integer not greater than* x.

SOLUTION. From the given function, we have

$$
\begin{aligned}
y = f(x) &= 0, \quad \text{when } 0 \le x < 1 \\
&= 1, \quad \text{when } 1 \le x < 2 \\
&= 2, \quad \text{when } 2 \le x < 3 \\
&= -1, \quad \text{when } -1 \le x < 0 \\
&= -2, \quad \text{when } -2 \le x < -1 \text{ etc.}
\end{aligned}
$$

On the convenient scale we draw the graph of each segment:

$$-1 \le x < 0, -2 \le x < -1, 0 \le x < 1, 1 \le x < 2 \text{ etc.}$$

In each segment y has a constant value.

e.g., for

$$
\begin{aligned}
-1 \le x < 0, &\quad y \text{ has the constant value } -1 \\
-2 \le x < -1, &\quad y \text{ has the constant value } -2 \\
0 \le x < 1, &\quad y \text{ has the constant value } 0, \text{ etc.}
\end{aligned}
$$

The graph (Fig. 5.11) thus consists of a number of parallel line segments, all parallel to the x-axis. These line segments (drawn in bold) look like steps, hence the function is called a *step-function*. There is a break at every integral value of x i.e., the function is not continuous at $x = 0, \pm1, \pm2$, etc.

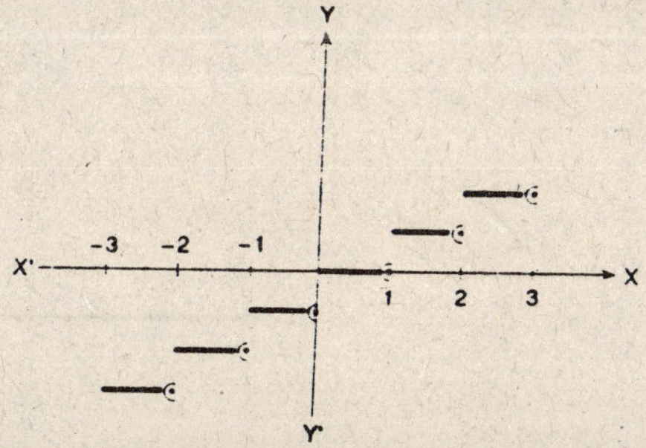

Fig 5.11

EXAMPLE 6. *Draw the graph of the following function*

$$
\begin{aligned}
y = f(x) &= 1 \quad \text{for } x \ge 0 \\
&= -1 \text{ for } x < -3
\end{aligned}
$$

SOLUTION. The graph (Fig. 5.12) consists of (a) a line parallel to x-axis in the first quadrant at a height 1 above the x-axis, the point $(0, 1)$ is included; (b) another line parallel to x-axis in the third quadrant at a depth 1 below the x-axis, the point $(-3, 1)$ is not included; (c) the function has not been defined for $-3 \le x < 0$ and hence, we do not get the corresponding y's i.e., there is no graph of the function in this interval.

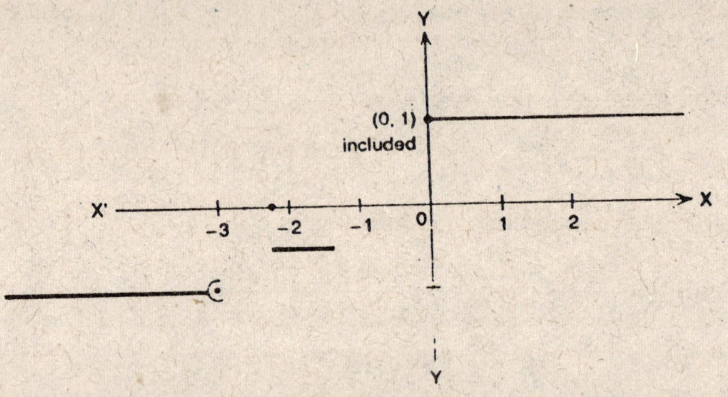

Fig 5.12

EXAMPLE 7. *Draw the graph of the following function:*

$$y = 2x + 1 \text{ when } x \ge 1$$
$$= 2x - 1 \text{ when } x < 1.$$

SOLUTION. Some of the values of x and y are tabulated below:

$x =$	0	$\frac{1}{2}$	$\frac{3}{4}$	1	$\frac{3}{2}$	2	3	−1	−2
$y =$	−1	0	$\frac{1}{2}$	3	4	5	7	−3	−5

Thus, when $x \ge 1$ we shall use the formula $y = 2x + 1$ and when $x < 1$ we use $y = 2x - 1$.

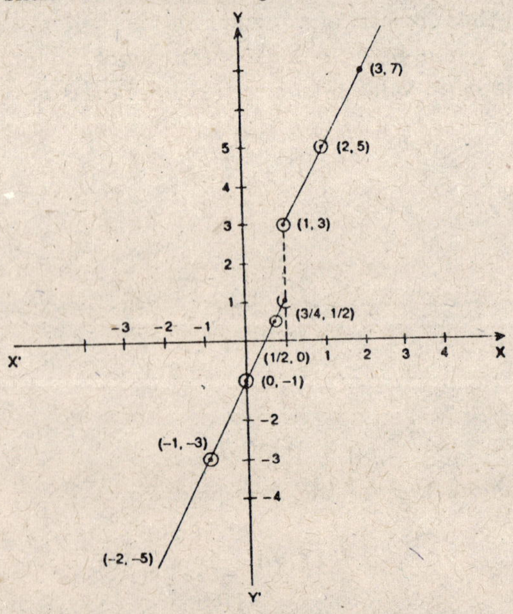

Fig 5.13

The graph (Fig. 5.13) consists of two half lines one in the first quadrant intersecting the line $x = 1$ at the point $(1, 3)$ and the other lies in first, and third quadrant intersecting the x-axis at the point $\left(\frac{1}{2}, 0\right)$ and y-axis at the point $(0, -1)$. The origin is not included here. The graph has a break at $x = 1$. So we say that the function is not continuous at $x = 1$.

EXAMPLE 8. *Sketch the graph of the function defined by*

$$\begin{aligned} f(x) &= x - 1 \text{ when } x > 0 \\ &= \frac{1}{2} \text{ when } x = 0 \\ &= x + 1 \text{ when } x < 0 \end{aligned}$$

SOLUTION. We tabulate some values of x and y.

x	1	−1	0	2	−2	3	−3
y	0	0	$\frac{1}{2}$	1	−1	2	−2

Thus, when $x > 0$ we shall use the formula $y = x - 1$ and when $x < 0$ we use $y = x + 1$.

On the axes of x and y we take a certain scale (say 2 small squares on graph paper may be taken as number 1).

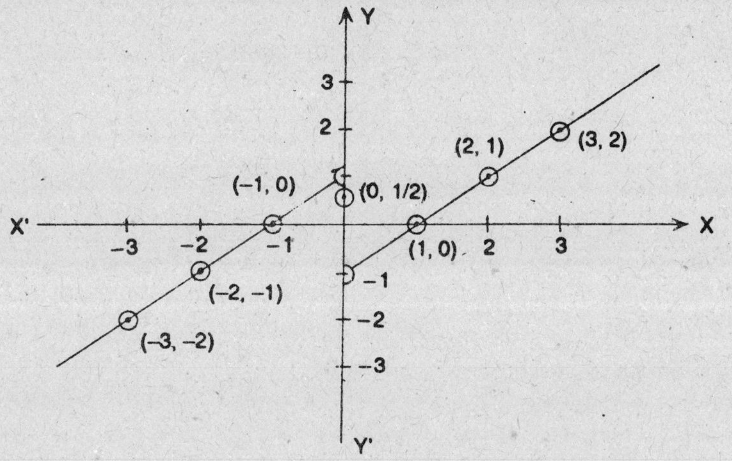

Fig 5.14

Hence, the graph (Fig. 5.14) consists of two half lines and a point $\left(0, \frac{1}{2}\right)$. One half line lies in the first and fourth quadrant intersecting the x-axis at the point $(1, 0)$ and the other lies in the second and third quadrant cutting the x-axis at the point $(-1, 0)$; the point $\left(0, \frac{1}{2}\right)$ is included in the graph, it is an isolated point. Here the graph has a break at $x = 0$. So the function $f(x)$ is not continuous there.

EXAMPLE 9. *A function $f(x)$ is defined by $f(x) = |x - 2| + 1$ over all real values of x. Show that $f(x)$ is continuous at $x = 2$.* **[ICWAI June 1983]**

SOLUTION. Now $f(x) = |x - 2| + 1$ over all real values of x can be written as

$$\begin{aligned} f(x) &= x - 2 + 1 = x - 1 \text{ when } x > 2, \\ f(x) &= 1 \text{ when } x = 2 \\ \text{and } f(x) &= -x + 2 + 1 = 3 - x \text{ when } x < 2. \end{aligned}$$

We tabulate some values of x and y.

x	0	1	2	3	4	−1	−2	−3
y	3	2	1	2	3	4	5	6

Thus, when $x \geq 2$ we shall use the formula $y = x - 1$ and when $x \leq 2$ we use $y = 3 - x$.

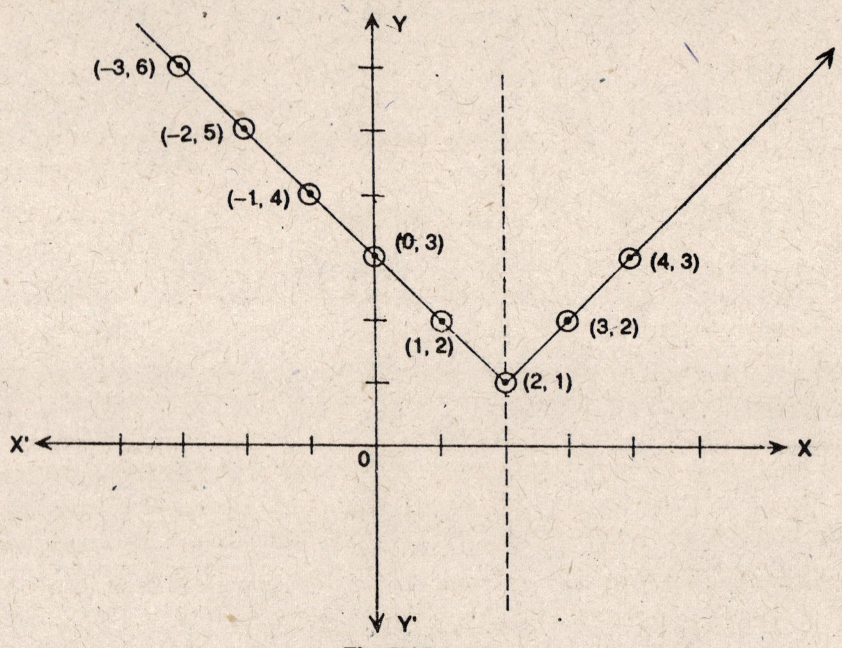

Fig 5.15

The graph (Fig. 5.15) consists of two half lines, one in the left side of the line $x = 2$ and other in the right side of the line $x = 2$, both intersect the line $x = 2$ at the point (2, 1). The point (2, 1) is included in the graph (see Fig. 5.15). There is no break i.e., the graph is continuous at $x = 2$.

EXAMPLE 10. *Draw the graph of the function:*

$$y = x \text{ if } x \leq 0 \text{ and } y = x^2 \text{ if } 0 < x \leq 2.$$

SOLUTION. We have

$$y = x, \quad \text{if } x \leq 0 \qquad (1)$$

$$\text{and} \quad y = x^2, \text{ if } 0 < x \leq 2 \qquad (2)$$

From (1), we have

x	0	−1	−2	−3	...
y	0	−1	−2	−3	...

These points are plotted with reference to $X'OX$ and $Y'OY$ as axes of co-ordinates and joined. The graph of equation (1) is a *straight line in the third quadrant bisecting the angle* $\angle X'OY'$.

From (2), we have

x	.5	1	1.5	2	...
y	.25	1	2.25	4	...

These points are plotted and joined. The graph of (2) is *half a parabola in the first quadrant up to the point* (2, 4).

The graph is shown in Fig. 5.16.

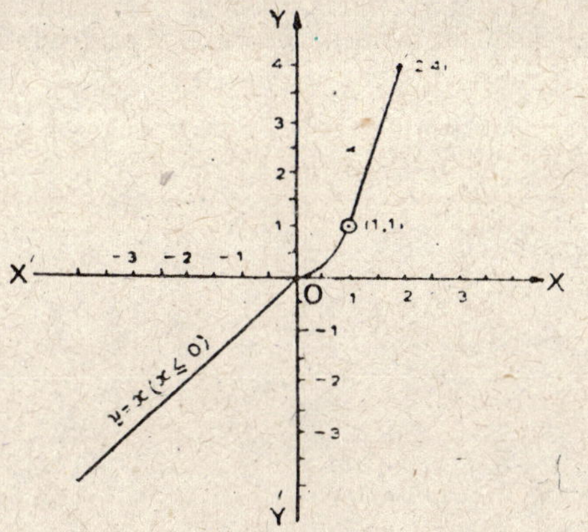

Fig 5.16

EXAMPLE 11. *Draw the graph of the function* $y = \frac{1}{x}$, *or*, $xy = 1$.

SOLUTION. If $x = 0, y$ is *undefined* and if $y = 0, x$ is undefined. $[\because \quad x = 1/y]$.

From the given equation, we see that (i) the graph passes through the points (1, 1) and $(-1, -1)$, (ii) if $x > 0, y > 0$ and if $x < 0, y < 0$; (iii) if x increases, y decreases and vice versa.

We construct a table of values of x and the corresponding values of y as follows:

x	$\frac{1}{4}$	$\frac{1}{2}$	1	2	3	4	-1	$-\frac{1}{2}$	$-\frac{1}{4}$	-2	-4
y	4	2	1	$\frac{1}{2}$	$\frac{1}{3}$	$\frac{1}{4}$	-1	-2	-4	$-\frac{1}{2}$	$-\frac{1}{4}$

[As $x \to 0^+, y \to \infty$ and as $x \to \infty, y \to 0^+$; again as $x \to 0^-, y \to -\infty$ and as $x \to -\infty$, $y \to 0^-$.]

Thus, we get *two branches of the curve, one in the first quadrant and the other in third quadrant*. As we take positive values of x nearer and nearer to zero, the values of y become larger and larger and ultimately infinitely large. Again when x takes negative values nearer and nearer to zero, the values of y becomes numerically larger and larger and ultimately infinitely large.

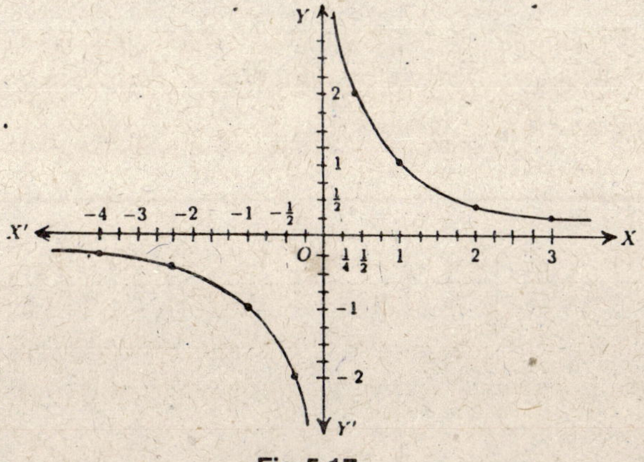

Fig 5.17

The graph of the given function is drawn in Fig. 5.17.

EXAMPLE 12. *Draw the graph of the function $y = x^3$.*

SOLUTION. $y = x^3$, for $-\infty < x < \infty$.

x	0	.5	1	$-.5$	-1	...
y	0	.125	1	$-.125$	-1	...

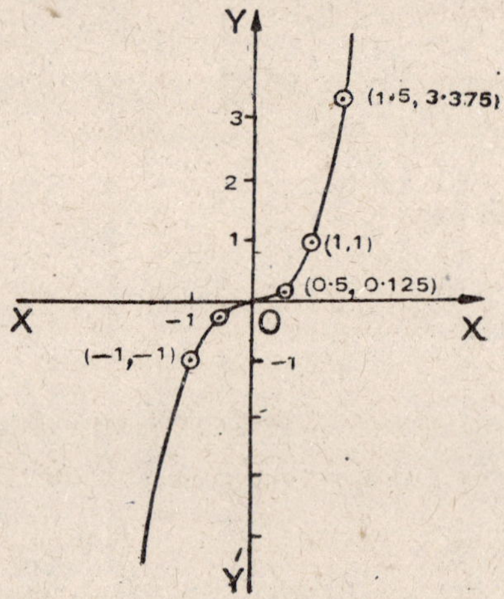

Fig 5.18

The graph is shown in the first and the third quadrant and it passes through the origin (0, 0). It is symmetrical about the origin O. [See Fig. 5.18.]

Exercise 5 (II)

[Graph of Functions]

1. Draw the graphs of the following linear functions:

(i) $x = 3$; (ii) $y = 6$; (iii) $y = -x$; (iv) $y = 2x + 3$.

[The domain of x in each case is the set of all real numbers.]

2. Draw the graph of each of the following functions:

(i) $\frac{x}{4} + \frac{y}{5} = 1$; (ii) $y = 3 - 2x$; (iii) $2y = 3x + 1$.

3. Draw the graph of each of the following functions:

(i) $\left.\begin{aligned} y &= 1, \text{ if } x \geq 0 \\ &= 0, \text{ if } x < 0 \\ &= -1, \text{ if } x < 0 \end{aligned}\right\}$; (ii) $\left.\begin{aligned} y &= 3 \text{ if } x \geq 0 \\ &= -3 \text{ if } x < 0 \end{aligned}\right\}$

(iii) $\left.\begin{aligned} f(x) &= x \text{ when } x \geq 0 \\ &= -x \text{ when } x < 0 \end{aligned}\right\}$; (iv) $f(x) = |x|$.

4. Draw the graph of each of the following functions:

(i) $\begin{aligned} y &= 2x, \text{ if } x > 0 \\ &= 0, \text{ if } x = 0 \\ &= -2x, \text{ if } x < 0. \end{aligned}$ (ii) $\begin{aligned} f(x) &= -x, \text{ when } x \leq 0, \\ &= x, \text{ when } 0 < x < 1. \end{aligned}$

From the graph find the value of $f(x)$ at $x = -\frac{1}{2}$.

5. Draw the graph of each of the following functions:

(i) $\left.\begin{aligned} f(x) &= x - 1, \text{ when } x > 0 \\ &= -\frac{1}{2}, \text{ when } x = 0 \\ &= x + 1, \text{ when } x < 0 \end{aligned}\right\}$; (ii) $\left.\begin{aligned} f(x) &= x, \text{ when } x < 1 \\ &= 1 + x, \text{ when } x > 1 \\ &= \frac{3}{2}, \text{ when } x = 1. \end{aligned}\right\}$.

From the graph find $f(1)$ and $f(\frac{1}{2})$.

[HINTS. See worked out Ex. 7 and 8.]

6. A function $f(x)$ is defined as:

$$\begin{aligned} f(x) &= 1 + 2x, \text{ when } x \leq 1 \\ &= 3 - x, \text{ when } x > 1. \end{aligned}$$

Draw the graph of the function.

7. Draw a neat diagram of the function:

$$f(x) = |x - 4| - 2.$$

[HINTS. $|x - 4| = x - 4$, if $x \geq 4$, $= 4 - x$, if $x < 4$

$\therefore$ $f(x) = x - 4 - 2 = x - 6$ if $x \geq 4$ and $f(x) = 4 - x - 2 = 2 - x$ if $x < 4$. Now draw the graph of $y = x - 6$ if $x \geq 4$ and $y = 2 - x$ if $x < 4$.]

8. Draw the graph of each of the following functions.

(i) $f(x) = \frac{|x|}{x}$; (ii) $g(x) = \frac{x}{|x|}$ **[CU 1986]**

[HINTS. $f(x) = \frac{x}{x} = 1$, if $x > 0$, and $f(x) = -\frac{x}{x} = -1$ if $x < 0$ and $f(x)$ is undefined at $x = 0$. See worked out Ex. 2 and for (i) and (ii); exclude the origin from the graph.]

9. Draw the graph of each of the following functions:

(i) $y = x^2$ (take at least ten points on the graph).

(ii) $y = \frac{4}{x}$ or $xy = 4$ (take at least five positive and five negative values of x and y)

(iii) $\begin{aligned} y &= 1 \text{ if } x \leq 0 \\ &= x^2 + 1 \text{ if } 0 < x < 2. \end{aligned}$

10. Draw the graph of the function: $y = 2x^2 - 10x + 15, x \in R$.

Chapter 6

LIMITS OF ALGEBRAIC FUNCTIONS

6.1. INTRODUCTION

The concept of *limit* is the foundation of Calculus and this concept plays an important role throughout the whole structure of Calculus. In this Chapter, we shall discuss both analytical and graphical ideas of *limit* with the concepts of a continuous variable x and a function $f(x)$ of x. Every attempt will be made to make the ideas clear from intuitive approach.

6.2. MEANING OF 'X TENDS TO a' : LIMIT OF A FUNCTION

If x be a real variable and 'a' be a fixed number, then by 'x tends to a' (written as '$x \to a$'), we mean that x assumes successively values (either greater than a or less than a) whose numerical differences from a i.e., $|x - a|$ becomes smaller and smaller and can ultimately be taken to be less than any small positive quantity we can name (i.e., less than any pre-assigned positive quantity δ, however small). In this case, x is very close to a (but $x \neq a$) and we say that 'x approaches a'.

If x approaches 'a' only through values greater than 'a' such that $x - a$ becomes smaller and smaller, then we say that 'x tends to a from the right side' and we express it by '$x \to a^+$'. In this case, x is very close to a and greater than a.

Similarly, if x approaches 'a' through values less than a such that $a - x$ becomes smaller and smaller, then we say hat 'x tends to a from the left side' and we express it by '$x \to a^-$'. In this case, x is very close to a and less than a.

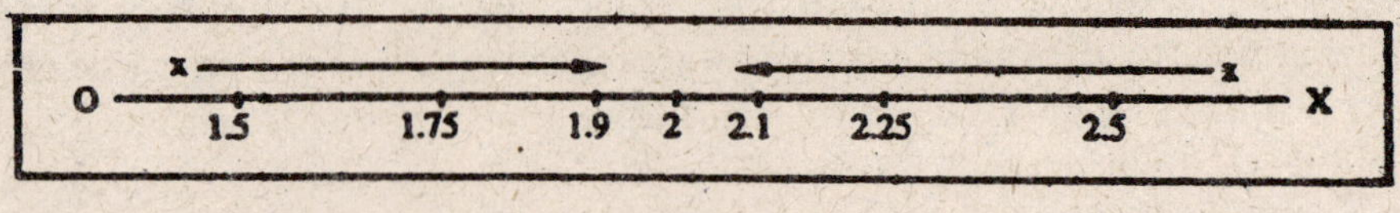

Fig 6.1

ILLUSTRATION 1. Let x be a real variable such that x assumes successively the values 2.1, 2.01, 2.001, 2.0001, $\cdots$. Then the difference $x-2$ becomes smaller and smaller and x becomes closer and closer to 2. In this case, we say that 'x tends to 2 from the right side' and we write $x \to 2^+$ or $x \to 2+0$.

Next let x assume successively the values $1.9, 1.99, 1.999, 1.999, \cdots$.

Then the difference $2-x$ becomes smaller and smaller and x becomes closer and closer to 2. In this case, we say that x tends to 2 from the left side and we write $x \to 2^-$ or $x \to 2-0$.

If $x = 2\cdot1, 2\cdot01, 2\cdot001, \cdots$ or, $x = 1\cdot9, 1\cdot99, 1\cdot999, \cdots$, then we say that x approaches 2 from either side and we write $x \to 2$. In this case, $|x-2| < \delta$ where δ is a pre-assigned positive number, however small.

ILLUSTRATION 2. By '$x \to 2+$', we mean that x assumes successively the values $2\cdot5$, $2\cdot25$, $2\cdot1$, $2\cdot01$, $2\cdot001$, $2\cdot0001, \cdots$. In this case, $x-2 < \delta$, where $\delta = a$ pre-assigned positive number, however small.

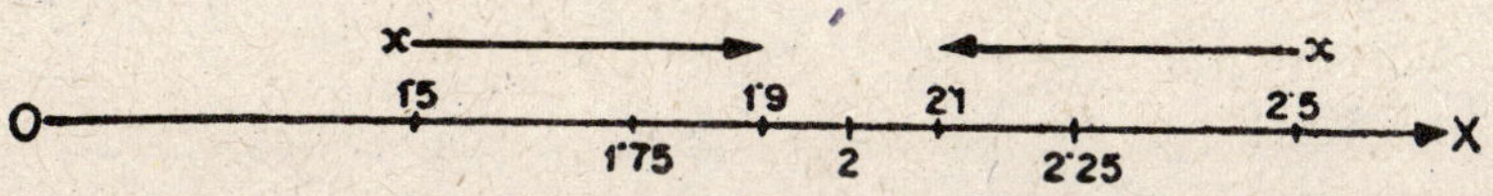

Fig 6.2

By '$x \to 2-$' we mean that x assumes successively the values $1\cdot5$, $1\cdot75$, $1\cdot9$, $1\cdot99$, $1\cdot999$, $1\cdot9999, \cdots$. In this case, $2-x < \delta$. If x approaches 2 either through values greater than 2 or through values less than 2 such that $|x-2| < \delta$, where δ is a pre-assigned positive number, however small, then we say that $x \to 2$.

Geometric idea of 'x → a'

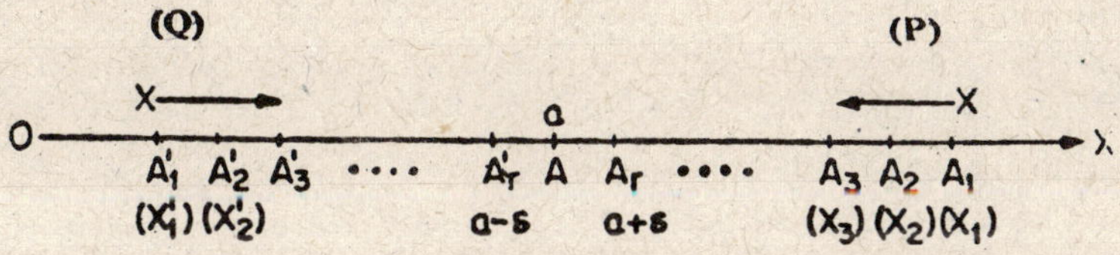

Fig 6.3

Like us take a point A on the number axis OX corresponding to the number 'a'. We take a value x_1 of x greater than a and plot it to the right of a, say at A_1. Next we take a value x_2 of x so that the corresponding point A_2 on OX lies between A and A_1 and, in this case, the value x_2 is nearer to a than x_1. We next take another value x_3 of x which corresponds to the point A_3 on OX lying between A and A_2 and in this case, the value x_3 is more close to a than x_2. Proceeding in this way we see that x remaining greater than a comes nearer and nearer to a. In this case, we say that the moving point P corresponding to x is approaching A from the right side or we say that x is approaching the fixed number a from the right side. If the process is continued indefinitely, P comes closer and closer to A without ever reaching it. Let A_r be an arbitrary point on the right of A and let A_r corresponds to the value $a+\delta$ of x (where δ is a positive number, no matter how small). If the successive values of x be such that the corresponding points ultimately cross A_r and remain within (A, A_r), then we say that the moving point $P \to A$ from the right or we say that x *tends to 'a' from the right* and we write $x \to a^+$ or $x \to a+0$.

Similarly, we may start from A_1' on the left of A corresponding to the value x_1' of x (less than a) and take the point A_2' between A and A_1' corresponding to the value x_2' which is nearer to a than x_1' so that the moving point Q comes nearer to A than A_1' and the process is continued as before until we cross A_r' corresponding to $x = a - \delta$. If the successive values of x be such that the corresponding points ultimately cross A_r' and remain within (A_r', A), then we say that the moving point $Q \to A$ from the left or we say that x *tends to 'a' from the left* and we write $x \to a^-$ or $x \to a - 0$.

NOTE. By $x \to a$, we mean that (i) $x \to a^+$ and $x \to a^-$; (ii) the successive values of x ultimately remain within an internal $(a-\delta, a+\delta)$ but $x \neq a$. This may be written as $0 < |x-a| < \delta$, where δ is an arbitrary poistive number, however small.

Mathematically, by $x \to a$, we mean.

Given any positive number δ, however small, the successive values of x ultimately satisfy the relation

$$0 < |x-a| < \delta, \quad \text{or,} \quad a-\delta < x < a+\delta \ (x \neq a).$$

Meaning of $x \to \infty$ and $x \to -\infty$

If x assumes positive values only and the successive values of x ultimately become and remain greater than any pre-assigned positive number N, however large, then we say that x *tends to infinity* or x *has an infinite limit* and denote it by $x \to \infty$.

If x assumes negative values only and the successive values of $-x$ ultimately become and remain greater than any pre-assigned positive number N, however large, then we say that $x \to -\infty$ or x *has a limit* $-\infty$.

6.3. LIMIT OF A FUNCTION

Let f be a real function; if $f(x)$ is defined for all real values of x in a neighbourhood of a fixed number 'a' and $f(x)$ approaches a fixed number 'l' as x approaches 'a' from either side of a, then 'l' is called the limit of f as $x \to a$ and we write

$$\underset{x \to a}{\text{Lt}}\ f(x) = l \quad \text{or} \quad \lim_{x \to a} f(x) = l$$

In this case 'l' is also called the **limiting value** of $f(x)$ when $x \to a$.

REMARKS. If $f(x) \to l$ as $x \to a$, then l is the limit of f as $x \to a$ (or the limit of the function at a). If no such l exists, then we say that $\lim_{x \to a} f(x)$ does not exist or the limit at a does not exist.

ILLUSTRATION 3. Suppose we have to evaluate $\lim_{x \to 2} f(x)$, where $f(x) = 2x + 3$.

$x \to 2+$	$2 \cdot 1$	$2 \cdot 01$	$2 \cdot 001$	$2 \cdot 0001$	$2 \cdot 00001$	$2 \cdot 000001$	$\cdots$
$f(x) \equiv 2x+3$	$7 \cdot 2$	$7 \cdot 02$	$7 \cdot 002$	$7 \cdot 0002$	$7 \cdot 00002$	$7 \cdot 000002$	$\cdots$

From the above table, we see that as $x \to 2^+$, $f(x) \to 7$. Here 7 is called the *right hand limit* of $f(x)$ as $x \to 2^+$. [We can write $\lim_{x \to 2^+} f(x) = 7$.]

Again,

$x \to 2-$	$1 \cdot 9$	$1 \cdot 99$	$1 \cdot 999$	$1 \cdot 9999$	$1 \cdot 99999$	$\cdots$
$f(x) \equiv 2x+3$	$6 \cdot 8$	$6 \cdot 98$	$6 \cdot 998$	$6 \cdot 9998$	$6 \cdot 99998$	$\cdots$

From this table, we see that as $x \to 2^-, f(x) \to 7$.

Here 7 is called the *left hand limit of* $f(x)$ as $x \to 2^-$.

Thus, we find that as $x \to 2$ from either side, $f(x) \to 7$. [We can write $\lim\limits_{x \to 2^-} f(x) = 7$.]

Hence $\lim\limits_{x \to 2} f(x) = 7$.

NOTE. If we put $x = a$ in $f(x)$, we get the functional value $f(a)$. In general $f(a) \neq l$. Even if $f(a)$ is undefined, the limiting value l of $f(x)$ when $x \to a$ may be a definite finite number.

As the concept of limit is abstract, we shall provide various types of worked out examples to enable the students to grasp the concept. We first discuss the process of finding limits of some simple functions.

EXAMPLE 1. *Evaluate each of the following limits:*

(i) $\lim\limits_{x \to 0} (2x^2 + 3x + 4)$; (ii) $\lim\limits_{x \to 2} (x^2 + 1)$.

SOLUTION.

(i) $\lim\limits_{x \to 0} (2x^2 + 3x + 4)$.

Since $x \to 0$, x is very close to 0 and, therefore, it is negligibly small.

$\therefore$ $2x^2$ and $3x$ are also negligibly small.

Hence $\lim\limits_{x \to 0} (2x^2 + 3x + 4) = 0 + 0 + 4 = 4$.

(ii)

$$\lim_{x \to 2} (x^2 + 1)$$

Put $x = 2 + h$, then as $x \to 2, h \to 0$, since $(x - 2)$ is negligibly small.

$$= \lim_{h \to 0} \{(2+h)^2 + 1\} = \lim_{h \to 0} \{4 + 4h + h^2 + 1\}$$

$$= \lim_{h \to 0} (5 + 4h + h^2) = 5 + 0 + 0 = \mathbf{5}.$$

EXAMPLE 2. *Find each of the following:*

(i) $\lim\limits_{x \to 2} \frac{x^2-1}{x+3}$; (ii) $\lim\limits_{x \to 3} \frac{x^2-9}{x-3}$. **[C.U. B.Com 1988, 1990]**

SOLUTION.

(i) $\lim\limits_{x \to 2} \frac{x^2-1}{x+3}$.

In this case, we find the limits of the numerator and denominator separately and then the limit of the given function.

$$\lim_{x \to 2} (x^2 - 1) = \lim_{h \to 0} \{(2+h)^2 - 1\} = \lim_{h \to 0} (3 + 4h + h^2) \quad [\text{putting } x = 2 + h]$$

$$= 3 [\text{since } h \to 0, 4h \text{ and } h^2 \text{ are negligibly small}]$$

and $\lim\limits_{x \to 2} (x + 3) = \lim\limits_{h \to 0} (2 + h + 3) = \lim\limits_{h \to 0} (5 + h) = 5 \quad \therefore \quad \lim\limits_{x \to 2} \dfrac{x^2 - 1}{x + 3} = \dfrac{3}{5}$.

(ii) In this case, the above method cannot be used.

For, $\lim_{x\to 3} x^2-9 = \lim_{h\to 0}\{(3+h)^2-9\} = \lim_{h\to 0}(6h+h^2) = 0$, $\lim_{x\to 0}(x-3) = \lim_{h\to 0}\{(3+h)-3\} = \lim_{h\to 0} h = 0$ and the given limit $= \frac{0}{0}$ which is undefined.

To evaluate the given limit we proceed as follows:

Put $x = 3 + h$ in the given function; then as $x \to 3, h \to 0$.

$$\therefore \quad \frac{x^2-9}{x-3} = \frac{(3+h)^2-9}{3+h-3} = \frac{6h+h^2}{h} = \frac{h(6+h)}{h} = 6+h \qquad [\because \ h \neq 0]$$

Hence, $\lim_{x\to 3}\frac{x^2-9}{x-3} = \lim_{h\to 0}(6+h) = 6.$

Second Method

$$x^2-9 = x^2-3^2 = (x+3)(x-3)$$

$$\therefore \quad \lim_{x\to 3}\frac{x^2-9}{x-3} = \lim_{x\to 3}\frac{(x+3)(x-3)}{(x-3)} = \lim_{x\to 3}(x+3) = 3+3 = 6. \qquad [\because \ x \neq 3]$$

EXAMPLE 3. *Evaluate:* $\lim_{x\to 2}\frac{x^2-3x+2}{x^2+x-6} = \frac{1}{5}$.

SOLUTION. We have

$$x^2-3x+2 = x^2-2x-x+2 = x(x-2)-1(x-2) = (x-2)(x-1)$$

$$\text{and} \quad x^2+x-6 = x^2+3x-2x-6 = x(x+3)-2(x+3) = (x+3)(x-2)$$

$$\therefore \quad \lim_{x\to 2}\frac{x^2-3x+2}{x^2+x-6} = \lim_{x\to 2}\frac{(x-2)(x-1)}{(x+3)(x-2)} = \lim_{x\to 2}\frac{x-1}{x+3} = \frac{2-1}{2+3} = \frac{1}{5}. \qquad [\because \ x \neq 2]$$

6.3.1. Graphical Approach

EXAMPLE 4. *Evaluate:* $\lim_{x\to 1}\frac{x^2-1}{x-1}$ *with the help of the graph of the function* $y = \frac{x^2-1}{x-1}$.

SOLUTION. Let us draw the graph of the function $y = \frac{x^2-1}{x-1}$. From the graph we shall find the limit of y (if it exists) as $x \to 1$.

We have $y = \frac{x^2-1}{x-1} = x+1$ when $x \neq 1$, and y is undefined at $x = 1$.

On the x-axis OX, the point A corresponds to 1 and on the y-axis the point C corresponds to 2. B is the point $(1, 2)$ on the graph.

Let $x \to 1$ from the right. Then the moving point P corresponding to x passes through the successive positions $A_1, A_2, \cdots$ and comes nearer and nearer to A from the right.

Corresponding to the points $A_1, A_2, \cdots$ on OX, let $P_1, P_2, \cdots$ be the points on the graph of $y = f(x) = \frac{x^2-1}{x-1}$ and $C_1, C_2, \cdots$ be the points on the y-axis. Then as $x \to 1^+$ passing through the points $A_1, A_2, \cdots$, from the graph of Fig. 6.4 we see that the corresponding moving point on the graph approaches the point B passing through the points $P_1, P_2, \cdots$ along the line $y = x+1$ and consequently the corresponding moving point on the y-axis approaches the point C passing through the points $C_1, C_2, \cdots$ from above.

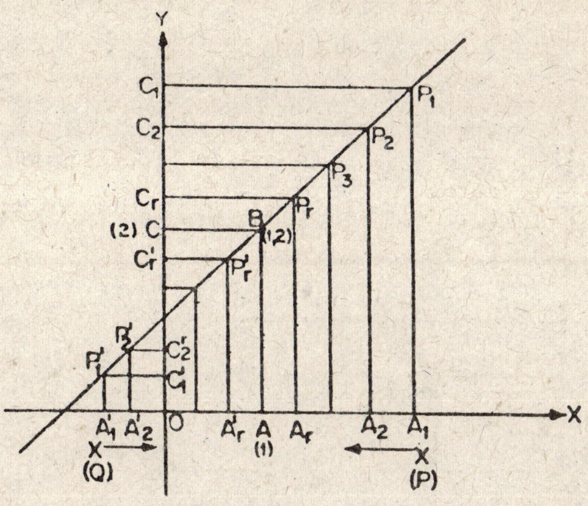

Fig 6.4

Next let $x \to 1$ from the left (i.e., let $x \to 1^-$). Then the moving point Q corresponding to x passess through the points A'_1, $A'_2, \cdots$ and comes closer and closer to B from the left. Corresponding to A'_1, $A'_2, \cdots$, let P'_1, $P'_2, \cdots$ be the points on the graph of $y = \frac{x^2-1}{x-1}$ and $C'_1, C'_2, \cdots$ be the points on the y-axis. Then as $x \to 1^-$ passing through the points $A'_1, A'_2, \cdots$, we see that the corresponding points on the graph appproach B and consequently the corresponding points on the y-axis approach C from below.

Since the moving point on the y-axis approaches $C(y = 2)$ both from above and below, we say that $y \to 2^+$ and $y \to 2^-$ as $x \to 1$ from the right and from the left.

Hence, $\mathbf{y \to 2}$ **as** $\mathbf{x \to 1}$**, or** $\lim\limits_{\mathbf{x \to 1}} \mathbf{y = 2}$**, or** $\lim\limits_{\mathbf{x \to 1}} \frac{\mathbf{x^2-1}}{\mathbf{x-1}} = \mathbf{2}$.

When $y \to 2$ as $x \to 1^+$, the limit is called the **right-hand limit**, and when $y \to 2$ as $x \to 1^-$, the limit is called the **left-hand limit**.

Note that in the above problem, $f(1)$ *does not exist, but* $\lim\limits_{x \to 1} f(x)$ *exists and is equal to* 2.

Analytical or Precise definition of limit of a function [(δ, ϵ) definition]

Mathematically, if corresponding to an arbitrary positive number ϵ, however small, we can find a positive numbers δ (depending on ϵ) such that

$$|f(x) - l| < \epsilon, \text{ when } 0 < |x - a| < \delta,$$

then we say that $f(x) \to l$ as $x \to a$ and we write $\lim\limits_{x \to a} f(x) = l$.

NOTE. Here $|f(x) - l| < \epsilon$ when $0 < |x - a| < \delta$ means that $f(x)$ lies between $l - \epsilon$ and $l + \epsilon$ for all x in $a - \delta < x < a + \delta$, but $x \neq a$.

ILLUSTRATION 4. *Using (δ, ϵ) definition, we shall show that* $\lim\limits_{x \to 1} (2x + 3) = 5$.

Here $f(x) = 2x + 3, l = 5, a = 1$.

Let ϵ be a given arbitrary positive number, however small. Then '5' will be the limiting value of $2x + 3$ as $x \to 1$ if we can find a positive number δ depending on ϵ such that $|(2x + 3) - 5| < \epsilon$ when $|x - 1| < \delta$.

$$\text{Now,} \quad |(2x + 3) - 5| < \epsilon \text{ when } |2x - 2| < \epsilon,$$

$$\text{or,} \quad 2|x - 1| < \epsilon, \text{ or, } |x - 1| < \epsilon/2.$$

Taking $\delta = \epsilon/2$, we obtain

$$|(2x+3)-5| < \epsilon \text{ when } |x-1| < \delta \text{ where } \delta = \epsilon/2$$

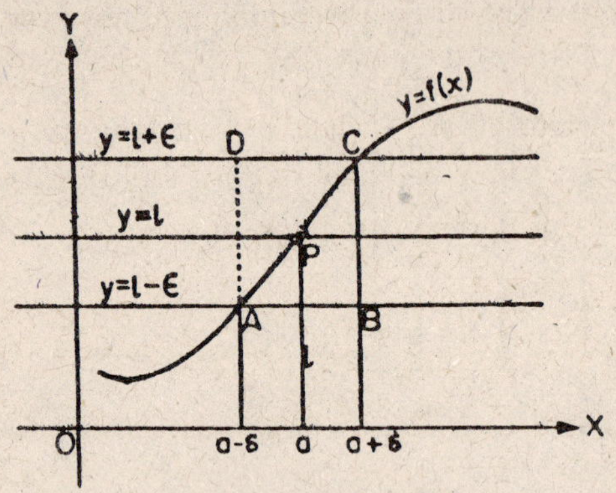

Fig 6.5

Hence $\lim_{x\to 1}(2x+3) = 5$.

Graphically, *the above* (δ, ϵ) *definition has the following meaning:*

When an arbitrary positive number ϵ is given, we draw three straight lines $y = l - \epsilon, y = l$ and $y = l + \epsilon$ parallel to the x-axis.

To establish $\lim_{x\to a} f(x) = l$, we have to find a positive number δ for each given ϵ such that the values of $f(x)$ for $a - \delta < x < a + \delta$ $(x \neq a)$ will lie within the rectangle $ABCD$ bounded by the lines $y = l - \epsilon, y = l + \epsilon, x = a - \delta, x = a + \delta$.

6.3.2. One Sided Limits : Right-hand and Left-hand Limits

If $f(x) \to l_1$ as $x \to a^+$ i.e., as x takes values very close to a, always remaining greater than a, then l_1 is called *the right-hand limit* or *right limit of f at a* and we write

$$\lim_{x\to a^+} f(x) = l_1.$$

Analytically, given an arbitrary positive number ϵ, however small; if it is possible to find a positive number δ such that

$$|f(x) - l_1| < \epsilon \text{ when } a < x < a + \delta,$$

then we say that l_1 is the **Right-hand limit** of $f(x)$ as $x \to a^+$ and we write $\lim_{x\to a^+} f(x) = l_1$]

If $f(x) \to l_2$ as $x \to a^-$ i.e., as x takes values very close to a, always remaining less than a, then l_2 is called the *left-hand limit* or *left limit of f* at a, and we write

$$\lim_{x\to a^-} f(x) = l_2.$$

[*Analytically,* given an arbitrary positive number ϵ, however small, if we can find a positive number δ such that

$$|f(x) - l_2| < \epsilon \text{ when } a - \delta < x < a,$$

then we say that l_2 is the Left-hand limit of $f(x)$ as $x \to a^-$ and we write $\lim_{x\to a^-} f(x) = l_2$]

Existence of $\lim_{x\to a} f(x)$

If the right-hand limit, i.e., $\lim_{x\to a^+} f(x)$ and the left-hand limit, i.e., $\lim_{x\to a^-} f(x)$, both exist and $\lim_{x\to a^+} f(x) = \lim_{x\to a^-} f(x)$, then $\lim_{x\to a} f(x)$ exists and is equal to the common value of the above two limits, i.e.,

$$\lim_{x\to a} f(x) = \lim_{x\to a^+} f(x) = \lim_{x\to a^-} f(x).$$

Distinction between $\lim_{x \to a} f(x)$ and $f(a)$

If we substitute $x = a$ in $f(x)$, we get the **functional value f(a)** i.e., $f(a)$ is the value of $f(x)$ when x is exactly equal to a. But $\lim_{x \to a} f(x)$ is the **limiting value of f(x)** when x approaches a from either side of a i.e., when $|x - a|$ can be made less than any pre-assigned positive number δ, however small, but $x \neq a$. In general $\lim_{x \to a} f(x) \neq f(a)$.

In fact, $f(a)$ may be undefined, but still the limiting value of $f(x)$ when $x \to a$ may be a definite finite number and vice-versa. As a special case, $\lim_{x \to a} f(x)$ may be equal to $f(a)$ and in this case, $f(x)$ is said to be *continuous* at $x = a$. We shall discuss this special case later on.

EXAMPLE 5. *Prove that* $\lim_{x \to 0} |x| = 0$, *but* $\lim_{x \to 0} \frac{|x|}{x}$ *does not exist.*

SOLUTION. We know that

$$\begin{aligned} |x| &= x \text{ if } x > 0 \\ &= 0 \text{ if } x = 0 \\ &= -x \text{ if } x < 0 \end{aligned}$$

$$\lim_{x \to 0+} |x| = \lim_{x \to 0+} x = 0 \qquad [\because \ |x| = x \text{ if } x > 0]$$

$$\text{and} \quad \lim_{x \to 0-} |x| = \lim_{x \to 0-} (-x) = 0 \qquad [\because \ |x| = -x \text{ if } x < 0]$$

$$\therefore \quad \lim_{x \to 0+} |x| = \lim_{x \to 0-} |x| = 0.$$

Hence $\lim_{x \to 0} |x| = 0$.

Second Part

$$\lim_{x \to 0+} \frac{|x|}{x} = \lim_{x \to 0+} \frac{x}{x} = \lim_{x \to 0+} 1 = 1 \qquad [\because \ |x| = x \text{ if } x > 0.]$$

$$\text{and} \quad \lim_{x \to 0-} \frac{|x|}{x} = \lim_{x \to 0^-} \frac{-x}{x} = \lim_{x \to 0^-} (-1) = -1. \qquad [\because \ |x| = -x \text{ if } x < 0.]$$

$$\therefore \quad \lim_{x \to 0+} \frac{|x|}{x} \neq \lim_{x \to 0-} \frac{|x|}{x}.$$

Hence $\lim_{x \to 0} \frac{|x|}{x}$ does not exist.

6.4. OTHER TYPES OF LIMITS

I. Function tending to infinity: Meaning of $f(x) \to \infty$ as $x \to a$

(i) Intuitively, by '$f(x) \to \infty$ as $x \to a$', we mean that when x approaches a from either side, $f(x)$ becomes larger and larger and ultimately exceeds any positive number we can name and in this case,

we write $\lim_{x \to a} f(x) = \infty$.

(ii) Using (δ, ϵ) definition, by '$f(x) \to \infty$ as $x \to a$', we mean that corresponding to any pre-assigned positive number N, however large, we can find a positive number δ, however small, such that

$$f(x) > N \quad \text{when} \quad 0 < |x - a| < \delta.$$

ILLUSTRATION 5. $\lim\limits_{x \to 0} \frac{1}{x^2} = \infty$.

(i) *Intuitively,* $\lim\limits_{x \to 0+} \frac{1}{x^2} = \infty$ *and* $\lim\limits_{x \to 0-} \frac{1}{x^2} = \infty$.

[Since as $x \to 0^+, x^2 \to 0$ and $\frac{1}{x^2} \to \infty$. Similarly for $x \to 0^-$.]

(ii) Using *Precise definition,* given any positive number G, we have to find δ such that

$$\frac{1}{x^2} > G \text{ when } 0 < |x - 0| < \delta.$$

$$\text{Now,} \quad \frac{1}{x^2} > G \text{ if } x^2 < \frac{1}{G}, \text{ i.e., if } |x| < \frac{1}{\sqrt{G}}$$

$$\text{i.e., if} \quad -\frac{1}{\sqrt{G}} < x < \frac{1}{\sqrt{G}}.$$

Taking $\delta = \frac{1}{\sqrt{G}}$, we have $\frac{1}{x^2} > G$ when $0 < |x| < \delta$.

Hence, $\lim\limits_{x \to 0} \frac{1}{x^2} = \infty$.

II. $\lim\limits_{x \to \infty} f(x) = 1$. (Independent variable x tends to infinity)

(i) *Intuitively,* by $f(x) \to l$ as $x \to \infty$, we mean that when x becomes larger and larger, $f(x)$ becomes closer and closer to l.

(ii) *Using (δ, ϵ) definition,* by $f(x) \to l$ as $x \to \infty$, we mean that corresponding to any pre-assigned positive number ϵ, however small, we can find a positive number N such that

$$|f(x) - l| < \epsilon \text{ for all } x > N.$$

ILLUSTRATION 6. $\lim\limits_{x \to \infty} \left(\frac{1}{x} + 1\right) = 1$.

(i) *Intuitively,* as $x \to \infty, \frac{1}{x} \to 0. \quad \therefore \quad \lim\limits_{x \to \infty} \left(\frac{1}{x} + 1\right) = 1$.

(ii) *Precisely,* let ϵ be any given arbitrary positive number, however small, we have to find a positive number N such that

$$\left|\left(\frac{1}{x} + 1\right) - 1\right| < \epsilon \text{ when } x > N.$$

$$\text{Now,} \quad \left|\left(\frac{1}{x} + 1\right) - 1\right| < \epsilon \text{ if } \left|\frac{1}{x}\right| < \epsilon \text{ i.e., if } \frac{1}{|x|} < \epsilon$$

$$\text{i.e., if} \quad |x| > \frac{1}{\epsilon} \text{ i.e., if } x > \frac{1}{\epsilon} \quad [\because \quad x \text{ is positive.}]$$

Taking $N = \frac{1}{\epsilon}$, we get $\left|\left(\frac{1}{x} + 1\right) - 1\right| < \epsilon$ when $x > N$.

Hence, $\lim_{x\to\infty}\left(\frac{1}{x}+1\right)=1$.

III. $\lim_{x\to\infty} f(x)=\infty$ (*Function* $\to\infty$ *as independent variable* $\to\infty$)

(i) *Intuitively,* as x becomes larger and larger, $f(x)$ also becomes larger and larger.

(ii) *Precisely,* given any positive number G, we can find another positive number N such that

$$f(x) > G \text{ when } x > N.$$

ILLUSTRATION 7. $\lim_{x\to\infty} x^2=\infty$ $[\because$ as $x\to\infty, x^2\to\infty.]$

IV. $\lim_{x\to a} f(x)=-\infty$ [*Finction tends to* $-\infty$ *when* $x\to\infty$.]

(i) *Intuitively,* as x approaches $a, -f(x)$ becomes larger and larger.

(ii) *Precisely,* given any positive number G, however large, we can find a positive number δ, no matter how small, such that

$$-f(x) > G \text{ when } 0<|x-a|<\delta.$$

EXAMPLE 6. *Does any of the following limits exist? Give reasons for your answer.*

(i) $\lim_{x\to 0}\frac{1}{x}$; (ii) $\lim_{x\to 0}\frac{1}{x^2}$; (iii) $\lim_{x\to 0}\frac{1}{x^3}$; (iv) $\lim_{x\to 0}\frac{1}{x^4}$

SOLUTION. (i) As $x\to 0^+, \frac{1}{x}\to+\infty$ and as $x\to 0^-, \frac{1}{x}\to-\infty$.

$\therefore$ $\lim_{x\to 0}\frac{1}{x}$ does not exist.

(ii) As $x\to 0^+, \frac{1}{x^2}\to+\infty$ and as $x\to 0^-, \frac{1}{x^2}\to+\infty$.

$\therefore$ $\lim_{x\to 0}\frac{1}{x^2}$ *exists,* but the limit is *infinite,* i.e., $\lim_{x\to 0}\frac{1}{x^2}=\infty$.

(iii) As in (i) the limit does not exist.

(iv) As in (ii), $\lim_{x\to 0}\frac{1}{x^4}=+\infty$.

6.5. THEOREMS ON LIMITS

To evaluate the limits of various functions, the following theorems will be frequently used.

Let $f(x)$ and $\phi(x)$ be two functions of a real variable x. If $\lim_{x\to a} f(x)=l$, and $\lim_{x\to a}\phi(x)=l'$, where l and l' are finite quantities, then

(1) $\lim_{x\to a}\{f(x)\pm\phi(x)\}=\lim_{x\to a} f(x)\pm\lim_{x\to a}\phi(x)=l\pm l'$;

(2) $\lim_{x\to a}\{f(x)\times\phi(x)\}=\lim_{x\to a} f(x)\times\lim_{x\to a}\phi(x)=l\times l'$;

(3) $\lim_{x\to a}\left\{\frac{f(x)}{\phi(x)}\right\}=\frac{\lim_{x\to a} f(x)}{\lim_{x\to a}\phi(x)}=\frac{l}{l'}$. [provided $l'\neq 0$]

(4) $\lim_{x\to a} C=C$, where C is a *constant,*

and $\lim_{x\to a} Cf(x)=C\lim_{x\to a} f(x)$

(5) If $\phi(x)\leq f(x)\leq\psi(x)$ and $\lim_{x\to a}\phi(x)=l$ and $\lim_{x\to a}\psi(x)=l$, then $\lim_{x\to a} f(x)=l$.

(6) If $f(x) < g(x)$ for all x, then $\lim_{x \to a} f(x) \leq \lim_{x \to a} g(x)$, provided both the limits exists.

Some Important Limits

We now state some important limits without proof. These limits will be useful in the latter part of this book.

1. $\lim_{x \to 0} \frac{e^x - 1}{x} = 1;$
2. $\lim_{x \to 0} \frac{1}{x} \log(1 + x) = 1;$
3. $\lim_{x \to 0} \frac{(1+x)^n - 1}{x} = n;$
4. $\lim_{n \to \infty} x^n = 0 \quad (-1 < x < 1);$
5. $\lim_{x \to 0} \frac{a^x - 1}{x} = \log_e a (a > 0);$
6. $\lim_{n \to \infty} \frac{x^n}{\underline{|n}} = 0;$
7. $\lim_{x \to \infty} \left(x + \frac{1}{x}\right)^x = e;$
8. $\lim_{x \to a} \frac{x^n - a^n}{x - a} = na^{n-1},$

where $a > 0$ and n is any rational number.

6.6. ILLUSTRATIVE EXAMPLES

Different types of problems on limits have been solved both analytically and graphically in this article. On going through these **worked-out examples,** students will have fair idea of solving problems on limits.

EXAMPLE 1. *Discuss the limit of $f(x)$ when $x \to 0$ where*

$$f(x) = 1, \text{ for } x \geq 0$$
$$= -1, \text{ for } x < 0.$$

[C.U. B.Com(Hons.) 1982]

SOLUTION. **1st method** (*Intuitive approach*)

$$\lim_{x \to 0^+} f(x) = \lim_{x \to 0^+} 1 = 1 \quad [\because \quad x > 0.]$$

and $$\lim_{x \to 0^-} f(x) = \lim_{x \to 0^-} (-1) = -1. \quad [\because \quad x < 0.]$$

Thus, we see that both $\lim_{x \to 0^+} f(x)$ and $\lim_{x \to 0^-} f(x)$ exist, but $\lim_{x \to 0^+} f(x) \neq \lim_{x \to 0^-} f(x)$.

Hence, $\lim_{x \to 0} f(x)$ **does not exist.**

[Note that $f(0) = 1$, but $\lim_{x \to 0} f(x)$ does not exist.]

NOTE. For the limit $\lim_{x \to 0} f(x)$ to exist, both the *right hand limit* $\lim_{x \to 0^+} f(x)$ and *the left hand limit* $\lim_{x \to 0^-} f(x)$ must exist and they *must be equal.* In the above problem, right hand limit $\neq$ left hand limit.

2nd method (*Graphical approach*)

The graph (See **Fig. 5.8** in **Fifth Chapter**) consists of two straight lines, one in the first quadrant parallel to the x-axis at a height of 1 unit from it and excluding the point $(0, 1)$ and the other in the third quadrant parallel to the x-axis at a depth of 1 unit from it and excluding the point $(0, -1)$.

From the graph we see that as $x \to 0$ from the right, the ordinate $y = f(x) \to 1$ (y being always equal to 1) and as $x \to 0$ from the left, the ordinate $y = f(x) \to -1$ (y being always equal to -1).

Thus, Right hand limit $= 1$ and Left hand limit $= -1$.

Hence, $\lim\limits_{x \to 0} f(x)$ **does not exist.**

EXAMPLE 2. *Prove that* $\lim\limits_{x \to 2} \frac{x^2-4}{x-2} = 4$.

SOLUTION. **1st method** (*Intuitive approach*)

$$\begin{aligned}\lim_{x \to 2} \frac{x^2-4}{x-2} &= \lim_{h \to 0} \frac{(2+h)^2-4}{2+h-2} \qquad \text{[Putting } x = 2+h, \text{ we see that as } x \to 2, h \to 0.] \\ &= \lim_{h \to 0} \frac{4+4h+h^2-4}{h} = \lim_{h \to 0} \frac{h(4+h)}{h} \\ &= \lim_{h \to 0} (4+h) \quad [\because \quad h \neq 0] = \lim_{h \to 0} 4 + \lim_{h \to 0} h \\ &= 4 + 0 = \mathbf{4}.\end{aligned}$$

2nd method [*Using* (δ, ϵ) *definition of limit*]

Here $f(x) = \frac{x^2-4}{x-2}$, $l = 4$ and $a = 2$.

Given an arbitrary positive number ϵ, however small, we have to find a positive number δ (depending on ϵ) such that

$$|f(x) - l| < \epsilon \text{ when } 0 < |x - a| < \delta.$$

Now $|f(x) - l| < \epsilon$ if $\left|\frac{x^2-4}{x-2} - 4\right| < \epsilon$

i.e., if

$\left|\frac{(x+2)(x-2)}{x-2} - 4\right| < \epsilon$ i.e., if $|x + 2 - 4| < \epsilon$ $[\because \quad x \neq 2]$

i.e., if $|x - 2| < \epsilon$, where $x \neq 2$

Taking $\delta = \epsilon$, we see that

$$\left|\frac{x^2-4}{x-2} - 4\right| < \epsilon \text{ when } 0 < |x - 2| < \delta$$

Hence, $\lim\limits_{x \to 2} \frac{x^2-4}{x-2} = \mathbf{4}$.

To solve this problem graphically, proceed as in **Example 4.**

EXAMPLE 3. *From the graph of the function* $f(x)$ *given by* $f(x) = x$, *when* $x > 0, f(x) = 0$, *when* $x = 0, f(x) = -x$, *when* $x < 0$, *decide whether* $\lim\limits_{x \to 0} f(x)$ *exists or not.*

[C.U. B.Com(Hons.) 1982]

SOLUTION. The graph of the given function is shown in the next page **Fig. 6.6** [the method of drawing this graph is discussed in **Example 3 (worked out)** in the **1st Chapter.**]

From the graph of the function, we see that as $x \to 0$ from the right passing through the points $A_1, A_2, \cdots, y \to 0$ passing through the corresponding points $C_1, C_2, \cdots$ from above.

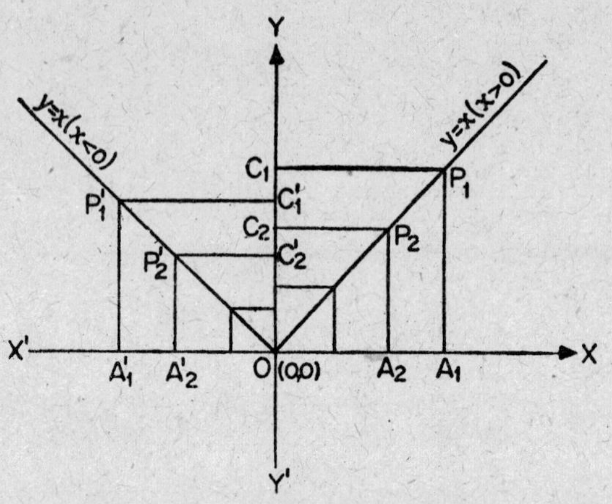

Fig 6.6

Again as $x \to 0$ from the left crossing the points $A'_1, A'_2, \cdots, y \to 0$ crossing the corresponding points $C'_1, C'_2, \cdots$ from above.

Thus, as $x \to 0$ from either side, $y \to 0$ from above.

Hence, $\lim\limits_{\mathbf{x}\to 0} \mathbf{f(x)}$ **exists** *and* $\lim\limits_{\mathbf{x}\to 0} \mathbf{f(x) = 0}$.

[**Intuitive Approach:**

$$\lim_{x\to 0^+} f(x) = \lim_{x\to 0^+} x = 0 \quad [\because \quad f(x) = x \text{ when } x > 0.]$$

$$\text{and} \quad \lim_{x\to 0^-} f(x) = \lim_{x\to 0^-} (-x) = 0. \quad [\because \quad f(x) = -x \text{ when } x < 0.]$$

Thus, $\lim\limits_{x\to 0^+} f(x)$ and $\lim\limits_{x\to 0^-} f(x)$ both *exist* and are *equal.*

Hence, $\lim\limits_{x\to 0} f(x) = 0.$]

EXAMPLE 4. *Evaluate the limit* $\lim\limits_{x\to 1} \frac{x^2-2x+3}{x+4}$. **[C.U. B.Com. (Hons.) 1983]**

SOLUTION. $\lim\limits_{x\to 1} \frac{x^2-2x+3}{x+4}$

$$= \lim_{h\to 0} \frac{(1+h)^2 - 2(1+h) + 3}{1+h+4} \quad \begin{array}{r}\text{Putting } x = 1+h, \text{ we see} \\ \text{that as } x \to 1, h \to 0.]\end{array}$$

$$= \lim_{h\to 0} \frac{1 + 2h + h^2 - 2 - 2h + 3}{h+5} = \lim_{h\to 0} \frac{h^2+2}{h+5} = \frac{0+2}{0+5} = \frac{\mathbf{2}}{\mathbf{5}}.$$

EXAMPLE 5. *Evaluate the following limits*

(i) $\lim\limits_{x\to 2} \frac{x^2-5x+6}{x^2-7x+10}$; (ii) $\lim\limits_{x\to 0} \frac{1-\sqrt{1-x^2}}{x^2}$. **[C.U. B.Com (Hons.) 1982]**

SOLUTION.

(i) $\lim_{x\to 2}\frac{x^2-5x+6}{x^2-7x+10}$ Put $x = 2 + h$; then as $x \to 2, h \to 0$.

$$= \lim_{h\to 0}\frac{(2+h)^2-5(2+h)+6}{(2+h)^2-7(2+h)+10}$$

$$= \lim_{h\to 0}\frac{4+4h+h^2-10-5h+6}{4+4h+h^2-14-7h+10} = \lim_{h\to 0}\frac{h^2-h}{h^2-3h}$$

$$= \lim_{h\to 0}\frac{h(h-1)}{h(h-3)} = \lim_{h\to 0}\frac{h-1}{h-3} \quad [\because \quad h \neq 0]$$

$$= \frac{\lim_{h\to 0}(h-1)}{\lim_{h\to 0}(h-3)} = \frac{\lim_{h\to 0}h - \lim_{h\to 0}1}{\lim_{h\to 0}h - \lim_{h\to 0}3} = \frac{0-1}{0-3} = \mathbf{\frac{1}{3}}.$$

(ii) $\lim_{x\to 0}\frac{1-\sqrt{1-x^2}}{x^2}$

$$= \lim_{x\to 0}\frac{(1-\sqrt{1-x^2})(1+\sqrt{1-x^2})}{x^2(1+\sqrt{1-x^2})} = \lim_{x\to 0}\frac{1-(\sqrt{1-x^2})^2}{x^2(1+\sqrt{1-x^2})}$$

$$= \lim_{x\to 0}\frac{1-(1-x^2)}{x^2(1+\sqrt{1-x^2})} = \lim_{x\to 0}\frac{x^2}{x^2(1+\sqrt{1-x^2})}$$

$$= \lim_{x\to 0}\frac{1}{1+\sqrt{1-x^2}} = \frac{1}{1+\sqrt{1-0}} = \frac{1}{1+1} = \mathbf{\frac{1}{2}}.$$

EXAMPLE 6. *Evaluate the limit:* $\lim_{x\to 0}\frac{\sqrt{2+3x}-\sqrt{2-5x}}{4x}$. **[C.U. B.Com (Hons.) 1982]**

SOLUTION.

$$\lim_{x\to 0}\frac{\sqrt{2+3x}-\sqrt{2-5x}}{4x}$$

$$= \lim_{x\to 0}\frac{(\sqrt{2+3x}-\sqrt{2-5x})(\sqrt{2+3x}+\sqrt{2-5x})}{4x(\sqrt{2+3x}+\sqrt{2-5x})}$$

$$= \lim_{x\to 0}\frac{(\sqrt{2+3x})^2-(\sqrt{2-5x})^2}{4x(\sqrt{2+3x}+\sqrt{2-5x})} = \lim_{x\to 0}\frac{(2+3x)-(2-5x)}{4x(\sqrt{2+3x}+\sqrt{2-5x})}$$

$$= \lim_{x\to 0}\frac{8x}{4x(\sqrt{2+3x}+\sqrt{2-5x})} = \lim_{x\to 0}\frac{2}{\sqrt{2+3x}+\sqrt{2-5x}}$$

$$= \frac{2}{\sqrt{2+3\cdot 0}+\sqrt{2-5\cdot 0}} = \frac{2}{\sqrt{2}+\sqrt{2}} = \frac{2}{2\sqrt{2}} = \mathbf{\frac{1}{\sqrt{2}}}.$$

EXAMPLE 7. *Evaluate the limit* $\lim_{x\to\infty}\frac{6-5x^2}{4x+15x^2}$. **[C.U. B.Com. (Hons.) 1983]**

SOLUTION. $\lim_{x\to\infty}\frac{6-5x^2}{4x+15x^2}$

$$= \lim_{x\to\infty}\frac{\frac{6}{x^2}-5}{\frac{4}{x}+15}$$ [Dividing both numerator and denominator by the highest power of x in the denominator.]

$$= \lim_{h\to 0}\frac{6h^2-5}{4h+15}$$ [Putting $\frac{1}{x} = h$, we see that as $x \to \infty, h \to 0$.]

$$= \frac{\lim_{h\to 0}(6h^2-5)}{\lim_{h\to 0}(4h+15)} = \frac{\lim_{h\to 0}6h^2 - \lim_{h\to 0}5}{\lim_{h\to 0}4h + \lim_{h\to 0}15} = \frac{6\cdot 0-5}{4\cdot 0+15}$$

$$= \frac{-5}{15} = -\mathbf{\frac{1}{3}}.$$

EXAMPLE 8. *Evaluate the limit* $\lim_{x\to 0}\frac{3x+|x|}{7x-5|x|}$, *if it exists.* **[Delhi U. B.Com. 1981]**

SOLUTION.

$$\lim_{x\to 0^+}\frac{3x+|x|}{7x-5|x|}.$$

We know that $|x| = x$, when $x>0$
$= 0$, when $x=0$
$= -x$, when $x<0$.

$$= \lim_{x\to 0^+}\frac{3x+x}{7x-5x} \qquad [\because \text{ when } x>0, |x|=x.]$$

$$= \lim_{x\to 0^+}\frac{4x}{2x} = \lim_{x\to 0^+} 2 = \mathbf{2}$$

and $$\lim_{x\to 0^-}\frac{3x+|x|}{7x-5|x|} = \lim_{x\to 0^-}\frac{3x-x}{7x-5(-x)} \qquad [\because |x|=-x, \text{ when } x<0]$$

$$= \lim_{x\to 0^-}\frac{2x}{12x} = \lim_{x\to 0^-}\frac{1}{6} = \frac{\mathbf{1}}{\mathbf{6}}. \qquad [\because x\neq 0]$$

Thus, we see that $\lim_{x\to 0^+}\frac{3x+|x|}{7x-5|x|} \neq \lim_{x\to 0^-}\frac{3x+|x|}{7x-5|x|}$

Hence, the given limit *does not exist.*

EXAMPLE 9. *Evaluate the limit* $\lim_{h\to 0}\frac{\sqrt{x+h}-\sqrt{x}}{h}$, *where* $x>0$.

[Delhi U. B.Com; Gau. U; C.U. B.Com.(Hons.) 1987]

SOLUTION.

$$\lim_{h\to 0}\frac{\sqrt{x+h}-\sqrt{x}}{h} = \lim_{h\to 0}\frac{(\sqrt{x+h}-\sqrt{x})(\sqrt{x+h}+\sqrt{x})}{h(\sqrt{x+h}+\sqrt{x})}$$

$$= \lim_{h\to 0}\frac{(\sqrt{x+h})^2-(\sqrt{x})^2}{h(\sqrt{x+h}+\sqrt{x})} = \lim_{h\to 0}\frac{x+h-x}{h(\sqrt{x+h}+\sqrt{x})}$$

$$= \lim_{h\to 0}\frac{h}{h(\sqrt{x+h}+\sqrt{x})} = \lim_{h\to 0}\frac{1}{\sqrt{x+h}+\sqrt{x}} \qquad [\because h\neq 0.]$$

$$= \frac{1}{\lim_{h\to 0}\sqrt{x+h}+\lim_{h\to 0}\sqrt{x}} = \frac{1}{\sqrt{x}+\sqrt{x}} = \frac{1}{2\sqrt{x}}$$

EXAMPLE 10. *Evaluate the limt:* $\lim_{x\to 1}\frac{x^2-1}{\sqrt{3x+1}-\sqrt{5x-1}}$ **[Bombay U.; C.U. 1991]**

SOLUTION.

$$\lim_{x\to 1}\frac{x^2-1}{\sqrt{3x+1}-\sqrt{5x-1}} = \lim_{x\to 1}\frac{(x^2-1)(\sqrt{3x+1}+\sqrt{5x-1})}{(\sqrt{3x+1}-\sqrt{5x-1})(\sqrt{3x+1}+\sqrt{5x-1})}$$

$$= \lim_{x\to 1}\frac{(x^2-1)(\sqrt{3x+1}+\sqrt{5x-1})}{(\sqrt{3x+1})^2-(\sqrt{5x-1})^2} = \lim_{x\to 1}\frac{(x^2-1)(\sqrt{3x+1}+\sqrt{5x-1})}{3x+1-5x+1}$$

$$= \lim_{x\to 1}\frac{(x+1)(x-1)(\sqrt{3x+1}+\sqrt{5x-1})}{-2(x-1)} = \lim_{x\to 1}\frac{(x+1)(\sqrt{3x+1}+\sqrt{5x-1})}{-2} \qquad [\because x\neq 1]$$

$$= -\frac{1}{2}\lim_{x\to 1}(x+1)(\sqrt{3x+1}+\sqrt{5x-1}) = -\frac{1}{2}(1+1)(\sqrt{3.1+1}+\sqrt{5.1-1})$$

$$= -\frac{1}{2}\times 2(2+2) = \mathbf{-4}.$$

EXAMPLE 11. *If* $f(x) = \frac{x+1}{+\sqrt{6x^2+3}+3x}$, *find* $\lim_{x\to -1} f(x)$ *and* $f(-1)$, *if they exist.*

[ICWAI (Final) December 1978, '82]

SOLUTION.

$$\lim_{x\to -1} f(x) = \lim_{x\to -1} \frac{x+1}{+\sqrt{6x^2+3}+3x} = \lim_{x\to -1} \frac{(x+1)(\sqrt{6x^2+3}-3x)}{(\sqrt{6x^2+3}+3x)(\sqrt{6x^2+3}-3x)}$$

$$= \lim_{x\to -1} \frac{(x+1)(\sqrt{6x^2+3}-3x)}{(6x^2+3)-(9x^2)} = \lim_{x\to -1} \frac{(x+1)(\sqrt{6x^2+3}-3x)}{3(1-x^2)}$$

$$= \lim_{x\to -1} \frac{(x+1)(\sqrt{6x^2+3}-3x)}{3(1-x)(1+x)} = \lim_{x\to -1} \frac{\sqrt{6x^2+3}-3x}{3(1-x)} \qquad [\because\ x \neq -1]$$

$$= \frac{\sqrt{6+3}+3}{3\cdot 2} = \frac{6}{6} = \mathbf{1},$$

and $f(-1) = \frac{0}{0}$ which is *undefined.*

6.7. CONTINUITY AT A POINT

The word *continuity* is used to indicate the absence of any *break* (or *gap*) in the graph of a function. If there is any *break* (or *gap*) at a point P corresponding to $x = a$, then we say that the function is *not continuous* (or discontinuous) at $x = a$.

DEFINITION. *A function $f(x)$ is said to be* **continuous at** $x = a$, *if*

(i) *$f(a)$ is defined and*

(ii) $\lim_{x\to a^+} \mathbf{f(x)} = \lim_{x\to a^-} \mathbf{f(x)} = \mathbf{f(a)}$.

Briefly, $f(x)$ is *continuous* at $x = a$ if $\lim_{x\to a} f(x) = f(a)$, provided $f(a)$ is finite and the limit exists.

If $x = a + h$, then as $x \to a, h \to 0$ and therefore,

$f(x)$ is *continuous* at $x = a$ if $\lim_{h\to 0} f(a+h) = f(a)$.

Cauchy's definition of Continuity

A function $f(x)$ is said to be **continuous** *at $x = a$ if $f(a)$ exists and corresponding to an arbitrary positive number ϵ, however small, we can find a positive number δ such that*

$$|f(x) - f(a)| < \epsilon, \textit{ whenever } |x - a| < \delta.$$

Continuity in an interval

A function $f(x)$ is said to be continuous in the interval $a < x < b$ if $f(x)$ is continuous at every point of the interval. If further $f(a) = \lim_{x\to a^+} f(x)$ and $f(b) = \lim_{x\to b^-} f(x)$, then $f(x)$ is said to be continuous in the closed interval $a \leq x \leq b$.

Properties of Continuous function

(i) The sum, difference and product of two functions which are continuous at a point (or in an interval) are continuous at that point (or in that interval).

(ii) The quotient of two functions which are continuous at a point (or in an interval) is continuous at that point (or in that interval), provided the denominator is not zero at the point (or in the interval).

(iii) A function of the type x^n where n is a positive real number is always continuous.

A polynomial: $f(x) = a_o x^n + a_1 x^{x-1} + a_2 x^{n-2} + \cdots + a_{n-1}x + a_n$ (where n is a point integer) is always continous.

(iv) A rational function: $\frac{f(x)}{g(x)}$ where $f(x)$ and $g(x)$ are two polynomials is also always continuous except at those points where the denominator of the function vanishes.

EXAMPLE 12. *Draw the graph of* $f(x) = \frac{x^2}{x}$ *and* $\phi(x) = x$.

From the graphs so drawn state which of the two functions is not continuous. What is the point of discontinuity? **[C.U. B.Com. (Hons.) 1983, Delhi U. B.Com.]**

SOLUTION. We first draw the graph of the function $y = f(x) = x^2/x$. Here $y = x$ when $x \neq 0$ and y is *undefined at* at $x = 0$; we have $x \neq 0$ and

x	1	2	3	-1	-2	·5	·25	$-\cdot 25$	$-\cdot 1$	$\cdots$
y	1	2	3	-1	-2	·5	·25	$-\cdot 25$	$-\cdot 1$	$\cdots$

We have drawn the graph of the function $y = x(x \neq 0)$ which is a straight line making an angle of 45° with the x-axis, the origin $(0, 0)$ being excluded from the line. (See Fig. 6.7).

From the graph, we see that as $x \to 0$ from the right passing through the points $A_1, A_2, \cdots$, $y \to 0$ passing through the corresponding points $C_1, C_2, \cdots$ from above and when $x \to 0$ from the left pssing through the points $A_1', A_2', \cdots$, again $y \to 0$ passing through the corresponding points $C_1', C_2', \cdots$ from below.

$\therefore$ Let $f(x)$ exists and $\lim_{x \to 0} f(x) = 0$

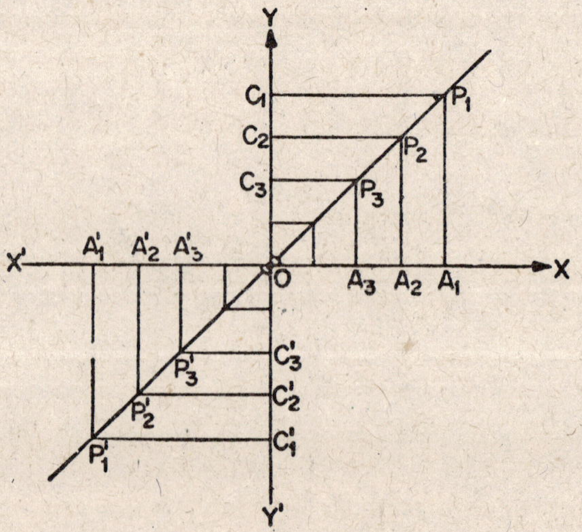

Fig 6.7

But $f(0)$ is *undefined*.

Hence $f(x)$ is **not continuous at $\mathbf{x = 0}$**.

The second function is $y = \phi(x) = x$, for all x.

We can draw the graph of this function exactly in the same way as we have done for the first function in Fig. 6.7. In this case, the only exception is that the line $y = x$ passes through the origin as $\phi(0) = 0$ is defined.

As before we can prove that $\lim_{x \to 0} \phi(x) = 0$. Also $\phi(0) = 0$.

$\because$ $\lim_{x \to 0} \phi(x) = \phi(0)$. Hence $\phi(x)$ is **continuous at $\mathbf{x = 0}$**.

Hence, $\phi(x)$ is *always continuous* and $f(x)$ *is continuous at all points except $x = 0$ i.e., the only point of discontinuity of $f(x)$ is $x = 0$.*

EXAMPLE 13. *A function $f(x)$ is defined as follows:*

$$\begin{aligned} f(x) &= 3 + 2x, \quad \text{for } -\frac{3}{2} \le x < 0 \\ &= 3 - 2x, \quad \text{for } 0 \le x < \frac{3}{2} \\ &= -3 - 2x, \text{ for } x \ge \frac{3}{2}. \end{aligned}$$

Discuss the continuity of $f(x)$ at $x = 0, \frac{3}{2}$. **[C.U. B.Sc]**

SOLUTION. *Continuity at $x = 0$*

$$\lim_{x \to 0+} f(x) = \lim_{x \to 0+} (3 - 2x) = 3 - 2 \cdot 0 = 3 \quad [\because \quad f(x) = 3 - 2x \text{ when } x > 0.]$$
$$\lim_{x \to 0-} f(x) = \lim_{x \to 0-} (3 + 2x) = 3 + 2 \cdot 0 = 3 \quad [\because \quad f(x) = 3 + 2x \text{ when } x < 0.]$$

At $x = 0, f(x) = 3 - 2x$; $\therefore$ $f(0) = 3 - 2 \cdot 0 = 3$.

Thus, $\lim_{x \to 0+} f(x) = \lim_{x \to 0-} f(x) = f(0)$.

Hence $f(x)$ is *continuous at $x = 0$*.

Continuity at $x = \frac{3}{2}$.

$$\lim_{x \to \frac{3}{2}^+} f(x) = \lim_{x \to \frac{3}{2}^+} (-3 - 2x) = -3 - 2 \times \frac{3}{2} = -6, \quad \left[\because \quad f(x) = -3 - 2x \text{ when } x > \frac{3}{2}.\right]$$
$$\lim_{x \to \frac{3}{2}^-} f(x) = \lim_{x \to \frac{3}{2}^-} (3 - 2x) = 3 - 2 \cdot \frac{3}{2} = 0. \quad \left[\because \quad f(x) = 3 - 2x \text{ when } x < \frac{3}{2}.\right]$$

Also at $x = \frac{3}{2}, f(x) = -3 - 2x$; $\therefore$ $f\left(\frac{3}{2}\right) = -3 - 2 \times \frac{3}{2} = -6$.

Thus, $\lim_{x \to \frac{3}{2}^+} f(x) \neq \lim_{x \to \frac{3}{2}^-} f(x) \neq f\left(\frac{3}{2}\right)$.

Hence $f(x)$ is *not continuous at $x = \frac{3}{2}$*.

EXAMPLE 14. *Is the following function continuous at* $x = 0$:

$f(x) = x$ *when* $x > 0, f(x) = 0$ *when* $x = 0, f(x) = -x$ *when* $x < 0$. **[C.U. B.Com (Hons.) 1982]**

SOLUTION. In the **worked out Example 3,** we have shown that $\lim_{x \to 0} f(x) = 0$.

Also given that $f(x) = 0$ when $x = 0$; $\therefore$ $f(0) = 0$.

$\therefore$ $\lim_{x \to 0} f(x) = f(0)$.

Hence, $f(x)$ is *continuous at* $x = 0$.

EXAMPLE 15. *Find the points of discontinuity of the function*

$$\frac{2x^2 + 6x - 5}{12x^2 + x - 20}$$ **[C.U. B.Com (Hons.) 1983]**

SOLUTION. The given function is undefined at the points where the denominator vanishes.

$\therefore$ The points of discontinuity of the function is given by

denominator $= 0$ i.e., $12x^2 + x - 20 = 0$

$$\begin{aligned}
\text{or,} \quad & 12x^2 + 16x - 15x - 20 = 0, \text{ or, } 4x(3x + 4) - 5(3x + 4) = 0, \\
\text{or,} \quad & (3x + 4)(4x - 5) = 0; \\
\therefore \quad & \text{Either } 3x + 4 = 0, \quad \text{or, } 4x - 5 = 0. \\
& \text{i.e., } \quad 3x = -4, \quad \text{or, } 4x = 5 \\
\therefore \quad & x = -\frac{4}{3} \quad \text{or, } x = \frac{5}{4}.
\end{aligned}$$

Hence, the **points of discontinuity** of the given function are $x = -\frac{4}{3}, \frac{5}{4}$.

EXAMPLE 16. *Using* (δ, ϵ) *definition, show that the function* $y = 3x + 2$ *is continuous at* $x = 5$.

SOLUTION. We have $y = f(x) = 3x + 2$; $\therefore$ $f(5) = 3 \cdot 5 + 2 = 17$.

Given an arbitrary positive number ϵ, however small, we have to find a positive number δ (depending on ϵ) such that

$$\begin{aligned}
& |f(x) - f(5)| < \epsilon \quad \text{when} \quad |x - 5| < \delta. \\
\text{Now,} \quad & |f(x) - f(5)| < \epsilon \quad \text{when} \quad |(3x + 2) - 17| < \epsilon, \\
\text{i.e., when} \quad & |3x - 15| < \epsilon \quad \text{i.e., when} \quad 3|x - 5| < \epsilon, \\
\text{i.e., when} \quad & |x - 5| < \frac{\epsilon}{3}.
\end{aligned}$$

Taking $\delta = \frac{\epsilon}{3}$, we find that $|f(x) - f(5)| < \epsilon$ when $|x - 5| < \delta$.

Hence, $f(x)$ i.e., the given function is continuous at $x = 5$.

NOTE. We can prove that the function $y = 3x + 2$ is continuous at every point of its domain of definition R which is the set of all real numbers.

Exercise 6

(Limits of Algebraic Functions)

A

1. Explain what do you mean by, (i) 'x tends to a'; (ii) 'x tends to infinity'.

Explain the statements: (i) $x \to 3$; (ii) $x \to 0$; (iii) $x \to -\infty$.

2. Define *the limit of a function* and illustrate it by an example.

3. Distinguish between $\lim\limits_{x \to a} f(x)$ and $f(a)$. **[C.U. B.Com(Hons.) 1981]**

4. Explain what do you mean by (i) $\lim\limits_{x \to a} f(x) = 5$;

(ii) $\lim\limits_{x \to 0} f(x) = 6$; (iii) $\lim\limits_{x \to 0} (x^2/x) = 0$. **[C.U. B.Sc 1980, '82]**

5. Show that

(i) $\lim\limits_{x \to 0} (4x + 5) = 5$; (ii) $\lim\limits_{x \to 3} \frac{x^2-9}{x-3} = 6$;

(iii) $\lim\limits_{x \to 3} \frac{x^2+x-12}{x-3} = 7$; (iv) $\lim\limits_{x \to 1} \frac{x^2-3x+2}{x^2-4x+3} = \frac{1}{2}$.

6. Using (δ, ϵ) definition, find δ from the following limits:

(i) $\lim\limits_{x \to 4} (2x - 3) = 5$; (ii) $\lim\limits_{x \to 2} \frac{x^2-4}{x-2} = 4$.

7. Prove that

(i) $\lim\limits_{x \to \infty} \frac{1}{x^2} = 0$; (ii) $\lim\limits_{x \to \infty} \left(\frac{2}{x^2} + 3\right) = 3$;

(iii) $\lim\limits_{x \to \infty} \frac{2x+3}{4x-5} = \frac{1}{2}$.

8. Using (δ, ϵ) definition (or otherwise), prove that

(i) $\lim\limits_{x \to 2} (3x + 2) = 8$; (ii) $\lim\limits_{x \to 1} \frac{x^2-1}{x-1} = 2$;

(iii) $\lim\limits_{x \to -2} \frac{x^2-4}{x+2} = -4$; **[C.U. 1975]** (iv) $\lim\limits_{x \to -\frac{1}{3}} \frac{9x^2-1}{3x-1} = -2$. **[Bangalore U. 1990]**

9. Draw the graph of the following function:

$f(x) = 1$ when $x > 0$, $f(x) = 0$ when $x = 0$, $f(x) = -1$ when $x < 0$. From the graph show that $\lim\limits_{x \to 0} f(x)$ does not exist.

10. Draw the graph of the following function:

$f(x) = 2x$ if $x > 0$, $f(x) = 0$ if $x = 0$ and $f(x) = -2x$ if $x < 0$.

Using the graph of the function, show that $\lim\limits_{x \to 0} f(x) = 0$.

11. Draw the graph of the function $f(x) = \frac{x^2-4}{x-2}$ and hence evaluate the limit $\lim\limits_{x \to 2} f(x)$, if it exists.

12. Evaluate the limit $\lim\limits_{x \to 0} f(x)$ if it exists, where

$$f(x) = 5 + 3x \text{ if } x \geq 0 \text{ and } f(x) = 5 - 3x \text{ if } x < 0.$$

13. A function $f(x)$ is defined as follows:

$$f(x) = 3 + 2x, \text{ when } x \leq 0$$
$$= 3 - 2x, \text{ when } x > 0.$$

Draw the graph of $f(x)$ and examine whether $\lim_{x \to 0} f(x)$ exists.

14. Draw the graph of the following function and examine whether $\lim_{x \to 0} f(x)$ exists.

$$f(x) = x - 1, \text{ when } x > 0$$
$$= -1/2, \text{ when } x = 0$$
$$= x + 1, \text{ when } x < 0.$$

15. Evaluate: (i) $\lim_{x \to 0} \frac{\sqrt{1+x}-1}{x}$ **[CA May 1991]**

(ii) $\lim_{x \to \infty} \frac{3-2x^2}{5x+4x^2}$; (iii) $\lim_{x \to \infty} \frac{e^x+2}{3e^x-1}$.

16. Discuss the existence of $\lim_{x \to \frac{3}{2}} f(x)$ if

$$f(x) = 3 + 2x, \text{ for } -\frac{3}{2} \leq x < 0$$
$$= 3 - 2x, \text{ for } 0 \leq x < \frac{3}{2}$$
$$= -3 - 2x \text{ for } x \geq \frac{3}{2}.$$

[HINTS. R.H. limit $= \lim_{x \to \frac{3}{2}^+} f(x)$ **[ICWAI June 1990]**

$= \lim_{x \to \frac{3}{2}^+} (-3 - 2x) = -6$ and L.H. limit $= \lim_{x \to \frac{3}{2}^-} f(x) = 0$.]

B

1. Give one example in each of the following cases:

(i) $f(a)$ does not exist, but $\lim_{x \to a} f(x)$ exists;

(ii) $f(a)$ exists, but $\lim_{x \to a} f(x)$ does not exist;

(iii) $f(a)$ and $\lim_{x \to a} f(x)$ both exist, but they are unequal;

(iv) $f(a)$ and $\lim_{x \to a} f(x)$ both exist and are equal;

(v) neither $f(a)$ nor $\lim_{x \to a} f(x)$ exists.

2. Explain the meaning of the statements:

(i) $f(x) \to \infty$ as $x \to a$; (ii) $f(x) \to l$ as $x \to \infty$.

3. Show that the function $y = \frac{1}{x}\{(1 + x)^2 - 1\}$ tends to 2 as x tends to zero and $y = 3/x^2$ tends to infinity as x tends to zero. **[C.U. B.Com (Hons.) 1980]**

4. Evaluate the following limits:

(i) $\lim_{x\to 1}\frac{x^2-2x+3}{3x+1}$; (ii) $\lim_{x\to 2}\frac{x^2-5x+6}{x^2-3x+2}$; (iii) $\lim_{x\to 0}\frac{3^x-1}{x}$;

(iv) $\lim_{x\to \frac{1}{2}}\frac{2x^2+3x-2}{2x^2+5x-3}$; (v) $\lim_{x\to 0}\frac{(1+x)^3-1}{x}$; (vi) $\lim_{x\to 0}\frac{4^{x+1}-4}{2x}$.

5. Do the following limits exist? If so, find their values:

(i) $\lim_{x\to 2}\frac{1}{x-2}$; (ii) $\lim_{x\to\infty}\left(\frac{3}{x^2}+5\right)$; (iii) $\lim_{x\to 0}\frac{1}{x^3}$;

(iv) $\lim_{x\to 1}\left\{\frac{(x-1)^2}{x-1}+(x^2-1)\right\}$; (v) $\lim_{x\to 3}\left(\frac{x}{x-3}-\frac{9}{x^2-3x}\right)$; (vi) $\lim_{x\to 0}\frac{a^x-1}{x}$.

[C.U. 1977] **[Bangalore U. 1991]**

6. A function $f(x)$ is defined as follows:

$$f(x) = x \text{ when } x \le 2$$
$$= 4 - x \text{ when } x > 2.$$

Find the value of $\lim_{x\to 2} f(x)$, if it exists.

7. (i) A function $f(x)$ is defined as follows:

$$f(x) = x^2 \text{ when } x < 1$$
$$= 2 \text{ when } x = 1$$
$$= x^2 + 1 \text{ when } x > 1.$$

Does $\lim_{x\to 1} f(x)$ exist?

(ii) Show that $\lim_{x\to 1} f(x)$ exists and is equal to $f(1)$,

where $f(x) = x + 1$ for $x \le 1$ and $f(x) = 3 - x^2$ for $x > 1$.

8. Find (if possible) $\lim_{x\to 0}\frac{e^{\frac{1}{x}}-1}{e^{\frac{1}{x}}+1}$ **[ICWAI December 1984]**

[HINTS. As $x \to 0^+$, $\frac{1}{x} \to \infty$ so that $e^{\frac{1}{x}} \to \infty$ and $\frac{1}{e^{\frac{1}{x}}} \to 0$.

$\therefore$ Right hand limit $= \lim_{x\to 0+}\frac{1-\frac{1}{e^{\frac{1}{x}}}}{1+\frac{1}{e^{\frac{1}{x}}}} = \frac{1-0}{1+0} = 1$.

Again as $x \to 0^-$, $\frac{1}{x} \to -\infty$ so that $e^{\frac{1}{x}} \to 0$ and L.H. limit $= -1$]

9. Find $\lim_{x\to 1}\frac{x-1}{\sqrt{x-1}+\sqrt{x+1}}$, if it exists. **[ICWAI June 1987]**

[HINTS. As $x \to 1^+$, $(x-1) \to 0$ and R.H. limit $= \frac{0}{0+\sqrt{2}} = 0$.

Again as $x \to 1^-$, $\sqrt{x-1}$ becomes imaginary (since $x < 1$).]

10. **Evaluate the following limits**

(i) $\lim_{x\to 0}\frac{1}{x}\{\sqrt{1+x}-\sqrt{(1-x)}$; (ii) $\lim_{x\to 0}\frac{a-\sqrt{a^2-x^2}}{x^2}$;

(iii) $\lim_{x\to 0}\frac{\sqrt{2+3x}-\sqrt{2(1-x)}}{4x}$; (iv) $\lim_{x\to 3}\frac{x-3}{\sqrt{x-2}-\sqrt{4-x}}$; (v) $\lim_{x\to 0}\frac{\sqrt{2+x^2}-\sqrt{2-x^2}}{x^2}$.

11. **If $f(x) = |x|$, find the Right-hand and the Left-hand limit of** $\frac{f(h)-f(0)}{h}$ as $h \to 0$ and show that $\lim_{h\to 0}\frac{f(h)-f(0)}{h}$ does not exist.

12. Evaluate the following limits:

(i) $\lim\limits_{x\to\infty}\frac{5-2x^2}{3x+5x^2}$; (ii) $\lim\limits_{x\to\infty}\frac{2x^2+7x+5}{4x^2+3x-1}$ **[C.U. B.Com (Hons.) 1981]**

(iii) $\lim\limits_{x\to\infty}\frac{1-\sqrt{x}}{1+\sqrt{x}}$; (iv) $\lim\limits_{n\to\infty}\frac{1^2+2^2+3^3+\cdots+n^2}{n^3}$

13. (i) If $f(x)=ax^2+bx+c$, show that $\lim\limits_{h\to0}\frac{f(x+h)-f(x)}{h}=2ax+b$.

(ii) If $f(t)=3t^3+4t$, find $\lim\limits_{h\to0}\frac{f(1+h)-f(1)}{h}$ **[ICWAI June 1992]**

14. Using (δ,ϵ) definition prove that $\lim\limits_{x\to5}\frac{2(x^2-25)}{x-5}=20$ and find the value of δ when $\epsilon=\cdot01$.

15. Verify that (i) $\lim\limits_{x\to\infty}\sqrt{x}(\sqrt{x+3}-\sqrt{x})=\frac{3}{2}$;

(ii) $\lim\limits_{x\to\infty}\sqrt{x}(\sqrt{x+4}-\sqrt{x})=2$ **[ICWAI June 1986]**

16. Show that $\lim\limits_{x\to\infty}(\sqrt[3]{x+1}-\sqrt[3]{x})=0$.

[HINTS. $\sqrt[3]{x+1}-\sqrt[3]{x}=\frac{\{(x+1)^{\frac{1}{3}}-x^{\frac{1}{3}}\}\{(x+1)^{\frac{2}{3}}+(x+1)^{\frac{1}{3}}\cdot x^{\frac{1}{3}}+x^{\frac{2}{3}}\}}{\{(x+1)^{\frac{2}{3}}+(x+1)^{\frac{1}{3}}\cdot x^{\frac{1}{3}}+x^{\frac{2}{3}}\}}$

$=\frac{(x+1)-x}{(x+1)^{\frac{2}{3}}+(x+1)^{\frac{1}{3}}\cdot x^{\frac{1}{3}}+x^{\frac{2}{3}}}$; as $x\to\infty,(x+1)^{\frac{2}{3}}\to\infty, x^{\frac{1}{3}}\to\infty, x^{\frac{2}{3}}\to\infty$.

$\therefore\quad (x+1)^{\frac{2}{3}}+(x+1)^{\frac{1}{3}}\cdot x^{\frac{1}{3}}+x^{\frac{2}{3}}\to\infty$ and $\frac{1}{(x+1)^{\frac{2}{3}}+(x+1)^{\frac{1}{3}}\cdot x^{\frac{1}{3}}+x^{\frac{2}{3}}}\to 0$]

17. If $f(x)=x^n$, where n is a positive integer, prove that

$$\lim_{h\to0}\frac{f(x+h)-f(x)}{h}=nx^{n-1}.$$

18. Examine whether the following limits exist:

(i) $\lim\limits_{x\to0}\frac{5x+|x|}{2x+|x|}$; (ii) $\lim\limits_{x\to0}\frac{4x+|x|}{3x-2|x|}$.

19. A function ϕ is defined by

$$\phi(x)=2-x,\ \text{when } 1\le x\le 2,$$
$$=x-\frac{1}{2}x^2,\ \text{when } x>2.$$

Obtain $\lim\limits_{h\to0^+}\frac{\phi(2+h)-\phi(2)}{h}$ and $\lim\limits_{h\to0^-}\frac{\phi(2+h)-\phi(2)}{h}$. **[ICWAI June 1984]**

20. Evaluate:

(i) $\lim\limits_{x\to0}\frac{5^x+3^x-2}{x}$; (ii) $\lim\limits_{x\to0}\frac{10^x-5^x-2^x+1}{x^2}$ **[ICWAI June 1985]**

[HINTS. (i) Given limit

$$=\lim_{x\to0}\frac{(5^x-1)+(3^x-1)}{x}=\lim_{x\to0}\frac{5^x-1}{x}+\lim_{x\to0}\frac{3^x-1}{x}=\text{etc.}$$

(ii) Given limit

$$=\lim_{x\to0}\frac{2^x\cdot5^x-5^x-2^x+1}{x^2}=\lim_{x\to0}\frac{(2^x-1)(5^x-1)}{x\times x}=\lim_{x\to0}\frac{2^x-1}{x}\times\lim_{x\to0}\frac{5^x-1}{x}=\text{etc.}]$$

21. Show that (i) $\lim\limits_{x\to 0} \frac{e^x-1}{\log(1+x)} = 1$; (ii) $\lim\limits_{x\to 0}\left\{\frac{(3^x-1)^2}{x\log_e(1+x)}\right\} = (\log_e 3)^2$.

[HINTS. (i) $\lim\limits_{x\to 0} \frac{e^x-1}{\log(1+x)} = \lim\limits_{x\to 0}\left\{\frac{e^x-1}{x} \times \frac{x}{\log_e(1+x)}\right\}$ = etc

(ii) $\lim\limits_{x\to 0} \frac{(3^x-1)^2}{x\log_e(1+x)} = \lim\limits_{x\to 0}\left\{\frac{(3^x-1)^2}{x^2} \times \frac{x}{\log(1+x)}\right\}$ = etc.]

22. Show that $\lim\limits_{x\to 1} f(x)$ exists and is equal to $f(1)$, where $f(x) = x+1$ for $x \le 1$, $f(x) = 3-x^2$ for $x > 1$. **[ICWAI June 1991]**

C

(Continuity)

1. What do you mean by continuity of $f(x)$ at $x = a$?

Or

Define the continuity of a function $f(x)$ at $x = a$.

[Delhi U. B.Com (Hons.) 1980; C.U. B.Com. (Hons.) 1982]

2. Explain what is meant by the continuity of a function in an interval.

3. Examine if the following statement is correct:

(i) $f(x)$ is continuous at $x = a$ if $\lim\limits_{x\to a} f(x)$ exists and $f(a)$ is a finite number.

(ii) $f(x)$ is continuous at $x = a$ if $f(a)$ exists and $\lim\limits_{h\to 0} f(a+h) = f(a)$.

4. (i) Using definition, show that $f(x) = 3x+5$ is continuous at $x = 2$.

(ii) Supposing $f(x) = x^2 - 1$, find $\lim\limits_{x\to 1} f(x)$ and show that $f(x)$ is continuous at $x = 1$.

[Bur. U. 1981]

5. Draw the graphs of the following functions and discuss from each graph the continuity of the function at $x = 0$:

(i) $f(x) = 2x+3$; (ii) $f(x) = |x|$; (iii) $f(x) = \frac{x^2}{x}$.

6. A function is defined as follows:

$$f(x) = 5 + 3x \text{ if } x \ge 0$$
$$= 5 - 3x \text{ if } x < 0.$$

Show that $f(x)$ is continuous at $x = 0$.

7. Given

$$\begin{aligned} f(x) &= -x, && \text{when } x \le 0 \\ &= x, && \text{when } 0 < x < 1 \\ &= 2 - x, && \text{when } x \ge 1. \end{aligned}$$

Discuss the continuity of $f(x)$ at $x = 0, 1$.

8. A function $f(x)$ is defined in $(0, 3)$ in the following way

$$\begin{aligned} f(x) &= x^2, && \text{when } 0 < x < 1 \\ &= x, && \text{when } 1 \le x < 2 \\ &= \frac{1}{4}x^3, && \text{when } 2 \le x < 3. \end{aligned}$$

Show that $f(x)$ is continuous at $x = 1$ and $x = 2$.

9. A function $f(x)$ is defined as follows:

$$\begin{aligned} f(x) &= \frac{1}{2} - x, \text{ when } 0 < x < \frac{1}{2}, \\ &= \frac{1}{2}, \quad \text{when } x = \frac{1}{2} \\ &= \frac{3}{2} - x, \text{ when } \frac{1}{2} < x < 1 \\ &= 1, \quad \text{when } x = 1. \end{aligned}$$

Discuss the continuity of $f(x)$ at $x = \frac{1}{2}$ and $x = 1$. **[ICWAI December 1982]**

10. Find the points of discontinuity of the following functions:

(i) $\frac{x^2+6x+8}{x^2-5x+6}$; (ii) $\frac{2x^2+5x-7}{10x^2+x-24}$.

11. If the function f is defined by

$$\begin{aligned} f(x) &= \frac{x^2 - 16}{x - 4} \text{ for } x \neq 4 \\ &= 10 \text{ for } x = 4, \end{aligned}$$

say, whether it is continuous at $x = 4$. If not, why? **[Delhi U. B.Com. (Hons.) 1982]**

12. A function $f(x)$ is defined as

$$\begin{aligned} f(x) &= \frac{1}{2} - x, \text{ for } 0 < x < \frac{1}{2} \\ &= 0, \text{ when } x = \frac{1}{2} \\ &= \frac{3}{2} - 3x, \text{ when } \frac{1}{2} < x < 1. \end{aligned}$$

Discuss its continuity at $x = \frac{1}{2}$. **[Delhi U. B.Com. (Hons.) 1981]**

13. (i) The function $f(x) = \frac{2x^2-8}{x-2}$ is undefined at $x = 2$.

What value should be assigned to $f(2)$ so that $f(x)$ is continuous at $x = 2$.

(ii) If $f(x) = \frac{x^2-5x+6}{x-2}$ and $g(x) = x - 3$, how do f and g differ? Is $f(x)$ continuous at all points? What about $g(x)$. **[Guru Nanak U. M.A. 1981]**

14. A function $f(x)$ is defined as follows:

$$\begin{aligned} f(x) &= x + 1, \text{ when } x \leq 1 \\ &= 3 - ax, \text{ when } x > 1. \end{aligned}$$

For what value of a will $f(x)$ be continuous at $x = 1$? With this value of a draw the graph of $f(x)$.

15. A function $f(x)$ is defined as follows:

$$\begin{aligned} f(x) &= x - 1, \text{ when } x > 0, \\ &= -\frac{1}{2}, \text{ when } x = 0, \\ &= x + 1, \text{ when } x < 0 \end{aligned}$$

Draw the graph of $f(x)$. From the graph find the value of $f(x)$ at $x = -\frac{1}{2}$ and state whether $f(x)$ is continuous at $x = 0$.

16. A function $f(x)$ is defined as follows:

$$\begin{aligned} f(x) &= 3 + 2x, \text{ when } x \leq 0 \\ &= 3 - 2x, \text{ when } x > 0. \end{aligned}$$

Draw the graph of $f(x)$ and examine whether $f(x)$ is continuous at $x = 0$.

17. A function is defined as follows:

$$\begin{aligned} f(x) &= x, \text{ when } x < 1 \\ &= 1 + x, \text{ when } x > 1 \\ &- \frac{3}{2}, \text{ when } x - 1. \end{aligned}$$

Draw the graph of $f(x)$ and examine whether $f(x)$ is continuous at $x = \frac{1}{2}$ and at $x = 1$.

18. Using (δ, ϵ) definition, prove that $f(x) = 3x + 7$ is continuous at $x = 5$. If $\epsilon = \cdot 003$, find the value of δ.

19. Consider the function $\frac{x}{|x|}$. Draw the graph of this function (Rough sketch only). Hence or otherwise prove that $f(x)$ is not continuous at $x = 0$. **[ICWAI December 1983]**

[HINTS. $f(x) = \frac{x}{|x|}$ where

$$\begin{aligned} |x| &= x \text{ if } x > 0 \\ &= 0 \text{ if } x = 0 \\ &= -x \text{ if } x < 0 \end{aligned}$$

$\therefore$ $f(x)$ is undefined at $x = 0$.

Thus, $\left.\begin{aligned} f(x) = {} & 1 \text{ if } x > 0 \\ = {} & -1 \text{ if } x < 0 \end{aligned}\right\}$; at $x = 0, f(x)$ is undefined and hence it is not continuous at $x = 0$.

Now draw the graph of $f(x)$.]

20. (i) A function $f(x)$ is defined by $f(x) = |x - 3| + 2$ over all real values of x. Show that $f(x)$ is continuous at $x = 3$.

[HINTS.

$$\begin{aligned} f(x) &= x - 3 + 2 = x - 1 \text{ if } x > 3 \\ &= 0 + 2 = 2 \text{ if } x = 3 \\ &= -(x - 3) + 2 = 5 - x \text{ if } x < 3. \end{aligned}$$

$$\therefore \quad \lim_{x \to 3^+} f(x) = \lim_{x \to 3^+} (x - 1) = 3 - 1 = 2, f(3) = 2$$

$$\text{and} \quad \lim_{x \to 3^-} f(x) = 2. \quad \text{Hence etc.]}$$

(ii) A function $f(x)$ is defined by $f(x) = |x - 2| + 1$ for all real values of x. Examine whether $f(x)$ is continuous at $x = 2$. **[ICWAI December 1983]**

21. The total cost C of producing x items is given by

$$C = 1000 + 5x, \quad \text{when } 0 \le x < 500$$
$$= 2,000 + 4x, \quad \text{when } 500 \le x \le 2,000.$$

Show that C is discontinuous at $x = 500$. **[ICWAI December 1991, '93]**

Answers

A

6. (i) $\delta = \epsilon/2$; (ii) $\delta = \epsilon$. **11.** 4. **12.** 5. **13.** 3 **14.** Limit does not exist. **15.** (i) $\frac{1}{2}$; (ii) $-\frac{1}{2}$; (iii) $\frac{1}{3}$. **16.** The limit does not exist.

B

1. (i) $\lim\limits_{x\to 1} \frac{x^2-1}{x-1}$ where $a = 1$; (ii) $\lim\limits_{x\to 0} f(x)$ where $f(x) = 1$ when $x > 0$, $f(x) = 0$ when $x = 0$ and $f(x) = -1$ when $x < 0$; (iii) $a = 0$ and $f(x) = x$ when $x \neq 0$ and $f(x) = 1$ when $x = 0$; (iv) $f(x) = |x|$ and $a = 0$; (v) $f(x) = \frac{1}{x}$ and $a = 0$. **4.** (i) 1/2; (ii) -1; (iii) $\log_e 3$; (iv) 5/7; (v) 3; (vi) $4\log_e 2$. **5.** (i) No; (ii) Yes, 5; (iii) No; (iv) Yes, 0; (v) 2; (vi) $\log_e a$. **6.** 2. **7.** No. **8.** The limit does not exist. **9.** The limit does not exist. **10.** (i) 1; (ii) $1/2a$; (iii) $5\sqrt{2}/16$; (iv) 1; (v) $\frac{1}{\sqrt{2}}$. **11.** R.H.Lt. = 1. and L.H.Lt. = -1. **12.** (i) $-2/5$; (ii) 1/2; (iii) -1; (iv) 1/3. **13.** (ii) 13. **14.** $\delta = \cdot 005$. **18.** (i) Does not exist; (ii) Does not exist. **19.** $-1, -1$. **20.** (i) $\log_e 15$; (ii) $\log_e 2 . \log_e 5$.

C

3. (i) No. Correct statement is $\lim\limits_{x\to a} f(x)$ and $f(a)$ both exist and are equal; (ii) Yes, correct. **4.** (ii) 0. **5.** (i) Continuous; (ii) Discontinuous. **7.** Continuous at $x = 0, 1$. **9.** Discontinuous at $x = \frac{1}{2}$ and $x = 1$. **10.** (i) $x = 2, 3$; (ii) $x = -\frac{8}{5}, \frac{3}{2}$. **11.** Not continuous, since $\lim\limits_{x\to 4} f(x) = 8$ and $f(4) = 10$. **12.** Continuous at $x = \frac{1}{2}$. **13.** (i) $f(2) = 8$; (ii) $f(x)$ is discontinuous at $x = 2$, but $g(x)$ is continuous at all points. **14.** $a = 1$. **15.** $\frac{1}{2}$; discontinuous. **16.** Continuous. **17.** Continuous at $x = \frac{1}{2}$; discontinuous at $x = 1$. **18.** $0 \cdot 001$. **20.** (ii) $f(x)$ is continuous at $x = 2$.

CHAPTER 7

DIFFERENTIATION OF ALGEBRAIC FUNCTIONS: MEANING OF DERIVATIVES

7.1. INTRODUCTION

The rate at which a function changes with respect to its independent variable is called the *derivative* of the function. In this chapter, we shall define the *derivative of a function* in terms of a *limit* involving the increments of the independent and the dependent variables, and using this definition, we shall show how to find the derivatives of various types of functions. We shall also acquaint the readers with the *standard rules for differentiation* and explain the *meaning of derivative* as a rate-measurer and, geometrically, as a slope of a tangent to the curve of the function.

7.2. INCREMENT

If the values of a variable x is changed from one value $x_\circ$ to another values x_1, then the difference $x_1 - x_\circ$ (i.e., final value—initial value) is called the **increment** of x and we denote this increment by Δx (read: delta x) or h. Thus, $\Delta x = x_1 - x_\circ$, or, $x_1 = x_\circ + \Delta x$. If x *increases* from $x_\circ$ to x_1, then $x_1 > x_\circ$ and the increment is *positive,* but if x decreases from $x_\circ$ to x_1, then the increment is *negative.* In both the cases, we shall use the term *increment* for Δx. Similarly, we shall denote the increment of y or $f(x)$ by Δy or $\Delta f(x)$.

If in a function $y = f(x)$, the independent variable x is given an increment Δx or h from $x = x_\circ$, then Δy or $\Delta f(x)$ will denote the corresponding increment of y and we have $y + \Delta y = f(x_\circ + \Delta x)$ where $y = f(x_\circ)$;

$$\therefore \quad \Delta y = f(x_\circ + \Delta x) - y = f(x_\circ + \Delta x) - f(x_\circ).$$

ILLUSTRATION 1. *Let* $y = 2x + 3$.

If x increases from 1 to 1.5, then $\Delta x = 1.5 - 1 = .5$ and y increases from $2 \times 1 + 3 = 5$ to $2 \times 1.5 + 3 = 6$, i.e., $\Delta y = 6 - 5 = 1$. If x decreases from 1 to .5, then $\Delta x = 0.5 - 1 = -.5$ and y decreases from 5 to $2 \times .5 + 3 = 4$, i.e., $\Delta y = 4 - 5 = -1$.

In this case, Δx and Δy have the *same sign.*

ILLUSTRATION 2. *Let* $y = \frac{2}{x}$. If x increases from 2 to 2.1, then $\Delta x = .1$ and y decreases from 1 to $\frac{2}{2.1}$ so that $\Delta y = \frac{2}{2.1} - 1 = \frac{-.1}{2.1} = -\frac{1}{21}$. If x decreases from 2 to 1.9, then $\Delta x = -.1$ and y increases from 1 to $\frac{2}{1.9}$ so that $\Delta y = \frac{2}{1.9} - 1 = \frac{.1}{1.9} = \frac{1}{19}$.

In this case, Δx and Δy have *opposite signs.*

From the above illustrations, we see that if x and y both increase or both decrease, then Δx and Δy will have the *same sign,* but if y decreases as x increases and vice versa, then Δx and Δy will have *opposite signs.*

Increment Ratio

If in a function $y = f(x), x$ is given an increment h (or Δx) from $x = x_\circ$, then as x changes from $x = x_\circ$ to $x = x_\circ + h, y = f(x)$ changes from $f(x_\circ)$ to $f(x_\circ + h)$.

$$\therefore \quad \Delta y = \text{ increment of } y = f(x_\circ + h) - f(x_\circ)$$

$$\therefore \quad \frac{\Delta y}{\Delta x} = \frac{f(x_\circ + h) - f(x_\circ)}{h} \qquad [\because \quad \Delta x = h]$$

The ratio $\frac{\Delta y}{\Delta x}$ or $\frac{f(x_\circ+h)-f(x_\circ)}{h}$ is called the **increment ratio.**

ILLUSTRATION 3. Let $y = f(x) = x^2$ and let $x_\circ = 2$.

Then $f(x_\circ) = f(2) = 2^2 = 4$. Let h (or Δx) be an increment of x. Then $2 + h$ is another value of x and the corresponding value of y is $f(2 + h) = (2 + h)^2$.

$$\therefore \quad \Delta y = \text{ increment of } y = f(2 + h) - f(2) = (2 + h)^2 - 4$$
$$= 4 + 4h + h^2 - 4 = 4h + h^2 = h(4 + h)$$

$\therefore$ The increment ratio $\frac{\Delta y}{\Delta x} = \frac{h(4+h)}{h} = 4 + h \qquad [\because \quad h \neq 0]$

We see that this *increment ratio is a function of h* (or Δx) i.e., *the ratio changes with h.* But when h becomes smaller and smaller, this ratio becomes nearer and nearer to 4 and ultimately when $h \to 0$, the increment ratio $\frac{f(2+h)-f(2)}{h} \to 4$. In this case, we say that the **derivative** of $f(x) = x^2$ w.r.t. x at the point $x = 2$ is 4.

7.3. DERIVATIVE (OR DIFFERENTIAL COEFFICIENT) OF A FUNCTION

DEFINITION. Let $y = f(x)$ be a function defined in a certain interval and x be a fixed interior point of this interval. Let Δx (or h) be an increment of x such that $x + \Delta x$ (or $x + h$) lies within the stated interval. Let Δy or $f(x + h) - f(x)$ be the corresponding increment of $y = f(x)$. Then the increment ratio

$$\frac{\Delta y}{\Delta x} = \frac{f(x + \Delta x) - f(x)}{\Delta x} \quad \text{or} \quad \frac{f(x + h) - f(x)}{h} \qquad [\because \quad \Delta x = h]$$

is a function of Δx (or h). If this ratio $\frac{\Delta y}{\Delta x}$ or $\frac{f(x+h)-f(x)}{h}$ tends to a *definite finite quantity* as Δx (or h) tends to zero, from either side, then this *finite quantity* is called the **derivative** or the **differential coefficient** of $f(x)$ *with respect to x 'at the point x'* and is denoted by $f'(x)$ or $\frac{d}{dx}\{f(x)\}$, or $\frac{dy}{dx}$.

Thus $\mathbf{f'(x)}$ **or** $\frac{dy}{dx} = \lim_{\Delta x \to 0} \frac{\Delta y}{\Delta x} = \lim_{h \to 0} \frac{f(x+h)-f(x)}{h}$, *provided this limit exists.* In this case we say that $f(x)$ is *derivable* w.r.t. x at the fixed point x.

REMARKS: (i) For the derivative $f'(x)$ to exist, the **Right-hand derivative**

$$Rf'(x) = \lim_{h \to 0+} \frac{f(x+h) - f(x)}{h}$$ and the **Left-hand derivative**

$$Lf'(x) = \lim_{h \to 0-} \frac{f(x+h) - f(x)}{h}$$ must both exist and must be equal.

(ii) The process of finding the derivative (or differential coefficient) is called **differentiation.** To differentiate $f(x)$ w.r.t. x means to find the derivative of $f(x)$ w.r.t. x.

(iii) The derivative of $f(x)$ at any fixed value 'a' of x is given by

$$f'(a) = \lim_{h \to 0} \frac{f(a+h) - f(a)}{h}, \text{ provided this limit exist,}$$

and the derivative of $f(x)$ at $x = 0$ is given by

$$f'(0) = \lim_{h \to 0} \frac{f(h) - f(0)}{h}, \quad \text{provided this limit exists.}$$

$f'(0)$ exists only when $Rf'(0) = \lim_{h \to 0+} \frac{f(h)-f(0)}{h}$ and $Lf(0) = \lim_{h \to 0-} \frac{f(h)-f(0)}{h}$ both exist and are equal.

Taking $x = a + h$, we have $h = x - a$ and as $h \to 0, x \to a$; we can define the **derivative of f(x) at x = a** as follows:

$$f'(a) = \lim_{x \to a} \frac{f(x) - f(a)}{x - a}, \quad \textit{provided the limit exists.}$$

PROPOSITION. *If $f(x)$ has a finite derivative at $x = a$, then $f(x)$ is continuous at $x = a$, but the converse is not always true.* **[Delhi U.; C.U. B.Com (Hons.) 1982]**

PROOF. Since $f(x)$ has a *finite derivative at* $x = a, f'(a)$ is *finite* and we have

$$f'(a) = \lim_{h \to 0} \frac{f(a+h) - f(a)}{h}$$

Now $$f(a+h) - f(a) = \frac{f(a+h) - f(a)}{h} \times h$$

$$\therefore \lim_{h \to 0} \{f(a+h) - f(a)\} = \lim_{h \to 0} \left\{ \frac{f(a+h) - f(a)}{h} \times h \right\}$$

or, $$\lim_{h \to 0} f(a+h) - \lim_{h \to 0} f(a) = \lim_{h \to 0} \frac{f(a+h) - f(a)}{h} \times \lim_{h \to 0} h$$

or, $$\lim_{h \to 0} f(a+h) - f(a) = f'(a) \times 0 = 0, \text{ since } f'(a) \text{ is finite.}$$

$$\therefore \lim_{h \to 0} f(a+h) = f(a).$$

This shows that $f(x)$ is *continuous* at $x = a$.

The converse is not always true.

Let us consider the function $f(x) = |x|$ i.e.,

$$\begin{aligned} f(x) &= x, \text{ when } x > 0 \\ &= 0, \text{ when } x = 0 \\ &= -x, \text{ when } x < 0. \end{aligned}$$

$$\lim_{x\to 0+} f(x) = \lim_{x\to 0+} x = 0 \qquad [\because \text{ when } x > 0, f(x) = x.]$$

and $$\lim_{x\to 0-} f(x) = \lim_{x\to 0-} (-x) = 0 \quad [\because \text{ when } x < 0, f(x) = -x.]$$

Also $f(0) = 0$. Thus, $\lim_{x\to 0+} f(x) = \lim_{x\to 0-} f(x) = f(0)$.

Hence $f(x)$ is *continuous at* $x = 0$.

Now $f'(0) = \lim_{h\to 0} \frac{f(h)-f(0)}{h}$, provided the limit exists.

$$\begin{aligned} Rf'(0) &= \lim_{h\to 0+} \frac{f(h)-f(0)}{h} = \lim_{h\to 0+} \frac{h-0}{h} \\ &= \lim_{h\to 0+} 1 = 1, \quad [\because \; f(x) = x \text{ when } x > 0.] \end{aligned}$$

and $$Lf'(0) = \lim_{h\to 0-} \frac{f(h)-f(0)}{h} = \lim_{h\to 0-} \frac{-h-0}{h}$$

$$[\because \; f(x) = -x \text{ when } x < 0.]$$

$$= \lim_{h\to 0-} (-1) = -1.$$

Thus, $Rf'(0) \neq Lf'(0)$; $\therefore$ $f'(0)$ does not exist.

$\therefore$ $f(x)$ is continuous at $x = 0$, but $f'(0)$ does not exist.

Hence, the theorem follows.

Derivatives using definition (Differentiation from first principles)

EXAMPLE 1. *Find from the first principles the derivative of the following function:*

$$y = x^3.$$ **[C.U. B.Com (Hons.) 1981]**

SOLUTION. Let $y = f(x) = x^3$. Then $f(x+h) = (x+h)^3$.

By definition, $f'(x) = \lim_{h\to 0} \frac{f(x+h)-f(x)}{h}$, provided the limit exists.

We have

$$\begin{aligned} f'(x) &= \lim_{h\to 0} \frac{(x+h)^3 - x^3}{h} = \lim_{h\to 0} \frac{x^3 + 3x^2h + 3xh^2 + h^3 - x^3}{h} \\ &= \lim_{h\to 0} \frac{h(3x^2 + 3xh + h^2)}{h} = \lim_{h\to 0} (3x^2 + 3xh + h^2) \qquad [\because \; h \neq 0] \\ &= \lim_{h\to 0} 3x^2 + \lim_{h\to 0} 3xh + \lim_{h\to 0} h^2 = 3x^2 + 3x.0 + 0 = \mathbf{3x^2}. \end{aligned}$$

EXAMPLE 2. *Differentiate from first principles the following functions:*

(i) $f(x) = x^2 + 3x$; **[C.U. B.Com (Hons.) 1982 (old)]**

(ii) $f(x) = \frac{1}{x^2} (x \neq 0)$; **[C.U. 1983; ICWAI June 1993]**

(iii) $f(x) = \sqrt{x} (x > 0)$. **[C.U. B.Com (Hons.) 1982; CA May 1981]**

SOLUTION. (i) We have $f(x) = x^2 + 3x$ and $f(x+h) = (x+h)^2 + 3(x+h)$. From first principles, we have

$$f'(x) = \lim_{h\to 0} \frac{f(x+h) - f(x)}{h}, \quad \text{provided the limit exists.}$$

$$= \lim_{h\to 0} \frac{(x+h)^2 + 3(x+h) - (x^2+3x)}{h} = \lim_{h\to 0} \frac{x^2 + 2xh + h^2 + 3x + 3h - x^2 - 3x}{h}$$

$$= \lim_{h\to 0} \frac{2xh + h^2 + 3h}{h} = \lim_{h\to 0} \frac{h(2x+3+h)}{h} = \lim_{h\to 0} (2x+3+h) \qquad [\because \ h \neq 0]$$

$$= 2x + 3 + 0 = \mathbf{2x+3}.$$

(ii) We have $f(x) = \frac{1}{x^2} (x \neq 0)$ and $f(x+h) = \frac{1}{(x+h)^2}$.

From first principles, we have

$$f'(x) = \lim_{h\to 0} \frac{f(x+h) - f(x)}{h}, \quad \text{provided the limit exists.}$$

$$= \lim_{h\to 0} \frac{\frac{1}{(x+h)^2} - \frac{1}{x^2}}{h} = \lim_{h\to 0} \frac{\frac{x^2 - (x+h)^2}{(x+h)^2 \cdot x^2}}{h}$$

$$= \lim_{h\to 0} \frac{-(2xh + h^2)}{x^2(x+h)^2} \times \frac{1}{h} = \lim_{h\to 0} \frac{-(2x+h)}{x^2(x+h)^2} \qquad [\because \ h \neq 0]$$

$$= -\frac{\lim_{h\to 0}(2x+h)}{\lim_{h\to 0} x^2(x+h)^2} = -\frac{2x+0}{x^2(x+0)^2} = -\frac{2x}{x^4} = -\frac{\mathbf{2}}{\mathbf{x^3}}.$$

(iii) We have $f(x) = \sqrt{x} (x > 0)$ and $f(x+h) = \sqrt{x+h}$.

From first principles, we get

$$f'(x) = \lim_{h\to 0} \frac{f(x+h) - f(x)}{h}, \quad \text{provided the limit exists.}$$

$$= \lim_{h\to 0} \frac{\sqrt{x+h} - \sqrt{x}}{h} = \lim_{h\to 0} \frac{(\sqrt{x+h} - \sqrt{x})(\sqrt{x+h} + \sqrt{x})}{h(\sqrt{x+h} + \sqrt{x})}$$

$$= \lim_{h\to 0} \frac{(\sqrt{x+h})^2 - (\sqrt{x})^2}{h(\sqrt{x+h} + \sqrt{x})} = \lim_{h\to 0} \frac{x+h-x}{h(\sqrt{x+h} + \sqrt{x})}$$

$$= \lim_{h\to 0} \frac{h}{h(\sqrt{x+h} + \sqrt{x})} = \lim_{h\to 0} \frac{1}{\sqrt{x+h} + \sqrt{x}} \qquad [\because \ h \neq 0]$$

$$= \frac{1}{\sqrt{x+0} + \sqrt{x}} = \frac{\mathbf{1}}{\mathbf{2\sqrt{x}}}.$$

EXAMPLE 3. *Using the first principle (and not otherwise) find the derivative of the function* $x^2 + \frac{1}{x} + 7$. **[ICWAI December 1991]**

SOLUTION. Let $f(x) = x^2 + \frac{1}{x} + 7$; then $f(x+h) = (x+h)^2 + \frac{1}{x+h} + 7$. By the *first principle*, we have

$$\begin{aligned} f'(x) &= \lim_{h\to 0} \frac{f(x+h)-f(x)}{h} = \lim_{h\to 0} \frac{(x+h)^2 + \frac{1}{x+h} + 7 - \left(x^2 + \frac{1}{x} + 7\right)}{h} \\ &= \lim_{h\to 0} \frac{x^2 + 2xh + h^2 + \frac{1}{x+h} + 7 - x^2 - \frac{1}{x} - 7}{h} = \lim_{h\to 0} \frac{2xh + h^2 + \frac{x-x-h}{(x+h)x}}{h} \\ &= \lim_{h\to 0} \frac{2xh + h^2 - \frac{h}{(x+h)x}}{h} = \lim_{h\to 0} \frac{h\left\{2x + h - \frac{1}{(x+h)x}\right\}}{h} \\ &= \lim_{h\to 0} \left\{2x + h - \frac{1}{(x+h)x}\right\} \qquad [\because \ h \neq 0] \\ &= 2x + 0 - \frac{1}{(x+0)\cdot x} = \mathbf{2x - \frac{1}{x^2}}. \end{aligned}$$

7.4. DERIVATIVES OF SOME STANDARD FUNCTIONS

I. *If n is any rational number, prove that* $\frac{d}{dx}(x^n) = nx^{n-1}$. **[Punjab U.]**

RROOF. Let $f(x) = x^n$; then $f(x+h) = (x+h)^n$.

By definition of derivative, we get

$$\begin{aligned} f'(x) &= \lim_{h\to 0} \frac{f(x+h)-f(x)}{h}, \text{ provided the limit exists} \\ &= \lim_{h\to 0} \frac{(x+h)^n - x^n}{h}. \end{aligned}$$

Now let $x + h = z$; then $h = z - x$ and as $h \to 0, z \to x$.

$$\therefore \quad f'(x) = \lim_{z\to x} \frac{z^n - x^n}{z - x} = nx^{n-1}$$

where n is any rational number and x is positive.

Hence, $\frac{d}{dx}(x^n) = nx^{n-1}$, *for all rational values of n and* $x > 0$.

ILLUSTRATION. $\frac{d}{dx}(x^5) = 5x^4$; $\frac{d}{dx}(x^{\frac{3}{2}}) = \frac{3}{2}x^{\frac{3}{2}-1} = \frac{3}{2}x^{\frac{1}{2}}$; $\frac{d}{dx}(x^{-\frac{1}{2}}) = -\frac{1}{2}x^{-\frac{3}{2}}$, etc.

NOTE. If n is a positive integer, the result can be easily proved by using Binomial theorem, i.e., writing $(x+h)^n = x^n + nx^{n-1}h + \frac{n(n-1)}{\lfloor 2}x^{n-2}h^2 + \cdots + h^n$.

If n is not a positive integer, the result can be proved by using Quotient Rule and Chain Rule. We shall discuss this case later.

II. *For all real x, prove that* $\frac{d}{dx}(e^x) = e^x$.

PROOF. Let $f(x) = e^x$; then $f(x+h) = e^{x+h}$.

From definition, we get

$$f'(x) = \lim_{h\to 0} \frac{f(x+h) - f(x)}{h}, \text{ provided the limit exists}$$

$$= \lim_{h\to 0} \frac{e^{x+h} - e^x}{h} = \lim_{h\to 0} \frac{e^x \cdot e^h - e^x}{h}$$

$$= \lim_{h\to 0} \frac{e^x \cdot (e^h - 1)}{h} = e^x \cdot \lim_{h\to 0} \frac{e^h - 1}{h} \qquad [\because\ e^x \text{ does not contain } h]$$

$$= e^x.1. \qquad \left[\because\ \lim_{h\to 0} \frac{e^h - 1}{h} = 1.\right]$$

$$= \mathbf{e^x}.$$

Hence $\frac{\mathbf{d}}{\mathbf{dx}}(\mathbf{e^x}) = \mathbf{e^x}$.

III. *For all values of x and $a > 0$, prove that* $\frac{\mathbf{d}}{\mathbf{dx}}(\mathbf{a^x}) = \mathbf{a^x.\log_e a}$.

SOLUTION. Let $f(x) = a^x (a > 0)$; then $f(x+h) = a^{x+h}$

By definition, we get

$$f'(x) = \lim_{h\to 0} \frac{f(x+h) - f(x)}{h} = \lim_{h\to 0} \frac{a^{x+h} - a^x}{h} = \lim_{h\to 0} \frac{a^x, a^h - a^x}{h} = a^x. \lim_{h\to 0} \frac{a^h - 1}{h}.$$

Now $a^h = e^{h \log_e a}$ $[\because\ \log_e a^h = \log_e e^{h \log_e a} \text{ or, } h \log_e a = h \log_e a]$

and $\lim_{h\to 0} \frac{a^h - 1}{h} = \lim_{h\to 0} \frac{e^{h \log_e a} - 1}{h}$ | Put $h \log_e a = z$; then as $h \to 0, z \to 0$ $h = z/\log_e a$.

$$= \lim_{z\to 0} \frac{e^z - 1}{z/\log_e a} = \log_e a \times \lim_{z\to 0} \frac{e^z - 1}{z} = \log_e a \cdot 1 \qquad \left[\because\ \lim_{z\to 0} \frac{e^z - 1}{z} = 1.\right]$$

$$= \log_e a.$$

$\therefore\ f'(x) = a^x \cdot \log_e a$, i.e., $\frac{\mathbf{d}}{\mathbf{dx}}(\mathbf{a^x}) = \mathbf{a^x.\log_e a}$.

ILLUSTRATION. $\frac{d}{dx}(2^x) = 2^x \log_e 2$, $\frac{d}{dx}(5^x) = 5^x \log_e 5$, etc.

IV. *Prove that* $\frac{\mathbf{d}}{\mathbf{dx}}(\mathbf{\log_e x}) = \frac{\mathbf{1}}{\mathbf{x}}$, *for all* $x > 0$.

SOLUTION. Let $f(x) = \log_e x$; then $f(x+h) = \log_e(x+h)$.

By definition of derivative, we get

$$f'(x) = \lim_{h\to 0} \frac{f(x+h) - f(x)}{h} = \lim_{h\to 0} \frac{\log_e(x+h) - \log_e x}{h} = \lim_{h\to 0} \frac{1}{h} \log_e\left(\frac{x+h}{x}\right)$$

$$= \lim_{h\to 0} \frac{1}{h} \log_e\left(1 + \frac{h}{x}\right) = \lim_{z\to 0} \frac{1}{zx} \log_e(1+z)$$ | Put $z = \frac{h}{x}$; then $h = zx$ and as $h \to 0, z \to 0$

$$= \frac{1}{x} \lim_{z\to 0} \frac{1}{z} \log_e(1+z) = \frac{1}{x} \cdot 1 \qquad \left[\because\ \lim_{z\to 0} \frac{1}{z} \log_e(1+z) = 1.\right]$$

$$= \frac{\mathbf{1}}{\mathbf{x}}.$$

Hence $\frac{\mathbf{d}}{\mathbf{dx}}(\mathbf{\log_e x}) = \frac{\mathbf{1}}{\mathbf{x}}$.

7.5. STANDARD RULES FOR DIFFERENTIATION

RULE 1. **Derivative of any constant c is zero i.e., $\frac{d}{dx}(c) = 0$.**

PROOF. Let $f(x) = c$; then $f(x+h) = c$

$$\therefore \quad f'(x) = \lim_{h \to 0} \frac{f(x+h) - f(x)}{h} = \lim_{h \to 0} \frac{c - c}{h} = 0.$$

ILLUSTRATION. $\frac{d}{dx}(1) = 0, \frac{d}{dx}(2) = 0, \frac{d}{dx}\left(\frac{2}{3}\right) = 0$, etc.

RULE 2. **If c is a constant and g(x) is a function such that g′(x) exists, then $\frac{d}{dx}\{cg(x)\} = c.\frac{d}{dx}\{g(x)\}$.**

PROOF. Let $f(x) = cg(x)$; then $f(x+h) = cg(x+h)$

$$f'(x) = \lim_{h \to 0} \frac{f(x+h) - f(x)}{h} = \lim_{h \to 0} \frac{cg(x+h) - cg(x)}{h}$$

$$= c \lim_{h \to 0} \frac{g(x+h) - g(x)}{h} = c \cdot \frac{d}{dx}\{g(x)\}.$$

$$\text{i.e.,} \quad \frac{d}{dx}\{cg(x)\} = c.\frac{d}{dx}\{g(x)\}.$$

ILLUSTRATION. $\frac{d}{dx}(2x^3) = 2\frac{d}{dx}(x^3) = 2.3x^2 = 6x^2$.

RULE 3. **The derivatives of the sum (or difference) of two functions is the sum (or difference) of their derivatives, provided both the derivatives exist,** i.e., if u, v be two functions of x, then

$$\frac{d}{dx}(u \pm v) = \frac{du}{dx} \pm \frac{dv}{dx}.$$

PROOF. Let $u = \phi(x), v = \psi(x)$ and $f(x) = u + v$.

Then, $f(x) = \phi(x) + \psi(x)$ and $f(x+h) = \phi(x+h) + \psi(x+h)$.

$$\therefore \quad f'(x) = \lim_{h \to 0} \frac{f(x+h) - f(x)}{h} = \lim_{h \to 0} \frac{\phi(x+h) + \psi(x+h) - \phi(x) - \psi(x)}{h}$$

$$= \lim_{h \to 0} \left[\frac{\phi(x+h) - \phi(x)}{h} + \frac{\psi(x+h) - \psi(x)}{h}\right]$$

$$= \lim_{h \to 0} \frac{\phi(x+h) - \phi(x)}{h} + \lim_{h \to 0} \frac{\psi(x+h) - \psi(x)}{h}$$

$$= \phi'(x) + \psi'(x) \text{ i.e., } \frac{d}{dx}(u+v) = \frac{du}{dx} + \frac{dv}{dx}.$$

Similarly, if $f(x) = u - v$, then, $\frac{d}{dx}(u - v) = \frac{du}{dx} - \frac{dv}{dx}$.

Hence, the result follows.

ILLUSTRATION. $\frac{d}{dx}(x^3 + e^x) = \frac{d}{dx}(x^3) + \frac{d}{dx}(e^x) = 3x^2 + e^x$.

RULE 4. **The derivatives of the product of two functions u and v is given by**

$$\frac{d}{dx}(u.v) = u\frac{dv}{dx} + v\frac{du}{dx} \quad \textbf{(Product Rule)}$$

where derivatives of u and v exist.

PROOF. Let $f(x) = u.v$, where $u = \phi(x)$ and $v = \psi(x)$.

Then $f(x) = \phi(x) \cdot \psi(x)$ and $f(x+h) = \phi(x+h).\psi(x+h)$.

$$\begin{aligned}
\therefore \quad f'(x) &= \lim_{h\to 0} \frac{f(x+h)-f(x)}{h} = \lim_{h\to 0} \frac{\phi(x+h)\cdot\psi(x+h) - \phi(x).\psi(x)}{h} \\
&= \lim_{h\to 0} \frac{\phi(x+h)\cdot\psi(x+h) - \phi(x+h).\psi(x) + \phi(x+h).\psi(x) - \phi(x).\psi(x)}{h} \\
&= \lim_{h\to 0} \left[\phi(x+h)\cdot \frac{\psi(x+h)-\psi(x)}{h} + \psi(x)\cdot \frac{\phi(x+h)-\phi(x)}{h}\right] \\
&= \lim_{h\to 0} \phi(x+h)\cdot \lim_{h\to 0} \frac{\psi(x+h)-\psi(x)}{h} + \psi(x)\cdot \lim_{h\to 0}\frac{\phi(x+h)-\phi(x)}{h} \\
&= \phi(x)\cdot\psi'(x) + \psi(x)\cdot\phi'(x).
\end{aligned}$$

Hence the result follows.

ILLUSTRATION.

$$\begin{aligned}
\frac{d}{dx}(e^x \cdot \log x) &= e^x \frac{d}{dx}(\log x) + \log x \frac{d}{dx}(e^x) \\
&= e^x \cdot \frac{1}{x} + \log x \cdot e^x = e^x \left(\frac{1}{x} + \log x\right).
\end{aligned}$$

EXTENSION. $\frac{d}{dx}(u.v.w) = vw\frac{du}{dx} + wu\frac{dv}{dx} + uv\frac{dw}{dx}$; and so on.

RULE 5. **The derivative of the quotient of two functions u and v is given by**

$$\frac{\mathbf{d}}{\mathbf{dx}}\left(\frac{\mathbf{u}}{\mathbf{v}}\right) = \frac{\mathbf{v}\cdot\frac{\mathbf{du}}{\mathbf{dx}} - \mathbf{u}\cdot\frac{\mathbf{dv}}{\mathbf{dx}}}{\mathbf{v^2}} \qquad \textbf{(Quotient Rule)}$$

PROOF. Let $f(x) = \frac{u}{v}$, where $u = \phi(x)$ and $v = \psi(x)$.

Then $f(x) = \frac{\phi(x)}{\psi(x)}$ and $f(x+h) = \frac{\phi(x+h)}{\psi(x+h)}$.

$$\begin{aligned}
\therefore \quad f'(x) &= \lim_{h\to 0} \frac{f(x+h)-f(x)}{h} = \lim_{h\to 0} \frac{\frac{\phi(x+h)}{\psi(x+h)} - \frac{\phi(x)}{\psi(x)}}{h} \\
&= \lim_{h\to 0} \frac{1}{h}\left\{\frac{\phi(x+h).\psi(x) - \psi(x+h).\phi(x)}{\psi(x+h).\psi(x)}\right\} \\
&= \lim_{h\to 0} \frac{1}{h}\left\{\frac{\phi(x+h).\psi(x) - \phi(x).\psi(x) + \phi(x).\psi(x) - \psi(x+h)\phi(x)}{\psi(x+h)\psi(x)}\right\} \\
&= \lim_{h\to 0} \frac{1}{\psi(x+h)\psi(x)}\left[\psi(x)\cdot\frac{\phi(x+h)-\phi(x)}{h} - \phi(x)\cdot\frac{\psi(x+h)-\psi(x)}{h}\right] \\
&= \frac{1}{\{\psi(x)\}^2}\ [\psi(x)\phi'(x) - \phi(x).\psi'(x), \quad \text{taking limits as} \quad h \to 0. \\
&= \frac{v\frac{du}{dx} - u\frac{dv}{dx}}{v^2}.
\end{aligned}$$

ILLUSTRATION.

$$\begin{aligned}
\frac{d}{dx}\left(\frac{x^2}{e^x}\right) &= \frac{e^x \cdot \frac{d}{dx}(x^2) - x^2 . \frac{d}{dx}(e^x)}{(e^x)^2} = \frac{e^x\cdot 2x - x^2\cdot e^x}{e^{2x}} \\
&= \frac{xe^x(2-x)}{e^{2x}} = \frac{x(2-x)}{e^x}.
\end{aligned}$$

RULE 6. **Function of a function : Chain Rule**

If y is a derivable function of z and z is itself a derivable function of x, then y is called a *function of a function of* x and y is also a *derivable function of* x. In this case, we have

$$\frac{\mathbf{dy}}{\mathbf{dx}} = \frac{\mathbf{dy}}{\mathbf{dz}} \times \frac{\mathbf{dz}}{\mathbf{dx}}. \qquad \textbf{[Chain Rule]}$$

ILLUSTRATION. (i) If $y = e^{x^2}$, then we can write $y = e^z$ where $z = x^2$.

Thus y is a function of z and z is a function of x and therefore, y is a *function of a function of* x.

$$\therefore \quad \frac{dy}{dx} = \frac{dy}{dz} \times \frac{dz}{dx} = \frac{d}{dz}(e^z) \times \frac{d}{dx}(x^2) = e^z \times 2x = 2xe^{x^2}.$$

(ii) If $y = (\log_e x)^3$, then we can write $y = z^3$, where $z = \log_e x$.

$$\therefore \quad \frac{dy}{dz} = 3z^{3-1} = 3z^2 \quad \text{and} \quad \frac{dz}{dx} = \frac{d}{dx}(\log_e x) = \frac{1}{x}.$$

By chain Rule,

$$\frac{dy}{dx} = \frac{dy}{dz} \times \frac{dz}{dx} = 3z^2 \cdot \frac{1}{x} = \frac{\mathbf{3(log_e x)^2}}{\mathbf{x}}.$$

This rule can be extended. If y is a function of z, z is a function of w and w is a function of x, then

$$\frac{dy}{dx} = \frac{dy}{dz} \times \frac{dz}{dw} \times \frac{dw}{dx}; \quad \text{and so on.}$$

A Special Case

We can write $\frac{\mathbf{dy}}{\mathbf{dx}} \times \frac{\mathbf{dx}}{\mathbf{dy}} = \mathbf{1}$, or, $\frac{\mathbf{dy}}{\mathbf{dx}} = \mathbf{1}/\frac{\mathbf{dx}}{\mathbf{dy}}$, if $\frac{dx}{dy} \neq 0$.

7.6. ILLUSTRATIVE EXAMPLES

EXAMPLE 1. *Find the derivative of*

(i) $x^4 + 2e^x + 3$; (ii) $2x^{3/2} - 3\log_e x + 6$.

SOLUTION.

(i) Let $y = x^4 + 2e^x + 3$.

Then

$$\begin{aligned}\frac{dy}{dx} &= \frac{d}{dx}(x^4 + 2e^x + 3) = \frac{d}{dx}(x^4) + 2\frac{d}{dx}(e^x) + \frac{d}{dx}(3)\\ &= 4x^{4-1} + 2.e^x + 0 = 4x^3 + 2e^x = \mathbf{2(2x^3 + e^x)}\end{aligned}$$

(ii) Let $y = 2x^{3/2} - 3\log_e x + 6$.

Then

$$\frac{dy}{dx} = 2\frac{d}{dx}(x^{3/2}) - 3\frac{d}{dx}(\log_e x) + \frac{d}{dx}(6) = 2.\frac{3}{2}x^{\frac{3}{2}-1} - 3.\frac{1}{x} + 0$$
$$= 3x^{1/2} - \frac{3}{x} = \mathbf{3\left(\sqrt{x} - \frac{1}{x}\right)}.$$

EXAMPLE 2. *Differentiate with respect to x each of the following:*

(i) $5^x.x^5$; (ii) $\frac{5}{1-3x}$; (iii) $\frac{2x^2+3}{\sqrt{x}}$; (iv) $\frac{a^2-x^2}{a^2+x^2}$. [C.U. 1982]

SOLUTION. (i) Let $y = 5^x.x^5$.

Then

$$\frac{dy}{dx} = \frac{d}{dx}(5^x.x^5) = 5^x.\frac{d}{dx}(x^5) + x^5.\frac{d}{dx}(5^x) = 5^x \cdot 5x^4 + x^5.5^x \log_e 5$$
$$= \mathbf{5^x.x^4(5 + x\log_e 5)}.$$

(ii) Let $y = \frac{5}{1-3x}$.

Then

$$\frac{dy}{dx} = \frac{d}{dx}\left(\frac{5}{1-3x}\right) = \frac{(1-3x).\frac{d}{dx}(5) - 5.\frac{d}{dx}(1-3x)}{(1-3x)^2}$$
$$= \frac{(1-3x).0 - 5.(0-3.1)}{(1-3x)^2} \qquad \left[\because \quad \frac{d}{dx}(x) = 1\right]$$
$$= \frac{0 - 5 \times -3}{(1-3x)^2} = \mathbf{\frac{15}{(1-3x)^2}}.$$

(iii) Let $y = \frac{2x^2+3}{\sqrt{x}}$.

Then

$$\frac{dy}{dx} = \frac{\sqrt{x}.\frac{d}{dx}(2x^2+3) - (2x^2+3)\frac{d}{dx}(\sqrt{x})}{(\sqrt{x})^2} = \frac{\sqrt{x}.(2.2x+0) - (2x^2+3).\frac{1}{2}x^{\frac{1}{2}-1}}{x}$$
$$= \frac{4x\sqrt{x} - (2x^2+3)\frac{1}{2\sqrt{x}}}{x} = \frac{8x^2 - (2x^2+3)}{2x\sqrt{x}} = \frac{6x^2-3}{2x\sqrt{x}} = \mathbf{\frac{3(2x^2-1)}{2x\sqrt{x}}}.$$

(iv) Let $y = \frac{a^2-x^2}{a^2+x^2}$.

Then

$$\frac{dy}{dx} = \frac{(a^2+x^2)\frac{d}{dx}(a^2-x^2) - (a^2-x^2)\frac{d}{dx}(a^2+x^2)}{(a^2+x^2)^2}$$
$$= \frac{(a^2+x^2).(0-2x) - (a^2-x^2)(0+2x)}{(a^2+x^2)^2}$$
$$= \frac{-2a^2x - 2x^3 - 2a^2x + 2x^3}{(a^2+x^2)^2} = \mathbf{-\frac{4a^2x}{(a^2+x^2)^2}}.$$

EXAMPLE 3. *Differentiate with respect to x:*

(i) $(1-5x)^6$; (ii) e^{3x^2-6x+2} **[C.U. B.Com (Hons.) 1982]**

SOLUTION. (i) Let $y=(1-5x)^6$. Then we can write $y=z^6$, where $z=1-5x$.

$$\therefore \quad \frac{dy}{dz}=6.z^{6-1}=6z^5 \quad \text{and} \quad \frac{dz}{dx}=0-5.1=-5.$$

Hence,

$$\frac{dy}{dx}=\frac{dy}{dz}\times\frac{dz}{dx}=6z^5\times -5=\mathbf{-30(1-5x)^5}.$$

(ii) Let $y=e^{3x^2-6x+2}$. Then we can write $y=e^z$, where $z=3x^2-6x+2$.

$$\therefore \quad \frac{dy}{dz}=e^z \quad \text{and} \quad \frac{dz}{dx}=3.2x-6.1=6(x-1).$$

Hence,

$$\frac{dy}{dx}=\frac{dy}{dz}\times\frac{dz}{dx}=e^z.6(x-1)=\mathbf{6(x-1)e^{3x^2-6x+2}}.$$

EXAMPLE 4. *A function $f(x)$ is defined by $f(x)=|x-2|+1$ over all real values of x. Obtain $\lim\limits_{x\to 2+}\frac{f(x)-f(2)}{x-2}$ and $\lim\limits_{x\to 2-}\frac{f(x)-f(2)}{x-2}$.*

What can you say about the derivative of $f(x)$ at $x=2$. **[ICWAI June 1983]**

SOLUTION. We have $f(x)=|x-2|+1$ for all real values of x,

$$\begin{aligned} \text{i.e.,}\quad f(x) &= x-2+1=x-1, \quad \text{when } x>2\\ &= 0+1=1, \quad \text{when } x=2 \qquad \therefore \quad \mathbf{f(2)=1}.\\ &= -(x-2)+1=3-x, \quad \text{when } x<2.\end{aligned}$$

$$\lim_{x\to 2+}\frac{f(x)-f(2)}{x-2}=\lim_{x\to 2+}\frac{(x-1)-1}{x-2}=\lim_{x\to 2+}\frac{x-2}{x-2}=\lim_{x\to 2+}1=1$$

$$\begin{aligned}\text{and}\quad \lim_{x\to 2-}\frac{f(x)-f(2)}{x-2}&=\lim_{x\to 2-}\frac{(3-x)-1}{x-2}=\lim_{x\to 2-}\frac{2-x}{x-2}\\ &=\lim_{x\to 2-}(-1)=-1.\end{aligned}$$

Since $\lim\limits_{x\to 2+}\frac{f(x)-f(2)}{x-2}\neq\lim\limits_{x\to 2-}\frac{f(x)-f(2)}{x-2}$, $f'(2)$ i.e., the derivative of $f(x)$ at $x=2$ *does not exist.*

EXAMPLE 5. *If $\lim\limits_{x\to c}\frac{f(x)-f(c)}{x-c}$ exists, then $f(x)$ has a derivative at $x=c$.*

Using this definition investigate whether $f(x)=\frac{1}{x}$ has a derivative at $x=2$ and obtain the derivative, if it exists. **[ICWAI December 1983]**

SOLUTION. We have

$$f'(c)=\lim_{x\to c}\frac{f(x)-f(c)}{x-c}, \quad \text{provided the limit exists.}$$

Here $f(x) = \frac{1}{x}$ and $c = 2$; $\therefore$ $f(2) = \frac{1}{2}$.

$$\therefore \quad f'(2) = \lim_{x\to 2} \frac{f(x) - f(2)}{x - 2} = \lim_{x\to 2} \frac{\frac{1}{x} - \frac{1}{2}}{x - 2} = \lim_{x\to 2} \frac{2 - x}{2x(x - 2)}$$
$$= \lim_{x\to 2} \frac{-(x - 2)}{2x(x - 2)} = \lim_{x\to 2} -\frac{1}{2x} \quad [\because \; x \neq 2]$$
$$= -\frac{1}{2 \times 2} = -\frac{1}{4}.$$

Since the limit $\lim_{x\to 2} \frac{f(x)-f(2)}{x-2}$ exists, $f(x) = \frac{1}{x}$ has a derivative at $x = 2$ and the derivative is $f'(2) = -\frac{1}{4}$.

EXAMPLE 6. *Obtain the derivative of* $x^2 . \log x$. **[ICWAI June 1981]**

SOLUTION. Let $y = x^2 \log x$.

Then

$$\frac{dy}{dx} = \frac{d}{dx}(x^2 . \log x) = x^2 . \frac{d}{dx}(\log x) + \log x . \frac{d}{dx}(x^2)$$
$$= x^2 . \frac{1}{x} + \log x . 2x = x + 2x \log x = \mathbf{x(1 + 2 \log x)}.$$

EXAMPLE 7. *Differentiate each of the following functions:*

(i) $\frac{3-5x}{3+5x}$; (ii) $\sqrt{2x} + 3^{2x}$; (iii) $(x^2 + 2)^5 (3x^4 - 5)^4$. **[C.U. 1982; ICWAI]**

SOLUTION. (i) Let $y = \frac{3-5x}{3+5x}$.

Then

$$\frac{dy}{dx} = \frac{(3 + 5x)\frac{d}{dx}(3 - 5x) - (3 - 5x).\frac{d}{dx}(3 + 5x)}{(3 + 5x)^2}$$
$$= \frac{(3 + 5x).(0 - 5.1) - (3 - 5x).(0 + 5.1)}{(3 + 5x)^2} = \frac{-15 - 25x - 15 + 25x}{(3 + 5x)^2} = \frac{\mathbf{-30}}{\mathbf{(3 + 5x)^2}}.$$

(ii) Let $y = \sqrt{2x} + 3^{2x}$.

Then $y = \sqrt{2}.x^{\frac{1}{2}} + 3^{2x}$

$$\therefore \quad \frac{dy}{dx} = \sqrt{2}.\frac{d}{dx}(x^{\frac{1}{2}}) + \frac{d}{dx}(3^{2x}) = \sqrt{2}.\frac{1}{2}.x^{(1/2)-1} + \frac{dz}{dx}, \text{ where } z = 3^{2x}$$

Now $z = 3^{2x} = 3^u$, where $u = 2x$

$$\therefore \quad \frac{dz}{du} = 3^u \log_e 3 \text{ and } \frac{du}{dx} = 2.1 = 2$$
$$\therefore \quad \frac{dz}{dx} = \frac{dz}{du} \times \frac{du}{dx} = 3^u \log_e 3 \times 2 = 2.3^{2x} . \log_e 3.$$
$$\therefore \quad \frac{dy}{dx} = \sqrt{2}.\frac{1}{2}.x^{-\frac{1}{2}} + 2.3^{2x} \log_e 3 = \frac{\mathbf{1}}{\mathbf{\sqrt{2x}}} + \mathbf{2.3^{2x} \log_e 3}$$

(iii) Let $y = (x^2+2)^5.(3x^4-5)^4$

$= u^5.v^4,$ where $u = x^2+2$ and $v = 3x^4-5$.

Then

$$\frac{du}{dx} = \frac{d}{dx}(x^2+2) = 2x, \text{ and } \frac{dv}{dx} = \frac{d}{dx}(3x^4-5) = 12x^3.$$

$$\therefore \quad \frac{dy}{dx} = u^5\frac{d}{dx}(v^4) + v^4\frac{d}{dx}(u^5) = u^5\frac{d}{dv}(v^4)\times\frac{dv}{dx} + v^4\frac{d}{du}(u^5)\times\frac{du}{dx}.$$

$$= u^5.4v^3 \times 12x^3 + v^4.5u^4 \times 2x = 48u^5v^3x^3 + 10u^4v^4x$$

$$= 2xu^4v^3(24ux^2+5v) = 2x(x^2+2)^4.(3x^4-5)^3\{24x^2(x^2+2)+5(3x^4-5)\}$$

$$= \mathbf{2x(x^2+2)^4(3x^4-5)^3(39x^4+48x^2-25)}$$

NOTE. If $y = f(v)$ and $v = \phi(x)$, we can write

$$\frac{dy}{dx} = \frac{dy}{dv}\times\frac{dv}{dx} = f'(v)\cdot\frac{dv}{dx}.$$

In the above problem, v^4 is a function of v and v is a function of x. Hence we can write

$$\frac{d}{dx}(v^4) = \frac{d}{dv}(v^4)\times\frac{dv}{dx} = 4v^3\cdot\frac{dv}{dx}.$$

Similarly,

$$\frac{d}{dx}(u^5) = \frac{d}{du}(u^5)\cdot\frac{du}{dx} = 5u^4\cdot\frac{du}{dx}.$$

[OTHERWISE. Taking logarithms of both sides, we get

$$\log_e y = 5\log_e(x^2+2) + 4\log_e(3x^4-5).$$

Differentiating both sides w.r.t. x, we get

$$\frac{d}{dx}(\log y) = 5\cdot\frac{d}{dx}\{\log(x^2+2)\} + 4\cdot\frac{d}{dx}\{\log(3x^4-5)\}$$

$$\text{or,} \quad \frac{1}{y}\cdot\frac{dy}{dx} = 5\cdot\frac{1}{x^2+2}\times(2x+0) + 4\cdot\frac{1}{3x^4-5}\times(12x^3-0)$$

$$= \frac{10x}{x^2+2} + \frac{48x^3}{3x^4-5} = \frac{78x^5+96x^3-50x}{(x^2+2)(3x^4-5)}$$

$$\therefore \quad \frac{dy}{dx} = \frac{y(78x^5+96x^3-50x)}{(x^2+2)(3x^4-5)} = \text{etc.}]$$

EXAMPLE 8. *Find* $\frac{dy}{dx}$ *if* $y = \log\left[e^x.\left(\frac{x-2}{x+2}\right)^{\frac{3}{4}}\right]$. **[CA May 1978]**

SOLUTION. We have

$$y = \log e^x + \frac{3}{4}\{\log(x-2) - \log(x+2)\} = x\log e + \frac{3}{4}\{\log(x-2) - \log(x+2)\}$$

$$= x + \frac{3}{4}\{\log(x-2) - \log(x+2)\} \qquad [\because \log e = 1]$$

$$\therefore \quad \frac{dy}{dx} = \frac{d}{dx}(x) + \frac{3}{4}\left[\frac{d}{dx}\{\log(x-2)\} - \frac{d}{dx}\{\log(x+2)\}\right]$$

$$= 1 + \frac{3}{4}\left[\frac{1}{x-2} \times (1-0) - \frac{1}{x+2} \times (1+0)\right]$$

[∵ $\log(x-2)$ and $\log(x+2)$ are functions of a function of x.]

$$= 1 + \frac{3}{4}.\left[\frac{x+2-x+2}{(x-2)(x+2)}\right] = 1 + \frac{3}{4} \times \frac{4}{x^2-2^2} = 1 + \frac{3}{x^2-4} = \frac{x^2-4+3}{x^2-4} = \frac{\mathbf{x^2-1}}{\mathbf{x^2-4}}.$$

7.7. LOGARITHMIC DIFFERENTIATION

If the power of a function of x is also a function of x (or a root) or if the function is a product of a number of functions, then it would be convenient for us if we first take logarithm w.r.t. the base e and then differentiate w.r.t. x. The following examples will make the idea clear.

Note that $\frac{d}{dx}(\log y) = \frac{d}{dy}(\log y) \cdot \frac{dy}{dx} = \frac{1}{y} \cdot \frac{dy}{dx}$.

EXAMPLE 9. *Find the derivative of the following functions:*

(i) $f(x) = \sqrt[3]{\frac{4+5x}{4-5x}}$; (ii) $\phi(x) = e^{\frac{x^2}{1+x^3}}$. **[ICWAI June 1979]**

SOLUTION. (i) We have $y = f(x) = \sqrt[3]{\frac{4+5x}{4-5x}} = \left(\frac{4+5x}{4-5x}\right)^{\frac{1}{3}}$

$\therefore \quad \log_e y = \frac{1}{3}[\log_e(4+5x) - \log_e(4-5x)]$

Differentiating both sides w.r.t. x, we get

$$\frac{1}{y} \cdot \frac{dy}{dx} = \frac{1}{3}\left[\frac{d}{dx}\{\log(4+5x)\} - \frac{d}{dx}\{\log(4-5x)\}\right]$$

$$= \frac{1}{3}\left[\frac{1}{4+5x} \times (0+5.1) - \frac{1}{4-5x} \times (0-5.1)\right]$$

$$= \frac{1}{3}\left[\frac{5}{4+5x} + \frac{5}{4-5x}\right] = \frac{5}{3} \cdot \left[\frac{4-5x+4+5x}{(4+5x)(4-5x)}\right]$$

$$= \frac{5}{3} \times \frac{8}{4^2-(5x)^2} = \frac{\mathbf{40}}{\mathbf{3(16-25x^2)}}$$

$$\therefore \quad \frac{dy}{dx} = \frac{40y}{3(16-25x^2)} = \frac{\mathbf{40}}{\mathbf{3(16-25x^2)}} \cdot \sqrt[3]{\frac{\mathbf{4+5x}}{\mathbf{4-5x}}}.$$

(ii) We have $y = \phi(x) = e^{\frac{x^2}{1+x^3}}$.

$\therefore \quad \log_e y = \frac{x^2}{1+x^3} \cdot \log_e e = \frac{x^2}{1+x^3} \quad [\because \quad \log_e e = 1]$

Differentiating both sides w.r.t. x, we get

$$\frac{1}{y} \cdot \frac{dy}{dx} = \frac{(1+x^3)\frac{d}{dx}(x^2) - x^2\frac{d}{dx}(1+x^3)}{(1+x^3)^2} = \frac{(1+x^3) \cdot 2x - x^2 \cdot (0+3x^2)}{(1+x^3)^2}$$

$$= \frac{2x+2x^4-3x^4}{(1+x^3)^2} = \frac{2x-x^4}{(1+x^3)^2} = \frac{x(2-x^3)}{(1+x^3)^2}$$

$$\therefore \quad \frac{dy}{dx} = y \cdot \frac{x(2-x^3)}{(1+x^3)^2} = \frac{\mathbf{x(2-x^3)}}{\mathbf{(1+x^3)^2}} \cdot \mathbf{e^{\frac{x^2}{1+x^3}}}.$$

EXAMPLE 10. *Find* $\frac{dy}{dx}$ *if* (i) $y = x^x$ **[CA November 1976; C.U. B.Com (Hons.) 1981, '85, '90]**

(ii) x^{e^x}. **[CA November 1975]**; (iii) x^{x^x} **[CA May 1975; Delhi U. 1981]**

SOLUTION. (i) Let $y = x^x$.

Then $\log_e y = x \log_e x$.

Differentiating both sides w.r.t. x, we get

$$\frac{1}{y} \cdot \frac{dy}{dx} = x \cdot \frac{d}{dx}(\log x) + \log x \cdot \frac{d}{dx}(x) = x \cdot \frac{1}{x} + \log x.1 = 1 + \log x$$

$$\therefore \quad \frac{dy}{dx} = y \cdot (1 + \log x) = \mathbf{x^x(1 + \log_e x)}.$$

(ii) Let $y = x^{e^x} = (x)^{e^x}$.

Then $\log_e y = e^x . \log_e x$.

Differentiating both sides w.r.t. x, we get

$$\frac{1}{y} \cdot \frac{dy}{dx} = e^x \cdot \frac{d}{dx}(\log x) + \log x \cdot \frac{d}{dx}(e^x) = e^x \cdot \frac{1}{x} + \log x . e^x = e^x \left(\frac{1}{x} + \log x\right);$$

$$\therefore \quad \frac{dy}{dx} = y . e^x \left(\frac{1}{x} + \log x\right) = \mathbf{x^{e^x} \cdot e^x \left(\frac{1}{x} + \log x\right)}$$

(iii) Let $y = x^{x^x} = (x)^{x^x}$.

Taking logarithms of both sides,

$$\log_e y = x^x . \log_e x.$$

Differentiating both sides w.r.t. x, we get

$$\frac{1}{y} \cdot \frac{dy}{dx} = x^x \cdot \frac{d}{dx}(\log x) + \log x \cdot \frac{d}{dx}(x^x) = x^x \cdot \frac{1}{x} + \log x . x^x (1 + \log x) \quad \text{[See (i) above]}$$

$$= x^{x-1} + x^x (1 + \log x) \log x$$

$$\therefore \quad \frac{dy}{dx} = y . [x^{x-1} + x^x (1 + \log x) \log x]$$

$$= \mathbf{x^{x^x} [x^{x-1} + x^x (1 + \log x) \log x]}, \text{ base being } e.$$

EXAMPLE 11. *If* $y = \frac{x}{\sqrt{1+x^2}}$, *prove that* $x^3 \frac{dy}{dx} = y^3$. **[ICWAI December 1983]**

SOLUTION. We have $y = \frac{x}{\sqrt{1+x^2}}$ (1)

$$\therefore \quad \frac{dy}{dx} = \frac{\sqrt{1+x^2} \cdot \frac{d}{dx}(x) - x \cdot \frac{d}{dx}(\sqrt{1+x^2})}{(\sqrt{1+x^2})^2} = \frac{\sqrt{1+x^2}.1 - x . \frac{1}{2}(1+x^2)^{\frac{1}{2}-1} . 2x}{1+x^2}$$

$$= \frac{\sqrt{1+x^2} - \frac{x^2}{\sqrt{1+x^2}}}{1+x^2} = \frac{\frac{1+x^2-x^2}{\sqrt{1+x^2}}}{1+x^2} = \frac{1}{\sqrt{1+x^2}} \times \frac{1}{1+x^2} = \frac{1}{\left(\sqrt{1+x^2}\right)^3}$$

From (1), $\sqrt{1+x^2} = \frac{x}{y}$; $\therefore$ $(\sqrt{1+x^2})^3 = \frac{x^3}{y^3}$.

$\frac{dy}{dx} = \frac{1}{x^3/y^3} = \frac{y^3}{x^3}$, or, $\mathbf{x^3 . \frac{dy}{dx} = y^3}$.

OTHERWISE. $\log y = \log x - \frac{1}{2}\log(1+x^2)$. Differentiating both sides w.r.t. x, we get

$$\frac{1}{y}\cdot\frac{dy}{dx} = \frac{1}{x} - \frac{1}{2}\cdot\frac{1}{1+x^2}\times(0+2x) = \frac{1}{x} - \frac{x}{1+x^2} = \frac{1+x^2-x^2}{x(1+x^2)}$$

$$= \frac{1}{x(1+x^2)}; \quad \therefore \quad \frac{dy}{dx} = \frac{y}{x(1+x^2)} = \frac{y}{x.x^2/y^2} = \frac{y^3}{x^3}, \quad \text{or,} \quad x^3.\frac{dy}{dx} = y^3.]$$

7.8. DIFFERENTIATION OF IMPLICIT FUNCTIONS

Sometimes the relation between two vaiables x and y is given by an equation of the form $f(x,y)=0$ and in such a case, none of the variables is directly expressed in terms of other. But the equation may define y as a function of x. In this case, y is called an **implicit function** of x, the relation being the *implicit function* of x and y.

ILLUSTRATION. $x^2+4y=8, x^2-2uy+3y^2=0$, etc. are implicit functions of x and y, each of which defines y as an *implicit function* of x.

To find $\frac{dy}{dx}$ when y is an implicit function of x, we differentiate each term of the equation with respect to x and then solve for $\frac{dy}{dx}$. The following examples will illustrate the process of obtaining $\frac{dy}{dx}$ from an implicit function.

EXAMPLE 12. (i) *Find $\frac{dy}{dx}$ if $x^2-2xy+y^2-2x=0$;*

(ii) *Find $\frac{dy}{dx}$ If $x^3+y^3=3axy$.* **[ICWAI December 1990]**

SOLUTION. (i) We have $x^2-2xy+y^2-2x=0$.

Differentiating each term w.r.t. x, we get

$$2x - 2(1.y + x.\frac{dy}{dx}) + 2y\frac{dy}{dx} - 2.1 = 0.$$

$$\text{or,} \quad x - y - x\frac{dy}{dx} + y\frac{dy}{dx} - 1 = 0, \quad \text{or,} \quad y\frac{dy}{dx} - x\frac{dy}{dx} = y - x + 1$$

$$\text{or,} \quad \frac{dy}{dx}(y-x) = y - x + 1; \quad \therefore \quad \mathbf{\frac{dy}{dx} = \frac{y-x+1}{y-x}}.$$

(ii) We have $x^3+y^3=3axy$ (1)

Differentiating both sides w.r.t. 'x', we get

$$3x^2 + 3y^2\cdot\frac{dy}{dx} = 3a\left(x\frac{dy}{dx} + 1.y\right) = 3ax\frac{dy}{dx} + 3ay$$

$$\text{or,} \quad x^2 + y^2\cdot\frac{dy}{dx} = ax\frac{dy}{dx} + ay, \quad \text{or,} \quad \frac{dy}{dx}(y^2 - ax) = ay - x^2$$

$$\text{or,} \quad \mathbf{\frac{dy}{dx} = \frac{ay^2 - x^2}{y^2 - ax}}.$$

EXAMPLE 13. *Find $\frac{dy}{dx}$ at $x=1, y=1$ if $x^3-2x^2y^2+5x+y-5=0$.*

[ICWAI December 1982]

SOLUTION. We have $x^3 - 2x^2y^2 + 5x + y - 5 = 0$.

Differentiating each term w.r.t. x, we get

$$3x^2 - 2\left(2xy^2 + x^2.2y\frac{dy}{dx}\right) + 5.1 + \frac{dy}{dx} - 0 = 0,$$

$$\text{or,}\quad \frac{dy}{dx} - 4x^2y.\frac{dy}{dx} = 4xy^2 - 3x^2 - 5$$

$$\text{or,}\quad \frac{dy}{dx}(1 - 4x^2y) = 4xy^2 - 3x^2 - 5$$

$$\text{or,}\quad \frac{dy}{dx} = \frac{4xy^2 - 3x^2 - 5}{1 - 4x^2y}.$$

At $x = 1, y = 1, \frac{dy}{dx} = \frac{4.1.1^2 - 3.1^2 - 5}{1 - 4.1^2.1} = \frac{-4}{-3} = \frac{4}{3}$.

EXAMPLE 14. *If* $x^y = e^{x-y}$, *prove that* $\frac{dy}{dx} = \frac{\log x}{(1+\log x)^2}$.

[CA May 1976; November 1978; C.U. 1981; ICWAI June 1985]

SOLUTION. We have $x^y = e^{x-y}$.

Taking logarithms of both sides, we get

$$y \log_e x = (x - y)\log_e e = (x - y).1 = x - y,$$

$$\text{or,}\quad y\log x + y = x, \quad \text{or,}\quad y(\log x + 1) = x,$$

$$\therefore\quad y = \frac{x}{\log x + 1}.$$

Differentiating both sides w.r.t. x, we get

$$\frac{dy}{dx} = \frac{(\log x + 1)\frac{d(x)}{dx} - x \cdot \frac{d}{dx}(\log x + 1)}{(\log x + 1)^2} = \frac{(\log x + 1)\cdot 1 - x \cdot \left(\frac{1}{x} + 0\right)}{(\log x + 1)^2}$$

$$= \frac{\log x + 1 - 1}{(\log x + 1)^2} = \frac{\mathbf{log\ x}}{(\mathbf{log\ x + 1})^2}.$$

EXAMPLE 15. *Find* $\frac{dy}{dx}$ *if* $e^{xy} - 4xy = 4$. **[ICWAI December 1989]**

SOLUTION. We have $e^{xy} - 4xy = 4$ (1)

Differentiating both sides w.r.t. 'x', we get

$$e^{xy} \cdot \frac{d}{dx}(xy) - 4\left(1.y + x.\frac{dy}{dx}\right) = 0$$

$$\text{or,}\quad e^{xy}\left(1.y + x\frac{dy}{dx}\right) - 4\left(y + x\frac{dy}{dx}\right) = 0$$

$$\text{or,}\quad \left(y + x\frac{dy}{dx}\right)\left(e^{xy} - 4\right) = 0$$

$$\therefore\quad \text{either}\quad y + x\frac{dy}{dx} = 0 \quad \text{or,}\quad e^{xy} - 4 = 0.$$

If $y + x\frac{dy}{dx} = 0$, then $x\frac{dy}{dx} = -y$, or, $\frac{dy}{dx} = -\frac{y}{x}$.

If $e^{xy} - 4 = 0$, then $e^{xy} = 4$ and from (1), we get $-4xy = 0$, or, $xy = 0$ *which is not possible.* For, then (1) becomes $e^{\circ} - 4.0 = 4$ i.e., $1 = 4$ which is absurd.

Hence $e^{xy} - 4 \neq 0$ and $\frac{dy}{dx} = -\frac{y}{x}$.

EXAMPLE 16. *If* $x^m y^n = (x+y)^{m+n}$, *prove that* $\frac{dy}{dx} = \frac{y}{x}$.

[C.U. May 1977, '86; ICWAI December 1980; C.U. B.Com (Hons.) 1983]

SOLUTION. We have $x^m y^n = (x+y)^{m+n}$.

Taking logarithm of both sides, w.r.t. the base e, we get

$$m \log x + n \log y = (m+n) \log(x+y).$$

Differentiating both sides w.r.t. x, we get

$$m \cdot \frac{1}{x} + n \cdot \frac{1}{y} \cdot \frac{dy}{dx} = (m+n).\frac{1}{x+y} \times \left(1 + \frac{dy}{dx}\right),$$

$$\text{or,} \quad \frac{m}{x} + \frac{n}{y} \cdot \frac{dy}{dx} = \frac{m+n}{x+y} + \frac{m+n}{x+y} \cdot \frac{dy}{dx},$$

$$\text{or,} \quad \frac{n}{y}.\frac{dy}{dx} - \frac{m+n}{x+y}.\frac{dy}{dx} = \frac{m+n}{x+y} - \frac{m}{x},$$

$$\text{or,} \quad \frac{dy}{dx}\left(\frac{n}{y} - \frac{m+n}{x+y}\right) = \frac{mx + nx - mx - my}{(x+y)x}$$

$$\text{or,} \quad \frac{dy}{dx}\left\{\frac{nx + ny - my - ny}{y(x+y)}\right\} = \frac{nx - my}{(x+y)x}$$

$$\text{or,} \quad \frac{dy}{dx}\left\{\frac{nx - my}{y(x+y)}\right\} = \frac{nx - my}{(x+y)x};$$

$$\therefore \quad \frac{dy}{dx} = \frac{nx - my}{(x+y)x} \times \frac{y(x+y)}{nx - my} = \frac{\mathbf{y}}{\mathbf{x}}.$$

7.9. TO FIND DERIVATIVE FROM PARAMETRIC EQUATIONS

In some cases, both the variables x and y concerning the equation of a curve are expressed in terms of a third variable t (or θ or α). The two relations which express x and y in terms of t (or θ or α) are together called the **parametric equations** of the curve. The third variable t (or θ or α) is called a **parameter.**

For example, $x = at^2$ and $y = 2at$ are the parametric equations of the parabola $y^2 = 4ax$.

In general, the parametric equations of a curve are taken as $\mathbf{x} = \phi(\mathbf{t})$ **and** $\mathbf{y} = \psi(\mathbf{t})$.

To find $\frac{dy}{dx}$ from *parametric equations*, we first calculate $\frac{dx}{dt}$ and $\frac{dy}{dt}$ and then write

$$\frac{\mathbf{dy}}{\mathbf{dx}} = \frac{\mathbf{dy}}{\mathbf{dt}} \times \frac{\mathbf{dt}}{\mathbf{dx}} = \frac{\mathbf{dy}}{\mathbf{dt}} \Big/ \frac{\mathbf{dx}}{\mathbf{dt}}, \text{ where } \frac{dx}{dt} \neq 0.$$

ILLUSTRATION. For the parabola $x = at^2, y = 2at$,

we have $\frac{dx}{dt} = 2at$ and $\frac{dy}{dt} = 2a$;

$$\therefore \quad \frac{dy}{dx} = \frac{dy}{dt} \Big/ \frac{dx}{dt} = \frac{2a}{2at} = \frac{1}{t}, \text{ where } t \neq 0.$$

EXAMPLE 17. *If $x = t \log t, y = \log t/t$, find $\frac{dx}{dt}$ and $\frac{dy}{dt}$. Now find $\frac{dy}{dx}$ when $t = 1$.*

[ICWAI June 1983]

SOLUTION. We have $x = t. \log t$ and $y = \frac{\log t}{t}$.

$$\therefore \quad \frac{dx}{dt} = \frac{d}{dt}(t \log t) = t \cdot \frac{d}{dt}(\log t) + \log t. \frac{d}{dt}(t)$$

$$= t \cdot \frac{1}{t} + \log t.1 = \mathbf{1 + \log t}.$$

$$\text{and} \quad \frac{dy}{dt} = \frac{d}{dt}\left(\frac{\log t}{t}\right) = \frac{t \frac{d}{dt}(\log t) - \log t \frac{d}{dt}(t)}{t^2}$$

$$= \frac{t \cdot \frac{1}{t} - \log t.1}{t^2} = \frac{\mathbf{1 - \log t}}{\mathbf{t^2}}$$

Now, $\frac{dy}{dx} = \frac{dy}{dt} \Big/ \frac{dx}{dt} = \frac{1-\log t}{t^2} \Big/ (1 + \log t) = \frac{1-\log t}{t^2(1+\log t)}$

At $t = 1$, $\frac{dy}{dx} = \frac{1-\log 1}{1^2(1+\log 1)} = \frac{1-0}{1(1+0)} = \mathbf{1}$.

Miscellaneous Examples

EXAMPLE 18. *If $y = x^{x^{x \cdots \infty}}$, prove that $x\frac{dy}{dx} = \frac{y^2}{1 - y \log x}$.* **[Punjab U. B.Com 1973]**

SOLUTION. We have $y = x^{x^{x \cdots \infty}} = x^y$, where $y = x^{x^{x \cdots \infty}}$

$\therefore \quad \log_e y = y \log_e x$.

Differentiating both sides w.r.t. x, we get

$$\frac{1}{y} \cdot \frac{dy}{dx} = y. \frac{d}{dx}(\log x) + \log x \frac{dy}{dx} = y. \frac{1}{x} + \log x \frac{dy}{dx}$$

$$\text{or,} \quad \frac{1}{y} \cdot \frac{dy}{dx} - \log x \frac{dy}{dx} = \frac{y}{x} \quad \text{or,} \quad \frac{dy}{dx}\left(\frac{1}{y} - \log x\right) = \frac{y}{x},$$

$$\text{or,} \quad x\frac{dy}{dx} = \frac{y}{\frac{1}{y} - \log x} = \frac{\mathbf{y^2}}{\mathbf{1 - y \log x}}.$$

EXAMPLE 19. *If $y = \log_e(x + \sqrt{x^2 + a^2})$, find $\frac{dy}{dx}$.*

[C.U. B.Com (Hons.) 1986, '94; Guru Nanak U. 1981; ICWAI December 1990]

SOLUTION. We have $y = \log_e(x + \sqrt{x^2 + a^2})$

$$\therefore \quad \frac{dy}{dx} = \frac{1}{x + \sqrt{x^2 + a^2}} \times \frac{d}{dx}(x + \sqrt{x^2 + a^2}) = \frac{1}{x + \sqrt{x^2 + a^2}} \times \left\{1 + \frac{1}{2}(x^2 + a^2)^{\frac{1}{2}-1} \times (2x + 0)\right\}$$

$$= \frac{1}{x + \sqrt{x^2 + a^2}} \times \left\{1 + \frac{x}{\sqrt{x^2 + a^2}}\right\} = \frac{1}{(x + \sqrt{x^2 + a^2})} \times \frac{(\sqrt{x^2 + a^2} + x)}{\sqrt{x^2 + a^2}} = \frac{\mathbf{1}}{\sqrt{\mathbf{x^2 + a^2}}}.$$

EXAMPLE 20. *If* $x = \frac{2t}{1+t^2}, y = \frac{1-t^2}{1+t^2}$, *prove that* $\frac{dy}{dx} + \frac{x}{y} = 0$. **[ICWAI June 1989]**

SOLUTION. We have $x = \frac{2t}{1+t^2}$ and $y = \frac{1-t^2}{1+t^2}$.

$$\therefore \quad \frac{dx}{dt} = \frac{(1+t^2)\cdot\frac{d}{dt}(2t) - 2t\cdot\frac{d}{dt}(1+t^2)}{(1+t^2)^2}$$
$$= \frac{(1+t^2).2.1 - 2t.(0+2t)}{(1+t^2)^2}$$
$$= \frac{2+2t^2-4t^2}{(1+t^2)^2} = \frac{2-2t^2}{(1+t^2)^2}$$

$$\text{and} \quad \frac{dy}{dt} = \frac{(1+t^2)\frac{d}{dt}(1-t^2) - (1-t^2)\frac{d}{dt}(1+t^2)}{(1+t^2)^2} = \frac{(1+t^2)\times -2t - (1-t^2)\times 2t}{(1+t^2)^2}$$
$$= \frac{-2t-2t^3-2t+2t^3}{(1+t^2)^2} = \frac{-4t}{(1+t^2)^2}$$

$$\therefore \quad \frac{dy}{dx} = \frac{\frac{dy}{dt}}{\frac{dx}{dt}} = \frac{\frac{-4t}{(1+t^2)^2}}{\frac{2-2t^2}{(1+t^2)^2}} = \frac{-4t}{2(1-t^2)} = -\frac{2t}{1-t^2}$$

$$\text{Now} \quad \frac{x}{y} = \frac{2t}{1+t^2}\times\frac{1+t^2}{1-t^2} = \frac{2t}{1-t^2}$$

$$\therefore \quad \frac{dy}{dx} = -\frac{x}{y}, \text{ or, } \mathbf{\frac{dy}{dx} + \frac{x}{y} = 0}..$$

EXAMPLE 21. *If* $y = \sqrt[5]{\frac{(x+1)(x-2)}{(x-3)(x+4)}}$, *find* $\frac{dy}{dx}$.

SOLUTION. We have $y = \left[\frac{(x+1)(x-2)}{(x-3)(x+4)}\right]^{\frac{1}{5}}$ (1)

Taking logarithm of both sides, we get

$$\log y = \frac{1}{5}[\log(x+1) + \log(x-2) - \log(x-3) - \log(x+4)]$$

Differentiating both sides w.r.t. x, we get

$$\frac{1}{y}\cdot\frac{dy}{dx} = \frac{1}{5}\left[\frac{d}{dx}\{\log(x+1)\} + \frac{d}{dx}\{\log(x-2)\} - \frac{d}{dx}\{\log(x-3)\} - \frac{d}{dx}\{\log(x+4)\}\right]$$
$$= \frac{1}{5}\left[\frac{1}{x+1}\times(1+0) + \frac{1}{x-2}\times(1-0) - \frac{1}{x-3}\times(1-0) - \frac{1}{x-4}\times(1+0)\right]$$
$$= \frac{1}{5}\left[\frac{1}{x+1} + \frac{1}{x-2} - \frac{1}{x-3} - \frac{1}{x+4}\right]$$

$$\therefore \quad \mathbf{\frac{dy}{dx} = \frac{y}{5}\left[\frac{1}{x+1} + \frac{1}{x-2} - \frac{1}{x-3} - \frac{1}{x+4}\right]}, \text{ where } y \text{ is given by (1).}$$

EXAMPLE 22. *If* $\sqrt{1-x^2} + \sqrt{1-y^2} = a(x-y)$, *show that* $\frac{dy}{dx} = \frac{\sqrt{1-y^2}}{\sqrt{1-x^2}}$.

[ICWAI (Final) December 1979]

SOLUTION. We have $\sqrt{1-x^2} + \sqrt{1-y^2} = a(x-y)$. (1)

Differentiating both sides w.r.t. x, we get

$$\frac{1}{2}(1-x^2)^{\frac{1}{2}-1}\times(0-2x)+\frac{1}{2}(1-y^2)^{\frac{1}{2}-1}\times\left(0-2y\cdot\frac{dy}{dx}\right)=a\left(1-\frac{dy}{dx}\right)$$

or, $$-\frac{x}{\sqrt{1-x^2}}-\frac{y}{\sqrt{1-y^2}}\cdot\frac{dy}{dx}=a-a\frac{dy}{dx}$$

or, $$a\frac{dy}{dx}-\frac{y}{\sqrt{1-y^2}}\cdot\frac{dy}{dx}=a+\frac{x}{\sqrt{1-x^2}}$$

or, $$\frac{dy}{dx}\left(a-\frac{y}{\sqrt{1-y^2}}\right)=a+\frac{x}{\sqrt{1-x^2}}$$

or, $$\frac{dy}{dx}\left(\frac{a\sqrt{1-y^2}-y}{\sqrt{1-y^2}}\right)=\frac{a\sqrt{1-x^2}+x}{\sqrt{1-x^2}}$$

$$\therefore\quad \frac{dy}{dx}=\frac{a\sqrt{1-x^2}+x}{a\sqrt{1-y^2}-y}\times\frac{\sqrt{1-y^2}}{\sqrt{1-x^2}} \qquad (2)$$

Now from (1), $a=\frac{\sqrt{1-x^2}+\sqrt{1-y^2}}{x-y}$,

and $$\frac{a\sqrt{1-x^2}+x}{a\sqrt{1-y^2}-y}=\frac{\left(\frac{\sqrt{1-x^2}+\sqrt{1-y^2}}{x-y}\right)\sqrt{1-x^2}+x}{\left(\frac{\sqrt{1-x^2}+\sqrt{1-y^2}}{x-y}\right)\sqrt{1-y^2}-y}$$

$$=\frac{1-x^2+\sqrt{(1-x^2)(1-y^2)}+x^2-xy}{\sqrt{(1-x^2)(1-y^2)}+1-y^2-xy+y^2}=\frac{\sqrt{(1-x^2)(1-y^2)}+1-xy}{\sqrt{(1-x^2)(1-y^2)}+1-xy}=1.$$

Hence from (2), $\frac{dy}{dx}=1\times\frac{\sqrt{1-y^2}}{\sqrt{1-x^2}}=\frac{\sqrt{1-y^2}}{\sqrt{1-x^2}}$.

[OTHERWISE. If we put $x=\sin\theta, y=\sin\phi$, then $\cos\theta+\cos\phi=a(\sin\theta-\sin\phi)$ which gives $\tan\frac{\theta-\phi}{2}=\frac{1}{a}$ or, $\theta-\phi=2\tan^{-1}\frac{1}{a}$; etc.]

Exercise 7(I)

[Derivatives]

[A]

1. Define the derivative of a function of one variable. **[C.U. B.Com (Hons.) 1980]**

2. (i) If $f(x)$ has a finite derivative at $x=a$, prove that $f(x)$ is continuous at $x=a$. **[C.U. B.Com (Hons.) 1981]**

(ii) Show by an example that if a function be continuous at a point, it is not necessarily derivable at the point. **[C.U. B.Com (Hons.) 1981]**

3. Find from the *first principles the derivative* of the following functions

(i) x; (ii) x^2; (iii) $3x+2$; (iv) $x^2-2x; 2x^2+3$;

(v) $\frac{1}{x}(x\neq 0)$; (vi) x^3+4x; (vii) $\sqrt{x}$; (viii) $\frac{1}{\sqrt{x}}(x>0)$;

(ix) $\sqrt[3]{x}$; (x) e^x; (xi) $\log_e x(x>0)$; (xii) 2^x.

4. Find, from first principle (i.e., using the definition of derivative) the derivative of

(i) x^3 at $x = 1$; (ii) $x^2 + 2x + 3$ at $x = 0$;

(iii) $\frac{1}{x^2}$ at $x = 2$; (iv) a^x at $x = 5$; (v) $\sqrt{x}$ at $x = 4$.

5. If $f(x) = |x|$ i.e., if $f(x) = x, 0, -x$ according as $x > 0, x = 0, x < 0$, then find $\lim_{h \to 0^+} \frac{f(h)-f(0)}{h}$ and $\lim_{h \to 0^-} \frac{f(h)-f(0)}{h}$, and show that $f'(0)$ does not exist.

6. Differentiate each of the following functions with respect to (w.r.t.) x:

(i) x^5; (ii) $2\sqrt{x}$; (iii) $4/\sqrt{x}$; (iv) $6/x^3$;

(v) $2x^3 + 3x^2 - 6x + 4$; (vi) $2\sqrt{x} - \frac{3}{x} + \frac{4}{x^2} - \frac{1}{x^3}$; (vii) $(x^2 - 2x)^2$; (viii) $\frac{(x-1)^3}{x^2}$;

(ix) $3x^{-2/3} + 4x^{-1/2} - 2$; (x) $3\sqrt[3]{x} - \frac{2}{\sqrt{x}} + 4x^2\sqrt{x}$; (xi) $3x^{2/3} - 4x^{3/4} + 5x^{4/5}$.

7. Differentiate with respect to x:

(i) e^{3x}; (ii) $2\log x$; (iii) 3^x;

(iv) $e^{-\frac{3}{2}x}$; (v) $e^{5x} + x$; (vi) $x^4 + 4^x + \log x$;

(vii) $2x^{\frac{3}{2}} - 3e^{\frac{1}{3}x} + 2^x$; (viii) $3\log x - 2\sqrt{x} + 5^x - 2$; (ix) $x^a + a^x + a^a + e^{ax}$.

8. Find the derivative of each of the following functions:

(i) xe^x; (ii) $x^2 \log x$; (iii) $4^x \cdot x^4$; (iv) $10^x \cdot x^{10}$;

(v) $x^3 e^{2x}$; (vi) $\sqrt{x} \cdot e^{3x}$; (vii) $x^n \log x$; (viii) $(2x - 3)(4x - 5)$;

(ix) $(x^2 - 2)(x^3 + 7)$; (x) $x^5 \cdot e^{2x} \cdot \log x$; (xi) $x^2 \cdot 5^{3x}$. **[C.U. B.Com (Hons.) 1984]**

9. Differentiate each of the following functions w.r.t. x:

(i) $\frac{x}{e^x}$; (ii) $\frac{\log x}{x}$; (iii) $\frac{e^{2x}}{2^x}$; (iv) $\frac{1}{2x-3}$;

(v) $\frac{3}{1-5x}$; (vi) $\frac{x^3}{\log x}$; (vii) $\frac{\log x}{e^{3x}}$; (viii) $\frac{3}{x^2+2}$;

(ix) $\frac{1+x}{1-x}$; (x) $\frac{5-3x}{5+3x}$; (xi) $\frac{a^2-x^2}{a^2+x^2}$; (xii) $\frac{2x^2+5x}{\sqrt{x}}$;

(xiii) $\frac{1+\sqrt{x}}{1-\sqrt{x}}$; (xiv) $\frac{e^{3x}-e^{2x}}{e^{3x}+e^{2x}}$; (xv) $\frac{x^2-2x-3}{x-1}$. **[C.U. B.Com (Hons.) 1984]**

10. Find the differential coefficient of each of the following:

(i) $(x^2 + 2x)^4$; (ii) $\log(3x + 7)$; (iii) e^{x^2+4x-5};

(iv) 7^{x^2+2x} **[C.U. 1988]**; (v) $(x^2 - 2x + 1)^{100}$; (vi) $\sqrt{x^2 + a^2}$ **[C.U. 1987; ICWAI]**;

(vii) x^x **[CA 1976]**; **[Bombay U. 1980]** (viii) $x^{\frac{1}{x}}$ **[ICWAI June 1999]**.

11. Find the derivative of each of the following functions:

(i) $x^x + x^2$; (ii) $x^{\log x}$; (iii) $(1 + x)^x$;

(iv) x^{1+x+x^2}; (v) $a^x \cdot x^x$ **[Bombay U. 1980]**;

(vi) $x^x + x^{\frac{1}{x}}$; (vii) 10^{10^x} **[ICWAI Dec. 1998]**.

12. Find $\frac{dy}{dx}$ from each of the following *implicit functions:*

(i) $x^2 + y^2 = 4$; (ii) $x^2 - 2xy + y^2 = 9$;

(iii) $3x^4 - x^2y + 2y^3 = 0$; (iv) $x^4 + x^2y^2 + y^4 = 0$.

13. Find $\frac{dy}{dx}$ from each of the following *parametric equations:*

(i) $x = at^2, y = 2at$; (ii) $x = ct, y = \frac{c}{t}$;

(iii) $3x = t^3, 2y = t^2$; (iv) $x = t^3, y = 3t$ at $t = 2$;

(v) $x = 6t - t^2, y = 2t + 3$ at $t = 0$; (vi) $x = \frac{2t}{1+t^2}, y = \frac{1-t^2}{1+t^2}$.

14. Find $\frac{dy}{dx}$ when (i) $x^y = y^x$. **[C.U. 1992; Guj. U. 1990]**

(ii) $x = y\log(xy)$; **[Mysore U. 1984]**; (iii) $x = y\log\left(\frac{x}{y}\right)$. **[C.U. 1992]**

[B]

1. (i) Given

$$f(x) = 3 + 2x, \text{ when } -\frac{3}{2} < x \le 0$$
$$= 3 - 2x, \text{ when } 0 < x < \frac{3}{2}.$$

Show that $f(x)$ is continuous at $x = 0$ but $f'(0)$ does not exist.

(ii) Is the function $f(x) = |x - 1|$ *derivable* at $x = 1$? **[Delhi U. 1981]**

2. Find the increment Δy of y corresponding to the increment Δx of x and also the increment ratio $\Delta y/\Delta x$ for the function $y = f(x) = \sqrt{x}$ at $x = 0$ and $\Delta x = 0.0001$. **[ICWAI December 1978]**

[HINTS. $f(x) = \sqrt{x}$; at $x = 0, f(0) = \sqrt{0} = 0$ and $f(0 + \Delta x) = \sqrt{\Delta x} = \sqrt{.0001} = .01$;
$\therefore\ \Delta y = f(0 + \Delta x) - f(0) = .01 - 0 = .01$, etc.]

3. Find from the *first principles the derivative* of the following functions:

(i) $\frac{1}{x^2}(x \ne 0)$; (ii) $x^3 + 6$; (iii) $\sqrt{x+3}$; (iv) $x + \frac{1}{x}$;

(v) $x^2 + 5x$ at $x = 1$; (vi) $\frac{1}{3x+2}$ at $x = 0$.

4. Differentiate each of the following functions w.r.t. x:

(i) $(1 - 3x)^6$; (ii) $(x^2 + 2x)^{\frac{3}{2}}$; (iii) $e^{2x^3-4x+3} \cdot e^{ax^2+bx+c}$;

(iv) $\log(x^2 - 3x + 2)$; (v) 5^{x^2-2x+5}; (vi) $\frac{(x+1)(x-3)}{(x-2)(x+4)}$;

(vii) $\sqrt{\frac{(x-2)(x-5)}{(x+3)(x-4)}}$.

5. Find $\frac{dy}{dx}$ for each of the following functions:

(i) $y = e^{x^2}$; (ii) $y = a^x + x^a + x^x + a^a$;

(iii) $y = (5 - 2x)(2x^3 + 3)$; **[Punjab U. M.A. 1978]** (iv) $y = x(1 + x)(1 + 2x)$; **[Punjab U. M.A. 1979]**

(v) $y = (x - 6)(2x^2 + 2x + 1)$; **[Guru Nanak U. 1974]** (vi) $y = \log\frac{ax+b}{cx+d}$;

(vii) $y = a^{x^2+x}$; (viii) $y = \frac{6x^2}{2x+1}$;

(ix) $y = \left(x + \frac{1}{x}\right)\left(\sqrt{x} + \frac{1}{\sqrt{x}}\right)$; (x) $y = x^2\sqrt{\frac{2x-1}{x+1}}$;

(xi) $y = \log_e\sqrt{\frac{1+x^2}{1-x^2}}$; (xii) $(3x - 1)^2\sqrt{x+3}$; **[Bombay U. 1974]**

6. If $y = 2w^2 + 1, w = 3z^2 + 2$ and $z = 2x + 3x^2$, find $\frac{dy}{dx}$.

7. Find $\frac{dy}{dx}$ if (i) $x^2 + y^2 - 2x = 0$; (ii) $\frac{x^2}{a^2} - \frac{y^2}{b^2} = 1$; $\frac{x^2}{a^2} + \frac{y^2}{b^2} = 1$;
(iii) $x^{\frac{3}{2}} + y^{\frac{3}{2}} = a^{\frac{3}{2}}$; (iv) $x^3 + 5x^2y + xy = 5$; (v) $x^3 + y^3 = 3axy$.

8. Find $\frac{dy}{dx}$ if (i) $x^{x^2+\log x}$; (ii) $(\log x)^{\log x}$;
(iii) e^{x^x}; (iv) x^{e^x}; (v) x^{x^x}; (vi) $(\log x)^{x^x}$

9. Find $\frac{dy}{dx}$ when $x = \frac{a(1-t^2)}{1+t^2}$ and $y = \frac{2bt}{1+t^2}$. **[Delhi U. B.Com 1980]**

10. Find $\frac{dy}{dx}$ if

(i) $y = \log_c \sqrt{a^2 + x^2}$; (ii) $\log_e(x + \sqrt{x^2 + 1})$;

(iii) $x^y = e^{x+y}$; (iv) $y = (x + \sqrt{1 + x^2})^m$;

(v) $y = \log_e \sqrt{(x + \sqrt{x^2 + a^2})}$; (vi) $y = \log \sqrt{2x + \sqrt{4x^2 + a^2}}$ **[ICWAI December 1984]**

11. Find the derivative of (i) x^5 w.r.t. x^2; (ii) $\log x$ w.r.t. $\frac{1}{x}$; (iii) 3^x w.r.t. e^x; (iv) e^{6x} w.r.t. $\log x$.

[HINTS. (i) Let $y = x^5, z = x^2$; then $\frac{dy}{dz} = \frac{dy}{dx} \Big| \frac{dz}{dx} = \frac{5x^4}{2x} = \frac{5}{2}x^3$.]

12. If $y(\log x + 1) = x$, prove that $\frac{dy}{dx} = \frac{\log x}{(\log x+1)^2}$.

13. (i) If $y = \sqrt{\frac{1-x}{1+x}}$, prove that $(1-x)^2\frac{dy}{dx} + y = 0$.

(ii) If $y = \left(\frac{1+x}{1-x}\right)^r$, prove that $(1 - x^2)\frac{dy}{dx} = 2ry$, where r is a given positive integer.

[ICWAI (Final) June 1984]

14. (i) Find $\frac{dy}{dx}$ if $x^y \cdot y^x = k$, when k is a constant. **[CA May 1988]**

(ii) Find $\frac{dy}{dx}$ if $e^{xy} - 4xy = 4$. **[C.U. B.Com. (Hons.) 1984; CA November 1979]**

15. Find $\frac{dy}{dx}$ if (i) $y = \sqrt[5]{\frac{3+2x}{3-2x}}$; (ii) $y = e^{x^2/(1+x^4)}$.

16. Given $x = t + t^{-1}$ and $y = t - t^{-1}$; find $\frac{dy}{dx}$ at $t = 2$. **[ICWAI (Final) December 1976]**

17. (i) If $x^5y^3 = (x + y)^8$, show that $y = x\frac{dy}{dx}$. **[ICWAI June 1992]**

(ii) If $x^3y^4 = (x + y)^7$, show that $\frac{dx}{dy} = \frac{x}{y}$. **[ICWAI June 1989]**

18. If $f(x) = \left(\frac{a+x}{b+x}\right)^{a+b+2x}$, show that

$$f'(0) = \left(2\log\frac{a}{b} + \frac{b^2 - a^2}{ab}\right)\left(\frac{a}{b}\right)^{a+b}$$ **[ICWAI December 1987, '91, '92]**

[HINTS. $\log_e f(x) = (a + b + 2x)\{\log_e(a + x) - \log_e(b + x)\}$

Differentiating both sides w.r.t. 'x', we get

$$\frac{1}{f(x)} \cdot f'(x) = 2 \cdot \{\log(a + x) - \log(b + x)\} + (a + b + 2x)\left\{\frac{1}{a+x} \times 1 - \frac{1}{b+x} \times 1\right\}$$

Putting $x = 0$, $\frac{f'(0)}{f(0)} = 2(\log a - \log b) + (a + b)\left(\frac{1}{a} - \frac{1}{b}\right) = 2\log\frac{a}{b} + \frac{(a+b)(b-a)}{ab}$

Also $f(0) = \left(\frac{a}{b}\right)^{a+b}$

Hence, $f'(0) = f(0) \cdot \left(2 \log \frac{a}{b} + \frac{b^2 - a^2}{ab}\right) = \text{etc.}]$

19. (i) If $y\sqrt{x^2+1} = \log(x + \sqrt{x^2+1})$, prove that

$$(x^2+1)\frac{dy}{dx} + xy - 1 = 0.$$

(ii) If $x\sqrt{1+y} + y\sqrt{1+x} = 0$, show that $(1+x)^2\frac{dy}{dx} + 1 = 0$.

20. If $y = x\sqrt{x^2+1} + \log(x + \sqrt{x^2+1})$, prove that

$$\frac{dy}{dx} = 2\sqrt{x^2+1}.$$

21. If $\sqrt{1-x^2} + \sqrt{1-y^2} = a(x-y)$, show that $\frac{dy}{dx} = \frac{\sqrt{1-y^2}}{\sqrt{1-x^2}}$ **[ICWAI (Final) December 1979]**

22. Find $\frac{dy}{dx}$ when

(i) $x^y + y^x = 1$. **[C.U. B.Com (Hons.) 1985]**

(ii) $x^y + xy = 8$. **[C.U. B.Com (Hons.) 1986]**

Answers

[A]

3. (i) 1; (ii) $2x$; (iii) 3; (iv) $2(x-1); 4x$;
(v) $-1/x^2$; (vi) $3x^3+4$; (vii) $1/(2\sqrt{x})$; (viii) $-1/(2\sqrt{x^3})$;
(ix) $1/(3\sqrt[3]{x^2})$; (x) e^x; (xi) $\frac{1}{x}$; (xii) $2^x \log_e 2$.

4. (i) 3; (ii) 2; (iii) -14; (iv) $a^5 \log_e a$; (v) $\frac{1}{4}$.

5. 1 and -1.

6. (i) $5x^4$; (ii) $1/\sqrt{x}$; (iii) $-2/\sqrt{x^3}$;
(iv) $-18/x^4$; (v) $6(x^2+x-1)$; (vi) $\frac{1}{\sqrt{x}} + \frac{3}{x^2} - \frac{8}{x^3} + \frac{3}{x^4}$;
(vii) $4x(x-1)(x-2)$; (viii) $1 - \frac{3}{x^2} + \frac{2}{x^3}$;
(ix) $-2(x^{-\frac{5}{3}} + x^{-\frac{3}{2}})$; (x) $x^{-\frac{2}{3}} + x^{-\frac{3}{2}} + 10x^{\frac{3}{2}}$; (xi) $2x^{-\frac{1}{3}} - 3x^{-\frac{1}{4}} + 4x^{-\frac{1}{5}}$.

7. (i) $3e^{3x}$; (ii) $2/x$; (iii) $3^x \log_e 3$;
(iv) $-\frac{3}{2}e^{-\frac{3}{2}x}$; (v) $5e^{5x}+1$; (vi) $4x^3 + 4^x \log_e 4 + \frac{1}{x}$;
(vii) $3\sqrt{x} - e^{\frac{1}{3}x} + 2^x \log_e 2$; (viii) $\frac{3}{x} - \frac{1}{\sqrt{x}} + 5^x \log_e 5$; (ix) $ax^{a-1} + a^x \log_e a + ae^{ax}$.

8. (i) $e^x(1+x)$; (ii) $x(1+2\log_e x)$; (iii) $4^x x^3(4 + x\log_e 4)$;
(iv) $10^x \cdot x^9(10 + x\log_e 10)$; (v) $x^2e^{2x}(2x+3)$; (vi) $e^{3x}\left(3\sqrt{x} + \frac{1}{2\sqrt{x}}\right)$;
(vii) $x^{n-1}(1 + n\log_e x)$; (viii) $16x - 22$; (ix) $5x^4 - 6x^2 + 14x$;
(x) $x^4e^{2x}(5\log_e x + 2x\log_e x + 1)$; (xi) $x5^{3x}.(2 + 3x\log_e 5)$.

9. (i) $\frac{1-x}{e^x}$; (ii) $\frac{1-\log_e x}{x^2}$; (iii) $\frac{e^{2x}(2-\log_e 2)}{2^x}$;

(iv) $-\frac{2}{(2x-3)^2}$; (v) $\frac{15}{(1-5x)^2}$; (vi) $\frac{x^2(3\log_e x-1)}{(\log x)^2}$;

(vii) $\frac{1-3x\log_e x}{xe^{3x}}$; (viii) $\frac{-6x}{(x^2+2)^2}$; (ix) $\frac{2}{(1-x)^2}$;

(x) $-\frac{30}{(5+3x)^2}$; (xi) $-\frac{4a^2x}{(a^2+x^2)^2}$; (xii) $\frac{6x+5}{2\sqrt{x}}$;

(xiii) $\frac{1}{\sqrt{x}(1-\sqrt{x})^2}$; (xiv) $\frac{2e^{5x}}{(e^{3x}+e^{2x})^2}$; (xv) $\frac{x^2-2x+5}{(x-1)^2}$.

10. (i) $8(x+1)(x^2+2x)^3$; (ii) $\frac{3}{3x+7}$; (iii) $2(x+2)e^{x^2+4x-5}$;

(iv) $2(x+1)\cdot 7^{x^2+2x}\cdot\log_e 7$; (v) $200(x-1)^{199}$; (vi) $\frac{x}{\sqrt{x^2+a^2}}$;

(vii) $x^x(1+\log_e x)$; (viii) $x^{\frac{1}{x}-2}\cdot(1-\log x)$.

11. (i) $x^x(1+\log_e x)+2x$; (ii) $2x^{\log_e x-1}\log_e x$;

(iii) $(1+x)^x\left\{\log(1+x)+\frac{x}{1+x}\right\}$; (iv) $x^{1+x+x^2}\left\{(1+2x)\log x+\frac{1+x+x^2}{x}\right\}$;

(v) $a^x x^x[1+\log_e(ax)]$; (vi) $x^x(1+\log_e x)+x^{\frac{1}{x}-2}(1-\log_e x)$;

(vii) $10^{10^x}\cdot 10^x(\log_e 10)^2$.

12. (i) $-\frac{x}{y}$; (ii) 1; (iii) $\frac{2x(y-6x^2)}{6y^2-x^2}$; (iv) $-\frac{x(2x^2+y^2)}{y(x^2+2y^2)}$.

13. (i) $\frac{1}{t}$; (ii) $-\frac{1}{t^2}$; (iii) $\frac{1}{t}$; (iv) $\frac{1}{4}$; (v) $\frac{1}{3}$; (vi) $-\frac{x}{y}$.

14. (i) $\frac{(x\log_e y-y)y}{(y\log\log_e x-x)x}$; (ii) $\frac{x-y}{x\{1+\log_e(xy)\}}$; (iii) $\frac{y-x}{x(1+\log_e y-\log_e x)}$.

[B]

1. (ii) $f(x)$ is not derivable at $x=1$ [since $Rf'(1)=1$ and $Lf'(1)=-1$.]

2. $\Delta y=.01$ and $\Delta y/\Delta x=.01$.

3. (i) $-\frac{2}{x^3}$; (ii) $3x^2$; (iii) $\frac{1}{2\sqrt{x+3}}$; (iv) $1-\frac{1}{x^2}$; (v) 7; (vi) $-\frac{3}{4}$.

4. (i) $-18(1-3x)^5$; (ii) $3(x+1)\sqrt{x^2+2x}$; (iii) $2(3x^2-2).\ e^{2x^3-4x+3}$; $(2ax+b)e^{ax^2+bx+c}$;

(iv) $\frac{2x-3}{x^2-3x+2}$; (v) $2(x-1)5^{x^2-2x+5}\cdot\log_e^5$; (vi) $\frac{(x+1)(x-3)}{(x-2)(x+4)}\cdot\left\{\frac{1}{x+1}+\frac{1}{x-3}-\frac{1}{x-2}-\frac{1}{x+4}\right\}$;

(vii) $\frac{1}{2}\sqrt{\frac{(x-2)(x-5)}{(x+3)(x-4)}}\left\{\frac{1}{x-2}+\frac{1}{x-5}-\frac{1}{x+3}-\frac{1}{x-4}\right\}$.

5. (i) $e^{x^2}.2x$; (ii) $a^x\log_e a+ax^{a-1}+x^x(1+\log_e x)$; (iii) $-16x^3+30x^2-6$;

(iv) $(1+x)(1+2x)+x(1+2x)+2x(1+x)$ or, $6x^2+6x+1$; (v) $6x^2-20x-11$;

(vi) $\frac{ad-bc}{(ax+b)(cx+d)}$; (vii) $(2x+1)a^{x^2+x}\log_e a$; (viii) $\frac{12x(x+1)}{(2x+1)^2}$;

(ix) $\left(1-\frac{1}{x}\right)\left\{\frac{2(x+1)^2+x^2+1}{2x\sqrt{x}}\right\}$; (x) $x^2\sqrt{\frac{2x-1}{x+1}}\left\{\frac{2}{x}+\frac{3}{2(2x-1)(x+1)}\right\}$;

(xi) $\frac{2x}{1-x^4}$; (xii) $\frac{12(3x-1)(x+3)+(3x-1)^2}{2\sqrt{x+3}}$.

6. $48(3z^2+2)^2(2x+3x^2)(1+3x)$, where $z=2x+3x^2$.

7. (i) $\frac{1-x}{y}$; (ii) $\frac{b^2x}{a^2y}$; $-\frac{b^2x}{a^2y}$; (iii) $-\sqrt{\frac{x}{y}}$; (iv) $-\frac{3x^2+10xy+y}{5x^2+x}$; (v) $\frac{ay-x^2}{y^2-ax}$.

8. (i) $\frac{(2(x^2+1)\log x+x^2)}{x}\cdot x^{x^2+\log x}$; (ii) $(\log x)^{\log x}\cdot\frac{1}{x}\{\log(\log x)+1\}$;

(iii) $e^{x^x}\cdot x^x(1+\log x)$; (iv) $x^{e^x}\cdot e^x\left(\frac{1}{x}+\log x\right)$;

(v) $x^{x^x}\cdot\{x^{x-1}+x^x(1+\log x)\log x\}$; (vi) $(\log x)^{x^x}\cdot x^x\cdot\left\{(1+\log x)\log(\log x)+\frac{1}{x\log x}\right\}$.

9. $-\frac{b(1-t^2)}{2at}$. **10.** (i) $\frac{x}{a^2+x^2}$; (ii) $\frac{1}{\sqrt{x^2+1}}$; (iii) $\frac{\log x-2}{(\log x-1)^2}$; (iv) $\frac{m(x+\sqrt{x^2+1})^m}{\sqrt{x^2+1}}$; (v) $\frac{1}{2\sqrt{x^2+a^2}}$; (vi) $\frac{1}{\sqrt{4x^2+a^2}}$.

11. (i) $\frac{5}{2}x^3$; (ii) $-x$; (iii) $3^x \log_e 3/e^x$; (iv) $6xe^{6x}$. **14.** (i) $-\frac{y(y+x\log y)}{x(y\log x+x)}$ or, $-\frac{y^2(1-\log x)}{x^2(1-\log y)}$; (iii) $-\frac{y}{x}$.

15. (i) $\sqrt[5]{\frac{3+2x}{3-2x}} \cdot \frac{12}{5(9-4x^2)}$; (ii) $\frac{x^2(3-x^4)}{(1+x^4)^2} \cdot e^{\frac{x^2}{1+x^4}}$. **16.** $\frac{5}{3}$.

22. (i) $-(yx^{y-1}+y^x\log y)/(x^y\log x+xy^{x-1})$; (ii) $-\frac{y(x^{y-1}+1)}{x(x^{y-1}\log x+1)}$.

7.10. SECOND AND HIGHER ORDER DERIVATIVES (SUCCESSIVE DIFFERENTIATION)

From our discussion of the derivatives of different types of functions, we see that the derivative of a function of x is also a function of x. Thus, the derivatives of $y = f(x)$ i.e., $f'(x)$ or $\frac{dy}{dx}$ is a function of x and $f'(x)$ may have a *derivative* which is denoted by by $f''(x)$ or $\frac{d^2y}{dx^2}$ and it is called the **second derivative** of $f(x)$. Similarly, the *derivative* of the second derivative is denoted by $f'''(x)$ or $\frac{d^3y}{dx^3}$ and it is called the *third derivative* of $f(x)$ and so on.

ILLUSTRATION. Suppose $y = x^3$; then $\frac{dy}{dx} = 3x^2$;

$$\frac{d^2y}{dx^2} = \frac{d}{dx}\left(\frac{dy}{dx}\right) = \frac{d}{dx}(3x^2) = 6x;$$
$$\frac{d^3y}{dx^3} = \frac{d}{dx}\left(\frac{d^2y}{dx^2}\right) = \frac{d}{dx}(6x) = 6; \frac{d^4y}{dx^4} = 0.$$

In general, nth derivative is denoted by $f^n(x)$ or $\frac{d^ny}{dx^n}$.

The first, second, third, etc. derivatives are also denoted by y_1, y_2, y_3, etc. respectively.

EXAMPLE 1. *If* $y = ae^{mx} + be^{-mx}$, *show that* $\frac{d^2y}{dx^2} = m^2y$. **[Delhi U. B.Com (Hons.) 1982]**

SOLUTION. We have

$$y = a\,e^{mx} + b\,e^{-mx}. \tag{1}$$

Differentiating w.r.t. x, we get

$$\frac{dy}{dx} = am.e^{mx} + b.(-m).e^{-mx} = ame^{mx} - bme^{-mx}$$

Differentiating again w.r.t. x, we have

$$\frac{d^2y}{dx^2} = am.me^{mx} - bm(-m).e^{-m}x = am^2e^{mx} + bm^2e^{-mx}$$
$$= m^2(ae^{mx} + be^{-mx}) = m^2y.$$

Hence $\mathbf{\frac{d^2y}{dx^2} = m^2y}$.

EXAMPLE 2. *If* $y = x^3 \log\frac{1}{x}$, *prove that* $x\frac{d^2y}{dx^2} - 2\frac{dy}{dx} + 3x^2 = 0$.

[CA May 1984; ICWAI December 1986]

SOLUTION. We have $y = x^3 \log \frac{1}{x} = x^3(\log 1 - \log x) = -x^3 \log x$.

$$\therefore \quad \frac{dy}{dx} = -\left(x^3 \cdot \frac{1}{x} + 3x^2 \cdot \log x\right) = -3x^2 \log x - x^2$$

$$\therefore \quad x\frac{dy}{dx} = -3x^3 \log x - x^3 = 3x^3 \log \frac{1}{x} - x^3 = 3y - x^3$$

Differentiating both sides again w.r.t. x, we get

$$x\frac{d^2y}{dx^2} + 1.\frac{dy}{dx} = 3\frac{dy}{dx} - 3x^2$$

$$\text{or,} \quad \mathbf{x\frac{d^2y}{dx^2} - 2\frac{dy}{dx} + 3x^2 = 0.}$$

EXAMPLE 3. *If* $y = \log(x + \sqrt{1 + x^2})$, *show that* $(1 + x^2)y_2 + xy_1 = 0$.

[Delhi U. B.Com 1982; CA May 1988]

SOLUTION. We have $y = \log(x + \sqrt{1 + x^2})$;

$$\therefore \quad \frac{dy}{dx} = \frac{1}{x + \sqrt{1 + x^2}} \times \left\{1 + \frac{1}{2}(1 + x^2)^{\frac{1}{2}-1} \times (0 + 2x)\right\}$$

$$= \frac{1}{x + \sqrt{1 + x^2}} \times \left\{1 + \frac{x}{\sqrt{1 + x^2}}\right\}$$

$$= \frac{x}{x + \sqrt{1 + x^2}} \times \frac{\sqrt{1 + x^2} + x}{\sqrt{1 + x^2}} = \frac{1}{\sqrt{1 + x^2}}$$

$$\text{or,} \quad \sqrt{1 + x^2}\frac{dy}{dx} = 1, \quad \text{or,} \quad (1 + x^2)\left(\frac{dy}{dx}\right)^2 = 1.$$

Differentiating both sides w.r.t. x, we get

$$(1 + x^2) \cdot 2\left(\frac{dy}{dx}\right)^{2-1} \cdot \frac{d^2y}{dx^2} + 2x \cdot \left(\frac{dy}{dx}\right)^2 = 0,$$

Dividing both sides by $2\frac{dy}{dx}$, we get

$$(1 + x^2)\frac{d^2y}{dx^2} + x\frac{dy}{dx} = 0, \text{ i.e., } \mathbf{(1 + x^2)y_2 + xy_1 = 0}.$$

EXAMPLE 4. *If* $st = c_1t^2 + \frac{c_2}{t}$, *show that* $t^2\frac{d^2s}{dt^2} + 2t\frac{ds}{dt} = 2s$ **[ICWAI June 1993]**

SOLUTION. We have $st = c_1t^2 + \frac{c_2}{t}$. (1)

Differentiating both sides w.r.t. 't', we get

$$s.1 + t.\frac{ds}{dt} = c_1.2t + c_2.\left(-\frac{1}{t^2}\right)$$

Differentiating again w.r.t. 't', we have

$$\frac{ds}{dt} + 1.\frac{ds}{dt} + t\frac{d^2s}{dt^2} = 2c_1.1 + \frac{2c_2}{t^3} = \frac{2}{t^2}\left(c_1t^2 + \frac{c_2}{t}\right)$$

$$\text{or,} \quad t\frac{d^2s}{dt^2} + 2\frac{ds}{dt} = \frac{2}{t^2} \times st = \frac{2s}{t} \quad \text{[By (1)]}$$

$$\text{or,} \quad t^2\frac{d^2s}{dt^2} + 2t\frac{ds}{dt} = 2s$$

EXAMPLE 5. *If* $2x = y^{\frac{1}{4}} + y^{-\frac{1}{4}}$, *then prove that* $(x^2-1)\frac{d^2y}{dx^2} + x\frac{dy}{dx} - 16y = 0$. **[CA May 1991]**

SOLUTION. We have $2x = y^{\frac{1}{4}} + y^{-\frac{1}{4}}$ (1)

Let $y^{\frac{1}{4}} = z$; then $\frac{1}{z} = y^{-\frac{1}{4}}$ and from (1), we get

$$2x = z + \frac{1}{z} = \frac{z^2+1}{z}$$

$$\text{or,} \quad z^2 + 1 = 2xz, \quad \text{or,} \quad z^2 - 2xz + 1 = 0$$

$$\therefore \quad z = \frac{2x \pm \sqrt{4x^2-4}}{2} = \frac{2(x \pm \sqrt{x^2-1})}{2} = x \pm \sqrt{x^2-1}$$

$$\therefore \quad y^{\frac{1}{4}} = x \pm \sqrt{x^2-1}, \quad \text{or,} \quad y = (x \pm \sqrt{x^2-1})^4 \qquad (2)$$

$$\therefore \quad \frac{dy}{dx} = 4(x \pm \sqrt{x^2-1})^{4-1} \cdot \frac{d}{dx}(x \pm \sqrt{x^2-1})$$

$$= 4(x \pm \sqrt{x^2-1})^3 \times \left\{1 \pm \frac{1}{2}(x^2-1)^{\frac{1}{2}-1} \times 2x\right\}$$

$$= 4(x \pm \sqrt{x^2-1})^3 \times \left(1 \pm \frac{x}{\sqrt{x^2-1}}\right) = 4(x \pm \sqrt{x^2-1})^3 \times \frac{\sqrt{x^2-1} \pm x}{\sqrt{x^2-1}}$$

$$\text{or,} \quad \frac{dy}{dx} = 4(x \pm \sqrt{x^2-1})^3 \times \pm\frac{(x \pm \sqrt{x^2-1}}{\sqrt{x^2-1}} = \pm\frac{4(x \pm \sqrt{x^2-1})^4}{\sqrt{x^2-1}} = \pm\frac{4y}{\sqrt{x^2-1}}$$

$$\therefore \quad \left(\frac{dy}{dx}\right)^2 = \frac{16y^2}{x^2-1}, \quad \text{or,} \quad (x^2-1)\left(\frac{dy}{dx}\right)^2 = 16y^2 \qquad (3)$$

Differentiating both sides of (3) w.r.t. 'x', we get

$$(x^2-1) \cdot 2\frac{dy}{dx} \cdot \frac{d^2y}{dx^2} + (2x-0)\left(\frac{dy}{dx}\right)^2 = 16.2y.\frac{dy}{dx}.$$

Dividing both sides by $2\frac{dy}{dx}$, we get

$$(x^2-1)\frac{d^2y}{dx^2} + x\frac{dy}{dx} = 16y, \quad \text{or,} \quad \mathbf{(x^2-1)\frac{d^2y}{dx^2} + x\frac{dy}{dx} - 16y = 0.}$$

EXAMPLE 6. *If* $y = (x + \sqrt{1+x^2})^m$, *prove that*

$$(1+x^2)\frac{d^2y}{dx^2} + x\frac{dy}{dx} - m^2y = 0.$$

[ICWAI December 1975, '80, '88; June 1982; Delhi U. 1982]

SOLUTION. We have $y = (x + \sqrt{1 + x^2})^m$

$$\therefore \quad \frac{dy}{dx} = m(x + \sqrt{1+x^2})^{m-1} \times \left\{1 + \frac{1}{2}(1+x^2)^{\frac{1}{2}-1} \times (0 + 2x)\right\}$$

$$= m(x + \sqrt{1+x^2})^{m-1} \times \left(1 + \frac{x}{\sqrt{1+x^2}}\right)$$

$$= m(x + \sqrt{1+x^2})^{m-1} \times \left(\frac{\sqrt{1+x^2} + x}{\sqrt{1+x^2}}\right)$$

$$= \frac{m(x + \sqrt{1+x^2})^m}{\sqrt{1+x^2}} = \frac{my}{\sqrt{1+x^2}}$$

$$\text{or,} \quad \left(\frac{dy}{dx}\right)^2 = \frac{m^2y^2}{1+x^2}, \quad \text{or,} \quad (1+x^2)\left(\frac{dy}{dx}\right)^2 = m^2y^2$$

Differentiating both sides w.r.t. x, we get

$$(1+x^2).2\frac{dy}{dx}.\frac{d^2y}{dx^2} + 2x\left(\frac{dy}{dx}\right)^2 = m^2.2y\frac{dy}{dx}$$

Dividing both sides by $2\frac{dy}{dx}$, we get

$$(1+x^2)\frac{d^2y}{dx^2} + x\frac{dy}{dx} = m^2y$$

$$\text{or,} \quad \mathbf{(1+x^2)\frac{d^2y}{dx^2} + x\frac{dy}{dx} - m^2y = 0.}$$

EXAMPLE 7. *Find $\frac{d^2y}{dx^2}$ from the equation $x^2 + y^2 = a^2$.*

SOLUTION. We have $x^2 + y^2 = a^2$.

Differentiating both sides, w.r.t. x, we get

$$2x + 2y\frac{dy}{dx} = 0 \quad \text{or,} \quad \frac{dy}{dx} = -\frac{x}{y}.$$

Differentiating again w.r.t. x, we get

$$\frac{d^2y}{dx^2} = -\frac{d}{dx}\left(\frac{x}{y}\right) = -\frac{y.1 - x.\frac{dy}{dx}}{y^2} = -\frac{y - x \times \left(-\frac{x}{y}\right)}{y^2}$$

$$= -\frac{y + \frac{x^2}{y}}{y^2} = -\frac{y^2 + x^2}{y^3} = -\frac{\mathbf{a^2}}{\mathbf{y^3}}.$$

EXAMPLE 8. *Given $x = t + t^{-1}$ and $y = t - t^{-1}$; find the value of $\frac{d^2y}{dx^2}$ at the point $t = 2$.*

[ICWAI December 1976]

SOLUTION. We have $x = t + \frac{1}{t}$ and $y = t - \frac{1}{t}$.

$$\therefore \quad \frac{dx}{dt} = 1 - \frac{1}{t^2} = \frac{t^2 - 1}{t^2}. \quad \text{and} \quad \frac{dy}{dt} = 1 + \frac{1}{t^2} = \frac{t^2+1}{t^2}.$$

$$\therefore \quad \frac{dy}{dx} = \frac{dy}{dt} \bigg/ \frac{dx}{dt} = \frac{t^2+1}{t^2-1}.$$

Now,

$$\frac{d^2y}{dx^2} = \frac{d}{dx}\left(\frac{dy}{dx}\right) = \frac{d}{dx}\left(\frac{t^2+1}{t^2-1}\right) = \frac{d}{dt}\left(\frac{t^2+1}{t^2-1}\right)\frac{dt}{dx}$$

$$= \frac{2t(t^2-1)-2t(t^2+1)}{(t^2-1)^2} \Big/ \frac{dx}{dt} = \frac{-4t}{(t^2-1)^2} \Big/ \left(\frac{t^2-1}{t^2}\right) = -\frac{4t^3}{(t^2-1)^3}$$

$\therefore$ At $t = 2 \cdot \dfrac{d^2y}{dx^2} = -\dfrac{4.2^3}{(2^2-1)^3} = -\dfrac{\mathbf{32}}{\mathbf{27}}.$

Exercise 7(II)

[Successive Differentiation]

1. Find $\frac{d^2y}{dx^2}$ and $\frac{d^3y}{dx^3}$ if (i) $y = x^4$; (ii) $y = e^{3x}$; (iii) $y = \log x$.

2. (i) If $y = e^{mx}$, prove that $\frac{d^2y}{dx^2} = m^2y$.

(ii) If $y = Ae^{ax} - Be^{-ax}$, prove that $\frac{d^2y}{dx^2} = a^2y$.

(iii) If $y = 2x + \frac{4}{x}$, prove that $x^2\frac{d^2y}{dx^2} + x\frac{dy}{dx} - y = 0$. **[ICWAI June 1990]**

3. If $y = x^4 - 3x^3 + 4x^2 - 7x$, find $\frac{d^2y}{dx^2}$ and $\frac{d^3y}{dx^3}$.

4. If $y = \sqrt{x} + \frac{1}{\sqrt{x}}$, find $\frac{d^2y}{dx^2}$ and $\frac{d^3y}{dx^3}$.

5. If $y = \frac{1+x}{1-x}$, prove that $\frac{d^2y}{dx^2} = \frac{4}{(1-x)^3}$.

6. (i) If $y = x^2 \log x$, prove that $\frac{d^2y}{dx^2} = 3 + 2\log x$.

(ii) Given $y = x\sqrt{x^2+9}$, find $\frac{d^2y}{dx^2}$ at $x = 4$.

(iii) If $u = v^3 \log \frac{1}{v}$, show that $v\frac{d^2u}{dv^2} - 2\frac{du}{dv} + 3v^2 = 0$. **[ICWAI June 1984]**

7. If $y = \frac{x}{x^2+a^2}$, prove that $\frac{d^2y}{dx^2} = \frac{2x(x^2-3a^2)}{(x^2+a^2)^3}$.

8. Find $\frac{d^2y}{dx^2}$ if (i) $y^2 = 4ax$; (ii) $\frac{x^2}{a^2} + \frac{y^2}{b^2} = 1$.

9. (i) If $ax^2 + 2h\,xy + by^2 = 1$, prove that $\frac{d^2y}{dx^2} = \frac{h^2-ab}{(hx+by)^3}$.

(ii) If $x^2 + xy + 2y^2 = 1$, show that $(x+2y)^3\frac{d^2y}{dx^2} + 6 = 0$.

(iii) If $xy = ax^2 + \frac{b}{x}$, show that $x^2y_2 + 2(xy_1 - y) = 0$.

10. (i) If $3x = t^3$ and $2y = t^2$, prove that $t^4\frac{d^2y}{dx^2} + 1 = 0$.

(ii) If $x = t^2 + 2$ and $y = t^4 - 3$, prove that $\frac{d^2y}{dx^2} = 2$.

11. If $x = 3t - t^3$ and $y = t + 1$, prove that at $t = 2$, $\frac{d^2y}{dx^2} = \frac{4}{81}$.

12. If $y = \sqrt{x+1} - \sqrt{x-1}$, prove that $(x^2-1)y_2 + xy_1 = \frac{1}{4}y$.

[Delhi U. B.Com (Hons.) 1981; ICWAI December 1985]

13. If $y = \log(x + \sqrt{x^2+a^2})$, prove that $(x^2+a^2)y_2 + xy_1 = 0$. **[CA May 1988]**

14. If $y = (x + \sqrt{a^2 + x^2})^p$, prove that $(a^2 + x^2)y_2 + xy_1 = p^2y$.

[ICWAI December 1988; CA November 1989]

15. $y = (x^2 - 1)^n$, prove that $(x^2 - 1)y_2 + 2(1 - n)xy_1 = 2ny$.

16. If $2x = y^{\frac{1}{m}} + y^{-\frac{1}{m}}$, prove that $(x^2 - 1)y_2 + xy_1 - m^2y = 0$. **[CA November 1982]**

[HINTS. See worked out Ex. 5.]

17. If $y^2 = P(x)$, a polynomial of degree ≥ 3, then obtain $2y^3\frac{d^2y}{dx^2} = y^2P''(x) - \frac{1}{2}\{P'(x)\}^2$.

[CA November 1992]

[HINTS. $y^2 = P(x)$; $\therefore$ $2y\frac{dy}{dx} = P'(x)$ i.e., $P'(x) = 2y\frac{dy}{dx}$

$$\therefore \quad P''(x) = 2\left[\frac{dy}{dx} \cdot \frac{dy}{dx} + y \cdot \frac{d^2y}{dx^2}\right] = 2\left(\frac{dy}{dx}\right)^2 + 2y\frac{d^2y}{dx^2}.$$

$$\therefore \quad \text{R.H.S.} \quad = y^2\left[2\left(\frac{dy}{dx}\right)^2 + 2y\frac{d^2y}{dx^2}\right] - \frac{1}{2} \times \left\{2y\frac{dy}{dx}\right\}^2 = \text{etc.}\Bigg]$$

Answers

1. (i) $12x^2, 24x$; (ii) $9e^{3x}, 27e^{3x}$; (iii) $-\frac{1}{x^2}, \frac{2}{x^3}$. **3.** $12x^2 - 18x + 8; 24x - 18$. **4.** $\frac{1}{4}x^{-\frac{3}{2}}(3x^{-1} - 1), \frac{3}{8}x^{-\frac{5}{2}}$ $(1 - 5x^{-1})$. **6.** (ii) $\frac{236}{125}$. **8.** (i) $-4a^2/y^3$; (ii) $-b^4/a^2y^3$.

7.11. MEANING OF DERIVATIVE

In this article, we shall give two meanings (or interpretations) of the derivative of a function: (i) *Derivative as a Rate-measurer* and (ii) *Derivative as the slope (or gradient) of a tangent to the curve of the function.*

Derivative as a Rate Measurer

Let $y = f(x)$ be a function of x and x_1 be a fixed value of x in the domain of definition of $f(x)$. Then the corresponding value of y is $y = f(x_1)$. Let Δx be an increment of x; then the new value of x is $x_1 + \Delta x$ and the corresponding value of y is $f(x_1 + \Delta x)$.

$\therefore$ $\Delta y =$ increment of $y = f(x_1 + \Delta x) - f(x_1)$

and $\frac{\Delta y}{\Delta x} =$ increment ratio $= \frac{f(x_1+\Delta x)-f(x_1)}{\Delta x}$ (1)

= **average rate of change of y w.r.t x when x changes from $\mathbf{x_1}$ to $\mathbf{x_1 + \Delta x}$.**

NOTE. We have $f(x + \Delta x) = f(x) + \Delta y = f(x) + \frac{\Delta y}{\Delta x} \cdot \Delta x$.

When $\Delta x \to 0, f(x + \Delta x) \to f(x) + f'(x)dx$.

ILLUSTRATION 1. Let us consider the function $y = x^2$ where $y = f(x)$.

Let us take a fixed value of x, say $x = 2$; then corresponding value of y is $2^2 = 4$.

Let us give an increment $\cdot 1$ to the value of x so that $\Delta x = \cdot 1$. Then the new value of x is $2 + \cdot 1 = 2.1$ and the corresponding new value of y is $f(2 \cdot 1) = (2 \cdot 1)^2 = 4 \cdot 41$.

∴ The corresponding increment of $y = \Delta y = f(2 \cdot 1) - f(2) = 4 \cdot 41 - 4 = \cdot 41$.

∴ Increment ratio $= \frac{\Delta y}{\Delta x} = \frac{\cdot 41}{\cdot 1} = 4 \cdot 1$.

In this case, we say that *the average rate of change of* y *w.r.t.* x *is* $4 \cdot 1$ *when* x *increases fr* 2 *to* $2 \cdot 1$, increment being $\cdot 1$.

Instantaneous Rate of Change of a function

From (1), we have $\frac{\Delta y}{\Delta x} = \frac{f(x_1+\Delta x)-f(x_1)}{\Delta x}$.

Now *let* Δx become smaller and smaller and ultimately $\Delta x \to 0$. Then *the limit* to which $\frac{\Delta y}{\Delta x}$ approaches as $\Delta x \to 0$ (if such a limit exists) is called the *instantaneous rate of change of* y *w.r.t.* x *at the value* $x = x_1$. But we know that

$\lim\limits_{\Delta x \to 0} \frac{f(x_1+\Delta x)-f(x_1)}{\Delta x}$ (if it exists), is **the derivative of y or $f(x)$ w.r.t. x at $x = x_1$.**

Hence $\frac{dy}{dx}$ *or* $f'(x)$ *at* $x = x_1$ *is the* **instantaneous rate of change** (*or simply, the rate of change*) *of* $y = f(x)$ *w.r.t.* x *at* $x = x_1$.

ILLUSTRATION 2. *If* $y = x^2$, *then* $\frac{dy}{dx} = 2x$.

At $x = 2$, the instantaneous rate of change of y is $2.2 = 4$ units for per unit change in x.

ILLUSTRATION 3. *Suppose* $C = f(Q)$ *where* C *is the total cost and* Q *the output; then the* **marginal cost** *is defined as the rate of change of total cost w.r.t. output.* If ΔQ be a small change in Q from Q_o to $Q_o + \Delta Q$ and ΔC the corresponding change in C, then $\Delta C/\Delta Q$ is the average marginal cost and

the marginal cost $= \lim\limits_{\Delta Q \to 0} \frac{\Delta C}{\Delta Q} = \frac{dC}{dQ}$.

If $C = Q^3 - 5Q^2 + 12Q + 60$, then $\frac{dC}{dQ} = 3Q^2 - 10Q + 12$ and the marginal cost at $Q = 5$ units is $3(5)^2 - 10 \times 5 + 12 =$ **37 units.**

ILLUSTRATION 4. *Let us consider the function* $y = \frac{500}{x}$. *Find the average rate of change of* y *w.r.t.* x *when* x *increases from* 20 *to* 20.5 *units. Find also the instantaneous rate of change of* y *at* $x = 20$.

Average rate of change of y w.r.t. x at $x = x_1$ is

$\frac{f(x_1+\Delta x)-f(x_1)}{\Delta x}$. Here $f(x) = \frac{500}{x}, x = 20$ and $\Delta x = .5$

$$\therefore \quad f(20) = \frac{500}{20} = 25, \quad f(20.5) = \frac{500}{20.5} = \frac{1000}{41}$$

∴ Average rate of change of y w.r.t. x at $x = 20$ is

$$\frac{f(20.5) - f(20)}{.5} = \frac{\frac{1000}{41} - 25}{.5} = \frac{1000 - 1025}{20.5}$$
$$= \frac{-25}{20.5} = -1.22 \quad \text{units per unit change in } x.$$

[The *negative sign* in the result indicates that y decreases per unit increase in x.]

$$\frac{dy}{dx} = -\frac{500}{x^2}, \text{ and at } x = 20, \frac{dy}{dx} = -\frac{500}{(20)^2} = -1.25,$$

i.e., *the instantaneous rate of change at* $x = 20$ *is* -1.25 *units per unit change in* x.

The *negative sign* indicates the *decrease rate of change* w.r.t. x.

Time-Rate of Change

The rate of change is called *the Time-rate of change* when the independent variable is **time** (t). If the dependent variable is the displacement s of a moving point at any instant of time t, then $s = f(t)$. Let Δt be a small increment of t and Δs the corresponding increment of s. Then

$$\frac{\Delta s}{\Delta t} = \frac{\text{increment of } s}{\text{increment of } t}$$
$$= \text{average velocity when } t \text{ increases from, say } t_o \text{ to } t_o + \Delta t.$$

Velocity

If Δt becomes smaller and smaller and ultimately $\Delta t \to 0$, then the limit to which $\frac{\Delta s}{\Delta t}$ approaches (if such a limit exists) is called the *instantaneous rate of change* of s w.r.t. t at $t = t_o$, i.e.,

$$\left(\frac{ds}{dt}\right)_{t=t_0} = \text{instantaneous rate of change of } s \text{ w.r.t. 't' at } t = t_o.$$
$$= \textbf{instantaneous velocity} \text{ (or simply, velocity) at } t = t_o.$$
$$= v_o(\text{say})$$

Thus, **velocity** *at any point is the time-rate of change of displacement at the point.*

Acceleration

Acceleration at any point is defined as the time-rate of change of velocity at that point i.e., *acceleration at* $t = t_o$ is $\left(\frac{dv}{dt}\right)_{t=t_o}$ or $\left(\frac{d^2s}{dt^2}\right)_{t=t_o}$

ILLUSTRATION 5. *A particle moves in a straight line in the same direction so that its distance s cm measured from a fixed point O on the line at time t secs is given by* $s = t^3 + 3t^2 - 4t$.

Find (i) *the velocity v at any time t;* (ii) *the velocity at the end of* 5 *seconds, and* (iii) *the average velocity while t changes from* 2 *to* 6 *seconds.*

(i) We have $s = t^3 + 3t^2 - 4t$; $\therefore$ $\frac{ds}{dt} = (3t^2 + 6t - 4)$ cm./sec.^{2} which is the velocity at any time t.

(ii) Velocity at the end of 5 seconds

$$= \left(\frac{ds}{dt}\right)_{t=5} = 3.5^2 + 6.5 - 4 = \mathbf{101cm./sec.}.$$

(iii) Average velocity while t changes from 2 to 6 secs.

$$= \frac{\Delta s}{\Delta t} = \frac{(6^3 + 3.6^2 - 4.6) - (2^3 + 3.2^2 - 4.2)}{6 - 2} = \frac{300 - 12}{4}$$
$$= \frac{288}{4} = \mathbf{72cm./sec.}$$

ILLUSTRATION 6. *For a particle moving in a straight line, the distance s cm. from a fixed point on the line described in t seconds is given by* $s = 2t^3 - 3t^2 + 5t$. *Find the velocity and the acceleration of the particle at the end of* 3 *seconds.*

We have $s = 2t^3 - 3t^2 + 5t$.

$$\therefore \quad \frac{ds}{dt} = 6t^2 - 6t + 5 \text{ and } \frac{d^2s}{dt^2} = 12t - 6.$$

At the end of 3 seconds, $t = 3$ and and hence

the velcoity of the particle $= \left(\frac{ds}{dt}\right)_{t=3} = 6.3^2 - 6.3 + 5 = 41$ cm./sec.

and the acceleration of the particle $= \left(\frac{d^2s}{dt^2}\right)_{t=3} = 12 \times 3 - 6 = 30$ cm./sec^2.

Related Rates of Change

In many problems, two or more variables (which are functions of time t) are involved. In such cases, we first find the relation (or relations) between the variables by using the given conditions and then differentiating both sides of the relation w.r.t. time t, we get the relation between their time-rates of change. The following example will illustrate this process.

EXAMPLE 1. *If the perimeter of a circle increases at a constant rate, prove that the rate of increase of the area varies as the radius of the circle.*

SOLUTION. If S be the perimeter and A the area of the circle of radius r, then $S = 2\pi r$ and $A = \pi r^2$

We have $S^2 = 4\pi^2 r^2 = 4\pi.A$, or, $A = S^2/4\pi$.

Differentiating both sides w.r.t. 't', we get

$$\frac{dA}{dt} = \frac{1}{4\pi} \cdot 2S \cdot \frac{dS}{dt} = \frac{1}{2\pi} \cdot 2\pi r \cdot \frac{dS}{dt} = r.\frac{dS}{dt} \tag{1}$$

Since perimeter S increases at a constant rate; $\therefore \; \frac{dS}{dt}$ = constant.

Hence from (1), $\frac{dA}{dt} \propto r$ i.e., the rate of increase of $A \propto r$.

EXAMPLE 2. *The side of a square sheet of metal is expanding at the rate of* 3 *cm. per minute, when heated. At what rate is the area of the sheet expanding when the side is* 10 *cm. long?*

[CA November 1992]

SOLUTION. Let the length of each side of the square at any time t be x cm.

Then $\quad \frac{dx}{dt}$ = the rate at which a side of the square is expanding

= 3 cm./min. (1)

If the area of the square at time t be A sq. cm., then

$$A = x^2; \quad \therefore \quad \frac{dA}{dt} = 2x\frac{dx}{dt} = 2x \times 3 = 6x \qquad \text{[by (1)]}$$

When the side is 10 cm. long, we have $x = 10$ cm.

$$\therefore \quad \frac{dA}{dt} = 6 \times 10 = 60.$$

Hence *the required rate at which the area of the sheet is expanding* = **60 sq. cm. per minute.**

EXAMPLE 3. *An inverted cone has a depth of* 10 *cms. and a base of radius* 5 *cms. Water is poured into it at the rate of* 1.5 *c.c. per minute. Find the rate at which the level of water in the cone is rising when the depth is* 4 *cms.* **[ICWAI December 1980]**

SOLUTION. At the end of t minutes, let r cm. be the radius of the circular water-surface when the depth of water is h cm. Let V be the volume of water at time t minutes. Then $V = \frac{1}{3}\pi r^2 h$. In the figure, $DE = r, OD = h, BC = 5$ cm. and $OC = 10$ cm.

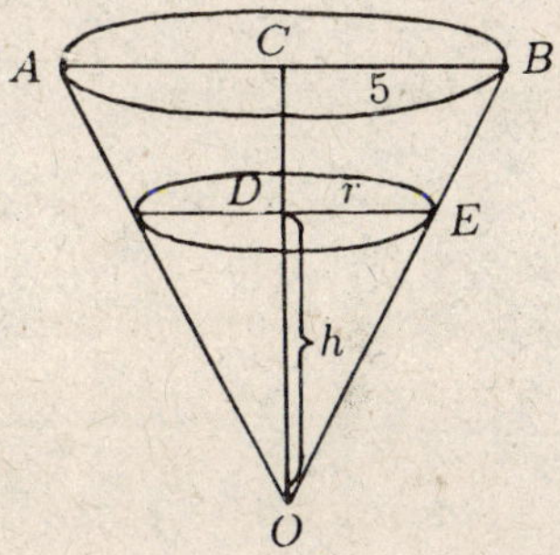

Fig 7.1

From the similar triangles ODE and OCB, we get

$$\frac{DE}{OD} = \frac{CB}{OC} = \frac{5}{10} = \frac{1}{2}, \text{ or, } \frac{r}{h} = \frac{1}{2}, \text{ or, } r = \frac{h}{2}.$$

$$\therefore \quad V = \frac{1}{3}\pi\left(\frac{h}{2}\right)^2 \cdot h = \frac{\pi}{12}h^3.$$

Differentiating both sides w.r.t. 't' we get

$$\frac{dV}{dt} = \frac{\pi}{12} \cdot 3h^2 \frac{dh}{dt} = \frac{\pi h^2}{4} \cdot \frac{dh}{dt}, \text{ or, } \frac{dh}{dt} = \frac{4}{\pi h^2} \cdot \frac{dV}{dt}.$$

Since water is poured at the rate of 1.5 c.c. per minute, $\frac{dv}{dt} = 1.5$

$$\therefore \quad \frac{dh}{dt} = \frac{4}{\pi h^2} \times 1.5$$

When $h = 4$ cm., $\frac{dh}{dt} = \frac{4}{\pi \cdot 4^2} \times 1.5 = \frac{1.5}{4\pi} = \frac{3}{8\pi}$.

Hence the rate at which the level of water is rising $= \frac{3}{8\pi}$ cm./min.

7.11.1. Derivative as the slope of a tangent to the curve $y = f(x)$

(*Geometrical Interpretation of the derivative at a point*)

Let $P(x, y)$ be any given point on the curve $y = f(x)$ with reference to the rectangular axes OX and OY, and Q be a neighbouring point $(x + \Delta x, y + \Delta y)$ on either side of P. Suppose $y = f(x)$ is continuous at P. Let PN, QM be perpendiculars to OX and PL perpendicular to QM. Then $PL = NM = OM - ON = x + \Delta x - x = \Delta x$ and $LQ = MQ - ML = MQ - NP = y + \Delta y - y = \Delta y$.

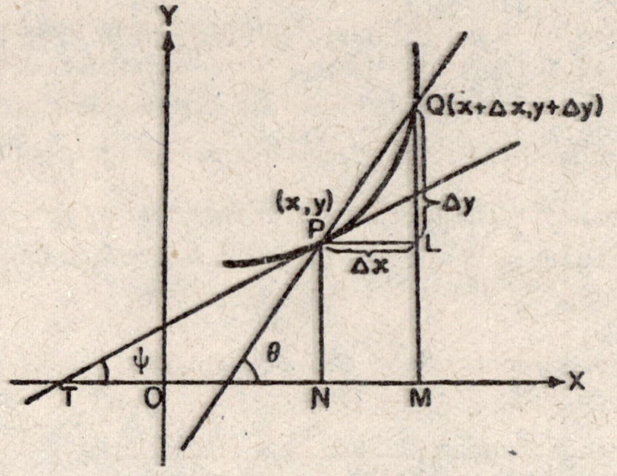

Fig 7.2

The slope of the chord PQ

$$= \frac{\text{Rise}}{\text{Run}} = \frac{LQ}{PL} = \frac{\Delta y}{\Delta x} = \frac{\text{increment of } y}{\text{increment of } x} = \frac{f(x+\Delta x)-f(x)}{\Delta x}. \tag{1}$$

Now let Q tend to P along the curve; then $\Delta x \to 0$ and the chord PQ may tend to a *difinite limiting position* PT (which is called the tangent to the curve at P) as $Q \to P$ from either side and

$$\lim_{\Delta x \to 0} \frac{f(x+\Delta x)-f(x)}{\Delta x} = \frac{dy}{dx} \text{ or, } f'(x).$$

Thus, in the limit when $\Delta x \to 0$, from (1) we have the slope of the tangent PT at $P = \frac{dy}{dx}$.

Hence *geometrically* $\frac{dy}{dx}$ *represents the slope (or gradient) of the tangent line to the curve* $y = f(x)$ *at the point* (x, y).

[If ψ be the inclination of the tangent line with the positive direction of the x-axis, then

$$\text{the slope of the line} = \tan\psi; \text{ i.e., } \frac{\mathbf{dy}}{\mathbf{dx}} = \tan\psi.]$$

If $\frac{dy}{dx} = 0$, *then slope* $= 0$. *This implies that the tangent line at* (x, y) *is* **parallel** *to the* x*-axis. If* $\frac{dx}{dy} = 0$, *then the tangent line at* (x, y) *is* **parallel** *to the* y*-axis.*

COROLLARY 1. From **Plane Analytic Geometry, the equation of the tangent** to the curve $y = f(x)$ at any point $P(x, y)$ is.

$\mathbf{Y - y = \frac{dy}{dx}(X - x)}$, *where* $\frac{dy}{dx}$ = *slope of the tangent at* P, *and* **the equation of the normal** *at* $P(x, y)$ *is*

$\mathbf{Y - y = -\frac{1}{\frac{dy}{dx}}(X - x)}$, *where* $\frac{dy}{dx} \neq 0$ *at* P, *or*, $\mathbf{(X - x) + (Y - y)\frac{dy}{dx} = 0}$.

Thus, the *equation of the tangent to the curve* $y = f(x)$ *at the point* (x_1, y_1) may be written as $y - y_1 = \left[\frac{dy}{dx}\right]_{(x_1, y_1)}(x - x_1)$, where *the slope of the tangent at* (x_1, y_1) is $\left[\frac{dy}{dx}\right]_{(x_1, y_1)}$.

Two tangents to the curve $y = f(x)$ will be (i) **parallel** if their *slopes are equal* and (ii) **perpendicular** to each other if the *product of their* slopes is -1.

2. If $\frac{dy}{dx}$ is *positive* at $P(x, y)$, i.e., if $f'(x) > 0$, then the tangent line at $P(x, y)$ makes an *acute angle* with the positive direction of the x-axis. But if $\frac{dy}{dx}$ is negative at $Q(x, y)$, i.e., if $f'(x) < 0$, then the tangent line at Q makes an *obtuse angle* with the positive direction of the x-axis.

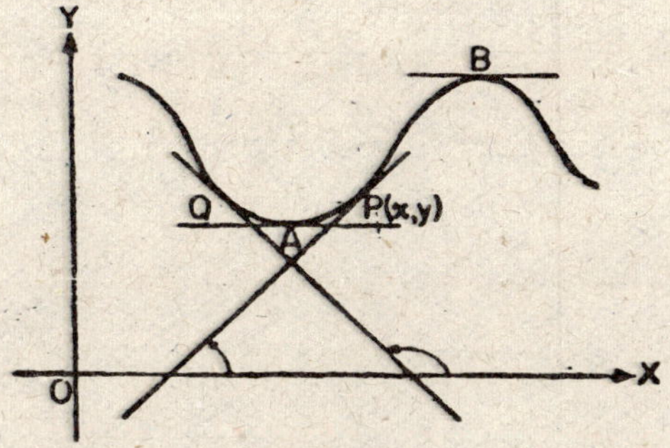

Fig 7.3

If $\frac{dy}{dx} = 0$ at (x, y), i.e., $f'(x) = 0$, then the tangent line is parallel to the x-axis. From the figure 7.3, we see that at A or B the tangent line is parallel to the x-axis, i.e., at A or B, $\frac{dy}{dx} = 0$.

EXAMPLE 4. *Find the slope of the curve* $y = x^2 - 3x + 4$ *when* $x = 1$ *and hence find the equation of the tangent at the point* $(1, 2)$.

SOLUTION. The equation of the curve is $y = x^2 - 3x + 4$ (1)

$$\therefore \quad \frac{dy}{dx} = 2x - 3. \text{ At } x = 1, \frac{dy}{dx} = 2.1 - 3 = -1.$$

Hence the slope of the curve (1) when $x = 1$ is $\mathbf{-1}$.

The required *equation of the tangent to the curve* (1) *at the point* $(1, 2)$ is

$$y - 2 = \left[\frac{dy}{dx}\right]_{(1,2)} (x - 1), \text{ or, } y - 2 = -1(x - 1)$$

$$\text{or,} \quad y - 2 = -x + 1 \text{ or, } \mathbf{x + y = 3}.$$

EXAMPLE 5. *Find the slope of the curve* $x^3 - 2x^2y^2 + 5x + y = 5$ *at the point* $(1, 1)$.

[ICWAI June 1994]

SOLUTION. The curve is $x^3 - 2x^2y^2 + 5x + y = 5$ (1)

Differentiating both sides with respect to 'x', we get

$$3x^2 - 2\left(2x.y^2 + x^2.2y\frac{dy}{dx}\right) + 5.1 + \frac{dy}{dx} = 0,$$

$$\text{or,} \quad 3x^2 - 4xy^2 - 4x^2y\frac{dy}{dx} + 5 + \frac{dy}{dx} = 0,$$

$$\text{or,} \quad \frac{dy}{dx}(1 - 4x^2y) = 4xy^2 - 3x^2 - 5,$$

$$\text{or,} \quad \frac{dy}{dx} = \frac{4xy^2 - 3x^2 - 5}{1 - 4x^2y}$$

At the point $(1,1)$, $\frac{dy}{dx} = \frac{4.1.1^2-3.1^2--3.1^2-5}{1-4.1^2.1} = \frac{4-3-5}{1-4} = \frac{-4}{-3} = \frac{4}{3}$.

EXAMPLE 6. *Find the slope of the curve* $y = \frac{x^2-12}{x-4}$ *at the point* $(0,3)$ *and determine the points where the tangent is parallel to the axis of* x. **[CA May 1984]**

SOLUTION. We have $y = \frac{x^2-12}{x-4}$. (1)

$$\therefore \quad \frac{dy}{dx} = \frac{(x-4)\cdot\frac{d}{dx}(x^2-12) - (x^2-12)\cdot\frac{d}{dx}(x-4)}{(x-4)^2}$$

$$= \frac{(x-4)\cdot 2x - (x^2-12).1}{(x-4)^2} = \frac{x^2-8x+12}{(x-4)^2}.$$

At the point $(0,3), x = 0$ and hence

$$\frac{dy}{dx} = \frac{0^2 - 8.0 + 12}{(0-4)^2} = \frac{12}{16} = \frac{3}{4}.$$

Hence, the slope of the curve at the point $(0,3)$ is $\frac{3}{4}$.

2*nd part:* The points at which the tangents are parallel to the axis of x is given by

$$\frac{dy}{dx} = 0, \text{ i.e., } x^2 - 8x + 12 = 0$$

$$\text{or,} \quad (x-2)(x-6) = 0; \quad \therefore \quad x = 2, 6.$$

If $x = 2$, from (1), $y = \frac{2^2-12}{2-4} = \frac{-8}{-2} = 4$; and if $x = 6, y = \frac{6^2-12}{6-4} = \frac{24}{2} = 12$.

Hence the points at which the tangents are parallel to the axis of x are $(2,4)$ and $(6,12)$.

Miscellaneous Examples

EXAMPLE 7. *Determine the coefficients* A *and* B *so that the curve* $y = Ax^2 + 3x + B$ *may pass through the point* $(0,1)$ *and have its tangent parallel to the axis of* x *at the point for which* $x = .75$.

[ICWAI December 1977]

SOLUTION. We have $y = Ax^2 + 3x + B$. (1)

Since the curve (1) passes through the point $(0,1)$, we have $1 = B$, i.e., $B = 1$.

Differentiating both sides of (1) w.r.t. x, we get

$$\frac{dy}{dx} = 2Ax + 3.$$

At $x = .75$, $\frac{dy}{dx} = 2A \times .75 + 3 = 1.5A + 3$.

Since the tangent at the point $x = .75$ is parallel to the axis of x, we have $1.5A + 3 = 0$ [$\because$ $\frac{dy}{dx}$ at $x = .75$ is 0.]

$$\text{or,} \quad 1.5A = -3, \text{ or, } A = -\frac{3}{1.5} = -2.$$

Hence, $\mathbf{A = -2}$ and $\mathbf{B = 1}$.

EXAMPLE 8. *Find the slope of the curve* $x = y^2 - 4y$ *at the points where it crosses the* y*-axis.*

[ICWAI June 1978]

SOLUTION. For the points of intersection of the curve with the y-axis we have $x = 0$ and $x = y^2 - 4y$; $\therefore$ $y^2 - 4y = 0$,

or, $y(y-4) = 0$; $\therefore$ $y = 0, 4$.

$\therefore$ The points of intersection of the curve and the y-axis are $(0,0)$ and $(0,4)$.

We have $\frac{dx}{dy} = 2y - 4 = 2(y-2)$;

$\therefore$ $\frac{dy}{dx} = 1\big/\frac{dx}{dy} = \frac{1}{2(y-2)}$.

$$\text{At} \quad (0,0), \frac{dy}{dx} = \frac{1}{2(0-2)} = -\frac{1}{4}.$$

$$\text{and at} \quad (0,4), \frac{dy}{dx} = \frac{1}{2(4-2)} = \frac{1}{4}.$$

Hence the required slopes are $-\frac{1}{4}$ and $\frac{1}{4}$.

EXAMPLE 9. *A man is walking at the rate of* 5 *km. per hour towards the foot of a towar* 30 *metres high. At what rate is he approaching the top of the towar when he is* 40 *metres from the foot of the tower?*

SOLUTION. Let AB be the tower of height 30 metres, B being its foot, and let O be the position of the man at any time t such that $OB = x$ metres. Let $OA = y$, then y is the distance of the man from the top of the tower at time t.

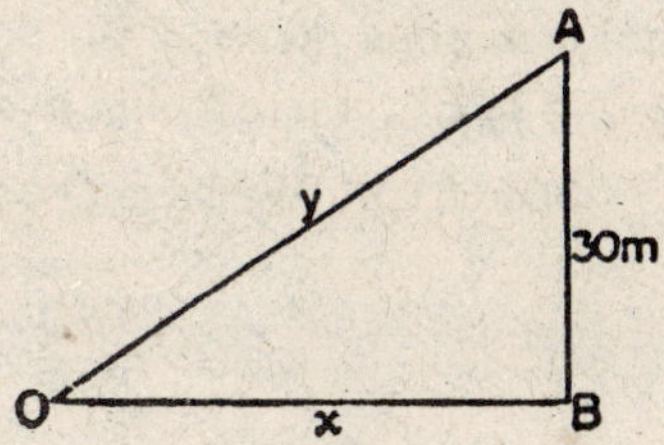

Fig 7.4

From, the right-angled ΔAOB, we have

$$y^2 = x^2 + (30)^2 \qquad (1)$$

Differentiating both sides with respect to 't', we get

$$2y\frac{dy}{dt} = 2x\frac{dx}{dt} + 0, \text{ or, } \frac{dy}{dt} = \frac{x}{y} \times \frac{dx}{dt} \qquad (2)$$

When $x = 40$ metres, from (1), $y^2 = (40)^2 + (30)^2 = 2500$; $\therefore$ $y = 50$ metres.

Since, the man is walking at the rate of 5 km. per hour;

$$\therefore \quad \frac{dx}{dt} = -5 \text{ km./hr.} \quad [\because \ x \text{ decrease as } t \text{ increases.}]$$

$\therefore$ From (2), when $x = 40$ m, we get

$$\frac{dy}{dt} = \frac{40}{50} \times -5 = -4 \text{ km./hr.}$$

[Negative sign indicates that y decreases when t increases.]

Hence, the man is approaching the top at the rate of **4 km./hr.**

EXAMPLE 10. *The rate of change of total cost (y) of a commodity per unit change of output (x) is called the marginal cost of the commodity. If there exists a relation between y and x in the form:*

$$y = 3x\left(\frac{x+7}{x+5}\right) + 5,$$

prove that the marginal cost falls continuously as the output increases. **[ICWAI June 1981]**

SOLUTION. We have $y = 3x\left(\frac{x+7}{x+5}\right) + 5 = 3 \cdot \frac{x^2+7x}{x+5} + 5$.

By the given definition,

$$\begin{aligned} \text{Marginal cost } &= \frac{dy}{dx} = 3 \cdot \frac{(x+5)(2x+7) - (x^2+7x)\cdot 1}{(x+5)^2} + 0 \\ &= 3 \cdot \left\{\frac{2x^2+17x+35-x^2-7x}{(x+5)^2}\right\} = 3 \cdot \left\{\frac{x^2+10x+35}{(x+5)^2}\right\} \\ &= 3 \cdot \left\{\frac{(x+5)^2+10}{(x+5)^2}\right\} = 3 \cdot \left\{1 + \frac{10}{(x+5)^2}\right\}. \end{aligned}$$

This shows that as x increases, $\frac{dy}{dx}$, i.e., the marginal cost decreases.

Hence the result follows:

EXAMPLE 11. *We define point elasticity of y with respect to x for a function $y = f(x)$ by the ratio $\left(\text{marginal function } \frac{dy}{dx}\right) : \left(\text{average function } \frac{y}{x}\right)$. Prove that the point elasticity of demand, given by $Q = k/P^n$, where k and n are constants, is independent of the price P.* **[ICWAI June 1983]**

SOLUTION. We have $Q = \frac{k}{P^n} = k.P^{-n}$

$$\therefore \quad \frac{dQ}{dP} = -kn.P^{-n-1}. \quad \text{Also} \quad \frac{Q}{P} = \frac{kP^{-n}}{P} = kP^{-n-1}.$$

By the definition of point elasticity of demand, we have the point elasticity of demand of Q w.r.t. P for the function $Q = \frac{k}{P^n}$

$= \frac{\frac{dQ}{dP}}{\frac{Q}{P}} = \frac{-kn.P^{-n-1}}{k.P^{-n-1}} = -n$ which is independepndnet of the price P.

Hence the result follows.

Exercise 7(III)

[Derivative as a rate-measurer and as the slope of a tangent]

[A]

1. For the function $y = 3x + 2$, find the average rate of change of y when x increases from 1.5 to 1.6.

2. If $y = 2x^2 + 3x$, find the instantaneous rate of change of y at $x = 4$.

3. If $y = \frac{300}{x}$, find the average rate of change of y w.r.t. x when x increases from 10 to 10.5 units. Find also the instantaneous rate of change of y at $x = 10$.

4. A particle moves in a straight line in the same direction so that its distance s cm. measured from a fixed point O on the line at time t secs. is given by $s = t^2 + 4t - 5$. Find (i) the velocity at any time t; (ii) the velocity at the end of 6 seconds, (iii) the average velocity while t changes from 3 to 5 seconds.

5. For a particle moving in a straight line, the distance s cm. from a fixed point on the line described in t seconds is given by $s = 4t^3 - 5t^2 + 6t$. Find the velocity and the acceleration of the particle at the end of 2 seconds.

6. If the rate of change of y w.r.t. x is 6 and x is changing at 4 units/sec., find the rate of change of y per second.

[HINTS. $\frac{dy}{dx} = 6$ and $\frac{dx}{dt} = 4$; Also $\frac{dy}{dx} = \frac{dy}{dt} \Big/ \frac{dx}{dt}$; find $\frac{dy}{dt}$.]

7. The side of an equilateral triangle is increasing at the rate of $\sqrt{3}$ cm./sec. How fast is the area increasing when its side is 5 cm.? **[Gau. U. 1977; Mag. U. 1981]**

[HINTS. If A sq. cm. be the area of the equilateral triangle of side a cm.,

$$\text{then} \quad \frac{da}{dt} = \sqrt{3} \text{ cm./sec. and } A = \frac{\sqrt{3}}{4}a^2$$

$$\therefore \quad \frac{dA}{dt} = \frac{\sqrt{3}}{2}a \cdot \frac{da}{dt} = \frac{\sqrt{3}}{2}a \cdot \sqrt{3} = \frac{3}{2}a = \frac{3}{2} \times 5 = \frac{15}{2} \text{ sq. cm./sec.}$$]

8. Using derivative as rate measurer prove the following statement: "If the area of a circle increases at a uniform rate, then the rate of increase of the perimeter varies inversely as the radius of the circle." **[ICWAI December 1979]**

9. A spherical balloon has a variable radius. Find the rate at which its volume is increasing with the radius at the instant when radius is 8 cm. (Take $\pi = \frac{22}{7}$)

10. A man is walking at the rate of 5 km. per hour towards the foot of a tower 60 metres high. At what rate is he approaching the top when he is 80 metres from the foot of the tower?

11. An inverted cone has a height of 15 cms. and a base of radius 7.5 cms. Water is poured into it at the rate of 2.2 c.c. per minute. Find the rate at which the level of water in the cone is rising when the depth is 7 cms.

12. Find the value of $\sqrt{6.33}$, given $\sqrt{6.25} = 2.5$, by the method of differential.

[HINTS. $f(x + \Delta x) = f(x) + f'(x)dx$; here $x = 6.25, \Delta x = 0.08, f(x) = \sqrt{x}, f'(x) = 1/2\sqrt{x}$.]

[B]

1. (i) Find the slope of the tangent line at the point $(0, 5)$ of the curve $y = \frac{1}{5}(x^2 + 10x - 15)$. At what point of the curve the slope of the tangent line is 8/5?

(ii) Find the gradient of the curve $y = 2x^3 - 3x^2 - 12x + 8$ when $x = 0$.

2. Find the slope of the tangent to the curve $y = \frac{x^2-15}{x-4}$ at the point $(0, 2)$ and determine the points where the tangent is parallel to the axis of x.

3. Determine the coefficients a and b so that the curve $y = ax^2 - 6x + b$ may pass through the point $(0, 2)$ and have its tangent parallel to the axis of x at the point for which $x = 1.5$.

4. (i) Find the slope of the curve $x = y^2 - 6y$ at the points where it crosses the y-axis.

(ii) Find the gradients of the tangents to the curve $y = x^2 - 8x$ at the points where it crosses the x-axis.

(iii) Find the slopes of the tangents at the three points where the curve $y = (x-1)(x^2-5x+6)$ cuts the x-axis.

5. Find the points at which the slope of the curve $y = x^3 - 6x^2 + 9x$ is (i) zero, (ii) 24.

6. (i) Find the slope of the curve $x^2 + xy + 2y^2 = 28$ at $x = 2, y = 3$. **[ICWAI December 1992]**

(ii) Find the gradient of the curve $\log(xy) = x^2 - y^2$ at the point $(1, 1)$.

[C.U. B.Com (Hons.) 1992]

7. If $y = 6x^2 - x^3$ and $\frac{dx}{dt} = \frac{1}{2}$ cm./sec., find how fast the slope of the curve is changing at the instant when $x = 3$ cm.

8. The curve $y = Ax^2 + Bx - 10$ passes through the point $(2, 0)$ and the gradient of the curve at this point is 3. Calculate the values of A and B.

9. Prove that curves $y = x^2 - 3x + 1$ and $x(y + 3) = 4$ intersect at right angles at the point $(2, -1)$.

[HINTS. Find the slopes of the tangents to the two curves at $(2, -1)$ and show that the product of the slopes $= -1$.]

10. At what points do the curves $y = x^2 - 1$ and $y = -2x^2 + 2$ intersect? Which curve is steeper at these points of intersection? **[ICWAI December 1975]**

11. Given $y = \frac{1}{3}x^3 - x^2 + 2$. Find the points where the direction of the curve is parallel to x-axis. **[ICWAI December 1993]**

[HINTS. Curve is

$$y = \frac{1}{3}x^3 - x^2 + 2 \tag{1}$$

$\therefore$ $\frac{dy}{dx} = x^2 - 2x = 0$ for the direction of the curve to be parallel to the x-axis.

or, $x(x - 2) = 0$, or, $\mathbf{x} = \mathbf{0}, \mathbf{2}$.

From (1), $\mathbf{y} = \mathbf{2}, \mathbf{\frac{2}{3}}$, etc.]

12. The rate of change of the total cost (y) of a commodity per unit change of output (x) is called the *marginal cost* of the commodity. Using this definition and considering the relation $y = 2x\left(\frac{x+4}{x+3}\right) + 3$, prove that the marginal cost falls continuously as the output increases.

[C]

1. Show that the instantaneous rate of change of the volume of a cube with respect to its edge x cm. is 48 cubic cm. when $x = 4$ cm.

2. The area of a circle is increasing at the uniform rate of 5 sq. cm. per minute. Calculate the rate, in centimetre per minute, at which the radius is increasing when the circumference of the circle is 40 cm.

3. A stone is dropped into a pond and the ripples widen at the rate of 14 cm./sec. What is the rate of increase of the circular area enclosed at the time when the radius of the circular ripple is 40 cm.?

4. A balloon contains a certain mass of gas whose volume is v cubic cm. and whose pressure is p newton per sq. cm., and it is known that p and v obey the law $pv = 1000$. If the volume increases at the rate of 50 cubic cm. per minute, find the rate of change of p when $v = 40$.

5. A man 5.6 ft. tall walks at a uniform rate of 3 miles per hour away from a lamp post 16.8 ft. high. Find the rate at which his shadow is increasing?

[HINTS. 3 m.p.h. $= 4.4$ ft./sec. If x be the distance of the man from the lamp post at any time t and s the length of the shadow, then $s/5.6 = (s+x)/16.8$, or, $2s = x$, etc.]

6. A spherical balloon is inflated by pumping in 168.10 c.c. of gas per second. Find the rate at which the radius of balloon is increasing when its original raidus is 20.5 cm.

7. A missile is through vertically upwards and it rises to a height s cm. in t secs., where $s = 380t(20-t)$. Find its velocity and acceleration after 6 secs. For what time does it continue to rise? What maximum height can it reach?

8. A circular cone, with semi-verical angle 45°, is fixed with its axis vertical and its vertex downwards. Water is poured into the cone at the rate of 4.4 cubic cm. per minute. Find the rate at which the depth of water is increasing when the depth is 6 cm.

Answers

[A]

1. 3. **2.** 19. **3.** $-2.857; -3$. **4.** (i) $(2t+4)$ cm./sec.; (ii) 16 cm./sec.; (iii) 12 cm./sec. **5.** 34 cm./sec. and 38 cm./sec.^{2}. **6.** 24 units/sec. **7.** 7.5 sq. cm./sec. **9.** 804.57 c.c./unit increase in radius. **10.** 4 km./hr. **11.** 4/70 cm./min. **12.** 2.516.

[B]

1. (i) $2, (-1, -24/5)$; (ii) -12. **2.** $15/16; (3,6), (5,10)$. **3.** $a = 2, b = 2$. **4.** (i) $-1/6, 1/6$; (ii) $-8, 8$; (iii) $2, -1, 2$. **5.** (i) $(1,4), (3,0)$; (ii) $(-1,-16), (5,20)$. **6.** (i) $-\frac{1}{2}$; (ii) $\frac{1}{3}$. **7.** 5.5 cm./sec. **8.** $A = -1$, $B = 7$. **10.** $(1,0), (-1,0)$; 2nd curve.

[C]

2. 1/8 cm./min. **3.** 3520 sq. cm./sec. **4.** 31.25 newton per sq. cm. per min. **5.** 2.2 ft./sec. **6.** $\frac{7}{220}$ cm./sec. **7.** 30.4 metres/sec.; -7.6 metres/sec.^{2}; 10 secs.; 380 metres. **8.** 7/180 cm. per min.

CHAPTER 8

PARTIAL DIFFERENTIATION

8.1. INTRODUCTION

In the previous chapter, we have discussed *differentiation* of functions of one variable. Now we shall consider functions of two or more independent variables and study the derivative of such functions with respect to an independent variable.

If there exists a relation between three variables x, y, z such that for every pair of values of x and y within a given domain, we get a definite value of z in a range, then z is called a function of the two independent variables x and y, and we write $z = f(x, y)$.

We can also define function of two independent variables x, y as the correspondence between two sets R and B, where R is the set of number pairs (x, y) and B is the set of real numbers represented by z.

ILLUSTRATION.

(i) If $z = 2x^2y$, and x, y are known, then we can find the value of z uniquely. Here we can say that z is a function of two independent variables x and y.

(ii) If $u = x^2 + 3xy + 2y^2$ and x, y are known in advance, then we can find the value of u uniquely. We can say that u is a function of two variables x and y and we can write $u = f(x, y)$.

(iii) If $v = x^2 + y^2 + z^2 + xy + yz + zx$ and x, y, z are known in advance, then we can determine v uniquely. Here we say that v is a function of three independent variables x, y, z and we write $v = f(x, y, z)$.

(iv) The area of a triangle is a function of two variables, its base and altitude; the volume of a parallelopiped is a function of three variables, its length, breadth and height, etc.

EXAMPLE 1. *If $f(x, y) = x^2 - 2xy + 3y^2 + 6$, find the values of $f(0, 0)$ and $f(2, 1)$.*

SOLUTION. $f(x, y) = x^2 - 2xy + 3y^2 + 6$

$\therefore f(0, 0) = 0^2 - 2.0.0 + 3.0^2 + 6 = 6$ and $f(2, 1) = 2^2 - 2.2.1 + 3.1^2 + 6 = 9$.

8.2. PARTIAL DERIVATIVES

Let $z = f(x, y)$ be a function of two independent variables x and y, and (x, y) be any point. Then the ordinary derivative of $f(x, y)$ with respect to x, keeping y constant, is called the **partial derivative** of $f(x, y)$ w.r.t. x and is denoted by the symbol $\frac{\partial f}{\partial x}$ or $\frac{\partial z}{\partial x}$ or $f_x(x, y)$ or z_x or f_x. Similarly, we can define *partial derivative* of $f(x, y)$ with respect to y.

Thus we have

$$\frac{\partial f}{\partial x} = \lim_{h\to 0} \frac{f(x+h, y) - f(x, y)}{h}, \text{ provided the limit exists,}$$

[Here y is fixed and h is the increment of x so that the new value of x is $x + h$ and the corresponding value of $f(x, y)$ is $f(x + h, y)$.]

$$\text{and} \quad \frac{\partial f}{\partial y} = \lim_{k\to 0} \frac{f(x, y+k) - f(x, y)}{k}, \text{ provided the limit exists.}$$

[Here x is fixed and k is the increment of y so that the new value of y is $y + k$ and the corresponding value of $f(x, y)$ is $f(x, y + k)$.]

The partial derivative of $f(x, y)$ w.r.t. x at the point (a, b) is given by $f_x(a, b) = \lim_{h\to 0} \frac{f(a+h,b)-f(a,b)}{h}$ provided the limit exists.

Similarly, we can define the partial derivative of $f(x, y)$ w.r.t. y at the point (a, b).

EXAMPLE 2. *If* $f(x, y) = x^2 + 3xy + 2y^2$, *find* $\frac{\partial f}{\partial x}$ *and* $\frac{\partial f}{\partial y}$.

SOLUTION. We have $f(x, y) = x^2 + 3xy + 2y^2$.

$$\therefore \quad \frac{\partial f}{\partial x} = 2x + 3.1.y + 0 = 2x + 3y. \quad \text{[differentiating w.r.t. } x\text{, keeping } y \text{ constant]}$$

$$\frac{\partial f}{\partial y} = 0 + 3x.1 + 2.2y = 3x + 4y. \quad \text{[differentiating w.r.t. } y\text{, keeping } x \text{ constant.]}$$

8.3. SUCCESSIVE PARTIAL DERIVATIVES

If $f(x, y)$ has partial derivatives at every point (x, y), then each of the partial derivatives $\frac{\partial f}{\partial x}$ and $\frac{\partial f}{\partial y}$ is, in general, a function of x and y and each of $\frac{\partial f}{\partial x}$ and $\frac{\partial f}{\partial y}$ may have partial derivatives w.r.t. x and y. These second derivatives are called the *second order partial derivatives of* $f(x, y)$ or z. These second order partial derivatives are denoted by

$$\frac{\partial}{\partial x}\left(\frac{\partial f}{\partial x}\right) = \frac{\partial^2 f}{\partial x^2} = f_{xx}, \quad \frac{\partial}{\partial y}\left(\frac{\partial f}{\partial y}\right) = \frac{\partial^2 f}{\partial y^2} = f_{yy},$$

$$\frac{\partial}{\partial x}\left(\frac{\partial f}{\partial y}\right) = \frac{\partial^2 f}{\partial x \partial y} = f_{xy}, \quad \frac{\partial}{\partial y}\left(\frac{\partial f}{\partial x}\right) = \frac{\partial^2 f}{\partial y \partial x} = f_{yx}.$$

NOTE. If f_{xy} and f_{yx} are continuous in a region R, then $f_{xy} = f_{yx}$ holds in R.

EXAMPLE 3. *If* $f(x, y) = x^3 + y^3 + 3xy$, *find* f_{xx}, f_{yy}, f_{xy} *and* f_{yx}.

SOLUTION. We have $f(x,y) = x^3 + y^3 + 3xy$.

$$\therefore \quad f_x = \frac{\partial f}{\partial x} = 3x^2 + 0 + 3.1.y = 3x^2 + 3y;$$
$$\therefore \quad f_{xx} = 3.2x + 0 = \mathbf{6x}.$$

Again

$$f_y = \frac{\partial f}{\partial y} = 0 + 3y^2 + 3x.1 = 3y^2 + 3x$$
$$\therefore \quad f_{yy} = 3.2y + 0 = \mathbf{6y}.$$
$$f_{xy} = \frac{\partial}{\partial x}\left(\frac{\partial f}{\partial y}\right) = \frac{\partial}{\partial x}(3y^2 + 3x) = 0 + 3.1 = 3.$$
$$f_{yx} = \frac{\partial}{\partial y}\left(\frac{\partial f}{\partial x}\right) = \frac{\partial}{\partial y}(3x^2 + 3y) = 0 + 3.1 = 3.$$

EXAMPLE 4. *If* $z = \log(x^2 + y^2)$, *prove that* $\frac{\partial^2 z}{\partial x^2} + \frac{\partial^2 z}{\partial y^2} = 0$.

SOLUTION. We have $z = \log(x^2 + y^2)$

$$\therefore \quad \frac{\partial z}{\partial x} = \frac{1}{x^2 + y^2} \times (2x + 0) = \frac{2x}{x^2 + y^2};$$
$$\therefore \quad \frac{\partial^2 z}{\partial x^2} = 2.\left[\frac{(x^2 + y^2).1 - x.2x}{(x^2 + y^2)^2}\right] = \frac{2(-x^2 + y^2)}{(x^2 + y^2)^2};$$
$$\frac{\partial z}{\partial y} = \frac{1}{x^2 + y^2} \times (0 + 2y) = \frac{2y}{x^2 + y^2}$$
$$\therefore \quad \frac{\partial^2 z}{\partial y^2} = 2\left[\frac{(x^2 + y^2).1 - y.2y}{(x^2 + y^2)^2}\right] = 2\frac{(x^2 - y^2)}{(x^2 + y^2)^2};$$
$$\therefore \quad \frac{\partial^2 z}{\partial x^2} + \frac{\partial^2 z}{\partial y^2} = \frac{2(-x^2 + y^2)}{(x^2 + y^2)^2} + \frac{2(x^2 - y^2)}{(x^2 + y^2)^2}$$
$$= \frac{-2x^2 + 2y^2 + 2x^2 - 2y^2}{(x^2 + y^2)^2} = 0.$$

EXAMPLE 5. *If* $f(x,y) = 3x^3 - 5x^2y + 2y^3$, *show that* $x\frac{\partial f}{\partial x} + y\frac{\partial f}{\partial y} = 3f(x,y)$.

[ICWAI December 1987]

SOLUTION. Given, $f(x,y) = 3x^3 - 5x^2y + 2y^3$. (1)

$$\therefore \quad \frac{\partial f}{\partial x} = 3.3x^2 - 5.2x.y + 0 = 9x^2 - 10xy$$
$$\text{and} \quad \frac{\partial f}{\partial y} = 0 - 5x^2.1 + 2.3y^2 = -5x^2 + 6y^2$$
$$\therefore \quad x\frac{\partial f}{\partial x} + y\frac{\partial f}{\partial y} = x(9x^2 - 10xy) + y(-5x^2 + 6y^2)$$
$$= 9x^3 - 10x^2y - 5x^2y + 6y^3 = 9x^3 - 15x^2y + 6y^3$$
$$= 3(3x^3 - 5x^2y + 2y^3) = \mathbf{3f(x,y)}$$

8.4. HOMOGENEOUS FUNCTIONS : EULER'S THEOREM

A function $f(x, y)$ of two independent variables x and y is said to be **homogeneous** *in x and y of degree n if it can be expressed in the form $x^n\phi\left(\frac{y}{x}\right)$ or $y^n\phi\left(\frac{x}{y}\right)$.*

ILLUSTRATION.

(i)
$$f(x,y) = ax^2 + by^2 + 2hxy = x^2\left\{a + b\left(\frac{y}{x}\right)^2 + 2h\left(\frac{y}{x}\right)\right\}$$
$$= x^2 \times \text{ a function of } \frac{y}{x} = x^2\phi\left(\frac{y}{x}\right).$$

$\therefore f(x, y)$ is a *homogeneous function* in x and y of degree 2.

[We may also express $f(x, y)$ in the form $f(x, y) = y^2\phi(\frac{x}{y})$.]

(ii)
$$f(x,y) = \frac{x^3 + 2x^2y + y^3}{x+y} = \frac{x^3\left\{1 + 2\left(\frac{y}{x}\right) + \left(\frac{y}{x}\right)^3\right\}}{x\left(1 + \frac{y}{x}\right)}$$
$$= x^2.\left\{\frac{1 + 2\left(\frac{y}{x}\right) + \left(\frac{y}{x}\right)^3}{1 + \frac{y}{x}}\right\} = x^2 \times \text{ a function of } \frac{y}{x} = x^2\phi\left(\frac{y}{x}\right).$$

$\therefore$ $f(x, y)$ is a *homogeneous function* in x and y of degree 2.

(iii)
$$f(x,y) = \frac{x^{\frac{1}{2}} + y^{\frac{1}{2}}}{x^{\frac{1}{4}} + y^{\frac{1}{4}}} = \frac{x^{\frac{1}{2}}\left\{1 + \left(\frac{y}{x}\right)^{\frac{1}{2}}\right\}}{x^{\frac{1}{4}}\left\{1 + \left(\frac{y}{x}\right)^{\frac{1}{4}}\right\}} = x^{\frac{1}{4}}\left\{\frac{1 + \left(\frac{y}{x}\right)^{\frac{1}{2}}}{1 + \left(\frac{y}{x}\right)^{\frac{1}{4}}}\right\}$$
$$= x^{\frac{1}{4}} \times \text{ a function of } \frac{y}{x} = x^{\frac{1}{4}}\phi\left(\frac{y}{x}\right).$$

$\therefore$ $f(x, y)$ is a *homogeneous function* in x and y of degree $\frac{1}{4}$.

An alternative definition

A function $f(x, y)$ of two independent variables x and y is said to be homogeneous in x and y of degree n when

$$f(tx, ty) = t^n f(x, y)$$

for any positive quantity t, where t is independent of x and y.

ILLUSTRATION. If $f(x, y) = \frac{x^4+y^4}{x+y}$, then

$$f(tx, ty) = \frac{t^4x^4 + t^4y^4}{tx + ty} = \frac{t^4(x^4 + y^4)}{t(x+y)} = \frac{t^3(x^4 + y^4)}{x+y} = t^3 f(x, y);$$

$\therefore$ $f(x, y)$ is a *homogeneous function* in x and y of degree 3.

Euler's Theorem on Homogeneous Functions of two variables.

If $f(x, y)$ be a homogeneous function of x and y of degree n having partial derivatives $\frac{\partial f}{\partial x}$ and $\frac{\partial f}{\partial y}$, then

$$\mathbf{x\frac{\partial f}{\partial x} + y\frac{\partial f}{\partial y} = nf(x, y).}$$

VERIFICATION. Since $f(x, y)$ is a *homogeneous function of degree n,* we can write

$$f(x, y) = x^n \phi\left(\tfrac{y}{x}\right)$$

$$\therefore \frac{\partial f}{\partial x} = nx^{n-1}\phi\left(\frac{y}{x}\right) + x^n\phi'\left(\frac{y}{x}\right) \times \frac{\partial}{\partial x}\left(\frac{y}{x}\right).$$

[where $\phi'\left(\frac{y}{x}\right)$ is the derivative $\phi\left(\frac{y}{x}\right)$ *w.r.t.* $\frac{y}{x}$.]

$$\text{i.e.,}\quad \frac{\partial f}{\partial x} = nx^{n-1}\phi\left(\frac{y}{x}\right) + x^n\phi'\left(\frac{y}{x}\right) \times -\frac{y}{x^2}$$

$$\therefore\quad x\frac{\partial f}{\partial x} = nx^n\phi\left(\frac{y}{x}\right) - x^n\phi'\left(\frac{y}{x}\right) \times \frac{y}{x} \tag{1}$$

$$\text{Again}\quad \frac{\partial f}{dy} = x^n\phi'\left(\frac{y}{x}\right) \times \frac{\partial}{\partial y}\left(\frac{y}{x}\right) = x^n\phi'\left(\frac{y}{x}\right) \times \frac{1}{x}$$

$$\therefore\quad y\frac{\partial f}{\partial y} = x^n\phi'\left(\frac{y}{x}\right) \times \frac{y}{x} \tag{2}$$

Adding (1) and (2), we get

$$x\frac{\partial f}{dx} + y\frac{\partial f}{\partial y} = nx^n\phi\left(\frac{y}{x}\right) = nf(x, y)$$

Hence the theorem is verified.

NOTE. This theorem can be extended for a homogeneous function of three or more variables. If $f(x, y, z)$ be a *homogeneous function* in x, y, z of *degree n, then*

$$x\frac{\partial f}{\partial x} + y\frac{\partial f}{\partial y} + z\frac{\partial f}{\partial z} = nf(x, y, z).$$

EXAMPLE 6. *Verify Euler's Theorem for the function $f(x, y) = 3x^4 - 2xy^3 + y^4$.*

[C.U. B.Com (Hons.) 1988]

SOLUTION. We have

$$f(x, y) = 3x^4 - 2xy^3 + y^4 = x^4(3 - 2\frac{y^3}{x^3} + \frac{y^4}{x^4})$$

$$= x^4\left\{3 - 2\left(\frac{y}{x}\right)^3 + \left(\frac{y}{x}\right)^4\right\} = x^4\phi\left(\frac{y}{x}\right)$$

$\therefore$ $f(x,y)$ is a *homogeneous function* in x, y of degree 4.

To verify *Euler's Theorem*, we have to show that $x\frac{\partial f}{\partial x} + y\frac{\partial f}{\partial y} = 4f(x,y)$.

Now

$$f(x,y) = 3x^4 - 2xy^3 + y^4 \tag{1}$$

$$\therefore \quad \frac{\partial f}{\partial x} = 3.4x^3 - 2.1.y^3 + 0 = 12x^3 - 2y^3$$

$$\text{and} \quad \frac{\partial f}{\partial y} = 0 - 2x.3y^2 + 4y^3 = -6xy^2 + 4y^3$$

$$\begin{aligned}\therefore \quad x\frac{\partial f}{\partial x} + y\frac{\partial f}{\partial y} &= x(12x^3 - 2y^3) + y(-6xy^2 + 4y^3)\\ &= 12x^4 - 2xy^3 - 6xy^3 + 4y^4 = 12x^4 - 8xy^3 + 4y^4\\ &= 4(3x^4 - 2xy^3 + y^4) = \mathbf{4f(x,y)}.\end{aligned}$$

Thus *Euler's Theorem is verified.*

EXAMPLE 7. *If* $f(x,y) = 2x^3 - 11x^2y + 3y^3$, *prove that*

$$x\frac{\partial f}{\partial x} + y\frac{\partial f}{\partial y} = 3f(x,y).$$

[C.U. B.Com (Hons.) 1983]

SOLUTION. We have

$$f(x,y) = 2x^3 - 11x^2y + 3y^3$$

$$\therefore \quad \frac{\partial f}{\partial x} = 2.3x^2 - 11.2x.y + 0 = 6x^2 - 22xy$$

$$\text{and} \quad \frac{df}{\partial y} = 0 - 11x^2.1 + 3.3y^2 = -11x^2 + 9y^2.$$

$$\begin{aligned}\therefore \quad x\frac{\partial f}{\partial x} + y\frac{\partial f}{\partial y} &= x.(6x^2 - 22xy) + y(-11x^2 + 9y^2)\\ &= 6x^3 - 22x^2y - 11x^2y + 9y^3 = 6x^3 - 33x^2y + 9y^3\\ &= 3(2x^3 - 11x^2y + 3y^3) = 3f(x,y).\end{aligned}$$

Hence the result follows.

8.5. MISCELLANEOUS PROBLEMS

EXAMPLE 8. *Show that the function* $z = \frac{2x-3y}{5y}$ *is homogeneous and prove that* $x\frac{\partial z}{\partial x} + y\frac{\partial z}{\partial y} = 0$.

[C.U. B.Com (Hons.) 1989]

SOLUTION. We have $z = \frac{2x-3y}{5y} = \frac{y\left(2.\frac{x}{y}-3\right)}{5y} = y^{\circ}.\left\{\frac{2\left(\frac{x}{y}\right)-3}{5}\right\}$.

This shows that z is a *homogeneous function* in x, y of degree 0.

Now

$$\frac{\partial z}{\partial x} = \frac{1}{5y}.\frac{\partial}{\partial x}(2x - 3y) = \frac{1}{5y}(2.1 - 0) = \frac{2}{5y} \qquad [\because \;\; y \text{ is fixed.}]$$

$$\text{and} \quad \frac{\partial z}{\partial y} = \frac{5y\frac{\partial}{\partial y}(2x-3y) - (2x-3y)\frac{\partial}{\partial y}(5y)}{(5y)^2} = \frac{5y.(0-3.1) - (2x-3y)5.1}{25y^2}$$

$$= \frac{-15y - 10x + 15y}{25y^2} = -\frac{10x}{25y^2} = \frac{-2x}{5y^2}$$

$$\therefore \quad x\frac{\partial z}{\partial x} + y\frac{\partial z}{\partial y} = x.\frac{2}{5y} + y.\left(-\frac{2x}{5y^2}\right) = \frac{2x}{5y} - \frac{2x}{5y} = \mathbf{0}.$$

EXAMPLE 9. *If* $f(x, y, z) = x^3 + y^3 + z^3 - 3xyz$, *prove that*

$$x\frac{\partial f}{\partial x} + y\frac{\partial f}{\partial y} + z\frac{\partial f}{\partial z} = 3f(x, y, z).$$

SOLUTION. We have

$$f(x, y, z) = x^3 + y^3 + z^3 - 3xyz.$$

$$\therefore \frac{\partial f}{\partial x} = 3x^2 - 3yz, \frac{\partial f}{\partial y} = 3y^2 - 3xz, \frac{\partial f}{\partial z} = 3z^2 - 3xy.$$

$$\therefore \quad x\frac{\partial f}{\partial x} + y\frac{\partial f}{\partial y} + z\frac{\partial f}{\partial z} = x(3x^2 - 3yz) + y(3y^2 - 3xz) + z(3z^2 - 3xy)$$

$$= 3x^3 - 3xyz + 3y^3 - 3xyz + 3z^3 - 3xyz$$

$$= 3x^3 + 3y^3 + 3z^3 - 9xyz = 3(x^3 + y^3 + z^3 - 3xyz)$$

$$= 3f(x, y, z).$$

Hence the result follows.

EXAMPLE 10. *If* $v = \log_e \frac{x^3+y^3}{x^2+y^2}$, *prove by Euler's theorem that* $x\frac{\partial v}{\partial x} + y\frac{\partial v}{\partial y} = 1$. **[C.U. B.Sc 1978]**

SOLUTION. We have

$$v = \log_e \frac{x^3 + y^3}{x^2 + y^2}; \qquad \therefore \quad e^v = \frac{x^2 + y^3}{x^2 + y^2}.$$

$$\text{If} \quad z = e^v, \text{ then } z = \frac{x^3 + y^3}{x^2 + y^2} = \frac{x^3\left(1 + \frac{y^3}{x^3}\right)}{x^2\left(1 + \frac{y^2}{x^2}\right)} = x.\left\{\frac{1 + \left(\frac{y}{x}\right)^3}{1 + \left(\frac{y}{x}\right)^2}\right\}$$

$\therefore$ z is a *homogeneous function* in x, y of degree 1.

Hence by Euler's theorem, $x\frac{\partial z}{\partial x} + y\frac{\partial z}{\partial y} = 1.z = z.$ (1)

Now $z = e^v$;

$$\therefore \quad \frac{\partial z}{\partial x} = e^v.\frac{\partial v}{\partial x} \text{ and } \frac{\partial z}{\partial y} = e^v\frac{\partial v}{\partial y}.$$

$\therefore$ From (1),

$$xe^v\frac{\partial v}{\partial x} + ye^v\frac{\partial v}{\partial y} = e^v, \quad \text{or,} \quad x\frac{\partial v}{\partial x} + y\frac{\partial v}{\partial y} = \mathbf{1}.$$

EXAMPLE 11. *If $v = \log r$ and $r^2 = x^2 + y^2 + z^2$, then prove that*

$$\frac{\partial^2 v}{\partial x^2} + \frac{\partial^2 v}{\partial y^2} + \frac{\partial^2 v}{\partial z^2} = \frac{1}{r^2}$$ **[C.U. B.Sc 1975]**

SOLUTION. We have $r^2 = x^2 + y^2 + z^2$; $\therefore$ $2\log r = \log(x^2 + y^2 + z^2)$
Again $v = \log r = \frac{1}{2}\log(x^2 + y^2 + z^2)$

$$\therefore \quad \frac{\partial v}{\partial x} = \frac{1}{2} \cdot \frac{1}{x^2 + y^2 + z^2} \times 2x = \frac{x}{x^2 + y^2 + z^2}$$

$$\frac{\partial^2 v}{\partial x^2} = \frac{(x^2 + y^2 + z^2).1 - x.2x}{(x^2 + y^2 + z^2)^2} = \frac{-x^2 + y^2 + z^2}{(x^2 + y^2 + z^2)^2}$$

Similarly,

$$\frac{\partial^2 v}{\partial y^2} = \frac{x^2 - y^2 + z^2}{(x^2 + y^2 + z^2)^2} \quad \text{and} \quad \frac{\partial^2 v}{\partial z^2} = \frac{x^2 + y^2 - z^2}{(x^2 + y^2 + z^2)^2}$$

$$\therefore \quad \frac{\partial^2 v}{\partial x^2} + \frac{\partial^2 v}{\partial y^2} + \frac{\partial^2 v}{\partial z^2} = \frac{-x^2 + y^2 + z^2}{(x^2 + y^2 + z^2)^2} + \frac{x^2 - y^2 + z^2}{(x^2 + y^2 + z^2)^2} + \frac{x^2 + y^2 - z^2}{(x^2 + y^2 + z^2)^2}$$

$$= \frac{-x^2 + y^2 + z^2 + x^2 - y^2 + z^2 + x^2 + y^2 - z^2}{(x^2 + y^2 + z^2)^2}$$

$$= \frac{x^2 + y^2 + z^2}{(x^2 + y^2 + z^2)^2} = \frac{1}{x^2 + y^2 + z^2} = \frac{\mathbf{1}}{\mathbf{r^2}}.$$

EXAMPLE 12. *If $z = f(x - cy) + F(x + cy)$ where f and F are any two functions and c is a constant, show that*

$$c^2 \frac{\partial^2 z}{\partial x^2} = \frac{\partial^2 z}{\partial y^2}.$$ **[C.U. B.Sc 1974]**

SOLUTION. We have $z = f(x - cy) + F(x + cy)$.

$$\therefore \quad \frac{\partial z}{\partial x} = f'(x - cy).\frac{\partial}{\partial x}(x - cy) + F'(x + cy).\frac{\partial}{\partial x}(x + cy)$$

$$= f'(x - cy) \times (1 - 0) + F'(x + cy) \times (1 + 0)$$

$$= f'(x - cy) + F'(x + cy)$$

Similarly,

$$\frac{\partial^2 z}{\partial x^2} = \frac{\partial}{\partial x}\left(\frac{\partial z}{\partial x}\right) = f''(x - cy) + F''(x + cy).$$

Again

$$\frac{\partial z}{\partial y} = f'(x - cy).\frac{\partial}{\partial y}(x - cy) + F'(x + cy).\frac{\partial}{\partial y}(x + cy)$$

$$= f'(x - cy) \times (0 - c.1) + F'(x + cy) \times (0 + c.1)$$

$$= -cf'(x - cy) + cF'(x + cy)$$

Similarly,

$$\frac{\partial^2 z}{\partial y^2} = -c \times -cf''(x-cy) + c \times cF''(x+cy) = c^2 f''(x-cy) + c^2 F''(x+cy)$$

$$= c^2[f''(x-cy) + F''(x+cy)] = c^2 \frac{\partial^2 z}{\partial x^2}.$$

Hence $c^2 \dfrac{\partial^2 z}{\partial x^2} = \dfrac{\partial^2 z}{\partial y^2}$.

Exercise 8

[Partial Differentiation]

1. If $f(x,y) = 2x^2 - 3xy + 5y^2 + 7$, find the values of $f(0,0)$ and $f(1,1)$.

2. If $f(x,y) = x^2 + 2xy + 3y^2$, find $\frac{\partial f}{\partial x}$ and $\frac{\partial f}{\partial y}$. Also show that $xf_x + yf_y = 2f(x,y)$.

3. If $f(x,y) = x^3 + y^3 + 2xy^2$, find f_{xx}, f_{yy}, f_{xy} and f_{yx}. Is f_{xy} equal to f_{yx}?

4. Find $\frac{\partial f}{\partial x}, \frac{\partial f}{\partial y}, \frac{\partial^2 f}{\partial x^2}, \frac{\partial^2 f}{\partial y^2}$ at $x = 2, y = 3$ if

(i) $f(x,y) = x^3 + y^3 - 3xy^2$; (ii) $f(x,y) = 2x^2 + 3y^2 - 8xy$.

5. If $u = x^3 + 3xy^2 + y^3$, show that $\frac{\partial^2 u}{\partial y \partial x} = \frac{\partial^2 u}{\partial x \partial y}$ **[Bombay U. B.Com 1980]**

6. Show that $f(x,y) = \frac{x^{\frac{1}{2}} + y^{\frac{1}{2}}}{x^{\frac{1}{3}} + y^{\frac{1}{3}}}$ is a homogeneous function of degree $\frac{1}{6}$.

7. Verify *Euler's theorem* for each of the following functions:

(i) $f(x,y) = x^2 + y^2 + 5xy$; (ii) $f(x,y) = x^3 + y^3 + 3xy^2$;

(iii) $f(x,y) = 2x^3 + 3y^3 - 5x^2y$;

(iv) $u = x^3 + x^2y + y^3$; **[Bombay U. B Com 1980; C.U. B.Com (Hons.) 1982]**

(v) $f(x,y) = x^3 + y^3 + 3x^2y + 3xy^2$; (vi) $f(x,y) = x^3 + 5x^2y + 2y^3$;

(vii) $f(x,y) = \frac{x^3+y^3}{x-y}$; **[C.U. B.Com (Hons.) 1994]** (viii) $z = \frac{x^2+y^2}{xy}$; **[Delhi U B Com (Hons) 1982]**

(ix) $f(x,y) = x^{\frac{2}{3}} + y^{\frac{2}{3}} - 3x^{\frac{1}{3}}y^{\frac{1}{3}}$; (x) $f(x,y) = \frac{x^3+y^3}{x^2+y^2}$.

8. (i) If $u = x^2y + y^2z + z^2x$, show that $\frac{\partial u}{\partial x} + \frac{\partial u}{\partial y} + \frac{\partial u}{\partial z} = (x+y+z)^2$ **[C.U. 1984]**

(ii) If $u = \log(x^2 + y^2)$, prove that $u_{xx} + u_{yy} = 0$

9. If $f = \frac{x+y}{x-y}$, find $x\frac{\partial f}{\partial x} + y\frac{\partial f}{\partial y}$. **[C.U. B.Sc 1982]**

10. If $f(x,y,z) = x^3 + y^3 + z^3 - 3x^2y + 3xy^2$, prove that $x\frac{\partial f}{\partial x} + y\frac{\partial f}{\partial y} + z\frac{\partial f}{\partial z} = 3f(x,y,z)$.

11. If $f(x,y) = x^2y^2/(x+y)$, prove that $x\frac{\partial f}{\partial x} + y\frac{\partial f}{\partial y} = 3f$.

12. If $u = x^2y + y^2x$, find the value of $x\frac{\partial u}{\partial x} + y\frac{\partial u}{\partial y}$ when $x = y = z = 1$.

[C.U. B.Com (Hons.) 1992]

13. If $f = \frac{x}{x^2+y^2}$, then find $\frac{\partial f}{\partial x}$ and $\frac{\partial f}{\partial y}$ and show that $x\frac{\partial f}{\partial x} + y\frac{\partial f}{\partial y} = -f$.

14. If $u = f(y/x)$, prove that $x\frac{\partial u}{\partial x} + y\frac{\partial u}{\partial y} = 0$.

15. If $v = \log \frac{x^2+y^2}{x+y}$, prove by Euler's theorem that $x\frac{\partial v}{\partial x} + y\frac{\partial v}{\partial y} = 1$.

16. If $u = \log\sqrt{x^2+y^2+z^2}$, then prove that $\frac{\partial^2 u}{\partial x^2} + \frac{\partial^2 u}{\partial y^2} + \frac{\partial^2 u}{\partial z^2} = \frac{1}{x^2+y^2+z^2}$.

17. If $u = f(y+ax) + g(y-ax)$ where f and g are any two functions and a is a constant, show that $\frac{\partial^2 u}{\partial x^2} = a^2\frac{\partial^2 u}{\partial y^2}$.

18. If $f = \sqrt{x^2+y^2+z^2}$, then prove that $f_{xx} + f_{yy} + f_{zz} = \frac{2}{f}$.

19. If $u = \log(x^3+y^3+z^3-3xyz)$, show that

(i) $\frac{\partial u}{\partial x} + \frac{\partial u}{\partial y} + \frac{\partial u}{\partial z} = \frac{3}{x+y+z}$;

(ii) $\frac{\partial^2 u}{\partial x^2} + \frac{\partial^2 u}{\partial y^2} + \frac{\partial^2 u}{\partial z^2} = -\frac{3}{(x+y+z)^2}$.

20. If $u = 1/\sqrt{x^2+y^2+z^2}$, then show that $\frac{\partial^2 u}{\partial x^2} + \frac{\partial^2 u}{\partial y^2} + \frac{\partial^2 u}{\partial z^2} = 0$. **[C.U. B.Sc 1976]**

[HINTS. $u_x = -\frac{1}{2}(x^2+y^2+z^2)^{-\frac{3}{2}} \times 2x = -x(x^2+y^2+z^2)^{-\frac{3}{2}}$,

$$u_{xx} = -(x^2+y^2+z^2)^{-\frac{3}{2}} + 3x^2(x^2+y^2+z^2)^{-\frac{5}{2}}.$$

Similarly, find u_{yy} and u_{zz};

$\therefore\ \ u_{xx} + u_{yy} + u_{zz} = -3(x^2+y^2+z^2)^{-\frac{3}{2}} + 3(x^2+y^2+z^2)(x^2+y^2+z^2)^{-\frac{5}{2}}$, etc.]

21. If $f(x,y) = x^2 - 3xy + y^2$, then prove that $\frac{\partial f}{\partial x} - \frac{\partial f}{\partial y} = (x-y)\left(\frac{\partial^2 f}{\partial x^2} - \frac{\partial^2 f}{\partial x \partial y}\right)$.

[ICWAI December 199

22. If $u = \frac{xy}{x+y}$, prove that $x^2u_{xx} + 2xyu_{xy} + y^2u_{yy} = 0$. **[ICWAI June 199**

Answers

1. 7 and 11. **2.** $2(x+y), 2(x+3y)$. **3.** $6x, 2(2x+3y), f_{xy} = f_{yx} = 4y$. **4.** (i) $-15, -9, 12, 6$; (ii) $-16, 2, 4, 6$
9. 0. **12.** 6. **13.** $(y^2-x^2)/(x^2+y^2)^2$ and $-2xy/(x^2+y^2)^2$.

CHAPTER 9

MAXIMA AND MINIMA OF ALGEBRAIC FUNCTIONS

9.1. INCREASING AND DECREASING FUNCTIONS

A function $y = f(x)$ is said to be an increasing function of x in a certain interval, say $a \leq x \leq b$, if y increases as x increases, i.e., if $a \leq x_1 < x_2 \leq b$, then $f(x_2) > f(x_1)$.

Geometrically, this means that as we move from left to right along the curve in $a \leq x \leq b$, the curve is **rising.** In this case, the increment Δx of x and the corresponding increment Δy of y *have the same sign* i.e., *they are either both positive or both negative so that $\Delta y/\Delta x$ is always positive.*

$\therefore$ In the limit when $\Delta x \to 0$, $\frac{\Delta y}{\Delta x} \to \frac{dy}{dx}$ so that the *derivative* $\frac{dy}{dx}$ *at any point P of the rising curve is positive* and the tangent line at P makes an *acute angle* with OX.

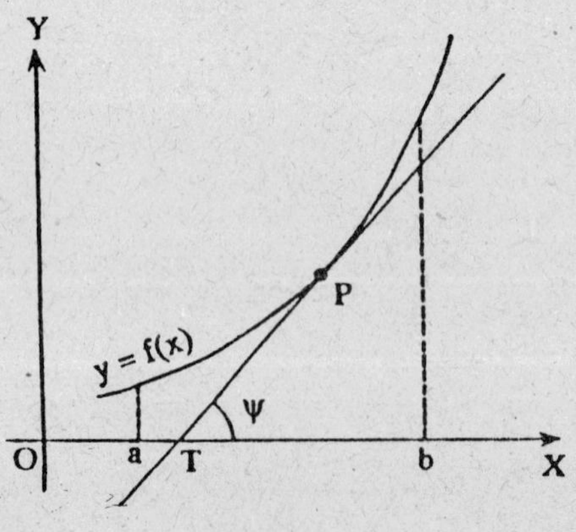

Fig 9.1

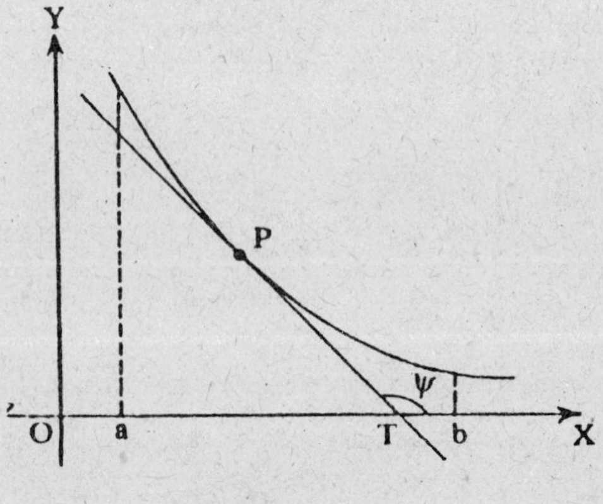

Fig 9.2

A function $y = f(x)$ is said to be a decreasing function of x in a certain interval, say $a \leq x \leq b$, if y decreases as x increases, i.e., if $a \leq x_1 < x_2 \leq b$, then $f(x_2) < f(x_1)$.

Geometrically, this means that as we move from left to right along the curve in $a \leq x \leq b$, the curve is **falling.** In this case, the increment Δx of x and the corresponding increment Δy of y have *opposite signs* so that $\Delta y/\Delta x$ is always *negative* and, in the limit, when $\Delta x \to 0$, $\frac{dy}{dx}$ at $P(x, y) = \lim_{\Delta x \to 0} \frac{\Delta y}{\Delta x}$ which is *negative.*

$\therefore$ The derivative $\frac{dy}{dx}$ *at any point P of the falling curve is negative and the tangent line at P makes an obtuse angle with OX.*

REMARK 1. From the above discussions, it follows that

(i) if $f'(c) > 0$, then $f(x)$ is increasing at c i.e., $f(x)$ has values greater than $f(c)$ on the right of $x = c$, and

(ii) if $f'(c) < 0$, then $f(x)$ is decreasing at c if i.e., $f(x)$ has values greater than $f(c)$ on the left of $x = c$.

REMARK 2. A function $y = f(x)$ may neither be an increasing nor a decreasing function of x at some point of the interval $[a, b]$. In such a case, $y = f(x)$ is called **stationary** at that point. At a stationary point, **the derivative $\mathbf{f'(x) = 0}$** and the tangent line is parallel to the x-axis (see Fig 9.3)

EXAMPLE 1. *If $y = x - \frac{1}{x}$, prove that y is an increasing function of x at all real x.*

SOLUTION. We have $y = x - \frac{1}{x}$.

$\therefore \quad \dfrac{dy}{dx} = 1 + \dfrac{1}{x^2} > 0$, for all real values of x, except $x = 0$.

Hence y is an increasing function of x at all real $x(x \neq 0)$.

EXAMPLE 2. *Show that $y = 1 + \frac{1}{x}$ is always a decreasing function of x.*

SOLUTION. We have $y = 1 + \dfrac{1}{x}$.

$\therefore \quad \dfrac{dy}{dx} = 0 - \dfrac{1}{x^2} = -\dfrac{1}{x^2} < 0$, for all real values of x, except $x = 0$.

Hence y is always a decreasing function of x for all real x (except $x = 0$).

EXAMPLE 3. *If $f(x) = 2x^3 + 3x^2 - 12x + 7$, find the stationary points of $f(x)$.*

SOLUTION. We have $f(x) = 2x^3 + 3x^2 - 12x + 7$.

$\therefore \quad f'(x) = 6x^2 + 6x - 12 = 6(x^2 + x - 2)$.

At the stationary points of $f(x)$, we have $f'(x) = 0$,

$$\begin{aligned} \text{i.e.,}\quad & 6(x^2 + x - 2) = 0, \quad \text{or,} \quad x^2 + x - 2 = 0, \\ \text{or,}\quad & x^2 + 2x - x - 2 = 0, \quad \text{or,} \quad x(x+2) - 1(x+2) = 0, \\ \text{or,}\quad & (x+2)(x-1) = 0; \quad \therefore \quad x = -2, 1. \end{aligned}$$

Hence the required stationary points are $\mathbf{x = -2, 1}$.

9.2. MAXIMA AND MINIMA OF A FUNCTION

DEFINITION. *A function $y = f(x)$ is said to have a* **relative maximum** (*or a local maximum*) *or simply* **maximum** *at $x = c$ if $f(c)$ be the greatest of all the values of $f(x)$ in some small neighbourhood of c, i.e., if we can find a positive number δ such that*

$$f(c) > f(x), \quad \text{for all x in } c - \delta < x < c + \delta \quad (x \neq c).$$

A function $y = f(x)$ is said to have a **relative minimum** (*or a local minimum*) *or simply* **minimum** *at $x = c'$ if $f(c')$ is the least of all the values of $f(x)$ in some small neighbourhood of c', i.e., if we can find a positive number δ such that*

$$f(c') < f(x), \quad \text{for all x in } c' - \delta < x < c' + \delta \quad (x \neq c').$$

The above definitions lead to the following conclusions:

(i) If $f(x)$ is increasing when $x < c$ but sufficiently close to c and $f(x)$ is decreasing when $x > c$ but sufficiently close to c, then $f(x)$ is maximum at $x = c$.

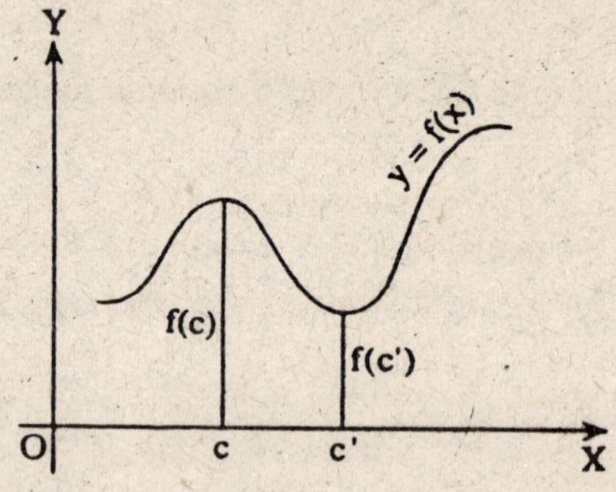

Fig 9.3

Graphically, $f(x)$ is maximum at $x = c$ if the curve $y = f(x)$ is rising on the left neighbourhood of c and falling on the right neighbourhood of c, i.e., if $f'(x) > 0$ for $x < c$ and $f'(x) < 0$ for $x > c$, x being sufficiently close to c in each case.

(ii) If $f(x)$ is decreasing when $x < c'$ but sufficiently close to c' and increasing when $x > c'$ but sufficiently close to c', then $f(x)$ is minimum at $x = c'$.

Graphically, $f(x)$ is minimum at $x = c'$ if the curve $y = f(x)$ is falling on the left neighbourhood of c' and rising on the right neighbourhood c', i.e., if $f'(x) < 0$ for $x < c'$ and $f'(x) > 0$ for $x > c'$, x being sufficiently close to c' in each case.

Extreme Value or Turning Value

By *Extreme Value or Turning Value* of a function we mean *maximum* as well as *minimum value* of the function. The points at which the function has an extreme value are called *Extreme points or Turning points.*

A Necessary Condition for Maxima and Minima

If $f(x)$ has an extreme value at $x = c$ and $f'(c)$ exists, then $f'(c) = 0$.

PROOF. Suppose $f(x)$ is maximum at $x = c$ and suppose $f'(c)$ exists.

If $f'(c) \neq 0$, then either $f'(c) > 0$ or $f'(c) < 0$.

Now if $f'(c) > 0$, then $f(x)$ will be increasing at c and, therefore, $f(x)$ will have values $> f(c)$ on the right of $x = c$ which contradicts our assumption that $f(x)$ is maximum at $x = c$.

Again, if $f'(c) < 0$, then $f(x)$ will be decreasing at c and, therefore, $f(x)$ will have values $> f(c)$ on the left of $x = c$ which again contradicts our assumption.

Hence $f'(c) = 0$.

If $f(x)$ is minimum at $x = c$ and $f'(c)$ exists, we can similarly prove that $f'(c) = 0$.

Hence the theorem follows.

First Derivative Test for Maxima and Minima

(*To find an extreme value by using definition*)

If $f'(c) = 0$, then $f(c)$ will be

(i) **a maximum value of f(x)** *if $f'(x)$ changes its sign from positive on the left of c to negative on the right;*

(ii) **a minimum value of f(x)** *if $f'(x)$ changes its sign from negative on the left of c to positive on the right;*

(iii) *neither a maximum nor a minimum value if $f'(x)$ has the same sign on both sides of c. Such a point is called a* **point of inflexion.**

EXAMPLE 4. *Show that the function $f(x) = x^3 - 6x^2 + 9x - 8$ has a maximum value at $x = 1$ and a minimum value at $x = 3$.* **[C.U. B.Com (Hons.) 1982]**

SOLUTION. We have

$$f(x) = x^3 - 6x^2 + 9x - 8.$$

$$\therefore \quad f'(x) = 3x^2 - 12x + 9 = 3(x^2 - 4x + 3) = 3(x-1)(x-3). \tag{1}$$

At $x = 1, f'(1) = 3 \times 0 \times -2 = 0$.

We see that when $x < 1$ but sufficiently close to $1, (x - 1)$ and $(x - 3)$ are both negative so that their product is positive and from (1), $f'(x) > 0$ i.e., the curve is rising on the left of $x = 1$.

When $x > 1$ but sufficiently close to $1, (x - 1)$ is positive and $(x - 3)$ is negative so that, from (1), $f'(x) < 0$ i.e., the curve is falling on the right of $x = 1$.

Hence $f(x)$ is maximum at $x = 1$.

At $x = 3, f'(3) = 3 \times 2 \times 0 = 0$.

When $x < 3$ but sufficiently close to $3, (x - 1)$ is positive and $(x - 3)$ is negative so that, from (1), $f'(x) < 0$ i.e., the curve is falling on the left of $x = 3$.

Again when $x > 3$ (but very close to 3), $(x - 1)$ and $(x - 3)$ are both positive so that, from (1), $f'(x) > 0$ i.e., the curve is rising on the right of $x = 3$.

Hence $f(x)$ is minimum at $x = 3$.

9.3. SECOND DERIVATIVE TEST FOR MAXIMA AND MINIMA

(A sufficient condition for a function $f(x)$ to have an extremum)

1. A function f(x) has a Maximum Value at x = c if

(i) $\mathbf{f'(c) = 0}$ *and* (ii) $\mathbf{f''(c) < 0}$, *provided* $\mathbf{f''(c)}$ *exists.*

Since $f(x)$ is maximum at $x = c$, (i) $f'(c) = 0$ and (ii) $f'(x)$ changes sign from positive on the left to negative on the right as x passes through c from left to right. This implies that $f'(x)$ is a decreasing function of x at $x = c$ and hence the derivative of $f'(x)$ at $x = c$ i.e., $f''(c) < 0$, provided $f''(c)$ exists.

2. A function f(x) has a Minimum Value at x = c if

(i) $\mathbf{f'(c) = 0}$ and (ii) $\mathbf{f''(c) > 0}$, provided $\mathbf{f''(c)}$ exists.

General Case : nth Derivative Test for Maxima and Minima

Let $\mathbf{f(x)}$ *be a function such that* $f'(c) = f''(c) = \cdots\cdots = f^{n-1}(c) = 0$ *and* $\mathbf{f^n(c) \neq 0}$. *Then* $\mathbf{f(x)}$ *has* (i) *a maximum at* $x = c$ *if* $f^n(c) < 0$ *and* n *is even,* (ii) *a minimum at* $x = c$ *if* $f^n(c) > 0$ *and* n *is even and* (iii) *neither a maximum nor a minimum at* $x = c$ *if* n *is odd.*

This Criterion involving the sign of the derivatives of second and higher orders will be used to find the extreme values of a function $f(x)$.

EXAMPLE 5. *Show that the function* $y = x^3 - 3x^2 + 5$ *has a maximum value at* $x = 0$ *and a minimum value at* $x = 2$.

SOLUTION. We have $y = x^3 - 3x^2 + 5$

$$\therefore \quad \frac{dy}{dx} = 3x^2 - 6x \quad \text{and} \quad \frac{d^2y}{dx^2} = 6x - 6.$$

At $x = 0, \frac{dy}{dx} = 0$ and $\frac{d^2y}{dx^2} = -6 < 0$.

Hence **y** is **maximum** at $\mathbf{x = 0}$.

At $x = 2, \frac{dy}{dx} = 12 - 12 = 0$ and $\frac{d^2y}{dx^2} = 12 - 6 = 6 > 0$.

Hence **y** is **minimum** at $\mathbf{x = 3}$.

EXAMPLE 6. *Find for what values of* x, *the following expression is maximum and minimum respectively:* $2x^3 - 21x^2 + 36x - 20$.

Find also the maximum and the minimum values. **[C.U. B.Com (Hons.) 1981]**

SOLUTION.

Let $f(x) = 2x^3 - 21x^2 + 36x - 20$.

Then $f'(x) = 6x^2 - 42x + 36$, and $f''(x) = 12x - 42$.

For the extreme values of $f(x)$, we must have

$$f'(x) = 0, \quad \text{i.e.,} \quad 6x^2 - 42x + 36 = 0$$

$$\text{or,} \quad x^2 - 7x + 6 = 0, \quad \text{or,} \quad x^2 - 6x - x + 6 = 0,$$

$$\text{or,} \quad x(x - 6) - 1(x - 6) = 0, \quad \text{or,} \quad (x - 6)(x - 1) = 0; \quad \therefore \quad \mathbf{x = 1, 6}.$$

At $x = 1, f''(1) = 12 - 42 = -30 < 0$.

Hence $\mathbf{f(x)}$ is **maximum** at $x = 1$ and the **maximum value** is

$$\mathbf{f(1)} = 2 - 21 + 36 - 20 = \mathbf{-3}.$$

At $x = 6, f''(6) = 12 \times 6 - 42 = 72 - 42 = 30 > 0$.

Hence $\mathbf{f(x)}$ is **minimum** at $\mathbf{x = 6}$ and the **minimum value** is

$$\mathbf{f(6)} = 2 \times 6^3 - 21 \times 6^2 + 36 \times 6 - 20 = 432 - 756 + 216 - 20 = \mathbf{-128}.$$

EXAMPLE 7. *Show that the function $x^3 - 9x^2 + 27x + 60$ is neither a maximum nor a minimum at $x = 3$.*

SOLUTION. Let $f(x) = x^3 - 9x^2 + 27x + 60$.

Then $f'(x) = 3x^2 - 18x + 27, f''(x) = 6x - 18$ and $f'''(x) = 6$.

At $x = 3$,

$$\begin{aligned} f'(3) &= 3.3^2 - 18.3 + 27 = 27 - 54 + 27 = 0 \\ f''(3) &= 6.3 - 18 = 18 - 18 = 0 \\ \text{and} \quad f'''(3) &= 6 \neq 0. \end{aligned}$$

Thus, $f'(3) = 0, f''(3) = 0$ and $f'''(3) \neq 0$.

Hence, $f(x)$ *has neither a maximum nor a minimum at* $x = 3$.

EXAMPLE 8. *A firm produces an output of x tonnes of a certain product at a total cost given by $c = Rs.(x^3 - 4x^2 + 7x)$. Find at what level of output average cost is minimum and what level will it be?* **[ICWAI June 1989]**

SOLUTION. We have $c = x^3 - 4x^2 + 7x$, where c is the total cost of x tonnes in rupees.

If $f(x)$ be the average cost in rupees, then

$$\begin{aligned} f(x) &= \frac{c}{x} = \frac{x^3 - 4x^2 + 7x}{x} = x^2 - 4x + 7 \\ \therefore \quad f'(x) &= 2x - 4 \quad \text{and} \quad f''(x) = 2. \end{aligned}$$

For average cost $f(x)$ to be *minimum,* we must have

$$f'(x) = 0, \quad \text{or,} \quad 2x - 4 = 0, \quad \text{or,} \quad 2x = 4, \quad \text{or,} \quad x = 2.$$

$$\text{At } x = 2, \quad f''(2) = \mathbf{2 > 0}.$$

Hence $f(x)$ *is minimum at $x = 2$ i.e.,* **average cost is minimum at output level of 2 tonnes.** The minimum average cost is $f(2) = 2^2 - 4.2 + 7 =$ **Rs. 3.**

EXAMPLE 9. *The cost function $C(x)$ for producing x units of a commodity is given by $C(x) = \frac{1}{3}x^3 - 5x^2 + 75x + 10$. At what level of output the marginal cost $\left(i.e., \frac{dC}{dx}\right)$ attains its minimum? What is the Marginal Cost of this level of production?*

[C.U. B.Com (Hons.) 1984; CA November 1991]

SOLUTION. The cost function $c(x)$ for producing x units is given by

$$c(x) = \frac{1}{3}x^3 - 5x^2 + 75x + 10 \qquad (1)$$

If $f(x)$ be the marginal cost, then

$$f(x) = \frac{dc}{dx} = \frac{1}{3}.3x^2 - 5.2x + 75.1 = x^2 - 10x + 75$$

$$\therefore \quad f'(x) = 2x - 10.1 + 0 = 2x - 10 \quad \text{and} \quad f''(x) = 2.1 - 0 = 2.$$

For the marginal cost $f(x)$ to be *minimum*, we must have

$$f'(x) = 0 \quad \text{i.e.,} \quad 2x - 10 = 0, \quad \text{or,} \quad 2x = 10, \quad \text{or,} \quad x = 5$$

$$\text{At } x = 5, \quad f''(5) = 2 > 0 \quad \text{i.e.,} \quad \mathbf{f''(5) > 0}.$$

Hence the *marginal cost* $f(x)$ *is* **minimum** *at output level of* **5 units** and the **minimum marginal cost at this level** $= f(5) = 5^2 - 10.5 + 75 = 25 - 50 + 75 = \mathbf{50}$.

EXAMPLE 10. *A firm produces x units of output per week at a total cost of Rs.* $(\frac{1}{3}x^3 - x^2 + 5x + 3)$. *Find the level at which the marginal cost and the average variable cost attain their respective minima.* **[C.U. B. Com (Hons.) 1965]**

SOLUTION. If $c(x)$ be the total cost of x units in rupees, then

$$c(x) = \frac{1}{3}x^3 - x^2 + 5x + 3$$

If $f(x)$ be the marginal cost in rupees, then

$$f(x) = \frac{dc}{dx} = \frac{1}{3}.3x^2 - 2x + 5.1 + 0 = x^2 - 2x + 5.$$

$$\therefore \quad f'(x) = 2x - 2.1 + 0 = 2x - 2$$

$$\text{and} \quad f''(x) = 2.1 - 0 = 2.$$

For the marginal cost $f(x)$ to be minimum, we must have

$$f'(x) = 0 \quad \text{i.e.,} \quad 2x - 2 = 0, \quad \text{or,} \quad 2x = 2, \quad \text{or,} \quad \mathbf{x = 1}$$

$$\text{At } x = 1, \quad f''(1) = 2 > 0 \quad \text{i.e.,} \quad \mathbf{f''(1) > 0}.$$

Hence *the marginal cost* $f(x)$ is **minimum** at $x = 1$ i.e., at output level of **1 unit.**

If $g(x)$ be the *average variable cost* (AVC) in rupees, then

$$g(x) = \frac{\text{variable cost}}{x} = \frac{\frac{1}{3}x^3 - x^2 + 5x}{x} = \frac{1}{3}x^2 - x + 5$$

$$\therefore \quad g'(x) = \frac{1}{3}.2x - 1 + 0 = \frac{2}{3}x - 1 \quad \text{and} \quad g''(x) = \frac{2}{3}.1 - 0 = \frac{2}{3}.$$

For AVC $g(x)$ to be *minimum,* we must have

$$g'(x) = 0 \quad \text{i.e.,} \quad \frac{2}{3}x - 1 = 0, \quad \text{or,} \quad \frac{2}{3}x = 1, \quad \text{or,} \quad x = \frac{3}{2},$$

$$\text{At } \mathbf{x} = \frac{\mathbf{3}}{\mathbf{2}}, \mathbf{g}''\left(\frac{\mathbf{3}}{\mathbf{2}}\right) = \frac{2}{3} > 0 \quad \text{i.e.,} \quad \mathbf{g}''\left(\frac{\mathbf{3}}{\mathbf{2}}\right) > \mathbf{0}.$$

Hence *AVC $g(x)$ attains its* **minima at $\mathbf{x = \frac{3}{2}}$ i.e., at output level of $\mathbf{\frac{3}{2}}$ units.**

EXAMPLE 11. *Let the cost function of a firm be given by the equation: $C(x) = 300x - 10x^2 + \frac{1}{3}x^3$ where $C(x)$ stands for cost function and x for output. Calculate* (i) *output at which marginal cost is minimum;* (ii) *output at which average cost is minimum;* (iii) *output at which average cost is equal to marginal cost.* **[CA November 1987; ICWAI June 1991]**

SOLUTION. We have $C(x) = 300x - 10x^2 + \frac{1}{3}x^3$.

(i) If $f(x)$ be the marginal cost (MC), then

$$f(x) = \frac{dC}{dx} = 300.1 - 10.2x + \frac{1}{3} \cdot 3x^2 = x^2 - 20x + 300$$

$$\therefore \quad f'(x) = 2x - 20 \quad \text{and} \quad f''(x) = 2.$$

For $f(x)$ i.e., MC to be **minimum,** we must have

$$f'(x) = 0, \quad \text{or,} \quad 2x - 20 = 0, \quad \text{or,} \quad x = 10.$$

At $x = 10, f''(x) = 2 > 0$, i.e., $f''(10) > 0$.

Hence $f(x)$, i.e., **MC is minimum at x = 10, i.e., at output level of 10 units.**

(ii) If $g(x)$ be the average cost (AC), then $g(x) = \frac{C(x)}{x} = 300 - 10x + \frac{1}{3}x^2$.

$\therefore \quad g'(x) = -10 + \frac{2}{3}x$ and $g''(x) = \frac{2}{3}$.

For $g(x)$, i.e., **AC to be minimum,** we must have

$$g'(x) = 0, \quad \text{or,} \quad -10 + \frac{2}{3}x = 0, \quad \text{or,} \quad x = 10 \times \frac{3}{2} = 15.$$

At $x = 15, g''(x) = \frac{2}{3} > 0$, i.e., $g''(15) > 0$.

Hence $g(x)$, i.e., **AC is minimum at x = 15,** i.e., **at output level of 15 units.**

(iii) Since average cost = marginal cost;

$$\therefore \quad 300 - 10x + \frac{1}{3}x^2 = x^2 - 20x + 300, \quad \text{or,} \quad \frac{2}{3}x^2 - 10x = 0, \quad \text{or,} \quad x\left(\frac{2}{3}x - 10\right) = 0.$$

But $x \neq 0$; $\quad \therefore \quad \frac{2}{3}x - 10 = 0, \quad$ or, $\quad x = 15$.

Hence the **required output** at which $AC = MC$ is **15 units.**

EXAMPLE 12. *The total cost function of a firm is $C = \frac{1}{3}x^3 - 5x^2 + 28x + 10$, where C is the total cost and x is the output. A tax at the rate of Rs. 2 per unit of output is imposed and the* *producer adds it to his cost. If the demand function is given by $p = 2530 - 5x$, where Rs. p is the price per unit of output, find the profit maximizing output and the price at the level.*

[CA May 1990]

SOLUTION. The total cost function $C(x)$ of x units including tax @ Rs. 2 per unit of output is given by

$$C(x) = \left(\frac{1}{3}x^3 - 5x^2 + 28x + 10\right) + 2x = \frac{1}{3}x^3 - 5x^2 + 30x + 10.$$

If $R(x)$ be the total revenue, then

$$R(x) = px = (2530 - 5x)x = 2530x - 5x^2.$$

If $P(x)$ be the profit on sale of x units, then

$$P(x) = R(x) - C(x) = 2530x - 5x^2 - \left(\frac{1}{3}x^3 - 5x^2 + 30x + 10\right) = 2500x - \frac{1}{3}x^3 - 10.$$

$\therefore \quad \dfrac{dP}{dx} = 2500 - x^2$ and $\dfrac{d^2P}{dx^2} = -2x.$

For $P(x)$, i.e., **profit to be maximum,** we must have

$$\frac{dP}{dx} = 0, \quad \text{or,} \quad 2500 - x^2 = 0, \quad \text{or,} \quad x^2 = 2500; \quad \therefore \quad x = 50$$

At $x = 50, \dfrac{d^2P}{dx^2} = -2 \times 50 = -100 < 0$, i.e., $P(50) < 0$.

Hence $P(x)$, i.e., **profit is maximum at x = 50,** i.e., **at output level of 50 units and the price p at x = 50** is given by

$$p = 2530 - 5 \times 50 = \textbf{Rs. 2,280}.$$

EXAMPLE 13. *A radio manufacturer produces x sets per week at a total cost of Rs. $(x^2 + 78x + 2500)$. He is a monopolist and the demand function for his product is $x = \frac{600-p}{8}$; when the price is Rs. p per set. Show that the maximum net revenue (i.e., profit) is obtained when 29 sets are produced per week. What is the monopoly price?* **[C.U. B. Com (Hons.) 1986]**

SOLUTION. If Rs. C be the total cost of x sets and Rs. R the total revenue, then $C = x^2 + 78x + 2500$ and $R = px$, where p is given by $x = \frac{600-p}{8}$, or, $p = 600 - 8x$

$$\therefore \quad R = (600 - 8x)x = 600x - 8x^2.$$

If P be the net revenue (i.e., profit), then

$$P = R - C = 600x - 8x^2 - (x^2 + 78x + 2500) = 522x - 9x^2 - 2500.$$

$\therefore \quad \dfrac{dP}{dx} = 522 - 18x$ and $\frac{d^2P}{dx^2} = -18.$

For P i.e., **profit to be maximum,** we must have

$$\frac{dP}{dx} = 0, \quad \text{or,} \quad 522 - 18x = 0, \quad \text{or,} \quad x = 522/18 = 29.$$

At $x = 29, \dfrac{d^2P}{dx^2} = -18 < \mathbf{0}$.

Hence P i.e., **profit is maximum at x = 29,** i.e., **when 29 sets are produced per week.**

Monopoly price is the price at which profit is maximum.

$\therefore$ Price p at $x = 29$ (i.e., monopoly price) is given by

$$p = 600 - 8 \times 29 = 600 - 232 = \textbf{Rs. 368}.$$

EXAMPLE 14. *Find for what values of x the function $x^2(x-1)^3$ has a maximum or a minimum. Write down the maximum and the minimum values.* **[C.U. B.Com (Hons.) 1983]**

SOLUTION. We have $f(x) = x^2(x-1)^3$.

$$\begin{aligned} \therefore \quad f'(x) &= 2x(x-1)^3 + 3x^2(x-1)^2. \\ f''(x) &= 2(x-1)^3 + 6x(x-1)^2 + 6x(x-1)^2 + 6x^2(x-1) \\ &= 2(x-1)^3 + 12x(x-1)^2 + 6x^2(x-1) \qquad (1) \end{aligned}$$

For the extreme values of $f(x)$, we must have $f'(x) = 0$

$$\begin{aligned} \text{i.e.,} \quad & 2x(x-1)^3 + 3x^2(x-1)^2 = 0 \\ \text{or,} \quad & x(x-1)^2\{2x - 2 + 3x\} = 0, \\ \text{or,} \quad & x(x-1)^2(5x-2) = 0; \\ \therefore \quad & x = 0, 1, 2/5. \end{aligned}$$

At $x = 0, f''(0) = 2(-1)^3 + 0 + 0 = -2 < 0$.

Hence f(x) is maximum at x = 0 and **the maximum value is f(0) = 0.**

At $x = 1, f''(1) = 2 \times 0 + 12 \times 1 \times 0 + 6 \times 1 \times 0 = 0$

From (1), $f'''(x) = 6(x-1)^2 + 12(x-1)^2 + 24x(x-1) + 12x(x-1) + 6x^2$.

At $x = 1, f'''(1) = 0 + 0 + 0 + 0 + 6.1^2 = 6 \neq 0$.

Thus we see that the odd order (3rd order) derivative is non-zero at $x = 1$.

Hence, **f(x) has neither a maximum nor a minimum at x = 1.**

$$\begin{aligned} \text{At} \quad x = \frac{2}{5}, f''\left(\frac{2}{5}\right) &= 2\left(\frac{-3}{5}\right)^3 + 12 \times \frac{2}{5}\left(\frac{-3}{5}\right)^2 + 6 \times \frac{4}{25}\left(\frac{-3}{5}\right) \\ &= -\frac{54}{125} + \frac{216}{125} - \frac{72}{125} = \frac{90}{125} > 0. \end{aligned}$$

Hence **f(x) is minimum at x = 2/5** *and* **the minimum value is**

$$f\left(\frac{2}{5}\right) = \left(\frac{2}{5}\right)^2\left(\frac{2}{5} - 1\right)^3 = \frac{4}{25} \times -\frac{27}{125} = -\mathbf{\frac{108}{3125}}.$$

9.4. CONCAVITY AND CONVEXITY : POINT OF INFLEXION

Let $P(x, y)$ be any point on the curve $y = f(x)$. Then the slope of the tangent line at P varies with $P(x, y)$.

When the tangent line PT is below the curve, the arc (or curve) is concave upward or convex downward (see fig 9.4); but when the curve is below the tangent line PT, the arc (or curve) is concave downward or convex upward (see fig 9.5)

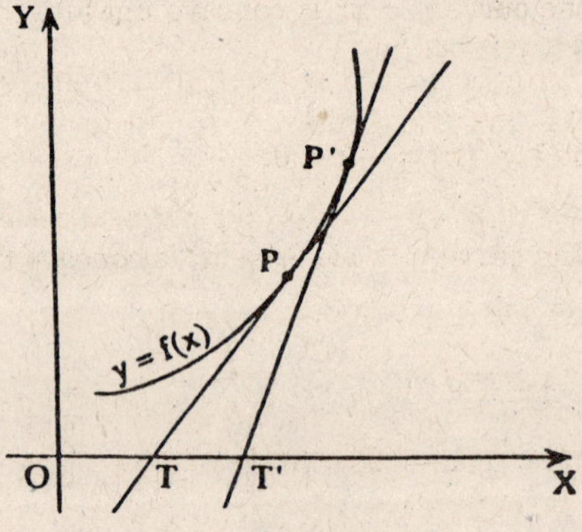

Fig 9.4

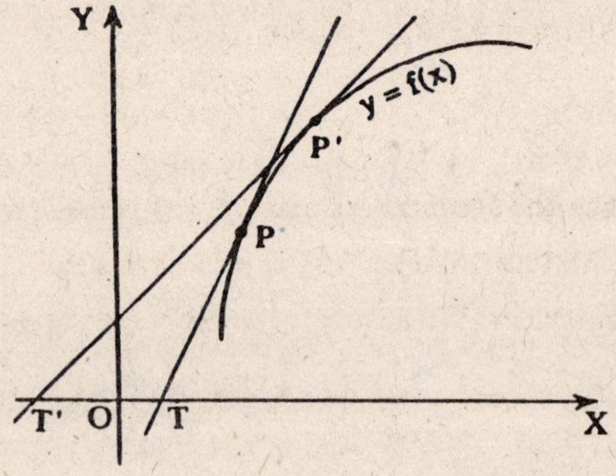

Fig 9.5

In fig 9.4, slope increases as x increases i.e., $f'(x)$ is an increasing function of x. Hence $f''(x)$ is positive. In fig 9.5, the slope of the tangent decreases as x increases i.e., $f'(x)$ is a decreasing function of x. Hence $f''(x)$ is negative.

Hence the curve $y = f(x)$ will be (i) concave upward (or convex downward) if the second derivative $f''(x)$ is positive, and concave downward (or convex upward) if $f''(x)$ is negative.

Point of Inflexion

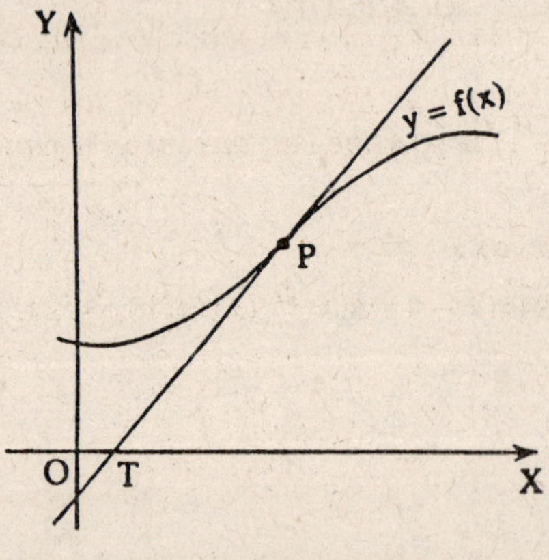

Fig 9.6

A point P of a curve $y = f(x)$ will be called a **point of inflexion** if the tangent line at P crosses the curve i.e., if P separates arcs having opposite directions of bending (see fig 9.6). This means that the curve on one side of P is concave upward and on the other side it is concave downward or vice versa.

On the two sides (left and right sides) of a point of inflexion P, the second derivative $f''(x)$ will have opposite signs, and hence $f''(x) = 0$ at P, provided $f''(x)$ is continuous at P.

The *condition for a point P to be a point of inflexion on the curve $y = f(x)$ is that*

$$\text{at } \mathbf{P}, \mathbf{f''(x) = 0} \quad \textit{and} \quad \mathbf{f'''(x) \neq 0}.$$

REMARKS. If $f'(x)$ is *infinite* at P, then P will be a *point of inflexion if at P*, $\frac{d^2x}{dy^2} = 0$ *and* $\frac{d^3x}{dy^3} \neq 0$.

EXAMPLE 15. *Show that* (i) $y = x^2$ *is concave upward, and* (ii) $y = 4 - 2x - x^2$ *is concave downward.*

SOLUTION.

(i) $y = x^2$ i.e., $f(x) = x^2$.

$$\therefore \quad f'(x) = 2x \quad \text{and} \quad f''(x) = 2 > 0.$$

Since the second derivative $f''(x)$ is positive, the curve $y = x^2$ is concave upward.

(ii) $y = 4 - 2x - x^2$, i.e., $f(x) = 4 - 2x - x^2$.

$$\therefore \quad f'(x) = -2 - 2x \quad \text{and} \quad f''(x) = -2 < 0.$$

Since the second derivative $f''(x)$ is negative, the curve $y = 4 - 2x - x^2$ is concave downward.

EXAMPLE 16. *Find the points of inflexion of the curve* $y = 2x^4 - 4x^3 + 3$.

SOLUTION. We have $f(x) = 2x^4 - 4x^3 + 3 \quad [\because \quad y = f(x)]$

$$\therefore \quad f'(x) = 8x^3 - 12x^2 \quad \text{and} \quad f''(x) = 24x^2 - 24x = 24x(x-1).$$

For the points of inflexion of the curve, we have

$$f''(x) = 0, \quad \text{i.e.,} \quad 24x(x-1) = 0; \quad \therefore \quad x = 0, 1.$$

CASE 1. When $x < 0$, but sufficiently close to $0, f''(x)$ is *positive, i.e., the curve is concave upward for* $x < 0$.

When $x > 0$, but sufficiently close to $0, f''(x)$ is negative i.e., the *curve is concave downward for* $x > 0$,

Hence **x = 0 is a point of inflexion of the curve.**

CASE 2. When $x < 1$, but sufficiently close to $1, f''(x) = 24x(x-1)$ is *negative* i.e., the curve is concave downward for $x < 1$.

When $x > 1$, but sufficiently close to $1, f''(x) = 24x(x-1)$ is *positive* i.e., *the curve is concave upward for* $x > 1$.

Hence **x = 1 is also a point of inflexion of the curve.**

[OTHERWISE. (Instead of Case 1 and Case 2) $f''(x) = 24x(x-1)$ and $f'''(x) = 48x - 24$.

At $x = 0, f''(0) = 0$ and $f'''(0) = -24 \neq 0$.

Hence $x = 0$ *is a point of inflexion of the curve.*

At $x = 1, f''(1) = 0$ and $f'''(1) = 48 - 24 = 24 \neq 0$.

Hence $x = 1$ *is also* a **point of inflexion** *of the curve.*]

EXAMPLE 17.

(i) *Show that* $x = 2$ *is a point of inflexion on the curve given by* $f(x) = x^3 - 6x^2 + 12x - 5$.

[CA May 1990]

(ii) *Find the points of inflexion on the curve* $y = x^4 - 6x^2 + 8x - 1$. **[CA November 1988]**

SOLUTION.

(i) We have $f(x) = x^3 - 6x^2 + 12x - 5$. (1)

$$\therefore \quad f'(x) = 3x^2 - 12x + 12, f''(x) = 6x - 12 \quad \text{and} \quad f'''(x) = 6.$$

At $x = 2, f'(x) = 3.2^2 - 12.2 + 12 = 12 - 24 + 12 = 0$, i.e., $f'(2) = 0$,

$f''(2) = 6.2 - 12 = 0$ and $f'''(2) = 6 \neq 0$

Thus $f''(2) = 0$ and $f'''(2) \neq 0$.

Hence, $\mathbf{x = 2}$ is a **point of inflexion** on the curve (1).

(ii) We have $y = x^4 - 6x^2 + 8x - 1$ (1)

$$\therefore \quad \frac{dy}{dx} = 4x^3 - 12x + 8, \frac{d^2y}{dx^2} = 12x^2 - 12 \quad \text{and} \quad \frac{d^3y}{dx^3} = 24x.$$

For the *points of inflexion* on the curve (1), we have

$$\frac{d^2y}{dx^2} = 0, \quad \text{or,} \quad 12x^2 - 12 = 0, \quad \text{or,} \quad x^2 = 1; \quad \therefore \quad x = \pm 1.$$

At $x = 1, \dfrac{d^3y}{dx^3} = 24 \cdot 1 = 24 \neq 0$ and at $x = -1; \dfrac{d^3y}{dx^3} = 24 \times -1 = -24 \neq 0$.

If $x = 1$, then from (1), $y = 1 - 6.1 + 8.1 - 1 = 2$,

and if $x = -1$, then $y = (-1)^4 - 6.(-1)^2 + 8.(-1) - 1 = 1 - 6 - 8 - 1 = -14$.

Thus at the point $(1, 2)$ and at the point $(-1, -14)$, we have

$$\frac{d^2y}{dx^2} = 0 \quad \text{and} \quad \frac{d^3y}{dx^3} \neq 0.$$

Hence $(1, 2)$ and $(-1, -14)$ are the required **points of inflexion** on the curve (1).

EXAMPLE 18. *Show that the curve* $y = x^2(3 - x)$ *has a point of inflexion at the point* $(1, 2)$.

[CA May 1991]

SOLUTION. We have $y = x^2(3 - x) = 3x^2 - x^3$ (1)

$$\therefore \quad \frac{dy}{dx} = 6x - 3x^2, \frac{d^2y}{dx^2} = 6 - 6x \quad \text{and} \quad \frac{d^3y}{dx^3} = -6.$$

For the *points of inflexion* on the curve (1), we have

$$\frac{d^2y}{dx^2} = 0, \quad \text{or,} \quad 6 - 6x = 0, \quad \text{or,} \quad x = 1.$$

$$\text{At } x = 1, \frac{d^3y}{dx^3} = -6 \neq 0 \quad \text{i.e.,} \quad \left(\frac{d^3y}{dx^3}\right)_{x=1} \neq 0.$$

Also if $x = 1$, from (1), $y = 3.1^2 - 1^3 = 2$.

Thus at the point $(1, 2)$, we have $\frac{d^2y}{dx^2} = 0$ and $\frac{d^3y}{dx^3} \neq 0$.

Hence the curve (1) has a **point of inflexion at the point (1, 2).**

EXAMPLE 19. *If the sides of a rectangle be x and y, express the perimeter P and the area A in terms of x and y. Prove (by the method of Calculus) that among all the rectangles with fixed perimeter P, the square is the one with maximum area.* **[ICWAI June 1980]**

SOLUTION. Perimeter of the rectangle $= 2(x + y)$ units,

and area of the rectangle = Length × breadth $= xy$ sq. units;

$$\therefore \quad P = 2(x + y), \qquad (1)$$

$$\text{and} \quad A = xy, \qquad (2)$$

where P is fixed.

From (1), $x + y = \frac{P}{2}$, or, $y = \frac{P}{2} - x$

$\therefore$ From (2), $A = xy = x\left(\frac{P}{2} - x\right) = \frac{Px}{2} - x^2$; $\therefore$ $\frac{dA}{dx} = \frac{P}{2} - 2x$. [$\because$ P is fixed]

For the maximum value of A,

$$\frac{dA}{dx} = 0, \quad \text{or,} \quad \frac{P}{2} - 2x = 0, \quad \text{or,} \quad 2x = \frac{P}{2}, \quad \text{or,} \quad x = \frac{P}{4}; \quad \therefore \quad y = \frac{P}{2} - \frac{P}{4} = \frac{P}{4}.$$

$$\frac{d^2A}{dx^2} = 0 - 2.1 = -2 < 0.$$

$\therefore$ A is **maximum** when $x = \frac{P}{4}$ and $y = \frac{P}{4}$ i.e., when $x = y$.

Hence among all the rectangles with fixed perimeter, **the square is the one with maximum area.**

EXAMPLE 20. *A watermelon grower wishes to send his products to the city market as early as possible in the season to catch the prices. He can send now 6 tons at a profit of Rs. 60 per ton. By waiting he estimates that he can add 3 tons per week to what he can send now, but then the profit will be reduced by Rs. 5 per ton per week. How long should he wait for the maximum profit? (Use the method of Calculus.)* **[ICWAI June 1979]**

SOLUTION. Let the watermelon grower wait x weeks for maximum profit. Then the quantity of products that can be sent to the city market $= (6 + 3x)$ tons and profit per ton = Rs. $(60 - 5x)$.

If $f(x)$ be the total profit in rupees, then

$$f(x) = (6 + 3x)(60 - 5x) = 360 + 150x - 15x^2.$$

$\therefore$ $f'(x) = 150 - 30x = 30(5 - x)$ and $f''(x) = -30$.

For the total profit $f(x)$ to be maximum, we have $f'(x) = 0$, i.e., $30(5 - x) = 0$, or, $x = 5$.

At $x = 5, f''(5) = -30 < 0$.

Hence the watermelon grower should **wait for 5 weeks for the maximum profit.**

EXAMPLE 21. *Assuming that the petrol burnt (per hour) in driving a motor boat varies as the cube of its velocity, show that the most economical speed when going against a current of c kms./hour is $\frac{3}{2}c$ kms./hour.* **[ICWAI December 1979]**

SOLUTION. Speed will be *most economical* when the petrol burnt to cover a given distance is *minimum.*

Let v be the velocity of the boat in km./hour and d km. be the distance to be covered. Then the velocity of the boat against the current $= (v - c)$ kms./hour and the time required to cover d km. $= d/(v - c)$ hours.

Petrol burnt per hour $= kv^3$ where k is a constant. If $f(x)$ be the *total amount of petrol burnt,* then

$$f(x) = kv^3 \times \frac{d}{v-c} = \frac{kdv^3}{v-c}.$$

$$\therefore \quad f'(x) = kd\left\{\frac{(v-c).3v^2 - v^3.1}{(v-c)^2}\right\} = \frac{kd(2v^3 - 3cv^2)}{(v-c)^2}$$

$$\text{and} \quad f''(x) = kd.\left\{\frac{(6v^2 - 6cv)(v-c)^2 - (2v^3 - 3cv^2).2(v-c)}{(v-c)^4}\right\}$$

$$= kd\left\{\frac{6v(v-c)^2 - 2v^2(2v-3c)}{(v-c)^3}\right\} \quad \text{[cancelling } (v-c) \text{ from numerator and denominator]}$$

For $f(x)$ to be minimum, we must have $f'(x) = 0$,

i.e., $2v^3 - 3cv^2 = 0$, or, $v^2(2v - 3c) = 0$.

But $v \neq 0$; $\therefore$ $2v - 3c = 0$, or, $\mathbf{v = 3c/2}$.

$$\text{At} \quad v = \frac{3c}{2}, f''(x) = kd\left\{\frac{6 \times \frac{3c}{2}\left(\frac{c}{2}\right)^2 - 2 \cdot \frac{9c^2}{4} \cdot (3c - 3c)}{\left(\frac{c}{2}\right)^3}\right\} = kd \times \frac{9c^3}{4} \Big/ \frac{c^3}{8}$$

$$= 18kd > 0. \quad [\because \ k \text{ and } d \text{ are positive.}]$$

Hence the *most economical speed for which the petrol burnt $f(x)$ is* **minimum** $= \frac{3c}{2}$ **km./hour.**

Exercise 9

[Maxima and Minima]

[A]

1. Prove that $y = x^3$ is always an increasing function of x.

2. Show that $y = \frac{1}{x}$ is always a decreasing function of x.

3. If $f(x) = x^3 + 3x^2 - 24x + 10$, find the stationary points of $f(x)$.

4. If $y = 2x^3 - 9x^2 + 12x + 25$, find the values of x for which $\frac{dy}{dx} = 0$.

[C.U. B.Com (Hons.) 1981]

5. Using the sign of the derivative $f''(x)$, show that the function (i) $f(x) = x^2 - 4x + 4$ is minimum at $x = 2$; (ii) $f(x) = 6 + 4x - x^2$ is maximum at $x = 2$.

6. Show that the function $y = x^3 - 3x^2 + 15$ has a maximum value at $x = 0$ and a minimum value at $x = 2$.

7. Show that the function $x^3 - 6x^2 + 12x + 30$ is neither a maximum nor a minimum at $x = 2$.

8. Find for what values of x the expression $2x^3 - 15x^2 + 24x - 15$ is maximum and minimum respectively. Find also the maximum and minimum values.

9. The cost C of manufacturing a certain article is given by the formula : $C = 5 + \frac{48}{x} + 3x^2$, where x is the number of articles manufactured. Find the minimum value of C.

[C.U. B.Com (Hons.) 1988]

10. Show that the local maximum value of $x + \frac{1}{x}$ is less than its local minimum value.

[C.U. B.Com (Hons.) 1986; ICWAI December 1994]

11. A firm produces an output of x tonnes of a certain product at a total cost given by $C =$ Rs. $(x^3 - 4x^2 + 7x)$. Find at what level of output average cost is minimum and what level will it be? **[ICWAI June 1989]**

12. Find the maximum and minimum values of $f(x) = \frac{1}{2}x^4 - x^2 + 1$. **[CA May 1988]**

13. If the total cost (C) and total revenue (R) for a company are given by $C = 20 + 4x$, $R = 30x - x^2$, where x is the output, find the output at which the profit is maximum. What is the maximum profit. **[Bombay U. B.Com 1990]**

[HINTS. If P be the total profit, then $P = R - C = 26x - x^2 - 20$.]

14. A manufacturer can sell x items $(x \geq 0)$ at a price of Rs. $(330 - x)$ each. The cost of producing x items is Rs. $(x^2 + 10x + 12)$. How many items should he sell to make the maximum profit? Determine also the maximum profit. **[CA May 1993]**

[HINTS. Here $C(x) =$ total cost $= x^2 + 10x + 12$, $R(x) =$ total $S.P. = (330 - x)x$

$\therefore$ $P(x) =$ total profit $= R(x) - C(x) =$ etc.]

15. The efficiency E of a small manufacturing concern depends on the number of workers W and is given by $10E = -\frac{W^3}{40} + 30W - 392$. Find the strength of the workers which gives maximum efficiency. **[CA May 1986]**

[HINTS. $10\frac{dE}{dW} = -\frac{3}{40}W^2 + 30$ and $10\frac{d^2E}{dW^2} = -\frac{3}{20}W$, $\frac{dE}{dW} = 0$ gives $3W^2 = 1200$, or, $W = \pm 20$. But W cannot be negative.

$\therefore$ $W = 20$ and at $W = 20$, $\frac{d^2E}{dW^2} = -\frac{3}{10} < 0$, etc.]

16. A steel plant produces x tonnes of steel per week at a total cost of Rs. $(\frac{1}{3}x^3 - 7x^2 + 111x + 50)$. Find the output level at which the marginal cost attains its minimum. (Use the concept of sign of derivative as used in finding extreme values.) **[C.U. B.Com (Hons.) 1983]**

17. A firm produces x tonnes of output at a total cost $C =$ Rs. $(\frac{1}{10}x^3 - 5x^2 + 10x + 5)$.

At what level of output will the marginal and the average variable cost attain their respective minima?

18. The demand function for a particular commodity is $y = 15e^{-\frac{x}{5}}$ for $0 \leq x \leq 8$, where y is the price per unit and x is the number of units demanded. Determine the price and the quantity for which revenue is maximum. **[CA November 1989]**

[HINTS. If R be the total Revenue, then $R = xy = 15xe^{-\frac{x}{3}}$.

$$\therefore \quad \frac{dR}{dx} = 15\left[1.e^{\frac{-x}{3}} + x.e^{\frac{-x}{3}}.\left(-\frac{1}{3}\right)\right] = 15e^{-\frac{x}{3}}\left(1-\frac{x}{3}\right)$$

$$\text{and} \quad \frac{d^2R}{dx^2} = 15 \times -\frac{1}{3}e^{\frac{-x}{3}}\left(1-\frac{x}{3}\right) + 15e^{\frac{-x}{3}} \times -\frac{1}{3} = -5e^{-\frac{x}{3}}\left(2-\frac{x}{3}\right).$$

Now apply second derivative test for maxima.]

19. The total cost function of a firm is $C = \frac{1}{3}x^3 - 4x^2 + 22x + 9$ where C is the total cost and x is the output. A tax at the rate of Rs. 3 per unit of output is imposed and the producer adds it to his cost. If the demand function is given by $p = 1625 - 4x$, where Rs. p is the price per unit of output, find the profit maximizing output and the price at the level.

20. A radio manufacturer finds that he can sell x radios per week at Rs. p each, where $p = 2(100 - \frac{x}{4})$. His cost of production of x radios per week is Rs. $(120x + \frac{x^2}{2})$. Show that his profit is maximum when the production is 40 radios per week. Find also his maximum profit per week.

[C.U. B.Com (Hons.) 1985]

[HINTS. R = total revenue = Rs. px = Rs. $2(100 - \frac{x}{4})x$ = Rs. $(200x - \frac{x^2}{2})$ and Total cost (TC) = Rs. $(120x + \frac{x^2}{2})$

$\therefore \quad P$ = total profit $= R - TC$ = Rs. $(200x - \frac{x^2}{2})-$ Rs. $(120x + \frac{x^2}{2})$ = Rs. $(80x - x^2)$.

$\therefore \quad \frac{dP}{dx} = 80 - 2x$ and $\frac{d^2P}{dx^2} = -2$, etc.]

[B]

1. Show that (i) $y = x^2 + 2x - 3$ is concave upward and (ii) $y = 5 - 3x - x^2$ is concave downward.

2. Show that (i) $x = 1$ is a point of inflexion on the curve $y = x^3 - 3x^2 + 3x - 5$, (ii) $x = 2$ is a point of inflexion of the curve $f(x) = x^4 - 4x^2 + 2x + 3$.

3. Show that $y = x^3 - 8$ has neither a maximum nor a minimum value. Does the curve have a point of inflexion? **[C.U. B.Com (Hons.) 1982]**

4. Show that the function $f(x) = x^2 + \frac{250}{x}$ has a minimum value at $x = 5$.

[C.U. B.Com (Hons.) 1982]

5. Find the maximum and minimum values of the function

(i) $x^3 - 3x + 1$ **[C.U. B.Com (Hons.) 1989]**

(ii) $2x^3 + 3x^2 - 36x + 10$, **[Delhi U. B.Com (Hons.) 1981]**

(iii) $f(x) = x^4 - 8x^3 + 22x^2 - 24x + 1$. **[Delhi U. B.Com (Hons.) 1980]**

6. Investigate the following function for maximum and minimum: $y = \frac{1}{3}x^3 - 2x^2 + 3x + 1$.

[ICWAI December 1983]

7. Prove that the curve given by $3y = x^3 - 3x^2 - 9x + 11$ has a maximum at $x = -1$, minimum at $x = 3$ and a point of inflexion at $x = 1$. **[ICWAI June 1982]**

8. Find the maximum and minimum values of the function $x^5 - 5x^4 + 5x^3 - 1$. Discuss its nature at $x = 0$. **[CA November 1986]**

9. (i) Find the points of inflexion on the curve $y = x^4 - 6x^2 + 8x - 1$. **[CA November 1988]**

(ii) Show that the curve $y = x^2(3 - x)$ has a point of inflexion at the point $(1, 2)$.

[CA May 1991]

10. $p = \frac{150}{q^2+2} - 4$ represents the demand function for a product where p is the price per unit for q units. Determine the marginal revenue function.

[HINTS. If R be the total revenue for q units, then $R = pq = \frac{150q}{q^2+2} - 4q$.

$\therefore$ Marginal Revenue $= \frac{dR}{dq} =$ etc.]

11. (i) A manufacturer can sell x items per month at a price $p = (300 - 2x)$ rupees. Manufacturer's cost of production, Rs. y, of x items is given by $y = 2x + 1000$. Find the number of items to be produced per month to yield the maximum profit. **[C.U. B.Com (Hons.) 1987]**

(ii) The price p per unit at which a company can sell all that it produces is given by the function $P(x) = 300 - 4x$. The cost function is $C(x) = 500 + 28x$ where x is the number of units produced. Find x so that the profit is maximum. **[CA November, 1987]**

[HINTS. $P(x)$ = Profit function = Revenue − Cost $= px - C(x) = 300x - 4x^2 - (500 + 28x) =$ etc.]

12. A firm produces x tonnes of output at a total cost $C = Rs.\left(\frac{1}{10}x^3 - 5x^2 + 10x + 5\right)$. At what level of output will the marginal cost and the average variable cost attain their respective minima? **[C.U. B.Com (Hons.) 1980]**

13. The total cost C of output q is given by $C = 300q - 10q^2 + \frac{1}{3}q^3$. Find the output levels at which the marginal cost and the average cost attain their respective minima. **[ICWAI June 1991]**

[HINTS. See worked out Example 8, 9.]

14. If n be the number of workers employed, the average cost of production is given by $C = 24n + \frac{3}{2(n-4)}$. Show that $n = 4\frac{1}{4}$ will make C minimum. Will you then advice to employ 4 or 5 workers? **[ICWAI June 1990]**

[HINTS. $\frac{dC}{dn} = 24 - \frac{3}{2(n-4)^2}$ and $\frac{d^2C}{dn^2} = \frac{3}{(n-4)^3}$

$\therefore$ C will be minimum when $\frac{dC}{dn} = 0$ and $\frac{d^2C}{dn^2} > 0 \cdot \frac{dC}{dn} = 0$ gives $n = 4\frac{1}{4}$ or $3\frac{3}{4}$.

At $C = 4\frac{1}{4}, \frac{d^2C}{dn^2} = 3/(\frac{1}{4})^3 > 0$, but at $C = 3\frac{3}{4}, \frac{d^2C}{dn^2} < 0$.

Hence C is minimum at $n = 4\frac{1}{4}$ and $C_{\min} = 102 + 6 = 108$ and at $n = 5, C = 121.5$.

Hence either 5 workers or 4 full-time and some part-time workers are to be employed.]

15. A firm has revenue function given by $R = 8D$ (where R is gross revenue and D is quantity sold) and a production cost function given by $C = 15000 + 60\left(\frac{D}{900}\right)^2$. Find the total profit function and the number of units to be sold to get the maximum profit. **[ICWAI December 1987]**

16. Prove that the maximum value of $\left(\frac{1}{x}\right)^x$ is $e^{\frac{1}{e}}$. **[ICWAI December 1992]**

[HINTS. Let $y = \left(\frac{1}{x}\right)^x$; then $\log y = x \log \frac{1}{x} = -x \log x$. $\therefore \frac{1}{y} \cdot \frac{dy}{dx} = -(\log x + 1)$, or, $\frac{dy}{dx} = -y(\log x + 1)$; $\therefore \frac{d^2y}{dx^2} = -\frac{dy}{dx}(\log x + 1) - \frac{y}{x}$, etc.]

[C]

1. The sum of two positive numbers is 16. Find the numbers if their product is maximum.

[CA May 1987]

[HINTS. Let one number be x; then the other number is $16 - x$. Let $y =$ product of the two numbers $= x(16 - x) = 16x - x^2$. Then $\frac{dy}{dx} = 16 - 2x$ and $\frac{d^2y}{dx^2} = -2$, etc.].

2. If the sum of two numbers be 12, find the maximum value of their product.

3. Find the two positive numbers whose product is 64, having minimum sum.

4. Show that among the rectangles of given perimeter the square has the greatest area.

5. The cost of fuel in running a locomotive is proportional to the square of the speed and is Rs. 48 per hour for a speed of 16 km. per hour. Other expenses amount to Rs. 300 per hour. What is the most economical speed? **[ICWAI June 1978]**

6. The cost of fuel consumed per hour in running an engine is proportional to the cube of its speed (in kms./hour). When the speed is 25 kms. per hour, the expenses of fuel are Rs. 125 per hour. Other expenses amount to Rs. 2,000 per hour. Find the most economical seed.

[CA November 1990]

[HINTS. If Rs. c be the cost of fuel per hour where the speed is v kms./hr., then $c \alpha v^3$, or, $c = kv^3$; given $c = 125$ when $v = 25$; $\therefore$ $k = \frac{1}{125}$; $\therefore$ $c = \frac{1}{125}v^3$. If s kms. be the total distance traversed, then time $= \frac{s}{v}$ hours. Total cost per hour $= \frac{1}{125}v^3 + 2000$. If Rs. T be the total cost to cover s kms., then $T = \left(\frac{1}{125}v^3 + 2000\right) \times \frac{s}{v} = s\left(\frac{1}{125}v^2 + \frac{2000}{v}\right)$. Now apply second derivative test *for T to be maximum to find v.*]

7. An open tank with a square base and vertical sides is to be constructed of sheet metal so as to hold a given quantity of water. Show that the cost of material will be least when the depth is half of the width. **[ICWAI June 1982]**

8. Determine the most economical dimensions of an open-air swimming pool of volume 32 cubic metres with a square bottom so that the facing of its walls and bottom require least quantity of materials.

9. A sheet of paper for a poster is to contain an area of 16 sq.m. The margin at the top and at the bottom are to be each 50 cm. and those on each side is $\frac{1}{3}$ metre. What will be the dimensions of the paper if the printed area is to be a maximum? Give your answer correct to two places of decimals. **[ICWAI June 1977]**

10. A square sheet of tin (each side $=a$ cm.) is to be used to make an open-top box by cutting a small square of tin from each corner and bending up the sides. How large a square should be cut from each corner in order that the box shall have as large a volume as possible?

[ICWAI December 1976]

(A rough diagram is essential.)

Answers

[A]

3. $x = -4, 2$. **4.** $x = 1, 2$. **8.** $x = 1, 4$; Max. value $= -4$, Min. value $= -31$. **9.** 41. **11.** 2 tonnes; Rs. 3. **12.** Max. value $= 1$ and Min. value $= \frac{1}{2}$. **13.** 13 units; 149. **14.** 80 units; Rs. 12,788. **15.** 20. **16.** 7 tonnes. **17.** $\frac{50}{3}$ tonnes; 25 tonnes. **18.** $\frac{15}{e}$; 3 units. **19.** 40 units; Rs. 1,465. **20.** Rs. 1,600.

[B]

3. Yes, at $x = 0$. **5.** (i) $2, -1$; (ii) $91, -34$; (iii) $-7, -8$. **6.** Max. at $x = 1$ and Max. value $= 2\frac{1}{3}$; Min. at $x = 3$ and Min. value $= 1$. **8.** Max. at $x = 1$ and Max. value $= 0$; Min. at $x = 3$ and Min. value $= -28$; $x = 0$ is a point of inflexion. **9.** (i) $(1, 2)$ and $(-1, -14)$. **10.** $\frac{150(2-q^2)}{(q^2+2)^2} - 4$. **11.** (i) 75; (ii) $x = 34$. **12.** $\frac{50}{3}$ tonnes; 25 tonnes. **13.** 10 units; 15 units. **14.** 5 workers or 4 full time and some part-time workers are to employed. **15.** $P(D) = 8D - 1,50,000 - 60\left(\frac{D}{900}\right)^2$; 54,000.

[C]

1. 8, 8. **2.** 36. **3.** 8, 8. **5.** 40 km./hr. **6.** 50 km./hr. **8.** Length = breadth = 4m. and hight = 2m. **9.** Length = 4.90 m and breadth = 3.27m. **10.** Square of side $\frac{a}{6}$.

9.5. EXTREME VALUES OF A FUNCTION OF TWO INDEPENDENT VARIABLES

The *necessary conditions* for a function $f(x, y)$ to have an extreme value are $f_x = 0$ and $f_y = 0$ which give the values of x and y. If $x = a$ and $y = b$ be a solution of these two equations, then we first find $f_{xx}(a, b)$, $f_{yy}(a, b)$ and $f_{xy}(a, b)$.

I. *If at (a, b), $f_{xx} \cdot f_{yy} - f_{xy}^2 > 0$ and $f_{xx} < 0$, then $f(x, y)$ is maximum at (a, b) and the maximum value is $f(a, b)$.*

II. *If at (a, b), $f_{xx} \cdot f_{yy} - f_{xy}^2 > 0$ and $f_{xx} > 0$, then $f(x, y)$ is minimum at (a, b) and the minimum values is $f(a, b)$.*

III. *If at (a, b), $f_{xx} \cdot f_{yy} - f_{xy}^2 < 0$, then $f(x, y)$ is neither a maximum nor a minimum at (a, b).*

CHAPTER 10

INTEGRATION : INTEGRATION BY SUBSTITUTION AND BY PARTS

10.1. INTEGRATION

DEFINITION 1. **Integration as the inverse (or reverse) of Differentiation.**

If $f(x)$ be the **derivative** *of a function $F(x)$ for all real x in a certain interval, i.e., if $\frac{d}{dx}\{F(x)\} = f(x)$, or, $d\{F(x)\} = f(x)\,dx$, then $F(x)$ is called an* **integral** *or an* **indefinite integral** *of $f(x)$ w.r.t. x and symbolically, we write*

$$\int \mathbf{f(x)\,dx = F(x)}.$$

Integration is the process of finding an integral of a function.

Here the symbol $\int$ stands for integration of the function $F(x)$ and dx after $f(x)$ indicates that x is the *variable of integration.* The function $f(x)$ which is to be integrated is called the *integrand.*

But if $\frac{d}{dx}\{F(x)\} = f(x)$, we can also write $\frac{d}{dx}\{F(x) + C\} = f(x)$, where C is an arbitrary constant. [$\because \frac{d}{dx}(C) = 0$.]

Hence we can always write $\int \mathbf{f(x)\,dx = F(x) + C}$,

where C is an *arbitrary constant* or, in other words, *the constant of integration.* As the value of C is not definitely known to us, the integral is called an *indefinite integral.*

ILLUSTRATION 1. *Since $\frac{d}{dx}(x^3) = 3x^2$, $\frac{d}{dx}(x^3+2) = 3x^2$, $\frac{d}{dx}(x^3-4) = 3x^2$, $\frac{d}{dx}(x^3+C) = 3x^2$, we can write $\int 3x^2\,dx = x^3 + C$, where C is an arbitrary constant.*

ILLUSTRATION 2. *Since* $\frac{d}{dx}(e^x) = e^x$; $\therefore$ $\int e^x\,dx = e^x + C$.

ILLUSTRATION 3. *Since* $\frac{d}{dx}(\log x) = \frac{1}{x}$; $\therefore$ $\int \frac{1}{x}\,dx = \log x + C$ $(x > 0)$.

ILLUSTRATION 4. *Since* $\frac{d}{dx}\{\frac{2^x}{\log_e 2}\} = 2^x$; $\int 2^x\,dx = \frac{2^x}{\log_e 2} + C$.

Rules of Integration

I. $\int\{f(x) \pm \phi(x)\}\,dx = \int f(x)\,dx \pm \int \phi(x)\,dx$.

II. $\int Cf(x)\,dx = C\int f(x)\,dx$, where C is a constant.

DEFINITION 2. **Definite Integral as the inverse of Differentiation.**

If $f(x)$ be the derivative of a function $F(x)$ for all x in $a \le x \le b$, then $F(x)$ is called a primitive or an **indefinite integral** *of $f(x)$ in $a \le x \le b$. Now, if $F(x)$ changes continuously from $F(a)$ to $F(b)$ as x changes from a to b, then $F(b) - F(a)$ is called the* **definite integral** *of $f(x)$ between the limits a and b and we denote this by*

$$\int_{\mathbf{a}}^{\mathbf{b}} \mathbf{f(x)\,dx}.$$

Thus $\int_{\mathbf{a}}^{\mathbf{b}} \mathbf{f(x)\,dx = F(b) - F(a) = [F(x)]_{x=a}^{x=b}}$.

In short, *if $\frac{d}{dx}\{F(x)\} = f(x)$ for all x in $a \le x \le b$, then $\int_a^b f(x)\,dx = F(b) - F(a)$ is the* **definite integral** *of $f(x)$ from a to b. Here 'a' is called the lower limit and 'b' the upper limit of the definite integral.*

ILLUSTRATION. *Since* $\frac{d}{dx}(\frac{x^2}{2}) = x$ *for all x in* $2 \le x \le 5$.

$\therefore$ $\int_2^5 x\,dx = \frac{5^2}{2} - \frac{2^2}{2} = \frac{25}{2} - \frac{4}{2} = \frac{21}{2}$ $[\because\ F(x) = \frac{x^2}{2}.]$

We shall discuss *Definite Integral* later, in details.

10.2. FUNDAMENTAL INTEGRALS

1. $\int \mathbf{x^n\,dx = \frac{x^{n+1}}{n+1} + C\ (n \ne -1)}$ $\left[\because\ \frac{d}{dx}(\frac{x^{n+1}}{n+1}) = x^n.\right]$

ILLUSTRATION 1. $\int x\,dx = \frac{x^{1+1}}{1+1} + C = \frac{x^2}{2} + C$.

ILLUSTRATION 2. $\int \sqrt{x}\,dx = \int x^{\frac{1}{2}}\,dx = \frac{x^{\frac{1}{2}+1}}{\frac{1}{2}+1} + C = \frac{2x^{\frac{3}{2}}}{3} + C$.

ILLUSTRATION 3. $\int \frac{1}{x^2} = \int x^{-2}\,dx = \frac{x^{-2+1}}{-2+1} + C = -\frac{1}{x} + C$.

ILLUSTRATION 5. $\int dx = \int x^\circ\,dx = \frac{x^{0+1}}{0+1} + C = x + C$.

If $n = -1$, the integral **1** becomes $\int x^{-1}\,dx = \int \frac{1}{x}\,dx$ which is considered below.

2. (i) $\int \mathbf{\frac{1}{x}\,dx = \log_e|x| + C}$; (ii) $\int \mathbf{\frac{1}{x \pm a}\,dx = \log|x \pm a| + C}$.

$[\because$ If $x > 0, \log_e x$ is real and $\frac{d}{dx}(\log x) = \frac{1}{x}$ and if $x < 0, \log(-x)$ is real and

$$\frac{d}{dx}\{\log(-x)\} = \frac{1}{-x} \times -1 = \frac{1}{x}.]$$

3. (i) $\int \mathbf{e^x\,dx = e^x + C}$ $\quad [\because \ \frac{d}{dx}(e^x + C) = e^x.]$

(ii) $\int \mathbf{e^{mx}\,dx = \frac{e^{mx}}{m} + C}$ $\quad \left[\because \ \frac{d}{dx}\left(\frac{e^{mx}}{m}\right) = \frac{1}{m} \cdot me^{mx} = e^{mx}.\right]$

ILLUSTRATION 1. (i) $\int e^{2x}\,dx = \frac{e^{2x}}{2} + C$; (ii) $\int e^{\frac{1}{2}x}\,dx = \frac{e^{\frac{1}{2}x}}{\frac{1}{2}} + C = 2e^{\frac{1}{2}x} + C.$

4. (i) $\int \mathbf{a^x\,dx = \frac{a^x}{\log_e a} + C\ (a > 0)}$ $\quad \left[\because \ \frac{d}{dx}\left(\frac{a^x}{\log_e a}\right) = \frac{1}{\log_e a} \cdot a^x \log_e a = a^x.\right]$

(ii) $\int \mathbf{a^{mx}\,dx = \frac{a^{mx}}{m\log_e a} + C}$ $\quad \left[\because \ \frac{d}{dx}\left(\frac{a^{mx}}{m\log_e a}\right) = \frac{1}{m\log_e a} \cdot a^{mx} \cdot m\log_e a = a^{mx}.\right]$

ILLUSTRATION 1. (i) $\int 3^x\,dx = \frac{3^x}{\log_e 3} + C$; (ii) $\int 3^{2x}\,dx = \frac{3^{2x}}{2\cdot\log_e 3} + C.$

10.3. ILLUSTRATIVE EXAMPLES

EXAMPLE 1. *Evaluate each of the following integrals:*

(i) $\int (4x^3 - \frac{3}{x} + 5e^{5x} - 2)\,dx$; (ii) $\int (\sqrt{x} - \frac{2}{\sqrt[3]{x}} + 3^x)\,dx$.

SOLUTION.

(i)
$$\int \left(4x^3 - \frac{3}{x} + 5e^{5x} - 2\right) dx = 4\int x^3\,dx - 3\int \frac{1}{x}\,dx + 5\int e^{5x}\,dx - 2\int dx$$
$$= 4 \cdot \frac{x^{3+1}}{3+1} - 3 \cdot \log|x| + 5 \cdot \frac{e^{5x}}{5} - 2 \cdot x + C$$
$$= \mathbf{x^4 - 3\log|x| + e^{5x} - 2x + C},$$

where C is an arbitrary constant.

(ii)
$$\int \left(\sqrt{x} - \frac{2}{\sqrt[3]{x}} + 3^x\right) dx = \int x^{\frac{1}{2}}\,dx - 2\int x^{-\frac{1}{3}}\,dx + \int 3^x\,dx$$
$$= \frac{x^{\frac{1}{2}+1}}{\frac{1}{2}+1} - 2 \times \frac{x^{-\frac{1}{3}+1}}{-\frac{1}{3}+1} + \frac{3^x}{\log_e 3} + C$$
$$= \frac{2}{3}x^{\frac{3}{2}} - 2 \times \frac{3}{2} \cdot x^{\frac{2}{3}} + \frac{3^x}{\log_e 3} + C$$
$$= \frac{2}{3}x^{\frac{3}{2}} - 3x^{\frac{2}{3}} + \frac{3^x}{\log_e 3} + C.$$

EXAMPLE 2. *Evaluate:*

(i) $\int (x^a + a^x + a^a)\,dx$; (ii) $\int (3^x + x^3 + e^{\frac{1}{2}x})\,dx$.

SOLUTION.

(i)
$$\int (x^a + a^x + a^a)\,dx = \int x^a\,dx + \int a^x\,dx + \int a^a\,dx$$
$$= \mathbf{\frac{x^{a+1}}{a+1} + \frac{a^x}{\log_e a} + a^a \cdot x + C} \qquad [\because \ \text{a is constant.}]$$

(ii)
$$\int \left(3^x + x^3 + e^{\frac{1}{2}x}\right) dx = \int 3^x\,dx + \int x^3\,dx + \int e^{\frac{1}{2}x}\,dx$$
$$= \mathbf{\frac{3^x}{\log_e 3} + \frac{x^4}{4} + \frac{e^{\frac{1}{2}x}}{\frac{1}{2}} + C = \frac{3^x}{\log_e 3} + \frac{1}{4}x^4 + 2e^{\frac{1}{2}x} + C},$$

where C is an arbitrary constant.

EXAMPLE 3. *Evaluate:* $\int (2\sqrt[3]{x} - 5x^{3.4} + 2x^{-0.3} + x^7 + 3)\, dx$ **[ICWAI June 1974]**

SOLUTION.

$$\int (2\sqrt[3]{x} - 5x^{3.4} + 2x^{-0.3} + x^7 + 3)\, dx = 2\int x^{\frac{1}{3}}\, dx - 5\int x^{3.4}\, dx + 2\int x^{-0.3}\, dx + \int x^7\, dx + 3\int dx$$

$$= 2\frac{x^{\frac{1}{3}+1}}{\frac{1}{3}+1} - 5\cdot\frac{x^{3.4+1}}{3.4+1} + 2.\frac{x^{-0.3+1}}{-0.3+1} + \frac{x^{7+1}}{7+1} + 3x + C.$$

$$= \mathbf{\frac{3}{2}x^{\frac{4}{3}} - \frac{5}{4.4}x^{4.4} + \frac{20}{7}x^{0.7} + \frac{1}{8}x^8 + 3x + C},$$

where C is an arbitrary constant.

EXAMPLE 4. *Evaluate each of the following integrals:*

(i) $\int \frac{(1-x)^3}{x}\, dx$; **[C.U. B. Com. (Hons.) 1982]** (ii) $\int \left\{(e^{2x})^2 + (a^{2x})^2\right\} dx$; **[ICWAI June 1975]**
(iii) $\int \frac{(x+1)(x-4)}{\sqrt{x}}\, dx$.**[Bombay U. B.Com 1980]**

SOLUTION.

(i)
$$\int \frac{(1-x)^3}{x}\, dx = \int \frac{(1 - 3x + 3x^2 - x^3)}{x}\, dx = \int \left(\frac{1}{x} - 3 + 3x - x^2\right) dx$$

$$= \int \frac{1}{x}\, dx - 3\int dx + 3\int x\, dx - \int x^2\, dx$$

$$= \mathbf{\log|x| - 3x + \frac{3}{2}x^2 - \frac{x^3}{3} + C}.$$

(ii)
$$\int \{(e^{2x})^2 + (a^{2x})^2\}\, dx = \int (e^{4x} + a^{4x})\, dx = \int e^{4x}\, dx + \int a^{4x}\, dx$$

$$= \mathbf{\frac{e^{4x}}{4} + \frac{a^{4x}}{4\log_e a} + C}.$$

(iii)
$$\int \frac{(x+1)(x-4)}{\sqrt{x}}\, dx = \int \frac{x^2 - 3x - 4}{\sqrt{x}}\, dx = \int \frac{x^2}{\sqrt{x}}\, dx - 3\int \frac{x}{\sqrt{x}}\, dx - 4\int \frac{1}{\sqrt{x}}\, dx$$

$$= \int x^{\frac{3}{2}}\, dx - 3\int x^{\frac{1}{2}}\, dx - 4\int x^{-\frac{1}{2}}\, dx$$

$$= \frac{x^{\frac{5}{2}}}{\frac{5}{2}} - 3\cdot\frac{x^{\frac{3}{2}}}{\frac{3}{2}} - 4\cdot\frac{x^{\frac{1}{2}}}{\frac{1}{2}} + C$$

$$= \frac{2}{5}x^{\frac{5}{2}} - 2x^{\frac{3}{2}} - 8x^{\frac{1}{2}} + C,$$ *where C is an arbitrary constant.*

EXAMPLE 5. *Evaluate each of the following integrals:*

(i) $\int \sqrt{x}(x^2 + 3x + 4)\, dx$; **[Bombay U. B.Com 1980]**

(ii) $\int \left(x - \frac{1}{x}\right)^3 dx, x > 0.$ **[Punjab U. 1977]**

SOLUTION.

(i) $$\int \sqrt{x}(x^2+3x+4)\,dx = \int (x^{\frac{1}{2}}\cdot x^2 + 3\cdot x^{\frac{1}{2}}\cdot x + 4\cdot x^{\frac{1}{2}})\,dx$$
$$= \int x^{\frac{5}{2}}\,dx + 3\int x^{\frac{3}{2}}\,dx + 3\int x^{\frac{3}{2}}\,dx + 4\int x^{\frac{1}{2}}\,dx$$
$$= \frac{x^{\frac{5}{2}+1}}{\frac{5}{2}+1} + 3\cdot\frac{x^{\frac{3}{2}+1}}{\frac{3}{2}+1} + 4\cdot\frac{x^{\frac{1}{2}+1}}{\frac{1}{2}+1} + C = \mathbf{\frac{2}{7}x^{\frac{7}{2}} + \frac{6}{5}x^{\frac{5}{2}} + \frac{8}{3}x^{\frac{3}{2}} + C}$$

(ii) $$\int \left(x-\frac{1}{x}\right)^3 dx = \int \left(x^3 - 3x^2\cdot\frac{1}{x} + 3\cdot x\cdot\frac{1}{x^2} - \frac{1}{x^3}\right) dx$$
$$= \int x^3\,dx - 3\int x\,dx + 3\int \frac{1}{x}\,dx - \int x^{-3}\,dx$$
$$= \mathbf{\frac{x^4}{4} - 3\cdot\frac{x^2}{2} + 3\log|x| - \left(\frac{x^2}{-2}\right) + C}$$
$$= \mathbf{\frac{1}{4}x^4 - \frac{3}{2}x^2 + 3\log|x| + \frac{1}{2x^2} + C.}$$

EXAMPLE 6. *Evaluate:*

(i) $\int \frac{x^3}{x-1}\,dx$; **[C.U. B.Com (Hons.) 1983]** (ii) $\int \frac{x^2}{x+2}\,dx$.**[Bombay U. B.Com 1980]**

SOLUTION.

(i) $$\int \frac{x^3}{x-1}\,dx = \int \left(x^2+x+1+\frac{1}{x-1}\right) dx$$
$$= \int x^2\,dx + \int x\,dx + \int 1\,dx + \int \frac{1}{x-1}\,dx$$
$$= \mathbf{\frac{x^3}{3} + \frac{x^2}{2} + x + \log|x-1| + C,}$$
where C is an arbitrary constant

$$\begin{array}{r|l} x-1) & x^3 \quad (x^2+x+1 \\ & \underline{x^3-x^2} \\ & \quad x^2 \\ & \quad \underline{x^2-x} \\ & \qquad x \\ & \qquad \underline{x-1} \\ & \qquad\quad 1 \end{array}$$

(ii) $$\int \frac{x^2}{x+2}\,dx = \int \left(x-2+\frac{4}{x+2}\right) dx$$
$$= \int x\,dx - 2\int dx + 4\int \frac{1}{x+2}\,dx$$
$$= \mathbf{\frac{x^2}{2} - 2x + 4\cdot\log|x+2| + C.}$$

$$\begin{array}{r|l} x+2) & x^2 \quad (x-2 \\ & \underline{x^2+2x} \\ & \quad -2x \\ & \quad \underline{-2x-4} \\ & \qquad 4 \end{array}$$

EXAMPLE 7. *Evaluate:* $\int \frac{3x+4}{6x+7}\,dx$.

SOLUTION.

$$\int \frac{3x+4}{6x+7}\,dx = \int \left(\frac{1}{2} + \frac{\frac{1}{2}}{6x+7}\right) dx$$

$$= \frac{1}{2}\int dx + \frac{1}{2}\int \frac{1}{6x+7}\,dx$$

$$= \frac{1}{2}x + \frac{1}{2}\cdot\frac{1}{6}\int \frac{1}{x+\frac{7}{6}}\,dx + C$$

$$= \mathbf{\frac{1}{2}x + \frac{1}{12}\log\left|x+\frac{7}{6}\right| + C}, \quad \left[\because \int \frac{1}{x+a}\,dx = \log|x+a|\right]$$

$$6x+7)\ 3x+4\ (\tfrac{1}{2}$$
$$\underline{3x+\tfrac{7}{2}}$$
$$\tfrac{1}{2}$$

Exercise 10 (I)

(Integration)

1. Define *Integration* as the inverse process of *Differentiation*. Give three illustrations.

2. What do you mean by the *constant of integration*? Is its value fixed?

3. State for what value of n, the formula $\int x^n\,dx = \frac{x^{n+1}}{n+1} + C$, where C is constant, is not true. Find the value of the integral for that particular value of n.

4. Using the definition of Indefinite Integral, show that:

(i) $\int e^{5x}\,dx = \frac{1}{5}e^{5x} + C$; (ii) $\int x^3\,dx = \frac{1}{4}x^4 + C$;
(iii) $\int 3^x\,dx = \frac{3^x}{\log_e 3} + C$; (iv) $\int 5^{3x}\,dx = \frac{5^{3x}}{3\log_e 5} + C$
(v) $\int(\sqrt{x} + 3x)\,dx = \frac{2}{3}x^{\frac{3}{2}} + \frac{3}{2}x^2 + C$.

5. Integrate the following functions with respect to 'x':

(i) $2x+3$; (ii) $\sqrt{x}$; (iii) $\frac{1}{\sqrt[3]{x}}$; (iv) $\frac{2}{x^2}$;
(v) $\frac{3}{x}$; (vi) $\frac{2}{x^{\frac{2}{3}}}$; (vii) $3^x \log_e 3$; (viii) $5e^{5x}$.

6. Evaluate each of the following integrals:

(i) $\int(x^3 - \frac{2}{x} + e^x - 1)\,dx$; (ii) $\int(2^x - \frac{1}{x^2} + 3e^{3x})\,dx$;
(iii) $\int\left(1 + \frac{2}{\sqrt{x}} + \frac{3}{x}\right) dx$; (iv) $\int\left(3^x + \frac{4}{x} - \frac{1}{\sqrt[3]{x}}\right) dx$.

7. Evaluate the following integrals:

(i) $\int(\sqrt[3]{x} - \frac{5}{x} + 3^{2x})\,dx$; (ii) $\int \frac{(1+x)^2}{x^2}\,dx$; (iii) $\int \frac{(x-1)^3}{x^2}\,dx$;
(iv) $\int \frac{(e^x+1)^3}{e^{2x}}\,dx$; (v) $\int \frac{(x+1)(x-4)}{\sqrt{x}}\,dx$. **[Bombay U. B.Com 1980]**

8. Evaluate:

(i) $\int(x+1)(2x+3)\,dx$; (ii) $\int(x^a + a^x + a^a)\,dx$; (iii) $\int \sqrt{x}(x^3 + \frac{4}{x})\,dx$;
(iv) $\int \frac{1+x^3}{1+x}\,dx$; (v) $\int \frac{x^4+1}{x+1}\,dx$; (vi) $\int \sqrt[3]{x}.(x^2 - 2x + 3)\,dx$.

[HINTS.

(v) $\int \frac{x^4+1}{x+1}\,dx = \int(x^3 - x^2 + x - 1 + \frac{2}{x+1})\,dx = \frac{1}{4}x^4 - \frac{1}{3}x^3 + \frac{1}{2}x^2 - x + 2\log|x+1| + C$]

9. Evaluate:

(i) $\int \frac{(x^2+2)^3}{x^6}\,dx$; [C.U. B.Com (Hons.) 1989] (ii) $\int \frac{x\,dx}{x+1}$ [C.U. B.Com (Hons.) 1987, '89];

(iii) $\int \frac{x^2}{x+2}\,dx$. [Bombay U. B.Com (Hons.) 1981]

10. Evaluate:

(i) $\int \frac{x^3}{x-1}\,dx$; [C.U. B.Com (Hons.) 1983] (ii) $\int \frac{x^2+5x+2}{x+2}\,dx$; [CA November 1987]

(iii) $\int \frac{2x+5}{4x+9}\,dx$; (iv) $\int \frac{3x+4}{6x+7}\,dx$.

Answers

(The constant of integration C, which is not written, is to be added to each answer.)

5. (i) x^2+3x; (ii) $\frac{2}{3}x^{\frac{3}{2}}$; (iii) $\frac{3}{2}x^{\frac{2}{3}}$; (iv) $-\frac{2}{x}$; (v) $3\log|x|$; (vi) $-\frac{4}{\sqrt{x}}$; (vii) 3^x; (viii) e^{5x}. **6.** (i) $\frac{1}{4}x^4 - 2\log|x| + e^x - x$; (ii) $\frac{2^x}{\log_e 2} + \frac{1}{x} + e^{3x}$; (iii) $x + 4\sqrt{x} + 3\log|x|$; (iv) $\frac{3^x}{\log_e 3} + 4\log|x| - \frac{3}{2}x^{\frac{2}{3}}$. **7.** (i) $\frac{1}{2}x^{\frac{4}{3}} - 5\log|x| + \frac{3^{2x}}{2\log_e 3}$; (ii) $x - \frac{1}{x} + 2\log|x|$; (iii) $\frac{1}{2}x^2 - 3x + 3\log|x| + \frac{1}{x}$; (iv) $e^x + 3x - 3e^{-x} - \frac{1}{2}e^{-2x}$; (v) $\frac{2}{5}x^{\frac{5}{2}} - 2x^{\frac{3}{2}} - 8x^{\frac{1}{2}}$. **8.** (i) $\frac{2}{3}x^3 + \frac{5}{2}x^2 + 3x$; (ii) $\frac{x^{a+1}}{a+1} + \frac{a^x}{\log_e a} + a^a \cdot x$; (iii) $\frac{2}{9}x^{\frac{9}{2}} + 8x^{\frac{1}{2}}$; (iv) $x - \frac{1}{2}x^2 + \frac{1}{3}x^3$; (v) $\frac{1}{4}x^4 - \frac{1}{3}x^3 + \frac{1}{2}x^2 - x + 2\log(x+1)$; (vi) $\frac{3}{10}x^{\frac{10}{3}} - \frac{6}{7}x^{\frac{7}{3}} + \frac{9}{4}x^{\frac{4}{3}}$. **9.** (i) $-\frac{1}{x^5}\left(\frac{1}{2}x^3 + 2x^2 + 3x + \frac{8}{5}\right)$; (ii) $x - \log|x+1|$; (iii) $\frac{1}{2}x^2 - 2x + 4\log|x+2|$. **10.** (i) $\frac{1}{3}x^3 + \frac{1}{2}x^2 + x + \log|x-1|$; (ii) $\frac{1}{2}x^2 + 3x - 4\log|x+2|$; (iii) $\frac{1}{2}x + \frac{1}{8}\log\left|x + \frac{9}{4}\right|$; (iv) $\frac{1}{2}x + \frac{1}{12}\log\left|x + \frac{7}{6}\right|$.

10.4. INTEGRATION BY SUBSTITUTION : CHANGE OF VARIABLE

Often the given function, i.e., the integrand is neither in the simple (or standard) form nor it can be integrated by mere inspection. In such a case, we use any one or more of the following methods to evaluate the given integral.

1. **Integration by Substitution;**
2. **Integration by Parts;**
3. **Integration by resolving into Partial Fractions.**

In this article we shall show how various types of integrals can be reduced to the *standard forms* by the *method of substitution.*

EXAMPLE 1. *Prove that*

(i) $\int f(ax+b)\,dx = \frac{1}{a}\int f(z)\,dz$;

(ii) $\int \{f(x)\}^n \cdot f'(x)\,dx = \frac{\{f(x)\}^{n+1}}{n+1}$;

(iii) $\int \frac{f'(x)}{f(x)}\,dx = \log|f(x)|$.

SOLUTION.

(i) $$\int f(ax+b)\,dx = \int f(z)\cdot\frac{1}{a}\,dz = \frac{1}{a}\int f(z)\,dz.$$

Put $ax+b=z$; then $\frac{dz}{dx}=a$; or, $a\,dx = dz$, or, $dx = \frac{1}{a}\,dz$.

NOTE. For integrals of the types: $\int(ax+b)^n\,dx$, $\int \sqrt[n]{ax+b}\,dx$ and $\int \frac{dx}{(a+bx)^n}$, suitable substitution is $ax+b=z$.

(ii) $$\int \{f(x)\}^n \cdot f'(x)\,dx = \int z^n\,dz = \frac{z^{n+1}}{n+1} + C.$$ | Put $f(x)=z$; then $\frac{dz}{dx}=f'(x)$ or, $f'(x)\,dx = dz$.

$$= \frac{\mathbf{\{f(x)\}^{n+1}}}{\mathbf{n+1}} + \mathbf{C}, \text{ where } C \text{ is an arbitrary constant.}$$

(iii) $$\int \frac{f'(x)}{f(x)}\,dx = \int \frac{dz}{z} = \int \frac{1}{z}\,dz$$ | Put $f(x)=z$; then $\frac{dz}{dx}=f'(x)$ or, $f'(x)\,dx = dz$.

$$= \log|z| + C = \mathbf{\log|f(x)| + C}.$$

NOTE. The results of the above three integrals will be used as formulae to solve many problems.

EXAMPLE 2. *Evaluate*

(i) $\int(2x+3)^5\,dx$; (ii) $\int(x^2-3x+5)^4\cdot(2x-3)\,dx$

(iii) $\int \frac{(4x-5)\,dx}{2x^2-5x+6}$; (iv) $\int\sqrt{5+3x}\,dx$ **[Bombay U. B.Com 1981]**

SOLUTION.

(i) $$\int (2x+3)^5\,dx$$ | Put $2x+3=z$; then $(2.1+0)\,dx = dz$, or, $dx = \frac{1}{2}\,dz$

$$= \int z^5 \cdot \frac{1}{2}\,dz = \frac{1}{2}\int z^5\,dz$$

$$= \frac{1}{2}\cdot\frac{z^{5+1}}{5+1} + C = \frac{1}{12}z^6 + C = \mathbf{\frac{1}{12}(2x+3)^6 + C}, \quad \textit{where } C \textit{ is an arbitrary constant.}$$

(ii) $$\int (x^2-3x+5)^4\cdot(2x-3)\,dx$$ | Put $x^2-3x+5=z$; then $(2x-3)\,dx = dz$

$$= \int z^4\cdot dz = \frac{z^5}{5} + C = \mathbf{\frac{1}{5}(x^2-3x+5)^5 + C}$$

(iii) $$\int \frac{(4x-5)\,dx}{2x^2-5x+6}$$ | Put $2x^2-5x+6=z$; then $(4x-5)\,dx = dz$

$$= \int \frac{dz}{z} = \log|z| + C = \mathbf{\log|2x^2-5x+6| + C}.$$

(iv) $$\int \sqrt{5+3x}\,dx$$ | Put $5+3x=z$; then $3\,dx = dz$, or, $dx = \frac{1}{3}\,dz$

$$= \int \sqrt{z}\cdot\frac{1}{3}\,dz = \frac{1}{3}\int z^{\frac{1}{2}}\,dz = \frac{1}{3}\cdot\frac{z^{\frac{1}{2}+1}}{\frac{1}{2}+1} + C = \frac{2}{9}z^{\frac{3}{2}} + C$$

$$= \mathbf{\frac{2}{9}(5x+3x)^{\frac{3}{2}} + C}.$$

EXAMPLE 3. *Evaluate the following integrals:*

(i) $\int \frac{dx}{(2x-3)^2}$; (ii) $\int(2x+3)\sqrt{x^2+3x-1}\,dx$; (iii) $\int \frac{(x-2)\,dx}{\sqrt[3]{x^2-4x+5}}$.

[C.U. B.Com 1982] **[C.U. B. Com (Hons.) 1983]**

SOLUTION.

(i) $$\int \frac{dx}{(2x-3)^2} = \frac{1}{2}\int \frac{dz}{z^2} = \frac{1}{2}\int z^{-2}\,dz$$ | Put $2x-3=z$; then $\frac{dz}{dx}=2$, or, $2\,dx = dz$, or, $dx = \frac{1}{2}\,dz$.

$$= \frac{1}{2}\times\frac{z^{-2+1}}{-2+1} + C = -\frac{1}{2z} + C = -\mathbf{\frac{1}{2(2x-3)} + C}$$

(ii) $$\int (2x+3)\sqrt{x^2+3x-1}\cdot dx = \int \sqrt{x^2+3x-1}\cdot(2x+3)\,dz$$ | Put $x^2+3x-1=z$ $\therefore\ (2x+3)\,dx = dz$

$$= \int \sqrt{z}\cdot dz = \int z^{\frac{1}{2}}\,dz = \frac{z^{\frac{1}{2}+1}}{\frac{1}{2}+1} + C$$

$$= \frac{2}{3}z^{\frac{3}{2}} + C = \mathbf{\frac{2}{3}(x^2+3x-1)^{\frac{3}{2}} + C.}$$

(iii) $$\int \frac{(x-2)\,dx}{\sqrt[3]{x^2-4x+5}} = \int \frac{\frac{1}{2}dz}{\sqrt[3]{z}} = \frac{1}{2}\int z^{-\frac{1}{3}}\,dz$$ | Put $x^2-4x+5=z$; then $(2x-4)\,dx = dz$

$$= \frac{1}{2}\times\frac{z^{-\frac{1}{3}+1}}{-\frac{1}{3}+1} + C = \frac{1}{2}\times\frac{3}{2}\times z^{\frac{2}{3}} + C$$ | or, $2(x-2)\,dx = dz$, or, $(x-2)\,dx = \frac{1}{2}\,dz$

$$= \frac{3}{4}z^{\frac{2}{3}} + C = \mathbf{\frac{3}{4}(x^2-4x+5)^{\frac{2}{3}} + C.}$$

EXAMPLE 4. *Evaluate:*

(i) $\int \frac{x\,dx}{(x^2+3)^2}$; **[Bombay U. B.Com 1980]**

(ii) $\int \frac{x^3\,dx}{(x^2+1)^3}$. **[Delhi U. B.Com 1982; CA November 1987]**

SOLUTION.

(i) $$\int \frac{x\,dx}{(x^2+3)^2} = \int \frac{\frac{1}{2}dz}{z^2} = \frac{1}{2}\int z^{-2}\,dz$$ | Put $x^2+3=z$; then $2x\,dx = dz$, or, $x\,dx = \frac{1}{2}\,dz$

$$= \frac{1}{2}\times\frac{z^{-2+1}}{-2+1} + C = -\frac{1}{2z} + C = -\mathbf{\frac{1}{2(x^2+3)} + C.}$$

(ii) $$\int \frac{x^3\,dx}{(x^2+1)^3} = \int \frac{x^2\cdot x\,dx}{(x^2+1)^3}$$ | Put $x^2+1=z$; then $2x\,dx = dz$, or, $x\,dx = \frac{1}{2}\,dz$

$$= \int \frac{(z-1)\cdot\frac{1}{2}dz}{z^3} = \frac{1}{2}\int\left(\frac{z}{z^3}-\frac{1}{z^3}\right)dz = \frac{1}{2}\left\{\int z^{-2}\,dz - \int z^{-3}\,dz\right\}$$

$$= \frac{1}{2}\left\{\frac{z^{-2+1}}{-2+1} - \frac{z^{-3+1}}{-3+1}\right\} + C = \frac{1}{2}\left(-z^{-1}+\frac{1}{2}z^{-2}\right) + C$$

$$= \mathbf{\frac{1}{2}\left(-\frac{1}{Z}+\frac{1}{2z^2}\right) + C = \frac{1}{2}\left\{\frac{1}{2(x^2+1)^2} - \frac{1}{x^2+1}\right\} + C.}$$

EXAMPLE 5. *Evaluate:*

(i) $\int x\sqrt{x^2-1}\,dx$ **[C.U. B.Com (Hons.) 1988]**

(ii) $\int 3x^2\sqrt{6x^3+11}\,dx$. **[C.U. B.Com (Hons.) 1993]**

SOLUTION.

(i) $\int x\sqrt{x^2-1}\,dx$ | Put $x^2-1=z$; then $2x\,dx = dz$, or, $x\,dx = \frac{1}{2}\,dz$

$$= \int \sqrt{x^2-1}\cdot x\,dx = \int \sqrt{z}\cdot\frac{1}{2}\,dz = \frac{1}{2}\int z^{\frac{1}{2}}\,dz = \frac{1}{2}\cdot\frac{z^{\frac{1}{2}+1}}{\frac{1}{2}+1}+C$$

$$= \frac{1}{2}\times\frac{2}{3}z^{\frac{3}{2}}+C = \mathbf{\frac{1}{3}(x^2-1)^{\frac{3}{2}}+C.}$$

(ii) $\int 3x^2\sqrt{6x^3+11}\,dx$ | Put $6x^3+11=z$; then $18x^2\,dx = dz$ or, $3x^2\,dx = \frac{1}{6}\,dz$

$$= \int \sqrt{z}\cdot\frac{1}{6}\,dz = \frac{1}{6}\int z^{\frac{1}{2}}\,dz = \frac{1}{6}\cdot\frac{z^{\frac{1}{2}+1}}{\frac{1}{2}+1}+C = \frac{1}{6}\times\frac{2}{3}z^{\frac{3}{2}}+C$$

$$= \mathbf{\frac{1}{9}(6x^3+11)^{\frac{3}{2}}+C.}$$

EXAMPLE 6. *Evaluate:*

(i) $\int \frac{1}{x\log x}\,dx$ **[Madras U. 1977]** (ii) $\int \frac{e^x-e^{-x}}{e^x+e^{-x}}\,dx$ **[Bhopal U. 1981, '83]**

SOLUTION.

(i) $\int \frac{1}{x\log x}\,dx$ | Put $\log x = z$; then $\frac{1}{x}\,dx = dz$

$$= \int \frac{1}{\log x}\cdot\frac{1}{x}\,dx = \int \frac{1}{z}\,dz = \log|z|+C = \mathbf{\log|\log x|+C.}$$

(ii) $\int \frac{e^x-e^{-x}}{e^x+e^{-x}}\,dx$ | Put $e^x+e^{-x}=z$; then $(e^x-e^{-x})\,dx = dz$

$$= \int \frac{dz}{z} = \log|z|+C = \mathbf{\log(e^x+e^{-x})+C.}$$

EXAMPLE 7. *Evaluate each of the following integrals:*

(i) $\int \frac{1-x}{\sqrt{1+x}}\,dx$; **[ICWAI June 1992]** (ii) $\int \frac{x+2}{\sqrt{x-2}}\,dx$. **[C.U. B.Com (Hons.) 1994]**

SOLUTION.

(i) $\int \frac{1-x}{\sqrt{1+x}}\,dx$ | Put $1+x=z^2$; then $dx = 2z\,dz$ and $z=(1+x)^{\frac{1}{2}}, x = z^2-1$.

$$= \int \frac{1-(z^2-1)}{\sqrt{z^2}}\cdot 2z\,dz = \int \frac{2-z^2}{z}\cdot 2z\,dz$$

$$= 2\int (2-z^2)\,dz = 2\left[2z-\frac{z^3}{3}\right]+C = 4z-\frac{2}{3}z^3+C$$

$$= \mathbf{4\sqrt{1+x}-\frac{2}{3}(1+x)^{\frac{3}{2}}+C.}$$

(ii) $\displaystyle\int \frac{x+2}{\sqrt{x-2}}\,dx$ | Put $x-2=z^2$; then $dx = 2z\,dz$ and $x = z^2+2,\ z = (x-2)^{\frac{1}{2}}$.

$$= \int \frac{(z^2+2)+2}{\sqrt{z^2}} \cdot 2z\,dz = 2\int \frac{z^2+4}{z}\cdot z\,dz = 2\int (z^2+4)\,dz$$

$$= 2\left[\frac{z^3}{3}+4z\right] + C = \frac{2}{3}z^3 + 8z + C = \mathbf{\frac{2}{3}(x-2)^{\frac{3}{2}} + 8\sqrt{x-2} + C}$$

EXAMPLE 8. *Evaluate:*

(i) $\int \frac{x\,dx}{\sqrt{x}+1}$; **[C.U. B.Com (Hons.) 1990; ICWAI]** (iii) $\int \frac{x^{\frac{1}{4}}}{1+x^{\frac{1}{4}}}\,dx$ **[ICWAI December 1992]**

SOLUTION.

(i) $\displaystyle\int \frac{x\,dx}{\sqrt{x}+1}$ | Put $x = z^2$; then $dx = 2z\,dz$ and $z = x^{\frac{1}{2}} = \sqrt{x}$

$$= \int \frac{z^2\cdot 2z\,dz}{\sqrt{z^2}+1} = 2\int \frac{z^3}{z+1}\,dz = 2\int \frac{(z^3+1-1)}{z+1}\,dz = 2\int \left(z^2 - z + 1 - \frac{1}{z+1}\right)dz$$

$$= 2\left[\frac{z^3}{3} - \frac{z^2}{2} + z - \log|z+1|\right] + C = \mathbf{2\left[\frac{1}{3}x^{\frac{3}{2}} - \frac{1}{2}x + \sqrt{x} - \log|\sqrt{x}+1|\right] + C.}$$

(ii) $\displaystyle\int \frac{x^{\frac{1}{4}}}{1+x^{\frac{1}{4}}}\,dx$ | Put $x = z^4$; then $dx = 4z^3\,dz$ and $z = x^{\frac{1}{4}}$.

$$= \int \frac{z}{1+z}\cdot 4z^3\,dz = 4\int \frac{z^4}{z+1}\,dz$$

$$= 4\int \left(z^3 - z^2 + z - 1 + \frac{1}{z+1}\right)dz$$

$$= 4\left[\frac{z^4}{4} - \frac{z^3}{3} + \frac{z^2}{2} - z + \log|z+1|\right] + C$$

$$= z^4 - \frac{4}{3}z^3 + 2z^2 - 4z + 4\log|z+1| + C$$

$$= \mathbf{x - \frac{4}{3}x^{\frac{3}{4}} + 2x^{\frac{1}{2}} - 4x^{\frac{1}{4}} + 4\log|x^{\frac{1}{4}}+1| + C.}$$

$$\begin{array}{l}
z+1)\ z^4 \qquad (z^3 - z^2 + z - 1 \\
\quad\ \ \underline{z^4 + z^3} \\
\qquad\quad -z^3 \\
\qquad\quad \underline{-z^3 - z^2} \\
\qquad\qquad\ z^2 \\
\qquad\qquad\ \underline{z^2 + z} \\
\qquad\qquad\quad -z \\
\qquad\qquad\quad \underline{-z - 1} \\
\qquad\qquad\qquad 1
\end{array}$$

EXAMPLE 9. *Evaluate:* $\displaystyle\int \frac{x^8}{(1-x^3)^{\frac{1}{3}}}\,dx.$ **[CA May 1987]**

SOLUTION.

$$\int \frac{x^8}{(1-x^3)^{\frac{1}{3}}}\,dx = \int \frac{x^6 \cdot x^2\,dx}{(1-x^3)^{\frac{1}{3}}}$$
Put $1 - x^3 = z^3$; then $-3x^2\,dx = 3z^2\,dz$

$$= \int \frac{(1-z^3)^2 \times -z^2\,dz}{(z^3)^{\frac{1}{3}}}$$
or, $x^2\,dx = -z^2\,dz$. Also $x^3 = 1 - z^3$ and $z = (1-x^3)^{\frac{1}{3}}$

$$= -\int \frac{(1-z^3)^2 \cdot z^2\,dz}{z} = -\int (1 - 2z^3 + z^6) z\,dz$$

$$= -\int (z - 2z^4 + z^7)\,dz = -\left(\frac{z^2}{2} - \frac{2z^5}{5} + \frac{z^8}{8}\right) + C$$

$$= -\frac{\mathbf{1}}{\mathbf{2}}(\mathbf{1}-\mathbf{x}^{\mathbf{3}})^{\frac{2}{3}} + \frac{\mathbf{2}}{\mathbf{5}}(\mathbf{1}-\mathbf{x}^{\mathbf{3}})^{\frac{5}{3}} - \frac{\mathbf{1}}{\mathbf{8}}(\mathbf{1}-\mathbf{x}^{\mathbf{3}})^{\frac{8}{3}} + \mathbf{C}.$$

EXAMPLE 10. *Evaluate:* $\int \frac{dx}{\sqrt{x+1}-\sqrt{x}}$. **[ICWAI June 1983]**

SOLUTION.

$$\int \frac{dx}{\sqrt{x+1}-\sqrt{x}} = \int \frac{(\sqrt{x+1}+\sqrt{x})\,dx}{(\sqrt{x+1}-\sqrt{x})(\sqrt{x+1}+\sqrt{x})}$$

$$= \int \frac{\sqrt{x+1}+\sqrt{x}}{x+1-x}\,dx = \int (\sqrt{x+1}+\sqrt{x})\,dx = \int \sqrt{x+1}\,dx + \int \sqrt{x}\,dx$$

$$= \int \sqrt{z}\,dz + \int \sqrt{x}\,dx, \quad \text{where} \quad x+1 = z \quad \text{and} \quad dx = dz$$

$$= \frac{z^{\frac{1}{2}+1}}{\frac{1}{2}+1} + \frac{x^{\frac{1}{2}+1}}{\frac{1}{2}+1} + C = \frac{2}{3}z^{\frac{3}{2}} + \frac{2}{3}x^{\frac{3}{2}} + C$$

$$= \frac{\mathbf{2}}{\mathbf{3}}(\mathbf{x}+\mathbf{1})^{\frac{3}{2}} + \frac{\mathbf{2}}{\mathbf{3}}\mathbf{x}^{\frac{3}{2}} + \mathbf{C}.$$

RULE. To evaluate integrals of the form $\int \frac{dx}{\sqrt{ax+b}+\sqrt{cx+d}}$, *rationalise the denominator first and then use the method of substitution.*

EXAMPLE 11. *Evaluate:* $\int \frac{dx}{\sqrt{2x+3}+\sqrt{2x-3}}$.

SOLUTION.

$$\int \frac{dx}{\sqrt{2x+3}+\sqrt{2x-3}} = \int \frac{(\sqrt{2x+3}-\sqrt{2x-3})\,dx}{(\sqrt{2x+3}+\sqrt{2x-3})(\sqrt{2x+3}-\sqrt{2x-3})}$$

$$= \int \frac{(\sqrt{2x+3}-\sqrt{2x-3})\,dx}{2x+3-(2x-3)} = \frac{1}{6}\int \{(2x+3)^{\frac{1}{2}} - (2x-3)^{\frac{1}{2}}\}\,dx$$

$$= \frac{1}{6}\int (2x+3)^{\frac{1}{2}}\,dx - \frac{1}{6}\int (2x-3)^{\frac{1}{2}}\,dx$$
Put $2x+3 = z$ and $2x-3 = t$. Then $2\,dx = dz$ and $2\,dx = dt$

$$= \frac{1}{6}\int z^{\frac{1}{2}} \cdot \frac{1}{2}\,dz - \frac{1}{6}\int t^{\frac{1}{2}} \cdot \frac{1}{2}dt$$

$$= \frac{1}{12} \times \frac{z^{\frac{1}{2}+1}}{\frac{1}{2}+1} - \frac{1}{12} \times \frac{t^{\frac{1}{2}+1}}{\frac{1}{2}+1} + C = \frac{1}{12} \times \frac{2}{3}z^{\frac{3}{2}} - \frac{1}{12} \times \frac{2}{3}t^{\frac{3}{2}} + C$$

$$= \frac{1}{18}(z^{\frac{3}{2}} - t^{\frac{3}{2}}) + C = \frac{\mathbf{1}}{\mathbf{18}}\{(\mathbf{2x}+\mathbf{3})^{\frac{3}{2}} - (\mathbf{2x}-\mathbf{3})^{\frac{3}{2}}\} + \mathbf{C}.$$

10.5. INTEGRATION BY PARTS—INTEGRATION OF A PRODUCT OF TWO FUNCTIONS

RULE. *If u and v be two functions of x such that u is differentiable and v is integrable, then*

$$\int (\mathbf{u}\cdot\mathbf{v})\,\mathbf{dx} = \mathbf{u}\int \mathbf{v}\,\mathbf{dx} - \int\left\{\frac{\mathbf{du}}{\mathbf{dx}}\cdot\int \mathbf{v}\,\mathbf{dx}\right\}\mathbf{dx},$$

i.e., the integral of the product of two functions = 1st function × Integral of the 2nd function—

Integral of [the derivative of the 1st × integral of the 2nd function.]

PROOF. We have $\frac{d}{dx}(u\cdot z) = \frac{du}{dx}\cdot z + u\cdot\frac{dz}{dx}$, where u, z are two differentiable functions of x.

Integrating both sides w.r.t. x, we get

$$uz = \int\left(\frac{du}{dx}\cdot z\right)dx + \int\left(u\cdot\frac{dz}{dx}\right)dx, \quad \text{or,} \quad \int\left(u\cdot\frac{dz}{dx}\right)dx = uz - \int\left(\frac{du}{dx}\cdot z\right)dx. \qquad (1)$$

Now if $\frac{dz}{dx} = v$, then $dz = v\,dx$; $\therefore\ z = \int v\,dx$.

Hence from (1), $\int(u\cdot v)\,dx = u\int v\,dx - \int\{\frac{du}{dx}\cdot\int v\,dx\}\,dx$.

EXAMPLE 12. *Evaluate:*

(i) $\int xe^x\,dx$; **[CA May 1975]** (ii) $\int x^2e^{ax}\,dx$; **[CA May 1980]**

(iii) $\int x\log x\,dx$. **[CA November 1976]**

SOLUTION.

(i) $$\int xe^x\,dx = x\int e^x\,dx - \int\left\{\frac{d}{dx}(x)\cdot\int e^x\,dx\right\}dx \quad \text{[integrating by parts]}$$

$$= xe^x - \int(1\cdot e^x)\,dx + C = xe^x - e^x + C = \mathbf{e^x(x-1)+C}.$$

(ii) $$\int x^2e^{ax}\,dx = x^2\int e^{ax}\,dx - \int\left\{\frac{d}{dx}(x^2)\cdot\int e^{ax}\,dx\right\}dx \quad \text{[integrating by parts]}$$

$$= x^2\cdot\frac{e^{ax}}{a} - \int\left(2x\cdot\frac{e^{ax}}{a}\right)dx + C = \frac{x^2e^{ax}}{a} - \frac{2}{a}\int xe^{ax}\,dx + C$$

$$= \frac{x^2e^{ax}}{a} - \frac{2}{a}\left[x\int e^{ax}\,dx - \int\left\{\frac{d}{dx}(x)\cdot\int e^{ax}\,dx\right\}\right]dx + C$$

$$= \frac{x^2e^{ax}}{a} - \frac{2}{a}\left[x\cdot\frac{e^{ax}}{a} - \int\left(1\cdot\frac{e^{ax}}{a}\right)dx\right] + C$$

$$= \frac{x^2e^{ax}}{a} - \frac{2}{a}\left[x\frac{e^{ax}}{a} - \frac{1}{a}\cdot\frac{e^{ax}}{a}\right] + C = \mathbf{\frac{x^2e^{ax}}{a} - \frac{2e^{ax}}{a^2}\left(x-\frac{1}{a}\right)+C}.$$

(iii) $$\int x\log x\,dx = \int \log x\cdot x\,dx$$

$$= \log x\int x\,dx = \int\left\{\frac{d}{dx}(\log x)\cdot\int x\,dx\right\} \quad \text{[integrating by parts]}$$

$$= \log x\cdot\frac{x^2}{2} - \int\left(\frac{1}{x}\cdot\frac{x^2}{2}\right)dx + C = \frac{x^2}{2}\log x - \frac{1}{2}\int x\,dx + C$$

$$= \frac{x^2}{2}\log x - \frac{1}{2}\cdot\frac{x^2}{2} + C = \mathbf{\frac{x^2}{2}\left(\log x - \frac{1}{2}\right)+C}.$$

NOTE. In the above problem, if we take x as the first function and $\log x$ as the 2nd function, we cannot evaluate the integral. But if we interchange the two functions x and $\log x$ in their positions, i.e., if we take $\log x$ as the first function and x as the second function, we can easily find the value of the integral as shown above.

EXAMPLE 13. *Evaluate:*

(i) $\int x \log(1+x)\,dx$; **[C.U. B.Com (Hons.) 1994]**

(ii) $\int x^n \log x\,dx$. **[CA May 1976; Delhi U. B.Com 1982]**

SOLUTION.

(i)
$$\begin{aligned}
\int x \log(1+x)\,dx &= \int \log(1+x)\cdot x\,dx \\
&= \log(1+x)\cdot\int x\,dx - \int\left[\frac{d}{dx}\{\log(1+x)\}\cdot\int x\,dx\right]dx \\
&= \log(1+x)\cdot\frac{x^2}{2} - \int\left[\frac{1}{1+x}\times 1\times\frac{x^2}{2}\right]dx + C \\
&= \frac{x^2}{2}\log(1+x) - \frac{1}{2}\int\frac{x^2}{1+x}\,dx + C \\
&= \frac{x^2}{2}\log(1+x) - \frac{1}{2}\int\left(x-1+\frac{1}{1+x}\right)dx + C \\
&= \mathbf{\frac{x^2}{2}\log(1+x) - \frac{1}{2}\left\{\frac{x^2}{2} - x + \log(1+x)\right\} + C}
\end{aligned}$$

(ii)
$$\begin{aligned}
\int x^n \log x\,dx &= \int \log x\cdot x^n\,dx \\
&= \log x\int x^n\,dx - \int\left\{\frac{d}{dx}(\log x).\int x^n\,dx\right\}dx \quad \text{[integrating by parts]} \\
&= \log x\cdot\frac{x^{n+1}}{n+1} - \int\left(\frac{1}{x}\cdot\frac{x^{n+1}}{n+1}\right)dx + C = \frac{x^{n+1}}{n+1}\cdot\log x - \frac{1}{n+1}\int x^n\,dx + C \\
&= \frac{x^{n+1}}{n+1}\log x - \frac{1}{n+1}\cdot\frac{x^{n+1}}{n+1} + C = \mathbf{\frac{x^{n+1}}{n+1}\left(\log x - \frac{1}{n+1}\right) + C.}
\end{aligned}$$

EXAMPLE 14. *Evaluate:*

(i) $\int \frac{\log x}{x^2}\,dx$; **[CA May 1983, 1988]** (ii) $\int(\log x)^2\,dx$. **[CA May 1982]**

SOLUTION.

(i)
$$\begin{aligned}
\int\frac{\log x}{x^2}\,dx &= \int\log x\cdot\frac{1}{x^2}\,dx = \log x\int\frac{1}{x^2}\,dx - \int\left\{\frac{d}{dx}(\log x)\cdot\int\frac{1}{x^2}\,dx\right\}dx \\
&= \log x\cdot\left(-\frac{1}{x}\right) - \int\left(\frac{1}{x}\times-\frac{1}{x}\right)dx + C \\
&= -\frac{\log x}{x} + \int\frac{1}{x^2}\,dx + C = -\frac{\log x}{x} - \frac{1}{x} + C = \mathbf{-\frac{1}{x}(\log x + 1) + C.}
\end{aligned}$$

(ii) $$\int (\log x)^2\,dx = \int (\log x)^2 \cdot 1 \cdot dx = (\log x)^2 \cdot \int 1\,dx - \int \left\{\frac{d}{dx}(\log x)^2 \cdot \int 1 \cdot dx\right\} dx$$

$$= x(\log x)^2 - \int \left(2 \cdot \log x \cdot \frac{1}{x} \cdot x\right) dx = x(\log x)^2 - 2\int \log x \cdot 1\,dx + C$$

$$= x(\log x)^2 - 2\left[\log x \int 1 \cdot dx - \int \left\{\frac{d}{dx}(\log x) \cdot \int 1\,dx\right\} dx + C\right.$$

$$= x(\log x)^2 - 2\left[\log x \cdot x - \int \left(\frac{1}{x} \cdot x\right) dx\right] + C$$

$$= x(\log x)^2 - 2[x\log x - \int 1 \cdot dx] + C = x(\log x)^2 - 2[x \log x - x] + C$$

$$= \mathbf{x\{(\log x)^2 - 2x(\log x - 1)\} + C}.$$

10.5.1 An Important Integral: $\int \mathbf{e^x\{f(x) + f'(x)\}\,dx = e^x f(x) + C}$.

We have

$$\int e^x\{f(x) + f'(x)\}\,dx = \int e^x f(x)\,dx + \int e^x f'(x)\,dx$$

$$= \int f(x) \cdot e^x\,dx + \int e^x f'(x)\,dx$$

$$= f(x) \cdot \int e^x\,dx - \int \left\{\frac{d}{dx}\{f(x)\} \cdot \int e^x\,dx\right\} dx + \int e^x f'(x)\,dx$$

[integrating the first integral by parts]

$$= f(x) \cdot e^x - \int e^x \cdot f'(x)\,dx + \int e^x f'(x)\,dx + C$$

$$= \mathbf{e^x f(x) + C}. \qquad [\because \text{ two integrals cancel each other}]$$

EXAMPLE 15. *Evaluate:* $\int \frac{e^x}{x}(1 + x\log x)\,dx$. **[ICWAI June 1987]**

SOLUTION.

$$\int \frac{e^x}{x}(1 + x \log x)\,dx = \int \frac{e^x}{x}\,dx + \int e^x \log x\,dx$$

$$= e^x \int \frac{1}{x}\,dx - \int \left\{\frac{d}{dx}(e^x) \cdot \int \frac{1}{x}\,dx\right\} dx + \int e^x \log x\,dx$$

$$= e^x \log x - \int e^x \cdot \log x\,dx + \int e^x \log x\,dx + C$$

$$= \mathbf{e^x \log x + C}.$$

EXAMPLE 16. *Evaluate:* $\int \frac{xe^x}{(x+1)^2}\,dx$.

[ICWAI December 1980, June 1991; CA May 1976, 1986; November 1984, 1989]

SOLUTION.

$$\int \frac{xe^x}{(x+1)^2}\,dx = \int \frac{(x+1-1)e^x}{(x+1)^2}\,dx = \int \frac{e^x}{x+1}\,dx - \int \frac{e^x}{(x+1)^2}\,dx$$
$$= \frac{1}{x+1}\int e^x\,dx - \int\left\{\frac{d}{dx}\left(\frac{1}{x+1}\right)\cdot\int e^x\,dx\right\}dx - \int \frac{e^x\,dx}{(x+1)^2}$$
$$= \frac{1}{x+1}\cdot e^x - \int -\frac{1}{(x+1)^2}\cdot e^x\,dx - \int \frac{e^x\,dx}{(x+1)^2} + C$$
$$= \frac{e^x}{x+1} + \int \frac{e^x\,dx}{(x+1)^2} - \int \frac{e^x\,dx}{(x+1)^2} + C = \mathbf{\frac{e^x}{x+1} + C}.$$

Exercise 10 (II)

(Integration by Substitution and by Parts)

A

1. Evaluate each of the following integrals:

(i) $\int (4x+3)^4\,dx$; (ii) $\int \sqrt{5+3x}\,dx$; (iii) $\int (2x+3)(x^2+3x)^2\,dx$; (iv) $\int (x^2-5x+3)^6\cdot(2x-5)\,dx$; (v) $\int \frac{1}{(2x+1)^2}\,dx$; (vi) $\int (2x-5)\sqrt{x^2-5x+6}\,dx$; (vii) $\int \frac{(6x-5)\,dx}{3x^2-5x+7}$.

2. Integrate the following functions:

(i) $\frac{x-1}{\sqrt{2x^2-4x+5}}$; **[C.U. B.Com (Hons.) 1990]** (ii) $\frac{x}{(x^2+3)^2}$; **[Bombay U. B.Com 1980]**

(iii) $\frac{3x^2-5}{e^{x^3-5x+7}}$.

3. Evaluate the following integrals:

(i) $\int \frac{dx}{x\log x}$; (ii) $\int \frac{(2x+3)\,dx}{(x^2+3x-5)^3}$; (iii) $\int \frac{(2x+5)\,dx}{\sqrt[3]{x^2+5x+7}}$; (iv) $\int \frac{3x+2}{\sqrt{x+1}}\,dx$; (v) $\int \frac{2x-3}{\sqrt{4x-1}}\,dx$.

4. Evaluate:

(i) $\int \frac{x^2dx}{(x^3+2)^3}$; (ii) $\int \frac{x^3\,dx}{(x^2+2)^5}$; (iii) $\int \frac{t^3dt}{\sqrt[3]{t^4+3}}$.

5. Evaluate:

(i) $\int \frac{x^3}{(x^2+1)^3}\,dx$; (ii) $\int \frac{x^8}{(1-x^3)^{\frac{1}{3}}}\,dx$. **[CA May 1987]**

[HINTS. See worked out Examples 4 and 9.]

6. Evaluate:

(i) $\int \frac{dx}{\sqrt{x-1}+\sqrt{x}}$; (ii) $\int \frac{dx}{\sqrt{x+1}+\sqrt{x+2}}$; (iii) $\int \frac{dx}{\sqrt{2x+5}-\sqrt{2x-5}}$.

7. Integrate each of the following functions:

(i) $\frac{(\log x)^2}{x}$; (ii) $\frac{1}{x(1+\log x)^3}$; (iii) $\frac{(\log x+3)^5}{x}$; (iv) $\frac{1-x}{\sqrt{1+x}}$.

[HINTS. (i) Put $\log x = z$; (ii) Put $1+\log x = z$; (iii) $\log x + 3 = z$; (iv) Put $1+x = z^2$.]

B

1. Evaluate:

(i) $\int xe^x\,dx$; (ii) $\int x\log x\,dx$; (iii) $\int \log x\,dx$; (iv) $\int x\cdot 3^x\,dx$.

[HINTS. See worked out Example 12. (iii) $\int \log x\,dx = \int \log x\cdot 1\,dx = \log x\cdot\int 1\,dx - \int\left\{\frac{d}{dx}(\log x)\cdot\int 1\,dx\right\}dx = x\log x - \int\left(\frac{1}{x}\cdot x\right)dx + C =$ etc.

(iv) $\int x\cdot 3^x\,dx = x\int 3^x\,dx - \int\left\{\frac{d}{dx}(x)\cdot\int 3^x\,dx\right\}dx = x\cdot\frac{3^x}{\log 3} - \int\left(1\cdot\frac{3^x}{\log 3}\right)dx + C$

$= \frac{3^x\cdot x}{\log 3} - \frac{1}{\log 3}\cdot\frac{3^x}{\log 3} + C = \frac{3^x}{\log_e 3}\left(x - \frac{1}{\log_e 3}\right) + C.$]

2. Evaluate each of the following:

(i) $\int x^2e^x\,dx$; (ii) $\int x^2\log\,x\,dx$; (iii) $\int(\log x)^2\,dx$; (iv) $\int\frac{\log x}{x^2}\,dx$.

3. Integrate the following functions:

(i) $\log(2x+3)$; (ii) $x^n\log\,x$; (iii) $(x+1)^2\log\,x$.

4. Evaluate: $\int(2x+3)\log(x^2+3x+4)\,dx$ **[Delhi U. B.Com (Hons.) 1982]**

[HINTS. Put $x^2+3x+4=z$; then $(2x+3)\,dx = dz$

$\therefore\quad \int(2x+3)\log(x^2+3x+4)\,dx = \int\log z\,dz = \int\log\ z.1\,dz$. Now see Hints of Example 1(iii).]

5. Evaluate:

(i) $\int e^x\left(\frac{1}{x}-\frac{1}{x^2}\right)dx$; (ii) $\int\frac{e^x}{x}(x\log\,x+1)\,dx$. **[ICWAI June 1987]**

[HINTS. Given integral $= \int e^x\cdot\frac{1}{x}\,dx - \int e^x\cdot\frac{1}{x^2}\,dx$]

6. Evaluate: $\int\frac{xe^x}{(x+1)^2}\,dx$. **[ICWAI December 1980; June 1991; CA May 1986]**

[HINTS. See worked out Example 16.]

7. Evaluate: $\int\frac{e^x(x^2+1)}{(x+1)^2}\,dx$ **[CA November 1990]**

[HINTS. Integrand $= \frac{e^x\{(x+1)^2-2x\}}{(x+1)^2} = e^x - 2\cdot\frac{xe^x}{(x+1)^2}$; see worked out Example 16.]

8. Evaluate: $\int\frac{xe^{2x}}{(2x+1)^2}\,dx$ **[CA Foundation June 1993]**

[HINTS.

$$\int\frac{xe^{2x}}{(2x+1)^2}\,dx = \int\frac{\left\{\frac{1}{2}(2x+1)-\frac{1}{2}\right\}}{(2x+1)^2}\cdot e^{2x}\,dx$$

$$= \frac{1}{2}\left[\int\frac{e^{2x}}{2x+1}\,dx - \int\frac{e^{2x}}{(2x+1)^2}\,dx\right]$$

Now, $$\int\frac{e^{2x}}{2x+1}\,dx = \frac{1}{2x+1}\int e^{2x} - \int\left\{\frac{d}{dx}\left(\frac{1}{2x+1}\right)\int e^{2x}\,dx\right\}dx = \text{etc.}$$]

Answers

(The constant of integration C, which is not written, is to be added to each answer.)

A

1. (i) $\frac{1}{20}(4x+3)^5$; (ii) $\frac{2}{9}(5+3x)^{\frac{3}{2}}$; (iii) $\frac{1}{3}\ (x^2+3x)^3$; (iv) $\frac{1}{7}(x^2-5x+3)^7$; (v) $-\frac{1}{2(2x+1)}$; (vi) $\frac{2}{3}(x^2-5x+6)^{\frac{3}{2}}$; $\log(3x^2-5x+7)$. 2. (i) $\frac{1}{2}\sqrt{2x^2-4x+5}$; (ii) $-\frac{1}{2(x^2+3)}$; (vi) $-e^{-(x^3-5x+7)}$. 3. (i) $\log\log x$;

(ii) $-\frac{1}{2(x^2+3x-5)^2}$; (iii) $\frac{3}{2}(x^2+5x+7)^{\frac{2}{3}}$; (iv) $2x\sqrt{x+1}$; (v) $\frac{1}{12}(4x-1)^{\frac{3}{2}}-\frac{5}{4}(4x-1)^{\frac{1}{2}}$. **4.** (i) $-\frac{1}{6(x^3+2)^2}$; (ii) $-\frac{1}{6(x^2+2)^3}+\frac{1}{4(x^2+2)^4}$; (iii) $\frac{3}{8}(t^4+3)^{\frac{2}{3}}$. **5.** (i) $\frac{1}{4(x^2+1)^2}-\frac{1}{2(x^2+1)}$; (ii) $-\frac{1}{2}(1-x^3)^{\frac{2}{3}}+\frac{2}{5}(1-x^3)^{\frac{5}{3}}-\frac{1}{8}(1-x^3)^{\frac{8}{3}}$. **6.** (i) $\frac{2}{3}\{x^{\frac{3}{2}}-(x-1)^{\frac{3}{2}}\}$; (ii) $\frac{2}{3}\{(x+2)^{\frac{3}{2}}-(x+1)^{\frac{3}{2}}\}$; (iii) $\frac{1}{30}\{(2x+5)^{\frac{3}{2}}+(2x-5)^{\frac{3}{2}}\}$. **7.** (i) $\frac{1}{3}(\log x)^3$; (ii) $-\frac{1}{2(1+\log x)^2}$; (iii) $\frac{1}{6}(\log x+3)^6$; (iv) $4\sqrt{1+x}-\frac{2}{3}(1+x)^{3/2}$.

B

1. (i) $e^x(x-1)$; (ii) $\frac{x^2}{2}\left(\log x-\frac{1}{2}\right)$; (iii) $x(\log x-1)$; (iv) $\frac{3^x}{\log_e 3}\left(x-\frac{1}{\log_e 3}\right)$. **2.** (i) $x^2e^x-2e^x(x-1)$; (ii) $\frac{x^3}{3}\left(\log x-\frac{1}{3}\right)$; (iii) $x(\log x)^2-2x(\log x-1)$; (iv) $-\frac{1}{x}(\log x+1)$. **3.** (i) $\left(x+\frac{3}{2}\right)\log|2x+3|-x$; (ii) $\frac{x^{n+1}}{n+1}\left(\log x-\frac{1}{n+1}\right)$; (iii) $\frac{1}{3}\{(x+1)^3\log x-\frac{1}{3}x^3-\frac{3}{2}x^2-3x-\log x\}$. **4.** $(x^2+3x+4)\{\log(x^2+3x+4)-1\}$. **5.** (i) $\frac{1}{x}e^x$; (ii) $e^x\log x$. **6.** $\frac{1}{x+1}e^x$. **7.** $e^x\left(\frac{x-1}{x+1}\right)$. **8.** $\frac{1}{4}\cdot\frac{e^{2x}}{2x+1}$.

10.6. SOME SPECIAL INTEGRALS

1. $\int\frac{dx}{x^2-a^2}=\frac{1}{2a}\log\left|\frac{x-a}{x+a}\right|+C$; **2.** $\int\frac{dx}{a^2-x^2}=\frac{1}{2a}\log\left|\frac{a+x}{a-x}\right|+C$;

3. $\int\frac{\mathbf{dx}}{\sqrt{\mathbf{x^2\pm a^2}}}=\mathbf{\log|x+\sqrt{x^2\pm a^2}|+C}$.

PROOF.

1.
$$\int\frac{dx}{x^2-a^2}=\int\frac{dx}{(x+a)(x-a)}=\int\frac{1}{2a}\left\{\frac{(x+a)-(x-a)}{(x+a)(x-a)}\right\}dx=\int\frac{1}{2a}\left(\frac{1}{x-a}-\frac{1}{x+a}\right)dx$$
$$=\frac{1}{2a}\{\log|x-a|-\log|x+a|\}+C=\frac{1}{2a}\log\left|\frac{x-a}{x+a}\right|+C.$$

Hence $\int\frac{dx}{x^2-a^2}=\frac{1}{2a}\log\left|\frac{x-a}{x+a}\right|+C$.

2.
$$\int\frac{dx}{a^2-x^2}=\int\frac{dx}{(a+x)(a-x)}=\int\frac{1}{2a}\left\{\frac{1}{a+x}+\frac{1}{a-x}\right\}dx$$
$$=\frac{1}{2a}\{\log|a+x|-\log|a-x|\}+C=\mathbf{\frac{1}{2a}\log\left|\frac{a+x}{a-x}\right|+C}$$

Hence $\int\frac{\mathbf{dx}}{\mathbf{a^2-x^2}}=\mathbf{\frac{1}{2a}\log\left|\frac{a+x}{a-x}\right|+C}$

3. $\int\frac{dx}{\sqrt{x^2\pm a^2}}$ | Put $x+\sqrt{x^2\pm a^2}=z$; then

$$\left\{1+\frac{1}{2}(x^2\pm a^2)^{\frac{1}{2}-1}\times 2x\right\}dx=dz$$

or, $\left(1+\frac{x}{\sqrt{x^2\pm a^2}}\right)dx=dz$, or, $\frac{\sqrt{x^2\pm a^2}+x}{\sqrt{x^2\pm a^2}}dx=dz$

or, $\frac{z}{\sqrt{x^2\pm a^2}}dx=dz$, or, $\frac{dx}{\sqrt{x^2\pm a^2}}=\frac{dz}{z}$.

$$\therefore\quad\int\frac{dx}{\sqrt{x^2\pm a^2}}=\int\frac{dz}{z}=\log|z|+C=\log|x+\sqrt{x^2\pm a^2}|+C$$

Hence $\int\frac{\mathbf{dx}}{\sqrt{\mathbf{x^2\pm a^2}}}=\mathbf{\log|x+\sqrt{x^2\pm a^2}|+C}$.

REMARKS. If we replace x by $x+m$ or $x-m$, where m is a constant, then the corresponding results obtained in the above integrals are also true. For example,

$\int \frac{dx}{(x\pm m)^2-a^2} = \frac{1}{2a}\log\left|\frac{(x\pm m)-a}{(x\pm m)+a}\right| + C;$ [∵ if we put $x \pm m = z$, then $dx = dz$]

Similarly, $\int \frac{dx}{a^2-(x\pm m)^2} = \frac{1}{2a}\log\left|\frac{a+(x\pm m)}{a-(x\pm m)}\right| + C.$

and $\int \frac{dx}{\sqrt{(x\pm m)^2+a^2}} = \log|(x\pm m) + \sqrt{(x\pm m)^2 \pm a^2}| + C.$

EXAMPLE 1. *Evaluate each of the following integrals:*

(i) $\int \frac{dx}{x^2-16}$; (ii) $\int \frac{dx}{4-x^2}$; (iii) $\int \frac{dx}{\sqrt{x^2+6^2}}$; (iv) $\int \frac{dx}{\sqrt{x^2-64}}$.

SOLUTION.

(i) $$\int \frac{dx}{x^2-16} = \int \frac{dx}{x^2-4^2}, \text{ which is of the form } \int \frac{dx}{x^2-a^2}.$$
$$= \frac{1}{2.4}\log\left|\frac{x-4}{x+4}\right| + C = \mathbf{\frac{1}{8}\log\left|\frac{x-4}{x+4}\right| + C}$$

(ii) $$\int \frac{dx}{4-x^2} = \int \frac{dx}{2^2-x^2}, \text{ which is of the form } \int \frac{dx}{a^2-x^2}.$$
$$= \frac{1}{2.2}\log\left|\frac{2+x}{2-x}\right| + C = \mathbf{\frac{1}{4}\log\left|\frac{2+x}{2-x}\right| + C.}$$

(iii) $$\int \frac{dx}{\sqrt{x^2+36}} = \int \frac{dx}{\sqrt{x^2+6^2}}, \text{ which is of the form } \int \frac{dx}{\sqrt{x^2+a^2}}$$
$$= \log|x + \sqrt{x^2+6^2}| + C = \mathbf{\log|x + \sqrt{x^2+36}| + C.}$$

(iv) $$\int \frac{dx}{\sqrt{x^2-64}} = \int \frac{dx}{\sqrt{x^2-8^2}}, \text{ which is of the form } \int \frac{dx}{\sqrt{x^2-a^2}}$$
$$= \log|x + \sqrt{x^2-8^2}| + C = \mathbf{\log|x + \sqrt{x^2-64}| + C}$$

EXAMPLE 2. *Evaluate:* (i) $\int \frac{dx}{x^2+4x-5}$; (ii) $\int \frac{dx}{7+6x-x^2}$.

SOLUTION.

(i) $$\int \frac{dx}{x^2+4x-5} \quad \Big| \quad x^2+4x-5 = x^2+4x+4-9 = (x+2)^2-3^2$$
$$= \int \frac{dx}{(x+2)^2-3^3} \quad \left[\because \text{ the integral is of the form } \int \frac{dx}{x^2-a^2}\right]$$
$$= \frac{1}{2.3}\log_e\left|\frac{x+2-3}{x+2+3}\right| + C = \mathbf{\frac{1}{6}\log_e\left|\frac{x-1}{x+5}\right| + C.}$$

(ii) $7+6x-x^2 = 7-(x^2-6x) = 7-(x^2-6x+9-9) = 7+9-(x-3)^2$
$= (4)^2-(x-3)^2.$

$$\therefore \int \frac{dx}{7+6x-x^2} = \int \frac{dx}{(4)^2-(x-3)^2} \quad \left[\text{which is of the form } \int \frac{dx}{a^2-x^2}\right]$$
$$= \frac{1}{2.4}\log_e\left|\frac{4+x-3}{4-(x-3)}\right| + C = \mathbf{\frac{1}{8}\log_e\left|\frac{1+x}{7-x}\right| + C.}$$

EXAMPLE 3. Evaluate: (i) $\int \frac{dx}{\sqrt{x^2-2x+5}}$; (ii) $\int \frac{dx}{\sqrt{4x^2+16x-20}}$.

SOLUTION.

(i) $$\int \frac{dx}{\sqrt{x^2-2x+5}} = \int \frac{dx}{\sqrt{(x-1)^2+2^2}} = \log\{(x-1)+\sqrt{(x-1)^2+2^2}\}+C$$

$$= \mathbf{\log_e\{(x-1)+\sqrt{x^2-2x+5}\}+C.}$$

(ii) $$\int \frac{dx}{\sqrt{4x^2+16x-20}} = \int \frac{dx}{\sqrt{4(x^2+4x-5)}} = \int \frac{dx}{2\sqrt{(x+2)^2-9}} = \frac{1}{2}\int \frac{dx}{\sqrt{(x+2)^2-3^2}}$$

$$= \frac{1}{2}\log_e\{(x+2)+\sqrt{(x+2)^2-3^2}\}+C$$

$$= \mathbf{\frac{1}{2}\log_e\{x+2+\sqrt{x^2+4x-5}\}+C.}$$

EXAMPLE 4. *Evaluate:* (i) $\int \frac{dx}{x^2-3x+1}$ **[C.U. B.Com (Hons.) 1984]**

(ii) $\int \frac{dx}{x\{10+7\log x+(\log x)^2\}}$ **[C.U. B.Com (Hons.) 1989]**

SOLUTION.

(i) $$\int \frac{dx}{x^2-3x+1}$$

| $x^2-3x+1 = x^2-2.x.\frac{3}{2}+\left(\frac{3}{2}\right)^2-\frac{9}{4}+1$ $= \left(x-\frac{3}{2}\right)^2-\left(\frac{\sqrt{5}}{2}\right)^2$

$$= \int \frac{dx}{\left(x-\frac{3}{2}\right)^2-\left(\frac{\sqrt{5}}{2}\right)^2}, \text{ which is of the form } \int \frac{dx}{x^2-a^2}$$

$$= \frac{1}{2\cdot\frac{\sqrt{5}}{2}}\cdot\log\left|\frac{\left(x-\frac{3}{2}\right)-\frac{\sqrt{5}}{2}}{\left(x-\frac{3}{2}\right)+\left(\frac{\sqrt{5}}{2}\right)}\right|+C$$

$$= \mathbf{\frac{1}{\sqrt{5}}\log\left|\frac{2x-3-\sqrt{5}}{2x-3+\sqrt{5}}\right|+C.}$$

(ii) $$\int \frac{dx}{x\{10+7\log x+(\log x)^2\}}$$

| Put $\log x = z$; then $\frac{1}{x}\,dx = dz$

$$= \int \frac{dz}{10+7z+z^2}$$

| $z^2+7z+10$ $= \left(z+\frac{7}{2}\right)^2-\left(\frac{3}{2}\right)^2$

$$= \int \frac{dz}{\left(z+\frac{7}{2}\right)^2-\left(\frac{3}{2}\right)^2}, \text{ which is of the form } \int \frac{dx}{x^2-a^2}$$

$$= \frac{1}{2.\frac{3}{2}}\log\left|\frac{\left(z+\frac{7}{2}\right)-\frac{3}{2}}{\left(z+\frac{7}{2}\right)+\frac{3}{2}}\right|+C = \frac{1}{3}\log\left|\frac{z+2}{z+5}\right|+C$$

$$= \mathbf{\frac{1}{3}\log\left|\frac{\log x+2}{\log x+5}\right|+C.}$$

10.7. INTEGRATION BY PARTIAL FRACTIONS

If the numerator and the denominator of an integrand be polynomials in x, say $f(x)$ and $g(x)$ respectively, and the numerator $f(x)$ is of lower degree than the denominator $g(x)$, then we can break up the integrand into partial fractions by adopting different methods depending on the nature of the factors of $g(x)$.

TYPE 1. Suppose the denominator $g(x)$ of the integrand is the product of non-repeated linear factors $(x-a), (x-b)$, etc.

Then we can write

$$\frac{f(x)}{g(x)} = \frac{A}{x-a} + \frac{B}{x-b} + \cdots$$

where $A, B, \cdots$ are constants. These constants can be easily determined as shown in the following example.

EXAMPLE 5. *Integrate the functions:*

(i) $\frac{x}{(x+1)(2x+1)}$; **[CA November 1978]** (ii) $\frac{1}{2t^2+3t+1}$; **[C.U. 1983]** (iii) $\frac{2x-1}{(x-1)(x-2)(x-3)}$.

SOLUTION.

(i) We can write $$\frac{x}{(x+1)(2x+1)} = \frac{A}{x+1} + \frac{B}{2x+1} = \frac{A(2x+1)+B(x+1)}{(x+1)(2x+1)}$$

$$\therefore \quad x \equiv A(2x+1) + B(x+1) \tag{1}$$

Substituting $x = -1, -\frac{1}{2}$ successively, we get

$$-1 = A\cdot(-2+1) + B\cdot 0 \text{ and } -\frac{1}{2} = A\cdot 0 + B\cdot\left(-\frac{1}{2}+1\right);$$

$$\therefore \quad \mathbf{A = 1 \text{ and } B = -1}.$$

$$\therefore \quad \int \frac{x}{(x+1)(2x+1)}\,dx = A\int\frac{dx}{x+1} + B\int\frac{dx}{2x+1}$$

$$= 1.\log|x+1| - 1.\int\frac{\frac{1}{2}dz}{z}, \text{ where } 2x+1 = z \text{ and } dx = \frac{1}{2}dz.$$

$$= \log|x+1| - \frac{1}{2}\log|z| + C = \mathbf{\log|x+1| - \frac{1}{2}|2x+1| + C}.$$

[OTHERWISE. Since $(2x+1)-(x+1) = x$, by inspection, $\frac{x}{(x+1)(2x+1)} = \frac{1}{x+1} - \frac{1}{2x+1}$.]

(ii) We have $2t^2 + 3t + 1 = 2t^2 + 2t + t + 1$

$$= 2t(t+1) + 1(t+1) = (t+1)(2t+1)$$

Let $$\frac{1}{(t+1)(2t+1)} = \frac{A}{t+1} + \frac{B}{2t+1}$$

$$\therefore \quad 1 \equiv A(2t+1) + B(t+1) \tag{1}$$

Substituting $t = -1, -\frac{1}{2}$ successively, we get $A = -1$ and $B = 2$.

$$\therefore \quad \int\frac{dt}{2t^2+3t+1} = A\int\frac{dt}{t+1} + B\int\frac{dt}{2t+1}$$

$$= -\log|t+1| + 2\cdot\frac{1}{2}\log|2t+1| + C$$

$$= \mathbf{\log\left|\frac{2t+1}{t+1}\right| + C}.$$

(iii) We can write

$$\frac{2x-1}{(x-1)(x-2)(x-3)} = \frac{A}{x-1} + \frac{B}{x-2} + \frac{C}{x-3}$$
$$= \frac{A(x-2)(x-3) + B(x-1)(x-3) + C(x-1)(x-2)}{(x-1)(x-2)(x-3)}$$
$$\therefore \quad 2x - 1 \equiv A(x-2)(x-3) + B(x-1)(x-3) + C(x-1)(x-2)$$

Substituting $x = 1, 2, 3$ successively, we get

$$1 = A(-1)(-2), 3 = B \cdot (1) \cdot (-1) \quad \text{and} \quad 5 = C.2.1.$$
$$\therefore \quad A = \frac{1}{2}, B = -3, \quad \text{and} \quad C = \frac{5}{2}.$$
$$\therefore \quad \frac{2x-1}{(x-1)(x-2)(x-3)} = \frac{1}{2} \cdot \frac{1}{x-1} - \frac{3}{x-2} + \frac{5}{2} \cdot \frac{1}{x-3}$$
$$\therefore \quad \int \frac{(2x-1)\,dx}{(x-1)(x-2)(x-3)} = \frac{1}{2}\int \frac{1}{x-1}\,dx - 3\int \frac{1}{x-2}\,dx + \frac{5}{2}\int \frac{1}{x-3}\,dx$$
$$= \mathbf{\frac{1}{2}\log|x-1| - 3\log|x-2| + \frac{5}{2}\log|x-3| + C_1}.$$

TYPE 2. Suppose the denominator $g(x)$ of the integrand contain linear factors, some of which are repeated. If $(x-a)$ is repeated, say three times, then for the factor $(x-a)^3$ in the denominator, there should be three partial fractions of the form

$$\frac{A}{x-a} + \frac{B}{(x-a)^2} + \frac{C}{(x-a)^3},$$

where A, B, C are contants that can be easily determined as shown below.

EXAMPLE 6. *Evaluate:* $\int \frac{3x^2+5x}{(x-1)(x+1)^2}\,dx$. **[ICWAI June 1980]**

SOLUTION. We can write

$$\frac{3x^2+5x}{(x-1)(x+1)^2} = \frac{A}{x-1} + \frac{B}{x+1} + \frac{C}{(x+1)^2} = \frac{A(x+1)^2 + B(x-1)(x+1) + C(x-1)}{(x-1)(x+1)^2} \quad (1)$$
$$\therefore \quad 3x^2 + 5x \equiv A(x+1)^2 + B(x-1)(x+1) + C(x-1) \quad (2)$$

Substituting $x = 1$, and $x = -1$, we get $8 = A.4$ and $-2 = C \times -2$; $\therefore$ $A = 2$ and $C = 1$.

Equating the coefficients of x^2 from both sides of (2), we get

$$3 = A + B, \quad \text{or,} \quad B = 3 - A = 3 - 2 = 1$$

$\therefore$ From (1), $\frac{3x^2+5x}{(x-1)(x+1)^2} = \frac{2}{x-1} + \frac{1}{x+1} + \frac{1}{(x+1)^2}$.

Hence $\int \frac{(3x^2+5x)\,dx}{(x-1)(x+1)^2} = 2\int \frac{dx}{x-1} + \int \frac{dx}{x+1} + \int \frac{dx}{(x+1)^2} = \mathbf{2\log|x-1| + \log|x+1| - \frac{1}{x+1} + C_1}$.

TYPE 3. Suppose the denominator of the integrand contain non-repeated quadratic factors like $ax^2 + bx + c$. For each such non-repeated quadratic factor, there should be a partial fraction of the form $\frac{Ax+B}{ax^2+bx+c}$, where A and B are constants that can be determined as follows.

EXAMPLE 7. *Evaluate the integral:* $\int \frac{x^2-4x-9}{(x-2)(x^2+9)}\,dx$.

SOLUTION.

$$\text{Let}\quad \frac{x^2-4x-9}{(x-2)(x^2+9)} = \frac{A}{x-2} + \frac{Bx+C}{x^2+9} = \frac{A(x^2+9)+(Bx+C)(x-2)}{(x-2)(x^2+9)}$$

$$\therefore\quad x^2-4x-9 \equiv A(x^2+9)+(Bx+C)(x-2) \qquad (1)$$

Substituting $x = 2$, we get $4-8-9 = A(4+9)$, or, $A = -1$.

Equating the coefficients of x^2 and the constant terms from both sides of (1), we get

$$1 = A+B \quad \text{and} \quad -9 = 9A-2C;$$

$$\text{or,}\quad 1 = -1+B \quad \text{and} \quad -9 = -9-2C; \quad \therefore \quad B = 2 \quad \text{and} \quad C = 0$$

$$\therefore\quad \frac{x^2-4x-9}{(x-2)(x^2+9)} = \frac{-1}{x-2} + \frac{2x}{x^2+9}$$

$$\therefore\quad \int \frac{(x^2-4x-9)\,dx}{(x-2)(x^2+9)} = -\int \frac{1}{x-2}\,dx + \int \frac{2x}{x^2+9}\,dx = -\log|x-2| + \log(x^2+9) + C_1$$

$$= \mathbf{\log\left|\frac{x^2+9}{x-2}\right| + C_1}.$$

EXAMPLE 8. *Evaluate:*

(i) $\int \frac{(2x+5)dx}{x^3+x^2-4x-4}$; **[CA November 1990]** (ii) $\int \frac{dx}{x(x^3+1)}$. **[CA November 1988]**

SOLUTION.

(i) $x^3+x^2-4x-4 = x^2(x+1)-4(x+1) = (x+1)(x^2-4)$, and we can write

$$\frac{2x+5}{x^3+x^2-4x-4} = \frac{2x+5}{(x+1)(x^2-4)} = \frac{A}{x+1} + \frac{Bx+C}{x^2-4} = \frac{A(x^2-4)+(Bx+C)(x+1)}{(x+1)(x^2-4)}$$

$$\therefore\quad 2x+5 \equiv A(x^2-4)+(Bx+C)(x+1) \qquad (1)$$

Substituting $x = -1$, we get $3 = A(1-4)+0 = -3A$; $\therefore$ $A = -1$.

Equating coefficients of x^2 and the constant terms from both sides of (1), we get $0 = A+B$ and $5 = -4A+C$; or, $B = -A = 1$ and $C = 5+4A = 1$.

$$\therefore\quad \frac{2x+5}{x^3+x^2-4x-4} = -\frac{1}{x+1} + \frac{x+1}{x^2-4}$$

$$\therefore\quad \int \frac{(2x+5)\,dx}{x^3+x^2-4x-4} = -\int \frac{dx}{x+1} + \int \frac{x+1}{x^2-4}\,dx$$

$$= -\log|x+1| + \frac{1}{2}\int \frac{2x}{x^2-4} + \int \frac{dx}{x^2-2^2} + C$$

$$= -\log|x+1| + \frac{1}{2}\log|x^2-4| + \frac{1}{2.2}\cdot\log\left|\frac{x-2}{x+2}\right| + C$$

$$= \mathbf{\frac{1}{2}\log|x^2-4| - \log|x+1| + \frac{1}{4}\log\left|\frac{x-2}{x+2}\right| + C}$$

[OTHERWISE. Since $(x+1)^2-(x^2+1)=2x$, by inspection, $\frac{x}{(x^2+1)(x+1)}=\frac{1}{2}\left(\frac{x+1}{x^2+1}-\frac{1}{x+1}\right)$. Sometimes it is difficult to resolve the intergrand into partial fractions by inspection. So the students are advised to adopt the first method.]

(ii) $$\int \frac{dx}{x(x^3+1)}=\int \frac{x^2\,dx}{x^3(x^3+1)}$$ | Put $x^3=z$; then $3x^2\,dx=dz$, or, $x^2\,dx=\frac{1}{3}\,dz$

$$=\int \frac{\frac{1}{3}\,dz}{z(z+1)}=\frac{1}{3}\int \frac{1}{z(z+1)}\,dz.$$

Let $\frac{1}{z(z+1)}=\frac{A}{z}+\frac{B}{z+1}=\frac{A(z+1)+Bz}{z(z+1)}$

$$\therefore \quad 1\equiv A(z+1)+Bz \tag{1}$$

Substituting $z=0,-1$ successively in (1), we get

$1=A(0+1)+B.0$ and $1=A.0+B.(-1)$; $\therefore$ **A = 1** and **B = −1**.

$$\therefore \quad \int \frac{1}{z(z+1)}\,dz=A\int \frac{1}{z}\,dz+B\int \frac{1}{z+1}\,dz=\log|z|-\log|z+1|+C_1.$$

Hence $\int \frac{dx}{x(x^3+1)}=\frac{1}{3}\{\log|x^3|-\log|x^3+1|\}+C=\mathbf{\frac{1}{3}\log\left|\frac{x^3}{x^3+1}\right|+C}$.

10.8. TWO STANDARD INTEGRALS

1. $\int \sqrt{x^2+a^2}\,dx\equiv\frac{x\sqrt{x^2+a^2}}{2}+\frac{a^2}{2}\log|x+\sqrt{x^2+a^2}|+C.$
2. $\int \sqrt{x^2-a^2}\,dx=\frac{x\sqrt{x^2-a^2}}{2}-\frac{a^2}{2}\log|x+\sqrt{x^2-a^2}|+C.$

[Delhi U. B.Com 1981; CA November 1983]

PROOF.

1. Let $I=\int \sqrt{x^2+a^2}\,dx$; then

$$I=\int \sqrt{x^2+a^2}\cdot 1\,dx$$

$$=\sqrt{x^2-a^2}\cdot\int 1.\,dx-\int\left\{\frac{d}{dx}(\sqrt{x^2+a^2}).\int 1.dx\right\}dx \quad \text{[Integrating by parts]}$$

$$=x\sqrt{x^2+a^2}-\int\left(\frac{x}{\sqrt{x^2+a^2}}\cdot x\right)dx=x\sqrt{x^2+a^2}-\int\frac{x^2+a^2-a^2}{\sqrt{x^2+a^2}}\,dx$$

$$=x\sqrt{x^2+a^2}-\int\sqrt{x^2+a^2}\,dx+a^2\cdot\int\frac{dx}{\sqrt{x^2+a^2}}$$

$$=x\sqrt{x^2+a^2}-I+a^2\cdot\log\left|x+\sqrt{x^2+a^2}\right|$$

or, $$2I=x\sqrt{x^2+a^2}+a^2\log\left|x+\sqrt{x^2+a^2}\right|.$$

$$\therefore \quad I=\frac{x\sqrt{x^2+a^2}}{2}+\frac{a^2}{2}\log|x+\sqrt{x^2+a^2}|+C.$$

Hence $\int \sqrt{\mathbf{x^2+a^2}}\,\mathbf{dx} = \frac{\mathbf{x\sqrt{x^2+a^2}}}{\mathbf{2}} + \frac{\mathbf{a^2}}{\mathbf{2}}\,\mathbf{\log|x+\sqrt{x^2+a^2}|+C}$.

2. Let $I = \int \sqrt{x^2-a^2}\,dx = \int \sqrt{x^2-a^2}\cdot 1\,dx$.

Integrating by parts and proceeding as above, we get

$$I = \frac{x\sqrt{x^2-a^2}}{2} - \frac{a^2}{2}\log\left|x+\sqrt{x^2-a^2}\right| + C.$$

EXAMPLE 9. *Evaluate:*

(i) $\int \sqrt{x^2+9}\,dx$; (ii) $\int \sqrt{x^2-4}\,dx$; (iii) $\int \sqrt{x^2+2x+5}\,dx$.

SOLUTION.

(i)
$$\int \sqrt{x^2+9}\,dx = \int \sqrt{x^2+3^2}\,dx = \frac{x\sqrt{x^2+9}}{2} + \frac{3^2}{2}\cdot\log\left|x+\sqrt{x^2+9}\right| + C$$
$$= \frac{x\sqrt{x^2+9}}{2} + \frac{9}{2}\log\left|x+\sqrt{x^2+9}\right| + C$$

(ii)
$$\int \sqrt{x^2-4}\,dx = \int \sqrt{x^2-2^2}\,dx$$
$$= \frac{x\sqrt{x^2-2^2}}{2} - \frac{2^2}{2}\log\left|x+\sqrt{x^2-2^2}\right| + C$$
$$= \frac{x\sqrt{x^2-4}}{2} - 2\log\left|x+\sqrt{x^2-4}\right| + C$$

(iii)
$$\int \sqrt{x^2+2x+5}\,dx = \int \sqrt{x^2+2\cdot x\cdot 1+1^2+4}\,dx = \int \sqrt{(x+1)^2+2^2}\,dx$$
$$= \frac{(x+1)\sqrt{(x+1)^2+2^2}}{2} + \frac{2^2}{2}\log\left|x+1+\sqrt{(x+1)^2+2^2}\right| + C$$
$$= \frac{(x+1)\sqrt{x^2+2x+5}}{2} + 2\log\left|x+1+\sqrt{x^2+2x+5}\right| + C.$$

EXAMPLE 10. *Evaluate:*

(i) $\int \sqrt{34-6x+x^2}\,dx$; (ii) $\int \sqrt{9x^2+9x-18}\,dx$.

SOLUTION.

(i)
$$\int \sqrt{34-6x+x^2}\,dx \qquad \left|\begin{array}{l} 34-6x+x^2 \\ =(x-3)^2+5^2 \end{array}\right.$$
$$= \int \sqrt{(x-2)^2+5^2}\,dx$$
$$= \frac{(x-1)\sqrt{(x-2)^2+5^2}}{2} + \frac{5^2}{2}\log\left|(x-2)+\sqrt{(x-2)^2+5^2}\right| + C$$
$$= \frac{(x-2)\sqrt{34-6x+x^2}}{2} + \frac{25}{2}\cdot\log\left|x-2+\sqrt{34-6x+x^2}\right| + C$$

(ii) $\int \sqrt{9x^2+9x-18}\,dx$ $\quad\Bigg|\quad 9x^2+9x-18 = 9(x^2+x-2) = 9\left\{\left(x+\frac{1}{2}\right)^2-\left(\frac{3}{2}\right)^2\right\}$

$$= \int \sqrt{9\left\{\left(x+\frac{1}{2}\right)^2-\left(\frac{3}{2}\right)^2\right\}}\,dx$$

$$= 3\int \sqrt{\left(x+\frac{1}{2}\right)^2-\left(\frac{3}{2}\right)^2}\,dx$$

$$= 3\left[\frac{\left(x+\frac{1}{2}\right)\sqrt{\left(x+\frac{1}{2}\right)^2-\left(\frac{3}{2}\right)^2}}{2} - \frac{\left(\frac{3}{2}\right)^2}{2}\cdot\log\left|\left(x+\frac{1}{2}\right)+\sqrt{\left(x+\frac{1}{2}\right)^2-\left(\frac{3}{2}\right)^2}\right|\right]+C$$

$$= \mathbf{\frac{3}{2}\left(x+\frac{1}{2}\right)\sqrt{x^2+x-2} - \frac{27}{8}\log\left|x+\frac{1}{2}+\sqrt{x^2+x-2}\right|+C.}$$

Exercise 10 (III)

(Integration by Standard Formulae and Partial Fractions)

A

1. Evaluate each of the following integrals:

(i) $\int \frac{dx}{x^2-4}$; (ii) $\int \frac{dx}{x^2-9}$; (iii) $\int \frac{dx}{16-x^2}$; (iv) $\int \frac{dx}{\sqrt{x^2+4}}$; (v) $\int \frac{dx}{\sqrt{x^2-36}}$

2. Evaluate :

(i) $\int \frac{dx}{\sqrt{x^2+5}}$; (ii) $\int \frac{dx}{\sqrt{x^2-8}}$; (iii) $\int \frac{dx}{x^2-3}$; (iv) $\int \frac{dx}{7-x^2}$.

3. Evaluate the following integrals:

(i) $\int \frac{dx}{x^2+2x-3}$; (ii) $\int \frac{dx}{5+4x-x^2}$; (iii) $\int \frac{dx}{\sqrt{x^2-8x+25}}$.

4. Evaluate:

(i) $\int \frac{dx}{\sqrt{x^2-6x+13}}$; (ii) $\int \frac{dx}{\sqrt{x^2+8x-9}}$.

5. Evaluate:

(i) $\int \frac{dx}{e^x-e^{-x}}$; (ii) $\int \frac{x\,dx}{1-x^4}$; (iii) $\int \frac{dx}{x\sqrt{x}-\sqrt{x}}$.

[HINTS.

(i) $\int \frac{e^x\,dx}{e^x(e^x-e^{-x})} = \int \frac{e^x\,dx}{e^{2x}-1}$; put $e^x = z$; then $e^x\,dx = dz$; etc.

(ii) Put $x^2 = z$; then $2x\,dx = dz$, or, $x\,dx = \frac{1}{2}\,dz$ and $1-x^4 = 1-z^2$; etc.

(iii) Put $\sqrt{x} = z$; then $\frac{1}{2\sqrt{x}}\,dx = dz$, or, $\frac{1}{\sqrt{x}}\,dx = \frac{dz}{2}$ and integral $= \frac{1}{2}\int \frac{dz}{z^2-1}$; etc.]

6. Evaluate:

(i) $\displaystyle\int \frac{e^x dx}{e^{2x}+6e^x+5}$; (ii) $\displaystyle\int \frac{dx}{x\{10+7\log x+(\log x)^2\}}$.

[HINTS. (i) Put $e^x = z$; (ii) Put $\log\,x = z$.]

7. Evaluate: $\int \frac{dx}{(1+x)\sqrt{1-x^2}}$. **[CA May 1993; C.U. B.Com (Hons.) 1994]**

[HINTS. Put $1+x=\frac{1}{z}$; then $dx=-\frac{1}{z^2}\,dz$ and $x=\frac{1}{z}-1=\frac{1-z}{z}$

$$\therefore \quad \int \frac{dx}{(1+x)\sqrt{1-x^2}} = \int \frac{-\frac{1}{z^2}\,dz}{\frac{1}{z}\sqrt{1-\frac{(1-z)^2}{z^2}}} = -\int \frac{dz}{\sqrt{2z-1}} = \text{etc.}]$$

B

1. Integrate the following functions:

(i) $\frac{1}{x(x+1)}$; (ii) $\frac{1}{(x-1)(x-2)}$; (iii) $\frac{2x}{(x-1)(x+3)}$.

2. Evaluate each of the following integrals:

(i) $\int \frac{x}{(x-1)(2x+1)}\,dx$; **[CA November 1976]** (ii) $\int \frac{2x}{(x-1)(2x+1)}\,dx$. **[CA November 1977]**

3. Evaluate:

(i) $\int \frac{x\,dx}{(2x+3)(x-3)}$; **[D.U. B. Com. 1980, 1982]** (ii) $\int \frac{x\,dx}{(x-a)(x-b)}$; **[D.U. B. Com. 1981]**

(iii) $\int \frac{(2-x^2)\,dx}{(x-3)(x-4)^2}$. **[ICWAI December 1979]**

4. Evaluate:

(i) $\int \frac{(3x^2+5x)\,dx}{(x-1)(x+1)^2}$; **[ICWAI June 1980]** (ii) $\int \frac{5x^2-27x+60}{(x-3)^2(x+5)}\,dx$. **[CA May 1983]**

5. Evaluate:

(i) $\int \frac{x}{x^3+x^2-x-1}\,dx$; (ii) $\int \frac{dx}{x(x^4+1)}$; **[CA May 1984]** (iii) $\int \frac{2x^3\,dx}{(x-1)(x-2)(2x+1)}$.

[HINTS. See worked out Example 8.]

6. Evaluate: (i) $\int \frac{e^x\,dx}{(2+e^x)(3+e^x)}$; (ii) $\int \frac{dx}{x\{2(\log x)^2+\log x-1\}}$

[HINTS. See worked out Example 4.]

7. Evaluate:

(i) $\int \sqrt{x^2+4}\,dx$; (ii) $\int \sqrt{x^2-9}\,dx$; (iii) $\int \sqrt{x^2-4x}\,dx$.

8. Evaluate the following integrals:

(i) $\int \sqrt{4x^2-9}\,dx$; (ii) $\int \sqrt{5-2x+x^2}\,dx$; (iii) $\int \sqrt{4x^2-20x+29}\,dx$.

[HINTS. See worked out Example 10.]

Answers

A

(The constant of integration C is to be added to each answer)

1. (i) $\frac{1}{4}\log\left|\frac{x-2}{x+2}\right|$; (ii) $\frac{1}{6}\log\left|\frac{x-3}{x+3}\right|$; (iii) $\frac{1}{8}\log\left|\frac{4+x}{4-x}\right|$; (iv) $\log\left|x+\sqrt{x^2+4}\right|$; (v) $\log\left|x+\sqrt{x^2-36}\right|$. **2.** (i) $\log\left|x+\sqrt{x^2+5}\right|$; (ii) $\log\left|x+\sqrt{x^2-8}\right|$; (iii) $\frac{1}{2\sqrt{3}}\log\left|\frac{x-\sqrt{3}}{x+\sqrt{3}}\right|$; (iv) $\frac{1}{2\sqrt{7}}\log\left|\frac{\sqrt{7}+x}{\sqrt{7}-x}\right|$. **3.** (i) $\frac{1}{4}\log\left|\frac{x-1}{x+3}\right|$; (ii) $\frac{1}{6}\log\left|\frac{1+x}{5-x}\right|$; (iii) $\log\left|(x-4)+\sqrt{x^2-8x+25}\right|$. **4.** (i) $\log\left|(x-3)+\sqrt{x^2-6x+13}\right|$;

(ii) $\log\,|(x+4)+\sqrt{x^2+8x-9}|$. **5.** (i) $\frac{1}{2}\log\left(\frac{e^x-1}{e^x+1}\right)$; (ii) $\frac{1}{4}\log\left|\frac{1+x^2}{1-x^2}\right|$; (iii) $\frac{1}{4}\log\left|\frac{\sqrt{x}-1}{\sqrt{x}+1}\right|$. **6.** (i) $\frac{1}{4}\cdot\log\left(\frac{e^x+1}{e^x+5}\right)$; (ii) $\frac{1}{3}\log\left|\frac{\log\,x+2}{\log\,x+5}\right|$. **7.** $-\sqrt{\frac{1-x}{1+x}}$.

B

1. (i) $\log\left|\frac{x}{x+1}\right|$; (ii) $\log\left|\frac{x-2}{x-1}\right|$; (iii) $\frac{1}{2}\log|x-1|+\frac{3}{2}\log|x+3|$. **2.** (i) $\frac{1}{3}\{\log|x-1|+\frac{1}{2}\log|2x+1|\}$; (ii) $\frac{2}{3}\{\log|x-1|+\frac{1}{2}\log|2x+1|\}$. **3.** (i) $\frac{1}{3}\{\frac{1}{2}\log|2x+3|+\log|x-3|\}$; (ii) $\frac{1}{a-b}\{a\log\,|x-a|-b\log|x-b|\}$; (iii) $-7\log|x-3|+6\log|x-4|+\frac{14}{x-4}$. **4.** (i) $2\log|x-1|+\log|x+1|-\frac{1}{x+1}$; (ii) $5\log|x+5|-\frac{3}{x-3}$. **5.** (i) $\frac{1}{4}\log\left|\frac{x-1}{x+1}\right|-\frac{1}{2(x+1)}$; (ii) $\frac{1}{4}\log\left(\frac{x^4}{x^4+1}\right)$. **6.** (i) $\log\left(\frac{2+e^x}{3+e^x}\right)$; (ii) $\frac{1}{3}\log\left|\frac{2\log\,x-1}{\log\,x+1}\right|$. **7.** (i) $\frac{x\sqrt{x^2+4}}{2}+2\log|x+\sqrt{x^2+4}|$; (ii) $\frac{x\sqrt{x^2-9}}{2}-\frac{9}{2}\log|x+\sqrt{x^2-9}|$; (iii) $\frac{(x-2)\sqrt{x^2-4x}}{2}-2\log|(x-2)+\sqrt{x^2-4x}|$. **8.** (i) $\frac{x}{2}\sqrt{4x^2-9}-\frac{9}{4}\log\left|x+\sqrt{x^2-\frac{9}{4}}\right|$; (ii) $\frac{(x-1)\sqrt{5-2x+x^2}}{2}+2\log|x-1+\sqrt{5-2x+x^2}|$; (iii) $\frac{(2x-5)\sqrt{(4x^2-20x+29)}}{2}+2\log|2x-5+\sqrt{4x^2-20x+29}|$.

CHAPTER 11

DEFINITE INTEGRALS: AREAS AND VOLUMES

11.1. DEFINITE INTEGRALS

We have already defined *integration as the inverse of differentiation.* Now, we shall define *integration as a process of summation or definite integral as the limit of a sum.* We shall also define definite integral as an area.

Integration as the Limit of a Sum

DEFINITION 1. Let $f(x)$ be a *single-valued continuous function* defined in a closed interval $a \leq x \leq b, a$ and b being both finite. Then $f(x)$ is bounded in $[a, b]$. Let us divide the interval $a \leq x \leq b$ into n equal sub-intervals, each of length h, such that

$$a < a+h < a+2h < \cdots < a+(r-1)h < a+rh < \cdots < a+(n-1)h < a+nh = b.$$

Now we form the sum

$$\begin{aligned}
&hf(a) + hf(a+h) + hf(a+2h) + \cdots + hf(a+rh) + \cdots + hf\{a+(n-1)h\} \\
&= h[f(a) + f(a+h) + f(a+2h) + \cdots + f(a+rh) + \cdots + f\{a+(n-1)h\}] \\
&= h\sum_{r=0}^{n-1} f(a+rh), \quad \text{where } a+nh = b, \text{ or, } nh = b-a.
\end{aligned}$$

Then the limit $\lim_{h \to 0} h \sum_{r=0}^{n-1} f(a+rh)$, if it exists, is called the **definite integral** of $f(x)$ w.r.t. x between the limits a and b and we denote it by the symbol $\int_a^b f(x)\, dx$.

Thus $\displaystyle \mathbf{\int_a^b f(x)\, dx = \lim_{h \to 0} h \sum_{r=0}^{n-1} f(a+rh)}$, **where** $\mathbf{nh = b - a}$.

REMARKS 1. Instead of the sum as stated above, we may form the following sum:

$$hf(a+h) + hf(a+2h) + \cdots + hf(a+nh)$$

$$= h\sum_{r=1}^{n} f(a+rh), \quad \text{where } nh = b - a, \text{ and in this case we have}$$

$$\mathbf{\int_a^b f(x)\, dx = \lim_{h \to 0} h \sum_{r=1}^{n} f(a+rh), \quad \text{where } nh = b - a.}$$

REMARKS 2. If we put $a = 0$ and $b = 1$ so that $nh = 1 - 0 = 1$, we obtain

$$\mathbf{\int_0^1 f(x)\, dx = \lim_{h \to 0} h \sum_{r=1}^{n} f(rh), \quad \text{where } nh = 1.}$$

EXAMPLE 1. *Evaluate from first principle* $\int_0^1 x^2 dx$. **[C.U. 1982]**

SOLUTION.

Here $f(x) = x^2, a = 0, b = 1$;

$\therefore \quad f(rh) = (rh)^2 = r^2h^2$, and $nh = b - a = 1 - 0 = 1$.

Using the definition, $\int_0^1 f(x)dx = \lim_{h \to 0} h \sum_{r=1}^{n} f(rh)$, where $nh = 1$, we get

$$\int_0^1 x^2 dx = \lim_{h \to 0} h \sum_{r=1}^{n} (r^2h^2) = \lim_{h \to 0} h[1^2h^2 + 2^2h^2 + \cdots + n^2h^2]$$

$$= \lim_{h \to 0} h \cdot h^2[1^2 + 2^2 + \cdots + n^2]$$

$$= \lim_{h \to 0} h^3 \cdot \frac{n(n+1)(2n+1)}{6} \quad \left[\because \quad 1^2 + 2^2 + \cdots + n^2 = \frac{n(n+1)(2n+1)}{6}\right]$$

$$= \lim_{h \to 0} \frac{nh(nh+h)(2nh+h)}{6} = \lim_{h \to 0} \frac{1 \cdot (1+h)(2.1+h)}{6} \quad [\because \quad nh = 1.]$$

$$= \frac{1 \cdot (1+0)(2+0)}{6} = \frac{2}{6} = \mathbf{\frac{1}{3}}.$$

EXAMPLE 2. *Evaluate by the method of summation:* $\int_1^2 5x dx$ **[C.U. B.Com (Hons.) 1994]**

SOLUTION. Here $f(x) = 5x, a = 1$ and $b = 2$;

$$\therefore \quad f(a+rh) = f(1+rh) = 5(1+rh) \quad \text{and} \quad nh = b - a = 2 - 1 = 1.$$

By the definition of definite integrals, we have

$$\begin{aligned}
\int_1^2 5x\,dx &= \lim_{h\to 0} h \sum_{r=1}^{n} f(a+rh) = \lim_{h\to 0} h \sum_{r=1}^{n} 5(1+rh) \\
&= \lim_{h\to 0} 5h \left[\sum_{r=1}^{n} 1 + h \sum_{r=1}^{n} r\right] = 5 \lim_{h\to 0} h \left[n + h \cdot \frac{n(n+1)}{2}\right] \\
&= 5 \lim_{h\to 0} \left[nh + \frac{nh(nh+h)}{2}\right], \text{ where } nh = 1 \\
&= 5 \lim_{h\to 0} \left[1 + \frac{1\cdot(1+h)}{2}\right] = 5\left[1 + \frac{1\cdot(1+0)}{2}\right] \\
&= 5 \times \frac{3}{2} = \mathbf{\frac{15}{2}}.
\end{aligned}$$

EXAMPLE 3. *Evaluate from the definition the integral* $\int_{-1}^{2} x^3 dx$.

SOLUTION. Here $f(x) = x^3, a = -1$ and $b = 2$;

$$\therefore \quad f(a+rh) = f(-1+rh) = (-1+rh)^3 \text{ and } nh = b - a = 2 - (-1) = 3.$$

$$\begin{aligned}
\therefore \quad \int_{-1}^{2} x^3 dx &= \lim_{h\to 0} h \sum_{r=1}^{n} f(a+rh) = \lim_{h\to 0} h \sum_{r=1}^{n} (-1+rh)^3 \\
&= \lim_{h\to 0} h \sum_{r=1}^{n} (-1 + 3rh - 3h^2r^2 + r^3h^3) \\
&= \lim_{h\to 0} h \left[-\sum_{r=1}^{n} 1 + 3h \sum_{r=1}^{n} r - 3h^2 \sum_{r=1}^{n} r^2 + h^3 \sum_{r=1}^{n} r^3\right] \\
&= \lim_{h\to 0} h \left[-n + 3h \cdot \frac{n(n+1)}{2} - 3h^2 \cdot \frac{n(n+1)(2n+1)}{6} + h^3 \left\{\frac{n(n+1)}{2}\right\}^2\right] \\
&= \lim_{h\to 0} \left[-nh + \frac{3}{2} \cdot nh(nh+h) - \frac{1}{2} \cdot nh(nh+h)(2nh+h) + \left\{\frac{nh(nh+h)}{2}\right\}^2\right] \\
&= \lim_{h\to 0} \left[-3 + \frac{3}{2} \times 3(3+h) - \frac{1}{2} \times 3(3+h)(2\cdot 3+h) + \left\{\frac{3\cdot(3+h)}{2}\right\}^2\right] \\
&= -3 + \frac{3}{2} \times 3(3+0) - \frac{1}{2} \times 3(3+0)(6+0) + \left\{\frac{3\cdot(3+0)}{2}\right\}^2 \\
&= -3 + \frac{27}{2} - \frac{54}{2} + \frac{81}{4} = \frac{-12 + 54 - 108 + 81}{4} = \mathbf{\frac{15}{4}}.
\end{aligned}$$

11.2. DEFINITE INTEGRAL AS AN AREA

Let $y = f(x)$ be a monotone increasing continuous function of x in $a \le x \le b$, a and b being both finite and $b > a$. Let PQ be the continuous curve for $y = f(x)$.

Let AC and BE be the ordinates at the points $x = a$ and $x = b$ respectively. Thus $OA = a$ and $OB = b$ so that $AB = b - a$.

Let us divide AB (i.e., the interval $a \le x \le b$) into n equal parts each of length h so that $nh = b - a$, or, $b = a + nh$.

Let us draw ordinates A_1D_1, $A_2D_2, \cdots$ at the points $x = a + h$, $a + 2h, \cdots$

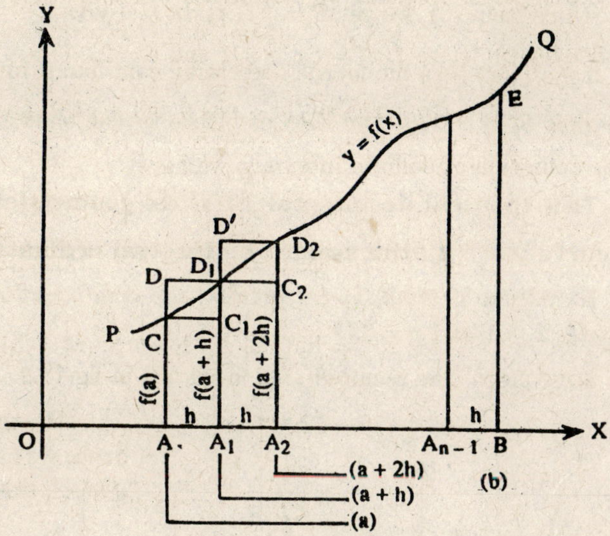

Fig 11.1

Let S denote the area enclosed by the curve $y = f(x)$, the x-axis and the two ordinates $x = a$ and $x = b$. If S_1 be the sum of the inner rectangles $ACC_1A_1, A_1D_1C_2A_2, \cdots$, then clearly

$$S_1 < S \quad \text{[see Fig 11.1] and} \tag{1}$$

$$S_1 = hf(a) + hf(a+h) + \cdots + hf(a + \overline{n-1}\cdot h) = h\sum_{r=0}^{n-1} f(a+rh).$$

$[\because$ area of $ACC_1A_1 = hf(a)$, area of $A_1D_1C_2A_2 = hf(a+h)$, etc.$]$

If S_2 be the sum of the outer rectangles $ADD_1A_1, A_1D'D_2A_2, \cdots$, then

$$S_2 > S \quad \text{[see Fig 11.1] and} \tag{2}$$

$$S_2 = hf(a+h) + hf(a+2h) + \cdots + hf(a+nh) = h\sum_{r=1}^{n} f(a+rh)$$

$$= h\sum_{r=0}^{n-1} f(a+rh) - hf(a) + hf(b) \quad [\because \; f(a+nh) = f(b)]$$

From (1) and (2), we have

$$S_1 < S < S_2. \tag{3}$$

Now let $n \to \infty$ i.e., the no. of sub-divisions of AB increases indefinitely; then the length h of each sub-division $\to 0$, so that $hf(a) \to 0, hf(b) \to 0$ and $S_1 \to \lim\limits_{h\to 0} h\sum\limits_{r=0}^{n-1} f(a+rh) = \int\limits_a^b f(x)\,dx$

and $S_2 \to \lim\limits_{h\to 0} h\sum\limits_{r=0}^{n-1} f(a+rh) = \int\limits_a^b f(x)\,dx \quad [\because \; hf(a) \to 0$ and $hf(b) \to 0]$.

Hence from (3), we get $\mathbf{S} = \int_a^b \mathbf{f(x)\,dx} = \int_a^b \mathbf{y dx}$.

If $y = f(x)$ be a monotone decreasing continuous function of x in $a \leq x \leq b$, then we can first prove that $S_1 > S > S_2$ and then as before we can show that $S = \int_a^b f(x)\,dx$.

Thus the definite integral $\int_a^b f(x)\,dx$ geometrically represents the area bounded by the curve $y = f(x)$, the x-axis and the two ordinates at $x = a$ and $x = b$.

EXAMPLE 4. *Find, by integration, the area bounded by the curve $y = x^2$, the x-axis and the ordinates $x = 1$ and $x = 3$.* **[C.U. B.Com (Hons.) 1982]**

SOLUTION. The required area is shaded in fig 11.2.

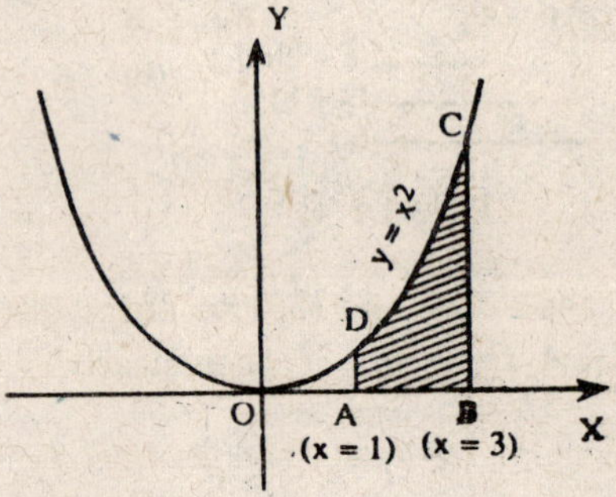

Fig 11.2

By the definition of **definite integral as an area,** we have the required area bounded by the curve $y = x^2$, the x-axis and the ordinates $x = 1$ and $x = 3$.

$$= \int_1^3 y\,dx = \int_1^3 x^2\,dx$$

$$= \left[\frac{x^3}{3}\right]_1^3 = \frac{3^3}{3} - \frac{1^3}{3} = \frac{27}{3} - \frac{1}{3}$$

$$= \frac{26}{3} = \mathbf{8\frac{2}{3}\ \text{sq. units.}}$$

NOTE. Areas under plane curves bounded by x-axis and area between two curves will be discussed later in details.

11.3. FUNDAMENTAL THEOREM OF INTEGRAL CALCULUS—EVALUATION PROCESS OF DEFINITE INTEGRAL

If (i) $\int_a^b f(x)dx$ *exists and* (ii) *there exists a function* $F(x)$ *such that* $F'(x) = f(x)$ *for every* x *in* $a \leq x \leq b$, *then*

$$\int_a^b \mathbf{f(x)\,dx} = \left[\mathbf{F(x)}\right]_a^b = \mathbf{F(b) - F(a)}.$$

The proof of this theorem is beyond the scope of this book.

ILLUSTRATION. *Evaluate* $\int_2^5 x^2dx$ *by using Fundamental Theorem.*

We have $f(x) = x^2$ and $\frac{d}{dx}(\frac{x^3}{3}) = x^2$ so that $F(x) = \frac{x^3}{3}$.

$\therefore \quad \int_2^5 x^2dx = F(5) - F(2) = \frac{5^3}{3} - \frac{2^3}{3} = \frac{117}{3} = \mathbf{39}.$

Thus the *process* is as follows:

First evaluate the indefinite integral $\int x^2 dx$ *and then substitute the upper limit* 5 *and lower limit* 2 *in the indefinite integral and subtract the second value so obtained from the first to get the required value of the definite integral.*

REMARK. The result of the Fundamental Theorem may be written as

$$\int_a^b f(x)\,dx = \int_a^b F'(x)\,dx = \Big[F(x)\Big]_a^b = F(b) - F(a).$$

[We omit the constant of integration as it will be cancelled in the process of finding the value of the definite integral.]

EXAMPLE 5. *Evaluate the following integrals:*

(i) $\int_1^4 (2x+5)\,dx$; (ii) $\int_1^2 \frac{2x}{1+x^2}\,dx$; (iii) $\int_0^4 \sqrt{3x+4}\,dx$.

SOLUTION.

(i) $$\int_1^4 (2x+5)\,dx = \left[2\cdot\frac{x^2}{2} + 5x\right]_1^4 = \Big[x^2 + 5x\Big]_1^4 = (4^2 + 5.4) - (1^2 + 5.1)$$

$$= 36 - 6 = \mathbf{30}.$$

(ii) $$\int_1^2 \frac{2x}{1+x^2}\,dx = \int_2^5 \frac{dz}{z} = \Big[\log_e z\Big]_2^5$$

| Put $1+x^2 = z$; then $2x\,dx = dz$ If $x = 1, z = 2$ and if $x = 2$, then $z = 5$.

$$= \log_e 5 - \log_e 2 = \mathbf{\log_e \frac{5}{2}}.$$

(iii) $$\int_0^4 \sqrt{3x+4}\,dx = \int_4^{16} \sqrt{z}\cdot\frac{1}{3}\,dz$$

| Put $3x+4 = z$; then $3dx = dz$ or, $dx = \frac{1}{3}\,dz$ If $x = 0, z = 4$ and if $x = 4, z = 16$.

$$= \frac{1}{3}\int_4^{16} \sqrt{z}\,dz = \frac{1}{3}\int_4^{16} z^{\frac{1}{2}}\,dz = \frac{1}{3}\left[\frac{2}{3}z^{\frac{3}{2}}\right]_4^{16}$$

$$= \frac{1}{3}\times\frac{2}{3}\left[(16)^{\frac{3}{2}} - (4)^{\frac{3}{2}}\right] = \frac{2}{9}[64-8] = \frac{2}{9}\times 56 = \frac{112}{9}.$$

EXAMPLE 6. *Evaluate each of the following integrals:*

(i) $\int_0^3 \frac{2x+3}{x+1}\,dx$; (ii) $\int_0^1 \frac{(x+1)(x-4)}{\sqrt{x}}\,dx$. **[B.U. 1980]**

SOLUTION.

(i) $$\int_0^3 \frac{2x+3}{x+1}\,dx = \int_0^3 \left(2 + \frac{1}{x+1}\right)dx = \Big[2x + \log(x+1)\Big]_0^3$$

| $x+1)\ 2x+3\ (2$; $2x+2$; 1

$$= (6 + \log 4) - (0 + \log 1) = \mathbf{6 + 2\log_e 2}.$$

(ii) $$\int_0^1 \frac{(x+1)(x-4)}{\sqrt{x}}\,dx = \int_0^1 \frac{(x^2-3x-4)}{\sqrt{x}}\,dx = \int_0^1 (x^{\frac{3}{2}} - 3x^{\frac{1}{2}} - 4x^{-\frac{1}{2}})\,dx$$

$$= \left[\frac{2}{5}x^{\frac{5}{2}} - 3\cdot\frac{2}{3}x^{\frac{3}{2}} - 4.2x^{\frac{1}{2}}\right]_0^1 = \left(\frac{2}{5} - 2 - 8\right) - 0 = -\mathbf{\frac{48}{5}}.$$

EXAMPLE 7. *Evaluate:* (i) $\int_4^6 \frac{dx}{x^2-9}$ **[ICWAI June 19**

(ii) $\int_0^1 \frac{dx}{(1+x)(2+x)}$. **[CA Foundation June 19**

SOLUTION.

(i) $$\int_4^6 \frac{dx}{x^2-3^2} = \frac{1}{2.3}\left[\log\left(\frac{x-3}{x+3}\right)\right]_4^6 = \frac{1}{6}\left(\log\frac{3}{9} - \log\frac{1}{7}\right)$$

$$= \frac{1}{6}\left(\log\frac{1}{3} - \log\frac{1}{7}\right) = \mathbf{\frac{1}{6}\log_e\frac{7}{3}}.$$

(ii) $$\int_0^1 \frac{dx}{(1+x)(2+x)} = \int_0^1 \left(\frac{1}{1+x} - \frac{1}{2+x}\right)dx$$

[Let $$\frac{1}{(1+x)(2+x)} = \frac{A}{1+x} + \frac{B}{2+x} = \frac{A(2+x)+B(1+x)}{(1+x)(2+x)}$$

$$\therefore \quad 1 \equiv A(2+x) + B(1+x).$$

Putting $x=-1, A=1$ and putting $x=-2, B=-1$.]

$$\therefore \quad \int_0^1 \frac{dx}{(1+x)(2+x)} = \Big[\log(1+x) - \log(2+x)\Big]_0^1$$

$$= (\log 2 - \log 3) - (\log 1 - \log 2) = 2\log 2 - \log 3$$

$$= \log 2^2 - \log 3 = \mathbf{\log_e\left(\frac{4}{3}\right)}.$$

EXAMPLE 8. *Evaluate:* $\int_1^e \frac{dt}{t(1+\log t)^2}$ **[ICWAI June 19**

SOLUTION.

$$\int_1^e \frac{dt}{t(1+\log t)^2}$$

Put $1+\log t = z$; then $\frac{1}{t}dt = dz$
If $t=1$, then $z = 1+\log 1 = 1+0 = 1$,
and if $t=e$, then $z = 1+\log e = 1+1 = 2$.

$$= \int_1^e \frac{1}{(1+\log t)^2}\cdot\frac{1}{t}dt$$

$$= \int_1^2 \frac{1}{z^2}dz = \left[-\frac{1}{z}\right]_1^2 = -\left(\frac{1}{2}-1\right) = \mathbf{\frac{1}{2}}.$$

EXAMPLE 9. *Evaluate:* $\int_0^1 t^2 e^t dt$ **[ICWAI June 1992]**

SOLUTION.

$$\begin{aligned}\int t^2 e^t dt &= t^2 \int e^t dt - \int \left\{\frac{d}{dt}(t^2) \cdot \int e^t dt\right\} dt \\ &= t^2 e^t - \int (2t \cdot e^t) dt + C = t^2 e^t - 2\int t e^t dt + C \\ &= t^2 e^t - 2\left[t \int e^t dt - \int \left\{\frac{d}{dt}(t) \cdot \int e^t dt\right\} dt\right] + C \\ &= t^2 e^t - 2\left[t e^t - \int (1 \cdot e^t) dt\right] + C \\ &= t^2 e^t - 2te^t + 2e^t + C = e^t(t^2 - 2t + 2) + C\end{aligned}$$

$$\therefore \quad \int_0^1 t^2 e^t dt = \left[e^t(t^2 - 2t + 2)\right]_0^1 \quad \text{[omitting } C\text{]}$$

$$= e(1 - 2 + 2) - 2e^0 = \mathbf{e - 2}.$$

EXAMPLE 10. *Evaluate* $\int_0^3 \frac{\sqrt{x+1}-1}{\sqrt{x+1}+1}\, dx.$ **[CA May 1989]**

SOLUTION.

$$\int_0^3 \frac{\sqrt{x+1}-1}{\sqrt{x+1}+1} dx = \int_1^2 \frac{z-1}{z+1} \cdot (2z\, dz)$$

Put $x + 1 = z^2$; then $dx = 2z\, dz$.
If $x = 0$, then $z = 1$ and if $x = 3$, then $z = 2$.

$$= 2\int_1^2 \frac{z^2 - z}{z+1} dz = 2\int_1^2 \left(z - 2 + \frac{2}{z+1}\right) dz$$

$$\begin{array}{r|l} z+1) & z^2 - z \;(z - 2 \\ & \underline{z^2 + z} \\ & -2z \\ & \underline{-2z - 2} \\ & 2 \end{array}$$

$$\begin{aligned} &= 2\left[\frac{z^2}{2} - 2z + 2\log(z+1)\right]_1^2 \\ &= 2\left[\left\{\frac{2^2}{2} - 2.2 + 2\log(2+1)\right\} - \left\{\frac{1^2}{2} - 2.1 + 2\log(1+1)\right\}\right] \\ &= 2\left[(2 - 4 + 2\log 3) - \left(\frac{1}{2} - 2 + 2\log 2\right)\right] = 2\left(-\frac{1}{2} + 2\log 3 - 2\log 2\right) \\ &= -1 + 4(\log 3 - \log 2) = \mathbf{4\log\frac{3}{2} - 1}. \end{aligned}$$

EXAMPLE 11. *Show that* $\int_\beta^\alpha \frac{\log u}{u} du = \frac{1}{2}\log(\alpha\beta)\cdot\log\left(\frac{\alpha}{\beta}\right)$. **[ICWAI June 1987; December 1991]**

SOLUTION.

$$\int_\beta^\alpha \frac{\log u}{u}\,du = \int_\beta^\alpha \log u \cdot \frac{1}{u}du$$

Put $\log u = z$; then $\frac{1}{u}du = dz$
If $u=\alpha, z = \log\alpha$ and if $u=\beta$,
then $z=\log\beta$

$$= \int_{\log\beta}^{\log\alpha} z\,dz = \left[\frac{z^2}{2}\right]_{\log\beta}^{\log\alpha} = \frac{1}{2}\left[(\log\alpha)^2 - (\log\beta)^2\right]$$

$$= \frac{1}{2}\left[(\log\alpha+\log\beta)(\log\alpha-\log\beta)\right] = \frac{1}{2}\log(\alpha\beta)\cdot\log\left(\frac{\alpha}{\beta}\right).$$

EXAMPLE 12. *Show that* $\int_8^{15} \frac{du}{(u-3)\sqrt{1+u}} = \frac{1}{2}\log\frac{5}{3}$. **[ICWAI December 1989]**

SOLUTION.

$$\int_8^{15} \frac{du}{(u-3)\sqrt{1+u}} = \int_3^4 \frac{2zdz}{(z^2-1-3)\cdot z}$$

Put $1+u=z^2$; then $du = 2z\,dz$
If $u=8$, then $z^2=9$; $\therefore\ z=3$.
If $u=15$, then $z^2=16$; $\therefore\ z=4$.
Also $u=z^2-1$.

$$= 2\int_3^4 \frac{dz}{z^2-2^2} = 2\cdot\frac{1}{2\cdot 2}\left[\log\frac{z-2}{z+2}\right]_3^4 = \frac{1}{2}\left[\log\frac{2}{6}-\log\frac{1}{5}\right]$$

$$= \frac{1}{2}\log\left(\frac{1}{3}\times\frac{5}{1}\right) = \mathbf{\frac{1}{2}\log\frac{5}{3}}.$$

EXAMPLE 13. *Evalute:* $\int_3^9 \frac{x+7}{(x+2)(x+3)^2}dx$. **[ICWAI December 1988]**

SOLUTION. Let

$$\frac{x+7}{(x+2)(x+3)^2} = \frac{A}{x+2}+\frac{B}{x+3}+\frac{C}{(x+3)^2}$$
$$= \frac{A(x+3)^2+B(x+2)(x+3)+C(x+2)}{(x+2)(x+3)^2}$$

Then

$$x+7 \equiv A(x+3)^2+B(x+2)(x+3)+C(x+2) \tag{1}$$

Putting $x=-2,-3$ successively, we get

$$5 = A \text{ and } 4 = C\times -1 \text{ or, } C=-4.$$

Equating coefficients of x^2 from both sides of (1), we get

$$0 = A+B, \quad \text{or,} \quad B=-A=-5.$$

$$\therefore \quad \frac{x+7}{(x+2)(x+3)^2} = \frac{5}{x+2} - \frac{5}{x+3} - \frac{4}{(x+3)^2}$$

Integrating in $[3, 9]$, we get

$$\int_3^9 \frac{x+7}{(x+2)(x+3)^2}dx = 5\int_3^9 \left(\frac{1}{x+2} - \frac{1}{x+3}\right)dx - 4\int_3^9 \frac{1}{(x+3)^2}dx$$

$$= 5\big[\log(x+2) - \log(x+3)\big]_3^9 - 4\left[-\frac{1}{x+3}\right]_3^9$$

$$= 5\big[(\log 11 - \log 12) - (\log 5 - \log 6)\big] - 4\left[-\frac{1}{12} + \frac{1}{6}\right]$$

$$= 5\left[\log\frac{11}{12} - \log\frac{5}{6}\right] - 4 \times \frac{1}{12}$$

$$= 5\log\left(\frac{11}{12} \times \frac{6}{5}\right) - \frac{1}{3} = \mathbf{5\ log}\left(\frac{\mathbf{11}}{\mathbf{10}}\right) - \frac{\mathbf{1}}{\mathbf{3}}.$$

EXAMPLE 14. *If $f'(u) = u^3 - 3u^2 + 1$ and $f(1) = 2$, find $f(u)$.*

SOLUTION. We have $f'(u) = u^3 - 3u^2 + 1$, where $f'(u) = \frac{d}{du}\{f(u)\}$.

Integrating both sides with respect to u, we get

$$f(u) = \frac{u^4}{4} - 3 \cdot \frac{u^3}{3} + u + C, \quad \text{i.e.,} \quad f(u) = \frac{u^4}{4} - u^3 + u + C \tag{1}$$

where C is an arbitrary constant.

Now given $f(1) = 2$ i.e., $f(u) = 2$ when $u = 1$;

$$\therefore \quad 2 = f(1) = \frac{1^4}{4} - 1^3 + 1 + C = \frac{1}{4} + C, \quad \text{or,} \quad C = 2 - \frac{1}{4} = \frac{7}{4}.$$

Hence from (1), we get $\mathbf{f(u) = \frac{u^4}{4} - u^3 + u + \frac{7}{4}}$.

EXAMPLE 15. *The marginal cost function of a product is given by*

$$\frac{dC}{dx} = 10 - 0.01x + 0.0009x^2.$$

Find the total cost function if the cost of producing 10 *units is* 105. **[CA November 1993]**

SOLUTION. We have $\frac{dC}{dx} = 10 - 0.01x + 0.0009x^2$, where C is the total cost function of x units denoted by $C(x)$.

Integrating both sides w.r.t. 'x', we get

$$C = 10x - 0.01 \times \frac{x^2}{2} + 0.0009 \times \frac{x^3}{3} + k \tag{1}$$

where k is an arbitrary constant.

Now given $C = 105$ when $x = 10$.

$$\therefore \quad 105 = 10 \times 10 - 0.01 \times \frac{(10)^2}{2} + 0.0003 \times (10)^3 + k$$
$$= 100 - 0.5 + 0.3 + k = 100 - 0.2 + k$$
$$\text{or,} \quad k = 5 + 0.2 = 5.2.$$

Hence from (1), the required total cost function is

$$\mathbf{C(x) = 5.2 + 10x - 0.005x^2 + 0.0003x^3}.$$

11.4. SUMMATION OF SERIES WITH THE HELP OF DEFINITE INTEGRALS

We shall use *the definition of the definite integral as the limit of a sum* to evaluate the limits of the sums of some series when the no. of terms $n \to \infty$.

By the definition of definite integral, we have

$$\int_a^b f(x)dx = \lim_{h\to 0} h \sum_{r=1}^{n} f(a+rh), \qquad \left| \begin{array}{l} \text{where } nh = b - a; \\ \text{or,} \quad h = \frac{b-a}{n} \end{array} \right.$$

$$= \lim_{n\to\infty} \frac{b-a}{n} \sum_{r=1}^{n} f\left(a + r \cdot \frac{b-a}{n}\right)$$

$$\text{i.e.,} \quad \lim_{n\to\infty} \frac{b-a}{n} \sum_{r=1}^{n} f\left(a + r.\frac{b-a}{n}\right) = \int_a^b f(x)dx.$$

A special case: If $a = 0$ and $b = 1$, then $nh = b - a = 1 - 0 = 1$,

$$\text{and} \quad \int_0^1 f(x)\,dx = \lim_{h\to 0} h \sum_{r=1}^{n} f(rh), \qquad \left| \begin{array}{l} \text{where } nh = 1, \text{ or, } n = \frac{1}{h} \\ \text{As } h \to 0, n \to \infty. \end{array} \right.$$

$$\text{or,} \quad \lim_{h\to 0} h \sum_{r=1}^{n} f(rh) = \int_0^1 f(x)dx. \tag{1}$$

To write the integral $\int_0^1 f(x)dx$ *from the limit on the left side, we replace* rh *by* x, h *by* dx *and take the lower and upper limits as* 0 *and* 1.

Putting $h = \frac{1}{n}$ on the left side of (1), we get

$$\lim_{n\to\infty} \frac{1}{n} \sum_{r=1}^{n} f\left(\frac{r}{n}\right) = \int_0^1 f(x)\,dx$$

To write the integral on the right side from the limit on the left side, we replace $\frac{r}{n}$ by x, $\frac{1}{n}$ by dx and take the limits as 0 *and* 1.

EXAMPLE 16. *Express the sum* $\lim\limits_{n\to\infty}\left[\frac{1^2}{n^3+1^3}+\frac{2^2}{n^3+2^3}+\cdots+\frac{n^2}{2n^3}\right]$ *as a definite integral and hence find its value.* **[C.U. B.Sc 1984]**

SOLUTION.

$$\lim_{n\to\infty}\left[\frac{1^2}{n^3+1^3}+\frac{2^2}{n^3+2^3}+\cdots+\frac{n^3}{2n^3}\right]=\lim_{n\to\infty}\frac{1}{n^3}\left[\frac{1^2}{1+\frac{1^3}{n^3}}+\frac{2^2}{1+\frac{2^3}{n^3}}+\cdots+\frac{n^2}{1+\frac{n^3}{n^3}}\right]$$

$$=\lim_{n\to\infty}\frac{1}{n}\left[\frac{\frac{1^2}{n^2}}{1+\frac{1^3}{n^3}}+\frac{\frac{2^2}{n^2}}{1+\frac{2^3}{n^3}}+\cdots+\frac{\frac{n^2}{n^2}}{1+\frac{n^3}{n^3}}\right]$$

$$=\lim_{h\to0}h\left[\frac{1^2h^2}{1+1^3h^3}+\frac{2^2h^2}{1+2^3h^3}+\cdots+\frac{n^2h^2}{1+n^3h^3}\right]$$

[where $\frac{1}{n}=h$ or, $nh=1$; as $n\to\infty, h\to0$]

$$=\lim_{h\to0}h\sum_{r=1}^{n}\frac{r^2h^2}{1+r^3h^3}$$

$$=\lim_{h\to0}h\sum_{r=1}^{n}\frac{(rh)^2}{1+(rh)^3}=\int_0^1\frac{x^2}{1+x^3}\,dx$$

Put $1+x^3=z$; then $3x^2dx=dz$ or, $x^2dx=\frac{1}{3}dz$. If $x=0, z=1$ and if $x=1, z=2$.

$$=\int_1^2\frac{\frac{1}{3}dz}{z}=\frac{1}{3}\int_1^2\frac{1}{z}dz$$

$$=\frac{1}{3}\left[\log z\right]_1^2=\frac{1}{3}\left[\log 2-\log 1\right]=\mathbf{\frac{1}{3}\log 2}.$$

EXAMPLE 17. *Evaluate the limit* $\lim\limits_{n\to\infty}\frac{1^p+2^p+\cdots+n^p}{n^{p+1}}$, *where* $p>-1$.

SOLUTION.

$$\lim_{n\to\infty}\frac{1^p+2^p+\cdots+n^p}{n^{p+1}}=\lim_{n\to\infty}\frac{1}{n}\left[\frac{1^p+2^p+\cdots+n^p}{n^p}\right]$$

$$=\lim_{n\to\infty}\frac{1}{n}\left[\left(\frac{1}{n}\right)^p+\left(\frac{2}{n}\right)^p+\cdots+\left(\frac{n}{n}\right)^p\right]$$

$$=\lim_{h\to0}h[(1h)^p+(2h)^p+\cdots+(nh)^p]$$

$\left[\text{where } \frac{1}{n}=h, \text{ or, } nh=1;\ \text{as } n\to\infty, h\to0.\right]$

$$=\lim_{h\to0}h\sum_{r=1}^{n}(rh)^p=\int_0^1x^pdx=\left[\frac{x^{p+1}}{p+1}\right]_0^1$$

$$=\frac{1}{p+1}-0=\mathbf{\frac{1}{p+1}}.$$

EXAMPLE 18. *Prove that* $\lim\limits_{n\to\infty}\left\{\left(1+\frac{1}{n}\right)\left(1+\frac{2}{n}\right)\cdots\left(1+\frac{n}{n}\right)\right\}^{\frac{1}{n}}=\frac{4}{e}$.

SOLUTION. Let $A=\left\{\left(1+\frac{1}{n}\right)\left(1+\frac{2}{n}\right)\cdots\left(1+\frac{n}{n}\right)\right\}^{\frac{1}{n}}$;

$$\text{then} \quad \log A = \frac{1}{n}\left\{\log\left(1+\frac{1}{n}\right)+\log\left(1+\frac{2}{n}\right)+\cdots+\log\left(1+\frac{n}{n}\right)\right\}$$

$$= \frac{1}{n}\sum_{r=1}^{n}\log\left(1+\frac{r}{n}\right);$$

$$\therefore \lim_{n\to\infty} \log A = \lim_{n\to\infty}\frac{1}{n}\sum_{r=1}^{n}\log\left(1+\frac{r}{n}\right)$$

$$= \lim_{h\to 0} h\sum_{r=1}^{n}\log(1+rh) \quad \left[\text{where } \frac{1}{n} = h \text{ or, } nh = 1, \text{ as } n\to\infty, h\to 0.\right]$$

$$= \int_{\circ}^{1}\log(1+x)\,dx$$

$$= \left[\log(1+x)\cdot x\right]_{\circ}^{1} - \int_{\circ}^{1}\left[\frac{d}{dx}\{\log(1+x)\}.\int 1\cdot dx\right]$$

[Using the rule for integration by parts.]

$$= \log 2 - \int_{\circ}^{1}\frac{1}{1+x}\times x\,dx$$

$$= \log 2 - \int_{\circ}^{1}\left(1-\frac{1}{1+x}\right)dx = \log 2 - \left[x-\log(1+x)\right]_{\circ}^{1}$$

$$= \log 2 - [(1-\log 2)-(0-\log 1)]$$

$$= \log 2 - 1 + \log 2 = 2\log 2 - \log e = \log\frac{4}{e}$$

$$\text{or,} \quad \log\lim_{n\to\infty} A = \log\frac{4}{e}; \quad \therefore \lim_{n\to\infty} A = \frac{\mathbf{4}}{\mathbf{e}}.$$

Exercise 11 (I)

(Definite Integrals)

1. Evaluate from definition each of the following integrals:

(i) $\int_{\circ}^{1} 3dx$; (ii) $\int_{\circ}^{1} x\,dx$; (iii) $\int_{\circ}^{1}(2x+3)\,dx$.

2. Evaluate the following integrals from first principle:

(i) $\int_{\circ}^{1} 2x^2dx$; **[C.U. 1991]** (ii) $\int_{\circ}^{1} x^3\,dx$; (iii) $\int_{\circ}^{1}(1+2x+3x^2)dx$. **[C.U. 1992]**

3. Evaluate each of the following integrals by the method of summation:

(i) $\int_a^b x\,dx$; (ii) $\int_1^5 3x dx$; (iii) $\int_2^3 (2x^2+5)dx$.

4. Evaluate by the method of summation and verify the result with the help of the Fundamental Theorem of Integral Calculus:

(i) $\int_0^1 (ax+b)\,dx$; (ii) $\int_a^b e^{kx}\,dx$; (iii) $\int_2^4 e^{3x}dx$.

5. Evaluate the following integrals:

(i) $\int_1^3 (3x^2+2x-5)dx$; (ii) $\int_2^5 \left(e^{2x}+\frac{3}{x}-4\right)dx$;

(iii) $\int_0^1 (2^x+x^2-e^{-x})dx$; (iv) $\int_2^{10} \sqrt{2x+5}dx$.

6. Evaluate each of the following integrals:

(i) $\int_2^3 \frac{2x}{1+x^2}dx$; (ii) $\int_1^2 \frac{(1+x)^2}{x}dx$; (iii) $\int_2^3 \frac{(1-x)^3}{x^2}dx$;

(iv) $\int_1^2 \frac{t^2+2t+5}{t}dt$. **[ICWAI June 1990]**

7. Evaluate

(i) $\int_0^1 \frac{1-x}{1+x}dx$; **[ICWAI June 1993]** (ii) $\int_1^4 \left(\sqrt{x}+\frac{1}{\sqrt{x}}\right)dx$;

(iii) $\int_0^1 x^3\sqrt{1+3x^4}dx$; (iv) $\int_0^{\frac{1}{3}} \sqrt{1-3x}dx$. **[ICWAI December 1993]**

8. Evaluate each of the following:

(i) $\int_1^{e^2} \frac{dx}{x(1+\log x)^2}$; (ii) $\int_0^1 \frac{2xdx}{(x^2+1)^3}$; (iii) $\int_0^1 x\,e^x dx$;

[C.U. 1990, '94; ICWAI December 1983]

(iv) $\int_0^1 \frac{xdx}{(1+x^2)^{\frac{3}{2}}}$; (v) $\int_1^2 x^2\log x\,dx$; (vi) $\int_1^{\sqrt{e}} x\log x\,dx$.

9. Evaluate:

(i) $\int_0^1 \frac{\log(1+x)}{1+x}dx$; **[Kanpur 1989]** (ii) $\int_7^{14} \frac{du}{(u-2)\sqrt{2+u}}$;

(iii) $\int_{C_1}^{C_2} \frac{\log t}{t}dt$; **[ICWAI December 1991]** (iv) $\int_e^{e^2} \frac{dx}{x\log x}$. **[ICWAI June 1988, 89]**

[HINTS. (i) Put $\log(1+x)=z$; (ii) Put $2+u=z^2$; (iii) $\log t = z$.]

10. Evaluate the value of the following integrals:

(i) $\int_2^3 \frac{2x+6}{(x^2+6x-9)^2}dx$; (ii) $\int_0^1 \frac{xdx}{\sqrt{1+x^2}}$; (iii) $\int_0^{\frac{\sqrt{3}}{2}} \frac{xdx}{\sqrt{1-x^2}}$;

(iv) $\int_0^{\log 2} \frac{e^x}{1+e^x}dx$; (v) $\int_4^6 \frac{dx}{x^2-9}$; (vi) $\int_0^1 \frac{dx}{(2+x)(3+x)}$.

11. Evaluate:

(i) $\int_0^3 \frac{x\,dx}{\sqrt{x+1}+\sqrt{5x+1}}$; (ii) $\int_0^1 \frac{3x^2+7x}{(x+1)(x+2)(x+3)}dx$;

(iii) $\int_4^8 \frac{dx}{(x-3)(x+1)^2}$. **[ICWAI June 1985]**

12. Evaluate:

(i) $\int_0^8 \frac{x^{\frac{1}{3}}}{1+x^{\frac{1}{3}}}dx$; (ii) $\int_0^8 \frac{dx}{\sqrt{(x-1)(x-5)}}$;

(iii) $\int_8^{15} \frac{du}{(u-3)\sqrt{1+u}}$. **[ICWAI December 1981; '89]**

[HINTS. (i) Put $x^{\frac{1}{3}} = z$; (ii) Put $x - 1 = z^2$.]

13. Evaluate the following limits:

(i) $\lim_{n\to\infty} \left\{\frac{1}{n+1} + \frac{1}{n+2} + \cdots + \frac{1}{n+n}\right\}$;

(ii) $\lim_{n\to\infty} \left\{\frac{1}{n+m} + \frac{1}{n+2m} + \cdots + \frac{1}{n+mn}\right\}$;

(iii) $\lim_{n\to\infty} \left\{\frac{1}{n^2+1^2} + \frac{2}{n^2+2^2} + \cdots + \frac{n}{n^2+n^2}\right\}$;

(iv) $\lim_{n\to\infty} \left\{\frac{1^2}{n^3+1^3} + \frac{2^2}{n^3+2^3} + \cdots + \frac{n^2}{2n^3}\right\}$;

(v) $\lim_{n\to\infty} \left\{\frac{1^m+2^m+\cdots+n^m}{n^{m+1}}\right\}$;

(vi) $\lim_{n\to\infty} \left\{\frac{1^4+2^4+3^4+\cdots+n^4}{n^5}\right\}$;

(vii) $\lim_{n\to\infty} \left\{\frac{1}{n} + \frac{n^2}{(n+1)^3} + \frac{n^2}{(n+2)^3} + \cdots + \frac{1}{8n}\right\}$;

(viii) $\lim_{n\to\infty} \left[\left(1+\frac{1^2}{n^2}\right)\left(1+\frac{2^2}{n^2}\right)^2 \cdots \left(1+\frac{n^2}{n^2}\right)^n\right]^{\frac{1}{n^2}}$.

14. Evaluate: $\int_2^3 (x+1)(x+2)(x+3)dx$. **[Bombay U. 1981]**

15. Evaluate each of the following:

(i) $\int_e^{e^2} (\log x)^2 dx$; (ii) $\int_0^1 \frac{(x+1)e^x}{(x+2)^2}dx$; (iii) $\int_1^2 \frac{e^x(x^2+1)dx}{(x+1)^2}$;

(iv) $\int_0^1 \frac{2x\,dx}{(x^2+2)(x^2+3)}$; (v) $\int_0^1 \frac{x^3 dx}{(x^4+3)(x^4+4)}$.

16. Find the area bounded by the curve $y = 3x^2$, the x-axis and the ordinates $x = 1$ and $x = 3$.

17. (i) If $f'(x) = 3x^2 + 2$ and $f(0) = 0$, find $f(2)$. **[CA Foundation June 1993]**

(ii) If $f'(x) = \log x$ and $f(1) = 0$, find $f(x)$. **[ICWAI December 1991]**

18. If $F'(x) = e^x\{f(x) + f'(x)\}$, find $F(x)$ where $F(0) = f(0)$. **[ICWAI June 1993]**

Answers

1. (i) 3; (ii) $\frac{1}{2}$; (iii) 4. **2.** (i) $\frac{2}{3}$; (ii) $\frac{1}{4}$; (iii) 3. **3.** (i) $\frac{1}{2}(b^2 - a^2)$; (ii) 36; (iii) $\frac{53}{3}$. **4.** (i) $\frac{1}{2}\ (a + 2b)$; (ii) $\frac{1}{k}(e^{kb} - e^{ka})$; (iii) $\frac{1}{3}e^6(e^6 - 1)$. **5.** (i) 24; (ii) $\frac{1}{2}e^4(e^5 - 1) + 3\log\frac{5}{2} - 12$; (iii) $\frac{1}{\log_e 2} + \frac{1}{e} - \frac{2}{3}$; (iv) $\frac{98}{3}$. **6.** (i) $\log_e 2$; (ii) $\log_e 2 + \frac{7}{2}$; (iii) $3\log_e \frac{2}{3} + \frac{2}{5}$; (iv) $\frac{7}{2} + 5\log 2$. **7.** (i) $2\log 2 - 1$ or $\log\frac{4}{e}$; (ii) $\frac{20}{3}$; (iii) $\frac{7}{18}$; (iv) $\frac{2}{9}$. **8.** (i) $\frac{2}{3}$; (ii) $\frac{3}{8}$; (iii) 1; (iv) $1 - \frac{1}{\sqrt{2}}$; (v) $\frac{8}{3}\log 2 - \frac{7}{9}$; (vi) $\frac{1}{4}$. **9.** (i) $\frac{1}{2}(\log 2)^2$; (ii) $\frac{1}{2}\log\left(\frac{5}{3}\right)$; (iii) $\frac{1}{2}\log(c_1c_2)\log\left(\frac{c_2}{c_1}\right)$. (iv) $\log 2$. **10.** (i) $\frac{11}{126}$; (ii) $\sqrt{2} - 1$; (iii) $\frac{1}{2}$; (iv) $\log\frac{3}{2}$; (v) $\frac{1}{6}\log\frac{7}{3}$; (vi) $\log\left(\frac{9}{8}\right)$. **11.** (i) $\frac{14}{15}$; (ii) $\log\frac{4}{3}$; (iii) $\frac{1}{8}\log\frac{5}{3} - \frac{1}{45}$. **12.** (i) $8 - 3\log 3$; (ii) $2\log\frac{4+\sqrt{15}}{3+\sqrt{8}}$; (iii) $\frac{1}{2}\log\frac{5}{3}$. **13.** (i) $\log 2$; (ii) $\frac{1}{m}\log(1 + m)$; (iii) $\frac{1}{2}\log 2$; (iv) $\frac{1}{3}\log 2$; (v) $\frac{1}{m+1}$; (vi) $\frac{1}{5}$; (vii) $\frac{3}{8}$; (viii) $\frac{4}{e}$. **14.** $\frac{351}{4}$. **15.** (i) $e(2e - 1)$; (ii) $\frac{e}{3} - \frac{1}{2}$; (iii) $\frac{e^2}{3}$; (iv) $\log\frac{9}{8}$; (v) $\frac{1}{4}\log\frac{16}{15}$. **16.** 26 sq. units. **17.** (i) 12; (ii) $x\log x - x + 1$. **18.** $e^x f(x)$.

11.5. PROPERTIES OF DEFINITE INTEGRALS

We shall use *Fundamental Theorem of Integral Calculus* to prove some general properties of Definite Integrals:

1. $\int_a^b f(x)\,dx = \int_a^b f(z)\,dz$.

PROOF. Let $\int f(x)\,dx = F(x)$; then $\int f(z)\,dz = F(z)$.

$$\text{L.H.S.} = \int_a^b f(x)\,dx = \Big[F(x)\Big]_a^b = F(b) - F(a)$$

and $$\text{R.H.S.} = \int_a^b f(z)\,dz = \Big[F(z)\Big]_a^b = F(b) - F(a).$$

Hence L.H.S. = R.H.S.

2. $\int_a^b f(x)\,dx = -\int_b^a f(x)\,dx$.

PROOF. Let $\int f(x)\,dx = F(x)$; then L.H.S. $= \Big[F(x)\Big]_a^b = F(b) - F(a)$

and R.H.S. $= -\Big[F(x)\Big]_b^a = -\{F(a) - F(b)\} = F(b) - F(a)$.

Hence L.H.S. = R.H.S.

3. $\int_a^b f(x)\,dx = \int_a^c f(x)\,dx + \int_c^b f(x)\,dx$, where $a < c < b$.

PROOF. Let $\int f(x)\,dx = F(x)$; then $\int_a^b f(x)\,dx = F(b) - F(a)$

and R.H.S. $= \Big[F(x)\Big]_a^c + \Big[F(x)\Big]_c^b = F(c) - F(a) + F(b) - F(c) = F(b) - F(a)$.

Hence L.H.S. = R.H.S.

4. $\int_0^a f(x)\,dx = \int_0^a f(a - x)\,dx$. **[CA November 1987]**

PROOF.

$$\text{R.H.S.} = \int_0^a f(a-x)\,dx \qquad \left| \begin{array}{l}\text{Put } a-x=z, \text{ then } dx=-dz \\ \text{If } x=0, z=a \text{ and if } x=a, z=0.\end{array}\right.$$

$$= \int_a^0 f(z)\times -dz = -\int_a^0 f(z)\,dz = \int_0^a f(z)\,dz = \int_0^a f(x)\,dx$$

[By property 2 and 1.]

5. (i) $\int_0^{2a} \mathbf{f(x)\,dx} = \int_0^a \mathbf{f(x)\,dx} + \int_0^a \mathbf{f(2a-x)\,dx}$;

(ii) $\int_0^{2a} f(x)\,dx = 2\int_0^a f(x)\,dx$, if $f(2a-x) = f(x)$, **[CA November 1986]**

and $\int_0^{2a} \mathbf{f(x)\,dx = 0}$, if $f(2a-x) = -f(x)$.

PROOF.

(i)

$$\int_0^a f(2a-x)\,dx = \int_{2a}^a f(z)\times -dz \qquad \left| \begin{array}{l}\text{Put } 2a-x=z; \text{ then } dx=-dz. \\ \text{If } x=0, z=2a \text{ and if } x=a, z=a.\end{array}\right.$$

$$= -\int_{2a}^a f(z)\,dz = \int_a^{2a} f(z)\,dz = \int_a^{2a} f(x)\,dx.$$

$$\therefore \text{R.H.S.} = \int_0^a f(x)\,dx + \int_a^{2a} f(x)\,dx = \int_0^{2a} f(x)\,dx \quad \text{[by property 3.]}$$

(ii) If $f(2a-x) = f(x)$, then $\int_0^a f(2a-x)\,dx = \int_0^a f(x)\,dx$.

Hence from (i), $\int_0^{2a} f(x) = \int_0^a f(x)\,dx + \int_0^a f(x)\,dx = 2\int_0^a f(x)\,dx$.

Again if $f(2a-x) = -f(x)$, then $\int_0^a f(2a-x)\,dx = -\int_0^a f(x)\,dx$ and from (i),

$$\int_0^{2a} f(x)\,dx = \int_0^a f(x)\,dx - \int_0^a f(x)\,dx = 0.$$

6. (i) $\int_{-a}^{a} \mathbf{f(x)\,dx} = \int_0^a \mathbf{\{f(x) + f(-x)\}\,dx}$.

(ii) $\int_{-a}^{a} \mathbf{f(x)\,dx = 2}\int_0^a \mathbf{f(x)\,dx}$, if $f(-x) = f(x)$

$\mathbf{= 0}$, if $f(-x) = -f(x)$.

PROOF.

(i) $\int_{-a}^{a} f(x)\,dx = \int_{-a}^{0} f(x)\,dx + \int_0^a f(x)\,dx$ (1)

Put $x = -z$ in the first integral on the R.H.S.; then $dx = -dz$ and if $x = -a, z = a$ and if $x = 0, z = 0$.

$$\therefore \int_{-a}^{0} f(x)\, dx = \int_{a}^{0} f(-z) \times -dz = -\int_{a}^{0} f(-z)\, dz = \int_{0}^{a} f(-z)\, dz = \int_{0}^{a} f(-x)\, dx.$$

$\therefore$ From (1), $\int_{-a}^{a} f(x)\, dx = \int_{0}^{a} f(-x)\, dx + \int_{0}^{a} f(x)\, dx = \int_{0}^{a}\{f(x) + f(-x)\}\, dx.$

(ii) If $f(-x) = f(x)$ i.e., if $f(x)$ is an *even function* of x, then by (i),

$$\int_{-a}^{a} f(x)\, dx = \int_{0}^{a}\{f(x) + f(x)\}\, dx = 2\int_{0}^{a} f(x)\, dx.$$

If $f(-x) = -f(x)$ i.e., if $f(x)$ is an *odd function* of x, then by (i)

$$\int_{-a}^{a} f(x)\, dx = \int_{0}^{a}\{f(x) - f(x)\}\, dx = 0.$$

EXAMPLE 1. *Evaluate:* $\int_{1}^{8} \frac{dx}{(9-x)^{\frac{2}{3}}}$.

SOLUTION.

$$\int_{1}^{8} \frac{dx}{(9-x)^{\frac{2}{3}}} = \int_{8}^{1} \frac{-dz}{z^{\frac{2}{3}}} = -\int_{8}^{1} \frac{dz}{z^{\frac{2}{3}}}$$

Put $9 - x = z$; then $-dx = dz$, or, $dx = -dz$
If $x = 1, z = 8$ and if $x = 8, z = 1$.

$$= \int_{1}^{8} z^{\frac{-2}{3}}\, dz \quad \text{[by Property 2]}$$

$$= \left[\frac{z^{-\frac{2}{3}+1}}{-\frac{2}{3}+1}\right]_{1}^{8} = 3\left[z^{\frac{1}{3}}\right]_{1}^{8} = 3\left[(8)^{\frac{1}{3}} - (1)^{\frac{1}{3}}\right] = 3(2-1) = \mathbf{3}.$$

EXAMPLE 2. *Evaluate* $\int_{0}^{2} \frac{Vx dx}{Vx+\sqrt{2-x}}$. **[ICWAI 1984]**

SOLUTION.

$$I = \int_{0}^{2} \frac{\sqrt{x}\, dx}{\sqrt{x} + \sqrt{2-x}} = \int_{0}^{2} \frac{\sqrt{2-x}}{\sqrt{2-x} + \sqrt{2-(2-x)}}\, dx \quad \text{[By property 4]}$$

$$= \int_{0}^{2} \frac{\sqrt{2-x}}{\sqrt{2-x} + \sqrt{x}}\, dx = \int_{0}^{2} \frac{\sqrt{2-x}}{\sqrt{x} + \sqrt{2-x}}\, dx$$

$$\therefore \quad 2I = I + I = \int_{0}^{2} \frac{\sqrt{x}}{\sqrt{x} + \sqrt{2-x}}\, dx + \int_{0}^{2} \frac{\sqrt{2-x}}{\sqrt{x} + \sqrt{2-x}}\, dx$$

$$= \int_{0}^{2} \frac{\sqrt{x} + \sqrt{2-x}}{\sqrt{x} + \sqrt{2-x}}\, dx = \int_{0}^{2} 1 \cdot dx = \left[x\right]_{0}^{2} = 2 - 0 = 2.$$

Hence $I = 1$ i.e., $\displaystyle\int_0^2 \frac{\sqrt{\mathbf{x}}}{\sqrt{\mathbf{x}}+\sqrt{\mathbf{2-x}}}\,\mathbf{dx} = \mathbf{1}$.

EXAMPLE 3. *Evaluate:* $\int_{-1}^{1} \frac{x^5}{a^6-x^6}dx$, *where* $a > 1$.

SOLUTION. We have $f(x) = \frac{x^5}{a^6-x^6}$, where $a > 1$.

$$\therefore\quad f(-x) = \frac{(-x)^5}{a^6-(-x)^6} = \frac{-x^5}{a^6-x^6} = -f(x).$$

$\therefore$ *$f(x)$ is an odd function of x.*

Hence, by Property 6(ii), we have

$$\int_{-1}^{1} f(x)dx = 0 \quad \text{i.e.,} \quad \int_{-1}^{1} \frac{\mathbf{x^5}}{\mathbf{a^6-x^6}}\mathbf{dx} = \mathbf{0}.$$

EXAMPLE 4. *Evaluate:* $\int_{-2}^{2} \frac{x^4}{a^{10}-x^{10}}\,dx$, *where* $a > 2$.

SOLUTION. We have $f(x) = \frac{x^4}{a^{10}-x^{10}}$, where $a > 2$.

$$\therefore\quad f(-x) = \frac{(-x)^4}{a^{10}-(-x)^{10}} = \frac{x^4}{a^{10}-x^{10}} = f(x).$$

$\therefore$ *$f(x)$ is an even function of x.*

Hence, by Property 6(ii), we have

$$\int_{-2}^{2} \frac{a^4}{a^{10}-x^{10}}dx = 2\int_0^2 \frac{x^4}{a^{10}-x^{10}}dx$$

Put $x^5 = z$; then $5x^4dx = dz$
or, $x^4dx = \frac{1}{5}dz$
If $x = 0, z = 0$ and if $x = 2, z = 32$.

$$= 2\int_0^{32} \frac{\frac{1}{5}dz}{a^{10}-z^2} = \frac{2}{5}\int_0^{32}\frac{dz}{(a^5)^2-z^2}$$

$$= \frac{2}{5}\times\frac{1}{2a^5}\cdot\left[\log\frac{a^5+z}{a^5-z}\right]_0^{32} = \frac{1}{5a^5}\left[\log\frac{a^5+32}{a^5-32} - \log\frac{a^5}{a^5}\right]$$

$$= \frac{\mathbf{1}}{\mathbf{5a^5}}\log\left(\frac{\mathbf{a^5+32}}{\mathbf{a^5-32}}\right) \qquad \left[\because\ \log\frac{a^5}{a^5} = \log 1 = 0.\right]$$

Exercise 11 (II)

(Properties of Definite Integrals)

1. Show that

(i) $\int_0^8 f(8-x)dx = \int_0^8 f(x)dx$; (ii) $\int_0^a f(a-x)dx = \int_0^a f(x)dx$. **[CA November 1987]**

2. Prove that $\int_a^b \frac{dx}{(a+b-x)^{\frac{2}{3}}} = 3(\sqrt[3]{b} - \sqrt[3]{a})$

[HINTS. Put $a + b - x = z$.]

3. Prove that $\int_{a+c}^{b+c} f(x-c)dx = \int_a^b f(x)dx$ and hence show that

$$\int_{a+c}^{b+c} \frac{dx}{(x-c)^3} = \frac{1}{2}\left[\frac{1}{a^2} - \frac{1}{b^2}\right].$$

4. Evaluate the following integrals:

(i) $\int_0^1 \frac{x^2 dx}{x^2+(1-x)^2}$; (ii) $\int_0^3 \frac{\sqrt{x}dx}{\sqrt{x}+\sqrt{3-x}}$; (iii) $\int_0^a \frac{\sqrt[3]{x}dx}{\sqrt[3]{a-x}+\sqrt[3]{x}}$.

5. Evaluate each of the following integrals:

(i) $\int_{-1}^1 x^3(1-x^2)^5 dx$; (ii) $\int_{-2}^2 x\sqrt{4-x^2}dx$.

6. Evaluate the integrals:

(i) $\int_{-2}^2 x^2(1-x^2)dx$; (ii) $\int_{-1}^1 \frac{x^2 dx}{a^6-x^6} (a > 1)$.

7. Evaluate each of the following:

(i) $\int_{-a}^a \frac{x^5 dx}{a^8-x^8}$; (ii) $\int_0^a \frac{x^5 dx}{x^5+(a-x)^5}$; (iii) $\int_{-2}^2 \frac{x^4 dx}{a^{10}-x^{10}} (a > 2)$.

Answers

4. (i) $\frac{1}{2}$; (ii) $\frac{3}{2}$; (iii) $\frac{a}{2}$. **5.** (i) 0; (ii) 0. **6.** (i) $-\frac{112}{5}$; (ii) $\frac{1}{3a^3} \log \frac{a^3+1}{a^3-1}$. **7.** (i) 0; (ii) $\frac{a}{2}$; (iii) $\frac{1}{5a^5} \log \frac{a^5+32}{a^5-32}$.

11.6. AREA UNDER PLANE CURVES

We have already shown in Art. 11.2 that *the definite integral* $\int_a^b f(x)dx$ *geometrically represents the area bounded by the curve* $y = f(x)$, *the* x-*axis and the two ordinates at* $x = a$ *and* $x = b$.

Similarly, we can show that $\int_c^d f(y)dy$ represents the area bounded by the curve $x = f(y)$, the y-axis and two abscissae $y = c$ and $y = d$.

Formulae to calculate area.

I. Area bounded by a plane curve y = f(x), the x-axis and two ordinates x = a and x = b.

$$= \int_a^b f(x)dx = \int_a^b ydx$$

II. Area bounded by a plane curve x = f(y), the *y*-axis and two abscissae y = c and y = d.

$$= \int_c^d f(y)dx = \int_c^d xdy.$$

To find the required area by using the formulae as stated above, we first draw a rough sketch of the given curve, shade the region whose area is to be determined and find the limits of integration. Then we set up a definite integral for the area and finally evaluate the integral. The final result will be in square units.

Illustrative Examples

EXAMPLE 1. *Find the area bounded by the curve $y^2 = 9x$, the x-axis and the ordinates $x = 1$ and $x = 4$.*

[C.U. B.Com (Hons.) 1994]

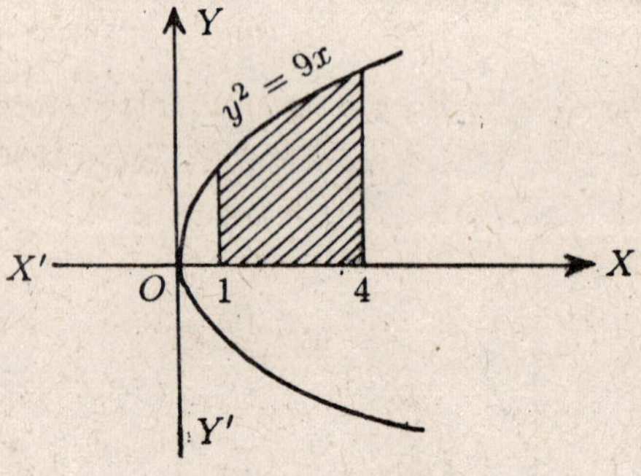

Fig 11.3

SOLUTION. The given curve is

$$y^2 = 9x \tag{1}$$

which is a parabola of the form $y^2 = 4ax$. Parabola (1) passes through the origin $(0, 0)$ and it is symmetrical about the x-axis.

Using (1), we find some points on the parabola as follows:

x	0	1	4	...
y	0	± 3	± 6	...

With these ideas we draw a rough sketch of the parabola. The required area is shaded in fig. 11.3.

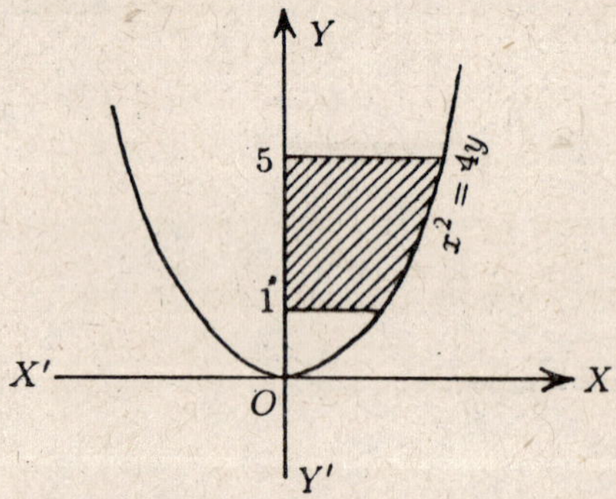

Fig 11.4

Hence the required area

$$= \int_1^4 ydx, \text{ where } y^2 = 9x, \quad \text{or, } y = \sqrt{9x} = 3\sqrt{x}$$

$$= \int_1^4 3\sqrt{x}dx = 3\int_1^4 x^{\frac{1}{2}}dx = 3\left[\frac{x^{\frac{1}{2}+1}}{\frac{1}{2}+1}\right]_1^4 = 3 \times \frac{2}{3}\left[x^{\frac{3}{2}}\right]_1^4$$

$$= 2\left[(4)^{\frac{3}{2}} - (1)^{\frac{3}{2}}\right] = 2(8-1) = \mathbf{14 \text{ sq. units}}.$$

EXAMPLE 2. *Find the area bounded by the parabola $x^2 = 4y$, the y-axis and the abscissae $y = 1$ and $y = 5$.*

SOLUTION. The equation of the parabola is $x^2 = 4y$ (1)

The parabola (1) passes through the origin $(0, 0)$ and it is symmetrical about the y-axis. Using (1), we construct the following table giving some points on the parabola.

x	0	± 2	± 4	± 1	$\cdots$
y	0	1	4	$\frac{1}{4}$	$\cdots$

With these ideas we draw a rough sketch of the parabola (1).

The required area is shaded in fig. 11.4.

Hence the required area

$$= \int_1^5 x\,dy, \quad \text{where } x^2 = 4y, \text{ or, } x = \sqrt{4y} = 2\sqrt{y}$$

$$= \int_1^5 2\sqrt{y}\,dy = 2\int_1^5 y^{\frac{1}{2}}dy = 2\cdot\left[\frac{y^{\frac{1}{2}+1}}{\frac{1}{2}+1}\right]_1^5$$

$$= 2\times\frac{2}{3}\left[y^{\frac{3}{2}}\right]_1^5 = \frac{4}{3}(5^{\frac{3}{2}}-1) = \mathbf{\frac{4}{3}(5\sqrt{5}-1)\ sq.\ units.}$$

EXAMPLE 3. *Find the area enclosed by the curve $y = 4x^3 - 3x^2$, the x-axis and the ordinates $x = 1$ and $x = 2$.* **[ICWAI June 1986]**

SOLUTION. The given curve is

$$y = 4x^3 - 3x^2 \qquad (1)$$

If $x = 0, y = 0$ i.e., the curve passes through the origin $(0,0)$.

Using (1), some points on the curve are tabulated below:

x	0	1	$1\frac{1}{4}$	$1\frac{1}{2}$	$1\frac{3}{4}$	2
y	0	1	$3\frac{1}{8}$	$6\frac{3}{4}$	$12\frac{1}{4}$	20

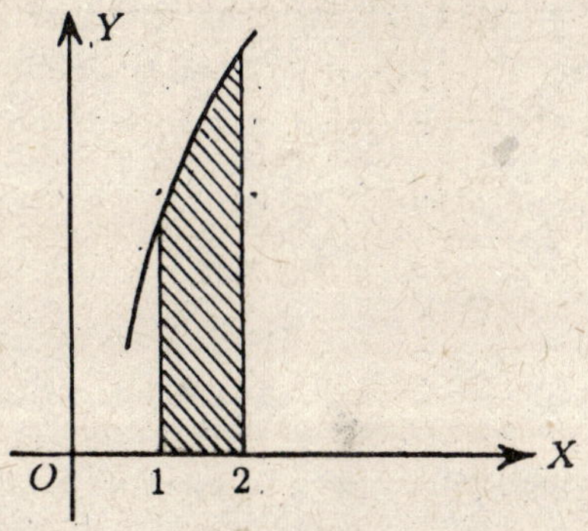

Fig 11.5

A rough sketch of the curve is drawn in fig. 11.5 and the required area is shaded.

Hence, the required area

$$= \int_a^b y dx = \int_1^2 (4x^3 - 3x^2)dx = \left[4\times\frac{x^4}{4} - 3\times\frac{x^3}{3}\right]_1^2 = \left[x^4 - x^3\right]_1^2$$

$$= (2^4 - 2^3) - (1^4 - 1^3) = (16-8) - 0 = \mathbf{8\ sq.\ units.}$$

11.6.1. Area between two curves

Let $y = f(x)$ and $y = g(x)$ be two given curves.

I. Suppose the two given curves intersect at two points, and $x = a, x = b$ are the ordinates of these two points. [See Fig. 11.6 (i)]

$y = f(x)$ represents the curve PQR and $y = g(x)$ represents the curve PSR.

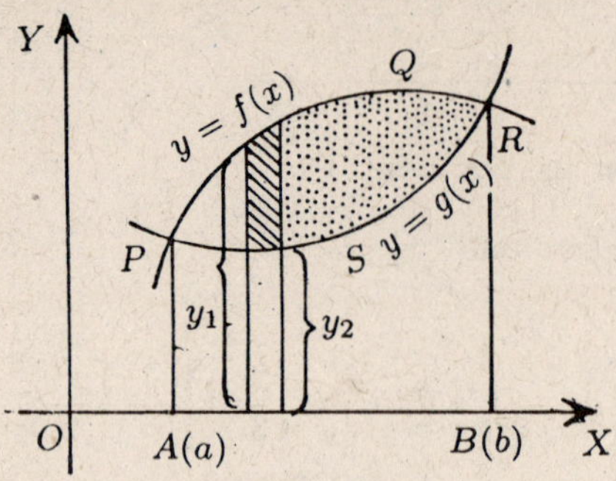

Fig 11.6 (i)

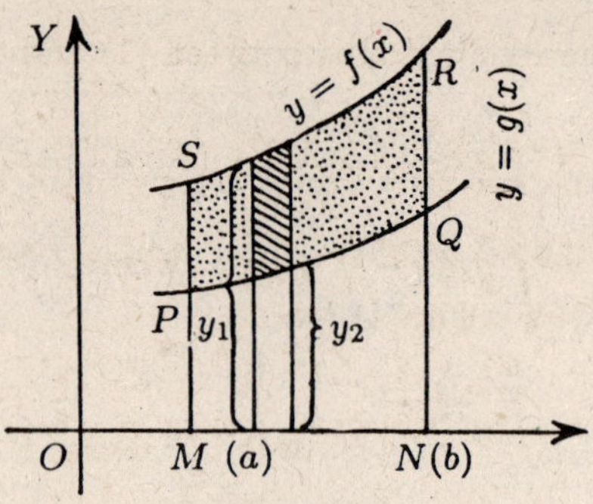

Fig 11.6(ii)

Then the required area between the curves

$$= \text{Area } PSRQP = \text{ Area } APQRB - \text{ Area } APSRB$$
$$= \int_a^b f(x)dx - \int_a^b g(x)dx = \int_a^b \{f(x) - g(x)\}dx = \int_a^b (y_1 - y_2)dx.$$

where $y_1 = f(x)$ and $y_2 = g(x)$ at the same abscissa x.

II. Suppose along with the two curves two ordinates, say $x = a$ and $x = b$ are also given. [See Fig. 11.6 (ii)]. Then the required area bounded by the two given curves $y = f(x)$ and $y = g(x)$ and the two given ordinates $x = a$ and $x = b$.

$$= \text{ Area } PQRSP = \text{Area } MSRN - \text{ Area } MPQN$$
$$= \int_a^b f(x)dx - \int_a^b g(x)dx = \int_a^b \{f(x) - g(x)\}dx = \int_a^b (y_1 - y_2)dx.$$

where $y_1 = f(x)$ and $y_2 = g(x)$ at the same abscissa x.

EXAMPLE 4. *Shade the area bounded by $y^2 = 8x$ and $y = x$ along positive direction of x-axis and use integration to find the area of that part.*

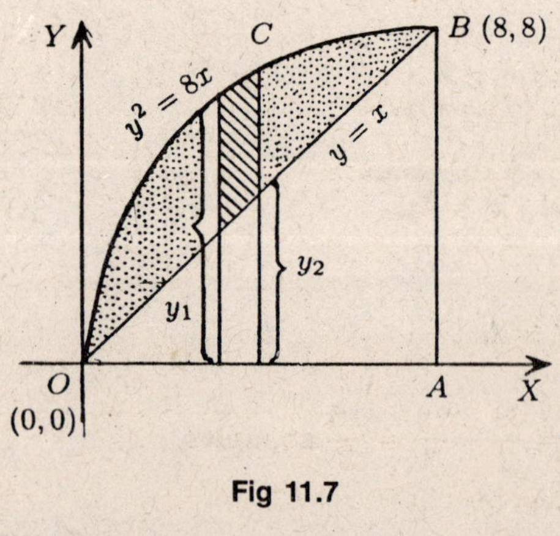

Fig 11.7

SOLUTION. We have

$$y^2 = 8x \tag{1}$$

and

$$y = x \tag{2}$$

Putting $y = x$ in (1), we get $x^2 = 8x$,

or, $x(x - 8) = 0$, $\therefore \; x = 0, 8$.

From (2), $y = 0, 8$.

$\therefore$ (1) and (2) intersect at the points $(0, 0)$ and $(8, 8)$. The area bounded by (1) and (2) has been shaded by dots. The dotted region is the rquired area between (1) and (2) in which x varies from 0 to 8.

Hence the required area between (1) and (2)

$$= (\text{Area } OABCO) - (\text{Area } OAB)$$

$$= \int_0^8 y_1 dx - \int_0^8 y_2 dx, \quad \text{where} \quad y_1^2 = 8x \quad \text{and} \quad y_2 = x$$

$$= \int_0^8 \sqrt{(8x)}\, dx - \int_0^8 x\, dx = \sqrt{8} \int_0^8 x^{\frac{1}{2}} dx - \int_0^8 x\, dx = \sqrt{8}\left[\frac{2}{3} x^{\frac{3}{2}}\right]_0^8 - \left[\frac{x^2}{2}\right]_0^8$$

$$= \frac{2\sqrt{8}}{3}(8\sqrt{8}) - \frac{1}{2} \times 64 = \frac{128}{3} - 32 = \mathbf{\frac{32}{3}} \textbf{ sq. units.}$$

EXAMPLE 5. *Shade the area enclosed by the two parabolas $y^2 = 4x$ and $x^2 = 4y$ and find by integration, the area of the shaded region.* **[C.U. 1986]**

SOLUTION. We have

$$y^2 = 4x \qquad (1)$$

and

$$x^2 = 4y \qquad (2)$$

From (2), $y = \frac{x^2}{4}$. Substituting this value of y in (1), we get

$$\frac{x^4}{16} = 4x, \quad \text{or,} \quad x(x^3 - 64) = 0;$$

$$\therefore \quad x = 0, 4 \quad \text{and from (2),} \quad y = 0, 4.$$

Hence, the two parabolas (1) and (2) intersect at the points $(0, 0)$ and $(4, 4)$.

We have shaded the area enclosed by the two parabolas (1) and (2). In this shaded portion x varies from 0 to 4 i.e., the limits of integration are 0 and 4.

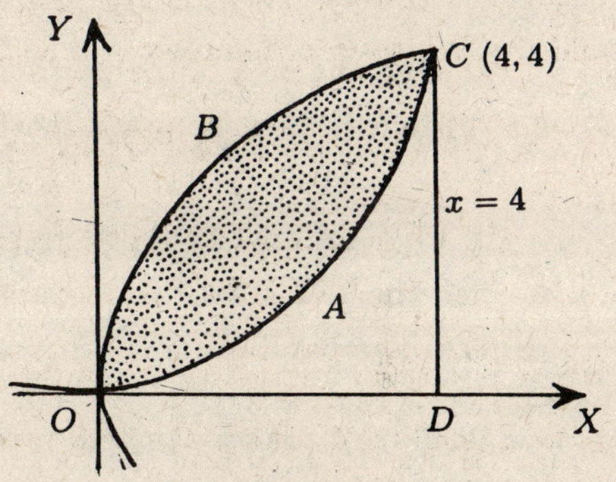

Fig 11.8

Hence, the required area enclosed by (1) and (2)

$$= \text{Area } OACBO = (\text{Area } OBCDO) - (\text{Area } OACDO)$$

$$= \int_0^4 y_1 dx - \int_0^4 y_2 dx, \quad \text{where} \quad y_1^2 = 4x \quad \text{and} \quad x^2 = 4y_2$$

$$= \int_0^4 \sqrt{(4x)} dx - \int_0^4 \frac{x^2}{4} dx = 2 \int_0^4 x^{\frac{1}{2}} dx - \frac{1}{4} \int_0^4 x^2 dx$$

$$= 2 \cdot \frac{2}{3}\left[x^{\frac{3}{2}}\right]_0^4 - \frac{1}{4} \cdot \frac{1}{3}\left[x^3\right]_0^4 = \frac{4}{3} \cdot 8 - \frac{1}{12} \cdot 64 = \frac{32}{3} - \frac{16}{3} = \mathbf{\frac{16}{3}} \textbf{ sq. units.}$$

Exercise 11 (III)

(Area under plane curves)

A

1. What is the geometrical meaning of $\int_a^b f(x)dx$? **[G.U. 1974; '77, '78]**

2. Find by integration the area bounded by the straight lines $y = 3x, y = 0, x = 2$ and $x = 5$. **[Gau. U. 1974; Mag. U. 1981]**

3. Find by integration the area of the triangle formed by the straight lines $3x - 5y = 0, x = 5$ and $y = 0$.

4. (i) Find by integration the area bounded by the curve $y = x^2$, the x-axis and the ordinates $x = 2$ and $x = 4$. **[ICWAI December 1993]**

(ii) Find the area bounded by $2y = x^2, y = 0$ and $x = 3$.

5. Find the area bounded by the parabola $x^2 = 6y$, the y-axis and the abscissae $y = 1$ and $y = 4$.

6. Find the area bounded by the curve $y^2 = 4x$, the x-axis and the ordinates $x = 1$ and $x = 4$. **[C.U. 1983]**

7. (i) Find the area bounded by the parabola $y^2 = 16x$, the x-axis and the ordinate $x = 4$. **[C.U. 1984]**

(ii) Find the area of the portion bounded by $y^2 = 4x$ and $x = 4$.

8. (i) Find the area bounded by the curve $y^2 = 4x$, the x-axis and the ordinate $x = 4$. **[C.U. B.Com (Hons.) 1990]**

(ii) Find the area bounded by the curve $xy = 2$, the x-axis and ordinates $x = 2$ and $x = 10$.

9. Find the area cut off from the parabola $y^2 = 12x$ by its latus rectum. **[ICWAI June 1989]**

[HINTS. The parabola is $\quad y^2 = 12x \quad$ (1)

where $4a = 12$, or, $a = 3$.

$\therefore$ The co-ordinates of the focus S are $(a, 0) = (3, 0)$ and the equation of the latus rectum is $x = 3$.

Hence the required area $= 2\int_0^3 ydx$, where $y^2 = 12x$.]

10. Find the area enclosed by the curve $y = 4x^3 - 3x^2$, the x-axis and the ordinates at $x = 1$ and $x = 2$. **[ICWAI June 1986]**

11. A plane area is bounded by the curve $y = x(5 - x)$ and the x-axis. Find its area.

12. (i) Find the area bounded by $y = 3(x - 1)(5 - x)$ and the x-axis. **[C.U. 1988]**

(ii) Draw a rough sketch of the curve $3y = (2x + 1)(x - 2)$ and find the area bounded by the curve and the axis of x.

13. Find the area bounded by the curve $x^2 = 4y$ and the line $y = x$. **[ICWAI December 1986, June 1990]**

14. Find the area of the plane portion bounded by $y^2 = 16x$ and $y = x$.

15. Find the area included between $y^2 = 9x$ and $y = x$. **[C.U. 1986]**

16. Find the area enclosed by the curves $y = 2x$ and $y = x^2$. **[G.U. 1976]**

17. Find the area bounded by the parabolas $y^2 = 4x$ and $x^2 = 4y$. **[C.U. B.Com (Hons.) 1987]**

18. Find the area of the region common to the curves $y^2 = 2x$ and $x^2 = 2y$.

19. (i) Shade the area enclosed by the parabolas $y^2 = 8x$ and $x^2 = y$ and use the method of integration to find the area so enclosed.

(ii) Find the area between the parabolas $y^2 = 4ax$ and $x^2 = 4ay$.

20. Find the area of the region bounded by the curves $6y = x^2$ and $6x = y^2$.

[ICWAI June 1993]

Answers

2. 20 sq. units. **3.** 7.5 sq. units. **4.** (i) $\frac{56}{3}$ sq. units; (ii) 4.5. **5.** $\frac{14\sqrt{6}}{3}$ sq. units. **6.** $\frac{28}{3}$ sq. units. **7.** (i) $\frac{64}{3}$ sq. units; (ii) $\frac{64}{3}$ sq. units. **8.** (i) $\frac{32}{3}$ sq. units. (ii) $2\log 5$ sq. units. **9.** 24 sq. units. **10.** 8 sq. units. **11.** $\frac{125}{6}$ sq. units. **12.** (i) 33 sq. units; (ii) $\frac{125}{72}$ sq. units. **13.** $\frac{8}{3}$ sq. units. **14.** $42\frac{2}{3}$ sq. units. **15.** $\frac{27}{2}$ sq. units. **16.** $\frac{4}{3}$ sq. units. **17.** $\frac{16}{3}$ sq. units. **18.** $\frac{4}{3}$ sq. units. **19.** (i) $\frac{8}{3}$ sq. units; (ii) $\frac{16a^2}{3}$ sq. units. **20.** 12 sq. units.

11.7. VOLUME OF A SOLID OF REVOLUTION

To find the volume of a solid formed by the revolution of an area bounded by the curve $y = f(x)$, the x-axis and the ordinates $x = a, x = b$ about the x-axis.

Let the equation $y = f(x)$ represent the curve CD between the ordinates $x = a$ and $x = b$. Let the curve CD be rotated about the x-axis OX so as to form a solid of revolution. This solid can be considered to be composed of an infinite number of elementary circular slices made by planes perpendicular to OX. Let $P(x, y)$ be any point on the curve $y = f(x)$ and $P'(x + \Delta x, y + \Delta y)$ be a neighbouring point on it and let $PQ, P'Q'$ be the corresponding ordinates. If Δx be the thickness of the elementary slice corresponding to P and P', then its volume $= \pi y^2 \cdot \Delta x$.

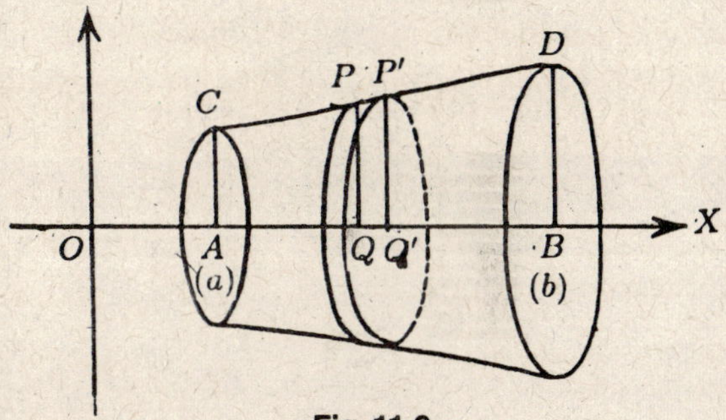

Fig 11.9

Hence, the *required volume of the solid of revolution*

$$= \lim_{\Delta x \to 0} \sum \pi y^2 \cdot \Delta x = \int_a^b \pi y^2 dx = \pi \int_a^b y^2 dx,$$

and the final result will be in the *cubic units*.

EXAMPLE 1. *Find the volume of a sphere of radius a.*

SOLUTION. A sphere is a solid of revolution *generated* by rotating a semi-circular area about its bounding diameter.

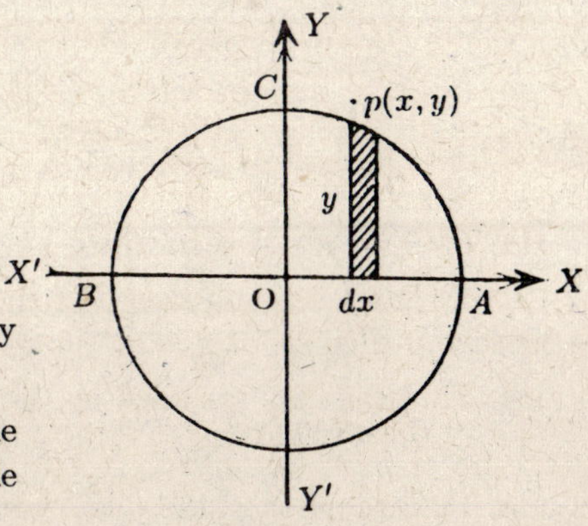

Fig 11.10

With reference to the centre O of the semi-circle as the origin, its diameter BA as the x-axis, the equation of the circle is

$$x^2 + y^2 = a^2 \quad \text{or,} \quad y^2 = a^2 - x^2.$$

The required volume of the sphere

$$= \int_{-a}^{a} \pi y^2 dx = \pi \int_{-a}^{a} y^2 dx = \pi \int_{-a}^{a} (a^2 - x^2) dx$$

$$= 2\pi \int_{0}^{a} (a^2 - x^2) dx \quad [\because \quad (a^2 - x^2) \quad \text{is an even function of } x.]$$

$$= 2\pi \left[a^2 x - \frac{x^3}{3} \right]_0^a = 2\pi \left[\left(a^3 - \frac{a^3}{3} \right) - 0 \right] = 2\pi \times \frac{2a^3}{3}$$

$$= \frac{4\pi a^3}{3} \text{ cubic units.}$$

EXAMPLE 2. *Find the volume of the solid of revolution formed by revolving the area enclosed between $y^2 = -x^2 + 4x$, the x-axis and the ordinates $x = 1$ and $x = 3$.*

SOLUTION. We have $y^2 = -x^2 + 4x = 4 - (x^2 - 4x + 4) = 4 - (x - 2)^2$, or, $(x - 2)^2 + y^2 = 2^2$, which is a circle of radius 2 with its centre at the point $(2, 0)$.

To find the required volume, we have to rotate the dotted area between the ordinates $x = 1$ and $x = 3$ about the x-axis.

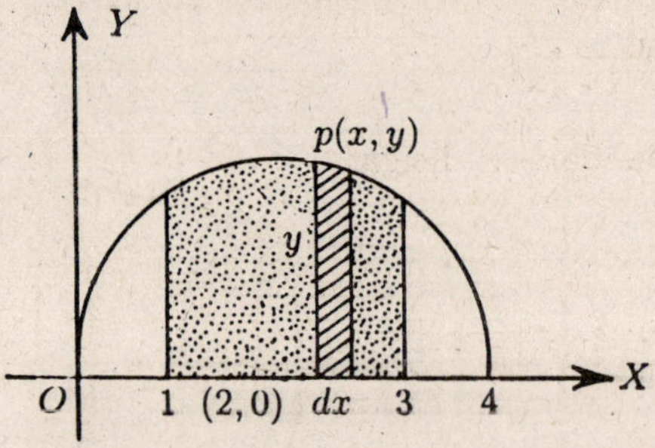

Fig 11.11

Hence, the required volume of the solid of revolution

$$= \int_{1}^{3} \pi y^2 dx = \pi \int_{1}^{3} (-x^2 + 4x) dx$$

$$= \pi \left[-\frac{x^3}{3} + 4 \cdot \frac{x^2}{2} \right]_1^3$$

$$= \pi \left[(-9 + 18) - \left(-\frac{1}{3} + 2 \right) \right] = \pi \left(7 + \frac{1}{3} \right)$$

$$= \frac{22\pi}{3}$$

EXAMPLE 3. *Find the volume of the paraboloid of revolution formed by revolving the parabola $y^2 = 8x$ about the x-axis from $x = 0$ to $x = 6$.*

SOLUTION. The equation of the parabola is $y^2 = 8x$.

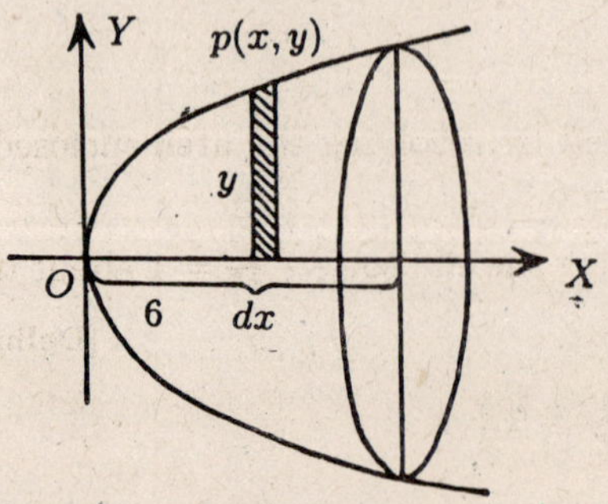

Fig 11.12

The paraboloid is formed by the rotation of the area enclosed between the parabola $y^2 = 8x$, the x-axis and the ordinates $x = 0, x = 6$.

Hence the required volume

$$= \int_{0}^{6} \pi y^2 dx = \pi \int_{0}^{6} 8x dx$$

$$= 8\pi \int_{0}^{6} x dx = 8\pi \left[\frac{x^2}{2} \right]_0^6 = 8\pi \times \frac{1}{2} [6^2 - 0^2]$$

$$= 4\pi \times 36 = 144\pi \text{ cubic units.}$$

EXAMPLE 4. *Find the volume of the right circular cone obtained by revolving a right-angled triangle about a side which is not the hypotenuse.*

SOLUTION. Let a be the radius of the base of a right circular cone of hight h. If α be the semi-vertical angle of the cone, $P(x, y)$ be any point on the cone, and PN perpendicular to the axis OX, then

$$\frac{PN}{ON} = \tan\alpha \quad \text{or,} \quad \frac{y}{x} = \tan\alpha = \frac{a}{h},$$

or, $y = \frac{a}{h}x$.

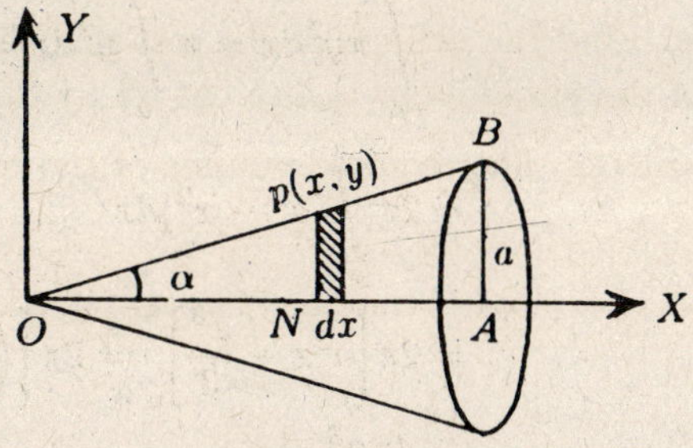

Fig 11.13

The right circular cone is formed by revolving the right-angled ΔOAB enclosed by the line $OB : y = \frac{a}{h}x$, the x-axis and the ordinate $x = h$.

Hence, the required volume of the right circular cone

$$= \int_0^h \pi y^2 dx = \pi \int_0^h \left(\frac{a}{h}x\right)^2 dx = \frac{\pi a^2}{h^2} \int_0^h x^2 dx$$

$$= \frac{\pi a^2}{h^2}\left[\frac{x^3}{3}\right]_0^h = \frac{\pi a^2}{h^2}\left[\frac{h^3}{3} - 0\right] = \frac{\pi a^2}{h^2} \times \frac{h^3}{3}$$

$$= \frac{1}{3}\pi a^2 h = \frac{1}{3} \times \text{(area of the box)} \times \text{height.}$$

Exercise 11 (IV)

(Volumes of Solids of Revolution)

1. (i) Find the volume of a sphere of radius 3 cms.

(ii) Show that the volume of a hemisphere of radius r is $\frac{2}{3}\pi r^3$.

2. Show that the volume of the paraboloid of revolution formed by rotating the area enclosed by $y^2 = 4ax$, the x-axis and the ordinates $x = 0$ and $x = h$ is $2\pi ah^2$.

[HINTS. Required volume $\int_0^h \pi y^2 dx$, where $y^2 = 4ax$.]

3. Find the volume of the solid of revolution formed by revolving the area enclosed between $y^2 = 8x - x^2$, the x-axis and the ordinates $x = 2$ and $x = 6$.

4. Find the volume of the solid generated by revolving the ellipse $\frac{x^2}{a^2} + \frac{y^2}{b^2} = 1$ about the x-axis.

[Delhi U. 1989]

[HINTS. Required volume $= \int_{-a}^{a} \pi y^2 dx$ where $\frac{x^2}{a^2} + \frac{y^2}{b^2} = 1$.]

5. Find the volume of the solid of revolution formed by rotating the area enclosed by $\frac{x^2}{16} + \frac{y^2}{9} = 1$, the x-axis and the ordinates $x = 2$ and $x = 3$ about the x-axis.

[HINTS. The required volume $= \int_2^3 \pi y^2 dx$ where $\frac{y^2}{9} = 1 - \frac{x^2}{16}$.]

6. Find the volume of the reel-shaped solid formed by the rovolution about the y-axis, of the part of the parabola $y^2 = 4ax$ cut off by the latus rectum. **[Ranchi U. 1986]**

[HINTS. The required volume of the reel-shaped solid

$$= \int_{-2a}^{2a} \pi x^2 dy = \pi \int_{-2a}^{2a} \left(\frac{y^2}{4a}\right)^2 dy = \frac{2\pi}{16a^2} \int_{o}^{2a} y^4 dy.]$$

Answers

1. (i) 36π cubic cms. **3.** $\frac{176\pi}{3}$ cubic units. **4.** $\frac{4}{3}\pi ab^2$ cubic units. **5.** $\frac{87\pi}{16}$ cubic units. **6.** $\frac{4\pi a^3}{5}$ cubic units.

CHAPTER 12

OPTIMISATION OF FUNCTIONS UNDER CONSTRAINTS: LINEAR PROGRAMMING : SIMPLEX METHOD

12.1. INTRODUCTION : INEQUALITIES

If a is any *real number,* then a is either positive or *negative* or *zero.* When a is *positive,* we write $a > 0$ which is read as 'a is greater than zero'. When a is *negative,* we write $a < 0$ which is read as 'a is less than zero'. If a is *zero,* we write $a = 0$ and in this case a is neither *positive* nor *negative.*

If $a \neq b$ (i.e., a is not equal to b), then either a is greater than b or a is less than b. (i) *a is said to be greater than b when $a - b$ is positive* and (ii) *a is said to be less than b when $a - b$ is negative.* We write these two statements as follows:

(i) $a > b$ when $a - b > 0$, and (ii) $a < b$ when $a - b < 0$.

ILLUSTRATION.

(i) $3 > 2$, because $3 - 2 = 1 > 0$;

(ii) $-2 > -3$, because $-2 - (-3) = -2 + 3 = 1 > 0$;

(iii) $0 > -1$, because $0 - (-1) = 1 > 0$.

If $a \not< b$ (i.e., a is not less than b), then either $a > b$ or $a = b$. The two relations $a > b$ and $a = b$ can be written together as $a \geq b$, where the symbol '$\geq$' means 'greater than or equal to'. Similarly if $a \not> b$ (i.e., a is not greater than b), then can write $a \leq b$, where the symbol '$\leq$' means 'less than or equal to'.

The symbols '$>$', '$<$', '$\geq$', '$\leq$' are called *the signs of inequalities.*

EXAMPLE 1.

(i) *If $a > 0$, then show that $-a < 0$;* (ii) *If $a > b$, then prove that $-a < -b$.*

SOLUTION.

(i) Since $a > 0$, a *is positive;* $-a$ is *negative.* Hence $-\mathbf{a} < \mathbf{0}$.

(ii) Since $a > b, a - b$ is *positive*; $\therefore$ $b - a$ is *negative*. Now $-a - (-b) = -a + b = b - a$ which is *negative*. Hence $-\mathbf{a} < -\mathbf{b}$.

EXAMPLE 2. *If a, b are both positive real numbers and $a > b$, then prove that $\frac{1}{a} < \frac{1}{b}$.*

SOLUTION. Since $a > b$; $\therefore$ $b < a$ and $b - a$ is *negative*. Now $\frac{1}{a} - \frac{1}{b} = \frac{b-a}{ab}$ which is *negative*, since a, b are both positive and $b - a$ is *negative*. Hence $\frac{1}{\mathbf{a}} < \frac{1}{\mathbf{b}}$.

Linear Inequalities (or Inequations) in Two Variables

Suppose x and y are two variables (or unknowns) *such that their sum is less than* 20; then we can write $x + y < 20$ which is an **inequality** or **inequation** in two variables (or unknowns) x and y of the *first degree*. It is called a **linear inequality** or **inequation** *in two variables x and y*. If x and y are two variables such that *their sum is not greater than* 20, we write $x + y \leq 20$ which is also a *linear inequation in two variables x and y*.

Similarly, if two variables x and y be such that their sum is (i) *greater than* 10, (ii) *not less than* 10, then in case (i), we write $x + y > 10$ and in case (ii), $x + y \geq 10$. Both $x + y > 10$ and $x + y \geq 10$ are also *linear inequations in two variables x and y*.

In general, a *linear inequation* in two variables x and y is of the form:

$ax + by + c < 0$ or $ax + by + c > 0$ or $ax + by + c \leq 0$ or $ax + by + c \geq 0$.

Linear inequations play a very important role in *Linear Programming*. In *Linear Programming*, linear inequations are called *linear constraints* which restrict our freedom of choice of the values of the variables x and y.

12.2. GRAPHS OF LINEAR INEQUATIONS—SOLUTION SETS

Graphs of the Inequalities $x > 3$ and $x \geq 3$

We know that the graph of $x = 3$ is a straight line , say $\overleftrightarrow{AB}$, parallel to y-axis at a distance 3 from it i.e., the x-coordinate of any point on this graph is 3.

Now to draw the graph of the inequality $x > 3$, we see that the line $x = 3$ i.e., $\overleftrightarrow{AB}$ divides the plane (Euclidean plane) into two parts, one lying on the right side of $\overleftrightarrow{AB}$ and the other on the left side of it. The x-coordinate of any point lying in the region on the right side of $\overleftrightarrow{AB}$ is greater than 3 and no point of this region lie on $\overleftrightarrow{AB}$.

Since for all points on the plane region lying on the right side of $\overleftrightarrow{AB}$, we have $x > 3$, *this plane region* (shown in Fig 12.1) *extended to the right of $\overleftrightarrow{AB}$ (no point of this region lying on $\overleftrightarrow{AB}$) is the graph of the inequality* $x > 3$. The graph is called the *solution set* of the inequality $x > 3$.

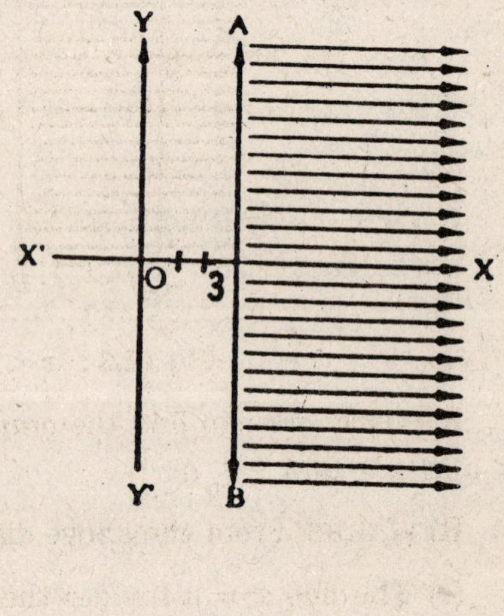

Fig 12.1

To draw the graph of the inequality $x \geq 3$, we see that it consists of $x > 3$ and $x = 3$. The equality $x = 3$ is true for all points lying on the line $\overleftrightarrow{AB}$. Thus all points lying on the line $\overleftrightarrow{AB}$ and to the right of $\overleftrightarrow{AB}$ satisfy the inequality $x \geq 3$.

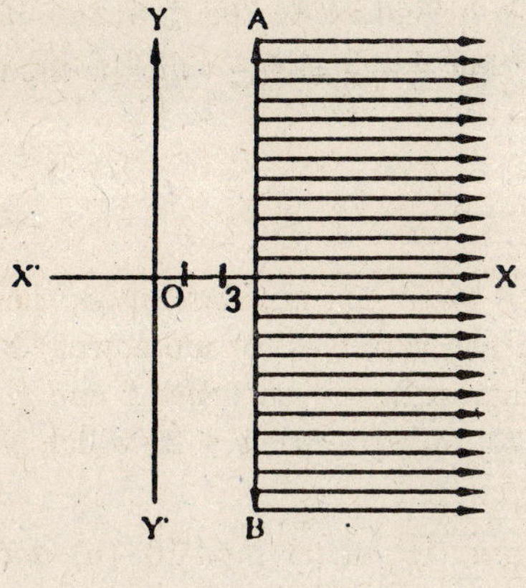

Fig 12.2 : $x \geq 3$

Hence *the plane region* (shown in Fig. 12.2) *extended from* $\overleftrightarrow{AB}$ *to the right of it is the graph of the inequality* $x \geq 3$ *and the* region is called the *solution set* of $x \geq 3$.

The graph (or the solution set) of the inequation $x > 3$ (or $x \geq 3$) may also be obtained as follows:

We see that any straight line not passing through the origin (0, 0) divides the plane (Euclidean plane) into two regions of which the region containing the origin is called the *origin side* and the other region not containing the origin is called the *non-origin side* of the line.

Clearly, the point (0, 0) does not satisfy the inequality $x > 3$ (or $x \geq 3$), since $0 < 3$. This indicates that the *non-origin side of the line* $x = 3$ *excluding the points lying on the line is the graph* (or *solution set*) *of the inequality* $x > 3$ *and the non-origin side of the line* $x = 3$ *including the points lying on the line is the graph* (or *solution set*) *of the inequality* $x \geq 3$.

Similarly, *the graph* (or *solution set*) *of the inequality* $x < 3$ *is the plane region on the left side of* $\overleftrightarrow{AB}$ *excluding the points lying on* $\overleftrightarrow{AB}$ *which is the origin side of the line* $\overleftrightarrow{AB}$. *The graph* (or *solution set*) *of the inequality* $x \leq 3$ *is the plane region* (shown in Fig. 12.4) *extended from* $\overleftrightarrow{AB}$ *to the left side of it which is the origin side of the line* $x = 3$ *including the points lying on the line.*

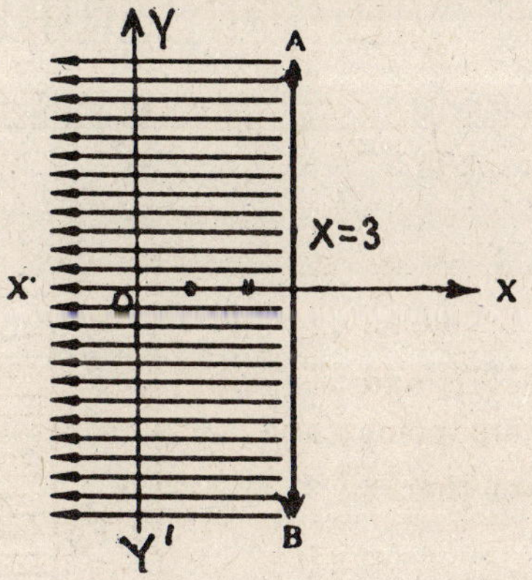

Fig 12.3 : $x < 3$

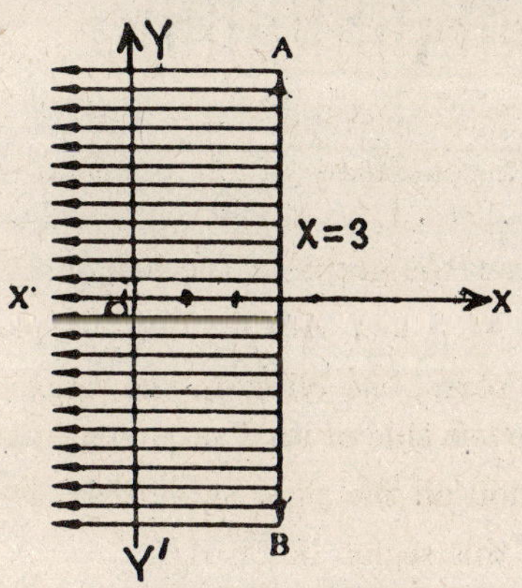

Fig 12.4 : $x \leq 3$

Similarly, we can find the *graph* (or *solution set*) of any other *inequation* of the form $x > a$ or $x < a$ or $x \geq a$ or $x \leq a$.

REMARKS. From the above discussion it follows that

(i) The line $x = a$ divides the Euclidean plane into two regions of which one region lying on the right side of the line is the graph (or solution set) of the inequation $x > a$ and the other lying on the left side of it is the graph (or solution set) of $x < a$, the points on the line being the graph (or solution set) of the line $x = a$.

(ii) The solution set or graph of the inequation $x > 0$ is the *half-plane* on the right side of the y-axis ($x = 0$) and the graph (or solution set) of the inequality (or inequation) $x < 0$ is the *other half-plane* on the left side of the y-axis.

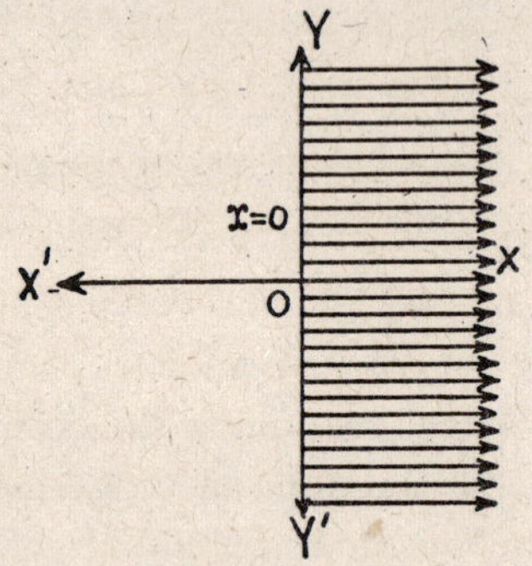

Fig 12.5 : $x \geq 0$

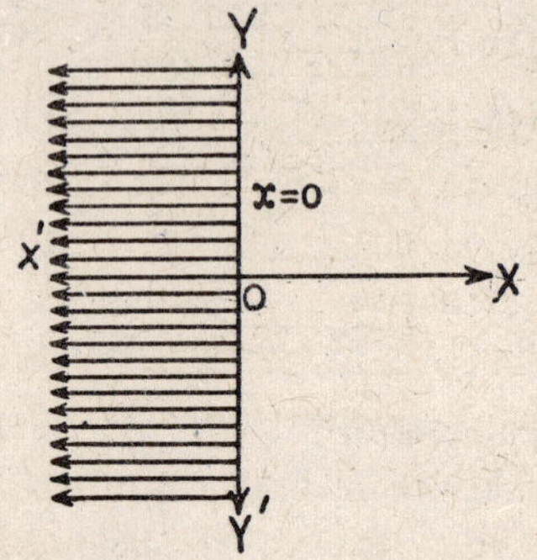

Fig 12.6 : $x \leq 0$

(iii) The line $y = b$ divides the plane into two regions of which one region lying above the line $y = b$ is the solution set or graph of the inequality $y > b$ and the other lying below the line $y = b$ is the graph (or solution set) of the inequality $y < b$.

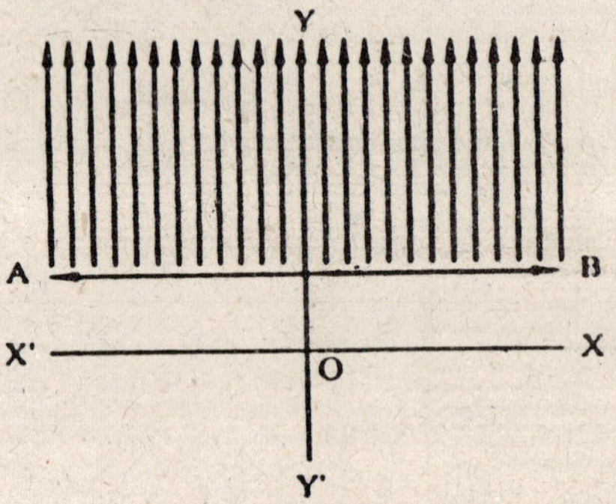

Fig 12.7 : $y > b$

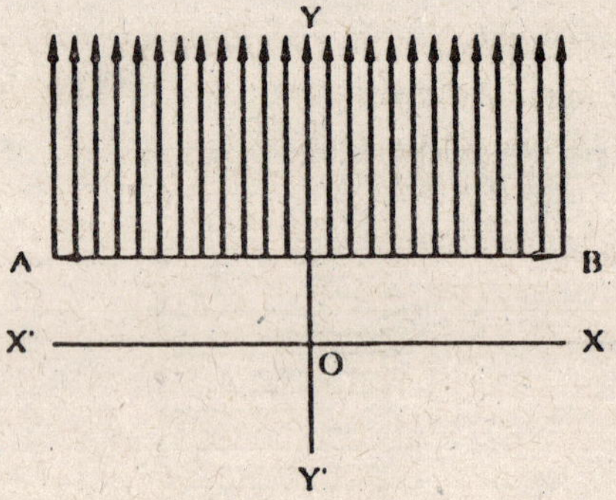

Fig 12.8 : $y \geq b$

(iv) The graph (or solution set) of the inequation $y > 0$ is the half-plane above the x-axis and the graph (or solution set) of $y < 0$ is the other half-plane below the x-axis.

Graphs of Linear Inequalities (or Inequations) in Two Variables

To obtain the graph of an inequality (or inequation) of the form

$$ax + by + c \geq 0 \quad \text{or} \quad ax + by + c \leq 0,$$

we first draw the straight line

$$ax + by + c = 0. \qquad (1)$$

The line (1) divides the plane into two regions of which one region is the graph (or solution set) of

$$ax + by + c > 0 \tag{2}$$

and the other is the graph (or solution set) of

$$ax + by + c < 0. \tag{3}$$

To find the graph (or solution set) of (2) and (3) we take any point of the plane not lying on (1) and substitute its co-ordinates in the given inequation. If the inequation is satisfied, then out of the two regions, the graph (or solution set) is that region which contains the point. But if the inequation is not satisfied, then the graph (or solution set) is the region which does not contain the point.

In particular, if origin (0, 0) does not lie on (1), then we take a point (0, 0) and substitute in the given inequation. If (0, 0) satisfy the inequation, then the region on the origin side of the line is the *graph* (or *solution set*) of the inequation. Otherwise the region on the non-origin side of the line is the *graph* or *solution set.*

EXAMPLE 1. *Draw the graphs of the inequations* (or *inequalities*): (i) $2x + 5y \leq 10$; *(ii)* $4x - 5y \geq 20$.

SOLUTION. (i) We have

$$2x + 5y \leq 10 \tag{1}$$

The equation corresponding to the inequation (1) is

$$2x + 5y = 10, \quad \text{or,} \quad \frac{x}{5} + \frac{y}{2} = 1 \tag{2}$$

The graph AB of the line (2) is first drawn with reference to $X'OX$ and $Y'OY$ as the rectangular axes of co-ordinates.

The line AB divides the plane into two regions one of which will satisfy the inequation

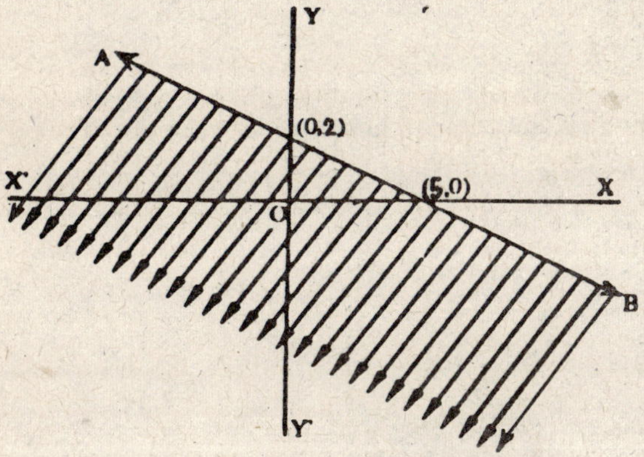

Fig 12.9 : $2x + 5y \leq 10$

$$2x + 5y < 10 \tag{3}$$

Let us take a point (0, 0) not lying on (2). Substituting $x = 0, y = 0$ in (3), we get $2.0+5.0 < 10$ which is true.

∴ The co-ordinates of the point (0, 0) satisfy the inequation (3). Hence the graph or solution set is the region on the origin side of the line i.e., the region below the line AB which contains the origin including the points on AB. [see Fig. 12.9]

(ii) We have

$$4x - 5y \geq 20 \qquad (1)$$

The equation corresponding to the inequation (1) is

$$4x - 5y = 20 \qquad (2)$$

or, $5y = 4x - 20$, or, $y = \frac{4}{5}x - 4$.

We have

x	0	5	−5
y	−4	0	−8

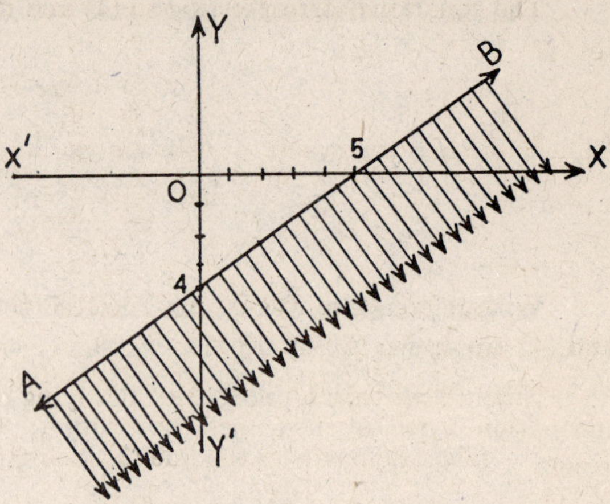

Fig 12.10 : $4x - 5y \geq 20$

We first draw the graph AB of the line (2) with reference to $X'OX$ and $Y'OY$ as rectangular axes of co-ordinates. Then the line $\overleftrightarrow{AB}$ divides the plane into two regions one of which is the graph of solution set of the inequation

$$4x - 5y > 20 \qquad (3)$$

Consider a point (0, 0) not lying on (2). Putting $x = 0$ and $y = 0$ in (3), we get $4.0 - 5.0 > 6$ which is *not true*.

∴ The point $(0, 0)$ does not satisfy the inequation (3).

Hence the graph (or solution set) is the region on the non-origin side of the line (i.e., the region below the line $\overleftrightarrow{AB}$) including the points on $\overleftrightarrow{AB}$ [see Fig. 12.10]

12.2.1. Graphs of System of Linear Inequations

If two or more linear inequalities (or inequations) have a common solution set, then the inequalities (or inequations) are called *simultaneous inequalities* (or *inequations*) or *system of inequalities* (or *inequations*). The solution set of a system of inequations can be found by drawing the graphs of the given inequations. The procedure is shown below with the help of a few worked out examples.

EXAMPLE 2. *Draw the graphs of the following system of inequations and indicate the solution set:* $3x + 5y \leq 15$ *and* $3x + 2y \leq 6$.

SOLUTION. The given inequations are

$$3x + 5y \leq 15 \qquad (1)$$

$$\text{and} \quad 3x + 2y \leq 6 \qquad (2)$$

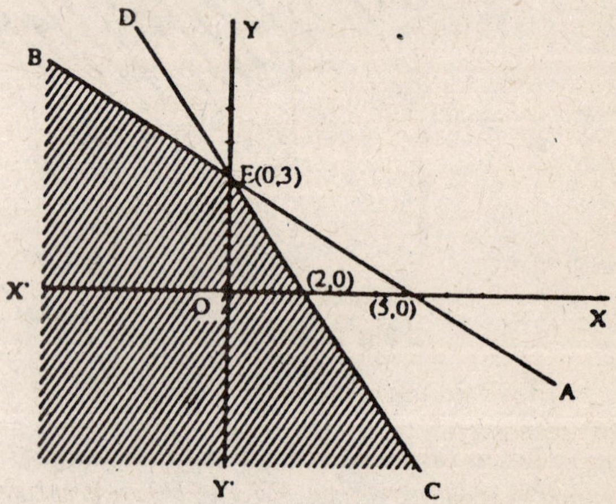

Fig 12.11

The equations corresponding to (1) and (2) are respectively

$$3x + 5y = 15 \quad \text{and} \quad 3x + 2y = 6.$$

$$\text{or,} \quad \frac{x}{5} + \frac{y}{3} = 1 \tag{3}$$

$$\text{and} \quad \frac{x}{2} + \frac{y}{3} = 1 \tag{4}$$

With reference to $X'OX$ and $Y'OY$ as the axes of co-ordinates, the graphs $\overleftrightarrow{AB}$ and $\overleftrightarrow{CD}$ of (3) and (4) are drawn in Fig. 12.11.

Now we see that a point $(0, 0)$ not lying on (3) satisfies $3x + 5y \leq 15$.

$\therefore$ The origin side of the line (3) including all points lying on $\overleftrightarrow{AB}$ is the graph or solution set of (1).

Again a point $(0, 0)$ not lying on (4) satisfies $3x + 2y \leq 6$.

$\therefore$ The origin side of the line (4) including all points lying on $\overleftrightarrow{CD}$ is the graph or solution set of (2).

The *common solution set or graph of* (1) *and* (2) *is shaded in* Fig. 12.11.

EXAMPLE 3. *Draw the graphs of the following simultaneous inequations and indicate the solution set:* $x + 2y \leq 6, 5x + 3y \leq 15, x \geq 0, y \geq 0$.

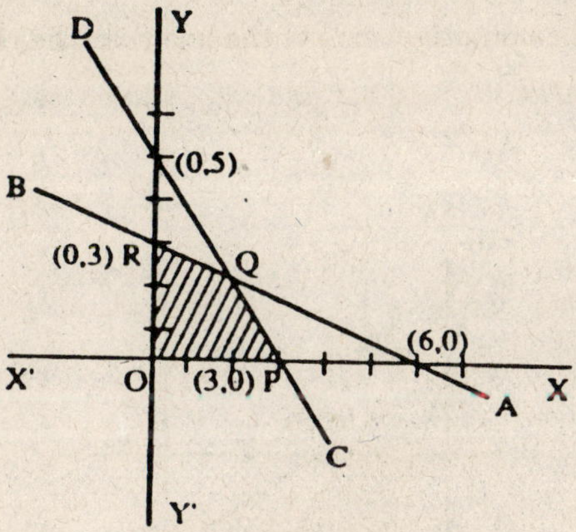

Fig 12.12

SOLUTION. The given inequations are

$$x + 2y \leq 6 \tag{1}$$

$$5x + 3y \leq 15 \tag{2}$$

$$x \geq 0 \tag{3}$$

$$\text{and} \quad y \geq 0 \tag{4}$$

and the corresponding equations are

$$x + 2y = 6 \tag{5}$$

$$5x + 3y = 15 \tag{6}$$

$$x = 0 \tag{7}$$

$$\text{and} \quad y = 0 \tag{8}$$

Referred to rectangular axes $X'OX$ and $Y'OY$, let us draw the graphs $\overleftrightarrow{AB}$ and $\overleftrightarrow{CD}$ of (5) and (6) respectively.

All points lying on $\overleftrightarrow{AB}$ and below it satisfy the inequation (1) and all points lying on CD and below it satisfy the inequation (2). [$\because$ $(0, 0)$ satisfy both (1) and (2).]

Also all points lying on the y-axis and to the right of it satisfy (3) and all points lying on the x-axis and above it satisfy (4).

Hence the *common solution set (or graph) of the given simultaneous inequations is the shaded region OPQR* in fig. 12.12.

EXAMPLE 4. *Draw the graphs of the following system of inequations and indicate the solution set:* $2x + 3y \geq 6, 2x + y \geq 4, x \leq 4$ *and* $y \leq 3$.

SOLUTION. The inequations are

$$2x + 3y \geq 6 \quad (1)$$

$$2x + y \geq 4 \quad (2)$$

$$x \leq 4 \quad (3)$$

$$\text{and} \quad y \leq 3 \quad (4)$$

The equations corresponding to (1), (2), (3) and (4) are respectively

$$2x + 3y = 6 \quad (5)$$

$$2x + y = 4 \quad (6)$$

$$x = 4 \quad (7)$$

$$\text{and} \quad y = 3 \quad (8)$$

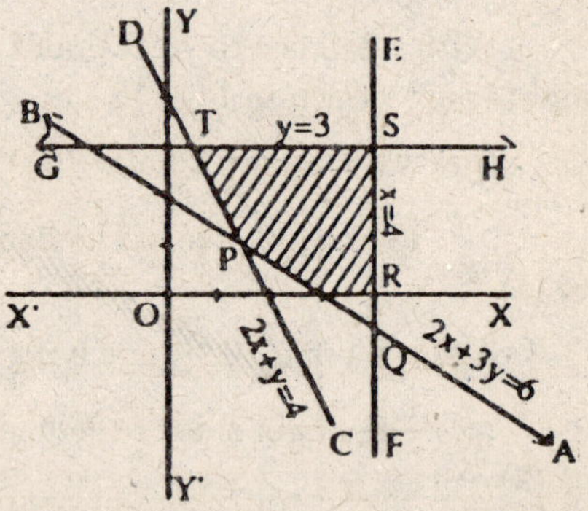

Fig 12.13

The graphs $\overleftrightarrow{AB}$, $\overleftrightarrow{CD}$, $\overleftrightarrow{EF}$ and $\overleftrightarrow{GH}$ of the lines (5), (6), (7) and (8) are drawn in fig. 12.13.

All points on $\overleftrightarrow{AB}$ and above $\overleftrightarrow{AB}$ satisfy (1), all points on $\overleftrightarrow{CD}$ and to the right of $\overleftrightarrow{CD}$ satisfy (2), all points on $\overleftrightarrow{EF}$ and to the left of $\overleftrightarrow{EF}$ satisfy (3) and all points on $\overleftrightarrow{GH}$ and below $\overleftrightarrow{GH}$ satisfy (4). Hence the *common solution set of the given system of inequations is the shaded region PQRST.*

EXAMPLE 5. *Draw the graphs of the following linear inequations and the solution set: (i.e. common portion)* : $x + y \leq 4, 3x + y \geq 3, x + 4y \geq 4, x \leq 3, y \leq 2$.

SOLUTION. The inequations are

$$x + y \leq 4 \quad (1)$$

$$3x + y \geq 3 \quad (2)$$

$$x + 4y \geq 4 \quad (3)$$

$$x \leq 3 \quad (4)$$

$$\text{and} \quad y \leq 2 \quad (5)$$

The equations corresponding to (1), (2), (3), (4) and (5) are respectively,

$$x + y = 4 \quad (6)$$

$$3x + y = 3 \quad (7)$$

$$x + 4y = 4 \quad (8)$$

$$x = 3 \quad (9)$$

$$y = 2 \quad (10)$$

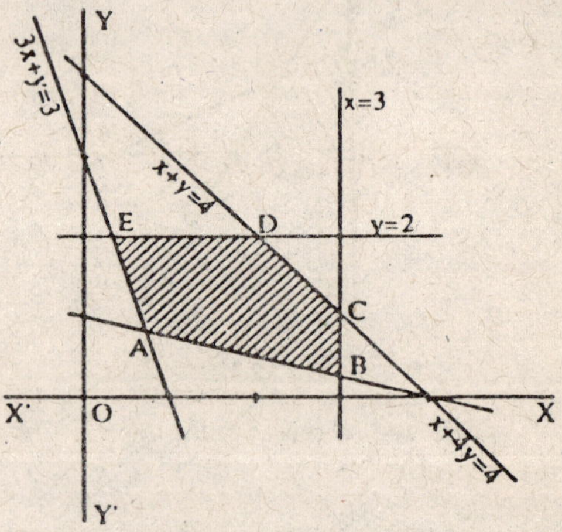

Fig 12.14

The graphs of (6), (7), (8), (9) and (10) are drawn and then the common solution set $ABCDE$ of (1), (2), (3), (4) and (5) is shaded. [See fig 12.14]. This *shaded region is a polygon bounded by straight line segments* AB, BC, CD, DE *and* EA.

EXAMPLE 6. *Draw the graphs of the following inequations and shade the solution set, if any:* $3x + 5y \geq 15, y \geq 1$ *and* $x \geq 1$.

SOLUTION. The given inequations are

$$3x + 5y \geq 15 \quad (1)$$

$$y \geq 1 \quad (2)$$

$$\text{and} \quad x \geq 1 \quad (3)$$

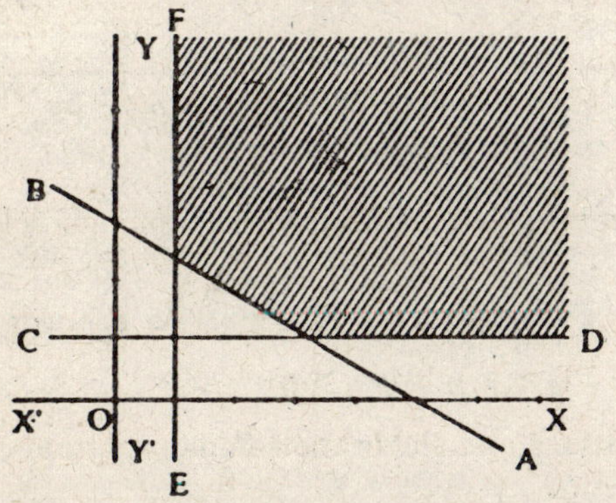

Fig 12.15

The equations corresponding to (1), (2) and (3) are respectively

$$3x + 5y = 15 \quad (4)$$

$$y = 1 \quad (5)$$

$$\text{and} \quad x = 1 \quad (6)$$

The graphs $\overleftrightarrow{AB}$, $\overleftrightarrow{CD}$ and $\overleftrightarrow{EF}$ of (4), (5) and (6) are drawn.

The common graph or solution set of (1), (2) and (3) is shaded in fig 12.15. It is not a closed region, but it is unbounded in the first quadrant, since the inequalities (1), (2), (3) are satisfied by arbitrarily large positive values of x and y.

EXAMPLE 7. *Find the linear inequalities (or inequations) for which the solution set (i.e. common portion of the graphs) is the shaded region in the figure given below.*

SOLUTION. The given shaded area is bounded by the lines

$$3x + 2y = 6 \quad (1)$$

$$y = 1 \quad (2)$$

$$5x + 6y = 30 \quad (3)$$

$$\text{and} \quad 3y - 2x = 6 \quad (4)$$

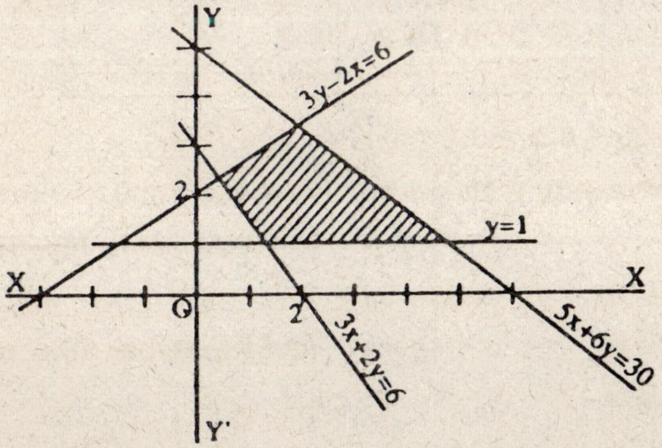

Fig 12.16

Clearly, any point of the given shaded region satisfy the inequations $3x + 2y \geq 6$, $y \geq 1, 5x + 6y \leq 30$ and $3y - 2x \leq 6$.

Hence the required linear inequations are $\mathbf{3x + 2y \geq 6}$, $\mathbf{y \geq 1}$, $\mathbf{5x + 6y \leq 30}$ and $\mathbf{3y - 2x \leq 6}$.

Exercise 12 (I)

(Graphs of Linear Inequalities)

1. Draw the graphs of the following inequalities:

(i) $x > 1$; (ii) $x \geq 3$; (iii) $x < 3$; (iv) $x \leq 1$; (v) $y \leq 2$; (vi) $y > 3$; (vii) $-2 < x < 2$; (viii) $-3 \leq x \leq 2$; (ix) $-1 \leq y \leq 4$.

2. Draw the graphs of the following inequalities:

(i) $4x + 3y \leq 12$; (ii) $2x + 3y \geq 6$; (iii) $5x + 4y > 20$; (iv) $3x - 5y \geq 15$; (v) $4x - 5y < 0$; (vi) $5x + 2y > 15$.

3. Draw the graphs of the following system of linear inequations and shade the common solution set:

(i) $-3 \leq x \leq 4, 1 \leq y \leq 5$; (ii) $x + y \leq 6, x \geq 0, y \geq 0$; (iii) $4x + 3y \leq 12, 2x + 5y \leq 10$; (iv) $2x + 3y \geq 6, x \leq 5, y \leq 3$; (v) $x + 2y \leq 6, 2x + y \leq 8, x \geq 0, y \geq 0$.

4. Draw the graphs of the following linear inequations and shade the common portion of the graphs:

(i) $x \leq 4$ and $y \geq -2$; (ii) $2x - 4y \leq 4, 3x + 4y \geq 6, y \leq 2$; (iii) $2x + 3y \leq 6, 5x + 2y \leq 10, x \geq 0, y \geq 0$; (iv) $3x + 5y \leq 10, 5x + 3y \leq 15, x \geq 0, y \geq 0$; (v) $x + y \leq 1, 3x + y \geq 3, x \geq 0, y \geq 0$.

5. A company produces two types of presentation goods A and B that require gold and silver. Each unit of type A requires 3 gms. of silver and 1 gm. of gold while that of B requires 1 gm. of silver and 2 gms. of gold. The company can procure at most 9 gms. of silver and 8 gms. of gold. If x be the number of units of type A to be produced and y be the number of units of type B, represent the above information by inequations and then draw the graphs of the same.

[HINTS. The given information may be stated as follows:

Goods	No. of units produced	Materials used per unit (in gms.)	
		Silver	Gold
A	x	3	1
B	y	1	2
Materials available	—	9	8

Hence the inequations are $3x + y \leq 9, x + 2y \leq 8, x \geq 0, y \geq 0$.]

6. Draw the graph of the linear inequalities $x + 2y \leq 10, x + y \geq 1, y \leq 4, x, y \geq 0$.

[CA Foundation June 1993]

7. Draw the graph of the linear inequalities $2x + y \geq 4, 3x + 5y \geq 15, x \geq 0, y \geq 0$.

[CA Foundation June 1993]

8. Draw the graph of the linear inequalities:

$$x - 2y \leq 0, 2x - y \leq 3, x \geq 0, y \geq 0.$$

Indicate the common region also. **[CA Foundation December 1993]**

12.3. LINEAR PROGRAMMING : MEANING

The term *programming* means "*planning*" i.e., the process of determining a particular program (or plan of action). *Linear Programming* is a mathematical technique to find the *optimum* (i.e., maximum or minimum) solution to an *objective function* of two or more variables (called *decision variables*) subject to a set of *linear constraints.* The term *linear* means that all relations among the variables i.e., in the constraints and in the objective function must be *linear* (i.e., indices of all the variables involved are all unity). The linear function which is to be optimised is called the *objective function.* Linear Programming Problems (LPP) deal with maximising profit or minimizing cost of production in a business (or an industry) under several linear constraints i.e., they deal with situations where a number of resources, such as men, materials, machines and land are available, and are to be combined to yield one or more products.

The general form of the *objective function in two variables x and y is*

$$z = c_1x + c_2y$$

where c_1 and c_2 are coefficients for the *decision variables* x and y. Here z may represent profit, cost or quantities produced and variables involved, in the objective function represent men, materials, machines, lands, etc.) and they can be manipulated in a decision-making environment. In every decision problem, there are certain restrictions on the decision variables i.e., freedom of choice of the values of the variables is restricted by given conditions. Such restrictions are expressed by *linear inequations* and *equations* which are called *constraints.* All decision variables are restricted to be non-negative i.e., $x \geq 0$ and $y \geq 0$ which are called *non-negativity constraints.*

Linear Programming Model

I. The *general linear programming model* for a *Linear Programming Problem* (*LPP*) in *two decision variables* x, y with *three constraints* is:

Optimise $\mathbf{z = c_1x + c_2y}$ subject to

$$\mathbf{a_{11}x + a_{12}y \leq b_1}$$
$$\mathbf{a_{21}x + a_{22}y \leq b_2}$$
$$\mathbf{a_{31}x + a_{32}y \leq b_3},$$

the non-negativity constraints being $\mathbf{x \geq 0, y \geq 0}$.

In all the above three constraints, "$\leq$" sign is taken. For, inequality $ax + by \geq c$ can always be written as $-ax - by \leq -c$. The number of constraints in an LPP may be two or three or four or any other number depending on the nature of the problem. The constraints other than the non-negativity constraints are called *structural constraints.*

II. The *general LP model for an LPP in n decision variables* $x_1, x_2, \cdots, x_n$ *with m constraints is:*

Optimize $z = c_1x_1 + c_2x_2 + \cdots + c_nx_n$

$$\text{subject to} \quad a_{11}x_1 + a_{12}x_2 + \cdots + a_{1n}x_n (\leq, =, \geq) b_1$$
$$a_{21}x_1 + a_{22}x_2 + \cdots + a_{2n}x_n (\leq, =, \geq) b_2$$
$$\cdots\cdots\cdots\cdots\cdots\cdots\cdots\cdots$$
$$a_{m1}x_1 + a_{m2}x_2 + \cdots + a_{mn}x_n (\leq, =, \geq) b_m$$
$$\text{and} \quad x_1 \geq 0, x_2 \geq 0, \cdots\cdots\cdots, x_n \geq 0,$$

where $a_{ij}(i = 1, 2, \cdots, m, j = 1, 2, \cdots, n)$ are *constants* called *activity parameters* and $b_i(i = 1, 2, \cdots, m)$ are *constants* called *requirement parameters.*

Thus, a Linear Programming Problem has three components:

(ii) Objective Function, (ii) Structural Constraints, and (iii) Non-negativity restrictions.

Feasible Region

By the *feasible region* of an LPP, we mean the set of points i.e., the set of values of the decision variables which simultaneously satisfy all the constraints of the LPP. Thus, any point in the feasible region is feasible (i.e., allowable) solution of an LPP.

12.3.1 Formulation of Linear Programming Problem

To formulate an LPP i.e., to state mathematically the *objective function* and the *linear constraints* from the verbal description of a decision making environment, we first construct a table showing the informations given in the description and then form the LP model considering limited resources at our desposal. The whole procedure is illustrated below with the help of few worked out examples.

EXAMPLE 1. *A company manufactures two types of souveniers made of plywood. Souveniers of type A require* 5 *minutes each for cutting and* 10 *minutes each for assembling. Souveniers of type B require* 8 *minutes for cutting and* 8 *minutes each for assembling. There are* 3 *hours and* 20 *minutes available for cutting and* 4 *hours available for assembling. The profit is* 50 *paise for type A and* 60 *paise for type B each of sourvenier. Give a mathematical formulation of the aforesaid Linear Programming Problem in terms of maximizing the profit.* **[CA May 1993]**

SOLUTION. Let the company manufacture x souveniers of type A and y sourveniers of type B. Let z denote total profit in paise. Then the informations supplied in the given problem may be stated in the form of a table as follows.

Table 12.1 Informations given in the problem

Type of souveniers	Numbers of souveniers	Manufacturing Time		Profit (in paise)
		Cutting	Assembling	
A	x	5	10	50
B	y	8	8	60
Time available (in minutes)	—	200	240	—

From the above table, we see that $z = 50x + 60y$, the constraint for cutting is $5x + 8y \leq 200$ and the constraint for assembling is $10x + 8y \leq 240$.

Again the number of souveniers manufactured cannot be negative.

$\therefore \quad x \geq 0$ and $y \geq 0$.

Thus, the *mathematical formulation of the given linear programming problem* is stated below:

Maximize $\quad \mathbf{z = 50x + 60y}$

subject to the constraints $\mathbf{5x + 8y \leq 200, 10x + 8y \leq 240}$, and $\mathbf{x \geq 0, y \geq 0}$.

EXAMPLE 2. "*A carpenter has* 90, 80 *and* 50 *running feet respectively of teak, plywood and rosewood. The product A requires* 2, 1 *and* 1 *running feet and the product B requires* 1, 2 *and* 1 *running feet of teak, plywood and rosewood respectively. If A would sell for Rs.* 48 *and B would sell for Rs.* 40 *per unit, how much of each should he make and sell in order to obtain the maximum gross income out of his stock of wood?"*

Give a mathematical formulation to this linear programming problem in terms of maximizing gross income. **[CA November 1988]**

SOLUTION. Let the carpenter make x units of the product A and y units of the product B. Then the informations given in the problem may be tabulated as follows.

Table 12.2 Informations given in the problem

Type of the product	No. of units	Running feet			Selling price (in Rs.)
		Teak	Plywood	Rosewood	
A	x	2	1	1	48
B	y	1	2	1	40
Total running feet available		90	80	50	—

Let Rs. z be the gross income in selling x units of A and y units of B.

Then, from the above table, the required *mathematical formulation of the given linear programming problem* is stated below:

Maximize $\mathbf{z = 48x + 50y}$

subject to the constraints $\mathbf{2x + y \leq 90, x + 2y \leq 80, x + y \leq 50,}$ **and** $\mathbf{x \geq 0, y \geq 0.}$

EXAMPLE 3. *A firm manufacturing two types of clectrical items A and B, can make a profit of Rs.* 20 *per unit of A and Rs.* 30 *per unit of B. But A and B make use of two essential components, a motor and a transformer.*

Each unit of A requires 3 *motors and* 2 *tranformers, and each unit of B requires* 2 *motors and* 4 *transformers.*

The total supply of components per month is restricted to 210 *motors and* 300 *transformers. Type B is an export model requiring a voltage stabiliser, restricted to* 65 *units per month.*

How many each of A and B should the firm manufacture per month in order to maximise its profit?

Give mathematical formulation of this Linear Programming Problem in terms of maximizing profit. **[CA May 1991]**

SOLUTION. Let the firm manufacture x units of type A of electrical items and y units of type B per month. Let z be the total profit in rupees. Then the informations given in the problem may be stated in a tabular form as follows:

Table 12.3 Informations given in the problem

Type of Electrical items	No. of units	Components required (No. of units)			Profit (in Rs.)
		Motors	Transformers	Voltage Stabilizer	
A	x	3	2	—	20
B	y	2	4	1	30
Total no. of components available		210	300	65	

From the above table, we give the *mathematical formulation of the linear programming problem* as follows:

Maximize $z = 20x + 30y$

subject to the constraints $3x + 2y \le 210, 2x + 4y \le 300, y \le 65,$ **and** $x \ge 0, y \ge 0.$

[See worked out Ex. 14.]

12.3.2 Graph of Constraints and Feasible Region

The graphs of linear constraints (i.e., linear inequations) in two variables x and y and the corresponding solution sets are already discussed in Art. 12.2.1. To find the *optimal solution of a linear programming problem,* we have to consider the *feasible region* (i.e., the solution set satisfying all the constraints). An illustrative example indicating the *feasible region* of an LPP is given below.

EXAMPLE 4. *A linear programming model is given below. Draw the graph of the constraints for the problem and indicate the feasible region.*

Maximise $z = 5x + 7y$, *subject to* $3x + 2y \le 12, 2x + 3y \le 13, x, y \ge 0.$

[C.U. BA/B.Sc 1982, '85]

SOLUTION. The given linear constraints are

$$3x + 2y \le 12 \quad (1)$$

$$2x + 3y \le 13 \quad (2)$$

$$\text{and} \quad x \ge 0, y \ge 0 \quad (3)$$

The equations corresponding to (1), (2) and (3) are respectively

$$3x + 2y = 12 \quad (4)$$

$$2x + 3y = 13 \quad (5)$$

$$x = 0 \quad (6)$$

$$\text{and} \quad y = 0 \quad (7)$$

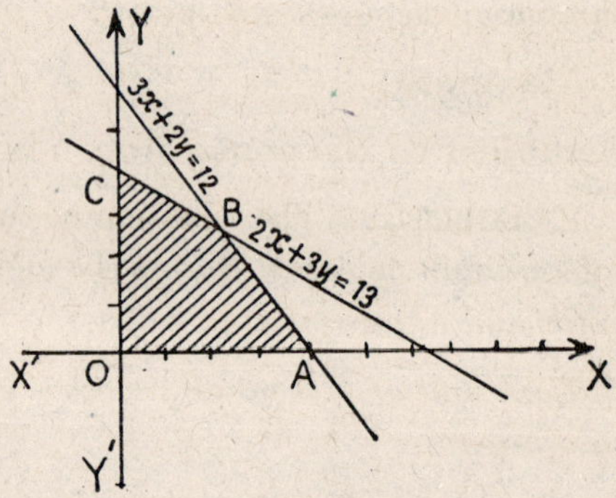

Fig 12.17

Referred to $X'OX$ and $Y'OY$ as the axes of co-ordinates, the graphs $\overleftrightarrow{AB}$ and $\overleftrightarrow{CB}$ of (1) and (2) are drawn in fig. 12.17. From the graph we see that any point in the shaded region (quadrilateral $OABC$) satisfies all the four constraints (1), (2) and (3).

Hence the required graph of all the constraints of the given LPP is the shaded region $OABC$.

Again, since any point in the shaded region $OABC$ satisfies all the given constraints of the LPP, the shaded region $OABC$ is the required **feasible region** of the LPP.

NOTE. The *common solution set* of all the linear inequations (i.e., all the linear constraints in an LPP) is the *feasible region.*

12.4. GRAPH OF THE OBJECTIVE FUNCTION : ISO-PROFIT LINES

The objective function of a Linear Programming Problem (LPP) in two variables x and y is

$$z = c_1x + c_2y \quad \text{(i)}$$

where c_1, c_2 are objective function coefficients for x and y, and z is the objective function value to be optimized.

Here c_1, c_2 are constants which are specified by the decision-maker during formulation of LP model and z changes when x and y are manipulated for solving the problem. Our main purpose is to find the values of x and y which will maximize or minimize z within the limitations of the given constraints.

From (1), $c_2 y = z - c_1 x$, or, $y = \left(-\frac{c_1}{c_2}\right)x + \frac{z}{c_2}$.

We see that the slope $\left(-\frac{c_1}{c_2}\right)$ is constant, since c_1 and c_2 are pre-specified constants.

$\therefore$ $z = c_1 x + c_2 y$ represents a series of parallel straight lines in which y-intercept varies as z changes. This series of parallel straight lines are called **iso-lines** for the objective function. Any one of these iso-lines may be obtained by arbitrarily selecting a value of z. When dealing with the problems of maximizing the objective function (which may be profit or sales volume or Revenue) in a LPP, the iso-lines are called **iso-profit lines.**

EXAMPLE 5. *Draw any three iso-profit lines for the objective function of the following linear programming problem and interpret it.*

Maximize $z = x + 3y$ *subject to:*

$2x + y \le 20, x + 2y \le 20, x \ge 0, y \ge 0.$

SOLUTION. The equation of the family of iso-profit lines for this problem is of the form

$$z = x + 3y \qquad (1)$$

in which we can select a value of z arbitrarily. If we choose $z = 12$, then from (1) the equation of the corresponding iso-profit line is $x + 3y = 12$ and its graph is drawn in the figure as the line AB. All points (x, y) lying on this iso-profit line lead to a profit of 12.

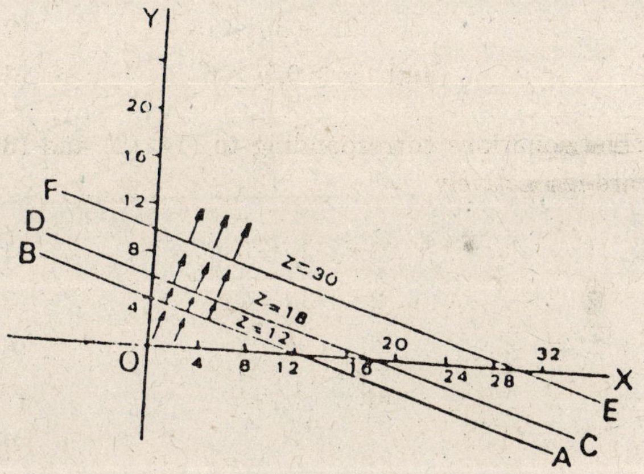

Fig 12.18

Similarly, taking $z = 18, 30$, we get the corresponding iso-profit lines CD and EF. In this way we can find a series of parallel iso-profit lines. The figure 12.18 shows that the farther away is the iso-profit line from the origin, the greater is the profit generated.

12.5. DETERMINATION OF OPTIMAL SOLUTION

If we draw a number of iso-profit lines for different values of z on the same graph, we can find the direction of improvement or increase in profit. This will help us to obtain the *optimal solution*. The *optimal solution is that point in the feasible region which yields the maximum profit (or minimum cost)*. This point can be found graphically as follows:

First draw the feasible region (i.e., the common solution set of all the constraints). Then draw the graphs of the iso-profit (or iso-cost) lines for different values of z, moving them in the direction of improvement until they reach a point beyond which no points of the feasible region lie on the iso-profit (or iso-cost) lines.

EXAMPLE 6. *Solve the following linear programming problem graphically :*

maximize $z = x + 3y$ *subject to* $2x + y \leq 20, x + 2y \leq 20, x \geq 0, y \geq 0$, *where* z *represents profit depending on two decision variables* x *and* y.

SOLUTION. First we draw the graph of the given linear constraints. From the figure, we see that the *feasible region* is the *polygon OPQR* which is a quadrilateral.

Now we draw iso-profit lines for $z = 12, 18, 24, \cdots$ moving them in the direction of improvement of profit (i.e., outward as indicated by arrows) until one line passes through the point R for which $x = 0$ and $y = 10$.

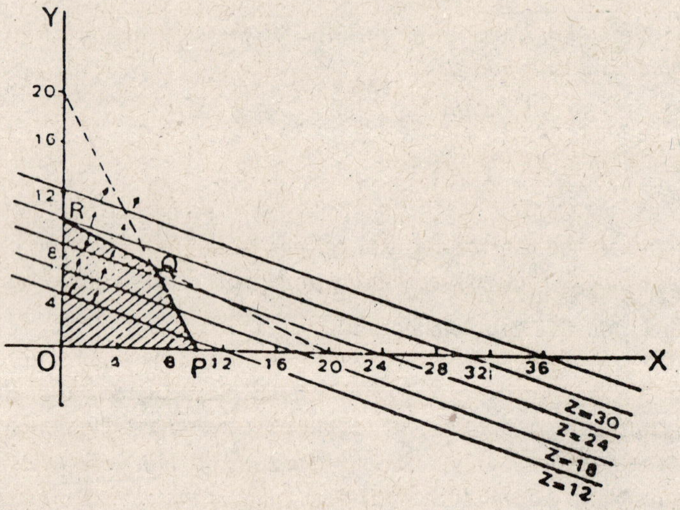

Fig 12.19

If we draw more iso-profit lines, say for $z = 36$, 40, etc. we find that they do not pass through any point lying in the feasible region i.e., they are completely outside the feasible region.

Thus, the point in the feasible region which yields the maximum profit is given by $x = 0$ and $y = 10$ and this is the *optimal solution* of the LPP and maximum value of z (i.e., maximum profit).

$$= 0 + 3 \times 10 = 30.$$

12.6. CONVEX SET : OPTIMAL VALUE OF THE OBJECTIVE FUNCTION

A region or a set C in the Euclidean plane is called a convex set if C contains the line segment joining any two points of C. Thus, the feasible region (or the set of feasible solutions) is a **convex set** or *convex polygon.* The regions shown below are convex sets.

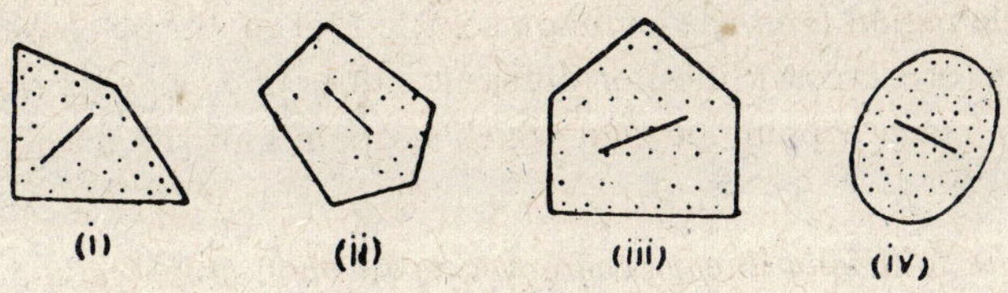

Fig 12.20

The figures given below are not convex sets.

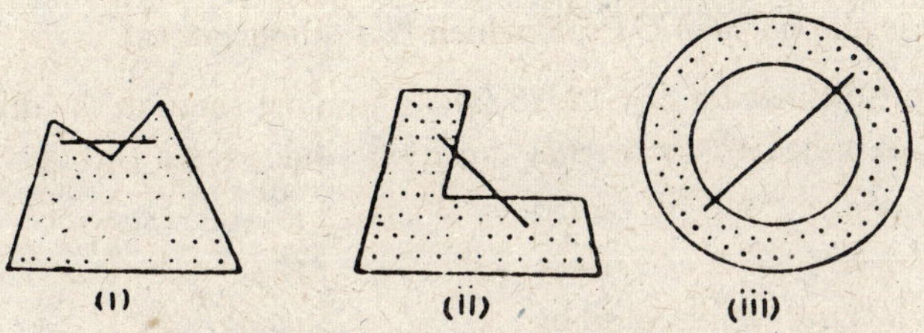

Fig 12.21

Optimal Value of the Objective Function

In worked out Example 4 of Art. 12.3.2, we have seen that the *feasible region* (i.e., the *common solution set* of all the constraints) is a *polygon in the first quadrant* [$\because$ $x \geq 0$ and $y \geq 0$]. Thus, *feasible region in many linear programming problem is a closed figure bounded by straight line segments.*

To solve an LPP graphically, we find a point (or points) in the convex polygon which will make the value of the *objective function maximum or minimum.* It is found from higher mathematics that the *optimal value of an objective function is attained at the vertices of a convex polygon.* So we have to find the values of the objective function at the vertices of the convex polygon (i.e., the feasible region). The largest of these values is the *maximum value of the objective function* and the *smallest of these values is its minimum value.* If the optimal value (i.e., maximum or minimum value) is attained at two vertices, then it is attained at every point on the line segment joining them.

Procedure to solve an LPP graphically

Steps to be followed to solve an LPP graphically when it contains two decision variables are stated below:

1. Write the linear equations corresponding to all the linear constraints and draw the straight lines corresponding to these linear equations in a graph.

2. Determine the feasible region (or the convex polygon) satisfying the given linear constraints.

3. Find the co-ordinates of the vertices (i.e., the corner points) of the convex polygon or feasible region by inspection of the graph and by solving the equations indicating the corners.

4. Calculate the value of the objective function at each vertex. The largest (or smallest) of these values is the maximum (or minimum) value of the objective function.

EXAMPLE 7. *Draw the graph of linear inequations and on the same graph indicate the feasible region of the following linear programming problem:*

Minimize $z = 2x + y$

subject to the constraints:

$$x + 2y \leq 10, x + y \geq 1, y \leq 4, x \geq 0 \quad \text{and} \quad y \geq 0.$$

[CA Foundation June 1994; CA Inter May 1992]

SOLUTION. The equations corresponding to the linear constraints (i.e., inequations) are

$$x + 2y = 10 \quad (1)$$

$$x + y = 1 \quad (2)$$

$$y = 4 \quad (3)$$

We draw the straight lines represented by (1), (2) and (3).

Note that $\frac{x}{10} + \frac{y}{5} = 1$ gives a point $(10, 0)$ on the x-axis and another point $(0, 5)$ on the y-axis.

From the graph, we see that the *feasible region* satisfying all the given constraints is the *convex polygon ABCDE*.

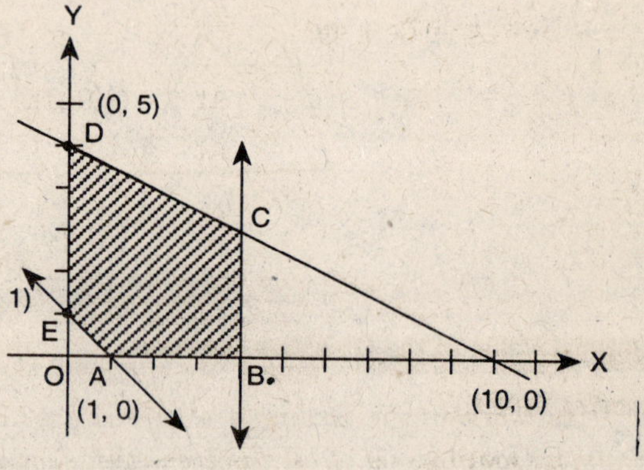

Fig 12.22

Hence the *required feasible region of the given LPP is the shaded* **convex polygon ABCDE.**

EXAMPLE 8. *Represent graphically the set of constraints in the following LPP, indicate the feasible region and hence find the optimal solution:*

Maximize $z = 7x + 4y$

subject to $x + 2y \leq 6, 3x + 2y \leq 12, x \geq 0, y \geq 0.$

SOLUTION. The equations corresponding to the linear structural constraints are

$$x + 2y = 6 \quad (1)$$

$$\text{and} \quad 3x + 2y = 12 \quad (2)$$

Let us first draw the straight lines (1) and (2) in the same graph. Note that $\frac{x}{6} + \frac{y}{3} = 1$ and $\frac{x}{4} + \frac{y}{6} = 1$.

Then we shade the feasible region $OABC$ satisfying all the given constraints

$x + 2y \leq 6, 3x + 2y \leq 12, x \geq 0$ and $y \geq 0$.

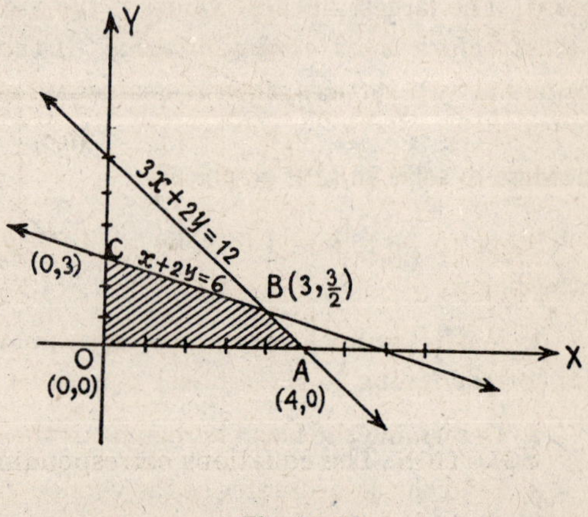

Fig 12.23

From the graph (see Fig. 12.23), we get by inspection the co-ordinates of the three vertices as $O(0,0), A(4,0)$ and $C(0,3)$.

For the other vertex B, we solve

$$x + 2y = 6 \qquad (1)$$

$$\text{and} \quad 3x + 2y = 12 \qquad (2)$$

Subtracting (1) from (2), $2x = 6$, or, $x = 3$.

Substituting $x = 3$ in (1), we get

$$3 + 2y = 6, \quad \text{or,} \quad 2y = 3; \quad \therefore \quad y = \frac{3}{2}.$$

$\therefore$ The other vertex B is the point $\left(3, \frac{3}{2}\right)$.

Now, $z = 7x + 4y$.

$$\begin{array}{lll} \text{At} & O(0,0), & z = 7.0 + 4.0 = 0. \\ \text{At} & A(4,0), & z = 7 \times 4 + 4 \times 0 = 28. \\ \text{At} & B\left(3, \frac{3}{2}\right), & z = 7 \times 3 + 4 \times \frac{3}{2} = 27. \\ \text{At} & C(0,3), & z = 7 \times 0 + 4 \times 3 = 12. \end{array}$$

From the above values, we see that the *maximum value of z is* 28 and *it is attained at the vertex* $A(4,0)$.

EXAMPLE 9. *Solve the following linear programming problem graphically: Minimize* $z = x_1 + 7x_2$ *subject to* $-x_1 + 2x_2 \le 8, x_1 - x_2 \le 4, 2x_1 + x_2 \ge 2, x_1 \ge 0, x_2 \ge 0$.

[C.U. BA/B.Sc 1992]

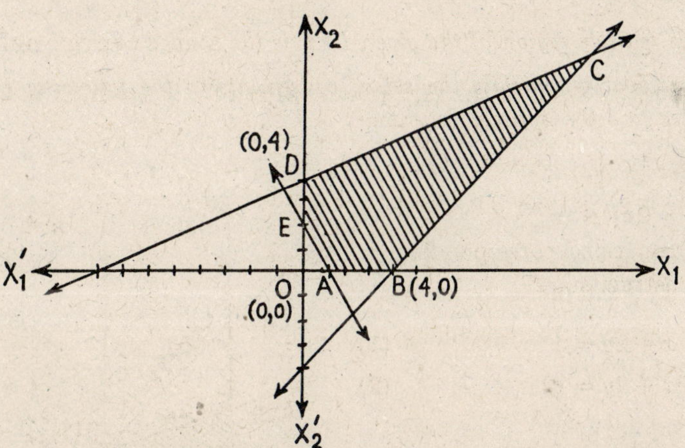

Fig 12.24

SOLUTION. The equations corresponding to the linear constraints are

$$-x_1 + 2x_2 = 8 \qquad (1)$$

$$x_1 - x_2 = 4 \qquad (2)$$

$$\text{and} \quad 2x_1 + x_2 = 2. \qquad (3)$$

Referred to $X_1'OX_1$ and $X_2'OX_2$ as rectangular axes, the straight lines (1), (2) and (3) are drawn on the same graph (See Fig. 12.24).

Note that

$$\frac{x_1}{-8} + \frac{x_2}{4} = 1$$
$$\frac{x_1}{4} + \frac{x_2}{-4} = 1$$
$$\text{and} \quad \frac{x_1}{1} + \frac{x_2}{2} = 1$$

The shaded region $ABCDE$ is the *feasible* region satisfying all the given constraints

$$-x_1 + 2x_2 \leq 8, x_1 - x_2 \leq 4, 2x_1 + x_2 \geq 2, \; x_1 \geq 0 \quad \text{and} \quad x_2 \geq 0.$$

From the graph, by inspection, the co-ordinates of the four corners A, B, D, E are $(1, 0)$, $(4, 0)$, $(0, 4)$ and $(0, 2)$ respectively.

For the other vertex C, we solve (1) and (2) for x_1 and x_2. Adding (1) and (2), we get $x_2 = 12$; $\therefore$ From (2), $x_1 = 4 + 12 = 16$.

$\therefore$ The co-ordinates of C are $(16, 12)$.

$$\begin{array}{lll} \text{At} & A(1,0), & z = 1 + 7 \times 0 = 1. \\ \text{At} & B(4,0), & z = 4 + 7 \times 0 = 4. \\ \text{At} & C(16,12), & z = 16 + 7 \times 12 = 100 \\ \text{At} & D(0,4), & z = 0 + 7 \times 4 = 28. \\ \text{At} & E(0,2), & z = 0 + 7 \times 2 = 14. \end{array}$$

From the above values we see that the **minimum value of z is 1 which is attained at the vertex $\mathbf{A(1, 0)}$.**

EXAMPLE 10. *Solve graphically:*

Maximize $\quad z = 2x_1 + 5x_2$

subject to the constraints $4x_2 - 3x_1 \leq 12$, $x_1 + x_2 \geq 2$, $x_1 \leq 4, x_1, x_2 \geq 0$. **[Madras U. 1983]**

SOLUTION. The equations corresponding to the constraints of the LPP are

$$4x_2 - 3x_1 = 12 \qquad (1)$$
$$x_1 + x_2 = 2 \qquad (2)$$
$$\text{and} \quad x_1 = 4 \qquad (3)$$

We first draw the straight lines (1) and (2) with reference to $X_1'OX_1$ and $X_2'OX_2$ as the axes of co-ordinates on the same graph. Note that

$$\frac{x_1}{-4} + \frac{x_2}{3} = 1 \quad \text{and} \quad \frac{x_1}{2} + \frac{x_2}{2} = 1.$$

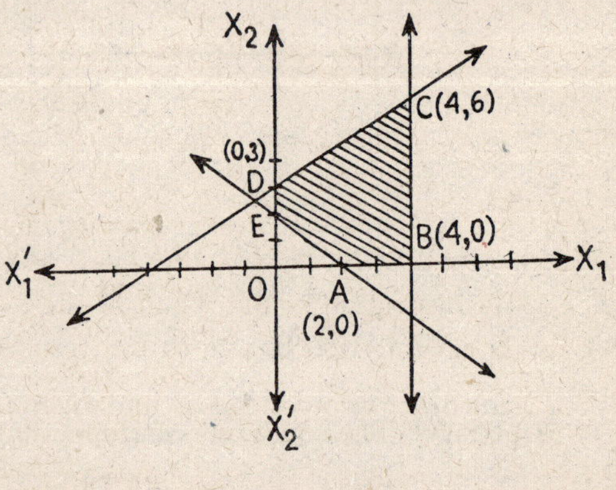

Fig 12.25

From the graph, by inspection, we see that the co-ordinates of three vertices are respectively $O(0,0), A(\frac{25}{4},0)$ and $C(0,5)$.

For the other vertex B, we solve (1) and (2).

$$16x + 32y = 160$$
$$16x + 12y = 100$$
$$\therefore \quad 20y = 60, \quad \text{or,} \quad y=3.$$

From (1)
$$16x + 12 \times 3 = 100$$
$$\text{or,} \quad 16x = 64, \quad \text{or,} \quad x = 4.$$

$\therefore$ The co-ordinates of the vertex B are $(4,3)$.

$$\text{At} \quad O(0,0), \quad z = 25 \times 0 + 20 \times 0 = 0.$$
$$\text{At} \quad A\left(\frac{25}{4},0\right), \quad z = 25 \times \frac{25}{4} + 20 \times 0 = \frac{625}{4} = 156.25.$$
$$\text{At} \quad B(4,3), \quad z = 25 \times 4 + 20 \times 3 = 160.$$
$$\text{At} \quad C(0,5), \quad z = 25 \times 0 + 20 \times 5 = 100.$$

From the above values, we see that **the maximum value of z is 160** *which is attained at the vertex B*$(4,3)$ *i.e., Mr. Natrajan should make* **4 tables and 3 book-cases** *to use the left over wood most profitably.*

EXAMPLE 13. *A carpenter has* 90, 80 *and* 50 *running feet respectively of teak, plywood and rosewood. The product A requires* 2, 1 *and* 1 *running feet and product B requires* 1, 2 *and* 1 *running feet of teak, plywood and rosewood respectively. If A would sell for Rs.* 48 *and B would sell for Rs.* 40 *per unit, how much of each should he make and sell in order to obtain the maximum gross income out of his stock of wood?*

(i) *Give a mathematical formulation to this linear programming problem.*

(ii) *Use graphical method to solve the problem.*

(iii) *Indicate clearly the feasible region on a graph.* **[CA November 1988]**

SOLUTION. Let the no. of units of the product A to be made be x and that of the product B to be made be y. Then the informations given in the problem may be stated as follows:

Table 12.5 Informations given in the problem

Product	No. of units to be made	Wood used per unit (ft.)			Income per unit (Rs.)
		Teak	Plywood	Rosewood	
A	x	2	1	1	48
B	y	1	2	1	40
Available stock	—	90	80	50	—

Let z be the gross income in rupees.

Mathematical formulation of the LPP:

Maximize $z = 48x + 40y$

subject to the constraints: $2x + y \leq 90, x + 2y \leq 80, x + y \leq 50, x \geq 0, y \geq 0$.

Feasible region

We first draw the straight lines represented by the equations $2x+y = 90, x+2y = 80, x+y = 50$.

From the graph, we see that the *feasible region* satisfying all the constraints of the problem is the *convex polygon OABCD*.

Graphical Solution of the Problem

By inspection of the graph of the constraints we obtain the co-ordinates of the three vertices O, A, D as $(0,0), (45,0), (0,40)$ respectively.

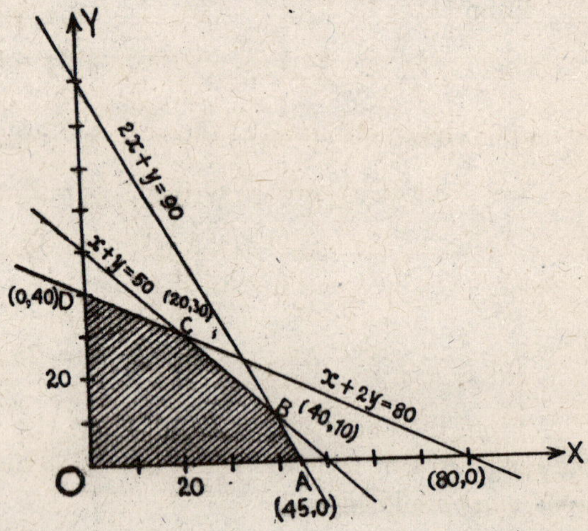

Fig 12.28

For the vertex B, we solve

$$2x + y = 90 \quad (1)$$

$$\text{and} \quad x + y = 50 \quad (2)$$

Subtracting (2) from (1),

$x = 40$. $\therefore$ From (2), $y = 50-40 = 10$.

$\therefore$ B is the point $(40, 10)$.

Again, for the vertex C, we solve

$$x + 2y = 80 \quad (3)$$

$$\text{and} \quad x + y = 50 \quad (4)$$

Subtracting (4) from (3), $y = 30$. From (4), $x = 50 - 30 = 20$.

$\therefore$ C is the point $(20, 30)$.

At $O(0,0)$, the value of z is $48 \times 0 + 40 \times 0 = 0$.
At $A(45,0)$, the value of z is $48 \times 45 + 40 \times 0 = 2160$.
At $B(40,10)$, the value of z is $48 \times 40 + 40 \times 10 = 2320$.
At $C(20,30)$, the value of z is $48 \times 20 + 40 \times 30 = 2160$.
At $D(0,40)$, the value of z is $48 \times 0 + 40 \times 40 = 1600$.

We see that the *maximum value of z is Rs.* **2320** *and it is attained at the vertex* $B(40, 10)$.

Hence for maximum profit, *the carpenter should make* 40 *units of product A and* 10 *units of product B*.

EXAMPLE 14. *A firm manufacturing two types of electrical items A and B, can make a profit of Rs.* 20 *per unit of A and Rs.* 30 *per unit of B. Both A and B make use of two essential components, a motor and a transformer. Each unit of A requires* 3 *motors and* 2 *transformers, and each unit of B requires* 2 *motors and* 4 *transformers. The total supply of components per month is restricted to* 210 *motors, and* 300 *transformers. Type B is an export model requiring a voltage stabiliser, restricted to* 65 *units per month. How many each of A and B should the firm manufacture per month in order to maximize its profit?*

(i) *Use graphical method to solve this problem.*

(ii) *Indicate the feasible region on the graph paper.* [CA May 1991]

SOLUTION. In Example 3 (worked out) we have shown the mathematical formulation of this linear programming problem which is

maximize $z = 20x + 30y$

subject to the constraints

$$3x + 2y \leq 210, 2x + 4y \leq 300, y \leq 65, \quad \text{and} \quad x \geq 0, y \geq 0.$$

The equations corresponding to the constraints are

$$3x + 2y = 210 \tag{1}$$

$$2x + 4y = 300 \tag{2}$$

$$\text{and} \quad y = 65 \tag{3}$$

We first draw the straight lines (1), (2) and (3) on the same graph. Note that

$$\frac{x}{70} + \frac{y}{105} = 1, \frac{x}{150} + \frac{y}{75} = 1 \quad \text{and} \quad y = 65.$$

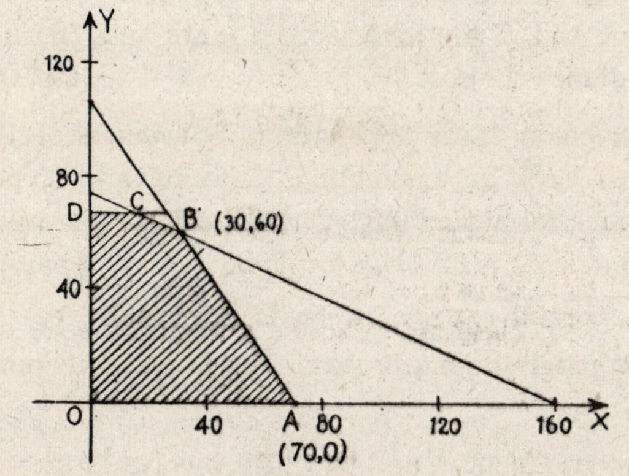

Fig 12.29

The *feasible region OABCD is shaded in the graph in which all the linear constraints of the LPP are satisfied.*

From the graph, by inspection, we see that the co-ordinates of the *vertices* O, A, D *are respectively* $O(0,0)$, $A(70,0)$ *and* $D(0,65)$. To find the vertex B, we solve (1) and (2).

$$6x + 4y = 420$$

$$2x + 4y = 300$$

$$4x = 120, \quad \text{or}, \quad x=30.$$

From (1), $2y = 210 - 90 = 120$, or, $y = 60$.

To find C, we have $y = 65$. From (2), $2x + 260 = 300$, or, $x = 20$.

$\therefore$ The co-ordinates of B *and* C *are respectively* $(30, 60)$ *and* $(20, 65)$.

At $O(0,0)$, $z = 20 \times 0 + 30 \times 0 = 0$.

At $A(70,0)$, $z = 20 \times 70 + 30 \times 0 = 1400$.

At $B(30,60)$, $z = 20 \times 30 + 30 \times 60 = 2400$.

At $C(20,65)$, $z = 20 \times 20 + 30 \times 65 = 2350$.

At $D(0,65)$, $z = 20 \times 0 + 30 \times 65 = 1950$.

From the above values, we see that the **maximum value of z is 2400** *which is attained at the vertex* $B(30, 60)$.

Hence *the firm should manufacture* **30 units of A** *and* **60 units of B** *per month to make maximum profit of* Rs. 2,400.

Exercise 12 (II)

(Graphical Method to solve an LPP)

[A]

1. What is a Linear Programming Problem? What are the assumptions in formulating an LPP? **[ICWAI (Final) June 1985]**

2. A machine producing either product A or B can produce A by using 2 units of chemicals and 1 unit of a compound and can produce B by using 1 unit of chemicals and 2 units of the compound. Only 800 units of chemicals and 1000 units of the compound are available. The profits available per unit of A and B are respectively Rs. 30 and Rs. 20. Give a mathematical formulation of this linear programming problem in terms of maximizing the profit.

3. Food X contains 6 units of vitamin A and 7 units of vitamin B per gram and costs 12 paise/gm. Food Y contains 8 units and 12 units of A and B per gram respectively and costs 20 paise/gm. The daily requirements of vitamin A and B are at least 100 units and 120 units respectively. Formulate the above as an LPP to minimize the cost. **[CU 1986]**

4. A company manufactures two types of souveniers made of plywood. Souveniers of Type A require 6 minutes each for cutting and 12 minutes each for assembling. Souveniers of Type B require 10 minutes each of cutting and 10 minutes each for assembling. There are 4 hours available for cutting and 5 hours available for assembling. The profit is 60 paise for Type A and 80 paise for Type B each of Souvenier.

Give a mathematical formulation of this linear programming problem in terms of maximizing the profit.

5. A factory is engaged in manufacturing two products A and B which involve lathe work, grinding and assembling. The cutting, grinding and assembling times required for one unit of A are 2, 1 and 1 hours respectively and for one unit of B are 3, 1 and 3 hours respectively. The profits on each unit of A and B are Rs. 2 and Rs. 3 respectively. Assuming that 300 hours of lathe time, 300 hours of grinding time and 240 hours of assembling time are available, pose a linear programming problem in terms of maximizing the profit on the items manufactured.

6. A furniture manufacturer wishes to find the number of tables and chairs to be made by him in order to optimise the use of his available resources. These products utilize two different types of timber and he has on hand 1,500 board feet of the first type and 1,000 board feet of the second type. He has 800 man-hours available for the total job. Each table and chair requires 5 and 1 board feet respectively, of the first type of timber and 2 and 3 board feet of second type. 3 man-hours are required to make a table and 2 man-hours are needed to make a chair. The manufacturer makes a profit of Rs. 12 on a table and Rs. 5 on a chair. Write out the Complete Linear Programming formulation of the problem in terms of maximizing the profit.

[B]

1. Find graphically the feasible region, if any, of the following LPP;

(i) Maximize $z = 5x + 7y$ subject to $3x + 2y \le 12, 2x + 3y \le 13, x \ge 0, y \ge 0$.

[C.U. 1982, '85]

(ii) Maximize $z = 9x + 7y$ subject to $x + 2y \le 7, x - y \le 4, x, y \ge 0$. **[C.U. 1987]**

2. Solve the following LPP graphically:

Maximize $z = 5x_1 + 3x_2$ subject to $3x_1 + 5x_2 \le 15, 5x_1 + 2x_2 \le 10$ and $x_1 \ge 0, x_2 \ge 0$.

[C.U. BA/B.Sc 1993]

3. Make a graphical representation of the set of constraints in the following LPP:

Maximize $z = 2x_1 + x_2$

subject to $x_1 + 3x_2 \le 15, 3x_1 - 4x_2 \le 12, x_1 \ge 0, x_2 \ge 0$, and find the extreme points of the convex set of feasible solutions.

4. Make the graphical representation of the set of constraints in the following LPP:

Maximize $z = 10x_1 + 15x_2$ subject to $x_1 + x_2 \ge 2$, $3x_1 + 2x_2 \le 6, x_1 \ge 0, x_2 \ge 0$ and find the extreme points of the convex set of feasible solutions. Find the maximum value of the objective function. **[C.U. 1983]**

5. Solve the following LPP graphically, indicating the feasible regions:

(i) Maximize $z = 4x_1 + 3x_2$ subject to $x_1 + x_2 \le 50$, $x_1 + 2x_2 \le 80$. $2x_1 + x_2 \ge 20$, $x_1 \ge 0, x_2 \ge 0$.

(ii) Maximize $z = 2x_1 + 4x_2$ subject to $2x_1 + 3x_2 \le 48$, $x_1 + 3x_2 \le 42, x_1 + x_2 \le 21$, $x_1 \ge 0, x_2 \ge 0$. **[C.U. BA/B.Sc 1993]**

6. Make a graphical representation of the set of constraints in the following LPP and then solve the problem:

Maximize $z = 2x + y$ subject to $4x + 3y \le 12, 4x + y \le 8, 4x - y \le 8, x \ge 0, y \ge 0$. **[C.U. 1988]**

[HINTS. Draw the straight lines $4x + 3y = 12, 4x + y = 8, 4x - y = 8$ and shade the feasible region satisfying all the given constraints. Note that the constraint $4x - y \le 8$ is redundant.]

7. Make a graphical representation of all the constraints in the following LPP, indicate the feasible region and then solve the problem:

(i) Minimize $z = 3x_1 + 2x_2$ subject to $3x_1 + 4x_2 \le 12$, $x_1 + x_2 \ge 2, x_1 \ge 0, x_2 \ge 0$.

(ii) Minimize $z = 3x - y$ subject to the constraints

$$x + y \le 6, 2x + y \le 8, 3x + 2y \le 6, x \ge 0, y \ge 0.$$

8. "Minimize $z = 4x + 2y$ subject to $3x + y \ge 27, -x - y \le -21, x + 2y \ge 30, x \ge 0, y \ge 0$". Solve this LPP.

9. Solve the following LPP graphically:

(i) Minimize $z = 20x_1 + 10x_2$ subject to $x_1 + 2x_2 \le 40, 3x_1 + x_2 \ge 30, 4x_1 + 3x_2 \ge 60$; $x_1 \ge 0, x_2 \ge 0$.

(ii) Maximize $z = 3x_1 + 2x_2$ subject to $-2x_1 + x_2 \leq 1, x_1 \leq 2, x_1 + x_2 \leq 3$, and $x_1, x_2 \geq 0$.

[C.U. BA/B.Sc 1989, 90]

(iii) Maximize $z = 2x_1 + x_2$ subject to $x_1 + x_2 \geq 5, 2x_1 + 3x_2 \leq 20$, $4x_1 + 3x_2 \leq 25$, and $x_1 \geq 0, x_2 \geq 0$. [C.U. BA/B.Sc 1991]

10. A company produces two types of presentation goods A and B that require gold and silver. Each unit of type A requires 3 gms of silver and 1 gm of gold while that of B requires 1 gm of silver and 2 gms. of gold. The company can procure 9 gms. of silver and 8 gms. of gold. If each unit of type A brings a profit of Rs. 40 and that of type B Rs. 50, determine the number of units of each type that should be produced to maximise the profit.

Indicate the feasible region on a graph paper. [CA May 1989]

11. A company produces two types of goods A and B that require gold and silver. Each unit of type A requires 2 gms. of silver and 1 gm of gold while one unit of type B requires 1 gm. of silver and 2 gms. of gold. The company has only 90 gms. of silver and 80 gms. of gold. If each unit of type A brings a profit of Rs. 400 and that of type B brings a profit of Rs. 500, find the number of units of each type the company should produce to maximise the profit.

(i) You are to give a mathematical formulation to this linear programming problem.

(ii) In order to solve the problem you are to use graphical method of solving a linear programming problem.

(iii) Indicate the feasible region on the graph paper. [CA November 1990]

12. A company manufactures two types of souveniers made of plywood. Souveniers of type A require 5 minutes each for cutting and 10 minutes each for assembling. Souveniers of type B require 8 minutes for cutting and 8 minutes each for assembling. There are 3 hours and 20 minutes available for cutting and 4 hours available for assembling.

The profit is 50 paise for Type A and 60 paise for Type B each souvenier. How many sourveniers of each type should the company manufacture in order to maximise the profit?

(i) Give a mathematical formulation of the aforesaid linear programming problem.

(ii) Indicate clearly the feasible region.

(iii) Use the graphical method to solve the problem. [CA May 1993]

13. A retailer deals in two items only—item A and item B. He has Rs. 50,000 to invest and a space to store at the most 60 pieces. An item A costs him Rs. 2,500 and B costs him Rs. 500. A net profit to him on item A is Rs. 500 and on item B is Rs. 150. If he can sell all the items that he purchases, how should he invest his amount to have a maximum profit?

(i) Give a mathematical formulation to this linear programming problem.

(ii) Use graphical method to solve the problem.

(iii) Indicate the feasible region on a graph paper. [CA May 1990]

14. A confectioner manufactures two types of biscuits—One Regular type and the other Non-regular type.

The Regular type sells at a profit of Rs. 40 per box and the Non-regular type sells at a profit of Rs. 50 per box.

The biscuits are processed in three main operations: Blending, Cooking and Packaging.

The average time taken in minutes for each box, for each of the processing operations is given below:

	Blending	Cooking	Packaging
Regulars	1 min.	5 min.	3 min.
Non-regulars	2 min.	4 min.	1 min.

The Blending equipment is available for a maximum of 12 hours, the cooking facilities for 30 hours at the most, and Packaging equipment for maximum 15 hours.

Determine how many boxes of each type the confectioner should manufacture in order to maximise his profit.

(i) Give a mathematical formulation of this Linear Programming Problem.

(ii) Use Graphical Method to solve the problem.

(iii) Indicate clearly the feasible region on the graph paper. **[CA November 1991]**

15. Give a mathematical formulation of the following linear programming problem:

The standard weight of a special purpose brick is 5 kg. and it contains two basic ingredients B_1 and B_2. B_1 costs Rs. 5 per kg. and B_2 costs Rs. 8 per kg. Strength considerations dictate that the brick contains not more than 4 kg. of B_1 and at least 2 kg of B_2. Determine the amount of ingredients B_1 and B_2 so that the cost of the brick may become minimum.

Solve this problem graphically.

[HINTS. The formulation of the LPP is

Minimise $z = 5x + 8y$ subject to $x + y = 5, x \leq 4, y \geq 2$, and $x \geq 0, y \geq 0$, where x and y are the weights of ingradients B_1 and B_2.

Now draw the straight lines $x + y = 5, x = 4$ anmd $y = 2$ in one graph. Note that the *feasible region is a line segment from* $(0, 5)$ *to* $(3, 2)$ and, therefore, the vertices (or extreme points) are $(0, 5)$ and $(3, 2)$.]

Answers

[A]

2. Maximize $z = 30x + 20y$ subject to the constraints $2x + y \leq 800, x + 2y \leq 1000, x \geq 0, y \geq 0$. **3.** Minimize $z = 12x + 20y$ subject to $6x + 8y \geq 100, 7x + 12y \geq 120, x \geq 0, y \geq 0$. **4.** Maximize $z = 60x + 80y$ subject to the constraints $6x + 10y \leq 240, 12x + 10y \leq 300$ and $x \geq 0, y \geq 0$. **5.** Maximize $z = 2x + 3y$ subject to $2x + 3y \leq 300, x + y \leq 300, x + 3y \leq 240$, and $x \geq 0, y \geq 0$. **6.** Maximize $z = 12x + 5y$ subject to $5x + y \leq 1500, 2x + 3y \leq 1000, 3x + 2y \leq 800$, and $x \geq 0, y \geq 0$.

[B]

2. $z_{\max} = 12\frac{7}{19}$ attained at $\left(\frac{20}{19}, \frac{45}{19}\right)$. **3.** $(0, 0), (4, 0), \left(\frac{96}{13}, \frac{33}{13}\right)$. **4.** $(0, 2), (0, 3), (2, 0)$; $z_{\max} = 45$ attained at $(0, 3)$. **5.** (i) $z_{\max} = 200$ attained at $(50, 0)$; (ii) 60 at $(6, 12)$. **6.** $z_{\max} = 5$ attained at $\left(\frac{3}{2}, 2\right)$. **7.** (i) $z_{\min} = 4$ attained at $(0, 2)$; (ii) $z_{\min} = -6$ attained at $(0, 6)$. **8.** $z_{\min} = 48$ attained at $(3, 18)$.

7. (i) $z_{\min} = 4$attained at $(0,2)$; (ii) $z_{\min} = -6$ attained at $(0,6)$. **8.** $z_{\min} = 48$ attained at $(3,18)$. **9.** (i) $z_{\min} = 240$ attained at $(6,12)$; (ii) $z_{\max} = 8$ at $(2,1)$; (iii) $z_{\max} = \frac{25}{2}$ at $\left(\frac{25}{4},0\right)$. **10.** 2 units of type A and 3 units of type B and $z_{\max} =$ Rs. 230. **11.** Maximize $z = 400x + 500y$ subject to the constraints $2x + y \leq 90, x + 2y \leq 80$, and $x \geq 0, y \geq 0; z_{\max} =$ Rs. 25,000 attained at $\left(\frac{100}{3},\frac{70}{3}\right)$. **12.** Maximize $z = 50x + 60y$ subject to $5x + 8y \leq 200, 10x + 8y \leq 240$, and $x \geq 0, y \geq 0$; $z_{\max} =$ 1600 paise = Rs. 16 attained at $(8,20)$. **13.** Maximize $z = 500x + 150y$ subject to $2500x + 500y \leq 50,000, x + y \leq 60$ and $x \geq 0, y \geq 0; z_{\max} =$ Rs. 12,500 attained at $(10,15)$ i.e., to get maximum profit he should invest in 10 units of A and 50 units of B. **14.** Maximise $z = 40x + 50y$ subject to $x + 2y \leq 720, 5x + 4y \leq 1800, 3x + y \leq 900, x \geq 0, y \geq 0; z_{\max} =$ Rs. 19,800 at $(120,300)$, i.e., the confectioner should manufacture 120 boxes of Regular type and 300 boxes of Non-regular type. **15.** $z_{\min}=$ Rs. 31 at $(3,2)$, i.e., 3 kg. of B_1 is to be mixed with 2 kg. of B_2.

12.7. SIMPLEX METHOD

This is a *matrix method* (or an iterative algorithm) which is a systematic repetitive solution procedure to obtain best possible solution under the given constraints (or restrictions). In every repetitive step, the method indicates whether the solution obtained is optimal, if not, it specifies how to find an improved solution. *Simplex method* can be used to solve all types of *LPP* involving any number of variables. As this is a long method, the whole procedure will be discussed step by step.

In this method, the basic requirements are:

(i) all constraints (i.e., inequations) must be expressed as equations, (ii) the right side of a constraint cannot be negative, (iii) all variables are restricted to non-negative values.

Slack and Surplus Variables

If a constraint in an *LPP* appears with "$\leq$" sign, then a non-negative variable is added to the left side of the inequation to convert it into an equation. Such a variable is called a *slack variable.* For example, if the constraint be $2x_1 + 3x_2 \leq 6$, then a non-negative variable x_3 is added to the left side to convert it into the equation $2x_1 + 3x_2 + x_3 = 6$. Here x_3 is a *slack variable.*

Similarly, a constraint in an *LPP* with "$\geq$" sign can be converted into an equation by subtracting a non-negative variable from the left side. Such a variable is called a *surplus variable.* For example, a constraint of the type $x_1 + 2x_2 \geq 8$ can be written as $x_1 + 2x_2 - x_3 = 8$, where x_3 is a *surplus variable.*

The right side say b_i, of a constraint must be *positive.* If b_i is negative, then both sides of the constraint is multiplied by (-1) to make the right side positive. In such a case, the sign of inequality is changed from "$\leq$" to "$\geq$" and *vice-versa.* For example, $x - 2y \leq -5$ may be written as $-x + 2y \geq 5$ and $2x - y \geq -3$ may be written as $-2x + y \leq 3$.

We first explain the whole procedure of Simplex method step by step with the help of a worked out example.

EXAMPLE 1. *Solve the following linear programming problem by using simplex method:*

$$\begin{aligned} \text{Maximize} \quad & z = 4x + 2y \\ \text{subject to} \quad & x + 2y \leq 15 \\ & 2x - y \leq 5 \\ & x, y \geq 0. \end{aligned}$$

[ICWAI December 1994]

SOLUTION. We solve this problem step by step showing the whole procedure of simplex method.

STEP 1. Two linear constraints $x + 2y \le 15$ and $2x - y \le 5$ are first converted into *equations* by adding slack variables u and v on the left sides of these two constraints and the given linear programming problem (LPP) is written as follows:

$$\text{Maximize} \quad z = 4x + 2y + 0.u + 0.v \tag{1}$$

$$\text{subject to} \quad x + 2y + 1.u + 0.v = 15 \tag{2}$$

$$2x - y + 0.u + 1.v = 5 \tag{3}$$

$$\text{Equation (1) may be written as} \quad z - 4x - 2y - 0.u - 0.v = 0 \tag{4}$$

STEP 2. The *initial simplex matrix* consisting of the number coefficients of (2), (3) and (4), omitting the symbol z and ignoring the non-negativity constraints, is the augmented matrix given below:

$$\left[\begin{array}{cccc|c} x & y & u & v & b_i \\ 1 & 2 & 1 & 0 & 15 \\ \boxed{2} & -1 & 0 & 1 & 5 \\ -4 & -2 & 0 & 0 & 0 \end{array}\right] \begin{array}{l} \textbf{Ratio} \\ 15/1 = 15 \\ 5/2 = 2.5 \leftarrow \\ \\ \end{array}$$

$$\uparrow$$

The last row is the *objective row* which corresponds to

$$z - 4x - 2y = 0, \quad \text{or,} \quad z = 4x + 2y.$$

STEP 3. From the objective row, we see that negative number with the largest absolute value is -4 which indicates that the first column containing -4 is the *pivotal* (*or key*) *column*. Now the ratios 15/1, 5/2 are formed for the positive elements 1 and 2 of the key column, these being b_i/positive x. The least of these two ratios is 5/2 and the corresponding row (i.e., 2nd row) is the key (or pivotal) row. The entry 2 at the intersection of the key column and key row is the *key-element* or *pivot*.

STEP 4. We divide the key row (2nd row) by the pivot 2 and then add suitable multiples of this new row to each of the other rows so that each entry except the pivot in the key column (1st column) becomes zero. This process is called *pivoting*. The new matrix after pivoting is shown below.

$$\left[\begin{array}{cccc|c} x & y & u & v & b_i \\ 0 & \boxed{\frac{5}{2}} & 1 & -\frac{1}{2} & \frac{25}{2} \\ 1 & -\frac{1}{2} & 0 & \frac{1}{2} & \frac{5}{2} \\ 0 & -4 & 0 & 2 & 10 \end{array}\right] \begin{array}{l} \textbf{Ratio} \\ \frac{25}{2}/\frac{5}{2} = 5 \leftarrow \\ \\ \\ \end{array} \quad \begin{array}{l} \textbf{Operations} \\ R_1' = R_1 - R_2' \\ R_2' = \frac{1}{2}R_2 \\ R_3' = R_3 + 4R_2' \end{array}$$

$$\uparrow$$

[Here R_i' denotes the ith row of this matrix and R_i the ith row of the matrix in Step 2.]

We see that the objective row (last row) contains one *negative element* -4.

$\therefore$ The solution from this matrix is *not optimal*.

STEP 5. We repeat the procedure of Step 3 and Step 4 until all the elements in the objectiv row are *non-negative.* Negative element -4 in the last row indicates that *second column* is the *ke (or pivotal) column* and the ratio $\frac{25}{2}/\frac{5}{2}$ corresponding to the positive element $\frac{5}{2}$ in the second colum shows that the *first row is the key (or pivotal) row* and $\frac{5}{2}$ *is the pivot.* Pivoting the above matrix we get the *final simplex matrix* as follows.

$$\begin{bmatrix} x & y & u & v & b_i \\ 0 & 1 & \frac{2}{5} & -\frac{1}{5} & 5 \\ 1 & 0 & \frac{1}{5} & \frac{2}{5} & 5 \\ 0 & 0 & \frac{8}{5} & \frac{6}{5} & 30 \end{bmatrix} \begin{matrix} \textbf{Operations} \\ R_1'' = \frac{2}{5}R_1' \\ R_2'' = R_1' + \frac{1}{2}R_1'' \\ R_3'' = R_3' + 4R_1'' \end{matrix}$$

Since all the elements in the objective row (last row) are *non-negative,* this is the *final simplex matrix.*

STEP 6. (*Optimal Solution*). The *last entry* in the objective (last) row is 30 which is the *maximum value* of the objective function $z = 4x + 2y$. The values of the variables x and y for which z is maximum are obtained as follows.

If in a column one element is 1 (unity) and the other elements are all zeros, then the *last entry* in the row containing 1 is the value of the corresponding variable. Otherwise the value of the variable is zero.

From the final simplex matrix, we find that

$$x = 5, y = 5, u = 0, v = 0.$$

Hence, *the maximum value of z is* **30** *which is obtained when* $x = 5$ *and* $y = 5$.

EXAMPLE 2. *Solve the following linear programming problem by simplex method:*

$$\begin{aligned} \text{Maximize} \quad & z = x_1 + 3x_2 \\ \text{subject to} \quad & 3x_1 + 6x_2 \leq 8 \\ & 5x_1 + 2x_2 \leq 10 \\ & x_1, x_2 \geq 0. \end{aligned}$$

[C.U. 1991]

SOLUTION.

STEP 1. Adding two slack variables x_3 and x_4 to the left sides of the two linear constraints, the corresponding equations are

$$3x_1 + 6x_2 + 1.x_3 + 0.x_4 = 8$$
$$5x_1 + 2x_2 + 0.x_3 + 1.x_4 = 10$$

Also, $$z - x_1 - 3x_2 + 0.x_3 + 0.x_4 = 0.$$

STEP 2. The *intitial simplex matrix*, omitting z and ignoring non-negativity constraints, is

$$\left[\begin{array}{cccc|c} x_1 & x_2 & x_3 & x_4 & b_i \\ 3 & \boxed{6} & 1 & 0 & 8 \\ 5 & 2 & 0 & 1 & 10 \\ -1 & -3 & 0 & 0 & 0 \end{array}\right] \begin{array}{l} \textbf{Ratio} \\ 8/6 = \frac{4}{3} \leftarrow \\ 10/2 = 5 \\ \\ \end{array}$$

$$\uparrow$$

The negative number with largest absolute value in the objective row (last row) is -3 which shows that the second column is *the key (or pivotal) column*. Now the *least* of the two ratios is $\frac{4}{3}$ which corresponds to the first row which is the *key (or pivotal) row*. The entry 6 common to the key column and key row is the *pivot*.

STEP 3. Pivoting the above matrix i.e., dividing the first row by 6 and then adding suitable multiples of this row to each of the other rows so that each entry except the pivot becomes zero, we obtain the following matrix:

$$\left[\begin{array}{cccc|c} x_1 & x_2 & x_3 & x_4 & b_i \\ \frac{1}{2} & 1 & \frac{1}{6} & 0 & \frac{4}{3} \\ 4 & 0 & -\frac{1}{3} & 1 & \frac{22}{3} \\ \frac{1}{2} & 0 & \frac{1}{2} & 0 & 4 \end{array}\right] \begin{array}{l} \textbf{Operations} \\ R_1' = \frac{1}{6}R_1 \\ R_2' = R_2 - 2R_1' \\ R_3' = R_3' + 3R_1' \end{array}$$

Here R_i' is the ith row of this matrix and R_i is the ith row of the matrix in Step 2.

We see that the objective row (the last row) contains no negative elements and hence this is the *final simplex matrix*.

STEP 4. The *last entry* 4 *in the objective row is the maximum value of* z. The values of the variables for which z is maximum are given by

$$x_1 = 0, \quad x_2 = \frac{4}{3}, \quad x_3 = 0, \quad x_4 = \frac{22}{3}.$$

Hence the *maximum value of* z *is* 4 *which is obtained when* $x_1 = 0$ *and* $x_2 = \frac{4}{3}$.

REMARKS. If in Step 3, the objective row contains a negative entry, then we have to repeat the procedure shown in Step 2 and Step 3 until all the entries in the objective row (last row) are non-negative (i.e., positive or zero).

12.7.1. Procedure to solve an LPP by Simplex Method

If all the linear constraints of an *LPP* appear with '$\leq$' sign, then the procedure to solve the problem by Simplex method is stated below.

(i) *Conversion of inequations into equations:* We introduce *slack* variables and rewrite the inequations and the objective function as *equations*.

(ii) *Initial simplex matrix:* We write the *initial simplex matrix* omitting z and ignoring the non-negativity constraints.

(iii) *Pivot:* Considering the negative entry with the largest absolute value in the objective row (last row), we find the *key column.* Then considering the *least* of the ratios which are (entries in the last column): (*positive* entries in the key column), ignoring the ratios corresponding to negative entries in the key column, we find the key row. *The* entry at the intersection of the key column and key row is the *pivot.*

(iv) *Pivoting:* Dividing the key row by the *pivot,* we add (or subtract) suitable multiples of this new key row to (or from) each of the other rows to make each entry (except the pivot 1) zero.

(v) *Final Simplex Matrix:* If the objective row contains any *negative entry,* then we repeat the steps (iii) and (iv) until all the entries in the objective are *non-negative numbers* and *the final simplex matrix is obtained.*

(vi) *Conclusion:* If the *final simplex matrix* is obtained in which *the objective row has no negative entries,* then the *last entry* in the objective row is **the maximum value of the objective function z.**

EXAMPLE 3. *Solve the following LPP by simplex method*

$$\begin{aligned} \text{Maximize} \quad & z = 7x_1 + 5x_2 \\ \text{subject to the constraints:} \quad & x_1 + 2x_2 \leq 6 \\ & 4x_1 + 3x_2 \leq 12 \\ & x_1, x_2 \geq 0. \end{aligned}$$

[Delhi U. 1979; Ranchi U. 1982]

SOLUTION. Introducing slack variables x_3 and x_4, we rewrite the two linear constraints and the objective function (ignoring the non-negativity constraints) as equations as follows:

$$x_1 + 2x_2 + 1.x_3 + 0.x_4 = 6 \tag{1}$$

$$4x_1 + 3x_2 + 0.x_3 + 1.x_4 = 12 \tag{2}$$

$$z - 7x_1 - 5x_2 + 0.x_3 + 0.x_4 = 0 \tag{3}$$

The *initial simplex matrix* consisting of the number coefficients of (1), (2) and (3), omitting z, is the *augmented matrix* given by

$$\left[\begin{array}{rrrr|r} x_1 & x_2 & x_3 & x_4 & b_i \\ 1 & 2 & 1 & 0 & 6 \\ \boxed{4} & 3 & 0 & 1 & 12 \\ -7 & -5 & 0 & 0 & 0 \end{array}\right] \begin{array}{l} \textbf{Ratio} \\ 6/1 = 6 \\ 12/4 = 3 \leftarrow \text{least} \\ \\ \end{array}$$

$$\uparrow$$

The last row is the *objective row.*

We see that the first column is the *key column* and the *second row* corresponding to the least ratio is the *key row.* Clearly, 4 is the *pivot* (or *key element*), since 4 lies at the intersection of the key column and key row. *Pivoting this matrix* i.e., dividing the second row by the pivot 4 and then adding (or, subtracting) suitable multiples of this new row to (or from) each of the other rows to make each entry (except the pivot) in the key column zero we obtain the following matrix:

$$\left[\begin{array}{cccc|c} x_1 & x_2 & x_3 & x_4 & b_i \\ 0 & \frac{5}{4} & 1 & -\frac{1}{4} & 3 \\ 1 & \frac{3}{4} & 0 & \frac{1}{4} & 3 \\ 0 & \frac{1}{4} & 0 & \frac{7}{4} & 21 \end{array}\right] \begin{array}{l} \textbf{Operations} \\ R_1' = R_1 - R_2' \\ R_2' = \frac{1}{4}R_2 \\ R_3' = R_3 + 7R_2' \end{array}$$

From last row, we see that all the entries in the objective row are *non-negative*. Hence this is the *final simplex matrix* and the **maximum value of the objective function is 21** *which is obtained when $x_1 = 3$ and $x_2 = 0$.*

EXAMPLE 4. *Using simplex method, solve the following LPP*:

$$\begin{aligned} \text{Minimize} \quad & z = x_2 - 3x_3 + 2x_5 \\ \text{subject to the constraints:} \quad & 3x_2 - x_3 + 2x_5 \leq 7 \\ & -2x_2 + 4x_3 \leq 12 \\ & -4x_2 + 3x_3 + 8x_5 \leq 10 \\ & x_2, x_3, x_5 \geq 0. \end{aligned}$$

[Madras IIT 1979; B.H.U. 1980; Meerut U. 1987]

SOLUTION. To minimize $z = x_2 - 3x_3 + 2x_5$

means to maximize z^* or $-z = -x_2 + 3x_3 - 2x_5$.

Introducing slack variables S_1, S_2 and S_3, we rewrite the linear constraints and the objective function as follows:

$$\begin{aligned} 3x_2 - x_3 + 2x_5 + 1.S_1 + 0.S_2 + 0.S_3 &= 7 \\ -2x_2 + 4x_3 + 0.x_5 + 0.S_1 + 1.S_2 + 0.S_3 &= 12 \\ -4x_2 + 3x_3 + 8x_5 + 0.S_1 + 0.S_2 + 1.S_3 &= 10 \\ z^* + x_2 - 3x_3 + 2x_5 + 0.S_1 + 0.S_2 + 0.S_3 &= 0. \end{aligned}$$

The *initial simplex matrix* of the given *LPP* is written below.

$$\left[\begin{array}{cccccc|c} x_2 & x_3 & x_5 & S_1 & S_2 & S_3 & b_i \\ 3 & -1 & 2 & 1 & 0 & 0 & 7 \\ -2 & \boxed{4} & 0 & 0 & 1 & 0 & 12 \\ -4 & 3 & 8 & 0 & 0 & 1 & 10 \\ 1 & -3 & 2 & 0 & 0 & 0 & 0 \end{array}\right] \begin{array}{l} \textbf{Ratio} \\ \\ 12/4 = 3 \leftarrow \\ 10/3 = 3\frac{1}{3} \\ \\ \end{array}$$
$$\qquad\uparrow$$

The last row of this matrix is the *objective row.*

The negative entry -3 in the objective row indicates that the second column is the *key column* and the least ratio 3 shows that the second row is the *key row.* The entry 4 at the intersection of the key column and key row is the *pivot* (or *key element*). Pivoting this matrix, we get the following matrix:

x_2	x_3	x_5	S_1	S_2	S_3	b_i	Ratio	Operations
$\boxed{\frac{5}{2}}$	0	2	1	$\frac{1}{4}$	0	10	$10/\frac{5}{2} = 4 \leftarrow$	$R_1' = R_1 + R_2'$
$-\frac{1}{2}$	1	0	0	$\frac{1}{4}$	0	3		$R_2' = \frac{1}{4}R_2$
$-\frac{5}{2}$	0	8	0	$-\frac{3}{4}$	1	1		$R_3' = R_3 - 3R_2'$
$-\frac{1}{2}$	0	2	0	$\frac{3}{4}$	0	9		$R_4' = R_4 + 3R_2'$
↑								

From the objective row, we see that the first column is the key column and from the ratio, we find that the first row is the key row. The entry $\frac{5}{2}$ at the intersection of the key column and the key row is the *pivot* (or *key element*). Pivoting this matrix, we obtain the *final simplex matrix* given below.

x_2	x_3	x_5	S_1	S_2	S_3	b_i	Operations
1	0	$\frac{4}{5}$	$\frac{2}{5}$	$\frac{1}{10}$	0	4	$R_1'' = \frac{2}{5}R_1'$
0	1	$\frac{2}{5}$	$\frac{1}{5}$	$\frac{3}{10}$	0	5	$R_2'' = R_2' + \frac{1}{2}R_1''$
0	0	10	1	$-\frac{1}{2}$	1	11	$R_3'' = R_3' + \frac{5}{2}R_1''$
0	0	$\frac{12}{5}$	$\frac{1}{5}$	$\frac{4}{5}$	0	11	$R_4'' = R_4' + \frac{1}{2}R_1''$

From the last row, we see that all the entries in the objective row are *non-negative*. Hence this is the *final simplex matrix.*

$\therefore$ The *maximum value of* z^* *is* 11 *which is obtained when* $x_2 = 4, x_3 = 5$ *and* $x_5 = 0$.

Hence the **minimum value of the objective function z** = *maximum value of* $-z = $ **−11** which is obtained when $x_2 = 4, x_3 = 5$ and $x_5 = 0$.

12.8. SIMPLEX METHOD INTRODUCING SLACK, SURPLUS AND ARTIFICIAL VARIABLES

To solve a linear programming problem by simplex method, we first rewrite an *LP* model (see Art.12.3) into simplex format by introducing *slack, surplus* and *artificial variables.* In a constraint with '$\leq$' sign a non-negative *slack variable* is added on the left side to convert the linear inequation into an equation. For each '$\geq$' constraint, a non-negative *surplus variable* is subtracted from the left side to convert the inequation into an equation.

In *LP* models, each constraint after conversion into an equation must contain at least one variable with coefficient (+1), in every other constraint the coefficient of the variable being 0. For a '$\leq$' constraint a slack variable is used and this condition is satisfied. But in a '$\geq$' constraint, a surplus variable is used, its coefficient being (−1), and the condition is not satisfied if there is no term with coefficient (+1). For '=' constraint also this condition is not satisfied. For '$\geq$' and for '=' constraints, an additional non-negative variable is added to the left side of each constraint. Such a variable is called an **artificial variable** which has no real meaning in the problem, it only provides a convenient starting point for the method. For the constraint $2x_1 + 5x_2 \geq 30$, we can write $2x_1 + 5x_2 - x_3 + x_4 = 30$ where x_3 is a *surplus variable* and x_4 is an *artificial variable.* For the constraint $3x_1 - 2x_2 = 12$, we can write $3x_1 - 2x_2 + x_3 = 12$ where x_3 is an *artificial* variable.

In a general LP model, we have m linear constraints in n variables and, therefore, in the *simplex format* of the LPP, there are m linear equations in n variables which include decision, slack, surplus and artificial variables, where $m \leq n$. To solve these m equations, we set $(n - m)$ of the variables equal to zero for an iteration and solve the other m equations for the remaining m variables which *form a basis for the iteration.* These m variables are *basic variables* and the remaining $(n - m)$ variables are *non-basic* variables. A solution obtained by setting $(n - m)$ variables equal to zero and solving the other m-equations for the m basic variables is called a *basic solution* and if these values are the first set of solution, then the solution is the *initial basic solution.* A set of values of n variables satisfying both the structural and non-negativity constraints is called *feasible solution.* A basic solution satisfying the non-negativity constraints is called a *basic feasible solution.*

12.8.1. Procedure to solve an LPP introducing slack, surplus and artificial variables

(i) If any value b_i is negative, we make it *positive* multiplying both sides of the corresponding constraint by (-1) and adjusting the sign of inequality (or equality) accordingly.

(ii) The given inequations are converted into equations by introducing *slack*, surplus and artificial variables. We rewrite the objective function taking 0 as the coefficient of slack and surplus variables and $(-M)$ as that of the artificial variable, where M is large.

(iii) Initial simplex table including the initial basic feasible solution is constructed.

(iv) We find $z_j = \Sigma c'_j a_{ij}$, where c'_j is the entry in the extreme left column representing the coefficients of the basic variables (slack and/or artificial) and a_{ij} is the corresponding constraint coefficients.

(v) We find the quantity $z_j - c_j$ in the index row.

(vi) Now test for the optimal value of z. If all $(z_j - c_j)$ are non-negative, then the solution is *optimal.*

(vii) If $z_j - c_j < 0$ for at least one j and $a_{ij} \leq 0$ for all $i = 1, 2, \cdots, m$, then we leave it here. In this case, the given LPP will have unbounded solution.

(viii) If an initial solution is not optimal and also it is not unbounded, then we proceed as follows.

(ix) We find the non-basic variable with the highest negative value in the index row as the new variable to be entered into the basis. The corresponding column is called the *key* (or *pivotal*) *column.*

(x) To find the variable to be removed from the basis, we calculate for each $a_{ik} (> 0)$ in the key column the ratio $R = b_i / a_{ik}$ and then find the basic variable associated with the row having the *least value of* R as the departing variable from the basis. The row associated with the least R is the key (or pivotal) row.

(xi) We find the key element (or pivot) lying at the intersection of the key column and key row.

(xii) We divide each entry in the key row by the pivot and use transformations to obtain the new solution.

(xiii) If $z_j - c_j$ is not non-negative for all j, we repeat the steps (ix) to (xii) until $z_j - c_j \geq 0$ for all j.

Removal of Artificial Variable

Price associated with each artificial variable is taken as $(-M)$, where M is large. An artificial variable has no real meaning in an LPP and we can eliminate it by the simplex method. If it is removed from the basis, we forget about it and drop it along with all its entries from the next iteration. We now illustrate the whole procedure with the help of worked out problems.

EXAMPLE 5. *Solve the following LPP by simplex method:*

$$\begin{aligned} \text{Maximize} \quad & z = x_1 + 4x_2 + 5x_3 \\ \text{Subject to} \quad & 2x_1 + x_2 + 3x_3 \leq 36 \\ & x_1 + 2x_2 + x_3 \leq 42 \\ & x_1, x_2, x_3 \geq 0. \end{aligned}$$

SOLUTION. Introducing two slack variables x_4 and x_5, we rewrite the given LPP in the *simplex format* given below.

[*Simplex format* is an LP model in which all the structural constraints are converted into equations by introducing slack, surplus and artificial variables depending on the nature of inequality (or equality) signs in the constraints.]

$$\begin{aligned} \text{Maximize} \quad & z = x_1 + 4x_2 + 5x_3 + 0.x_4 + 0.x_5 \qquad (1) \\ \text{subject to} \quad & 2x_1 + x_2 + 3x_3 + 1.x_4 + 0.x_5 = 36 \\ & x_1 + 2x_2 + x_3 + 0.x_4 + 1.x_5 = 42 \\ & x_1, x_2, x_3, x_4, x_5 \geq 0. \end{aligned}$$

We first construct an initial simplex table of the above LPP as follows:

Table 1

		c_j	1	4	5	0	0	**Ratio**
c'_j	X_B	b_i	x_1	x_2	x_3	x_4	x_5	
0	x_4	36	2	1	[3]	1	0	$36/3 = 12 \leftarrow$ key row
0	x_5	42	1	2	1	0	1	$42/1 = 42$
		z_j	0	0	0	0	0	
	$z_j - c_j$		-1	-4	-5	0	0	
					↑ key column			

In the above table, c'_j-column consists of the coefficients of the slack variables x_4 and x_5 in the objective function (1), X_B-column consists of the slack variables x_4 and x_5, first row (c_j-row) represents the coefficients of the objective function (1), b_i-column represents the numbers on the right sides of the two constraint equations, and x_1-, x_2-, x_3- columns represent the corresponding coefficients of x_1, x_2, x_3, x_4, x_5 in the constraint equations. z_j-row represents the sum of the products of the entries in c'_j-column and the corresponding entries in the x_j column [e.g., $z_1 = 0.2 + 0.1 = 0, z_2 = 0.1 + 0.2 = 0$, etc.].

From the last row, we see that $z_j - c_j = -1, -4, -5$ which are < 0 and, therefore, this table *does not give the optimal solution.*

The highest negative value of $z_j - c_j$ is -5 which corresponds to x_3-column. Therefore, x_3-column is the *key column* and x_3 is the new *entering variable* to the basis. Now we compute the ratio b_i/a_{ik} i.e., 36/3 and 42/1. The least these two ratios is 36/3 which indicates that x_4 is the variable to be removed from the basis and the first row is the *key row.* The entry 3 at the intersection of the key column and key row is the *pivot* or *key element.* Now replace 0 and x_4 of key row by 5 and x_3 respectively. We decide the key row by the pivot 3 and construct a new table as follows.

Table 2

		c_j	1	4	5	0	0	Ratio	Operations
c'_j	X_B	b_i	x_1	x_2	x_3	x_4	x_5		
5	x_3	12	$\frac{2}{3}$	$\frac{1}{3}$	1	$\frac{1}{3}$	0	$12/\frac{1}{3} = 36$	$R'_1 = \frac{1}{3}R_1$
0	x_5	30	$\frac{1}{3}$	$\boxed{\frac{5}{3}}$	0	$-\frac{1}{3}$	1	$30/\frac{5}{3} = 18 \leftarrow$ key row	$R'_2 = R_2 - R'_1$
		z_j	$\frac{10}{3}$	$\frac{5}{3}$	5	$\frac{5}{3}$	0	[Here R_i denote the ith row of Table 1	
	$z_j - c_j$		$\frac{7}{3}$	$-\frac{7}{3}$	0	$\frac{5}{3}$	0	R'_i that of Table 2]	
				↑ key column					

We see that $(z_j - c_j)$-row contains one negative entry $-\frac{7}{3}$ and hence this table does not give the optimal solution. We repeat the above operations until $z_i - c_j \geq 0$ for all j and construct table 3 given below. In this case $\frac{5}{3}$ is the *pivot*, x_2 is the new entering variable and x_5 is the variable to be removed from the basis.

Table 3

		c_j	1	4	5	0	0	Operations
c'_j	X_B	b_i	x_1	x_2	x_3	x_4	x_5	Performed
5	x_3	6	$\frac{3}{5}$	0	1	$\frac{2}{5}$	$-\frac{1}{5}$	$R''_1 = R'_1 - \frac{1}{3}R''_2$
4	x_2	18	$\frac{1}{5}$	1	0	$-\frac{1}{5}$	$\frac{3}{5}$	$R''_2 = \frac{3}{5}R'_2$
		z_j	$\frac{19}{5}$	4	5	$\frac{6}{5}$	$\frac{7}{5}$	[Here R''_i denotes the
	$z_j - c_j$		$\frac{14}{3}$	0	0	$\frac{6}{5}$	$\frac{7}{5}$	ith row of Table 3]

We see that the *index row i.e.,* $(z_j - c_j)$*-row contains no negative entries* and, therefore, Table 3 gives the *optimal solution* which is given by

$$x_1 = 0, \quad x_2 = 18, \quad x_3 = 6, \quad x_4 = 0, \quad x_5 = 0.$$

Hence, the maximum value of $Z = 0 + 4 \times 18 + 5 \times 6 = \mathbf{102}$.

EXAMPLE 6. *Solve the following linear programming problem by simplex method:*

$$\begin{aligned} \text{Maximize} \quad & z = 2x_1 + 3x_2 \\ \text{subject to} \quad & x_1 + x_2 \leq 8 \\ & x_1 + 2x_2 = 5 \\ & 2x_1 + x_2 \leq 8 \\ & x_1, x_2 \geq 0. \end{aligned}$$

[C.U. 1991]

SOLUTION. Introducing slack and artificial variables, we rewrite the given LPP in the *simplex format* as follows.

$$\begin{aligned} \text{Maximize} \quad & z = 2x_1 + 3x_2 + 0.x_3 + (-M)x_4 + 0.x_5 \\ \text{subject to} \quad & x_1 + x_2 + 1.x_3 + 0.x_4 + 0.x_5 = 8 \\ & x_1 + 2x_2 + 0.x_3 + 1.x_4 + 0.x_5 = 5 \\ & 2x_1 + x_2 + 0.x_3 + 0.x_4 + 1.x_5 = 8 \\ & x_1, x_2, x_3, x_4, x_5 \geq 0, \quad \text{where } M \text{ is large.} \end{aligned}$$

The initial simplex table of the above LPP is constructed below:

Table 1

		c_j	2	3	0	$-M$	0	**Ratio**
c'_j	X_B	b_i	x_1	x_2	x_3	x_4	x_5	
0	x_3	8	1	1	1	0	0	$8/1 = 8$
$-M$	x_4	5	1	[2]	0	1	0	$5/2 = 2.5 \leftarrow$ key row
0	x_5	8	2	1	0	0	1	$8/1 = 8$
		z_j	$-M$	$-2M$	0	$-M$	0	
	$z_j - c_j$		$-M-2$	$-2M-3$	0	0	0	
				↑ key column				

From Table 1, we see that 2 is the *pivot,* x_2 is the entering variable and x_4 is the variable to be removed from the basis X_B. The new simplex Table 2 is constructed on the next page.

Table 2

		c_j	2	3	0		0	Ratio
c'_j	X_B	b_i	x_1	x_2	x_3		x_5	
0	x_3	$\frac{11}{2}$	$\frac{1}{2}$	0	1	Dropped	0	$\frac{11}{2}/\frac{1}{2}=11$
3	x_2	$\frac{5}{2}$	$\frac{1}{2}$	1	0		0	$\frac{5}{2}/\frac{1}{2}=5$
0	x_5	$\frac{11}{2}$	$\boxed{\frac{3}{2}}$	0	0		1	$\frac{11}{2}/\frac{3}{2}=3\frac{2}{3}$ ← key row
		z_j	$\frac{3}{2}$	3	0		0	
	$z_j - c_j$		$-\frac{1}{2}$	0	0		0	
			↑ key column					

Note that in the above table the *artificial variable x_4 is removed and the corresponding column is dropped.*

From the last row of the above table we see that $-\frac{1}{2}$ is a negative entry in $(z_j - c_j)$-row and, therefore, this table does not give the optimal solution. x_1 is the entering varaible and x_5 is the variable to be removed, $\frac{3}{2}$ being the *pivot.* The new simplex table 3 is constructed below.

Table 3

		c_j	2	3	0		0
c'_j	X_B	b_i	x_1	x_2	x_3		x_5
0	x_3	$\frac{11}{3}$	0	0	1	Dropped	$-\frac{1}{3}$
3	x_2	$\frac{2}{3}$	0	1	0		$-\frac{1}{3}$
2	x_1	$\frac{11}{3}$	1	0	0		$\frac{2}{3}$
		z_j	2	3	0		$\frac{1}{3}$
	$z_j - c_j$		0	0	0		$\frac{1}{3}$

From the last row of this table, we see that $z_j - c_j \geq 0$ for all j and hence Table 3 gives the optimal solution which is given by

$$x_1 = \frac{11}{3}, \quad x_2 = \frac{2}{3}, \quad x_3 = \frac{11}{3}, \quad x_5 = 0.$$

Hence, **the maximum value of z** is $2 \times \frac{11}{3} + 3 \times \frac{2}{3} = \mathbf{\frac{28}{3} = 9\frac{1}{3}}$

EXAMPLE 7. *Solve the following LPP by simplex method:*

$$\begin{aligned} \text{Maximize} \quad & z = 3x_1 - x_2 \\ \text{subject to} \quad & 2x_1 + x_2 \geq 2, \\ & x_1 + 3x_2 \leq 3, \\ & x_2 \leq 4; \\ & x_1, x_2 \geq 0. \end{aligned}$$

[C.U. B.A./B.Sc 1992]

SOLUTION. Introducing slack, surplus and artificial variables, we rewrite the given *LPP* in the *simplex format* as follows.

$$\begin{aligned}
\text{Maximize}\quad & z = 3x_1 - x_2 + 0.x_3 + Mx_4 + 0.x_5 + 0.x_6 \\
\text{Subject to}\quad & 2x_1 + x_2 - x_3 + x_4 + 0.x_5 + 0.x_6 = 2, \\
& x_1 + 3x_2 + 0.x_3 + 0.x_4 + 1.x_5 + 0.x_6 = 3, \\
& 0.x_1 + 1.x_2 + 0.x_3 + 0.x_4 + 0.x_5 + 1.x_6 = 4, \\
& x_1, x_2, x_3, x_4, x_5, x_6 \geq 0.
\end{aligned}$$

In the above simplex format, x_3 is a surplus variable, x_4, x_5 are slack variables and x_6 is an artificial variable, where M is large. From the simplex format, we construct the simplex tables successively as shown below.

		c_j	3	-1	0	$-M$	0	0	**Ratio**
c_j	X_B	b_i	x_1	x_2	x_3	x_4	x_5	x_6	
$-M$	x_4	2	$\boxed{2}$	1	-1	1	0	0	$2/2 = 1 \leftarrow$ key row
0	x_5	3	1	3	0	0	1	0	$3/1 = 3$
0	x_6	4	0	1	0	0	0	1	
		$z_j \rightarrow$	$-2M$	$-M$	M	$-M$	0	0	
		$z_j - c_j \rightarrow$	$-2M - 3$	$-M + 1$	M	0	0	0	
			↑ key column						

3	x_1	1	1	$\frac{1}{2}$	$-\frac{1}{2}$		0	0	
0	x_5	2	0	$\frac{5}{2}$	$\boxed{\frac{1}{2}}$		1	0	$2/\frac{1}{2} = 4 \leftarrow$ key row
0	x_6	4	0	1	0		0	1	
		z_j	3	$\frac{3}{2}$	$-\frac{3}{2}$		0	0	
		$(z_j - c_j) \rightarrow$	0	$\frac{5}{2}$	$-\frac{3}{2}$		0	0	
					↑ key column				

3	x_1	3	1	3	0		1	0
0	x_3	4	0	5	1		2	0
0	x_6	4	0	1	0		0	1
		z_j	3	9	0		3	0
		$(z_j - c_j) \rightarrow$	0	10	0		3	0

From the last row, we see that $z_j - c_j \geq 0$ for all j.

$\therefore$ The last part of the above table gives optimal solution which is given by $x_1 = 3, x_2 = 0$, $x_3 = 4, x_5 = 0, x_6 = 4$. Hence the maximum value of $z = 3 \times 3 - 0 = \mathbf{9}$.

EXAMPLE 8. *Solve the following Linear Programming Problem by simplex method:*

$$\begin{aligned} \text{Maximize} \quad & z = x_1 + x_2 \\ \text{Subject to} \quad & 2x_1 + 3x_2 \leq 22, \\ & 2x_1 + x_2 \leq 14, \\ & x_1 - x_2 \leq 4, \\ & 3x_1 - 2x_2 \geq -6, \\ & x_1, x_2 \geq 0. \end{aligned}$$

[C.U. B.A./B.Sc 1994]

SOLUTION. The given LPP may be written as

$$\begin{aligned} \text{Maximize} \quad & z = x_1 + x_2 \\ \text{subject to} \quad & 2x_1 + 3x_2 \leq 22, \\ & 2x_1 + x_2 \leq 14, \\ & x_1 - x_2 \leq 4, \\ & -3x_1 + 2x_2 \leq 6; \\ & x_1, x_2 \geq 0. \end{aligned}$$

Introducing slack variables x_3, x_4, x_5, x_6, we can rewrite the above LPP as follows:

$$\begin{aligned} \text{Maximize} \quad & z = x_1 + x_2 + 0.x_3 + 0.x_4 + 0.x_5 + 0.x_6 \\ \text{subject to} \quad & 2x_1 + 3x_2 + 1.x_3 + 0.x_4 + 0.x_5 + 0.x_6 = 22 \\ & 2x_1 + x_2 + 0.x_3 + 1.x_4 + 0.x_5 + 0.x_6 = 14 \\ & x_1 - x_2 + 0.x_3 + 0.x_4 + 1.x_5 + 0.x_6 = 4 \\ & -3x_1 + 2x_2 + 0.x_3 + 0.x_4 + 0.x_5 + 1.x_6 = 6; \\ & x_1, x_2, x_3, x_4, x_5, x_6 \geq 0. \end{aligned}$$

From the above *simplex format,* we construct simplex tables successively as shown in the next page.

		c_j	1	1	0	0	0	0	Ratio
c'_j	X_B	b_i	x_1	x_2	x_3	x_4	x_5	x_6	
0	x_3	22	2	3	1	0	0	0	$22/2 = 11$
0	x_4	14	2	1	0	1	0	0	$14/2 = 7$
0	x_5	4	[1]	−1	0	0	1	0	$4/1 = 4 \leftarrow$ key row
0	x_6	6	−3	2	0	0	0	1	
		$z_j \rightarrow$	0	0	0	0	0	0	
		$z_j - c_j$	−1	−1	0	0	0	0	
			↑ key column						

Note: Since there is a *tie* in the highest negative value in the index row (last row), we can select any one of the two columns (usually the column farthest to the left).

									Ratio
0	x_3	14	0	5	1	0	−2	0	$14/5 = 2.8$
0	x_4	6	0	[3]	0	1	−2	0	$6/3 = 2 \leftarrow$
1	x_1	4	1	−1	0	0	1	0	
0	x_6	18	0	−1	0	0	3	1	
		$z_j \rightarrow$	1	−1	0	0	1	0	
		$(z_j - c_j) \rightarrow$	0	−2	0	0	1	0	
				↑					

									Ratio
0	x_3	4	0	0	1	$-\frac{5}{3}$	[$\frac{4}{3}$]	0	$4/\frac{4}{3} = 3 \leftarrow$ key row
1	x_2	2	0	1	0	$\frac{1}{3}$	$-\frac{2}{3}$	0	—
1	x_1	6	1	0	0	$\frac{1}{3}$	$\frac{1}{3}$	0	$6/\frac{1}{3} = 18$
0	x_6	20	0	0	0	$\frac{1}{3}$	$\frac{7}{3}$	1	$60/7 = 8\frac{4}{7}$
		$z_j \rightarrow$	1	1	0	$\frac{2}{3}$	$-\frac{1}{3}$	0	
		$(z_j - c_j) \rightarrow$	0	1	0	$\frac{2}{3}$	$-\frac{1}{3}$	0	
							↑ key column		

0	x_5	3	0	0	$\frac{3}{4}$	$-\frac{5}{4}$	1	0
1	x_2	4	0	1	$\frac{1}{2}$	$-\frac{1}{2}$	0	0
1	x_1	5	1	0	$-\frac{1}{4}$	$\frac{3}{4}$	0	0
0	x_6	13	0	0	$-\frac{7}{4}$	$\frac{13}{4}$	0	1
		$z_j \rightarrow$	1	1	$\frac{1}{4}$	$\frac{1}{4}$	0	0
		$(z_j - c_j) \rightarrow$	0	0	$\frac{1}{4}$	$\frac{1}{4}$	0	0

From the last row (Index row), we see that $z_j - c_j \geq 0$ for j and, therefore, the last part of the table gives *optimal solution which is given by* $x_1 = 5, x_2 = 4$.

Hence, **the maximum value of** Z *is* $5 + 4 = $ **9**.

Exercise 12 (III)

(Simplex Method of Solution of an LPP)

1. What do you mean by *slack* and *surplus variables*? What is an *artificial variable*? Give one example for each.

2. State the general form of an *LPP* indicating the objective function and the decision variables.

3. Convert the following linear constraints into constraint equations by introducing slack and surplus variables:

$$\text{(i)}\quad \left.\begin{aligned} 3x_1+2x_2 &\le 12,\\ 2x_1+5x_2 &\ge 6,\\ x_1,x_2 &\ge 0 \end{aligned}\right\};\qquad \text{(ii)}\quad \left.\begin{aligned} 2x_1-x_2 &\le 10\\ x_1+4x_2 &\ge 7\\ x_1,x_2 &\ge 0 \end{aligned}\right\}$$

4. Introducing slack, surplus and artificial variables rewrite the following *LPP* in the simplex format:

(i) Maximize $z = 2x_1 + 3x_2$ subject to

$$x_1 + 2x_2 \le 8, 3x_1 + x_2 \le 6, x_1, x_2 \ge 0.$$

(ii) Maximize $z = 4x_1 + 7x_2$ subject to

$$x_1 + 3x_2 \le 10, \quad x_1 - x_2 \ge -2, \quad x_2 \le 3, \quad x_1, x_2 \ge 0.$$

(iii) Maximize $z = 5x_1 - 2x_2$ subject to

$$2x_1 + x_2 \le 9, \quad 3x_1 - x_2 \ge 5, \quad x_1 + x_2 \ge 6, x_1, x_2 \ge 0.$$

(iv) Maximize $z = 2x_1 + 5x_2 + 3x_3$ subject to

$$2x_1 + 3x_2 + x_3 \le 4, \quad x_1 + 2x_2 + x_3 \le 2, \quad x_1, x_2, x_3 \ge 0.$$

5. Solve the following linear programming problem (*LPP*) by simplex method:

(i) Maximize $z = 2x + 3y$ subject to

$$x + y \le 1, \quad 3x + y \le 4, \quad x, y \ge 0.$$

(ii) Maximize $z = 5x_1 + 3x_2, x_1 \ge 0, x_2 \ge 0$ subject to

$$3x_1 + 5x_2 \le 15, \quad 5x_1 + 2x_2 \le 0.$$

[Viswa Bharati 1983; C.U. 1985, '93]

6. Solve the following *LPP* by the simplex method:

(i) Maximize $z = 3x_1 + 6x_2 + 2x_3$ subject to

$$3x_1 + 4x_2 + x_3 \le 2, \quad x_1 + 3x_2 + 2x_3 \le 1, \quad x_1, x_2, x_3 \ge 0.$$

(ii) Maximize $z = x_1 + 4x_2 + 5x_3$ subject to

$$2x_1 + x_2 + 3x_3 \le 36, \quad x_1 + 2x_2 + x_3 \le 42, x_1, x_2, x_3 \ge 0.$$

(iii) Maximize $z = 3x_1 + 6x_2 + 2x_3$ subject to

$$3x_1 + 4x_2 + x_3 \le 2, x_1 + 3x_2 + 2x_3 \le 1, \quad x_1, x_2, x_3 \ge 0.$$ **[C.U. 1990]**

7. Solve the following *LPP* by simplex method:

Minimize $z = x_1 - 3x_2 + 2x_3$ subject to

$$3x_1 - x_2 + 2x_3 \le 7, \quad -2x_1 + 4x_2 \le 12, \quad -4x_1 + 3x_2 + 8x_3 \le 10, \quad x_1, x_2, x_3 \ge 0.$$

8. Solve the following linear programming problem by simplex method:

(i) Maximize $z = 2x_1 + 3x_2$ subjec to

$$x_1 + x_2 \le 8, \quad x_1 + 2x_2 = 5, 2x_1 + x_2 \le 8, \quad x_1, x_2 \ge 0.$$

(ii) Minimize $z = 4x_1 + 3x_2$ subject to

$$x_1 + 2x_2 \ge 8, \quad 3x_1 + 2x_2 \ge 12, \quad x_1, x_2 \ge 0.$$ **[C.U. 1989]**

9. Using simplex method solve the following *LPP*:

Maximize $z = 5x_1 + 2x_2 + 10x_3$ subject to

$$x_1 - x_2 \le 10, \quad x_2 - x_3 \ge 10, \quad x_1 + x_2 + x_3 \le 10, \quad x_1, x_2, x_3 \ge 0.$$ **[ICWAI (Final) June 1985]**

10. Food *A* contains 20 units of Vitamin *X* and 40 units of Vitamin *Y* per gram. Food *B* contains 30 units each of Vitamin *X* and *Y*. The daily minimum human requirements of Vitamin *X* and *Y* are 900 units and 1200 units respectively. How many grams of each type of food should be consumed so as to minimise the cost, if food *A* costs 60 paise per gram and food *B* costs 80 paise per gram? **[ICWAI (Final) December, 1986]**

[HINTS. Let Food *A* consist of x_1 grams and Food *B* of x_2 grams. Let z be the total cost in rupees. Then information (or conditions) given in the problem may be stated as follows.

Food	No. of Grams	Vitamin contents		Cost per gram (in paise)
		X	*Y*	
A	x_1	20	40	60
B	x_2	30	30	80
Daily minimum requirement of vitamin		900	1200	

From this table, we formulate the *LPP* as follows:

Minimize $z = 60x_1 + 80x_2$ subject to

$$20x_1 + 30x_2 \ge 900, 40x_1 + 30x_2 \ge 1200 \quad \text{where} \quad x_1, x_2 \ge 0.$$

Now solve the problem by simplex method.]

Answers

3. (i) $3x_1 + 2x_2 + x_3 = 12, 2x_1 + 5x_2 - x_4 = 6$; here x_3 is a slack and x_4 is a simplex variable; (ii) $2x_1 - x_2 + x_3 = 10, x_1 + 4x_2 - x_4 = 7$.

4. (i) Maximize $z = 2x_1 + 3x_2 + 0.x_3 + 0.x_4$ subject to

$$x_1 + 2x_2 + x_3 = 8, \quad 3x_1 + x_2 + x_4 = 6, \quad x_1, x_2, x_3, x_4 \geq 0$$

Here x_3, x_4 are slack variables.

(ii) Maximize $z = 4x_1 + 7x_2 + 0.x_3 + 0.x_4 + 0.x_5$ subject to

$$x_1 + 3x_2 + x_3 = 10, \quad -x_1 + x_2 + x_4 = 2, \quad x_2 + x_5 = 3, \quad x_1, x_2, x_3, x_4, x_5 \geq 0.$$

(iii) Maximize $z = 5x_1 - 2x_2 + 0.x_3 + 0.x_4 + (-M)x_5 + 0.x_6 + (-M)x_7$ subject to

$$2x_1 + x_2 + x_3 = 9,\ 3x_1 - x_2 - x_4 + x_5 = 5,\ x_1 + x_2 - x_6 + x_7 = 6.\ x_1, x_2, x_3, x_4, x_5, x_6, x_7 \geq 0.$$

(iv) Maximize $z = 2x_1 + 5x_2 + 3x_3 + 0.x_4 + 0.x_5$ subject to

$$2x_1 + 3x_2 + x_3 + x_4 = 4, \quad x_1 + 2x_2 + x_3 + x_5 = 2, \quad x_1, x_2, x_3, x_4, x_5 \geq 0.$$

5. (i) $z_{\text{max}} = 3$ at $x = 0, y = 1$; (ii) $z_{\text{max.}} = \frac{235}{19}$ at $x_1 = \frac{20}{19}, x_2 = \frac{45}{19}$.

6. (i) $z_{\text{max}} = 102$ at $x_1 = 0, x_2 = 18, x_3 = 6$; (iii) $z_{\text{max}} = \frac{12}{5}$ at $x_1 \frac{2}{5}, x_2 = \frac{1}{5}, x_3 = 0$.

7. $z_{\text{min}} = -11$ at $x_1 = 4, x_2 = 5, x_3 = 0$.

8. (i) $z_{\text{max}} = \frac{28}{3}$ at $x_1 = \frac{11}{5}, x_2 = \frac{2}{3}$; (ii) $z_{\text{min}} = 17$ at $x_1 = 2, x_2 = 3$.

9. $z_{\text{max}} = 20$ at $x_1 = 0, x_2 = 10, x_3 = 0$.

10. Minimum cost = Rs. 25 when Food $A = 15$ units and Food $B = 20$ units.

Appendix to Chapter 9

Linear Programming

Linear Programming (L.P.) is a widely used mathematical optimization technique which was developed in 1947 by George B. Dantzig for solving planning problems of the U.S. Air Force. Though computer 'programming' is not related to L.P., the development of computer has greatly contributed to the success of L.P. In L.P. linear equations are solved again and again, each time changing one variable, till we arrive at the final solution. In actual industrial problems the constraints are too many and sometimes more than hundred linear equations are formed, the solutions of which are practically impossible without the aid of a computer.

A great number of economic business decisions, eg., best product mix of a firm, advertising budget funds allocation among competing media, selection of best production process, etc., can be analysed and solved by L.P. All business concerns have certain objectives, eg., maximization of profit, output, sales, minimization of cost, etc. The algebraic expression of the objective is called an objective function which must be linear. The optimization of the linear objective function must be subject to constraints, which are also linear algebraic expression in the form of either equalities or, inequalities. Such constraints have to obey 'non-negativity restrictions' as the variables cannot have negative values. The translation of the firm's problems into objective function and a set of linear constraints is called 'Formulation of the L.P.' A problem, once formulated, can be solved by using a number of different techniques of which the 'Graphical Solution' and the 'Simplex Method' are very popular. In this chapter we seek to explain the process of maximization and minimization of such objective functions with examples.

Applications of L.P.

Economic and business decisions often deal with the allocation of scarce resources, eg., raw material, money, time, space, people, etc. among competing projects either to maximize some objectives, eg., output, return on investment profit, market share, etc., or, minimize some objectives, eg., cost, waste, pollution, etc., L.P. can be applied for solving the following practical problems of industry:

Product Mix Problems

The optimum product mix to be produced with company's scarce manpower, plant capacity, raw-materials, finance, etc., can be analysed and solved by L.P. Let us take a food processing plant producing tomato products, eg., stewed tomato, tomato paste, tomato soup, ketchup, tomato juice, canned tomatoes, etc. It can produce any or all of these products simultaneously, but it has limited supply of tomatoes, time, labour, sugar, etc. Each product has different profit contribution and, hence, it becomes a problem for the management to decide how much of each product to be produced. Moreover, the management may be interested in knowing how much they can pay for extra units of the factors limited in supply. These questions can be answered by using the L.P. technique.

Diet Problems

Animal feeds are produced by mixing a number of ingredients each of which contains different proportions of protein, vitamins, minerals, etc. The animal feeds produced must meet certain nutritional levels as specified by the Government, at the lowest cost. The producers may like to know the increase in cost when the nutritional level of the feed is increased. This problem is also associated with pharmaceutical, fertilizer, lawn seed and pet food industries. L.P. is an answer to such problems.

Advertising Budget Allocation

A firm has limited funds for advertising budget allocation, eg., T.V., radio, newspaper, magazines, bill broads, neon-advertisements, etc. and it would like to know how much money should be allocated to which medium for getting the maximum benefit. T.V. advertising may again be split as day or evening shows, depending on the type of audiences. The fund allocation problem can be solved by L.P.

Process Selection

This problem is similar to diet problems. It deals with product that can be produced by using any one (or, more) of several processes, each involving different proportions of vairous inputs. A firm would like to produce the product by combining two or more processes and inputs in such a way that production costs are minimized. L.P. can suggest an answer to such problems.

Distribution Problems

Many firms have two or more plants where a certain product is produced and several warehouses at different locations for storing the products before sending them to various retail outlets. The distribution costs also differ for various routes used from production plant to warehouse and to sales outlet. Management must decide the shipping assignments, i.e., how many units should go from each sales outlet, with a minimizing view to shipping cost. Such problems can be solved by transportation and L.P. techniques.

Oil Processing and Transportation Problems

Large petroleum firms receive crude oil from different sources which they transport to several refineries where various products are produced jointly in the cracking process. L.P. is used to find out the optimum product-mix, the best method of allocation of crude oil from different sources to the various refineries and transportation of products to sales outlets. Thus L.P. is widely used in petroleum industry.

Personnel Assignment Problems

These problems are similar to distribution problems. An accounting firm would like to find out the best method of assigning audit staff personnel to various audit activities within the audit office constraints, and simultaneously meeting the professional and economic objectives of the offices. L.P. and assignment techniques can be used for solution of such problems.

Long-range Capacity Planning for Electric Utilities

Good long-range planning models are necessary for energy related complicated problems. Demand projections for future years and information relating to operation and investment costs should be incorporated in such models. John R. McNamara developed one such capacity planning model for electric utilities based on L.P. to minimize the costs of satisfying projected demands. The model is simple, user-oriented, and can be used to solve problems quickly.

Besides these, L.P. can be applied to various other fields of decision-making.

Assumptions of the L.P. Model

An L.P. model is based on the following assumptions:

1. There must be an objective which a firm wants to maximize, or minimize. The objective function (algebraic) must be linear. Multiple objectives may also be incorporated in the analysis.
2. There must be alternatives available as no decision is required when a firm is faced with a single course of action, eg., if a product can be produced by one process only, no decision is required.
3. The linear objective function must be optimized subject to some structural constraints, eg., materials, time, money, etc., (resources), plant capacity, contractual agreements, legal considerations, marketing quotas, etc. These constraints may be expressed algebraically, either as linear inequalities or, linear equations. Like the objective function, the constraints must also be linear functions.
4. Variables do not take negative values and, hence, this is known as non-negativity restriction, i.e., the value of the decision variables will be either zero or positive.

Formulation of the L.P. Problem

Let us now consider a product mix problem. A firm manufactures two types of boxes, Type A and Type B. The processing time in minutes of welding, press and plating on these boxes are given below. The capacities of these departments and contributions of these boxes are also given.

	Type A Box	Type B Box	Available hours
Welding	3 mins.	3 mins.	60 mins.
Press	6 mins.	2 mins.	60 mins.
Plating	8 mins.	0 mins.	60 mins.
Contribution	30 P.	20 P.	

How many of A and B boxes are to be produced to get maximum contribution?

The process of formulating L.P. problems involve transformation of the descriptive information regarding the situations into mathematical statements.

The following example illustrates the point:

Problem 1

Let x_1 = number of type A boxes, x_2 = number of type B boxes. The objective function becomes maximizing $Z = 30x_1 + 20x_2$ where Z represents profit and 30 and 20 are the contribution of Type A and Type B boxes, respectively.

The next step in formulating a problem is to specify the constraints. As x_1 and x_2 both take 3 mins. for welding operation and the total available mins. in welding department is 60 mins., the constraint equation will be as follow:

$$3x_1 + 3x_2 \leq 60 \quad \text{(Welding Department)}$$

i.e., the total mins. required for producing x_1 and x_2 boxes should be either less than, or equal to, 60 mins.

Similarly, other constraint equations are:

$$\begin{aligned} 6x_1 + 2x_2 &\leq 60 \quad \text{(Press shop)} \\ 8x_1 + 0x_2 &\leq 60 \quad \text{(Planting shop)} \\ x_1 \text{ and } x_2 &\geq 0 \end{aligned}$$

If there are only two variables, the problem can be solved by a simple graphical method. Where more than two variables are involved, we apply the 'Simplex Method'.

Graphic Solution (Maximisation)

Let us solve the same problem graphically. Here only two decision variables, i.e., x_1 and x_2, are involved. These variables are plotted along x-axis (horizontal) and y-axis (vertical).

To plot the constraints on a graph, these are expressed in the form of the following equations:

$$3x_1 + 3x_2 = 60 \qquad (9.A.1)$$

$$6x_1 + 2x_2 = 60 \qquad (9.A.2)$$

$$8x_1 = 60 \qquad (9.A.3)$$

Now, from (1) we get $\frac{x_1}{x_2}\left|\frac{0}{20}\right|\frac{20}{0}\right|$, and from (2) $\frac{x_1}{x_2}\left|\frac{0}{30}\right|\frac{10}{0}\right|$. Now $OABCD$ in fig. 9.1 is the convex region and the points in O, A, B, C, D are called the feasible solutions to the L.P. problem. There is a fundamental theorem of L.P. which states that the objective function is optimized at one of the corner points, i.e., O, A, B, C, D. Thus, for maximum profit—only these corner points, also called basic feasible solutions are to be evaluated.

Moreover, the solution lies in the first quadrant as $x_1 \geq 0$ and $x_2 \geq 0$.

Now from (1) and (2), we have

$$\begin{aligned} 6x_1 + 6x_2 &= 120 \\ -6x_1 + 2x_2 &= 60 \\ 4x_2 &= 60 \quad \Rightarrow \quad x_2 = 15 \text{ and } x_1 = 5. \end{aligned}$$

Again, from (2) and (3), we have

$$x_1 = 7.5 \quad \text{and} \quad x_2 = 7.5.$$

Thus the coordinates of B and C are $(5, 15)$ and $(7.5, 7.5)$.

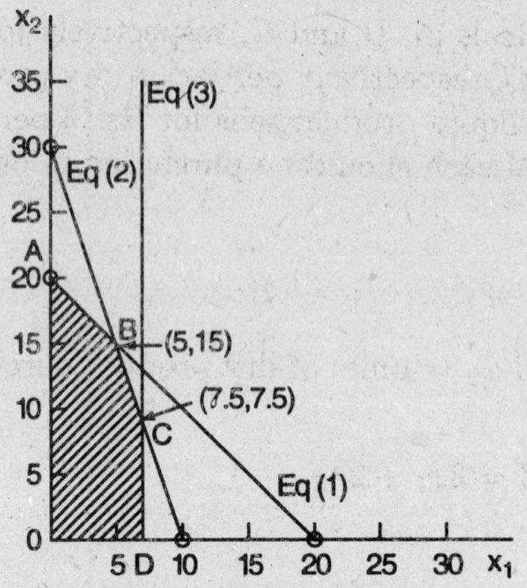

Fig 9.1 The Feasible Solution

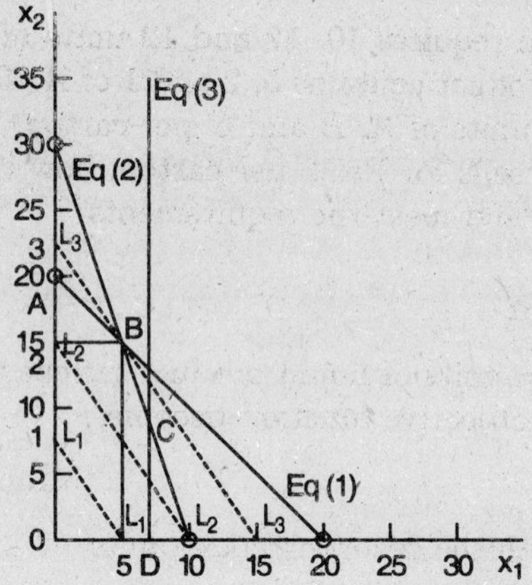

Fig 9.2 The Alternative Method

The points can also be directly obtained from the graph.

Now $z = 30x_1 + 20x_2$.

At 0, $Z = 30 \times 0 + 20 \times 0 = 0$.

At A, $Z = 30 \times 0 + 20 \times 20 = 400$.

At B, $Z = 30 \times 5 + 20 \times 15 = 450$.

At C, $Z = 30 \times \frac{15}{2} + 20 \times \frac{15}{2} = 375$.

At D, $Z = 30 \times \frac{15}{2} + 20 \times 0 = 225$.

Here $Z =$ Rs. 450 (maximum at B when $x_1 = 5$ and $x_2 = 15$).

An alternative method for obtaining the optimal basic feasible solution is shown in fig. 9.2, which is same as fig. 9.1 with several dotted iso-profit lines, i.e., L_1L_1, L_2L_2, L_3L_3, etc. An iso-profit line is a graphical representation of all possible combinations of two products which give the same profit. These are parallel lines having the same slope. There may be infinite number of such lines. The further an iso-profit line is from the origin, the greater is the profit.

Here we select a reasonable profit and draw the objective function line relating to this profit. Next we pull the iso-profit line out of the solution space gradually till it touches the solution space at one extreme point only. Now we can find the optimum profit and the values of the decision variable from the graph.

$Z = 30x_1 + 20x_2$ (objective function) is a linear equation of first degree. If we take different values of Z, eg., 150, 300, 600 etc. and plot them on the graph, the lines will be parallel:

$$30x_1 + 20x_2 = 150 \quad \therefore \quad \begin{array}{c|c|c} x_1 & 0 & 5 \\ \hline x_2 & 7.5 & 0 \end{array}$$

Again, $30x_1 + 20x_2 = 30$

$$\therefore \quad \begin{array}{c|c|c} x_1 & 0 & 10 \\ \hline x_2 & 15 & 0 \end{array} \quad \text{and so on.}$$

L_1L_1, L_2L_2, L_3L_3, are the iso-profit lines. L_3L_3 is touching the solution space $OABCD$ at one point, i.e., $B(5, 15)$.

$\therefore$ $Z =$ Rs. 450 (optimum profit) and $x_1 = 5$ and $x_2 = 15$ (optimum product mix).

Graphic Solution : Minimisation

Let us discuss a minimization problem.

Problem 2

A person requires 10, 12 and 12 units of chemicals A, B and C, respectively for his garden. A liquid product contains 5, 2 and 1 of A, B and C, respectively per jar. A dry product contains 1, 2 and 4 units of A, B and C per carton. If the liquid product sells for Rs. 3 per jar and the dry product sells for Rs. 2 per carton, how many of each should be purchased in order to minimize the cost and meet the requirements?

Solution

Let x_1 = units of liquid product purchased and x_2 = units of dry product purchased.

The objective function becomes:

$$\text{Minimize } Z = 3x_1 + 2x_2 \qquad (9.A.4)$$

subject to the following constraints

$$5x_1 + x_2 \geq 10 \quad \text{(for Chemical } A\text{)} \qquad (9.A.5)$$

$$2x_1 + 2x_2 \geq 12 \quad \text{(for Chemical } B\text{)} \qquad (9.A.6)$$

$$x_1 + 4x_2 \geq 12 \quad \text{(for Chemical } C\text{)} \qquad (9.A.7)$$

$$\text{and} \quad x_1, x_2 \geq 0 \qquad (9.A.8)$$

To plot the constraints on a graph, these are expressed in the form of the following equations:

$$5x_1 + x_2 = 10 \qquad (9.A.9)$$

$$2x_1 + 2x_2 = 12 \qquad (9.A.10)$$

$$x_1 + 4x_2 = 12 \qquad (9.A.11)$$

From (9) $\frac{x_1}{x_2}\left|\frac{0}{10}\right|\frac{2}{0}$.

From (10) $\frac{x_1}{x_2}\left|\frac{0}{6}\right|\frac{6}{0}$.

From (11) $\frac{x_1}{x_2}\left|\frac{0}{3}\right|\frac{12}{0}$.

Let us now draw an iso-profit line

$$3x_1 + 2x_2 = 42 \text{ (say)} \quad (9.A.12)$$

$$\therefore \quad \frac{x_1}{x_2}\left|\frac{0}{21}\right|\frac{14}{0}$$

Here the solution area lies beyond the lines (9)', (10)' and (11)' as shown by the shaded area in fig. 9.3.

Next we move the iso-profit line towards the origin till the last point on the boundary of the solution area is reached, i.e., B (here). The coordinates of B can also be obtained by solving equations (9)' and (10)', as follows:

$$10x_1 + 2x_2 = 20$$

$$10x_1 + 10x_2 = 60$$

$$\therefore \quad -8x_2 = -40$$

$$\therefore \quad x_2 = 5 \quad \text{and} \quad x_1 = 1.$$

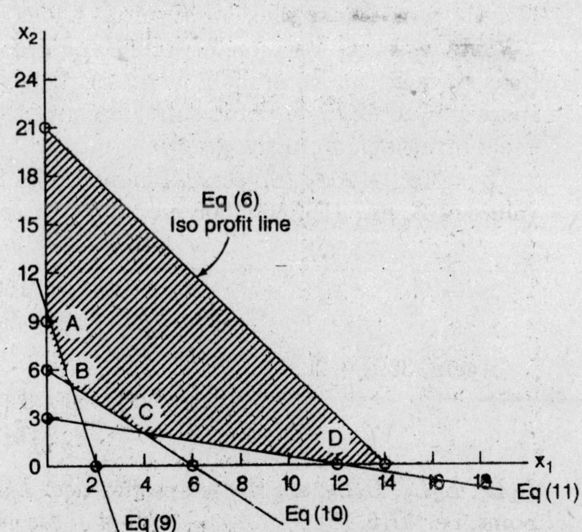

Fig 9.3 An Iso-Profit Line

Now Z is minimum at $B = 3 \times 1 + 2 \times 5$ = Rs. 13. The coordinates of B can also be obtained from the graph directly.

The Simplex Method

Complex L.P. problems cannot be solved by graphic solutions. For such problems we use the simplex method. Let us discuss a simple maximization problem.

Problem 1

The *ABC* Manufacturing Company can make two products P_1 and P_2. Each of the products requires time on a cutting machine and a finishing machine:

	Product	
	P_1	P_2
Cutting hours (per unit)	2	1
Finishing hours (per unit)	3	3
Profit per unit	Rs. ??	Rs. 4

The number of cutting hours available per week is 390, the number of finishing hours available per week is 810.

How much of each product should be produced in order to achieve maximum profit for the company?

Solution

Let

$$x_1 = \text{Output of product } P_1;$$
$$x_2 = \text{Output of product } P_2;$$
$$x_3 = \text{Slack variable, i.e., unused cutting hours;}$$
$$x_4 = \text{Slack variable, i.e., unused finishing hours;}$$
$$\text{and} \quad Z = \text{Optimum profit.}$$

Now the objective function becomes: Maximize $Z = 6x_1 + 4x_2 + 0x_3 + 0x_4$ subject to the constraints:

$$2x_1 + x_2 \leq 390$$
$$3x_1 + 3x_2 \leq 810$$
$$\text{and} \quad x_1, x_2, x_3, x_4 \geq 0$$
$$\text{or, maximize} \quad Z = 6x_1 + 4x_2 + 0x_3 + 0x_4 \qquad \text{(9.A.13)}$$

subject to constraints:

$$2x_1 + x_2 + x_3 = 390 \qquad \text{(9.A.14)}$$
$$3x_1 + 3x_2 + x_4 = 810 \qquad \text{(9.A.15)}$$
$$\text{and} \quad x_1, x_2, x_3 \;\&\; x_4 \geq 0$$

As all the values of $(C_j - z_j)$, i.e., index row of Pass II are either zero, or, negative, the optimum solution has been obtained.

The manufacturers must produce 120 units per week and 150 units per week of P_1 and P_2, respectively, to get the maximum contribution, i.e., Rs. 1,320.

Calculations

The process of calculation follows a few steps. These are explained below.

Table 9.1 : The Simplex Method

		A′	B′	C′	D′	E′	F′	G′	
	A	Gain	C_j	a_{io}	6	4	0	0	
	B	Gain C_i	Basic Variable		x_1	x_2	x_3	x_4	
Key Row →	C	0	x_3	390	(2) Pivot	1	1	0	Starting Table
	D	0	x_4	810	3	3	0	1	Starting Table
	E	Z_j		0	0	0	0	0	Starting Table
	F	$C_j - Z_j$			Key col. 6 ↑	4	0	0	← Index Row
	G	6	x_1	195	1	1/2	1/2	0	Pass I
Key Row →	H	0	x_4	225	0	3/2	(– 3/2) Pivot	1	Pass I
	I	Z_j		1,170	6	3	3	0	Pass I
	J	$C_j - Z_j$			0	Key col. 1 ↑	– 3	0	← Index Row
	K	6	x_1	120	1	0	1	1/3	Pass II
	L	4	x_2	150	0	1	– 1	2/3	Pass II
	M	Z_1		1,320	6	4	2	2/3	Pass II
	N	$C_j - Z_j$			0	0	– 2	– 2/3	Index Row

Starting Table

Put the r.h.s. of equations (14) and (15) in CC' and DC' squares, respectively. Put the coefficients of x_1, x_2, x_3 and x_4 in equation (14) in CD', CE', CF' and CG' squares, respectively. Similarly, put the coefficients of x_1, x_2, x_3 and x_4 in equation (15) in DD', DE', DF' and DG' squares respectively. Put the slack variables, x_3 and x_4, and their coefficients 0 and 0, as shown in equation (13) in CB', DB', CA' and DA' squares, respectively.

<u>Z_j row calculations</u>

EC' square $= 390 \times 0 + 810 \times 0 = 0$

ED' square $= 2 \times 0 + 3 \times 0 = 0$ and so on.

$C_j - Z_j$ row calculations

FD' square $= 6 - 0 = 6$ (i.e., $AD' - FD'$)

FE' square $= 4 - 0 = 4$ and so on.

Pass I Calculations

To find the pivot put a vertical arrow in FD' square having maximum contribution, i.e., 6. Next we find out $\frac{CC'}{CD'}$, i.e., $\frac{390}{2} = 195$ and $\frac{DC'}{DD'}$, i.e., $\frac{810}{3} = 270$. As 195 is the minimum value, we put a horizontal arrow in the CA' square, and put a circle round (2) placed in CD' square, i.e., at the crossing of the arrows. This (2) is called 'pivot' for pass I. The horizontal and vertical arrows in the starting table indicate the x_3 with contribution 0 is thrown out and x_1 with contribution 6 comes in Pass I. All other figures in the G' row of Pass I is obtained by dividing the respective figures of the first row of the starting table by the pivot, i.e., $GA' = 6$, $GB' = x_1$, $GC' = \frac{390}{2} = 195$, $GD' = \frac{2}{2} = 1$, $GE' = \frac{1}{2}$, $GF' = \frac{1}{2}$ and $GG' = \frac{0}{2} = 0$.

In the H-row of Pass I, the figures in HA' and HB' will remain unchanged, i.e., 0 and x_4. $HC' = DC' - \frac{CC'}{CD'} \times DD' = 810 - \frac{390}{2} \times 3 = 225$; $HD' = 0$ [As this is in the same column of pivot (2)]; $HE' = DE' - \frac{CE'}{CD'} \times DD' = 3 - \frac{1}{2} \times 3 = \frac{3}{2}$; $HF' = DF' - \frac{CF'}{CD'} \times DD' = 0 - \frac{1}{2} \times 3 = -\frac{3}{2}$ and so on.

Z_j, or I-row calculations

$$IC' = 195 \times 6 + 225 \times 0 \text{ (i.e., } GC' \times GA' + HC' \times HA') = 1,170$$
$$ID' = 1 \times 6 + 0 \times 0 \text{ (i.e., } GD' \times GA' + HD' \times HA') = 6 \text{ and so on.}$$
$$C_j = Z_j, \text{ or } J\text{-row calculations}$$
$$JD' = 6 - 6 \text{ (i.e., } AD' - ID') = 0$$
$$JE' = 4 - 3 \text{ (i.e., } AE' - IE') = 1 \text{ and so on.}$$

Pass II Calculations

Similar to Pass I: The index row (i.e., $C_j - Z_j$) values in Pass II for the slack variables, i.e., X_3 and X_4, have a significant economic interpretation. Their absolute values, i.e., 2 and $\frac{2}{3}$ here, show the amount of change in the optimal value of the objective function which would occur from relaxing the corresponding constraint by one unit. This value is known as the 'shadow price'. Hence we can say that if one more hour of cutting time were available, ABC manufacturing company could increase the profit by Rs. 2, i.e., the shadow price for cutting time is Rs. 2. Similarly, the shadow price for finishing time is Rs. $\frac{2}{3}$.

Additional Aspects of the Simplex Method

Big-M Method

So far we have discussed about less than or equal to type constraints. But many problems have constraints of equalities, or, greater than or equal to inequalities. Let us take a problem and solve it.

Problem 1

Maximize the profit function and give your comment:

$$Z = 26x_1 + 39x_2 + 13x_3 \text{ (objective function)}$$
$$x_1 + x_2 + x_3 \leq 2,000$$
$$x_1 + \frac{3}{2}x_2 + \frac{3}{4}x_3 \leq 2,400$$
$$x_2 = 1,000$$
$$x_1, x_2, x_3 \geq 0.$$

Solution

Introducing slack variables x_4 and x_5 and artificial variable x_6, we have the objective function:

$$\text{Maximize } Z = 26x_1 + 39x_2 + 13x_3 + 0x_4 + 0x_5 - Mx_6 \tag{9.A.16}$$

subject to constraints

$$x_1 + x_2 + x_3 + x_4 = 2,000 \tag{9.A.17}$$

$$x_1 + \frac{3}{2}x_2 + \frac{3}{4}x_3 + x_5 = 2,400 \tag{9.A.18}$$

$$x_2 + x_6 = 1,000 \tag{9.A.19}$$

$$\text{and} \quad x_1,\ x_2,\ x_3,\ x_4,\ x_5,\ x_6 \geq 0.$$

When the constraint is of the $\geq$ type, we must subtract a slack variable to get an equality constraint. To generate an initial basic feasible solution with such $\geq$ constraints, an "artificial variable"is added to each such constraint. Unlike slack variables, artificial variables have no economic meaning and are only used to establish an initial basic feasible solution. As this variable has no economic meaning, we do not want it to appear in the final solution mix. Accordingly we assign a very large negative value in the objective function. In our Equation (16), M is an arbitrary large positive number.

Now see Table 9.2. As all the values of the final index $(C_j - Z_j)$ row are either negative, or zero, optimum solution has been reached.

$\therefore$ $x_1 = 900$, $x_2 = 1,000$, $x_3 = 0$ and Z (maximum) = 62,400.

Calculations are similar to the previous problem.

Table 9.2 : Simplex Method

	Gain C_j	C_j Basic variable	a_{io}	26 x_1	39 x_2	13 x_3	0 x_4	0 x_5	–M x_6	
	0	x_4	2,000	1	1	1	1	0	0	
	0	x_5	2,400	1	3/2	3/4	0	1	0	
Key Row →	–M	x_6	1,000	0	① Pivot	0	0	0	1	Starting Table
	Z_j		–1,000M	0	–M	0	0	0	–M	
	$C_j - Z_j$			26	Key col. 39 + M ↑	13	0	0	0	Index Row
	0	x_4	1,000	1	0	1	1	0	x	
Key Row →	0	x_5	900	① Pivot	0	3/4	0	1	x	Pass I. Drop x_6 with all its entries
	39	x_2	100	0	1	0	0	0	x	
	Z_j		39,000	0	39	0	0	0	x	
	$C_j - Z_j$			Key col. 26 ↑	0	13	0	0	x	Index Row
	0	x_4	100	0	0	1/4	1	–1	x	
	26	x_1	900	1	0	3/4	0	1	x	
	39	x_2	1,000	0	1	0	0	0	x	
	Z_1		62,400	26	39	39	0	26	x	Pass II
	$C_j - Z_j$			0	0	–13/2	0	-26	x	Index Row

Problem 2

Use Big-M method to maximize $Z = 6x_1 + 4x_2$ subject to constraints

$$2x_1 + 3x_2 \leq 30$$
$$3x_1 + 2x_2 \leq 24$$
$$x_1 + x_2 \geq 3$$
$$\text{and} \quad x_1, x_2 \geq 0$$

Give two different solutions, if the solution is not unique.

Solution

Introducing slack variables x_3 and x_4, surplus variable x_5 and artificial variable x_6, we get the constraints as

$$2x_1 + 3x_2 + x_3 = 30$$
$$3x_1 + 2x_2 + x_4 = 24$$
$$x_1 + x_2 - x_5 + x_6 = 3$$
$$x_1, x_2, x_3, x_4, x_5 \text{ and } x_6 \geq 0$$

and the objective function is: Maximize $Z = 6x_1 + 4x_2 + 0x_3 + 0x_4 + 0x_5 - Mx_6$.

Now get the solution by eliminating big-M.

Minimisation Problem

So long we have discussed about maximization problems. But in many practical situations, the objective function has to be minimized. Here we convert the minimization problem into a maximization problem by using the following expression:

Minimize $Z = -$ Maximize $(-Z)$.

Next we maximize $(-Z)$ as before and take the negative value of maximize $(-Z)$.

Problem 3

Use Big-M method to minimize $Z = 15x_1 + 12x_2$ subject to the constraints:

$$4x_1 + 2x_2 \geq 32; x_1 + 3x_2 \geq 9 \quad \text{and} \quad x_1, x_2 \geq 0$$

Solution

Introducing surplus variables x_3 and x_4 and artificial variables x_5 and x_6, we get

$$\text{Minimize } Z = 15x_1 + 12x_2 + 0x_3 + 0x_4 + Mx_5 + Mx_6$$

subject to constraints

$$4x_1 + 2x_2 - x_3 + x_5 = 32$$
$$x_1 + 3x_2 - x_4 + x_6 = 9$$
$$x_1, x_2, x_3, x_4, x_5 \quad \text{and} \quad x_6 \geq 0$$

Now, Minimize $Z = -$ Maximize $(-Z)$. Here, Maximize $(-Z) = -15x_1 - 12x_2 - 0x_3 - 0x_4 - Mx_5 - Mx_6$.

Next apply Big-M method to solve maximize $(-Z)$. The optimum value of minimize $Z =$ the negative value of maximize $(-Z)$.

The General Mathematical Statement of L.P. Model

Optimize $Z = C_1x_1 + C_2x_2 + \cdots + C_nx_n$, the objective function, where $(C_1, C_2, \cdots, C_n)$ are constants and $(x_1, x_2, \cdots, x_n)$ are the decision variables subject to the constraints

$$\begin{aligned}
a_{11}x_1 + a_{12}x_2 + \cdots + a_{1j}x_j + \cdots + a_{1n}x_n &= b_1 \\
a_{21}x_1 + a_{22}x_2 + \cdots + a_{2j}x_j + \cdots + a_{2n}x_n &= b_2 \\
\vdots \qquad\qquad \vdots \qquad\qquad & \vdots \\
a_{i1}x_1 + a_{i2}x_2 + \cdots + a_{ij}x_j + \cdots + a_{in}x_n &= b_i \\
\vdots \qquad\qquad \vdots \qquad\qquad & \vdots \\
a_{m1}x_1 + a_{m2}x_2 + \cdots + a_{mj}x_j + \cdots + a_{mn}x_n &= b_m
\end{aligned}$$

$$\text{and} \quad x_1, x_2, \cdots, x_n \geq 0.$$

The above constraints have all been written in equality form. Here $a_{11}, a_{12}, \cdots, a_{mn}$ are the constants.

Here $n > m$ and, hence, a set of undetermined equations are available.

The statement may now be summarised as follows:

Optimize $Z = \Sigma_j C_j x_j$ where $j = 1, 2, \cdots, n$, subject to, $\Sigma_j a_{ij} x_j = l_i$ where $i = 1, 2, \cdots, m$.

The Dual

Every linear programming problem has a second complementary L.P. problem which is known as the 'dual'. The original problem is called 'primal'. The solution of the 'primal' can be obtained by solving either 'dual', or 'primal'. If the 'primal' is a maximization problem, 'dual' is a minimization problem, and vice versa.

Relationship between the Primal and the Dual	
Primal	*Dual*
1. Constants in constraints	1. Co-efficients of objective function
2. Co-efficients of objective function	2. Constants in constraints
3. Inequality signs in constraints	3. Inequality signs reversed
4. Constraints row coefficients	4. Constraints column coefficients

Problem 1

Primal Problem

Maximize $Z = 60x_1 + 80x_2$, subject to constraints

$$\begin{aligned}
5x_1 + 10x_2 &\leq 400 \\
10x_1 + 15x_2 &\leq 450 \quad \text{and} \quad x_1, x_2 \geq 0.
\end{aligned}$$

Dual of the above 'primal' will be Minimize $\alpha = 400y_1 + 450y_2$ subject to constraints

$$\begin{aligned}
5y_1 + 10y_2 &\geq 60 \\
10y_1 + 15y_2 &\geq 80 \quad \text{and} \quad y_1, y_2 \geq 0.
\end{aligned}$$

In both the cases, Z (max.) $= \alpha$ (min.), y_1 and y_2 are the 'dual' variables. We can solve the 'dual' problems by graphic or simplex method as explained earlier.

Sensitivity Analysis

After getting the optimum solution of a L.P. problem, we may study the changes in the optimum solution with changes in the parameters of the problem. The following changes can be made:

(1) Change coefficients of the objective function.
(2) Change coefficients of the variables on the l.h.s. of the constraints.
(3) Change the numbers on the r.h.s. of the constraints.
(4) Add/subtract new variables and
(5) Add/subtract constraints, etc.

This study is significant as it shows how sensitive is the current optimum solution to the changes in parameters. Management may be willing to know the range of variation of the parameters which does not affect the optimum solution under study. This study of a L.P. problem is called "Sensitivity Analysis".

Most of the analysis is done by computer codes. We should be able to interpret the output from such codes, e.g., LPGOGO Code, etc.

Questions and Problems

1. Solve the following L.P. problems using the graphic method:

(a) Maximize $Z = 5x_1 + 10x_2$ subject to:

$$2x_1 + 10x_2 \leq 60;$$
$$0.625x_1 + x_2 \leq 5 \quad \text{and} \quad x_1, x_2 \geq 0.$$

(b) Minimize $Z = 24x_1 + 6x_2$ subject to:

$$2x_1 + x_2 \geq 10;$$
$$2x_1 + 3x_2 \geq 24 \quad \text{and} \quad x_1, x_2 \geq 0.$$

Show the set of feasible solutions by shading, and circle the basic feasible solutions.

2. What is linear programming? Discuss the application of this technique in the real commercial world.

Appendix to Chapter 10

Other Operations Research Techniques

In the earlier chapters of this title we have tried to cover some important aspects of the theory of decision-making. Nowadays a part of this theory has come to be known as operations research (O.R.). O.R., by itself, is a heterogeneous collection of decision-making tools. We have, in fact, covered some of these tools (e.g., linear programming, forecasting, etc.) in others parts of the book. The purpose of this chapter is to touch on those parts of O.R. which have not been so covered. We shall briefly deal with the following topics: (1) Queueing Models, (2) Simulation and (3) Game Theory.

Most management decisions involve allocating limited company resources so as to fulfil particular objectives. For example, in pursuing a profit-target the manager of a multi-product company must decide how much of each product to produce, that is, he must decide how much scarce resources like labour, capital equipment, factory space, and so on, to devote to each product. The same manager examining his stockholding costs will have to decide how much stock of each good to carry in order to service his customers.

Managers seeking optimum solutions to such problems would formulate their objectives in more stringent terms; they would seek the combination of product outputs which maximizes profit or contribution; and the level of stock which would minimize their stock costs. Such optimum solutions are rarely achieved if managers rely upon intuition or subjective judgments' in making decisions. Decisions based upon various convenient 'rules of thumb' are rarely adequate except for small, repetitive decisions, for only by chance will they produce an optimum solution. To arrive at an optimum solution thorough analysis is required.

Operations research provides just such a thorough analysis. An operation-research approach entails constructing mathematical models to represent the essentials of a real-life problem, and then manipulating these models to obtain a solution which is 'best' in terms of meeting the objective. In this sense one could regard operations research as the technology of economics, bearing much the same relationship to economics as engineering does to physics, with economic theory providing the basic philosophy of optimization, and operations research applying this philosophy to business problems.

Application of O.R. to Business Problems

Application of operations research to a business problem involves a number of stages:

1. The problem must be identified and formulated in precise terms prior to seeking solution. This is not easy, for often the operations researcher may not too familiar with the firm's operations and procedures, and communications difficulties between himself and the line managers who do possess this knowledge may combine with limited or inaccurate data to make problem-definition a difficult task. In relation to this first stage we may note that a particular O.R. study starts with fairly limited aims—to provide an optimum solution to a particular problem. Since this problem often relates to only one small part of the firm's total operations, then a solution which is optimum for this small part may not be optimum from the point of view of the company as a whole. Where this occurs the operational analyst is sub-optimizing rather than achieving an overall optimum solution. For example, a company may minimize the costs of carrying stocks of finished goods, but if this is done subject to an unrealistic service-level constraint, then stock may be inadequate and customers can be lost.

2. In seeking an optimum solution it is essential to have clear and precise criteria to use. This requires that the objectives of the business in relation to a particular problem be made explicit and be clearly formulated: for example, 'Minimize stock costs; maximize contribution.'

3. For any particular problem there will be constraints within which an optimum solution must be found. These constraints relate mainly to the avilability of a particular resource or resources. For example, in planning production of only per 4,000 week, and this will limit the amounts of products which can be made. Other constraints may arise directly out of management decisions; for example, an investment trust seeking to maximize expected returns by allocating its funds between various industrial shares might impose a constraint upon the proportion of total funds to be invested in any one company, so as to avoid the risks inherent in tying its fortunes too closely to those of any one company.

4. The next stage of an O.R. study involves constructing a methematical model or models to represent the problem as defined. These mathematical models are abstract representations of the physical situation, and they consist of mathematical expressions representing the factors involved and their inter-relationships.

6. The solution obtained must then be validated against the real problem to ensure that it is reasonable before it can finally be implemented.

For some problems the facts of the situation are known for certain in advance, for example, the amount of available machine-capacity. Such problems are *deterministic* and can be represented by a mathematical model. Often problems are *probabilistic* in so far as future outcomes are not known for certain, and only information about the likelihood of possible outcomes is available. For example, the exact number of customers who will arrive at a supermarket checkout during a particular hour on some future Friday is not known for certain. However, by studying records of customer attendances on a number of previous Fridays it is possible to gain some idea of the range of possible customer attendances, and the likelihood of particular attendance figures occurring within that range. Where problems are probabilistic, models must be constructed which contain both mathematical and statistical expressions.

Every business problem will have certain special characteristics, and the operations researcher attempting to solve a specific problem will need to construct a model which is a reasonable representation of that problem. However, business problems can be classified on the basis of their common characteristics, so that we can talk, for example, about inventory problems or queueing problems. For each of these groups of problems set of standard-solution techniques have been devised, and the bulk of this chapter will be devoted to examining some of them.

1. Queueing: In queueing problem the question is how many sercice channels to provide in order to ensure that customers do not have to wait an 'excessive' time for service. For example, how many runways are needed for aircraft, how many unloading berths for oil-tankers, how many telephone operators for subscribers, and how many hospital beds to serve patients? In the

same way that stock-outs can be virtually eliminated by carrying a sufficiently large safety-stock, queues can be virtually eliminated by providing a large enough service facility. However, in the same way that carrying a large safety-stock involves high costs for the firm, the provision of numerous service facilities involes large investment in physical facilities such as tanker berths, or large labour-costs, as in the case of supermarket checkout staff.

Thus the problem is one of balancing costs—on the one hand the cost of the resources used to provide service; and on the other hand the cost of the time lost by customers while waiting for service. Sometimes the company must bear the queueing costs directly, as would be the case where maintenance and production staff must wait at the stores for material or components, or where oil-tankers must wait for berths. In the former case a reduction of stores personnel would reduce stores costs but would mean more idle queueing time for production and maintenance workers. In the latter case a small number of unloading berths would keep the cost of these facilities low, but would entail long unproductive delays for the company's oil tankers. Often the company does not have to bear queueing costs directly, as would be the case where shoppers experience long delays at checkouts or customers have long waits for service at bank counters. However, costs still exist here, for if customers experience long delays they will become dissatisfied and will tend to turn to other supermarkets or banks. The question, then, is: what level of service should be provided in order to minimize the sum of service-cost and waiting-cost?

1. **Queueing Models:** Suppose that a firm is trying to decide how many service channels it should provide in order to ensure that its customers do not have to wait for too long a time. When customers wait for service, queues form. Queues can always be eliminated by providing a large enough service facility. But investment in service facilities is costly. Thus, the cost of servicing the customer has to be weighted against the cost of time lost by customers when they wait in the queue. (If the waiting time is too long, customers at the back of the queue will leave, inflicting a loss on the firm).

One may be tempted to think that in the long run it is possible to guess, on the basis of experience, how many customers a firm will get on the average and how long it will take to service each customer. It will then be possible to decide on the suitable level of investment in service facilities so that the length of the queue of customers does not go out of control. For instance, the manager of a supermarket may find from experience that it takes 2 minutes on the average to service a customer. The market can then handle 30 customers in an hour. Thus, if 90 customers arrive at the store in an hour on the average, the store must keep at least 3 cash counters if queue formation is to be prevented (or if queues are to be prevented from growing, assuming that there was a queue to begin with).

The argument may be correct under certain circumstances and there is no doubt that some businessmen actually apply this kind of logic to their decision-making problems. However, the problem is not always so simple. If the 90 customers in an hour, in the above example, arrive at an even rate of 3 customers in every 2 minutes, the three cash counters can handle all of them. But suppose that all the 90 customers arrive in the very first minute. Then, obviously, a queue will form even if there are three cash counters. The last person in the queue will have to wait for about an hour before being serviced. If this waiting time is too long for him, he may leave the store without making his purchase. That is a loss to the store.

Queueing problems, of course, arise in a wider variety of circumstances than just in supermarket management. How many runways to build at an airport, how many berths to build in a port, how many beds to provide for in a nursing home—these are all queueing problems. To complicate matters, queues can be of many different types. Specifically, they can vary with respect to customer, queue discipline and service characteristics. Customer differenences are easy to explain. In some cases, as in a supermarket, we can speak of a single, homogeneous group of customers. In a port, however, a supertanker will need quite different types of service facilities from a small ship. A port, therefore, will have a heterogeneous group of 'customers', i.e., ships. Queue disciplines may differ. There may be only one queue although there are many service channels, or there may be a number of parallel queues. Service characteristics also may take different forms. Customers may be attended to on a 'first-come-first-served' basis, or they can be served at random. Sometimes, specific groups of customers may be given preferences.

Correspondingly, queueing models vary in their complexities. For simple situations we can build simple queueing models. For instance, if A is the average time gap between the arrivals of successive customers, if B is the average service time and if customers arrive in a completely random fashion, then the average number of customers in the queue is $\frac{B}{A-B}$. The probability of the event that a customer will have to wait for service is $\frac{B}{A}$ and the average time a customer spends in the queue is $\frac{B^2}{A-B}$. Whether the customers consider this average waiting time to be too long can be found from experience or by the method of directly interviewing the customers. If it is considered to be tolerable, the manager will judge the service facilities to be adequate. If it is considered to be too long, B has to be brought down by expanding the service facilities. The amount of funds to be invested in the construction of new facilities can be decided by noting which value of $\frac{B^2}{A-B}$ is considered to be tolerable by the customers.

[How did we get the mathematical expressions of the previous paragraphs? We assumed that customer arrivals have a Poisson probability distribution. The chances of 0, 1, 2, 3, ... arrivals in a unit of time is given by the Poisson formula :

Probability $(c) = \frac{e^{-\lambda}.\lambda^c}{c!} \quad (c = 0, 1, 2, ...)$

It can be shown that λ would then be the mean number of arrival in a unit of time. (The average time between successive arrives is, therefore, $\frac{1}{\lambda}$. This was our A). Similarly, we implicitly assumed that the number of services per unit of time has a Poisson distribution. The chances 0, 1, 2, 3, ... services per unit of time is given by the formula :

Probability $(d) = \frac{e^{-\theta}\theta^d}{d!} \quad (d = 0, 1, 2, ...)$

θ would then be the mean number of services per unit time. (The average service-times, therefore, is $\frac{1}{\theta}$. This was our B). It can be shown that under these circumstances the mean time that a customer has to spend on the queue will be $\frac{\rho^2}{\theta(1-P)}$ where $\rho = \frac{\lambda}{\theta}$. This can be easily seen to be the same as $\frac{B^2}{A-B}$.]

For more complicated situations, queueing models get quite complicated. In these situations one usually takes recourse to the method of simulation. We describe this method briefly in the next subsection.

2. Simulation. Complex decision-making situations involving stochastic elements are difficult to solve by exact mathematical methods. For instance, in our example of the queueing problem we implicity made the assumption of a Poisson distribution of arrival and service times. This was just a simplifying assumption. There is no *a priori* reason why it should be true in practice. Indeed, queueing models get quite complicated if we insist that the mathematical forms of the probability distributions correspond exactly to what happens in reality.

As an alternative we can simulate the system, i.e., we can construct a typical life story of the system based upon a model representing the rules of operation of the system. In our queueing example we would construct probability distributions of customer arrivals and services based upon long-term historical experiences of the values. From these distributions we can draw samples of the variables. Thus we shall get typical sequences of customer arrivals and services. These values can then be used for the purpose of determining when a typical customer arrives and departs.

Obviously this process will tell us how effectively the present servicing facilities are coping with the problem of customer servicing. We can also make repeated use of a sample. The possible effects of changes in the operational mechanism of the system can be gauged by re-using the same sample values with the necessary changes in the model. Therefore, it is possible to determine ways of improving the performance of service facilities without tampering with the actual physical facilities in existence. In fact, if dependable probability distributions from the important variables are available from the experiences of similar other systems; it is indeed possible to simulate the operation of the system on paper and determine the best service facilities even before the actual facilities are constructed at all. Finally, it is clear that although we have touched our remarks in term of the queueing models, simulation methods have a much wider applicability. Wherever decision-making under uncertainty is involved, we can arrive at practical decisions by drawing samples from a simulated model of the operation of the system.

In truth complex resource-allocation problems which involve probabilistic elements such as stockholding and queueing situations often cannot be solved completely by exact analysis. As an alternative, it is possible to simulate the operation of a system—to create a typical life-history of the system based upon a mathematical model representing the actual system and its rules of operation. In the case of a queueing problem, customer arrival-rate and service-time would be key variables in such a model, and probability distributions for these variables based upon long-term historical experience of the values and frequencies of these variables would have to be included. From these distributions it is possible to generate sample values of the variables—sampling from the arrival-rate distribution to give a typical sequence of customer arrivals, and from the service-time distribution to give a typical sequence of the time taken for each customer to be served. These pairs of sample values can then be applied to the model, working out step by step when each customer arrives, is served, and departs.

From the sample sequence it is possible to note how well the existing service facilities are coping with customers, and the extent to which existing service capacity is utilized. Also it is possible to re-use the simulation, repeating the sample values with changes in the operating system in order to predict the likely effects of the changes. Thus it is possible to experiment with the simulation in order to investigate the effects of such changes as increasing the number of service channels of changing the arrangement of channels from a parallel to a sequential one. In this way it becomes possible to discover methods of improving the performance of the system without having to experiment with the actual system, make changes in its operating characteristics and discover the best characteristics from the point of view of performance before the actual system is constructed at all, provided that meaningful probability distributions for variables are available based upon the experience of other similar systems.

To illustrate the above discussion we shall take a simple simulation example of a queueing problem, that of a garage near a trunk road which at the moment has a single block of petrol pumps and employs one attendant to serve motorists. On the basis of past experience it is known that roughly half the vehicles which arrive will take about 1 minute to serve, while the other half will take 2 minutes to serve. Thus the probability distribution of service-time will be as shown in Figure 10.1(a), and from this we can deduce that over the course of a typical hour it will take on average $1\frac{1}{2}$ minutes to serve a customer. During a typical hour it is also known that for half the time no vehicles will be arriving for petrol, for one-third of the time one vehicle will arrive, and for one-sixth of the hour the attendant will be faced with two vehicles arriving more or less simultaneously for service. The probability distribution for vehicle arrival rates based on this experience is shown in Fig. 10.1(b). It shows that the number of vehicles arriving per minute will be zero on half of all possible occasions, one vehicle per minute on a third of occasions, and that the likelihood of two vehicles arriving during any 1 minute is only a sixth. From this information we can calculate the average rate at which vehicles arrive during the course of an hour by multiplying each arrival rate by the number of minutes in an hour for which that rate is likely to be experienced, thus:

zero vehicles per minute × 30 minutes = 0
one vehicle per minute × 20 minutes = 20
two vehicles per minute × 10 minutes = 20
40 vehicles per hour

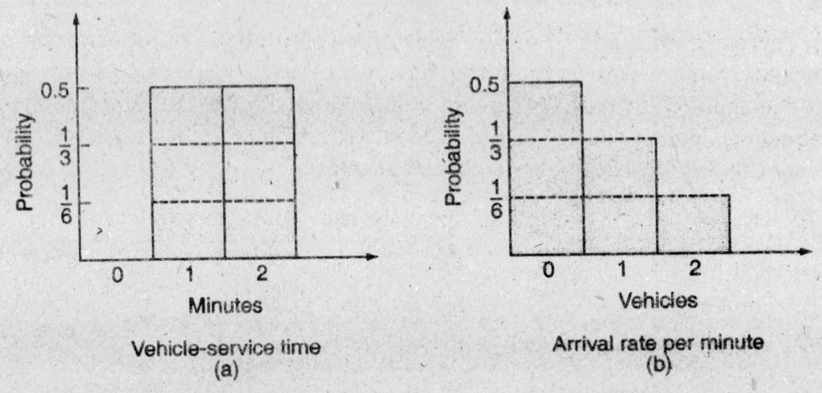

Fig. 10.1 Simulation example: probability distributions.

Now we can proceed to build up an arrival and service pattern for a typical working hour, based upon the above probability distributions. Let us start with service times. Although we know that on average a vehicle will take $1\frac{1}{2}$ minutes to serve, we do not know wether any individual vehicle arriving will take 1 or 2 minutes to serve. However, we do know that there is an equal likelihood of a vehicle taking 1 or 2 minutes, so we can determine at random whether a particular vehicle will take 1 or 2 minutes to service. We can do this by designating the head of a coin as 'vehicle takes 2 minutes to serve' and the reverse side as 'vehicle takes 1 minute to serve', then flipping the coin for each successive vehicle to determine the length of time the vehicle is being serviced. For example, the first few flips may give the result: H, T, T, H, H, H, T, etc., so that we know that the first vehicle will take 2 minutes to serve, the next two vehicles will each take 1 minute, the next three 2 minutes each, and so on.

Now we can turn to the distribution of arrivals. If we divide our typical hour into sixty discrete 1 minute perods, then taking any single minute the number of vehicles—none, one or two—which will arrive in that minute is completely random. Yet although the number of vehicles arriving in any 1 minute is random, the frequency with which any of the three arrival rates occurs will be dictated by the probability distribution (Figure 10.1(b)). If we take vehicle arrivals over a long period, even though we cannot predict what number of vehicles will arrive in any particular minute we do know that on half of the occasions no vehicle will arrive; on one-third of occasions, one vehicle; and on one-sixth of occasions, two vehicles. In order to generate random number which accord with this distribution we can use a die. Since on half or three-sixths of occasions we expect no vehicles to arrive then we allow the faces 1, 2 and 3 to represent zero vehicle-arrivals, and whenever one of there three faces turns up on a throw then no vehicles arrive in that minute. On one-third or two-sixths of occasions we expect one vehicle to arrive, so we allow faces 4 and 5 to represent one vehicle. Finally, on one-sixth of occasions we expect two vehicles to arrive, so that 6 faces of the die is taken to represent two vehicles. The first few throws of the die might generate values as follows:

1st minute	face 1	No arrival
2nd minute	face 1	No arrival
3rd minute	face 3	No arrival
4th minute	face 2	No arrival
5th minute	face 6	Two arrivals
6th minute	face 5	One arrival
7th minute	face 4	One arrival
and so on.		

If sixty such throws were made—one for each minute—and the number of 'no arrival', 'one arrival' and 'two arrivals' counted, then the number of each group occurring should closely approximate to the number of each group we would expect from the probability distribution. The sample frequencies generated in the sample distribution are shown below, and as can be seen, they correspond closely to the expected distribution.

Event	Sample of sixty throws	number expected
no arrival	33	30 $(\frac{1}{2})$
one arrival	17	20 $(\frac{1}{3})$
two arrivals	10	10 $(\frac{1}{6})$
	60	60

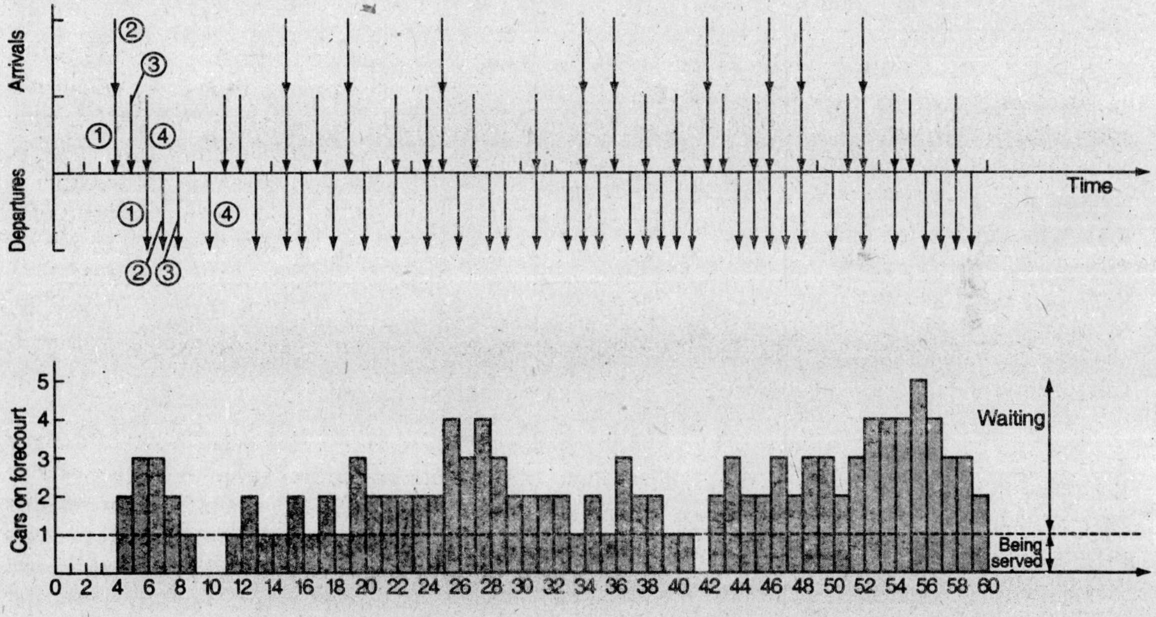

Fig 10.2 Simulation of garage operations.

These sample values of arrivals and service times can be incorporated into a simulation of sixty-minutes' garage operations, as shown in fig. 10.2. The top part of this figure shows the pattern of arrivals, service completions, and departures from the garage. In the first 4 minutes of operation no vehicles arrive, then at the beginning of the fifth minute two vehicles arrive. The first of these is served immediately, and since it takes 2 minutes to serve it departs at the end of the sixth minute. The second must wait for 2 minutes while the first vehicle is being served, and starts being served at the beginning of the seventh minute. It takes 1 minute to serve, and thus departs at the end of the seventh minute. At the beginning of the sixth minute one vehicle arrives. This must wait 2 minutes while the first vehicle completes service and the second vehicle is served. It will start to be served at the beginning of the eighth minute, and since it takes 1 minute to serve it departs at the end of the eighth minute. One further vehicle arrives at the beginning of the seventh minute—this must wait until the second and third vehicle are served, begins to be served at the end of the eighth minute, and departs at the end of the tenth minute. Since no further vehicle arrive until the beginning of the twelfth minute then during the eleventh minute no vehicles will be awaiting service or being served and the attendant will be free. The rest of the period is simulated in the same way.

The lower part of fig. 10.2 shows the number of cars on the garage forecourt in any minute and it is derived from the top part of the figure. It shows both vehicles being served and vehicles queueing. As can be seen, in a few time-peroids such as the first four minutes and the eleventh minute no vehicles are using the garage. The maximum number of vehicles on the forecourt is five—one being served and four waiting—and this occurs only once, in the fifty-sixth minute.

The simulation represents only 1 hour's operations, of course, and if there are significant variations in average arrival rates between different hours of the day or different days of the week then it may be desirable to simulate a whole day's or even a whole week's operations. For such larger simulations dice or coins are inappropriate for generating sample values and random-number tables or a computer need to be used. However, even from such a simple simulation as that above, a great deal of information can be derived. For example, we know that the garage facilities are unused on a total of 6 out of 60 minutes; so that service facilities are utilized 90% of the time. The average number of cars on the forecourt at any time is approximately two, and an average of approximately one car is waiting for service at any time. Further, the avearage time a car has to wait before it begins to be serviced is about 2 minutes.

Having derived this information it is possible to repeat the simulation with changed conditions. A simulation with two banks of petrol pumps and two attendants would show the effects of adding extra service facilities in terms of reducing the length of queues and waiting time while reducing the percentage utilization of service facilities. Or an examination of vehicle arrivals may show that vans and lorries have a longer average service time than cars, so that it becomes worth while to separate the arriving vehicle population into two groups—private cars and commercial vehicles—and construct a probability disturbution for each. Each arriving vehicle could then be randomly designated private or commercial, and a simulation undertaken. Thus it would become possible to investigate by simulation the effects of providing separate banks of pumps and attendants—one for private vehicles and one for commercial ones.

3. Game(s) Theory: In seeking the most effective way to achieve a particular market-share a company needs to decide upon the relative importance to attach to price and the various non-price marketing variables. But where there exists interdependence between firms of the kind discussed under oligopolistic markets in Chapter 11, the company's choice of marketing policies must be competitors as well. The company needs to assess competitors' reactions to its own marketing policies in order that the 'pay-off' from any particular marketing action may be estimated. Game(s) theory presents one such technique which may aid in this estimation.

Game(s) theory is a technique using logical deduction to explore the consequences of the various strategies which might be adopted by competing players. As such, it can be used to represent the problems involved in formulating marketing strategy in a competitive situation. Consider a struggle for share of the market between two firms where the total market-size is fixed, so that every percentage increase in the market-share of one firm is necessarily lost to the other. This situation is called a two-person zero-sum game. It is called zero-sum because no matter what is done by either competitor the total market-size cannot be increased, so that the interests of the competitors are diametrically opposed.

Suppose company X has three strategy choices under consideration, a price reduction for its product indicated by P; a new advertising compaign A; and an increase in its sale-force S. Company Y has the same three strategies available, and a fourth strategy, R which it might adopt, namely, introduction of a restyled product. Assume that each firm can only adopt one of its alternative strategies at a time. Any pair of strategies open to the two companies would result in a particular division of the market between them. For example, if X were to adopt its strategy P and reduce price, and Y were to choose strategy A and initiate an advertising campaigh, then company X might gain 70% of the market and company Y 30%. This 70% market-share could be described as X's pay-off.

All such market-share information can be summarized in the form of a *pay-off matrix,* as in fig. 10.3, which shows what company X will receive by way of market-share for each possible combination of strategy choice by himself and his competitor. For example, the 70% figure recorded in the space at the junction of firm X's strategy P and firm Y's strategy A indicates that X will receive 7-% of the market, and so by implication Y must receive 30%.

Firm X's Strategy \ Firm Y's Strategy	P	A	S	R
P	50 %	70 %	(22 %)	25 %
A	27 %	(17 %)	19 %	75 %
S	64 %	30 %	(15 %)	20 %

Fig 10.3 Pay-off matrix

We assume that both X and Y are acquainted with all the information contained in this table. Using these data, each player must decide on his best stategy without knowing the counter-move which will be made by his opponent. the choice of strategy will depend upon the decision criterion used by each player. If the players adopt a cautious approach then they will assume the worst and act accordingly. Applying this pessimistic approach to the pay-off matrix, if firm X were to adopt its strategy P its management would assume that firm Y would employ its strategy S, thereby reducing firm X's pay-off from its strategy P to its minimum value, 22%. Similarly the fatalistic view of X's strategy A is that Y will employ its strategy A so that X will obtain ony 17% of the market. The minimum market-share pay-off for X's strategy S is 15%. These minimum pay-offs from X's various strategies are marked in fig. 10.3 with circles.

With this pessimistic view firm X can make the best of the situtation by aiming at the highest of these minimum pay-offs, that is, firm X will choose that one among its strategies for which the circled figure is highest. This decision rule is called a maximin strategy, since it leads to choosing the maximum from among the various minimum pay-offs available, and it would lead here to choice of strategy P by firm X, with a market-shapre pay-off of 22%.

Firm Y could employ a similar strategy. However, for Y to assume the worst means that X receives a large market-share, so that Y is residually left with very little. Thus if Y employs its strategy P its worst possible pay-off is 36% of the market (64% going to X), and this market by underlying the 64% in the matrix. If firm Y were to employ its strategy A its worst possible pay-off would be 30% of the market (70% going to X), and this is similarly market by underlining the appropriate matrix figure, and so on. The best of these pessimistic pay-offs for Y is the lowest of these underlined figures (the lowest percentage going to X). The best of these choices is called Y's minimax strategy, the minimum of the various maximum pay-offs going to X: in this case it is strategy S, giving firm X only 22% of the market.

The outcome of this particular competitive situation is determinate. Firm X will choose its strategy P and firm Y its strategy S, and neither firm would be inclined to alter its choice of strategy. However, the game ony has a determinate solution because the matrix contains a unique saddle-point at the intersection of X's strategy P and Y's strategy S, where the pay-off value of 22% is the highest of all the row minima and at the same time is the lowest of the column maxima.

Simple game-theory models such as the one above serve to emphasize the problems faced by a company such as X in choosing its marketing strategy where its market-share depends not only on its own strategy but on its competitor's strategy as well. Thus each firm must decide on a strategy without knowing the counter-move which will be made by rivals. However, such a simple model cannot completely represent the real-life strategy-choice problems involved in a competitive market situation. In reality firms will not know for certain the exact pay-offs or market-shares which result from pursuing various strategies and encountering particular counter-moves. As the number of firms increases beyond two the matrix become very complicated. Firms in real life have not just three or four strategies available, but an infinite number of strategies; for example, they can consider many different degrees of price-cut, and many different sizes of advertising campaign using various media. Games need not be constant-sum ones, for the market may be growing under the influence of various marketing strategies. Games need not involve a unique saddle-point, so that a determinate solution may not emerge. Firms do not have only one strategy which they can adopt at a time, they may in fact employ mixed strategies, involving, say, a price reduction and an advertising campaign. Companies need not always compete, but may settle for co-operative behaviour. Finally, firms may not adopt a cautious approach as their decision criterion but may adopt a more adventurous apporach in formulating strategies. Though game-theory models can be extended to take account of some of these complication, it remains true that they can do little more than give insight into the competitive market process.

Appendix : Further Note on Game Theory

The two-firm oligopoly behaviour can be analysed with the aid of game theory developed by Von Neumann and O. Morgensten. Here the outcome of the game depends on the behaviour patterns of the competitors. The game is not one of chance, but one of strategy.

Let us consider a simple duopoly (two firms) situation. The two firms are X and Y. Each has the objective of maximizing its own market share and each has three possible courses of action (different possible combinations of decision variables), for example, strategy 1 may be high-price and aggressive marketing. We can now construct a pay-off matrix, showing the market share of firm A resulting from different combinations of strategies.

A \ B	1	2	3	min
1	50	65	45	45
2	55	60	65	55
3	45	50	60	45
max	55	65	65	

The problem for both A and B is to choose an optimal strategy, i.e., the strategy which maximises market share. Needless to say, the total market share is 100 so that if A gets X per cent, B must get $(100 - X)$ per cent. A knows that B is also trying to maximise his market share, so A expects that whichever choice he makes, B will react to minimise the market share of A. This offers a clue for solving the problem. Since A expects the worst possible reaction from B. A adopts a maximum criterion. To do this A considers what is the worst that could happen for each choice. If he chooses strategy 1, his worst possible market share is 45%, for strategy 2, 55%, and for stretegy 3, 45%. Assuming logically that B will do his best, A would choose strategy 2, where the worst that can happen is a 55% share.

Here B decides in an identical manner, only now a minimax strategy is adopted, since B whishes to minimise the market share of A (and therefore, maximise hiw own share). He, therefore, selects the least of the column maximum. If he chooses strategy 1, the worst than can happen is that A gets a 55% share.

In this situation, both strategies result in the same expected outcome, a market share for A of 55%. This equilibrium solution is called a *saddle point,* and represents a position where neither A nor B would wish to change their decisions. Such saddle-points, where the row minimum equals the column maximum, need not always exist. Where there is no such point, the optimal choice will be a mix of strategies, where different choices are made in fixed proportions.

The choice of strategy could now be easily simplified. However B reacts, for A, choice 2 is always better than choice 3 (results in a higher market share). Therefore, A will never choose strategy 3, and is said to be dominated by 2. From B's point of view, strategy 1 is always better than strategy 2, since 1 always results in a lower market share for A (higher share for B).

To calculate the optimum strategy when there is no saddle-point, we may consider the general 2×2 pay-off matrix shown below:

Let the proportion of times A plays strategy I be p_1. Then if p_2 is the proportion of times A plays strategy II, $p_2 = 1 - p_1$. Similarly, let p_3 and p_4 represent the mixed proportions for B playing I and II, and therefore, $p_3 + p_4 = 1$.

	I	II	III	IV
I	2	−2	6	3
II	4	−2	4	5
III	5	2	3	0
IV	−4	0	8	4

The problem simply boils down to finding $p_1, \cdots, p_4$. To do this we need the concept of the expected value of a game (V). This is simply the net result of the game when only optimum strategies are adopted. In terms of our notation, the expected value of the game $[E(V)]$ is expressed as:

$$E(V) = a_1p_1p_3 + a_2p_1p_4 + b_1p_2p_3 + b_1p_2p_4.$$

The problem ca now be expressed as:

Maximize $E(V)$ subject to the constraints $p_1 + p_2 = 1$; $p_3 + p_4 = 1$.

This can be solved by forming the following Lagrangian function thus:

$$\max := E(V) + \lambda_1(p_1 + p_2 - 1) + \lambda_2(p_3 + p_4 - 1).$$

Taking the partial derivatives with respect to $p_1, ...p_4$ and setting them equal to zero, we get, the first order conditions as:

$$\frac{\partial L}{\partial p_1} = a_1p_3 + a_2p_4 + \lambda_1 = 0 \tag{10.A.1}$$

$$\frac{\partial L}{\partial p_2} = b_1p_3 + b_2p_4 + \lambda_1 = 0 \tag{10.A.2}$$

$$\frac{\partial L}{\partial p_3} = a_1p_1 + b_1p_2 + \lambda_2 = 0 \tag{10.A.3}$$

$$\frac{\partial L}{\partial p_4} = a_2p_1 + b_2p_2 + \lambda_2 = 0 \tag{10.A.4}$$

$$\frac{\partial L}{\partial \lambda_1} = p_1 + p_2 - 1 = 0 \tag{10.A.5}$$

$$\frac{\partial L}{\partial \lambda_2} = p_3 + p_4 - 1 = 0. \tag{10.A.6}$$

The six simultaneous equations can now be solved for six values $p_1, ..., p_4$ and λ_1, λ_2 (for obtaining solutions we have added two artificial variables).

If, for instance, (1) is multiplied by b_1, and (2) is multiplied by a_1, we get

$$a_1b_1p_3 + a_2b_1p_4 + b_1\lambda_1 = 0$$

$$\text{and} \quad a_1b_1p_3 + a_1b_2p_4 + a_1\lambda_1 = 0.$$

After subtraction, we get

$$p_4(a_2b_1 - a_1b_2) + \lambda_1(b_1 - a_1) = 0.$$

$$\therefore\ p_4 = \frac{\lambda_1(a_1 - b_1)}{(a_2b_1 - a_1b_2)}.$$

Likewise, for p_3, we get

$$p_3 = \frac{\lambda_1(b_2 - a_2)}{(a_2b_1 - a_1b_2)}.$$

Now if we let

$$C = \frac{\lambda_1}{a_2b_1 - a_1b_2},$$

then we get

$$p_4 = C(a_1 - b_1)$$

$$p_3 = C(b_2 - a_2).$$

Now, from equation (6), $p_3 + p_4 = 1$, we get

$$C(a_1 - b_1) + C(b_2 - a_2) = 1,$$

$$\text{or,} \quad C = \frac{1}{(a_1 - b_1) + (b_2 - a_2)}$$

$$\text{and} \quad p_3 = \frac{(b_2 - a_2)}{(a_1 - b_1) + (b_2 - a_2)}$$

$$p_4 = \frac{(a_1 - b_1)}{(a_1 - b_1) + (b_2 - a_1)}$$

In a similar way we get the following solutions:

$$p_1 = \frac{(b_2 - b_1)}{(a_1 - a_2) + (b_2 - b_1)}$$

$$p_2 = \frac{(a_1 - b_1)}{(a_1 - b_1) + (b_2 - a_2)}$$

This is known as the method of oddments which can simply be stated as follows:

The proportion of times A plays strategy 1, is simply the ratio of the absolute value of the other row difference to the absolute value of *that row* difference. (In terms of our notation, if A plays I and II in the ratio $x : y$, $p_1 = x/(x + y)$ and $p_2 = y/(x + y)$.

Thus, the proportion of times B plays his strategy I is the ratio of the absolute value of the ***other column*** difference to the absolute value of ***that column*** difference.

Properties of Saddle Points

The maximin or minimax strategies have a number of important properties. W.J. Baumol has identified the following two properties of such equilibrium (saddle) points as the most important of all.

Property 1. This was called by Baumol the protective power of maximin strategies. According to Baumol, maximin strategy offers both parties a measure of protection in that A's maximum strategy gives him the largest share of market which B can be prevented from reducing any further, and B's minimax startegy offers B the lowest share of market for A, which A can be prevented from increasing any further. A has set up the highest absolutely defensible floor under his earnings. Thus, when A plays strategy I, anything B does will either leave his market share at its maximum level, or raise it above that figure. Similarly, B's use of his minimax strategy places the lowest possible ceiling over A's pay-off.

By contrast, suppose A had chosen strategy II instead of his maximin strategy I. It is true if B miscalculates and plays strategy I or IV, this offers A a greater market share than the maximin pay-off, 18. But B then has available a better counterstrategy. He can choose strategy II, which (with A using his strategy II) will confine A to a 5 percent share of market. In other words, by choosing a strategy other than his maximin strategy, A has left himself unprotected against a countermove by B which gives him, A, less then his maximum-security-level share. Thus, the maximin or minimax strategy is designed to offer both sides maximum protection—it may well be described as the coward's (or if one prefers, the predunt man's) strategy.

Property 2. Where the pay-off matrix possesses saddle point, a maximin strategy is the most advantageous strategy available to the one firm *if the other firm chooses a minimax strategy*. This explains why the coincident pay-off matrix entry of the minimax-maximin strategy combination, is called an *equilibrium* or *saddle point*. The implication, in Baumol's words, is that if one of the two firms plays its minimax (maximin) strategy, the other is motivated to employ its maximin (minimax) strategy because that is how it can achieve its largest market share. Equilibrium points therefore, possess an element of inner stability in that if one player adopts a strategy consistent with the attainment of such a point, the other player is also motivated to do so.

Example. Determine the optimal strategies for each player in the following games. Also find out the value of each game to player X :

	I	II	III	IV	V
I	3	0	1	4	−2
II	1	−4	0	7	4
III	5	2	3	4	6
IV	−4	1	−1	3	5
V	2	1	−1	0	1

	I	II	III	IV
I	2	−2	6	3
II	4	−2	4	5
III	5	2	3	0
IV	−4	0	8	4

[**Hints.** (i) X plays III, Y play II, value of game = 2 (ii) X plays II and III in the proportions 1/4, 3/4, while Y plays I and II in the porportions 1/4, 3/4. The value of the game = −1/2]

This property can be illustrated with the aid of our pay-off matrix. If B plays its minimax strategy III, the most which A can obtain is an 18 percent share of the market, which he tests by playing his maximin strategy I. The reason this is so is that since 18% is also B's minimax pay-off, it must represent the largest figure in column 3 (the worst market share for B when he plays strategy III). Similarly we see that if A employes his maximum strategy I, the best B can do in response is to employ his maximin strategy III, because any other strategy will give A more than 18 percent of the market.

Property 3. All equilibrium pairs are minimax-maximin strategies. A pair of strategies a and b (where a is any one of the strategies open to firm A and b is one of those open to B) is defined as an *equilibrium pair* if, whenever firm A choose a, B's most profitable countermove is b, and vice-versa.

The previous property of minimax strategies, stated in this terminology, is that the minimax-maximin strategy combination constitutes an equilibrium pair. In addition, we may now assert that the converse of that proposition is also valid, i.e., that any equilibrium pairs of strategies are necessarily minimax-maximin strategies.

Property 4. Equality of pay-offs of different equilibrium pairs. A pay-off table may possess more than one equilibrium pair of strategies. Suppose we call them (a, b) and (a', b'). However, since by the preceding property, both a and a' must be maximin strategies for A, they must yield the same security pay-off to A. Similarly b and b' must yield the same secruity value to B. In other words, any of the *four* strategy combinations $(a, b), (a', b'), (a, b'), (a'b)$ must yield the same pay-offs. Therefore, if there are several equilibrium pairs of strategies, and if one of the players picks any such strategy, then the other player can achieve the same degree of protection (minimum pay-off) no matter which of these he chooses.

Property 5. Maximin strategies may be poor countermoves to non-minimax strategies. The minimax strategy also has an important unattractive feature. Suppose one of the firms is run by managers who are poorly informed or are not very clever, or who simply are willing to take risks, and who, for any of those reasons, do not employ a maximin strategy. Then, the maximin strategy is likely to be unprofitable to the other firm. For example, if B employs strategy I, then it will be strategy III which yields A its highest market share (64 percent) and A's maximin startegy I, will not do as well. In other words, the prudent maximin strategy is only guaranteed to be good when playing against another predunt man!

Exercises

Consider the following statements for a pay-off matrix in a two-person zero-sum game possessing a Saddle Point solution.

(a) Saddle Point solutions are equilibrium solutions;

(b) All equilibrium solutions are Saddle Point solutions.

Do you think that these two statements are identically equivalent? Are both the statements are identically equivalent? Are both the statement simultaneously valid for a two-person, zero-sum game? What do you mean by the 'protective property' of a Saddle Point solution? Why is the solution so called?

Part II

STATISTICAL TECHNIQUES

CHAPTER 1

PROBABILITY AND EXPECTED VALUE

1.1. INTRODUCTION

The first foundation of the *Theory of Probability* was laid in the middle of the seventeenth century. It originated in problems dealing with games of chance played by tossing coins, drawing cards, throwing dice, etc. The notion of Probability is now used in almost all disciplines—Statistics, Economics, Business, Industry, Engineering; etc. The Probability Theory deals with uncertain situations regarding the occurrence of given phenomena, i.e., it is the study of events which are neither absolutely certain nor impossible. In this chapter, we will study the definition of Probability, Set Theoretic Approach and Total and Compound Probability. We first explain some important terms which will be used in defining Probability.

Experiment (or Random Experiment)

It is an operation that results in two or more outcomes. Although we know the set of all different outcomes of an experiment, it is not possible to predict which one of the set will occur at any particular execution of the experiment. For example: (i) *'Tossing a fair coin'* is an *experiment*, because if a coin is tossed, either head or tail will turn up, i.e., we have two possible outcomes. (ii) *Casting an unbiased die* is an *experiment,* because if a die is cast, then there are six possible outcomes, i.e., appearance of 1 or 2 or 3 or 4 or 5 or 6 on the die. (iii) Drawing a card from a well-shuffled pack of 52 cards is an experiment. (iv) Drawing a ball from a bag containing, say, 5 red and 4 white balls is an experiment.

1.2. EVENTS

The results (or outcomes) of experiments or observations are called *events*. Events may be either **elementary** (i.e., simple) or **composite.** Elementary events cannot be decomposed further, while composite events can be decomposed into elementary events. For example, 'Getting Head on tossing a coin' is an elementary event while 'throwing 8 points by a single cast of two dice' is a composite event. Here 8 points may be obtained by throwing (2, 6) or (3, 5) or (4, 4) or (5, 3) or (6, 2), each of which is an elementary event.

Equally likely events

A number of events are said to be *equally likely* (or equally probable) if, having taken into account all the conditions, we have no reason to expect any one of the events in preference to the others. For example, (i) as a result of drawing a card from a well-shuffled pack of 52 cards, any card may appear in the draw so that the 52 different cases (elementary events) are equally likely; (ii) If a fair die (i.e., unbiased die) is cast, all the six possible outcomes 1, 2, 3, 4, 5, 6 are *equally likely,* i.e., we have no reason to expect any one of these in preference to the others; (iii) In tossing a perfect coin (i.e., unbiased coin), the two possible outcomes, *Head and Tail, are equally likely,* i.e., we have no reason to expect that Heads will appear more often than Tails or vice versa.

Mutually exclusive (or incompatible) events

Events are said to be *mutually exclusive* (*or incompatible*) when only one of the events can occur and two (or more) events cannot happen simultaneously, i.e., occurrence of one of the events prevents the occurrence of others. On the contrary, events are compatible (i.e., not mutually exclusive) if it is possible for them to happen simultaneously. The events of 'getting Head and Tail' in the case of tossing a coin are mutually exclusive, because if Head turns up, we cannot get Tail and vice versa, i.e., Head and Tail cannot occur simultaneously. Similarly, when a die (unbiased) is cast, then the outcomes 1, 2, 3, 4, 5, 6 are all *mutually exclusive,* because the occurrence of any one of these six outcomes implies non-occurrence of the others. But if A be the event that an *even number* will appear on top, and B that a *number less than* 4 will appear, then clearly A and B are not *mutually exclusive,* since when 2 appears on top, both A and B occur.

Exhaustive

Events are said to be *exhaustive* when they include all possible cases. The events of getting Head and Tail in the case of tossing a coin are exhaustive. In casting a die, there are 6 exhaustive events (or cases), since any one of all the six numbers 1, 2, 3, 4, 5, 6 may appear on top.

At random

At random means without giving any preference or priority to any (i.e., without bias for any) case so that every one may get an equally likely possibility of occurrence.

Meaning of Probability

In every day life, we come accross the statements like. He is probably wrong, 'The chances of his winning are fifty-fifty.' 'It is very *likely* that that it will rain tonight.' These are not mathematically precise statements in the sense that we cannot form any definite idea about the occurrence or non-occurrence of the events. But they give an idea of a *varying degree of Probability* of occurrence or non-occurrence of the events. Again 'Death of an animal' or 'Failling down of a fruit from a tree' is an *Absolute Certainty* and 'Swimming across of the Indian Ocean' is an *Absolute Impossibility.* The vaguencess of statements stated above has been removed by introducing a device for measuring the degree of Probability of which the *highest* in degree is the *Absolute Certainty* and the lowest the *Absolute Impossibility.* Now, whatever may be the chance of happening of the event, it cannot be worse that Absolute Impossibility or brighter than Absolute Certainty. Mathematically, in the case of Absolute Impossibility, $p = 0$, p standing for probability, and for Absolute Certainty, $p = 1$. Any Chance or Probability can then be represented by a fraction lying between 0 and 1. Hence, mathematically the Probability or Chance of happening of an event lies between 0 and 1 and is, therefore, a positive proper fraction.

1.3. DEFINITION OF PROBABILITY

We shall now give three definitions of Probability:

(i) **Classical or Mathematical (or a Priori) definition.**

(ii) **Empirical or Statistical definition.**

(iii) **Subjective Approach to Probability.**

Classical or Mathematical Definition of Probability

DEFINITION. *If there are n mutually exclusive, exhaustive and equally likely cases, and m of them are favourable to a certain event A, then the probability (or chance) of the occurrence of A is defined as the ratio m/n.*

Symbolically,

$$\mathbf{P(A) = \frac{m}{n} = \frac{No.\ of\ favourable\ cases}{Total\ no.\ of\ all\ equally\ likely\ cases}},$$

where $P(A)$ denotes the probability of occurrence of the event A.

The Probability (or Chance) of non-occurrence of the event A

$$\mathbf{= \frac{n - m}{n} = \frac{No.\ of\ unfavourable\ cases}{Total\ no.\ of\ all\ equally\ likely\ cases}}$$

Symbolically, if $\bar{A}$ or A^c denotes the non-occurrence of A, then

$$P(\bar{A}) = \frac{n-m}{n} = \frac{n}{n} - \frac{m}{n} = 1 - \frac{m}{n} = 1 - P(A) \qquad \left[\because \ \frac{m}{n} = P(A)\right],$$

$$\text{i.e.,} \quad P(A^c) = 1 - P(A), \quad \text{or,} \quad P(A) + P(A^c) = 1.$$

ODDS. (i) The **odds in favour** of the event A are as $m : (n - m)$

= (no. of favourable cases) : (no. of unfavourable cases), and

(ii) The **odds against** the event A are as $(n - m) : m$

= (no. of unfavourable cases) : (no. of favourable cases).

If the *odds in favour of an event A* be $m : n$, then $P(A) = \frac{m}{m+n}$ and $P(A^c) = \frac{n}{m+n}$.

If the *odds against the event B* be $u : v$, then $P(B) = \frac{v}{u+v}$ and $P(B^c) = \frac{u}{u+v}$.

NOTE 1. The probability as defined above is clearly a number lying between 0 and 1. When the occurrence of the event is an absolute certainty, $m = n$, and therefore, the probability of its occurrence, i.e., $P(A) = n/n = 1$. When the occurrence of the event is an absolute impossibility, $m = 0$, and therefore, the probability of its occurrence $=0/n = 0$. Thus for a certain event, $p = 1$ and for an impossible event $p = 0$, where $p =$ probability (or chance).

Again, $0 \leq m \leq n$, or, $0 \leq m/n \leq 1$, or, $\mathbf{0 \leq P(A) \leq 1}$.

NOTE 2. The *classical definition of Probability* is based on two assumptions, viz. (1) all the outcomes (i.e., all the n mutually exclusive cases) are **equally likely** and (2) the total number of exhaustive cases (i.e., n) is **finite.** If any one of these two assumptions does not hold, *classical definition* fails, i.e., we cannot apply classical definition of Probability.

Illustrative Examples

EXAMPLE 1. *A bag contains three white and five black balls. What is the chance that a ball drawn at random will be black? Also find the odds in favour of the event and against the event.*

SOLUTION. The total number of balls $= 3 + 5 = 8$.

1 ball can be drawn out of these 8 balls in ${}^8C_1$ ways $= 8$ ways.

∴ The total number possible cases for the event $= 8$.

Again, one black ball can be drawn out of 5 black balls in ${}^5C_1 = 5$ ways;

∴ the total number of cases favourable to the event $= 5$.

∴ the *chance* that the ball drawn is black $= \frac{5}{8}$.

2ND PART. Total number of cases unfavourable to the event $= 8 - 5 = 3$.

∴ The *odds* in favour of the event are as **5 : 3**,

and the *odds* against the event are as **3 : 5**.

NOTE. The chance that the ball drawn is white = the chance that the ball drawn is not black $= 1 - \frac{5}{8} = \frac{3}{8}$. This result can also be obtained by the direct method.

The odds in favour of the ball being white = 3 : 5,

and the odds against the ball being white = 5 : 3.

EXAMPLE 2. *A (six-faced) die is thrown, find the chance that* (i) *an ace turns up;* (ii) *any one of* 1, 2, 3 *turns up.*

SOLUTION. A die has six faces; if it is thrown, then either 1 or 2 or 3 or 4 or 5 or 6 will appear on the uppermost face of the die.

∴ Total number of all possible cases = 6.

(i) Ace (i.e., 1) will turn up in 1 way only.

∴ No. of cases favourable to the event of getting an ace = 1.

Hence, the required chance that an ace turns up $= \mathbf{\frac{1}{6}}$.

(ii) Any one of 1, 2, 3 turns up in 3 ways.

$\therefore$ No. of cases favourable to any one of 1, 2, 3 is 3.

Hence, the required chance that any one of 1, 2, 3 turns up $= \frac{3}{6} = \frac{1}{2}$.

EXAMPLE 3. *If a coin is tossed, what is the chance of a 'head'?*

SOLUTION. Either 'head' or 'tail' may turn up when a coin is tossed.

$\therefore$ There are 2 equally likely cases, of which only 1 is in favour of showing a 'head'.

Hence, the required chance $= \frac{1}{2}$.

EXAMPLE 4. *Three coins are tossed. What is the probability that they all fall heads?*

SOLUTION. Each coin can fall in 2 different ways, showing head or tail;

$\therefore$ 3 coins can fall in $2 \times 2 \times 2$ different ways.

$\therefore$ The total number of possible cases for the event $= 2 \times 2 \times 2 = 8$.

Now 3 coins can fall to show all heads in only 1 way.

$\therefore$ Out of 8 possible cases only 1 is in favour of the event of showing all heads.

Hence, the required probability that they all fall heads $= \frac{1}{8}$.

EXAMPLE 5. *If one card is drawn at random from a well-shuffled pack of* 52 *cards, find the chance that the card is* (i) *a diamond,* (ii) *not a diamond,* (iii) *an ace,* (iv) *neither a spade nor a heart.*

SOLUTION. One card can be drawn out of 52 in ${}^{52}C_1$ ways = 52 ways.

$\therefore$ Total no. of all possible equally likely cases = 52.

(i) One diamond can be drawn out of 13 in ${}^{13}C_1$ ways = 13 ways.

$\therefore$ Total no. of favourable cases = 13.

Hence, the required chance that the card is a diamond $= \frac{13}{52} = \frac{1}{4}$.

(ii) The required chance that the card is not a diamond $= 1 - \frac{1}{4} = \frac{3}{4}$.

(iii) An ace can be drawn out of 4 in ${}^{4}C_1$ ways = 4 ways.

$\therefore$ No. of favourable cases = 4.

Hence, required chance that the card is an ace $= \frac{4}{52} = \frac{1}{13}$.

(iv) There are 13 spades and 13 hearts in a pack 52 of cards.

$\therefore$ Either a spade or a heart can be drawn in ${}^{26}C_1$ ways = 26 ways.

$\therefore$ The chance that the card is either a spade or a heart $= \frac{26}{52} = \frac{1}{2}$.

Hence, the required chance that the card is neither a spade nor a heart $= 1 - \frac{1}{2} = \frac{1}{2}$.

EXAMPLE 6. *A man draws at random* 3 *balls from a bag containing* 6 *red and* 5 *white balls. What is the chance of getting the balls all red?* **[C.U. B. Com. 1979]**

SOLUTION. Total no. of balls $= 6 + 5 = 11$.

3 balls can be drawn out of 11 in ${}^{11}C_3$ ways $= \frac{11.10.9}{3.2.1} = 165$ ways.

$\therefore$ Total number of possible cases for the event = 165.

Again, 3 red balls can be drawn out of 6 in ${}^{6}C_3$ ways $= \frac{6.5.4}{3.2.1} = 20$ ways.

$\therefore$ Total number of cases favourable to the event = 20.

Hence, the required chance of getting the balls all red $= \frac{20}{165} = \frac{4}{33}$.

EXAMPLE 7. *Three balls are drawn at random from a bag containing* 6 *blue and* 4 *red balls. What is the chance that two balls are blue and one is red?* **[B.U. B. Com. 1977]**

SOLUTION. Total no. of balls $= 6 + 4 = 10$.

3 balls can be drawn out of 10 in ${}^{10}C_3$ ways $= \frac{10 \cdot 9 \cdot 8}{3 \cdot 2 \cdot 1} = 120$ ways.

$\therefore$ Total no. of cases for the event $= 120$.

Again, 2 blue balls can be drawn out of 6 in ${}^6C_2$ ways and 1 red ball can be drawn out of 4 in ${}^4C_1$ ways.

$\therefore$ 2 blue balls and 1 red ball jointly can be drawn in ${}^6C_2 \times {}^4C_1$ ways $= \frac{6.5}{2.1} \times \frac{4}{1} = 60$ ways.

$\therefore$ total no. of favourable cases for the event $= 60$.

Hence, the required chance of drawing 2 blue and 1 red balls $= \frac{60}{120} = \frac{1}{2}$.

EXAMPLE 8. *What is the chance that a leap year selected at random will contain*

(i) 53 Sundays; **[Delhi U. M. Com. 1975]**

(ii) 53 Thursdays or 53 Fridays? **[CA May 1988]**

SOLUTION. A leap year consists of 366 days in which there are 52 complete weeks and 2 more consecutive days. 52 weeks contain 52 Sundays, 52 Thursdays and 52 Fridays.

(i) A leap year will contain 53 Sundays if these two consecutive days contain one Sunday.

2 *consecutive* days can be selected from the 7 days in a week in the following possible ways:

(Sunday, Monday), (Monday, Tuesday), (Tuesday, Wednesday), (Wednesday, Thursday), (Thursday, Friday), (Friday, Saturday), (Saturday, Sunday). (1)

We see that out of the above 7 possibilities, 2 (the first and the last) contain 'Sunday', i.e., no. of favourable cases = 2.

Hence, the required chance that a leap year will contain 53 Sundays $= \frac{2}{7}$.

(ii) Again from (1) we see that *out of the* 7 *outcomes,* (i.e., possibilities) 3 *are favourable* to the event of 53 Thursdays or 53 Fridays and they are (Wednesday, Thursday), (Thursday, Friday) and (Friday, Saturday).

[Note that by "either 53 Thursdays or 53 Fridays, we mean that either Thursday or Friday or both Thursday and Friday.]

Hence, the required chance that a leap year will contain either 53 Thursdays or 53 Fridays $= \frac{3}{7}$.

NOTE. If by the event "either 53 Thursdays or 53 Fridays" we mean "Thursdays or Fridays" and exclude the case Thursday and Friday, then the required chance will be $\frac{2}{7}$.

EXAMPLE 9. *Find the probability that in a game of bridge a hand of* 13 *cards will contain all the* 4 *aces.*

SOLUTION. There are 52 cards in all.

A hand of 13 cards can be made up out of 52 in ${}^{52}C_{13}$ ways.

$\therefore$ Total number of equally likely cases $= {}^{52}C_{13}$.

Roughly speaking subjective probability may be considered as the odds one would give in betting on an event.

The mathematical theory of probability deals with objective probabilities, its origin being in the prediction of results in gambling. Business and administration deals with both objective and subjective probabilities. We shall now discuss objective probabilities in detail.

1.4. SET THEORETIC APPROACH

We know that the results of an experiment which cannot be decomposed further are called *elementary* events or outcomes. 'Getting head' on tossing a coin is an elementary event. The set S of all possible elementary events (or outcomes) of a given experiment is called the **Sample Space** of the experiment. A particular elementary event or outcome which is an element of S is called a *Sample Point* or simply a *Sample*. A *composite event* A is a set of elementary events (or outcomes) of S, and A is a subset of the sample space S. We shall call the null set ϕ, the *impossible event*, and the sample space S, the *certain or sure event*. We shall now explain some set operations combining two or more events $A, B, \cdots$.

(i) The event $A \cup B$ will denote the occurrence of either A or B or both A and B, i.e., occurrence of at least one of A and B.

(ii) The event $A \cap B$ will denote the simultaneous occurrence of A and B. Similarly, $A \cap B \cap C \cap \cdots$ will denote the simultaneous occurrence of $A, B, C, \cdots$.

(iii) The event A^c (or A') will denote the non-occurrence of A.

(iv) The event $A - B$ will denote the occurrence of A and the non-occurrence of B. Clearly, $A - B = A \cap B^c$.

(v) Two events of A and B are said to be mutually exclusive if they are disjoint, i.e., if $A \cap B = \phi$.

EXAMPLE (Experiment). *Toss a die and observe the number appearing on top. Notice that the possible outcomes or sample points are* 1, 2, 3, 4, 5, 6 *and the sample space S consists of these six sample points, i.e.,* $S = \{1, 2, 3, 4, 5, 6\}$.

Let A be the event that an *even number* appears and B that an *odd number* appears and C that a *number less than* 4 appears. Then

$$A = \{2, 4, 6\}, B = \{1, 3, 5\}, C = \{1, 2, 3\}.$$

$A \cap B = \{1, 2, 3, 4, 5, 6\} = S$ which is the certain event, since either an even number or an odd number must appear.

$A \cap B = \phi$, i.e., an even number and an odd number cannot occur simltaneously. In other words, A and B are mutually exclusive events.

$A^c = \{1, 3, 5\}$ = the event that an even number does not occur.

$B \cup C = \{1, 2, 3, 5\}$ = the event that an odd number or a number less than 4 occurs.

$B \cap C = \{1, 3\}$ = the event that an odd number less than 4 appears.

NOTE. The number of all possible sample points in the sample space S will be denoted by the symbol $n(S)$ and the no. of sample points in any event A by $n(A)$.

Definition of Probability (Classical Definition)

Set Theoretic treatment of Probability Theory will be based on two assumption, viz. (1) the total no. of elementary events in the sample space S is finite, say N, and (2) the experiment is such that the N elementary events are equally likely. Then, if m is the number of elementary events favourable to an event A (i.e., A occurs when any one of the elementary events occurs and conversely), the probability $P(A)$ of the event A is defined by

$$P(A) = \frac{m}{N} = \frac{n(A)}{n(S)},$$

where $n(A)$ = no. of sample points in A and

$n(S)$ = Total no. of sample points in S.

Properties of P(A)

(i) Since $0 \leq m \leq N$, dividing by N we have $0 \leq m/N \leq 1$, i.e., $0 \leq P(A) \leq 1$.

(ii) If A is an impossible event, then $m = 0$. $\therefore \quad P(A) = 0/N = 0$.

(iii) If A is a certain event, then $m = N$. $\therefore \quad P(A) = N/N = 1$.

(iv) If the occurrence of A implies the occurrence of B (the occurrence of B may not imply the occurrence of A), then $P(A) \leq P(B)$.

EXAMPLE 1. *Three fair coins are tossed once. Construct the sample space of the outcomes of the random experiment. Find the probability of* (i) *at least one head,* (ii) *exactly one tail.*

[ICWAI June 1993]

SOLUTION. If S be the required sample space, H represents head and T represents tail, then S is the set of all possible outcomes given by

$$S = \{HHH, HHT, HTH, HTT, THH, THT, TTH, TTT\}.$$

(i) $n(S) = 8$. If A be the event that at least one head appears, then

$$A = \{HHH, HHT, HTH, HTT, THH, THT, TTH\};$$

$$\therefore \quad n(A) = 7; \quad \therefore \quad P(A) = \frac{n(A)}{n(S)} = \frac{7}{8}.$$

(ii) If B be the event that exactly one tail appear, then

$$B = \{HHT, HTH, THH\}$$

$$\therefore \quad n(B) = 3; \quad \therefore \quad P(B) = \frac{n(B)}{n(S)} = \frac{3}{8}.$$

EXAMPLE 2. *If a die is tossed, what is the probability that the number appearing on top is* (i) *even,* (ii) *less than* 4, (iii) *not an even number,* (iv) *either an even or an odd number,* (v) *an odd number less than* 4.

SOLUTION. If a die is tossed, the possible sample points are $1, 2, 3, 4, 5, 6$ and, therefore, the sample space consists of these 6 sample points,

$$\text{i.e.,} \quad S = \{1, 2, 3, 4, 5, 6\}; \quad \therefore \quad n(S) = 6.$$

Let A be the event that an even number appears, B that an odd number appears and C that a number less than 4 appears. Then

$$A = \{2, 4, 6\}, \ B = \{1, 3, 5\}, \ C = \{1, 2, 3\}, \ A^c = \{1, 3, 5\}$$
$$A \cup B = \{1, 2, 3, 4, 5, 6\} = S, \ B \cap C = \{1, 3\}.$$
$$\therefore \quad n(A) = 3, \ n(C) = 3, \ n(A^c) = 3, \ n(A \cup B) = 6, \ n(B \cap C) = 2.$$

(i) The probability that the number appearing on top is even, is

$$P(A) = \frac{n(A)}{n(S)} = \frac{3}{6} = \mathbf{\frac{1}{2}}.$$

(ii) The probability tnat the number appearing on top is less than 4, is

$$P(C) = \frac{n(C)}{n(S)} = \frac{3}{6} = \mathbf{\frac{1}{2}}.$$

(iii) The probability that the number appearing on top is not an even number, is

$$P(A^c) = \frac{3}{6} = \mathbf{\frac{1}{2}}. \qquad [\text{Also } P(A^c) = 1 - P(A) = 1 - \tfrac{1}{2} = \tfrac{1}{2}.]$$

(iv) The probability that the number appearing on top is either an even or an odd number, is

$$P(A \cup B) = \frac{n(A \cup B)}{n(S)} = \frac{6}{6} = \mathbf{1}.$$

(v) The probability that the number appearing on top is an odd number less than 4, is

$$P(B \cap C) = \frac{n(B \cap C)}{n(S)} = \frac{2}{6} = \mathbf{\frac{1}{3}}.$$

EXAMPLE 3. *What is the probability of getting* 3 *white balls in a draw of* 3 *balls from a box containing* 5 *white and* 4 *black balls?* **[CA May 1976]**

SOLUTION. Total no. of balls is $5 + 4 = 9$.

3 balls can be drawn out of 9 in ${}^9C_3$ ways $= \frac{9.8.7}{3.2.1} = 84$ ways.

$\therefore$ Total no. of possible outcomes $= 84$.

$\therefore$ The sample space S consists of 84 sample points, i.e., $n(S) = 84$.

Let A be the event that 3 white balls are drawn. Then

$n(A)$ = the possible no. of ways in which 3 white balls can be drawn out of 5 is

$$^5C_3 = \frac{5.4.3}{3.2.1} = 10.$$

Hence, the required probability that 3 white balls are drawn from the box is

$$\frac{n(A)}{n(S)} = \frac{10}{84} = \mathbf{\frac{5}{42}}.$$

EXAMPLE 4. *A sample of 3 items is selected at random from a box of 12 items of which 3 are defective. Find the possible number of defective combinations of the said 3 selected items along with probability of a defective combination.* **[CA May 1989]**

SOLUTION. 3 items can be selected from the box containing 12 items in $^{12}C_3$ ways $= \frac{12.11.10}{3.2.1}$ = 220 ways.

∴ Total no. of cases = 220.

No. of non-defective items in the box = 12 − 3 = 9.

∴ 3 non-defective items can be selected out of 9 in $^9C_3$ ways $= \frac{9.8.7}{3.2.1}$ = 84 ways.

∴ Possible number of non-defective combinations = 84.

∴ Possible number of defective combinations = 220 − 84 = 136.

Hence, the required probability of a defective combination $= \frac{136}{220} = \frac{34}{55}$.

[OTHERWISE. 1 defective and 2 non-defective items can be selected in $^3C_1 \times {}^9C_2$ ways, 2 defectives and 1 non-defective items can be selected in $^3C_2 \times {}^9C_1$ ways, and 3 defective items can be selected in $^3C_3$ ways.]

∴ No. of defective combinations $= {}^3C_1 \times 9C_2 + {}^3C_2 \times {}^9C_1 + {}^3C_3 = 136$.]

EXAMPLE 5. *In a family there are 3 children. Find the probability that all of them will have different birthdays.*

SOLUTION. The birthday of the first child may fall on any one of the 365 days, the second child's birthday may occur on any one of the 365 days and similarly for the third child.

∴ The total no. of all possible ways in which the 3 children can have their birthdays = 365 × 365 × 365, i.e., $n(S) = 365 \times 365 \times 365$.

For the no. of favourable cases, we see that the first child can have his birthday on any one of the 365 days and then the second child has a different birthday on any one of the remaining 364 days in the year, and similarly the third child can have a different birthday on any of the remaining 363 days.

∴ The number of cases favourable to the event A ('different birthdays') is 365 × 364 × 363, i.e., $n(A) = 365 \times 364 \times 363$.

Hence, the required probability that all the 3 children will have different birthdays is

$$\frac{n(A)}{n(S)} = \frac{365 \times 364 \times 363}{365 \times 365 \times 365} = 0.99179 = \mathbf{0.99\ (approx)}.$$

1.5. THEOREMS OF TOTAL PROBABILITY (THE RULE OF ADDITION)

We shall now prove two theorems on Total Probability which will enable us to find the probability of the union of a set of events. First we consider the case of a set of mutually exclusive events.

THEOREM 1. *If A and B be two mutually exclusive events, then $P(A \cup B) = P(A) + P(B)$, i.e., the probability that either A or B occurs is the sum of the probabilities of the events A and B.*

EXTENSION. *For r mutually exclusive events $A_1, A_2, \cdots, A_r$,*

$$P(A_1 \cup A_2 \cup \cdots \cup A_r) = P(A_1) + P(A_2) + \cdots + P(A_r).$$

PROOF. Let the total number of all possible elementary events be N out of which m_1 are favourable to A and m_2 are favourable to B. Then the number of elementary events that are favourable to either A or B is $m_1 + m_2$. [Since A and B are two mutually exclusive events.]

Hence, $P(A \cup B)$ = Probability that either A or B occurs

$$= \frac{m_1 + m_2}{N} = \frac{m_1}{N} + \frac{m_2}{N} = P(A) + P(B)$$

$$\left[\because \ \tfrac{m_1}{N} = P(A) \text{ and } \tfrac{m_2}{N} = P(B), \text{ by definition}\right]$$

$$\text{i.e.,} \quad \mathbf{P(A \cup B) = P(A) + P(B)}. \tag{1}$$

EXTENSION.

$$P(A_1 \cup A_2 \cup A_3 \cup \cdots \cup A_r) = P(A_1 \cup [A_2 \cup A_3 \cup \cdots \cup A_r])$$

$$= P(A_1) + P(A_2 \cup A_3 \cup \cdots \cup A_r) \quad \text{[using the result (1)]}$$

$$= P(A_1) + P(A_2) + P(A_3 \cup A_4 \cup \cdots \cup A_r) \quad \text{[proceeding as before]}$$

$$= \cdots\cdots\cdots\cdots\cdots\cdots\cdots\cdots$$

$$= P(A_1) + P(A_2) + \cdots + P(A_r)$$

Hence, the theorem follows.

COROLLARY 1. *If $A_1, A_2, \cdots, A_r$ are exhaustive, i.e., one of them must occur, then $A_1 \cup A_2 \cup \cdots \cup A_r$ is a certain event and, therefore,*

$$P(A_1 \cup A_2 \cup \cdots \cup A_r) = 1, \quad \text{or,} \quad P(A_1) + P(A_2) + \cdots + P(A_r) = 1$$

[$\because$ $A_1, A_2, \cdots, A_r$ are *mutually exclusive* events.]

In particular, the event A and its complement, i.e., A and A^c are exhaustive and mutually exclusive.

$$\therefore \quad P(A) + P(A^c) = 1$$

$$\text{or,} \quad \mathbf{P(A) = 1 - P(A^c)}, \quad \text{or,} \quad \mathbf{P(A^c) = 1 - P(A)}.$$

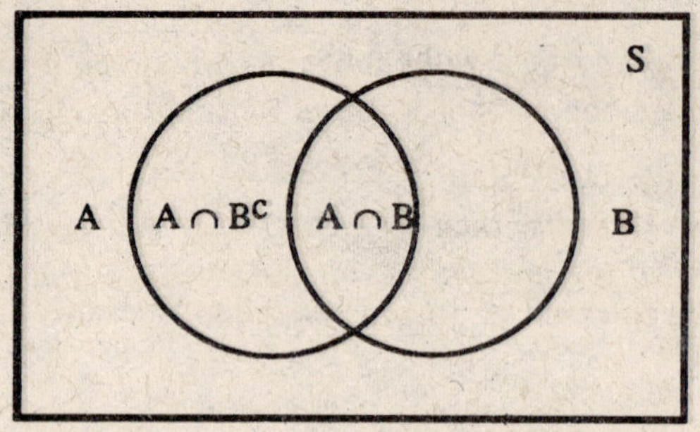

Fig 1.1

COROLLARY 2. *If A and B are two events, not mutually exclusive, connected with a random experiment, then A will occur if and only if any one of the mutually exclusive events $A \cap B$ and $A \cap B^c$ occurs. Therefore, by theorem I.*

$$\mathbf{P(A) = P(A \cap B) + P(A \cap B^c)}.$$

Similarly,

$$\mathbf{P(B) = P(A \cap B) + P(A^c \cap B)}.$$

THEOREM 2. *If A and B be any two events (not necessarily mutually exclusive), then $P(A \cup B)$, i.e., the probability that at least one of the two events A and B occurs is given by*

$$\mathbf{P(A \cup B) = P(A) + P(B) - P(A \cap B)}.$$

PROOF. Let S be the sample space and A, B be any two events of S.

We have

$$P(A \cup B) = \frac{n(A \cup B)}{n(S)} \tag{1}$$

where $n(A \cup B)$ = the number of sample points (or elements) in $A \cup B$ and $n(S)$ = the total no. of all possible sample points in S.

From *Set Theory* we know that $n(A \cup B) = n(A) + n(B) - n(A \cap B)$.

$$\therefore \text{ From (1)}, \quad P(A \cup B) = \frac{n(A) + n(B) - n(A \cap B)}{n(S)} = \frac{n(A)}{n(S)} + \frac{n(B)}{n(S)} - \frac{n(A \cap B)}{n(S)}$$
$$= P(A) + P(B) - P(A \cap B).$$

Hence, the theorem follows.

COROLLARY. *If A and B are two mutually exclusive events, then $A \cap B = \phi$;*

$\therefore \; n(A \cap B) = 0; \quad \therefore \; P(A \cap B) = 0$. Hence, $\mathbf{P(A \cup B) = P(A) + P(B)}$.

GENERALISATION. We know that for any three events, A, B, C,

$n(A \cup B \cup C) = n(A) + n(B) + n(C) - n(A \cap B) - n(B \cap C) - n(A \cap C) + n(A \cap B \cap C)$ and $P(A \cup B \cup C) = \frac{n(A \cup B \cup C)}{n(S)}$.

Hence, $P(A \cup B \cup C) = P(A) + P(B) + P(C) - P(A \cap B) - P(B \cap C) - P(A \cap C) + P(A \cap B \cap C)$.

Similarly, we can write the formulae for the probabilities of four or more events.

EXAMPLE 1. *From a set of* 17 *balls marked* $1, 2, 3, \cdots, 16, 17$, *one is drawn at random.* (a) *What is the chance that its number is a multiple of* 3 *or of* 7? (b) *What is the probability that its number is an even number greater than* 9? **[CA November 1985]**

SOLUTION. Let S be the sample space connected with the drawing.

Then $S = \{1, 2, 3, \cdots, 16, 17\}; \quad \therefore \; n(S) = 17$.

(a) Let A be the event that the number of the ball is a multiple of 3, and B be the event that its number is a multiple of 7.

Then $A = \{3, 6, 9, 12, 15\}$ and $B = \{7, 14\}$; $\therefore$ $n(A) = 5$ and $n(B) = 2$.

$$\therefore \quad P(A) = \frac{n(A)}{n(S)} = \frac{5}{17} \quad \text{and} \quad P(B) = \frac{n(B)}{n(S)} = \frac{2}{17}.$$

Since A and B are mutually exclusive events, by the theorem of Total Probability, we have

$$P(A \cup B) = P(A) + P(B) = \frac{5}{17} + \frac{2}{17} = \frac{7}{17}.$$

Hence, the required chance that its number is a multiple of 3 or of 7 is

$$P(A \cup B) = \mathbf{\frac{7}{17}}.$$

(b) Let C be the event that the number of the ball is an even number greater than 9. Then $C = \{10, 12, 14, 16\}$; $\therefore$ $n(C) = 4$.

Hence, the required probability that its number is an even number greater than $9 = \mathbf{\frac{4}{17}}$.

EXAMPLE 2. *A fair die is thrown. Write down the sample space. What is the chance that either an odd number or a number greater than* 4 *will turn up?* **[C.U. B. Com. (Hons.) 1986]**

SOLUTION. Let S be the sample space connected with the throwing of the die. Then

$$S = \{1, 2, 3, 4, 5, 6\}; \quad \therefore \quad n(S) = 6.$$

If A be the event that an odd number will turn up and B, the event that a number greater than 4 will turn up, then

$$A = \{1, 3, 5\} \quad \text{and} \quad B = \{5, 6\}. \quad \text{Also} \quad A \cap B = \{5\}.$$

$\because$ A and B are not mutually exclusive events.

Now $n(A) = 3, n(B) = 2$ and $n(A \cap B) = 1$.

$\therefore$ $P(A) = \frac{n(A)}{n(S)} = \frac{3}{6} = \frac{1}{2}, P(B) = \frac{n(B)}{n(S)} = \frac{2}{6} = \frac{1}{3}$, and $P(A \cap B) = \frac{n(A \cap B)}{n(S)} = \frac{1}{6}$.

$\therefore$ By the theorem of total probability, we have

$$\begin{aligned} P(A \cup B) &= P(A) + P(B) - P(A \cap B) \\ &= \frac{1}{2} + \frac{1}{3} - \frac{1}{6} = \frac{3 + 2 - 1}{6} = \frac{4}{6} = \frac{2}{3}. \end{aligned}$$

Hence, the required chance $= \mathbf{\frac{2}{3}}$.

EXAMPLE 3. *The probability that a contractor will get a plumbing contract is* $2/3$ *and the probability that he will not get an electric contract is* $5/9$. *If the probability of getting at least one contract is* $4/5$, *what is the probability that he will get both the contracts?* **[CA May 1979]**

SOLUTION. Let A be the event that the contractor will get the plumbing contract and B, that he will get the electric contract. Then

$$P(A) = \frac{2}{3}, P(B^c) = \frac{5}{9} \quad \text{and} \quad P(A \cup B) = \frac{4}{5}.$$

We have to find the value of $P(A \cap B)$.

We have $P(B) = 1 - P(B^c) = 1 - \frac{5}{9} = \frac{4}{9}$.

By the theorem of Total Probability, we have

$$P(A \cup B) = P(A) + P(B) - P(A \cap B);$$
$$\therefore \quad \frac{4}{5} = \frac{2}{3} + \frac{4}{9} - P(A \cap B) = \frac{10}{9} - P(A \cap B), \quad \text{or,} \quad P(A \cap B) = \frac{10}{9} - \frac{4}{5} = \frac{50-36}{45} = \frac{14}{45}.$$

Hence, the required probability $= \mathbf{\frac{14}{45}}$.

EXAMPLE 4. *A and B are two events, not mutually exclusive, connected with a random experiment E. If $P(A) = \frac{1}{4}$, $P(B) = \frac{2}{5}$ and $P(A \cup B) = \frac{1}{2}$, find the values of the following probabilities:*

(i) $P(A \cap B)$; (ii) $P(A \cap B^c)$; (iii) $P(A^c \cup B^c)$

where c stands for the complement. **[C.U. B. Com. (Hons.) 1980]**

SOLUTION. We have $P(A \cup B) = P(A) + P(B) - P(A \cap B)$, where A and B are two events, not mutually exclusive.

$$\text{or,} \quad \frac{1}{2} = \frac{1}{4} + \frac{2}{5} - P(A \cap B), \quad \text{or,} \quad P(A \cap B) = \frac{1}{4} + \frac{2}{5} - \frac{1}{2} = \frac{5+8-10}{20} = \mathbf{\frac{3}{20}}.$$

(ii) Event A will occur if and only if any one of the two mutually exclusive events $A \cap B$ and $A \cap B^c$ occurs.

$$\therefore \quad P(A) = P(A \cap B) + P(A \cap B^c),$$
$$\text{or,} \quad \frac{1}{4} = \frac{3}{20} + P(A \cap B^c), \quad \text{or,} \quad P(A \cap B^c) = \frac{1}{4} - \frac{3}{20} = \frac{5-3}{20} = \mathbf{\frac{1}{10}}.$$

(iii) **By De Morgan's Law,** $(A \cap B)^c = A^c \cup B^c$.

$$\therefore \quad P(A^c \cup B^c) = P[(A \cap B)^c] = 1 - P(A \cap B) = 1 - \frac{3}{20} = \mathbf{\frac{17}{20}}.$$

EXAMPLE 5. *If a pair of dice is thrown, find the probability that the sum is neither* 7 *nor* 11.

[CA November 1988]

SOLUTION. If S be the sample space connected with the throwing of the pair of dice, then $S = \{(1,1), (1,2), (1,3), (1,4), (1,5), (1,6), (2,1), (2,2), (2,3), \cdots, (6,6)\}$.

$\therefore \quad n(S) = 6 \times 6 = 36.$

If A be the event that the sum is 7 and B the event that the sum is 11, then

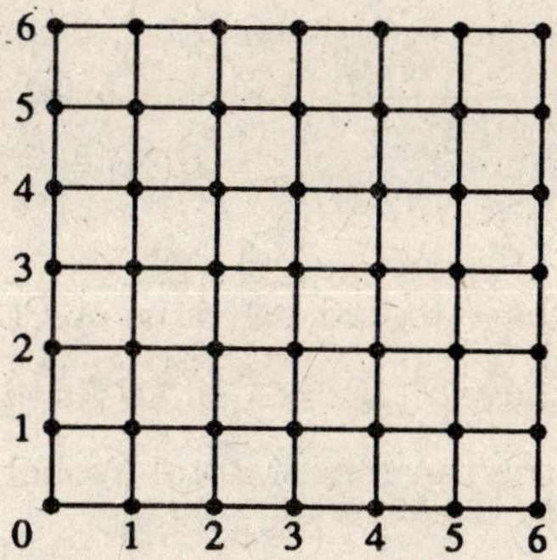

$$A = \{(1,6),(2,5),(3,4),(4,3),(5,2),(6,1)\}$$

and $B = \{(5,6),(6,5)\}$.

$\therefore \quad n(A) = 6 \quad \text{and} \quad n(B) = 2.$

$$\therefore \quad P(A) = \frac{n(A)}{n(S)} = \frac{6}{36} = \frac{1}{6}$$

and $$P(B) = \frac{n(B)}{n(S)} = \frac{2}{36} = \frac{1}{18}.$$

$\therefore$ The probability that the sum is either 7 or 11

$$= P(A \cup B) = P(A) + P(B) \quad [\because \ A \text{ and } B \text{ are mutually exclusive events.}]$$

$$= \frac{1}{6} + \frac{1}{18} = \frac{4}{18} = \frac{2}{9}.$$

Hence, the required probability that the sum is neither 7 nor 11 $= 1 - P(A \cup B) = 1 - \frac{2}{9} = \frac{7}{9}$.

1.6. COMPOUND PROBABILITY : CONDITIONAL PROBABILITY

The probability of the simultaneous occurrence of two or more events is called **compound probability** and is denoted by $P(A \cap B)$ for two events A and B, and by $P(A_1 \cap A_2 \cap \cdots \cap A_r)$ for r events $A_1, A_2, \cdots, A_r$.

The probability of the occurrence of the event B assuming that the event A has actually occurred is called the **conditional probability** of B and is denoted by $P(B/A)$ or $P(B, A)$, which is read as the probability of B given A.

Theorem of Compound Probability (The Rule of Multiplication)

The probability of simultaneous occurrence of A and B is given by the product of the unconditional probability of the event A by the conditional probability of B, assuming that A has actually occurred.

Symbolically, $\mathbf{P(A \cap B) = P(A) \cdot P(B/A)}$.

PROOF. Let A be a subset of the sample space S such that $n(A) \neq 0$, i.e., the event A occurs.

Let us consider, together with $n(A)$, the number of elementary events $n(A \cap B)$ which are favourable to both A and B. Then $n(A)$ is the no. of all possible elementary events for the conditional event B/A, assuming that A has actually occurred, out of which $n(A \cap B)$ are favourable to B/A. [In this case, A is the reduced sample space, due to which occurrence of B is restricted to $A \cap B$].

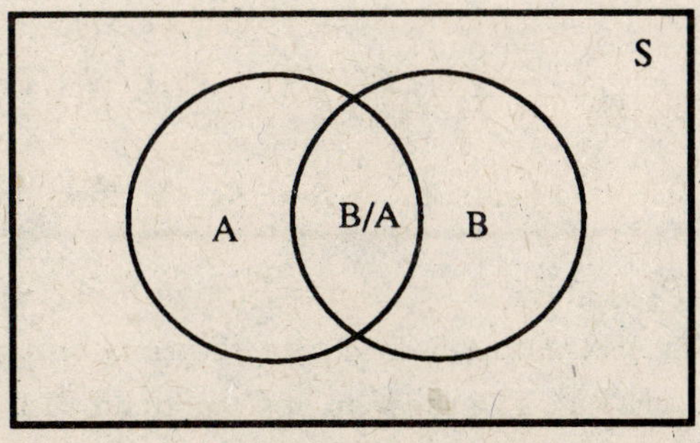

Fig 1.2

$$\therefore \quad \frac{n(A \cap B)}{n(A)} = \text{the conditional probability of } B \text{ assuming that } A \text{ has actually occurred.}$$

$$= P(B/A),$$

$$\text{or,} \quad P(B/A) = \frac{n(A \cap B)}{n(A)} = \frac{n(A \cap B)/n(S)}{n(A)/n(S)} = \frac{P(A \cap B)}{P(A)},$$

$$\text{or,} \quad \mathbf{P(A \cap B) = P(A) \cdot P(B/A)}. \tag{1}$$

Hence, the theorem follows.

[OTHERWISE. Let N be the total no. of all equally likely cases and m of them are favourable to the event A. Then the cases favourable to both A and B are all included in the m cases favourable to A. Let their number be m_1. The probability $P(A \cap B)$ that both A and B will occur is given by

$$P(A \cap B) = \frac{m_1}{N} = \frac{m}{N} \cdot \frac{m_1}{m} \tag{1}$$

Now, $\frac{m}{N} = \frac{\text{No. of cases favourable to } A}{\text{Total no. of all possible cases}} = P(A)$.

Also assuming the occurrence of A, there are only m equally likely cases left for B (the remaining $N - m$ cases becoming impossible to B), out of which m_1 cases are favourable to B. Hence, the ratio $\frac{m_1}{m}$ represents the conditional probability $P(B/A)$ of B, assuming that A has actually occurred, i.e.,

$$\frac{m_1}{m} = P(B/A).$$

$\therefore$ From (1), we get $P(A \cap B) = P(A) \cdot P(B/A)$.

Hence, the theorem follows.]

GENERALISATION. *For three events, A, B and C, we have*

$$\mathbf{P(A \cap B \cap C) = P(A) \cdot P(B/A) \cdot P(C/A \cap B)}.$$ [C.U. B. Com. (Hons.) 1992]

PROOF.

$$P(A \cap B \cap C) = P(A \cap D), \quad \text{where} \quad D = B \cap C$$
$$= P(A) \cdot P(D/A) = P(A) \cdot P\{(B \cap C)/A\} = P(A) \cdot P(B/A) \cdot P(C/A \cap B).$$

For r events $A_1, A_2, \cdots, A_r$, the formula becomes

$$P(A_1 \cap A_2 \cap \cdots \cap A_r) = P(A_1) \cdot P(A_2/A_1) \cdot P(A_3/A_1 \cap A_2) \cdots P(A_r/A_1 \cap A_2 \cap \cdots \cap A_{r-1}).$$

NOTE. The theorem of Compound Probability enables us to find a formula for the calculation of Conditional Probability $P(B/A)$. Since $A \cap B = B \cap A$, interchanging A and B in (1), we get $P(B \cap A) = P(B) \cdot P(A/B)$, and hence,

$$P(A \cap B) = P(A) \cdot P(B/A) = P(B) \cdot P(A/B).$$

COROLLARY. *If two events are independent, the occurrence of one of them will not affect the probability of occurrence of the other. If A and B are independent events, then* $P(B/A) = P(B)$. *Thus for two independent events A and B, the theorem of Compound Probability becomes*

$$\mathbf{P(A \cap B) = P(A) \cdot P(B)}.$$

For r mutually independent events $A_1, A_2, \cdots, A_r$, we have

$$P(A_1 \cap A_2 \cap \cdots \cap A_r) = P(A_1) \cdot P(A_2) \cdots P(A_r).$$

Dependent and Independent Events **[ICWAI December 1984]**

Two events A and B are said to be *independent* if the occurrence of one of them, say A, does not affect the probability of occurrence of the other event B. In other words, A and B are *independent* if and only if

$$P(B/A) = P(B) \quad \text{and} \quad P(A/B) = P(A), \quad \text{i.e.,} \quad P(A \cap B) = P(A) \cdot P(B).$$

Otherwise, they are said to be *dependent* (or *interdependent*) events. For dependent events, the occurrence or non-occurrence of one of them affects the probability of occurrence of the other events. If A and B are two *dependent events,* then

$$P(A \cap B) = P(A)P(B/A), \quad \text{or,} \quad P(B)P(A/B).$$

ILLUSTRATION 1. *When a coin is tossed twice in succession, the result (say 'getting a head') of the first tossing does not affect the result (say 'getting a tail') of the second tossing. Hence, the two events are independent.*

ILLUSTRATION 2. *When a die is thrown twice, the result of the first throw does not affect the result (and hence, probability) of the second throw.*

ILLUSTRATION 3. *If a card is drawn from a pack of* 52 *cards and replaced, and then a card is again drawn from the pack, the two events are independent. But if the first card is not replaced before the second drawing, the probability of drawing the second card is affected by the first event and hence, in this case the two events are dependent.*

NOTE. When events are *not independent,* we have to use *conditional probability,* since the result of the second event is conditional, depending on the result of the first event.

EXAMPLE 1.

(i) *If* $P(A) = 2/5, P(B) = 1/3$ *and* $P(A \cup B) = 1/2$, *find* $P(A/B)$ *and* $P(B/A)$.

(ii) *If A and B are two independent events and* $P(A) = 2/3, P(B) = 3/5$, *find* $P(A \cup B)$.

SOLUTION.

(i) We have $P(A \cup B) = P(A) + P(B) - P(A \cap B)$

or, $\frac{1}{2} = \frac{2}{5} + \frac{1}{3} - P(A \cap B)$, or, $P(A \cap B) = \frac{2}{5} + \frac{1}{3} - \frac{1}{2} = \frac{7}{30}$.

We know that $P(A \cap B) = P(A) \cdot P(B/A) = P(B) \cdot P(A/B)$

$$\therefore \quad P(A/B) = \frac{P(A \cap B)}{P(B)} = \frac{7}{30} \Big/ \frac{1}{3} = \mathbf{\frac{7}{10}}.$$

$$\text{and} \quad P(B/A) = \frac{P(A \cap B)}{P(A)} = \frac{7}{30} \Big/ \frac{2}{5} = \frac{7}{30} \times \frac{5}{2} = \mathbf{\frac{7}{12}}.$$

(ii) Since A and B are two independent events,

$$\therefore \quad P(A \cap B) = P(A) \cdot P(B) = \frac{2}{3} \times \frac{3}{5} = \frac{2}{5}.$$

We have $P(A \cup B) = P(A) + P(B) - P(A \cap B)$

$$= \frac{2}{3} + \frac{3}{5} - \frac{2}{5} = \frac{10 + 9 - 6}{15} = \mathbf{\frac{13}{15}}.$$

EXAMPLE 2. *In an examination, 30% of the students have failed in Mathematics, 20% of the students have failed in chemistry and 10% have failed in both Mathematics and Chemistry. A student is selected at random:*

(i) *What is the probability that the student has failed in Mathematics if it is known that he has failed in Chemistry?*

(ii) *What is the probability that the student has failed either in Mathematics or in Chemistry?*

[CA May 1989]

SOLUTION. Let M and C be the events that a student selected at random 'fail in Mathematics' and 'fail in Chemistry' respectively.

Then $P(M) = \frac{30}{100} = 0.3, P(C) = \frac{20}{100} = 0.2$ and $P(M \cap C) = \frac{10}{100} = 0.1$.

(i) The required probability that the student selected has *failed in Mathematics given that he has failed in Chemistry* $= P(M/C) = \frac{P(M \cap C)}{P(C)} = \frac{0.1}{0.2} = \frac{1}{2} = \mathbf{0.5}$.

(ii) The required probability that the student selected at random has failed *either in Mathematics or in Chemistry* $= P(M \cup C) = P(M) + P(C) - P(M \cap C) = 0.3 + 0.2 - 0.1 = \mathbf{0.4}$.

EXAMPLE 3. *The personnel department of a company has records which show the following analysis of its 200 engineers:*

Age	Bachelors degree only	Masters degree	Total
Under 30	90	10	100
30 to 40	20	30	50
Over 40	40	10	50
Total	150	50	200

If one engineer is selected at random from the company, find:

(a) *The probability that he has only a bachelor's degree.*

(b) *The probability that he has a master's degree, given that he is over* 40.

(c) *The probability that he is under* 30, *given that he has only a bachelor's degree.*

[Delhi U. MBA 1977]

SOLUTION. Let A be the event that an engineer has only a bachelor's degree, B, that he is over 40 years of age, C, that he has master's degree and D, that he is under 30 years of age.

(a) The probability that he has only a bachelor's degree is

$$P(A) = \frac{150}{200} = \frac{\mathbf{3}}{\mathbf{4}}.$$

(b) The probability that an engineer has a master's degree, given that he is over 40 is

$$P(C/B) = \frac{P(C \cap B)}{P(B)} = \frac{\frac{10}{200}}{\frac{50}{200}} = \frac{10}{50} = \frac{\mathbf{1}}{\mathbf{5}}.$$

(c) The probability that an engineer is under 30, given that he has only a bachelor's degree is

$$P(D/A) = \frac{P(D \cap A)}{P(A)} = \frac{\frac{90}{200}}{\frac{150}{200}} = \frac{90}{150} = \frac{\mathbf{3}}{\mathbf{5}}.$$

EXAMPLE 4. *If A and B be two independent events, prove that* (i) *A and B^c,* (ii) *A^c and B^c are also independent.*

SOLUTION.

(i) For any two events A and B, we have

$$P(A) = P(A \cap B) + P(A \cap B^c), \quad \text{or,} \quad P(A \cap B^c) = P(A) - P(A \cap B) \tag{1}$$

Since A and B are two independent events, $P(A \cap B) = P(A) \cdot P(B)$.

$\therefore$ From (1), $P(A \cap B^c) = P(A) - P(A) \cdot P(B) = P(A)\{1 - P(B)\}$,

or, $P(A \cap B^c) = P(A) \cdot P(B^c)$ $\quad [\because \; 1 - P(B) = P(B^c)]$.

This shows that A and B^c are also *independent.*

(ii) By **De Morgan's Law,** $A^c \cap B^c = (A \cup B)^c$;

$$\begin{aligned} \therefore \quad P(A^c \cap B^c) &= P\{(A \cup B)^c\} = 1 - P(A \cup B) = 1 - \{P(A) + P(B) - P(A \cap B)\} \\ &= 1 - P(A) - P(B) + P(A) \cdot P(B) \\ &\qquad [\because \; A \text{ and } B \text{ are two independent events}] \\ &= \{1 - P(A)\} - P(B)\{1 - P(A)\} = \{1 - P(A)\}\{1 - P(B)\} = P(A^c) \cdot P(B^c), \end{aligned}$$

i.e., $P(A^c \cap B^c) = P(A^c) \cdot P(B^c)$.

This shows that A^c and B^c are also *independent events.*

EXAMPLE 5. *A problem in statistics is given to three students, A, B, C, whose chances of solving it are $\frac{1}{2}, \frac{1}{3}$ and $\frac{1}{4}$ respectively. If they try it independently, what is the probability that the problem will be solved?*

SOLUTION. Let A be the event that student A will slove the problem. Similarly B and C be the events for the students B and C respectively, to solve the problem.

Then $P(A) = \frac{1}{2}, P(B) = \frac{1}{3}, P(C) = \frac{1}{4}$.

$\therefore \quad P(A^c) =$ Probability that A will not solve the problem.

$$= 1 - P(A) = 1 - \tfrac{1}{2} = \tfrac{1}{2}.$$

Similarly, $P(B^c) = 1 - \frac{1}{3} = \frac{2}{3}$, and $P(C^c) = 1 - \frac{1}{4} = \frac{3}{4}$.

$\therefore$ The probability that none of the students A, B, C, will solve the problem
$= P(A^c) \cdot P(B^c) \cdot P(C^c) = \frac{1}{2} \times \frac{2}{3} \times \frac{3}{4} = \frac{1}{4}$.

[$\because$ A, B, C are independent events, A^c, B^c, C^c are also independent events]

Hence, the required probability that the problem will be solved (i.e., at least one of A, B, C will solve the problem) $= 1 - \frac{1}{4} = \frac{3}{4}$.

[OTHERWISE.

$$P(A \cup B \cup C) = P(A) + P(B) + P(C) - P(A \cap B) - P(B \cap C) - P(A \cap C) + P(A \cap B \cap C).$$

$$= \tfrac{1}{2} + \tfrac{1}{3} + \tfrac{1}{4} - (\tfrac{1}{2} \times \tfrac{1}{3} + \tfrac{1}{3} \times \tfrac{1}{4} + \tfrac{1}{2} \times \tfrac{1}{4}) + \tfrac{1}{2} \times \tfrac{1}{3} \times \tfrac{1}{4}$$

($\because$ $A, B.C$ are independent events)

$$= \tfrac{13}{12} - \tfrac{9}{24} + \tfrac{1}{24} = \tfrac{18}{24} = \tfrac{3}{4}.]$$

EXAMPLE 6. *A bag contains* 8 *red balls and* 5 *white balls. Two successive draws of* 3 *balls are made without replacement. Find the probability that the first drawing will give* 3 *white balls and the second,* 3 *red balls.* **[CA May 1978]**

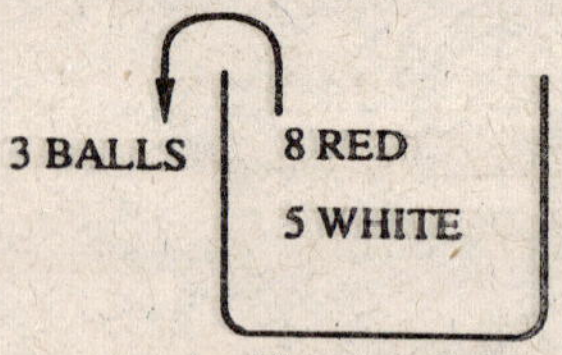

First drawing

SOLUTION. Let A be the event that the 3 balls in the first drawing are all white, and B, that the 3 balls in the second drawing are all red.

Total number of balls in the bag is $8 + 5 = 13$.

3 balls can be drawn out of 13 in ${}^{13}C_3$ ways

$= \frac{13 \cdot 12 \cdot 11}{3 \cdot 2 \cdot 1} = 286$ ways.

$\therefore \quad n(S) = 286.$

3 white balls can be drawn out of 5 in ${}^{5}C_3$ ways $= \frac{5 \cdot 4 \cdot 3}{3 \cdot 2 \cdot 1} = 10$ ways.

$$\therefore \quad n(A) = 10; \qquad \therefore \quad P(A) = \frac{n(A)}{n(S)} = \frac{10}{286} = \frac{5}{143}.$$

If the 3 white balls are not replaced, we are left with 8 red and 2 white balls. We have to find the conditional probability $P(B/A)$ where A has actually occurred.

In this case, total no. of balls is $8 + 2 = 10$.

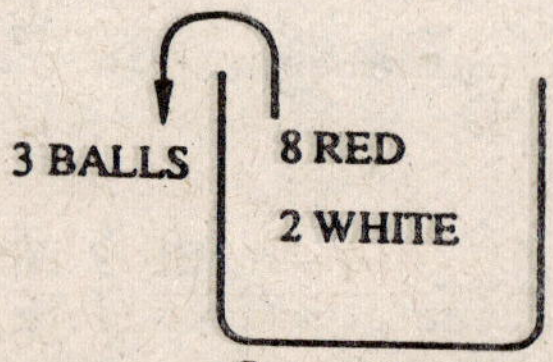

Second drawing

3 balls can be drawn out of 10 in ${}^{10}C_3$ ways

$= \frac{10 \cdot 9 \cdot 8}{3 \cdot 2 \cdot 1} = 120$ ways

and 3 red balls can be drawn out of 8 in ${}^{8}C_3$ ways

$= \frac{8 \cdot 7 \cdot 6}{3 \cdot 2 \cdot 1} = 56$ ways.

$\therefore \quad P(B/A) = \frac{56}{120} = \frac{7}{15}.$

Hence, by the theorem of Compound Probability,

$$P(A \cap B) = P(A) \cdot P(B/A) = \frac{5}{143} \times \frac{7}{15} = \mathbf{\frac{7}{429}}.$$

EXAMPLE 7. *Two sets of candidates are competing for the positions on the Board of Directors of a Company. The probabilities that the first and second sets will win are* 0.6 *and* 0.4 *respectively. If the first set wins, the probability of introducing a new product is* 0.8, *and the corresponding probability, if the second set wins, is* 0.3. *What is the probability that the new product will be introduced?*

[CA November 1978]

SOLUTION. Let A be the event that the first set will win, B, that the second set will win and C, that the new product will be introduced.

Then C occurs if and only if one of the two mutually exclusive events $A \cap C$ and $B \cap C$ occurs. Therefore,

$$P(C) = P(A \cap C) + P(B \cap C),$$

$$\text{i.e.,} \quad P(C) = P(A) \cdot P(C/A) + P(B) \cdot P(C/B) \qquad (1)$$

Given $P(A) = 0.6, P(B) = 0.4, P(C/A) = 0.8$ and $P(C/B) = 0.3$.

$\therefore$ From (1), $P(C) = 0.6 \times 0.8 + 0.4 \times 0.3 = 0.48 + 0.12 = 0.60$.

Hence, the required probability is **0.60**.

EXAMPLE 8. *The odds against student X solving a Business Statistics problem are* 8 *to* 6, *and odds in favour of student Y solving the same problem are* 14 *to* 16.

(i) *What is the chance that the problem will be solved if they both try independently of each other?*

(ii) *What is the probability that neither solves the problem?* **[CA November 1979]**

SOLUTION. Let A be the event that the first student X will solve the problem and B, that the second student Y will solve the problem. Then clearly

$$P(A) = \frac{6}{8+6} = \frac{6}{14} = \frac{3}{7} \quad \text{and} \quad P(B) = \frac{14}{14+16} = \frac{14}{30} = \frac{7}{15}.$$

[$\because$ odds against an event = no. of unfavourable cases: no. of favourable cases, and odds in favour = no. of favourable cases : no. of unfavourable cases.]

(i) The required probability that the problem will be solved if they both try independently of each other is $P(A \cup B)$.

$$P(A \cap B) = P(A) \cdot P(B) \qquad [\because \ A \text{ and } B \text{ are independent events}]$$
$$= \frac{3}{7} \times \frac{7}{15} = \frac{1}{5}.$$

$$\therefore \quad P(A \cup B) = P(A) + P(B) - P(A \cap B) = \frac{3}{7} + \frac{7}{15} - \frac{1}{5} = \frac{45 + 49 - 21}{105} = \mathbf{\frac{73}{105}}.$$

(ii) The probability that X cannot solve the problem is

$$P(A^c) = 1 - P(A) = 1 - \frac{3}{7} = \frac{4}{7}.$$

Similarly, $P(B^c) = 1 - \frac{7}{15} = \frac{8}{15}$.

Hence, the required probability that neither solves the problem is

$$P(A^c \cap B^c) = P(A^c) \times P(B^c) \qquad [\because \ A^c \text{ and } B^c \text{ are independent events}]$$
$$= \frac{4}{7} \times \frac{8}{15} = \mathbf{\frac{32}{105}}.$$

[OTHERWISE. The required probability that neither solves the problem

$$= 1 - (\text{Probability that at least one of } X \text{ and } Y \text{ will solve the problem})$$
$$= 1 - P(A \cup B) = 1 - \tfrac{73}{105} = \tfrac{32}{105}.]$$

EXAMPLE 9. *There are three men aged 60, 65 and 70 years. The probability to live 5 years more is 0.8 for a 60 year old, 0.6 for a 65 year old and 0.3 for a 70 year old person. Find the probability that at least two of the three persons will remain alive 5 years hence.*

[C.U. B. Com. (Hons.) 1981]

SOLUTION. Let A be the event that the man aged 60 years will live 5 years more. Similarly, events B and C denote the same thing for the other two men aged 65 and 70 years respectively. Then

$$P(A) = 0.8, P(B) = 0.6, P(C) = 0.3;$$
$$\therefore \quad P(A^c) = 1 - P(A) = 1 - 0.8 = 0.2, P(B^c) = 0.4 \quad \text{and} \quad P(C^c) = 0.7.$$

Clearly, A, B, C are three *independent events.*

$\therefore$ A^c, B^c, C^c are also *independent events.*

The required probability that at least two of the three persons will remain alive 5 years hence,

$$= P(A \cap B \cap C^c) + P(A \cap B^c \cap C) + P(A^c \cap B \cap C) + P(A \cap B \cap C).$$
$$= P(A) \cdot P(B) \cdot P(C^c) + P(A) \cdot P(B^c) \cdot P(C) + P(A^c) \cdot P(B) \cdot P(C) + P(A) \cdot P(B) \cdot P(C).$$

[$\because$ A, B, C, A^c, B^c, C^c are all *independent events.*]

$$= 0.8 \times 0.6 \times 0.7 + 0.8 \times 0.4 \times 0.3 + 0.2 \times 0.6 \times 0.3 + 0.8 \times 0.6 \times 0.3$$
$$= 0.336 + 0.096 + 0.036 + 0.144 = \mathbf{0.612}.$$

1.7. BAYES' THEOREM

We can revise probabilities when new (or additional) information concerning a random experiment is available. The procedure for revising probabilities due to a specific cause is known as *Bayes' theorem* and it was originally developed by Rev. Thomas Bayes. It gives a probability law relating a *posteriori probability to a priori probability.*

STATEMENT. *An event A can occur only if any one of the set of exhaustive and mutually exclusive events $B_1, B_2, \cdots, B_n$ occurs. The probabilities $P(B_1), P(B_2), \cdots, P(B_n)$ and the conditional probabilities $P(A/B_i); i = 1, 2, \cdots, n$, for A to occur are known. Then the conditional probability $P(B_i/A)$ when A has actually occurred is given by*

$$P(B_i/A) = \frac{P(B_i)P(A/B_i)}{P(B_1)\cdot P(A/B_1) + P(B_2)\cdot P(A/B_2) + \cdots + P(B_n)\cdot P(A/B_n)}.$$

ALTERNATIVE STATEMENT. *If $B_1, B_2, \cdots, B_n$, are mutually disjoint events with $P(B_i) \neq 0$; $i = 1, 2, \cdots, n$, then for any event A which is a subset of $B_1 \cup B_2 \cup \cdots \cup B_n$ such that $P(A) > 0$, we have*

$$\mathbf{P(B_i/A) = \frac{P(B_i)P(A/B_i)}{\sum_{i=1}^{n} P(B_i)P(A/B_i)}}.$$

PROOF. Since $B_1, B_2, \cdots, B_n$ are mutually exclusive events and since A occurs only when any one of $B_1, B_2, \cdots, B_n$ occurs, therefore, A occurs in any one of the mutually exclusive events

$$A \cap B_1, A \cap B_2, \cdots, A \cap B_n.$$

$\therefore$ By the *theorem of total probability,* we have

$$\begin{aligned} P(A) &= P(A \cap B_1) + P(A \cap B_2) + \cdots + P(A \cap B_n) \\ &= P(B_1 \cap A) + P(B_2 \cap A) + \cdots + P(B_n \cap A) \\ &= P(B_1)\cdot P(A/B_1) + P(B_2)\cdot P(A/B_2) + \cdots + P(B_n)\cdot P(A/B_n). \end{aligned}$$

[By the theorem of compound probability]

Again by the theorem of compound probability, we have

$$P(A \cap B_i) = P(A)\cdot P(B_i/A) \text{ and } P(B_i \cap A) = P(B_i)\cdot P(A/B_i)$$

$$\therefore \quad P(A)\cdot P(B_i/A) = P(B_i)\cdot P(A/B_i) \qquad [\because \quad P(A \cap B_i) = P(B_i \cap A)]$$

$$\text{or,} \quad P(B_i/A) = \frac{P(B_i)\cdot P(A/B_i)}{P(A)}$$

$$= \frac{P(B_i)\cdot P(A/B_i)}{P(B_1)\cdot P(A/B_1) + P(B_2)\cdot P(A/B_2) + \cdots + P(B_n)\cdot P(A/B_n)}.$$

Hence, the theorem follows.

EXAMPLE 1. *There are two identical boxes containing respectively 4 white and 3 red balls, and 3 white and 7 red balls. A box is chosen at random and a ball is drawn from it. If the ball is white, what is the probability that it is from the first box?* **[C.U. B. Sc. (Hons.) 1967]**

SOLUTION. Let A be the event that the ball drawn is white and let B_1, B_2 be the events of choosing the first and the second boxes respectively.

Then $P(B_1)$ = Probability of selecting the first box = $\frac{1}{2}$

and $P(B_2)$ = Probability of selecting the second box = $\frac{1}{2}$.

$P(A/B_1)$ = Probability of selecting 1 white ball from the first box = $\frac{^4C_1}{^7C_1} = \frac{4}{7}$.

Similarly, $P(A/B_2) = \frac{3}{10}$.

By Bayes' Theorem, we get

$P(B_1/A)$ = the required probability that if the ball is white, then it is from the first box

$$= \frac{P(B_1) \cdot P(A/B_1)}{P(B_1) \cdot P(A/B_1) + P(B_2) \cdot P(A/B_2)}$$

$$= \frac{\frac{1}{2} \times \frac{4}{7}}{\frac{1}{2} \times \frac{4}{7} + \frac{1}{2} \times \frac{3}{10}} = \frac{4}{14} \times \frac{140}{61} = \mathbf{\frac{40}{61}}.$$

NOTE. $P(B_2/A)$ = Probability that if the ball is white, it is from the 2nd box

$$= \frac{P(B_2) \cdot P(A/B_2)}{P(B_1) \cdot P(A/B_1) + P(B_2) \cdot P(A/B_2)} = \frac{\frac{1}{2} \times \frac{3}{10}}{\frac{61}{140}} = \mathbf{\frac{21}{61}}.$$

EXAMPLE 2. *In a bolt factory, machines M_1, M_2, M_3 manufacture respectively* 25, 35 *and* 40 *per cent of the total ouput. Of their output,* 5, 4 *and* 2 *per cent respectively, are defective bolts. One bolt is drawn at random from the product and is found to be defective. What is the probability that it is manufactured in the machine M_2?* **[C.U. B. Sc. (Hons.) 1964]**

SOLUTION. Let B_1, B_2, B_3 be the events that the bolt drawn at random is manufactured by machines M_1, M_2, M_3 respectively, and let A be the event that the bolt drawn is defective.

Then $P(B_1)$ = Probability that the bolt drawn was manufactured by $M_1 = \frac{25}{100} = \frac{1}{4}$.

Similarly, $P(B_2) = \frac{35}{100} = \frac{7}{20}$ and $P(B_3) = \frac{40}{100} = \frac{2}{5}$.

$P(A/B_1)$ = the probability of drawing a defective bolt from the lot of bolts manufactured by $M_1 = \frac{5}{100} = \frac{1}{20}$.

Similarly, $P(A/B_2) = \frac{4}{100} = \frac{1}{25}$ and $P(A/B_3) = \frac{2}{100} = \frac{1}{50}$.

By Bayes' Theorem, we have

$$P(B_2/A) = \frac{P(B_2) \cdot P(A/B_2)}{P(B_1) \cdot P(A/B_1) + P(B_2) \cdot P(A/B_2) + P(B_3) \cdot P(A/B_3)}$$

$$= \frac{\frac{7}{20} \times \frac{1}{25}}{\frac{1}{4} \times \frac{1}{20} + \frac{7}{20} \times \frac{1}{25} + \frac{2}{5} \times \frac{1}{50}} = \frac{\frac{7}{500}}{\frac{25+28+16}{2000}} = \frac{7}{500} \times \frac{2000}{69} = \frac{28}{69}.$$

Hence, the required probability that the defective bolt drawn is manufactured by machine $M_2 = \mathbf{\frac{28}{69}}$.

NOTE. The probability that the defective bolt drawn is manufactured by machine M_1

$$= P(B_1/A) = \frac{P(B_1) \cdot P(A/B_1)}{\sum_{i=1}^{3} P(B_i) \cdot P(A/B_i)} = \frac{\frac{1}{80}}{\frac{69}{2000}} = \mathbf{\frac{25}{69}}$$

and the probability that the defective bolt drawn is manufactured by machine M_3

$$= P(B_3/A) = \frac{P(B_3) \cdot P(A/B_3)}{\sum_{i=1}^{3} P(B_i) \cdot P(A/B_i)} = \frac{\frac{1}{125}}{\frac{69}{2000}} = \mathbf{\frac{16}{69}}.$$

1.8. PROBABILITY : AXIOMATIC APPROACH

Let S be a sample space and let A be any event in S (i.e., $A \subseteq S$). We define a function P on S [for any event A, the functional value $P(A)$ is a real number] and call it a probability function on the sample space S if the following three axioms hold:

1. *For any event A in S, $P(A) \geq 0$.*
2. $P(S) = 1$.
3. *If $A_1, A_2, \cdots$ be any sequence of mutually exclusive events in S, then*

$$P(A_1 \cup A_2 \cup \cdots) = P(A_1) + P(A_2) + \cdots$$

We can now prove a number of theorems directly from the axioms.

THEOREM 1. *For every event A, $P(A^c) = 1 - P(A)$, where A^c is the complement of A.*

PROOF. For every event A, the sample space S can be decomposed into the two mutually exclusive events A and A^c, i.e., $S = A \cup A^c$.

Therefore, $P(S) = P(A \cup A^c) = P(A) + P(A^c)$, by *Axiom* 3.

Again, by *Axiom* 2, $P(S) = 1$.

$\therefore \quad P(A) + P(A^c) = 1$.

Hence, $P(A^c) = 1 - P(A)$.

THEOREM 2. *For every event A in S, $0 \leq P(A) \leq 1$.*

PROOF. By *Axiom* 1, $P(A) \geq 0$ and $P(A^c) \geq 0$.

Since $P(A^c) = 1 - P(A)$; $\quad \therefore \quad 1 - P(A) \geq 0$, or, $1 \geq P(A)$.

Thus $0 \leq P(A)$ and $P(A) \leq 1$.

Hence, $0 \leq P(A) \leq 1$.

THEOREM 3. *If ϕ is the null set, then $P(\phi) = 0$.*

PROOF. For any event A, $A \cup \phi = A$, where ϕ is the null set (i.e., impossible event).

$\therefore \quad P(A) = P(A \cup \phi) = P(A) + P(\phi)$, by *Axiom* 3.

[$\because$ A and ϕ are two mutually exclusive events.]

Hence, $P(\phi) = 0$.

THEOREM 4. *If $A \subseteq B$, then $P(A) \leq P(B)$.*

PROOF. If $A \subseteq B$, then B can be decomposed into the two mutually exclusive events A and $B - A$, i.e., $B = A \cup (B - A)$.

$\therefore \quad P(B) = P[A \cup (B - A)] = P(A) + P(B - A)$, by *Axiom* 3.

Since by *Axiom* 1, $P(B - A) \geq 0$, we get $P(B) \geq P(A)$.

THEOREM 5. *If A and B are any two events, then $P(A - B) = P(A) - P(A \cap B)$.*

PROOF. If A and B are any two events, then A can be decomposed into the mutually exclusive events $A - B$ and $A \cap B$, i.e., $A = (A - B) \cup (A \cap B)$.

By *Axiom* 3, $P(A) = P[(A - B) \cup (A \cap B)] = P(A - B) + P(A \cap B)$.

Hence, $P(A - B) = P(A) - P(A \cap B)$.

THEOREM 6. *If A and B be any two events, then $P(A \cup B) = P(A) + P(B) - P(A \cap B)$.*

PROOF. Event $A \cup B$ can be decomposed into the mutually exclusive events $A - B$ and B, i.e., $A \cup B = (A - B) \cup B$.

By *Axiom* 3, $P(A \cup B) = P(A - B) + P(B)$, and by *Theorem* 5, $P(A - B) = P(A) - P(A \cap B)$.

Hence, $P(A \cup B) = P(A) - P(A \cap B) + P(B) = P(A) + P(B) - P(A \cap B)$.

COROLLARY. *Using the result of Theorem 6, we can prove that for any three events A, B, C,*

$$P(A \cup B \cup C) = P(A) + P(B) + P(C) - P(A \cap B) - P(B \cap C) - P(A \cap C) + P(A \cap B \cap C).$$

Finite Probability Space : Equiprobable Space

Let S be a finite sample space consisting of N elementary events (called sample points), i.e., $S = \{a_1, a_2, \cdots, a_N\}$. Then a finite probability space is obtained by assigning to each sample point a_i of S a real number p_i called the probability of a_i satisfying (i) $p_i \geq 0$ and (ii) $p_1 + p_2 + \cdots + p_N = 1$. The probability $P(A)$ of any event A of S is defined as the sum of the probabilities of the sample points in A. If A is made up of m elementary events $A_1, A_2, \cdots, A_m$, then $A = A_1 \cup A_2 \cup \cdots \cup A_m$ and, therefore,

$$P(A) = P(A_1) + P(A_2) + \cdots + P(A_m), \quad \text{by } \textit{Axiom } 3.$$

In particular, if all elementary events, say $A_1, A_2, \cdots, A_N$, of the sample space S be assigned *equal probabilities,* then the sample space S is said to be **equiprobable** or **uniform space** in which the probability of each elementary event is $1/N$. In this case

$$P(A) = \frac{1}{N} + \frac{1}{N} + \cdots \text{to} \quad m \text{ terms} = \frac{m}{N} = \frac{\text{no. of elements in } A}{\text{no. of elements in } S}$$
$$= \frac{n(A)}{n(S)}, \quad \text{which is the classical definition of probability.}$$

1.9. MISCELLANEOUS PROBLEMS

EXAMPLE 1. *Three horses A, B and C are in a race : A is twice as likely to win as B and B is twice as likely to win as C. What are the respective probabilities of winning?* **[CA May 1988]**

SOLUTION. Let the probability of the event that C will win $= p$, i.e., $P(C) = p$.

Then the probability that B will win $= 2p$, i.e., $P(B) = 2p$

and the probability that A will win $= 2 \times 2p = 4p$ i.e., $P(A) = 4p$.

Since either A or B or C will win the race; $\quad \therefore \quad P(A) + P(B) + P(C) = 1$.

$\therefore \quad p + 2p + 4p = 1$, or, $7p = 1$, or, $p = \frac{1}{7}$.

Hence, $P(A) = 4p = \frac{4}{7}, P(B) = 2p = \frac{2}{7}$ and $P(C) = p = \frac{1}{7}$.

EXAMPLE 2. *There are* 100 *students in a college class of which* 36 *are boys studying Statistics and* 13 *are girls not studying Statistics. If there are* 55 *girls in all, find the probability that a boy picked up at random is not studying Statistics.* **[CA May 1990]**

SOLUTION. Total number of boys in the college class $= 100 - 55 = 45$.

1 boy can be selected out of 45 boys in $^{45}C_1$ ways $= 45$ ways.

$\therefore$ Total number of all possible cases for the event $= 45$.

Now 1 boy studying Statistics can be selected out of 36 in $^{36}C_1$ ways $= 36$ ways.

$\therefore$ No. of cases favourable to the event A that the boy packed up at random is studying Statistics $= 36$.

$\therefore \quad P(A) =$ Probability that the boy picked up is *studying Statistics* $= \frac{36}{45} = \frac{4}{5}$.

Hence, the required probability that the boy picked up at random is *not studying Statistics* $= P(A^c) = 1 - P(A) = 1 - \frac{4}{5} = \frac{1}{5}$.

[OTHERWISE. Total number of boys not studying Statistics $= 45 - 36 = 9$.

1 boy can be selected out of 9 boys $= {}^9C_1$ ways $= 9$ ways.

$\therefore$ No. of favourable cases for the event that a boy picked up at random is not studying Statistics $= 9$. Hence, the required probability $= \frac{9}{45} = \frac{1}{5}$.]

EXAMPLE 3. *A packet of* 10 *electronic components is known to include* 3 *defectives. If* 4 *components are randomly chosen and tested, what is the probability of finding among them not more than one defective?* **[C.U. B. Com. (Hons.) 1980]**

SOLUTION. 4 components can be chosen out of 10 in $^{10}C_4$ ways.

$\therefore$ Total no. of all possible cases $= {}^{10}C_4 = \frac{10.9.8.7}{4.3.2.1} = 210$, i.e., $n(S) = 210$.

Now among 4 components drawn, not more than one defective can occur in the following two mutually exclusive events:

(i) A: getting 1 defective component and 3 non-defective components.

(ii) B: getting no defective component, i.e., 4 non-defective components.

1 defective component can be drawn out of 3 in $^3C_1$ ways and 3 non-defective components can be drawn out of 7 in $^7C_3$ ways.

$\therefore \quad n(A) =$ no. of cases favourable to $A = {}^3C_1 \times {}^7C_3 = 3 \times 35 = 105$.

Similarly, $n(B) =$ no. of cases favourable to $B = {}^7C_4 = 35$.

$$\therefore \quad P(A) = \frac{n(A)}{n(S)} = \frac{105}{210} = \frac{1}{2} \quad \text{and} \quad P(B) = \frac{n(B)}{n(S)} = \frac{35}{210} = \frac{1}{6}.$$

Hence, by the theorem of Total Probability, the required probability

$$= P(A \cup B) = P(A) + P(B) = \tfrac{1}{2} + \tfrac{1}{6} = \tfrac{\mathbf{2}}{\mathbf{3}}.$$

EXAMPLE 4. *Boxes* 1 *and* 2 *contain respectively* 4 *white,* 3 *red and* 3 *blue balls; and* 5 *white,* 4 *red and* 3 *blue balls. If one ball is drawn at random from each box, what is the probability that both the balls are of the same colour?* [C.U. B. Com. (Hons.) 1980]

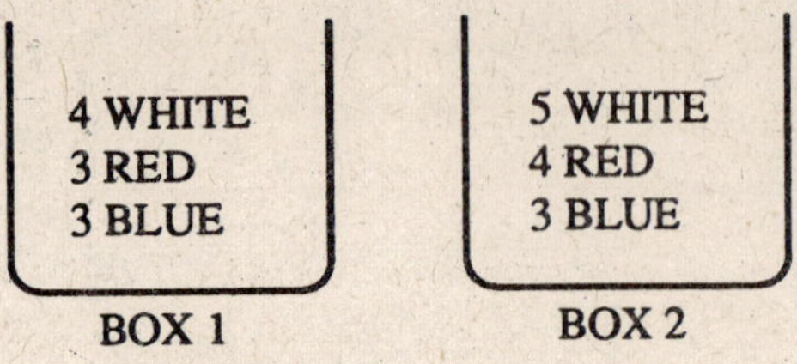

SOLUTION. Both the balls will be of the same colour if they are either (i) both white or (ii) both red, or (iii) both blue. Let A, B, C be the events that both the balls are white, red and blue, respectively.

1 ball can be drawn out of 10 from box 1 in ${}^{10}C_1$ ways = 10 ways and 1 white ball can be drawn out of 4 in ${}^{4}C_1$ ways = 4 ways.

$\therefore \quad P(A_1)$ = Probability of drawing 1 white ball from box 1 $= \frac{4}{10} = \frac{2}{5}$.

Similarly, $P(A_2)$ = Probability of drawing 1 white ball from box 2 $= \frac{{}^{5}C_1}{{}^{12}C_1} = \frac{5}{12}$.

Since A_1 and A_2 are two independent events, $\therefore \quad P(A) = P(A_1) \times P(A_2) = \frac{2}{5} \times \frac{5}{12} = \frac{1}{6}$.

Similarly, $P(B)$ = Probability that both the balls are red $= \frac{{}^{3}C_1}{{}^{10}C_1} \times \frac{{}^{4}C_1}{{}^{12}C_1} = \frac{3}{10} \times \frac{4}{12} = \frac{1}{10}$

and $P(C)$ = Probability that both the balls are blue $= \frac{{}^{3}C_1}{{}^{10}C_1} \times \frac{{}^{3}C_1}{{}^{12}C_1} = \frac{3}{10} \times \frac{3}{12} = \frac{3}{40}$.

Since A, B and C are three mutually exclusive events, by the theorem of Total probability, the required probability that both the balls are of the same colour $= \frac{1}{6} + \frac{1}{10} + \frac{3}{40} = \frac{20+12+9}{120} = \frac{41}{120}$.

EXAMPLE 5. *If* $P(A \cap B^c) = 1/3$ *and* $P(A \cup B) = 2/3$, *find* $P(B)$.

What is $P(A)$ *if* $P(A \cap B) = 1/6$.

SOLUTION. By **De Morgan's Law,** $(A \cup B)^c = A^c \cap B^c$.

$\therefore \quad P(A^c \cap B^c) = P[(A \cup B)^c] = 1 - P(A \cup B) = 1 - 2/3 = 1/3.$

Event B^c will occur if and only if any one of the two mutually exclusive events $A \cap B^c$ and $A^c \cap B^c$ occurs.

$$\therefore \quad P(B^c) = P(A \cap B^c) + P(A^c \cap B^c) = \frac{1}{3} + \frac{1}{3} = \frac{2}{3}.$$

Hence, $P(B) = 1 - P(B^c) = 1 - \frac{2}{3} = \frac{1}{3}$.

2ND PART. Event A will occur if and only if any one of the two mutually exclusive events $A \cap B$ and $A \cap B^c$ occurs.

$$\therefore \quad P(A) = P(A \cap B) + P(A \cap B^c) = \frac{1}{6} + \frac{1}{3} = \frac{1+2}{6} = \frac{1}{2}$$

EXAMPLE 6. *A candidate is selected for interview for three posts. For the first post there are* 3 *candidates, for the second there are* 4, *and for the third there are* 2. *What is the chance of his getting at least one post?* [CA May 1980]

SOLUTION. Let A be the event that the candidate gets the first post, B be the event that he gets the second post, and C that he gets the third post.

Then $P(A) = \frac{1}{3}$, $P(B) = \frac{1}{4}$ and $P(C) = \frac{1}{2}$.

$\therefore \quad P(A^c) = 1 - \frac{1}{3} = \frac{2}{3}$, $P(B^c) = 1 - \frac{1}{4} = \frac{3}{4}$, $P(C^c) = 1 - \frac{1}{2} = \frac{1}{2}$.

Since A, B, C are independent, therefore, A^c, B^c, C^c are also independent.

$\therefore$ The chance that the candidate does not get any post $= P(A^c)\cdot P(B^c)\cdot P(C^c) = \frac{2}{3}\times\frac{3}{4}\times\frac{1}{2} = \frac{1}{4}$.

Hence, the required chance that he gets at least one post $= 1 - \frac{1}{4} = \frac{3}{4}$.

[OTHERWISE. The required chance $= P(A\cup B\cup C) = P(A)+P(B)+P(C)-P(A\cap B)-P(B\cap C)$ $-P(A\cap C)+P(A\cap B\cap C)$. Here $P(A)=\frac{1}{3}$, $P(B)=\frac{1}{4}$, $P(C)=\frac{1}{2}$; $P(A\cap B)=P(A)\cdot P(B) = \frac{1}{3}\times\frac{1}{4}=\frac{1}{12}$, $P(B\cap C)=P(B)\cdot P(C)=\frac{1}{4}\times\frac{1}{2}=\frac{1}{8}$, $P(A\cap C)=P(A)\cdot P(C)=\frac{1}{3}\times\frac{1}{2}=\frac{1}{6}$ and $P(A\cap B\cap C)=\frac{1}{3}\times\frac{1}{4}\times\frac{1}{2}=\frac{1}{24}$, since A, B, C are independent.

Hence, the required chance $= \frac{1}{3}+\frac{1}{4}+\frac{1}{2}-\frac{1}{12}-\frac{1}{8}-\frac{1}{6}+\frac{1}{24}=\frac{3}{4}$.]

EXAMPLE 7. *A, B, C and D are four mutually exclusive and exhaustive events. If the odds against the events B, C, D are respectively* 7 : 2, 7 : 5 *and* 13 : 5, *find the odds in favour of the event A.*

SOLUTION. Odds against an event = (no. of unfavourable cases) : (no. of favourable cases).

Since the odds against the events B, C and D are 7 : 2, 7 : 5 and 13 : 5 respectively,

$$\therefore\quad P(B)=\frac{2}{7+2}=\frac{2}{9},\quad P(C)=\frac{5}{7+5}=\frac{5}{12},\quad P(D)=\frac{5}{13+5}=\frac{5}{18}.$$

Again, since A, B, C and D are four mutually exclusive and exhaustive events:

$$\therefore\quad P(A\cup B\cup C\cup D)=P(A)+P(B)+P(C)+P(D)\quad\text{and}\quad P(A\cup B\cup C\cup D)=1.$$

$$\therefore\quad P(A)+P(B)+P(C)+P(D)=1,\quad\text{or,}\quad P(A)+\frac{2}{9}+\frac{5}{12}+\frac{5}{18}=1;$$

$$\therefore\quad P(A)=1-\left(\frac{2}{9}+\frac{5}{12}+\frac{5}{18}\right)=1-\frac{11}{12}=\frac{1}{12}\quad\text{and}\quad P(A^c)=1-\frac{1}{12}=\frac{11}{12}.$$

Hence, the required odds in favour of the event $A = P(A) : P(A^c) =$ **1 : 11**.

EXAMPLE 8. *Two persons A and B stand in a line with* 10 *other persons. What is the probability that there are* 3 *persons between A and B?* **[C.U. B. Sc. (Hons.) 1970]**

SOLUTION. Total no. of persons = 2 + 10 = 12.

12 persons can be arranged in a line in $|\underline{12}$ ways.

$\therefore$ Total no. of all possible equally likely cases $= |\underline{12}$.

To find the no. of favourable cases, let the 1st, 2nd, 3rd, ..., 12th places be represented by 1, 2, 3, ..., 12. There will be 3 persons between A and B if they occupy the following 8 pairs of places $(1,5),(2,6),(3,7),(4,8),(5,9),(6,10),(7,11),(8,12)$. When A and B occupy places 1 and 5 respectively, the remaining 10 places can be filled up by the other 10 persons in $|\underline{10}$ ways. But A and B can be interchanged in their positions in $|\underline{2}$ ways.

$\therefore$ The no. of arrangements when A and B occupy the 1st and 5th places $= |\underline{2}\times|\underline{10}$.

Similarly, the no. of arrangements when A and B occupy any one of the other 7 pairs of places $= |\underline{2}\times|\underline{10}$.

$\therefore$ The no. of favourable cases $= 8\times|\underline{2}\times|\underline{10}$.

Hence, the required probability that there are 3 persons between A and $B = \dfrac{8\times|\underline{2}\times|\underline{10}}{|\underline{12}} = \mathbf{\dfrac{4}{33}}$.

[OTHERWISE. A and B can occupy any two of the 12 places in ${}^{12}C_2$ ways $= \frac{12.11}{2.1} = 66$ ways.

$\therefore$ Total no. of all possible equally likely cases = 66.

There will be 3 persons between A and B if A and B occupy the pairs of places $(1,5)$, $(2,6)$, $(3,7)$, $(4,8)$, $(5,9)$, $(6,10)$, $(7,11)$, $(8,12)$, i.e., the number of favourable cases = 8.

Hence, the required probability that there will be 3 persons between A and $B = \frac{8}{66} = \mathbf{\frac{4}{33}}$.]

EXAMPLE 9. *A box contains* 20 *tickets of identical appearance, the tickets being numbered* $1, 2, 3, \cdots, 20$. *If* 3 *tickets are chosen at random, find the probability that the numbers on the drawn tickets are in arithmetic progression.* **[C.U. 1971]**

SOLUTION. 3 tickets can be chosen out of 20 in ${}^{20}C_3$ ways.

$\therefore$ The total number of all possible equally likely cases $= {}^{20}C_3 = \frac{20\times19\times18}{3\times2\times1} = 1140$.

The three numbers on the three drawn tickets will be in A.P. if there is a common difference of either 1, or 2, or 3, or ..., or 9 in the three numbers. (If the common difference is 9, the three numbers are 1, 10, 19 or 2, 11, 20). With a common difference 1, the sets of three numbers are $\{1,2,3\}, \{2,3,4\}, \{3,4,5\}, \cdots, \{18,19,20\}$, i.e., there are 18 such sets.

With common difference 2, the sets of three numbers are $\{1,3,5\}, \{2,4,6\}, \{3,5,7\}, \cdots,$ $\{16,18,20\}$, i.e., there are 16 such sets.

With common difference 3, the sets of three numbers are $\{1,4,7\}, \{2,5,8\}, \{3,6,9\}, \cdots,$ $\{14,17,20\}$, i.e., there are 14 such sets and so on.

Finally, with a common difference 9, the sets of three numbers are $\{1,10,19\}, \{2,11,20\}$, i.e., there are 2 such sets.

$\therefore$ The number of favourable cases $= 18 + 16 + 14 + \cdots + 2 = \frac{9}{2}\{2 \times 18 + (9-1) \times -2\} = 90$ $[\because \ 18 + (n-1) \times -2 = 2, n = 9]$.

Hence, the required probability $= \frac{90}{1140} = \mathbf{\frac{3}{38}}$.

EXAMPLE 10. *Four different objects* $1, 2, 3, 4$ *are distributed at random on four places marked* $1, 2, 3, 4$. *What is the probability that none of the objects occupies the place corresponding to its number?*

SOLUTION. 4 objects can be distributed on the four places in $\lfloor 4$ ways = 24 ways.

$\therefore$ Total number of all possible equally likely cases = 24.

Number of ways in which all the four objects can occupy the places corresponding to their numbers = 1.

If three objects occupy their places, then the 4th object will also occupy its place and this is already considered.

If two objects occupy their places, the remaining two can go wrong by occupying each other's place, i.e., in only 1 way, and 2 objects can be selected out of 4 in ${}^4C_2$ ways.

$\therefore$ The number of ways in which only two objects can occupy their places $= 1 \times {}^4C_2 = 6$.

If one object occupies its place, any one of the remaining 3 objects can go wrong in 2 ways by occupying the positions of the other two, and 1 object can be chosen out of 4 in ${}^4C_1$ ways.

$\therefore$ The number of ways in which only one object can occupy its place $= 2 \times {}^4C_1 = 8$.

$\therefore$ Total no. of ways in which at least one object can occupy its place = 1 + 6 + 8 = 15.

$\therefore$ Probability that at least one object occupies its place $= \frac{15}{24} = \frac{5}{8}$.

Hence, the required probability that none of the objects occupies its place $= 1 - \frac{5}{8} = \mathbf{\frac{3}{8}}$.

[OTHERWISE. The Total number of cases $= \lfloor 4 = 24$.

The number of ways in which none of the objects occupy its position
$= \lfloor 4 \left\{1 - \frac{1}{\lfloor 1} + \frac{1}{\lfloor 2} - \frac{1}{\lfloor 3} + \frac{1}{\lfloor 4}\right\} = 24\left\{1 - 1 + \frac{1}{2} - \frac{1}{6} + \frac{1}{24}\right\} = 24 \times \frac{12-4+1}{24} = 9.$

[$\because$ The number of ways in which none of the n objects numbered 1, 2, 3, ..., n occupies the place corresponding to its number $= \lfloor n \left\{1 - \frac{1}{\lfloor 1} + \frac{1}{\lfloor 2} - \frac{1}{\lfloor 3} + \cdots + (-1)^n \cdot \frac{1}{\lfloor n}\right\}$.]

Hence, the required probability $= \frac{9}{24} = \mathbf{\frac{3}{8}}$.]

EXAMPLE 11. *There are two bags. The first contain* 2 *red and* 1 *white balls whereas the second bag has only* 1 *red and* 2 *white balls. One ball is taken out at random from the first bag and is put in the second bag. Then a ball is chosen at random from the second bag. What is the probability that this last ball is red?* **[CA November 1987]**

SOLUTION. The ball transferred from the first to the second bag may either be red or white.

CASE 1. 1 red ball is transferred from the first to the second bag.

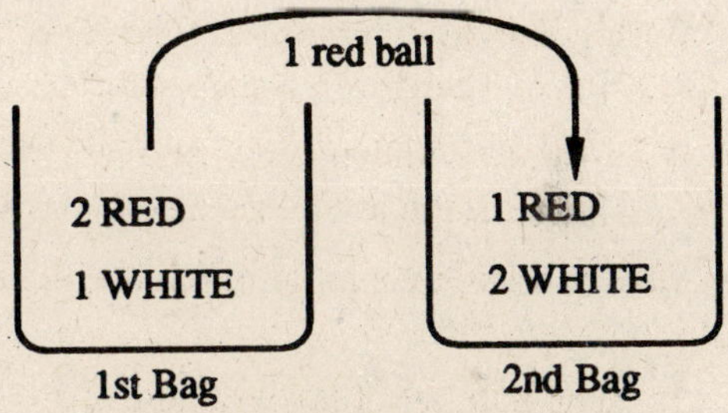

CASE 1

Probability of transferring 1 red ball from the first to the second bag $= \frac{^2C_1}{^3C_1} = \frac{2}{3}$.

After 1 red ball is transferred, the no. of red balls in the second bag $= 1 + 1 = 2$ and the total no. of balls in the second bag $= 2 + 2 = 4$.

$\therefore$ Probability of drawing 1 red ball from the second bag $= \frac{^2C_1}{^4C_1} = \frac{2}{4} = \frac{1}{2}$.

$\therefore$ Probability of first transferring 1 red ball and then drawing 1 red ball from the second bag $= \frac{2}{3} \times \frac{1}{2} = \frac{1}{3}$.

CASE 2. 1 white ball is transferred from the first to the second bag.

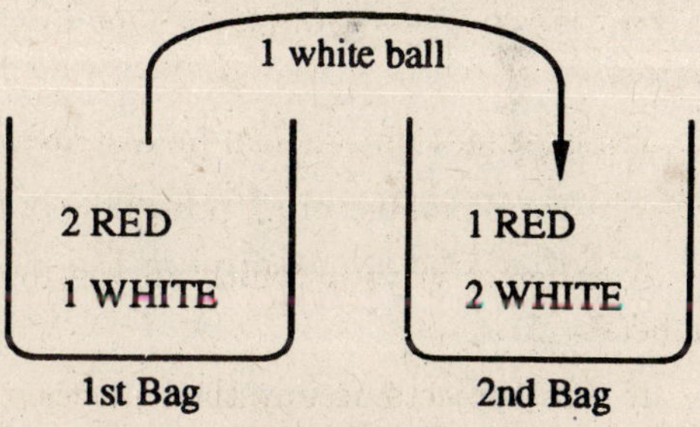

CASE 2

Probability of transferring 1 white ball from the first to the second bag $= \frac{^1C_1}{^3C_1} = \frac{1}{3}$.

As in Case 1, probability of drawing 1 red ball from the second bag $= \frac{^1C_1}{^4C_1} = \frac{1}{4}$.

$\therefore$ Probability of first transferring 1 white ball and then drawing 1 red ball from the second bag $= \frac{1}{3} \times \frac{1}{4} = \frac{1}{12}$.

Hence, by the theorem of total probability (mutually exclusive events), the required probability $= \frac{1}{3} + \frac{1}{12} = \frac{4+1}{12} = \mathbf{\frac{5}{12}}$.

EXAMPLE 12. *What is the probability that over a two day period the number of requests would either be* 11 *or* 12, *if at a motor garage, the records of service requests with their probabilities, are as given below?*

Daily Demand :	5	6	7
Probability :	0.25	0.65	0.10

[CA November 1990]

SOLUTION. Let A, B, C be the events that the daily demands (i.e., the number of requests) are 5, 6, 7 respectively.

Then $P(A) = 0.25$, $P(B) = 0.65$ and $P(C) = 0.10$.

The number of requests over a two-day period will be 11 if either (i) the demand in the first day is 5 and in the second day is 6 or (ii) the demand in the first day is 6 and in the second day is 5.

$\therefore$ Probability of 11 service requests over a two-day period $= P(A) \times P(B) + P(B) \times P(A)$ $= 0.25 \times 0.65 + 0.65 \times 0.25 = 0.1625 + 0.1625 = 0.3250$.

Again the number of requests over a two-day period will be 12 if the demands on the first and second day respectively, are (i) 5 and 7 or (ii) 7 and 5 or (iii) 6 and 6.

$\therefore$ Probability of 12 service requests over a two-day period $= P(A) \times P(C) + P(C) \times P(A) + P(B) \times P(B) = 0.25 \times 0.10 + 0.10 \times 0.25 + 0.65 \times 0.65 = 0.025 + 0.025 + 0.4225 = 0.4725$.

Hence, the required probability of 11 or 12 service requests over a two-day period $= 0.3250 + 0.4725 =$ **0.7975**.

Exercise 1(I)

Theory

1. Explain the following terms with a suitable example for each:

(i) Events, (ii) Elementary and compound events, (iii) Equally likely events, (iv) Mutually exclusive events, (v) Sample space, (vi) Outcome, (vii) Exhaustive set of events.

[C.U. B. Com. (Hons.) 1984]

2. Write down the Classical Definition of Probability and point out its limitations.

[Agra U. M. Com. 1989]

3. State and prove the Theorem of Total Probability for two mutually exclusive events. How is the result modified when the events are not mutually exclusive. **[B.U. Econ. (Hons.) 1974]**

4. Define Conditional Probability. State and prove the theorem of Compound Probability.

[C.U. B. Com. (Hons.) 1981, 1983, 1985]

5. (i) Explain with examples the rules of Addition and Multiplication in Theory of Probability.

[CA November 1977; C.U. M. Com. 1975; Econ. (Hons.) 1979; G.U. 1978]

(ii) If A and B be any two events, show that $P(A \cup B) = P(A) + P(B) - P(A \cap B)$. What will happen if A and B are mutually exclusive? **[ICWAI June 1993]**

6. (a) Define (i) mutually exclusive events and (ii) independent events.

[ICWAI December 1984; C.U. B. Com. (Hons.) 1980; 1983; CA May 1987]

(b) State Bayes' theorem of conditional probability. **[C.U. M. Com. 1985]**

7. Define independent and mutually exclusive events. Can the two events be mutually exclusive and independent simultaneously? Support your answer with examples.

[C.U. B. Com. (Hons.) 1983; D.U. M. Com. 1978]

8. A and B are two given events; what conclusion can be made in each of the following cases:

(i) $P(A) = P(B)$; (ii) $P(A \cup B) = 1$; (iii) $P(A \cup B) = P(A) + P(B)$; (iv) $P(A \cap B) = P(A) \cdot P(B)$; (v) $P(A \cup B) = P(A) + P(B) - P(A \cap B)$.

9. Let A, B, C be three events connected with an experiment. Under what conditions will the events be exhaustive and mutually exclusive?

10. If A and B be two events, prove that

(i) $P(A \cup B) \leq P(A) + P(B)$; **[ICWAI June 1990]**

(ii) $P(A \cap B) \geq P(A) + P(B) - 1$. **[ICWAI December 1991]**

[HINTS. (i) $P(A \cup B) = P(A) + P(B) - P(A \cap B) \leq P(A) + P(B)$ $[\because \ P(A \cap B) \geq 0]$;

(ii) $P(A) + P(B) - P(A \cap B) = P(A \cup B) \leq 1$, or, $P(A) + P(B) - 1 \leq P(A \cap B)$.]

11. Examine the validity of the following statements:

(i) If $P(A \cup B) = P(B)$, then $P(A \cap B) = P(A)$. **[ICWAI June 1992]**

(ii) If A and B are independent events, then $\bar{A}$ and $\bar{B}$ are also independent, where $\bar{A}, \bar{B}$ are the complements of A and B respectively. **[ICWAI December 1990]**

[**Ans.** (i) Vaid; (ii) Valid.]

[A]

1. A bag contains 3 green and 8 white balls. If one ball is drawn from it at random, find the chance that the ball drawn is green.

2. If a coin is tossed, what is the chance of a 'Tail'? If three coins are tossed, find the chance that they are all Tails.

3. If a die is tossed, what is the chance of getting (i) an even number, (ii) a number greater than 2 and (iii) an even number greater than 2.

4. From a pack of 52 cards, 1 card is drawn at random. Find the chance that the card is (i) red, (ii) an ace, (iii) a spade and (iv) either a king or an ace.

5. (i) What is the chance of picking a spade, or an ace not of spade, from a pack of 52 cards? **[C.U. B. Com. 1965]**

(ii) Out of 5 players of which two are members of a certain club, three are to be selected to represent the country at an international tournament. Find the probability that less than two of those selected to represent are members of the club. **[CA May 1984]**

6. (i) From a well-shuffled pack of 52 cards, one card is drawn at random. Find the chance that the card is (i) either a king or a knave, (ii) neither a king nor a knave, (iii) neither a heart nor a diamond, (iv) neither an ace, nor a king, nor a queen, nor a knave.

(ii) Two letters are drawn at random from the word HOME. Write down the sample space. Now find the probability that (i) both the letters are vowels; (ii) at least one is a vowel; (iii) one of the letters chosen is M. **[C.U. B. Com. (Hons.) 1984]**

7. From a bag containing 7 white and 5 red balls, 4 balls are drawn at random. What is the probability that they are all white? **[C.U. B. Com. 1977]**

8. (i) In a single cast with two dice, find the chance of throwing 7 (i.e., of throwing two numbers whose sum is 7). **[B.U. B. Com. 1976]**

(ii) If 4 unbiased coins are tossed, find the probability that there should be two heads.

9. Two balls are drawn at random from a bag containing 6 white balls and 4 black balls. Find the chance that one is white and the other is black. **[B.U. B. Com. 1975]**

10. Four balls are drawn at random from a bag containing 5 red and 7 white balls. Compute the probability of getting (i) 4 red balls, (ii) 2 red and 2 white balls, (iii) 3 white balls and 1 red ball.

11. Four balls are drawn at random from a bag containing 5 black and 8 white balls. What are the odds in favour of the balls being all white?

12. (i) Find the chance of not throwing an ace, two or three, in a single throw with a die.

(ii) There are 17 balls numbered from 1 to 17 in a bag. If a person selects one at random, what is the probability that the number printed on the ball will be an even number greater than 9?

[CA November 1985]

13. (i) What are the odds against throwing ace or six in a single throw with a die? And what are the odds in favour?

(ii) Two unbiased dice are thrown. Find the probability that the sum of the faces is not less than 10. **[ICWAI December 1987]**

[HINTS. If S be the sample space connected with the throwing of two dice, then

$S = \{(1,1), (1,2), \cdots, (6,6)\}$ and $n(S) = 36$ = total no. of all possible cases.

If A be the event that the sum of the faces is not less than 10, then

$$A = \{(4,6), (5,5), (6,4), (5,6), (6,5), (6,6)\}; \quad \therefore \quad n(A) = 6.$$

Hence the required probability $= \frac{n(A)}{n(S)} = \frac{6}{36} = \frac{1}{6}$.]

14. Given below are the weekly wages (in Rs.) of six workers in a factory: 62, 90, 78, 85, 79 and 68.

If two of these workers are selected at random to serve as representatives, what is the probability that at least one will have a wage lower than the average. **[CA May 1984]**

15. Five men in a company of 20 are graduates. If 3 men are picked out of the 20 at random, what is the probability that (i) they are all graduates? (ii) there is no graduate? What is the probability of at least one graduate?

16. A bag contains 10 rupee coins, 7 fifty-paise coins and 4 twenty-five paise coins. Find the probability of drawing (i) a rupee-coin; (ii) three rupee-coins; and (iii) three coins, one of each type.

[C.U. M. Com. 1978]

17. Consider four events: A, NOT A, B, NOT B. It is given that $P(B) = 0.4, P(A$ but NOT $B)$ $= 0.3$, P (NOT $A) = 0.7$. Prove that A and B are mutually exclusive and hence, find $P(A \cup B)$.

[C.U. B. Com. (Hons.) 1984]

18. Let E denote the experiment of tossing a coin three times in succession. Construct the samples space S. Write down the elements of the 2 events E_1 and E_2, where E_1 is the event that the number of heads exceeds the number of tails and E_2 is the event of getting head in the first trial. Find the probabilities $P(E_1)$ and $P(E_2)$ assuming that all the elements of S are equally likely to occur. **[ICWAI June 1984]**

19. A, B and C are three mutually exclusive and exhaustive events. Find $P(B)$, if $\frac{1}{8}P(C) = \frac{1}{2}P(A) = P(B)$. **[ICWAI June 1987]**

20. The probability that the teacher in Statistics will take a sudden test on any day of a week is $\frac{2}{5}$. A student abstains for 2 days in a week. What is the probability that he will miss at least one test?

[HINTS. Probability that he will not miss a test on any of two days $= \frac{3}{5} \times \frac{3}{5}$.

$\therefore$ Required Probability $= 1 - \frac{9}{25} = \frac{16}{25}$.]

21. If a random arrangements of the letters of the word **'Commerce'**, find the probability that all the vowels come together. **[Delhi U. B. Com. (Hons.) 1984]**

[HINTS. Total no. of the arrangements $= \dfrac{\lfloor 8}{\lfloor 2 \times \lfloor 2 \times \lfloor 2} = 5040$ and the no. of the favourable cases $= \dfrac{\lfloor 6}{\lfloor 2 \times \lfloor 2} \times \dfrac{\lfloor 3}{\lfloor 2} = \mathbf{540}$.]

22. A pair of dice is rolled. Find the probability that an odd sum is obtained.

[ICWAI June 1994]

[HINTS. If A be the event that an odd sum is obtained, then $A = \{(1,2), (2,1), (1,4), (2,3), (3,2), (4,1), (1,6), (2,5), (3,4), (4,3), (5,2), (6,1), (3,6), (4,5), (5,4), (6,3), (5,6), (6,5)\}$;

$\therefore$ $n(A) = \mathbf{18}$, etc.]

[B]

1. Two cards are drawn from a well-shuffled pack of 52 cards. Find the probability that (i) both are spades, (ii) both are kings, (iii) one is a spade and is a other heart.

2. A sub-committee of 6 members is to be formed out of a group consisting of 7 men and 4 ladies. Calculate the probability that the sub-committee will consist of (i) exactly 2 ladies, and (ii) at least 2 ladies. **[C.U. Econ. (Hons.) 1975]**

3. An article manufactured by a company consists of two parts, A and B. In the process of manufacture of part A, 9 out of 100 are likely to be defective. Similarly, 5 out of 100 are likely to be defective in the manufacture of part B. Calculate the probability that the assembled article will not be defective. **[CA November 1976]**

4. There are four balls in a bag—white, red, green and blue. If a ball is drawn out at random three times in succession, what is the chance that all the three would be white? (Assume that the ball is replaced after each drawing.)

5. (i) A coin is tossed three times in succession. What is the probability of the tosses coming in the order:

(a) Head, tail, head; (b) Head, head, head; (c) Two heads and one tail?

[C.U. B. Com. 1966]

(ii) Find the chance of throwing head and tail alternately in three successive tossings of coin. **[C.U. B. Com. 1965]**

6. From a bag containing 5 green, 6 blue and 4 red balls, 7 balls are drawn at random. Find the chance that 2 green, 3 blue and 2 red balls are drawn. What are the odds against drawing 2 green, 3 blue and 2 red balls?

7. (i) If a die is thrown twice, what is the chance that the first throw does not show less than 4 and the second does not show more than 4?

(ii) A pair of dice is tossed together. What is the probability that the sum of points on the two dice is (a) 6? (b) more than 8? [ICWAI December 1994]

8. In a single cast with 2 dice (i) what are the odds against throwing 8, i.e., against two numbers the sum of which is 8, (ii) what is the chance of throwing more than 8, and what is the chance of throwing less than 8?

9. In a single cast with 3 dice, what is the chance of throwing (i) three fives, (ii) two-four-six, (iii) five-six-six? What are the odds against the events?

10. Three cards are drawn from a pack of 52 cards, each card being replaced before the next one is drawn. Compute the probability that all are (i) spades; (ii) aces; and (iii) red.

11. One bag contains 4 red and 2 black balls; another bag contains 3 red and 5 black balls. If one ball is drawn from each bag, determine the probability that (i) both are red, (ii) both are black, (iii) one is red and one is black.

12. (i) One counter is drawn at random from a bag containing 70 counters marked with the first 70 numerals. Find the chance that it is multiple of 8 or 9.

(ii) From a set of 18 balls marked $1, 2, 3, \cdots, 17, 18$, one is drawn at random. What is the chance that its number is either a multiple of 3 or of 4?

13. An investment consultant predicts that odds against the price of a certain stock will go up during the next week are 2 : 1 and the odds in favour of the price remaining the same are 1 : 3. What is the probability that the price of the stock will go down during the next week?

[CA May 1987]

[HINTS. If A be the event that 'price will go up', and B be the event that 'price will remain the same', then $P(A) = \frac{1}{2+1} = \frac{1}{3}$ and $P(B) = \frac{1}{1+3} = \frac{1}{4}$; $\therefore \quad P(A \cup B) = P(A) + P(B) = \frac{7}{12}$.

$\therefore$ Probability that the price will go down $= 1 - P(A \cup B) =$ etc.]

14. A bag contains 4 green and 6 red balls. A ball is drawn at random and then, without replacing it, a second ball is drawn. What is the chance that a green ball is drawn each time?

15. Two drawings, each of 4 balls, are made from a bag containing 6 red and 5 black balls, the balls not being replaced before the second trial; find the chance that the first drawing gives 4 red balls and the second gives 1 red and 3 black balls.

16. A problem in Statistics is given to three students, A, B, C, whose chances of solving it are $\frac{1}{3}, \frac{1}{4}, \frac{1}{5}$ respectively. What is the probability that the problem will be solved?

17. The independent probabilities that the three sections of a costing department will encounter a computer error are 0.1, 0.3 and 0.3, each week respectively. Calculate the probability that there will be : (i) at least one computer error; (ii) one and only one computer error encountered by the costing department next week. [C.U. M. Com. 1985]

18. A bag contains 4 red and 3 blue balls. Two drawings of 2 balls are made. Find the probability of drawing first 2 red balls and second 2 blue balls (i) if the balls are returned to the bag after the first draw, (ii) if the balls are not returned after the first draw. [ICWAI Decmber 1990]

[C]

1. If $P(A) = \frac{1}{4}, P(B) = \frac{2}{5}, P(A \cup B) = \frac{1}{2}$, find $P(A \cap B), P(A/B)$ and $P(B/A)$.

2. If A and B are two independent events and $P(A) = \frac{3}{5}, P(B) = \frac{2}{3}$, find $P(A \cap B)$ and $P(A \cup B)$.

3. If $P(A) = \frac{1}{2}, P(B) = \frac{2}{5}, P(A \cap B) = \frac{1}{3}$, find $P(A \cup B), P(A^c \cap B^c), P(A^c \cup B^c), P(A \cap B^c)$ and $P(A^c \cap B)$.

4. A construction company is bidding for two contracts, A and B. The probability that the company will get contract A is $\frac{3}{5}$, the probability that the company will get contract B is $\frac{1}{3}$ and the probability that the company will get both the contracts is $\frac{1}{8}$. What is the probability that the company will get at least one contract?

5. The probability that a contractor will get an electric contract is $\frac{3}{5}$, and the probability that he will not get a plumbing contract is $\frac{7}{10}$. If the probability of getting at least one contract is $\frac{4}{7}$, what is the probability that he will get both the contracts?

6. The probability that a Management Accountant's job applicant has a post-graduate degree is 0.30, that he has had some work experience as a Chief Accountant is 0.70, and that he has both is 0.20. Out of 400 applicants, what number would have either a post-graduate degree or some professional work experience or both?

7. (i) A bag contains 10 red and 6 green balls. Two successive drawings of 3 balls are made without replacement. Find the probability that the first drawing will give 3 red balls and the second will give 3 green balls.

(ii) A bag contains 6 white and 9 black balls. Four balls are drawn at a time. Find the probability for the first draw to give 4 white balls and the second to give 4 black balls when the balls are not replaced before the second draw. [C.U. B. Com. (Hons.) 1983]

8. A bag contains 5 red and 3 black balls and the second bag contains 4 red and 5 black balls. One of these is selected at random and a draw of two balls is made from it. What is the probability that one of them is red and the other is black?

*9. There are two identical boxes containing 5 white and 3 red balls and 4 white and 6 red balls. A box is chosen at random and a ball is drawn from it. If the ball is white, what is the probability that it is from the second box?

[HINTS. Use Bayes' Theorem.]

*10. In a bolt factory, machines X, Y, Z manufacture respectively 20, 35 and 45 per cent of the total output. Of their output, 8, 6 and 5 per cent respectively, are defective bolts. One bolt is drawn at random from the product and is found to be defective. What is the probability that it is manufactured in the machine Z?

[HINTS. Use Bayes' Theorem.]

11. A box contains 4 defective and 6 good electronic calculators. Two calculators are drawn out one by one without replacement. (i) What is the probability that the two calculators so drawn are good? (ii) One of the two calculators so drawn is tested and found to be good. What is the probability that the other one is also good? [CA May 1985]

12. A cost accountant has applied to three companies A, B and C for a job. It is known that his chances of receiving offers from A, B, C, A and B both, A and C both, and B and C both are

0.47, 0.29, 0.22, 0.08, 0.06 and 0.07 respectively. It is also known that his chances of getting offers from all the three companies is 0.03. What is the probability that he will (i) get at least one offer? (ii) not get any offer from C? and (iii) not get any offer? **[ICWAI June 1994]**

[HINTS. $P(A) = 0.47$, $P(B) = 0.29$, $P(C) = 0.22$, $P(A \cap B) = 0.08$, $P(A \cap C) = 0.06$, $P(B \cap C) = 0.07$ and $P(A \cap B \cap C) = 0.03$. Now find $P(A \cup B \cup C)$, $P(C')$ and $1 - P(A \cup B \cup C)$.]

[D]

1. If 2 balls are drawn one after another from a bag containing 3 white and 5 black balls, what is the probability that (i) the first ball is white and the second is black; (ii) one ball is white and the other is black?

2. One urn contains 2 white and 2 black balls; a second urn contains 2 white and 4 black balls. (i) If one ball is chosen from each urn, what is the probability that they will be of the same colour? (ii) If an urn is selected at random and one ball is drawn from it, what is the probability that it will be a white ball?

3. X and Y stand in a line at random with 8 other persons. What is the probability that there are 3 persons between X and Y?

4. Given that $P(A) = \frac{3}{8}$, $P(B) = \frac{5}{8}$ and $P(A \cup B) = \frac{3}{4}$, find $P(A/B)$ and $P(B/A)$. Are A and B independent? **[ICWAI June 1991]**

5. What is the probability that (i) a leap year selected at random will contain 53 Sundays, (ii) a non-leap year selected at random will contain 53 Sundays?

6. If n biscuits are distributed at random among N beggars, show that the probability that a particular beggar receives $r(< n)$ biscuits is $\frac{{}^nC_r(N-1)^{n-r}}{N^n}$.

7. In a group of equal number of men and women 10% men and 45% women are unemployed. What is the probability that a person selected at random is employed?

8. An urn contains 4 white and 5 black balls. A second urn contains 5 white and 4 black balls. One ball is transferred from the first to the second urn; then a ball is drawn from the second urn. What is the probability that it is white?

9. Three groups of children contain 3 girls and 1 boy, 2 girls and 2 boys and 3 boys and 1 girl. One child is selected at random from each group. Show that the chance that the three selections consist of 1 girl and 2 boys is 13/32.

10. A speaks truth in 60% and B in 75% of the cases. In what percentage of cases are they likely to contradict each other in stating the same fact?

11. A six faced die is so biased that it is twice as likely to show an even number as an odd number when thrown. It is thrown twice. What is the probability that the sum of the two numbers thrown is even?

12. A, B and C, in order, toss a coin. The first one to throw a head wins. What are their respective chances of winning, assuming that the game may continue indefinitely?

13. From a pack of 52 cards, an even number of cards is drawn. Show that the probability that these consist of half red and half black cards is $\left\{\frac{\underline{|52}}{(\underline{|26})^2} - 1\right\} \Big/ (2^{51} - 1)$.

14. A and B throw with a pair of dice. A wins if he throws 6 before B throws 7, and B wins if he throws 7 before A throws 6. If A begins, show that his chance of winning is 30/61.

15. There are three men aged 60, 65 and 70 years. The probability to live 5 years more is 0.8 for a 60 year old, 0.6 for a 65 year old and 0.3 for a 70 year old person. Find the probability that at least two of the three persons will remain alive 5 years hence.

16. If $P(A) = \frac{1}{3}, P(B) = \frac{1}{2}, P(A/B) = \frac{1}{6}$, find $P(B/A)$ and $P(B/\bar{A})$.
[HINTS. $P(A \cap B) = P(B), P(A/B) = \frac{1}{2} \times \frac{1}{6} = \frac{1}{12}$; $\therefore\ P(B/A) = \frac{1}{12}/\frac{1}{3} = \frac{1}{4}$.
$P(B) = P(A \cap B) + P(\bar{A} \cap B) \Rightarrow P(\bar{A} \cap B) = \frac{1}{2} - \frac{1}{12} = \frac{5}{12}$.
$\therefore\ P(B/\bar{A}) = \frac{P(B\cap\bar{A})}{P(\bar{A})} = \frac{\frac{5}{12}}{1-\frac{1}{3}} = \frac{5}{8}$.]

[E]

1. (i) Can the following represent measures of probability?

(a) $P(A) = 0.2, P(B) = 0.7, P(C) = 0.1$;

(b) $P(A) = 0.4, P(B) = 0.6, P(C) = 0.2$;

where $A \cup B \cup C = S$ (the sample space) and A, B, C are mutually exclusive events.

(ii) Three fair coins are tossed once. Construct the sample space of the outcomes of the random experiment. Mention two mutually exclusive events. Find the probability of (i) at least one head, (ii) exactly one tail. **[C.U. B. Com. (Hons.) 1982; 1985]**

2. If A and B are events connected with a random experiment such that $P(A) = \frac{1}{2}, P(B) = \frac{1}{3}$ and $P(A \cap B) = \frac{1}{4}$, find (i) $P(A \cup B)$; (ii) $P(A/B)$; (iii) $P(A^c \cap B^c)$; (iv) $P(A^c \cup B^c)$ and (v) $P(A^c \cap B)$.

3. Let A and B be events with $P(A \cup B) = \frac{7}{8}, P(A \cap B) = \frac{1}{4}$ and $P(A^c) = \frac{5}{8}$. Find $P(A), P(B)$ and $P(A \cap B^c)$.

4. Let A and B be two events connected with a random experiment such that $P(A) = \frac{1}{2}$, $P(A \cup B) = \frac{3}{4}$, and $P(B^c) = \frac{5}{8}$. Find $P(A \cap B), P(A^c \cap B^c), P(A^c \cup B^c)$ and $P(B \cap A^c)$.

5. The nine digits 1, 2, 3, 4, 5, 6, 7, 8, 9 are arranged in random order to form a nine-digit number. Find the probability that 1, 2 and 3 appear as neighbours in the order mentioned.

[C.U. Econ. (Hons.) 1972]

6. In a family there are 4 children. Find the probability that (i) all of them will have different birthdays, (ii) two of them will have the same birthday. (1 year = 365 days).

7. A bag contains 5 red and 4 black balls. A ball is drawn at random from the bag and put into another bag which contains 3 red and 7 black balls. A ball is drawn randomly from the second bag. What is the probability that it is red? **[C.U. Econ. (Hons.) 1970]**

8. One shot is fired from each of three guns. Let A, B, C denote the events that the target is hit by the first, second and the third gun respectively. Assuming that A, B, C are mutually independent events and that $P(A) = 0.5, P(B) = 0.6, P(C) = 0.8$, find the probability that at least one hit is registered. **[C.U. Maths. (Hons.) 1975]**

9. What is the chance of getting at least one defective item, if 3 items are drawn randomly from a lot containing 10 items, of which just 2 are defective?

10. There are 5 persons in a room. Find the probability that at least 2 of them will have the same birthday in the same calender month of a year.

11. Mr X is called for interview for 3 separate posts. At the first interview there are 5 candidates; at the second, 4 candidates; at the third 6 candidates. If selection of each candidate is equally likely, find the probability that Mr X will be selected for (i) at least one post; (ii) at least two posts. **[C.U. Econ. (Hons.) 1974]**

12. In a bridge game, North and South have 9 spades between them. Find the probability that either East or West has no spades.

(There are only 13 spades in a pack of 52 cards and each player has 13 cards. The players are designated by the positions they occupy, viz. North, South, East, West.)

13. It was found that a league match in football ends in WIN, LOSS or DRAW. A club is supposed to play 22 matches. Being a supporter of the club, what is the probability that you can predict 18 correct results?

[HINTS. Total no. of cases $= 3^{22}$, and no. of the favourable cases $= {}^{22}C_{18} \times 2^4$.]

14. There are 100 applicants for a job in a factory. Some of them are commerce graduates and some are not; some of them have at least five years' experience and some have not, with the exact break down being

	Commerce graduate	Not Commerce graduate
At least 5 years' experience	22	11
Less than 5 years' experience	38	29

If the order in which the applicants are interviewed by the factory manager is random, C is the event that the first applicant interviewed is a commerce graduate, and E is the event that the first applicant interviewed has at least five years' experience, calculate the following probabilities:

(i) $P(C)$, (ii) $P(E')$, (iii) $P(C' \cap E')$, (iv) $P(C|E)$, (v) $P(E'|C')$. **[ICWAI December 1993]**

[HINTS. Total no. of commerce graduates $= 22 + 38 = 60$ and total no. of non-commerce graduates $= 11 + 29 = 40$.

$P(C) = \frac{60}{100} = 0.6, \quad P(E) = \frac{22+11}{100} = 0.33; \quad \therefore \; P(E') = 1 - 0.33 = 0.67.$

$P(C' \cap E') = \frac{29}{100} = 0.29, \quad P(C \cap E) = \frac{22}{100} = 0.22$, etc.]

Answers

[A]

1. $\frac{3}{11}$. **2.** $\frac{1}{2}, \frac{1}{8}$. **3.** (i) $\frac{1}{2}$; (ii) $\frac{2}{3}$, (iii) $\frac{1}{3}$. **4.** (i) $\frac{1}{2}$; (ii) $\frac{1}{13}$; (iii) $\frac{1}{4}$; (iv) $\frac{2}{13}$. **5.** (i) $\frac{4}{13}$; (ii) $\frac{7}{10}$. **6.** (i) (a) $\frac{2}{13}$; (b) $\frac{11}{13}$; (c) $\frac{1}{2}$; (d) $\frac{9}{13}$; (ii) $S = \{HO, HM, HE, OM, OE, ME\}$; $1/6; 5/6; 1/2$. **7.** $\frac{7}{99}$. **8.** (i) $\frac{1}{6}$; (ii) $\frac{3}{8}$. **9.** $\frac{8}{15}$. **10.** (i) $\frac{1}{99}$; (ii) $\frac{14}{33}$; (iii) $\frac{35}{99}$. **11.** 14 : 129. **12.** (i) $\frac{1}{2}$; (ii) $\frac{4}{17}$. **13.** 2 : 1; 1 : 2. **14.** $\frac{3}{5}$. **15.** $\frac{1}{114}, \frac{91}{228}, \frac{137}{228}$. **16.** (i) $\frac{10}{21}$; (ii) $\frac{12}{133}$; (iii) $\frac{4}{19}$. **17.** 0.7. **18.** $S = \{HHH, HHT, HTH, THH, HTT, THT, TTH, TTT\}, E_1 = \{HHT, HTH, THH\}, E_2 = \{HHH, HHT, HTH, HTT\}$; $\frac{3}{8}, \frac{1}{2}$ **19.** $\frac{1}{6}$. **20.** $\frac{16}{25}$. **21.** $\frac{3}{28}$. **22.** $\frac{1}{2}$.

[B]

1. (i) $\frac{1}{17}$; (ii) $\frac{1}{221}$; (iii) $\frac{13}{102}$. **2.** (i) $\frac{5}{11}$; (ii) $\frac{53}{66}$. **3.** 0.8645. **4.** $\frac{1}{64}$. **5.** (a) (i) $\frac{1}{8}$; (ii) $\frac{1}{8}$; (iii) $\frac{3}{8}$. (b) $\frac{1}{4}$. **6.** $\frac{80}{429}$; 349 : 80. **7.** (a) $\frac{1}{3}$; (b) (i) $\frac{5}{36}$; (ii) $\frac{5}{18}$. **8.** (i) 31 : 5; (ii) $\frac{5}{18}$; (iii) $\frac{7}{12}$. **9.** (i) $\frac{1}{216}$, 215 : 1; (ii) $\frac{1}{36}$, 35 : 1; (iii) $\frac{1}{72}$, 71 : 1. **10.** (i) $\frac{1}{64}$; (ii) $\frac{1}{2197}$; (iii) $\frac{1}{8}$. **11.** (i) $\frac{1}{4}$; (ii) $\frac{5}{24}$; (iii) $\frac{13}{24}$. **12.** (i) $\frac{3}{14}$; (ii) $\frac{1}{2}$. **13.** $\frac{5}{12}$. **14.** $\frac{2}{15}$. **15.** $\frac{2}{77}$. **16.** $\frac{3}{5}$. **17.** (i) 0.559; (ii) 0.427. **18.** (i) $\frac{2}{49}$; (ii) $\frac{3}{25}$.

[C]

1. $\frac{3}{20}, \frac{3}{8}, \frac{3}{5}$. **2.** $\frac{2}{5}, \frac{13}{15}$. **3.** $\frac{23}{30}, \frac{7}{30}, \frac{2}{3}, \frac{1}{6}, \frac{4}{15}$. **4.** $\frac{97}{120}$. **5.** $\frac{23}{70}$. **6.** 320. **7.** (i) $\frac{15}{1001}$; (ii) $\frac{3}{715}$. **8.** $\frac{275}{504}$. **9.** $\frac{16}{41}$. **10.** $\frac{45}{119}$. **11.** (i) $\frac{1}{3}$; (ii) $\frac{5}{9}$. **12.** 0.80; 0.78; 0.20.

[D]

1. (i) $\frac{15}{56}$; (ii) $\frac{15}{28}$. **2.** (i) $\frac{1}{2}$; (ii) $\frac{5}{12}$. **3.** $\frac{2}{15}$. **4.** $\frac{2}{5} : \frac{2}{3}$; A and B are not independent [$\because \; P(A \cap B) \neq P(A) \cdot P(B)$]. **5.** (i) $\frac{2}{7}$; (ii) $\frac{1}{7}$. **7.** $\frac{29}{40}$. **8.** $\frac{49}{90}$. **10.** 45% of the cases. **11.** $\frac{5}{9}$. **12.** $\frac{4}{7}$; $\frac{2}{7}$; $\frac{1}{7}$. **15.** 0.612. **16.** $\frac{1}{4}$; $\frac{5}{8}$.

[E]

1. (a) (i) Yes; (ii) No; (b) $S = \{HHH, HHT, HTH, THH, HTT, THT, TTH, TTT\}$; HHH, TTT; $\frac{7}{8}$; $\frac{3}{8}$ **2.** (i) $\frac{7}{12}$; (ii) $\frac{3}{4}$; (iii) $\frac{5}{12}$; (iv) $\frac{3}{4}$; (v) $\frac{1}{12}$. **3.** $\frac{3}{8}, \frac{3}{4}, \frac{1}{8}$. **4.** $\frac{1}{8}, \frac{1}{4}, \frac{7}{8}, \frac{1}{4}$. **5.** $\frac{1}{72}$. **6.** (i) $\frac{364 \times 363 \times 362}{(365)^3}$; (ii) $\frac{6 \times 364 \times 363}{(365)^3}$. **7.** $\frac{32}{99}$. **8.** 0.96. **9.** $\frac{8}{15}$. **10.** $1 - \frac{364 \times 363 \times 362 \times 361}{(365)^4}$. **11.** (i) $\frac{1}{2}$; $\frac{13}{120}$. **12.** $\frac{11}{115}$. **13.** $\frac{{}^{22}C_{18} \times 2^4}{3^{22}}$. **14.** 0.6, 0.67, 0.29, $\frac{2}{3}, \frac{29}{40}$.

1.10. RANDOM VARIABLE (OR STOCHASTIC VARIABLE)

We know that 'tossing a coin', 'throwing a die', 'drawing a card from a pack of 52 cards', etc., are all experiments. If a coin is tossed, either 'head ' or 'tail' turns up and the chance of a head is $\frac{1}{2}$ and the chance of a tail is also $\frac{1}{2}$. Similarly, when a die is cast, the possible outcomes (i.e., the numbers that will appear on top) are 1, 2, 3, 4, 5, 6 each of which occurs with probability (or chance) $\frac{1}{6}$. The experiments whose results (or outcomes) depend on chance are called *Random Experiments.* The definition of a *random variable* is based on the results of a random experiment.

DEFINITION. *A variable whose numerical value is determined by the outcome (or result) of a random experiment is called a random variable or a chance variable.*

A random variable X can also be regarded as a real-valued function defined on the sample space S of a random experiment such that for each point x of the sample space, $f(x)$ is the probability of occurrence of the event represented by x.

ILLUSTRATION. *Consider a random experiment of tossing* 3 *coins. Then the sample space S is given by $S = \{HHH, HHT, HTH, HTT, THH, THT, TTH, TTT\}$.*

Let X denote the number of heads observed. Then $X = 0$ if the outcome is $TTT, X = 1$ if the outline is HTT or THT or $TTH, X = 2$ if the outcome is HHT or HTH or THH, and finally $X = 3$ if the outcome is HHH.

$\therefore$ X is a random variable whose values are determined by the outcomes of the random experiment of tossing 3 coins, and it is a function with domain S and range $\{0, 1, 2, 3\}$. We can write

$$\begin{cases} X(TTT) = 0, & X(THT) = 1, & X(TTH) = 1, & X(HTT) = 1, \\ X(THH) = 2, & X(HTH) = 2, & X(HHT) = 2, & X(HHH) = 3. \end{cases}$$

A random variable may either be *discrete* or *continuous.*

Discrete and Continuous Random Variables

DEFINITION. *If a variable can assume only a discrete set of values, i.e., a finite set of values (as in the case of 'casting a die') or at most an enumerably infinite set of values (as in Poisson distribution discussed in the next chapter), then it is called a* **discrete random variable.**

ILLUSTRATION 1. *The number appearing on top of a die when it is cast.*

ILLUSTRATION 2. *The number of defectives in a sample of electric bulbs.*

ILLUSTRATION 3. *The number of printing mistakes per page of a book.*

ILLUSTRATION 4. *The number of telephone calls received per day, etc.*

If a random variable can assume all real values at a given interval, it is called a **continuous random variable.** *In this case no enumeration of favourable and total cases is possible. Heigths, weights, temperature, time, etc. are examples of continuous random variables.*

In this chapter, we shall discuss topics concerned with discrete random variables.

Probability Function (or Density Function) of A Random Variable

If a random variable X assumes the discrete set of a values $x_1, x_2, \cdots, x_n$, then the fucntion f defined by

$$\begin{aligned} f(x_i) &= P(X = x_i) \\ &= \textit{Probabilty that } X \textit{ assumes the value } x_i = p_i \text{ (say)} \end{aligned}$$

is called Probability Function (or Density Function or Probability Mass Function) of X. This function gives the probabilities corresponding to the different values $x_1, x_2, \cdots, x_n$ of the variable X and satisfies the following two conditions:

$$\text{(i)} \;\; f(x_i) \geq 0, \; \textit{for } i = 1, 2, \cdots, n; \quad \text{(ii)} \;\; \sum_{i=1}^{n} f(x_i) = 1.$$

ILLUSTRATION. *If x is the number appearing on top of a die when it is cast, then $f(x) = \frac{1}{6}$; $x = 1, 2, 3, 4, 5, 6$. In this case, the probability function is a constant function.*

Discrete Probability Distribution

If a random variable x can assume a discrete set of values $x_1, x_2, \cdots, x_n$ with respective probabilities $p_1, p_2, \cdots, p_n$ where $p_1 + p_2 + \cdots + p_n = 1$, then the occurrence of the values x_i with their probabilities p_i, $(i = 1, 2, \cdots, n)$, is called the **discrete probability distribution of x.**

ILLUSTRATION. *If x represents the number appearing on top of a die when it is cast, then the values of x are* 1, 2, 3, 4, 5, 6 *which occur with respective probabilities $\frac{1}{6}, \frac{1}{6}, \frac{1}{6}, \frac{1}{6}, \frac{1}{6}, \frac{1}{6}$, where $\frac{1}{6} + \frac{1}{6} + \frac{1}{6} + \frac{1}{6} + \frac{1}{6} + \frac{1}{6} = 1$. Thus the values of x with their respective probabilities define the discrete probability distribution of x:*

x :	1	2	3	4	5	6	Total
p :	1/6	1/6	1/6	1/6	1/6	1/6	1

EXAMPLE 1. *X is a dicrete random variate having the following probability distribution:*

x :	0	1	2	3	4	5	6	7
$P(X=x)$:	0	k	$2k$	$2k$	$3k$	k^2	$2k^2$	$7k^2+k$

(i) *Determine the constant k;* (ii) *find $P(X<6)$;* (iii) *what will be $P(X \geq 6)$ and $P(0<X<5)$?*

SOLUTION. The probability function $f(x) = P(X = x)$ must satisfy the conditions (i) $f(x) \geq 0$ and (ii) $\Sigma f(x) = 1$.

By (ii), we have

$$0 + k + 2k + 2k + 3k + k^2 + 2k^2 + 7k^2 + k = 1,$$

$$\text{or,}\quad 10k^2 + 9k - 1 = 0, \quad \text{or,}\quad 10k^2 + 10k - k - 1 = 0,$$

$$\text{or,}\quad 10k(k+1) - 1(k+1) = 0, \quad \text{or,}\quad (k+1)(10k-1) = 0; \qquad \therefore\ k = -1,\ \tfrac{1}{10}.$$

By (i), $k \neq -1$. For if $k = -1$, then $f(1), f(2), f(3), f(4)$, become negative which contradicts the condition (i).

Hence, $\mathbf{k = \frac{1}{10} = 0.1}$.

(ii) $$P(X<6) = f(0) + f(1) + f(2) + f(3) + f(4) + f(5) = 0 + k + 2k + 2k + 3k + k^2$$
$$= 8k + k^2 = 8 \times 0.1 + (0.1)^2 = 0.8 + 0.01 = \mathbf{0.81}.$$

(iii) $$P(X \geq 6) = 1 - P(X<6) \qquad [\because\ \Sigma f(x) = 1.]$$
$$= 1 - 0.81 = \mathbf{0.19}$$

and $$P(0<X<5) = P(1) + P(2) + P(3) + P(4) = k + 2k + 2k + 3k$$
$$= 8k = \tfrac{8}{10} = \mathbf{0.8}.$$

1.11. EXPECTATION OF A RANDOM VARIABLE (OR EXPECTED VALUE OR MATHEMATICAL EXPECTATION)

DEFINITION. *If a discrete random variable x assumes the discrete set of values $x_1, x_2, \cdots, x_n$ with respective probabilities $p_1, p_2, \cdots, p_n$ where $p_1 + p_2 + \cdots + p_n = 1$, then the* **expectation** *or* **expected value** *or* **mathematical expectation** *of x, written as* $\mathbf{E(x)}$, *is defined by*

$E(x) = p_1x_1 + p_2x_2 + \cdots + p_nx_n = \sum_{i=1}^{n} p_ix_i$, *or Σpx, i.e., it is the sum of the product of the different possible values of x and the corresponding probabilities.*

If in this expectation the probabilities p_i are replaced by relative frequencies f_i/N where $N = \Sigma f_i$, then $E(x) = \Sigma fx/N =$ Mean. As N becomes larger and larger, the relative frequencies f_i/N approach the probabilities p_i. [See Empirical Definition of Probability]

We shall take **E(x) as the Mean of the probability distribution of x,** which is a characteristic of the random variable x.

The expected value of x^2 is defined by $E(x^2) = \Sigma p_ix_i^2$, and the expected value of x^r is defined by $E(x^r) = \Sigma p_ix_i^r$.

EXAMPLE 2. *If x is a random variable and c is a constant, show that*

(i) $E(c) = c$; (ii) $E(cx) = cE(x)$; (iii) $E(x - \bar{x}) = 0$.

SOLUTION.

(i) $E(c) = \Sigma p_i c = c\Sigma p_i = c.1 = c.$ $\quad [\because \quad \Sigma p_i = 1]$

(ii) $E(cx) = \Sigma p_i c x_i = c\Sigma p_i x_i = c.E(x).$

(iii) $E(x - \bar{x}) = \Sigma p_i(x_i - \bar{x}) = \Sigma p_i x_i - \Sigma p_i \bar{x} = E(x) - \bar{x}\Sigma p_i$ $\quad [\because \quad \bar{x}$ is fixed]

$= \bar{x} - \bar{x}.1 = 0.$

We shall use these results as **formulae.**

EXAMPLE 3. *If x denotes the number of points on a die, find the expection of x.*

SOLUTION. Since x represents the number of points on a die, the different values of x are 1, 2, 3, 4, 5, 6, each having the same probability $\frac{1}{6}$.

By definition,

$$E(x) = \sum p_i x_i = \frac{1}{6}\cdot 1 + \frac{1}{6}\cdot 2 + \frac{1}{6}\cdot 3 + \frac{1}{6}\cdot 4 + \frac{1}{6}\cdot 5 + \frac{1}{6}\cdot 6 = \frac{1}{6}(1+2+3+4+5+6)$$
$$= \frac{1}{6}\cdot\frac{6(6+1)}{2} = \frac{7}{2} = \mathbf{3.5}.$$

We state below two theorems on expected values without proofs.

THEOREM I. *The expectation of the sum of two discrete random variables is the sum of their expectations.*

Symbolically, $E(x+y) = E(x) + E(y)$.

COROLLARY 1. *For three discrete random variables x, y, z, $E(x+y+z) = E(x)+E(y)+E(z)$.*

We have similar results for any number of random variables.

COROLLARY 2. *If $y = a + bx$, where a and b are constans, then $E(y) = a + bE(x)$.*

$E(y) = E(a+bx) = E(a) + E(bx) = a + bE(x)$.

THEOREM II. *The mathematical expectation of the product xy of two independent random variables x and y, is equal to the product of their expectations.*

Symbolically, $E(xy) = E(x)E(y)$.

EXAMPLE 4. *Find the mathematical expectation of the sum of points on n dice.*

SOLUTION. Let x_i denote the number of points on the ith die and S denote the sum of the points on n dice. Then $S = x_1 + x_2 + \cdots + x_n$.

$$\therefore \quad E(S) = E(x_1 + x_2 + \cdots + x_n) = E(x_1) + E(x_2) + \cdots + E(x_n).$$

But for a single die, x_i has the six different values 1, 2, 3, 4, 5, 6, each of which occurs with the same probability $\frac{1}{6}$ and, therefore,

$$E(x_i) = \frac{1}{6}\cdot 1 + \frac{1}{6}\cdot 2 + \frac{1}{6}\cdot 3 + \frac{1}{6}\cdot 4 + \frac{1}{6}\cdot 5 + \frac{1}{6}\cdot 6$$
$$= \frac{1}{6}(1+2+3+4+5+6) = \frac{7}{2}, \quad \text{for } i = 1, 2, \cdots, n.$$

Hence, $E(S) = \frac{7}{2} + \frac{7}{2} + \cdots$ to n terms $= \mathbf{\frac{7n}{2}}$.

EXAMPLE 5. *A number is chosen at random from the set $1, 2, 3, \cdots, 100$, and another number is chosen at random from the set $1, 2, \cdots, 50$. What is the expected value of the product?*

[C.U. B. Com. (Hons.) 1981]

SOLUTION. Let x be the number chosen at random from the set $1, 2, 3, \cdots, 100$. Then x is a discrete random variable whose probability distribution is given by

x :	1	2	3	...	100	Total
p :	1/100	1/100	1/100	...	1/100	1

$$\therefore \quad E(x) = \sum p_i x_i = \frac{1}{100} \times 1 + \frac{1}{100} \times 2 + \frac{1}{100} \times 3 + \cdots + \frac{1}{100} \times 100$$
$$= \frac{1}{100}(1 + 2 + 3 + \cdots + 100) = \frac{1}{100} \cdot \frac{100(100+1)}{2} = \frac{101}{2}.$$

If y be the number chosen at random from the set $1, 2, \cdots, 50$, then the probability distribution of y is given by

y :	1	2	3	...	50	Total
p' :	1/50	1/50	1/50	...	1/50	1

$$\therefore \quad E(y) = \sum p'_i y_i = \frac{1}{50} \times 1 + \frac{1}{50} \times 2 + \frac{1}{50} \times 3 + \cdots + \frac{1}{50} \times 50$$
$$= \frac{1}{50}(1 + 2 + 3 + \cdots + 50) = \frac{1}{50} \cdot \frac{50(50+1)}{2} = \frac{51}{2}.$$

Clearly x and y are two *independent random variables*. Hence, expected value of the product $= E(xy) = E(x) \cdot E(y) = \frac{101}{2} \times \frac{51}{2} = \frac{5151}{4}$.

1.12. VARIANCE AND STANDARD DEVIATION OF A RANDOM VARIABLE

Like *Mean*, **Variance** is a characteristic of a random variable x and it is used to measure dispersion (or variation) of x.

Variance

The **Variance** *of a random variable x is the expected value of $(x - \bar{x})^2$ where $\bar{x}$ is the mean of x, i.e., Variance of x or* $\text{var}(x) = E(x - \bar{x})^2$.

We can show that $\text{var}(x) = E(x^2) - \{E(x)\}^2$. **[C.U. B. Com. (Hons.) 1983]**

PROOF.

$$\text{var}(x) = E(x - \bar{x})^2 = E(x^2 - 2x\bar{x} + \bar{x}^2) = E(x^2) - 2\bar{x}E(x) + E(\bar{x}^2)$$
$$= E(x^2) - 2\bar{x}^2 + \bar{x}^2 \qquad [\because \; E(x) = \bar{x}]$$
$$= E(x^2) - \bar{x}^2 = E(x^2) - \{E(x)\}^2.$$

Standard Deviation (σ)

The Stanard Deviation (S.D.) of a random variable x is the positive square-root of the variance of x, i.e., S.D. $(\sigma) = \sqrt{\text{var}(x)} = \sqrt{E(x^2) - \{E(x)\}^2}$.

EXAMPLE 6. *A random variable x has the following probability distribution:*

x :	0	1	2	3
Probability :	1/8	3/8	3/8	1/8

Find the variance and hence, determine the standard deviation of the distribution.

SOLUTION. Variance of $x = E(x^2) - \{E(x)\}^2$.

$$\text{Now} \quad E(x) = \sum p_i x_i = \frac{1}{8} \times 0 + \frac{3}{8} \times 1 + \frac{3}{8} \times 2 + \frac{1}{8} \times 3 = \frac{3+6+3}{8} = \frac{12}{8} = \frac{3}{2} = 1.5$$

$$\text{and} \quad E(x^2) = \sum p_i x_i^2 = \frac{1}{8} \times 0^2 + \frac{3}{8} \times 1^2 + \frac{3}{8} \times 2^2 + \frac{1}{3} \times 3^2 = 0 + \frac{3}{8} + \frac{12}{8} + \frac{9}{8} = \frac{24}{8} = 3.$$

$\therefore$ Variance $= 3 - (1.5)^x = 3 - 2.25 = \mathbf{0.75}$.

Standard deviation $= \sqrt{\text{var}\,(x)} = \sqrt{0.75} = \mathbf{0.87}$ (approx.)

EXAMPLE 7. *A random variable has the following probability distribution:*

x :	4	5	6	8
Probability :	0.1	0.3	0.4	0.2

Find the expectation and the standard deviation of the random variable.

[C.U. B. Com. (Hons.) 1980, 1988]

SOLUTION. We have

x_i :	4	5	6	8	Total
p_i :	0.1	0.3	0.4	0.2	1

By definition,

$$\begin{aligned}
\text{Expectation of } x = E(x) &= \Sigma p_i x_i = 0.1 \times 4 + 0.3 \times 5 + 0.4 \times 6 + 0.2 \times 8 \\
&= 0.4 + 1.5 + 2.4 + 1.6 = \mathbf{5.9}. \\
\text{var}\,(x) &= E(x^2) - \{E(x)\}^2, \quad \text{and S.D.} = \sqrt{\text{var}\,(x)}. \\
E(x^2) &= \Sigma p_i x_i^2 = 0.1 \times 4^2 + 0.3 \times 5^2 + 0.4 \times 6^2 + 0.2 \times 8^2 \\
&= 0.1 \times 16 + 0.3 \times 25 + 0.4 \times 36 + 0.2 \times 64 \\
&= 1.6 + 7.5 + 14.4 + 12.8 = 36.3 \\
\therefore \quad \text{var}\,(x) &= 36.3 - (5.9)^2 = 36.3 - 34.81 = 1.49.
\end{aligned}$$

Hence, standard deviation $= \sqrt{1.49} = \mathbf{1.22}$ (approx).

EXAMPLE 8. *A bag contains* 5 *white and* 7 *black balls. Find the expectation of a man who is allowed to draw two balls from the bag and who is to receive one rupee for each black ball and two rupees for each white ball drawn.* **[C.U. B. Com. (Hons.) 1982]**

SOLUTION. 2 balls can be drawn out of 12 in ${}^{12}C_2$ ways and 2 black balls can be drawn out of 7 in ${}^{7}C_2$ ways.

$\therefore$ P_i = probability of drawing 2 black balls $= \frac{{}^7C_2}{{}^{12}C_2} = \frac{7}{22}$.

Similarly, p_2 = Probability of drawing 1 black and 1 white ball $= \frac{{}^5C_1 \times {}^7C_1}{{}^{12}C_2} = \frac{35}{66}$ and p_3 = Probability of drawing 2 white balls $= \frac{{}^5C_2}{{}^{12}C_2} = \frac{5}{33}$.

If x be the amount of money received in a draw, then the *probability distribution of* x is given by

Result	2 black balls	1 black and 1 white ball	2 white balls	Total
x	Rs. 2	Rs. 2 + Re. 1 = Rs. 3	Rs. 2 × 2 = Rs. 4	
p	7/22	35/66	5/33	1

Hence, the required expectation of the man $= E(x) = \Sigma p_i x_i = \frac{7}{22} \times \text{Rs.}2 + \frac{35}{66} \times \text{Rs.}3 + \frac{5}{33} \times \text{Rs.}4$ $= \text{Rs.}\frac{187}{66} =$ **Rs.2.83**.

EXAMPLE 9. *A and B play for a prize of* Rs. 99. *The prize is to be won by a player who first throw a '3' with one die. A first throws and if he fails, B throws and if he fails, A again throws and so on. Find their respective expectations.* **[CA November 1981]**

SOLUTION. The probability of throwing '3' with a die $= \frac{1}{6}$ and the probability of not throwing '3' with a die $= 1 - \frac{1}{6} = \frac{5}{6}$.

A will win the prize if he throws '3' in the first casting, or A fails in the first, B fails in the second and A throws '3' in the third casting, or A fails, B fails and again A fails, B fails and then A throws '3' in the fifth casting, and so on. This may continue indefinitely.

Hence, the probability that A will win the prize

$$= \frac{1}{6} + \frac{5}{6} \times \frac{5}{6} \times \frac{1}{6} + \frac{5}{6} \times \frac{5}{6} \times \frac{5}{6} \times \frac{5}{6} \times \frac{1}{6} + \cdots$$

$$= \frac{1}{6}\left[1 + \left(\frac{5}{6}\right)^2 + \left(\frac{5}{6}\right)^4 + \cdots \text{to } \infty\right]$$

$$= \frac{1}{6} \times \frac{1}{1 - \left(\frac{5}{6}\right)^2} \quad [\because \text{ For an infinite G.P., sum} = \tfrac{a}{1-r}, \text{ where } -1 < r < 1.]$$

$$= \frac{1}{6} \times \frac{36}{11} = \mathbf{\frac{6}{11}}.$$

B will win the prize if A fails to throw '3' in the first casting, and B throws '3' in the second casting or A fails, B fails and again A fails and then B throws '3' in the 4th casting and so on. This may continue indefinitely.

Hence, the probability that B will win the prize

$$= \frac{5}{6} \times \frac{1}{6} + \frac{5}{6} \times \frac{5}{6} \times \frac{5}{6} \times \frac{1}{6} + \frac{5}{6} \times \frac{5}{6} \times \frac{5}{6} \times \frac{5}{6} \times \frac{5}{6} \times \frac{1}{6} + \cdots$$

$$= \frac{5}{6} \times \frac{1}{6}\left[1 + \left(\frac{5}{6}\right)^2 + \left(\frac{5}{6}\right)^4 + \cdots \text{to } \infty\right]$$

$$= \frac{5}{36} \times \frac{1}{1 - \left(\frac{5}{6}\right)^2} = \frac{5}{36} \times \frac{36}{11} = \mathbf{\frac{5}{11}}.$$

Hence, A's expectation = Rs. $99 \times \frac{6}{11} =$ **Rs.54** and B's expectation = Rs. $99 \times \frac{5}{11} =$ **Rs.45**.

EXAMPLE 10. *An unbiased coin is tossed four times. If x denotes the number of heads, form the distribution of x by writing down all the possible outcomes and hence calculate the expected value and variance of x.* **[ICWAI December 1984]**

SOLUTION. If p denotes the probability of getting x heads, then probability distribution of x is given by

x :	0	1	2	3	4	Total
p :	1/16	1/4	3/8	1/4	1/16	1

$[\because \; P(x=0) = \frac{^4C_0}{2^4} = \frac{1}{16}; P(x=1) = \frac{^4C_1}{2^4} = \frac{4}{16} = \frac{1}{4};$ etc.]

Expected value of $x = E(x) = \Sigma p_i x_i = \frac{1}{16} \times 0 + \frac{1}{4} \times 1 + \frac{3}{8} \times 2 + \frac{1}{4} \times 3 + \frac{1}{16} \times 4$ $= 0 + \frac{1}{4} + \frac{3}{4} + \frac{3}{4} + \frac{1}{4} = \frac{8}{4} = \mathbf{2}$.

Now $E(x^2) = \sum p_i x_i^2 = \frac{1}{16} \times 0^2 + \frac{1}{4} \times 1^2 + \frac{3}{8} \times 2^2 + \frac{1}{4} \times 3^2 + \frac{1}{16} \times 4^2$

$$= 0 + \frac{1}{4} + \frac{3}{2} + \frac{9}{4} + 1 = \frac{1+6+9+4}{4} = \frac{20}{4} = 5.$$

$\therefore$ Variance of $x =$ var $(x) = E(x^2) - \{E(x)\}^2 = 5 - (2)^2 = \mathbf{1}$.

EXAMPLE 11.

(i) *If 'a' is a constant, then* var $(a) = 0$ *and* var $(ax) = a^2$ var (x);

(ii) *If* a *and* b *are constants, then* var $(a + bx) = b^2$ var (x).

SOLUTION.

(i) var $(a) = E(a^2) - \{E(a)\}^2$.

Since 'a' is a constant, $E(a) = a, E(a^2) = a^2$.

$$\therefore \quad \text{var}\,(a) = a^2 - a^2 = \mathbf{0}.$$

$$\text{var}\,(ax) = E(a^2x^2) - \{E(ax)\}^2 = a^2E(x^2) - \{aE(x)\}^2 = a^2E(x^2) - a^2\{E(x)\}^2$$
$$= a^2[E(x^2) - \{E(x)\}^2] = \mathbf{a^2\,var(x)}.$$

(ii) Let $y = a + bx$; then $\bar{y} = E(y) = E(a + bx) = a + bE(x)$, i.e., $\bar{y} = a + b\bar{x}$

[$\because \quad \bar{x} =$ Mean $= E(x)$].

$\therefore \quad y - \bar{y} = bx - b\bar{x} = b(x - \bar{x})$.

By definition,

$$\text{var}\,(y) = E(y - \bar{y})^2 = E[b(x - \bar{x})]^2 = E[b^2(x - \bar{x})^2] = b^2E(x - \bar{x})^2 = b^2\,\text{var}\,(x).$$

Hence, $\mathbf{var(a + bx) = b^2 var(x)}$.

For two independent random variables x and y we have var $(ax + by) = a^2$ var $(x) + b^2$ var (y).

1.13. REPEATED TRIALS : BERNOULLI TRIALS

By the word 'trial', we mean an attempt to produce an event A which is neither certain nor impossible. 'Tossing a coin' is a trial and 'getting a head' is an event, say A. The outcome (or result) of a trial is called a 'success' if the event A occurs, and a 'failure' if A fails to occur.

If a trial is repeated, we get a series of trials. A series of trials will be said to be independent with respect to an event A *if the probability of this event in any trial remains the same, whether the results of any number of other trials are known or not.*

Repeated independent trials are called *Bernoulli* trials or Bernoullian series of trials if there are only two possible outcomes (success or failure, yes or no, hit or miss, etc.) for each trial and their probabilities remain the same throughout the trials.

THEOREM. *Prove that the probability of* r *successes in a series of* n *independent trials* $(r \leq n)$ *is* $\mathbf{{}^nC_r p^r q^{n-r}}$, *where* p *is the probability of a success and* $q(1 = 1 - p)$ *is the probability of a failure in a single trial.*

PROOF. Let 'S' denote a successes and 'F' denote a failure. Let us first find the probability that the first r trials are successes and the remaining $(n - r)$ trials are failures, i.e., the probability of

$$\underbrace{SS\cdots S}_{\text{1st } r \text{ trials}} \quad \underbrace{FF\cdots F}_{(n-r) \text{ trials}}$$

Since n trials are independent, by the theorem of compound probability, the probability of r successes is $\underbrace{p \times p \times \cdots \times p}_{r \text{ times}} = p^r$, and the probability of $(n - r)$ failures is $\underbrace{q \times q \times \cdots \times q}_{(n-r) \text{ times}} = q^{n-r}$.

$\therefore$ The probability that the first r trials are successes and the remaining $(n-r)$ trials are failures is $p^r q^{n-r}$ where $q = 1 - p$. Similarly, the probability of obtaining r successes and $(n-r)$ failures in any other definite specified order is also $p^r q^{n-r}$.

But we are interested in finding the probability that in n independent trials any r trials are successes [and, therefore, remaining $(n-r)$ trials are failures]. r trials can be selected out of n in ${}^nC_r$ mutually exclusive ways in each of which the proabability of r successes is $p^r q^{n-r}$.

Hence, by *the theorem of total probability,* the probability $f(r)$ of r successes (regardless of their order) in a series of n independent trials is $f(r) = {}^n C_r p^r q^{n-r}$, where $q = 1 - p$.

EXAMPLE 12. *Four coins are tossed simultaneously. What is the probability of getting* 2 *heads and* 2 *tails?* [CA May 1977]

SOLUTION. We know that tossing 4 coins simultaneously once is the same thing as tossing one coin 4 times, provided all the coins are unbiased.

Let 'getting head' by tossing a coin represent a 'success'. Then 'getting tail' will be a 'failure'. $\therefore\ p = \frac{1}{2}$ and $q = \frac{1}{2}$.

Thus we have 4 independent trials in which 2 trials are successes and 2 failures, i.e., $n = 4, r = 2, p = \frac{1}{2}, q = \frac{1}{2}$.

Hence, the required probability of getting 2 heads and 2 tails $= {}^4C_2 \left(\frac{1}{2}\right)^2 \left(\frac{1}{2}\right)^{4-2} = \frac{4.3}{2.1} \times \frac{1}{4} \times \frac{1}{4} = \mathbf{\frac{3}{8}}$.

EXAMPLE 13. *Four unbiased coins are tossed simultaneously. Let X be the random variable denoting the number of heads obtained. Obtain the probability distribution of X. Find $E(X)$ and* var(X). [Symbols have their usual meanings.] [C.U. B. Com. (Hons.) 1987]

SOLUTION. The probability distribution of X is given by

x :	0	1	2	3	4	Total
$f(x)$:	1/16	4/16	6/16	4/16	1/16	1

[$\because$ 1 head can be obtained in ${}^4C_1$ ways = 4 ways, 2 heads can be obtained in ${}^4C_2$ ways = 6 ways, etc.]

$$\therefore\ E(X) = \sum x f(x) = 0 \times \frac{1}{16} + 1 \times \frac{4}{16} + 2 \times \frac{6}{16} + 3 \times \frac{4}{16} + 4 \times \frac{1}{16}$$
$$= \frac{0+4+12+12+4}{16} = \frac{32}{16} = \mathbf{2}.$$
$$E(X^2) = \sum x^2 f(x) = 0^2 \times \frac{1}{16} + 1^2 \times \frac{4}{16} + 2^2 \times \frac{6}{16} + 3^2 \times \frac{4}{16} + 4^2 \times \frac{1}{16}$$
$$= \frac{0+4+24+36+16}{16} = \frac{80}{16} = 5.$$
$$\therefore\ \text{var}\ (X) = E(X^2) - \{E(X)\}^2 = 5 - 2^2 = \mathbf{1}.$$

EXAMPLE 14. 13 *cards are drawn simultaneously from a pack of* 52 *cards. If aces count* 1, *face cards* 10 *each, and others according to their denominations, find the expectation of the total score on the* 13 *cards.*

SOLUTION. Let S be the total score on the 13 cards and x_i be the number on the ith card drawn. Then

$$S = \sum_{i=1}^{13} x_i \quad \text{and} \quad E(S) = E(x_1 + x_2 + \cdots + x_{13}) = E(x_1) + E(x_2) + \cdots + E(x_{13}).$$

Now

$$E(x_i) = 1 \cdot \frac{4}{52} + 2 \cdot \frac{4}{52} + \cdots + 10 \cdot \frac{4}{52} + 10 \cdot \left(\frac{4}{52} + \frac{4}{52} + \frac{4}{52}\right)$$
$$= \frac{4}{52}(1 + 2 + \cdots + 10) + 3.10 \cdot \frac{4}{52} = \frac{1}{13} \times \frac{10(10+1)}{2} + \frac{30}{13} = \frac{85}{13}.$$
$$\therefore \quad E(x_i) = \frac{85}{13} \quad \text{for } i = 1, 2, \cdots, 13.$$

Hence, $E(S) = \frac{85}{13} + \frac{85}{13} + \cdots$ to 13 terms $= \frac{85}{13} \times 13 = \mathbf{85}$.

Exercise 1(II)

Theory

1. Define 'Random Variable'. How do you distinguish between 'discrete' and 'continuous' random variables? Illustrate your answer with suitable examples. **[C.U. B. Com. (Hons.) 1980, 1981]**

2. What do you mean by 'Discrete Probability Distribution' and 'Probability Function'? Give one example for each.

3. (i) What do you understand by the 'the expectation of a random variable'? Explain as clearly as you can. **[C.U. Econ. (Hons.) 1976]**

(ii) Define mathematical expectation of a random variable. **[ICWAI June 1985]**

4. Define 'Expectation' and 'Variance' of a random variable. Prove that

$$E(x - \bar{x})^2 = E(x^2) - \{E(x)\}^2.$$

5. Write notes on: (i) Random Variable, (ii) Dependent and Independent events.

[C.U. B. Com. (Hons.) 1980]

6. Define 'Bernoulli Trials' and give an example. Prove that the probability of r successes in a series of n independent trials if ${}^nC_r p^r q^{n-r}$ where p is the probability of a success in a single trial and $q = 1 - p$.

Problems

[A]

1. If x is a random variable, show that

(i) $E(1) = 1$; (ii) $E(3x) = 3E(x)$; (iii) $E(2 + 3x) = 2 + 3E(x)$.

2. A random variable X has the following probability distribution:

X :	-1	0	1	2
Probability :	1/3	1/6	1/6	1/3.

Compute the expectation of X. **[C.U. Econ. (Hons.) 1977]**

3. Find the mathematical expectation of the sum of points on 10 dice.

4. A random variable x has the following probability distribution:

x :	1	2	3	4	5	6
Probability :	1/6	1/6	1/6	1/6	1/6	1/6

Find the variance and hence determine the standard deviation of the distribution.

5. (i) For what value of a will the function $f(x) = ax; x = 1, 2, \cdots, n$, be the probability mass function of a discrete random variable x? Find the mean and variance of x.

[HINTS. $\Sigma f(x) = 1$ gives $a\Sigma x = 1$, or, $a \cdot \frac{n(n+1)}{2} = 1$, etc. $E(x) = \Sigma x f(x) = a\Sigma x^2 =$ etc. and $E(x^2) = \Sigma x^2 f(x) =$ etc.]

(ii) A random variable X has the following probability function:

Values of X :	0	1	2	3	4	5	6	7
$P(X)$:	0	$2k$	$3k$	k	$2k$	k^2	$7k^2$	$2k^2 + k$

Find the value of k and then evaluate $P(X < 6), P(X \geq 6)$ and $P(0 < X < 5)$.

[CA May 1991]

[HINTS. See worked out Example 1.]

6. Evaluate k if $f(x) = k, x = 1, 2, 3, 4, 5, 6,$

$= 0$, elsewhere

is a probability mass function. Also find its mean and standard deviation. **[ICWAI December 1991]**

[HINTS. $\Sigma f(x) = 1$ gives $6k = 1$, or, $k = 1/6$. The probability distribution of x is given by

x :	1	2	3	4	5	6	Total
$f(x)$:	1/6	1/6	1/6	1/6	1/6	1/6	1

Now find $E(x) = \Sigma x f(x)$ and $E(x^2) = \Sigma x^2 f(x)$. See worked out Examples 6 and 7.]

7. A random variable has the following probability distribution:

x :	4	6	7	10
Probability :	0.2	0.4	0.3	0.1

Find the expectation and the standard deviation of the random variable.

8. Prove that: (i) var (2) = 0; (ii) var $(3x) = 9\,\text{var}\,(x)$; (iii) var $(3 + 4x) = 16\,\text{var}\,(x)$.

9. Find the expected value and variance of the following probability distribution:

x :	-10	-20	30	75	80
$p(x)$:	1/5	3/20	1/2	1/10	1/20

10. (a) In a business venture a man can make a profit of Rs. 2,000 with a probability of 0.4 or have a loss of Rs. 1,000 with a probability of 0.6. What is his expected profit?

(b) A box contains 15 electric bulbs of which 5 are defectives. A man selects 3 bulbs at random. Find the expected number of defective bulbs in his selection.

(c) A player tosses 3 coins. He wins Rs. 16 if 3 heads appear, Rs. 8 if 2 heads appear, Rs. 4 if 1 head appears and Rs. 2 if no head appears. Find his expected amount of winning.

(d) Three coins, whose faces are marked 1 and 2, are tossed. What is the expectation of the total value of number on their faces? **[CA November 1982]**

[HINTS. If X denote the total value of numbers on the faces of the three coins, then the probability distribution of X is given by

x_i :	3	4	5	6	Total
$P(x_i)$:	1/8	3/8	3/8	1/8	1

[∵ Total value 4 occurs when the outcomes are (1, 1, 2), (1, 2, 1), (2, 1, 1).]
Now find $E(X) = \Sigma x_i P(x_i)$.]

11. A coin is tossed until a head appears. What is the expected number of tosses?

[ICWAI June 1985]

[HINTS. If x denote the no. of tosses until a head appears, then

x_i :	1	2	3	4	⋯	Total
p_i :	1/2	1/4	1/8	1/16	⋯	1

$$\therefore \quad E(x) = \Sigma p_i x_i = \frac{1}{2} \times 1 + \frac{1}{4} \times 2 + \frac{1}{8} \times 3 + \frac{1}{16} \times 4 + \cdots$$
$$= \frac{1}{2}\left\{1 + 2 \times \frac{1}{2} + 3 \times \left(\frac{1}{2}\right)^2 + 4 \times \left(\frac{1}{2}\right)^3 + \cdots\right\} = \frac{1}{2}\left(1 - \frac{1}{2}\right)^{-2}.]$$

12. The monthly demand for radios is known to have the following probability distribution:

Demand :	1	2	3	4	5	6
Probability :	0.10	0.15	0.20	0.25	0.20	0.10

Determine the expected demand for radios. Also find the variance. If the cost (Rs. C) of producing (n) radios is given by $C = 1000 + 200n$, determine the expected cost.

13. A number is chosen at random from the set $1, 2, 3, \cdots, 100$ and another number is chosen at random from the set $1, 2, 3, \cdots, 50$. What is the expected value of their product.

[C.U. B. Com. (Hons.) 1981]

[HINTS. Assume that the two random variables which can assume values from the first and the second sets respectively are independent of each other.]

14. Five coins are tossed simultaneously. What is the probability of getting 3 heads and 2 tails?

15. Eight coins are thrown simultaneously. Find the probability of obtaining (i) exactly 6 heads; (ii) at least 6 heads.

16. If a sample of 5 items is drawn randomly from a lot containing 10% defective items, what is the probability of getting not more than one defective item? **[MBA 1977]**

17. Let x denote the profit that a man makes in a business. He may earn Rs. 2,800 with probability 0.5; he may lose Rs. 5,500 with probability 0.3 and he may neither earn nor lose with probability 0.2. Calculate the mathematical expectation of x.

18. (i) A person tosses a coin once and is to receive Rs. 4 for head and is to pay Rs. 2 for tail. Find expectation and variance of his gain.

(ii) A person tosses two coins simultaneously and is to receive Rs. 8 for two heads, Rs. 2 for one head and he is to pay Rs. 6 for no head. Find his expectation.

19. A man draws 2 balls from a bag containing 3 white and 5 black balls. If he is to receive Rs. 14 for every white ball and Rs. 7 for every black ball drawn, what is his expectation?

20. (i) The probability that there is at least one error in an accounts statement prepared by A is 0.2, for B and C they are 0.25 and 0.4 respectively. A, B and C prepared 10, 16 and 20 statements respectively. Find the expected number of correct statements in all. **[CA May 1980]**

[HINTS. If A, B, C be the events that there is at least one error in an accounts statement prepared by A, B, C respectively, then $P(A) = 0.2, P(B) = 0.25, P(C) = 0.4$ so that $P(A^c) =$

0.8, $P(B^c) = 0.75, P(C^c) = 0.6$. Hence, the expected no. of corrected statements $= 0.80 \times 10 + 0.75 \times 16 + 0.6 \times 20 = 32$.]

(ii) The probability that there is at least one error in an account statement prepared by A is 0.3 and for B and C, they are 0.4 and 0.45 respectively. A, B and C prepared 20, 10, 40 statements respectively. Find the expected number of correct statements in all. **[CA November 1991]**

21. If a person gains or loses an amount equal to the number appearing when a balanced die is rolled once, according to whether the number is even or odd, how much money can he expect per game in the long run? **[C.U. Econ. (Hons.) 1982]**

22. A box contains 8 tickets. 3 of the tickets carry a prize of Rs. 5 each and the other 5 carry a prize of Rs. 2.

(i) If one ticket is drawn, what is the expected value of the prize?

(ii) If two tickets are drawn, what is the expected value of the game? **[ICWAI December 1985]**

[HINTS.

(i) If x be the value of the prize in rupees and p the corresponding probability, then

x :	2	5	Total
p :	5/8	3/8	1

Hence, etc.

(ii)

x :	4	7	10	Total
p :	${}^5C_1/{}^8C_2$	${}^5C_1 \times {}^3C_1/{}^8C_2$	${}^3C_2/{}^8C_2$	1

Hence, etc.]

23. An unbiased coin is tossed four times. If x denotes the number of heads, form the distribution of x by writing down all the possible outcomes and hence calculate the expected value and variance of x. **[ICWAI December 1984]**

24. 10,000 tickets are sold in a lottery in which there is a first prize of Rs. 5,000, two second prizes of Rs. 1,000 each and ten consolation prizes of Rs. 100 each. One ticket cost Re. 1. Find the expected net gain or loss if you buy a ticket.

[HINTS. If Rs. x be the net gain or loss and p the corresponding probability, then the prob. distribution of x is

x	Rs. 4,999	Rs. 999	Rs. 99	– Re. 1	Total
p	1/10,000	2/10,000	10/10,000	9987/10,000	1

Hence, etc.]

25. A and B toss in turn an ordinary die for a prize of Rs. 55. The first to toss a six wins. If A has the first throw, what is his expectation? **[ICWAI June 1986]**

[HINTS. See worked out Example 9.]

[B]

1. The p.m.f. of a random variable (X) is given by

$$\begin{aligned} f(x) &= 2p \text{ for } x = 1 \\ &= p \text{ for } x = 2 \\ &= 4p \text{ for } x = 3 \\ &= 0 \text{ otherwise} \end{aligned}$$

Find the value of p and $E(X)$. Also calculate $P(X > 1)$. **[ICWAI December 1983; June 1994]**

[HINTS. $\Sigma f(x) = 1$ gives $7p = 1$, or, $p = \frac{1}{7}$.

$E(X) = \Sigma p_i x_i = 1 \times 2p + 2 \times p + 3 \times 4p = 16p = \frac{16}{7}$.

$P(X > 1) = P(2) + P(3) = f(2) + f(3) =$ etc.]

2. If it rains, a taxi driver can earn Rs. 100 per day. If it is fair, he can lose Rs. 10 per day. If the probability of rain is 0.4, what is his expectation? **[ICWAI December 1989]**

3. Throwing 2 unbiased coins simultaneously, Mr. X bets with Mrs. X that he will receive Rs. 4 from her if he gets 2 heads and he will give Rs. 4 to her otherwise. Find Mr. X's expectation.

[ICWAI June 1991]

4. A player tosses 3 fair coins. He wins Rs. 10 if 3 heads appear, Rs. 6 if 2 heads appear and Rs. 2 if 1 head appears. On the other hand he losses Rs. 25 if 3 tails appear. Find the expected gain of the player. **[ICWAI December 1990]**

5. Three marbles are drawn without replacement from an urn containing 4 red and 6 white marbles. If x is a random variable which denotes the total number of red marbles drawn, construct a table showing the probability distribution of x. Also find $E(x)$. **[ICWAI December 1993]**

[HINTS. Clearly $x = 0, 1, 2, 3; p_1 = {}^6C_3/{}^{10}C_3 = \frac{1}{6}, p_2 = {}^4C_1/{}^6C_2/{}^{10}C_3 = \frac{1}{2}$, etc.]

6. A man runs an ice cream parlour in a holiday resort. If the summer is mild he can sell 2500 cups of ice-cream if it is hot, he can sell 4000 cups; if it is very hot, he can sell 5000 cups. It is known that the probability in any year for the summer to be mild is 1/7 and hot is 4/7. A cup of ice cream costs Rs. 2 and sold for Rs. 3.50. What is his expectation? **[ICWAI June 1990]**

[HINTS. Profit per cup = Rs. 1.50, p' = the probability that the Summer is very hot = $1 - (\frac{1}{7} + \frac{4}{7}) = \frac{2}{7}$. If x be amount of profit in Rs. and p the corresponding probability, then

x	3750	6000	7500	Total
p	$\frac{1}{7}$	$\frac{4}{7}$	$\frac{2}{7}$	1]

Answers

[A]

2. 1/2. **3.** 35. **4.** 2.92; 1.71. **5.** (i) $\frac{2}{n(n+1)}$; $\frac{2n+1}{3}$; $\frac{n^2+n-2}{18}$; (ii) $\frac{1}{10}, 0.81, 0.19, 0.8$. **6.** $\frac{1}{6}; 3.5, \frac{\sqrt{35}}{2\sqrt{3}}$ or 1.71. **7.** 6.3; 1.62. **9.** 21.5; 950.25. **10.** (a) Rs. 200; (b) 1; (c) Rs. 6.75, (d) 4.5. **11.** 2. **12.** 3.60; 2.14; Rs. 1,720. **13.** $\frac{5151}{4}$. **14.** 5/16; **15.** 7/64, 37/256. **16.** 45, 927/50,000. **17.** Rs. 250 (Loss). **18.** (i) Re. 1, Rs. 9; (ii) Rs. 1.50. **19.** Rs. 19.25. **20.** (i) 32; (ii) 42. **21.** 50 paise. **22.** Rs. 3.125 or Rs. 3.13; and Rs. 6.25. **23.** 2; 1 **24.** 20 paise (loss). **25.** Rs. 30.

[B]

1. $\frac{1}{7}, \frac{16}{7}, \frac{5}{7}$. **2.** Rs. 34. **3.** Rs. 2, i.e., Mr. X will give Rs. 2. **4.** Rs. 1.13. **5.** 1.2. **6.** Rs. 6, 107.14.

CHAPTER 2

ELEMENTS OF THEORETICAL DISTRIBUTIONS: BINOMIAL, POISSON AND NORMAL

2.1. INTRODUCTION

We know that Frequency Distributions are based on actual observations. We shall now discuss another important type of Distribution known as *Theoretical* or *Expected Frequency Distribution.* Often we can mathematically deduce the Expected Frequency Distributions of certain populations on the basis of theoretical considerations. Such Distributions are known as *Theoretical Distributions* or *Probability Distributions.* For these Distributions, a random experiment is theoretically assumed to serve as model and the probabilities are given by a function of the random variable called *Probability function* (see Art. 1.10). In this chapter, we shall discuss three important theoretical (or Probability) Distributions, viz., (1) **Binomial Distribution,** (2) **Poisson Distribution** and (3) **Normal Distribution.** Of these, the first two are *Discrete Probability Distributions* and the third is a *Continuous Probability Distribution.*

2.2. BINOMIAL DISTRIBUTION (OR BERNOULLI DISTRIBUTION)

Binomial Distribution (or Bernoulli Distribution) is the most fundamental and important Discrete Probability Distribution in Statistics and is defined by the Probability function

$$\mathbf{f(x) = {}^{n}C_{x}p^{x}q^{n-x}}, \quad \mathbf{(x = 0, 1, 2, \cdots, n)} \tag{1}$$

which gives the probability of x successes in a series of n independent trials ($x \leq n$) where p is the constant probability of success in a single trial and $q = 1 - p$. [For proof of (1) see Art. 4.13.]

If n and p are constants, the above function $f(x)$ represents a Discrete Probability Distribution given by

x	0	1	2	$\cdots$	n
$f(x)$	q^n	${}^nC_1p^1q^{n-1}$	${}^nC_2p^2q^{n-2}$	$\cdots$	p^n

It is called *Binomial Distribution,* because for $x = 0, 1, 2, \cdots, n$, it gives the successive terms of the Binomial expansion $(q+p)^n = q^n + {}^nC_1p^1q^{n-1} + {}^nC_2p^2q^{n-2} + \cdots + p^n$.

Clearly $\sum_{x=0}^{n} f(x) = (q+p)^n = 1^n = 1 \quad [\because \quad q = 1-p, \text{ or, } p+q=1.]$

The two independent constants n and p are called *parameters of the Binomial Distribution* and the Distribution is completely known when the values of p and n are known.

Conditions of Binomial Distribution

The Binomial Distribution holds under the following conditions:

(1) Trials are repeated under identical conditions for a fixed number of times, say n times.

(2) There are only two possible outcomes, viz., success or failure for each trial.

(3) The probability of success in each trial remains constant and does not change from trial to trial.

(4) The trials are independent, i.e., the probability of an event in any trial is not affected by the results of any other trial.

Properties of Binomial Distribution

(1) Binomial Distribution is a Discrete Probability Distribution in which the random variable x (the no. of successes) assumes the values 0, 1, 2, $\cdots$, n where n is finite.

(2) Mean $= np$, Variance $= npq$, S.D. $(\sigma) = \sqrt{npq}$, Skewness $= (q-p)/\sqrt{npq}$ and Kurtosis $= (1-6pq)/npq$ where $q = 1-p$.

(3) The mode of the Binomial Distribution is that value of x which occurs with the largest probability. It may have either one of two modes.

(4) If two independent random variables x and y follow Binomial Distribution with parameters (n_1, p) and (n_2, p) respectively, their sum $(x+y)$ also follows Binomial Distribution with parameters (n_1+n_2, p).

EXTENSION. If n independent trials are repeated N times, we get N sets of n trials and the expected frequency of x successes is $N \cdot {}^nC_xp^xq^{n-x}$. The expected frequencies of $0, 1, 2, \cdots, n$ successes are the successive terms of the Binomial expansion of $N(q+p)^n$.

2.2.1. Illustrative Examples

EXAMPLE 1. *Six coins are tossed simultaneously. What is the probability of getting* (i) 2 *heads,* (ii) *at least two heads and* (iii) *more than* 2 *heads?*

SOLUTION. Let 'getting a head by tossing a coin' be a 'success'.

Then $p = \frac{1}{2}, q = 1-p = \frac{1}{2}$. Here $n = 6$.

The probability function is

$$f(x) = {}^nC_x p^x q^{n-x} = {}^6C_x \left(\frac{1}{2}\right)^x \left(\frac{1}{2}\right)^{6-x}. \tag{1}$$

(i) Putting $x = 2$ in (1), we get the probability $f(2)$ of 2 heads given by

$$f(2) = {}^6C_2 \left(\frac{1}{2}\right)^2 \left(\frac{1}{2}\right)^{6-2} = 15 \cdot \frac{1}{4} \cdot \frac{1}{16} = \mathbf{\frac{15}{64}}.$$

(ii) Probability of at least two heads

$$= 1 - \{f(0) + f(1)\} = 1 - \left\{{}^6C_0 \left(\frac{1}{2}\right)^0 \left(\frac{1}{2}\right)^{6-0} + {}^6C_1 \left(\frac{1}{2}\right)^1 \left(\frac{1}{2}\right)^{6-1}\right\}$$

$$= 1 - \left\{1.1 \cdot \frac{1}{64} + 6 \cdot \frac{1}{2} \cdot \frac{1}{32}\right\} - 1 - \frac{7}{64} - \mathbf{\frac{57}{64}}.$$

(iii) Probability of getting more than 2 heads

$$= 1 - (\text{Probability of getting not more than 2 heads})$$

$$= 1 - \{f(0) + f(1) + f(2)\} = 1 - \left\{\frac{1}{64} + \frac{6}{64} + \frac{15}{64}\right\} = 1 - \frac{22}{64} = \frac{42}{64} = \mathbf{\frac{21}{32}}.$$

EXAMPLE 2. *Eight coins are thrown simultaneously. Show that the probability of getting at least* 6 *heads is* $\frac{37}{256}$. **[ICWAI (Final) June 1974]**

SOLUTION. Let 'the occurrence of head' by tossing a coin be a 'success'. Then p = constant probability of a success $= \frac{1}{2}, q = 1 - p = \frac{1}{2}$. The probability function $f(x)$ of x successes is given by

$$f(x) = {}^nC_x p^x q^{n-x} = {}^8C_x \left(\frac{1}{2}\right)^x \left(\frac{1}{2}\right)^{8-x}$$

∴ The required probability of getting at least 6 heads (i.e., at least 6 successes)

$$= f(6) + f(7) + f(8) = {}^8C_6 \left(\frac{1}{2}\right)^6 \left(\frac{1}{2}\right)^{8-6} + {}^8C_7 \left(\frac{1}{2}\right)^7 \left(\frac{1}{2}\right)^{8-7} + {}^8C_8 \left(\frac{1}{2}\right)^8 \left(\frac{1}{2}\right)^{8-8}$$

$$= 28 \times \frac{1}{256} + 8 \times \frac{1}{256} + 1 \times \frac{1}{256} = \mathbf{\frac{37}{256}}.$$

EXAMPLE 3. *The screws produced by a certain machine were checked by examining samples of* 12. *The following table shows the distribution of* 128 *samples according to the no. of defective items they contained.*

No. of defectives in a sample of 12 :	0	1	2	3	4	5	6	7	Total
No. of Samples :	7	6	19	35	30	23	7	1	128

Fit a Binomial Distribution and find the expected frequencies if the chance of the machine being defective is $\frac{1}{2}$. *Find the mean and variance of the fitted distribution.* **[Delhi U. M. Com. 1978]**

SOLUTION. Let the occurrence of a defective screw be a success.

Here $n = 7, p = \frac{1}{2}, q = 1 - p = \frac{1}{2}, x = 0, 1, 2, \cdots, 7; N = 128$.

x	Binomial Law: $N \cdot {}^nC_x \cdot p^x q^{n-x}$	Expected Freq. f_e	Observed Freq. f_o
0	$128 \times {}^7C_0(\frac{1}{2})^0 \cdot (\frac{1}{2})^7 = 128 \times \frac{1}{128} = 1$	1	7
1	$128 \times {}^7C_1(\frac{1}{2})^1 \cdot (\frac{1}{2})^6 = 128 \times \frac{7}{128} = 7$	7	6
2	$128 \times {}^7C_2(\frac{1}{2})^2 \cdot (\frac{1}{2})^5 = 128 \times \frac{21}{128} = 21$	21	19
3	$128 \times {}^7C_3(\frac{1}{2})^3 \cdot (\frac{1}{2})^4 = 128 \times \frac{1}{128} = 35$	35	35
4	$128 \times {}^7C_4(\frac{1}{2})^4 \cdot (\frac{1}{2})^3 = 35$	35	30
5	$128 \times {}^7C_5(\frac{1}{2})^5 \cdot (\frac{1}{2})^2 = 21$	21	23
6	$128 \times {}^7C_6(\frac{1}{2})^6 \cdot (\frac{1}{2})^1 = 7$	7	7
7	$128 \times {}^7C_7(\frac{1}{2})^7 \cdot (\frac{1}{2})^0 = 1$	1	1
	Total	128	128

$$\text{Mean} = \Sigma f_e x / N = \frac{1 \times 0 + 7 \times 1 + 21 \times 2 + 35 \times 3 + 35 \times 4 + 21 \times 5 + 7 \times 6 + 1 \times 7}{128}$$

$$= \frac{7 + 49 + 147 + 245}{128} = \frac{448}{128} = \mathbf{3.5}.$$

$$\text{Variance} = \frac{\Sigma f_e x^2}{N} - \left(\frac{\Sigma f_e x}{N}\right)^2 = 14 - (3.5)^2 = 14 - 12.25 = \mathbf{1.75}.$$

$$\left[\because \frac{\Sigma f_e x^2}{N} = \frac{49 + 259 + 609 + 875}{128} = \frac{1792}{128} = 14.\right]$$

[OTHERWISE. Mean $= np = 7 \times \frac{1}{2} = \mathbf{3.5}$ and Variance $= npq = 7 \times \frac{1}{2} \times \frac{1}{2} = \mathbf{1.75}$.]

EXAMPLE 4. *If the probability of defective bolts be* $\frac{1}{10}$, *find the following for the Binomial Distribution of defective bolts in a total of* 400 :

(i) *the mean;* (ii) *the standard deviation;* (iii) *the moment coefficient of skewness.*

[ICWAI (Final) June 1977, 1980]

SOLUTION. Here $n = 400, p = \frac{1}{10} = 0.1, q = 1 - p = 0.9$.

(i) Mean of the Binomial Distribution $= np = 400 \times 0.1 = \mathbf{40}$.

(ii) S.D. $(\sigma) = \sqrt{npq} = \sqrt{400 \times 0.1 \times 0.9} = \sqrt{36} = \mathbf{6}$.

(iii) Moment coefficient of skewness $= \frac{q-p}{\sqrt{npq}} = \frac{0.9-0.1}{6} = \frac{0.8}{6} = \mathbf{0.133}$.

EXAMPLE 5. *What is the probability of guessing correctly at least six of the ten answers in a* TRUE-FALSE *objective test?* **[ICWAI (Final) December 1979]**

SOLUTION. We have $f(x) = {}^nC_x p^x q^{n-x}$, where $q = 1 - p$.

Here $n = 10, p = \frac{1}{2}, q = 1 - \frac{1}{2} = \frac{1}{2}, x = 6, 7, 8, 9, 10$.

Hence the required probability

$$= f(6) + f(7) + f(8) + f(9) + f(10)$$

$$= {}^{10}C_6\left(\frac{1}{2}\right)^6\left(\frac{1}{2}\right)^{10-6} + {}^{10}C_7\left(\frac{1}{2}\right)^7\left(\frac{1}{2}\right)^{10-7} + {}^{10}C_8\left(\frac{1}{2}\right)^8\left(\frac{1}{2}\right)^{10-8}$$

$$+ {}^{10}C_9\left(\frac{1}{2}\right)^9\left(\frac{1}{2}\right)^{10-9} + {}^{10}C_{10}\left(\frac{1}{2}\right)^{10}\left(\frac{1}{2}\right)^{10-10}$$

$$= \left(\frac{1}{2}\right)^{10}\left\{{}^{10}C_6 + {}^{10}C_7 + {}^{10}C_8 + {}^{10}C_9 + {}^{10}C_{10}\right\}$$

$$= \left(\frac{1}{2}\right)^{10}\left\{{}^{10}C_4 + {}^{10}C_3 + {}^{10}C_2 + {}^{10}C_1 + 1\right\}$$

$$= \frac{1}{1024}(210 + 120 + 45 + 10 + 1) = \frac{386}{1024} = \mathbf{\frac{193}{512}}.$$

EXAMPLE 6.

(i) *Determine the Binomial Distribution for which the mean is* 4 *and standard deviation is* $\sqrt{3}$. **[CA May 1992]**

(ii) *Point out the fallacy, if any, in the following statement: "The mean of a Binomial Distribution is* 10 *and its standard deviation is* 4*".* **[CA November 1988]**

SOLUTION.

(i) For the *Binomial Distribution,*

$$np = \text{Mean} = 4 \qquad (1)$$

$$\sqrt{npq} = \text{Standard deviation} = \sqrt{3}, \quad \text{or,} \quad npq = 3 \qquad (2)$$

Substituting $np = 4$ in (2), we get $4 \cdot q = 3$, or, $\mathbf{q = \frac{3}{4}}$.

$\therefore \quad p = 1 - q = 1 - \frac{3}{4} = \mathbf{\frac{1}{4}}$.

Substituting $p = \frac{1}{4}$ in (1), we get $n \cdot \frac{1}{4} = 4$, or, $\mathbf{n = 16.}$

Hence the required *probability function of Binomial Distribution* is

$$f(x) = {}^nC_x \cdot p^x \cdot q^{n-x}, \quad \text{where } q = 1 - p$$

$$= {}^{16}C_x \cdot \left(\frac{1}{4}\right)^x \cdot \left(\frac{3}{4}\right)^{16-x}, \quad \text{where } x = 0, 1, 2, 3, \cdots, 16.$$

(ii) For the *given Binomial Distribution,* np = mean = 10 (1)

and $\sqrt{npq}$ = standard deviation = 4, or, $npq = 16$. (2)

Dividing (2) by (1), we get $q = \frac{16}{10} = 1.6 > 1$, which is *absurd,* since $0 < q < 1$.

Hence the statement cannot be true.

EXAMPLE 7. *A Binomial random variable* X *satisfies the relation* $9P(X = 4) = P(X = 2)$ *when* $n = 6$. *Find the value of the parameter 'p'.* **[CA November 1991]**

SOLUTION. For a *Binomial Distribution,* the probability function is

$$f(x) = {}^nC_x \cdot p^x \cdot q^{n-x} = {}^6C_x \cdot p^x \cdot q^{6-x}, \quad \text{where } q = 1-p.$$

$$\therefore \quad P(X=4) = f(4) = {}^6C_4 p^4 q^{6-4} = {}^6C_2 p^4 q^2$$

$$\text{and} \quad P(X=2) = f(2) = {}^6C_2 p^2 q^{6-2} = {}^6C_2 p^2 q^4.$$

By the given condition,

$$9P(X=4) = P(X=2), \quad \text{or,} \quad 9 \cdot {}^6C_2 p^4 q^2 = {}^6C_2 p^2 q^4,$$

$$\text{or,} \quad 9p^2 = q^2 = (1-p)^2 = 1 - 2p + p^2,$$

$$\text{or,} \quad 8p^2 + 2p - 1 = 0, \quad \text{or,} \quad 8p^2 + 4p - 2p - 1 = -0,$$

$$\text{or,} \quad 4p(2p+1) - 1(2p+1) = 0, \quad \text{or,} \quad (2p+1)(4p-1) = 0.$$

But p cannot be negative; $\therefore$ $4p - 1 = 0$, or, $\mathbf{p = \frac{1}{4} = 0.25}$.

EXAMPLE 8. *In a Binomial Distribution consisting of* 5 *independent trials, probabilities of* 1 *and* 2 *successes are* 0.4096 *and* 0.2048 *respectively. Find the parameter 'p' of the distribution.*

[CA November 1988]

SOLUTION. For a *Binomial Distribution,* the probability of x successes in a series of n independent trials is given by

$$f(x) = {}^nC_x \cdot p^x \cdot q^{n-x}.$$

Here $n = 5$; $\therefore$ $f(x) = {}^5C_x \cdot p^x \cdot q^{5-x}$.

$\therefore$ $f(1) = {}^5C_1 \cdot p \cdot q^{5-1} = 5pq^4$ and $f(2) = {}^5C_2 \cdot p^2 \cdot q^{5-2} = 10p^2q^3$, where $q = 1-p$. It is given that $f(1) = 0.4096$ and $f(2) = 0.2048$.

$$\therefore \quad 5pq^4 = 0.4096 \tag{1}$$

$$\text{and} \quad 10p^2q^3 = 0.2048 \tag{2}$$

Dividing (2) by (1), we get

$$\frac{10p^2q^3}{5pq^4} = \frac{0.2048}{0.4096}, \quad \text{or,} \quad \frac{2p}{q} = \frac{1}{2}, \quad \text{or,} \quad 4p = q = 1-p,$$

$$\text{or,} \quad 5p = 1, \quad \text{or,} \quad \mathbf{p = \frac{1}{5} = 0.2}.$$

EXAMPLE 9. *The overall percentage of failures in a certain examination is* 40. *What is the probability that out of a group of* 6 *candidates at least* 4 *passed the examination?*

[ICWAI (Final) December 1974]

SOLUTION. Let 'the event of a candidate passing the examination' be a 'success'. Then

$q =$ Probability of failure of a candidate in the examination $= 40\%$ (given) $= \frac{40}{100} = \frac{2}{5}$.

$\therefore$ $p =$ Probability of success (i.e., passing in the examination) in a single trial $= 1 - q = 1 - \frac{2}{5} = \frac{3}{5}$.

Here $n =$ Number of independent trials = No. of candidates in the group = 6.

The probability function $f(x)$ of x successes in Binomial Distribution is

$$f(x) = {}^nC_x p^x q^{n-x} = {}^6C_x \left(\frac{3}{5}\right)^x \left(\frac{2}{5}\right)^{6-x} \quad (1)$$

$\therefore$ The required probability = the probability of at least 4 successes in 6 independent trials

$$= f(4) + f(5) + f(6)$$

$$= {}^6C_4\left(\frac{3}{5}\right)^4\left(\frac{2}{5}\right)^{6-4} + {}^6C_5\left(\frac{3}{5}\right)^5\left(\frac{2}{5}\right)^{6-5} + {}^6C_6\left(\frac{3}{5}\right)^6\left(\frac{2}{5}\right)^{6-6}$$

[Using (1)]

$$= 15 \times \frac{81}{625} \times \frac{4}{25} + 6 \times \frac{243}{3125} \times \frac{2}{5} + 1 \times \frac{729}{15625} \times 1$$

$$= \frac{4860 + 2916 + 729}{15625} = \frac{8505}{15625} = \mathbf{\frac{1701}{3125}}.$$

EXAMPLE 10. *Five coins are tossed* 3200 *times. Find the expected frequencies of the distribution of heads and tails and tabulate the result. Calculate the mean number of heads and standard deviation.* **[CA (Inter) May 1977]**

SOLUTION. Let 'getting a head by tossing a coin' be a success. Then $p =$ constant probability of success $= \frac{1}{2}, q = 1 - p = \frac{1}{2}$.

The expected frequencies are the successive terms of the Binomial expansion of $N(q+p)^n$.

Here $n = 5, N = 3200, p = \frac{1}{2}, q = \frac{1}{2}$.

The Binomial expansion of $N(q+p)^n$, i.e., of 3200 $(\frac{1}{2} + \frac{1}{2})^5$

$$= 3200\left[\left(\frac{1}{2}\right)^5 + {}^5C_1\left(\frac{1}{2}\right)^{5-1}\left(\frac{1}{2}\right)^1 + {}^5C_2\left(\frac{1}{2}\right)^{5-2}\left(\frac{1}{2}\right)^2 + {}^5C_3\left(\frac{1}{2}\right)^{5-3}\left(\frac{1}{2}\right)^3 + {}^5C_4\left(\frac{1}{2}\right)^{5-4}\left(\frac{1}{2}\right)^4 + {}^5C_5\left(\frac{1}{2}\right)^{5-5}\left(\frac{1}{2}\right)^5\right]$$

$$= 3200\left[\left(\frac{1}{2}\right)^5 + 5\left(\frac{1}{2}\right)^5 + 10\left(\frac{1}{2}\right)^5 + 10\left(\frac{1}{2}\right)^5 + 5\left(\frac{1}{2}\right)^5 + \left(\frac{1}{2}\right)^5\right]$$

$$= 3200 \times \left(\frac{1}{2}\right)^5 [1 + 5 + 10 + 10 + 5 + 1]$$

$$= 100[1 + 5 + 10 + 10 + 5 + 1] = 100 + 500 + 1000 + 1000 + 500 + 100.$$

Success (x): (No. of heads)	0	1	2	3	4	5	Total
Failures: (No. of tails)	5	4	3	2	1	0	
Frequency (f) :	100	500	1000	1000	500	100	3200

Mean number of success $(\bar{x}) = \frac{\Sigma fx}{\Sigma f} = \frac{8000}{3200} = \mathbf{2.5}$.

[OTHERWISE. Mean $= np = 5 \times \frac{1}{2} = 2.5$.]

S.D. $(\sigma) = \sqrt{npq} = \sqrt{5 \times \frac{1}{2} \times \frac{1}{2}} = \frac{\sqrt{5}}{2} = \mathbf{1.12}$.]

EXAMPLE 11. *If a variable is binomially distributed (with parameters n and p), determine its mean, variance and standard deviation. Find the probability that in a family of five children there will be* (i) *at least one boy;* (ii) *at least one boy and one girl* (Assume that the probability of a female birth is $\frac{1}{2}$). **[ICWAI (Final) December 1976, '92; C.U. B. Com. (Hons.) 1994]**

SOLUTION. The probability function of Binomial Distribution is
$f(x) = {}^nC_x p^x q^{n-x}; x = 0, 1, 2, \cdots, n$ where n is finite.

$$\text{Mean} = E(x) = \sum_{x=0}^{n} x f(x) = \sum_{x=0}^{n} x \cdot {}^nC_x p^x q^{n-x}$$
$$= 0 \cdot {}^nC_0 p^0 q^n + 1 \cdot {}^nC_1 p^1 q^{n-1} + 2 \cdot {}^nC_2 p^2 q^{n-2} + 3 \cdot {}^nC_3 p^3 q^{n-3} + \cdots + n \cdot {}^nC_n p^n q^0$$
$$= 0 + npq^{n-1} + 2 \cdot \frac{n(n-1)}{1 \times 2} \cdot p^2 q^{n-2} + 3 \cdot \frac{n(n-1)(n-2)}{1 \times 2 \times 3} \cdot p^3 q^{n-3} + \cdots + np^n$$
$$= np\left[q^{n-1} + \frac{(n-1)}{1} pq^{n-2} + \frac{(n-1)(n-2)}{1 \times 2} p^2 q^{n-3} + \cdots + p^{n-1}\right]$$
$$= np\left[q^{n-1} + {}^{n-1}C_1 p^1 q^{(n-1)-1} + {}^{(n-1)}C_2 p^2 q^{(n-1)-2} + \cdots + p^{n-1}\right]$$
$$= np(q+p)^{n-1} = np(1)^{n-1} \qquad [\because \quad q + p = 1]$$
$$= \mathbf{np}. \qquad \therefore \quad \textbf{Mean} = \mathbf{np}.$$

Variance $= E(x^2) - \{E(x)\}^2$.

$$\text{Now } E(x^2) = \sum_{x=0}^{n} x^2 f(x) = \sum_{x=0}^{n} \{x(x-1) + x\} f(x) = \sum_{x=0}^{n} x(x-1) f(x) + \sum_{x=0}^{n} x f(x)$$
$$= \sum_{x=0}^{n} x(x-1) {}^nC_x p^x q^{n-x} + E(x)$$
$$= 0 + 0 + 2.1 \cdot {}^nC_2 p^2 q^{n-2} + 3.2 \cdot {}^nC_3 p^3 q^{n-3} + 4.3 \cdot {}^nC_4 p^4 q^{n-4} + \cdots + n(n-1) {}^nC_n p^n q^0 + E(x)$$
$$= 2 \cdot \frac{n(n-1)}{1 \times 2} p^2 q^{n-2} + 3.2 \cdot \frac{n(n-1)(n-2)}{1 \times 2 \times 3} p^3 q^{n-3} + 4.3 \cdot \frac{n(n-1)(n-2)(n-3)}{1 \times 2 \times 3 \times 4} p^4 q^{n-4} + \cdots + n(n-1)p^n + E(x)$$
$$= n(n-1)p^2\left[q^{n-2} + \frac{(n-2)}{1} p^1 q^{n-3} + \frac{(n-2)(n-3)}{1 \times 2} p^2 q^{n-4} + \cdots + p^{n-2}\right] + E(x)$$
$$= n(n-1)p^2\left[q^{n-2} + {}^{n-2}C_1 p^1 q^{n-3} + {}^{n-2}C_2 p^2 q^{n-4} + \cdots + p^{n-2}\right] + E(x)$$
$$= n(n-1)p^2(q+p)^{n-2} + E(x) = n(n-1)p^2(1)^{n-2} + np = n(n-1)p^2 + np.$$

$\therefore$ Variance $= n(n-1)p^2 + np - (np)^2 = n^2p^2 - np^2 + np - n^2p^2 = np(1-p) = \mathbf{npq}$.

$\therefore$ Standard deviation $= \sqrt{npq}$. **[C.U. M. Com. 1985]**

2ND PART. Let the event of a child being a boy be a 'success'. Then the occurrence of a female would be a 'failure'.

Here $q = \frac{1}{2}, p = 1 - q = 1 - \frac{1}{2} = \frac{1}{2}$, and $n = 5$.

(i) The probability that there will be no boy $= {}^5C_0 (\frac{1}{2})^0 (\frac{1}{2})^5 = \frac{1}{32}$.

Hence the required probability that there will be at least one boy $= 1 - \frac{1}{32} = \frac{31}{32}$.

(ii) In a family of 5 children, at least one boy and one girl can occur in the following mutually exclusive forms: (1) 1 boy and 4 girls; (2) 2 boys and 3 girls; (3) 3 boys and 2 girls; (4) 4 boys and 1 girl.

Hence the required probability of at least 1 boy and 1 girl

$$= {}^5C_1 \left(\frac{1}{2}\right)^1 \left(\frac{1}{2}\right)^4 + {}^5C_2 \left(\frac{1}{2}\right)^2 \left(\frac{1}{2}\right)^3 + {}^5C_3 \left(\frac{1}{2}\right)^3 \left(\frac{1}{2}\right)^2 + {}^5C_4 \left(\frac{1}{2}\right)^4 \left(\frac{1}{2}\right)^1$$

$$= 5 \times \frac{1}{32} + 10 \times \frac{1}{32} + 10 \times \frac{1}{32} + 5 \times \frac{1}{32} = \frac{30}{32} = \mathbf{\frac{15}{16}}.$$

2.3. POISSON DISTRIBUTION

Poisson Distribution is a discrete (countably infinite) probability distribution and is defined by the probability function

$$\mathbf{f(x) = \frac{e^{-m} m^x}{\lfloor x}}, \quad \mathbf{(x = 0, 1, 2, 3, \cdots)} \tag{1}$$

where m is a positive constant called the parameter of the distribution and $e = 2.71828$ *approximately.* $\left[e = 1 + \frac{1}{\lfloor 1} + \frac{1}{\lfloor 2} + \frac{1}{\lfloor 3} + \cdots \text{ to } \infty.\right]$

It was discovered by a French mathematician S.D. Poisson in 1837. It is widely used in statistical work. Poisson distribution is the limiting form of the Binomial Distribution when the number of trials n becomes sufficiently large and the probability p of success in a trial very small, where $np = m$ is a positive constant. [For proof see Art. 5.3.1.]

Examples of Poisson Distribution

(i) The number of telephone calls per minute at a switch board.

(ii) The number of printing mistakes per page in a large text.

(iii) The number of cars passing a certain point in one minute.

(iv) The number of particles emitted by a radio-active substance.

(v) The number of persons born blind per year in a large city.

(vi) The number of typographical errors made by a typist in a large number of pages.

(vii) The number of defective electric bulbs manufactured by a reputed company.

EXTENSION. If a series of trials is repeated N times, the expected frequency of x successes is $Nf(x) = N \cdot \frac{e^{-m} \cdot m^x}{\lfloor x}$.

2.3.1. Poisson Distribution as a Limit of the Binomial Distribution

If in the Binomial Distribution, the number of trials n becomes very large and the probability p of success in a trial very small where $np = m$ remains constant (i.e., if $n \to \infty, p \to 0$, where $np = m =$ constant), then the Binomial Distribution tends to Poisson Distribution as shown below.

In case of Binomial Distribution, the probability $P(x)$ of x successes in a series of n independent trials is given by

$$P(x) = {}^nC_x p^x q^{n-x}, \quad \text{where } p + q = 1$$
$$= \frac{n(n-1)(n-2)\cdots(n-x+1)}{\lfloor x} \cdot p^x q^{n-x}.$$

$$\text{Let } np = m, \text{ or, } p = \frac{m}{n}; \quad \therefore \quad q = 1 - p = 1 - \frac{m}{n}.$$

$$\therefore \quad P(x) = \frac{n(n-1)(n-2)\cdots(n-x+1)}{\lfloor x} \cdot \left(\frac{m}{n}\right)^x \cdot \left(1 - \frac{m}{n}\right)^{n-x}$$
$$= \frac{1\cdot(1-\frac{1}{n})(1-\frac{2}{n})\cdots(1-\frac{x-1}{n})}{\lfloor x} \cdot m^x \cdot \frac{(1-\frac{m}{n})^n}{(1-\frac{m}{n})^x}.$$

Now, let $n \to \infty$, then since x, m are fixed and $\frac{1}{n} \to 0$,

$\therefore \quad 1-\frac{1}{n}, 1-\frac{2}{n}, \cdots, (1-\frac{x-1}{n}), (1-\frac{m}{n})^x$ all tend to 1, and $\lim\limits_{n\to\infty}(1-\frac{m}{n})^n = \lim\limits_{N\to-\infty}(1+\frac{1}{N})^{-mN}$ $= \left\{\lim\limits_{N\to-\infty}(1+\frac{1}{N})^N\right\}^{-m} = e^{-m}$, where $-\frac{m}{n} = \frac{1}{N}$, or, $N = -\frac{n}{m}$ and $N \to -\infty$ as $n \to \infty$.

Hence, in the limit, when $n \to \infty$ $(p \to 0, np = m)$, we get

$$\lim_{n\to\infty} \cdot P(x) = \frac{m^x}{\lfloor x} \cdot e^{-m} = \frac{e^{-m} \cdot m^x}{\lfloor x}.$$

Writing $f(x)$ for $\lim\limits_{n\to\infty} P(x)$, we have

$$\mathbf{f(x) = \frac{e^{-x} \cdot m^x}{\lfloor x}}, \quad \textbf{where } \mathbf{x = 0, 1, 2, 3, \cdots}$$

Poisson Distribution which is a discrete probability distribution in which the variable x assumes an *infinite set of values* $0, 1, 2, 3, \cdots$ with probabilities $f(0), f(1), f(2), f(3), \cdots$ is given by

x	0	1	2	3	$\cdots$	Total
$f(x)$	e^{-m}	$(e^{-m} \cdot m)/3\lfloor 1$	$(e^{-m} \cdot m^2)/3\lfloor 2$	$(e^{-m} \cdot m^3)/3\lfloor 3$	$\cdots$	1

NOTE. The distribution is completely known when the value of the parameter m is known. The value of m usually lies between 0.1 and 10.

The Poisson Distribution explains the behaviour of those discrete random variables for which the probability of occurrence of an event is *small* and the total number of possible cases is *very large*.

2.3.2. Properties of Poisson Distribution

1. *Poisson Distribution is a discrete probability distribution* in which the random variable x assumes the infinite set of values 0, 1, 2, 3, ...

2. Mean $= m =$ parameter of the distribution, Variance $= m$, S.D. $(\sigma) = \sqrt{m}$, Skewness $= \frac{1}{\sqrt{m}}$ and Kurtosis $= \frac{1}{m}$.

3. The mode of Poisson Distribution is that value of x which occurs with the largest probability. It may have either one or two modes. If m is not an integer, the mode is the integral value between $m-1$ and m. But if m is an integer, then there are two modes which are $m-1, m$.

4. If x and y be two independent Poisson variates with parameters m_1 and m_2 respectively, then their sum $x+y$ is also a Poisson variate with parameter m_1+m_2.

5. The first, second, and third raw moments are respectively m, m^2+m, m^3+3m^2+m.

EXAMPLE 12. *A random variables x follows Poisson Distribution with parameter* 4. *Find the probabilities that x assumes the values* (i) 0, 1, 2, 4; (ii) *less than* 2; (iii) *at least* 3.
[Given then $e^{-4} = 0.0183$.]

SOLUTION. For the Poisson Distribution with parameter m, the probability $f(x)$ of x successes is

$$f(x) = \frac{e^{-m} \cdot m^x}{\lfloor x} = \frac{e^{-4} \cdot 4^x}{\lfloor x} \quad [\because \quad m = 4].$$

(i) Here $x = 0, 1, 2, 4$.

$$\therefore \quad f(0) = \frac{e^{-4} \cdot 4^0}{\lfloor 0} = \frac{e^{-4} \cdot 1}{1} = \mathbf{0.0183}; \qquad f(2) = \frac{e^{-4} \cdot 4^2}{\lfloor 2} = \frac{0.0183 \times 16}{2} = \mathbf{0.1464};$$

$$f(1) = \frac{e^{-4} \cdot 4^1}{\lfloor 1} = \frac{0.0183 \times 4}{1} = \mathbf{0.0732}; \qquad f(4) = \frac{e^{-4} \cdot 4^4}{\lfloor 4} = \frac{0.0183 \times 32}{3} = \mathbf{0.1952}.$$

(ii) Here "less than 2" means "either 0 or 1", i.e., $x = 0$, or 1. Hence the required probability $= f(0) + f(1) = 0.0183 + 0.0732 = \mathbf{0.0915}$.

(iii) Here "at least 3" means "either 3, or 4, or 5, or ...".
Hence the required probability that x assumes at least 3 is

$$\begin{aligned} &= f(3) + f(4) + f(5) + \cdots \\ &= 1 - \{f(0) + f(1) + f(2)\} \qquad [\because \quad f(0) + f(1) + f(2) + f(3) + \cdots = 1] \\ &= 1 - (0.0183 + 0.0732 + 0.1464) = 1 - 0.2379 = \mathbf{0.7621}. \end{aligned}$$

EXAMPLE 13. *If* 5% *of the electric bulbs manufactured by a company are defective, use Poisson Distribution to find the probability that in a sample of* 100 *bulbs* (i) *none is defective,* (ii) 5 *bulbs will be defective.* [Given $e^{-5} = 0.007$.] **[ICWAI (Final) December 1979]**

SOLUTION. Let the occurrence of a defective bulb be a success. Then $p = \frac{5}{100} = 0.05$ (small) and $n = 100$ (large).

$\therefore \quad m = np = 100 \times 0.05 = 5$ which is the parameter of Poisson Distribution.

For Poisson Distribution with parameter $m = 5$, the probability of x successes is

$$f(x) = \frac{e^{-m} \cdot m^x}{\lfloor x} = \frac{e^{-5} \cdot 5^x}{\lfloor x}.$$

(i) Since none is defective; $\therefore \quad x = 0$.

Hence the required probability that none is defective $= f(0) = \frac{e^{-5}.5^{\circ}}{\lfloor 0} = \frac{e^{-5}\,1}{1} = e^{-5} = \mathbf{0.007}$.

(ii) Since 5 bulbs will be defective; $\therefore\quad x = 5$.

Hence the required probability that 5 bulbs will be defective $= f(5) = \frac{e^{-5}.5^5}{\lfloor 5} = \frac{0.007 \times 625}{24}$ $= \mathbf{0.182}$.

EXAMPLE 14. *Records show that the probability is* 0.00002 *that a car will have a flat tyre while driving over a certain bridge. Use the Poisson probability distribution to determine the probability that among* 20,000 *cars driven over this bridge, not more than one will have a flat tyre.*
[Given $e^{-0.2} = 0.819, e^{-0.4} = 0.670$.] **[CA May 1990]**

SOLUTION. Here $p = 0.00002$ and $n = 20,000$ so that m = parameter $= np = 0.00002 \times 20,000$ $= 0.4$.

$\therefore$ The Poisson probability function is

$$f(x) = \frac{e^{-m} \cdot m^x}{\lfloor x} = \frac{e^{-0.4} \cdot (0.4)^x}{\lfloor x}, \quad \text{where } x = 0, 1, 2, 3.$$

The required probability that not more than one will have a flat tyre $= f(0) + f(1)$

$$= \frac{e^{-0.4} \cdot (0.4)^{\circ}}{\lfloor 0} + \frac{e^{-0.4} \cdot (0.4)^1}{\lfloor 1} = \frac{0.670 \times 1}{1} + \frac{0.670 \times 0.4}{\lfloor 1}$$
$$= 0.670 + 0.2680 = 0.9380 = \mathbf{0.938}.$$

EXAMPLE 15. *Find the probability that at most* 5 *defective bolts will be found in a box of* 200 *bolts, if it is known that* 2 *percent of such bolts are expected to be defective.* (*You may take the distribution to be Poisson*). *Take* $e^{-4} = 0.0183$. **[ICWAI (Final) June 1980]**

SOLUTION. Let the occurrence of a defective bolt be a success.

Then p = Probability that a bolt drawn at random is defective $= \frac{2}{100} = 0.02$ which is small and n = total no. of bolts in the box = 200 which is large.

Also $m = np = 200 \times 0.02 = 4$ which is a finite constant.

$\therefore$ The number of defective bolts (i.e., x) approximately follows Poisson Distribution. The probability $f(x)$ of x successes (i.e., defectives) is given by

$$f(x) = \frac{e^{-m} \cdot m^x}{\lfloor x} = \frac{e^{-4} \cdot 4^x}{\lfloor x}.$$

By "at most 5" we mean "either 0, or 1, or 2, or 3, or 4, or 5", i.e., $x = 0$, or 1, or 2, or 3, or 4, or 5.

Hence the required probability that at most 5 bolts are defective

$$= f(0) + f(1) + f(2) + f(3) + f(4) + f(5)$$
$$= \frac{e^{-4} \cdot 4^{\circ}}{\lfloor 0} + \frac{e^{-4} \cdot 4^1}{\lfloor 1} + \frac{e^{-4} \cdot 4^2}{\lfloor 2} + \frac{e^{-4} \cdot 4^3}{\lfloor 3} + \frac{e^{-4} \cdot 4^4}{\lfloor 4} + \frac{e^{-4} \cdot 4^5}{\lfloor 5}$$
$$= e^{-4}\left(1 + \frac{4}{1} + \frac{16}{2} + \frac{64}{6} + \frac{256}{24} + \frac{1024}{120}\right)$$
$$= 0.0183\left(1 + 4 + 8 + \frac{32}{3} + \frac{32}{3} + \frac{128}{15}\right) = 0.0183 \times \frac{643}{15} = \mathbf{0.784}.$$

EXAMPLE 16. *The probability that a man aged 45 years will die within a year is* 0.012. *What is the probability that out of* 10 *such men at least* 9 *will reach their forty-sixth birthday?* [Given $e^{-0.12} = 0.88692$.] **[ICWAI December 1991]**

SOLUTION. Since the probability $p = 0.012$ that a man aged 45 years will die within a year is very small, we have to use *Poisson distribution,* m = parameter = $np = 10 \times 0.012 = 0.12$.

For the *Poisson Distribution,* the probability function $f(x)$ is given by

$$f(x) = \frac{e^{-m} \cdot m^x}{\underline{|x}} = \frac{e^{-0.12} \cdot (0.12)^x}{\underline{|x}},$$

where x is the no. of men that will die within a year.

$$f(0) = \frac{e^{-0.12} \cdot (0.12)^\circ}{\underline{|0}} = \frac{0.88692 \times 1}{1} = 0.88692$$

$$\text{and} \quad f(1) = \frac{e^{-0.12} \cdot (0.12)^1}{\underline{|1}} = \frac{0.88692 \times 0.12}{\underline{|1}} = 0.10643.$$

Hence the required probability that at least 9 out of 10 men will reach their 46th birthday

= Probability that 9 will not die + Probability that 10 will not die
= Probability that 1 man will die + Probability that nobody will die
= $f(1) + f(0) = 0.10643 + 0.88692 =$ **0.99335**.

[OTHERWISE. Use *Binomial Distribution:* $f(x) = {}^{10}C_x \cdot p^x \cdot q^{n-x}$; here $p = 1 - 0.012 = 0.988$, $q = 0.012, x = 9, 10$.]

EXAMPLE 17. *Between the hours of* 2 *and* 4 *p.m. the average number of phone calls per minute coming into the switch board of a company is* 2.5. *Find the probability that during one particular minute there will be no phone call at all.* [Given $e^{-2} = 0.13523$ and $e^{-0.5} = 0.60650$.]

[ICWAI (Final) June 1976]

SOLUTION. Let the random variable x represent the number of phone calls received per minute between 2 and 4 p.m. Then x follows Poisson Distribution with parameter, say m. For a Poisson Distribution, m = parameter = mean, or average; $\therefore \; m = 2.5$.

The probability of x phone calls is

$$f(x) = \frac{e^{-m} \cdot m^x}{\underline{|x}} = \frac{e^{-2.5} \cdot (2.5)^x}{\underline{|x}}.$$

Here $x = 0$; $\therefore \; f(0) = \frac{e^{-2.5} \cdot (2.5)^\circ}{\underline{|0}} = e^{-2.5} = e^{-2+(-0.5)} = e^{-2} \cdot e^{-0.5} = 0.13534 \times 0.60650$ $= 0.082083$.

Hence the required probability that there will be no phone call $= f(0) =$ **0.082083**.

EXAMPLE 18. *If a random variable x follows a Poisson Distribution such that probability $(x = 1)$ = probability $(x = 2)$, find the mean and variance. Find also probability $(x = 0)$.*

[ICWAI; C.U. B. Com. (Hons.) 1982]

SOLUTION. For Poisson Distribution, the probability function is $f(x) = \frac{e^{-m} \cdot m^x}{\lfloor x}$.

$\therefore \quad P(x=1) = f(1) = \frac{e^{-m} \cdot m^1}{\lfloor 1} = me^{-m}$ and $P(x=2) = f(2) = \frac{e^{-m} \cdot m^2}{\lfloor 2} = \frac{m^2 e^{-m}}{2}$.

Since $P(x=1) = P(x=2)$; $\therefore \quad me^{-m} = \frac{m^2 e^{-m}}{2}$, or, $\frac{m}{2} = 1$, or, $\mathbf{m = 2}$.

$\therefore$ **Mean = m = 2** and **Variance = m = 2.**

Hence $P(x=0) = f(0) = \frac{e^{-m} \cdot m^\circ}{\lfloor 0} = \frac{e^{-m} \cdot 1}{1} = e^{-2}$.

EXAMPLE 19. *If X is a Poisson variable such that $P(X=2) = 9P(X=4) + 90P(X=6)$, find the mean and the variance of X.* **[CA May 1989]**

SOLUTION. For Poisson Distribution, the probability function is $f(x) = \frac{e^{-m} \cdot m^x}{\lfloor x}$, where m is mean (parameter) of the distribution.

Now $P(X=2) = f(2) = \frac{e^{-m} \cdot m^2}{\lfloor 2}$, $P(X=4) = f(4) = \frac{e^{-m} \cdot m^4}{\lfloor 4}$ and $P(X=6) = f(6) = \frac{e^{-m} \cdot m^6}{\lfloor 6}$.

Since $P(X=2) = 9P(X=4) + 90P(X=6)$, we have

$$\frac{e^{-m} \cdot m^2}{\lfloor 2} = 9 \cdot \frac{e^{-m} \cdot m^4}{\lfloor 4} + 90 \cdot \frac{e^{-m} \cdot m^6}{\lfloor 6}, \quad \text{or,} \quad \frac{1}{\lfloor 2} = \frac{9m^2}{\lfloor 4} + \frac{90m^4}{\lfloor 6}$$

$$\text{or,} \quad \frac{1}{2} = \frac{3m^2}{8} + \frac{m^4}{8}, \quad \text{or,} \quad m^4 + 3m^2 - 4 = 0, \quad \text{or,} \quad (m^2+4)(m^2-1) = 0.$$

$\therefore$ Either $m^2 + 4 = 0$, or, $m^2 - 1 = 0$. But m cannot be imaginary.

$\therefore$ $m^2 = 1$, or, $m = 1$, taking positive sign.

Hence **mean = m = 1** and **Variance = m = 1.**

EXAMPLE 20. *Assuming that the probability of a fatal accident in a factory during the year is $\frac{1}{1200}$. Calculate the probability that in a factory employing* 300 *workers, there will be at least two fatal accidents in a year.* ($e^{0.25} = 0.7788$). **[ICWAI December 1984]**

SOLUTION. Here p = probability of a fatal accident during the year $= \frac{1}{1200}$, and $n = 300$.

Let the occurrence of a fatal accident be a success.

Then m = the parameter of Poisson Distribution $= np = 300 \times \frac{1}{1200} = \frac{1}{4} = 0.25$.

For Poisson Distribution with parameter $m = 0.25$, the probability of x successes (i.e., x fatal accidents) is

$$f(x) = \frac{e^{-m} \cdot m^x}{\lfloor x} = \frac{e^{-0.25} \cdot (0.25)^x}{\lfloor x} \qquad (1)$$

$\therefore$ The required probability that there will be at least two fatal accidents in a year

$$= f(2) + f(3) + f(4) + \cdots = 1 - \{f(0) + f(1)\} = 1 - \left\{\frac{e^{-0.25}(0.25)^\circ}{\lfloor 0} + \frac{e^{-0.25}(0.25)^1}{\lfloor 1}\right\}$$

$= 1 - \{e^{-0.25} + e^{-0.25}(0.25)\}$ [Using (1)]

$= 1 - e^{-0.25}(1 + 0.25) = 1 - 0.7788 \times 1.25 = 1 - 0.9735 = \mathbf{0.0265}$.

EXAMPLE 21. *Using Poisson approximation to the Binomial Distribution, solve the following problem:*

If the probability that an individual suffers a bad reaction from a particular injection is 0.001, *determine the probability that out of* 2,000 *individuals* (i) *exactly, three,* (ii) *more than two individuals will suffer a bad reaction.* [Given $e^2 = 7.4$.] **[ICWAI (Final) June 1975]**

SOLUTION. Let the random variable x represent the number of individuals who suffers from bad reaction. Then x follows Binomial Distribution with $n = 2,000$ and $p = 0.001$. But since p is small and n is large, and $m = np = 2000 \times 0.001 = 2$ is positive constant, the Binomial Distribution can be approximated to Poisson Distribution with parameter $m = 2$.

For Poisson Distribution, the probability function is $f(x) = \frac{e^{-m} \cdot m^x}{\lfloor x} = \frac{e^{-2} \cdot 2^x}{\lfloor x}$.

(i) Since exactly 3 individuals suffer bad reaction; $\therefore \quad x = 3$.

Hence the probability that exactly 3 individuals suffer a bad reaction $= f(3) = \frac{e^{-2} \cdot 2^3}{\lfloor 3} = \frac{8}{6e^2}$ $= \frac{4}{3 \times 7.4} =$ **0.18018**.

(ii) Here $x = 3$, or 4, or 5, or 6, or ...

Hence the required probability that more than two individuals suffer bad reaction

$$\begin{aligned}
&= f(3) + f(4) + f(5) + \cdots \\
&= 1 - \{f(0) + f(1) + f(2)\} \\
&= 1 - \left\{\frac{e^{-2} \cdot 2^0}{\lfloor 0} + \frac{e^{-2} \cdot 2^1}{\lfloor 1} + \frac{e^{-2} \cdot 2^2}{\lfloor 2}\right\} \\
&= 1 - \left\{\frac{1}{e^2} + \frac{2}{e^2} + \frac{2}{e^2}\right\} = 1 - \frac{5}{e^2} \\
&= 1 - \frac{5}{7.4} = \frac{2.4}{7.4} = \mathbf{0.3243}.
\end{aligned}$$

EXAMPLE 22. *Obtain the Mean and Variance of Poisson Distribution.*

[C.U. M. Com. 1974; B. Com. (Hons.) 1995]

SOLUTION. For Poisson Distribution, the probability function is

$$f(x) = \frac{e^{-m} \cdot m^x}{\lfloor x}; \quad x = 0, 1, 2, 3, \cdots, \infty.$$

$$\begin{aligned}
\text{Mean} = E(x) &= \sum_{x=0}^{\infty} x f(x) = \sum_{x=0}^{\infty} x \cdot \frac{e^{-m} \cdot m^x}{\lfloor x} = e^{-m} \sum_{x=0}^{\infty} \frac{x \cdot m^x}{\lfloor x} \\
&= e^{-m}\left[0 + \frac{1 \cdot m^1}{\lfloor 1} + \frac{2 \cdot m^2}{\lfloor 2} + \frac{3 \cdot m^3}{\lfloor 3} + \cdots + \frac{r \cdot m^r}{\lfloor r} + \cdots\right] \\
&= e^{-m}\left[m + \frac{m^2}{\lfloor 1} + \frac{m^3}{\lfloor 2} + \cdots + \frac{m^r}{\lfloor r-1} + \cdots\right] \\
&= me^{-m}\left[1 + \frac{m}{\lfloor 1} + \frac{m^2}{\lfloor 2} + \cdots + \frac{m^{r-1}}{\lfloor r-1} + \cdots\right] \\
&= me^{-m} \cdot e^m = me^0 = \mathbf{m}.
\end{aligned}$$

$$\text{Variance} = E(x^2) - \{E(x)\}^2.$$

$$\text{Now } E(x^2) = \sum_{x=0}^{\infty} x^2 f(x) = \sum_{x=0}^{\infty} \{x(x-1)+x\} \cdot \frac{e^{-m} \cdot m^x}{\underline{|x}}$$

$$= \sum_{x=0}^{\infty} x(x-1)\frac{e^{-m} \cdot m^x}{\underline{|x}} + \sum_{x=0}^{\infty} x\frac{e^{-m}m^x}{\underline{|x}}$$

$$= \sum_{x=0}^{\infty} x(x-1)\frac{e^{-m} \cdot m^x}{\underline{|x}} + m, \qquad [\because \; E(x) = m]$$

$$= e^{-m}\sum_{x=0}^{\infty} \frac{x(x-1)m^2 \cdot m^{x-2}}{x(x-1)\underline{|x-2}} + m = e^{-m} \cdot m^2 \sum_{x=2}^{\infty} \frac{m^{x-2}}{\underline{|x-2}} + m$$

$$= m^2 e^{-m}\left[\frac{m^\circ}{\underline{|0}} + \frac{m^1}{\underline{|1}} + \frac{m^2}{\underline{|2}} + \frac{m^3}{\underline{|3}} + \cdots\right] + m$$

$$= m^2 e^{-m}\left[1 + \frac{m}{\underline{|1}} + \frac{m^2}{\underline{|2}} + \frac{m^3}{\underline{|3}} + \cdots\right] + m$$

$$= m^2 e^{-m} \cdot e^m + m = m^2 + m.$$

$\therefore$ Variance $= m^2 + m - (m)^2 = \mathbf{m}$.

2.4. CONTINUOUS PROBABILITY DISTRIBUTION

In discrete probability distributions (viz., Binomial and Poisson Distributions) the random variable can assume either a finite set of values or at most an enumerably (or countably) infinite set of values. But a continuous distribution is one in which the random variable x can assume any value between certain limits a and b. The number of all possible values is then uncountably infinite and it is useless to speak of the probability of any particular value, since we cannot associate a finite probability with each value. In this case, we consider the probability that the value of the variable will fall within a specified interval in the range of the continuous random variable. If the probability that the value of the variable x falling in an infinitesimal interval $x - \frac{1}{2}dx$ to $x + \frac{1}{2}dx$ can be expressed as $f(x)dx$, or $P(x - \frac{1}{2}dx \leq X \leq x + \frac{1}{2}dx) = f(x)dx$, then the continuous function $f(x)$ defines the continuous probability distribution of the random variable x. $f(x)$ is called the *probability density function* or *simply density function* of x and it satisfies the conditions: (i) $f(x) \geq 0$ for all x and (ii) $\int_{-\infty}^{\infty} f(x)dx = 1$, i.e., the total area under the curve $y = f(x)$ bounded by the x-axis $= 1$.

The probability that x lies in the interval $c \leq x \leq d$ is denoted by the symbol $P(c \leq x \leq d)$ and is defined by $P(c \leq x \leq d) = \int_c^d f(x)dx$ which represents the area under the curve $y = f(x)$ bounded by the x-axis and the ordinates $x = c$ and $x = d$.

The expectation (*or mean*) of x is defined by $E(x)$ = Expectation or Mean = $\int_{-\infty}^{\infty} xf(x)dx$, where the integral exists.

Expectation of $x^2 = E(x^2) = \int_{-\infty}^{\infty} x^2 f(x)dx$, and *Variance of* $x = E(x^2) - \{E(x)\}^2$ $= \int_{-\infty}^{\infty} x^2 \, f(x)dx - \{\int_{-\infty}^{\infty} xf(x)dx\}^2$, where all the integrals exist.

EXAMPLE 23. *Find the mean and variance of the p.d.f. given by* $f(x) = 12x^2(1-x)$ *for* $0 \leq x \leq 1, f(x) = 0$ *otherwise.* **[ICWAI June 1991]**

SOLUTION.

$$\text{Mean} = E(x) = \int_{-\infty}^{\infty} xf(x)dx = \int_{0}^{1} x \cdot 12x^2(1-x)dx \qquad [\because \ f(x) = 0 \text{ elsewhere}]$$

$$= 12\int_{0}^{1}(x^3 - x^4)dx = 12\left[\frac{x^4}{4} - \frac{x^5}{5}\right]_0^1 = 12\left(\frac{1}{4} - \frac{1}{5}\right) = 12 \times \frac{1}{20} = \frac{3}{5} = \mathbf{0.6}.$$

$$E(x^2) = \int_{-\infty}^{\infty} x^2 f(x)dx = \int_{0}^{1} x^2 \cdot 12x^2(1-x)dx = 12\int_{0}^{1}(x^4 - x^5)dx$$

$$= 12\left[\frac{x^5}{5} - \frac{x^6}{6}\right]_0^1 = 12\left(\frac{1}{5} - \frac{1}{6}\right) = 12^\circ \times \frac{1}{30} = \frac{2}{5} = 0.4.$$

$\therefore$ Variance of $x = E(x^2) - \{E(x)\}^2 = 0.4 - (0.6)^2 = 0.4 - 0.36 = \mathbf{0.04}$.

2.4.1. Normal Distribution (or Gaussian Distribution)

Normal (or Gaussian) Distribution is the most important continuous probability distribution in statistics and is defined by the probability density function (or simply density function)

$$\mathbf{f(x)} = \frac{\mathbf{1}}{\sigma\sqrt{\mathbf{2}\pi}} \cdot \mathbf{e}^{-[(\mathbf{x}-\mathbf{m})^2/2\sigma^2]}; \quad (-\infty < \mathbf{x} < \infty) \tag{1}$$

where m = mean, σ = standard deviation, $\pi = 3.1416$ or $\frac{22}{7}$, and $e = 2.71828$ approximately.

The curve representing the Normal Distribution (1) is called the *normal curve* and the total area bounded by the curve and the x-axis is one, i.e., $\int_{-\infty}^{\infty} f(x)dx = 1$.

The area under the curve between the ordinates $x = a$ and $x = b$, where $a < b$, represents the probability that x lies between a and b, i.e., $P(a < x < b)$.

Thus $\mathbf{P(a < x < b)}$ = area under the normal curve between the vertical lines $\mathbf{x = a}$ and $\mathbf{x = b}$, which is $\int_a^b \mathbf{f(x)dx}$.

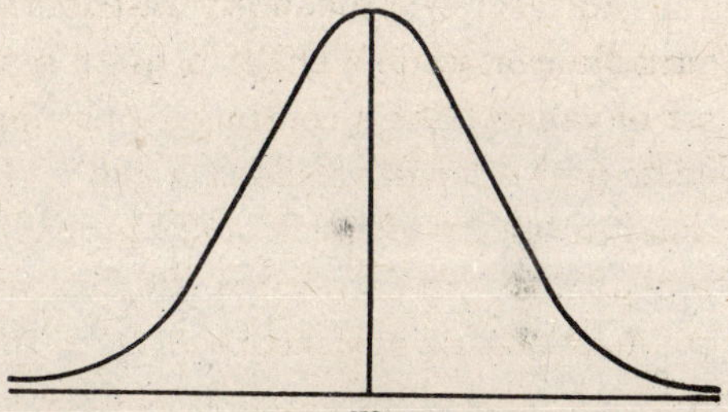

Fig 2.1

The curve is *symmetrical* about the mean (m) and bell-shaped and the two tails on the right and the left sides of the mean (m) extends to infinity. Clearly, Mean = Median = Mode.

Standard Normal Distribution

If we take $\frac{x-m}{\sigma} = z$ in (1), we obtain the **Standard Normal Distribution** with **mean zero** and S.D. (σ) = **1** defined by the **density function.**

$$p(z) = \frac{1}{\sqrt{2\pi}} \cdot e^{-(z^2/2)}; \quad (-\infty < z < \infty).$$

Here z is called the **standard normal variable** *with mean 0 and standard deviation 1 and in short, we say that $p(z)$ is $N(0,1)$.*

Area under Standard Normal Curve

A graph of the standard normal curve $y = p(z)$ is shown in the adjoining figure. The percentage distribution of area under the curve is also indicated in the figure.

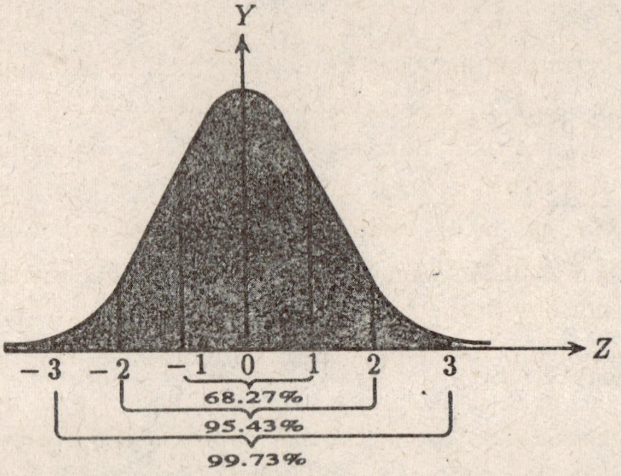

Fig 2.2

The areas included between the vertical lines $z = -1$ and $z = +1; z = -2$ and $z = +2, z = -3$ and $z = +3$ are respectively 68.27%, 95.45% and 99.73% of the total area which is 1.

Let $\phi(z)$ = area under the standard normal curve to the left of the ordinate $z = \int_{-\infty}^{z} p(z)dz$ or $\int_{-\infty}^{z} \frac{1}{\sqrt{2\pi}} e^{-\frac{1}{2}z^2}$ then $\phi(-z)$ = area under the standard normal curve to the left of the ordinate $(-z) = \int_{-\infty}^{-z} p(z)dz = \frac{1}{\sqrt{2\pi}} \int_{-\infty}^{-z} e^{-\frac{1}{2}z^2} \cdot dz$ = area under the standard normal curve to the right of the ordinate z [From symmetry of the standard normal curve about $z = 0$] $= 1 - \phi(z) = 1 - \int_{-\infty}^{z} p(z)dz$.

[$\because$ Sum of the areas under the standard normal curve to the left and to the right of the ordinate z is 1.]

The values of $\phi(z)$ for positive values of z only (i.e., the areas under this curve bounded by the ordinates at $z = 0$ and any positive value of z) are given in the Statistical Table at the end of the book.

From symmetry of the standard normal curve about $z = 0$, we have

(Area between z = − c and z = 0) = (area between z = 0 and z = c).

$P(c < z < d)$ = area under the standard normal curve between the lines $z = c$ and $z = d$ is $\int_{c}^{d} p(z)dz = \frac{1}{\sqrt{2\pi}} \int_{c}^{d} e^{-\frac{1}{2}z}dz$.

For the *Normal Distribution*, $P(c < x < d)$ = probability that x lies between c and $d = \phi(\frac{d-m}{\sigma}) - \phi(\frac{c-m}{\sigma}) = \phi(d') - \phi(c')$ where $c' = \frac{c-m}{\sigma}$ and $d' = \frac{d-m}{\sigma}$ [using the relation $z = \frac{x-m}{\sigma}$].

Hence c' and d' are called the *standardized values* of c and d.

Properties of Normal Distribution

1. Normal Distribution is a continuous probability distribution having two parameters m and σ.

2. Mean $= m$; Standard Deviation $= \sigma$; Skewness = 0; Kurtosis = 0; Mean = Median = Mode $= m$.

3. The normal curve is bell-shaped and symmetrical about the line $x = m$, and the two tails of the curve on both sides of $x = m$ extends to infinity.

4. The quartiles Q_1 and Q_3 are equidistant from the mean m and $Q_1 = m - 0.67\sigma$, $Q_3 = m + 0.67\sigma$ approximately. Quartile Deviation $= 0.67\sigma$ and Mean Deviation $= 0.80\sigma$.

5. All odd order central moments are zero, i.e., $m_1 = m_3 = m_5 = \cdots = 0$.

Mean $(m) = A + m_1'$.

Even order moments are given by $m_{2r} = 1.3.5...(2r-1) \cdot \sigma^{2r}; r = 1, 2, 3, \cdots$; clearly $m_2 = 1 \cdot \sigma^2 = \sigma^2, m_4 = 1 \cdot 3\sigma^4 = 3\sigma^4$, etc.

Importance of the Normal Distribution

Normal Distribution plays a very important role in Statistical Theory and, in particular, in Sampling Theory. It has been found that:

1. Data obtained from Psychological, Physical and Biological measurements approximately follow Normal Distribution.

2. Distribution like Binomial, Poisson, etc., can be approximated to Normal Distribution.

3. For large samples, any statistic (i.e., sample mean, sample S.D., etc.) approximately follows Normal Distribution and as such it can be studied with the help of normal curve.

4. Normal curve is used to find confidence limits of the population parameters.

5. Normal Distributions are largely applied in statistical quality control in industry for finding control limits.

6. The theory of errors of observations in physical measurements are based on Normal Distribution.

EXAMPLE 24. *Find the area under the normal curve in the following cases using table:*

(i) *between* $z = 0$ *and* $z = 1.4$; (ii) *between* $z = -0.56$ *and* $z = 0$;
(iii) *between* $z = -0.45$ *and* $z = 2.42$; (iv) *between* $z = 0.75$ *and* $z = 1.96$.

SOLUTION.

(i) In the table given at the end of the book, proceed downward under column marked z on top until 1.4 is reached, and then proceed right, to column marked 0 on top.

The result obtained is **0.4192** which is the required area. Here 0.4192 represents the probability that z lies between 0 and 1.4, i.e., $P(0 \leq z \leq 1.4) = 0.4192$.

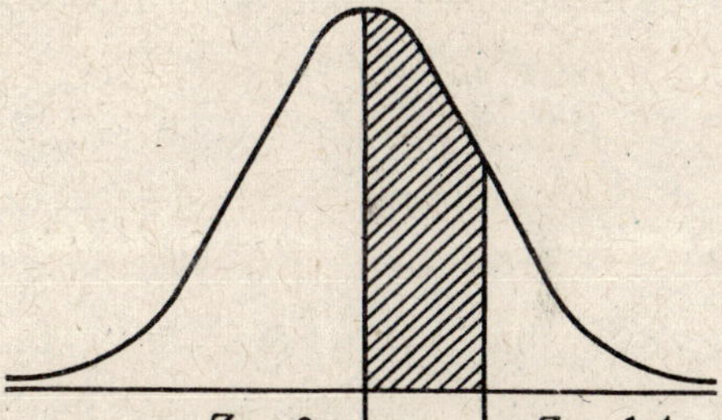

Fig 2.3

(ii) Required area = (area between $z = -0.56$ and $z = 0$) = (area between $z = 0$ and $z = 0.56$).

[by Symmetry]

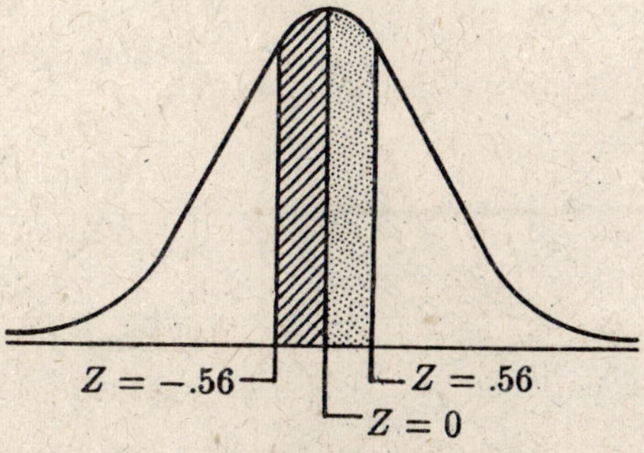

Fig 2.4

To find the area between $z = 0$ and $z = 0.56$ from the table I given at the end of the book, proceed downward under column marked z until 0.5 is reached. Then proceed right to column marked 6 on top.

The result obtained is **0.2123** which is the required area and it represents the probability that z lies between -0.56 and 0, i.e., $P(-0.56 \leq z \leq 0) = 0.2123$.

(iii) Required area = (area between $z = -.45$ and $z = 0$)+ (area between $z = 0$ and $z = 2.42$) = (area between $z = 0$ and $z = 0.45$) + (area between $z = 0$ and $z = 2.42$) [by Symmetry] = 0.1736 + 0.4922 [from table] = **0.6658.**

[Clearly, $P(-0.45 \leq z \leq 2.42) = 0.6658$.]

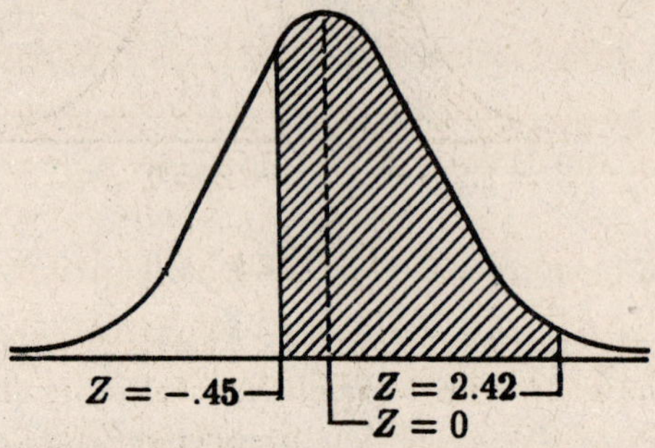

Fig 2.5

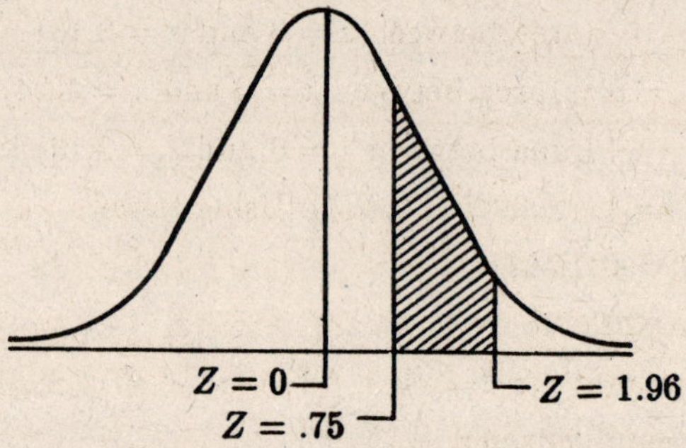

Fig 2.6

(iv) Required area = (area between $z = 0$ and $z = 1.96$) – (area between $z = 0$ and $z = 0.75$) = 0.4750 – 0.2734 [from table] = **0.2016.**

[Clearly, $P(0.75 \leq z \leq 1.96) = 0.2016$.]

EXAMPLE 25. *Find the probability that the standard normal variate is* (i) *less than* –0.8; (ii) *greater than* 1.76; (iii) *greater than* 2.13 *but less than* –1.24.

SOLUTION.

(i) Since the standard normal curve is symmetrical about $z = 0$;

∴ (area under the normal curve to the left of $z = 0$) = (area under the normal curve to the right of $z = 0$) = $\frac{1}{2}$ = 0.5.

Required probability $P(z < -0.8)$

= area under the normal curve to the left of $z = -0.8$

= (area to the left $z = 0$) – (area between $z = -0.8$ and $z = 0$)

= 0.5 – (area between $z = 0$ and $z = 0.8$) [by Symmetry]

= 0.5 – 0.2881 = **0.2119.**

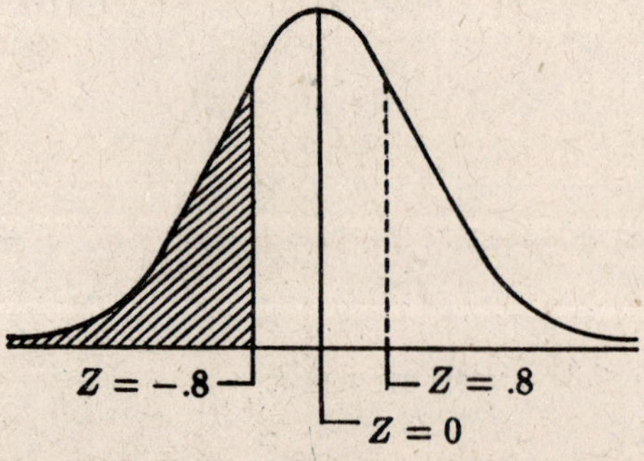

Fig 2.7

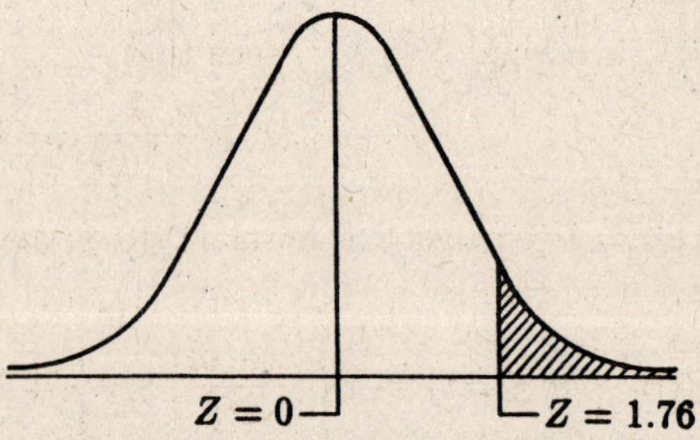

Fig 2.8

(ii) Required probability $P(z > 1.76)$ = area under the normal curve to the right of $z = 1.76$ = (area to the right of $z = 0$) – (area between $z = 0$ and $z = 1.76$) = 0.5 – 0.4607 = **0.0392.**

(iii) Required Probability

$= P(z > 2.13 \text{ and } z < -1.24)$

= total area under the standard normal curve

– (area between $z = -1.24$ and $z = 0$)

– (area between $z = 0$ and $z = 2.13$)

= 1 – (area between $z = 0$ and $z = 1.24$)

– (area between $z = 0$ and $z = 2.13$)

= 1 – 0.3925 – 0.4834 [Using table]

= **0.1241.**

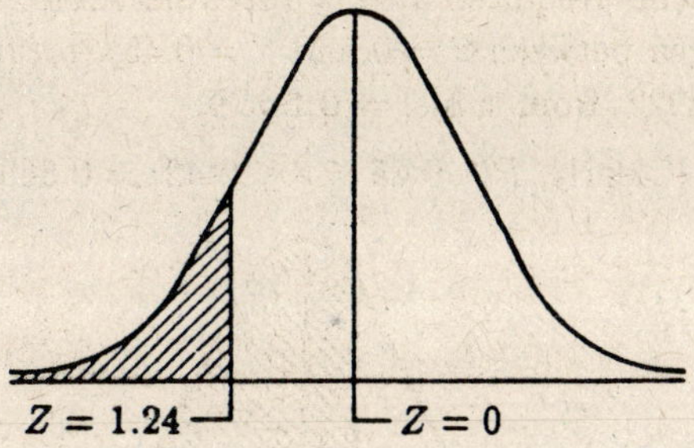

Fig 2.9

EXAMPLE 26.

(i) *Show that* $f(x) = \frac{5}{\sqrt{\pi}}e^{-25x^2}, -\infty < x < \infty$, *is the p.d.f. of a Normal Distribution with mean zero and variance* $\frac{1}{50}$. **[ICWAI December 1991]**

(ii) *For a Normal Distribution* $N(m, \sigma^2)$, *evaluate* $P\{|x - m| \leq 3\sigma\}$.
[*Given* $\int_0^3 \frac{1}{\sqrt{2\pi}}e^{-\frac{1}{2}t^2}\,dt = 0.4986$.] **[ICWAI December 1991]**

SOLUTION.

(i) The p.d.f. of a Normal Distribution $N(m, \sigma)$ is

$$f(x) = \frac{1}{\sigma\sqrt{2\pi}}e^{-\frac{(x-m)^2}{2\sigma^2}}; \quad -\infty < x < \infty. \tag{1}$$

By the question,

$$f(x) = \frac{5}{\sqrt{\pi}}e^{-25x^2}; \quad -\infty < x < \infty. \tag{2}$$

Comparing (1) and (2), we get

$$\frac{1}{\sigma\sqrt{2\pi}} = \frac{5}{\sqrt{\pi}} \quad \text{and} \quad \frac{(x-m)^2}{2\sigma^2} = 25x^2, \quad \text{or,} \quad \frac{1}{\sigma\sqrt{2}} = 5 \quad \text{and} \quad (x-m)^2 = 50\sigma^2x^2$$

$$\therefore \quad \sigma^2 = \frac{1}{25 \times 2} = \frac{1}{50} \quad \text{and} \quad (x-m)^2 = 50 \times \frac{1}{50} \times x^2 = x^2. \tag{3}$$

From (3), $x - m = x$, taking positive sign, or, $\mathbf{m = 0}$.

Hence $f(x) = \frac{5}{\sqrt{\pi}}e^{-25x^2}, -\infty < x < \infty$ is *the p.d.f. of a Normal Distribution with mean zero and variance* $\frac{1}{50}$.

(ii) x is normal $N(m, \sigma^2)$ such that

$$f(x) = \frac{1}{\sigma\sqrt{2\pi}}e^{-\frac{(x-m)^2}{2\sigma^2}}; \quad -\infty < x < \infty.$$

Let $z = \frac{x-m}{\sigma}$; then z is normal $N(0, 1)$ and $p(z) = \frac{1}{\sqrt{2\pi}}e^{-\frac{1}{2}z^2}; -\infty < z < \infty$.

Now

$$P\{|x - m| \leq 3\sigma\} = P\left\{\left|\frac{x-m}{\sigma}\right| \leq 3\right\} = P(|z| \leq 3) = P(-3 \leq z \leq 3)$$

$$= P(-3 \leq z \leq 0) + P(0 \leq z \leq 3) = 2P(0 \leq z \leq 3), \quad \text{from symmetry}$$

$$= 2\int_0^3 \frac{1}{\sqrt{2\pi}}e^{-\frac{1}{2}t^2}\,dt = 2 \times 0.4986 = \mathbf{0.9972}.$$

EXAMPLE 27. *The mean weight of* 500 *male students at a certain college is* 151 *lb. and the standard deviation is* 15 *lb. Assuming that the weights are normally distributed, find how many students weigh* (i) *between* 119.5 *and* 155.5 *lb.,* (ii) *more than* 160 *lb.*

SOLUTION. Here m = mean = 151 lb., σ = S.D. = 15 lb.

We have $z = \frac{x-m}{\sigma}$ = Value of x in standard units (or standardized value of x).

(i) 119.5 lb. in standard units $= \frac{119.5-151}{15} = -2.10$

and 155.5 lb. in standard units $= \frac{155.5-151}{15} = 0.30$.

∴ Proportion of students whose weights lie between 119.5 and 155.5 lb

= (area under the standard normal curve between $z = -2.10$ and $z = 0.30$)

= (area between $z = -2.10$ and $z = 0$) + (area between $z = 0$ and $z = 0.30$)

= (area between $z = 0$ and $z = 2.10$) + (area between $z = 0$ and $z = 0.30$)

= 0.4821 + 0.1179 [Using table] = 0.6000.

Hence the required number of students whose weights lie between 119.5 and 155.5 lb. = 0.6000 × 500 = **300.**

(ii) 160 lb. in standard units $= \frac{160-151}{15} = \frac{9}{15} = 0.60$.

∴ Proportion of students whose weights are more than 160 lb.

= area under the standard normal curve to the right of $z = 0.60$

= (area to the right of $z = 0$) – (area between $z = 0$ and $z = 0.60$)

= 0.5 – 0.2258 [Using table] = 0.2742.

Hence, the required number of students weighing more than 160 lb. = 0.2742 × 500 = **137** (approximately).

EXAMPLE 28. *A sample of* 100 *dry battery cells tested to find the length of life produced the following results :* $\bar{x} = 12$ *hours,* $\sigma = 3$ *hours.*

Assuming that the data are normally distributed, what percentage of battery cells are expected to have life: (i) *more than* 15 *hours,* (ii) *less than* 6 *hours and* (iii) *between* 10 *and* 14 *hours?*

Given z :	2.5	2	1	0.67
Area :	0.4938	0.4772	0.3413	0.2487

[ICWAI (Final) June 1979]

SOLUTION. We know that standardized value of x is $z = \frac{x-m}{\sigma}$.

Here m = mean = 12 hours, σ = S.D. = 3 hours.

∴ Standardized value of 15 $= \frac{15-12}{3} = +1$;

Standardized value of 6 $= \frac{6-12}{3} = -2$;

Standardized value of 10 $= \frac{10-12}{3} = -0.67$;

Standardized value of 14 $= \frac{14-12}{3} = 0.67$.

∴ Probability that the life of a battery cell is more than 15 hours

= area under the standard normal curve to be right of $z = 1$

= (area to the right of $z = 0$) – (area between $z = 0$ and $z = 1$)

= 0.5 – 0.3413 = 0.1587 = **15.87%.**

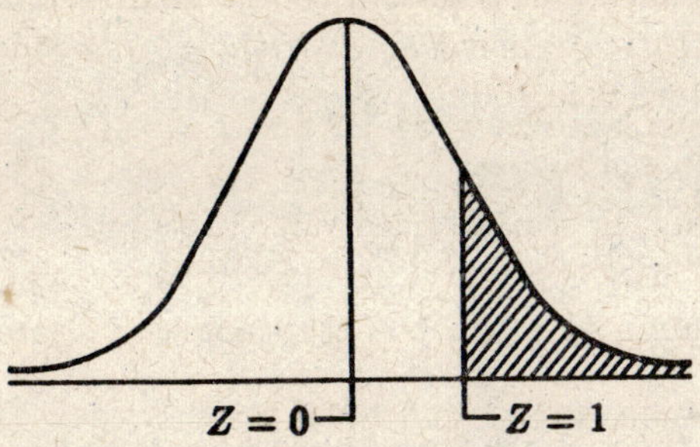

Fig 2.10

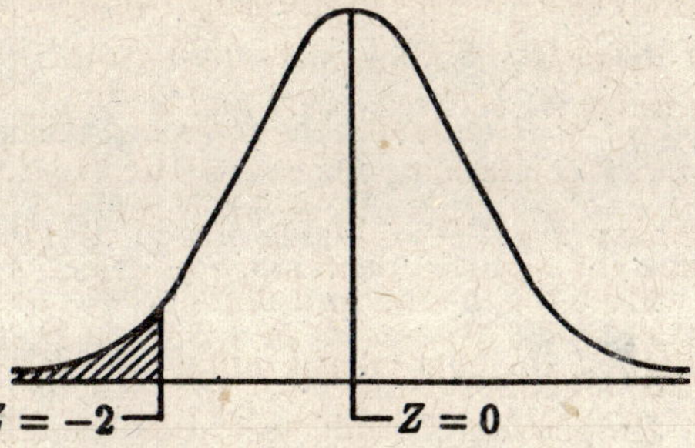

Fig 2.11

Probability that the life of a battery cell is less than 6 hours

= area under the normal curve to the left of $z = -2$

= area to the right of $z = +2$ [by Symmetry]

$= 0.5 - 0.4772 = 0.0228 =$ **2.28%**.

Probability that the life lies between 10 and 14 hours

= area under the normal curve btween $z = -0.67$ and $z = 0.67$

= 2 (area between $z = 0$ and $z = 0.67$) $= 2 \times 0.2487 = 0.4974 =$ **49.74%**.

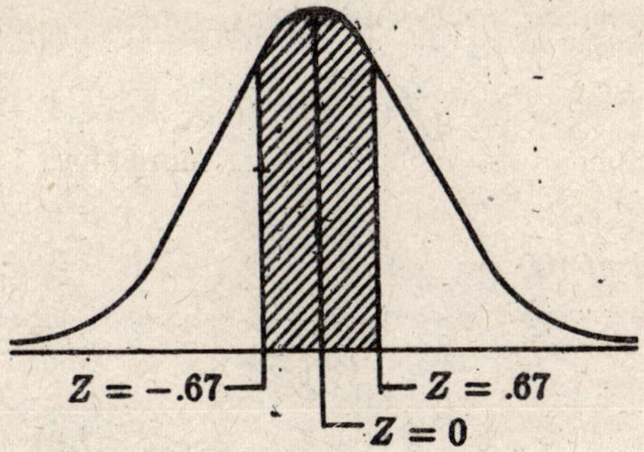

Fig 2.12

Hence the required percentage of battery cells with life (i) more than 15 hours is **15.87,** (ii) less than 6 hours is **2.28,** and (iii) between 10 and 14 hours is **49.74.**

EXAMPLE 29. *The mean of the inner diameters (in inch) of a sample of* 200 *tubes produced by a machine is* 0.502 *and the standard deviation is* 0.005. *The purpose for which these tubes are intended allows a maximum tolerance in the diameter of* 0.496 *to* 0.508 *(i.e., otherwise the tubes are considered defective). What percentage of the tubes produced by the machine is defective if the diameters are found to be normally distributed?*

[*Area under the standard normal curve between* $z = 0$ *and* $z = 1.2$ *is* 0.3849].

[ICWAI (Final) June 1980]

SOLUTION. Here m = mean of the inner diameters = 0.502 inch. σ = Standard deviation = 0.005 inch.

The tolerance limits of non-defective tubes are 0.496 inch and 0.508 inch.

Standardized value of 0.496 $= \frac{x-m}{\sigma} = \frac{0.496-0.502}{0.005} = -1.2$;

Standardized value of 0.508 $= \frac{0.508-0.502}{0.005} = +1.2$.

$\therefore$ Proportion of non-defective tubes

$= $ Area under the standard normal curve between $z = -1.2$ and $z = +1.2$

$= 2$ (Area between $z = 0$ and $z = 1.2$) $= 2 \times 0.3849 = 0.7698 = 76.98\%$.

Hence the required percentage of defective tubes $= 100\% - 76.98\% =$ **23.02%.**

EXAMPLE 30. *The mean of a Normal Distribution is* 50 *and* 5% *of the values are greater than* 60. *Find the standard deviation of this distribution.*

(*Given: The area under standard normal curve between* $z = 0$ *and* $z = 1.64$ *is* 0.45.)

[ICWAI (Final) December 1979]

SOLUTION. Here m = mean = 50, σ = S.D. = ?, $z = \frac{x-m}{\sigma}$ = standardised value of x, and $P(x > 60) = \frac{5}{100} = 0.05$.

$\therefore$ Standardised value of 60 is $\frac{60-50}{\sigma} = \frac{10}{\sigma}$; $\therefore$ $P(z > 10/\sigma) = 0.05$.

By the condition of the problem, 0.05 must be the area under the standard normal curve to the right of $z = \frac{10}{\sigma}$.

Again, given that the area between $z = 0$ and $z = 1.64$ is 0.45.

$\therefore$ Area to the right of $z = 1.64$

$=$ (area to the right of $z = 0$) $-$ (area between $z = 0$ and $z = 1.64$) $= 0.5 - 0.45 = 0.05$.

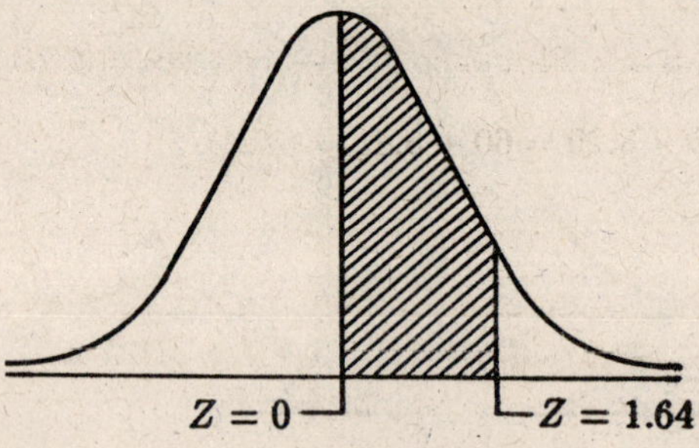

Fig 2.13

Thus 0.05 is the area to the right of $z = \frac{10}{\sigma}$ as well as to the right of $z = 1.64$.

Hence $\frac{10}{\sigma} = 1.64$, or, $\sigma = \frac{10}{1.64} = \frac{1000}{164} =$ **6.1**.

EXAMPLE 31. *In a large group of men, it is found that* 5% *are under* 60 *inches and* 40% *are between* 60 *and* 65 *inches in height. Assuming the distribution to be exactly normal, find the mean and the standard deviation of height.* (*For area of the standard normal curve* 0.05 *and* 0.45 *between* 0 *and a specified value, the z values are approximately* 0.125 *and* 1.645 *respectively*).

[CA November 1991]

SOLUTION. By the given condition, $P(x < 60) = \frac{5}{100} = 0.05$ and $P(60 < x < 65) = 0.40$, where x represents the height in inches.

$$\therefore \quad P(x < 65) = P(x < 60) + P(60 < x < 65) = 0.05 + 0.40 = 0.45.$$

Now standardised value of x (i.e., z-value) is $z = \frac{x-m}{\sigma}$ where m = mean and σ = S.D.

$\therefore$ Standardised value of 60 (i.e., z-value) is $\frac{60-m}{\sigma}$ and that of 65 is $\frac{65-m}{\sigma}$.

But $P(X < 60) = 0.05$ and $P(X < 65) = 0.45$ indicates that 60 and 65 both lie on the leftside of m and, therefore z-values $\frac{60-m}{\sigma}$ and $\frac{65-m}{\sigma}$ are both *negative*.

$\therefore$ $P(z < \frac{60-m}{\sigma}) = 0.05$ and $P(z < \frac{65-m}{\sigma}) = 0.45$ and from symmetry we can write

$$P\left(z > -\frac{60-m}{\sigma}\right) = 0.05 \qquad (1)$$

$$\text{and} \quad P\left(z > -\frac{65-m}{\sigma}\right) = 0.45 \qquad (2)$$

From (1), $P(z > 0) - P(0 < z < -\frac{60-m}{\sigma}) = 0.05$, or, $0.5 - 0.05 = P(0 < z < \frac{m-60}{\sigma})$, or, $P(0 < z < \frac{m-60}{\sigma}) = 0.45$.

Similarly, from (2), we get

$$P\left(0 < z < \frac{m-65}{\sigma}\right) = 0.5 - 0.45 = 0.05$$

$$\therefore \quad \frac{m-60}{\sigma} = 1.645 \quad \text{and} \quad \frac{m-65}{\sigma} = 0.125 \text{ (given);}$$

$$\text{or,} \quad m - 60 = 1.645\sigma \qquad (3)$$

$$\text{and} \quad m - 65 = 0.125\sigma. \qquad (4)$$

Subtracting (4) from (3), $5 = 1.52\sigma$, or, $\sigma = \frac{5}{1.52} = 3.289 = \mathbf{3.29}$.

From (3), $m = 60 + 1.645 \times 3.29 = 60 + 5.41 = \mathbf{65.41}$.

Exercise 2

Theory

1. Explain the concept of *'Theoretical Distribution'* with reference to a discrete random variable. Define *'Binomial Distribution'*, and state the conditions under which the distribution holds.

[ICWAI (Final) June 1974]

2. Write down the expressions for the Binomial Distribution clearly explaining the meaning of the symbols used. Find the mean of the Binomial Distribution. **[ICWAI (Final) December 1975]**

3. (i) If a variable is binomially distributed (with parameters n and p), determine its mean, variance with standard deviation. **[ICWAI (Final) December 1976]**

(ii) Write down the p.m.f., mean and variance of a Binomial Distribution. Under what conditions this distributons tends to *Poisson Distribution?* **[ICWAI June 1992]**

4. (i) Write down the expressions for Binomial and for Poisson Distributions.

[ICWAI (Final) June 1975, 1979; December 1981]

(ii) State the properties of Binomial Distribution. **[ICWAI December 1983]**

(iii) Point out the salient features of Binomial and Normal Probability Distributions.

[CA November 1985; May 1988]

5. (i) If a random variable follows Poisson Distribution, find its mean and variance.

(ii) Write short notes on Poisson Probability Distribution. **[CA May 1990]**

6. (i) Define a Poisson random variable and give five physical situations illustrating Poisson Distributions. **[ICWAI December 1977; June 1983]**

(ii) What is Poisson distributon? Explain with an example and state the conditions under which this distribution is used. **[CA May 1992]**

7. (i) Define *Normal Distribution* and deduce the standardised form. Draw a rough sketch of the standardised normal curve. In the latter case what are the values of mean and standard deviation? **[ICWAI (Final) June 1976, 1978]**

(ii) State the properties of the Normal Distribution. **[CA May 1991]**

(iii) What are the properties of a normal curve. **[CA May 1983]**

8. What is a random variable? Write down the expressions which define Binomial, Poisson and Normal Probability Distributions. Give three physical situations illustrating a Poisson random variable. **[ICWAI (Final), June 1977]**

9. Obtain the *Poisson Distribution* as a limit of the *Binomial Distribution* stating clearly the hypothesis you make.

10. (i) Define probability density function of a continuous random variable. **[ICWAI June 1983]**

(ii) Write down the probability density function of a *normal variate.* What is the ordinate of the curve of the above Distribution at its mean? **[ICWAI (Final) December 1980, 1981]**

11. Obtain the variance of a Binomial Distribution and show that the variance cannot exceed $\frac{n}{4}$.

[ICWAI June 1983]

12. A random variable X with mean μ and variance σ^2 has a Normal Distribution. Write down its probability density function $f(x)$. Write the expression in terms of the standard normal variate z. Give a rough sketch of the Standard Normal curve and then its salient features.

[ICWAI December 1982]

Problems

[A]

1. A student obtained the following results. Comment on the accuracy of his results:

(i) For a Binomial Distribution, mean = 4, variance = 3.

(ii) For a Poisson Distribution, mean = 10, S.D. = 5.

(iii) For a Normal Distribution, mean = 50, median = 52. **[ICWAI December 1980]**

2. Examine the validity of the following statements:

(i) The mean of binomial distribution is 10 and s.d. is 4. **[ICWAI December 1993]**

(ii) The mean of a binomial distribution is 3 and variance is 9. **[ICWAI June 1989]**

3. Determine the Binomial Distribution for which the mean is 4 and standar deviation is $\sqrt{3}$.

[CA May 1992]

4. The probability density function of a *continuous random variable* x is given by;

$$f(x) = kx(2-x), \quad 0 < x < 2$$
$$= 0, \text{ elsewhere.}$$

Calculate the value of the constant k and $E(x)$. **[ICWAI December 1986]**

[HINTS. $\int_{-\infty}^{\infty} f(x)dx = 1$, or, $\int_{0}^{2} f(x)dx = 1$, or, $\int_{0}^{2} kx(2-x)dx = 1$, etc. $E(x) = \int_{0}^{2} xf(x)dx$ = etc.]

5. Five coins are tossed simultaneously. What is the probability of (i) 3 heads, (ii) at least three heads, and (iii) more than 3 heads?

6. A machine produces 2% of defectives on an average. If 4 articles are chosen randomly, what is the probability that there will be exactly 2 defective articles?

7. (i) For a Binomial Distribution the mean is 3 and the variance is 2. Find the values of n and p.

(ii) For a Binomial Distribution, mean = 20 and S.D. = 4. Calculate n, p and q.

8. (i) In a shooting competition, the probability of a man hitting a target is $\frac{1}{5}$. If he fires 5 times, what is the probability of hitting the target at least twice?

(ii) Assume that the probability that a bomb dropped from an aeroplane will strike a target is $\frac{1}{5}$. If 6 bombs are dropped, find the probability that (a) exactly 2 will strike the target, (b) at least 2 will strike the target.

9. For a Binomial Distribution, the mean and the standard deviation are respectively 5 and 2. Find the probability of getting a non-zero value from this distribution.

[HINTS. $np = 5, npq = 4$; $\therefore$ $q = \frac{4}{5}$ and $n = 25, p = \frac{1}{5}$; find $1 - f(0)$.]

10. (i) If the probability of a defective bulb be $\frac{1}{5}$, find the following for the Binomial Distribution of defective bulbs in a total of 400 bulbs: (a) the mean; (b) the standard deviation; (c) the moment coefficient of skewness.

(ii) Is the following statement true? Give reasons for your answer:

"The mean of a Binomial Distribution is 3 and the standard deviation is 2."

11. (i) The overall percentage of failures in a certain examination is 60. What is the probability that out of a group of 6 candidates at least 5 passed the examination?

(ii) 20% of the bolts produced by a machine are defective. Deduce the probability distribution of the number of defectives in a sample of 5 bolts chosen at random. **[ICWAI June 1984]**

[HINTS. p = probability of a defective bolt (success) $= \frac{20}{100} = \frac{1}{5}$ and $q = 1 - p = 1 - \frac{1}{5} = \frac{4}{5}$. $f(x) = {}^nC_x p^x q^{n-x} = {}^5C_x (\frac{1}{5})^x (\frac{4}{5})^{5-x}$.

$\therefore$ The probability distribution of x is given by

x	0	1	2	3	4	5	Total
$f(x)$	1024/3125	256/625	123/625	32/625	4/625	1/3125	1]

12. 8 coins are tossed 256 times. Find the expected frequencies of success (i.e., getting head). Tabulate the results obtained. Calculate the mean number of success and S.D.

13. In 10 independent throws of a defective die, the probability that an even number will appear 5 times is twice the probability that an even number will appear 4 times. Find the probability that an even number will not appear at all in 10 independent throws of the die.

[HINTS. ${}^{10}C_5 p^5 q^5 = 2 \times {}^{10}C_4 p^4 q^6$, or, $3p = 5q = 5(1 - p)$; $\therefore$ $p = \frac{5}{8}, q = \frac{3}{8}$.]

14. Suppose that the half the population of a town are consumers of rice. 100 investigators are appointed to find out its truth. Each investigator interview 10 individuals. How many investigators do you expect to report that three or less of the people interviewed are consumers of rice.

[ICWAI June 1979]

[HINTS. Required number of investigators $= 100\times$ the probability that the investigators report that 3 or less of the people interviewed are consumers of rice.]

15. The incidence of occupational disease in an industry is such that the workmen have a 20% chance of suffering from it. What is the probability that out of 6 workmen, 4 or more will contract the disease?

16. (i) Find the probability that in a family of 4 children there will be : (a) at least 1 boy, (b) at least 1 boy and 1 girl. Assume that the probability of a male birth is $\frac{1}{2}$.

(ii) Out of 2000 families with 4 children each, how many would you expect to have (a) at least 1 boy, (b) at least 1 boy and 1 girl, (c) 2 girls?

17. From the past experience a stock broker finds that 70% of the telephone calls he receives during the business hours, are orders and the remaining are for other business. What is the probability that out of first 8 telephone calls during a day (i) exactly 5 calls are order calls? (ii) atleast 6 are order calls? **[ICWAI December 1994]**

[HINTS. p probability that a telephone call received is an order $= \frac{70}{100} = \frac{7}{10}$; $\therefore q = 1 - p = \frac{3}{10}$. Also $n = 8$. $f(x) = {}^8C_x \left(\frac{7}{10}\right)^x \left(\frac{3}{10}\right)^{8-x}$; (i) $f(5) = {}^8C_5 \left(\frac{7}{10}\right)^5 \left(\frac{3}{10}\right)^3 =$ etc., (ii) $f(6) + f(7) + f(8) =$ etc.]

18. Assuming that half the cost accountants are commerce graduates, so that the chance of a cost accountant being a commerce graduate is $\frac{1}{2}$ and assuming that 100 investigators each take 10 accountants to see whether they are commerce graduates, how many investigators would you expects to report that three accountants or less were commerce graduates?

[HINTS. $p = \frac{1}{2}$, $q = 1 - p = 1 - \frac{1}{2} = \frac{1}{2}$, $n = 10$, $N = 100$, $x = 3, 2, 1, 0$. Required no. of investigators $= \Sigma N f(x)$ when $x - 3, 2, 1, 0. = 100 \sum_{x=0}^{3} {}^{10}C_x (\frac{1}{2})^x \cdot (\frac{1}{2})^{10\ \ x} =$ etc.]

[B]

1. (i) A random variable x follows Poisson Distribution with parameter 3. Find the probabilities that x assumes the values (a) 0, 1, 2, 3; (b) less than 2; (c) at least 3. [Given $e^{-3} = 0.0498$).

(ii) If X be a Poisson variate with parameter 1, find $P(3 < X < 5)$. [Given $e^{-1} = 0.36783$].

[ICWAI June 1983]

[HINTS. In $3 < X < 5, X = 4$, find $P(X = 4)$.]

2. If 3% of the bolts manufactured by a company are defective, what is the probability that in a sample of 200 bolts, 5 will be defective? [Given $e^{-6} = 0.00248$]

3. (i) The variance of a Poisson Distribution is 4. Find the probability that $x = 3$. [Given $e^{-4} = 0.0183$]

(ii) The standard deviation of a Poisson variate x is $\sqrt{3}$. Find the probability that $x = 2$. [Given $e^{-3} = 0.0498$]

(iii) The standard deviation of a Poisson Distribution is 2. Find the probability that $x = 3$. [Given $e^{-4} = 0.0183$] **[ICWAI December 1981]**

4. Examine the validity of the following statements giving briefly the reasons for your answer:

(i) For a Poisson distribution, mean = 3 and standard deviation = 4.

[ICWAI December 1992]

(ii) If $P(X = 1) = P(X = 2)$ for a Poisson variate, then $E(X) = 2$.

[ICWAI December 1989]

(iii) If $P(X = 0) = P(X = 1)$ for a Poisson variate X, then $P(X > 0) = \frac{1}{e}$.

[HINTS. (i) For a Poisson distribution, mean = Variance. But here $m = 3$, Variance = 16.

(ii) $P(X = 1) = P(X = 2) \Rightarrow \frac{e^{-m} \cdot m^1}{\lfloor 1} = \frac{e^{-m} \cdot m^2}{\lfloor 2}$, or, $m = 2$, i.e., $E(X) = 2$, etc.

(iii) $P(X = 0) = P(X = 1) \Rightarrow m = 1$; $\therefore$ $P(X > 0) = 1 - P(X = 0) =$ etc.]

5. (i) If the probability that an individual suffers a bad reaction from a particular injection is 0.01, find the probability that out of 500 individuals (a) exactly two, (b) more than two individuals will suffer a bad reaction. [Given $e^{-5} = 0.00674$].

(ii) In a company manufacturing toys, it is found that 1 in 500 is defective. Find the probability that there will be at the most two defectives in a sample of 2,000 units. [Given $e^{-4} = 0.0183$] **[ICWAI June 1990]**

[HINTS. See Example 15. Here $m = np = 2000 \times \frac{1}{500} = 4$. Required probability $= f(0) + f(1) + f(2) =$ etc.]

6. (i) If 2% of the items made by a factory are defective, find the probability that there are 3 defective items in a sample of 100 items.

(ii) If 2% of electric bulbs manufactured by a certain company are defective, find the probability that in a sample of 200 bulbs, (a) less than 2 bulbs, (b) more than 3 bulbs, are defective. [Given $e^{-4} = 0.0183$] **[ICWAI December 1985]**

(iii) Experience has shown that, on the average, 2% of an airline's flights suffer a minor equipment failure in an aircraft. Estimate the probability that the no. of minor equipment failures in the next 50 flights will be (i) zero, (ii) at least two. **[C.U. M. Com. 1985]**

7. (i) For a Poisson Distribution, $f(0) = f(1)$. Find $f(x > 0)$. [Given $e = 2.718$]

[ICWAI December 1990]

(ii) If for a Poisson variate $x, P(x = 1) = P(x = 2)$, find $P(x = 1 \text{ or } x = 2)$. Also find its mean and standard deviation. **[ICWAI June 1993; CA November 1993]**

8. (i) A random variable x follows Poisson law such that $P(x = k) = P(x = k + 1)$. Find its mean and variance. **[ICWAI December 1986]**

[HINTS. See Example 18.]

(ii) If a random variable x follows a Poisson Distribution such that probability $(x = 1) =$ probability $(x = 2)$, find the mean and variance. Find also probability $(x = 0)$.

[C.U. B. Com. (Hons.) 1982]

9. (i) Between 4 and 5 p.m. the average number of phone calls per minute coming into the switchboard of a company is 3. Find the probability that during one particular minute there will be ( ) no phone call, (b) exactly 2 phone calls. [Given $e^{-3} = 0.0498$]

(ii) Between the hours 2 p.m. and 4 p.m. the average number of phone calls per minute coming into the switchboard of a company is 2.35. Find the probability that during one particular minute there will be at most 2 phone calls. [Given $e^{-2.35} = 0.095374$] **[ICWAI June 1984]**

[HINTS. See worked out Example 17; find $f(x), f(0), f(1)$ and $f(2)$. Required probability $= f(0) + f(1) + f(2) =$ etc.]

10. Assuming that 4% of the output of a factory making certain parts is defective and that 100 units are in a package , what is the probability that at most 3 defective parts may be found in a package? [Given $e^{-4} = 0.0183$]

11. (i) It is found that the number of accident occurring in a factory follows Poisson Distribution with a mean of 2 accidents per week. Find the probability that (a) no accident occurs in a week, (b) the number of accidents in a week exceeds 2. [Given $e^{-2} = 0.135$]

(ii) The number of accidents in a year attributed to taxi drivers in a city follows Poisson Distribution with mean 3. Out of 1000 taxi drivers, find approximately the number of drivers with (a) no accident in a year and (b) more than 3 accident in a year.
[Given that $e^{-1} = 0.3679, e^{-2} = 0.1353, e^{-3} = 0.0498$] **[CA November 1988]**

[HINTS. For the Poisson Distribution, the probability function is $f(x) = \frac{e^{-m} \cdot m^x}{\underline{|x}}$, where m is the mean. $\therefore$ $f(x) = \frac{e^{-3} \cdot 3^x}{\underline{|x}}; f(0) = e^{-3}, f(1) = e^{-3} \cdot 3, f(2) = \frac{e^{-3} \cdot 9}{2}$ and $f(3) = \frac{e^{-3} \cdot 27}{6} = \frac{9e^{-3}}{2}$. Now find $P(X > 3) = 1 - \{f(0) + f(1) + f(2) + f(3)\}$. (i) No. of drivers $= f(0) \times 1000$ and (ii) No. of drivers $= P(X > 3) \times 1000$.]

12. The average number of misprints per page of a book is 1.5. What is the probability that a particular page is free from misprints? If the book contains 800 pages, how many of these contain more than 1 misprints? [Given $e^{-1.5} = 0.22$]

13. If the chance of being killed by flood during a year is $\frac{1}{3000}$, use Poisson Distribution to calculate the probability that out of 3000 persons living in a village at least one would die in flood in a year. **[C.U. M. Com. 1976]**

14. A radioactive source emits on the average 2.5 particles per second. Calculate the probability that 2 or more particles will be emitted in an interval of 4 seconds. **[ICWAI June 1991]**

[HINTS. $f(x) = \frac{e^{-m} m^x}{\underline{|x}}$, where $m = 2.5 \times 4 = 10$; $\therefore$ $f(x) = \frac{e^{-10} \cdot 10^x}{\underline{|x}}$. Required probability $= f(2) + f(3) + \cdots = 1 - \{f(0) + f(1)\} = 1 - (e^{-10} + 10e^{-10}) =$ etc.]

15. In turning out certain toys in a manufacturing process in a factory, the average number of defectives is 10%. What is the probability of getting exactly 3 defectives in a sample of 10 toys chosen at random, by using Poisson approximation to the Binomial Distribution? [Take $e = 2.72$]

[ICWAI December 1978]

16. One-fifth per cent of the blades produced by a blade-manufacturing factory turn out to be defective. The blades are supplied in packets of 10. Use Poisson Distribution to calculate the approximate number of packets containing no defective, one defective and two defective blades respectively in a consignment of 1,00,000 packets. [Given $e^{-0.02} = 0.9802$]

[ICWAI December 1977]

17. A manufacturer of blades knows that 5% of his product is defective. If he sells blades in boxes of 100 and guarantees that not more than 10 blades will be defective, what is the probability (approximately) that a box will fail to meet the guaranteed quantity?

[HINTS. Since the probability of defective blades is small, you may use Poisson Distribution.]

18. A local electrical appliances shop has found from experience that the demand for tube lights is distributed as Poisson with a mean of 4 tube light per week. If the shop keeps 6 tubes during a particular week, what is the probability that the demand will exceed the supply during that week? [Given $e^{-4} = 0.0183$] **[ICWAI June 1985]**

19. Number of road accidents on a highway during a month follows a Poisson Distribution with mean 6. Find the probability that in a certain month number of accidents will be (i) not more than 3, (ii) between 2 and 4. [Given $e^{-6} = 0.00248$] **[ICWAI June 1986]**

20. A manufacturer who produces medicine bottles, finds that 0.1% of the bottles are defective. The bottles are packed in boxes containing 500 bottles. A drug manufacturer buys 100 boxes from the producer of bottles. Using Poisson Distribution, find how many boxes will contain: (i) no defectives, (ii) at least two defectives. [Given $e^{-0.5} = 0.6065$] **[CA May 1986]**

[HINTS. $p = \frac{0.1}{100}, n = 500, N = 100; \quad \therefore \quad m = np = 0.5$. Expected frequency of x successes = $Nf(x)$.]

21. The probability that a Poisson variate x takes a positive value is $(1 - e^{-1.5})$. Find the variance and also the probability that x lies between -1.5 and 1.5.

[C]

1. A random variable X has a Normal Distribution with mean μ, and variance σ^2. Write down the expression for its density function. Express this density function in terms of the standard normal variable. In the latter case, what are the values of mean and standard deviation?

[ICWAI June 1978]

2. Find the mean and variance of the p.d.f. given by

$$\begin{aligned} f(x) &= 12x^2(1-x), \quad \text{for } 0 \le x \le 1 \\ &= 0, \quad \text{otherwise.} \end{aligned}$$

[ICWAI June 1992]

[HINTS. Mean $= E(x) = \int_{-\infty}^{\infty} x\, f(x)\, dx = \int_0^1 x \cdot 12x^2(1-x)\, dx =$ etc.

Variance $= E(x^2) - \{E(x)\}^2 = \int_0^1 x^2 \cdot 12x^2(1-x)\, dx - \{E(x)\}^2 =$ etc.]

3. Find the area under the normal curve (i.e., the probabilities) in the following cases using table: (i) between $z = 0$ and $z = 1.8$; (ii) between $z = -0.78$ and $z = 0$; (iii) between $z = 0.85$ and $z = 2.15$, where z is a standard normal variate.

4. Find the probability that the standard normal variate is (i) less than – 1.3; (ii) greater than 0.95; (iii) greater than 1.65 but less than – 1.32.

5. The mean height of 1000 students at a certain college is 165 cms and S.D. 10 cms. Find the number of students whose height is (i) less than 172 cms; (ii) between 159 and 178 cms; and (iii) more than 173.2 cms.

6. (i) If X follows a Normal Distribution with mean 12 and variance 16, find $P(X \geq 20)$.

[ICWAI December 1990]

[Given $\int_{-\infty}^{2} \frac{1}{\sqrt{2\pi}} \cdot e^{-\frac{1}{2}t^2} dt = 0.97725$]

[HINTS. $z = \frac{x-m}{\sigma} = \frac{x-12}{4}$; if $x = 20, z = \frac{20-12}{4} = 2$,

$\therefore \quad P(X \geq 20) = P(Z \geq 2) = 1 - P(Z < 2) = 1 - \int_{-\infty}^{2} \frac{1}{\sqrt{2\pi}} \cdot e^{-\frac{1}{2}t^2} dt =$ etc.]

(ii) If z is normally distributed with mean 0 and variance 1, find (a) $P(z \geq -1.64)$; (b) $P(-1.96 \leq z \leq 1.96)$ and (c) $P(|z| \geq 1)$.

(iii) For a certain normal variate x, the mean is 12 and s.d. $= 4$. Find (i) $P_r(x \geq 20)$, (ii) $P_r(x \leq 12)$. [Given area under the normal curve from $z = 0$ to $z = 2$ is 0.4772.]

[ICWAI December 1993]

7. The diameters of ball bearings are normally distributed with mean 0.6140 inches and S.D. 0.0025 inches. Calculate the percentage of ball bearings with diameters (i) between 0.610 and 0.618 inches, (ii) greater than 0.617 inches, (iii) less than 0.608 inches.

8. (i) The mean of a Normal Distribution is 60 and 6% of the values are greater than 70. Find the standard deviation of this distribution.

[Given: The area under the standard normal curve between $z = 0$ and $z = 1.56$ is 0.44.]

(ii) A grinding machine is set so that its production of shafts has an average diameter of 10.10 cms. and a standard deviation of 0.20 cms. The product specifications call for shaft diameters between 10.05 cms. and 10.20 cms. What proportion of output meets the specifications presuming Normal Distribution?

[CA November 1985]

9. For a certain Normal Distribution, the first moment about 10 is 40 and the fourth moment about 50 is 48. What is the arithmetic mean and standard deviation of the distribution?

[ICWAI (Final) December 1978]

[HINTS. Mean $= A + m_1' = 10 + 40 = 50$, and $m_4 = 48 \quad (\because \quad \text{Mean} = 50)$.]

10. For a Normal Distribution $N(m, \sigma^2)$, evaluate $P(|x - m| \leq 3\sigma$. Given $\int_0^3 \frac{1}{\sqrt{2\pi}} e^{-\frac{1}{2}t^2} dt =$ 0.4986.

[ICWAI December 1991]

[HINTS. $f(x) = \frac{1}{\sigma\sqrt{2\pi}} e^{-\frac{(x-m)^2}{2\sigma^2}}; -\infty < x < \infty$. Let $z = \frac{x-m}{\sigma}$; then $p(z) = \frac{1}{\sqrt{2\pi}} e^{-\frac{1}{2}z^2}$

$P(|x - m| \leq 3\sigma) = P(|z| \leq 3) = 2P(0 \leq z \leq 3) = 2 \times 0.4986 =$ etc.]

11. For a Normal Distribution of 100 items, the lower quartile Q_1 is 73 and σ is 15. Find (i) median, (ii) limits for central 50% of the distribution and (iii) mean deviation.

[HINTS. For a Normal Distribution, Mean = Median and $Q_1 = m - 0.67\sigma, Q_3 = m + 0.67\sigma$ and Mean Deviation = 0.80σ.]

12. Assuming that the height distribution of a group of men is normal, find the mean and the standard deviation, if 84% of the men have heights less than 65.2 inches and 68% have heights lying between 65.2 and 62.8 inches. **[ICWAI (Final) June 1978]**

13. Supoose that we have a wholesale electrical warehouse. Past sale records indicate a mean of daily sales for a certain type of transformer equal to 5 units. Demand for this item is distributed to a Poisson Distribution given by the formula $f(x) = \frac{\lambda^x e^{-\lambda}}{\lfloor x}(e^{-5} = 0.00674)$. Suppose we have only 3 transformers in stock. What is the probability that the demand will be greater than what we have on hand? **[ICWAI December 1983]**

14. In a certain factory blades are manufactured in packets of 10. There is a 0.2% probability for any blade to be defective. Using Poisson Distribution calculate approximately the number of packets containing two defective blades in a consignment of 20,000 packets.
[Given $e^{-0.02} = 0.9802$]? **[ICWAI June 1981]**

15. For a random variable the probability density function is expressed as,
$f(x) = \sqrt{\frac{2}{\pi}} \cdot e^{-2(x-3)^2}, [-\infty < x < \infty]$. (i) Identify the distribution; (ii) Give the values of mean and standard deviation of the distribution; (iii) Write down two important properties of the distribution.?

[ICWAI June 1983]

[HINTS. We can write $f(x) = \frac{1}{\frac{1}{2}\sqrt{2\pi}} \cdot e^{-\frac{1}{2}\cdot\left(\frac{x-2}{1/2}\right)^2}$, $-\infty < x < \infty$ which is a Normal Distribution with mean = 3, S.D. = $\frac{1}{2}$, etc.]

16. A factory turns out an article by mass production methods. From past experience it appears that 20 articles on an average are rejected out of every batch of 100. Find the variance of the number of rejects in a batch. What is the probability that the number of rejects in a batch exceeds 30? [Given : Area under a normal curve between $z = 0$ and $z = 2.5$ is 0.4938]

[ICWAI December 1981]

[D]

1. Fit a Poisson Distribution to the following data and calculate the theoretical frequencies [given $e^{-0.5} = 0.61$] :

No. of Deaths :	0	1	2	3	4
Frequency :	122	60	15	2	1

[ICWAI June 1982]

[HINTS. m = mean of the Poisson Distribution = $\frac{\Sigma fx}{N} = \frac{100}{200} = 0.5$.

Hence $f(x) = \frac{e^{-m} \cdot m^x}{\lfloor x} = \frac{e^{-0.5} \cdot (0.5)^x}{\lfloor x}$, where $x = 0, 1, 2, 3, \cdots$

x :	0	1	2	3	4	5 and more
$f(x)$:	0.61	0.305	0.076	0.0131	0.002	0

Here $Nf(x)$ = expected frequency = 122, 61, 15, 2, 0.]

2. The Distribution of typing mistakes committed by a typist is given below. Assuming a Poisson Model, find the expected frequencies:

Mistakes per Page :	0	1	2	3	4	5
No. of Pages :	76	74	29	17	3	1

[C.U. M. Com. 1981]

[HINTS. $m = \Sigma fx/N = 1$; take $e = 2.718$ and find $f(0), f(1), \cdots f(5)$. Then expected frequencies $= Nf(x) = 200f(x) =$ etc. for $x = 0, 1, \cdots, 5$.]

3. A certain hospital usually admits 50 patients per day. On an avarage, 4 patients in 100 require special facilities found in special rooms of the hospital. On the morning of a certain day, it is found that there are four such rooms available. Assuming that 50 patients will be admitted, find the probability that more than 4 patients will require such special rooms.
[Given $e^{-2} = 0.13534$] **[C.U. M. Com. 1980]**

[HINTS. Here $n = 50, p = \frac{4}{100} = 0.04, m = np = 2$. Using Poisson Distribution as a limit of the Binomial Distribution, we get $Pr(x > 4) = 1 - Pr(x \leq 4) = 1 - e^{-2}(1 + 2 + \frac{2^2}{\underline{|2}} + \frac{2^3}{\underline{|3}} + \frac{2^4}{\underline{|4}}) = 1 - 7e^{-2}$ $= 1 - 7 \times 0.13534 = 0.05262$.]

4. For a normal distribution with mean 3 and variance 16, find the value of y of the variate such that the probability of the variate lying in the interval $(3, y)$ is 0.4772. [You are given $P(z \leq 2)$ $= 0.9772$]. **[ICWAI June 1991]**

[HINTS. $z = \frac{x-m}{\sigma} = \frac{x-3}{4}$. If $x = 3, z = 0$ and if $x = y, z = \frac{y-3}{4}$. Given $P(3 \leq x \leq y) = 0.4772$, or, $P(0 \leq z \leq \frac{y-3}{4}) = 0.4772$. Also $P(z \leq 0) = 0.5$.

$\therefore \quad P(z \leq \frac{y-3}{4}) = 0.9772 = P(z \leq 2)$. Hence $\frac{y-3}{4} = 2$, or, $y = 11$.]

5. The weekly wages of 1,000 workers are normally distributed around a mean of Rs. 70 and with a standard deviation of Rs. 5. Estimate the number of workers whose weekly wages will be (i) between Rs. 70 and Rs. 72; (ii) between Rs. 69 and Rs. 72; (iii) more than Rs. 75; (iv) less than Rs. 63 and (v) more than Rs. 80.

Also estimate the lowest weekly wages of the 100 highest paid workers.

[Delhi U. Econ. (Hons.) 1977]

6. In a sample of 120 workers in a factory the mean and S.D. of wages were Rs. 11.35 and Rs. 3.03 respectively. Find the percentage of workers getting wages between Rs. 9 and Rs. 17 in the whole factory, assuming that the wages are normally distributed. **[CA May 1981]**

7. Find the mean and standard deviation of a normal distribution of marks in an examination where 44% of the candidates obtained marks below 55 and 6% got above 80 marks.

[Given $\int_0^{1.555} \phi(t)dt = 0.44$, $\int_0^{0.15} \phi(t)dt = 0.06$] **[ICWAI June 1985]**

[HINTS. At $x = 55, z = \frac{55-m}{\sigma}$ and at $x = 80, z = \frac{80-m}{\sigma}$.

$\therefore \quad P(z < \frac{55-m}{\sigma}) = .44, \quad \text{or,} \quad P(0 < z < \frac{m-55}{\sigma}) = .5 - .44 = .06.$

$\therefore \quad \frac{m-5}{\sigma} = 0.15, \quad \text{or,} \quad m - 55 = 0.15\sigma.$ (1)

$P(z > \frac{80-m}{\sigma}) = .06, \quad \text{or,} \quad P(0 < z < \frac{80-m}{\sigma}) = .44.$

$\therefore \quad \frac{80-m}{\sigma} = 1.555, \quad \text{or,} \quad 80 - m = 1.555\sigma.$ (2)

Solving (1) and (2), $m = 57.2$ and $\sigma = 14.66$.]

8. In a business, it is assumed that the average daily sales (in Rs.) follows a normal distribution. It is given that the probability that the average daily sales is less than Rs. 124 is .0287 and the probability that it exceeds Rs. 270 is .4599. Find the mean and S.D. of the distribution.

[C.U. M. Com. 1985]

9. If a random variable x follows normal distribution with mean 10 and standard deviation 50, write down its p.d.f. Also calculate $P(X \leq -108), P(|X| \geq 108), P(10 < X \leq 108)$, and $P(X \leq 108/X > 10)$.

[Given $\phi(1.96) = 0.9750021, \phi(2.36) = 0.9908625$, where $\phi(x) = \int_{-\infty}^{x} \frac{e^{\frac{-t^2}{2}}}{\sqrt{2\pi}} dt$]

[HINTS. m = mean = 10, σ = S.D. = 50. The p.d.f. of x is $f(x) = \frac{1}{\sigma\sqrt{2\pi}} e^{-\frac{(x-m)^2}{2\sigma^2}}; (-\infty < x < \infty) = \frac{1}{50\sqrt{2\pi}} e^{-\frac{(x-10)^2}{2(50)^2}}; (-\infty < x < \infty)$, or, $f(z) = \frac{1}{\sqrt{2\pi}} e^{-\frac{z^2}{2}}$, where $z = \frac{x-10}{50}$ and $-\infty < z < \infty$.

If $x = -108, z = \frac{-108-10}{50} = -2.36$; if $x = 108$, then $z = 1.96$; if $x = 0, z = 0$.

$$P(X \leq -108) = P(z \leq -2.36) = P(z \geq 2.36) = 1 - P(z \leq 2.36)$$
$$= 1 - \phi(2.36) = 1 - 0.9908625 = 0.0091375.$$
$$P(|X| \geq 108) = P(X \geq 108) + P(X \leq -108) = P(z \geq 1.96) + P(z \leq -2.36)$$
$$= 1 - \phi(1.96) + 0.009175 = \text{etc.}]$$

10. If a random variable X follows a normal distribution with mean 18 and variance 625, find: (i) $P(-31 < X < 67)$ and (ii) $P(X < 67/X > 18)$. **[ICWAI June 1990]**

[Given $\frac{1}{\sqrt{2\pi}} \int_{-\infty}^{1.96} e^{-\frac{1}{2}t^2} dt = 0.9750021$]

[SOLUTION.

(i) $z = \frac{x-m}{\sigma} = \frac{x-18}{25}$; if $x = -31, z = -\frac{49}{25} = -1.96$ and if $x = 67, z = \frac{49}{25} = 1.96$. If $x = 18, z = 0$.

$\therefore \quad P(-31 < X < 67) = P(-1.96 < z < 1.96) = \int_{-1.96}^{1.96} e^{-\frac{1}{2}t^2} dt = \frac{2}{\sqrt{2\pi}} \int_{\circ}^{1.96} e^{-\frac{1}{2}t^2} dt$ $= \frac{2}{\sqrt{2\pi}} \left\{ \int_{-\infty}^{1.96} e^{-\frac{1}{2}t^2} dt - \int_{-\infty}^{\circ} e^{-\frac{1}{2}t} dt \right\} = 2\{0.9750021 - 0.5\} = 2 \times 0.4750021 = 0.9500042.$

(ii) $P(X < 67/X > 18) = \frac{P(X<67 \cap X>18)}{P(X>18)} \quad [\because \quad P(B/A) = \frac{P(A \cap B)}{P(A)}] = \frac{P(18<X<67)}{P(X>18)} = \frac{P(0<z<1.96)}{P(z>0)}$ $= \frac{1}{\sqrt{2\pi}} \int_{\circ}^{1.96} e^{-\frac{1}{2}t^2} dt \Big/ 0.5 = \frac{0.4750021}{0.5} = 0.9500042.]$

11. The p.d.f. of a normal variate X is $f(x) = \frac{\sqrt{2}}{100\sqrt{\pi}}e^{-\frac{1}{50}(\frac{x-10}{10})^2}$; $-\infty < x < \infty$.

Calculate: (i) $P(|X| \geq 108)$ and (ii) $P(X \leq 108/x > 10)$. [Given: $P(z \leq 1.96) = 0.98$ and $P(z \leq 2.36) = 0.99$, where z is a $N(0,1)$ variate.] **[ICWAI June 1994]**

[HINTS. $f(x) = \frac{\sqrt{2}}{100\sqrt{\pi}}e^{-\frac{1}{50}(\frac{x-10}{10})^2}, -\infty < x < \infty$. Also $f(x) = \frac{1}{\sigma\sqrt{2\pi}}e^{-\frac{(x-m)^2}{2\sigma^2}}, -\infty < x < \infty$.

$\therefore \ \frac{\sqrt{2}}{100\sqrt{\pi}} = \frac{1}{\sigma\sqrt{2\pi}}$ and $\frac{1}{50}(\frac{x-10}{10})^2 = \frac{(x-m)^2}{2\sigma^2} \Rightarrow \sigma = 50, m = 10$.

$\therefore \ z = \frac{x-m}{\sigma} = \frac{x-10}{50}$; if $x = 108, z = 1.96$ and if $x = 10, z = 0$, etc.]

Answers

[A]

1. (i) $p = \frac{1}{4}, q = \frac{3}{4}, n = 16$. Nothing to comment against the results; (ii) The results are inconsistent; (iii) The results are inconsistent. **2.** (i) The statement is not valid; (ii) The statement is valid. **3.** $f(x) = {}^{16}C_x(\frac{1}{4})x(\frac{3}{4})^{16-x}; x = 0, 1, 2, \cdots, 16$. **4.** $\frac{3}{4}, 1$. **5.** (i) $\frac{5}{16}$; (ii) $\frac{1}{2}$; (iii) $\frac{3}{16}$. **6.** $6(0.02)^2(0.98)^2$, or, 0.00230496. **7.** (i) $n = 9, p = \frac{1}{3}$; (ii) $n = 100, p = \frac{1}{5}, q = \frac{4}{5}$. **8.** (i) $\frac{821}{3125}$; (ii) $\frac{768}{3125}, \frac{2048}{3125}$. **9.** $1 - (0.8)^{25}$. **10.** (i) (a) 80, (b) 8, (c) 0.075. (ii) Not true. **11.** (i) $\frac{3645}{15625}$; (ii)

x :	0	1	2	3	4	5	Total
$f(x)$:	1024/3125	256/625	128/625	32/625	4/625	1/3125	1

12. 1, 8, 28, 56, 70, 56, 28, 8, 1; Mean = 4; S.D. = 1.4142. **13.** $(\frac{3}{8})^{10}$. **14.** 17. **15.** $\frac{53}{3125}$.16. (i) (a) $\frac{15}{16}$; (b) $\frac{7}{8}$; (ii) (a) 1875, (b) 1750, (c) 750.

[B]

1. (i) (a) 0.0498, 0.1494, 0.2241, 0.2241; (b) 0.1992; (c) 0.5767; (ii) 0.0153. **2.** 0.16. **3.** (i) 0.1952; (ii) 0.2241; (iii) 0.1952. **4.** (i) Not valid; (ii) Valid; (iii) Not valid. **5.** (i) (a) 0.08425; (b) 0.87531; (ii) 0.2379. **6.** (i) 0.180; (ii) 0.0915, 0.5669; (iii) 0.368, 0.264. **7.** (i) 0.6321; (ii) $4e^{-2}; 2, \sqrt{2}$. **8.** (i) $k + 1, k + 1$; (b) 2; 2; e^{-2}. **9.** (i) (a) 0.0498; (b) 0.2241; (ii) 0.582854. **10.** 0.4331. **11.** (i) (a) 0.135; (b) 0.325; (ii) (a) 50; (b) 353. **12.** (i) 0.22; (ii) 360. **13.** $1 - e^{-1}$. **14.** $1 - 11e^{-10}$. **15.** 0.061. **16.** 98020, 1960, 20. **17.** $1 - e^{-5}(1 + \frac{5}{\lfloor 1} + \frac{5^2}{\lfloor 2} + \cdots + \frac{5^{10}}{\lfloor 10})$ where $e^{-5} = 0.0067$. **18.** 0.1114. **19.** (i) 0.15128; (ii) 0.08928. **20.** (i) 61; (ii) 9. **21.** $1.5; 2.5/e^{1.5}$.

[C]

1. $f(x) = \frac{1}{\sigma\sqrt{2\pi}} e^{-\frac{(x-\mu)}{2}\sigma^2}; (-\infty < x < \infty); p(z) = \frac{1}{\sqrt{2\pi}} e^{-\frac{1}{2}z^2}$, where $z = \frac{x-\mu}{\sigma}$ and $-\infty < z < \infty$. Mean = 0. S.D. −1. **2.** 0.6; 0.04. **3.** (i) 0.4641; (ii) 0.2823; (iii) 0.1819. **4.** (i) 0.0968; (ii) 0.1711; (iii) 0.1429. **5.** (i) 258; (ii) 629; (iii) 206. **6.** (i) 0.02275; (ii) (a) 0.9495; (b) 0.9500; (c) 0.6826. **7.** (i) 93%; (ii) 8.1%; (iii) 0.47%. **8.** (i) 6.41; (ii) 29.02%. **9.** 50, 2. **10.** 0.9972. **11.** (i) 83.05; (ii) $Q_1 = 73$ and $Q_3 = 93.10$; (iii) Mean Deviation = 12. **12.** Mean = 64.0 inches, S.D. = 1.2 inches. **13.** 0.73492. **14.** 3.9208, or 4. **16.** 16; 0.0062.

[D]

2. 73.6, 73.6, 36.8, 12.3, 3.0, 0.7. **3.** 0.05262. **4.** 11. **5.** 155, 235, 159, 81, 23; Rs. 76.40. **6.** 75.1%. **7.** $m = 57.2; \sigma = 14.66$. **8.** $m = 262.7; \sigma = 73$. **9.** $\frac{1}{\sqrt{2\pi}} e^{-\frac{1}{2}z^2}$, where $z = \frac{x-10}{5}$ and $-\infty < z < \infty$; 0.0091375; 0.0341354, 0.4750021, 0.9500042. **10.** (i) 0.9500042; (ii) 0.9500042. **11.** 0.96; 0.96.

CHAPTER 3

SAMPLING THEORY: DIFFERENT METHODS OF SAMPLING AND SIMULATED SAMPLING

3.1. INTRODUCTION

We have already defined *population* and *Sample* and discussed the two ways of collection of statistical data, *viz.* by *Complete Enumeration* (or *Census*) and *Sample Survey.* **Population** (or *Universe*) *is the aggregate or totality of statistical data forming a subject of investigation,* e.g., (i) the population of books in the National Library, (ii) the population of the heights of Indians, (iii) the population of Nationalised Banks in India, etc. A **Sample** *is a portion of the population which is examined with a view to estimating the characteristics of the population,* e.g., (i) to assess the quality of a bag of rice, we examine only a portion of it. The portion selected from the bag is called a *sample,* while the whole quantity of rice in the bag is the *population,* (ii) to estimate the proportion of defective articles in a large consignment, only a portion (i.e., a few of them) is selected and examined. The portion selected is a *sample.*

When information is collected in respect of every individual item, the enquiry is said to be done by *Complete Enumeration* or *Census;* e.g., during the *Census of Population* (which is done every ten years in India), information in respect of each individual person residing in India is collected. This method gives information for each and every unit of the population with greater accuracy. But this method involves huge amount of money, long time and much effort. In most cases of statistical inquiry, because of limitations of time and cost, only a portion (i.e., a sample) of the available source of information is examined, and the data collected from them. This process of partial enumeration is known as **Sample Survey.** The results and findings are then generalised and made applicable to the whole field of inquiry. This is known as **Sampling.** The process of sampling is based on two important principles of statistics:

1. Law of Statistical Regularity, *which states that a moderately large number of items selected at random from a given population exhibits nearly the same composition and characteristics of the population.*

2. Law of Inertia of Large Numbers, *which states that, other things remaining the same, the larger the size of the sample, the more accurate is the result obtained. This is nothing but a corollary to the Law of Statistical Regularity.*

3.2. DIFFERENT METHODS OF SAMPLING

The different methods of **Sampling** are discussed below under two separate heads.

A. Random Sampling Methods

1. **Random Sampling** (or *Probability Sampling*)
2. **Stratified Sampling** (or *Stratified Random Sampling*)
3. **Systematic Sampling** (or *Quasi-random Sampling*)
4. **Multi-stage Sampling** (or *Multi-stage Random Sampling*)

B. Non-random Sampling Methods

1. **Purposive Sampling** (or *Judgment Sampling*)
2. **Quota Sampling**
3. **Convenience Sampling**
4. **Cluster Sampling** (or *Block Sampling*)
5. **Sequential Sampling**

I. Random Sampling (or Probability Sampling) **[CA May 1991]**

Random Sampling is the process of drawing a sample from a population in such a way that each member of the population has an equal chance of being included in the sample. The sample obtained by the process of random sampling is called a *random sample.*

In the words of W. M. Harper:

"A random sample is a sample selected in such a way that every item in the population has an equal chance of being included."

ILLUSTRATION 1. *A hand of cards dealt from a well shuffled pack of cards is a random sample.*

ILLUSTRATION 2. *Winning tickets, in a lottery are drawn at random by taking numbers out of a revolving drum. The drawn tickets form a random sample.*

EXPLANATION. The lottery tickets identical in all respects and each bearing a number of the tickets sold, are placed in a drum and thoroughly mixed. Then one ticket is drawn from the drum without looking at it. After the first ticket is drawn the rest of the tickets in the drum are again thoroughly shaken and mixed. Another ticket is then drawn. The process of alternate shuffling and drawing a ticket is continued until the required number of tickets, equal to the number of prizes to be awarded, are drawn. The drawn tickets then form a random sample. Since the tickets are similar in all respects except that they bear different numbers, and these are thoroughly mixed before a drawing, all the tickets have the same chance of being drawn. We cannot suspect in this case that any ticket has been drawn in preference to another.

Random Sampling is the simplest and most important among the various sampling techniques, and it is free from personal bias. Selection of items in a random sample depends entirely on chance.

Often every unit of the population is assigned a number and slips bearing these numbers (or names) are placed in a drum or box and thoroughly mixed. Then we can draw a sample (or required number) of slips as explained in the above illustration by using a table of random numbers. Random sampling is free from personal bias. Selection of items in a random sample depends entirely on chance.

There are two types of *random sampling*:

(i) **Simple Random Sampling with Replacement (SRSWR):** If units of a sample are drawn one by one from the population in such a way that after each drawing the selected units are returned to the population and that each time a drawing is made every number of the population has an equal chance of being drawn, then the *sampling* is called *simple random sampling with replacement.* If the population size is *finite,* the process is most suitable.

(ii) **Simple Random Sampling without Replacement (SRSWR):** If the units of a sample are drawn one by one from the population such that after each drawing the selected unit is not returned to the population and that each time a drawing is made, every one of the remaining members has an equal chance of being drawn, then the sampling is called *simple random sampling without replacement.* When the population is infinitely large (like *normal population*), random sampling without (or with) replacement is used.

Cases may sometimes arise, where it may so happen that the members constituting the population are so bulky or heavy or fragile that they cannot be put in a drum and mixed for the purpose of drawing a sample. Sometimes the members of the population may be immovable things. In such cases, random sampling is done by using a *table of random numbers* which consists of numbers of (say) two or four or five digits compiled by some random process.

ILLUSTRATION 1. *To select a random sample of* 5 *bags of rice from a shipload containing* 10, 000 *bags.*

ILLUSTRATION 2. *To choose a random sample o patients from a hospital in order to test the efficacy of a certain newly-invented drug.*

ILLUSTRATION 3. *To select randomly* 15 *words from a dictionary.*

ILLUSTRATION 4. *To select* 500 *plots of land in a State in a random way.*

Let us take illustration 1 and see how to draw random sample of 5 bags from the whole shipload. The method is as follows:

All the rice bags are first serially numbered from 1 to 10,000. Each of these numbers are then written on 10,000 small identical cards. The cards are placed inside a box, and 5 amongst them are chosen as in the lottery. The bags bearing the numbers corresponding to those on the drawn cards then comprise our random sample from the whole lot.

In this case, our problem of choosing 5 bags of rice is reduced to choosing 5 numbers between 1 and 10,000. This may, however, be done in an alternative way without bothering much about 10,000 identical cards and choosing cards one by one from the box. This is done with the help of so-called *random numbers.* Tables of random numbers are available, which show series of figures with the digits $0, 1, 2, 3, 4, \cdots, 9$ arranged in rows and columns in a purely haphazard manner (random fashion). The following is an extract from one of these two-digit series.

43	10	53	74	35	08	90	61	18	37	44	10
50	32	40	43	62	23	50	05	10	03	22	11
51	94	05	17	58	53	78	80	59	01	94	32
13	99	75	53	08	70	94	25	12	58	41	54

The 10,000 bags of rice of the ship are numbered $1, 2, \cdots, 99, 100, 101, \cdots, 999, 1000, \cdots, 9998, 9999, 10000$. From a page of random numbers we now select any row and column and take 5 four-digit figures successively as they occur. Thus, if we start from the digit in the first row and first column of the above series in random numbers and move horizontally, our selected numbers will be 4310, 5374, 3508, 9061, 1837. In other words, the bags bearing the above numbers will be our random sample from the whole shipload. Sometimes, it may so happen that a particular number appears more than once. In this case, the number is retained only once. If 0000 appeared, the bag bearing the number 10,000 would have been included in the sample.

In the case of choosing words at random from a dictionary or plots of land within a State, random numbers may be used as above.

There are different *random number series* (*or tables*) which are commonly used in practice.

(i) **Tippet's random number tables** which consist of 10,400 numbers of four digits selected at random from the British census reports.

(ii) **Fisher and Yates' tables** which was constructed by drawing numbers at random from A.S. Thomson's 20-figure logarithmic tables.

(iii) **Kendal and R. Smith's series** (or *random tables*) which consist of 25,000 random numbers of four digits.

(iv) **Rand corporation random number tables** which consist of 2,00,000 random numbers of five digits.

(v) **Indian Statistical Institute's random number tables.**

When the population is homogeneous in regard to a particular characteristics being studied, random samples are always expected to yield better results than by any other type of sample.

Random Sampling is a scientific process in which sampling error can be measured. It is economical in that it saves time, money and labour.

II. Stratified Sampling (or Stratified Random Sampling) [CA May 1990]

Stratified Sampling is generally used when the population is heterogeneous. In this case, the population is first sub-divided into several parts (or small groups) called *strata* according to some relevant characteristics so that each stratum is more or less homogeneous. Each stratum is called a sub-population. Then a small sample (called sub-sample) is selected from each stratum at random. All the sub-samples combined together form the *stratified sample.* This represents the population properly. The process of obtaining and examining a stratified sample with a view to estimating the characteristic of the population is known as **Stratified Sampling.**

ILLUSTRATION. *Let us select a stratified sample of* 100 *families from a city with a view to studying their economic conditions. For this purpose, the city area is divided into a number of strata, according to economic condition of their inhabitants, as measured by annual income (say). Thus, localities mostly inhabited by people with more or less similar annual income may be included under one stratum. A few families are then chosen at random from each so that the sum total of all the families from all the strata is* 100.

If proper stratification can be made so that the strata differ from each other as much as possible, but there is much homogeneity within each stratum, then a stratified sample will give better estimates of the population characteristics than a random sample of the same size.

III. Systematic Sampling (or Quasi-Random Sampling)

This means forming the sample in some systematic manner, usually by taking items at regular intervals. In this case, all the units of the population are arranged in some order. If the population size is finite, all the units are first serially listed and arranged in order. Then from the first k items, one unit is selected at random. This unit and every kth unit of the serially listed population combined together constitute a *systematic sample*. This type of sampling is known as *Systematic Sampling*.

ILLUSTRATION. *Suppose it is desired to select a systematic sample of* 500 *villages from a state having* 40,000 *villages. A list of all the villages which is our population, is first prepared and these are serially numbered. In this case the population size is* 80 *times the sample size. A number between* 1 *and* 80, *say* 57, *is selected at random with the help of random numbers. Then the village with serial number* 57 *is the first member of our sample. After the first member is drawn, every subsequent* 80*th village in the list, i.e., those with serial numbers* 137, 217, 297, 377, 457, $\cdots$ *etc. are included in the sample.*

It is thus seen that, as in the case of a random sample, listing of the population units is essential before a systematic sample is drawn. The difference however, lies in the fact that in the case of a random sample *all* the members have to be chosen randomly, whereas in the case of a systematic sample *only the first member has to be chosen at random.* Thus a systematic sample is much easier to choose than a random sample of the same size.

In the illustration above, the list of villages may be prepared in two ways. *Firstly,* the villages within a subdivision are consecutively written and after this is done, another subdivision within the same district is chosen and all its villages listed. The process is continued until all the villages in a district are included in the list. Then another district is chosen and all its villages are similarly listed. The complete list of villages is then serially numbered. In this list all the villages under one subdivision or district occupy a particular portion of the list. *Secondly,* all the villages within the State are alphabetically arranged and given a serial number. It is worth noting that since the alphabetical order of the villages has no relation with their relative geographical position, a systematic sample from the alphabetical list will be equivalent to a ramdom sample.

Similarly, while articles are being produced in a factory every item say, 5th or 18th or 47th produced may be taken out to form a sample and examined for any possible defect in the shape or size or any quality of the product. If the periodicity of production does not coincide with the sampling interval, i.e., 5 or 18, or 47, as quoted above, then the systematic sample is expected to be equivalent to a ramdom one. But, if we go on examining every 50th item during production and it is found that the machine is to be fed with raw materials everytime 50 or 100 or 150 or any multiple of 50 articles are produced, then the systematic sample is certainly *not* to be treated as a random or a representative sample.

IV. Multi-Stage Sampling

In this method, the sampling procedure is carried out in several stages. The population is first divided into large groups called first-stage units. These first-stage units are then divided into smaller groups, called second-stage units, and second-stage units are divided into third-stage units, and so on until we come to the ultimate units or a sample of desired size. At first, a sample of the first stage units is chosen by any suitable method. Then a sample of second-stage units is selected from each of the selected first-stage units and the process is repeated from stage to stage until we reach the ultimate units.

ILLUSTRATION. *Let us try to choose* 500 *villages from West Bengal with a total number of* 38,471 *villages. The whole of the State may firstly be supposed to be composed of Police Stations, nearly* 300 *in number; and it is not at all difficult to choose a few amongst them. The Police Stations thus comprise our first stage sampling units. These Police Stations are composed of several Unions, and we choose a number of Unions from each of the selected Police Stations. The Unions are our second stage sampling units. From each of the Unions thus selected, we finally choose our required number of villages. These villages are our third stage of basic sampling units.*

The advantage in choosing the multi-stage sample of 500 villages over a random sample of the same size is that all the 38,471 villages are not required to be listed or numbered. Only the 300 Police Stations first require listing for selection. After the selection of Police Stations is done, only those Unions which lie within the jurisdiction of the selected Police Stations need be listed for selection of second stage units. Finally, only a list of those villages which lie within the selected Unions has to be prepared for selection of the villages.

Multi-stage sampling is useful in cases where the survey is contemplated over a wide area and journey from one part to the other is rather difficult and expensive.

In all the sampling procedures mentioned above, it is possible to forecast the accuracy of the estimate.

ILLUSTRATION. *In forecasting the yield of jute, say, we may select some villages and therefrom choose a large number of plots of land by the procedure of multi-stage sampling. If only these selected plots of land are visited and the yield of jute crop estimated, it is possible to forecast the total yield of jute for the whole of the State subject to a small percentage of error. The actual yield, may not be exactly the same as estimated by sample survey methods. But the maximum possible difference between the actual and the estimated values may be calculated and stated in terms of probability.*

3.3. NON-RANDOM SAMPLING METHODS

I. Purposive Sampling (or Judgment Sampling)

When the choice of the individual items of a sample entirely depends on the discretion (i.e., individual judgment) of the investigator (or sampler), it is called a *Purposive* or *Judgment Sampling.*

In this type, the members constituting the sample are chosen not according to some definite scientific procedure, but according to *convenience and personal choice* of the individual, who selects the sample. Two or more such independent purposive samples may give widely different estimates of the same population. In this method, the investigator must have a good deal of experience and a thorough knowledge of the population. Purposive selection is always subject to some kind of bias. This method is suitable when the sample is small.

ILLUSTRATION. *If a sample of* 10 *students is to be selected from a class of* 80 *to analyse the extra-curricular activities of the students of the class, the investigator would select* 10 *students who, in his judgment, would represent the class.*

II. Quota Sampling

In this method, the interviewers (or investigators) are assigned definite quotas according to certain criteria. They are instructed to obtain the required number of interviews to fill in each quota. The interviewers select the individuals (i.e., sample items) for interviews on their personal judgments within the quotas. When all or a part of the whole quota is not available or approachable, the quota is completed by supplementing new respondents. Quota Sampling is a type of Judgment Sampling It is cheap and easy, but it is open to various types of errors and bias. This method is often used in marketing research studies.

III. Convenience Sampling

In this type of sampling, a sample is selected from readily available lists (or source) like, Telephone directories, Automobile registration records, Stock Exchange directories, etc. Such a sample is called a *convenience* sample and it is a convenient slice (or fraction) of the population. Convenience sampling is useful in public opinion surveys, making pilot studies, and to audit accounts.

IV. Cluster Sampling (or Block Sampling)

This method is useful when the population is widely dispersed and consists of an unequal concentration of individual units. In this type of sampling, we first form suitable clusters or blocks of units of higher concentration. Then we survey all the units of some clusters selected by any suitable sampling method. It is also called *area sampling.* Though this method has some advantages, it is not scientific as it is subject to personal bias. Cluster sampling is used for geographical studies of many kinds.

V. Sequential Sampling

This method consists of a number (or a sequence) of samples drawn one after another from the population depending on the results of previous samples. If the result of the first sample leads to a decision that it is not at all acceptable, the lot from which the sample was drawn is rejected. But if the result indicates that the first sample is acceptable, no new sample is drawn. However, if the first sample leads to no clear decision, second sample is drawn and, as before, if required a third sample is drawn to arrive at a final decision to accept or reject the lot. This sampling method is widely used in connection with Statistical quality control.

VI. Use of Statistical Methods in Accounts and Auditing [CA May 1984]

Statistical methods are popularly used in the field of accounting and auditing, particularly when the area of enquiry is fairly large. Statistical methods may be used in the following ways.

(i) It is used for proper classification of accounts.

(ii) It is used for finding trend in respect of financial results over a period of time.

(iii) It is used for showing the correlation or relationship between the variables like production and sales or future price and cost of production.

(iv) It is used for the inflation accounting by using *Price Indices.*

The main object of auditing is to verify accounts with documentary and other evidences and to report whether the final accounting statements are true and fair. As the volume of transactions in a business is very large, it is often impossible to verify each and every transaction in detail. In such a situation, an auditor makes use of sampling techniques in carrying out his work. He may perform his duties by conducting *test checking or pilot survey or sample survey.* This technique will save time, cost and energy. On the basis of the result obtained from the analysis of a sample, the auditor becomes aware of the extent of audit risk and then arrive at a valid conclusion.

3.4. PILOT SURVEY

Before conducting a large-scale exercise in a statistical enquiry, it is always better to run a small exploratory or **pilot survey** in the fie' of enquiry. Such a *pilot survey* will be useful in the following ways.

(i) It can reveal deficiencies in the sampling frame and the sample design.

(ii) It can reveal whether the postal or the interview method is better.

(iii) It can indicate the likely response rate in a larger survey; it may also identify the main sources of non-response and indicate how they should be dealt with in the main survey.

(iv) It will analyse the first draft of the questionnaire and reveal the defects, if any.

(v) It will provide insights into the problems faced by the interviewers.

(vi) It can provide guidance as to the best form of administrative set-up for the survey.

Use of Statistical Methods in Accounts and Auditing **[CA May 1984]**

Statistical methods are popularly used in the field of accounting and auditing, particularly when the area of enquiry is fairly large. Statistical methods may be used in the following ways.

(i) It is used for proper classification of accounts.

(ii) It is used for finding trend in respect of financial results over a period of time.

(iii) It is used for showing the correlation or relationship between the variables like production and sales or future price and cost of production.

(iv) It is used for the inflation accounting by using *Price Indices.*

The main object of auditing is to verify accounts with documentary and other evidences and to report whether the final accounting statements are true and fair. As the volume of transactions in a business is very large, it is often impossible to verify each and every transaction in detail. In such a situation, an auditor makes use of sampling techniques in carrying out his work. He may perform his duties by conducting *test checking* or *pilot survey* or *sample survey.* This technique will save time, cost and energy. On the basis of the result obtained from the analysis of a sample, the auditor becomes aware of the extent of audit risk and then arrive at a valid conclusion.

3.5. ABSOLUTE AND RELATIVE ERRORS **[CA May 1981,1983]**

In Statistics errors occur in measurement, counting, approximation, sampling, etc. To guard ourselves against arriving at wrong conclusions due to errors occuring beyond certain limits, we should measure errors and express them in absolute and relative terms. Some errors do not affect the validity of our conclusions.

Absolute error *in statistics is defind as the actual difference between the true value and the estimated (or observed) value, i.e., Absolute error = True value ~ Estimated value*; e.g., if 5.01 kg. is taken as 5 kg., then Absolute error = 5.01 − 5 = .01.

Relative error *in statistics is defined as the ratio of the absolute error to the true value, often expressed as a percentage i.e.,*

$$\text{Relative error} = \frac{\text{Absolute error}}{\text{True value}} \quad \text{or} \quad \frac{\text{Absolute error}}{\text{True value}} \times 100\%;$$

e.g., If 5.01 kg. is taken as 5 kg., then Relative error $= \frac{.01}{5.01} = \frac{1}{501}$ or .2%.

Sampling and Non-sampling Errors **[CA November 1983]**

A *Parameter* is a statistical measure like population mean, population S.D., etc. based on all the units of the units of the population. *Statistic* is also a statistical measure like sample mean, sample S.D. etc., based only on the units selected in the sample.

A sample is a part of the population from which it is drawn. Therefore, it cannot be expected generally to supply full information about the population, though any information obtained from the sample is taken as a characteristic of the population. There will, therefore, be in most cases difference between *Statistics* and *Parameters*. These differences (or errors) are called *Sampling Errors*.

In all surveys (sample survey or census) some errors may occur during collection of the actual information. These errors are called *non-sampling errors*. Non-sampling errors cannot be measured.

3.6. SIMULATION

About 30 years ago Prof. J. V. Neumann and Prof. S. M. Ulam first used *Simulation Technique* in solving the nuclear-shielding problems which were too complicated for analysis and too expensive for experimental solution.

Simulation *is a quantitative technique used for conducting a series of organized trial and error experiments (alternative to analytical treatment) on a model of a system (or process) to predict the behaviour of the system (or process) over a period of time. In fact, simulation is a method of making decisions under conditions of uncertainty, particularly where the mathematical formulation of the problem is not possible.* It is a device to provide solutions to various business problems where either all values of the variables are not known in advance or there is no easy way to find such values. Many real-life business problems are so complicated that it is often impossible to transcribe them in mathematical equations or to solve the equations even when they could be so transcribed. In such cases, (when analytical methods either fail or become complicated), *Simulation Technique* is used to find solutions to such problems.

For *Simulation*, we first formulate a mathematical model describing the operation of the system which represents an image of reality and then perform sampling experiment on the model of the system.

There are two types of *Simulation*:

1. **Monte Carlo Method.**
2. **System Simulation Method.**

Of the above two methods, *Monte Carlo Simulation* is widely used as an alternative to analytical (or mathematical) evaluation of a model for many types of problems. Analytical solution gives the optimal or correct answer, while *Monte Carlo Simulation* yields a solution which is very close to the optimal but not necessarily the exact (or correct) solution. However, simulated solution converges to the optimal (or correct) solution as the number of simulated trials become indefinitely large. This is possible only with high-speed computers. In practice, it is necessary to truncate the simulation process after a finite (or limited) number of trials.

System Simulation Method is the reproduction of the operating environment which is too complicated and too costly. We explain here **Monte Carlo Simulation.**

3.7. MONTE CARLO SIMULATION BASED ON RANDOM NUMBERS

For *Monte Carlo Simulation*, we develop a model which describes the operation of the system under study. The first step is to define the problem and structure it in a quantitative format without concerning ourselves whether it is to be solved by simulation or by analytical methods. The model developed needs to be complete and realistic representation of all important (or essential) aspects of the system under study. All models are not suitable for Monte Carlo Simulation. Only models under uncertainty can be evaluated by the Monte Carlo Technique, because this technique is based on the continued observation of the system over a long period of experience. Theoretically, we draw on a large number of samples from the model and through these observations examine the behaviour of the system.

The Monte Carlo Method used to simulate a sample is based on the use of *random numbers.* The random numbers are numbers selected in such a way that every number has an equal chance of being drawn. After selecting a random number we convert it into an observation drawn from the probability distribution specified by the model.

Let us consider an easy example to illustrate the basic concept of *Monte Carlo Simulation.*

EXAMPLE. *Suppose we build a model of a production line which on an average produces* 7% *defective items that occur at random. Items are packed for sale in the lots of five. Suppose we like to know what percentage of the lots contains no defective.*

Using *analytical methods*, the answer is

$$^5C_0(.07)^0(.93)^{5-0} = (.93)^5 = 0.6957 \text{ or } 0.70.$$

Let us now use Monte Carlo Simulation to answer the same question. We can use four-digit random numbers 0000 to 9999 where the random numbers 0000 to 0699 represent defective items and 0700 to 9999 represent good (i.e., non-defective) items. Let us now generate random numbers by the *mid-square technique* (due to J.V. Neumann and Metropolis) as follows:

Take a four-digit number and square it. From the result take the four-digit starting with the third from the left. This is the first random number. To find the second random number start with the new four-digit number (i.e., the first random number) and repeat the process. Such a procedure will generally produce 10^5 random numbers. For our example, suppose we start with the number 4835. The first random number is 3772 [$\because$ $(4835)^2 = 23377225$] and, therefore, the first item sampled is *good*, since random numbers 0700 to 9999 represent good items. The second random number is 2279 [$\because$ $(3772)^2 \doteq 14227984$] and, therefore, the second item is also good. Similarly, the third, fourth and fifth random numbers are respectively 9384, 0594 and 2836 and, therefore, the third item is good, the fourth item is defective, and the fifth item is good. Thus, the first lot of five items sampled at random contains one defective item. Repeating this process we draw 8 lots the results of which are tabulated in the following table. If the simulated item is good, we represent it by G. Similarly, defective item is represented by D.

Table 3.1 **Results of the Simulated Lots drawn**

Lot	Random Numbers	Simulated items	Number of defective items in Lot
1	3772, 2279, 9384, 0594, 2836	G, G, G, D, G	1
2	4289, 3955, 6420, 2164, 8289	G, G, G, G, G	0
3	7075, 0556, 9136, 4664, 7528	G, D, G, G, G	1
4	6707, 9838, 7862, 8110, 7721	G, G, G, G, G	0
5	6138, 6750, 5625, 6406, 0368	G, G, G, G, D	1
6	5424, 4197, 6148, 7979, 6644	G, G, G, G, G	0
7	1427, 3632, 1914, 6339, 1829	G, G, G, G, G	0
8	4524, 4665, 7622, 0948, 8704	G, G, G, G, G	0

From the above table we see that on the basis of the simulated sample of 8 lots, the expected percentage of good lots is $\frac{5}{8}$ i.e., 0.625. This does not equal the analytical answer 0.70 found earlier. The result of simulated items in Table 3.1 is based on only 8 samples. With the help of computers we could increase the number of samples from 8 to 8000 in a few minutes of computer time, and concurrently the accuracy of our answer would also increase. Monte Carlo Simulation gives only an approximate answer. If the number of simulated replications is large and the model is good, the approximation will be excellent.

The *mid-square technique* shown above is one of the various methods that are used for generating random numbers. Whenever we use a method, we must be careful to ensure that *the numbers generated are random and the result in observations follows the probability distribution specified in the model.* This is very important in *Monte Carlo Simulation.* Instead of generating random numbers, in many cases of simulation we may use published tables of *random numbers* (or *random digits*).

Monte Carlo Methods are used to study traffic flow on proposed freeways, to conduct war games, to study the spread of epidemics or human behaviour during natural disaster (i.e., flood or earthquake, etc.). In business research, such methods are also used to solve inventory problems, production scheduling, and to study many other situations involving over-all planning and organization.

Monte Carlo Technique used in *Sampling* is called **Sampling Simulation** or **Simulated Sampling.** It provides a good deal of insight into the sampling process, and into the imaginative ways that a statistician can use computers. Sampling by repeated hand calculations is a lengthy and time consuming process. In practice, a computer is much better and is popularly used for repetitive calculations. A computer can easily draw a sample and calculate its mean, then repeat this procedure over and over, hundreds of times in a second. It takes only a few minutes to build up a frequency distribution that very closely approximates a probability distribution. The process is called *computer Monte Carlo* or *Sampling Simulation.*

Monte Carlo Techniques are commonly used to check theoretical results. It is used to estimate sampling distributions in cases where theoretical sampling distributions are too difficult to derive.

Exercise 3

(Sampling Theory: Different methods of Sampling)

1. Distinguish between *complete enumeration* and *sample survey*. How far is the latter more advantageous than the former and why?

2. What do you mean by *Sampling*? What are the various types of sampling?

3. Define the terms *Population* and *Sample*. Give one example for each.

4. What is sampling? Give its objects and name the two laws which form the basis of sampling.

5. Explain the terms: (a) Random Sampling; (b) Law of Statistical Regularity; (c) Sample Survey.

6. (a) Distinguish clearly between *Stratified* and *Cluster Sampling*.

(b) Distinguish between random sampling and stratified sampling. Give one illustration of each. **[ICWAI Dec 1985]**

7. (i) Describe the different types of sampling known to you. Illustrate your answer with suitable examples. **[CA Nov 1982]**

(ii) Describe briefly any three types of sampling commonly used. **[CA Nov 1981]**

8. What do you mean by *Stratified Random Sampling*? Discuss the advantages of stratified sampling over simple random sampling.

9. Explain the terms: (a) Systematic Sampling; (b) Multi-stage Sampling; (c) Purposive Sampling; (d) Quota Sampling; (e) Cluster Sampling; (f) Convenience Sampling; (g) Sequential Sampling.

10. Write short notes on the following:

(a) Random Sampling. **[CA Nov 1980]**

(b) Stratified Sampling. **[CA May 1980,'86; Nov 1983; ICWAI June 1994]**

(c) Sampling and its uses. **[CA May 1981,'82]**

(d) Application of Sampling in the Audit Accounts. **[CA Nov 1978]**

(e) Use of Statistical methods in Accounts and Auditing **[CA May 1984]**

(f) Absolute and Relative errors. **[CA May 1981, '83]**

(g) Sampling and Non-sampling errors. **[CA May 1978; Nov 1983]**

11. What do you mean by *Simulation*? What is *Monte Carlo Simulation*?

12. Write short notes on *Monte Carlo Simulation* and illustrate it by an example.

13. "There are many different ways of selecting a sample". Describe the important sampling methods pointing out the characteristics of each. **[CA May 1987]**

14. Write short notes on "Stratified Random Sampling" and "Sequential Sampling".

[CA Foundation June 1994]

CHAPTER 4

SAMPLING DISTRIBUTION: STATISTICAL ESTIMATION AND TESTING OF HYPOTHESIS

4.1. INTRODUCTION

We know that **population** (or *universe*) is the aggregate of statistical data forming a subject of investigation and a **sample** is a portion of the population which is examined with a view to estimating the characteristics of the population. *Sampling theory* is the study of relationships between a population and samples drawn from the population and it is applicable to random samples only. In this chapter, our main object will be to obtain the maximum information about the population with the help of samples, i.e. to estimate the true value of the population parameters (e.g. population mean, population S.D. and population proportion, etc.) by using *sample statistics* like sample mean, sample S.D., sample proportion, etc. and to find the limits of accuracy of estimates based on samples. Sampling theory helps us to determine whether the differences between two samples are actually due to chance variation or whether they are really significant. It is also useful in **testing of hypothesis** *and* **significance** which is important in the *theory of decisions.*

Parameter

It is a statistical measure based on all the units of a population. For example, population mean, population S.D., proportion of defectives in the population are **parameters.**

Statistic

Sample statistic on simply *statistic is a statistical measure based only on all the units* (*or observations*) *selected in a sample.* For example, sample mean, sample S.D., proportion of defectives in the sample are **statistics.**

29

NOTE. As the units (or observations) selected in two or more samples drawn from a population are not the same, the value of a *statistic* varies from sample to sample, but the *parameter* always remains constant (since all the units in a population always remain the same). The variation in the value of a *statistic* is called *sampling fluctuation*. A *parameter* has no sampling fluctuation. Usually, *statistic* is used to estimate the value of an unknown *parameter*.

4.2. SAMPLING DISTRIBUTION OF A STATISTIC

Let us consider a population of size N (i.e. a population containing N units) and let us draw all possible random samples of a given size n. We get $N_{C_n} = k$ (say) samples each of size n. For each of these k samples, we compute a statistic (i.e., sample mean or S.D. or proportion of defectives, etc.). The value of a statistic t may vary from sample to sample. Let $t_1, t_2, \cdots, t_k$ be the values of statistic t for the k samples. Each of these values occurs with a definite probability. Thus we can construct a table showing the set of values $t_1, t_2, \cdots, t_k$ of t with their respective probabilities. This *probability distribution* of t is known as the **Sampling Distribution** of t.

If N is large, the number k of all possible samples is also large ($\because\ k > N$). In such a case, the values $t_1, t_2, \cdots, t_k$ of t may be arranged in the form of a relative frequency distribution and the limiting form of this relative frequency distribution when the number of samples k becomes infinitely large (i.e., when $k \to \infty$), is called the **sampling distribution** of *statistic* t. A *statistic* (i.e., sample mean, sample S.D., sample proportion of defectives, etc.) has always a *sampling distribution*, but a *parameter* (i.e. population mean, population S.D., population proportion, etc.) has no sampling distribution.

NOTE. In simple sampling, each unit of the population has an equal chance of being included in the sample and, therefore, it must be done *with replacement when the population is finite.* But if the population is *infinite, no replacement is necessary.* In simple random sampling, a member x_i of a sample can assume any one of the N units of the population with the same probability.

Central Limit Theorem (*Two important Sampling Distributions*)

I. *If $\bar{x}$ be the mean of a random sample of size n drawn from a population having mean μ and S.D. σ, then the sampling distribution of the sample mean $\bar{x}$ is approximately a normal distribution with mean μ and S.D. = S.E. of $\bar{x}$, provided the sample size n is sufficiently large* ($n \geq 30$).

II. *If p be the proportion of defectives in a random sample of size n drawn from a population having the proportion of defectives P, then the sampling distribution of the sample proportion of defectives p is approximately a normal distribution with mean P and S.D. = S.E. of p, provided the sample size n is sufficiently large* ($n \geq 30$).

Usually a sample of size 30 or more is considered as a 'large sample'. However, the larger the value of n, the better is the approximation.

4.3. STANDARD ERROR (S.E.) OF A STATISTIC

The standard error of a statistic t (i.e., S.E. of sample mean, or sample S.D. or sample proportion of defectives, etc.) is the standard deviation of the sampling distribution of the statistic. Thus S.E. of sample mean $\bar{x}$ is the S.D. of the sampling distribution of sample mean. It will play a very important role in the sampling theory.

S.E. is used as a tool in *tests of hypotheses or tests of significance.* It gives an idea about the reliability and precision of a sample. It helps in determining the limits (confidence limits) within which the parameters are expected to lie.

The formulae (without proof) for the standard errors (S.E.) of some well-known statistics for random samples are given below. In this chapter, we shall denote population mean by μ, population

S.D. by σ, population proportion by P (where $Q = 1 - P$), sample size by n, sample mean by $\bar{x}$, sample S.D. by s and sample proportion by p (where $q = 1 - p$).

Formulae for S.E.

1. S.E. of sample mean $\bar{x}(\hat{\sigma}_{\bar{x}}) = \frac{\sigma}{\sqrt{n}}$.

2. S.E. of sample proportion $p = \sqrt{\frac{PQ}{n}}$, where $Q = 1 - P$.

3. S.E. of sample S.D. (s) $= \sqrt{\frac{\sigma^2}{2n}}$ or $\frac{\sigma}{\sqrt{2n}}$.

4. S.E. of the difference of two sample means $\bar{x}_1$ and $\bar{x}_2$, i.e., S.E. of $(\bar{x}_1 - \bar{x}_2) = \sqrt{\frac{\sigma_1^2}{n_1} + \frac{\sigma_2^2}{n_2}}$, where $\bar{x}_1$ *and* $\bar{x}_2$ *are the means of two random samples of sizes* n_1 *and* n_2 *drawn from two populations with* S.D. σ_1 *and* σ_2 *respectively.*

5. S.E. of $(p_1 - p_2) = \sqrt{\frac{P_1Q_1}{n_1} + \frac{P_2Q_2}{n_2}}$, *where* p_1 *and* p_2 *are the proportions of two random samples of sizes* n_1 *and* n_2 *drawn from two populations with proportions* P_1 *and* P_2 *respectively.*

6. S.E. of $(s_1 - s_2)$ = S.E. of diff. of two sample S.D. $= \sqrt{\frac{\sigma_1^2}{2n_1} + \frac{\sigma_2^2}{2n_2}}$.

For a **finite population** *of size* N, **when a sample is drawn without replacement,** *we have*

(i) **S.E. of sample mean $= \frac{\sigma}{\sqrt{n}} \cdot \sqrt{\frac{N-n}{N-1}}$.**

(ii) **S.E. of sample proportion $= \sqrt{\frac{PQ}{n}} \cdot \sqrt{\frac{N-n}{N-1}}$.**

If the sample size is *large,* we can assume the sampling distribution to be **normal**. Again if the value of the sampling fraction n/N is greater than 0.05, then *finite population correction factor* $\sqrt{\frac{N-n}{N-1}}$ is used.

For an infinite population when the sample is drawn without replacement, Formulae 1 and 2 remain the same.

Uses of S.E.

1. S.E. is used to find the *precision* of the sample estimate of a population parameter. If a statistic t is used to estimate the parameter θ, then precision of $t = \frac{1}{\text{S.E. of } t}$.

2. S.E. is used to test whether the difference $(t - \theta)$ between the sample statistic and the population parameter is *significant* or it is due to sampling fluctuations.

3. It is used to test whether the difference between two independent sample estimates of the same population parameter is *significant.*

4. It is used to test the equality of two population parameters (i.e., population means, population proportions).

5. It is used to determine the *point estimates* of a population parameter.

6. It is used to find *the interval estimate* of a population parameter.

PROPOSITION. *The mean and* S.E. *of sample mean* $\bar{x}$ (*i.e., mean and* S.D. *of the sampling distribution of* $\bar{x}$) *when samples of the same size* n *are drawn from a population having mean* μ *and* S.D. σ *are given by* **Mean of $\bar{x} = E(\bar{x}) = \mu$ and S.E. of $\bar{x} = \sigma/\sqrt{n}$.**

PROOF Let $x_1, x_2, \cdots, x_n$ be the units (or observations) selected in a simple random sample from a finite population of N units $X_1, X_2, \cdots, X_N$.

Then $\bar{x} = \frac{x_1+x_2+\cdots+x_n}{n}$ and $\mu = \frac{X_1+X_2+\cdots+X_N}{N}$.

In simple random sampling, each sample member x_i can assume any one of the N units of the population with the same probability 1/N. Therefore, x_i is a random variable with the probability distribution given by

x_i :	X_1	X_2	$\cdots$	X_N	Total
p_i :	$1/N$	$1/N$	$\cdots$	$1/N$	1

$$\therefore E(x_i) = \frac{1}{N}X_1 + \frac{1}{N}X_2 + \cdots + \frac{1}{N}X_N = \frac{X_1 + X_2 + \cdots + X_N}{N} = \mu$$

i.e., $\mathbf{E(x_i) = \mu}$, **for** $\mathbf{i = 1, 2, \cdots, n}$.

and Var $(x_i) = E\{x_i - E(x_i)\}^2 = E(x_i - \mu)^2 =$ population variance $= \sigma^2$.

Now

$$E(\bar{x}) = E\left\{\frac{x_1 + x_2 + \cdots + x_n}{n}\right\} = \frac{1}{n}E(x_1 + x_2 + \cdots + x_n)$$

$$= \frac{1}{n}\{E(x_1) + E(x_2) + \cdots + E(x_n)\} = \frac{1}{n}(\mu + \mu + \cdots \text{to } n \text{ terms}) = \frac{1}{n} \cdot n\mu = \mu$$

$$\text{and Var }(\bar{x}) = E\{\bar{x} - E(\bar{x})\}^2 = E(\bar{x} - \mu)^2 = E\left\{\frac{\Sigma x}{n} - \frac{n\mu}{n}\right\}^2 = E\left\{\frac{\Sigma(x-\mu)}{n}\right\}^2$$

$$= \frac{1}{n^2}E\left\{\sum(x - \mu)\right\}^2 = \frac{1}{n^2}E\left\{\sum_{i=1}^{n} E(x_i - \mu)^2 + 2\sum_{\substack{i,j=1\\(i<j)}}^{n} E(x_i - \mu)E(x_j - \mu)\right\}.$$

[$\because x_i$ and x_j are independent random variables, as the samples are drawn *with replacement.*]

$= \frac{1}{n^2}\{n\sigma^2 + 2.\Sigma 0.0.\}[\because E(x_i - \mu) = E(x_i) - E(\mu) = \mu - \mu = 0$ and $E(x_i - \mu)^2 = \sigma^2; i = 1, 2, \cdots, n.]$

$$= \frac{1}{n^2} \times n\sigma^2 = \frac{\sigma^2}{n}.$$

Hence S.E. of $\bar{\mathbf{x}} = \sqrt{\text{Var }(\bar{x})} = \sqrt{\frac{\sigma^2}{n}} = \frac{\sigma}{\sqrt{\mathbf{n}}}$.

4.3.1. Illustrative Examples

EXAMPLE 1. *A population consists of the four numbers* 3, 4, 2, 5. *Consider all possible distinct samples of size two and verify that the population mean is equal to the mean of the sample means.*

SOLUTION. The population mean $(\mu) = \frac{3+4+2+5}{4} = 3.5$.

All possible distinct samples of size two and the corresponding sample means are shown in the following table:

TABLE 4.1 SAMPLES OF SIZE TWO AND THEIR SAMPLE MEANS

Sample No. (1)	Samples (2)	Total of the sample values (3)	Sample mean [Col. 3 ÷ 2] (4)
1	3,4	7	3.5
2	3,2	5	2.5
3	3,5	8	4.0
4	4,2	6	3.0
5	4,5	9	4.5
6	2,5	7	3.5
Total	...	...	21.0

[Sampling used in the above table is *random sampling without replacement* and *the no. of samples* = $^4C_2 = 6$].

Mean of sample means $= \frac{21.0}{6} = \frac{7}{2} = \mathbf{3.5}$.

Hence, the population mean $= \mathbf{3.5} =$ the mean of the sample means.

EXAMPLE 2.

(i) *A simple random sample of size* 36 *is drawn from a finite population consisting of* 101 *units. If the population* S.D. *is* 12.6, *find the standard error of sample mean when the sample is drawn* (a) *with replacement,* (b) *without replacement.*

(ii) *If a random sample of size* 5 *is drawn from a finite population of* 41 *units without replacement, then find the standard error of the sample mean, if the population* S.D. *is* 10.

[ICWAI June 1992]

SOLUTION.

(i) (a) If the sample is drawn with replacement, then

$$\text{S.E. of sample mean } \bar{x} = \frac{\sigma}{\sqrt{n}} = \frac{12.6}{\sqrt{36}} = \frac{12.6}{6} = \mathbf{2.1}.$$

(b) If the sample is drawn without replacement, then

$$\text{S.E. of sample mean } \bar{x} = \frac{\sigma}{\sqrt{n}} \cdot \frac{\sqrt{N-n}}{N-1}.$$

Here $\sigma = 12.6, n = 36, N = 101$.

$$\therefore \quad \text{S.E. of sample mean } \bar{x} = \frac{12.6}{6} \cdot \sqrt{\frac{101-36}{101-1}} = 2.1 \times \sqrt{\frac{65}{100}} = 2.1 \times \sqrt{0.65} = 2.1 \times 0.806$$
$$= 1.6926 = \mathbf{1.69}.$$

(ii) S.E. of the sample mean $\bar{x} = \frac{\sigma}{\sqrt{n}} \cdot \sqrt{\frac{N-n}{N-1}}$.

Here $n = 5, N = 41, \sigma = 10$.

$$\therefore \quad \text{S.E. of } \bar{x} = \frac{10}{\sqrt{5}} \cdot \sqrt{\frac{41-5}{41-1}} = \frac{10}{\sqrt{5}} \cdot \sqrt{\frac{36}{40}} = \frac{6}{2} \cdot \frac{10}{\sqrt{5}} \cdot \frac{1}{\sqrt{10}} = 3 \cdot \frac{\sqrt{10}}{\sqrt{5}} = \mathbf{3\sqrt{2}}.$$

EXAMPLE 3. *A random sample of* 500 *oranges was taken from a large consignment and* 65 *were found to be defective. Show that the* S.E. *of the proportion of bad ones in a sample of this size is* 0.015. **[ICWAI June 1984]**

SOLUTION. Here $n = 500, p =$ sample proportion of defectives $= \frac{65}{500} = 0.13$.

Since the population proportion P is not known, we take the value of p for P.

$$\therefore \quad \text{S.E. of } p = \sqrt{\frac{PQ}{n}} = \sqrt{\frac{pq}{n}} \text{ (approximately)}, \quad \text{where } q = 1 - p$$
$$= \sqrt{\frac{0.13 \times (1-0.13)}{500}} = \sqrt{\frac{0.13 \times 0.87}{500}} = \sqrt{0.000226} = \mathbf{0.015 \text{ (approx.)}}.$$

EXAMPLE 4. *A simple random sample of size* 9 *is drawn without replacement from a finite population consisting of* 25 *units. If the number of defective units in the population be* 5, *find the* S.E. *of the sample proportion of defectives.*

SOLUTION. S.E. of the sample proportion of defectives $= \sqrt{\frac{PQ}{n}} \cdot \sqrt{\frac{N-n}{N-1}}$;

Here $N = 25, n = 9, P = \frac{5}{25} = \frac{1}{5}, Q = 1 - P = 1 - \frac{1}{5} = \frac{4}{5}$.

$$\therefore \quad \text{S.E. of the sample proportion of defectives} = \sqrt{\frac{\frac{1}{5} \times \frac{4}{5}}{9}} \cdot \sqrt{\frac{25-9}{25-1}} = \frac{\frac{2}{5}}{3} \times \sqrt{\frac{16}{24}} = \frac{2}{15}\sqrt{\frac{2}{3}}$$

$$= \frac{2}{15} \times 0.8165 = \mathbf{0.1088}.$$

EXAMPLE 5. *Let the five numbers* 3, 4, 5, 6, 7 *constitute a universe. Select all samples of size three. Compute their means. Compare the mean of the sample means with the mean of the Universe.*

[C.U. M. Com. 1966]

SOLUTION. The mean μ of the Universe (i.e., population mean) is given by

$$\mu = \frac{3+4+5+6+7}{5} = \frac{25}{5} = 5.$$

All possible samples of size three (the no. of samples $= {}^5C_3 = 10$) and their means are shown in the following table:

TABLE 4.2 SAMPLES OF SIZE THREE AND THEIR SAMPLE MEANS

Sample No. (1)	Sample Values (2)	Total of the Sample Values (3)	Sample Mean [Col. 3 ÷ 3] (4)
1	3, 4, 5	12	4
2	3, 4, 6	13	$4\frac{1}{3}$
3	3, 4, 7	14	$4\frac{2}{3}$
4	3, 5, 6	14	$4\frac{2}{3}$
5	3, 5, 7	15	5
6	3, 6, 7	16	$5\frac{1}{3}$
7	4, 5, 6	15	5
8	4, 5, 7	16	$5\frac{1}{3}$
9	4, 6, 7	17	$5\frac{2}{3}$
10	5, 6, 7	18	6
Total	...	...	50

Mean of sample means $= \frac{50}{10} = 5$.

Thus **mean of sample means = mean of the universe.**

NOTE. In Example 5, random sampling without replacement is implied. When a unit, say 3, is drawn, without replacing it, we draw two more units 4, 5, to obtain the sample $\{3, 4, 5\}$ or 4, 6, to obtain the sample $\{3, 4, 6\}$ etc. In random sampling without replacement, each member (or unit) of a population cannot be selected more than once in a sample (but in random sampling with replacement a unit may be chosen more than once in a sample) and in such a case we can prove as in Example 1 or Example 5 that mean of sample means = population mean.

EXAMPLE 6. *A population consists of the four members* 3, 7, 11, 15. *Consider all possible samples of size two which can be drawn with replacement from this population. Find* (i) *the population mean,* (ii) *the population* S.D., (iii) *the mean of the sampling distribution of means;* (iv) S.D. *of the sampling distribution. Verify* (iii) *and* (iv) *by using* (i) *and* (ii) *and by use of suitable formulae. Solve this problem if sampling is without replacement.* **[ICWAI December 1976; June 1992]**

SOLUTION.

(i) μ = Population mean $= \frac{\Sigma x}{N} = \frac{3+7+11+15}{4} = \frac{36}{4} = 9.$

(ii) σ = Population S.D. $= \sqrt{\frac{\Sigma(x-\mu)^2}{N}} = \sqrt{\frac{(-6)^2+(-2)^2+(2)^2+(6)^2}{4}} = \sqrt{\frac{80}{4}} = \sqrt{20}.$

(iii) **Simple Random Sampling with replacement (SRSWR).** All possible random samples of size two *with replacement* (in this case the no. of samples $= N^n = 4^2$), and their sample means are shown in the following table:

TABLE 4.3 SAMPLES OF SIZE TWO AND THEIR SAMPLE MEANS

Sl. No.	Sample Values	Total	Sample Mean	Sl. No.	Sample Values	Total	Sample Mean
1	3, 3	6	3	9	11, 3	14	7
2	3, 7	10	5	10	11, 7	18	9
3	3, 11	14	7	11	11, 11	22	11
4	3, 15	18	9	12	11, 15	26	13
5	7, 3	10	5	13	15, 3	18	9
6	7, 7	14	7	14	15, 7	22	11
7	7, 11	18	9	15	15, 11	26	13
8	7, 15	22	11	16	15, 15	30	15

In the above table, we have shown in all 4^2, i.e., 16 possible samples of size two with replacement. Hence, each of the 16 sample means occurs with probability 1/16. But each of 5 and 13 is repeated *twice* and each of 7 and 11 is repeated *thrice*. Therefore, 5, 13, 7, 11 occur with respective probabilities $1/8, 1/8, 3/16, 3/16$. Similarly, 9 occurs with probability 1/4. The *probability distribution of the sample mean* $\bar{x}$ (i.e., **the sampling distribution of $\bar{\mathbf{x}}$**) is given below:

Sample mean ($\bar{x}$) :	3	5	7	9	11	13	15	Total
Probability (p) :	1/16	1/8	3/16	1/4	3/16	1/8	1/16	1

Mean of the sampling distribution of means

$$= E(\bar{x}) = \Sigma p_i \bar{x}_i$$
$$= \frac{1}{16} \times 3 + \frac{1}{8} \times 5 + \frac{3}{16} \times 7 + \frac{1}{4} \times 9 + \frac{3}{16} \times 11 + \frac{1}{8} \times 13 + \frac{1}{16} \times 15$$
$$= \frac{3+10+21+36+33+26+15}{16} = \frac{144}{16} = \mathbf{9}.$$

(iv) $\text{var}(\bar{x}) = E(\bar{x}^2) - \{E(\bar{x})\}^2$

$$E(\bar{x}^2) = \frac{1}{16} \times 3^2 + \frac{1}{8} \times 5^2 + \frac{3}{16} \times 7^2 + \frac{1}{4} \times 9^2 + \frac{3}{16} \times 11^2 + \frac{1}{8} \times 13^2 + \frac{1}{16} \times 15^2$$
$$= \frac{9+50+147+324+363+338+225}{16} = \frac{1456}{16} = 91.$$

$\therefore\ \text{var}(\bar{x}) = 91 - (9)^2 = 91 - 81 = \mathbf{10}.$

Hence, S.D. of the sampling distribution of means $= \sqrt{\text{var}(\bar{x})} = \sqrt{\mathbf{10}}.$

5TH PART. Using the formulae: $E(\bar{x}) = \mu$ and S.E. of $\bar{x} = \frac{\sigma}{\sqrt{n}}$, we get the mean of the sampling distribution of means $= E(\bar{x}) = \mu = \mathbf{9}$, and S.E. of the sampling distribution of means = S.E. of $\bar{x} = \sigma/\sqrt{n} = \sqrt{20}/\sqrt{2} = \sqrt{10}.$

Hence, the results of (iii) and (iv) are verified by using the results of (i) and (ii).

6TH PART. **Simple Random Sampling without replacement (SRSWOR):**

All possible samples of size two without replacement and their sample means with probability of their occurrence are given below:

TABLE 4.4 SAMPLING WITHOUT REPLACEMENT

Sl. No.	Sample Values	Total	Sample Mean	Probability
1	3, 7	10	5	1/6
2	3, 11	14	7	1/6
3	3, 15	18	9	1/6
4	7, 11	18	9	1/6
5	7, 15	22	11	1/6
6	11, 15	26	13	1/6

Since 9 occurs twice, its probability of occurrence $= \frac{2}{6} = \frac{1}{3}$.

Each of the other sample means occurs only once with probability $\frac{1}{6}$.

Sampling distribution of $\bar{x}$ without replacement is given below:

Sample mean ($\bar{x}$) :	5	7	9	11	13	Total
Probability (p) :	1/6	1/6	1/3	1/6	1/6	1

Mean of this sampling distribution of means $= E(\bar{x})$

$$= \frac{1}{6} \times 5 + \frac{1}{6} \times 7 + \frac{1}{3} \times 9 + \frac{1}{6} \times 11 + \frac{1}{6} \times 13 = \frac{5+7+18+11+13}{6} = \frac{54}{6} = \mathbf{9}. \quad (1)$$

$$\text{var}(\bar{x}) = E(\bar{x}^2) - \{E(\bar{x})\}^2 = \frac{1}{6} \times 5^2 + \frac{1}{6} \times 7^2 + \frac{1}{3} \times 9^2 + \frac{1}{6} \times 11^2 + \frac{1}{6} \times 13^2 - (9)^2$$

$$= \frac{25+49+162+121+169}{6} - 81 = \frac{526-486}{6} = \frac{40}{6} = \frac{20}{3}.$$

$$\text{S.D. of the sampling distribution of means} = \sqrt{\text{var}(\bar{x})} = \sqrt{\frac{20}{3}}. \quad (2)$$

Using the formulae: $E(\bar{x}) = \mu$ and S.E. of $\bar{x} = \frac{\sigma}{\sqrt{n}}\sqrt{\frac{N-n}{N-1}}$, we get $E(\bar{x}) = \mu = 9$ and S.E. of $\bar{x} = \frac{\sqrt{20}}{\sqrt{2}} \cdot \sqrt{\frac{4-2}{4-1}} = \sqrt{10} \cdot \sqrt{\frac{2}{3}} = \sqrt{\frac{20}{3}}$.

These results are identical with (1) and (2).

4.4. STATISTICAL ESTIMATION

The principles of sampling theory are used in **statistical inference** which is defined by W. A. Spur and C. P. Bonini as *"the process by which we draw a conclusion about some measure of a population based on a sample value. The measure might be a variable, such as the mean,* S.D. *etc. The purpose of sampling is to estimate some characteristics for the population from which the sample is selected."*

One of the important problems of *statistical inference* is the *estimation of population parameters* (or simply *parameters,* i.e., population mean, population S.D., etc.) from the corresponding *sample statistics* (or simply *statistics,* i.e., sample mean, sample S.D., etc.).

Unbiased and Biased Estimates

A statistic is called an *unbiased estimator* of the corresponding parameter if the mean of the sampling distribution of the statistic is equal to the corresponding population parameter. Otherwise, the statistic is called a *biased estimator* of the corresponding parameter. The values of such statistics in the above two cases are called *unbiased* and *biased estimates* respectively.

Analytically, a statistic t which is a function of the sample values $x_1, x_2, \cdots, x_n$ is an *unbiased estimator* of population parameter θ if $E(t) = \theta$, i.e., E (statistic) $=$ parameter.

Otherwise, the statistic t is a *biased estimator* of θ and the bias is given by Bias $= E(t) - \theta$.

ILLUSTRATION. *Since* $E(\bar{x}) = \mu$, *the sample mean* $\bar{x}$ *is an unbiased estimator of population mean* μ.

Again since $E(s^2) = (\frac{n-1}{n})\sigma^2 \neq \sigma^2$ [see Example 7], *the sample variance* s^2 *is a biased estimator of the population variance* σ^2. But if we take $S^2 = (\frac{n}{n-1})s^2$, then we have $E(S^2) = \frac{n}{n-1}E(s^2) = \frac{n}{n-1} \times \frac{n-1}{n} \cdot \sigma^2 = \sigma^2$ and hence, S^2 *is an unbiased estimator of* σ^2. **The unbiased estimator of S.E. of sample mean is** $\frac{S}{\sqrt{n}} = \frac{1}{\sqrt{n}} \times \frac{\sqrt{n}}{\sqrt{n-1}}s = \frac{s}{\sqrt{n-1}}$ $\quad [\because \quad$ S.E. of $\bar{x} = \frac{\sigma}{\sqrt{n}}]$.

4.4.1. Point Estimation and Interval Estimation

If an estimate of a population parameter is given by a *single value* (a specific observed value of a statistic), then the estimate is called a *point estimate* of the parameter. But if an estimate of a population parameter be given by two distinct numbers between which the parameter may be considered to lie, then the estimate is called an *interval estimate* of the parameter. As the value of a point estimate fluctuates from sample to sample, interval estimates are preferable to point estimates. Also the interval estimate indicates the accuracy (or precision) of an estimate.

A statement of the error of an estimate is called its *reliability*.

ILLUSTRATION. *If the height of a man is measured as* 5.75 *ft., then the measurement gives a point estimate, but if the height is given as* (5.75 ± 0.02) *ft., i.e., the height lies between* 5.73 *and* 5.77 *ft., then the measurement gives an interval estimate.*

The sample mean $\bar{x}$ is a point estimate of population mean μ, sample variance s^2 is a point estimate of population variance σ^2.

EXAMPLE 7. *If* $x_1, x_2, \cdots, x_n$ *is a random sample from an infinite population with variance* σ^2, *and* $\bar{x}$ *is the sample mean, show that* $\sum_{i=1}^{n}(x_i - \bar{x})^2/n$ *is a biased estimate of* σ^2, *but the bias becomes negligible for large* n. *Give an unbiased estimate of* σ^2. **[C.U. Econ. (Hons.); Delhi U.]**

SOLUTION. Let μ be the population mean. Then $E(x_i) = \mu$ and $\text{var}(x_i) = E\{x_i - \mu\}^2 = \sigma^2$, for $i = 1, 2, \cdots, n$. [See proposition in Art. 4.3.1]

If s be the sample S.D., then $s^2 = \frac{\Sigma(x_i - \bar{x})^2}{n}, i = 1, 2, \cdots, n$.

$$\text{Now} \quad s^2 = \frac{\Sigma(x_i - \bar{x})^2}{n} = \frac{\Sigma x_i^2}{n} - 2\bar{x}\frac{\Sigma x_i}{n} + \bar{x}^2 = \frac{\Sigma x_i^2}{n} - 2\bar{x}^2 + \bar{x}^2 = \frac{\Sigma x_i^2}{n} - \bar{x}^2 \qquad \left[\because \quad \frac{\Sigma x_i}{n} = \bar{x}\right]$$

$$= \frac{\Sigma(x_i - \mu)^2}{n} - (\bar{x} - \mu)^2 \qquad [\because \quad s^2 \text{ is independent of any change of origin.}]$$

$$\left[\text{Also} \quad \frac{\Sigma(x_i - \mu)^2}{n} - (\bar{x} - \mu)^2 = \frac{\Sigma x_i^2}{n} - 2\mu\frac{\Sigma x_i}{n} + n\frac{\mu^2}{n} - (\bar{x}^2 + \mu^2 - 2\bar{x}\mu) = \frac{\Sigma x_i^2}{n} - \bar{x}^2.\right]$$

$$\therefore \quad E(s^2) = E\left\{\frac{\Sigma(x_i-\mu)^2}{n} - (\bar{x}-\mu)^2\right\} = E\left\{\frac{\Sigma(x_i-\mu)^2}{n}\right\} - E(\bar{x}-\mu)^2$$

$$= \frac{\Sigma E(x_i-\mu)^2}{n} - E(\bar{x}-\mu)^2 = \frac{\Sigma \operatorname{var}(x_i)}{n} - \operatorname{var}(\bar{x}) \quad \text{[See Art. 4.3.1]}.$$

$$= \frac{\Sigma\sigma^2}{n} - \frac{\sigma^2}{n} = \frac{n\sigma^2}{n} - \frac{\sigma^2}{n} = \sigma^2\left(1-\frac{1}{n}\right) = \frac{n-1}{n}\sigma^2$$

Thus $E(s^2) = \frac{n-1}{n}\cdot\sigma^2 \neq \sigma^2$.

Hence, s^2 is a biased estimator of σ^2 and bias $= E(s^2) - \sigma^2 = \frac{n-1}{n}\sigma^2 - \sigma^2 = -\frac{\sigma^2}{n}$.

When n increases, bias numerically decreases and when $n \to \infty$, bias$\to 0$. Hence, bias becomes negligible for large n.

Let us consider $S^2 = \frac{ns^2}{n-1} = \frac{\Sigma(x_i-\bar{x})^2}{n-1}$.

Then $E(S^2) = E\{\frac{ns^2}{n-1}\} = \frac{n}{n-1}E(s^2) = \frac{n}{n-1}\times\frac{n-1}{n}\cdot\sigma^2 = \sigma^2$.

Hence, $S^2 = \frac{\Sigma(x_i-\bar{x})^2}{n-1}$ *is an unbiased estimator of* σ^2.

EXAMPLE 8. *The following observations constitute a random sample from an unknown population. Estimate the mean and* S.D. *of the population. Also find the estimate of* S.E. *of sample mean:* 14, 19, 17, 20, 25. **[MBA 1979; ICWAI]**

SOLUTION. We know that the unbiased estimates of the population mean (μ) and the population variance (σ^2) are respectively the values of $\bar{x} = \frac{\Sigma x_i}{n}$ and $S^2 = \frac{\Sigma(x_i-\bar{x})^2}{n-1}$.

$$\text{Here} \quad n = 5, \bar{x} = \frac{14+19+17+20+25}{5} = \frac{95}{5} = 19,$$

$$\text{and} \quad \Sigma(x_i-\bar{x})^2 = (14-19)^2 + (19-19)^2 + (17-19)^2 + (20-19)^2 + (25-19)^2$$

$$= 25 + 0 + 4 + 1 + 36 = 66.$$

$$\therefore \quad S^2 = \frac{\Sigma(x_i-\bar{x})^2}{n-1} = \frac{66}{5-1} = \frac{66}{4} = 16.5.$$

$$\therefore \quad S = \sqrt{16.5} = 4.06.$$

Hence, the estimate of μ is 19 and that of σ is $S = 4.06$.

S.E. of $\bar{x} = \frac{\sigma}{\sqrt{n}} = \frac{S}{\sqrt{5}}$ [$\because$ σ is not known, its estimate S is taken]

$\therefore$ Estimate of S.E. of $\bar{x} = \frac{\sqrt{16.5}}{\sqrt{5}} = \sqrt{\frac{16.5}{5}} = \sqrt{3.3} = 1.82$ (approx.).

4.5. CONFIDENCE INTERVAL ESTIMATES OF PARAMETERS

In an interval estimation of the population parameter θ, if we can find two quantities t_1 and t_2 based on sample observations drawn from the population such that the unknown parameter θ is included in the interval $[t_1, t_2]$ in a specified percentage of cases, then this interval is called a **confidence interval** for the parameter θ. The lower limit t_1 and the upper limit t_2 of this interval are called **confidence limits** of θ. The confidence interval has a *specified confidence or probability* of correctly estimating the true value of the population parameter. In this case, $P(t_1 \le \theta \le t_2) = c$, where c is a given (specified) probability.

The computation of *confidence interval* and *confidence limits* is based on the sampling distribution of a statistic. We know that the *sampling distribution of the sample mean* $\bar{x}$ *of a random sample of size* $n (n \ge 30)$ *drawn from a population having mean* μ *and* S.D. σ *is approximately a normal distribution with mean* μ *and* S.D. = S.E. *of* $\bar{x} = \sigma/\sqrt{n}$.

$\therefore\quad z = \frac{\bar{x}-\mu}{\sigma/\sqrt{n}}$ has a **standard normal distribution** with mean = 0 and S.D. = 1. [See Art 5.4.1.]

From the distribution of area under a standard normal curve, it is known that 95.45% of the area lies between the ordinates $z = \pm 2$, i.e., $P(-2 \le z \le 2) = 95.45\% = 0.9545$, where $z = \frac{\bar{x}-\mu}{\sigma/\sqrt{n}}$, i.e., the inequality $-2 \le \frac{\bar{x}-\mu}{\sigma/\sqrt{n}} \le 2 \quad \cdots(1)$ holds in 95.45% of cases and it does not hold in only 4.55% of the cases.

From (1), we have $-\frac{2\sigma}{\sqrt{n}} \le \bar{x} - \mu \le \frac{2\sigma}{\sqrt{n}}$, or, $\bar{x} - \frac{2\sigma}{\sqrt{n}} \le \mu \le \bar{x} + \frac{2\sigma}{\sqrt{n}}$,
or, $\bar{\mathbf{x}} - \mathbf{2}$ **(S.E. of** $\bar{\mathbf{x}}$**)** $\le \mu \le \bar{\mathbf{x}} + \mathbf{2}$ **(S.E. of** $\bar{\mathbf{x}}$**)**. $\left[\because \quad \frac{\sigma}{\sqrt{n}} = \text{S.E. of } \bar{x}.\right]$

This interval is called the 95.45% **confidence interval** for the population mean μ and $\bar{x} \pm 2$ (S.E. of $\bar{x}$) are called the 95.45% **confidence limits for** μ. Here 2 is the *confidence coefficient* or z-value.

Again 99.73% of the area under the standard normal curve lies between the ordinates $z = \pm 3$, i.e., $P(-3 \le z \le 3) = 0.9973$.

Proceeding as before, 99.73% *confidence interval* and *confidence limits for* μ are respectively $\bar{x} - 3$ (S.E. of $\bar{x}$) $\le \mu \le \bar{x} + 3$ (S.E. of $\bar{x}$), and $\bar{x} \pm 3$ (S.E. of $\bar{x}$).

Similarly, 95% *confidence interval* and *confidence limits for* μ are respectively
$\bar{x} - 1.96$ (S.E. of $\bar{x}$) $\le \mu \le \bar{x} + 1.96$ (S.E. of $\bar{x}$), and $\bar{x} \pm 1.96$ (S.E. of $\bar{x}$).

Using *the table for the area under standard normal curve,* we can find the *confidence interval* and *confidence limits* corresponding to any specified percentage.

Since the sampling distribution of the sample proportion p of a large random sample of size $n(n \ge 30)$ drawn from a population having population proportion P, is approximately *a normal distribution with* mean P and S.D. = S.E. of p, we can find the *confidence interval and confidence limits for the population proportion* P, proceeding as in the case for the sampling distribution of sample mean $\bar{x}$.

For small samples $(n < 30)$ drawn from a normal population, t-distribution (discussed later) is used to find the confidence interval of the population mean if σ is not known.

The formulae for the confidence limits of some well-known statistics for large random samples are given below:

I. Confidence Limits for Population Mean μ

(i) 95% confidence limits are $\bar{x} \pm 1.96$ (S.E. of $\bar{x}$);
(ii) 95.45% confidence limits are $\bar{x} \pm 2$ (S.E. of $\bar{x}$);
(iii) 99% confidence limits are $\bar{x} \pm 2.58$ (S.E. of $\bar{x}$);
(iv) 99.73% confidence limits are $\bar{x} \pm 3$ (S.E. of $\bar{x}$).

Of the above confidence limits, the last one is the almost sure limits.

II. Confidence Limits for Population Proportion P

(i) 95% confidence limits are $p \pm 1.96$ (S.E. of p);
(ii) 95.45% confidence limits are $p \pm 2$ (S.E. of p);
(iii) 99% confidence limits are $p \pm 2.58$ (S.E. of p);
(iv) 99.73% confidence limits are $p \pm 3$ (S.E. of p).

III. Confidence Limits for the Difference $\mu_1 - \mu_2$ of Two Population Means μ_1 and μ_2

(i) 95% confidence limits are $(\bar{x}_1 - \bar{x}_2) \pm 1.96$ (S.E. of $\bar{x}_1 - \bar{x}_2$);

(ii) 95.45% confidence limits are $(\bar{x}_1 - \bar{x}_2) \pm 2$ (S.E. of $\bar{x}_1 - \bar{x}_2$);

(iii) 99% confidence limits are $(\bar{x}_1 - \bar{x}_2) \pm 2.58$ (S.E. of $\bar{x}_1 - \bar{x}_2$);

(iv) 99.73% confidence limits are $(\bar{x}_1 - \bar{x}_2) \pm 3$ (S.E. of $\bar{x}_1 - \bar{x}_2$).

IV. Confidence Limits for the Difference $P_1 - P_2$ of Two Population Proportions

(i) 95% confidence limits are $(p_1 - p_2) \pm 1.96$ (S.E. of $p_1 - p_2$);

(ii) 95.45% confidence limits are $(p_1 - p_2) \pm 2$ (S.E. of $p_1 - p_2$);

(iii) 99% confidence limits are $(p_1 - p_2) \pm 2.58$ (S.E. of $p_1 - p_2$);

(iv) 99.73% confidence limits are $(p_1 - p_2) \pm 3$ (S.E. of $p_1 - p_2$).

REMARKS. The 99.73% confidence limits in the above cases may be taken as the almost sure limits without mentioning the degree of confidence. In calculating S.E. if population parameters are not known, corresponding sample statistics are used to find an approximate value of S.E. For example, if the population S.D. σ is not known, the S.E. of $\bar{x}$ is calculated by using sample S.D. s in place of σ.

4.5.1. Determination of Proper Sample Size

Determination of proper sample size is important for testing of hypothesis in business problems. The size of sample should neither be two small nor be too large. If it is too small, then it may not help us to arrive at a valid conclusion. Again if it is too large, then there may be loss of time and money without arriving at the desired result.

Sample Size for Estimating Population Mean

Let $\bar{x}$ be the *mean of a random sample* drawn from a population having mean μ and S.D. σ. Let the sampling distribution of the sample mean $\bar{x}$ be approximately a normal distribution with mean μ and S.D. σ. If E be the permissible sampling error, then $E = \bar{x} - \mu$.

Again the confidence interval for the population mean μ is $\bar{x} \pm z$ (S.E. of $\bar{x}$) $= \bar{x} \pm E$ where z = confidence coefficient or z-value (which is 1.96 at 5% level of significance) and $E = z$ (S.E. of $\bar{x}$) $= z \cdot \frac{\sigma}{\sqrt{n}}$, n being the *sample size.*

Thus $E = \frac{z\sigma}{\sqrt{n}}$, or, $\sqrt{n} = \frac{z\sigma}{E}$; $\quad \therefore \quad \mathbf{n} = (\frac{z\sigma}{E})^2$, which gives the **required sample size.**

Sample Size for Estimating Population Proportion

Let p be *sample proportion* and P be the *population proportion.* Then, as before, E = permissible sampling error $= p - P$ and the confidence interval for the population proportion P is $p \pm z$ (S.E. of p) $= p \pm E$, where $E = z$ (S.E. of p) $= z \cdot \sqrt{\frac{PQ}{n}}$, n being the sample size, or, $E^2 = \frac{z^2PQ}{n}$, or, $n = \frac{z^2PQ}{E^2}$, where $Q = 1 - P$.

EXAMPLE 9. *A random sample of the heights of* 100 *students from a large population of students in a University having* S.D. *of* 0.75 *ft. has an average height of* 5.6 *ft. Find* (i) 95% *and* (ii) 99% *confidence limits for the average height of all the students of the University.*

SOLUTION. Here $\bar{x}$ = sample mean = 5.6 ft., σ = population S.D. = 0.75 ft. n = size of the sample = 100.

$$\text{S.E. of } \bar{x} = \frac{\sigma}{\sqrt{n}} = \frac{0.75}{\sqrt{100}} = \frac{0.75}{10} = 0.075.$$

(i) 95% confidence limits for the population mean are $\bar{x} \pm 1.96$ (S.E. of $\bar{x}$) $= 5.6 \pm 1.96 \times 0.075 = 5.6 \pm 0.147 = \mathbf{5.453}$ and $\mathbf{5.747}$.

(ii) 99% confidence limits for the population mean are $\bar{x} \pm 2.58$ (S.E. of $\bar{x}$) $= 5.6 \pm 2.58 \times 0.075 = 5.6 \pm 0.1935 =$ **5.4065** and **5.7935**.

EXAMPLE 10. *A sample of* 100 *measurements of breaking strength of cotton threads gave a mean of* 7.4 *ounces and a* S.D. *of* 1.2 *ounces. Find* 95% *confidence limits for the mean breaking strength.* **[ICWAI December 1983]**

SOLUTION. Here n = sample size = 100, $\bar{x} = 7.4$ and s = sample S.D. = 1.2.

$$\therefore \quad \text{S.E. of } \bar{x} = \frac{\sigma}{\sqrt{n}} = \frac{s}{\sqrt{n}} \text{ (approximately).} \qquad [\because \ \sigma \text{ is not known, we take } s \text{ for } \sigma.]$$

$$= \frac{1.2}{\sqrt{100}} = \frac{1.2}{10} = 0.12.$$

Hence, 95% confidence limits for the population mean are $\bar{x} \pm 1.96$ (S.E. of $\bar{x}$) $= 7.4 \pm 1.96 \times 0.12 = 7.4 \pm 0.2352 =$ **7.1648** and **7.6352.**

EXAMPLE 11. *In a large consignment of oranges a random sample of* 500 *oranges revealed that* 65 *oranges were bad. Prove that* 99.73% *of bad oranges in the consignment certainly lies between* 8.5% *and* 17.5%. (*You may use normal approximation to binomial distribution*).

[ICWAI June 1978, 1982; B.U. B. Com. 1974]

SOLUTION. Here p = sample proportion of bad oranges $= \frac{65}{500} = \frac{13}{100} = 0.13$; $\quad q = 1 - p = 0.87$.

$$\text{S.E. of } p = \sqrt{\frac{PQ}{n}} = \sqrt{\frac{pq}{n}} \qquad [\because \ P \text{ is not known, we take } p \text{ for } P.]$$

$$= \sqrt{\frac{0.13 \times 0.87}{500}} = \sqrt{0.0002262} = 0.015.$$

$\therefore$ The 99.73% confidence limits for the population proportion P of bad oranges are $p \pm 3$ (S.E. of p) $= 0.13 \pm 3 \times 0.015 = 0.13 \pm 0.045 = 0.085$ and 0.175, i.e., **8.5% and 17.5%.**

Hence, the result follows.

EXAMPLE 12. *A random sample of* 160 *people is taken and* 120 *were in favour of liberalising licensing regulations. With* 95% *confidence, what proportion of all people are in favour?* (z-*value with* 95% *confidence is* 1.96). **[CA November 1989]**

SOLUTION. Here $n = 160, p = \frac{120}{160} = 0.75, q = 1 - p = 1 - 0.75 = 0.25$.

$$\therefore \quad \text{S.E. of } p = \sqrt{\frac{PQ}{n}} = \sqrt{\frac{pq}{n}} = \sqrt{\frac{0.75 \times 0.25}{160}} = \sqrt{\frac{0.1875}{160}} = 0.03423.$$

$\therefore$ 95% confidence limits for the population proportion are $p \pm 1.96$ (S.E. of p)
$= 0.75 \pm 1.96 \times 0.03423 = 0.75 \pm 0.067$, i.e., the confidence limits are 0.683 and 0.817

Hence, the required proportion of people in favour of liberalising licensing regulations with 95% confidence lies between 0.683 and 0.817.

EXAMPLE 13. *A sample of size* 64 *was drawn from a population consisting of* 128 *units. The sample mean of the measurements on a certain characteristic was found to be* 28. *Set up* 96% *confidence limits for the population mean, if it is known that the population* S.D. *for the characteristic is* 4. **[C.U. M. Com.]**

SOLUTION. 96% confidence limits for the population mean are approximately $\bar{x} \pm 2.05$ (S.E. of $\bar{x}$). Here $\bar{x} = 28, n = 64, N = 128$ and $\sigma = 4$.

$$\text{S.E. of } \bar{x} = \frac{\sigma}{\sqrt{n}} \cdot \sqrt{\frac{N-n}{N-1}} = \frac{4}{\sqrt{64}} \cdot \sqrt{\frac{128-64}{128-1}} = \frac{4}{8} \times \sqrt{\frac{64}{127}} = \frac{4}{11.27} = 0.355.$$

Hence, the required 96% confidence limits are $\bar{x} \pm 2.05$ (S.E. of $\bar{x}$), i.e., $28 \pm 2.05 \times 0.355 = 28 \pm 0.72775 = 28 \pm 0.728 =$ **28.728** and **27.272**.

EXAMPLE 14. *A random sample of* 100 *articles taken from a batch of* 2000 *articles shows that the average diameter of the articles* = 0.354 *with* S.D. = 0.048. *Find* 95% *confidence interval for the average diameter of this batch of* 2000 *articles.* **[ICWAI December 1979; C.U. M. Com. 1972]**

SOLUTION. Suppose the sample is drawn without replacement from the batch of 2000 (finite) articles. Then $\bar{x}$ = sample mean = 0.354 and S.E. of $\bar{x} = \frac{\sigma}{\sqrt{n}}\sqrt{\frac{N-n}{N-1}}$.

Here $N = 2000, n = 100$; as σ is not known, we replace σ by the sample S.D. $= s = 0.048$.

$$\therefore \quad \text{S.E. of } \bar{x} = \frac{0.048}{\sqrt{100}} \cdot \sqrt{\frac{2000-100}{2000-1}} = \frac{0.048}{10} \cdot \sqrt{\frac{1900}{1999}}$$
$$= 0.0048 \times \sqrt{0.95} = 0.0048 \times 0.975 = 0.00468.$$

$\therefore$ The 95% confidence limits are $\bar{x} \pm 1.96$ (S.E. of $\bar{x}$), i.e., $0.354 \pm 1.96(0.00468)$
$= 0.354 + 0.0091728 = 0.354 \pm 0.0092 =$ **0.3632** and **0.3448**.

Hence, the required **95% confidence interval is [0.3448, 0.3632].**

EXAMPLE 15. *A simple random sample of size* 66 *was drawn in the process of estimating the mean annual income of* 950 *families of a certain township. The mean and the standard deviation of the sample were found to be* Rs. 4,730 *and* Rs. 7.65 *respectively. Find a* 95% *confidence interval for the population mean.* [*Table value of z for confidence level at* 95% *is* 1.96.]

[CA November 1991]

SOLUTION. We have n = sample size = 66 (large), $N = 950; \bar{x} = 4730, s = 7.65$.

Since the sample is *large*, we can assume the sampling distribution to be **normal**.

$$\therefore \quad \text{S.E. of } \bar{x} = \frac{\sigma}{\sqrt{n}} \cdot \sqrt{\frac{N-n}{N-1}}$$

[$\because \ \frac{n}{N} = \frac{66}{950} = 0.06947 > 0.05$, finite population correction factor is used.]

$$= \frac{s}{\sqrt{n-1}} \cdot \sqrt{\frac{N-n}{N-1}} \quad [\because \ \sigma \text{ is not known, unbiased estimator is used.}]$$

$$= \frac{7.65}{\sqrt{66-1}} \times \sqrt{\frac{950-66}{950-1}} = \frac{7.65}{\sqrt{65}} \times \sqrt{\frac{884}{949}} = 0.9158 = 0.916.$$

$\therefore$ 95% confidence interval is given by $\bar{x} \pm 1.96$ (S.E. of $\bar{x}$) $= 4730 \pm 1.96 \times 0.916 = 4730 \pm 1.795$.

$\therefore$ 95% *confidence limits for the population mean* μ *are* $4730 - 1.795$ and $4730 + 1.795$, i.e., **4728.205** and **4731.795**.

Hence, the *required* 95% *confidence interval is* **Rs. 4728.21** $\leq \mu \leq$ **Rs. 4731.80**.

If σ is replaced by s only, then S.E. of $\bar{x}$ will be 0.909.

EXAMPLE 16. *A random sample of* 100 *articles taken from a batch of* 2696 *articles contains* 5 *defective articles. Find* 95% *confidence interval for the proportion of defective articles in the whole batch.* **[ICWAI (Final) June 1974]**

SOLUTION. Here $n = 100, N = 2696$ and $p = 5/100 = 0.05$.

Since the population size $N = 2696$ (finite), the Standard Error (S.E.) of p is given by

$$\text{S.E. of } p = \sqrt{\frac{PQ}{n}} \cdot \sqrt{\frac{N-n}{N-1}} = \sqrt{\frac{pq}{n}} \cdot \sqrt{\frac{N-1}{N-1}} \quad \text{(approximately)}$$

$$= \sqrt{\frac{0.05(1-0.05)}{100}} \cdot \sqrt{\frac{2696-100}{2696-1}} \quad [\because \ q = 1-p]$$

$$= \sqrt{\frac{0.05 \times 0.95}{100}} \times \sqrt{\frac{2596}{2695}} = 0.022 \times 0.98 = 0.02156.$$

$\therefore$ 95% confidence limits are $p \pm 1.96$ (S.E. of p), i.e., $0.05 \pm 1.96 \times 0.02156 = 0.05 \pm 0.0422576$ $= 0.05 \pm 0.0423 = 0.0923$ and 0.0077.

Hence, the required **95%** confidence interval is [**0.0077, 0.0923**].

EXAMPLE 17. *Find the sample size such that the probability of the sample mean differing from the population mean by not more than* $\frac{1}{10}$*th of standard deviation is* 0.95. **[ICWAI June 1991]**

SOLUTION. Let $\bar{x}$ be the mean of the sample of size n, μ the population mean and σ the population standard deviation. Then by the given condition,

$$P\left(|\bar{x}-\mu| \leq \frac{1}{10}\sigma\right) = \frac{95}{100}, \quad \text{or,} \quad P\left(\frac{|\bar{x}-\mu|}{\sigma/\sqrt{n}} \leq \frac{\frac{1}{10}\sigma}{\sigma/\sqrt{n}}\right) = 0.95$$

$$\text{or,} \quad P\left(|Z| \leq \frac{\sqrt{n}}{10}\right) = 0.95 = P(|Z| \leq 1.96) \quad \left[\because \ \frac{|\bar{x}-\mu|}{\sigma/\sqrt{n}} = Z.\right]$$

$$\therefore \quad \frac{\sqrt{n}}{10} = 1.96, \quad \text{or,} \quad \sqrt{n} = 19.6; \quad \therefore \quad n = 384.16 = 384 \text{ (approx)}.$$

Hence, the required sample size is 384.

[OTHERWISE. E = permissible sampling error $= \bar{x} \sim \mu \simeq \frac{1}{10}\sigma$, z-value $= 1.96$.

$\therefore$ The required sample size $(n) = (\frac{z\sigma}{E})^2 = (\frac{1.96\sigma}{\frac{1}{10}\sigma})^2 = (19.6)^2 = 384.16 \simeq$ **384**.]

EXAMPLE 18. *A pathologist wants to determine on the basis of sample study, the mean time required to complete a certain analysis so that he may be* 98% *confident that the mean may remain within* ± 3 *days of the true mean. As per the available record, the population variance is* 81 *days. What must be the size of the sample for his study? How large a sample would be required if the precision is to be doubled?* (*Table value of z corresponding to* 98% *confidence interval is* 2.33)

[CA May 1992]

SOLUTION. By the given conditions, E = permissible sampling error = 3, z=2.33, $\sigma^2 = 81$; $\therefore \quad \sigma = \sqrt{81} = 9$. Let n be the required size of the sample.

Then $n = (\frac{Z\sigma}{E})^2 = (\frac{2.33 \times 9}{3})^2 = (2.33 \times 3)^2 = (6.99)^2 = 48.86 \simeq 49$.

Hence, the *required size of the sample is* **49**.

2ND PART. If the precision (exactness) is doubled, then E is halved so that $E = 3/2 = 1.5$. In this case, if n be the sample size, then $n = (\frac{2.33 \times 9}{1.5})^2 = (2.33 \times 6)^2 = 195.44 \simeq$ **196**.

[Note that if we take $n = 195$, precision may not be doubled as E will be > 1.5.]

Exercise 4(I)

Theory

(Sampling, Sampling Distribution and Estimation)

1. (i) Distinguish between (a) *Population* and *Sample*; (b) *Complete Enumeration* and *Sample Survey.*

(ii) What do you mean by *Sampling*? What are the various types of *Sampling*?

2. Explain the terms: (i) Random Sampling, (ii) Law of Statistical Regularity. (iii) Simple Random Sampling. **[ICWAI June 1991]**

3. Distinguish between *random sampling* and *stratified sampling.* Give one illustration of each. **[ICWAI December 1985, '93]**

4. (i) Describe the different types of *sampling* known to you. Illustrate your answer with suitable examples. **[CA November 1982]**

(ii) Describe briefly any three types of *sampling* commonly used. **[CA November 1981]**

5. Write short notes on each of the following:

(i) Random sampling; **[CA November 1980]**

(ii) Sampling and its uses; **[CA May 1981, 1982]**

(iii) Stratified sampling; **[CA May 1980, 1986, 1990; ICWAI June 1994]**

(iv) Probability sampling; **[CA May 1991]**

(v) Non-probability sampling; **[CA May 1992]**

(vi) Sampling of Accounting records; **[CA May 1989; November 1986, 1991]**

(vii) Use of statistical methods in Accounts and Auditing. **[CA May 1984]**

6. (i) Distinguish between a *parameter* and a *statistic.* **[ICWAI June 1973, 1979]**

(ii) What do you mean by the *sampling distribution of a statistic* and its *standard error*? **[ICWAI June 1984, 1986; December 1991]**

7. Bring out the importance of *sampling distribution* and the concept of *standard error* in statistical application. **[CA May 1986]**

8. Write short notes on each of the following:

(i) Statistics and parameters; **[CA November 1983]**

(ii) Sampling distribution; **[CA May 1983, 1985; ICWAI December 1983]**

(iii) Standard Error; **[CA May 1988]**

(iv) Central limit theorems;

(v) Confidence Interval of a parameter.

Problems

[A]

1. A population consists of the four numbers 2, 4, 3, 5. Consider all possible distinct samples of size two and verify that the population mean is equal to the mean of the sample means.

2. A population consists of 5 units only. The values of a certain charactersistic for those units are 2, 1, 3, 4 and 6. Take all possible distinct samples of size two and verify that the population mean is equal to the mean of sample mean.

3. A simple random sample of size 64 is drawn from a finite population consisting of 122 units. If the population S.D. is 16.8, find the standard error of sample mean when the sample is drawn (i) with replacement, (ii) without replacement.

4. A simple random sample of size 16 is drawn without replacement from a finite population consisting of 50 units. If the number of defective units in the population be 5, find the standard error of the sample proportion of defectives.

5. A random sample of 400 oranges was taken from a large consignment and 52 were found to be defective. Show that the standard error of the proportion of defective ones in a sample of this size is nearly 0.017.

6. The values of a characteristic x of a population containing six units are given by 2, 6, 5, 1, 7, 3. Take all possible samples of size two and verify that the mean of the population is exactly equal to the mean of the sample means. **[C.U. M. Com. 1971, 1973, 1985]**

7. (i) A population consists of 5 numbers 2, 3, 6, 8, 11. Consider all possible samples of size two which can be drawn with replacement from this population. Calculate the S.E. of sample means.

[ICWAI June 1978]

(ii) A population consists of four values 3,7,11,15. Draw all possible samples of size two with replacement. Verify that the population mean is equal to the mean of the sample means. Construct the sampling distribution of sample means and calculate the standard deviation of the sampling distribution. **[ICWAI December 1976, '93; June 1992]**

8. Compute the Standard Error of the mean and construct the sampling distribution of the mean for simple random samples of two families each from a population of 5 families which is given below:

Family :	A	B	C	D	E
Family :	4	3	2	5	7

[C.U. M. Com. 1974]

[HINTS. Here the population values are 4,3, 2, 5, 7; $n = 5$; S.E. $= \frac{\sigma}{\sqrt{n}}\sqrt{\frac{N-n}{N-1}}$.]

9. Ages of 5 persons have been recorded (in years) as 14, 19, 17, 20, 25. For random samples of size 3 drawn without replacement from this population, obtain the sampling distribution of $\bar{x}$. Show that the mean of sample means $(\bar{x})$ equals the population mean and obtain the S.E. of $\bar{x}$, directly from the sampling distribution and also by using the formula.

[HINTS. See Worked out Example 6.]

10. A simple random sample of size 5 is drawn without replacement from a finite population consisting of 41 units. If the population S.D. is 6.25, find the standard error of sample mean. (Use finite population correction.) **[ICWAI June 1991]**

11. If $x_1, x_2, \cdots, x_n$ be a random sample drawn from an infinite population with variance σ^2, and $\bar{x}$ is the sample mean, show that $\sum_{i=1}^{n}(x_i - \bar{x}_i)^2/n$ is a biased estimate of σ^2, but the bias becomes negligible for large n. Give an unbiased estimate of σ^2.

12. The following observations constitute a random sample from an unknown population. Estimate the mean and S.D. of the population. Also find the estimate of S.E. of sample mean: 15, 18, 16, 21, 25.

13. A random sample of the heights of 81 students from a large population of students in a University having S.D. of 0.72 ft. has an average height of 5.5 ft. Find (i) 95% and (ii) 99% confidence limits for the average height of all the students of the University.

14. In a large consignment of oranges, a random sample of 400 oranges revealed that 52 oranges were bad. Find 95% and 99% confidence limits for the proportion of defective oranges in the whole consignment.

15. (i) If a sample of size 16 drawn from a normal population with unknown mean and variance 144 has mean 40, then show that 95% interval estimate of the population mean is (34.12, 45.88).

[ICWAI June 1990, '93]

(ii) A sample of 100 measurements of breaking strength of cotton threads gave a mean of 7.4 ounces and a S.D. of 1.2 ounces. Find 95% confidence limits for the mean breaking strength.

[ICWAI December, 1983]

[HINTS. $n = 100, \bar{x} = 7.4, s = 1.2$, S.E. of $\bar{x} = \frac{\sigma}{\sqrt{n}} = \frac{s}{\sqrt{n}} = 0.12$ etc.]

16. A random sample of size 10 from a normal population gives the values 64, 72, 65, 70, 68, 71, 65, 62, 66, 67. If the standard error of the sample mean is $\sqrt{0.7}$, find 95% confidence interval for the population mean. Also find the population variance. **[ICWAI December 1987]**

[HINTS. $\bar{x} = (64 + 72 + 65 + 70 + 68 + 71 + 65 + 62 + 66 + 67) \div 10 = 67, n = 10$, S.E. of $\bar{x} = \sqrt{0.7}$. Hence, 95% confidence interval is [$\bar{x}$ − 1.96 (S.E. of $\bar{x}$), $\bar{x}$ + 1.96 (S.E. of $\bar{x}$), i.e., $67 - 1.96\sqrt{0.7}, 67 + 1.96\sqrt{0.7}$; etc. Again $\sigma/\sqrt{n} = \sqrt{0.7}$, or, $\sigma/\sqrt{10} = \sqrt{0.7}$.]

[B]

1. For a population of six units, the values of a characteristic X are given below: 3, 9, 6, 5, 7, 10. Consider all possible samples of size two from the above population and show that the mean of the sample means is exactly equal to the population mean. **[C.U. M. Com. 1973]**

2. In a random sample of size 100 taken from a population of size 1,000, the mean and S.D. of a sample characteristic are found to be 4.8 and 1.1 respectively. Find the 95% confidence interval for the population mean. **[C.U. M. Com. 1970]**

3. A sample of 600 screws is taken from a large consignment and 75 are found to be defective. Estimate the percentage of defectives in the consignment and assign limits within which the percentage lies. **[ICWAI June 1975]**

4. A random sample of 100 articles is taken from a large batch of articles contain 5 defective articles. Set up 96 per cent confidence limits for the proportion of defective articles in the batch. If the batch contains 2696 articles, set up 95% confidence interval for the proportion of defective articles. **[C.U. M. Com. 1967]**

5. (i) A random sample of 100 ball bearings selected from a shipment of 2000 ball bearings has an average diameter of 0.354 inches with a S.D. = 0.048 inches. Find 95% confidence interval for the average diameter of these 2000 ball bearings. **[ICWAI December 1979]**

(ii) The mean weight of a random sample of size 100 from a student's population is 65.8 kgs. and the standard derivation is 4 kgs. Set up 95% confidence limits of the mean weight of the students' population. **[CA Foundation June 1993]**

6. 10 Life Insurance Policies in a sample of 200 taken out of 50,000 were found to be insured for less than Rs. 5,000. How many policies can be reasonably expected to be insured for less than Rs. 5,000 in the whole lot at 95% confidence level? **[CA November 1980]**

[HINTS. $p = 10/200 = 0.05, q = 0.95, n = 200$; S.E. $(p) = 0.01541$; 95% confidence limits are $p \pm 1.96$ (S.E. of p) $= 0.05 \pm 0.0302036$, i.e., 0.0197964 and 0.0802036. Required No. of policies lies between 989.82 and 4010.18, i.e., **990** and **4010**.]

6. A random sample of 160 people is taken and 120 were in favour of liberalising licensing regulations. With 95% confidence, what proportion of all people are in favour? (z-value with 95% confidence is 1.96). **[CA November 1989]**

8. Find the sample size such that the probability of the sample mean differing from the population mean by not more that $\frac{1}{5}$th of the standard deviation is 0.95.

9. With a sample size of 400, the calculated standard error of mean is 2 with a mean of 120. What sample size would be required so that we could be 95% confident that the population mean is within ±3.5 of the sample mean? (z-value with 95% confidence is 1.96). **[CA November 1989]**

[HINTS. Since $n = 400$ and S.E. of $\bar{x} = 2$; $\therefore$ $\frac{\sigma}{\sqrt{n}} = 2$, or, $\frac{\sigma}{\sqrt{400}} = 2$, or, $\sigma = 40$.

$\therefore$ Required sample size $= (\frac{z\sigma}{E})^2 = (\frac{1.96 \times 40}{3.5})^2 =$ etc.]

10. A simple random sample of size 100 has mean 15, the population variance being 25. Find an interval estimate of the population mean with a confidence level of (i) 99% and (ii) 95%.

If the population variance is not given, then what should be done to find out the required interval estimates? **[CA November 1988]**

[HINTS. **2nd Part.** If σ^2 is not given, we have to find the unbiased estimate of σ^2 which is $s/\sqrt{n-1}$.]

Answers

[A]

1. $\mu = 3.5$. **2.** $\mu = 3.2$. **3.** (i) 2.1; (ii) 1.45. **4.** 0.0625. **6.** $\mu = 4$. **7.** (i) $\mu = 6$, S.E. = 2.32; (ii) $(3,3)$ $(3,7)$, $(3,11)$, $(3,15)$, $(7,3)$, $(7,7)$, $(7,11)$, $(7,15)$, $\cdots$, $(15,15)$;

$\bar{x}$:	3	5	7	9	11	13	15	Total
p :	$\frac{1}{16}$	$\frac{1}{8}$	$\frac{3}{16}$	$\frac{1}{4}$	$\frac{3}{16}$	$\frac{1}{8}$	$\frac{1}{16}$	1

8. S.E. = 1.053;

Mean :	2.5	3	3.5	4	4.5	5	5.5	6
Probability :	0.1	0.1	0.2	0.1	0.2	0.1	0.1	0.1

9. S.E. = 1.48. **10.** 2.65. **11.** $S^2 = \Sigma(x_i - \bar{x})^2/(n-1)$. **12.** 19, 4.06 and 1.82. **13.** (i) 5.3432 and 5.6568; (ii) 5.2936 and 5.7064. **14.** 0.09668 and 0.163320, 0.08614 and 0.17386. **15.** 7.1648 and 7.6352. **16.** [65.39, 68.64]; 7.

[B]

1. $\mu = 20/3$. **2.** [4.60, 5]. **3.** 12.5%, 8.45% and 16.35%. **4.** 0.005 and 0.095; 0.008 and 0.092. **5.** (i) [0.3448, 0.3632]; (ii) 65.016 and 66.584 kgs. **6.** 990 and 4010. **7.** The proportion lies between 0.683 and 0.817. **8.** 96. **9.** 502. **10.** (i) [13.71, 16.29]; (ii) [14.02, 15.98].

4.6. TESTING OF HYPOTHESIS

The main object of the Sampling Theory is the study of the Tests of Hypothesis or Tests of Significance.

In many circumstances, we are to make decisions about population on the basis of only sample information. For example, on the basis of sample data, (i) a quality control manager is to determine whether a process is working properly, (ii) a drug chemist is to decide whether a new drug is really effective in curing a disease, (iii) a statistician has to decide whether a given coin is biased, etc. Such decisions are called statistical decisions (or simply decisions).

Statistical Hypothesis : Null Hypothesis and Alternative Hypothesis

In attempting to arrive at decisions about the populations on the basis of sample information, it is necessary to make *assumptions* or *guesses* about the population parameters involved. Such an assumption (or statement) is called a *statistical hypothesis* which may or may not be true. The procedure which enables us to decide on the basis of sample results whether a *hypothesis* is true or not, is called Test of Hypothesis or Test of Significance. There are two hypotheses: (1) *Null Hypothesis* and (2) *Alternative Hypothesis.*

In Tests of Hypothesis we always begin with an assumption or hypothesis (i.e., assumed value of a population parameter). This is called **Null Hypothesis.** *The Null Hypothesis asserts that there is no (significant) difference between the statistic and the population parameter and whatever observed difference is there, is merely due to fluctuations in sampling from the same population.* Null Hypothesis is usually denoted by the symbol H_o. The null (or no difference) attitude on the part of a statistician before drawing any sample is the basis of Null Hypothesis.

R. A. Fisher defined *Null Hypothesis* as "the Hypothesis which is tested for possible rejection under the assumption that it is true".

Any hypothesis which contradicts the Null Hypothesis H_o is called an **Alternative Hypothesis** and is denoted by the symbol H_1.

The two hypotheses H_o and H_1 are such that if one is true, the other is false and vice versa.

For example, if we have to test whether the population mean μ has a specified value μ_o, then (1) the *Null Hypothesis* is $H_o : \mu = \mu_o$ and (2) the *Alternative Hypothesis* may be (i) $H_1 : \mu \neq \mu_o$ (i.e., $\mu > \mu_o$ or $\mu < \mu_o$), or (ii) $H_1 : \mu > \mu_o$, or (iii) $H_1 : \mu < \mu_o$.

The Alternative Hypothesis in (i) is known as a *two-tailed alternative* and the Alternative Hypothesis in (ii) and (iii) are known as *right-tailed* and *left-tailed alternatives* respectively. The corresponding tests of hypotheses are called *two-tailed* (or *two-sided*), *right-tailed* (*one-sided*) and *left-tailed* (*one-sided*) *tests* respectively.

4.6.1. Errors of Sampling : Type I and Type II Errors

If a statistical hypothesis is tested, we may get the following four possible cases:

(i) the null hypothesis H_o is true but it is rejected by test procedure;

(ii) the null hypothesis is false but it is accepted by test,

(iii) the null hypothesis is true and it is accepted by test,

(iv) the null hypothesis is false and it is rejected by test.

Clearly the first two cases lead to errors which are called *errors of sampling.* The error made in (i) [i.e., when H_o is true, it is rejected] is called *Type I Error.* The error comitted in (ii) [i.e., when H_o is false, it is accepted] is called *Type II Error.* In either case a wrong decision is taken.

4.6.2. Level of Significance and Critical Region

In testing a hypothesis, the maximum probability with which we are willing to risk a Type I Error is called the *level of significance of the test.* The level of significance is generally specified before a test procedure so that the results obtained may not influence our decision.

In practice we take either 5% (i.e., .05) or 1% (i.e., .01) level of significance, although other levels such as 2%, $\frac{1}{2}$% etc. may also be used. When we choose 5% level of significance in a test procedure, there are about 5 cases in 100 that we would reject the hypothesis when it should be accepted, i.e., we are about 95% confident that we have made the right decision. Similarly, if we choose 1% level of significance in testing a hypothesis, then there is only 1 case in 100 that we would reject the hypothesis when it should be accepted, i.e., we are about 99% confident that we have made the right decision.

Suppose that under a given hypothesis the sampling distribution of a statistic t is approximately a normal distribution with mean $E(t)$ and S.D. $= \sigma_t =$ S.E. of t.

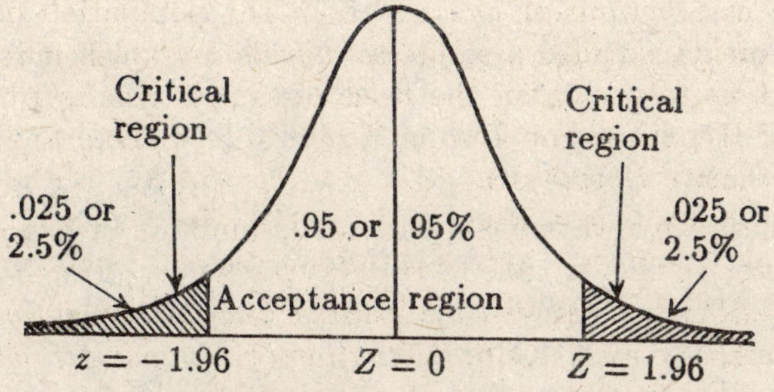

Fig 4.1 Two-tailed test

Then $z = \frac{t-E(t)}{\sigma_t} = \frac{\text{Observed value} - \text{Expected value}}{\text{S.E. of } t}$ is called the *standardized normal variable* or *test statistic* or *z-score,* and its distribution is the *standardized normal distribution with mean* 0 *and* S.D. 1, the graph of which is shown in fig 4.1. The total area under the normal curve is 1 which is 100%.

From fig 4.1, we see that if the test statistic z of a sample statistic t lies between -1.96 and 1.96, then we are 95% confident that the hypothesis is true [since the area under the normal curve between $z = -1.96$ and $z = 1.96$ is .95 which is 95% of the total area, i.e., $P(-1.96 \leq z \leq 1.96) = 0.95$].

But if for a simple random sample we find that the test statistic (or z-score) z lies outside the range -1.96 to 1.96, i.e., if $|z| > 1.96$, we would say that such an event could happen with *probability of only* .05 (total shaded area in the fig 4.1) if the given hypothesis were true. In this case we say that *z-score differed significantly* from the value expected under the hypothesis and hence, the hypothesis is to be rejected at 5% (or .05) level of significance. Here the total shaded area .05 in fig 4.1 represents the probability of our being wrong in rejecting the hypothesis, i.e., .05 is the probability of making a Type I Error. *Thus if* $|z| > 1.96$, *we say that the hypothesis is rejected at a .05 (i.e., 5%) level of significance.*

The set of z scores outside the range -1.96 and 1.96, i.e., $|z| > 1.96$ constitutes the **critical region or region of rejection of the hypothesis or the region of significance.** Thus **critical region** is the area under the sampling distribution in which the test statistic value has to fall for the null hypothesis to be rejected. On the other hand the set of z scores inside the range -1.96 to 1.96 is called the **region of acceptance of the hypothesis.** *The values* -1.96 *and 1.96 are called* **critical values** *at 5% level of significance.*

Similarly, we can define *critical region* at any other (i.e., 1%, 5%, etc.) level of significance.

Decision Rule (Two-sided Tests)

From the above discussion we can formulate the following rule of decisions:

I. (i) Reject the null hypothesis at 5% level of significance if the test statistic z lies outside the range -1.96 to 1.96, i.e., if $|z| > 1.96$.

(ii) Accept the null hypothesis at 5% level of significance if $|z| \not> 1.96$, i.e., if $|z| \leq 1.96$.

II. (i) Reject the null hypothesis at 1% level of significance if the test statistic z lies outside the range -2.58 to 2.58, i.e., if $|z| > 2.58$.

(ii) Accept the null hypothesis at 1% level of significance if $|z| \not> 2.58$, i.e., if $|z| \leq 2.58$.

4.6.3. One-Tailed and Two-Tailed Tests

If the *Alternative Hypothesis* (H_1) in a test of a statistical hypothesis be **one-tailed** (either *right-tailed* or *left-tailed*), then the test is called a **one-tailed test.** For example, to test whether the population mean $\mu = \mu_o$, we have $H_o : \mu = \mu_o$ against the Alternative Hypothesis H_1 given by

$$\mathbf{H_1} : \mu > \mu_o \quad \text{(Right-tailed) or} \quad \mathbf{H_1} : \mu < \mu_o \quad \text{(Left-tailed).}$$

In this case, the test is a *single-tailed* or *one-tailed test.* In the right-tailed test where $H_1 : \mu > \mu_o$, the *critical region* (or *rejection region*) $z > z_\alpha$ lies entirely in the right tail of the sampling distribution of sample mean $\bar{x}$ with area equal to *the level of significance* α. Similarly, in the left-tailed ($H_1 : \mu < \mu_o$), the critical region $z < -z_\alpha$ lies entirely in the left tail of the sampling distribution of $\bar{x}$ with area equal to the *level of significance* α. [See figs 4.2 and 4.3].

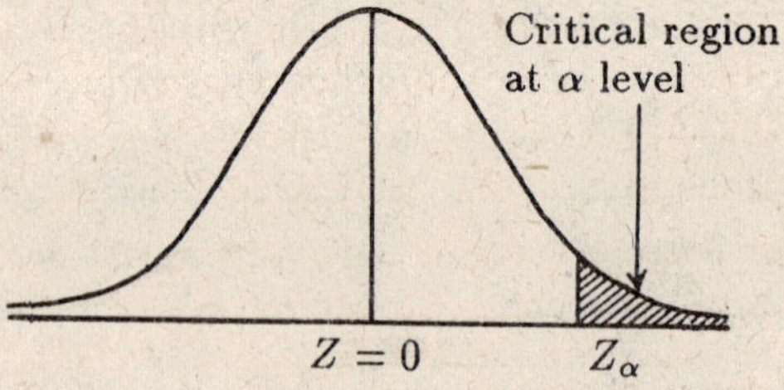

Fig 4.2 Right-tailed test

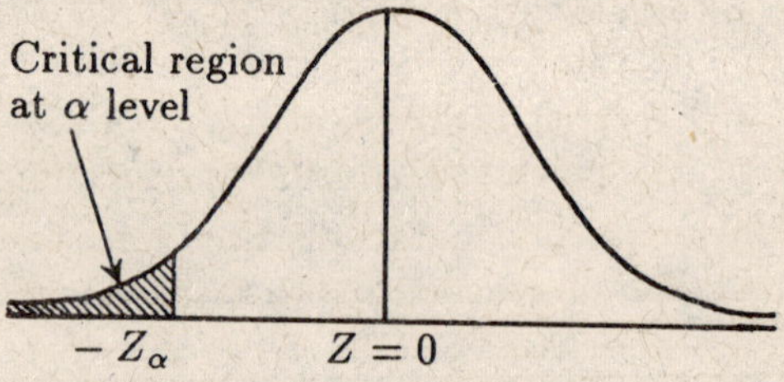

Fig 4.3 Left-tailed test

If the Alternative Hypothesis H_1 in a test be *two-tailed* or *two-sided* (*both right* and *left tailed*), i.e., $H_1 : \mu \neq \mu_o$ (i.e., $\mu > \mu_o$ and $\mu < \mu_o$), then *the test is called two-tailed test* and in such a case the *critical region* lies in both the right and left tails of the sampling distribution of the test statistic, with total area equal to the *level of significance* [See fig 4.1].

In practice, the type of the tests to be applied depends entirely on the nature of the Alternative Hypothesis H_1. We apply two-tailed or one-tailed test according as H_1 is two-tailed or one-tailed.

Critical values of z for both two-tailed and one-tailed tests at 1%, 5% and 10% level of significance are given below:

TABLE 4.5 CRITICAL VALUES OF Z

Level of significance (α)	1%	5%	10%
Critical values for two-tailed tests	$\|z_\alpha\| = 2.58$	$\|z_\alpha\| = 1.96$	$\|z_\alpha\| = 1.645$
Critical values for Right-tailed tests	$z_\alpha = 2.33$	$z_\alpha = 1.645$	$z_\alpha = 1.28$
Critical value for Left-tailed tests	$z_\alpha = -2.33$	$z_\alpha = -1.645$	$z_\alpha = -1.28$

4.6.4. Procedure for Testing of Hypothesis

Procedure (i.e., various steps) for testing of Hypothesis is given below:

1. Set up the *Null Hypothesis* H_o.

2. Set up the *Alternative Hypothesis* H_1 which is complementary to H_o. From the nature of H_1 decide whether *one-tailed* (*right* or *left tail*) *test* or *two-tailed test is to be applied.*

3. Choose an appropriate *level of significance* (a) depending on the reliability and risk of the estimates. Usually α is given in a problem.

4. Calculate the value of *the test statistic* z under the null hypothesis by using the formula $z = \frac{t - E(t)}{\text{S.E. of } t}$, where t is the sample statistic.

5. *Compare the computed value of z with the critical value z_α at the given* (or *chosen*) *level of significance α.* **If $|z| > z_\alpha$, reject the null hypothesis H_o at α level of significance. But if $|z| \le z_\alpha$, we accept H_o at α level of significance.**

4.7. LARGE SAMPLE TESTS

For large samples (for $n \ge 30$), the sampling distributions of many statistics are approximately *normal distributions*. In such cases, we can use the results of TABLE 4.5 to formulate decision rules. Some special tests are given below.

I. Test for a Specified Mean

A *random sample of size $n (n \ge 30)$ has a sample mean $\bar{x}$. To test the hypothesis that the population mean μ has a specified value μ_o.*

The Null Hypothesis is $H_o : \mu = \mu_o$.

The Alternative Hypothesis is (i) $H_1 : \mu \ne \mu_o$ (i.e., $\mu > \mu_o$ or $\mu < \mu_o$), or, (ii) $H_1 : \mu > \mu_o$, or (iii) $H_1 : \mu < \mu_o$. Since n is large, the sampling distribution of $\bar{x}$ is approximately *normal.*

$\therefore$ If H_o is true, the test statistic $z = \frac{\bar{x}-\mu_o}{\text{S.E. of } \bar{x}}$ or $\frac{\bar{x}-\mu}{\text{S.E. of } \bar{x}}$ has approximately a *standard normal distribution.* The **critical region** for z depending on the nature of H_1 and level of significance α is given below:

TABLE 4.6 REJECTION RULE FOR $H_o : \mu = \mu_o$

Level of significance (α)	1%	5%	10%
Critical region for $\mu \ne \mu_o$ (Two-tailed test)	$\|z\| > 2.58$	$\|z\| > 1.96$	$\|z\| > 1.645$
Critical region for $\mu > \mu_o$ (Right-tailed test)	$z > 2.33$	$z > 1.645$	$z > 1.28$
Critical region for $\mu < \mu_o$ (Left-tailed test)	$z < -2.33$	$z < -1.645$	$z < -1.28$

NOTE. Without any reference to the level of significance, we may reject the null hypothesis H_o when $|z| > 3$.

EXAMPLE 1. *The mean life of a sample of* 100 *electric bulbs produced by a company is found to be* 1570 *hours with a* S.D. *of* 120 *hours. If μ is the mean life time of all the bulbs produced by the company, test the hypothesis $\mu = 1600$ hours against the alternative hypothesis $\mu \ne 1600$ hours, using a level of significance of* 0.05.

(*At this level, for a two-tailed test, the critical values are* -1.96 *and* $+1.96$).

[ICWAI June 1976, 1983, 1984]

SOLUTION. The Null Hypothesis is $H_o : \mu = 1600$ hours, (here $\mu_o = 1600$), and the Alternative Hypothesis is $H_1 : \mu \ne 1600$ hours.

Since H_1 is two-tailed (i.e., two-sided), we are to use two-tailed test.

Let us assume that H_o is true. The test statistic is $z = \frac{\bar{x}-\mu}{\text{S.E. of } \bar{x}}$, where S.E. of $\bar{x} = \frac{\sigma}{\sqrt{n}}$.

Here $\bar{x}$ = sample mean = 1570 hours, $n = 100 (> 30), \mu = 1600$. Since the sample size n is large, $\bar{x}$ is *approximately normally distributed* with mean μ and S.D. $= \frac{\sigma}{\sqrt{n}}$,

$$\therefore \quad \text{S.E. of } \bar{x} = \frac{\sigma}{\sqrt{n}} = \frac{s}{\sqrt{100}} \quad \text{(approximately)} \qquad [\because \text{ population S.D. } \sigma \text{ is not known.}]$$

$$= \frac{120}{10} = 12 \text{ hours.}$$

$$\therefore \quad z = \frac{1570 - 1600}{12} = \frac{-30}{12} = -2.5$$

and $|z| = |-2.5| = 2.5 > 1.96$.

This shows that $z = -2.5$ lies in the critical region $|z| > 1.96$.

(Actually $z = -2.5$ lies in the left-tail $z \leq -1.96$ of the sampling distribution of z.)

Hence, *the Null Hypothesis H_o is rejected at 5%, i.e., 0.05 level of significance and we conclude that* **the mean life of the population of electric bulbs cannot be taken as 1600 hours.**

EXAMPLE 2. *A random sample of* 900 *members is found to have a mean of* 4.45 *cms. Can it be reasonably regarded as a sample from a large population whose mean is* 5 *cms. and variance is* 4 *cms. squared?* **[CA May 1984]**

SOLUTION. Let us suppose that the Null Hypothesis is $H_o : \mu = 5$ cms.

Then the Alternative Hypothesis is $H_1 : \mu \neq 5$ cms.

Since H_1 is two-tailed ($\mu > 5$ or $\mu < 5$), we shall have to use two-tailed test.

Here $n = 900$ (large), $\bar{x} = 4.45, \sigma = \sqrt{\text{variance}} = \sqrt{4} = 2$.

Let us assume that H_o is true. The test statistic z is

$$z = \frac{x - \mu}{\text{S.E. of } \bar{x}} \quad \text{where S.E. of } \bar{x} = \frac{\sigma}{\sqrt{n}} = \frac{2}{\sqrt{900}} = \frac{2}{30} = \frac{1}{15}$$

$$= \frac{4.45 - 5}{1/15} = -0.55 \times 15 = -8.25$$

$$\therefore \quad |z| = |-8.25| = 8.25 > 3.$$

We reject the Null Hypothesis and conclude that the given sample cannot be regarded as a sample from the given population.

NOTE. Since, $|z| > 3$ and level of significance is not given, we may reject H_o at 5%, 1% or $\frac{1}{2}$% level of significance. In the above problem, the *Null Hypothesis is rejected without mentioning any level of significance.*

EXAMPLE 3. *The mean breaking strength of the cables supplied by a manufacturer is* 1800 *with a* S.D. 100. *By a new technique in the manufacturing process it is claimed that the breaking strength of the cables have increased. In order to test this claim a sample of* 50 *cables is tested. It is found that the mean breaking strength is* 1850. *Can we support the claim at* 0.01 *level of signifance?*

[ICWAI December 1980, 1983]

SOLUTION. Let us assume that the Null Hypothesis is $H_o : \mu = 1800$, (i.e., we assume that there is no significant change in the mean breaking strength of the cables).

The Alternative Hypothesis is $H_1 : \mu > 1800$. $[\because \quad 1850 > 1800]$

Since H_1 is *one-tailed* (*right-tailed*), we use *one-tailed* (*right-tailed*) *test*. Let us assume that H_o is true.

Here $\bar{x} = 1850, \mu = 1800, \sigma = 100$ and $n = 50$.

$\therefore \quad$ S.E. of $\bar{x} = \frac{\sigma}{\sqrt{n}} = \frac{100}{\sqrt{50}}$.

The test statistic is

$$z = \frac{\bar{x} - \mu}{\text{S.E. of } \bar{x}} = \frac{1850 - 1800}{100/\sqrt{50}} = \frac{50\sqrt{50}}{100} = \frac{1}{2}\sqrt{50} = \frac{1}{2} \times 7.071 = 3.54.$$

We see that $z = 3.54 > 2.33$.

Hence, *we reject the Null Hypothesis at* 1%, *i.e.,* 0.01 *level of significance and conclude that* **the claim is justified.**

EXAMPLE 4. *A manufacturer of ball-point pens claims that a certain pen he manufactures has a mean writing life of* 400 *pages with a standard deviation of* 20 *pages. A purchasing agent selects a sample of* 100 *pens and puts them for test. The mean writing life for the sample was* 390 *pages. Should the purchasing agent reject the manufacturer's claim at* 5% *level?* **[CA May 1991]**

SOLUTION. Here the sample size 100 is *large.* Let us apply large sample test.

The Null Hypothesis is $H_o : \mu = 400$, (here $\mu_o = 400$) and the Alternative Hypothesis is $H_1 : \mu < 400$.

Since H_1 is one (left) sided, we use one-tailed (left-tailed) test. Let us assume that H_o is true. The *test statistic* is $z = \frac{\bar{x}-\mu}{\text{S.E. of } \bar{x}}$, where S.E. of $\bar{x} = \frac{\sigma}{\sqrt{n}}$.

Here $\bar{x}$ = sample mean = 390 pages, $n = 100(> 30), \mu = 400$.

Since the sample size n is large, $\bar{x}$ is approximately normally distributed with mean μ and S.D. $= \sigma/\sqrt{n}$.

$$\therefore \quad \text{S.E. of } \bar{x} = \frac{\sigma}{\sqrt{n}} = \frac{20}{\sqrt{100}} = \frac{20}{10} = 2 \text{ pages}$$

$$\therefore \quad z = \frac{390 - 400}{2} = \frac{-10}{2} = -5 < -1.645.$$

[The table value of z at 5% level of significance for left-tailed test is -1.645.]

Since the calculated value -5 of z falls in the critical (i.e., rejected) region, the purchasing agent *rejects the null hypothesis at 5% level,* i.e., *he rejects the manufacturer's claim at* 5% *level.*

II. Test for a Specified Proportion (Large Sample Test)

A random sample of size $n(n \geq 30)$ has a sample proportion p of members possessing a certain attribute (i.e., proportion of successes). To test the hypothesis that the proportion P in the population has a specified value P_o.

The Null Hypothesis is $H_o : P = P_o$.

The Alternative Hypothesis is (i) $H_1 : P \neq P_o$ (i.e., $P > P_o$ or $P < P_o$), or (ii) $H_1 : P > P_o$, or (iii) $H_1 : P < P_o$.

Since n is large, the sampling distribution of p is *approximately normal.*

$\therefore$ If H_o is true, the test statistic $z = \frac{p-P_o}{\text{S.E. of } p}$ or $\frac{p-P}{\text{S.E. of } p}$ is *approximately normally distributed.*

The *critical region* for z depending on the nature of H_1 and level of significance α is given in the following table.

TABLE 4.7 REJECTION RULE FOR $H_o : P = P_o$

Level of Significance	1%	5%	10%
Critical region for $P \neq P_o$ (Two-tailed test)	$\lvert z\rvert > 2.58$	$\lvert z\rvert > 1.96$	$\lvert z\rvert > 1.645$
Critical region for $P > P_o$ (Right-tailed test)	$z > 2.33$	$z > 1.645$	$z > 1.28$
Critical region for $P < P_o$ (Left-tailed test)	$z < -2.33$	$z < -1.645$	$z < -1.28$

NOTE. Without any reference to the level of significance, we may reject the null hypothesis H_o when $|z| > 3$.

EXAMPLE 5. *A coin is tossed* 900 *times and head appears* 490 *times. Does it support the hypothesis that the coin is unbiased?*

SOLUTION. If P be the probability of getting a head by tossing an unbiased coin, then $P = \frac{1}{2} = 0.5$.

Let the Null Hypothesis H_o be that the *coin is unbiased,* i.e., $H_o : P = \frac{1}{2}$. (Here $P_o = \frac{1}{2}$).

The Alternative Hypothesis is $H_1 : P \neq \frac{1}{2}$.

If p be the observed (sample) proportion of heads, then $p = \frac{490}{900} = 0.544$.

S.E. of $p = \sqrt{\frac{PQ}{n}} = \sqrt{\frac{\frac{1}{2}(1-\frac{1}{2})}{900}} = \frac{1}{60}$. $[\because \quad Q = 1 - P]$

Assuming that H_o is true, the test statistic is

$$z = \frac{p - P}{\text{S.E. of } p} = \frac{0.544 - 0.5}{\frac{1}{60}} = 0.044 \times 60 = 2.64 > 1.96.$$

Thus calculated value of $z >$ the table value of z, at 5% level of significance. Hence, we reject H_o and conclude that *the coin is not unbiased,* i.e., the *coin is biased.*

EXAMPLE 6. *A die was thrown* 9000 *times and of these* 3220 *yielded a* 3 *or* 4. *Is this consistent with the hypothesis that the die was unbiased?* **[ICWAI June 1983]**

SOLUTION. The probability of obtaining a 3 or 4 from an unbiased die $= \frac{2}{6} = \frac{1}{3}$.

Let the Null Hypothesis H_o be that the *die is unbiased,* i.e., $H_o : P = \frac{1}{3}$. Here $P_o = \frac{1}{3}$.

The Alternative Hypothesis is $H_1 : P \neq \frac{1}{3}$.

Here H_1 is two-tailed (i.e., $P > \frac{1}{3}$ or $P < \frac{1}{3}$). Let us use two-tailed test.

Assuming that H_o is true, the test statistic is $z = \frac{p - P_o}{\text{S.E. of } p}$ where S.E. of $p = \sqrt{\frac{PQ}{n}}, Q = 1 - P$.

Here $n = 9000, P = \frac{1}{3} = .3333, Q = 1 - P = 1 - \frac{1}{3} = \frac{2}{3}$ and $p =$ observed proportion of successes $= \frac{3220}{9000} = 0.3578$;

$$\therefore \quad \text{S.E. of } p = \sqrt{\frac{PQ}{n}} = \sqrt{\frac{\frac{1}{3} \times \frac{2}{3}}{9000}} = \sqrt{\frac{2}{81000}} = \sqrt{0.0000246} = 0.00496.$$

$$\therefore \quad z = \frac{0.3578 - 0.3333}{0.00496} = \frac{0.0245}{0.00496} = \frac{2450}{496} = 4.94.$$

Thus $|z| = 4.94 > 3$.

Hence, *we reject H_o and conclude that the die* **is not unbiased,** i.e., **the die is biased.** In this case the level of significance may be 5%, 1% or $\frac{1}{2}$%.

EXAMPLE 7. *In a sample of* 400 *parts manufactured by a factory, the number of defective parts was found to be* 30. *The company, however, claimed that only* 5% *of their product is defective. Is the claim tenable?* **[ICWAI June 1975]**

SOLUTION. $P_o =$ expected proportion of defective parts $= \frac{5}{100} = 0.05$, and $p =$ observed proportion of defective parts $= \frac{30}{400} = 0.075$.

Let us assume that the Null Hypothesis is $H_o : P = 0.05$, i.e., the claim is tenable.

Then the Alternative Hypothesis is $H_1 : P > 0.05$. $[\because \quad 0.075 > 0.05.]$

Since H_1 is *one-tailed* (*right-tailed*), we use *one-tailed test* (*right-tailed test*). Let us assume that H_o is true.

$$\therefore \quad \text{S.E. of } p = \sqrt{\frac{PQ}{n}} = \sqrt{\frac{0.05 \times 0.95}{400}} = \sqrt{0.0001187} = 0.0109. \quad [\because \quad Q = 1 - P.]$$

The test statistic is

$$z = \frac{p - P_o}{\text{S.E. of } p} = \frac{0.075 - 0.05}{0.0109} = \frac{0.025}{0.0109} = \frac{250}{109} = 2.294.$$

Thus we see that $z = 2.294 > 1.645$.

Hence, we reject the Null Hypothesis H_o at 5% level of significance and conclude that **the claim of the company is not tenable.**

EXAMPLE 8. *In a sample of* 500 *articles manufactured by a company, the number of defective articles was observed to be* 20. *The purchaser, however, claimed that* 5% *of their product is defective. Is the claim justified? (Use* 5% *level of significance.)*

SOLUTION. We have P_o = expected proportion of defective articles $= \frac{5}{100} = 0.05$, and p = observed proportion of defective articles $= \frac{20}{500} = 0.04$.

Let the Null Hypothesis be $H_o : P = 0.05$.

Then the Alternative Hypothesis is $H_1 : P < 0.05$. $[\because \; 0.04 < 0.05]$.

Since H_1 is *one-tailed* (*left-tailed*), we use one-tailed (left-tailed) test. Let us assume that H_o is true.

$$\text{S.E. of } p = \sqrt{\frac{PQ}{n}} = \sqrt{\frac{0.05 \times 0.95}{500}} = \sqrt{0.000095} = 0.00975.$$

The test statistic is

$$z = \frac{p - P_o}{\text{S.E. of } p} = \frac{.04 - .05}{.00975} = -\frac{.01}{.00975} = -\frac{1000}{975} = -1.026.$$

Thus we see that $z = -1.026 > -1.645$.

Hence, we accept the Null Hypothesis H_o at 5% level of significance and conclude that the claim of the purchaser is justified.

III. Test for Equality of Two Means (Large Samples)

Let $\bar{x}_1$ and $\bar{x}_2$ be the sample means of two independent large random samples of sizes n_1 and n_2 drawn from two populations having means μ_1 and μ_2 and standard deviations σ_1 and σ_2. To test whether the two population means are equal.

Let the Null Hypothesis be $H_o : \mu_1 = \mu_2$.

Then the Alternative Hypothesis is $H_1 : \mu_1 \neq \mu_2$.

[If the null hypothesis is *not rejected*, we say that the *two samples are drawn from the same population* and there is *no significant difference in the sample means.*]

$$\text{S.E. of } (\bar{x}_1 - \bar{x}_2) = \sqrt{\frac{\sigma_1^2}{n_1} + \frac{\sigma_2^2}{n_2}}$$

where σ_1 and σ_2 are S.D. of the two populations.

Assuming that H_o is true, the test statistic $z = \frac{\bar{x}_1 - \bar{x}_2}{\text{S.E. of } (\bar{x}_1 - \bar{x}_2)}$ is approximately normally distributed with mean 0 and S.D. 1.

Rejection Rule for $H_o : \mu_1 = \mu_2$

1. If $|z| > 1.96$, then reject H_o at 5% level of significance.
2. If $|z| > 2.58$, then reject H_o at 1% level of significance.
3. If $|z| > 1.645$, then reject H_o at 10% level of significance.

Otherwise, we accept H_o.

NOTE. If S.D. σ_1 and σ_2 of the two populations are not known, we shall use sample S.D. S_1 and S_2 as estimates of σ_1 and σ_2. For one-tailed test, the critical regions are the same as in TABLE 4.6.

For small samples ($n < 30$), we can use *normal distribution to test for a specified population mean or equality of two means as in large sample tests only, if the sample is drawn from a normal population whose* S.D. σ *is known.*

EXAMPLE 9. *The means of two large samples of sizes* 1000 *and* 2000 *are* 67.5 *and* 68.0 *respectively. Test the equality of means of the two populations each with* S.D. 2.5. (*No. credit if the null and alternative hypothesis are not stated. Assumptions should be stated clearly.*)

[ICWAI June 1982]

SOLUTION. Let μ_1 and μ_2 be the means of the two populations.

Let the Null Hypothesis be $H_\circ : \mu_1 = \mu_2$.

Then the Alternative Hypothesis is $H_1 : \mu_1 \neq \mu_2$.

Let us assume that $H_\circ$ is true, i.e., there is no difference between μ_1 and μ_2.

Since the sample sizes are large, the test statistic

$$z = \frac{\bar{x}_1 - \bar{x}_2}{\text{S.E. of } (\bar{x}_1 - \bar{x}_2)}, \quad \text{where S.E. of } (\bar{x}_1 - \bar{x}_2) = \sqrt{\frac{\sigma_1^2}{n_1} + \frac{\sigma_2^2}{n_2}},$$

is approximately normally distributed with mean 0 and S.D. 1.

Here $\bar{x}_1 = 67.5, \bar{x}_2 = 68.0, \sigma_1 = \sigma_2 = 2.5, n_1 = 1000, n_2 = 2000$.

$$\therefore \quad \text{S.E. of } (\bar{x}_1 - \bar{x}_2) = \sqrt{\frac{\sigma_1^2}{n_1} + \frac{\sigma_2^2}{n_2}} = \sqrt{\frac{(2.5)^2}{1000} + \frac{(2.5)^2}{2000}} = \sqrt{0.00625 + 0.003125}$$

$$= \sqrt{0.009375} = 0.097.$$

$$\therefore \quad z = \frac{\bar{x}_1 - \bar{x}_2}{\text{S.E. of } (\bar{x}_1 - \bar{x}_2)} = \frac{67.5 - 68.0}{0.097} = \frac{-0.5}{0.097} = -\frac{500}{97} = -5.15.$$

$\therefore \quad |z| = |-5.15| = 5.15 > 3$, i.e., the difference is highly significant.

Hence, *we reject the Null Hypothesis and conclude that the* **two population means are not equal.**

EXAMPLE 10. *The sales manager of a large company conducted a sample survey in States A and B taking* 400 *sample salesmen in each case. The results were:*

	State A (in Rs.)	State B (in Rs.)
Average Sales	2,500	2,200
Standard Deviation	400	550

Test whether the average sales is the same in the two states at 1% *level.* **[CA May 1984]**

SOLUTION. Let the average sales in the two states be μ_1 and μ_2.

We set the Null Hypothesis $H_\circ$ as $H_\circ : \mu_1 = \mu_2$.

Then the Alternative Hypothesis is $H_1 : \mu_1 \neq \mu_2$.

Let us assume that $H_\circ$ *is true,* i.e., there is *no significant difference between* μ_1 and μ_2. The test statistic is

$$z = \frac{\bar{x}_1 - \bar{x}_2}{\text{S.E. of } (\bar{x}_1 - \bar{x}_2)} \quad \text{where S.E. of } (\bar{x}_1 - \bar{x}_2) = \sqrt{\frac{\sigma_1^2}{n_1} + \frac{\sigma_2^2}{n_2}}.$$

Here $n_1 = n_2 = 400, \bar{x}_1 = 2,500, \bar{x}_2 = 2,200, \sigma_1 \simeq S_1 = 400$, and $\sigma_2 \simeq S_2 = 550$.

$$\therefore \quad \text{S.E. of } (\bar{x}_1 - \bar{x}_2) = \sqrt{\frac{(400)^2}{400} + \frac{(550)^2}{400}} = \sqrt{400 + 756.25} = \sqrt{1156.25} = 34 \text{ (approximately)}.$$

$$\therefore \quad z = \frac{2500 - 2200}{34} = \frac{300}{34} = 8.82 > 2.58.$$

Since the computed value of $z > 2.58$, *we reject the Null Hypothesis at 1% level of significance and conclude that the* **two average sales are significantly different,** i.e., *they are not the same in the two states.*

EXAMPLE 11. *Random samples drawn from two places gave the following data relating to the heights of adult males:*

	Place A	Place B
Mean height (in inches)	68.50	68.58
Standard deviation (inches)	2.5	3.0
Number of items in samples	1200	1500

Test at 5% *level, that the mean height is the same for adults in the two places,* (*Table value of* z *at* 5% *level for two tailed test is* 1.96). **[CA May 1989]**

SOLUTION. Let the mean height in the two places be μ_1 and μ_2 respectively.

We set the Null Hypothesis H_o as $H_o : \mu_1 = \mu_2$.

Then the Alternative Hypothesis is $H_1 : \mu_1 \neq \mu_2$.

Let us assume that H_o is true, i.e., *there is no significant difference between* μ_1 *and* μ_2. The test statistic is

$$z = \frac{\bar{x}_1 - \bar{x}_2}{\text{S.E. of } (\bar{x}_1 - \bar{x}_2)}, \quad \text{where S.E. of } (\bar{x}_1 - \bar{x}_2) = \sqrt{\frac{\sigma_1^2}{n_1} + \frac{\sigma_2^2}{n_2}}$$

Here $\bar{x}_1 = 68.50, \bar{x}_2 = 68.58, \sigma_1 = 2.5, \sigma_2 = 3.0, n_1 = 1200, n_2 = 1500$.

$$\therefore \quad \text{S.E. of } (\bar{x}_1 - \bar{x}_2) = \sqrt{\frac{(2.5)^2}{1200} + \frac{(3.0)^2}{1500}} = \sqrt{0.00521 + 0.006} = \sqrt{0.01121} = 0.10588$$

$$\therefore \quad z = \frac{68.50 - 68.58}{0.10588} = -\frac{0.08}{0.10588} = -0.7556$$

$$\therefore \quad |z| = 0.7556 < 1.96.$$

Since the *computed value of z is less than the table value, we cannot reject the null hypothesis at* 5% *level and conclude that* **the mean is the same for adults in the two places.**

EXAMPLE 12. *In a certain factory there are two different processes of manufacturing the same item. The average weight in a sample of* 250 *items produced from one process is found to be* 120 *grammes with a* S.D. *of* 12 *grammes; the corresponding figures in a sample of* 400 *items from the other process are* 124 *and* 14. *Compute the* S.E. *of the difference between the two sample means. Is this difference significant at* 1% *level? Also find* 99% *confidence limits for the difference in the average weights of items produced by the two processes.*

[ICWAI December 1978; Delhi U. M. Com. 1975]

SOLUTION. Let μ_1 and μ_2 be the mean weights of items produced from the first and the second processes respectively.

Let the Null Hypothesis be $H_o : \mu_1 = \mu_2$.

Then the Alternative Hypothesis is $H_1 : \mu_1 \neq \mu_2$.

Let us assume that H_o is true. Then the test statistic is

$$z = \frac{\bar{x}_1 - \bar{x}_2}{\text{S.E. of } (\bar{x}_1 - \bar{x}_2)}, \quad \text{where S.E. of } (\bar{x}_1 - \bar{x}_2) = \sqrt{\frac{\sigma_1^2}{n_1} + \frac{\sigma_2^2}{n_2}}.$$

Here $n_1 = 250, n_2 = 400, \bar{x}_1 = 120, \bar{x}_2 = 124, s_1 = 12, s_2 = 14$.

Since σ_1 and σ_2 are not known, we take the values of sample S.D. s_1 and s_2 for σ_1 and σ_2 in computing S.E. of $(\bar{x}_1 - \bar{x}_2)$.

$$\therefore \text{ S.E. of } (\bar{x}_1 - \bar{x}_2) = \sqrt{\frac{(12)^2}{250} + \frac{(14)^2}{400}} = \sqrt{\frac{144}{250} + \frac{196}{400}} = \sqrt{\frac{2132}{2000}} = \sqrt{1.066} = \mathbf{1.032}.$$

$$\therefore \quad z = \frac{120 - 124}{1.032} = \frac{-4}{1.032} = -3.876.$$

$$\therefore \quad |z| = 3.876 > 2.58.$$

Hence, *we reject the Null Hypothesis at* 1% *level of significance and conclude that the difference between the mean weights of the items produced by the two processes is significant.*

The 99% confidence limits for $\mu_1 - \mu_2$ are $(\bar{x}_1 - \bar{x}_2) \pm 2.58$ [S.E. of $(\bar{x}_1 - \bar{x}_2)$]
$= (120 - 124) \pm 2.58 \times 1.032 = -4 \pm 2.66 = -1.34$ and -6.66.

Hence, the 99% *confidence limits for* $\mu_1 - \mu_2$ *are* **1.34 gms. and 6.66 gms.**

IV. Test for Equality of Two Proportions (Large Samples)

Let p_1 *and* p_2 *be the proportions in two large random samples of sizes* n_1 *and* n_2 *drawn from two populations having proportions* P_1 *and* P_2. *To test whether the two population proportions* P_1, P_2 *are equal.*

Let us set the Null Hypothesis H_o as $H_o : P_1 = P_2$.

Then the Alternative Hypothesis is $H_1 : P_1 \neq P_2$.

Assuming that H_o is true, we have $P_1 = P_2 = P$ (say), and the sampling distribution of $p_1 - p_2$ is approximately normal with mean = 0 and S.D. = $\sqrt{pq(\frac{1}{n_1} + \frac{1}{n_2})}$, where $p = \frac{n_1p_1+n_2p_2}{n_1+n_2}$ and $q = 1 - p$.

$$\therefore \quad \text{S.E. of } (\mathbf{p_1 - p_2}) = \sqrt{\mathbf{pq}\left(\frac{\mathbf{1}}{\mathbf{n_1}} + \frac{\mathbf{1}}{\mathbf{n_2}}\right)}.$$

Since the sample sizes n_1 and n_2 are large, the test statistic $z = \frac{p_1 - p_2}{\text{S.E. of } (p_1 - p_2)}$ **is approximately normally distributed with mean 0 and S.D. 1.**

Rejection Rule for $\mathbf{H_o : P_1 = P_2}$

1. If $|z| > 1.96$, then reject H_o at 5% level of significance.
2. If $|z| > 2.58$, then reject H_o at 1% level of significance.
3. If $|z| > 1.645$, then reject H_o at 10% level of significance.

For one-tailed test, the critical regions are the same as in TABLE 4.7.

EXAMPLE 13. *In a certain district A,* 450 *persons were considered regular consumers of tea out of a sample of* 1000 *persons. In another district B,* 400 *were regular consumers of tea out of a sample of* 800 *persons. Do these facts reveal a significant difference between the two districts as far as tea-drinking habit is concerned? (Use* 5% *level.)* **[CA November 1975]**

SOLUTION. Let P_1 and P_2 be the population proportions of persons who are regular consumers of tea in the districts A and B respectively.

We set the Null Hypothesis H_o as $H_o : P_1 = P_2$.

Then the Alternative Hypothesis is $H_1 : P_1 \neq P_2$.

We have $p = \frac{n_1p_1+n_2p_2}{n_1+n_2}$ and S.E. of $(p_1 - p_2) = \sqrt{pq(\frac{1}{n_1} + \frac{1}{n_2})}$.

Here $n_1 = 1000, p_1 = \frac{450}{1000} = 0.45, n_2 = 800, p_2 = \frac{400}{800} = 0.5$.

$\therefore \quad p = \frac{1000\times0.45+800\times0.5}{1000+800} = \frac{450+400}{1800} = 0.47$ and $q = 1 - 0.47 = 0.53$ and S.E. of $(p_1 - p_2)$ $= \sqrt{0.47 \times 0.53(\frac{1}{1000} + \frac{1}{800})} = \sqrt{\frac{0.47\times0.53\times18}{8000}} = \sqrt{0.00056} = 0.0237$.

Assuming that H_o is true, the test statistic is

$$z = \frac{p_1 - p_2}{\text{S.E. of } (p_1 - p_2)} = \frac{0.45 - 0.5}{0.0237} = \frac{-0.05}{0.0237} = -2.1097.$$

$\therefore \quad |z| = 2.1097 > 1.96$.

Hence, *we reject the Null Hypothesis at* 5% *level of significance and conclude that there is a* **significant difference** *between the two districts as far as tea-drinking habit is concerned.*

EXAMPLE 14. *Two groups A and B consist of* 100 *people each who have a disease. A serum is given to group A but not to group B. It is found that in groups A and B,* 75 *and* 65 *people respectively recover from the disease. Test the hypothesis that the serum helps to cure the disease.*

[ICWAI December 1983; June 1984]

SOLUTION. Let P_1 and P_2 be the population proportions of people in groups A and B respectively who recover from the disease.

Let the Null Hypothesis be $H_o : P_1 = P_2$.

Then the Alternative Hypothesis is $H_1 : P_1 \neq P_2$.

We have $p = \frac{n_1p_1+n_2p_2}{n_1+n_2}$ and S.E. of $(p_1 - p_2) = \sqrt{pq(\frac{1}{n_1} + \frac{1}{n_2})}$.

Here $n_1 = n_2 = 100, p_1 = \frac{75}{100} = 0.75, p_2 = \frac{65}{100} = 0.65$;

$\therefore \quad p = \frac{100\times0.75+100\times0.65}{100+100} = \frac{140}{200} = 0.7, q = 1 - p = 0.3$ and S.E. of $(p_1 - p_2)$ $= \sqrt{0.7 \times 0.3(\frac{1}{100} + \frac{1}{100})} = \sqrt{\frac{0.42}{100}} = \sqrt{0.0042} = 0.065$.

Assuming that H_o is true, the test statistic is

$$z = \frac{p_1 - p_2}{\text{S.E. of } (p_1 - p_2)} = \frac{0.75 - 0.65}{0.065} = \frac{0.10}{0.065} = 1.54 < 1.96.$$

Since $z < 1.96$, **we accept the Null Hypothesis at 5% level of significance** and **conclude that there is no difference in P_1 and P_2, i.e., the serum does not help to cure the disease.** (Note that there is no significant difference between the proportion of people in group A *who are given the serum* and the proportion of people in group B who *are not given the serum.*)

EXAMPLE 15. *A machine produced* 20 *defective articles in a batch of* 400. *After overhauling it produced* 10 *defectives in a batch of* 300. *Has the machine improved?* **[CA November 1981]**

SOLUTION. Let P_1 and P_2 be the proportions of defective articles in the population of articles manufactured by the machine before and after overhauling, respectively.

Let the Null Hypothesis be $H_o : P_1 = P_2$.

The Alternative Hypothesis is $H_1 : P_1 > P_2$.

$$p_1 = \frac{20}{400} = 0.05 \text{ and } p_2 = \frac{10}{300} = 0.0333 \text{ and } p_1 > p_2.$$

We have $p = \frac{n_1p_1+n_2p_2}{n_1+n_2}$ and S.E. of $(p_1 - p_2) = \sqrt{pq(\frac{1}{n_1} + \frac{1}{n_2})}$

Here $n_1 = 400, n_2 = 300, p_1 = 0.05, p_2 = 1/30$

$\therefore \quad p = \frac{400\times 3+0.05+300\times 1/30}{400+300} = \frac{30}{700} = \frac{3}{70}, q = 1 - p = \frac{67}{70};$

$$\therefore \quad \text{S.E. of } (p_1 - p_2) = \sqrt{\frac{3}{70} \times \frac{67}{70}\left(\frac{1}{400} + \frac{1}{300}\right)} = \sqrt{\frac{201}{4900} \times \frac{7}{1200}} = \sqrt{\frac{201}{840000}}$$

$$= \sqrt{0.0002392} = 0.0155.$$

Assuming that H_o is true, the test statistic is

$$z = \frac{p_1 - p_2}{\text{S.E. of } (p_1 - p_2)} = \frac{0.05 - 0.0333}{0.0155} = \frac{0.0167}{0.0155} = 1.077.$$

Since $z = 1.077 < 1.645$, *we cannot reject the Null Hypothesis at* 5% *level of significance.* In other words, *we accept the Null Hypothesis at* 5% *level and conclude that the* **machine has not improved.**

EXAMPLE 16. *A company has the head office at Calcutta and a branch at Bombay. The personnel director wanted to know if the workers at the two places would like the introduction of a new plan of work and a survey was conducted for this purpose. Out of a sample of* 500 *workers at Calcutta* 62% *favoured the new plan. At Bombay out of a sample of* 400 *workers* 41% *were against the new plan. Is there any significant difference between the two groups in their attitude towards the new plan at* 5% *level?* **[CA May 1983]**

SOLUTION. Let P_1 and P_2 be the population proportions in Calcutta and Bombay respectively who favour the new plan.

Let the Null Hypothesis be $H_o : P_1 = P_2$.

The Alternative Hypothesis is $H_1 : P_1 \neq P_2$.

We have $p = \frac{n_1p_1+n_2p_2}{n_1+n_2}$ and S.E. of $(p_1 - p_2) = \sqrt{pq(\frac{1}{n_1} + \frac{1}{n_2})}$.

Here $n_1 = 500, p_1 = 0.62, n_2 = 400, p_2 = (100 - 41)\% = 0.59$.

$$\therefore \quad p = \frac{500 \times 0.62 + 400 \times 0.59}{500 + 400} = \frac{546}{900} = 0.607, q = 1 - p = 0.393.$$

$$\text{S.E. of } (p_1 - p_2) = \sqrt{0.607 \times 0.393\left(\frac{1}{500} + \frac{1}{400}\right)} = \sqrt{\frac{0.607 \times 0.393 \times 9}{2000}} = \sqrt{0.00107} = 0.0327.$$

Assuming that H_o is true, the test statistic is

$$z = \frac{p_1 - p_2}{\text{S.E. of } (p_1 - p_2)} = \frac{0.62 - 0.59}{0.0327} = \frac{0.03}{0.0327} = 0.917 < 1.96.$$

Since $z < 1.96$, **we accept the Null Hypothesis at** 5% *level of significance and conclude that* **there is no significant difference** *between the two groups in their attitude towards the new plan.*

Exercise 4(II)

Theory

(Tests of Hypotheses)

1. Explain very briefly the terms: (i) Sampling distribution of a statistic; (ii) Type II Error, and (iii) Level of significance. **[ICWAI June 1984]**

2. Explain the following terms (mention only the essential points): (i) Statistic and Parameter; (ii) Critical Region; (iii) Standard Error. **[ICWAI June 1983; CA 1975]**

3. Explain clearly the procedure generally followed in testing of a hypothesis. Point out the difference between one-tailed and two-tailed tests. **[Delhi U. M. Com. 1982; ICWAI June 1987]**

4. How do you test the significance of the difference between the means of the two samples.

5. Define : Type I error and standard error. **[ICWAI December 1990]**

Explain clearly the procedure generally followed in testing of a hypothesis.

[ICWAI June 1987]

6. Explain the terms :

(i) Level of significance; **[ICWAI June 1986]**

(ii) One tailed test; **[CA November 1990]**

(iii) Two-tailed test.

7. Write short notes on the following:

(i) Standard Error and Tests of Significance. **[CA November 1982]**

(ii) Level of Significance. **[CA May 1982; ICWAI June 1984, 1986]**

(iii) Null Hypothesis. **[H.P.U. MBA 1982; B.U. B. Com. 1979]**

(iv) Null and Alternative Hypothesis. **[CA May 1989]**

(v) Errors in Hypothesis Testing. **[CA November 1990]**

Problems

(Tests of Hypotheses)

[A]

1. The mean life of a sample of 64 electric bulbs produced by a company is found to be 1375 hours with a S.D. of 80 hours. If μ is the mean life time of all bulbs produced by the company, test the hypothesis $\mu = 1400$ hours against the alternative hypothesis $\mu \neq 1400$ hours, using 5% level of significance. [At 5% levels for two-tailed test the critical values are -1.96 and $+1.96$.]

2. (i) A sample of 400 items has mean 4.6. Can the sample be regarded as drawn from a large population whose mean is 5.1 and variance is 4?

(ii) Is it likely that a sample of size 300 whose mean is 12, is a random sample from a large population with mean 12.8 and S.D. 5.2? **[ICWAI December 1992]**

[HINTS. $\bar{x} = 12, n = 300, \mu = 12.8, \sigma = 5.2$; S.E. of $\bar{x} = \frac{\sigma}{\sqrt{n}} = \frac{5.2}{\sqrt{300}} = 0.3$ and $|z| = \left|\frac{12-12.8}{0.3}\right| = \frac{8}{3} = 2.67 > 1.96$, etc.]

3. A sample of 400 male students is found to have a mean height of 171.38 cms. Can it be reasonably regarded as a sample from a large population with mean height 171.17 cms and S.D. 3.30 cms.? **[ICWAI June 1980]**

4. (i) A coin is tossed 900 times and heads appear 490 times. Does this result support the hypothesis that the coin is unbiased? **[ICWAI December 1974; June 1989, 92]**

(ii) A coin is tossed 400 times and it turns head 216 times. Is it reasonable to assume that the coin is unbiased? **[ICWAI December 1990]**

5. A die was thrown 400 times and 'six' resulted 80 times. Do the data justify the hypothesis of an unbiased die? **[B.U. 1970; ICWAI June 1977]**

6. An automatic machine was designed to pack exactly 2.0 kg of Vanaspati. A sample of 100 tins was examined to test the machine. The average weight was found to be 1.94 kg with S.D. 0.10 kg. Is the machine working properly? **[CA May 1968]**

[HINTS. Here $\mu = 2$ kg, $n = 100, \bar{x} = 1.94$ kg, $S =$ sample S.D. $= 0.10$ kg.]

7. Before an increase in excise duty on tea, 400 people out of a sample of 500 persons were found to be tea drinkers. After an increase in duty, 400 people were tea drinkers in a sample of 600 people. Using standard error of proportion, state whether there is a sufficient decrease in the consumption of tea. **[CA May 1977]**

8. A random sample of size 10 drawn from a normal population has a mean 48. Test the hypothesis that the population mean is 50, its variance being given to be 4. Also obtain 99% confidence interval for the population mean. [z-value at 1% level = 2.58.] **[ICWAI December 1990]**

[HINTS. S.E. of $\bar{x} = \sigma/\sqrt{n} = 2/\sqrt{10} = 0.63$

$\therefore \quad z = \frac{\bar{x}-\mu}{\text{S.E. of } \bar{x}} = \frac{48-50}{0.63} = -3.17$ and $|z| = 3.17 > 2.58$.

99% confidence interval for μ is

$[\bar{x} - 2.58(\text{S.E. of } \bar{x}), \bar{x} + 2.58(\text{S.E. of } \bar{x})] = [48 - 2.58 \times 0.63, 48 + 2.58 \times 0.63.]$

9. In a hospital, 138 females and 162 males were born in a week. Do these figures conform to the hypothesis that the sexes are born in *equal proportion*?

[HINTS. Apply the test for a specified proportion $P_o = \frac{1}{2} = 0.5 =$ probability of equal proportion. Here $p =$ proportion of females born $= 138/300 = 0.46$.]

10. Past records show that the average grade of students taking a particular accountancy course is 65 marks with S.D. of 16 marks. A new method of teaching is to be tested and a random sample of 64 students is chosen. At the end of the course the average marks for this group of students is 69. Test the hypothesis that the new teaching method has improved the average performance of students. Discuss any assumptions that you make and whether additional information would help you evaluate the experiment. **[C.U. M. Com. 1985]**

[HINTS. $H_o : \mu = 65; H_1 : \mu > 65$. Use Right-Tail test. $\sigma/\sqrt{n} = 2, z = (69 - 65)/2 = 2 > 1.645$ at 5% level and < 2.33 at 1% level, etc.]

11. Two independent random samples of sizes 10 and 15 from two independent normal populations having variances 4 and 9 were found to have means 48 and 46 respectively. Test at 5% significance level whether the two population means may be taken to be equal. What assumptions do you make in applying the test?

Also find 95% confidence limits for the difference of the population means.

[ICWAI December 1988]

[HINTS. Since the two small samples are drawn from two independent normal populations having known variances (i.e., known S.D.), we can use the formulae given in Art. 4.7.2 to test the hypothesis. Calculate $z = \frac{\bar{x}_1 - \bar{x}_2}{\text{S.E. of } (\bar{x}_1 - \bar{x}_2)}$, where S.E. of $\bar{x}_1 - \bar{x}_2 = \sqrt{\frac{\sigma_1^2}{n_1} + \frac{\sigma_2^2}{n_2}} = \sqrt{0.4 + 0.6} = \sqrt{1} = 1$, $\bar{x}_1 = 48, \bar{x}_2 = 46$.]

[B]

1. (i) A random sample of 400 flower stems has an average length of 10 cm. Can this be regarded as a sample from a large population with mean of 10.2 cm and a standard deviation of 2.25 cm? **[Delhi U. B.A. Econ. (Hons.) 1982]**

(ii) A random sample of 200 tins of coconut oil gave an average weight of 4.95 kgs. with a standard deviation 0.21. Do we accept the hypothesis of net weight of 5 kgs. per tin at 1% level? **[ICWAI December 1985]**

[HINTS. $n = 200, \bar{x} = 4.95, \sigma \simeq S = 0.21, m_o = 5$ kgs.]

2. (i) A sample of size 400 was drawn and the sample mean was found to be 99. Test whether this sample could have come from a normal population with mean 100 and variance 64 at 5% level of significance. **[Delhi U. M. A. (Econ.) 1977]**

(ii) A sample of 900 items has mean 8.4 and standard deviation 2.61. Can the sample be regarded as drawn from a population with mean 3.25 at 5% level of significance? **[ICWAI December 1989]**

3. The mean life time of a sample of 100 fluorescent light tubes produced by a company is computed to be 1,570 hours with a standard deviation of 120 hours. The company claims that the average life of the tubes produced by company is 1,600 hours. Using the level of significance of 0.05, is the claim acceptable? **[Delhi U. 1979; ICWAI June 1977]**

4. A dice is thrown 49152 times and of these 25145 yielded either 4 or 5 or 6. Is this consistent with the hypothesis that the dice must be unbiased? **[ICWAI June 1980]**

5. (i) Is it likely that a sample of 300 items whose mean is 16.0 is a random sample from a large population whose mean is 16.1 and standard deviation 5.2? [ICWAI June 1973; MBA 1978]

(ii) In a sample of 500 parts manufactured by a company, the number of defective parts was found to be 42. The company, however, claimed that 6% of their product is defective. Is the claim tenable?

(iii) In a sample of 600 parts manufactured by a factory, the number of defective parts was found to be 45. The company, however, claimed that only 5 percent of their product is defective. Is the claim tenable? **[ICWAI June 1986]**

[HINTS. See Example 7 in Art. 4.7.1.]

6. A company producing glass fly-rods by a new process claimed that there would be 25 defective per hundred. When a sample of 500 was taken, the number of defectives found was 150. Test the correctness of the company's claim at 5% level of significance, stating clearly the null hypothesis with which you start.

7. The means of two large samples of sizes 800 and 1600 are 74.5 and 75.0 respectively. Test the equality of means of the two populations each with S.D. 2.4 at 5% level of significance.

8. In a certain district A, 560 persons were regular consumers of tea out of a sample of 1000 persons. In another district B, 500 out of 800 persons were regular consumers of tea. Do these facts reveal a significant difference between the two districts as far as tea-drinking habit is concerned? (Use 5% level of significance.)

9. Electric bulbs manufactured by X and Y companies gave the following results:

	X Co.	Y Co.
No. of bulbs used	100	100
Mean life in hours	1300	1248
S.D. in hours	82	93

Using standard error of the difference between means, state whether there is any significant difference in the mean life of the two makes. **[R.U. M. Com. 1979; CA May 1975]**

10. Two groups A and B consist of 100 people each who have a disease. A serum is given to group A but not to group B. It is found that in groups A and B, 70 and 60 people respectively recover from the disease. Test the hypothesis that the serum helps to cure the disease.

11. In an infantile paralysis epidemic 500 persons contracted the disease. 300 received no serum treatment and of those 75 became paralysed. Of those who did receive serum treatment, 65 became paralysed. Was the serum treatment effective? **[CA November 1979]**

12. In order to test whether a coin is perfect, the coin is tossed 5 times. The null hypothesis of perfectness is rejected if and only if more than 4 heads are obtained. What is the probability of Type I error? Find the probability of Type II error when the corresponding probability of head is 0.2.

[C]

1. A manufacturer of steel bars claims that his products have a mean breaking strength of 48 units. For a sample of 144 bars produced by his firm, the mean breaking strength is 46.2 units and the standard deviation is 8.7 units. Make a test at the 5% level of significance and state whether this evidence supports his claim.

2. A machine part was designed to withstand an average pressure of 120 units. A random sample of size 100 from a large batch was tested and it was found that the average pressure which these parts can withstand is 105 units with a standard deviation of 20 units. Test whether the batch meet the specification. **[C.U. M. Com. 1972]**

[HINTS. $H_o : \mu = 120$ and $H_1 : \mu < 120, z = -7.5 < -1.645$. Hence, etc.]

3. A sample of size 600 persons selected at random from a large city shows that percentage of male in the sample is 53%. It is believed that male to total population ratio in the city is $\frac{1}{2}$. Test whether this belief is confirmed by the observation. **[C.U. M. Com. 1971]**

4. A manufacturer claimed that at least 95% of the equipments which he supplied to a factory conformed to specifications. An examination of a sample of 200 pieces of equipments revealed that 18 were faulty. Test his claim at a significance level of (i) 0.05; (ii) 0.01.

[ICWAI December 1977; CA December 1979]

5. A sample of 100 iron bars is said to be drawn from a large number of bars whose lengths are normally distributed with mean 4 ft. and S.D. 0.6 ft. If the sample mean is 4.2 ft., can the sample be regarded as a truly random sample? (Null hypothesis and assumptions should be stated clearly).

[ICWAI June 1982]

6. A random sample of 100 days shows an average daily sale of Rs. 50 with a S.D. of Rs. 10 in a particular shop. Assuming a normal distribution, construct a 95% confidence interval for the expected sale per day. **[C.U. Econ. (Hons.) 1982]**

7. (i) Intelligence tests on two groups—one group consisting of 121 girls and the other group consisting of 81 boys—give the following results:

Group of Girls :	Mean = 84	S.D. = 10
Group of Boys :	Mean = 81	S.D. = 12

Examine if the difference is significant. **[ICWAI December 1981]**

(ii) The mean yield of wheat from a district A was 210 lbs. with S.D. = 10 lbs. per acre from a sample of 100 plots. In another district B, the mean yield was 220 lbs. with S.D. = 12 lbs. from a sample of 150 plots. Assuming that the standard deviation of yield in the entire state was

11 lbs., test whether there is any significant difference between the mean yield of crops in the two districts. **[CA May 1976]**

8. 400 women shoppers are chosen at random in market A. Their average weekly expenditure on food is found to be Rs. 250 with a S.D. of Rs. 40. These figures are Rs. 220 and Rs. 55 respectively in the market B where also 400 women shoppers are chosen at random. Test at 1% level of significance whether the average weekly food expenditure of the two populations of shoppers are equal. **[ICWAI June 1979]**

9. A random sample of 1,000 workers from South India shows that their mean wages are Rs. 47 per week with a S.D. of Rs. 28. A random sample of 1,500 workers from North India gives a mean wage of Rs. 49 per week with a S.D. of Rs. 40. Is there any significant difference between their mean level of wages? **[ICWAI December 1979]**

10. (i) In a simple sample of 600 men from a certain city, 450 men are found to be smokers. In a sample of 900 from another city, 450 are found to be smokers. Do the data indicate that the two cities are significantly different with respect to the prevalence of smoking among men? **[ICWAI June 1978]**

(ii) In a sample of 500 people in Kerala, 280 are tea drinkers and the rest are coffee drinkers. Can we assume that both coffee and tea are equally popular in this State at 1% level of significance? **[CA May 1978]**

11. In a sample of 600 students in a certain college 400 are found to use dot pens. In another college from a sample of 900 students 450 were found to use dot pens. Test whether the two colleges are significantly different with respect to the habit of using dot pens. (Null and Alternative hypotheses should be stated clearly.) **[ICWAI December 1982]**

12. A person buys 100 electric tubes of each of two well-known makes, taken at random from stocks for testing purpose. He finds that 'make A' has a mean life of 1300 hours with a S.D. of 82 hours, and 'make B' has mean life of 1,248 hours with a S.D. of 93 hours. Discuss the significance of these results. Which make of electric tubes should the person buy? **[Delhi U. M. Com. 1982]**

[HINTS. $H_o : \mu_1 = \mu_2; H_1 : \mu_1 \neq \mu_2, z = 4.2 > 2.58$. Since $\bar{x}_1 > \bar{x}_2$, make A of electric bulbs should be preferred.]

13. An examination was given to 50 students at college A and to 60 students at college B. At A, the mean grade was 75 with a S.D. of 9. At B, the mean grade was 79 with a S.D. of 7. Is there a significant difference between the performance of the students at A and those at B, given that $\alpha = 0.05? \alpha = 0.01$?

14. The mean height of 50 male students who showed above average participation in college athletics was 68.2 inches with a standard deviation of 2.5 inches; while 50 male students who showed no interest in such participation had a mean height of 67.5 inches with a standard deviation of 2.8 inches. Test the hypothesis that male students who participate in college athletics are taller than other male students. **[Delhi U. 1981]**

15. From the following data, obtained from a sample of 1,000 persons, calculate the standard error of the mean:

Earnings (in Rs.) :	0–10	10–20	20–30	30–40	40–50	50–60	60–70	70–80
No. of Persons :	50	100	150	200	200	100	100	100

If the average of the population was Rs. 42.00, what conclusion can you arrive at about the reliability of the sample? **[CA November 1976]**

[HINTS. $\bar{x} = 41, S =$ sample S.D. $= 19.34$, S.E. $= \frac{\sigma}{\sqrt{n}} \simeq \frac{s}{\sqrt{n}} = \frac{19.34}{\sqrt{1000}} = 0.61; H_o : \mu = 42; H_1 : \mu \neq 42; z = 1/0.61 = -1.64$, or $|z| = 1.64 < 1.96$. Hence, etc.]

16. The average number of defective articles in a certain factory is claimed to be less than the average for all the factories. The average for all the factories is 30.5. A random sample of 100 defective articles showed the following distribution:

Class limits :	16–20	21–25	26–30	31–35	36–40
Number :	12	22	20	30	16

Calculate the mean and standard deviation of the sample and use it to claim that the average is less than the figure for all the factories at 5% level of significance. Given $z(-1.645) = 0.95$.

[U.U. M. Com. 1981; CA May 1979]

[HINTS. $\bar{x} = 28.80, s = 6.35; H_o : \mu = 30.5$ and $H_1 : \mu < 30.5$ (One tailed i.e., left-tailed test). S.E. $= \frac{\sigma}{\sqrt{n}} \simeq \frac{s}{\sqrt{n}} = \frac{6.35}{10} = 0.635$ and $z = -1.7/0.635 = -2.68 < -1.645$. Hence, etc.]

Answers

[A]

1. No, since $|z| = 2.5 > 1.96$ at 5% level. **2.** (i) No, since $|z| = 5 > 3$; (ii) No, since $|z| = 2.67 > 1.96$ at 5% level. **3.** Yes, since $|z| = 1.27 < 1.96$. **4.** (i) No, since $|z| = 2.67$; (ii) Yes; since $|z| = 1.60 < 1.96$. **5.** Yes, since $|z| = 1.77 < 1.96$. **6.** No, since $|z| = 6 > 2.58$ at 1% level. **7.** Significant decrease in the consumption of tea, since $z = 4.94 > 2.33$ at 1% level. **8.** Population mean is not 50; 99% confidence interval is [46.37, 49.63]. **9.** Yes, the sexes are born in equal proportions. **10.** At 5% level, H_o is rejected and at 1% level H_o is accepted i.e., at 5% level the new method does not improve the average performance while at 1% level it improves the average performance. **11.** Two population means cannot be equal; 0.04, 3.96.

[B]

1. (i) Yes, since $|z| = 1.777 < 1.96$; (ii) No, since $|z| = 3.367 > 2.58$. **2.** (i) No, since $|z| = 2.5 > 1.96$; (ii) Yes, $z = 1.72 < 1.96$. **3.** No, since $|z| = 2.5 > 1.96$. **4.** No, since $|z| = 5.14 > 2.58$. **5.** (i) No, since $|z| > 1.96$; (ii) No, since $|z| = 2.264$; (iii) No, the claim is not tenable. **6.** Not correct; since $|z| = 2.6 > 1.96$ or 1.645. **7.** Not equal, since $|z| = 4.8 > 1.96$. **8.** Yes, since $|z| = 2.83 > 1.96$. **9.** Significant difference, since $|z| = 4.19 > 3$. **10.** Does not help, since $|z| = 1.49 < 1.96$. **11.** The serum treatment is not effective, since $|z| = 1.875 < 2.58$ at 1% level of significance. **12.** $1/32 = 0.03125; 1 - (0.2)^5 = 0.99968$.

[C]

1. Does not support the manufacturer's claim, since $|z| = 2.5 > 1.96$. **2.** Does not meet the specification, since $z = -7.5 < -1.645$. **3.** Confirmed, since $|z| = 1.47 < 1.96$. **4.** (i) Claim not justified at 05 level, since $z = -2.60 < -1.645$; (ii) claim not justified at .01 level, since $z = -2.60 < -2.33$. **5.** No; since $|z| = 3.33 > 2.58$ at 1% level. **6.** [Rs. 48.04, Rs. 51.96]. **7.** (i) Not significant; since $|z| = 1.86 < 1.96$; (ii) significant difference, since $|z| = 7.04 > 2.58$ at 1% level. **8.** Not equal; since $|z| = 8.82 > 2.58$ at 1% level. **9.** No; since $|z| = 1.47 < 1.96$ at 5% level.

10. (i) Yes; since $z = 9.6 > 2.58$; (ii) No; since $|z| = 2.68 > 2.58$. **11.** Significantly different at 1% level, since $|z| = 6.42 > 2.58$. **12.** The result is significant at 1% level, since $|z| = 4.2 > 2.58$. **13.** Yes, since $|z| = 2.56 > 1.96$ at 5% level. (Note that at 1% level, H_o may be accepted, since $|z| < 2.58$). **14.** No significant difference in the heights, since $|z| = 1.32$. **15.** Mean $(\bar{x}) = 28.8$, S.D. $(s) = 6.35$, $z = -2.68 < -1.645$ at 5% level. H_o is rejected and hence, $\mu < \mu_o$.

4.8. SMALL SAMPLE TESTS

We have so far discussed large sample tests in each of which the sample size n is ≥ 30 and the sampling distribution of the statistic is approximately normal. Now we shall consider samples of size $n < 30$. Such samples (in which $n < 30$) are called *small samples.* For a *small sample* $(n < 30)$, we can use *normal distribution to test for a specified population mean, or equality of two means as in large sample tests* **only if the sample is drawn from a normal population whose S.D. σ is known.** But if σ is not known, we cannot proceed as above. In this section, we shall discuss the situation in which the sample is small $(n < 30)$ and the population is normally distributed but σ is not known. *If a population is normally distributed, the sampling distribution of the mean of any sample size is also normally distributed, whether σ is known or not.* In small sample tests, we shall first discuss a very useful distribution known as **Student's t distribution** (or simply **t distribution**), which involves an important expression—**degrees of freedom.**

Degrees of Freedom (d.f. or df or dof)

The **degrees of freedom** (*df*) *is a* **number** *which tells us how many of the values* (or *numbers*) *may be independently* (or *freely*) *chosen.* For example, if we are allowed to pick *any five* numbers, then there is no restriction on any of the *five* numbers (or values). We may choose 12, 5, 13, 4, 7 or any other set of five numbers. Since all the *five numbers* have the *freedom to vary,* we say that the *degrees of freedom* (i.e., the total number of values that may freely vary) is **5**.

If we impose a restriction on the numbers such as the *mean is* 10 (or the *sum is* 50), we can no longer freely pick all the five numbers. We can choose the first four numbers independently (i.e., freely), but the fifth number must be such that the total is 50. If the first four numbers selected freely be 12, 5, 13, 4, then the fifth number would have to be 16 for the sum of the five numbers to be 50. In this case, we say that we have only 4 *degrees of freedom,* i.e., (5-1) *degrees of freedom.* In general, if we have one sample of n numbers (or observations) with a *specified mean,* then we have $(n-1)$ *degrees of freedom.* But if we have two samples of sizes n_1 and n_2 with specified means $\bar{x}_1$ and $\bar{x}_2$, then we have $(n_1 + n_2 - 2)$ *degrees of freedom.*

Student's t Distribution (or Simply t-Distribution)

Student's t distribution is an important continuous probability distribution, first introduced by W. S. Gosset who wrote under the pen-name 'Student', and it is used for testing of hypothesis on *small samples.*

DEFINITION. *If $x_1, x_2, \cdots, x_n$ be any random sample of size n drawn from a normal (or approximately normal) population with mean μ and variance σ^2, then the student's t is defined by the test statistic $t = \frac{\bar{x}-\mu}{S/\sqrt{n}}$, where $\bar{x}$ = sample mean and $S^2 = \frac{1}{n-1}\sum_{i=1}^{n}(x_i - \bar{x})^2$ is an unbiased estimate of σ^2.* [See worked out Example 7 in Art. 4.4.1]

If s^2 be the sample variance, then $s^2 = \frac{\Sigma(x_i-\bar{x})^2}{n}$ so that $\frac{S^2}{s^2} = \frac{n}{n-1}$, or, $S = \sqrt{\frac{n}{n-1}} \cdot s$, or, $S/\sqrt{n} = s/\sqrt{n-1}$.

An unbiased estimate of S.E. of $\bar{x}$ is $s/\sqrt{n-1}$. $\therefore$ $t = \frac{\bar{x}-\mu}{S/\sqrt{n}} = \frac{\bar{x}-\mu}{s/\sqrt{n-1}}$.

This test statistic t follows t distribution with $(n-1)$ degrees of freedom (d.f.). Thus d.f. is $n-1$, i.e., (sample size) -1.

[As S^2 is an unbiased estimate of σ^2, and to find S^2 we have to compute $\Sigma(x_i - \bar{x})^2$ which involves $x_1 - \bar{x}, x_2 - \bar{x}, \cdots, x_n - \bar{x}$, where $\Sigma(x_i - \bar{x}) = 0$, we can choose only $(n-1)$ of the n values $x_i - \bar{x}(i = 1, 2, \cdots, n)$ independently, and hence, d.f. is $n - 1$.]

The probability density function (p.d.f.) of t with $\nu = (n-1)$ d.f. is

$$f(t) = K\left(1 + \frac{t^2}{\nu}\right)^{-(\nu+1)/2} \quad ; \quad -\infty < t < \infty$$

where K is a constant.

Properties of t-Distribution

(i) t-distribution (i.e., the probability curve) is *symmetrical* about the line $t = 0$.

(ii) t-distribution is *asymptotic* to the t-axis, i.e., the two tails of the curve on both sides of $t = 0$ extends to infinity.

(iii) The form of the probability curve varies with the degrees of freedom (d.f.), i.e., with the sample size.

(iv) t-distribution has a *greater dispersion* (i.e., spread) than the standard normal distribution.

(v) It is unimodal with Mean = Median = Mode.

Test for a Specified Mean (S.D. σ unknown)

A random sample of size $n(n < 30)$ has a sample mean $\bar{x}$. To test the hypothesis that the population mean μ has a specified value μ_o when population S.D. *σ is not known.*

Let the Null Hypothesis be $H_o : \mu = \mu_o$.

Then the Alternative Hypothesis is $H_1 : \mu \neq \mu_o$.

Assuming that H_o is true, the test statistic t given by

$$t = \frac{\bar{x} - \mu}{s/\sqrt{n-1}}, \quad \text{where } s = \text{sample S.D.}$$

follows t-distribution with $\nu = (n-1)$ degrees of freedom. We calculate the value of $|t|$ and compare this value with tabulated value of t (value from the tables of t) at α level of significance. If the calculated value > the tabulated value, we reject H_o at α level. Otherwise, we accept H_o. (At 5% level, for *two-tail t-test,* we take $\alpha = 0.025$.)

[In the above test, three cases may arise: (i) $\mu \neq \mu_o$. (ii) $\mu > \mu_o$ and (iii) $\mu < \mu_o$. The respective rejection regions in the three cases are (i) $|t| > t_{\alpha/2}$, (ii) $t > t_\alpha$ and (iii) $t < -t_\alpha$ with $(n-1)$ d.f.]

95% confidence limits for the population mean μ are $\bar{x} \pm t_\alpha s/\sqrt{n-1}$, where $\alpha = .025$.

For *two-tail test,* the value of $\alpha/2$ is taken for α.

Test for Equality of Two Means (σ_1, σ_2 are unknown)

Let $\bar{x}_1$ and $\bar{x}_2$ be the sample means of two independent random samples of sizes n_1 and n_2 drawn from two normal populations having means μ_1 and μ_2. To test whether the two population means are equal. $(n_1 < 30, n_2 < 30)$ [or *to test whether the difference $\bar{x}_1 - \bar{x}_2$ is significant.*]

Let the Null Hypothesis be $H_o : \mu_1 = \mu_2$.

Then the Alternative Hypothesis is $H_1 : \mu_1 \neq \mu_2$.

If the two population S.D. σ_1 and σ_2 are equal, then $\sigma_1 = \sigma_2 = \sigma$ (say) and an unbiased estimate S^2 of the common variance σ^2 is given by $S^2 = \frac{n_1 s_1^2 + n_2 s_2^2}{n_1 + n_2 - 2}$, where s_1^2, s_2^2 are the two sample variances.

S.E. of $(\bar{x}_1 - \bar{x}_2) = S\sqrt{\frac{1}{n_1} + \frac{1}{n_2}}$, where $S = \sqrt{\frac{n_1 s_1^2 + n_2 s_2^2}{n_1 + n_2 - 2}}$.

We can write $n_1 s_1^2 = \Sigma(x_1 - \bar{x}_1)^2$ and $n_2 s_2^2 = \Sigma(x_2 - \bar{x}_2)^2$.

[An unbiased estimate S^2 of the common variance is sometimes given by $S^2 = \frac{(n_1-1)s_1^2+(n_2-1)s_2^2}{n_1+n_2-2}$.]

Assuming that H_o is true, the test statistic t given by

$$t = \frac{\bar{x}_1 - \bar{x}_2}{S\sqrt{\frac{1}{n_1} + \frac{1}{n_2}}}$$

follows t distribution with $(n_1 + n_2 - 2)$ degrees of freedom.

We calculate the value of $|t|$ at α level of significance and compare this value with the tabulated value of t at α level. If calculated value > tabulated value, reject the null hypothesis H_o at α level. Otherwise, we accept H_o.

95% confidence limits for the difference of population means are

$$(\bar{x}_1 - \bar{x}_2) \pm t_\alpha \cdot S\sqrt{\frac{1}{n_1} + \frac{1}{n_2}}, \quad \text{where } \alpha = 0.025.$$

[For two-tail test, the value of $\alpha/2$ is taken for α.]

Uses of t-Test

t-test is used when (i) the size n of the sample is *small* (i.e., $n < 30$), (ii) the variance (or σ) of the population is *not known,* (iii) the sample is a random one and (iv) the population is normal (or approximately normal). This test is used (1) to test for a specified mean, (2) to test for equality of two means of two independent samples drawn from two normal populations, S.D. of the populations being unknown, and (3) to test the significance of difference between the means of paired data.

EXAMPLE 1. *A machine is designed to produce insulating washers for electrical devices of average thickness of* .025 *cm. A random sample of* 10 *washers was found to have an average thickness of* .024 *cm. with a* S.D. *of* .002 *cm. Test the significance of the deviation. Value of* t *for* 9 *degrees of freedom at* 5% *level is* 2.262. **[CA November 1980]**

SOLUTION. We have $\mu = .025, n = 10, \bar{x} = .024, s = .002$, where s is the sample S.D.

Since the sample size is small and population S.D. σ is not known, we use t test.

Let the Null Hypothesis be $H_o : \mu = .025$.

Then the Alternative Hypothesis is $H_1 : \mu \neq .025$. The test statistic is

$$t = \frac{\bar{x} - \mu}{s/\sqrt{n-1}} = \frac{.024 - .025}{.002/\sqrt{10-1}} = \frac{-.001}{.002/3} = -\frac{.003}{.002} = -1.5.$$

Degrees of freedom $= n - 1 = 10 - 1 = 9$.

The tabulated value of t for 9 d.f. at 5% level = 2.262.

$\therefore \quad |t| = 1.5 < 2.262 \quad [\because$ for two-tail test, $\alpha/2$ is taken for α.]

Since the calculated value of $|t|$ < *the tabulated value, we accept the Null Hypothesis at* 5% *level and conclude that the* **deviation is not significant.**

EXAMPLE 2. *Two samples of* 6 *and* 5 *items respectively gave the following data:*

Mean of the first sample = 40, S.D. *of the first sample* = 8.

Mean of the second sample = 50, S.D. *of the 2nd sample* = 10.

Is the difference of the means significant? The value of t *for* 9 *d.f at* 5% *level is* 2.26. **[CA May 1981]**

SOLUTION. We have $n_1 = 6, \bar{x}_1 = 40, s_1 = 8$ and $n_2 = 5, \bar{x}_2 = 50, s_2 = 10$.

Since the sample sizes are small and σ_1, σ_2 are not known, we use t test. Let μ_1, μ_2 be the population means of the two populations.

An unbiased estimate S^2 of the common variance is given by

$$S^2 = \frac{n_1 s_1^2 + n_2 s_2^2}{n_1 + n_2 - 2} = \frac{6 \times 64 + 5 \times 100}{6 + 5 - 2} = \frac{884}{9} = 98.22;$$

$$\therefore \quad S = \sqrt{98.22} = 9.91.$$

Let the Null Hypothesis be $H_o : \mu_1 = \mu_2$.

Then the Alternative Hypothesis is $H_1 : \mu_1 \neq \mu_2$.

Assuming that H_o is true, the test statistic is

$$t = \frac{\bar{x}_1 - \bar{x}_2}{S\sqrt{\frac{1}{n_1} + \frac{1}{n_2}}} = \frac{40 - 50}{9.91\sqrt{\frac{1}{6} + \frac{1}{5}}} = \frac{-10}{9.91 \times 0.606} = -1.67.$$

Also d.f. $= 5 + 6 - 2 = 9$.

$\therefore \quad |t| = 1.67 < 2.26$ for 9 d.f., i.e., the calculated value of $|t| <$ the tabulated value at 5% level with 9 d.f.

Hence, *we accept the Null Hypothesis and conclude that the* **difference between the means is not significant.**

EXAMPLE 3. *Samples of two types of electric bulbs were tested for length of life and the following data were obtained:*

	Type I	Type II
Number in the sample	8	7
Mean of the sample (in hours)	1,134	1,024
Standard Deviation of the Sample (in hours)	35	40

Test at 5% *level, whether the difference in the sample mean is significant.* (*Table values of t for* 13 *d.f.* = 2.16, *for* 14 *d.f.* = 2.15 *and for* 15 *d.f.* = 2.13 *at* 5% *level for two-tailed areas and* 1.77, 1.76 *and* 1.75 *respectively for one-tailed area*). **[CA November 1991]**

SOLUTION. Here $n_1 = 8, \bar{x}_1 = 1134, s_1 = 35; n_2 = 7, \bar{x}_2 = 1024, s_2 = 40$.

Since the sample sizes are small and σ_1, σ_2 are not known, we use t-test. Let μ_1, μ_2 be the population means of the length of life of the Type I and Type II bulbs respectively.

Let the Null Hypothesis be $H_o : \mu_1 = \mu_2$.

Then the Alternative Hypothesis is $H_1 : \mu_1 \neq \mu_2$.

An unbiased estimate S of the common population S.D. is given by

$$S = \sqrt{\frac{n_1 s_1^2 + n_2 s_2^2}{n_1 + n_2 - 2}} = \sqrt{\frac{8 \times (35)^2 + 7 \times (40)^2}{8 + 7 - 2}} = \sqrt{\frac{8 \times 1225 + 7 \times 1600}{13}} = \sqrt{\frac{21000}{13}}$$

$$= \sqrt{1615.38} = 40.19.$$

$$\text{S.E. of } (\bar{x}_1 - \bar{x}_2) = S\sqrt{\frac{1}{n_1} + \frac{1}{n_2}} = 40.19\sqrt{\frac{1}{8} + \frac{1}{7}} = 40.19 \times 0.518 = 20.82.$$

Assuming that H_o is true, the test statistic is

$$t = \frac{\bar{x}_1 - \bar{x}_2}{S\sqrt{\frac{1}{n_1} + \frac{1}{n_2}}} = \frac{1134 - 1024}{20.82} = \frac{110}{20.82} = 5.283.$$

Also d.f. $= 8 + 7 - 2 = 13$.

Thus $t = 5.283 > 2.16$, i.e., the computed value of t is greater than the table value of t at 5% level with 13 d.f.

Hence, *we reject H_o and conclude that the two types of electric bulbs differ significantly in their means.*

EXAMPLE 4. *A group of* 5 *patients treated with medicine A weigh* 42, 39, 48, 60 *and* 41 *kgs.; a second group of* 7 *patients from the same Hospital treated with medicine B weigh* 38, 42, 56, 64, 68, 69 *and* 62 *kgs. Do you agree with the claim that medicine 'B' increases the weight significantly?* [*The value of 't' at* 5% *level of significance for* 10 *degrees of freedom is* 2.2281.] **[ICWAI June 1979]**

SOLUTION. Let the Null Hypothesis be $H_o : \mu_1 = \mu_2$, i.e., there is no significant difference between A and B as regards their effect on increase in weight.

Then the Alternative Hypothesis is $H_1 : \mu_1 < \mu_2$ (left-tailed), i.e., B increases the weight significantly.

Since the sample sizes are small and the population standard deviations are not known, we use t-test.

Let H_o be true. An unbiased estimate S^2 of the common population variance σ^2 is given by

$$S^2 = \frac{n_1 s_1^2 + n_2 s_2^2}{n_1 + n_2 - 2} \quad \text{and the test statistic is} \quad t = \frac{\bar{x}_1 - \bar{x}_2}{S\sqrt{\frac{1}{n_1} + \frac{1}{n_2}}}.$$

TABLE 4.8 CALCULATIONS OF S^2 AND t

Medicine A			Medicine B		
x_1	$x_1 - \bar{x}_1$	$(x_1 - \bar{x}_1)^2$	x_2	$x_2 - \bar{x}_2$	$(x_2 - \bar{x}_2)^2$
42	−4	16	38	−19	361
39	−7	49	42	−15	225
48	2	4	56	−1	1
60	14	196	64	7	49
41	−5	25	68	11	121
			69	12	144
			62	5	25
$230 = \Sigma x_1$	···	$290 = \Sigma(x_1 - \bar{x}_1)^2$	$399 = \Sigma x_2$	···	$926 = \Sigma(x_2 - \bar{x}_2)^2$

$$\bar{x}_1 = \frac{\Sigma x_1}{n_1} = \frac{230}{5} = 46; \quad \bar{x}_2 = \frac{\Sigma x_2}{n_2} = \frac{399}{7} = 57$$

$$n_1 s_1^2 = \Sigma(x_1 - \bar{x}_1)^2 = 290 \quad \text{and} \quad n_2 s_2^2 = 926.$$

$$\therefore \quad S^2 = \frac{290 + 926}{5 + 7 - 2} = \frac{1216}{10} = 121.6.$$

$$\therefore \quad S = \sqrt{121.6} = 11.03.$$

$$\therefore \quad t = \frac{46 - 57}{11.03\sqrt{\frac{1}{5} + \frac{1}{7}}} = \frac{-11}{11.03 \times 0.585} = \frac{-11}{6.45} = -1.71.$$

$$\therefore \quad |t| = 1.71 < 2.2281.$$

Since the calculated value of $|t| <$ the tabulated value of t at 5% level with 10 d.f., we accept the Null Hypothesis H_o and conclude that the medicines A and B do not differ significantly in increasing the weights of the patients.

NOTE. For a *left-tailed test,* $|t|$ at 5% level with 10 d.f. is 1.812.

EXAMPLE 5. *Following data show the cost per square foot of floor area concerning randomly selected* 7 *schools and* 5 *office blocks from those completed during the period* 1984 *to* 1989:

Building Type	Cost per Square foot (Rs.)						
Schools :	28	31	26	27	23	38	37
Office Blocks :-	37	42	34	37	35		

Do the data support the hypothesis that the cost per square foot for office blocks was greater than that for schools? Test at 5% *level of significance using 't' test.* **[CA November 1990]**

SOLUTION. Let x_1 and x_2 represent costs per square foot (Rs.) of school building and office building respectively.

Let the Null Hypothesis be $H_o : \bar{x}_1 = \bar{x}_2$.

Then the Alternative Hypothesis is $H_1 : \bar{x}_1 < \bar{x}_2$.

TABLE 4.9 CALCULATIONS FOR S^2 AND t

Sample of Schools			Sample of Office Blocks		
x_1	$x_1 - \bar{x}_1$	$(x_1 - \bar{x}_1)^2$	x_2	$x_2 - \bar{x}_2$	$(x_2 - \bar{x}_2)^2$
28	−2	4	37	0	0
31	1	1	42	5	25
26	−4	16	34	−3	9
27	−3	9	37	0	0
23	−7	49	35	−2	4
38	8	64			
37	7	49			
$210 = \Sigma x_1$	...	$192 = \Sigma(x_1 - \bar{x}_1)^2$	$185 = \Sigma x_2$		$38 = \Sigma(x_2 - \bar{x})^2$

$$\bar{x}_1 = \frac{\Sigma x_1}{n_1} = \frac{210}{7} = 30; \bar{x}_2 = \frac{\Sigma x_2}{n_2} = \frac{185}{5} = 37$$

$$n_1 s_1^2 = \Sigma(x_1 - \bar{x}_1)^2 = 192 \quad \text{and} \quad n_2 s_2^2 = \Sigma(x_2 - \bar{x}_2)^2 = 38$$

$\therefore$ An unbiased estimate S^2 of the common population variance is

$$S^2 = \frac{n_1 s_1^2 + n_2 s_2^2}{n_1 + n_2 - 2} = \frac{192 + 38}{7 + 5 - 2} = \frac{230}{10} = 23; \quad \therefore \quad S = \sqrt{23} = 4.796.$$

$\therefore$ The test statistic is $t = \dfrac{\bar{x}_1 - \bar{x}_2}{S\sqrt{\frac{1}{n_1} + \frac{1}{n_2}}} = \dfrac{30 - 37}{4.796\sqrt{\frac{1}{7} + \frac{1}{5}}} = \dfrac{-7}{4.796 \times 0.586}.$

$\therefore$ $|t| = 2.491 > 1.812. = -\frac{7}{2.81} = -2.491.$

Also d.f. $= n_1 + n_2 - 2 = 7 + 5 - 2 = 10.$

[The table value of 't' at 5% with 10 d.f. for one-tailed (left-sided) test is 1.812.] Since the calculated value of $|t| <$ the table value of t at 5% level with 10 d.f. for one-tailed test, we reject H_o and conclude that **cost per square foot of office blocks was greater than that of schools.**

4.8.1. Paired t-Test for the Difference of Means

Suppose a business concern is interested to know whether a particular media of promoting sales of a product is really effective or not. In this case we have to test whether the average sales before and after the sales promotion are equal.

Let $x_1, x_2, \cdots, x_n$ be the sales of a product in n departmental stores for a certain period before sales promotion and $y_1, y_2, \cdots, y_n$ the corresponding sales of the same product for the same period after the sales promotion.

Then $(x_1, y_1), (x_2, y_2), \cdots, (x_n, y_n)$ are the pairs of the sales data before and after the sales promotion in the n departmental stores.

To test the significance of the difference between the sales x and y we apply paired t test.

Let $d_i = x_i - y_i$ or $y_i - x_i, i = 1, 2, \cdots, n$.

[We shall choose the right side such that Σd_i is positive.]

Let the Null Hypothesis be $H_\circ : \mu_1 = \mu_2$, i.e., there is no difference between the average sales before and after the sales promotion.

Then the Alternative Hypothesis is $H_1 : \mu_1 \neq \mu_2$.

Assuming that $H_\circ$ is true, the test statistic

$$t = \frac{\bar{d}}{S/\sqrt{n}}, \quad \text{where} \quad \bar{d} = \frac{\Sigma d}{n}$$

$$\text{and} \quad S^2 = \frac{\Sigma(d - \bar{d})^2}{n-1} = \frac{1}{n-1}\left[\Sigma d^2 - \frac{(\Sigma d)^2}{n}\right] = \frac{\Sigma d^2 - (\bar{d})^2 \times n}{n-1}$$

$[\because \quad \bar{d} = \Sigma d/n.]$

follows t distribution with $(n-1)$ d.f.

EXAMPLE 6. *IQ test was administered to* 5 *persons before and after they were trained. The results are given below:*

Candidates :	I	II	III	IV	V
IQ before training :	110	120	123	132	125
IQ after training :	120	118	125	136	121

Test whether there is any change in IQ after the training programme $[t_{0.01}(4) = 4.6]$.

[CA May 1980]

SOLUTION. Let us apply paired t test.

Let the Null Hypothesis be $H_\circ : \mu_1 = \mu_2$, i.e., there is no significant effect of the training.

Then the Alternative Hypothesis is $H_1 : \mu_1 < \mu_2$.

Assuming that $H_\circ$ is true, the test statistic is

$$t = \frac{\bar{d}}{S/\sqrt{n}}, \quad \text{where} \quad \bar{d} = \frac{\Sigma d}{n}, d = y - x \quad \text{and} \quad S^2 = \frac{\Sigma(d - \bar{d})^2}{n-1} = \frac{\Sigma d^2 - (\bar{d})^2 \times n}{n-1}.$$

TABLE 4.10 CALCULATIONS FOR $\bar{d}$ AND s

Candidates (Persons)	*IQ* before training (x)	*IQ* after training (y)	$d = y - x$	d^2
I	110	120	10	100
II	120	118	– 2	4
III	123	125	2	4
IV	132	136	4	16
V	125	121	– 4	16
Total	. . .	. . .	$10 = \Sigma d$	$140 = \Sigma d^2$

$$\therefore \quad \bar{d} = \frac{\Sigma d}{n} = \frac{10}{5} = 2 \quad \text{and} \quad S^2 = \frac{140 - (2)^2 \times 5}{5-1} = \frac{140-20}{4} = 30; \qquad \therefore \quad s = \sqrt{30}.$$

$$\therefore \quad t = \frac{\bar{d}}{s/\sqrt{n}} = \frac{2}{\sqrt{30}/\sqrt{5}} = \frac{2}{\sqrt{6}} = \frac{2}{2.45} = 0.82 \quad \text{and} \quad d.f. = n-1 = 5-1 = 4.$$

Thus $t = 0.82 < 4.6$ at 1% level with 4 d.f.

Since *the calculated value of* $t <$ *the tabulated value with 4 d.f. at 1% level,* **we accept H$_o$** *at 1% level and conclude that* **there is no significant change in IQ after the training programme.**

EXAMPLE 7. *A certain stimulus administered to each of the* 12 *patients resulted in the following increase of blood pressure:* $5, 2, 8, -1, 3, 0, -2, 1, 5, 0, 4$ *and* 6.

Can it be concluded that the stimulus will, in general, be accompanied by an increase in blood pressure? (*Given for* 11 *d.f.,* $t_{0.01} = 2.2$). **[ICWAI December 1980]**

SOLUTION. Here $d = y - x = 5, 2, 8, -1, 3, 0, -2, 1, 5, 0, 4, 6$.

Let the Null Hypothesis be $H_o : \mu_1 = \mu_2$, i.e., there is *no significant difference* in blood pressure before and after administering the stimulus.

The Alternative Hypothesis is $H_1 : \mu_1 \neq \mu_2$.

Assuming that H_o is true, the test statistic is $t = \frac{\bar{d}}{S/\sqrt{n}}$ where $\bar{d} = \frac{\Sigma d}{n}$ and $S^2 = \frac{\Sigma d^2 - (\bar{d}^2) \times n}{n-1}$.
Now $d = 5, 2, 8, -1, 3, 0, -2, 1, 5, 0, 4, 6$ and $d^2 = 25, 4, 64, 1, 9, 0, 4, 1, 25, 0, 16, 36$.

$$\therefore \quad \bar{d} = \frac{\Sigma d}{n} = \frac{31}{12} = 2.58 \quad \text{and} \quad \Sigma d^2 = 185.$$

$$\therefore \quad S^2 = \frac{185 - (2.58)^2 \times 12}{12-1} = \frac{185 - 79.87}{11} = 9.55$$

$$\therefore \quad S = \sqrt{9.55} = 3.09.$$

$$\therefore \quad t = \frac{2.58}{3.09/\sqrt{12}} = \frac{2.58 \times \sqrt{12}}{3.09} = 2.90 > 2.2, \quad \text{and } d.f. = n-1 = 12-1 = 11.$$

Since *the calculated value of* $t >$ *the tabulated value with* 11 *d.f. at* 1% *level,* **we reject the Null Hypothesis H$_o$** *and conclude that* **the stimulus will, in general, be accompanied by an increase in blood pressure.**

4.9 CHI-SQUARE DISTRIBUTION : CHI-SQUARE TEST

Chi-Square Distribution is an important continuous probability distribution, first formulated by Helmert and then discovered by Karl Pearson.

DEFINITION. *If* x *is a normal variate (i.e., normally distributed) with mean* μ *and* S.D. σ, *then* $z = \frac{x-\mu}{\sigma}$ *is a standard normal variate with mean 0 and* S.D. *1, and* $z^2 = (\frac{x-\mu}{\sigma})^2$ *is a* **Chi-square variate with 1 degree of freedom.** *Chi-square variate is denoted by the symbol* χ^2.

If $x_1, x_2, \cdots, x_n$ *be n independent normal variates with means* $\mu_1, \mu_2, \cdots, \mu_n$ *and standard deviations* $\sigma_1, \sigma_2, \cdots, \sigma_n$ *respectively, then*

$$\chi^2 = \left(\frac{x_1 - \mu_1}{\sigma_1}\right)^2 + \left(\frac{x_2 - \mu_2}{\sigma_2}\right)^2 + \cdots + \left(\frac{x_n - \mu_n}{\sigma_n}\right)^2 = \sum_{i=1}^{n} \left(\frac{x_i - \mu_i}{\sigma_i}\right)^2$$

is a **Chi-square variate with n degrees of freedom.**

The *probability density function of Chi-square* (χ^2) *distribution with* $\nu = (n-1)$ *degrees of freedom is given by*

$$f(\chi^2) = K \cdot (\chi^2)^{\frac{1}{2}(\nu-2)} \cdot e^{-\frac{1}{2}\chi^2}; 0 < \chi^2 < \infty,$$

where K *is a constant and* $\nu = n - 1$ *is the number of degrees of freedom.* A variable which follows Chi-square distribution is called a *Chi-square variate.*

Some Properties of χ^2-Distribution

1. Mean = degrees of freedom ν, Mode = $\nu - 2$ and S.D. = $\sqrt{2\nu}$.

2. For $n > 1$, the χ^2 probability curve is positively skewed and starting from 0 extends to infinity on the right.

As d.f. increases, skewness decreases and the probability curve rapidly tends to symmetry. For large d.f. (i.e., if $\nu \to \infty$), the chi-square distribution tends to normal distribution.

3. If χ_1^2 and χ_2^2 be independent Chi-square variates with n_1 and n_2 degrees of freedom, then their sum $\chi_1^2 + \chi_2^2$ is also a Chi-square variate with $(n_1 + n_2)$ degrees of freedom.

4. If $x_1, x_2, \cdots, x_n$ be a random sample from a normal population with mean μ and variance σ^2, then

(i) $\sum_{i=1}^{n}(x_i - \mu)^2/\sigma^2$ follows Chi-square distribution with n degrees of freedom; and

(ii) $\sum_{i=1}^{n}(x_i - \bar{x})^2/\sigma^2$ follows Chi-square distribution with $(n-1)$ degrees of freedom, where $\bar{x}$ is the sample mean and $\sum(x_i - \bar{x}) = 0$.

χ^2 *distribution is used in both large and small sample tests.*

Observed and Expected Frequencies

In many cases we have seen that the results obtained in samples do not agree exactly with theoretical results expected according to rules of probability. For example, if we toss a fair coin 100 times, theoretically we may expect 50 heads and 50 tails, but it is rare to obtain these results in practice.

If, in a particular sample, a set of possible events, $A_1, A_2, \cdots, A_k$ are observed to occur with frequencies $O_1, O_2, \cdots, O_k$ and according to probability rules $A_1, A_2, \cdots, A_k$ are expected to occur with frequencies $E_1, E_2, \cdots, E_k$ (see TABLE 4.11), then $O_1, O_2, \cdots, O_k$ are called **observed** (or **experimental**) **frequencies** and $E_1, E_2, \cdots, E_k$ are called **expected** (or **theoretical**) **frequencies.**

TABLE 4.11 OBSERVED AND EXPECTED FREQUENCIES

Event :	A_1	A_2	A_3	......	A_k
Observed Frequency :	O_1	O_2	O_3	......	O_k
Expected Frequency :	E_1	E_2	E_3	......	E_k

Two-way classification tables or $h \times k$ tables in which observed frequencies occupy h rows and k columns, are called **contigency tables.** In a 2×2 contigency table, observed frequencies occupy 2 rows and 2 columns (See Table No. 6.13 or 6.15). Corresponding to each observed frequency (O_i) in a contigency table, we can find an expected frequency (E_i) subject to some hypothesis according to the rules of probability. These frequencies which occupy the *cells of a contigency table* are called *cell frequencies.*

Chi-Square Test (χ^2 test)

It is a very simple and widely used test. In Chi-square tests, χ^2 distribution is mainly used

(i) to test the goodness of fit,

(ii) to test the independence of attributes,

(iii) to test if the population has a specified value of the variance σ^2.

We shall discuss these tests one by one as applications of χ^2 distribution.

Chi-Square Test for Goodness of Fit

It is a very popular test given by Karl Pearson in 1900. This test is used to decide whether the discrepancy between theory and experiment is significant or not, i.e., *to test whether the difference between the theoretical and observed values can be attributed to chance or not.*

Let the *Null Hypothesis* H_o *be that there is no significant difference between the observed* (i.e., *experimental*) *values and the corresponding expected* (*or theoretical*) *values.*

The *Alternative Hypothesis* H_1 is that the above *difference is significant.*

If $O_1, O_2, \cdots, O_n$ be a set of observed (i.e., experimental) frequencies and $E_1, E_2, \cdots, E_n$ the corresponding set of expected (i.e., theoretical or hypothetical) frequencies, then Karl Pearson's test statistic is

$$\chi^2 = \sum_{i=1}^{n} \left[\frac{(O_i - E_i)^2}{E_i}\right] = \frac{(O_1 - E_1)^2}{E_1} + \frac{(O_2 - E_2)^2}{E_2} + \cdots + \frac{(O_n - E_n)^2}{E_n}.$$

Assuming that the Null Hypothesis H_o is true, the test statistic χ^2 follows Chi-square distribution with $(n-1)$ degrees of freedom, where $\sum_{i=1}^{n} O_i = \sum_{i=1}^{n} E_i$, i.e., $\Sigma(O_i - E_i) = 0$.

If the calculated value of $\chi^2 >$ tabulated value of χ^2 at α level, the Null Hypothesis H_o is rejected. Otherwise, H_o is accepted.

Degrees of Freedom (d.f.)

The degrees of freedom is the number of independent variates which make up the statistic χ^2.

The number of degrees of freedom is also defined as the total number of observations minus the number of independent constraints (i.e., *restrictions*) *imposed on the observations.*

For a contingency table with r rows and c columns, the degrees of freedom (d.f.) $= (r-1)(c-1)$.

For example, if a contingency table has 2 rows and 2 columns, then $\nu = d.f. = (2-1)(2-1) = 1$.

Expected frequency in a cell of a contingency table may be calculated by using the formula:

$$\textbf{Expected frequency} = \frac{\textbf{Row total} \times \textbf{Column total}}{\textbf{Grand Total}}$$

REMARKS. If the observed and expected frequencies be denoted by O_i and E_i, then $\sum_{i=1}^{n} O_i = \sum_{i=1}^{n} E_i = N$, where N is the total frequency. In this case, the observed and expected frequencies are subjected to a *linear constraint,* $\because$ $\Sigma(O_i - E_i) = \Sigma O_i - \Sigma E_i = N - N = 0$ is a linear constraint.

$\therefore$ Degrees of freedom $= n - 1$.

Conditions of Validity

χ^2 test can be used only when (i) N, i.e., total frequency is *large*, i.e., > 50, (ii) the observations are *independent*, (iii) the constraints on the cell frequencies, if any, are *linear*, (iv) no theoretical (or expected) frequency, is *small*, i.e., $E_i \not< 5$; if any $E_i < 5$, we use pooling technique, i.e., we add the small frequencies with the preceding or succeeding frequency to obtain the resulting sum > 5 and adjust d.f. accordingly.

EXAMPLE 8. *A die was thrown* 90 *times with the following results:*

Face :	1	2	3	4	5	6	Total
Frequency :	10	12	16	14	18	20	90

Are these data consistent with the hypothesis that the die is unbiased? (*Given* $\chi^2_{0.05} = 11.07$ *for* 5 *degrees of freedom.*)

SOLUTION. Let the Null Hypothesis H_o be that the die is unbiased. Then the Alternative Hypothesis H_1 is that the die is biased.

TABLE 4.12 CALCULATIONS FOR χ^2

Face	O_i	E_i	$(O_i - E_i)$	$(O_i - E_i)^2$	$(O_i - E_i)^2/E_i$
1	10	15	−5	25	25/15
2	12	15	−3	9	9/15
3	16	15	1	1	1/15
4	14	15	−1	1	1/15
5	18	15	3	9	9/15
6	20	15	5	25	25/15
Total	90	90	...	...	$70/15 = \Sigma[(O_i - E_i)^2/E_i]$

Expected frequency of each of 1, 2, 3, 4, 5, 6 is $\frac{1}{6} \times 90 = 15$.

Assuming that H_o is true, we have

$$\chi^2 = \sum \left[\frac{(O_i - E_i)^2}{E_i}\right] = \frac{70}{15} = 4.67.$$

Here no. of observations (or classes) is 6 and there is only *one linear constrain, viz.*, $\Sigma O_i = \Sigma E_i = 90$.

$\therefore$ Degrees of freedom = 6 − 1 = 5.

Since, *the calculated value of* χ^2 < *the tabulated value of* χ^2 *at* 5% *level with* 5 *d.f.*, **we accept the Null Hypothesis H$_o$** *and* **conclude that the die is unbiased.**

EXAMPLE 9. *The following figures show the distribution of digits in numbers chosen at random from a telephone directory:*

Digits :	0	1	2	3	4	5	6	7	8	9
Frequency :	1026	1107	997	966	1075	933	1107	972	964	853

Test at 5% *level whether the digits may be taken to occur equally frequently in the directory.*

(*The table value for Chi-square for* 9 *degrees of freedom* = 16.919) **[CA May 1988]**

SOLUTION. Let the Null Hypothesis H_o be that the digits occur equally frequently in the directory.

The Alternative Hypothesis is H_1: The digits do not occur equally frequently.

TABLE 4.13 CALCULATIONS FOR χ^2

Digit	O_i	E_i	$(O_i - E_i)$	$(O_i - E_i)^2$	$(O_i - E_i)^2/E_i$
0	1026	1000	26	676	0.676
1	1107	1000	107	11449	11.449
2	997	1000	−3	9	0.009
3	966	1000	−34	1156	1.156
4	1075	1000	75	5625	5.625
5	933	1000	−67	4489	4.489
6	1107	1000	107	11449	11.449
7	972	1000	−28	784	0.784
8	964	1000	−36	1296	1.296
9	853	1000	−147	21609	21.609
Total	10000	10000	—	—	58.542

Expected frequency of each of the ten digits $= \frac{1}{10} \times 10000 = 1000$.

Assuming that H_o is true, the test statistic is $\chi^2 = \Sigma\frac{(O_i - E_i)^2}{E_i} = 58.542$ with $d.f. = 10 - 1 = 9$.

The table value of χ^2 at 5% level 9 with d.f. is 16.919. $\therefore \quad \chi^2 = 58.542 > 16.919$.

Since the calculated value of $\chi^2 <$ the table value of χ^2 at 5% level with 9 d.f., *we reject H_o and conclude that the digits do not occur equally frequently in the directory.*

EXAMPLE 10. *A survey of* 320 *families with* 5 *children each revealed the following distribution:*

No. of boys :	5	4	3	2	1	0
No. of girls :	0	1	2	3	4	5
No. of families :	14	56	110	88	40	12

Is the result consistent with the hypothesis that male and female births are equally probable?

[Delhi U. M. Com. 1975; B.H.U. B. Com. 1981]

[Or *Fit a* **Binomial Distribution** *and test the goodness of fit.*]

SOLUTION. Let the Null Hypothesis H_o be that male and female births are equally probable, i.e., $p = q = \frac{1}{2}$.

The expected frequency x of female births is given by $f(x) = N \cdot {}^n C_x p^x q^{n-x}$ where $N = 320; n = 5, x = 0, 1, 2, 3, 4, 5$.

$$\therefore \quad f(0) = 320 \times {}^5C_o \times \left(\frac{1}{2}\right)^o \times \left(\frac{1}{2}\right)^{5-0} = 320 \times 1 \times 1 \times \frac{1}{32} = 10.$$

$$f(1) = 320 \times {}^5C_1 \times \left(\frac{1}{2}\right)^1 \times \left(\frac{1}{2}\right)^{5-1} = 320 \times 5 \times \frac{1}{32} = 50.$$

$$f(2) = 320 \times {}^5C_2 \times \left(\frac{1}{2}\right)^2 \times \left(\frac{1}{2}\right)^{5-2} = 320 \times 10 \times \frac{1}{32} = 100.$$

$$f(3) = 320 \times {}^5C_3 \times \left(\frac{1}{2}\right)^3 \times \left(\frac{1}{2}\right)^{5-3} = 320 \times 10 \times \frac{1}{32} = 100.$$

$$f(4) = 320 \times {}^5C_4 \times \left(\frac{1}{2}\right)^4 \times \left(\frac{1}{2}\right)^{5-4} = 320 \times 5 \times \frac{1}{32} = 50.$$

$$f(5) = 320 \times {}^5C_5 \times \left(\frac{1}{2}\right)^5 \times \left(\frac{1}{2}\right)^{5-5} = 320 \times 1 \times \frac{1}{32} = 10.$$

The Expected or theoretical (Binomial) frequencies of female births are:

x :	0	1	2	3	4	5
$f(x)$:	10	50	100	100	50	10

Let us now apply χ^2 *test to examine the goodness of fit* of the given data to the above *Binomial distribution.*

TABLE 4.14 CALCULATIONS FOR χ^2

No. of Families		$(O-E)$	$(O-E)^2$	$(O-E)^2/E$
Observed Frequency O	Expected Frequency E			
14	10	4	16	1.60
56	50	6	36	0.72
110	100	10	100	1.00
88	100	−12	144	1.44
40	50	−10	100	2.00
12	10	2	4	0.40
Total	...	...	...	7.16

$$\therefore \quad \chi^2 = \sum \left[\frac{(O-E)^2}{E}\right] = 7.16.$$

Degrees of freedom is $6-1=5$. [$\because$ No. of observation $=6$ and no. of linear constraints $=1$, as $\sum(O_i - E_i) = 0$.]

The tabulated value of χ^2 at 5% level with 5 d.f. is 11.07.

Since the calculated value of $\chi^2 <$ *the tabulated value, we accept the Null Hypothesis and conclude that the male and female births are equally probable.*

EXAMPLE 11. *The following mistakes per page were observed in a book:*

No. of Mistakes per Page :	0	1	2	3	4	Total
No. of Pages :	211	90	19	5	0	325

Fit a **Poisson distribution** *and test the goodness of fit.* [$e^{-0.44} = 0.644$.]

[Delhi U. M.A. (Econ.) 1972]

SOLUTION. If x be the random variable denoting the no. of mistakes per page, then the observed frequency distribution of x is

TABLE 4.15 CALCULATIONS FOR MEAN

x	f	fx
0	211	0
1	90	90
2	19	38
3	5	15
4	0	0
Total	$325 = N = \Sigma f$	$143 = \Sigma fx$

$\therefore \quad$ Mean $(m) = \frac{\Sigma fx}{N} = \frac{143}{325} = 0.44.$

The expected frequency of x mistakes per page is given by Poisson Law

$$f(x) = N \cdot \frac{e^{-m} \cdot m^x}{\lfloor x} = \frac{325 \cdot e^{-0.44}(0.44)^x}{\lfloor x}, \text{ where } x = 0, 1, 2, 3, 4.$$

$$\therefore \quad f(0) = \frac{325 \times 0.644 \times 1}{1} = 209.3, \quad f(1) = 209.3 \times 0.44 = 92.1, \quad f(2) = 209.3 \times \frac{(.44)^2}{2} = 20.3,$$

$$f(3) = 209.3 \times \frac{(.44)^3}{6} = 3.0, \quad f(4) = 209.3 \times \frac{(.44)^4}{24} = 0.3.$$

TABLE 4.16 CALCULATIONS FOR χ^2

O_i	E_i	$O_i - E_i$	$(O_i - E_i)^2$	$(O_i - E_i)^2/E_i$
211	209.3	1.7	2.89	0.0138
90	92.1	−2.1	4.41	0.0479
19, 5, 0 } 24	20.3, 3.0, 0.3 } 23.6	0.4	0.16	0.0068
325	325	$0 = \Sigma(O_i - E_i)$	...	0.0685

$$\therefore \quad \chi^2 = \sum \frac{(O_i - E_i)^2}{E} = 0.0685, \quad \text{d.f.} = 5 - 1 - 1 - 2 = 1.$$

[$\because$ $\Sigma(0_i - E_i) = 0$, and m is calculated from the given data and then used to find E_i, and the last two cell frequencies (being < 5) are added to the preceding one].

The tabulated value of χ^2 is 3.84 and $0.0685 < 3.84$.

Hence, *the Poission distribution is a good fit to the given data.*

4.9.1. Test for Independence of Attributes

Let the observations be classified according to two attributes and the frequencies O_i in the different categories be shown in a two-way table, called *Contingency Table.* We have to test on the basis of the cell frequencies whether the *two attributes are independent or not.*

Under the Null Hypothesis H_o that the two attributes are independent, the expected frequencies (E_i) of any cell $= \frac{\text{Row total} \times \text{Column total}}{\text{Grand total}}$.

The test statistic

$$\chi^2 = \sum_i \left[\frac{(O_i - E_i)^2}{E_i}\right] \tag{1}$$

approximately follows Chi-square distribution with ν = d.f. = (No. of rows −1) × (No. of columns −1).

If the calculated value of $\chi^2 >$ the tabulated value with ν d.f. at α level, we reject the Null Hypothesis H_o. Otherwise, we accept H_o.

2×2 Contingency Table

Under the Null Hypothesis of independence of attributes, 2 × 2 contingency table (or nine square table) with the four cell frequencies a, b, c, d is given below.

TABLE 4.17 CONTINGENCY TABLE

	A	$\bar{A}$	Total
B	a	b	$a + b$
$\bar{B}$	c	d	$c + d$
Total	$a + c$	$b + d$	$N = a + b + c + d$

The value of χ^2 is given by $\chi^2 = \frac{N(ad-bc)^2}{(a+b)(c+d)(a+c)(b+d)}$, where $N = a+b+c+d$, with ν = d.f. $=(2-1)\times(2-1)=1$.

If the expected frequencies are in fractions (or, decimals), then calculations for χ^2 become tedious. In such a case we use this formula to find χ^2. Otherwise, we use formula (1) to compute χ^2.

Yates' Correction for 1 d.f.

In a 2×2 contigency table, ν = d.f. = 1, and therefore, one of the four cell frequencies can be arbitrary if the row and column totals remain fixed. F. Yates corrected the formula for χ^2 to maintain its character of continuous Chi-square distribution as follows.

If $ad > bc, a$ and d are replaced by $a-\frac{1}{2}$ and $d-\frac{1}{2}$ and b and c are replaced by $b+\frac{1}{2}$ and $c+\frac{1}{2}$. But if $ad < bc$, then a, d are increased by $\frac{1}{2}$ and b, c are decreased by $\frac{1}{2}$.

After Yates' correction, the formula for χ^2 becomes

$$\chi^2 = \frac{N\left[\left(a\mp\frac{1}{2}\right)\left(d\mp\frac{1}{2}\right)-\left(b\pm\frac{1}{2}\right)\left(c\pm\frac{1}{2}\right)\right]^2}{(a+b)(c+d)(a+c)(b+d)}$$

$$\text{Now}\quad N\left[\left(a\mp\frac{1}{2}\right)\left(d\mp\frac{1}{2}\right)-\left(b\pm\frac{1}{2}\right)\left(c\pm\frac{1}{2}\right)\right]^2$$

$$=N\left[ad\mp\frac{1}{2}(a+d)+\frac{1}{4}-\left\{bc\pm\frac{1}{2}(b+c)+\frac{1}{4}\right\}\right]^2$$

$$=N\left[(ad-bc)\mp\frac{1}{2}(a+d)\mp\frac{1}{2}(b+c)\right]^2$$

$$=N\left[(ad-bc)\mp\frac{1}{2}(a+b+c+d)\right]^2 = N\left[|ad-bc|-\frac{N}{2}\right]^2$$

[$\because$ $-ve$ or $+ve$ sign is taken according as $ad > bc$ or $ad < bc$.]

$$\therefore\quad \chi^2\text{ (corrected)} = \frac{N\left[|ad-bc|-\frac{N}{2}\right]^2}{(a+b)(c+d)(a+c)(b+d)}.$$

EXAMPLE 12. *"A sample of* 300 *students of Under-graduate and* 300 *students of Post-graduate classes a University were asked to give their opinion towards the autonomous colleges.* 190 *of the Under-graduate and* 210 *of the Post-graduate students favoured the autonomous status".*

Present the above fact in the form a frequency table and test, at 5% *level, that opinions of Under-graduate and Post-graduate students on autonomous status of colleges are independent. (Table value of Chi-square at* 5% *level for* 1 *d.f. is* 3.84.) **[CA May 1989]**

SOLUTION. Let the Null Hypothesis H_o be that opinions of Under-graduate and Post-graduate students on autonomous states of colleges are independent.

Then the Alternative Hypothesis is H_1 : the opinions are not independent.

The contigency table of observed frequencies is given below:

TABLE 4.18 CONTINGENCY TABLE

	In Favour	Not in Favour	Total
Under-graduate	190 (A)	110 (C)	300
Post-graduate	210 (B)	90 (D)	300
Total	400	200	600

Expected frequency $= \frac{\text{Row total} \times \text{Column total}}{\text{Grand total}}$.

$\therefore$ Expected frequency of cell $A = \frac{400 \times 300}{600} = 200$,

Expected frequency of cell $B = 400 - 200 = 200$,

Expected frequency of cell $C = 300 - 200 = 100$,

and Expected frequency of cell $D = 300 - 200 = 100$.

TABLE 4.19 CALCULATIONS FOR χ^2

Cell	Observed Frequency O	Expected Frequency E	$(O-E)^2$	$(O-E)^2/E$
A	190	200	$(-10)^2 = 100$	$100/200 = 0.5$
B	210	200	$(10)^2 = 100$	$100/200 = 0.5$
C	110	100	$(10)^2 = 100$	$100/100 = 1$
D	90	100	$(-10)^2 = 100$	$100/100 = 1$
Total	—	—	—	$3 = \Sigma\{(O-E)^2/E\}$

Assuming that H_0 is true, the test statistic is

$$\chi^2 = \sum \frac{(O_i - E_i)^2}{E_i} = 3 < 3.84 \quad \text{and} \quad \nu = \text{d.f.} = (2-1)(2-1) = 1.$$

Since the calculated value of χ^2 is less than the table value at 5% level with 1 d.f., we accept H_0 and conclude that *opinions of Under-Graduate and Post-Graduate students on autonomous status of colleges are* **independent.**

EXAMPLE 13. *Out of* 800 *persons,* 25% *were literate and* 300 *had travelled beyond the limits of their district.* 40% *of the literates were among those who had not travelled. Prepare a* 2×2 *table and test at* 5% *level of significance whether there is any relation between travelling and literacy.*

[CA May 1990]

SOLUTION. Let the Null Hypothesis H_0 be that literacy and travelling are independent i.e., there is no association between them.

Then the Alternative Hypothesis is H_1 : literacy and travelling are not independent i.e., there exists association between them.

We present given information in a 2×2 table as follows.

TABLE 4.20 CONTINGENCY TABLE

	Travelled	Not travelled	Total
Literate	120(A)	80(C)	200
Illiterate	180(B)	420(D)	600
Total	300	500	800

The observed frequencies (O_i) in the cells A, B, C, D are respectively 120, 180, 80, 420. The corresponding expected frequencies (E_i) of the cells A, B, C, D are respectively

$$\frac{300 \times 200}{800}, \frac{300 \times 600}{800}, \frac{500 \times 200}{800}, \frac{500 \times 600}{800}, \quad \text{i.e., } 75, 225, 125, 375.$$

[After finding $E_1 = 75$ for cell A, we can find E_2, and E_3, subtracting 75 from 300 and 200. Then we can find E_4 by subtracting either E_2 from 600 or E_3 from 500.]

Assuming that H_o is true, the test statistic is

$$\chi^2 = \sum \frac{(O_i - E_i)^2}{E_i} = \frac{(120-75)^2}{75} + \frac{(180-225)^2}{225} + \frac{(80-125)^2}{125} + \frac{(420-375)^2}{375}$$

$$= \frac{2025}{75} + \frac{2025}{225} + \frac{2025}{125} + \frac{2025}{375} = 27 + 9 + 16.2 + 5.4 = 57.6$$

Also d.f. $= (2-1)(2-1) = 1$. The table value of χ^2 at 5% level with 1 d.f. $= 3.841$.

Thus $\chi^2 = 57.6 > 3.841$, i.e., calculated value of $\chi^2 >$ Table value of χ^2.

Hence, *we reject* H_o *at* 5% *level with* 1 *d.f. and conclude that there exists a relation between travelling and literacy.*

EXAMPLE 14. *Calculate the expected frequencies for the following data presuming the two attributes viz., condition of home and condition of child as independent:*

Condition of Home / Condition of child	Clean	Dirty
Clean	70	50
Fairly Clean	80	20
Dirty	35	45

Use Chi-square test at 5% *level to state whether the two attributes are independent.*

(*Table values of Chi-square at* 5% *for* 2 *d.f. is* 5.991 *and for* 3 *d.f. is* 7.815 *and for* 4 *d.f. is* 9.488). **[CA November 1989]**

SOLUTION. Let the Null Hypothesis be H_o : the two attributes are independent, i.e., there is no association between the attributes.

Then the Alternative Hypothesis is H_1: An association exists between the two attributes.

We present the given information in the form of a contigency table showing the observed frequencies (O_i) and calculate the corresponding expected frequencies (E_i).

TABEL 6.21 CONTINGENCY TABLE

Condition of Home / Condition of Child	Clean	Dirty	Total
Clean	70(A)	50(D)	120
Fairly Clean	80(B)	20(E)	100
Dirty	35(C)	45(F)	80
Total	185	115	300

The Expected frequencies (E_i) of the cells A, B, C, D, E, F are respectively

$$\frac{120 \times 185}{300}, \frac{100 \times 185}{300}, \frac{80 \times 185}{300}, \frac{120 \times 115}{300}, \frac{100 \times 115}{300}, \frac{80 \times 115}{300},$$

i.e., 74, 61.67, 49.33, 46, 38.33, 30.67.

Assuming that H_o is true, the test statistic is

$$\chi^2 = \sum \frac{(O_i - E_i)^2}{E_i} = \frac{(70-74)^2}{74} + \frac{(80-61.67)^2}{61.67} + \frac{(35-49.33)^2}{49.33} + \frac{(50-46)^2}{46} + \frac{(20-38.33)^2}{38.33} + \frac{(45-30.67)^2}{30.67}$$

$$= 0.216 + 5.448 + 4.163 + 0.348 + 8.766 + 6.695 = 25.636.$$

Also d.f. $= (3-1)(2-1) = 2 \times 1 = 2$.

Thus $\chi^2 = 25.636 > 5.991$ at 5% level with 2 d.f., i.e., calculated value of $\chi^2 >$ Table value of χ^2 at 5% level with 2 d.f.

Hence, *we reject* H_o *and conclude that the two attributes are independent.*

4.9.2. Test for a Specified Population Variance

Suppose that a random sample $x_1, x_2, \cdots, x_n$ is drawn from a normal population with mean μ and variance σ^2. To test the hypothesis that the population variance σ^2 has a specified value $\sigma_\circ^2$.

Let the Null Hypothesis be $H_\circ : \sigma^2 = \sigma_\circ^2$ [or $\sigma = \sigma_\circ$].

Then the Alternative Hypothesis is $H_1 : \sigma^2 \neq \sigma_\circ^2$ [or $\sigma^2 > \sigma_\circ^2$].

The test statistic is $\chi^2 = \Sigma\frac{(x_i - \bar{x})^2}{\sigma_\circ^2} = \frac{ns^2}{\sigma_\circ^2}$, where s^2 = sample variance $= \frac{\Sigma(x_i - \bar{x})^2}{n}$ and $ns^2 = (n-1)S^2$.

Assuming that $H_\circ$ is true, the test statistic χ^2 follows Chi-square distribution with $(n-1)$ degrees of freedom.

If the calculated value of $\chi^2 >$ the tabulated value, we reject the Null Hypothesis $H_\circ$. Otherwise, we accept $H_\circ$.

EXAMPLE 15. *Weights in kg. of* 10 *students are:* 38, 40, 45, 53, 47, 43, 55, 48, 52, 49. *Can we say that the variance of the distribution of weights of all students from which the above sample of* 10 *students was drawn, is equal to* 20 *square kgs.?*

[*At* 9 *d.f.*, $\chi^2_{0.05} = 16.92, \chi^2_{0.01} = 21.67$; *at* 10 *d.f.*, $\chi^2_{0.05} = 18.31, \chi^2_{0.01} = 23.21$.]

[CA November 1979]

SOLUTION. [Variance $\sigma^2 = 20$ square kg. and S.D. $\sigma = \sqrt{20}$ kg.]

Let the Null Hypothesis be $H_\circ : \sigma^2 = 20$.

The Alternative Hypothesis is $H_1 : \sigma^2 > 20$.

TABLE 4.22 CALCULATIONS FOR SAMPLE VARIANCE s^2

x_i (Wt. in kg.)	$x_i - \bar{x}$	$(x_i - \bar{x})^2$
38	−9	81
40	−7	49
45	−2	4
53	6	36
47	0	0
43	−4	16
55	8	64
48	1	1
52	5	25
49	2	4
$470 = \Sigma x_i$	···	$280 = \Sigma(x_i - \bar{x})^2$

Hence, $n = 10$.

$$\bar{x} = \text{sample mean} = \frac{\Sigma x_i}{n} = \frac{470}{10} = 47; \quad s^2 = \frac{\Sigma(x_i - \bar{x})^2}{n} = \frac{280}{10} = 28.$$

Assuming that $H_\circ$ is true, $\chi^2 = \frac{ns^2}{\sigma_\circ^2} = \frac{10 \times 28}{20} = 14$.

Degrees of freedom $= n - 1 = 10 - 1 = 9$.

Since *the calculated value* 14 *of* $\chi^2 <$ *the tabulated value* 16.92 *at* 5% *level with* 9 *d.f., we accept the Null Hypothesis at* 5% *level and conclude that* **the variance of the distribution of weights of all students in the population is 20 square kgs.**

4.10. SNEDECOR'S F-DISTRIBUTION

It is a continuous probability distribution, first tabulated by G. W. Snedecor and named F in honour of R. A. Fisher. It is used to test the equality of two population variances.

DEFINITION. *If χ_1^2 and χ_2^2 be two independent Chi-square variates with ν_1 and ν_2 degrees of freedom respectively, then $F = \frac{\chi_1^2/\nu_1}{\chi_2^2/\nu_2}$ follows Snedecor's F-distribution with (ν_1, ν_2) degrees of freedom.*

Thus F-distribution is the distribution of the ratio of two independent Chi-square variates divided by their respective degrees of freedom.

The *probability density function of F-distribution* is given by

$$f(F) = K \cdot (F)^{\frac{\nu_1}{2}-1}\left(1 + \frac{\nu_1}{\nu_2}F\right)^{-\frac{(\nu_1+\nu_2)}{2}} ; \quad 0 \leq F < \infty,$$

where K is a constant.

Some Properties of F-Distribution

1. The sampling distribution of F-distribution depends only on the degrees of freedom ν_1 and ν_2; it does not involve any population parameter.

2. Mean $= \frac{\nu_2}{\nu_2-2}$, S.D. $= \frac{\nu_2}{\nu_2-2} \cdot \sqrt{\frac{2(\nu_1+\nu_2-2)}{\nu_1(\nu_2-4)}}$, provided they are positive.

3. The F-distribution curve is *positively skewed* and starting from O it extends to infinity on the right.

Test for Equality of Two Population Variances

Let two independent random samples of sizes n_1 and n_2 be drawn from two normal populations. To test the hypothesis that the two population variances σ_1^2 and σ_2^2 are equal.

Let the Null Hypothesis be $H_\circ : \sigma_1^2 = \sigma_2^2$.

The Alternative Hypothesis is $H_1 : \sigma_1^2 \neq \sigma_2^2$.

The estimates of σ_1^2 and σ_2^2 are given by

$$S_1^2 = \left(\frac{n_1}{n_1 - 1}\right)s_1^2 = \frac{\Sigma(x_1 - \bar{x}_1)^2}{n_1 - 1} \quad \text{and} \quad S_2^2 = \left(\frac{n_2}{n_2 - 1}\right)s_2^2 = \frac{\Sigma(x_2 - \bar{x}_2)^2}{n_2 - 1},$$

where s_1^2 and s_2^2 are the variances of the two samples.

Assuming that $H_\circ$ is true, the test statistic $F = \frac{S_1^2}{S_2^2}$, or, $\frac{S_2^2}{S_1^2}$ according as $S_1^2 > S_2^2$, or, $S_2^2 > S_1^2$ follows F-distribution with $(n_1 - 1, n_2 - 1)$ degrees of freedom.

If the calculated value of $F >$ the tabulated value of F at 5% level, we reject the Null Hypothesis $H_\circ$ and conclude that the variances σ_1^2 and σ_2^2 are not equal. Otherwise, we accept the Null Hypothesis $H_\circ$.

NOTE. In numerical problems, we take the greater of the two estimates of variances S_1^2, S_2^2 in the numerator and the other in the denominator, i.e., if $S_2^2 > S_1^2$, then $F = \frac{S_2^2}{S_1^2}$.

EXAMPLE 16. *In a sample of* 8 *observations, the sum of the squared deviations of items from the mean was* 94.5. *In another sample of* 10 *observations, the value was found to be* 101.7 *Test whether the difference in variances is significant at* 5% *level.*

You are given that at 5% *level, critical value of F for $\nu_1 = 7$ and $\nu_2 = 9$ degrees of freedom is* 3.29, *and for $\nu_1 = 8$ and $\nu_2 = 10$ degrees of freedom, its value is* 3.07. **[CA May 1979]**

SOLUTION. Let the Null Hypothesis be $H_\circ : \sigma_1^2 = \sigma_2^2$, where σ_1^2, σ_2^2 are the variances of the two populations from which the samples are drawn.

The Alternative Hypothesis is $H_1 : \sigma_1^2 \neq \sigma_2^2$.

We have $S_1^2 = \frac{\Sigma(x_1-\bar{x}_1)^2}{n_1-1}$ and $S_2^2 = \frac{\Sigma(x_2-\bar{x}_2)^2}{n_2-1}$.

Here $n_1 = 8, \Sigma(x_1 - \bar{x}_1)^2 = 94.5; n_2 = 10, \Sigma(x_2 - \bar{x}_2)^2 = 101.7$.

$\therefore \quad S_1^2 = \frac{94.5}{8-1} = 13.5$ and $S_2^2 = \frac{101.7}{10-1} = 11.3$.

Let H_o be true.

Since $S_1^2 > S_2^2$, the test statistic is

$$F = \frac{S_1^2}{S_2^2} = \frac{13.5}{11.3} = 1.1947.$$

Degrees of freedom are $\nu_1 = n_1 - 1 = 8 - 1 = 7$ and $\nu_2 = n - 1 = 10 - 1 = 9$.

The table value of F at 5% level for $\nu_1 = 7$ and $\nu_2 = 9$ degrees of freedom is 3.29 and $1.1947 < 3.29$. Since the calculated value of $F <$ the table value, *we accept the Null Hypothesis* H_o *and conclude that the difference is not significant at* 5% *level.*

EXAMPLE 17. *In one sample of* 10 *observations from a normal population, the sum of the squares of the deviations of the sample values from sample mean is* 100.4 *and in another sample of* 12 *observations from another normal population, the sum of the squares of the deviations of the sample values from the sample mean is* 115.5. *Test at* 5% *level whether the populations have the same variance.* **[CA May 1991]**

SOLUTION. Let σ_1^2, σ_2^2 be the variances of the two normal populations from which the samples are drawn.

Let the null Hypothesis be $H_o : \sigma_1^2 = \sigma_2^2$.

Then the Alternative Hypothesis is $H_1 : \sigma_1^2 \neq \sigma_2^2$.

Now $n_1 = 10, \Sigma(x_1 - \bar{x}_1)^2 = 100.4$ and $n_2 = 12, \Sigma(x_2 - \bar{x}_2)^2 = 115.5$.

If S_1^2 and S_2^2 be the estimates of σ_1^2 and σ_2^2, then

$$S_1^2 = \frac{\Sigma(x_1 - \bar{x}_1)^2}{n_1 - 1} = \frac{100.4}{9} = 11.156 \quad \text{and} \quad S_2^2 = \frac{\Sigma(x_2 - \bar{x}_2)^2}{n_2 - 1} = \frac{115.5}{11} = 10.5.$$

Let H_o be true. Since $S_1^2 > S_2^2$, the test statistic is

$$F = \frac{S_1^2}{S_2^2} = \frac{11.156}{10.5} = 1.0625 \text{ (approx.)}$$

Degrees of freedom are $\nu_1 = n_1 - 1 = 10 - 1 = 9$ and $\nu_2 = n_2 - 1 = 12 - 1 = 11$.

The table value of F at 5% level for $\nu_1 = 9$ and $\nu_2 = 11$ degrees of freedom is 2.8962 and $F = 1.0625 < 2.8962$.

Since the calculated value of $F <$ the table value, *we accept* H_o *at* 5% *level with* 9 *and* 11 *degrees of freedom and conclude that* **the populations have the same variance.**

EXAMPLE 18. *Two sources of raw materials are under consideration by a company. Both sources seem to have similar characteristics, but the company is not sure about their respective uniformity. A sample of ten lots from source A yields a variance of* 225, *and a sample of eleven lots from source B yields a variance of* 200. *Is it likely that the variance of source A is significantly greater than the variance of source B.* $\alpha = 0.01$. **[Delhi U. M. Com. 1976]**

SOLUTION. Let the Null Hypothesis be $H_o : \sigma_1^2 = \sigma_2^2$, i.e., the variances of sources A and B are equal.

The Alternative Hypothesis is $H_1 : \sigma_1^2 > \sigma_2^2$

We have $s_1^2 = (\frac{n_1}{n_1-1})S_1^2$ and $s_2^2 = (\frac{n_2}{n_2-1})S_2^2$.

Here $n_1 = 10, S_1^2 = 225$ and $n_2 = 11, S_2^2 = 200$.

$$\therefore \quad s_1^2 = \left(\frac{10}{10-1}\right) \times 225 = \frac{10}{9} \times 225 = 250$$

$$\text{and} \quad s_2^2 = \left(\frac{11}{11-1}\right) \times 200 = \frac{11}{10} \times 200 = 220.$$

Assuming that H_o is true, the test statistic is

$$F = \frac{s_1^2}{s_2^2} = \frac{250}{220} \quad [\because \quad s_1^2 > s_2^2.]$$
$$= 1.136$$

Degrees of freedom are $\nu_1 = n_1 - 1 = 9, \nu_2 = 11 - 1 = 10$.

The table value of F with d.f. $\nu_1 = 9, \nu_2 = 10$ at 1% level is 4.94, and $F = 1.136 < 4.94$.

Since the calculated value of $F <$ the tabulated value, we accept the Null Hypothesis H_o at 1% level with $\nu_1 = 9, \nu_2 = 10$ and conclude that the two population variances are the same.

EXAMPLE 19. *Two samples are drawn from two normal populations. From the following data test whether the two samples have the same variance at 5% level:*

Sample 1	:	60	65	71	74	76	82	85	87		
Sample 2	:	61	66	67	85	78	63	85	86	88	91

[CA May 1983]

SOLUTION. Let the Null Hypothesis be $H_o : \sigma_1^2 = \sigma_2^2$, where σ_1^2 and σ_2^2 are the variances of the two populations.

The Alternative Hypothesis is $H_1 : \sigma_1^2 \neq \sigma_2^2$.

We have $s_1^2 = \frac{\Sigma(x_1 - \bar{x}_1)^2}{n_1 - 1}$ and $s_2^2 = \frac{\Sigma(x_2 - \bar{x}_2)^2}{n_2 - 1}$.

Here n_1 = size of sample 1 = 8 and n_2 = size of sample 2 = 10.

Let us assume that H_o is true.

TABLE 4.23 CALCULATIONS FOR SAMPLE VARIANCE

Sample I			Sample II		
x_1	$x_1 - \bar{x}_1$	$(x_1 - \bar{x}_1)^2$	x_2	$x_2 - \bar{x}_2$	$(x_2 - \bar{x}_2)^2$
60	−15	225	61	−16	256
65	−10	100	66	−11	121
71	−4	16	67	−10	100
74	−1	1	85	8	64
76	1	1	78	1	1
82	7	49	63	−14	196
85	10	100	85	8	64
87	12	144	86	9	81
			88	11	121
			91	14	196
$600 = \Sigma x_1$	...	$636 = \Sigma(x_1 - \bar{x}_1)^2$	$770 = \Sigma x_2$	...	$1200 = \Sigma(x_2 - \bar{x}_2)^2$

$$\bar{x}_1 = \frac{\Sigma x_1}{n_1} = \frac{600}{8} = 75, \quad \bar{x}_2 = \frac{\Sigma x_2}{n_2} = \frac{770}{10} = 77$$

$$s_1^2 = \frac{636}{8-1} = 90.857 \quad \text{and} \quad s_2^2 = \frac{1200}{10-1} = 133.33.$$

Since $s_2^2 > s_1^2$, the test statistic is $F = \frac{s_2^2}{s_1^2} = \frac{133.33}{90.857} = 1.467$ and degrees of freedom are $(n_2 - 1, n_1 - 1)$, i.e., (9, 7).

The tabulated value of F at 5% level with 9 and 7 degrees of freedom is 3.68 and $F = 1.467 < 3.68$.

Since the calculated value of F < tabulated value of F, **we accept the Null Hypothesis** *at 5% level with d.f.* (9, 7) *and conclude that* **the variances of the two populations is the same** *and, therefore, the two samples have the same variance.*

Exercise 4(III)

(Testing of Hypothesis : t, χ^2 and F-Tests)

Theory

1. What do you mean by *small sample tests*? How do they differ from *large sample tests*. Mention names of the well-known small sample tests.

2. Define each of the following distributions:

(i) Student's t distribution; (ii) Chi-square distribution; (iii) F-distribution.

3. Point out the various applications and properties of t-distributiion. **[CA May 1988]**

4. (i) Discuss the importance of χ^2 test. How is it used to test the association between attributes? **[CA November 1982]**

(ii) What are the purposes for which Chi-square test of significance is used? Explain and illustrate. **[CA November 1985]**

5. (i) State the assumptions underlying student's t-test and Snedecor's F-test when applied to both single and two-sample problems. **[CA May 1980]**

(ii) When and for what purposes 't' test of significance is used? **[CA May 1985]**

6. Describe a contingency table. How do you test the significance of the association of attributes? **[CA May 1981]**

7. State any two uses to which Chi-square test of significance can be put. **[CA November 1983]**

8. Write short notes on the following:

(i) Student's Test;

(ii) Chi-Square Test; **[CA November 1977, 1987]**

(iii) Snedecor's F-test; **[CA November 1979]**

(iii) Paired t-test for the difference of Means.

Problems

[A]

1. (i) A machine is designed to produce washers for electrical devices of average thickness .05 cm. A random sample of 17 washers was found to have an average thickness of .045 cm. with S.D. of .008 cm. Test the significance of the deviation. [Value of t for 16 degrees of freedom at 5% level is 2.12.]

(ii) For a random sample of size 10, the mean is 106 and S.D. is 10. Is if reasonable to assume that this sample came from a normal population with mean greater than 100? [Given; $t_{0.01} = 2.82$ for 9 d.f.;=2.76 for 10 d.f.] **[ICWAI June 1994]**

2. (i) A random sample of size 20 from a normal population gives a sample mean of 42 and sample S.D. of 6. Test the hypothesis that the population mean is 44. State clearly the alternative hypothesis you allow for and the level of significance adopted. **[CA November 1974]**

(ii) For a random sample of size 10 from a normal population, the mean is 12.1 and the standard deviation is 3.2. Is it reasonable to suppose that the population mean is 14.5? Test at 5% significance level. (Clearly state the null and alternative hypotheses and assumptions).

(Given $t_{0.025}$ at 9 d.f. = 2.262; $t_{0.05}$ at 9 d.f. = 1.833). **[ICWAI June 1989]**

[HINTS. See worked out Example 1]

3. A machinist is making engine parts, with axle diameter of 0.700 inch. A random sample of 10 parts shows a mean diameter of 0.742 inch with S.D. of 0.040 inch. Compute the statistic you would use to test whether the work is meeting the specification. Also state how you would proceed further. **[M.U. M. Com. 1982]**

4. (i) A company has been producing steel tubes of mean inner diameter of 2.00 cms. A sample of 10 tubes gives an inner diameter of 2.01 cms. and a variance of 0.004 cms. squared. Is the difference in the value of mean significant? (Value of t for 9 degrees of freedom at 5% level = 2.262.).

[CA November 1981]

(ii) A random sample of size 10 from a normal population gives a mean of 2.01 and variance of 0.004. Obtain a 95% confidence internal for the population mean. [Given: Value of t for 9 d.f. at 5% level=1.833.] **[ICWAI Dec 1992]**

5. (i) Two salesmen A and B are working in a certain district. From a sample survey conducted by the Head Office, the following results were obtained. State whether there is any significant difference in the average sales between the two salesmen:

	A	B
No. of sales	20	18
Average sales (in Rs.)	170	205
Standard deviation (in Rs.)	20	25

[CA November 1977]

(ii) Two batches of the same product are tested for their mean life. Assuming that lives of the product follow a normal distribution with an unknown variance, test the hypothesis that the mean life is the same for both the batches, given the following information.

Batch	Sample size	Mean life in hours ($\bar{X}$)	Standard Deviation (s)
I	10	750	12
II	8	820	14

Choose a significance level of 5%. **[CA May 1986]**

Values of t at 5% level.

d.o.f. :	14	15	16	17	18
t :	2.145	2.151	2.120	2.110	2.101

6. Two types of batteries are tested for their length of life and the following data are obtained:

	No. of sample	Mean life in hours	Variance
Type A	9	600	121
Type B	8	640	144

Is there a significant difference in the two means? Value of t for 15 degrees of freedom at 5% level is 2.131. **[CA November 1982]**

7. (i) A die was thrown 60 times with the following results:

Face :	1	2	3	4	5	6	Total
Frequency :	6	9	8	12	11	14	60

Are the data consistent with the hypothesis that the die is unbiased? (Given: $\chi^2_{.01} = 15.09$ for 5 degrees of freedom).

(ii) A die is thrown 150 times with the following results:

No. turned up :	1	2	3	4	5	6
Frequency :	19	23	28	17	32	31

Test the hypothesis that the die is unbiased. [Given $\chi^2_{0.05,5} = 11.07$] **[ICWAI December 1986]**

(iii) Four dice were thrown 112 times and the number of times 1, 3 or 5 was thrown were as under:

No. of dice throwing 1, 3 or 5 :	0	1	2	3	4
Frequency :	10	25	40	30	7

Find the value of Chi-square presuming that all dice were fair. **[CA May 1985]**

8. A survey of 640 families with 5 children each revealed the following distribution:

No. of Boys :	5	4	3	2	1	0
No. of Girls :	0	1	2	3	4	5
No. of Families :	28	112	220	176	80	24

Is the result consistent with the hypothesis that male and female births are equally probable?

9. A random sample of size 20 from a normal population gives a sample mean of 42 and a sample standard deviation of 6. Test the hypothesis that the population S.D. is 9.

[CA November 1974]

10. (i) Apply χ^2 (Chi-Square) test to find out if the following figures provide evidence of the effectiveness on inoculation.

	Attacked	Not attacked	Total
Inoculated	20	300	320
Not inoculated	80	600	680
Total	100	900	1,000

[Given, the value of χ^2 at 5% with 1 d.f. = 3.84.]

(ii) The table given below shows the data obtained during an epidemic of cholera;

	Attacked	Not attacked
Inoculated:	42	232
Not inoculated:	106	748

Test the effectiveness of inoculation in preventing the attack of cholera. [Given: $\chi_{0.05} = 3.841$ for 1 d.f.; 5.991 for 2 d.f.; 7.815 for 3 d.f.] **[ICWAI June 1994]**

[HINTS. Use $\chi^2 = \frac{N(ad-bc)^2}{(a+b)(c+d)(a+c)(b+d)}$, where $N = a+b+c+d$. Here $a = 42$, $b = 232$, $c = 106$. $d = 748$; etc.]

11. Out of a sample of 120 persons in a village, 76 persons were administered a new drug for preventing influenza and out of them, 24 persons were attacked by influenza. Out of those who were not administered the new drug, 12 persons were not affected by influenza. Prepare:

(a) 2×2 tables showing the actual and expected frequencies.

(b) Use Chi-Square Test for finding out whether the new drug is effective or not.

At 5% level for one degree of freedom the value of Chi-Square = 3.84. **[CA November 1975]**

12. In a sample of 10 observations, the sum of the squares of the deviations of items from their mean is 130.5. In another sample of 14 observations, the value is found to be 148.5. Test whether the difference is significant at 5% level. [You are given that at 5% level for 9 and 13 degrees of freedom the value of F is 2.71.]

13. Two sources of raw materials are under consideration by a company. Both sources seem to have similar characteristics, but the company is not sure about their respective uniformity. A sample of 10 lots from source A yields a variance of 270, and a sample of 13 lots from source B yields a variance of 192. Is it likely that the variance of source A is significantly greater than the variance of source B. ($\alpha = 0.01$.)

14. Two random samples are drawn from two normal populations and the following results were obtained:

Sample I :	16	17	18	19	20	21	22	24	26	27		
Sample II :	19	22	23	25	26	28	29	30	31	32	35	36

Obtain estimates of the variances of the two populations and test whether the two populations have the same variance. **[CA November 1981]**

[HINTS. Calculate s_1^2, s_2^2 and then use F-test.]

15. A random sample of size 7 from a normal population gave a mean 977.51 and a standard deviation 4.42. Find a 95% confidence interval for the population mean.
(Given: $t_{0.05;6} = 1.943, t_{0.05;7} = 1.895, t_{0.025;6} = 2.447, t_{0.025;7} = 2.365$).

(Find the values upto two places of decimal). **[ICWAI June 1988]**

[HINTS. Here $n = 7, \bar{x} = 977.51, S = 4.42$, d.f. $= 7 - 1 = 6, t_\alpha = t_{0.025;6} = 2.447$.

$\therefore \quad t_\alpha \cdot s/\sqrt{n-1} = 2.447 \times \frac{4.42}{\sqrt{6}} = 4.41$ (approx.). Hence, 95% confidence interval for population mean μ are $[\bar{x} - t_\alpha \cdot s/\sqrt{n-1}, \bar{x} + t_\alpha \cdot s/\sqrt{n-1}$ = etc.]

16. Two random samples were drawn from two normal populations and their values are:

A :	66	67	75	76	82	84	88	90	92		
B :	64	66	74	78	82	85	87	92	93	95	97

Test whether the two populations have the same variance at the 5% level of significance. [$F = 3.11$ at 5% level for $\nu_1 = 8$ and $\nu_2 = 10$.] **[CA May 1986]**

17. A random sample of size 20 from a normal population gives a mean of 42 and variance of 25; test the hypothesis that the population standard deviation is 8 at 5% level of significance. [Given: $\chi^2 = 30.14$ for 19 d.f.] **[ICWAI June 1993]**

[HINTS. $Chi^2 = \frac{ns^2}{\sigma_0^2} = \frac{20 \times 25}{(8)^2} = 7.8125$, d.f. $= n - 1 = 20 - 1 = 19$; etc.]

[B]

1. (i) The mean weekly sales of soap bars in departmental stores was 146.3 bars per store. After an advertising campaign the mean weekly sales in 22 stores for a typical week increased to 153.7 and showed a S.D. of 17.2. Was the advertising campaign successful? **[Delhi U. 1981]**

[HINTS. Use t-test for a specified mean; $H_o : \mu = 146.3$ and $H_1 : \mu > 146.3$ (right-tailed.), $t = 9.03 > 1.72$.]

(ii) In a sample of 26 items drawn from a population the mean was found to be 50. If the 90% confidence limits for the population mean were 46.584 and 53.416, find the standard deviation of the sample. **[ICWAI December 1988]**

[HINTS. Since the sample is small and S.D. is not known, we use t-distribution. 90% confidence limits for the population mean are $\bar{x} \pm t_\alpha s/\sqrt{n-1}$, or, $50 \pm 1.708 \times s/5$. $\therefore$ $50 + 1.708 \times s/5 = 53.416$. Now find s.]

2. (i) The height of 10 males of a given locality are found to be 70, 67, 62, 68, 61, 68, 70, 64, 64, 66 inches. Is it reasonable to believe that the average height is greater than 64 inches? Test at 5% significant level, assuming that for 9 degrees of freedom $P(t > 1.83) = 0.05$.

[C.U. Maths. (Hons.). 1978, 1981]

[HINTS. $H_o : \mu = 64; H_1 : \mu > 64; \bar{x} = 66, s^2 = 10, t = 2, d.f. = 9$.]

(ii) Certain pesticide is packed into bags by a machine. A random sample of 10 bags is drawn and their contents are found to weigh (in kgs.) as follows: 50, 49, 52, 44, 45, 48, 46, 45, 49, 45.

Test if the average packing can be taken to be 50 kgs. **[ICWAI December 1985]**

[HINTS. Use t-test for a specified mean; $\bar{x} = 47.3$ kgs.]

3. The following table gives the number of air-craft accidents that occurred during the various days of the week. Test whether the accidents are uniformly distributed over the week.

Days :	MON	TUE	WED	THU	FRI	SAT
No. of Accidents :	14	18	12	11	15	14

[M.U. 1976]

[HINTS. $\bar{x} = \frac{\Sigma x}{6} = \frac{84}{6} = 14$ which is the expected frequency of the accidents on each of the six days; $\chi^2 = \Sigma[(O-E)^2/E] = 2.14$.]

4. Pumpkins were grown under two experimental conditions. Two random samples of 9 and 11 pumpkins show the sample standard deviations of their weights as 0.8 and 0.5 respectively. Assuming that the weight distributions are normal, test the hypothesis that the true variances are equal at 5% level. [Assume $P(F_{10,8} \geq 3.35) = 0.05$ and $P(F_{8,10} \geq 3.07) = 0.05$.] **[IAS 1978]**

5. A soap manufacturing company was distributing a particular brand of soap through a large number of retail shops. Before a heavy advertisement campaign, the mean sales per week per shop was 140 dozens. After the campaign, a sample of 26 shops was taken and the mean sales was found to be 147 dozens with S.D. 16. Can you consider the advertisement effective? **[CA November 1978]**

6. The heights of 10 men taken at random from a normal population were 63, 64, 70, 68, 69, 67, 69, 65, 72 and 67 inches. Do these data support the hypothesis of a population mean of 66.1 inches?

7. Two laboratories carry out independent estimates of a particular chemical in a medicine produced by a certain firm. A sample is taken from each batch, halved and the separate halves sent to the two laboratories. The following data is obtained.

No. of samples = 10; Mean value of the difference in estimates = 0.6; Sum of the squares of the differences (from their mean) = 20.

Is the difference significant? (Value of t at 5% level for 9. d.f. is 2.262.) **[CA May 1982]**

8. A salesman is expected to effect an average sales of Rs. 3,500. A sample test revealed that a particular salesman had made the following sales:

Rs. 3,700, Rs. 2,500, Rs. 3,400, Rs. 5,200, Rs. 3,000 and Rs. 2,000. Using 0.05 level of significance conclude whether his work is below standard or not. **[CA May 1983]**

9. Two random samples gave the following results.

	Size(n)	Sample mean($\bar{x}$)	$\Sigma(x-\bar{x})^2$
Sample I	10	15	90
Sample II	12	14	108

Test whether the samples come from the same normal population.

[HINTS. Use F-test; $F = s_1^2/s_2^2 = 1.02$, and t-test for $H_o : \mu_1 = \mu_2; |t| = 0.742$.]

10. The foreman of ABC mining company has estimated the average quantity of iron ore extracted to be 36.8 tonnes per shift and the sample S.D. to be 2.8 tonnes per shift, based upon a random selection of 4 shifts. Construct a 90% confidence interval around this estimate. (At 10% level of significance the table value of t for 3 d.f. is 2.353.) **[CA November 1983]**

11. Two groups of 100 people each were taken for testing the use of a vaccine. 15 persons contracted the disease out of the inoculated persons, while 25 contracted the disease in the other group. Test the efficacy of the vaccine using χ^2 value. At 5% level, for 1 d.f., the value of $\chi^2 = 3.84$.

[CA November 1980]

12. The sales data of an item in six shops and after a special promotional campaign are as under:

Shops :	A	B	C	D	E	F
Before Campaign :	53	28	31	48	50	42
After Campaign :	58	29	30	55	56	45

Can the campaign be judged to be a success? Test at 5% level of significance.

[CA November 1983]

13. Two sets of the students selected at random from a college were taken; one was given memory tests as they were, and the other set was given a memory test after two weeks' training, and scores were given below:

Set A :	10	8	7	9	8	10	9	6	7	8
Set B :	12	8	8	10	8	11	9	8	9	9

Do you think there is any significant effect due to training?

(Null and Alternative hypothesis should be stated.)

[Given $t = 2.10$ at d.f. $= 18$, $\alpha = 0.05$.] **[ICWAI June 1985]**

14. (i) A certain diet newly introduced to each of the 12 pigs resulted in the following increase in body weight: $6, 3, 8, -2, 3, 0, -1, 1, 6, 0, 5$ and 4.

Can you conclude that the diet is effective in increasing the weight of pigs? (Given $t_{0.05} = 2.20$ with 11 d.f.). **[ICWAI December 1985]**

(ii) A drug is given to 10 patients, and the increments in their blood pressure were recorded to be 3, 6, −2, 4, −3, 4, 6, 0, 0, 2. Is it reasonable to believe that the drug has no effect on change of blood pressure? (Use 5% value of t for 9 d.f. = 2.26.) **[ICWAI December 1986]**

[HINTS. Similar to worked out example 7. Here $n = 10, \bar{d} = 2, s = \sqrt{10}$.]

15. In a survey of 200 boys, of which 75 were intelligent, 40 had skilled fathers; while 85 of the unintelligent boys had unskilled fathers. Do these figures support the hypothesis that skilled fathers have intelligent boys? Use χ^2 test. Value of χ^2 for 1 d.f. at 5% level is 3.84. **[CA November 1982]**

16. A fertiliser mixing machine is set to give 12 kg. of nitrate for every quintal bag of fertiliser. Ten 100 kg. bags are examined. The percentages of nitrate are as: 11, 14, 13, 12, 13, 12, 13, 14, 11, 12.

Is there reason to believe that the machine is defective? Value of t for 9 degrees of freedom is 2.262. **[CA November 1982]**

17. Out of 8,000 graduates in a town 800 are females; out of 1500 graduate employees 120 are females. Use χ^2 to determine if any distinction is made in appointment on the basis of sex. Value of χ^2 at 5% level for 1 d.f. is 3.84. **[CA November 1981]**

18. In a certain sample of 2,000 families, 1,400 people are consumers of tea. Out of the 1,800 Hindu families, 1,236 families consume tea. Use χ^2 test and state whether there is any significant difference between consumption of tea among Hindu and non-Hindu families. χ^2 values are given below:

Degree of freedom	$P = .05$	$P = .01$
1	3.84	2.71
2	5.99	4.60
3	7.82	6.25

[CA May 1978]

19. Out of 2,000 people exposed to small-pox in a village, 450 were attacked. Among the people 365 were vaccinated and out of them 50 were attacked. Form a Chi-square table and conclude therefrom whether vaccination can be regarded as a good preventive or not. **[CA May 1975]**

20. A sample of 400 items is taken from a normal population whose mean is 4 and whose variance is also 4. If the sample mean is 4.45, can the sample be regarded as a truly random sample? Give necessary justification for your conclusion. **[ICWAI December 1977]**

21. Of 160 offsprings of a certain cross between guinea pigs, 102 were red, 24 were black and 34 were white. According to a genetic model the probabilities of red, black and white are respectively 9/16, 3/16 and 1/4. Test at 5% significant level, if the data are consistent with the model. For 2 degrees of freedom $P(\chi^2 > 5.99) = 0.05$. **[C.U. B. Sc. (Maths.) 1977, 1979]**

22. The time taken by workers in performing a job by method I and method II is given below:

Method I :	20	16	26	27	24	22	
Method II :	27	33	42	35	31	34	36

Do the data show that the variances of time distribution in a population from which these samples are drawn do not differ significantly.

23. The results of a survey to know the educational attainment among 100 persons randomly selected in a locality are given below:

	Education			
	Middle	High School	College	Total
Male	10	15	25	50
Female	25	10	15	50
Total	35	25	40	100

Can you say that education depends on sex?

[Given $\chi^2 = 5.99$ at d.f. $= 2$, and $\alpha = 0.05$. (Null Hypothesis should be stated clearly.)]

[ICWAI December 1984]

24. To test the efficacy of a new drug a controlled experiment was conducted wherein 300 patients were administered the new drug and 200 other patients were not given the drug. The patients were monitored and the results were obtained as follows:

	Cured	Condition Worsened	No effect	Total
Given the Drug	200	40	60	300
Not given the Drug	120	30	50	200
Total	320	70	110	500

Use χ^2 test for finding the effect of the drug.

[Given d.f.	1	2	3
χ^2 at 5%	3.84	5.991	7.815.]

[CA May 1986]

25. In a laboratory experiment, two random samples gave the following results:

Sample	Size	Sample mean	Sum of squares of deviations from the mean
1	10	15	90
2	12	14	108

Test the equality of samples variances at 5% level of significance.

[Table values of F for $\nu_1 = 9$ and $\nu_2 = 11$ is 2.90 and for $\nu_1 = 11$ and $\nu_2 = 9$ is 3.10]

[CA November 1988]

[HINTS. See worked out Example 17.]

26. In a test given to two groups of students drawn from two normal populations, the marks obtained were as follows:

Group A :	18	20	36	50	49	36	34	49	41
Group B :	29	28	26	35	30	44	46		

Examine at 5% level whether the two populations have the same variance. **[CA May 1990]**

[HINTS. See worked out Example 19.]

Answers

[A]

1. (i) The deviation is significant at 5% level; since $|t| = 2.5 > 2.12$; (ii) no; population mean = 100. **2.** The population mean may be 44 at 5% level; since $|t| = 1.45 < t_{0.25} = 2.09$. The alternative Hypothesis is $H_1 : \mu \neq 44$. **3.** $t = 3.15$; since $t > 2.26$ for 9 d.f. at 5% level, H_o is rejected and hence, the work is meeting the specification. **4.** (i) No; since $t = 0.475 < 2.262$ at 5% level with 9 d.f; (ii) $[1.97, 2.05]$. **5.** (i) Yes; the difference in the average sales is significant. (ii) The mean life is not same for both the batches. **6.** Yes; since $|t| = 6.734 > 2.131$. **7.** (i) Yes; since $\chi^2 = 4.2 < 15.09$ at 1% level with 5 d.f.; (ii) The dice is unbiased, since $\chi^2 = 7.92 < 11.07$. (iii) $\chi^2 = 1.85$. **8.** Yes; since $\chi^2 = 3.58 < 11.07$ at 5% level with 5 d.f. **9.** The population S.D. may be 9 at 5% level; since $\chi^2 = 30.14$ at 5% level with 19 d.f. **10.** (i) The inoculation is quite effective; since $\chi^2 = 7.353$; (ii) $\chi^2 = 1.5477 < 3.841$; not effective. **11.** The drug is significantly effective; since $\chi^2 = 18.97$ with 1 d.f. **12.** The difference is not significant; since $F = 1.27 < 2.71$ at 5% level with $\nu_1 = 9$ and $\nu_2 = 13$. **13.** No; the variance of source A is equal to the variance of source B at 1% level; since $F = 1.44 < 4.39$ at 1% level with $\nu_1 = 9$ and $\nu_2 = 12$. **14.** Estimates of the two population variances are 14 and 27.1; the two populations have the same variance, since $F = 1.94 < 2.90$ at 5% level with (9,11) d.f. **15.** [973.10, 981.92]. **16.** The two populations have the same variance at 5% level with d.f. 8 and 10, since $F = 1.42 < 3.11$.**17.** H_0 is true i.e., the population S.D. is 8 at 5%level for 9 d.f.

[B]

1. (i) Yes; since $t = 9.03 > 1.72$ at 5% level for 21 d.f.; (ii) 10. **2.** (i) Yes; since $t = 2$ (right-tailed test) > 1.83 at 5% level with 9 d.f. (ii) The average packing cannot be taken to be 50 kgs. **3.** The accidents are uniformly distributed over the week, since $\chi^2 = 2.14$ for 5 d.f. $<$ the tabulated value 11.07 at 5% for 5 d.f. **4.** The true variances are equal, since $F = 2.62$ for $v_1 = 8$ and $v_2 = 10$ d.f. and table value of F is 3.07. **5.** Yes, since $t = 2.19 >$ the table value 1.71 (right-tailed) at 5% level with 25 d.f. **6.** Yes; since $|t| = 1.47 <$ the table value 2.26 for 9 d.f. **7.** No; since $t = 1.27$ (paired t test for difference of means) < 2.262 at 5% for 9 d.f. **8.** Upto to the standard, since $|t| = .44$ with d.f. 5. **9.** The samples are drawn from the same normal population. **10.** $[0.0342, 0.0558]$; since $s/\sqrt{n-1} = 0.0046$. **11.** Not effective; since $\chi^2 = 3.125 <$ less than the table value 3.84. **12.** Yes; since $t = 2.78 > 2.57$ (the table value at 5% for 5 d.f.). **13.** No significant effect. **14.** (i) Yes, effective; (ii) yes; since $t = 2 < 2.26$. **15.** Yes; since $\chi^2 = 8.89 > 3.84$ at 5% level for 1 d.f. **16.** No; since $t = 1.47 < 2.262$ at 5% for 9 d.f. **17.** Yes, distinction is made in appointment on the basis of sex; since $\chi^2 = 13.89 > 3.84$ at 5% level for 1 d.f. **18.** Yes, there is significant difference in the consumption of tea; since $\chi^2 = 15.22 > 3.84$ at 5% level with 1 d.f. **19.** Yes, vaccination is preventive; since $\chi^2 = 19.22 > 3.84$ at 5% level for 1 d.f. **20.** No; since $|z| = 4.5 > 1.96$ at 5% level. **21.** Yes, the data are consistent with the model; since $\chi^2 = 3.7 < 5.99$. **22.** Yes, since $F = 1.28 < 4.95$ at 5% level for $v_1 = 6$ and $v_2 = 5$. **23.** Yes, since $\chi^2_{0.05} = 11.56 > 5.99$. **24.** The drug has no effect, since the value of $\chi^2_{0.05}$ with d.f. 2 is $2.435 < 5.991$. **25.** Variances are equal, since $F = 1.018 < 2.90$. **26.** Same variance, since $F = 2.203 < 4.15$ (table value).

Chapter 5

ANALYSIS OF VARIANCE

5.1. INTRODUCTION

We know that *variance* of a series of observations is the mean (A.M.) of the squares of the deviations of the observations from their mean, and *variance* is used as a measure of variation. Student's t-test is used to test whether there is any significant difference (or variation) in the *means of two populations.* This test fails when we consider the *means of three or more populations.* The equality of several population means can be tested by comparing the *sample variances using F-distribution, i.e., by analysis of variance.* The *analysis of variance* is one of the most powerful tools of statistical analysis and this technique is used to test whether the difference between the means of three or more populations is significant or not. The systematic procedure of this statistical technique was first developed by R. A. Fisher and the F-distribution was named in his honour. Earlier, this technique was used in agricultural experiments. Now *analysis of variance* is widely used in natural, social and physical sciences. For example, (1) we can explain by using the technique of the analysis of variance whether different varieties of seeds or fertilizers or soils differ significantly or not as regards average yields of land; (2) a manager of a firm may use this technique to know whether there is a significant difference in the average sale figures of different salesmen employed by the firm; (3) the differences in various types of drugs manufactured by a company to cure a particular disease may be studied through this technique.

In this chapter our main object is *to test on the basis of sample observations whether the means of three or more populations are equal or not.* It may be observed that there are differences (or variation) in the observations *within each sample* and this variation arises due to chance. On examining means and variances of several samples, we can observe *variation between the different samples (or groups)*. The technique of analysis of variance split up the variance into its various components. Usually the variance (or total variance) is splitted into two parts:

(i) *variance between the sample (or groups)*;

(ii) *variance within the samples (or groups)*.

According to H.T. Hayslett:

The analysis of variance is a technique that separates the variation that is present into independent components; then these components are analysed in order to test certain hypothesis.

Assumptions in Analysis of Variance

The analysis of variance is based on the following *assumptions*:

(1) The samples are independently (or randomly) drawn from the populations;

(2) All the populations from which samples have been drawn are normally distributed;

(3) The variances of all the populations are equal.

5.2. THE TECHNIQUE OF ANALYSIS OF VARIANCE

The observations may be classified according to *one factor* (criterion) or *two factors*. The classifications according to *one factor* and *two factors* are respectively called *one-way classification* and *two-way classification*.

We shall discuss the technique of analysis of variance separately for: (1) **One-way classification** and (2) **Two-way classification.**

Variance and its different components may be obtained in each of the two types of classification by (a) Direct Method, (b) Short-cut Method, (c) Coding Method.

5.2.1. One-way Classification

In *one-way classification*, the observations (or data) are classified according to *one factor* (or *criterion*). For example, the yields of several plots of land may be classified according to one or more types of fertilisers.

Direct Method

Let the *Null Hypothesis* be $H_\circ : \mu_1 = \mu_2 = \cdots = \mu_k$ where $\mu_1, \mu_2, \cdots, \mu_k$ are the arithmetic means of the populations from which k samples are randomly drawn.

The *Alternative Hypothesis* is H_1 : all $\mu_i (i = 1, 2, \cdots, k)$ are not equal. The steps in carrying out the analysis are given below.

I. Calculation of Variance Between the Samples or Groups

(Calculation of the Sum of the Squares of Variations Between the Samples)

It is the sum of the squares of the deviations of the means of various samples (or groups) from the grand mean. To calculate *Variance Between the Samples,* we proceed, as follows:

(i) Calculate the *sample means* $\bar{X}_1, \bar{X}_2, \cdots, \bar{X}_k$ of all the k samples.

(ii) Calculate the *grand mean* $\bar{X}$ by using the formula: $\bar{X} = \frac{\bar{X}_1+\bar{X}_2+\cdots+\bar{X}_k}{k}$ or $\frac{T}{N}$, where T = Grand total of all observations and N = total no. of observations in all k samples = $\sum_{i=1}^{k} n_i$, where n_i is the size of the ith sample.

(iii) Find the deviations of the means of the different samples from the grand mean $\bar{X}$, i.e., find $\bar{X}_1 - \bar{X}, \bar{X}_2 - \bar{X}, \cdots, \bar{X}_k - \bar{X}$.

(iv) Square these deviations and multiply by the no. of items in the corresponding sample and then obtain the total. This total gives *the sum of the squares of the deviations for variance between the samples* (or *between the columns*) and it is denoted by SSB or SSC.

Thus $SSB = \sum_{i=1}^{k} n_i(\bar{X}_1 - \bar{X})^2$.

Variance or Mean Square Between Samples (MSB or MSC)

If we divide the total obtained in (iv) by the degrees of freedom $\nu_1 = (k-1)$, we get the *Variance or the Mean Square Between the Samples* which is denoted by MSB or MSC. In this case, the degrees of freedom ν_1 is the number of samples minus one. Thus for 4 samples, the degrees of freedom will be $4-1$, i.e., 3.

MSB indicates the degree of explained variance due to sampling fluctuations.

II. Calculation of Variance within the Samples

(Calculation of the Sum of the Squares of Variations Within the Samples)

Variance within the samples is the total of the sum of the squares of the deviations of the various items from the mean values of the respective samples, and its calculation is shown below.

(i) Calculate the sample means $\bar{X}_1, \bar{X}_2, \cdots, \bar{X}_k$ of all the k samples.

(ii) Find the deviations of the various items of k samples from the mean values of the respective samples.

(iii) Square all the deviations obtained in (ii) and find the total of these squared deviations. This total is the *Sum of the Square of Deviations Within the Samples* or *Sum of the Squares due to Error.* It is denoted by SSW or SSE.

Thus, $SSW = \Sigma(X_1 - \bar{X}_1)^2 + \Sigma(X_2 - \bar{X}_2)^2 + \cdots + \Sigma(X_k - \bar{X}_k)^2$.

Variance or Mean Square Within the Sample (MSW or MSE)

If we divide the total obtained in (iii) by the degrees of freedom $\nu_2 = (N - k)$, we get the *Variance* or the *Mean Square Within the Samples* which is denoted by MSW or MSE. In this case, the degrees of freedom is the total no. of items in all the samples minus the no. of samples. MSW indicates chance variation and it cannot be explained in terms of variation in the population.

III. Calculation of the Test Statistic F

When H_o is true, both the Mean Squares (or Variances) MSB and MSW are the independent unbiased estimates of the same population variance σ^2. Hence, the *test statistic* is

$$\mathbf{F} = \frac{\mathbf{MSB}}{\mathbf{MSW}}, \quad \text{or,} \quad \frac{\mathbf{MSC}}{\mathbf{MSE}}$$

which follows *F-distribution with degrees of freedom* $\nu_1 = k - 1$ *and* $\nu_2 = N - k$. In genral $MSB > MSW$. But if $MSB < MSW$, we shall take the inverse ratio for F, i.e., $F = MSW/MSB$.

The technique of *analysis of variance* is called ANOVA and a table showing the Source of Variation, Sum of Squares, Degrees of Freedoms, Mean Squares and Mean Square (or Variance) Ratio is called ANOVA Table.

IV. Decision

Compare the calculated value of F with the tabulated (critical) value of F for $(k - 1, N - k)$ degrees of freedom at $\alpha\%$ level (may be 5% or 1% level). *If the calculated value > the tabulated value, reject H_o and conclude that all the population means are not equal. Otherwise, accept H_o and conclude that the population means are all equal.*

Let us now summarise calculations for Sums of Squares together with the corresponding degrees of freedom, Mean Squares and Variance Ratio in an ANOVA Table.

TABLE 5.1 ANALYSIS OF VARIANCE (OR ANOVA) TABLE

Source of Variation	Sum of Squares (SS)	Degrees of Freedom ($d.f.$)	Mean Squares (MS)	Test Statistic (Variance Ratio)
Between (Col.)	SSB	$k-1$	$MSB = SSB/(k-1)$	
				$F = (MSB/MSW)$
Within (Errors)	SSW	$N-k$	$MSW = SSW/(N-k)$	
Total	SST	$N-1$	...	...

SST = Total sum of Squares of Variations = $SSB + SSW$. In the above table SSB and SSW may be replaced by SSC and SSE, and MSB and MSW may be replaced by MSC and MSE.

Check

To check up the calculations, the sum of the squares of the deviations for total variation should be calculated. The total variation is calculated by taking the squares of the deviations of all the individual items from the grand average. This total should be equal to $SSB + SSW$. This explains the additive property of the analysis of variation. The degrees of freedom ($d.f.$) for total variance $= N - 1 =$ (No. of items in all the samples) − 1.

5.2.2. Illustrative Examples

EXAMPLE 1. *Fill in the blanks of the following* ANOVA *table:*

Source	$d.f.$	SS	MSS	F
Between	2	*	5	
Within	*	14	*	*
	9	*		

[ICWAI June 1988]

SOLUTION. $d.f.$ within $= 9 - 2 = 7$, i.e., $k - 1 = \mathbf{2}$ and $N - k = \mathbf{7}$. [See TABLE 5.1]

Now, $MSB = \frac{SSB}{k-1}$, or, $5 = \frac{SSB}{2}$, or, $\mathbf{SSB = 10}$ and $MSW = \frac{SSW}{N-k} = \frac{14}{7} = 2$.

Total SS $= SSB + SSW = 10 + 14 = 24$; $F = \frac{MSB}{MSW} = \frac{5}{2} = 2.5$.

The required complete ANOVA table is given below.

TABLE 5.2 ANOVA TABLE

Source	$d.f.$	SS	MSS	F
Between	2	10	5	
Within	7	14	2	2.5
Total	9	24		

EXAMPLE 2. *The following data give the yields on* 12 *plots of land in three samples, each of of* 4 *plots, under three varieties of fertilizers* A, B *and* C.

A	B	C
25	20	24
22	17	26
24	16	30
21	19	20

Is there any significant difference in the average yields of land under the three varieties of fertilizers?

SOLUTION. Let the Null Hypothesis be H_o : there is no significant difference in the average yields under the three varieties.

The Alternative Hypothesis is H_1: the difference is significant.

The calculations for sample means, the Variance Between and Within the samples are shown below:

TABLE 5.3 CALCULATIONS FOR SAMPLE MEANS

Sample I X_1	Sample II X_2	Sample III X_3
25	20	24
22	17	26
24	16	30
21	19	20
$92 = \Sigma X_1$	$72 = \Sigma X_2$	$100 = \Sigma X_3$

$$\bar{X}_1 = \frac{\Sigma X_1}{n_1} = \frac{92}{4} = 23, \quad \bar{X}_2 = \frac{\Sigma X_2}{n_2} = \frac{72}{4} = 18, \quad \bar{X}_3 = \frac{\Sigma X_3}{n_3} = \frac{100}{4} = 25.$$

$$\text{Grand mean } (\bar{X}) = \frac{\bar{X}_1 + \bar{X}_2 + \bar{X}_3}{3} = \frac{66}{3} = 22.$$

SSB = Sum of the Squares Between the samples

$= \Sigma n_i(\bar{X}_i - \bar{X})^2 = 4(23-22)^2 + 4(18-22)^2 + 4(25-22)^2 \qquad [\because \ n_1 = n_2 = n_3 = 4.]$

$= 4 + 64 + 36 = 104,$

and ν_1 = degrees of freedom $= k - 1 = 3 - 1 = 2.$

$\therefore \ MSB$ = Mean Square Between the samples $= \dfrac{SSB}{\nu_1} = \dfrac{104}{2} = 52.$

TABLE 5.4 CALCULATIONS FOR SSW

Sample I		Sample II		Sample III	
X_1	$(X_1 - \bar{X}_1)^2$	X_2	$(X_2 - \bar{X}_2)^2$	X_3	$(X_3 - \bar{X}_3)^2$
25	4	20	4	24	1
22	1	17	1	26	1
24	1	16	4	30	25
21	4	19	1	20	25
Total	$10 = \Sigma(X_1 - \bar{X}_1)^2$	—	$10 = \Sigma(X_2 - \bar{X}_2)^2$	—	$52 = \Sigma(X_3 - \bar{X}_3)^2$

SSW = Sum of the Squares Within the samples

$= \Sigma(X_1 - \bar{X}_1)^2 + \Sigma(X_2 - \bar{X}_2)^2 + \Sigma(X_3 - \bar{X}_3)^2 = 10 + 10 + 52 = 72,$

and ν_2 = degrees of freedom $= N - k = 12 - 3 = 9.$

$\therefore \ MSW$ = Mean Square Within the samples $= \dfrac{SSW}{\nu_2} = \dfrac{72}{9} = 8.$

TABLE 5.5 ANALYSIS OR VARIANCE (ANOVA) TABLE

Source of Variation	Sum of Squares (SS)	Degrees of freedom ($d.f.$)	Mean Square (MS)	Test Statistic
Between Samples	104	2	52	
				$F = 52/8 = 6.5$
Within Samples	72	9	8	
Total	$176 = SST$	$11 = N - 1$	...	

From the table given at the end of the book, the value of F for $\nu_1 = 2$ and $\nu_2 = 9$ at 5% level is 4.26. We see that *the calculated value 6.5 of F is greater than the tabulated value* 4.26. Hence, *we reject the Null Hypothesis at* 5% *level and conclude that the difference in the average yields under the three varieties is* **significant.**

Short-cut Method

The procedure shown above in *Direct Method* is lengthy and time-consuming and hence, it is not generally used in practice. A *Short-cut Method* based on the sum of the squares of the individual values is usually used. In this method the computational work is considerably reduced and the method is more convenient when the sample means and the grand mean are fractions.

The various steps of *Short-cut Method* are given below.

(i) Calculate the *total T of all the observations in all k samples.*
Thus $T = \Sigma X_1 + \Sigma X_2 + \cdots + \Sigma X_k$.

(ii) Find the *Correction factor* by using the formula : Correction factor $= \frac{T^2}{N}$.

(iii) Calculate the sum of the squares of all the values (or observations) in k samples and subtract the correction factor $\frac{T^2}{N}$ from this sum to obtain the *Total sum of the Squares of deviations SST.* Thus

$$SST = \Sigma X_1^2 + \Sigma X_2^2 + \cdots + \Sigma X_k^2 - \frac{T^2}{N}.$$

(iv) Find the square of the total of each sample and divide each such squared value by the number of values of the corresponding sample and then calculate the total of all the results thus obtained and subtract the correction factor from this total. This final result gives the *Sum of the Squares of Deviations Between the Samples.* Thus

$$SSB = \left[\frac{(\Sigma X_1)^2}{n_1} + \frac{(\Sigma X_2)^2}{n_2} + \cdots + \frac{(\Sigma X_k)^2}{n_k}\right] - \frac{T^2}{N}.$$

(v) Calculate SSW, i.e., the *Sum of the Squares Within the samples by subtracting SSB from SST.* Thus

$$SSW = SST - SSB.$$

Now proceed as in Direct Method to obtain MSB, MSW and F and to arrive at the final decision. The procedure of Short-cut Method will be well-understood from the following illustration. [See Example 3.]

EXAMPLE 3. *Let us solve the previous problem (Example 2) by Short-cut* Method.

SOLUTION. **TABLE 5.6 CALCULATIONS FOR SHORT-CUT METHOD**

Sample I		Sample II		Sample III	
X_1	X_1^2	X_2	X_2^2	X_3	X_3^2
25	625	20	400	24	576
22	484	17	289	26	676
24	576	16	256	30	900
21	441	19	361	20	400
$92 = \Sigma X_1$	$2126 = \Sigma X_1^2$	$72 = \Sigma X_2$	$1306 = \Sigma X_2^2$	$100 = \Sigma X_3$	$2552 = \Sigma X_3^2$

T = Sum of all the values of the three samples $= \Sigma X_1 + \Sigma X_2 + \Sigma X_3 = 92 + 72 + 100 = 264.$

$$\text{Correction factor} = \frac{T^2}{N} = \frac{(264)^2}{12} = 5808. \qquad [\text{Here } N = 12.]$$

$$SST = \text{The Total Sum of Squares}$$

$$= \Sigma X_1^2 + \Sigma X_2^2 + \Sigma X_3^2 - \frac{T^2}{N} = 2126 + 1306 + 2552 - 5808 = 176.$$

$$SSB = \text{Sum of the Squares Between the Samples}$$

$$= \frac{(\Sigma X_1)^2}{n_1} + \frac{(\Sigma X_2)^2}{n_2} + \frac{(\Sigma X_3)^2}{n_3} - \frac{T^2}{N} = \frac{(92)^2}{4} + \frac{(72)^2}{4} + \frac{(100)^2}{4} - 5808$$

$$= 2116 + 1296 + 2500 - 5808 = 104;$$

$$\nu_1 = d.f. = k - 1 = 3 - 1 = 2.$$

$$SSW = \text{Sum of the Squares Within the samples}$$

$$= SST - SSB = 176 - 104 = 72$$

$$\nu_2 = d.f. = N - k = 12 - 3 = 9.$$

Now proceed as in Example 2 to arrive at the final decision.

Coding Method

The Short-cut Method becomes tedious when the magnitude of the given values is *large*. *Coding Method* simplifies the calculations involved in the Short-cut Method and is popularly used in practice. As the test statistic F in the *analysis of variance* is the variance ratio, its value does not change if all the given values are *coded, i.e., are either multiplied or divided by a common factor, or if a common figure is either subtracted from or added to each of the given values.* By this method, big figures are reduced in magnitude by subtraction or division, and work is simplified without altering the value of F. The procedure is shown in the following example.

EXAMPLE 4. *Three samples of five, four and five motor car tyres are drawn respectively from three brands A, B and C manufactured by three machines. The life-time of these tyres (in '000 miles) is given below. Test whether the average life-time of the three brands of tyres are equal or not.*

TABLE 5.10 ANOVA TABLE

Source of Variation	SS	d.f.	MS	F(Test Statistic)
Between Samples	168.5	2	84.25	
				$F = (84.25/22.83) = 3.69$
Within Samples	205.5	9	22.83	
Total	374.0	11		

The table value of F at 5% level with 2 and 9 d.f. is 4.26, and $3.69 < 4.26$, i.e., calculated value of $F <$ the table value.

Hence, *there is no significant difference in brands preference at 5% level.*

EXAMPLE 6. *The Amrit Merchandising Co. wishes to test whether its three salesmen A, B and C tend to make sales of the same size or whether they differ in their selling ability as measured by the average size of their sales. During the last week there have been* 14 *sale calls; A made* 5 *calls, B made* 4 *calls and C made* 5 *calls. Following are the weekly sales record (in* Rs.) of the three salesmen:

A :	300	400	300	500	0
B :	600	300	300	400	...
C :	700	300	400	600	500

Perform the analysis of variance and draw your conclusion. **[D.U. M.Com.]**

SOLUTION. Let the Null Hypothesis be H_o: *the three salesmen tend to make sales of the same size.*

Let us divide each observation by the common factor 100. Then the coded data and their squares are given in the following table:

TABLE 5.11 CALCULATIONS FOR ANALYSIS OF VARIANCE

Sample I		Sample II		Sample III	
X_1	X_1^2	X_2	X_2^2	X_3	X_3^2
3	9	6	36	7	49
4	16	3	9	3	9
3	9	3	9	4	16
5	25	4	16	6	36
0	0	...	...	5	25
$15 = \Sigma X_1$	$59 = \Sigma X_1^2$	$16 = \Sigma X_2$	$70 = \Sigma X_2^2$	$25 = \Sigma X_3$	$135 = \Sigma X_3^2$

$$T = \text{Sum of all the observations in the three samples}$$

$$= \Sigma X_1 + \Sigma X_2 + \Sigma X_3 = 15 + 16 + 26 = 56.$$

$$\text{Correction factor} = \frac{T^2}{N} = \frac{(56)^2}{14} = 224.$$

$$SST = \text{Total Sum of the Squares } = \Sigma X_1^2 + \Sigma X_2^2 + \Sigma X_3^2 - \frac{T^2}{N}$$

$$= 59 + 70 + 135 - 224 = 40.$$

SSB = Sum of the Squares Between the samples

$$= \frac{(\Sigma X_1)^2}{n_1} + \frac{(\Sigma X_2)^2}{n_2} + \frac{(\Sigma X_3)^2}{n_3} - \frac{T^2}{N} = \frac{(15)^2}{5} + \frac{(16)^2}{4} + \frac{25)^2}{5} - 224 = 10;$$

$\nu_1 = d.f. = k - 1 = 3 - 1 = 2.$

SSW = Sum of the Squares Within the samples $= SST - SSB = 40 - 10 = 30;$

$\nu_2 = d.f. = N - k = 14 - 3 = 11.$

$$\therefore \quad MSB = \frac{SSB}{\nu_1} = \frac{10}{2} = 5 \quad \text{and} \quad MSW = \frac{SSW}{\nu_2} = \frac{30}{11} = 2.73.$$

TABLE 5.12 ANALYSIS OF VARIANCE TABLE

Source of Variation	Sum of Squares (SS)	Degrees of Freedom ($d.f.$)	Mean Square (MS)	Test Statistic
Between Samples	10	2	5	
				$F = (5/2.73) = 1.83$
Within Samples	30	11	2.73	
Total	40	13		

The table value of F for $\nu_1 = 2$ and $\nu_2 = 11$ at 5% level is 3.98, and the calculated value 1.83 of $F <$ the tabulated value 3.98 at 5% level. Hence, *we accept the Null Hypothesis H_o at 5% level and conclude that the three salesmen tend to make sales of the same size.*

EXAMPLE 7. *An experimentor wished to study the effect of four fertilizers on the yield of a crop. He divided the field into 24 plots and assigned each fertilizer at random to 6 plots. Part of his calculations are shown below:*

Source	$d.f.$	SS	MS	F	$F_{5\%}$
Fertilizers	⋯	2940	⋯		
				⋯	3.10
Within Group	⋯	⋯	⋯		
Total	⋯	6212			

(a) *Complete the above table by filling in the values marked by...*

(b) *Test at 5% level to see whether the fertilizers differ significantly.* **[C.U.]**

SOLUTION.

(a) Here N = total no. of observation = 24, k = No. of samples = 4.

$\therefore$ Total $d.f. = N - 1 = 24 - 1 = 23; d.f.$ for Fertilizers (i.e., $d.f.$ for Between the groups) $= k - 1 = 4 - 1 = 3;$

$\therefore$ $d.f.$ for Within group $= N - k = 24 - 4 = 20.$

SSB = Sum of Squares Between Fertilizers = 2940

$\therefore$ SSW = Sum of Squares Within group $= SST - SSB = 6212 - 2940 = 3272.$

$$\therefore \quad MSB = \text{Mean Square Between Fertilizers} = \frac{SSB}{d.f.} = \frac{2940}{3} = 980$$

$$\text{and} \quad MSW = \text{Mean Square Within the groups} = \frac{SSW}{d.f.} = \frac{3272}{20} = 163.6.$$

$$F = \frac{MSB}{MSW} = \frac{980}{163.6} = 5.99.$$

The required completed table is given below.

TABLE 5.13 ANALYSIS OF VARIANCE TABLE

Source	$d.f.$	SS	MS	F	$F_{5\%}$
Fertilizers	3	2940	980		
				5.99	3.10
Within Group	20	3272	163.6		
	23	6213			

(b) We see that the calculated value of F, i.e., 5.99 > the tabulated value 3.10 of F at 5% level with $d.f.$ $\nu_1 = 3$ and $\nu_2 = 20$. Hence, *we conclude that the fertilizers differ significantly.*

5.3. TWO-WAY CLASSIFICATION

In *two-way classification,* statistical data are classified according to *two different factors* (or *criteria*). For example, the yield of a crop in several plots of land may be classified according to *different varieties of seeds* and *different varieties of fertilizers.*

The *Total variance* or the *Sum of Squares of variations in a two-way classification* consists of three parts: (i) SSC, i.e., *the Sum of Squares Between the columns or Variance between the columns,* (ii) SSR, i.e., *the Sum of Squares Between the rows or Variance between the rows and* (iii) SSE, i.e., *the Sum of Squares for the residuals or residual variance* (or the Sum of Squares due to errors). Thus

$$SST = SSC + SSR + SSE.$$

The total number of *degrees of freedom* $= cr - 1$, where c and r are the number of columns and the number of rows respectively.

Degrees of freedom between columns $= c - 1$.

Degrees of freedom between rows $= r - 1$.

Degrees of freedom between residuals $= (cr - 1) - (c - 1) - (r - 1) = (c - 1)(r - 1)$.

In *two-way classification,* the Analysis of Variance table or ANOVA table is shown below.

TABLE 5.14 ANALYSIS OF VARIANCE TABLE (ANOVA TABLE)

Source of Variation	Sum of Squares (SS)	Degrees of Freedom ($d.f.$)	Mean Square (MS)
Between Columns	SSC	$c - 1$	$MSC = SSC/(c-1)$
Between Rows	SSR	$r - 1$	$MSR = SSR/(r-1)$
Residual (or Error)	SSE	$(c-1)(r-1)$	$MSE = SSE/(c-1)(r-1)$
Total	SST	$N - 1$	

The *test statistic F for variance between columns* is given by

$$F = \frac{MSC}{MSE} = \frac{\text{Variance between columns}}{\text{Residual Variance}}.$$

After calculating the value of F, we find the corresponding table value of F at 5% for $c-1$ and $(c-1)(r-1)$ degrees of freedom. If the calculated value of $F >$ the tabulated value, then we reject the Null Hypothesis H_o and conclude that the difference between the column values is significant.

Note that if $MSE > MSC$, then we shall take $F = \frac{MSE}{MSC}$.

Again the *test statistic F for Variance between rows* is given by

$$F = \frac{MSR}{MSE} = \frac{\text{Variance between rows}}{\text{Residual Variance}}$$

If $MSE > MSR$, then we shall take $F = \frac{MSE}{MSR}$.

We calculate the value of F and compare this value with the tabulated value and finally conclude for the difference between the row values as before.

Analysis of Variance in two-way classification is illustrated below by an example.

EXAMPLE 8. *A company appoints four salesmen A, B, C and D and observes their sales in three seasons, summer, winter and monsoon. The figures (in lakhs) are given in the following table:*

Season	Salesmen				
	A	*B*	*C*	*D*	Total
Summer	36	36	21	35	128
Winter	28	29	31	32	120
Monsoon	26	28	29	29	112
Total	90	93	81	96	360

Carry out an analysis of variance. **[P.U. M. Com.]**

SOLUTION. Let the Null Hypothesis be H_o : *There is no significant difference between salesmen or between seasons.*

The given data are first *coded* by subtracting 30 from each observation and then classified according to *two factors*:

(i) Salesmen and (ii) Seasons in the following table.

TABLE 5.15 CALCULATIONS FOR ANALYSIS OF VARIANCE

Salesman / Seasons	*A*	*B*	*C*	*D*	Season total
Summer	6	6	−9	5	8
Winter	−2	−1	1	2	0
Monsoon	−4	−2	−1	−1	−8
Salesmen total	0	3	−9	6	$0 = T$ (Grand total)

Correction factor $= \frac{T^2}{N} = \frac{0^2}{12} = 0.$

$$\begin{aligned} SSC &= \text{Sum of Squares Between salesmen} \\ &= \frac{0^2}{3} + \frac{3^2}{3} + \frac{(-9)^2}{3} + \frac{6^2}{3} - \frac{T^2}{N} = 0 + 3 + 27 + 12 - 0 = 42 \end{aligned}$$

and $d.f. = c - 1 = 4 - 1 = 3.$

$$SSR = \text{Sum of Squares Between Seasons}$$

$$= \frac{(8)^2}{4} + \frac{0^2}{4} + \frac{(-8)^2}{4} - \frac{T^2}{N} = 16 + 0 + 16 - 0 = 32$$

and $d.f. = r - 1 = 3 - 1 = 2.$

$$SST = \text{Total Sum of Squares}$$

$$= \{6^2 + (-2)^2 + (-4)^2 + 6^2 + (-1)^2 + (-2)^2 + (-9)^2 + 1^2 + (-1)^2 + 5^2 + 2^2 + (-1)^2\} - \frac{T^2}{N}$$

$$= \{36 + 4 + 16 + 36 + 1 + 4 + 81 + 1 + 1 + 25 + 4 + 1\} - 0 = 210$$

and $d.f. = N - 1 = 12 - 1 = 11.$

$\therefore \quad SSE = SST - (SSC + SSR) = 210 - (42 + 32) = 136$

amd $d.f. = 11 - (3 + 2) = 6.$

The Analysis of Variance table is shown below.

TABLE 5.16 ANOVA TABLE

Source of Variation	Sum of Squares (SS)	Degrees of Freedom ($d.f.$)	Mean Square ($M.S.$)	Variance Ratio
Between Columns	42	3	14	
				$F_1 = (22.67/14) = 1.62$
Between Rows	32	2	16	
				$F_2 = (22.67/16) = 1.42$
Residual	136	6	22.67	
Total	210	11		

The table value of F for $\nu_1 = 6$ and $\nu_2 = 3$ degrees of freedom at 5% level is 8.94. Since the calculated value 1.62 < the tabulated value at 5% level, we conclude that there is no significant difference between the salesmen.

Again the table value of F for $\nu_1 = 6$ and $\nu_2 = 2$ degrees of freedom at 5% level is 19.33. *Since the calculated value of F < the tabulated value at 5%, we conclude that there is no significant difference between the seasons.*

EXAMPLE 9. *Set up a two-way* ANOVA *table for the data given below:*

Pieces of Field	Treatment			
	A	B	C	D
P	45	40	38	37
Q	43	41	45	38
R	39	39	41	41

(*Use coding method subtracting* 40 *from the given numbers*) **[CA May 1992]**

SOLUTION. Subtracting the *code* value 40 from the given values, we get the coded data and construct the following table.

TABLE 5.17 CALCULATIONS FOR ANALYSIS OF VARIANCE

Pieces of Field \ Treatment	A	B	C	D	Total
P	5	0	−2	−3	0
Q	3	1	5	−2	7
R	−1	−1	1	1	0
Total	7	0	4	−4	$7 = T$

$$\text{Correction factor} = \frac{T^2}{N} = \frac{(7)^2}{12} = \frac{49}{12}.$$

SSC = Sum of the Squares Between Treatment

$$= \frac{7^2}{3} + \frac{0^2}{3} + \frac{4^2}{3} + \frac{(-4)^2}{3} - \frac{T^2}{N} = \frac{49}{3} + 0 + \frac{16}{3} + \frac{16}{3} - \frac{49}{12} = 22.92,$$

and $d.f. = c - 1 = 4 - 1 = 3.$

SSR = Sum of the Squares Between Pieces of Fields

$$= \frac{0^2}{4} + \frac{7^2}{4} + \frac{0^2}{4} - \frac{T^2}{N} = \frac{49}{4} - \frac{49}{12} = 8.17$$

and $d.f. = r - 1 = 3 - 1 = 2.$

SST = Total Sum of squares

$$= \{5^2 + 3^2 + (-1)^2 + 0^2 + 1^2 + (-1)^2 + (-2)^2 + 5^2 + 1^2 + (-3)^2 + (-2)^2 + 1^2\} - \frac{T^2}{N}$$

$$= 25 + 9 + 1 + 0 + 1 + 1 + 4 + 25 + 1 + 9 + 4 + 1 - \frac{49}{12} = 76.92$$

and $d.f. = N - 1 = 12 - 1 = 11.$

$\therefore \quad SSE = SST - (SSC + SSR) = 76.92 - (22.92 + 8.17) = 45.83$

and $\quad d.f. = 11 - (3 + 2) = 6.$

Two-way ANOVA table for the given data is given below

TABLE 5.18 ANOVA TABLE

Source of Variation	Sum of Squares SS	$d.f.$	Mean Squares MS	F-Ratio
Between Columns	22.92	3	22.92/3= 7.64	
				$F_1 = (7.64/7.64) = 1$
Between Rows	8.17	2	4.08	
				$F_2 = (7.64/4.08) = 1.87$
Residual (or Errors)	45.83	6	7.64	
Total	76.92	11		

EXAMPLE 10. *Apply the technique of Analysis of Variance to the following data showing the yields of* 3 *varieties of a crop each from* 4 *blocks, and test whether the mean yields of the varieties are equal or not. Also test the equality of the block means.*

Varieties	Blocks			
	I	II	II	IV
A	4	8	6	8
B	5	5	7	8
C	6	7	9	5

Given $F_{.05} = 5.143, F_{.01} = 10.925$ *for d.f.* $(2,6); F_{.05} = 19.33$ *for d.f.* $(6,2)$ *and* $F_{.05} = 4.757, F_{01} = 9.779$ *for d.f.* $(3,6)$. **[C.U. B.Sc. 1979]**

SOLUTION. Let the Null Hypothesis be H_o: The mean yields of the varieties are equal or the block means are equal.

The given data are first coded by subtracting 5 from each observation and then classified according to two factors: i) Blocks and ii) Varieties.

TABLE 5.19 TWO-WAY CLASSIFICATION OF CODED DATA

Varieties \ Blocks	I	II	III	IV	Total
A	−1	3	1	3	6
B	0	0	2	3	5
C	1	2	4	0	7
Total	0	5	7	6	$18 = T$

$$\text{Correction factor} = \frac{T^2}{N} = \frac{(18)^2}{12} = 27.$$

$$SSC = \text{Sum of Squares Between Blocks (i.e., Between Columns)}$$
$$= \frac{0^2}{3} + \frac{5^2}{3} + \frac{7^2}{3} + \frac{6^2}{3} - \frac{T^2}{N} = 36.67 - 27 = 9.67,$$
and $d.f. = c - 1 = 4 - 1 = 3$.

$$SSR = \text{Sum of Squares Between Varieties (i.e., Between Rows)}$$
$$= \frac{6^2}{4} + \frac{5^2}{4} + \frac{7^2}{4} - \frac{T^2}{N} = 27.5 - 27 = .5$$
and $d.f. = r - 1 = 3 - 1 = 2$.

$$SST = \text{Total Sum of Squares}$$
$$= \{(-1)^2 + 0^2 + 1^2 + 3^2 + 0^2 + 2^2 + 1^2 + 2^2 + 4^2 + 3^2 + 3^2 + 0^2\} - \frac{T^2}{N}$$
$$= 54 - 27 = 27,$$
and $d.f. = N - 1 = 12 - 1 = 11$.

$\therefore \; SSE = SST - (SSC + SSR) = 27 - (9.67 + 5)$

and $d.f. = 11 - (3 + 2) = 6$.

TABLE 5.20 ANOVA TABLE

Source of Variation	Sum of Squares (*SS*)	Degrees of Freedom (*d.f.*)	Mean Square (*M.S.*)	Variance Ratio
Between Blocks	9.67	3	3.22	
				$F = (3.22/2.81) = 1.15$
Between Varieties	0.5	2	0.25	
				$F = (2.81/0.25) = 11.24$
Residual	16.83	6	2.81	
Total	27	11		

Since the calculated value of F (viz., 1.15) *is* < *the tabulated value* 4.757 *at* 5% *level for* (3, 6) *d.f. we conclude that the* **mean yields of the varieties are equal.**

Again *since the calculated value of F (viz.,* 11.24) *is* < *the tabulated value* 19.33 *at* 5% *level for* (6, 2) *d.f., we conclude that* **the block means are also equal.**

Exercise 5

(Analysis of Variance)

1. What assumptions need to be made while using the technique of analysis of variance.

[CA November 1986, 1991]

2. Discuss the various steps involved in the analysis of variance in one-way classification.

[CA May 1988]

3. What is the null hypothesis often investigated in analysis of variance? **[CA May 1987]**

4. Write short notes on the following:

(i) ANOVA table for one-way classification; **[ICWAI December 1991]**

(ii) ANOVA table for two-way classification;

(iii) Coding Method in Analysis of Variance.

5. The following data give the yields on 12 plots of land in three samples, each of 4 plots, under three varieties of seed A, B and C:

A :	32	35	31	30
B :	30	24	32	26
C :	26	27	25	30

Set-up one-way ANOVA table and use it to test whether difference in the average yields under the three varieties is significant or not.

6. Three different machines are used for a production. On the basis of the outputs, set up one-way ANOVA table and hence, test whether the machines are equally effective.

Outputs		
Machine 1	Machine 2	Machine 3
10	9	20
5	7	16
11	5	10
10	6	14

[Given: Value of F at 5% level of significance with (2, 9) $d.f. = 4.26$] **[ICWAI. June 1991]**

7. Three samples, each of size 5, were drawn from three uncorrelated normal populations with equal variances. Test the hypothesis that the population means are equal at 5% level.

Sample I	Sample II	Sample III
10	9	14
12	7	11
9	12	15
16	11	14
13	11	16

[ICWAI December 1988]

8. A consumer magazine was interested in determining whether any difference existed in the average life of four different brands of transistor batteries. A random sample of 4 batteries of each brand was tested with the following results (in hours):

Brand I	Brand II	Brand III	Brand IV
12	14	12	14
15	17	19	21
18	12	20	25
10	19	23	20

Perform an one-way ANOVA table and hence test whether there is any significant difference in the average life of the four brands at 5% level?

9. The following figures relate to production in Kg. of three varieties:

A :	14	16	18		
B :	14	13	15	22	
C :	18	16	16	19	20

Is there any significant difference in the production of the three varieties? **[B.U. B.A. 1976]**

10. An experimentor wanted to study the effect of 3 fertilisers on the yield of a crop. He divided the field into 12 plots and assigned each fertiliser at random to 4 plots. Part of his calculations are shown in the next page.

Source	$d.f.$	SS	MS	F	$F_{.05}$
Fertilisers	...	104	...		
					4.26
Within Group	...	...	...		
Total		176			

(a) Complete the above table by filling the gaps shown by ...

(b) Test at 5% level to see whether the fertilisers differ significantly.

11. The three samples given below have been obtained from three normal populations with equal variances. Test the hypothesis that the population means are equal at 5% level of significance.

Sample I	6	8	5	12	9
Sample II	5	3	8	7	7
Sample III	10	7	11	10	12

(Value of $F_{0.05}$ with 2, 14 $d.f.$ = 3.88) **[ICWAI December 1990]**

12. A manager of a mercantile firm wishes to test whether its three salesmen A, B, C tend to make sales of the same size or differ in their selling abilities. During a week there have been 14 sale calls—A made 5 calls, B made 4 calls and C made 5 calls. Following are the sales data for the week of the three salesmen:

A :	500	400	700	800	600
B :	300	700	400	600	
C :	500	300	500	400	300

Perform the analysis of variance and draw your conclusion.

13. Three varieties A, B, C of a crop are tested in a randomized block design with four replications. The yields are given below in pounds:

Variety	Replications				Total
	1	2	3	4	
A	6	4	8	6	24
B	7	6	6	9	28
C	8	5	10	9	32

Test whether there are differences between varieties. Test also whether yield of A differs significantly from that of B. **[B.U. B.Com. 1976]**

14. The following table gives the number of refrigerators sold by 4 salesmen of Kelvinator (India) Ltd., in three months January, February and March in the year 1978:

Month	A	B	C	D
January	50	40	48	39
February	46	48	50	45
March	39	44	40	39

Is there a significant difference in the sales made by the four salesmen? **[D.U. M.Com.]**

15. Four different manufacturing processes were tried at three different stations and the average measurement of a quality characteristic of the product by these processes obtained as in the following table. Perform the analysis of variance of the data and list for the difference between the processes.

Station	Processes			
	A	B	C	D
I	7	14	11	11
II	15	16	14	10
III	8	15	10	12

[C.U. M.Com. 1982]

16. Suppose that we are interested in establishing the yield producing ability of four types of soyabeans A, B, C and D. We have three blocks of land X, Y and Z which may be different in fertility. Each block of land is divided into four plots and the different types of soyabeans are assigned to the plots in each block by a random procedure. The following results are obtained:

Block \ Type	A	B	C	D
X	5	9	11	10
Y	4	7	8	10
Z	3	5	8	9

Test whether A, B, C and D are significantly different. **[AIMA January 1979]**

17. The following data give the number of units produced per day by 4 workers A, B, C, D using four different types of machines, M_1, M_2, M_3, M_4 :

	M_1	M_2	M_3	M_5
A	45	42	48	38
B	40	32	50	34
C	43	36	44	40
D	36	38	46	36

(a) Test whether the mean productions of the four different types of machines are equal.

(b) Test also whether the four workers differ with respect to mean productivity.

18. Set up ANOVA table for the following per hectare yield for three varieties of wheat, each grown on four plots:

Plot of Land	Per hectare yield (in '00 kgs.) Variety of Wheat		
	A_1	A_2	A_3
1	6	5	5
2	7	5	4
3	3	3	3
4	8	7	4

Also work out F-ratio. **[CA May 1985]**

19. Perform a two-way ANOVA on the data given below:

Plots of Land	Treatment			
	A	B	C	D
I	38	40	41	39
II	45	42	49	36
III	40	38	42	42

(Use coding method subtracting 40 from the given numbers.) **[CA May 1989]**

20. Perform a two-way ANOVA table on the data given below:

Treatment 2 \ Treatment 1	(i)	(ii)	(iii)
(i)	30	26	38
(ii)	24	29	28
(iii)	33	24	35
(iv)	36	31	30
(v)	27	35	33

(Use coding method subtracting 30 from the given numbers.) **[CA November 1985]**

Answers

[A]

5. Difference in the average yield under the three varieties are not significant; since $F = 3.704 >$ the tabulated value 4.26 at 5% level for $\nu_1 = 2$ and $\nu_2 = 9$.

6.

$d.f.$	SS	MS	F
2	145.60	72.75	
			$F = 7.91$
9	82.75	9.19	
11	228.25		

Conclusion: Machines are not equally effective.

7. The population means are not equal.

8. Yes, there is a significant difference, since $F = 4.088 > 3.49$ at 5% level with $\nu_1 = 3$ and $\nu_2 = 12$.

9. No, the three varieties do not differ significantly in production; since $F = 1.157 < 1.26$ at 5% level with $\nu_1 = 2$ and $\nu_2 = 9$.

10. (a) $\nu_1 = 2, \nu_2 = 9$; $SSW = 72$; $MSB = 52$, $MSW = 8$; $F = 6.5$.

(b) The fertilizers differ significantly at 5% with (2, 9) $d.f.$

11. All population means are not equal, since $F = 4 > 3.88$ (table value).

12. Three salesmen tend to make sales of the same size; since $F = 2.29 <$ the tabulated value 3.98 at 5% level with (2, 11) $d.f.$

13. There are no differences between varieties; since $F = 2.4 <$ the tabulated value at 5% level for (2, 6) $d.f.$

Also yield of A does not differ significantly from that of B, since $F = 3.6 <$ the tabulated value at 5% for (3, 6) $d.f.$

14. No, since $F = 1.55 <$ the tabulated value 8.85 at 5% level with $\nu_1 = 8$ and $\nu_2 = 3$.

15. There is no significant difference between the processes; since $F = 2.224 <$ the tabulated value 4.07 at 5% level with (3, 8) $d.f.$

16. A, B, C, D differ significantly; since $F = 9.32 >$ the tabulated value 4.07 at 5% level with (3, 8) $d.f.$

17. (a) The mean productions of the four different types of machines are not equal at 5% level; since $F = 5.52 >$ the tabulated value 3.86 for (3,9) $d.f.$

(b) The four workers do not differ significantly with respect to mean productivity; since $F = 1.63 < 3.86$ at 5% level with (3, 9) $d.f.$

[Note that at 1% level for (3, 9) $d.f.$ the tabulated value of F is 6.99 and both 5.52 and 1.63 are less than 6.99 and hence the mean productions by 4 machines as well by 4 workers are equal at 1% level.]

18.

$SSC = 8$	$k - 1 = 2$	$MSB = 4$	
			$F = 1.50.$
$SSE = 24$	$N - k = 9$	$MSW = 2.67$	

19.

$SSC = 42$	$c - 1 = 3$	$MSC = 14$	
			$F_1 = 1.312$
$SSR = 26$	$r - 1 = 2$	$MSR = 13$	
			$F_2 = 1.218$
$SSE = 64$	$(c - 1)(r - 1) = 6$	$MSE = 10.67$	
$SST = 132$	11		

20.

$SSC = 38.80$	$c - 1 = 2$	$MSC = 19.40$	
			$F_1 = 1.12$
$SSR = 52.93$	$r - 1 = 4$	$MSR = 13.23$	
			$F_2 = 1.64$
$SSE = 173.87$	$(c - 1)(r - 1) = 8$	$MSE = 21.73$	
$SST = 265.60$	$N - 1$ or $cr - 1 = 14$		

CHAPTER 6

CORRELATION AND REGRESSION

6.1. INTRODUCTION

In **Basic Statistics** for ICWAI Foundation Course, we have discussed *Measures of Central Tendency* and *Dispersion* involving the values of *one variable only.* But in many business problems we have to deal with *two variables.*

We shall now study two (or more) variables simultaneously and try to find the quantitative relationship between them. For example, the relationship between two variables like (1) income and expenditure, (2) height and weight, (3) rainfall and yield of crops, (4) price and demand, etc. will be examined in this chapter. The methods of expressing the relationship between two variables are due mainly to *Sir Francis Galton* and *Karl Pearson.*

6.2. CORRELATION

Correlation is a statistical measure for finding out the *degree* (*or strength*) *of association* between two (or more) variables. By 'association' we mean the tendency of the variables to move together. If two variables X and Y are so related that movements (or variations) in one, say X, tend to be accompanied by corresponding movements (or variations) in the other variable Y, then X and Y are said to be *correlated.* The movements may be in the same direction (i.e., either both X, Y increase or both of them decrease) or in the opposite directions (i.e., one, say X, increases and the other i.e., Y decreases). *Correlation is said to be positive or negative according as these movements are in the same or in the opposite directions.* If Y is unaffected by any change in X, then X and Y are said to be uncorrelated.

In the words of L.R. Conner :

"If two or more quantities vary in sympathy so that movements in the one tend to be accompanied by corresponding movements in the other, then they are said to be correlated."

Correlation may be linear or non-linear. If the amount of variation in X bears a constant ratio to the corresponding amount of variation in Y, then correlation between X and Y is said to be *linear.* Otherwise it is non-linear. *Correlation coefficient* or *Coefficient of correlation (r)* measures the **degree** of linear relationship, (i.e., linear correlation) between two variables.

6.3. DETERMINATION OF CORRELATION

Correlation between two variables may be determined by any one of the following methods :

(1) Two-way Frequency Table

(2) Scatter Diagram

(3) Co-variance Method or Karl Pearson's Method

(4) Rank Method.

(5) Concurrent Deviation Method.

Two-way Frequency Table (or Bivariate Frequency Table)

This is the simplest method of examining correlation between two variables. To construct a two-way frequency table we represent one variable, say X, along the vertical columns and the other variable Y along the horizontal rows. If there are m class-intervals for the X-series and n for the Y-series, we construct a table with m rows and n columns having $m \times n$ squares or cells. Each pair of observations is now shown by a tally mark (/) in the appropriate cell. When all the pairs of observations have been shown by tally marks in the two-way table, the cell frequencies are obtained by counting the tally marks of each cell. The type of correlation—positive or negative is roughly known by the nature of concentration of various cell frequencies. Two-way frequency table gives only a rough idea of the degree of correlation and, therefore, it is not generally used.

Method of construction of two-way frequency table will be clear from the example given below.

EXAMPLE 1. *The ages of twenty husbands and wives are given below. Form a two-way frequency table showing the relationship between the ages of husbands and wives with class-intervals* 20–25, 25–30, *etc.*

Sl. No.	1	2	3	4	5	6	7	8	9	10
Age of Husband :	28	37	42	25	29	47	37	35	23	41
Age of Wife :	23	30	40	26	25	41	35	25	21	38

Sl. No.	11	12	13	14	15	16	17	18	19	20
Age of Husband :	27	39	23	33	36	32	22	29	38	48
Age of Wife :	24	34	20	31	29	35	23	27	34	47

[CA May 1970]

SOLUTION.

TABLE 6.1 TWO-WAY FREQUENCY TABLE SHOWING AGES OF HUSBANDS AND WIVES

Age of wife in years ⟶

	20–25	25–30	30–35	35–40	40–45	45–50	Total
20–25	/// 3						3
25–30	// 2	/// 3					5
30–35			/ 1	/ 1			2
35–40		// 2	/// 3	/ 1			6
40–45				/ 1	/ 1		2
45–50					/ 1	/ 1	2
Total	5	5	4	3	2	1	20

NOTE. In the above table class-intervals 20–25, 25–30, etc. represent respectively 20 and above but below 25, 25 and above but below 30, etc. For the Sl. No. 1, the age of husband, 28 years, fall in the 2nd class-interval 25–30 and the age of wife, 23, fall in the 1st class-interval 20–25. Therefore, we draw a tally mark (/) in the 1st cell of 2nd row. Similarly, all other pairs of observations can be shown by tally marks in the appropriate cells.

6.3.1. Scatter Diagram

The existence of correlation can be shown graphically by means of a *scatter diagram.* Statistical data relating to simultaneous movements (or variations) of two variables can be graphically represented by points. One of the two variables, say X, is shown along the horizontal axis OX and the other variable Y along the vertical axis OY. All the pairs of values of X and Y are now shown by points (or dots) on the graph paper. This diagrammatic representation of bivariate data is known as *scatter diagram.*

The scatter diagram of these points as also the direction of the scatter reveals the nature and strength of correlation between the two variables. The following are some scatter diagrams showing different types of correlation between two variables.

In fig 6.1 and 6.3, the movements (or variations) of the two variables are in the same direction and the scatter diagram shows a *linear path.* In this case, correlation is *positive* and association between the variables is direct.

In fig 6.2 and 6.4, the movements of the two variables are in opposite directions and the scatter shows a linear path. In this case correlation is *negative,* i.e., association between the variables is *indirect.*

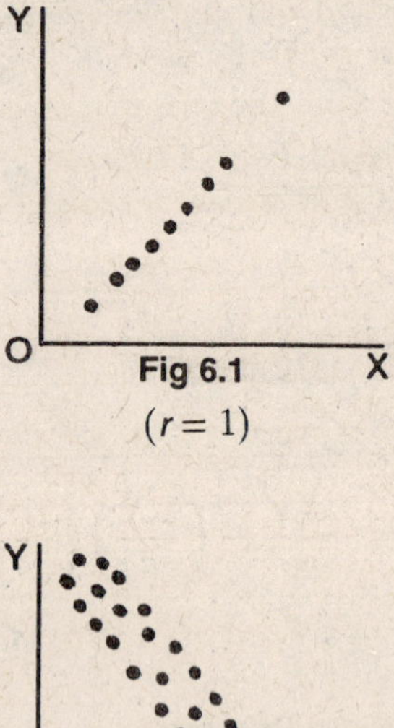

Fig 6.1
($r = 1$)

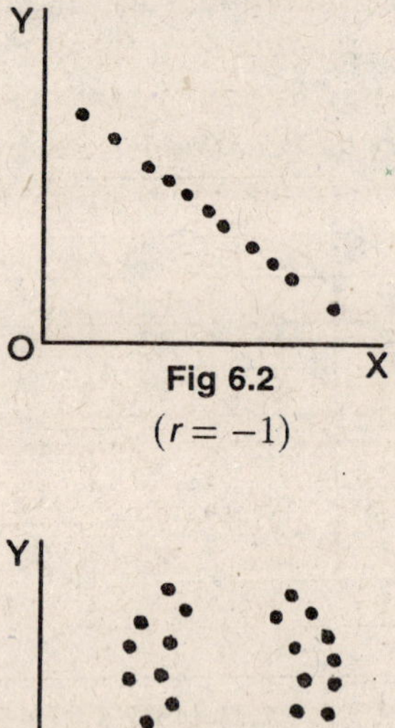

Fig 6.2
($r = -1$)

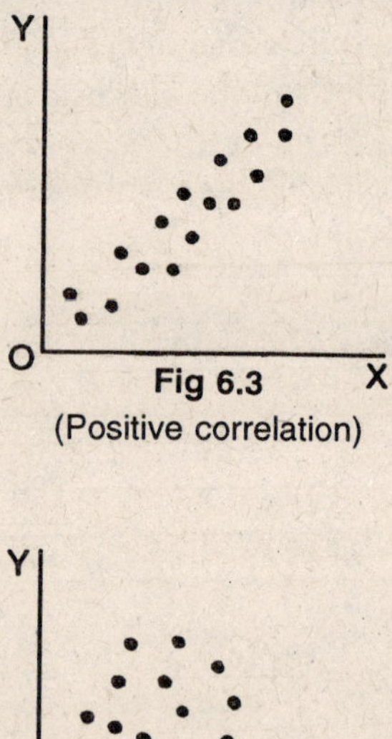

Fig 6.3
(Positive correlation)

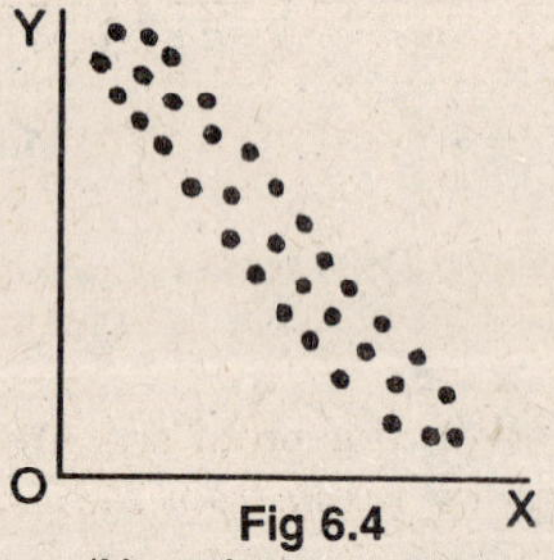

Fig 6.4
(Negative correlation)

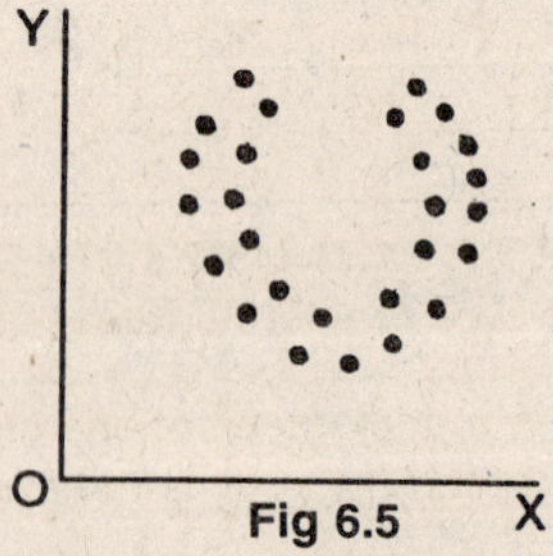

Fig 6.5
($r = 0$)

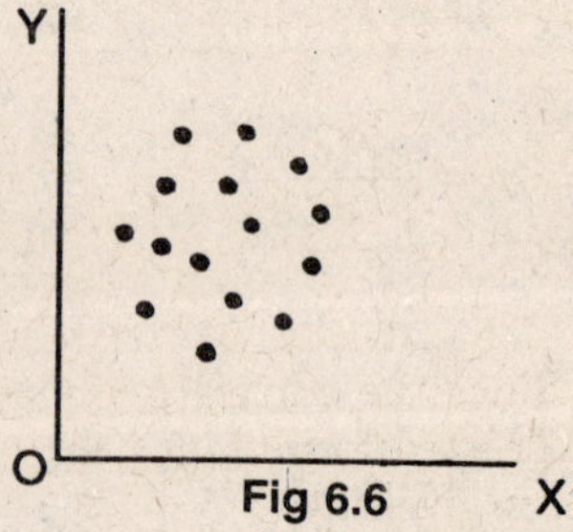

Fig 6.6
($r = 0$)

In fig 6.5 and 6.6, the points (or dots) instead of showing any linear path lie around a curve or form a swarm. In this case correlation is very small and we can take $r = 0$.

In fig 6.1 and 6.2, all the ponts lie on a straight line. In these cases correlation is perfect and $r = +1$ or -1 according as the correlation is positive or negative.

6.3.2. Correlation Coefficient by Covariance or Karl Pearson's Method

If $(X_1, Y_1), (X_2, Y_2), \cdots, (X_n, Y_n)$ be n pairs of observations on two variables X and Y, then the *covariance* of X and Y, written as cov (X, Y), is defined by

$$\text{cov }(X,Y) = \frac{1}{n}\Sigma(X-\bar{X})(Y-\bar{Y}).$$

Covariance indicates the joint variations between two variables.

The *correlation coefficient* or *the coefficient of correlation or product moment correlation coefficient* (r) between X and Y is defined by

$$r = \frac{\text{cov }(X,Y)}{\sigma_X\sigma_Y} = \frac{\Sigma[(X-\bar{X})(Y-\bar{Y})]}{n\sigma_X\sigma_Y}$$

where σ_X, σ_Y are standard deviations of X and Y respectively.

The formula for the Correlation Coefficient r may be written in different forms.

(i) If $x = X - \bar{X}$ = deviation of X from its mean and $y = Y - \bar{Y}$ = deviation of Y from its mean, then

$$r = \frac{\Sigma xy}{n\sigma_X\sigma_Y} \qquad (1)$$

[$\because$ S.D. is independent of ány change of origin.]

This formula was introduced by *Karl Pearson.*

$$\text{Now} \quad \sigma_X = \sqrt{\frac{\Sigma x^2}{n} - \left(\frac{\Sigma x}{n}\right)^2} = \sqrt{\frac{\Sigma x^2}{n}}, \qquad [\because \Sigma x = \Sigma(X-\bar{X}) = 0]$$

$$\text{Similarly,} \quad \sigma_Y = \sqrt{\frac{\Sigma y^2}{n}};$$

$$\therefore \text{ from (1)}, \quad r = \frac{\Sigma xy}{n\sqrt{\frac{\Sigma x^2}{n}} \times \sqrt{\frac{\Sigma y^2}{n}}} = \frac{\Sigma xy}{\sqrt{\Sigma x^2} \times \sqrt{\Sigma y^2}}.$$

(ii)
$$\begin{aligned}\text{cov }(X,Y) &= \frac{1}{n}\Sigma(X-\bar{X})(Y-\bar{Y}) = \frac{1}{n}\Sigma\{XY - X\bar{Y} - \bar{X}Y + \bar{X}\bar{Y}\}\\ &= \frac{\Sigma XY}{n} - \bar{Y}\frac{\Sigma X}{n} - \bar{X}\frac{\Sigma Y}{n} + \frac{n\bar{X}\bar{Y}}{n}\\ &= \frac{\Sigma XY}{n} - \bar{X}\bar{Y} - \bar{X}\bar{Y} + \bar{X}\bar{Y} = \frac{\Sigma XY}{n} - \bar{X}\bar{Y} = \frac{\Sigma XY}{n} - \left(\frac{\Sigma X}{n}\right)\left(\frac{\Sigma Y}{n}\right);\end{aligned}$$

$$\therefore \quad r = \frac{\text{cov }(X,Y)}{\sigma_X\sigma_Y} = \frac{\frac{\Sigma XY}{n} - \left(\frac{\Sigma X}{n}\right)\left(\frac{\Sigma Y}{n}\right)}{\sqrt{\frac{\Sigma X^2}{n} - \left(\frac{\Sigma X}{n}\right)^2} \times \sqrt{\frac{\Sigma Y^2}{n} - \left(\frac{\Sigma Y}{n}\right)^2}}.$$

Since the correlation coefficient is independent of the choice of origin [for proof see Art. 6.5], the corrected formula for correlation coefficient r, when the *deviations are taken from the assumed mean,* is given by

$$r = \frac{\frac{\Sigma xy}{n} - \frac{\Sigma x}{n} \times \frac{\Sigma y}{n}}{\sqrt{\frac{\Sigma x^2}{n} - \left(\frac{\Sigma x}{n}\right)^2} \times \sqrt{\frac{\Sigma y^2}{n} - \left(\frac{\Sigma y}{n}\right)^2}},$$

where $x = X - a$ and $y = Y - b$, a and b being assumed means of X and Y respectively.

This formula can also be written as

$$r = \frac{n\Sigma xy - (\Sigma x)(\Sigma y)}{\sqrt{n\Sigma x^2 - (\Sigma x)^2} \times \sqrt{n\Sigma y^2 - (\Sigma y)^2}} = \frac{\Sigma xy - \dfrac{(\Sigma x)(\Sigma y)}{n}}{\sqrt{\Sigma x^2 - \dfrac{(\Sigma x)^2}{n}} \times \sqrt{\Sigma y^2 - \dfrac{(\Sigma y)^2}{n}}}.$$

* (iii) *Karl Pearson's formula* for correlation coefficient r with frequencies of both the variables X and Y is given by

$$\frac{\dfrac{\Sigma f dxdy}{N} - \left(\dfrac{\Sigma f dx}{N}\right)\left(\dfrac{\Sigma f dy}{N}\right)}{\sqrt{\dfrac{\Sigma f dx^2}{N} - \left(\dfrac{\Sigma f dx}{N}\right)^2} \times \sqrt{\dfrac{\Sigma f dy^2}{N} - \left(\dfrac{\Sigma f dy}{N}\right)^2}} = \frac{\Sigma f dxdy - \dfrac{(\Sigma f dx)(\Sigma f dy)}{N}}{\sqrt{\Sigma f dx^2 - \dfrac{(\Sigma f dx)^2}{N}} \times \sqrt{\Sigma f dy^2 - \dfrac{(\Sigma f dy)^2}{N}}}.$$

where $dx = \frac{X-a}{c}$ and $dy = \frac{Y-b}{d}$.

EXAMPLE 2. *Find the coefficient of correlation from the following data:*

X :	1	2	3	4	5	6	7
Y :	6	8	11	9	12	10	14

SOLUTION.

TABLE 6.2 CALCULATIONS FOR COEFFICIENT OF CORRELATION

X	Y	$x = X - \bar{X}$	$y = Y - \bar{Y}$	x^2	y^2	xy
1	6	−3	−4	9	16	12
2	8	−2	−2	4	4	4
3	11	−1	1	1	1	−1
4	9	0	−1	0	1	0
5	12	1	2	1	4	2
6	10	2	0	4	0	0
7	14	3	4	9	16	12
$28 = \Sigma X$	$70 = \Sigma Y$	0	0	$28 = \Sigma x^2$	$42 = \Sigma y^2$	$29 = \Sigma xy$

$$\bar{X} = \frac{\Sigma X}{n} = \frac{28}{7} = 4 \quad \text{and} \quad \bar{Y} = \frac{\Sigma Y}{n} = \frac{70}{7} = 10.$$

Karl Pearson's coefficient of correlation (r) is given by

$$r = \frac{\Sigma xy}{\sqrt{\Sigma x^2} \times \sqrt{\Sigma y^2}} = \frac{29}{\sqrt{28} \times \sqrt{42}};$$

$$\therefore \quad \log r = \log 29 - \left(\frac{1}{2}\log 28 + \frac{1}{2}\log 42\right) = 1.4624 - \left(\frac{1}{2} \times 1.4472 + \frac{1}{2} \times 1.6232\right)$$

$$= 1.4624 - (.7236 + .8116) = 1.4624 - 1.5352 = \bar{1}.9272;$$

$$\therefore \quad r = \text{antilog } (\bar{1}.9272) = \mathbf{0.8457 \text{ (approx.)}}$$

EXAMPLE 3. *Karl Pearson's coefficient of correlation between two variables X and Y is* 0.28, *their covariance is* +7.6. *If the variance of X is* 9, *find the standard deviation of Y-series.*

[Agra U. 1970]

SOLUTION. Karl Pearson's coefficient of correlation r is given by

$$r = \frac{\text{cov}\ (X, Y)}{\sigma_X \sigma_Y} \tag{1}$$

Here $r = 0.28$, cov $(X, Y) = 7.6$ and $\sigma_X^2 = 9$; $\therefore\ \sigma_X = 3$. Using (1), $0.28 = \dfrac{7.6}{3\sigma_Y}$

$$\text{or,}\quad 0.84\sigma_Y = 7.6, \quad \text{or,}\quad \sigma_Y = \frac{7.6}{0.84} = \frac{760}{84} = 9.048.$$

Hence the standard deviation of Y-series is 9.048.

EXAMPLE 4. *Calculate the coefficient of correlation between X and Y series from the following data :*

$$\sum_{i=1}^{15}(X_i - \bar{X})^2 = 136, \quad \sum_{i=1}^{15}(Y_i - \bar{Y})^2 = 138, \quad \text{and} \quad \sum_{i=1}^{15}(X_i - \bar{X})(Y - \bar{Y}) = 122.$$

SOLUTION. We have

$$r = \frac{\Sigma xy}{\sqrt{\Sigma x^2} \times \sqrt{\Sigma y^2}} \quad \text{where } x = X - \bar{X},\ y = Y - \bar{Y}.$$

Here $\Sigma xy = 122$, $\Sigma x^2 = 136$ and $\Sigma y^2 = 138$;

$$\therefore\quad r = \frac{122}{\sqrt{136} \times \sqrt{138}};$$

$$\therefore\quad \log r = \log 122 - \frac{1}{2}(\log 136 + \log 138) = 2.0864 - \frac{1}{2}(2.1335 + 2.1399)$$

$$= 2.0864 - 2.1367 = \bar{1}.9497$$

$$r = \text{antilog}\ (\bar{1}.9497) = 0.8910 = \mathbf{0.89\ (approx.)}$$

EXAMPLE 5. *Calculate Pearson's coefficient of correlation between advertisement cost and sales as per the data given below :*

Advertisement cost in '000 Rs. :	39	65	62	90	82	75	25	98	36	78
Sales in lakh Rs. :	47	53	58	86	62	68	60	91	51	84

[CA November 1975]

SOLUTION. Karl Pearson's coefficient of correlation (r) is given by

$$r = \frac{\Sigma xy}{\sqrt{\Sigma x^2} \times \sqrt{\Sigma y^2}} \qquad \text{where } x = X - \bar{X} \text{ and } y = Y - \bar{Y}.$$

TABLE 6.3 CALCULATIONS FOR CORRELATION COEFFICIENT

X	Y	$x = X - \bar{X}$	$y = Y - \bar{Y}$	x^2	y^2	xy
39	47	−26	−19	676	361	494
65	53	0	−13	0	169	0
62	58	−3	−8	9	64	24
90	86	25	20	625	400	500
82	62	17	−4	289	16	−68
75	68	10	2	100	4	20
25	60	−40	−6	1600	36	240
98	91	33	25	1089	625	825
36	51	−29	−15	841	225	435
78	84	13	18	169	324	234
$650 = \Sigma X$	$660 = \Sigma Y$	0	0	$5398 = \Sigma x^2$	$2224 = \Sigma y^2$	$2704 = \Sigma xy$

$$\bar{X} = \frac{\Sigma X}{n} = \frac{650}{10} = 65; \quad \bar{Y} = \frac{\Sigma Y}{n} = \frac{660}{10} = 66, \qquad r = \frac{2704}{\sqrt{5398} \times \sqrt{2224}};$$

$$\therefore \quad \log r = \log 2704 - \frac{1}{2}(\log 5398 + \log 2224) = 3.4320 - \frac{1}{2}(3.7322 + 3.3472)$$

$$= 3.4320 - 3.5397 = \bar{1}.8923;$$

$$\therefore \quad r = \text{antilog } (\bar{1}.8923) = 0.7803 = \mathbf{0.78\ (approx.)}$$

EXAMPLE 6. *Calculate Pearson's coefficient of correlation from the following taking* 100 *and* 50 *as the assumed average of X and Y respectively :*

X :	104	111	104	114	118	117	105	108	106	100	104	105
Y :	57	55	47	45	45	50	64	63	66	62	69	61

[CA November 1976]

SOLUTION.

TABLE 6.4 CALCULATIONS FOR COEFFICIENT OF CORRELATION

X	Y	$x = X - a$	$y = Y - b$	x^2	y^2	xy
104	57	4	7	16	49	28
111	55	11	5	121	25	55
104	47	4	−3	16	9	−12
114	45	14	−5	196	25	−70
118	45	18	−5	324	25	−90
117	$50 = b$	17	0	289	0	0
105	64	5	14	25	196	70
108	63	8	13	64	169	104
106	66	6	16	36	256	96
$100 = a$	62	0	12	0	144	0
104	69	4	19	16	361	76
105	61	5	11	25	121	55
—	—	$96 = \Sigma x$	$84 = \Sigma y$	$1128 = \Sigma x^2$	$1380 = \Sigma y^2$	$312 = \Sigma xy$

Pearson's coefficient of correlation (r) is given by

$$r = \frac{\Sigma xy - \dfrac{(\Sigma x)(\Sigma y)}{n}}{\sqrt{\Sigma x^2 - \dfrac{(\Sigma x)^2}{n}} \times \sqrt{\Sigma y^2 - \dfrac{(\Sigma y)^2}{n}}} = \frac{312 - \dfrac{96 \times 84}{12}}{\sqrt{1128 - \dfrac{96 \times 96}{12}} \times \sqrt{1380 - \dfrac{84 \times 84}{12}}}$$

$$= \frac{312 - 672}{\sqrt{1128 - 768} \times \sqrt{1380 - 588}} = \frac{-360}{\sqrt{360 \times 792}}.$$

Let $A = \dfrac{360}{\sqrt{360 \times 792}}$;

$$\therefore \quad \log A = \log 360 - \frac{1}{2}(\log 360 + \log 792) = 2.5563 - \frac{1}{2}(2.5563 + 2.8987)$$

$$= 2.5563 - 2.7275 = \bar{1}.8288;$$

$$\therefore \quad A = \text{antilog } (\bar{1}.8288) = 0.6742;$$

$$\therefore \quad r = -0.6742 = \mathbf{-0.67 \text{ (approx.)}}$$

EXAMPLE 7. *A computer while calculating the correlation coefficient between two variables X and Y from 25 pairs of observations obtained the following results :* $n = 25, \Sigma X = 125, \Sigma Y = 100, \Sigma X^2 = 650, \Sigma Y^2 = 460$ *and* $\Sigma XY = 508$.

It was, however, discovered at the time of checking that two pairs of observations were not correctly copied. They were taken as $(6, 14)$ *and* $(8, 6)$, *while the correct values were* $(8, 12)$ *and* $(6, 8)$. *Prove that the correct value of the correlation coefficient should be* $\frac{2}{3}$.

[ICWAI Final, June 1977; Madras U. 1988]

SOLUTION. When the two incorrect pairs of observations are replaced by the correct pairs, the revised results for the whole series are :

$$\Sigma X = 125 - \text{(Sum of two incorrect values of } X) + \text{(Sum of two correct vlaues of } X)$$

$$= 125 - (6 + 8) + (8 + 6) = 125.$$

Similarly,

$$\Sigma Y = 100 - (14 + 6) + (12 + 8) = 100,$$

$$\Sigma X^2 = 650 - (6^2 + 8^2) + (8^2 + 6^2) = 650,$$

$$\Sigma Y^2 = 460 - (14^2 + 6^2) + 12^2 + 8^2 = 460 - 232 + 208 = 436,$$

$$\text{and} \quad \Sigma XY = 508 - (6 \times 14 + 8 \times 6) + (8 \times 12 + 6 \times 8) = 508 - 132 + 144 = 520;$$

$\therefore$ *Correct value of the* **correlation coefficient** (r) is

$$r = \frac{\Sigma XY - \dfrac{(\Sigma X)(\Sigma Y)}{n}}{\sqrt{\Sigma X^2 - \dfrac{(\Sigma X)^2}{n}} \times \sqrt{\Sigma Y^2 - \dfrac{(\Sigma Y)^2}{n}}}.$$

$$= \frac{520 - \dfrac{125 \times 100}{25}}{\sqrt{650 - \dfrac{(125)^2}{25}} \times \sqrt{436 - \dfrac{(100)^2}{25}}}$$

$$= \frac{20}{\sqrt{25 \times 36}} = \frac{20}{5 \times 6} = \mathbf{\frac{2}{3}}.$$

EXAMPLE 8. *Find the coefficient of correlation between the grouped frequency distribution of two variables (Profits and Sales) given below in the form of a two-way frequency table :*

Sales (in '0000 rupees) ⟶

	80–90	90–100	100–110	110–120	120–130	Total
50–55	1	3	7	5	2	18
55–60	2	4	10	7	4	27
60–65	1	5	12	10	7	35
65–70	—	3	8	6	3	20
Total	4	15	37	28	16	100

SOLUTION.

TABLE 6.5 CALCULATIONS FOR CORRELATION COEFFICIENT

Sales (in '0000 rupees) ⟶

		Class-intervals	80-90	90-100	100-110	110-120	120-130				
		Mid-values (x)	85	95	105	115	125				
Class inter-vals	Mid-Values (y)	dx / dy	−2	−1	0	1	2	Total f	fdy	fdy^2	$fdxdy$
50–55	52.5	−1	1 (2)	3 (3)	7 (0)	5 (−5)	2 (−4)	18	−18	18	−4
55–60	57.5	0	2 (0)	4 (0)	10 (0)	7 (0)	4 (0)	27	0	0	0
60–65	62.5	1	1(−2)	5 (−5)	12 (0)	10 (10)	7 (14)	35	35	35	17
65–70	67.5	2	0 (0)	3 (−6)	8 (0)	6 (12)	3 (12)	20	40	80	18
		Total f	4	15	37	28	16	100	57	133	31
		fdx	−8	−15	0	28	32	37			
		fdx^2	16	15	0	28	64	123			
		$fdxdy$	0	−8	0	17	22	31	Check		

The *correlation coefficient* (r) is given by

$$r = \frac{\Sigma f dx dy - \dfrac{(\Sigma f dx)(\Sigma f dy)}{N}}{\sqrt{\Sigma f dx^2 - \dfrac{(\Sigma f dx)^2}{N}} \times \sqrt{\Sigma f dy^2 - \dfrac{(\Sigma f dy)^2}{N}}} = \frac{31 - \dfrac{37 \times 57}{100}}{\sqrt{123 - \dfrac{(37)^2}{100}} \times \sqrt{133 - \dfrac{(57)^2}{100}}}$$

$$= \frac{31 - 21.09}{\sqrt{123 - 13.69} \times \sqrt{133 - 32.49}} = \frac{9.91}{\sqrt{109.31 \times 100.51}}$$

$$\therefore \quad \log r = \log 9.91 - \frac{1}{2}(\log 109.31 + \log 100.51) = 0.9961 - \frac{1}{2}(2.0386 + 2.0021)$$

$$= 0.9961 - 2.0204 = \bar{2}.9757;$$

$$\therefore \quad r = \text{antilog}\ (\bar{2}.9757) = 0.09456 = \mathbf{0.0946\ (approx).}$$

NOTE.

(1) $dx = \dfrac{x - 105}{10}$ and $dy = \dfrac{y - 57.5}{5}$.

(2) Number within brackets in each cell is the product of that cell frequency and the corresponding values of dx and dy.

(3) $fdxdy$ represents algebraic sum of the numbers within brackets in any row or column.

6.3.3. Rank Correlation (or Correlation by Rank Method)

Simple correlation coefficient (or product-moment correlation coefficient) is based on the magnitudes of the variable. But in many situations it is not possible to find the magnitudes of the variable at all. For example, we cannot measure beauty or intelligence quantitatively. In this case, it is possible to rank the individuals in some order. Rank correlation is based on the rank or the order and not on the magnitude of the variable. It is more suitable if the individuals (or variables) can be arranged in order of merit or proficiency. If the ranks assigned to individuals range from 1 to N, then the correlation coefficient between two series of ranks is called *Rank correlation coefficient. Edward Spearman's formula for Rank coefficient of correlation* (R) is given by

$$R = 1 - \frac{6\Sigma D^2}{N(N^2-1)} \quad \text{or} \quad 1 - \frac{6\Sigma D^2}{N^3 - N}$$

where D is the difference between the ranks of the two series and N is the number of individuals in each series.

EXAMPLE 9. *Ten students got the following percentage of marks in Mathematics and Statistics :*

Student (Roll No.) :	1	2	3	4	5	6	7	8	9	10
Marks in Mathematics :	78	36	98	25	75	82	90	62	65	39
Marks in Statistics :	84	51	91	60	68	62	86	58	53	47

Calculate the correlation coefficient. **[C.U. 1961; ICWAI June 1988]**

SOLUTION. In Mathematics, student with Roll No. 3 gets the highest mark 98 and is ranked 1; Roll No. 7 securing 90 marks has rank-2 and so on. Similarly, we can find the ranks of students in Statistics.

TABLE 6.6 CALCULATIONS FOR RANK CORRELAITON

Roll No.	Mathematics		Statistics		Rank Diff	D^2
	Marks	Rank (x)	Marks	Rank (y)	$D = x - y$	
1	78	4	84	3	1	1
2	36	9	51	9	0	0
3	98	1	91	1	0	0
4	25	10	60	6	4	16
5	75	5	68	4	1	1
6	82	3	62	5	− 2	4
7	90	2	86	2	0	0
8	62	7	58	7	0	0
9	65	6	53	8	− 2	4
10	39	8	47	10	− 2	4
Total	—	—	—	—	—	$30 = \Sigma D^2$

Applying *Edward Spearman's formula :*

$$R = 1 - \frac{6\Sigma D^2}{N(N^2-1)} \qquad [\text{here } N = 10, \quad \Sigma D^2 = 30]$$

$$= 1 - \frac{6 \times 30}{10(10^2-1)} = 1 - \frac{18}{99} = 1 - \frac{2}{11} = \frac{9}{11} = \mathbf{0.82}.$$

Edward Spearman's Formula for Tied Ranks

If in a series two or more individuals (or items) have the same score, then we find the average of the ranks of these individuals and allot this average rank to each of them. [In example 10, as the score 98 occurs three times, there is a tie for the 7th place and in this case, we find the average rank $\frac{7+8+9}{3} = 8$ of 7, 8, 9 and assign it to each 98.]

In such cases, *Edward Spearman's modified formula* is

$$R = 1 - \frac{6[\Sigma D^2 + \Sigma(t^3 - t)/12]}{N(N^2 - 1)}$$

where t is the number of individuals (or items) involved in a tie in the first or second series.

EXAMPLE 10. *Find the rank correlation coefficient of the following data :*

Series A :	115	109	112	87	98	120	98	100	98	118
Series B :	75	73	85	70	76	82	65	73	68	80

SOLUTION. In series A, the highest score is 120 and, therefore, its rank is 1; the rank of the second highest score 118 is 2. Proceedig in this manner, we find that the rank of 98 is 7 and 98 occurs three times. As there is a tie for the 7th place, we find the average rank $\frac{7+8+9}{3}$ i.e., 8 and assign 8 as rank to each of the three 98. The score next to 98 is 87 and its rank is 10. Similarly, we can find the ranks of individuals (or items) in series B.

TABLE 6.7 CALCULATIONS FOR THE RANK CORRELATION COEFFICIENT

Series A		Series B		Rank Difference $D = x - y$	D^2
Score	Rank (x)	Score	Rank (y)		
115	3	75	5	−2	4
109	5	73	6.5	−1.5	2.25
112	4	85	1	3	9
87	10	70	8	2	4
98	8	76	4	4	16
120	1	82	2	−1	1
98	8	65	10	−2	4
100	6	73	6.5	−0.5	0.25
98	8	68	9	−1	1
118	2	80	3	−1	1
Total	—	—	—	—	$42.50 = \Sigma D^2$

By *Edward Spearman's formula,*

$$R = 1 - \frac{6\left\{\sum D^2 + \sum\left(\frac{t^3 - t}{12}\right)\right\}}{N(N^2 - 1)}$$

where t = Number of individuals involved in a tie.

Here $\Sigma D^2 = 42.50, N = 10, t = 3, 2$ and

$$\sum \frac{t^3 - t}{12} = \frac{3^3 - 3}{12} + \frac{2^3 - 2}{12} = \frac{24}{12} + \frac{6}{12} = 2 + 0.5 = 2.5.$$

$$\therefore \quad R = 1 - \frac{6\{42.5 + 2.5\}}{10 \cdot (10^2 - 1)} = 1 - \frac{6 \times 45}{10 \times 99} = 1 - \frac{3}{11} = \frac{8}{11} = \mathbf{0.73}.$$

EXAMPLE 11. *The coefficient of rank correlation between the marks in Statistics and Mathematics obtained by a certain group of students is* $\frac{2}{3}$ *and the sum of the squares of the differences in ranks is* 55. *Find the number of students in the group.*

SOLUTION. *Edward Spearman's formula* for rank correlation coefficient is

$$R = 1 - \frac{6\Sigma D^2}{N(N^2-1)}$$

Here $R = \frac{2}{3}, \Sigma D^2 = 55, N = ?$

$$\therefore \quad \frac{2}{3} = 1 - \frac{6 \times 55}{N(N^2-1)} = 1 - \frac{330}{N(N^2-1)}, \quad \text{or,} \quad \frac{330}{N(N^2-1)} = 1 - \frac{2}{3} = \frac{1}{3}$$

$$\text{or,} \quad N(N^2-1) = 990, \quad \text{or,} \quad N(N-1)(N+1) = 990, \quad \text{or,} \quad (N-1)N(N+1) = 9.10.11.$$

Hence $N = 10$ i.e., the Number of students in the group = **10.**

EXAMPLE 12. *The coefficient of rank correlation of the marks obtained by* 10 *students in Mathematics and Statistics was found to be* 0.5. *It was then detected that the difference in ranks in the two subjects for one particular student was wrongly taken to be* 3 *in place of* 7. *What should be the correct rank correlation coefficient?* **[C.U. B. Com. (Hons.) 1983]**

SOLUTION. *Edward Spearman's formula* for the coefficient of rank correlation is

$$R = 1 - \frac{6\Sigma D^2}{N(N^2-1)}$$

Here $R = 0.5, N = 10, \Sigma D^2 = ?$

$$\therefore \quad 0.5 = 1 - \frac{6\Sigma D^2}{10(10^2-1)} = 1 - \frac{6\Sigma D^2}{10 \times 99} = 1 - \frac{\Sigma D^2}{165}$$

$$\text{or,} \quad \frac{\Sigma D^2}{165} = 1 - 0.5 = 0.5 = \frac{1}{2}, \quad \text{or,} \quad \Sigma D^2 = 82.5.$$

Now, correct value of ΣD^2

$= \text{Incorrect } \Sigma D^2 - (\text{incorrect difference in ranks})^2 + (\text{correct difference in ranks})^2$
$= 82.5 - (3)^2 + (7)^2 = 122.5.$

Hence the *correct rank correlation coefficient*

$$= 1 - \frac{6 \times 122.5}{10(10^2-1)} = 1 - \frac{122.5}{165} = \frac{42.5}{165} = \mathbf{0.2576}.$$

6.4. CONCURRENT DEVIATION METHOD

Let $(X_1, Y_1), (X_2, Y_2), \cdots, (X_{n+1}, Y_{n+1})$ be $n+1$ pairs of observations on two variables X and Y. Let C_X and C_Y represent the direction of change in X and Y respectively with reference to the preceding values. Then C_X represents the signs, plus (+) or minus (−), of $X_2 - X_1, X_3 - X_2, \cdots, X_{n+1} - X_n$ and C_Y represents the signs of $Y_2 - Y_1, Y_3 - Y_2, \cdots, Y_{n+1} - Y_n$.

If C be the *no. of concurrent deviations* i.e., *the no. of positive signs in $C_X \cdot C_Y$.*, then the *coefficient of concurrent deviations* r is given by

$$\mathbf{r} = \pm\sqrt{\pm\left(\frac{2C - n}{n}\right)}, \quad \text{where } n = \text{no. of pairs of deviations compared.}$$

If $\frac{2C-n}{n}$ is negative, then we take negative sign both inside and outside the square root. If $\frac{2C-n}{n}$ is positive, we take positive sign inside and outside the square root.

EXAMPLE 13. *Calculate the coefficient of correlation, using the method of concurrent deviations, between supply and demand given the following data. Also comment on your result:*

Year :	1980	1981	1982	1983	1984	1985	1986	1987	1988	1989
Supply ('000 tons) :	120	110	120	119	140	125	127	119	140	160
Demand ('000 tons) :	240	250	260	266	232	245	255	267	268	239

[CA November 1991]

SOLUTION.

TABLE 6.8 CALCULATIONS FOR THE COEFFICIENT OF CONCURRENT DEVIATIONS

Year	Supply X	Demand Y	Direction of change in X C_X	Direction of change in Y C_Y	$C_X \cdot C_Y$
1980	120	240			
1981	110	250	−	+	−
1982	120	260	+	+	+
1983	119	266	−	+	−
1984	140	232	+	−	−
1985	125	245	−	+	−
1986	127	255	+	+	+
1987	119	267	−	+	−
1988	140	268	+	+	+
1989	160	239	+	−	−

∴ Total no. of concurrent deviations (C) = 3 (i.e., total no. of positive signs in the last column).

The *coefficient of correlation by the concurrent deviation method* is given by

$$r = \pm\sqrt{\pm\left(\frac{2C - n}{n}\right)}, \quad \text{where } n = 10 - 1 = 9 \text{ and } C = 3$$

$$= \pm\sqrt{\pm\left(\frac{2 \times 3 - 9}{9}\right)} = \pm\sqrt{\pm\left(\frac{6 - 9}{9}\right)} = -\sqrt{- \times -\frac{1}{3}}$$

$$= -\sqrt{\frac{1}{3}} = \mathbf{-0.58\ (approx.)}.$$

6.5. THEOREM 1

Show that the correlation coefficient is independent of the origin of reference and the units of measurement.

PROOF. Let $(X_1, Y_1), (X_2, Y_2), \cdots, (X_n, Y_n)$ be the n pairs of observations relating to two variables X and Y. Let us change the origins of X and Y by a and b and the scales (or units of measurement) by c and d respectively.

$$\text{Let} \quad x_i = \frac{X_i - a}{c} \quad \text{and} \quad y_i = \frac{Y_i - b}{d},$$

where a, b, c, d are constants, c and d being positive.

The required results will be proved if we can show that $r_{XY} = r_{xy}$.

$$\text{Now} \quad x_i = \frac{X_i - a}{c}, \quad \text{or,} \quad X_i = a + cx_i;$$

$$\therefore \quad \bar{X} = \frac{\Sigma X_i}{n} = \frac{\Sigma(a + cx_i)}{n} = \frac{na + c\Sigma x_i}{n} = a + c\frac{\Sigma x_i}{n} = a + c\bar{x};$$

$$\therefore \quad X_i - \bar{X} = c(x_i - \bar{x}).$$

Similarly, $Y_i - \bar{Y} = d(y_i - \bar{y})$.

$$\sigma_X^2 = \frac{\Sigma(X_i - \bar{X})^2}{n} = \frac{\Sigma c^2(x_i - \bar{x})^2}{n} = c^2\sigma_x^2; \qquad \therefore \quad \sigma_X = c\sigma_x \quad [\because \quad c \text{ is positive}].$$

Similarly, $\sigma_Y = d\sigma_y$;

$$\therefore \quad r_{XY} = \frac{\Sigma[(X_i - \bar{X})(Y_i - \bar{Y})]}{n\sigma_X\sigma_Y} = \frac{\Sigma[c(x_i - \bar{x}) \cdot d(y_i - \bar{y})]}{n \cdot c\sigma_x \cdot d\sigma_y} = \frac{\Sigma[(x_i - \bar{x})(y_i - \bar{y})]}{n\sigma_x\sigma_y} = r_{xy}.$$

Hence the theorem follows.

REMARKS. In general, $\sigma_X = |c|\sigma_x$ and $\sigma_Y = |d|\sigma_y$ so that $r_{XY} = \frac{cd}{|c|\cdot|d|} \cdot r_{xy}$. Now $\frac{cd}{|c|\cdot|d|} = 1$ or -1 according as c, d have the same sign or opposite signs. $\therefore \quad r_{XY} = \pm r_{xy}$ according as c, d have the same or opposite signs i.e., the absolute value of the correlation coefficient is independent of any change of scale.

EXAMPLE 14. *If* $r_{xy} = 0.6$, *find* r_{uv} *where*

(i) $u = 3x + 5, v = 4y - 3$; (ii) $u = 3x + 5, v = -4y + 3$. **[C.U. B. Com. (Hons.) 1989]**

SOLUTION. We know that if $u = \frac{x-a}{c}$ and $v = \frac{y-b}{d}$, then $r_{uv} = r_{xy}$ or $-r_{xy}$ according as c, d are of the same or opposite signs.

(i) $u = 3x + 5 = 3(x + \frac{5}{3}) = (x + \frac{5}{3})/\frac{1}{3}$ and $v = 4y - 3 = (y - \frac{3}{4})/\frac{1}{4}$. Here $c = \frac{1}{3}$ and $d = \frac{1}{4}$ and c, d are both *positive* i.e., they have the same sign.

$$\therefore \quad r_{uv} = r_{xy} = 0.6.$$

(ii) $u = 3x + 5 = 3(x + \frac{5}{3}) = (x + \frac{5}{3})/\frac{1}{3}$ and $v = -4y + 3 = -4(y - \frac{3}{4}) = (y - \frac{3}{4})/-\frac{1}{4}$. Here $c = \frac{1}{3}$ and $d = -\frac{1}{4}$ and c, d have opposite signs.

$$\therefore \quad r_{uv} = -r_{xy} = -0.6.$$

THEOREM 2. *Prove that the correlation coefficient r lies between − 1 and + 1, i.e.,* $-1 \le r \le 1$.

[C.U. B. Com. (Hons.) 1981, 1987; ICWAI June 1988]

PROOF. Let $(X_1, Y_1), (X_2, Y_2), \cdots, (X_n, Y_n)$ be the n pairs of observations on two variables X and Y.

$$\text{Let} \quad x_i = \frac{X_1 - \bar{X}}{\sigma_X} \quad \text{and} \quad Y_i = \frac{Y_i - \bar{Y}}{\sigma_Y},$$

where σ_X, σ_Y are the standard deviations of X, Y respectively.

We have

$$\Sigma x_i^2 = \sum \left(\frac{X_i - \bar{X}}{\sigma_X}\right)^2 = \frac{\Sigma(X_i - \bar{X})^2}{\sigma_X^2} = \frac{n\sigma_X^2}{\sigma_X^2} = n.$$

Similarly, $\Sigma y_i^2 = n$.

$$\Sigma x_i y_i = \sum \left[\left(\frac{X_i - \bar{X}}{\sigma_X}\right)\left(\frac{Y_i - \bar{Y}}{\sigma_Y}\right)\right] = \frac{\Sigma[(X_i - \bar{X})(Y_i - \bar{Y})]}{\sigma_X \sigma_Y} = n\frac{\Sigma[(X_i - \bar{X})(Y_i - \bar{Y})]}{n\sigma_X \sigma_Y} = nr,$$

where r is the correlation coefficient between X and Y.

Since the square of a quantity is never negative, we have

$$\Sigma(x_i + y_i)^2 \geq 0 \qquad (1)$$

$$\text{and} \quad \Sigma(x_i - y_i)^2 \geq 0 \qquad (2)$$

From (1), $\Sigma(x_i^2 + y_i^2 + 2x_i y_i) \geq 0$, or, $\Sigma x_i^2 + \Sigma y_i^2 + 2\Sigma x_i y_i \geq 0$,

or, $n + n + 2nr \geq 0$, or, $2n + 2nr \geq 0$, $[\because$ n is positive],

or, $r \geq -1$, i.e., $-1 \leq r$.

From (2), $\Sigma(x_i^2 + y_i^2 - 2x_i y_i) \geq 0$, or, $\Sigma x_i^2 + \Sigma y_i^2 - 2\Sigma x_i y_i \geq 0$,

or, $2n - 2nr \geq 0$, or, $2n(1 - r) \geq 0$,

or, $1 - r \geq 0$, or, $1 \geq r$, i.e., $r \leq 1$.

Combining $-1 \leq r$ and $r \leq 1$, we get $\mathbf{-1 \leq r \leq 1}$.

Hence the theorem follows.

Uses of Correlation Coefficient

The correlation coefficient r is used to measure the strength (or degree) of relationship between two variables. If the scatter diagram of the values of the variables indicates a linear path, the correlation coefficient is considered as a useful measure for finding the strength of relationship between the variables. A positive value of r shows that the movements of the variables are in the same direction, i.e., high values of one variable are associated with high values of the other, or low values are associated with low values of the other. When r is negative, the movements are in the opposite directions, i.e., high values of one variable are associated with low values of the other.

Properties of Correlation Coefficient

The important properties of correlation coefficient r are as follows:

(i) it is independent of any change of origin of reference and the units of measurement;

(ii) its value lies between -1 and $+1$, i.e., $-1 \leq r \leq +1$;

(iii) it is a *pure number* and it measures the *strength of association* between two variables.

6.6. PROBABLE ERROR OF CORRELATION COEFFICIENT

Let $(X_1, Y_1), (X_2, Y_2), \cdots, (X_n, Y_n)$ be n pairs of observations on two variables X and Y and r be the correlation coefficient between X and Y. Then the *Standard Error* (S.E.) of r is given by

$$\mathbf{S.E.\ of\ r} = \frac{\mathbf{1 - r^2}}{\sqrt{\mathbf{n}}}$$

and the *Probable Error* (P.E.) of r is given by

$$\mathbf{P.E.\ of\ r = 0.6745 \times (S.E.\ of\ r) = 0.6745\left(\frac{1 - r^2}{\sqrt{n}}\right)}.$$

P.E. or S.E. of r is used to examine the existence of correlation between two variables.

If $r <$ P.E. of r, then the value of r is *insignificant* and there is no correlation between the variables.

If $r > 6$ (P.E. of r), the value of r is *significant* and there is correlation between the variables.

The upper and lower limits within which the coefficient of correlation in the population is expected to lie are r + P.E. and $r-$ P.E.

$$\textit{Coefficient of Determination} = (\textit{Coefficient of correlation})^2 = r^2.$$

EXAMPLE 15. *Calculate the correlation coefficient and its probable error from the following results:*

$$\sum_{i=1}^{100} x_i = 280, \sum_{i=1}^{100} y_i = 60, \sum_{i=1}^{100} x_i^2 = 2384, \sum_{i=1}^{100} y_i^2 = 117, \sum_{i=1}^{100} x_i y_i = 438$$

[ICWAI (Final), July 1971]

SOLUTION.

$$r = \frac{\dfrac{\Sigma xy}{n} - \dfrac{\Sigma x}{n} \cdot \dfrac{\Sigma y}{n}}{\sqrt{\dfrac{\Sigma x^2}{n} - \left(\dfrac{\Sigma x}{n}\right)^2} \cdot \sqrt{\dfrac{\Sigma y^2}{n} - \left(\dfrac{\Sigma y}{n}\right)^2}} = \frac{\dfrac{438}{100} - \left(\dfrac{280}{100}\right) \cdot \left(\dfrac{60}{100}\right)}{\sqrt{\dfrac{2384}{100} - \left(\dfrac{280}{100}\right)^2} \cdot \sqrt{\dfrac{117}{100} - \left(\dfrac{60}{100}\right)^2}}$$

$$= \frac{4.38 - 2.8 \times 0.6}{\sqrt{23.84 - 7.84} \times \sqrt{1.17 - 0.36}} = \frac{2.7}{\sqrt{16} \times \sqrt{0.81}} = \frac{2.7}{4 \times .9} = \mathbf{0.75}.$$

$$\text{P.E. of } r = 0.6745 \times \frac{1 - (0.75)^2}{\sqrt{100}} = 0.6745 \times \frac{0.4375}{10} = \mathbf{0.02951}.$$

EXAMPLE 16. *In a correlation analysis, the values of the Karl Pearson's coefficient of correlation and its probable error were found to be* 0.90 *and* 0.04 *respectively. Find the value of "n".*

[CA May 1991]

SOLUTION. The probable error (P.E.) is given by P.E. $= 0.6745 \cdot \left(\frac{1-r^2}{\sqrt{n}}\right)$.

Here $r = 0.90$ and P.E. $= 0.04$; $n = ?$

$$\therefore \quad 0.04 = 0.6745\left\{\frac{1 - (0.9)^2}{\sqrt{n}}\right\}, \quad \text{or,} \quad \sqrt{n} = \frac{0.6745 \times (1 - .81)}{0.04} = \frac{0.6745 \times 0.19}{0.04} = 3.204 \text{ (approx.)}$$

$$\therefore \quad n = (3.204)^2 = 10.2656.$$

But n i.e., the number of samples cannot be a fraction.

Hence **n = 10.**

6.7. REGRESSION

By *regression* (linear) we mean average relationship between two variables, and this relationship is used to estimate or predict the most likely values of one variable for specified values of the other variable. One of the variables is called *independent or the explained variable* and the other is called *dependent or the explaining* variable. In this case, the *coefficient of determination* which gives the percentage variation in the explaining variable is given by

$$\textbf{Coefficient of determination} = r^2 = \frac{\text{Explain variance}}{\text{Total variance}}.$$

In the words of M. M. Blair : "Regression is the measure of the average relationship between two or more variables in terms of the original units of the data." If there are two or more independent variables, then regression is called multiple regression.

If $r = 0.9$, then $r^2 = 0.81 = 81\%$, which indicates that only 81% of the total variation has been explained and remaining 19% of the total variation remain unexplained.

Regression Equations

Prediction or estimation of most likely values of one variable for specified values of the other is done by using suitable equations involving the two variables. Such equations are known as *Regression equations.*

Regression Equation of Y on X

In linear regression if we fit a straight line of the type $Y = a + bX$ to the given data by the method of least squares, we obtain the regression equation of Y on X.

Let $(X_1, Y_1), (X_2, Y_2), \cdots, (X_n, Y_n)$ be n pairs of observations and let the straight line to be fitted to these data be

$$Y = a + bX \tag{1}$$

Applying the method of least squares, we get the following normal equations :

$$\mathbf{\Sigma Y = na + b\Sigma x} \tag{2}$$

$$\text{and} \quad \mathbf{\Sigma XY = a\Sigma X + b\Sigma X^2} \tag{3}$$

Dividing (2) by n, $\frac{\Sigma Y}{n} = a + b\frac{\Sigma X}{n}$ or, $\bar{Y} = a + b\bar{X}$ (4)

Subtracting (4) from (1), we get

$$Y - \bar{Y} = b(X - \bar{X}) \tag{5}$$

Now multiplying (2) by ΣX and (3) by n and then subtracting, we have

$$(\Sigma X)(\Sigma Y) - n\Sigma XY = b(\Sigma X)^2 - nb\Sigma X^2$$

$$\text{or,} \quad b\{n\Sigma X^2 - (\Sigma X)^2\} = n\Sigma XY - (\Sigma X)(\Sigma Y)$$

$$\text{or,} \quad b = \frac{n\Sigma XY - (\Sigma X)(\Sigma Y)}{n\Sigma X^2 - (\Sigma X)^2} = \frac{\frac{\Sigma XY}{n} - \left(\frac{\Sigma X}{n}\right)\left(\frac{\Sigma Y}{n}\right)}{\frac{\Sigma X^2}{n} - \left(\frac{\Sigma X}{n}\right)^2} \tag{6}$$

Replacing b by b_{YX} in (5), the regression equation of Y on X is

$$Y - \bar{Y} = b_{YX}(X - \bar{X}) \tag{7}$$

where b_{YX} is given by (6). Equation (7) is the regression equation of Y on X and it is used to estimate the most likely values of Y for given values of X.

Regression equation of X on Y

The regression equation of X on Y is the equation of the best fitted straight line of the type $X = a' + b'Y$ to the given data by the method of least squares.

Applying the principle of least squares, we get the following two normal equations for determining a' and b' :

$$\Sigma X = na' + b'\Sigma Y \tag{8}$$

$$\text{and} \quad \Sigma XY = a'\Sigma Y + b'\Sigma Y^2 \tag{9}$$

Solving (8) and (9) for a' and b' and proceeding as before, the regression equation of X on Y is

$$X - \bar{X} = b_{XY}(Y - \bar{Y}) \tag{10}$$

$$\text{where} \quad b_{XY} = \frac{\dfrac{\Sigma XY}{n} - \left(\dfrac{\Sigma X}{n}\right)\left(\dfrac{\Sigma Y}{n}\right)}{\dfrac{\Sigma Y^2}{n} - \left(\dfrac{\Sigma Y}{n}\right)^2}. \tag{11}$$

Formulae (6) and (11) give the values of b_{YX} and b_{XY} by using the original values of the variables X and Y.

Equation (10) is used to estimate the most likely values of X for given values of Y.

Regression Coefficients

b_{YX} and b_{XY} defined by (6) and (11) are called the *regression coefficients* of the two regression lines (7) and (10)

The formula for b_{YX} and b_{XY} may be written in different forms.

(i) We have cov $(X,Y) = \frac{\Sigma XY}{n} - (\frac{\Sigma X}{n})(\frac{\Sigma Y}{n})$ and $r = \frac{\text{cov}(X,Y)}{\sigma_X \sigma_Y}$, or, cov $(X,Y) = r\sigma_X\sigma_Y$.

∴ From (6) and (11), we get

$$b_{YX} = \frac{\text{cov}(X,Y)}{\sigma_X^2} = \frac{r\sigma_X\sigma_Y}{\sigma_X^2} = \frac{r\sigma_Y}{\sigma_X} \tag{A}$$

$$\text{and} \quad b_{XY} = \frac{\text{cov}(X,Y)}{\sigma_Y^2} = \frac{r\sigma_X\sigma_Y}{\sigma_Y^2} = \frac{r\sigma_X}{\sigma_Y} \tag{B}$$

$$\text{In this case } b_{YX} \times b_{XY} = \frac{r\sigma_Y}{\sigma_X} \times \frac{r\sigma_X}{\sigma_Y} = r^2 \tag{C}$$

i.e., the product of the two regression coefficients $= r^2$.

From (C), we see that b_{YX} and b_{XY} are either both positive or both negative, otherwise r^2 will be negative which is impossible. Again from (A) and (B), we see that b_{YX} and b_{XY} have the same sign as that of r i.e., if b_{YX} and b_{XY} are both *positive*, then r is *positive*, or if b_{YX} and b_{XY} are both *negative*, then r is negative.

(ii) Since σ_X, σ_Y, r are all independent of the choice of the origin of reference, b_{YX} and b_{XY} are also independent of the choice of origin. The formula for b_{YX} and b_{XY}, when the deviations are taken from the assumed mean, are given by

$$b_{YX} = \frac{\frac{\Sigma xy}{n} - \left(\frac{\Sigma x}{n}\right)\left(\frac{\Sigma y}{n}\right)}{\frac{\Sigma x^2}{n} - \left(\frac{\Sigma x}{n}\right)^2} \quad \text{and} \quad b_{XY} = \frac{\frac{\Sigma xy}{n} - \left(\frac{\Sigma x}{n}\right)\left(\frac{\Sigma y}{n}\right)}{\frac{\Sigma y^2}{n} - \left(\frac{\Sigma y}{n}\right)^2}$$

where $x = X - a$ and $y = Y - b$, a and b being the assumed means of X and Y respectively.

(iii) If $x = X - \bar{X}$ = deviation of X from its mean, and $y = Y - \bar{Y}$ = deviation of Y from its mean, then

$$b_{YX} = \frac{\frac{\Sigma xy}{n}}{\frac{\Sigma x^2}{n}} = \frac{\Sigma xy}{\Sigma x^2} \qquad [\because \ \Sigma x = 0 \ \text{ and } \ \Sigma y = 0.]$$

Similarly, $b_{XY} = \dfrac{\Sigma xy}{\Sigma y^2}$.

NOTE. We have two regression lines :

$$Y - \bar{Y} = b_{YX}(X - \bar{X}) \qquad \text{(i)}$$

$$\text{and} \quad X - \bar{X} = b_{XY}(Y - \bar{Y}) \qquad \text{(ii)}$$

Equation (i) is used to find the best estimates of Y for given values of X and (ii) is used to obtain the best estimates of X for given values of Y. As the equations (i) and (ii) have been derived under *two different assumptions*, one equation cannot serve both the purposes.

Equations (i) and (ii) will be *identical* if their gradients b_{YX} and $\frac{1}{b_{XY}}$ are equal i.e., if

$$b_{YX} = \frac{1}{b_{XY}}, \quad \text{or,} \quad b_{YX} \cdot b_{XY} = 1, \quad \text{or,} \quad r^2 = 1, \quad \text{i.e.,} \quad \text{if } r = \pm 1.$$

EXAMPLE 17. *From the following data, find the two regression equations :*

X :	1	2	3	4	5	6	7
Y :	2	4	7	6	5	6	5

SOLUTION.

TABLE 6.9 CALCULATIONS FOR REGRESSION EQUATIONS

X	Y	$x = X - \bar{X} = X - 4$	$y = Y - \bar{Y} = Y - 5$	x^2	y^2	xy
1	2	−3	−3	9	9	9
2	4	−2	−1	4	1	2
3	7	−1	2	1	4	−2
4	6	0	1	0	1	0
5	5	1	0	1	0	0
6	6	2	1	4	1	2
7	5	3	0	9	0	0
$28 = \Sigma X$	$35 = \Sigma Y$	0	0	$28 = \Sigma x^2$	$16 = \Sigma y^2$	$11 = \Sigma xy$

$$\bar{X} = \frac{\Sigma X}{n} = \frac{28}{7} = 4, \quad \bar{Y} = \frac{\Sigma Y}{n} = \frac{35}{7} = 5;$$

$$\therefore \quad b_{YX} = \frac{\Sigma xy}{\Sigma x^2} = \frac{11}{28} = 0.39 \text{ (approx.)} \quad \text{and} \quad b_{XY} = \frac{\Sigma xy}{\Sigma y^2} = \frac{11}{16} = 0.69 \text{ (approx.)}$$

Hence the regression equation of Y on X is

$$Y - \bar{Y} = b_{YX}(X - \bar{X}), \quad \text{or,} \quad Y - 5 = 0.39(X - 4) = 0.39X - 1.56, \quad \text{or,} \quad \mathbf{Y = 0.39X + 3.44}$$

and the regression equation of X on Y is

$$X - \bar{X} = b_{XY}(Y - \bar{Y}), \quad \text{or,} \quad X - 4 = 0.69(Y - 5) = 0.69Y - 3.45, \quad \text{or,} \quad \mathbf{X = 0.69Y + 0.55}.$$

EXAMPLE 18. *From the following results, obtain the two regression equations and estimate the yield of crops when the rainfall is* 29 *cms. and the rainfall when the yield is* 600 *kg.*

	Y (Yield in kgs.)	X (Rainfall in cms.)
Mean	508.4	26.7
S.D.	36.8	4.6

Coefficient of correlation between yield and rainfall = 0.52. **[CA May 1976]**

SOLUTION. We have $\bar{X} = 26.7, \bar{Y} = 508.4, \sigma_X = 4.6, \sigma_Y = 36.8, r = 0.52$.

The regression equation of Y on X is

$$Y - \bar{Y} = b_{YX}(X - \bar{X}), \quad \text{where} \quad b_{YX} = r\frac{\sigma_Y}{\sigma_X}, \quad \text{or,} \quad Y - 508.4 = 0.52 \times \frac{36.8}{4.6}(X - 26.7)$$

or, $Y - 508.4 = 4.16(X - 26.7)$, or, $Y = 508.4 + 4.16X - 111.072$

or, $\mathbf{Y = 4.16X + 397.328}$.

When $X = 29, Y = 4.16 \times 29 + 397.328 =$ **517.968 kgs.**

The regression equation of X on Y is

$$X - \bar{X} = b_{XY}(Y - \bar{Y}), \quad \text{where} \quad b_{XY} = r\frac{\sigma_X}{\sigma_Y}, \quad \text{or,} \quad X - 26.7 = 0.52 \times \frac{4.6}{36.8}(Y - 508.4)$$

or, $X - 26.7 = 0.065(Y - 508.4) = 0.065Y - 33.046$, or, $X = 26.7 + 0.065Y - 33.046$

or, $\mathbf{X = 0.065Y - 6.346}$.

When $Y = 600, X = 0.065 \times 600 - 6.346 =$ **32.654 kgs.**

EXAMPLE 19. *You are given the data relating to purchases and sales. Obtain the two regression equations by the method of least squares and estimate the likely sales when the purchases equal* 100.

Purchases :	62	72	98	76	81	56	76	92	88	49
Sales :	112	124	131	117	132	96	120	136	97	85

[CA May 1975]

SOLUTION.

TABLE 6.10 CALCULATIONS FOR REGRESSION EQUATIONS

Purchases X	Sales Y	$x = X - \bar{X}$ $= X - 75$	$Y = Y - \bar{Y}$ $= Y - 155$	x^2	y^2	xy
62	112	−13	−3	169	9	39
72	124	−3	9	9	81	−27
98	131	23	16	529	256	368
76	117	1	2	1	4	2
81	132	6	17	36	289	102
56	97	−19	−19	361	361	361
76	120	1	5	1	25	5
92	136	17	21	289	441	357
88	97	13	−18	169	324	−234
49	85	26	−30	676	900	780
$750 = \Sigma X$	$1150 = \Sigma Y$	0	0	$2240 = \Sigma x^2$	$2690 = \Sigma y^2$	$753 = \Sigma xy$

$$\bar{X} = \frac{\Sigma X}{n} = \frac{750}{10} = 75 \quad \text{and} \quad \bar{Y} = \frac{\Sigma Y}{n} = \frac{1150}{10} = 115,$$

$$b_{YX} = \frac{\Sigma xy}{\Sigma x^2} = \frac{1753}{2240} = 0.78 \quad \text{and} \quad b_{XY} = \frac{\Sigma xy}{\Sigma y^2} = \frac{1753}{2690} = 0.652.$$

The regression equation of Y on X is

$$Y - \bar{Y} = b_{YX}(X - \bar{X}), \quad \text{or,} \quad Y - 115 = 0.78(X - 75) = 0.78X - 58.50, \quad \text{or,} \quad \mathbf{Y = 0.78X + 56.5}. \tag{1}$$

The regression equation of X on Y is

$$X - \bar{X} = b_{XY}(Y - \bar{Y}), \quad \text{or,} \quad X - 75 = 0.652(Y - 115) = 0.652Y - 74.98, \quad \text{or,} \quad \mathbf{X = 0.652Y + 0.02}.$$

When $X = 100$, from (1) Y is given by $Y = 0.78 \times 100 + 56.5 = \mathbf{134.5}$.

EXAMPLE 20. *The regression equations calculated from a given set of observations are* $x = -0.4y + 6.4$ *and* $y = -0.6x + 4.6$. *Calculate* $\bar{x}, \bar{y}$ *and* r_{xy}. **[C.U. B. Com. (Hons) 1981]**

SOLUTION. We have

$$x = -0.4y + 6.4 \tag{1}$$

$$\text{and} \quad y = -0.6x + 4.6 \tag{2}$$

Putting $x = -0.4y + 6.4$ in (2), we get

$$y = -0.6(-0.4y + 6.4) + 4.6 = 0.24y - 3.84 + 4.6$$

$$\text{or,} \quad y(1 - 0.24) = 0.76, \quad \text{or,} \quad 0.76y = 0.76; \quad \therefore \quad y = 1.$$

From (1), $x = -0.4 \times 1 + 6.4 = -0.4 + 6.4 = 6$

$\therefore$ $\mathbf{\bar{x} = 6}$ and $\mathbf{\bar{y} = 1}$. [$\because$ $(\bar{x}, \bar{y})$ is the point of intersection of (1) and (2).]

Clearly, (1) is the regression equation of x on y and (2) is the regression equation of y on x.

$$\therefore \quad b_{xy} = -0.4 \quad \text{and} \quad b_{yx} = -0.6$$

$$\therefore \quad r_{xy}^2 = b_{xy} \cdot b_{yx} = -0.4 \times -0.6 = 0.24; \quad \therefore \quad r_{xy} = \pm\sqrt{0.24}.$$

Since b_{xy} and b_{yx} are *both negative*, r_{xy} is *negative*.

$$\therefore \quad \mathbf{r_{xy} = -\sqrt{0.24}}.$$

EXAMPLE 21. *You are given variance of* $X = 9$. *The regression equations are* $8X - 10Y + 66 = 0$ *and* $40X - 18Y = 214$.

Find (i) *Average values of X and Y,*
(ii) *Correlation coefficient between the two variables,*
(iii) *Standard Deviation of Y.* **[CA November 1977]**

SOLUTION. The regression equations are

$$8X - 10Y = -66 \qquad (1)$$
$$40X - 18Y = 214 \qquad (2)$$

Since the point $(\bar{X}, \bar{Y})$ lies on both the lines of regression (1) and (2), the means $\bar{X}$ and $\bar{Y}$ of X and Y are given by

$$8\bar{X} - 10\bar{Y} = -66 \qquad (3)$$
$$40\bar{X} - 18\bar{Y} = 214 \qquad (4)$$

Multiplying (3) by 5, we get

$$40\bar{X} - 50\bar{Y} = -330$$
From (4), $$40\bar{X} - 18\bar{Y} = 214$$

Subtracting, we get $$-32\bar{Y} = -544$$

$$\therefore \quad \mathbf{\bar{Y} = 17}.$$

Substituting $\bar{Y} = 17$ in (1), we get

$$8\bar{X} - 10 \times 17 = -66, \quad \text{or,} \quad 8\bar{X} = 170 - 66 = 104; \qquad \therefore \quad \bar{X} = 13.$$

We know that $r = \pm\sqrt{b_{YX} \cdot b_{XY}}$, where b_{YX} and b_{XY} are the regression coefficients of the two lines of regression.

From (1), $8X + 66 = 10Y$, or, $Y = \frac{4}{5}X + \frac{33}{5}$; $\quad \therefore \quad b_{YX} = \frac{4}{5}$.

From (2), $40X = 18Y + 214$, or, $X = \frac{9}{20}Y + \frac{107}{20}$; $\quad \therefore \quad b_{XY} = \frac{9}{20}$.

Since the regression coefficients are positive, the correlation coefficient r is also positive.

Hence $r = +\sqrt{\frac{4}{5} \times \frac{9}{20}} = \sqrt{\frac{9}{25}} = \frac{3}{5} = 0.6$.

Again $\sigma_X^2 =$ Variance of $X = 9$; $\quad \therefore \quad \sigma_X = 3$.

We have $b_{YX} = r \cdot \frac{\sigma_Y}{\sigma_X}$, or, $\frac{4}{5} = \frac{3}{5} \times \frac{\sigma_Y}{3} = \frac{\sigma_Y}{5}$; $\quad \therefore \quad \sigma_Y = 4$.

NOTE. Both the regression coefficients obtained in the above problem are less than 1 and, therefore, their product $b_{YX} \cdot b_{XY} = r^2 < 1$. If we choose (i) as the regression equation of X on Y and (2) as the regression equation of Y on X, we would get $b_{XY} = \frac{5}{4}$ and $b_{YX} = \frac{20}{9}$ so that $b_{XY} \cdot b_{YX} > 1$ which is impossible.

EXAMPLE 22. *In trying to evaluate the effectiveness in its advertising campaign, a firm compiled the following information :*

Year	1968	1969	1970	1971	1972	1973	1974	1975
Advertising Expenditure ('000 Rs.)	12	15	15	23	24	38	42	48
Sales (lakh Rs.)	5.0	5.6	5.8	7.0	7.2	8.8	9.2	9.5

Calculate the regression equation of sales on advertising expenditure. Estimate the probable sales when advertisement expenditure is Rs. 60 thousand.

SOLUTION.

TABLE 6.11 CALCULATIONS FOR REGRESSION EQUATION

Advertising expenditure (in '000 Rs.) X	Sales (in lakh Rs.) Y	$x = X - a$ $= X - 25$	$y = Y - b$ $= Y - 7$	x^2	y^2	xy
12	5.0	−13	−2.0	169	4.00	26.0
15	5.6	−10	−1.4	100	1.96	14.0
15	5.8	−10	−1.2	100	1.44	12.0
23	7.0	−2	0	4	0	0
24	7.2	−1	.2	1	.04	−.2
38	8.8	13	1.8	169	3.24	23.4
42	9.2	17	2.2	289	4.84	37.4
48	9.5	23	2.5	529	6.25	57.5
Total	—	$17 = \Sigma x$	$2.1 = \Sigma y$	$1361 = \Sigma x^2$	$21.77 = \Sigma y^2$	$170.1 = \Sigma xy$

We have

$$\bar{X} = a + \frac{\Sigma x}{n} = 25 + \frac{17}{8} = 25 + 2.25 = 27.125,$$

$$\bar{Y} = b + \frac{\Sigma y}{n} = 7 + \frac{2.1}{8} = 7 + 0.26 = 7.26,$$

$$b_{XY} = \frac{\Sigma xy - \dfrac{(\Sigma x)(\Sigma y)}{n}}{\Sigma x^2 - \dfrac{(\Sigma x)^2}{n}} = \frac{170.1 - \dfrac{17 \times 2.1}{8}}{1361 - \dfrac{(17)^2}{8}} = \frac{170.1 - 4.463}{1361 - 36.125} = \frac{165.637}{1324.875} = 0.125.$$

The regression line of sales (Y) on advertising expenditure (X) is

$$Y - \bar{Y} = b_{YX}(X - \bar{X}), \quad \text{or,} \quad Y - 7.26 = 0.125(X - 27.125)$$

$$\text{or,} \quad Y = 7.26 + 0.125X - 3.39 = 0.125X + 3.87, \quad \text{i.e.,} \quad Y = 0.125X + 3.87.$$

When $X = 60, Y = 0.125 \times 60 + 3.87 = 11.37$

i.e., the probable sales = **Rs. 11.37 lakhs** when the advertisement expenditure is Rs. 60 thousand.

6.8. PROPERTIES OF LINEAR REGRESSION

1. The two regression lines $Y - \bar{Y} = b_{YX}(X - \bar{X})$ and $X - \bar{X} = b_{XY}(Y - \bar{Y})$ intersect at the point $(\bar{X}, \bar{Y})$ whose coordinates are the means of X and Y.

2. $b_{YX} \cdot b_{XY} = r^2$, or, $r = \pm\sqrt{b_{YX} \cdot b_{XY}}$, i.e., the correlation coeffieient is the *geometric mean* (G.M.) of the regression coefficients.

3. Since $b_{YX} = r \cdot \frac{\sigma_Y}{\sigma_X}$ and $b_{XY} = r \cdot \frac{\sigma_X}{\sigma_Y}$, if $r = 0$, then $b_{YX} = 0$ and $b_{XY} = 0$. Also r, b_{YX} and b_{XY} all *have the same sign,* since σ_X and σ_Y are always positive.

4. The two regression lines will be *identical* if $b_{YX} = \frac{1}{b_{XY}}$, i.e., if $b_{YX} \cdot b_{XY} = 1$, i.e., if $r^2 = 1$, i.e., $r = \pm 1$. If $r = 0$, the two lines of regression become $Y - \bar{Y} = 0$ and $X - \bar{X} = 0$ which are perpendicular to each other.

Exercise 6(I)

[A]

Theory

1. (i) Define the term correlation. **[ICWAI June 1975; June 1977]**

(ii) Define positive and negative correlation. **[CA November 1975]**

2. (i) What is a scatter diagram ? Indicate by means of suitable scatter diagrams different types of correlation that may exist between the variables in bivariate data.

[ICWAI June 1974; June 1976]

(ii) Distinguish between Variance and Co-variance. **[CA November 1986]**

3. (i) Briefly explain the concept of regression and its use. **[CA November 1977]**

(ii) Explain the terms : Coefficient of correlation and Regression coefficients.

[C.U. B. Com. 1982]

(iii) Define "Regression". Why are there two regression lines? **[ICWAI December 1984]**

(iv) Explain the distinction between Regression and Correlation. **[CA Foundation June 1994]**

4. Define Rank correlation. Write down Spearman's Formula for rank correlation coefficient R. What are the limits of R ? Interpret the case when R assumes the minimum value.

[ICWAI June 1975; December 1976; CA November 1985]

5. Write short notes on—

(i) Scatter diagram. **[CA November 1975; 1976; 1978; 1982]**

(ii) Rank correlation coefficient. **[CA November 1977; C.U. B. Com. 1983]**

(iii) Regression equations. **[C.U. B. Com. 1983; CA May 1978, 1985, 1986]**

(iv) Spearman's coefficient of correlation. **[CA November 1985]**

6. (i) What are regression coefficients ? Show that

$$r^2 = b_{XY} \cdot b_{YX},$$

where the symbols have their usual meaning. What can you say about the angle between the regression lines when (i) $r = 0$, (ii) $r = \pm 1$, (iii) r increases from 0 to 1 ? **[ICWAI December 1976]**

(ii) What are the coefficients of linear regression ? Prove that the coefficient of correlation is the geometric mean of the coefficients of regression. **[C.U. B. Com. (Hons.) 1991]**

7. What are regression lines ? Why is it necessary to consider two lines of regression ? In case the two lines are identical, prove that the correlation coefficient is either + 1 or − 1.

[ICWAI December 1977]

8. Explain the concept of 'correlation' between two variables. Prove that r is independent of the origin of reference and the units of measurement. [ICWAI June 1975; January 1972]

9. Prove that the correlation coefficient r lies between -1 and $+1$.

[C.U. B. Com. (Hons.) 1981, 1987; ICWAI June 1988]

10. Obtain the equations of the two lines of regression for a bivariate distribution.

[ICWAI July 1970; C.U. B. Com. (Hons.) 1985, 1987]

11. What does regression coefficients indicate? Is it possible that one coefficient has a positive value whereas the other happens to be negative? If not why? [CA November 1984]

12. What is Correlation Analysis? Explain the rank method of computation of the coefficient of correlation. [CA Foundation December 1993]

[B]

Correlation

1. (i) Find the *coefficient of correlation* from the following data:

X :	1	2	3	4	5
Y :	3	2	5	4	6

[C.U. B. Com. 1984, 1987]

(ii) Calculate the *coefficient of correlation* from the following data :

X :	1	2	3	4	5
Y :	6	8	11	8	12

[C.U. B. Com. 1985, 1991]

2. Karl Pearson's coefficient of correlation between two variables X and Y is 0.52, their covariance is $+ 7.8$. If the variance of X is 16, find the *standard deviation of Y series.*

3. Calculate the correlation Coefficient between X and Y series from the following data :

(i) $\sum_{i=1}^{12}(X_i - \bar{X})^2 = 360,\ \sum_{i=1}^{12}(Y_i - \bar{Y})^2 = 250$ and $\sum_{i=1}^{12}(X_i - \bar{X})(Y_i - \bar{Y}) = 225.$

(ii) $n = 12,\ \Sigma X = 120,\ \Sigma Y = 130,\ \Sigma(X - 8)^2 = 150,\ \Sigma(Y - 10)^2 = 200$ and $\Sigma(X - 8)(Y - 10) = 50.$ [CA May 1992]

4. (i) The heights and weights of 15 persons are given below. Form a *two-way frequency table* with class-intervals $60'' - 62'', 62'' - 64''$ and so on and 50–55 kgs, 55–60 kgs. and so on.

Sl. No. :	1	2	3	4	5	6	7	8	9	10	11	12	13	14	15
Height :	61	65	68	62	60	63	67	69	61	64	63	65	66	64	68
Weight :	62	55	70	60	58	50	53	65	54	73	64	66	68	73	67

(ii) Draw a scatter diagram for the following bivariate data :

X	1	2	3	4	5	6
Y	6	4	3	5	4	2

[C.U. B. Com. 1982]

5. State in each case whether you would expect to find a *positive correlation*, a *negative correlation* or *no correlation* :

(i) The ages of husbands and wives,

(ii) Shoe size and intelligence,

(iii) Years of education and income,

(iv) Insurance companies's profits and the number of claims they have to pay,

(v) Amount of rainfall and yield of crop. **[C.U. M. Com.]**

6. Calculate *Pearson's coefficient of correlation* between advertisement cost and sales as per the data given below :

Advertisement Cost in '000 Rs. :	40	65	60	90	85	75	35	90	34	76
Sales in lakh Rs. :	45	56	58	82	65	70	64	85	50	85

7. Find the *coefficient of correlation* from the following data :

X :	10	12	13	16	17	20	25
Y :	19	22	24	27	29	33	37

[C.U. B. Com. 1989]

8. Calculate the Pearson's coefficient of correlation from the followng data using 44 and 26 respectively as the origin of X and Y.

X :	43	44	46	40	44	42	45	42	38	40	42	57
Y :	29	31	19	18	19	27	27	29	41	30	26	10

[CA May 1978]

9. In order to find the correlation coefficient between two variables X and Y from 12 observations, the following calculations were made :

$$\Sigma X = 30, \quad \Sigma Y = 5, \quad \Sigma X^2 = 670, \quad \Sigma Y^2 = 285, \quad \Sigma XY = 334.$$

On subsequent verification it was found that the pair $(X = 11, Y = 4)$ was copied wrongly, the correct value being $(X = 10, Y = 14)$. Find the *correct value of correlation coefficient.*

[ICWAI June 1975]

10. Find the *coefficient of correlation* between the ages of husbands and the ages of wives given below, in the form of a two-way frequency table :

Ages of Husbands (in years)→

	20–25	25–30	30–35	35–40	Total
15–20	20	10	3	2	35
20–25	4	28	6	4	42
25–30	—	5	11	—	16
30–35	—	—	2	—	2
35–40	—	—	—	—	0
Total	24	43	22	6	95

11. (i) Compute the *correlation coefficient* between the corresponding values of X and Y in the following table :

X :	2	4	5	6	8	11
Y :	18	12	10	8	7	5

[C.U. B. Com. (Hons.) 1990]

(ii) Multiply each X-value in the table by 2 and add 6. Multiply each value of Y in the table by 3 and subtract 15. Find the *correlation coefficient* between the two new sets of values. Explain why you do or do not obtain the same result as in (i).

12. (i) Write down Spearman's formula for determining rank correlation coefficient R. For the two series, we have $\Sigma D^2 = 30$ and $N = 10$; find R. [C.U. B. Com. 1983]

(ii) The rankings of 10 individuals at the start and on the finish of a course of training are as follows :

Individuals :	A	B	C	D	E	F	G	H	I	J
Rank Before :	1	6	3	9	5	2	7	10	8	4
Rank After :	6	8	3	7	2	1	5	9	4	10

Calculate Spearman's coefficient of correlation. [B.U. B. Com. 1975]

13. (i) In a contest, two judges ranked eight candidates A, B, C, D, E, F, G and H in order of their performance, as shown in the following table. Find the rank correlation coefficient.

	A	B	C	D	E	F	G	H
First Judge :	5	2	8	1	4	6	3	7
Second Judge :	4	5	7	3	2	8	1	6

[ICWAI June 1975]

(ii) Calculate the coefficient of correlation from the following data by the method rank differences:

Rank of X:	10	4	2	5	8	5	6	9
Rank of Y:	10	6	2	5	8	4	5	9

[CA Foundation June 1994]

14. (i) Calculate the coefficient of rank correlation for the following data of marks obtained by 10 students in Book-keeping and Commercial Arithmetic at an examination :

Student No. :	1	2	3	4	5	6	7	8	9	10
Marks in Book-keeping (out of 60) :	43	29	35	18	40	11	49	10	5	22
Marks in Commercial-Arithmetic (out of 40) :	36	6	17	14	25	10	32	0	3	20

[B.U. B. Com. 1974]

(ii) Find the *Rank Correlation Coefficient* for the following data of marks obtained by 10 students in Mathematics and Statistics :

Student (Roll No.) :	1	2	3	4	5	6	7	8	9	10
Marks in Mathematics :	80	38	95	30	74	84	91	60	66	40
Marks in Statistics :	85	50	92	58	70	65	88	56	52	46

[C.U. B. Com. 1986]

[C]

Regression

1. From the following data, find the two regression equations :

X :	1	2	3	4	5
Y :	2	3	5	4	6

Find also the most probable value of Y when $X = 2.5$. [C.U. B. Com. 1983, 1985, 1989]

2. (i) Find the two regression equations from the following data:

X:	57	58	59	59	60	61	62	64
Y:	77	78	75	78	82	82	79	81

(ii) From the following data, obtain the two regression equations :

Sales :	91	97	108	121	67	124	51	73	111	57
Purchases :	71	75	69	97	70	91	39	61	80	47

[CA May 1977]

3. (i) If two regression coefficients are 0.9 and 0.2, what would be the value of the correlation coefficient r ?

(ii) Find out the value of r and σ_Y from the following data :

$$3X = Y, \quad 4Y = 3X \quad \text{and} \quad \sigma_X = 2.$$

4. For some bivariate data, the following results were obtained :

The mean value of $X = 53.2$, the mean value of $Y = 27.9$, the regression coefficient of Y on $X = -1.5$ and the regression coefficient of X on $Y = -0.2$.

Find (i) the most probable value of Y when $X = 60$, (ii) the coefficient of correlation between X and Y. **[C.U. M. Com. 1974]**

5. Find the regression equation of X on Y from the following data :

$$\Sigma X = 24, \quad \Sigma Y = 44, \quad \Sigma XY = 306, \quad \Sigma X^2 = 164, \quad \Sigma Y^2 = 574, \quad N = 4.$$

6. (a) You are given the following data :

	X	Y
Arithmetic Mean :	20	25
Standard Deviation :	5	4

Correlation Coefficient between X and Y is 0.6. Find the two *regression equations.*

[C.U. B. Com. 1986]

(b) You are given the following data :

Correlation coefficient between X and $Y = 0.66$.

	X	Y
Arithmetic Mean :	36	85
Standard Deviation :	11	8

(i) Find the two regression equations

(ii) Estimate the value of X when $Y = 75$. **[CA November 1978]**

7. (i) For certain X and Y series, which are correlated, the two lines of regression are

$$5X - 6Y + 90 = 0 \quad \text{and} \quad 15X - 8Y - 130 = 0.$$

Find which is the regression equation of Y on X and which is that of X on Y. Find the means of the two series and the correlation coefficient between them.

(ii) Two lines of regression are given by $x + 2y = 5$ and $2x + 3y = 8$ and $\sigma_x^2 = 12$. Calculate the values of $\bar{x}, \bar{y}, \sigma_x^2$ and r.

8. You are given variance of $Y = 16$. The regression equations are $4X - 5Y + 33 = 0$ and $20X - 9Y = 107$, find

(i) the average values of X and Y, (ii) correlation coefficient between X and Y, and (iii) Standard Deviation of X.

9. The following data are given for marks in English (X) and Mathematics (Y) at a certain examination :

	English	Mathematics
Mean Marks :	39.5	47.5
S.D. Marks :	10.8	16.8

Coefficient of correlation between marks in English and Mathematics = + 0.42. Find the two regression equations.

Using these regression equations estimate the value of Y for $X = 50$ and the value of X for $Y = 30$. **[Delhi U. M. Com. 1974]**

10. A department store gives in-service training to its salesmen which is followed by a test. It is considering whether it should terminate the services of any salesman who does not do well in the test. The following data give the test scores and sales made by nine salesmen during a certain period.

Test Scores :	14	19	24	21	26	22	15	20	19
Sales ('00 Rs.) :	31	36	48	37	50	45	33	41	39

Calculate the coefficient of correlation between the test scores and the sales. Does it indicate that the termination of services of low test scores is justified ? If the firm wants a minimum sales volume of Rs. 3,000.00, what is the minimum test score that will ensure continuation of service ?

[CA November 1974]

11. While calculating the coefficient of correlation between two variables X and Y the following results were obtained.

The number of observations = 25; $\Sigma X = 125; \Sigma Y = 100; \Sigma X^2 = 650; \Sigma Y^2 = 460; \Sigma XY = 508$. It was, however, later discovered at the time of checking that two pairs of observations (X, Y) were copied (6, 14) and (8, 6) while the correct values were (8, 12) and (6, 8) respectively. Determine the correct value of the coefficient of correlation.

Hence find the correct equations of the two lines of regression. **[ICWAI June 1978]**

12. Calculate the *coefficient of correlation, using the method of concurrent deviations*, between supply and demand given below. Also comment on your result:

Year :	1982	1983	1984	1985	1986	1987	1988	1989	1990	1991
Supply ('000 tons) :	140	130	135	128	150	132	138	128	159	168
Demand ('000 tons) :	260	270	280	290	246	252	264	275	278	247

[HINTS. See worked out Example 13.]

Answers

[B]

1. (i) + 0.8; (ii) 0.775. **2.** 3.75. **3.** (i) + 0.75; (ii) 0.215. **5.** (i) Positive correlation; (ii) No correlation; (iii) Positive correlation; (iv) Negative correlation; (v) Positive correlation. **6.** + 0.78. **7.** + 0.99. **8.** −0.73. **9.** + 0.78. **10.** + 0.61. **11.** (i) −0.92; (ii) −0.92. **12.** (i) 0.82; (ii) 0.394. **13.** (i) + $\frac{2}{3}$; (ii) 0.83. **14.** (i) +0.87, (ii) 0.82.

[C]

1. $Y = 0.9X + 1.3, X = 0.9Y - 0.6$, 3.55. **2.** (i) $Y = \frac{2}{3}X + 39; X = \frac{6}{11}Y + 16.9$; (ii) $Y = 0.61X + 15.1$ and $X = 1.36Y - 5.2$. **3.** (i) + 0.4; (ii) + 0.5, $\sigma_Y = 3$. **4.** (i) 17.7; (ii) −0.5477. **5.** $X = 0.467Y + 0.863, X = 3.7$. **6.** (a) $Y = 0.48X + 15.4$ and $X = 0.75Y + 1.25$; (b) $Y = 0.48X + 67.72, X = 0.9075Y - 41.1375$ and 26.925. **7.** (i) $5X - 6Y + 90 = 0, 10X - 8Y - 130 = 0$ and $\bar{X} = 30, \bar{Y} = 40, r = \frac{2}{3}$. (ii) $\bar{x} = 1, \bar{y} = 2, r = -3\frac{\sqrt{3}}{2} = -0.866$ and $\sigma_y^2 = 4$. **8.** $\bar{X} = 13, \bar{Y} = 17, r = +0.6$ and $\sigma_X = 3$. **9.** $X = 0.27Y + 26.675, Y = 0.653X + 21.693, X = 34.775$ and $Y = 54.343$. **10.** $r = 0.947$; the value 0.947 of r is high enough to justify the proposal; $Y = 1.61X + 7.8, X = 0.557Y - 2.4$, minimum test score that will ensure contiñuation of service = 14.3 or 14. **11.** $\frac{2}{3}, Y = 0.8X$ and $9X - 5Y = 25$. **12.** −0.58.

Exercise 6(II)

[A]

Correlation and Regression

1. Mention the correct value of correlation coefficient with reasons :

(i)

X :	2	3	5	8	9
Y :	4	6	10	16	18

(ii)

Rank of X :	1	2	3	4	5
Rank of Y :	5	4	3	2	1

2. Draw the scatter diagram of the following bivariate data :

X :	2	3	5	7	9	12	13
Y :	3	2	7	8	11	10	16

State the nature of correlation, if any, from the scatter diagram.

3. (i) If $N = 10$ and $\Sigma d^2 = 280$, what is the value of rank correlation coefficient?

(ii) If $R = 0.6$ and $N = 10$, find the value of ΣD^2, where D is the difference in ranks of the two series.

(iii) If $b_{xy} = -0.4$ and $b_{xy} = -0.9$, find r_{xy}.

4. From the data given below, find the number of items :

$$r = 0.5, \quad \Sigma xy = 120, \quad \Sigma x^2 = 80, \sigma_y = 9.$$

(Here x, y are the deviations from arithmetic average). [D.U. M. Com. 1972]

5. If $x = X - \bar{X}$ and $y = Y - \bar{Y}$ and $\Sigma x^2 = 10, \Sigma y^2 = 24$, $\Sigma xy = 12$, then find the coefficient of correlation between the two variables X and Y.

6. Calculate the coefficient of correlaiton from the folllowing data:

X :	1	2	3	4	5
Y :	6	8	11	8	12

7. Write down a formula the coefficient of correlation between two variables X and Y. Obtain the coefficient from the following data:

	X	Y
Number of observations:	15	15
Arithmetic mean:	25	18
Sum of the squares of deviations from mean:	136	138

Sum of the product of the deviations of X and Y series from their respective means $= 122$.

[Delhi U. B. Com. 1989]

8. (i) Calculate the correlation coefficient between the height of father and son from the given data :

Height of Father (in inches) :	64	65	66	67	68	69	70
Height of Son (in inches) :	66	67	65	68	70	68	72

[CA November 1980]

(ii) Find the correlation coefficient between X and Y from the following data:

X :	16	14	15	28	35	48
Y :	74	61	50	54	43	46

[Madras U. B. Com. 1984]

9. Consider the following data :

X :	1	2	3	4	5	6
Y :	6	4	3	5	4	2

(i) Draw a scatter diagram from the data.

(ii) From the scatter diagram guess whether the coefficient of correlation is closer to + 1, – 1 or zero.

(iii) Calculate r by using Pearson product-moment correlation coefficient formula.

(iv) Find the linear regression of Y on X by the method of least squares. Graph this line on the scatter diagram. Predict the value of Y if $X = 4$. **[ICWAI December 1982]**

10. The marks secured by a group of 10 students in the Written Selection Test (X) and in the Aptitude Test (Y) are given below :

X :	44	42	40	52	39	32	24	46	41	50
Y :	24	25	28	29	32	35	36	41	45	50

Calculate product moment correlation coefficient and rank correlation coefficient. Why the two coefficients differ ? **[ICWAI June 1982]**

11. In the estimation of regression equations of two variables X and Y the following results were obtained : $\bar{X} = 90, \bar{Y} = 70, N = 10, \Sigma x^2 = 6360, \Sigma y^2 = 2860, \Sigma xy = 3900$.

Obtain the two equations. **[CA May 1983]**

12. The marks obtained by 25 students in Statistics and Economics are given below. The first figure in brackets indicates the marks in Statistics and the second marks in Economics.

(14,12)	(0,2)	(1,5)	(7,3)	(15,9)
(2,8)	(12,18)	(9,11)	(5,3)	(17,13)
(19,18)	(11,7)	(10,13)	(13,16)	(16,14)
(6,10)	(4,1)	(11,14)	(8,3)	(9,15)
(13,11)	(14,17)	(10,10)	(11,7)	(15,15)

Prepare a two way table taking the magnitude of each class-interval as 4 marks, the first being equal to 0 and less than 4. **[CA May 1982]**

13. (i) Calculate coefficient of rank correlation of the following data of marks of eight students in Accountancy and Statistics :

Student's Number :	1	2	3	4	5	6	7	8
Marks in Statistics :	52	63	45	36	72	65	45	25
Marks in Accountancy :	62	53	51	25	79	43	60	33

[B.U. B. Com. 1979]

(ii) In a bivariate sample, the sum of the squares of differences between the ranks of observed values of two variables is 231 and the correlaiton coefficient between them is -0.4. Find the number of pairs. **[Gujarat U. 1982; ICWAI December 1987]**

14. Ten competitors in a beauty contest are ranked by three judges in the following order.

1st Judge :	1	6	5	10	3	2	4	9	7	8
2nd Judge :	3	5	8	4	7	10	2	1	6	9
3rd Judge :	6	4	9	8	1	2	3	10	5	7

Use the rank correlation coefficient to determine which pair of judges has the nearest approach to common tastes in beauty. **[P.U. B. Com. 1970; R.U. 1973]**

15. Find the coefficient of rank correlation between marks obtained in Mathematics and Statistics:

Students :	A	B	C	D	E	F	G	H	I	J
Marks in Mathematics :	30	20	40	50	30	20	30	50	10	0
Marks in Statistics :	15	40	40	45	20	30	15	50	20	10

16. The coefficient of rank correlation of the ranks obtained by 10 students in Statistics and Accountancy was found to be 0.5. It was later discovered that the difference in ranks in the two subjects obtained by one student was wrongly taken as 3 instead of 7. Find the correct coefficient of rank correlation. **[B.U. B. Com.]**

[HINTS. Using **Edward Spearman's formula,** find $\Sigma D^2 = 82.5$ and then find the correct value of $\Sigma D^2 = 82.5 - 3^2 + 7^2 = 122.5$ and then find the correct value of R]

17. Write down a formula for finding the coefficient of correlation between two variables X, Y and obtain the coefficient from the following data :

	X	Y
No. of observations :	15	15
Arithmetic Means :	25	18
Sum of the Squares of the Deviations from the Mean :	136	138

Sum of the product of the deviations of X and Y series from their respective means is 122.

[ICWAI June 1981]

18. (i) If $U = 2X + 11$ and $V = 3Y + 7$, what will be the correlation coefficient between U and V? Justify your statement. **[ICWAI June 1981]**

(ii) Calculate Pearson's coefficient of correlation from the following data :

X :	45	55	56	58	60	65	68	70	75	80	85
Y :	56	50	48	60	62	64	65	70	74	82	90

Take 65 and 70 as the assumed averages of X, Y : **[ICWAI June 1980]**

19. With the following data in 6 cities calculate the coefficient of correlation by Pearson's method between the density of population and *the death rate :*

Cities	Area in Square Miles	Population in '000	Number of Deaths
A	150	30	300
B	180	90	1440
C	100	40	560
D	60	42	840
E	120	72	1224
F	80	24	312

[HINTS. Density of population = Population ÷ Area = 200, 500, 400, 700, 600, 300 and Death rate per thousand = Death ÷ Population = 10, 16, 14, 20, 17, 13. Now find r].

20. (i) Two variables gave the following data : $\bar{x} = 20, \bar{y} = 15, \sigma_x = 4, \sigma_y = 3, r = 0.7$.

Obtain the two regression equations and find the most likely value of y when $x = 24$.

[CA November 1980]

(ii) The correlation coefficient between X and Y is 0.60. If the variance of $X = 2.25$, the variance of $Y = 4.00$, mean of $X = 10$ and mean of $Y = 20$, find the equations of the regression lines of (i) Y on X, (ii) X on Y. **[ICWAI December 1979]**

21. (i) If the average price of a commodity (per kg.) at Bombay and Madras are Rs. 2.40 and Rs. 2.79 respectively, estimate the most likely price at Bombay corresponding to the price of Rs. 2.33 at Madras. Given the S.D. of prices at Bombay and at Madras are 0.326 and 0.207 respectively and coefficient of correlation between the prices = 0.774.

(ii) The equations of two lines of regression obtained in a correlation analysis are the following:

$$2x + 3y - 8 = 0 \quad \text{and} \quad x + 2y - 5 = 0.$$

Obtain the value of the correlation coefficient and the variance of y, given that the variance of x is 12. **[ICWAI June 1981]**

22. (i) The equations of two regression lines in a correlation analysis are as follows :

$$3x + 2y = 26 \quad \text{and} \quad 6x + y = 31.$$

A student obtains the mean values $\bar{x} = 7, \bar{y} = 4$ and the value of the correlation coefficient $r = 0.5$. Do you agree with him ? If not, suggest your results. **[ICWAI June 1982]**

(ii) In a partially destroyed record the following data are available : Variance of $x = 25$, Regression equation of x upon y is $5x - y = 22$ and regression equation of y upon x is $64x - 45y = 25$. Find (i) Mean values of x and y, (ii) S.D. of y, (iii) Coefficient of correlation between x and y.

[CA November 1981]

23. The two regression lines are given by $3x + 2y = 6$ and $7x + 5y = 12$. (i) Estimate y when $x = 10$; (ii) Calculate the correlation coefficient value between x and y; (iii) What percentage of total variation remains unexplained by the regresion by y on x? **[ICWAI December 1994]**

[HINTS. If $3x + 2y = 6$ be the regression equation of x on y and $7x + 5y = 12$ be the regression equation of y on x, then $b_{xy} = -\frac{2}{3}$ and $b_{yx} = -\frac{7}{5}$ and $r^2 = b_{yx} \cdot b_{xy} = \frac{14}{15}(< 1)$.

$\therefore \quad r = -\sqrt{\frac{14}{15}}$. Percentage of the total variation remains explained $= r^2 = \frac{14}{15}$, etc.]

24. From the following tables find the correlation coefficient between age and playing habit of students:

Age (years):	15	16	17	18	19	20
No. of students:	250	200	150	120	100	80
Regular players:	200	150	90	48	30	12

What conclusion do you draw from the result? **[H.P. U. 1987; Delhi U. B. Com. 1989]**

[HINTS. If X and Y denote *age* (years) and percentage of regular players respectively, then $Y = \frac{200}{250} \times 100, \frac{150}{200} \times 100, \frac{90}{150} \times 100$, etc., i.e., $Y = 80, 75, 60, 40, 30, 15$. Now find r between X and Y.]

[B]

1. The following data show the marks of 10 students in Mathematics and Statistics in an examination:

Marks in Mathematics :	45	70	65	40	80	40	50	70	85	60
Marks in Statistics :	35	80	70	40	90	45	60	80	80	50

Find *Karl Pearson's coefficient of correlation* between the marks in Mathematics and Statistics and comment on the result. **[CA May 1989]**

[HINTS. See worked out Example 5.]

2. Calculate Karl Pearson's coefficient of correlation from the following data, using 20 as the working mean for price, and 70 as the working mean for demand:

Price :	14	16	17	18	19	20	21	22	23
Demand :	84	78	70	75	66	67	62	58	60

[CA May 1986]

3. Calculate *Spearman's coefficient of correlation* between marks assigned to ten students by judges X and Y in a certain competitive test as shown below:

Sl. No.	1	2	3	4	5	6	7	8	9	10
Marks by judge X	52	53	42	60	45	41	37	38	25	27
Marks by judge Y	65	68	43	38	77	48	35	30	25	50

[HINTS. See worked out Example 9] **[CA November 1988]**

4. Calculate *Rank correlation coefficient* from the following marks given out of 200 by two judges, X and Y, in a music competition to 8 participants:

Sl. No.	1	2	3	4	5	6	7	8
Marks awarded by X	74	98	110	70	65	85	88	59
Marks awarded by Y	121	133	170	102	90	152	160	85

Also give your comment on the computed coefficient. **[CA November 1990]**

[HINTS. See worked out Example 9.]

5. Compute the appropriate regression equation for the following data:

X (Independent Variable) :	2	4	5	6	8	11
Y (Dependent Variable) :	18	12	10	8	7	5

[CA November 1986]

[HINTS. Find the regresson equation of Y on X. See worked out Example 17.]

6. Using the following information you are required to:

(i) obtain the linear regression of Y on X;

(ii) estimate the level of defective parts delivered when inspection expenditure amounts to Rs. 28,000.

$\Sigma X = 424, \Sigma XY = 12815, \Sigma Y^2 = 15123, \Sigma Y = 363, \Sigma X^2 = 21926, n = 10.$

X means expenditure on inspection ('000 ruppes).

Y means defective parts delivered ('00). **[CA May 1990]**

[HINTS. $\bar{X} = \Sigma X/n = 42.4, \bar{Y} = \Sigma Y/n = 36.3, b_{YX} = \frac{1281.5-42.4\times 36.3}{2192.6-(42.4)^2} =$ etc.]

7. Given is the following information:

	X	Y
	Rs.	Rs.
Arithmetic average	6	8
Standard deviation	5	40/3

Coefficient of correlation between X and $Y = 8/15$.

Find (i) the regression coefficient of Y on X; (ii) the regression equation of X on Y; (iii) the most likely value of Y when $X = 100$ rupees. **[CA November 1987]**

[HINTS. See worked out Example 18.]

8. Given that the variance of $x = 9$ and the regression lines are $8x - 10y + 66 = 0, 40x - 18y = 214$, find the coefficient of correlation between x and y. Find also the Standard Deviation of y. **[CA May 1988]**

[HINTS. See worked out Example 21.]

9. Find the regression coefficient of Y on X from the following regression equations:

$$5X = 22 + Y$$
$$64X = 24 + 45Y.$$

Is it possible to calculate the standard deviation of Y from the given information? Answer with reason. **[CA November 1989]**

[HINTS. $b_{XY} = 1/5, b_{YX} = 64/45 = 1.42$, where $b_{XY} \cdot b_{YX} = 64/225 < 1$. See also worked out Example 21.]

10. Given below marks obtained in an examination by ten students in two subjects Mathematics Statistics:

Score in Math:	58	59	60	65	66	52	75	31	46	48
Score in Stat.:	56	87	89	46	93	65	44	54	78	68

Calculate the correlation coefficient. **[ICWAI June 1994]**

11. The bivariate frequency distribution based on monthly salary and age of 100 clerks working in some large scale commercial organisation is as under:

Monthly Salary (Rs.) / Age (Years)	600–700	700–800	800–900	900–1000
20 and less than 30	16	6	—	—
30 and less than 40	4	10	4	4
40 and less than 50	—	4	18	12
50 and less than 60	—	—	10	12

Compute Karl Pearson's coefficient of correlation between age and monthly salary of clerks and comment on it. **[CA May 1987]**

[HINTS. See worked out Example 8.]

12. Find the coefficient of correlation using the method of concurrent deviations from the following data:

Year :	1981	1982	1983	1094	1985	1986	1987	1988	1989
Supply :	250	260	271	284	270	280	285	294	288
Price :	380	370	350	338	365	354	336	290	310

Comment on your result.

Answers

[A]

1. (i) 1; (ii) −1. **3.** (i) −0.7; (ii) 66; (iii) −0.6. **4.** 10. **5.** 0.77. **6.** 0.77. **7.** 0.89. **8.** (i) 0.81; (ii) −0.758. **9.** (iii) $r = -0.68$; (iv) $Y + 0.514X = 5.8$, $X + 0.9Y = 7.1, 7.856$. **10.** 0.081, 0.018; difference due to some loss of information. **11.** $Y = 0.6132X - 14.812; X = 1.3636Y - 5.45$. **13.** 0.64. **14.** $R_{12} = -0.212, R_{23} = -0.297, R_{13} = 0.636$; The first and the 3rd Judge have the nearest approach to common tastes in beauty. **15.** 0.63. **16.** 0.258. **17.** 0.89. **18.** (i) $r_{UV} = r_{XY}$ since the correlation coefficient is independnt of any change of origin and scale; (ii) 0.92. **19.** 0.99. **20.** (i) $y = 0.52x + 4.5, x = 0.93y + 6.05; 17.1$; (ii) $Y = 0.8X + 12$ and $X = 0.45Y + 1$. **21.** (i) Rs. 1.90; (ii) $-\sqrt{\frac{3}{2}}, 4$. **22.** (i) No. $\bar{x} = 4, \bar{y} = 7$ and $r = -0.5$. (ii) $\bar{x} = 6, \bar{y} = 8, \sigma_y = \frac{40}{3}$ and $r = \frac{8}{15}$. **23.** $11.6; -\sqrt{\frac{14}{15}}$ or $-0.966; 6\frac{2}{3}\%$. **24.** −0.99; high negative correlation between age and playing habit of students.

[B]

1. 0.91; high positive correlation (i.e., strength of association is very high). **2.** −0.95. **3.** 0.54. **4.** 0.93; high degree of positive relationship. **5.** $Y = 18.04 - 1.34X$. **6.** $Y = 63.96 - 06525X; 4569$. **7.** 1.42, $X = 0.2Y + 4.4$, Rs. 141.48. **8.** 0.6, 4. **9.** 1.42; No, as σ_x is not known. **10.** −0.0124. **11.** 0.77; high correlation between age and monthly salary. **12.** $r = -1$, i.e., there is a perfect inverse association (or relationship) between supply and price.

CHAPTER 7

INDEX NUMBERS

7.1. INTRODUCTION

A very useful statistical tool for measuring changes in a variable or a group of related variables with respect to time, geographic location or other characteristic is *Index Number.* Index Number, in its simplest form, represents a special case of an average, generally weighted average, compiled from a sample of items judged to be representative of the whole. In this chapter, we shall study various types of Index Numbers, their uses, and the principles involved in the construction of Index Numbers.

7.2. INDEX NUMBER

An Index Number is a number which is used as a device for comparison between the price, quantity or value of a group of articles (related variables) in different situations, e.g., at a certain place or a period of time and that at another place or period of time. When the comparison is in respect of prices, it is called an Index Number of Prices; when in respect of physical quantities, it is termed as Index Number of Quantities. Other Index Numbers are defined in the same manner.

The period of time, usually a year and sometimes a week or a month, with whose prices the price of other periods are compared, is called the *Base period.* Thus, index numbers are meant for comparison of variations arising out of the difference in situations, e.g., change of time or change of place.

The statement that the Index Number of wholesale prices in Calcutta for the year 1989 was 150 compared to 1983, means that there was a net increase in the prices of wholesale commodities in the Calcutta market to the extent of 50 per cent. In comparing the prices in a given year with the price of a particular year called the *base year* (or base period), the price at the base year is taken as 100, and the price at the given period of time (called *current year*), for which the Index Number is required, is expressed as a percentage of the base year price. Thus, if for any item, p_1 be the current price (i.e., price in the current year) and p_o, the base price, then corresponding

$$\textbf{Index Number} = \frac{p_1}{p_o} \times 100 = \frac{\textbf{Current price}}{\textbf{Base price}} \times 100.$$

7.3. PRICE RELATIVE

A *Price-Relative* or simply a *Relative* is the ratio of the price of a certain commodity at the current year to the price at the base year, expressed as a percentage. So,

$$\text{Price-Relative} = \frac{\text{Current year's price}}{\text{Base year's price}} \times 100 \quad \text{or} \quad \frac{p_1}{p_o} \times 100.$$

Price-Relatives are thus the same as Index Numbers for prices.

7.4. SELECTION OF BASE

Every index number is associated with a base period. The base selected in constructing index numbers should suffer from no abnormalities, i.e., the base period (year, month or day) should be so selected that there is no war, famine, widespread earthquake or flood, etc., causing abnormalities (boom or depression) in the prices (or quantities) in that period.

Usually, bases are selected in three different ways, and according to these three types of base periods, the following are the three methods of constructing Index Numbers:

(a) *Fixed Base Method,* (b) *Chain Base Method* and (c) *Average Base Method.*

(a) Fixed Base Method: Simple and Composite Index Numbers

In Fixed Base Method, a year is fixed as base period and the prices during the base year are represented by 100. The Price-Relatives of the other years are then the required Index Numbers.

Simple Index Numbers

EXAMPLE 1.

TABLE 7.1 PRICE INDEX OF A SINGLE COMMODITY VIZ. RICE

Year	Price of Rice per Ql. (Rs.)	Index No. with 1960 as Base Year	Index No. with 1957 as Base Year
1957	40	$(40/50) \times 100 = 80$	100
1958	36	$(36/50) \times 100 = 72$	$(36/40) \times 100 = 90$
1959	48	96	$(48/40) \times 100 = 120$
1960	50	100	125
1961	44	88	110
1962	52	104	130
1963	46	92	115

These Index Numbers are Simple Index Numbers.

Composite Index Numbers

In the case of more than one item, their price-relatives with respect to a selected base are determined separately. The statistical average of these relatives is called a *Composite Index Number* or *simply an Index Number* in respect of the items. The *arithmetic mean* is the most popularly used average for the purpose.

EXAMPLE 2.

TABLE 7.2 PRICE INDEX OF RICE, WHEAT AND JAWAR (BASE YEAR: 1957)

Year	Price of Rice per Ql. (Rs.)	Price of Wheat per Ql. (Rs.)	Price of Jowar per Ql. (Rs.)	Index Numbers			Composite Index No.
				Rice	Wheat	Jowar	
1957	40	25	20	100	100	100	100
1958	36	21	24	90	84	120	98
1959	48	27	21	120	108	105	111
1960	50	26	22	125	104	110	113
1961	44	23	19	110	92	95	99
1962	52	28	23	130	112	115	119
1963	46	24	17	115	96	85	98.67

Here the simple (unweighted) arithmetic mean of the three price-relatives of the three commodities, in each year, has been taken as the Composite Index Number.

When weights are attached to different commodities, the weighted arithmetic mean of the Price-Relatives is to be determined for the Composite Index Number.

(b) Chain Base Method

When year to year comparison is desired, Index Numbers are determined by a method known as *Chain-Base Method.* In this method, each year is taken as the base for the immediately next year, the first year itself being its own base. For example, if Index Numbers for 1957, 1958, 1959, 1960 and 1961 are to be constructed, 1960 will be the base for 1961, 1959 for 1960, 1958 for 1959, 1957 for 1958 and 1957 itself for 1957.

Such indices are particularly found suitable for use in business, where changes with reference to immediate past are considered more important than a relative-change with remoter period. These indices are comparatively free from seasonal variations.

Some of the advantages of Chain-Base Index Numbers are: *new items may be readily included or old ones dropped in their calculations;* also *such indices are more free from seasonal variations than the Fixed Base Indices.*

EXAMPLE 3.

TABLE 7.3 PRICE INDEX OF RICE (CHAIN-BASE METHOD)

Year	Price of Rice per Ql. (Rs.)	Calculations	Chain-Base Index Numbers
1957	40	$\frac{40}{40} \times 100 =$	100
1958	36	$\frac{36}{40} \times 100 =$	90
1959	48	$\frac{48}{36} \times 100 =$	133.3
1960	50	$\frac{50}{48} \times 100 =$	104.2
1961	44	$\frac{44}{50} \times 100 =$	88
1962	52	$\frac{52}{44} \times 100 =$	118.2

The *Chain-Base Index Numbers are also known as Link Index Numbers.*

EXAMPLE 4.

TABLE 7.4 CONVERSION OF FIXED BASE INDEX NUMBERS OF RICE TO CHAIN-BASE INDEX NUMBERS

Year	Fixed Base Index No.	Conversion	Chain-Base Index Numbers
1958	90	$\frac{90}{90} \times 100 =$	100
1959	120	$\frac{120}{90} \times 100 =$	133.3
1960	125	$\frac{125}{120} \times 100 =$	104.2
1961	110	$\frac{110}{125} \times 100 =$	88
1962	130	$\frac{130}{110} \times 100 =$	118.2

EXAMPLE 5.

TABLE 7.5 CONVERSION OF CHAIN-BASE INDEX NUMBERS TO FIXED BASE INDEX NUMBERS

Year	Chain-Base Index No.	Conversion	Fixed Base Index No.
1957	120		120
1958	115	$\frac{120}{100} \times 155 =$	138
1959	75	$\frac{138}{100} \times 75 = \frac{207}{2} =$	103.5
1960	80	$\frac{207}{2 \times 100} \times 80 = \frac{414}{5} =$	82.8
1961	87.5	$\frac{414}{5 \times 100} \times \frac{175}{2} = \frac{1449}{20} =$	72.5

(c) Average Base Method

The *average of a number of years' prices* may be used as *base-price,* in determining index numbers. This has the effect of minimising the abnormalities of any particular year.

EXAMPLE 6. *Prepare index numbers of prices of rice for five years with the average price as base:*

Year :	1957	1958	1959	1960	1961
Rate per Rupee :	2.500 kg.	4 kg.	3.125 kg.	3.500 kg.	2.536 kg.

After converting the prices into rupees per Ql. (1 Ql. = 100 kg.) the whole working is as under:

TABLE 7.6 PRICE INDEX OF RICE WITH THE AVERAGE OF THE FIVE YEARS' PRICE AS BASE-PRICE

Year	Price per Ql. (Rs.)	Average Price (Base-Price) (Rs.)	Calculations	Index No.
1957	40		$\frac{40}{33} \times 100 =$	121.2
1958	25		$\frac{25}{33} \times 100 =$	75.8
1959	32	33	$\frac{32}{33} \times 100 =$	97.0
1960	28.57		$\frac{28.57}{33} \times 100 =$	86.6
1961	39.43		$\frac{39.43}{33} \times 100 =$	119.5

NOTE. Price of 2.5 kg. = Re. 1; $\therefore$ Price of 100 kg. $= \frac{100}{2.5}$ = Rs. 40.
Price of 4 kg. = Re. 1; $\therefore$ Price of 100 kg. $= \frac{100}{4}$ = Rs. 25, and so on.

7.5. Methods of Construction of Index Numbers

The following are the different methods of construction of *Index Numbers of Prices* of different commodities.

1. Fixed Base Method

A. Method of Aggregates

(1) Simple Aggregate of Prices;
(2) Weighted Aggregate of Prices.

B. Method of Relatives

(1) Simple Arithmetic Mean of Price Relatives
(2) Simple Geometric Mean of Price Relatives
(3) Weighted Arithmetic Mean of Price Relatives
(4) Geometric Mean of two weighted Aggregates of Prices (*Special case*).

2. Chain Base Method

Simple Arithmetic or Geometric Mean of Link Relatives (Chain Index).

Notations

For the purpose of showing the above modes of construction by mathemetical formulae, the following symbols will be used:

$p_o', p_o'', p_o''', \cdots =$ prices of items 1, 2, 3, ... respectively in the base year, say Y_o.
$q_o', q_o'', q_o''', \cdots =$ quantities of items 1, 2, 3, ... respectively in the base year, Y_o.
$p_1', p_1'', p_1''', \cdots =$ prices of items 1, 2, 3, ... respectively in the current year Y_1.
$q_1', q_1'', q_1''', \cdots =$ quantities of items 1, 2, 3, ... respectively in the current year Y_1.

Similar notations for prices and quantities of items 1, 2, 3, ... respectively in the years Y_2, Y_3 etc., will be used. However, p_o, q_o, and p_1, q_1 will generally refer to the price and quantity at the base year (Y_o) and at the current year (Y_1) respectively, without any specific mention about the different items

$I_{01} =$ Index Number for the year Y_1 with the year Y_o as base.
$I_{12} =$ Index Number for the year Y_2 with the year Y_1 as base, and so on.

A. Method of Aggregates

1. Simple Aggregate of Prices

The price per standard unit for each of the items included in the group is aggregated or totalled for the base year as well as for the current year separately. The total price for the current year expressed as a percentage of the total for the base year, gives the Index Number. Thus, symbolically,

Simple Aggregative Price Index

$$I_{01} = \frac{p_1' + p_1'' + p_1''' + \cdots}{p_o' + p_o'' + p_o'''} \times 100 = \frac{\Sigma p_1}{\Sigma p_o} \times 100.$$

EXAMPLE 1.

TABLE 7.7 DETERMINATION OF SIMPLE AGGREGATIVE INDEX NUMBER

Commodity	Base (1961) Price (Rs. per Ql.) p_o	Current (1965) Price (Rs. per Ql.) p_1
Rice	32	50
Wheat	25	25
Oil (edible)	90	100
Fish	120	140
Potato	35	40
Total	$302 = \Sigma p_o$	$355 = \Sigma p_1$

$$\therefore \text{ Simple aggregative index number } (I_{01}) = \frac{\Sigma p_1}{\Sigma p_o} \times 100 = \frac{355}{302} \times 100 = \mathbf{117.5}.$$

2. Weighted Aggregate of Prices

In this type, the prices in the current year and the base year are both weighted by some quantities (or weights). The weighted prices are then aggregated and the ratio of the aggregate for the current year to the aggregate for the base year, expressed as a percentage, gives the desired Index.

If $w', w'', ..., w^{(n)}$ are the respective weights, then the *weighted aggregative price index* is given by

Weighted Aggregative Price Index

$$I_{01} = \frac{p_1'w' + p_1''w'' + \cdots + p_1^{(n)}w^{(n)}}{p_o'w' + p_o''w'' + \cdots + p_o^{(n)}w^{(n)}} \times 100 = \frac{\Sigma p_1 w}{\Sigma p_o w} \times 100.$$

NOTE. Students should note that the same set of weights are to be used both for the base year and the current year.

EXAMPLE 2. *Find, by the weighted Aggregative Method, the Index Number from the following data:* [B.U. B. Com. 1966; N.B.U. B. Com. 1969]

TABLE 7.8 DETERMINATION OF WEIGHTED AGGREGATIVE INDEX NUMBER

Commodity	Base (1961) Price (Rs. per Ql.) (p_o)	Current (1965) Price (Rs. per Ql.) (p_1)	Weight (w)	$p_1 w$	$p_o w$
Rice	32	50	8	400	256
Wheat	25	25	6	150	150
Oil (edible)	90	100	7	700	630
Fish	120	140	3	420	360
Potato	35	40	5	200	175
Total	...	...	...	1,870	1,571

$\therefore$ Weighted aggregative index number $(I_{01}) = \dfrac{\Sigma p_1 w}{\Sigma p_o w} \times 100 = \dfrac{1870}{1571} \times 100 = \mathbf{119.03}$.

There are various ways of *weighting,* depending on the nature of weights used.

I. If base year quantities are used as weights, we have an Index Number known as **Laspeyre's Index.** Thus,

$$\textbf{Laspeyre's Index } (I_{01}) = \frac{p_1'q_o' + p_1''q_o'' + p_1'''q_o''' + \cdots}{p_o'q_o' + p_o''q_o'' + p_o'''q_o''' + \cdots} \times 100 = \frac{\Sigma p_1 q_o}{\Sigma p_o q_o} \times 100$$

$$= \frac{\text{Sum of prices of base period quantities at current prices}}{\text{Sum of prices of base period quantities at base prices}} \times 100.$$

II. If the *current year quantities are used as weights,* the Index Number arrived at is known as **Paasche's Index.**

$$\textbf{Paasche's Index } (I_{01}) = \frac{p_1'q_1' + p_1''q_1'' + p_1'''q_1''' + \cdots}{p_o'q_1' + p_o''q_1'' + p_o'''q_1''' + \cdots} \times 100 = \frac{\Sigma p_1 q_1}{\Sigma p_o q_1} \times 100$$

$$= \frac{\text{Sum of prices of current period quantities at current prices}}{\text{Sum of prices of current period quantities at base prices}} \times 100.$$

NOTE. 1. In Laspeyre's Index, the weights (base year quantities q_o) do not change from year to year. Thus only information on latest prices is to be collected. But in Paasche's Index, the weights being current year quantities q_1, the latest information on weights (i.e., quantities) as well as prices must be obtained. Thus computation of a Paasche's Index involves more labour in collection of data.

NOTE. 2. According to the *law of supply and demand* people tend to purchase more when prices are low and to purchase less when prices are high. This law is valid if the need for commodities is not absolutely essential. In Laspeyres' Index $\Sigma p_1 q_o$ will be somewhat higher than it should be by the law of supply and demand, so that total cost would be less than predicted by $\Sigma p_1 q_o$. Thus Laspeyres' Index $\frac{\Sigma p_1 q_o}{\Sigma p_o q_o}$ tends to be higher than it should be.

In Laspeyres' Index if q_o is replaced by q_1, we get Paasche's Index. This interchange of q_o and q_1 tends to make the Paasche's Index lower than it should be.

EXAMPLE 3. *Calculate the Index Number from the following data, by using Laspeyre's formula.*

TABLE 7.9 CALCULATION OF INDEX NUMBER (LASPEYRE'S FORMULA)

Commodity	Base Year (1957) Quantities (q_o)	Base Year (1957) Prices (Rs.) (p_o)	Current Year (1959) Prices (Rs.) (p_1)	($p_1 q_o$)	($p_o q_o$)
Rice	20	40	48	960	800
Wheat	16	25	27	432	400
Oil (edible)	8	95	105	840	760
Fish	10	110	120	1200	1100
Milk	6	80	100	600	480
Total	—	—	—	4,032	3,540

By Laspeyre's formula, required Index Number $= \dfrac{\Sigma p_1 q_o}{\Sigma p_o q_o} \times 100 = \dfrac{4032}{3540} \times 100 = 113.9.$

III. Another system of weighting makes use of both the base year quantities and the current year quantities. In fact, *the sum (or average) of both these quantities* is used as weight and we get an Index Number known as **Marshall-Edgeworth's Index.**

$$\textbf{Marshall-Edgeworth's Index } (I_{01}) = \frac{p_1'(q_o' + q_1') + p_1''(q_o'' + q_1'') + p_1'''(q_o''' + q_1''') + \cdots}{p_o'(q_o' + q_1') + p_o''(q_o'' + q_1'') + p_o'''(q_o''' + q_1''') + \cdots} \times 100$$

$$= \frac{\Sigma p_1(q_o + q_1)}{\Sigma p_o(q_o + q_1)} \times 100.$$

IV. Bowley's Index (I_{01}) : *The Arithmetic Mean of Laspeyre's Index and Paasche's Index is known as* **Bowley's Index.**

$$\text{Thus } \textbf{Bowley's Index } (I_{01}) = \frac{1}{2} \text{ (Laspeyre's Index + Paasche's Index)}$$

$$= \frac{1}{2}\left(\frac{\Sigma p_1 q_o}{\Sigma p_o q_o} + \frac{\Sigma p_1 q_1}{\Sigma p_o q_1}\right) \times 100.$$

B. Method of Relatives

1. Simple Arithmetic Mean of Price Relatives

Expressed in symbols, $100\dfrac{p_1'}{p_o'}$, $100\dfrac{p_1''}{p_o''}$, $100\dfrac{p_1'''}{p_o'''}, \cdots$

are the price relatives of items 1, 2, 3, ... respectively. The Index Number, calculated by this method is given by

$$I_{01} = \frac{1}{n}\left(100\frac{p_1'}{p_o'} + 100\frac{p_1''}{p_o''} + 100\frac{p_1'''}{p_o'''} + \cdots\right),$$

(where n is the number of items included in the group).

$$= \frac{100}{n}\left(\frac{p_1'}{p_o'} + \frac{p_1''}{p_o''} + \frac{p_1'''}{p_o'''} + \cdots\right) = \frac{100}{n}\sum\left(\frac{p_1}{p_o}\right).$$

2. Simple Geometric Mean of Price Relatives

The Index Number computed by this method is given by

$$I_{01} = \sqrt[n]{100\frac{p_1'}{p_o'} \times 100\frac{p_1''}{p_o''} \times 100\frac{p_1'''}{p_o'''} \times \cdots} = 100\sqrt[n]{\frac{p_1'}{p_o'} \times \frac{p_1''}{p_o''} \times \frac{p_1'''}{p_o'''} \times \cdots};$$

$$\therefore \quad \log I_{01} = \log 100 + \frac{1}{n}\Sigma \log \frac{p_1}{p_o}.$$

3. Weighted Arithmetic Mean of Price Relatives

When the weights $w_1, w_2, \cdots, w_n$ are attached to the respective commodities, the Index Number, calculated as the weighted arithmetic mean of price-relatives, is given by

$$I_{01} = \frac{100}{\Sigma w}\left(\frac{p_1' w_1}{p_o'} + \frac{p_1'' w_2}{p_o''} + \cdots + \frac{p_1^{(n)} w_n}{p_o^{(n)}}\right), \quad \text{i.e.,} \quad I_{01} = \frac{100}{\Sigma w}\sum\frac{p_1 w}{p_o}.$$

But, for all practical purposes, the weights adopted in this method are the values (= price × quantity) of items. There are several Index Number calculated as the weighted A.M. of price-relatives, depending on the nature of weights used.

1. The Index Number calculated as the *arithmetic mean of price-relatives weighted by the base year values* $p_o q_o$ is given by

$$I_{01} = \frac{\sum\left(100\frac{p_1}{p_o} \times p_o q_o\right)}{\Sigma p_o q_o} = \frac{\Sigma(100 p_1 q_o)}{\Sigma p_o q_o}, \quad \text{or,} \quad I_{01} = \frac{\Sigma p_1 q_o}{\Sigma p_o q_o} \times 100 \quad \text{which is } \textbf{Laspeyres' Index.}$$

2. The A.M. of price-relatives weighted by values of current year quantities at base year prices $p_o q_1$ is **Paasche's Index** given by

$$I_{01} = \frac{\sum\left(100\frac{p_1}{p_o} \times p_o q_1\right)}{\Sigma p_o q_1} = \frac{\Sigma p_1 q_1}{\Sigma p_o q_1} \times 100.$$

Weighted Geometric Mean of Price Relatives

The Index Number, calculated by this method, is not very much in use. It is given by

$$I_{01} = 100\left\{\left(\frac{p_1'}{p_o'}\right)^{w_1} \times \left(\frac{p_1''}{p_o''}\right)^{w_2} \times \cdots \times \left(\frac{p_1^{(n)}}{p_o^{(n)}}\right)^{w_n}\right\}^{1/\Sigma w},$$

where $w_1, w_2, \cdots, w_n$ are the weights attached to the respective commodities;

$$\therefore \quad \log I_{01} = \log 100 + \frac{1}{\Sigma w}\sum w \log \frac{p_1}{p_o}.$$

Weighted Harmonic Mean of Price Relatives

The Index Number calculated as the *Harmonic Mean* of price-relatives weighted by *current year values* $p_1 q_1$ is given by

$$I_{01} = \frac{\Sigma p_1 q_1}{\sum\left\{(p_1 q_1)\Big/\left(\frac{p_1}{p_o} \times 100\right)\right\}} = \frac{\Sigma p_1 q_1}{\Sigma p_o q_1} \times 100, \quad \text{which is } \textbf{Paasche's Index} \text{ Number.}$$

4. Special Index: Geometric Mean of Two Aggregative Price Index Numbers

The Geometric mean of Laspeyres' Index and Paasche's Index is known as Fisher's Ideal Index, after the name of Irving Fisher.

$$\textbf{Fisher's Ideal Index } (I_{01}) = \sqrt{\text{Laspeyre's Index} \times \text{Paasche's Index.}} = \mathbf{100}\sqrt{\frac{\Sigma p_1 q_o}{\Sigma p_o q_o} \times \frac{\Sigma p_1 q_1}{\Sigma p_o q_1}}.$$

NOTE.. Fisher's Ideal Index is of special importance, because geometric mean is useful in averaging ratios and percentages and Index Number shows percentage changes. Also Fisher's Ideal

Index Number obeys Time Reversal Test and Factor Reversal Test which are the tests for good Index Numbers.

General Index from Group Indices

The items (or commodities) included in construcing an Index Number are divided into some groups—similar or related items falling in the same group. Index Number for each group (called *Group Index*) is then determined. The **General Index** is the Arithmetic Mean of the group indices and it is given by the formula:

$$\textbf{General Index} = \frac{\Sigma wI}{\Sigma w}, \quad \text{where } I = \text{Group Index and } w = \text{group weight.}$$

7.6. ILLUSTRATIVE EXAMPLES

EXAMPLE 1. *Find, by the Arithmetic-mean method, the Index Number from the following data:*

Commodity	Base Price (Rs.)	Current Price (Rs.)
Rice	30	35
Wheat	22	25
Fish	54	64
Potato	20	25
Coal	15	18

[C.U. B. Com. 1976]

SOLUTION. The required Index Number I_{01}, by the *Arithmetic Mean Method,* is given by

$$I_{01} = \frac{100}{n}\Sigma\frac{p_1}{p_o} = \frac{100}{5}\left(\frac{35}{30}+\frac{25}{22}+\frac{64}{54}+\frac{25}{20}+\frac{18}{15}\right) = 20\left(\frac{7}{6}+\frac{25}{22}+\frac{32}{27}+\frac{5}{4}+\frac{6}{5}\right)$$

$$= \frac{70}{3}+\frac{250}{11}+\frac{640}{27}+25+24 = 23.333+22.727+23.704+49 = 118.764 = \mathbf{118.76}.$$

EXAMPLE 2. *Find, by Arithmetic Mean Method, the index number from the following data:*

Commodity	Base Price	Current Price	Weight
Rice	30	52	8
Wheat	25	30	6
Fish	130	150	3
Potato	35	49	5
Oil	70	105	7

[B.U. B. Com. 1974]

SOLUTION.

TABLE 7.10 CALCULATIONS OF WEIGHTED A.M. OF PRICE-RELATIVES

Commodity	Base Price (p_o)	Current Price (p_1)	Weight w	$\frac{p_1}{p_o}$	$\frac{p_1}{p_o} \times w$
Rice	30	52	8	1.73	13.84
Wheat	25	30	6	1.20	7.20
Fish	130	150	3	1.15	3.45
Potato	35	49	5	1.40	7.00
Oil	70	105	7	1.50	10.50
Total	—	—	$29 = \Sigma w$	—	$41.99 = \Sigma\left(\frac{p_1}{p_o} \times w\right)$

$\therefore$ The required Index Number I_{01} is given by $I_{01} = \frac{100}{\Sigma w}\Sigma\left(\frac{p_1 w}{p_o}\right) = \frac{100}{29} \times 41.99$

$$= \frac{4199}{29} = 144.793 = \mathbf{144.79}.$$

EXAMPLE 3. *The following table gives weights (base-year price × quantity) and price relatives for* 1929 *and* 1930 *with* 1928 *as base-year for four commodities:*

Commodity	Price Relatives		Weights
	1929	1930	
A	125	112.5	6
B	120	110	10
C	$83\frac{1}{3}$	$91\frac{2}{3}$	6
D	75	125	1

Calculate the index nuber for 1930, using unweighted Arithmetic Mean of the price-relatives.

[C.U. B. Com. 1966]

Find also the index number for 1929, using weighted A.M. of price-relatives.

SOLUTION. Using unweighted A.M. of the price-relatives,

$$\text{required index number } = \frac{1}{4}\left(112.5 + 110 + 91\frac{2}{3} + 125\right) = \frac{1}{4}\left(112\frac{1}{2} + 110 + 91\frac{2}{3} + 125\right)$$

$$= \frac{1}{4} \times \left(439\frac{1}{6}\right) = \frac{1}{4} \times \frac{2635}{6} = \frac{2635}{24} = \mathbf{109.79}.$$

Using weighted A.M. of the price-relatives, the required index number

$$= \frac{100}{\Sigma w}\sum\frac{p_1 w}{p_o} = \frac{1}{\Sigma w}\sum\left(\frac{p_1}{p_o} \times 100\right)w = \frac{1}{23}\left(125 \times 6 + 120 \times 10 + 83\frac{1}{3} \times 6 + 75 \times 1\right)$$

$$= \frac{1}{23}(750 + 1200 + 500 + 75) = \frac{1}{23} \times 2525 = \mathbf{109.78}.$$

EXAMPLE 4. *Prepare Index Numbers of prices for three years with the average prices as base from the following data:*

	Rate per Rupee		
	Wheat	Cotton	Oil
1st Year :	4 kg.	2 kg.	2 kg.
2nd Year :	3 kg.	1.500 kg.	1.250 kg.
3rd Year :	2.500 kg.	1 kg.	0.750 kg.

[S.U. B. Com.]

SOLUTION. After converting the prices into rupees per Ql. (1Ql. = 100 kg.) the working is as shown below:

TABLE 7.11 INDEX NUMBERS FOR THREE YEARS (AVERAGE BASE METHOD)

Commodities	Base-Price Average Price (per Ql.) Rs.	1st Year		2nd Year		3rd Year	
		Price (per Ql.) Rs.	Price Relatives	Price (per Ql.) Rs.	Price Relatives	Price (per Ql.) Rs.	Price Relatives
Wheat	32.78	25	76.27	33.33	101.68	40	122.03
Cotton	72.22	50	69.23	66.67	92.32	100	138.46
Oil	87.78	50	56.96	80	91.14	133.33	151.89
Total	—	—	202.46	—	285.14	—	412.38

∴ Applying simple Arithmetic-Mean method of Relatives, the required Index Numbers are:

$$= \frac{202.46}{3} = \mathbf{67.5 \text{ for 1st yr;}} \quad \frac{285.14}{3} = \mathbf{95.0 \text{ for 2nd yr;}} \quad \text{and} \quad \frac{412.38}{3} = \mathbf{137.5 \text{ for 3rd yr.}}$$

NOTE.. Base price for wheat $= (25+33.33 + 40) \div 3 = 32.78$, and price-relative for wheat $= (25 \div 32.78) \times 100 = 76.27$.

EXAMPLE 5. *From the table of group index number and group weights given below, calculate the cost of living index.*

Group	Group Index Number	Weight
Food	428	45
Clothing	240	15
Fuel and Light	200	8
House Rent	125	20
Others	170	12

[C.U. B. Com. 1978]

SOLUTION. The cost of living index (or general index from group indices) I_{01} is given by

$$I_{01} = \frac{\Sigma wI}{\Sigma w}, \quad \text{where } I = \text{group index and } w = \text{group weight}$$

TABLE 7.12 CALCULATIONS FOR THE COST OF LIVING INDEX

Group	Index I	Weight w	wI
Food	428	45	19260
Clothing	240	15	3600
Fuel and Light	200	8	1600
House Rent	125	20	2500
Others	170	12	2040
Total	—	$100 = \Sigma w$	$29000 = \Sigma wI$

$$\therefore \quad I_{01} = \frac{29000}{100} = \mathbf{290}.$$

EXAMPLE 6. *Calculate the Laspeyres' and the Paasche's Index Numbers for the following data:*

Commodity	Base Year		Current Year	
	Quantity	Price per lb. Rs. P.	Quantity	Price per lb. Rs. P.
A	10.00	0.80	11.0	0.70
B	8.0	0.85	9.0	0.90
C	5.0	1.30	5.5	0.80

[M.U. B. Com. 1976]

SOLUTION.

TABLE 7.13 CALCULATIONS FOR LASPEYRES' AND PAASCHE'S INDICES

Commodity	Base Year		Current Year		$p_o q_o$	$p_o q_1$	$p_1 q_o$	$p_1 q_1$
	Price p_o	Quantity q_o	Price p_1	Quantity q_1				
A	0.80	10.0	0.70	11.0	8.00	8.80	7.00	7.70
B	0.85	8.0	0.90	9.0	6.80	7.65	7.20	8.10
C	1.30	5.0	0.80	5.5	6.50	7.15	4.00	4.40
Total	—	—	—	—	21.30 $= \Sigma p_o q_o$	23.60 $= \Sigma p_o q_1$	18.20 $= \Sigma p_1 q_o$	20.20 $= \Sigma p_1 q_1$

$$\therefore \quad \text{Laspeyre's Index} = \frac{\Sigma p_1 q_o}{\Sigma p_o q_o} \times 100 = \frac{18.20}{21.30} \times 100 = 85.446 = \mathbf{85.45 \text{ (approx.)}}$$

$$\text{Paasche's Index} = \frac{\Sigma p_1 q_1}{\Sigma p_o q_1} \times 100 = \frac{20.20}{23.60} \times 100 = 85.593 = \mathbf{85.59 \text{ (approx.)}}$$

EXAMPLE 7. *Compute the Laspeyre's and Paasche's price index numbers for the year* 1987 *using the following data concerning four commodities:*

Quantity (kg.)	Commodity			
	A	B	C	D
in 1982	8	10	15	20
in 1987	6	5	10	15
Price per kg. (Rs.)				
in 1982	20	50	40	20
in 1987	40	60	50	20

[CA May 1989]

SOLUTION.

TABLE 7.14 CALCULATIONS FOR LASPEYRE'S AND PAASCHE'S INDEX NUMBERS

Commodity	1982		1987		$p_0 q_0$	$p_0 q_1$	$p_1 q_0$	$p_1 q_1$
	Price p_0	Quantity q_0	Price p_1	Quantity q_1				
A	20	8	40	6	160	120	320	240
B	50	10	60	5	500	250	600	300
C	40	15	50	10	600	400	750	500
D	20	20	20	15	400	300	400	300
Total					1660 $= \Sigma p_0 q_0$	1070 $= \Sigma p_0 q_1$	2070 $= \Sigma p_1 q_0$	1340 $= \Sigma p_1 q_1$

$$\therefore \quad \text{Laspeyre's Price Index} = \frac{\Sigma p_1 q_0}{\Sigma p_0 q_0} \times 100 = \frac{2070}{1660} \times 100 = \mathbf{124.7}$$

$$\text{and Paasche's Price Index} = \frac{\Sigma p_1 q_1}{\Sigma p_0 q_1} \times 100 = \frac{1340}{1070} \times 100 = \mathbf{125.23}.$$

EXAMPLE 8. *The following table gives the prices and quantities of four commodities A, B, C and D for the years* 1985 *and* 1988. *Calculate the price index for* 1988 *with* 1985 *as base by using Marshall-Edgeworth's method. Compare this index with Laspeyre's index number:*

Commodity	1985		1988	
	Price	Quantity	Price	Quantity
A	40	10	50	7
B	20	5	30	8
C	30	6	40	10
D	10	9	20	10

[CA May 1991]

SOLUTION.

TABLE 7.15 CALCULATIONS FOR MARSHALL-EDGEWORTH'S INDEX

Commodity	1985		1988		p_0q_0	p_0q_1	p_1q_0	p_1q_1
	Price p_0	Quantity q_0	Price p_1	Quantity q_1				
A	40	10	50	7	400	280	500	350
B	20	5	30	8	100	160	150	240
C	30	6	40	10	180	300	240	400
D	10	9	20	10	90	100	180	200
Total					770 $= \Sigma p_0q_0$	840 $= \Sigma p_0q_1$	1070 $= \Sigma p_1q_0$	1190 $= \Sigma p_1q_1$

$$\therefore \text{ Marshall-Edgeworth's Index} = \frac{\Sigma p_1(q_0+q_1)}{\Sigma p_0(q_0+q_1)} \times 100 = \frac{\Sigma p_1q_0 + \Sigma p_1q_1}{\Sigma p_0q_0 + \Sigma p_0q_1} \times 100$$

$$= \frac{1070+1190}{770+840} \times 100 = \frac{2260}{1610} \times 100 = 140.37.$$

$$\text{Laspeyre's Index Number} = \frac{\Sigma p_1q_0}{\Sigma p_0q_0} \times 100 = \frac{1070}{770} \times 100 = \frac{10700}{77} = \mathbf{138.96}$$

From the above results we see that *Marshall-Edgeworth's Index is slightly greater than Laspeyre's Index.*

EXAMPLE 9. *It is stated that the Marshall-Edgeworth's index number is a good approximation to the ideal index number, verify using the following data:*

Commodity	1970		1974	
	Price	Quantity	Price	Quantity
A	2	74	3	82
B	5	125	4	140
C	7	40	6	33

[B.U. B. Com. 1975]

SOLUTION.

TABLE 7.16 CALCULATIONS FOR MARSHALL-EDGEWORTH INDEX

Commodity	1970		1974		$p_o q_o$	$p_o q_1$	$p_1 q_o$	$p_1 q_1$
	Price p_o	Quantity q_o	Price p_1	Quantity q_1				
A	2	74	3	82	148	164	222	246
B	5	125	4	140	625	700	500	560
C	7	40	6	33	280	321	240	198
Total	—	—	—	—	1053 $= \Sigma p_o q_o$	1095 $= \Sigma p_o q_1$	962 $= \Sigma p_1 q_o$	1004 $= \Sigma p_1 q_1$

$$\textbf{Marshall-Edgeworth Index} = \frac{\Sigma p_1(q_o + q_1)}{\Sigma p_o(q_o + q_1)} \times 100 = \frac{\Sigma p_1 q_o + \Sigma p_1 q_1}{\Sigma p_o q_o + \Sigma p_o q_1} \times 100$$

$$= \frac{962 + 1004}{1053 + 1095} \times 100 = \frac{196600}{2146} = \mathbf{91.527}.$$

$$\textbf{Fisher's Ideal Index} = \sqrt{\frac{\Sigma p_1 q_o}{\Sigma p_o q_o} \times \frac{\Sigma p_1 q_1}{\Sigma p_o q_1}} \times 100 = \sqrt{\frac{962}{1053} \times \frac{1004}{1095}} \times 100 = \mathbf{91.523}.$$

From above we see that the Marshall Edgeworth's Index is a good approximation to Fisher's Ideal Index.

EXAMPLE 10. *Prepare Index Number for 1960, on the basis of 1950, from the following information:*

Year	Article I		Article II		ArticleIII	
	Price	Quantity	Price	Quantity	Price	Quantity
1950	5	10	8	6	6	3
1960	4	12	7	7	5	4

[A.U. M. Com.]

SOLUTION. The quantities for the Base year and the Current year being different, either *Marshall-Edgeworth's Index* or *Fisher's Ideal Index* may be constructed with the given data. Fisher's Ideal Index, being better, is determined here.

TABLE 7.17 COMPUTATION OF FISHER'S IDEAL INDEX

Article	1950		1960		$p_o q_1$	$p_1 q_o$	$p_o q_o$	$p_1 q_1$
	p_o	q_o	p_1	q_1				
I	5	10	4	12	60	40	50	48
II	8	6	7	7	56	42	48	49
III	6	3	5	4	24	15	18	20
Total	—	—	—	—	140	97	116	117

$\therefore$ Fisher's Ideal Index Number for 1960 on the basis of 1950 is

$$I = 100 \times \sqrt{\frac{\Sigma p_1 q_o}{\Sigma p_o q_o} \times \frac{\Sigma p_1 q_1}{\Sigma p_o q_1}} = \sqrt{\frac{97}{116} \times \frac{117}{140}} \times 100;$$

$$\therefore \quad \log I = \log 100 + \frac{1}{2}(\log 97 + \log 117 - \log 116 - \log 140) = 1.9222;$$

$$\therefore \quad I = \text{Antilog } 1.9222 = 83.6.$$

NOTE.. Index Numbers obtained in Examples 1–8 are all Price Index Numbers.

7.7. CHAIN BASE METHOD

In the *Chain Base Method* of computing Index Numbers, the price of each item in any year is compared with its price in the *preceding year,* and expressed as a percentage. These are known as **Link Relatives.** *The link relative is, thus, the ratio of the price of an article at any period to its price in the period just preceding it, expressed as a percentage.* The link relative for the first year $Y_\circ$ is arbitrarily taken as 100. The link relatives for the different items in other years are then averaged for each year separately (the arithmetic or the geometric mean is generally employed) to get the **Link Indices.**

These link indices for the successive years are then chained together by multiplication to obtain the *Chain Index Numbers,* relative to a common base.

The link relatives are shown below:

TABLE 7.18 LINK RELATIVES

Items ↓ / Year ⟶	$Y_\circ$	Y_1	Y_2	...	Y_k
1	100	$\frac{p_1'}{p_\circ'} \times 100$	$\frac{p_2'}{p_1'} \times 100$	...	$\frac{p_k'}{p_{k-1}'} \times 100$
2	100	$\frac{p_1''}{p_\circ''} \times 100$	$\frac{p_2''}{p_1''} \times 100$	...	$\frac{p_k''}{p_{k-1}''} \times 100$
⋮	⋮	⋮	⋮	...	⋮
⋮	⋮	⋮	⋮	...	⋮
n	100	$\frac{p_1^{(n)}}{p_\circ^{(n)}} \times 100$	$\frac{p_2^{(n)}}{p_1^{(n)}} \times 100$	...	$\frac{p_k^{(n)}}{p_{k-1}^{(n)}} \times 100$

If the arithmetic mean is used, then

Link Index for $Y_\circ$ = average of col. $Y_\circ = 100$

Link Index for Y_1 = average of col. Y_1, so that

$$I_{01}' = \frac{1}{n}\sum\left(\frac{p_1}{p_\circ} \times 100\right) = \frac{100}{n}\sum\left(\frac{p_1}{p_\circ}\right).$$

$$\text{Link Index for } Y_2, I_{12}' = \frac{1}{n}\sum\left(\frac{p_2}{p_1} \times 100\right) = \frac{100}{n}\sum\left(\frac{p_2}{p_1}\right).$$

$$\text{Link Index for } Y_3, I_{23}' = \frac{1}{n}\sum\left(\frac{p_3}{p_2} \times 100\right) = \frac{100}{n}\sum\left(\frac{p_3}{p_2}\right), \quad \text{and so on.}$$

The *Chain Index Numbers* are calculated as follows:

Chain Index for $Y_\circ = 100$,

Chain Index for Y_1 (as compared to $Y_\circ$), $I_{01} = I_{01}'$

Chain Index for Y_2 (as compared to $Y_\circ$), $I_{02} = \dfrac{I_{01} \times I_{12}'}{100}$

Chain Index for Y_3 (as compared to $Y_\circ$), $I_{03} = \dfrac{I_{02} \times I_{23}'}{100} = \dfrac{I_{01}' \times I_{12}' \times I_{23}'}{100^2}$ and so on.

$$\text{Thus Chain Index for any year} = \frac{\text{Link Index for that year} \times \text{Chain Index of previous year}}{100}.$$

Similarly, if geometric mean is used as the measure for averaging,

Link Index for $Y_o = 100$.

$$\text{Link Index for } Y_1, I'_{01} = \sqrt[n]{100\frac{p'_1}{p'_o} \times 100\frac{p''_1}{p''_o} \times 100\frac{p'''_1}{p'''_o} \times \cdots}$$

$$\text{Link Index for } Y_2, I'_{12} = \sqrt[n]{100\frac{p'_2}{p'_1} \times 100\frac{p''_2}{p''_1} \times 100\frac{p'''_2}{p'''_1} \times \cdots}$$

$$\text{Link Index for } Y_3, I'_{23} = \sqrt[n]{100\frac{p'_3}{p'_2} \times 100\frac{p''_3}{p''_2} \times 100\frac{p'''_3}{p'''_2} \times \cdots} \quad \text{and so on.}$$

The Chain Index Numbers with base Y_o are calculated from these indices in the same manner as shown above.

EXAMPLE 11. *Prepare index numbers* (1978 = 100) *from the Link Relatives given below:*

Year	1979	1980	1981	1982	1983	1984	1985
Link relatives	105	75	71	105	95	90	90

[CA November 1989]

SOLUTION. We have to find *Chain Index Numbers,* taking the Index Number of 1978 as 100, by using the formula:

$$\textbf{Chain Index for any year} = \frac{\textbf{Link Index for the year} \times \textbf{Chain Index of the previous year}}{\textbf{100}}.$$

[Here link relatives are the Link Indices].

TABLE 7.19 CALCULATION OF CHAIN INDEX NUMBERS

Year	Link Relatives	Chain Index Numbers
1978	100	100
1979	105	$\frac{105\times100}{100} = 105$
1980	75	$\frac{75\times105}{100} = 78.75$
1981	71	$\frac{71\times78.75}{100} = 55.71$
1982	105	$\frac{105\times55.91}{100} = 58.71$
1983	95	$\frac{95\times58.71}{100} = 55.77$
1984	90	$\frac{90\times55.77}{100} = 50.19$
1985	90	$\frac{90\times50.19}{100} = 45.17$

EXAMPLE 12. *Compute the Chain Index Numbers with* 1966 *prices as base, from the following table giving the average wholesale prices of the commodities, A, B, and C, for the years* 1966–1970:

AVERAGE WHOLESALE PRICES

Commodities	1966	1967	1968	1969	1970
A	20	16	28	35	21
B	25	30	24	36	45
C	20	25	30	24	30

SOLUTION.

TABLE 7.20 CALCULATION OF CHAIN INDEX NUMBERS WITH 1966 AS BASE

Commodities	Link Relative				
	1966	1967	1968	1969	1970
A	100	$\frac{16}{20} \times 100 = 80$	$\frac{28}{16} \times 100 = 175$	$\frac{35}{28} \times 100 = 125$	$\frac{21}{35} \times 100 = 60$
B	100	120	80	150	125
C	100	125	120	80	125
Total	300	325	375	355	310
Link Indices	$300 \div 3 = 100$	$325 \div 3 = 108.3$ (I'_{01})	$375 \div 3 = 125$ (I'_{12})	$355 \div 3 = 118.3$ (I'_{23})	$310 \div 3 = 103.3$ (I'_{34})
	100	$(I_{01} = I'_{01})$ $\frac{100 \times 108.3}{100} = 108.3$	$\left(I_{02} = \frac{I_{01} \times I'_{12}}{100}\right)$ $\frac{108.3 \times 125}{100} = 135.4$	$\left(I_{03} = \frac{I_{02} \times I'_{23}}{100}\right)$ $\frac{135.4 \times 118.3}{100} = 160.2$	$\left(I_{04} = \frac{I_{03} \times I'_{34}}{100}\right)$ $\frac{160.2 \times 103.3}{100} = 165.5$

Relation between Price Relative and Link Relative

If p_o, p_r, p_{r+1} be the prices per unit of a certain commodity in the base year (or 1st year) Y_o, and any two other consecutive years Y_r and Y_{r+1} respectively, then

$$\text{Price Relative for } Y_r = \frac{p_r}{p_o} \times 100, \quad \text{and} \quad \text{Price Relative for } Y_{r+1} = \frac{p_{r+1}}{p_o} \times 100.$$

$$\text{Again, Link Relative for } Y_{r+1} = \frac{p_{r+1}}{p_r} \times 100.$$

$$\therefore \quad \text{Link Relative for } Y_{r+1} = \frac{\frac{p_{r+1}}{p_o} \times 100}{\frac{p_r}{p_o} \times 100} \times 100 = \frac{\text{Price Relative for } Y_{r+1}}{\text{Price Relative for } Y_r} \times 100,$$

$$\text{i.e., Link Relative for any year} = \frac{\text{Price Relative for the year}}{\text{Price Relative for the previous year}} \times 100.$$

7.8. PROBLEMS IN THE CONSTRUCTION OF INDEX NUMBERS

The various problems in the construction of Index Numbers are:

(1) Determination of the exact purpose for which the proposed Index Numbers are constructed.

(2) Selection of items which are to be included in the group.

(3) Collection of data regarding prices and quantities and selection of sources from which such data are to be collected.

(4) Choice of the base period.

(5) Determination of weights to be employed.

(6) Selection of the measure of central tendency (or average) to be used. We shall discuss them one by one.

1. Determination of the Exact Purpose

Before starting to construct an Index Number, a clear idea as to the purpose and nature of its use is essential. All Index Numbers do not serve the same purpose. Thus, for constructing the Index Number of Wholesale Prices, the prices from retail dealers are not necessary, just as for construction of a Cost of Living Index, the quotations of cloth price ex-mill or prices of cotton yarn are useless. One must be sure of what changes the proposed Index Numbers are going to measure.

2. Selection of Items

It is not possible to include all the commodities in the construciton of an Index Number for reasons of economy and ease of calculation. The items included for the construction of an Index Number are the most important ones in each field, i.e., such articles whose price movements appear to be the most representative of the group. Inclusion of a very large number of items creates difficulty in the accurate collection of data regarding prices and quantities, apart from the increased cost. On the other hand, selection of too few items will make the Index Number unrepresentative of the general price level. The selection of items should be such in which vast majority of the people are generally interested and consequently those which are consumed in large quantities than others. With passageof time, the habits and tastes of people change and thus some new items gather importance while some other lose importance. Hence, the less important items should be replaced by new ones in conformity with their relative importance.

3. Collection of Data and Selection of Source

For a regular source of Index Numbers, a systematic collection of prices should be made from prominent business firms or standard retail stores located at different important centres, at regular intervals of time. The selected shops should be those which are visited by a large majority of customers. The average of the prices so collected from different centres is taken as the representative price. The average of the weekly price may be used for monthly indices, while yearly indices will be computed on the basis of the average of the monthly prices.

4. Choice of Base Period

The base period should be chosen carefully and be such a one when no abnormal increase or decrease in price was noticed. Once the base period is selected, all the subsequent indices are computed with reference to this fixed base period until, of course, after a long time it is found necessary to shift the base to a more recent period. Usually, a year is taken as base, preferably a year of some economic importance of the country.

Index Numbers are calculated in three ways according to the nature of base period: (a) Fixed Base Method, (b) Chain Base Method and (c) Average Base Method.

5. Determination of Weights

Most of the Index Numbers used at present are weighted averages of price-relatives or ratio of two weighted aggregates of prices. The weighting of prices is necessary because a change in the prices of some important articles affects the general price level to a large extent than does a similar change in the prices of some other less important items. For example, a middle class family in an urban area has to spend more than 50% of the total income on food, while about 15% only of the income is spent as house rent. A small percentage increase in the food prices will affect the family much more severely than a similar percentage increase in the house rent.

While computing Index Numbers, the system of weighting and particularly the allocation of weights to the individual items is of utmost importance. Different methods of weighting are used to obtain different types of Index Numbers. Price-relatives are weighted by values, prices by quantities, and quantities by prices.

In Laspeyre's Index $\left(=\frac{\Sigma p_1 q_o}{\Sigma p_o q_o}\right)$, the base year quantities are used as weights, while in Paasche's Index $\left(=\frac{\Sigma p_1 q_1}{\Sigma p_o q_1}\right)$, the weights are the current year quantities. Thus, Laspeyre's Index measures the relative change in cost in the current year of a set of goods which are consumed in the base year; while Paasche's Index measures the relative change in cost of a set of goods consumed in the current year as compared to the consumption of the same set of goods during base year. Since the pattern of consumption changes with the passage of time, both these methods are subject to some criticism.

In Marshall-Edgeworth's Index $= \frac{\Sigma p_1 (q_o + q_1)}{\Sigma p_o (q_o + q_1)}$, the sum or the average of the quantities used in the base and current year is used as weights.

When the weighted arithmetic mean of price relatives is used for computation of Index Numbers

$$I_{01} = \left(\frac{\sum 100\frac{p_1}{p_o} \times p_o q_o}{\sum p_o q_o}\right),$$

the weights used are the values (= price × quantity) or total outlay on each comodity.

6. Selecting the Average to be used

It is evident from our discussions that Index Numbers are actually averages of percentage changes in price of each of the commodities included in the group. The Arithmetic Means (Simple and Weighted) and Geometric Means are most frequently used for the purpose. In certain cases, median is also employed.

The A.M. is easy to compute and readily understood; but since it gives more weight to the items with high prices (although less important) and less to the ones whose per unit cost is low, the G.M. is preferred in many cases since it gives equal importance to equal ratios of change, and also is not very much affected by high or low prices. However, the computation of G.M. involves much labour in calculation, and hence it is employed not so often as the A.M.

7.9. QUANTITY (OR VOLUME) INDEX NUMBERS

All the formulae used for calculating the Price Index Numbers, discussed so far, may also be used to compute the Quantity Index Numbers. The only modification necessary is that prices (p) should be replaced by quantities (q) and vice versa. Thus, using the Simple Aggregative formula, we get

Simple Aggregative Index

For Price $= \frac{\Sigma p_1}{\Sigma p_o} \times 100$; For Quantity $= \frac{\Sigma q_1}{\Sigma q_o} \times 100$.

Using base year prices as weights, Quantity Index $= \frac{\Sigma q_1 p_o}{\Sigma q_o p_o} \times 100$.

Again, using Laspeyre's formula,

$$\text{Laspeyre's Price Index} = \frac{\Sigma p_1 q_o}{\Sigma p_o q_o} \times 100.$$

$$\text{Laspeyre's Quantity Index} = \frac{\Sigma q_1 p_o}{\Sigma q_o p_o} \times 100 = \frac{\Sigma p_o q_1}{\Sigma p_o q_o} \times 100.$$

$$\text{Fisher's Quantity Index} = 100 \times \sqrt{\frac{\Sigma q_1 p_o}{\Sigma q_o p_o} \times \frac{\Sigma q_1 p_1}{\Sigma q_o p_1}} = 100 \sqrt{\frac{\Sigma p_o q_1}{\Sigma p_o q_o} \times \frac{\Sigma p_1 q_1}{\Sigma p_1 q_o}}.$$

Similarly, we can write down other formulae for Quantity Index Numbers.

EXAMPLE 13. *From the following data prepare a Quantity Index Number for the year* 1953 *taking* 1948 *as the base year (use Fisher's Ideal Index Formula)* :

Year	Commodity I		Commodity II		Commodity III	
	Price	Quantity	Price	Quantity	Price	Quantity
1948	5	10	8	6	6	3
1953	4	12	7	7	5	4

[ICWAI (Final) June 1975]

SOLUTION.

TABLE 7.21 CALCUATIONS FOR QUANTITY INDEX NUMBER

Commodity	1948		1953		$p_o q_o$	$p_o q_1$	$q_o p_1$	$q_1 p_1$
	p_o	q_o	p_1	q_1				
I	5	10	4	12	50	60	40	48
II	8	6	7	7	48	56	42	49
III	6	3	5	4	18	24	15	20
Total	—	—	—	—	$116 = \Sigma q_o p_o$	$140 = \Sigma q_1 p_o$	$97 = \Sigma q_o p_1$	$117 = \Sigma q_1 p_1$

$$\text{Fisher's Quantity Index} = \sqrt{\frac{\Sigma q_1 p_o}{\Sigma q_o p_o} \times \frac{\Sigma q_1 p_1}{\Sigma q_o p_1}} \times 100 = \sqrt{\frac{140}{116} \times \frac{117}{97}} \times 100 = \mathbf{120.65}.$$

EXAMPLE 14. *For the following data, calculate quantity index number for the current year* (*i.e.*, Q_{01}) *by Fisher's formula:*

Commodity	Base Year		Current Year	
	Quantity	Price	Quantity	Price
I	6	5	8	6
II	8	3	10	2
III	12	2	10	4
IV	2	8	2	7
V	5	9	6	9

[CA November 1990]

SOLUTION.

TABLE 7.22 CALCULATIONS FOR QUANTITY INDEX NUMBER BY FISHER'S FORMULA

Commodity	Base year		Current year		p_0q_0	p_0q_1	p_1q_0	p_1q_1
	q_0	p_0	q_1	p_1				
I	6	5	8	6	30	40	36	48
II	8	3	10	2	24	30	16	20
III	12	2	10	4	24	20	48	40
IV	2	8	2	7	16	16	14	14
V	5	9	6	9	45	54	45	54
Total	–	–	–	–	$139 = \Sigma p_0q_0$	$160 = \Sigma p_0q_1$	$159 = \Sigma p_1q_0$	$176 = \Sigma p_1q_1$

Quantity Index Number by Fisher's Formula (Q_{01})

$$= \sqrt{\frac{\Sigma p_0q_1}{\Sigma p_0q_0} \times \frac{\Sigma p_1q_1}{\Sigma p_1q_0}} \times 100 = \sqrt{\frac{160 \times 176}{139 \times 159}} \times 100 = \mathbf{112.88}.$$

EXAMPLE 15. *Using Paasche's formula compute the Quantity Index and the Price Index Numbers for* 1970 *with* 1966 *as base year:*

Commodity	Quantity (in Units)		Value (in Rs.)	
	1966	1970	1966	1970
A	100	150	500	900
B	80	100	320	500
C	60	72	150	360
D	30	33	360	297

[ICWAI (Final) June 1975]

SOLUTION.

TABLE 7.23 CALCULATION FOR PAASCHE'S INDEX

Commodity	Quantity		Value (in Rs.)		$p_o = \frac{p_oq_o}{q_o}$	$p_1 = \frac{p_1q_1}{q_1}$	p_oq_1	p_1q_o
	q_o	q_1	p_oq_o	p_1q_1				
A	100	150	500	900	5	6	750	600
B	80	100	320	500	4	5	400	400
C	60	72	150	360	2.5	5	180	300
D	30	33	360	297	12	9	396	270
Total	—	—	—	2057 $= \Sigma p_1q_1$	—	—	1726 $= \Sigma p_oq_1$	1570 $= \Sigma q_op_1$

$$\text{Paasche's Quantity Index} = \frac{\Sigma q_1p_1}{\Sigma q_op_1} \times 100 = \frac{2057}{1570} \times 100 = 131.019 = \mathbf{131.02\ (approx.)}$$

$$\text{Paasche's Price Index} = \frac{\Sigma p_1q_1}{\Sigma p_oq_1} \times 100 = \frac{2057}{1726} \times 100 = 119.177 = \mathbf{119.18\ (approx.)}$$

7.10. COST OF LIVING INDEX OR CONSUMER PRICE INDEX NUMBER

Cost of Living Index Numbers also known as *Consumer Price Index Numbers* measure the relative (expressed as a percentage) amount of money necessary to derive equal satisfaction during two periods of time, after taking into consideration the fluctuations of the retail prices of consumer goods during these two periods.

Generally, the list of items consumed varies for different classes of people, (e.g., the rich, the poor and the middle class) at the same place of residence. Also people of the same class belonging to different geographical regions have different consumer-habits. Thus the Cost of Living Index always relates to a specified class of people and a specified geographical area, and it helps us in determining the effect of changes in prices on different classes of consumers living in different areas.

Construction of a Cost of Living Index

The first step in the construction of a Cost of Living Index is the decision about the class of people for whom the Index Number is meant, i.e., it should be clearly mentioned whether the Index Number relates to industrial workers or officers or teachers etc. It is also necessary to decide on the geographical area to be covered by the Index Number.

The second step is to conduct a *family budget enquiry* covering the class of people for whom the Index Number is intended. The enquiry should be conducted in the base year by the *process of random sampling.* This would give us information regarding the nature, quality and quantities of commodities consumed by an average family of the class and also the amount spent on different items of consumption. The items on which the money is spent are classified under five major groups: (a) Food, (b) Clothing, (c) Fuel and Light, (d) Housing, and (e) Miscellaneous.

Each of these groups includes a large number of important items. For example, the group *Food* includes Rice, Wheat, Fish, Milk, Egg, Sugar, etc. Among these only important items which are used by the majority of the class of people are included in the construction of a Cost of Living Index.

The next step is to collect *retail priccs* of the items from the localities in which the class of people concerned reside or from the markets where they usually make their purchases. Price quotations should be obtained at least once a week.

After the collection of retail prices, we would observe that each item will have a number of price quotations depending on qualities and markets. In this case, an average price for each item is calculated. Such average is first calculated for the base period of the Index, and later for every week, or month or year according as the Index is maintained on a weekly, monthly or yearly basis.

As the relative importance of various items for different classes of people is not the same, prices or price-relatives are always weighted and, therefore, the Cost of Living Index is always a *weighted Index.* Amount spent on each commodity by an average family gives the weights.

The percentage expenditure on an item constitutes *the weight of the item* and the percentage expenditure on the five groups constitute the *group weight.*

Laspeyre's Formula

$$I_{01} = \frac{\Sigma p_1 q_o}{\Sigma p_o q_o} \times 100$$

is widely employed for computing the Cost of Living Index.

The above formula may be written as

$$I_{01} = \frac{\Sigma\left(\dfrac{p_1}{p_o} \times 100 \times p_o q_o\right)}{\Sigma p_o q_o} = \frac{\Sigma I w}{\Sigma w},$$

where $I = \frac{p_1}{p_o} \times 100$ = price-relative of an item consumed, and $w = p_o q_o$ = base price of an item consumed, so that I_{01} = weighted arithmetic average of the price-relatives, weighted with the weights $p_o q_o$ representing the value, at base prices, of the items consumed in the base year.

If $\Sigma w = 100$, the formula reduces to

$$I_{01} = \frac{\Sigma I w}{100},$$

where I = price-relative, and w = percentage of family's budget spent on an item in the base year.

Separate index numbers are first of all determined for each of the five major groups, by calculating the weighted average of price relatives of the selected items in the group. The weights in this case are proportional to the expenditure of an average family on the different items in the group. These group-indices are weighted by the percentage of total family budget spent on each of these groups and the weighted average gives the final *Cost of Living Index Number.*

DEFLATION. Due to *inflation* (i.e., due to rise in prices) the value of a rupee is decreased (i.e., we can purchase less with the same amount of money). This means that the *purchasing power of money* is diminished. **Deflation** *is the technique of adjusting the rupee value figure at a time period dividing it by the appropriate price index (usually Cost of Living Index) of the same time period after considering changes in price level.* When prices increase, money wages are *deflated* by the price index to find the real wages. Thus *real wage is determined after deflating the money wage by the Cost of Living Index by using the formula:*

$$\text{Real Wage} = \frac{\text{Money (or Actual) wage}}{\text{Cost of Living Index}} \times 100.$$

The process of finding **real wage** by using *Cost of Living Index (C.L.I.)* is called **deflation.**

Equivalent wage in a year Y' relative to the year Y to maintain the same standard of living

$$= \frac{\text{C.L.I. for } Y'}{\text{C.L.I. for } Y} \times \text{actual wage in } Y.$$

Purchasing Power of a Rupee in any year, say Y, in terms of a particular year Y', is given by the formula:

$$\textbf{Purchasing Power} = \frac{\textbf{Index Number for Y}'}{\textbf{Index Number for Y}}$$

As $p_o q_o$ and $p_1 q_o$ are the aggregate expenditure in current and base periods respectively, the method of computing *Cost of Living Index* by the application of Laspeyre's formula is known as *Aggregate Expenditure Method* and the method of computation by the application of the formula $\frac{\Sigma I w}{\Sigma w}$ or $\frac{\Sigma I w}{100}$ is known as the *Family Budget Method.*

EXAMPLE 15. *During a certain period the cost of living index number goes up from* 110 *to* 200 *and the salary of a worker is also raised from* Rs. 325 *to* Rs. 500. *Does the worker really gain, and if so, by how much in real terms?* **[ICWAI December 1975; C.U. B. Com. (Hons) 1984, 1990]**

SOLUTION. We have

$$\text{Real Wage} = \frac{\text{Actual wage}}{\text{Cost of living Index}} \times 100$$

$$\therefore \quad \text{Real wage of Rs. } 325 = \frac{325}{110} \times 100 = \textbf{Rs.295.45} \text{ (approx.)}$$

$$\text{and} \quad \text{Real Wage of Rs. } 500 = \frac{500}{200} \times 100 = \textbf{Rs.250}.$$

Since the real wage of Rs. 500 is less than that of Rs. 325, *the worker does not really gain. Real wage decrease by* Rs. 295.45 – Rs. 250.00, i.e., Rs. 45.45.

EXAMPLE 16. *The following are the group index numbers and the group weights of an average working class family's budget. Construct the cost of living index number by assigning the given weights:*

Group	Index Number	Weight
Food	352	48
Fuel	220	10
Clothing	230	8
Rent	160	12
Miscellaneous	190	15

[ICWAI January 1970; June 1979; Kerala U. B. Com. 1989]

SOLUTION.

TABLE 7.24 CONSTRUCTION OF COST OF LIVING INDEX NUMBER

Group	Index Number (I)	Weight (w)	Iw
Food	352	48	16,896
Fuel	220	10	2,200
Clothing	230	8	1,840
Rent	160	12	1,920
Miscellaneous	190	15	2,850
Total	—	$93 = \Sigma w$	$25,706 = \Sigma Iw$

$$\therefore \text{ the cost of living Index No.} = \frac{\Sigma Iw}{\Sigma w} = \frac{25706}{93} = \mathbf{276.4}.$$

EXAMPLE 17. *Given below are the average wages in rupees per hour of unskilled workers of a factory during the years* 1975–1980. *Also shown is the Consumer Price Index for these years (taking* 1975 *as base year with Price Index* 100). *Determine the real wages of the workers during* 1975–1980 *compared with their wages in* 1975.

Year	1975	1976	1977	1978	1979	1980
Consumer Price Index	100	120.2	121.7	125.9	129.3	140
Average Wage (rupees/hour)	1.19	1.94	2.13	2.28	2.45	3.10

How much is the worth of the one rupee of 1975 in subsequent years ? **[ICWAI June 1982]**

SOLUTION. We have

$$\text{Real Wage} = \frac{\text{Actual Wage for a period}}{\text{Cost of Living Index for the period (or consumer Price Index).}} \times 100.$$

TABLE 7.25 CALCULATION OF REAL WAGES

Year	Consumer Price Index (Base: 1975)	Average Wage (Rs./Hour)	Real Wages of Workers (Rs./Hours)	Worth of Re.1 of 1975 (Rs.) 100 ÷ Col. 2
1975	100.0	1.19	(1.9 ÷ 100) × 100 = 1.19	1.00
1976	120.2	1.94	(1.94 ÷ 120.2) × 100 = 1.61	0.83
1977	121.7	2.13	(2.13 ÷ 121.7) × 100 = 1.75	0.82
1978	125.9	2.28	(2.28 ÷ 125.9) × 100 = 1.81	0.79
1979	129.3	2.45	(2.45 ÷ 129.3) × 100 = 1.89	0.77
1980	140.0	3.10	(3.10 ÷ 140) × 100 = 2.21	0.71

NOTE.. Purchasing power in a year of one rupee of 1975 $= \frac{\text{Index Number for 1975}}{\text{Index Number of the year}}$.

EXAMPLE 18. *The group indices and the corresponding weights for the working class Cost of Living Index numbers in an industrial city for the years* 1976 *and* 1980 *are given below:*

Group	Weight	Group Index	
		1976	1980
Food	71	370	380
Clothing	3	423	504
Fuel etc.	9	469	336
House Rent	7	110	116
Miscellaneous	10	279	283

Compute the cost of living indices for the two years 1976 *and* 1980. *If a worker was getting* 300 *per month in* 1976, *do you think that he should be given some extra allowance so that he can maintain his* 1976 *standard of living ? If so, what should be the minimum amount of this extra allowance ?* **[C.U. B. Com. (Hons.) 1982; ICWAI June 1981]**

SOLUTION. Cost of Living Index $= \frac{\Sigma Iw}{\Sigma w}$, where I = Group Index and w = group weight.

TABLE 7.26 CALCULATIONS FOR COST OF LIVING INDEX

Group	Weight w	Group Index		$I_1 w$	$I_2 w$
		1976 (I_1)	1980 (I_2)		
Food	71	370	380	26270	26980
Clothing	3	423	504	1269	1512
Fuel etc.	9	469	336	4221	3024
House Rent	7	110	116	770	812
Miscellaneous	10	279	283	2790	2830
Total	$100 = \Sigma w$	—	—	$35320 = \Sigma I_1 w$	$35158 = \Sigma I_2 w$

$$\text{Cost of Living Index for 1976} = \frac{\Sigma I_1 w}{\Sigma w} = \frac{35320}{100} = \mathbf{353.20}.$$

$$\text{Cost of Living Index for 1980} = \frac{\Sigma I_2 w}{\Sigma w} = \frac{35158}{100} = \mathbf{351.58}.$$

Since *Cost of Living Index* for 1980 is slightly less than the Cost of Living Index for 1976, the worker need not be given any extra allowance to maintain his 1976 standard of living.

[The cost of living Index for 1980 relative to that for 1976 $= \frac{351.58}{353.20}$, and to maintain the same standard of living as 1976, the workers needs $300 \times \frac{351.58}{353.20} = 298.62$. But he is already getting 300.]

7.11. TESTS FOR INDEX NUMBERS

The three common tests for a good index number formula are: (1) Time Reversal Test, (2) Factor Reversal Test, and (3) Circular Test.

1. Time Reversal Test

An index number formula satisfies this test if it works both ways, forward and backward, with respect to time. In other words, an index number I_{01} for the year Y_1 with base year Y_o, calculated by this formula, should be the reciprocal of the index number I_{10} for the year Y_o with base year Y_1. Symbolically, $I_{01} \times I_{10} = 1$, omitting the factor 100 from both the indices.

This test is satisfied by: (i) Simple Aggregative Index, (ii) Marshall-Edgeworth's Index, (iii) Fisher's Ideal Index, and (iv) Simple G.M. of Price Relatives.

2. Factor Reversal Test

An index number formula satisfies this test if the product of the Price Index and the Quantity Index gives the *true value ratio,* omitting the factor 100 from each index. Symbolically, an index number formula satisfies this test if

$$P_{01} \times Q_{01} = \frac{\Sigma p_1 q_1}{\Sigma p_o q_o} = \text{the true value ratio} = TVR$$

where P_{01} = Price Index for Y_1 with base year Y_o and Q_{01} = Quantity Index for Y_1 with base year Y_o, omitting the factor 100

Fisher's Ideal Index is the only formula which satisfies this test.

3. Circular Test

This test is based on the shifting of base in a circular fashion. It may be considered as an *extension of Time Reversal Test.* An index number formula is said to satisfy the *Circular Test* if it satisfies

$$I_{01} \times I_{12} \times I_{23} \times \cdots \times I_{(n-1)n} \times I_{no} = 1.$$

This test is concerned with the measurement of price changes over a period of years when the shiftability of the base is desirable.

This test is satisfied by: (i) Simple Aggregative Index, (ii) Simple Geometric Mean of Price Relatives and (iii) Weighted Aggregative Formula with fixed weights.

EXAMPLE 19. *Show that the simple aggregative formula and weighted aggregative formula (fixed weights) satisfy Circular Test. Does Fisher's Ideal Index satisfy this test?* **[CA May 1991]**

SOLUTION. For three years Y_o, Y_1, Y_2, using simple aggregative formula (omitting the factor 100), we get

$$I_{01} = \frac{\Sigma p_1}{\Sigma p_o}, \quad I_{12} = \frac{\Sigma p_2}{\Sigma p_1} \quad \text{and} \quad I_{20} = \frac{\Sigma p_o}{\Sigma p_2}; \qquad \therefore \quad I_{01} \times I_{12} \times I_{20} = \frac{\Sigma p_1}{\Sigma p_o} \times \frac{\Sigma p_2}{\Sigma p_1} \times \frac{\Sigma p_o}{\Sigma p_2} = 1.$$

Hence, the simple aggregative formula satisfies *Circular Test.*

Again, by weighted aggregative formula (fixed weights),

$$I_{01} = \frac{\Sigma p_1 w}{\Sigma p_o w}, \quad I_{12} = \frac{\Sigma p_2 w}{\Sigma p_1 w} \quad \text{and} \quad I_{20} = \frac{\Sigma p_o w}{\Sigma p_2 w}; \qquad \therefore \quad I_{01} \times I_{12} \times I_{20} = \frac{\Sigma p_1 w}{\Sigma p_o w} \times \frac{\Sigma p_2 w}{\Sigma p_1 w} \times \frac{\Sigma p_o w}{\Sigma p_2 w} = 1.$$

Hence, the weighted aggregative formula (fixed weights) also satisfies *Circular Test.*

Similarly, we can prove the result for four and more than four years.

By *Fisher's Ideal Index Formula* (omitting the factor 100), we get

$$I_{01} = \sqrt{\frac{\Sigma p_1 q_0}{\Sigma p_0 q_0} \times \frac{\Sigma p_1 q_1}{\Sigma p_0 q_1}}, \quad I_{12} = \sqrt{\frac{\Sigma p_2 q_1}{\Sigma p_1 q_1} \times \frac{\Sigma p_2 q_2}{\Sigma p_1 q_2}}, \quad I_{20} = \sqrt{\frac{\Sigma p_0 q_2}{\Sigma p_2 q_2} \times \frac{\Sigma p_0 q_0}{\Sigma p_2 q_0}}$$

$$\therefore \quad I_{01} \times I_{12} \times I_{20} = \sqrt{\frac{\Sigma p_1 q_0}{\Sigma p_0 q_0} \times \frac{\Sigma p_1 q_1}{\Sigma p_0 q_1} \times \frac{\Sigma p_2 q_1}{\Sigma p_1 q_1} \times \frac{\Sigma p_2 q_2}{\Sigma p_1 q_2} \times \frac{\Sigma p_0 q_2}{\Sigma p_2 q_2} \times \frac{\Sigma p_0 q_0}{\Sigma p_2 q_0}}$$

$$= \sqrt{\frac{\Sigma p_1 q_0 \times \Sigma p_2 q_1 \times \Sigma p_0 q_2}{\Sigma p_0 q_1 \times \Sigma p_1 q_2 \times \Sigma p_2 q_0}} \neq 1.$$

Hence, *Fisher's Ideal Index Formula does not satisfy Circular Test.*

EXAMPLE 20. *Show that neither Laspeyre's formula nor Paasche's formula obeys Time Reversal and Factor Reversal Tests of index numbers.* **[ICWAI June 1974]**

PROOF. Laspeyre's formula (omitting the factor 100) is

$$I_{01} = \frac{\Sigma p_1 q_o}{\Sigma p_o q_o}. \tag{i}$$

Interchanging the suffixes 0 and 1, we get

$$I_{10} = \frac{\Sigma p_o q_1}{\Sigma p_1 q_1}. \tag{ii}$$

Multiplying (i) and (ii), we have

$$I_{01} \times I_{10} = \frac{\Sigma p_1 q_o}{\Sigma p_o q_o} \times \frac{\Sigma p_o q_1}{\Sigma p_1 q_1} \neq 1.$$

Therefore, *Laspeyre's formula* does not obey Time Reversal Test which gives $I_{01} \times I_{10} = 1$.

Again, *Paasche's formula* (omitting the factor 100) is

$$I_{01} = \frac{\Sigma p_1 q_1}{\Sigma p_o q_1}. \tag{iii}$$

Interchanging the suffixes 0 and 1, we get

$$I_{10} = \frac{\Sigma p_o q_o}{\Sigma p_1 q_o}. \tag{iv}$$

Multiplying (iii) and (iv), we have

$$I_{01} \times I_{10} = \frac{\Sigma p_1 q_1}{\Sigma q_o p_1} \times \frac{\Sigma p_o q_o}{\Sigma p_1 q_o} \neq 1.$$

Thus, Paasche's formula also does not obey Time Reversal Test.

Factor Reversal Test is $P_{01} \times Q_{01} = \frac{\Sigma p_1 q_1}{\Sigma p_o q_o}$, where P_{01} = Price Index and Q_{01} = Quantity Index.

Laspeyre's Price Index P_{01} (omitting the factor 100) is

$$P_{01} = \frac{\Sigma p_1 q_o}{\Sigma p_o q_o}. \tag{v}$$

Interchanging p and q in (v), we get Laspeyre's Quantity Index

$$Q_{01} = \frac{\Sigma q_1 p_o}{\Sigma q_o p_o} = \frac{\Sigma p_o q_1}{\Sigma p_o q_o}. \tag{vi}$$

Multiplying (v) and (vi), we have

$$P_{01} \times Q_{01} = \frac{\Sigma p_1 q_o}{\Sigma p_o q_o} \times \frac{\Sigma p_o q_1}{\Sigma p_o q_o} \neq \frac{\Sigma p_1 q_1}{\Sigma p_o q_o}.$$

This shows that Laspeyre's formula does not obey Factor Reversal Test.

Again, Paasche's Price Index P_{01} is given by

$$P_{01} = \frac{\Sigma p_1 q_1}{\Sigma p_o q_1}. \tag{vii}$$

Interchanging p and q, Paasche's Quantity Index is

$$Q_{01} = \frac{\Sigma q_1 p_1}{\Sigma q_o p_1} = \frac{\Sigma p_1 q_1}{\Sigma p_1 q_o}. \tag{viii}$$

Multiplying (vii) and (viii), we get

$$P_{01} \times Q_{01} = \frac{\Sigma p_1 q_1}{\Sigma p_o q_1} \times \frac{\Sigma p_1 q_1}{\Sigma p_1 q_o} \neq \frac{\Sigma p_1 q_1}{\Sigma p_o q_o},$$

which shows that Paasche's formula does not obey Factor Reversal Test.

EXAMPLE 21. *Examine whether Fisher's Ideal Index Number satisfies the Time Reversal and Factor Reversal Tests.*

[C.U. B. Com. 1982, 1984; ICWAI July 1970, December 1975; CA May 1986, 1990]

SOLUTION. Fisher's Ideal Index Number (omitting the factor 100) is

$$I_{01} = \sqrt{\frac{\Sigma p_1 q_o}{\Sigma p_o q_o} \times \frac{\Sigma p_1 q_1}{\Sigma p_o q_1}}. \tag{i}$$

Interchanging the suffixes 0 and 1, we get

$$I_{10} = \sqrt{\frac{\Sigma p_o q_1}{\Sigma p_1 q_1} \times \frac{\Sigma p_o q_o}{\Sigma p_1 q_o}}. \tag{ii}$$

Multiplying (i) and (ii), we get

$$I_{01} \times I_{10} = \sqrt{\frac{\Sigma p_1 q_o}{\Sigma p_o q_o} \times \frac{\Sigma p_1 q_1}{\Sigma p_o q_1}} \times \sqrt{\frac{\Sigma p_o q_1}{\Sigma p_1 q_1} \times \frac{\Sigma p_o q_o}{\Sigma p_1 q_o}} = \sqrt{\frac{\Sigma p_1 q_o}{\Sigma p_o q_o} \times \frac{\Sigma p_1 q_1}{\Sigma p_o q_1} \times \frac{\Sigma p_o q_1}{\Sigma p_1 q_1} \times \frac{\Sigma p_o q_o}{\Sigma p_1 q_o}}$$
$$= \sqrt{1} = 1,$$

i.e., $I_{01} \times I_{10} = 1$, which shows that Fisher's Ideal Index Number satisfies the Time Reversal Test.

Again, Fisher's Price Index P_{01} is given by

$$P_{01} = \sqrt{\frac{\Sigma p_1 q_o}{\Sigma p_o q_o} \times \frac{\Sigma p_1 q_1}{\Sigma p_o q_1}}. \tag{iii}$$

Interchanging p and q, we get Fisher's Quantity Index

$$Q_{01} = \sqrt{\frac{\Sigma q_1 p_o}{\Sigma q_o p_o} \times \frac{\Sigma q_1 p_1}{\Sigma q_o p_1}} = \sqrt{\frac{\Sigma p_o q_1}{\Sigma p_o q_o} \times \frac{\Sigma p_1 q_1}{\Sigma p_1 q_o}}. \tag{iv}$$

Multiplying (iii) and (iv), we have

$$P_{01} \times Q_{01} = \sqrt{\frac{\Sigma p_1 q_o}{\Sigma p_o q_o} \times \frac{\Sigma p_1 q_1}{\Sigma p_o q_1} \times \frac{\Sigma p_o q_1}{\Sigma p_o q_o} \times \frac{\Sigma p_1 q_1}{\Sigma p_1 q_o}} = \sqrt{\frac{(\Sigma p_1 q_1)^2}{(\Sigma p_o q_o)^2}} = \frac{\Sigma p_1 q_1}{\Sigma p_o q_o}$$

= the true value ratio.

This shows that Fisher's Ideal Index Number satisfies Factor Reversal Test.

EXAMPLE 22. *Calculate Fisher's Ideal Index using the following data and check whether it satisfies the "Time Reversal Test".*

Commodities	1974		1975	
	Quantity	Price (Rs.)	Quantity	Price (Rs.)
X	50	32	50	30
Y	35	30	40	25
Z	55	16	50	18

[A.P.U. B. Com. 1976; C.U. B. Com. (Hons.) 1986]

SOLUTION.

TABLE 7.27 CALCULATIONS FOR FISHER'S IDEAL INDEX

Commodity	1974		1975		$p_o q_o$	$p_o q_1$	$p_1 q_o$	$p_1 q_1$
	q_o	p_o	q_1	p_1				
X	50	32	50	30	1600	1600	1500	1500
Y	35	30	40	25	1050	1200	875	1000
Z	55	16	50	18	880	800	990	900
Total	—	—	—	—	3530 $= \Sigma p_o q_o$	3600 $= \Sigma p_o q_1$	3365 $= \Sigma p_1 q_o$	3400 $= \Sigma p_1 q_1$

Fisher's Price Index (P_{01}) is given by

$$P_{01} = \sqrt{\frac{\Sigma p_1 q_o}{\Sigma p_o q_o} \times \frac{\Sigma p_1 q_1}{\Sigma p_o q_1}} \times 100 = \sqrt{\frac{3365}{3530} \times \frac{3400}{3600}} \times 100 = \sqrt{\frac{114410}{127080}} \times 100$$

$$= \sqrt{0.90029} \times 100 = \mathbf{94.88\ (approx.)}$$

2nd Part.

$$P_{01} = \sqrt{\frac{3365}{3530} \times \frac{3400}{3600}}, \quad \text{omitting the factor 100.}$$

$$\text{Again,} \quad P_{10} = \sqrt{\frac{\Sigma p_o q_1}{\Sigma p_1 q_1} \times \frac{\Sigma p_o q_o}{\Sigma p_1 q_o}} = \sqrt{\frac{3600}{3400} \times \frac{3530}{3365}}.$$

$$\therefore \quad P_{01} \times P_{10} = \sqrt{\frac{3365}{3530} \times \frac{3400}{3600} \times \frac{3600}{3400} \times \frac{3530}{3365}} = \sqrt{1} = 1.$$

This shows that Fisher's Index satisfies *Time Reversal Test*.

EXAMPLE 23. *Using the following data, show that Fisher's Ideal formula satisfies the Factor Reversal Test:*

Commodity	Price (in Rs.) per Unit		Number of Units	
	Base Period	Current Period	Base Period	Current Period
A	6	10	50	56
B	2	2	100	120
C	4	6	60	60
D	10	12	30	24
E	8	12	40	36

[ICWAI (Final) December 1974]

SOLUTION.

TABLE 7.28 CALCULATIONS FOR FISHER'S IDEAL INDEX

Commodity	Price		Quantity		$p_o q_o$	$p_o q_1$	$p_1 q_o$	$p_1 q_1$
	p_o	p_1	q_o	q_1				
A	6	10	50	56	300	336	500	560
B	2	2	100	120	200	240	200	240
C	4	6	60	60	240	240	360	360
D	10	12	30	24	300	240	360	288
E	8	12	40	36	320	288	480	432
Total	—	—	—	—	1360 $= \Sigma p_o q_o$	1344 $= \Sigma p_o q_1$	1900 $= \Sigma p_1 q_o$	1880 $= \Sigma p_1 q_1$

Omitting the factor 100, Fisher's Price Index P_{01} is given by

$$P_{01} = \sqrt{\frac{\Sigma p_1 q_o}{\Sigma p_o q_o} \times \frac{\Sigma p_1 q_1}{\Sigma p_o q_1}} = \sqrt{\frac{1900}{1360} \times \frac{1880}{1344}}.$$

Interchanging p and q Fisher's Quantity Index Q_{01} is

$$Q_{01} = \sqrt{\frac{\Sigma q_1 p_o}{\Sigma q_o p_o} \times \frac{\Sigma q_1 p_1}{\Sigma q_o p_1}} = \sqrt{\frac{1344}{1360} \times \frac{1880}{1900}}.$$

$$\therefore \quad P_{01} \times Q_{01} = \sqrt{\frac{1900}{1360} \times \frac{1880}{1344} \times \frac{1344}{1360} \times \frac{1880}{1900}} = \sqrt{\frac{(1880)^2}{(1360)^2}} = \frac{1880}{1360} = \frac{\Sigma p_1 q_1}{\Sigma p_o q_o}.$$

This shows that Fisher's Ideal Index satisfies *Factor Reversal Test.*

EXAMPLE 24. *When the cost of cigarette was increased by* 50%, *a smoker who maintained his former scale of consumption said that the rise of cigarette price had increased his cost of living by* 5%. *What per cent of his cost of living was due to buying cigarette before the change of price ?*

[ICWAI June 1983]

SOLUTION. Let his expenditure on cigarette before the change of price be Rs. x. Then his expenditure on cigarette after increase in price of cigarette $= x + 50\%$ of $x =$ Rs. $1.5x$.

$$\therefore \quad \text{Increase in expenditure} = 1.5x - x = \text{Rs. } 0.5x$$

If Rs. y be his former cost of living, then his cost of living after the increase in price of cigarette (other prices remaining fixed) $= y + 5\%$ of $y =$ Rs. $1.05y$.

$\therefore$ Increase in expenditure $= 1.05y - y =$ Rs. $0.05y$.

$$\therefore \text{ We have } 0.5x = 0.05y, \quad \text{or,} \quad x = \frac{0.05}{0.5}y = \frac{1}{10}y$$

Hence, the required expenditure on cigarette before the change of price, expressed as percentage of his cost of living $= \frac{x}{y} \times 100 = \frac{1}{10} \times 100 =$ **10%**.

[OTHERWISE. Let the required percentage be x. Then we have

Group	Weights (w)	% increase in price (i)	iw
(i) Cigarette	x	50	$50x$
(ii) Other items	$100 - x$	0	0
Total	$100 = \Sigma w$	—	$50x = \Sigma iw$

Average percentage increase for all items $= \frac{\Sigma iw}{\Sigma w}$, or, $5 = \frac{50x}{100}$, or, $50x = 500$;

$\therefore$ $x = 10$.]

7.12 Base Shifting

Sometimes it becomes necessary to shift the base period of a series of Index Numbers from one period to another.

If the base is too old, we shift the base to a more recent period to make the data more useful.

Base-shifting is also required if we are given two (or more) series of Index Numbers with different base periods. For example, if a series of Index Numbers with the base year 1976 is to be compared with another series whose base year is 1985, then it is necessary to convert either the former series into a new one with 1985 as the base year or the two series into new ones with any other year as the common base. This is done by using the formula:

Index Number for any year with a new base year

$$= \frac{\text{Old Index Number for the year}}{\text{Old Index Number for the new base year}} \times 100.$$

In this case, we take the index number of the new base year as 100.

EXAMPLE 25. *Shift the base period of the following series of index numbers from* 1978 *to* 1985 :

Year	1982	1983	1984	1985	1986	1987	1988
Index Number (Base 1978 = 100)	120	125	132	140	150	158	175

SOLUTION.

TABLE 7.29 SHIFTING OF BASE PERIOD FROM 1978 TO 1985

Year	Index Number with base 1978	Index Number with new base 1985
1982	120	$\frac{120}{140} \times 100 = 85.71$
1983	125	$\frac{125}{140} \times 100 = 89.29$
1984	132	$\frac{132}{140} \times 100 = 94.29$
1985	140	$\frac{140}{140} \times 100 = 100.00$
1986	150	$\frac{150}{140} \times 100 = 107.14$
1987	158	$\frac{158}{140} \times 100 = 112.86$
1988	175	$\frac{175}{140} \times 100 = 125.00$

EXAMPLE 26. *In* 1980, *an index number is* 100; *it rises* 5% *in* 1981, *falls* 2% *in* 1982, *and again rises* 4% *in* 1983 *and* 6% *in* 1984. *If rise and fall begin with respect to previous year, find the index numbers for the given years shifting the base to* 1983.

SOLUTION.

TABLE 7.30 Shifting of base period from 1980 to 1983

Year	Index Number (Base 1980)	Index Number (Base 1983)
1980	100.0	$\frac{100}{107} \times 100 = 93.46$
1981	$\frac{105}{100} \times 100 = 105.0$	$\frac{105}{107} \times 100 = 98.13$
1982	$\frac{98}{100} \times 105 = 102.9$	$\frac{102.9}{107} \times 100 = 96.17$
1983	$\frac{104}{100} \times 102.9 = 107.0$	$\frac{107}{107} \times 100 = 100.00$
1984	$\frac{106}{100} \times 107 = 113.4$	$\frac{113.4}{107} \times 100 = 105.98$

7.12.1. Splicing of Index Numbers

Sometimes, an old series of index numbers is discontinued and a new series of index numbers is constructed with a recent period as the base. As these two series have different base periods, they cannot be compared. To make them comparable, the two series of index numbers are *spliced together*, i.e., one continuous series of index numbers with a common base period is prepared. Thus *splicing is the technique* (i.e., *statistical procedure*) *of combining two* (*or more*) *series of index numbers with different base periods to obtain a continuous series of index numbers with a common base period.* We illustrate the whole procedure with the help of a worked out Example.

EXAMPLE 27. *Splice the following two series of index members with* (i) *base* 1970 *and* (ii) *base* 1975:

Year :	1970	1971	1972	1973	1974	1975	1976	1977	1978	1979	1980
Series A :	100	110	125	150	180	200	...	...	...	...	...
Series B :	...	...	...	...	...	100	105	90	120	140	160

SOLUTION. From the given data, we see that series A with base year 1970 is discontinued after 1975 and a new series is constructed with 1975 as base year. We have to splice (i) the series B to A

shifting the base of series B to 1970 and (ii) the series A to B shifting the base of A to 1975. The procedure is shown in the following table.

TABLE 7.31 SPLICING OF TWO SERIES OF INDEX NUMBERS

Year	Series A Index Number (Base 1970 = 100)	Series B Index Number (Base 1975 = 100)	New continuous Series (Spliced Index Numbers)	
			Base 1970 = 100	Base 1975 = 100
1970	100	...	100	$\frac{100}{200} \times 100 = \mathbf{50}$
1971	110	...	110	$\frac{100}{200} \times 110 = \mathbf{55}$
1972	125	...	125	$\frac{100}{200} \times 125 = \mathbf{62.5}$
1973	150	...	150	$\frac{100}{200} \times 150 = \mathbf{75}$
1974	180	...	180	$\frac{100}{200} \times 180 = \mathbf{90}$
1975	200	100	200	100
1976	...	105	$\frac{200}{100} \times 105 = \mathbf{210}$	105
1977	...	90	$\frac{200}{100} \times 90 = \mathbf{180}$	90
1978	...	120	$\frac{200}{100} \times 120 = \mathbf{240}$	120
1979	...	140	$\frac{200}{100} \times 140 = \mathbf{280}$	140
1980	...	160	$\frac{200}{100} \times 160 = \mathbf{320}$	160

EXAMPLE 28. *Due to change in prices, the cost of livng index for the working class in a city rose to* **225** *in April from* 180 *in March,* 1980. *The index of food became* 252 *from* 198, *that of clothing from* 185 *to* 205, *that of fuel and lighting from* 175 *to* 195 *and that of miscellaneous from* 138 *to* 212. *The index of rent, however, remained unchanged at* 150. *Find the weights of all the groups if the weights of clothing, fuel and lighting and rent were the same.* **[ICWAI June 1990]**

SOLUTION. Let the total weights $(\Sigma w) = 100$, where w_1 and w_2 are the weights of food and clothing respectively.

TABLE 7.32 CALCULATIONS FOR THE WEIGHTS OF THE DIFFERENT GROUPS

Group	Group Index		Weight (w)	For March I_1w	For April I_2w
	March (I_1)	April (I_2)			
Food	198	252	w_1	$198w_1$	$252w_1$
Clothing	185	205	w_2	$185w_2$	$205w_2$
Fuel and Light	175	195	w_2	$175w_2$	$195w_2$
Rent	150	150	w_2	$150w_2$	$150w_2$
Miscellaneous	138	212	$100 - w_1 - 3w_2$	$3800 - 138w_1 - 414w_2$	$21200 - 212w_1 - 636w_2$
Total	—	—	$100 = \Sigma w$	$60w_1 + 96w_2 + 13800 = \Sigma I_1 w$	$40w_1 - 86w_2 + 21200 = \Sigma I_2 w$

Since the Cost of Living Indices (C.L.I) for March and April are respectively 180 and 225;

$$\therefore \quad \text{CLI for March} = \frac{\Sigma I_1 w}{\Sigma w} = 180,$$

$$\text{or,} \quad \frac{60w_1 + 96w_2 + 13800}{100} = 180, \text{ or, } 5w_1 + 8w_2 = 350, \quad (1)$$

$$\text{and} \quad \text{CLI for April} = \frac{\Sigma I_2 w}{\Sigma w} = 225,$$

$$\text{or,} \quad \frac{40w_1 - 86w_2 + 21200}{100} = 225, \text{ or, } 20w_1 - 43w_2 = 650. \quad (2)$$

Solving (1) and (2), $w_1 = 54$ and $w_2 = 10$.

Hence, the required weights of the five groups are Food: 54, Clothing: 10, Fuel and Light: 10, Rent: 10 and Miscellaneous: 16.

7.13. USES OF INDEX NUMBERS

Index Numbers are widely used to study the relative positions of business and economic conditions. At the Government level, index numbers are used for wage policy, price policy, taxation and general economic policies.

Index Numbers were originally developed to measure the changes in prices of commodities. But they are now increasingly used to measure changes in physical quantities or total value of producton, the volume of trade, the intensity of business activity. We have, thus, the Index Number of Wholesale Prices, the Index Numbers of the Retail Prices, the Index Number of Industrial Production, the Cost of Living Index Number, the Index Number of Business Activity, and of many others. They are all useful in their own fields.

Index Numbers help in framing suitable economic and business policies. For example, the *Cost of Living Index* helps the employer to adjust wages and salaries, specially, Dearness Allowance of an employee in accordance with the cost of living. If the wages, salaries and Dearness Allowance are not adjusted in accordance with the cost of living, it leads very often to strikes and lock-outs causing considerable loss of production and the consequent loss of National Income.

The *Index Number of Industrial Production* is used to study the comparative position in production. The *Wholesale Price Index and the Retail-Price Index* indicate the changes that take place in the value of money. *Index Numbers of Stock Prices* help the speculators to forecast the future trend in the stock market.

Index Numbers are also useful in many other fields, e.g., Sociologists speak of *population indices;* Psychologists measure *Intelligence Quotients;* Health Authorities construct indices to display changes in the adequacy of the Hospital facilities; etc.

Index Numbers are very useful in *deflation.* The process of obtaining the *real wages* from the *nominal wages,* on adjustment by the Cost of Living Index, is known as *deflation.*

Limitations of Index Numbers

(i) Index numbers may be affected by errors like sampling error and formula error.

(ii) Index numbers are based on some selected items and, therefore, they indicate only the broad trend and not the real picture about trend.

(iii) The customs and habits of the consumers may change over a period of time. Also the distribution of income between different gorups of people may change. All these may affect the composition of the Index number.

(iv) There is no all-purpose Index Number. As various methods are used for constructing Index numbers, we get different results from these methods and these may create confusion.

Exercise 7

(Index Numbers)

Theory

1. What is meant by an Index Number ? **[C.U. B. Com. 1969, 1978, 1984; D.U. B. Com. 1972]** State the uses and limitations of Index Numbers.

[C.U. B. Com. 1976, 1984; CA November 1991]

Define Price-relative. **[B.U. B. Com. 1977; ICWAI (Final)]**

2. (i) What is "Index Number"? How it is prepared ? How it is weighted ?

(ii) What is index number ? State the importance of 'base year' in calculating index number.

[C.U. B. Com. (Hons.) 1991]

(iii) Write a critical note on Uses and Limitations of Index Numbers. **[CA November 1991]**

3. (i) Discuss the various problems in the construction of Index Numbers.

[C.U. B. Com. 1976; B.U. B. Com. 1974]

(ii) What are the problems faced in the construction of Index Numbers ? **[CA May 1986]**

(iii) Explain the problem faced in the construction of Cost of Living Index. **[CA May 1992]**

4. Discuss the importance and use of weights in the construction of Index Numbers.

[ICWAI (Final) 1971; C.U. M. Com. 1972]

5. Explain the different methods of construction of Index Numbers.

6. What is the Chain Base Method of construction of Index Numbers and how does it differ from the Fixed Base Method ? **[ICWAI (Final) December 1976; C.U. B. Com. (Hons.) 1983, 1990]**

7. Explain with formula, the construction of the following Index Numbers of Price:

(i) Laspeyre's Index; (ii) Paasche's Index; (iii) Marshall-Edgeworth's Index; (iv) Fisher's Ideal Index.

8. Define Laspeyre's and Paasche's Index Numbers. It is sometimes said that Laspeyre's Price Index tends to *overestimate* price changes while Peasche's Price Index tends to *underestimate* them. Put forward a possible explanation to substantiate this statement.

[G.U. M. Com. 1977; C.U. B. Com. (Hons.) 1985]

9. What weights are used in Laspeyre's, Paasche's and Marshall-Edgeworth's Price Index Numbers? Prove that Marshall-Edgeworth Price Index Number lies between the Laspeyre's and Paasche's Price Index Numbers. **[ICWAI (Final) June 1976]**

10. What are the tests prescribed for a good Index Number ? Describe the Index Number which satisfies these tests.

11. What are the tests to be satisfied by a good Index Number ? Examine how far they are met by Fisher's Ideal Index Number. **[C.U. B. Com. (Hons.) 1982; CA November 1988; May 1991]**

12. Explain the time Reversal Test and Factor Reversal Test of Index Numbers and examine whether the following Index Numbers satisfy the above tests:

Laspeyre's Index Number, Paasche's Index Number, Marshall-Edgeworth Index Number and Fisher's Ideal Index Number. **[ICWAI June 1982; C.U. B. Com. (Hons.) 1986]**

13. (i) What is a Cost of Living Index Number ? What does it measure ? How is it prepared ?

(ii) What is the *cost of living index number ?* Is it the same as the consumer price index number? **[ICWAI June 1979]**

(iii) Write short notes on "Chain Base Index Numbers". **[CA November 1985]**

14. What data are essential for the construction of an Index Number of Industrial Production? What are the weights used and how are they calculated ? Explain the method employed for construction of such an Index Number.

15. Write short notes on each of the following:

(i) Time Reversal Test; **[CA May 1990]**

(ii) Factor Reversal Test. **[CA November 1986]**

(iii) Shifting and splicing of Index numbers. **[CA Foundation June 1994]**

(iv) Cost of Living index. **[ICWAI June 1994]**

16. Distinguish between deflating and splicing the Index Numbers. **[CA November 1989]**

[A]

1. (i) The average price of mustard oil per quintal in the years 1974 to 1978 are given below:

PRICE OF MUSTARD OIL PER QUINTAL IN RS.

Year	Price
1974	585
1975	500
1976	635
1977	780
1978	895

Find the corresponding index numbers taking 1975 as the base year.

(ii) The average prices of Rice, Wheat and Jowar per quintal in the years 1972 to 1976 are given below:

AVERAGE PRICE PER QUINTAL IN RS.

Year	Rice	Wheat	Jowar
1972	150	82	80
1973	175	72	72
1974	200	90	80
1975	220	99	96
1976	198	81	88

Find the price Relatives of Rice, Wheat and Jowar and hence calculate the composite Index Numbers.

(Take 1974 as the base year).

(iii) In 1976, the average price of a commodity was 20% more than in 1975 but 20% less than in 1974; and moreover it was 50% more than 1977. Reduce the data to price relatives using 1975 as base (1975 Price Relative = 100). **[ICWAI December 1978]**

[HINTS. Price-relative of 1976 = 80% of price-relative of 1974, or, 120 = (80/100) $\times x$ or, $x = 150$.

Again price-relative of 1976 = 150% of price-relative of 1977, or, 120 = (150/100) $\times y$, or, $y = 80$. Hence, etc.]

2. From the arranged price of rice given below, find the Chain Base Index Numbers.

Year :	1970	1971	1972	1973	1974	1975
Price in Rs. (per quintal) :	108	96	120	144	132	180

3. From the fixed base index numbers given below, prepare chain base index numbers:

Year :	1966	1967	1968	1969	1970	1971
Index :	94	98	102	95	98	100

[A.U. B. Com.]

4. From the chain base index numbers given below, prepare fixed base index numbers:

Year :	1971	1972	1973	1974	1975
Index :	110	160	140	200	150

[D.U. B. Com. (Hons.) 1976]

5. Find (a) by the method of Aggregates and (b) by the Arithmetic-mean method, index number from the following data:

Commodity	Base Price	Current Price
Rice	30	36
Wheat	25	28
Oil	90	108
Potato	15	21
Fish	96	120

6. Find, by the Arithmetic mean method, the Index Number from the following data:

Commodity	Base Price	Current Price
Rice	30	35
Wheat	22	25
Fish	54	64
Potato	20	25
Coal	15	18

[C.U. B. Com. 1976]

7. Find the Index Number by (a) the method of relatives (using arithmetic mean) and (b) the method of aggregates from the following data:

Commodity	Base Price	Current Price
Rice	35	42
Wheat	30	35
Pulse	40	38
Fish	107	120

[C.U. B. Com. 1973]

8. Construct Laspeyre's price index number from the following data:

Commodity	Base Year		Current Year	
	Price	Quantity	Price	Quantity
A	2	8	4	6
B	5	10	6	5
C	4	14	5	10
D	2	19	2	13

[C.U. B. Com. (Hons.) 1988]

9. Find Laspeyre's and Fisher's price index numbers for the following data for the year 1990 with base year 1986:

Commodity	1986		1990	
	Price (Rs./kg.)	Quantity (kg.)	Price (Rs./kg.)	Quantity (kg.)
Wheat	4.0	20	5.5	20
Sugar	5.0	10	7.0	9
Edible oil	10.5	5	14.5	4
Vegetables	4.5	4	8.0	4

[ICWAI December 1994]

10. Using the following data (given in suitable units) calculate Fisher's Ideal Index Number for 1985 with 1984 as base and examine whether it satisfies the "Time Reversal Test."

Commodity	1984		1985	
	Quantity	Price	Quantity	Price
A	50	32	50	40
B	35	30	40	35
C	55	16	50	18

[C.U. B. Com. (Hons.) 1989]

11. Calculate the price index numbers by (a) Paasche's method, (b) Laspeyre's method, (c) Bowley's method, (d) Fisher's ideal formula.

Commodity	1979		1980	
	Price in Rs.	Quantity in Kgs.	Price in Rs.	Quantity in Kgs.
A	20	8	40	6
B	50	10	60	5
C	40	15	50	10
D	20	20	20	15

[ICWAI December 1980]

12. The data below show the percentage increases in price of a few selected food items and the weights attached to each of them. Calculate the index number for the food group.

Food items :	Rice	Wheat	Dal	Oil	Ghee	Spices	Milk	Meat	Veg.	Ref.
Weights :	40	8	10	7	2	3	7	8	12	3
% increase in Price :	200	150	105	225	300	450	200	400	250	175

(Here Ref. = Refreshment.) **[ICWAI December 1984]**

[HINTS. Current Index of an item (I) = 100 + Percentage increase in price. Calculate the current indices of all the food items and then find the index number by using the formula $I_{01} = \frac{\Sigma Iw}{\Sigma w}$]

13. (i) In calculating a certain cost of living index number the following weights were used: Food 15, Clothing 3, Rent 4, Fuel and light 2, Miscellaneous 1. Calculate the index for a date when the average percentage increases in prices of items in the various groups over the base period were 32, 54, 47, 78 and 58 respectively. **[ICWAI (Final) 1973]**

(ii) During a certain period the cost of living index goes up from 110 to 200 and the salary of a worker is also raised from Rs. 330 to Rs. 500. Does he really gain and if so, by how much in real terms? **[ICWAI December 1992]**

[HINTS. See worked out Example 15.]

14. The following table gives the index numbers for different groups together with their respective weights for 1990 (base year 1985):

Group	Group Index Number	Group Weight
Food	130	60
Clothing	280	5
Lighting and Fuel	190	7
Rent	300	9
Miscellaneous	200	19

(i) Find out the overall cost of living index number for the year 1990.

(ii) Suppose a person was earning Rs. 1,500 per month in 1985; what should be his salary in 1990, if his standard of livng in that year to be the same as in 1985? **[ICWAI December 1994]**

[HINTS. See worked out Example 18.]

[B]

1. Find, by weighted aggregative method, the index number of the following data:

Commodity	Base Price	Current Price	Weight
Rice	140	180	10
Oil	400	550	7
Sugar	100	250	6
Wheat	125	150	8
Fish	200	300	4

[B.U. B. Com. 1977]

2. Construct, by the method of weighted aggregate of prices, the index number for 1960 on the basis of 1952 from the following information:

Commodity	Average Price for 1952	Average Price for 1960	Weights
Rice	30	30	20
Pulse	35.50	32.50	6
Potato	12.50	10	4
Oil	90	100	3.5
Salt	8	10	1.5

3. Find, by Arithmetic Mean Method, the index number from the following data:

Commodity	Base Price	Current Price	Weight
Rice	25	28	20
Wheat	20	22	12
Oil	30	27	10
Fish	90	99	8

[B.U. B. Com. 1972]

4. Construct an index number for the following data using weighted average of price-relatives method:

Commodity	Current Year (1960)	Base Year (1970)	Weights
	Price in Rs.	Price in Rs.	
A	5.20	4.25	30
B	3.75	2.95	40
C	1.95	2.15	15
D	8.10	8.85	15

5. The following are the prices of commodities in 1970 and 1975. Calculate a price index based on price relatives, using the *Geometric mean:*

Year	Commodity					
	A	B	C	D	E	F
1970	45	60	20	50	85	120
1975	55	70	30	75	90	130

[B.U. B. Com. 1976]

6. Calculate, by the method of weighted Arithmetic mean of Price-Relatives, the index number of prices for 1960 on the basis of 1959 from the data given below:

Commodities	Weights	Price per unit	Price per unit
		1959	1960
A	40	16.00	20.00
B	25	40.00	60.00
C	5	0.50	0.50
D	20	5.12	6.25
E	10	2.00	1.50

7. Prepare Index Number for 1959 on the basis of 1949, by applying *Laspeyre's Method,* where the following information is given:

Commodity	1949		1959
	Price	Quantity	Price
Rice	4	50	10
Wheat	3	10	8
Jowar	2	5	4

8. Calculate *Paasche's Index Number for prices* from the following data taking 1968 as the base year:

Commodity	1968		1973	
	Price	Quantity	Price	Quantity
A	1	6	3	5
B	3	5	8	5
C	4	8	10	6

[B.U. 1974]

9. If the ratio of Laspeyres' index and Paasche's index is 28: 27, find the missing figure in the following table:

Commodity	Base Year		Current Year	
	Price	Quantity	Price	Quantity
X	1	10	2	5
Y	1	5	?	2

[ICWAI June 1987]

[HINTS. If p be the missing figure, then $\Sigma p_0q_0 = 15, \Sigma p_1q_0 = 20 + 5p, \Sigma p_0q_1 = 7$ and $\Sigma p_1q_1 = 10 + 2p$. Now use the given condition.]

10. Calculate Marshall-Edgeworth Index Number for prices from the following data, taking 1974 as the base year:

Commodity	1974		1975	
	Price	Quantity	Price	Quantity
A	2	74	3	82
B	5	125	4	140
C	7	40	6	33

11. Construct Fisher's Ideal Index for prices from the following data :

Commodity	1960 (Base Year)		1968 (Current Year)	
	Price	Quantity	Price	Quantity
A	8	6	12	5
B	10	5	11	6
C	7	8	8	5

12. "Marshall-Edgeworth's index number is a good approximation to the Fisher's Ideal Index Number"—Verify the truth of this statement from the following data:

Year	Rice		Wheat		Jowar	
	Price	Quantity	Price	Quantity	Price	Quantity
1970	9.3	100	6.4	11	5.1	5
1977	4.5	90	3.7	10	2.7	3

[ICWAI June 1980]

13. (i) The prices of a commodity in the years 1975 and 1980 were 25 and 30 respectively. Find the price relatives (i) taking 1975 as base year; (ii) taking 1980 as base year. Verify the truth of Time Reversal property. **[C.U. B. Com. 1984]**

(ii) From the following data find the index numbers for the current year and the base year based on each other and show that the G.M. makes it reversible but the A.M. does not.

Commodity	Prices	
	Base Year	Current Year
A	25	55
B	30	45

[ICWAI June 1985]

[SOLUTION.

For A, $\dfrac{p_1}{p_o} \times 100 = \dfrac{55}{25} \times 100 = 220;\quad \dfrac{p_o}{p_1} \times 100 = \dfrac{25}{55} \times 100 = \dfrac{500}{11}$

For B, $\dfrac{p_1}{p_o} \times 100 = \dfrac{45}{30} \times 100 = 150;\quad \dfrac{p_o}{p_1} \times 100 = \dfrac{30}{45} \times 100 = \dfrac{200}{3}$

I_{01} as A.M. of price-relatives $= \dfrac{220 + 150}{2} = 185$

I_{10} as A.M. of price-relatives $= \dfrac{1}{2}\left(\dfrac{500}{11} + \dfrac{200}{3}\right) = \dfrac{3770}{66} = 56.06.$

I_{01} as G.M. of price-relatives $= \sqrt{220 \times 150} = 181.66$

$I_{10} = \sqrt{\dfrac{500}{11} \times \dfrac{200}{3}} = 55.05$

For A.M., $I_{01} \times I_{10} = \dfrac{185}{100} \times \dfrac{56.06}{100} \neq 1$ and for G.M., $I_{01} \times I_{10} = \dfrac{181.66}{100} \times \dfrac{55.05}{100} = 1.$

Hence, the results follows.]

14. From the information gtiven below, find the Laspeyres' and Paasche's price index numbers for year II with year I as base:

Commodity	Price/Unit (in Rs.)		Commodity (in kg.)	Total value (in Rs.)
	Year I	Year II	Year I	Year II
A	24.09	12.30	5	184.50
B	20.66	10.17	8	122.04
C	18.60	16.42	16	295.56
D	9.45	10.21	25	189.00

Verify whether the above index numbers satisfy the Time Reversal Test. **[ICWAI June 1994]**

[HINTS. Total value $(p_1'q_1')$ in the year II = 184.50 and $p_1' = 12.30$;

$\therefore\ q_1' = \frac{184.50}{12.30} = 15$, etc. See worked out Example 15.]

15. From the following price of commodities given in rupees per unit, find chain base index numbers with 1980 as the base year:

Commodity \ Year	1980	1981	1982	1983	1984
A	2	3	4	5	6
B	8	10	12	15	18
C	4	5	8	10	12

[ICWAI December 1993]

[HINTS. See worked out Example 12.]

[C]

1. (i) Construct the cost of living index number from the following group data:

Group	Weights	Group Index Number for a given year
(1) Food	47	247
(2) Fuel and Light	7	293
(3) Clothing	8	289
(4) House Rent	13	100
(5) Miscellaneous	14	236

[ICWAI (Final) 1977; C.U. B. Com. (Hons.) 1986]

(ii) From the following data, calculate *the cost of living index number:*

Group	Weight	Index Number (Base: 1952–53 = 100)
Food	50	241
Clothing	2	221
Fuel and Light	3	204
Rent	16	256
Miscellaneous	29	179

[C.U. B. Com. (Hons.) 1991]

2. Annual production (in million tonnes) for four commodities is given below:

Commodity	Production in year			Weights
	1970	1974	1975	
A	160	200	266	20
B	24	42	45	30
C	50	72	68	13
D	250	168	156	17

Calculate quantity index numbers for the years 1974 and 1975 with 1970 as base year, using (i) simple arithmetic mean, and (ii) weighted arithmetic mean of the relatives.

[ICWAI (Final) 1976]

3. Find index numbers for the years 1961, 1962, 1963 by the chain base method, with base year 1960, from the following table:

Year :	1960	1961	1962	1963
Link Index :	100	110	95.5	109.5

[ICWAI (Final)]

4. Calculate quantity index for 1973 from the following data using (i) Laspeyre's formula, (ii) Paasche's formula and Fisher's formula with 1968 as the base year:

Commodity	1968		1973	
	Price	Quantity	Price	Quantity
A	1	6	5	4
B	3	5	8	5
C	4	8	10	6

5. Compute, by *Fisher's formula*, the Quantity Index Number from the data given below:

Article	1974		1976	
	Price (Rs.)	Total Value (Rs.)	Price (Rs.)	Total Value (Rs.)
A	5	50	4	48
B	8	48	7	49
C	6	18	5	20

[Delhi U. B. Com. (Hons.) 1977]

6. For the following data, calculate quantity index number for the current year (i.e., Q_{01}) by Fisher's formula:

Commodity	Base Year		Current Year	
	Quantity	Price	Quantity	Price
I	6	5	8	6
II	8	3	10	2
III	12	2	10	2
IV	2	8	2	7
V	5	9	6	9

[CA November 1990]

7. With the data given below, calculate the Price Index and Quantity Index by *Fisher's Ideal Formula* and then verify that Fisher's Ideal Formula satisfies the *Factor Reversal Test:*

Commodity	Base Year		Current Year	
	Price (Rs.)	Quantity ('000 tons)	Price (Rs.)	Quantity ('000 tons)
A	56	72	50	26
B	32	107	30	83
C	41	62	28	48

[ICWAI (Final) December 1977]

8. Using the following data, show that Fisher's Ideal Index satisfies both the Time Reversal Test and Factor Reversal Test:

Commodity	Base Year		Current Year	
	Price	Quantity	Price	Quantity
A	10	50	12	60
B	8	30	9	32
C	6	35	7	40

9. The price relatives and weights of a set of commodities are given in the following table:

Commodity :	A	B	C	D
Price Relative :	120	127	125	119
Weight :	$2w_1$	w_2	w_1	$w_2 + 3$

If the index for the set is 122 and the sum of the weights is 40, find w_1 and w_2.

[ICWAI December 1987, 1989]

[HINTS.

$$2w_1 + w_2 + w_1 + (w_2 + 3) = 40, \quad \text{or,} \quad 3w_1 + 2w_2 = 37 \tag{1}$$

$$122 = \text{Index No.} = \text{A.M. of Price relatives} = \frac{120 \times 2w_1 + 127w_2 + 125w_1 + 119(w_2 + 3)}{2w_1 + w_2 + w_1 + (w_2 + 3)}$$

$$= \frac{365w_1 + 246w_2 + 357}{40}, \quad \text{or,} \quad 365w_1 + 246w_2 = 4523 \tag{2}$$

Solve (1) and (2).]

10. The cost of living index uses the following weights: Food: 40, Rent: 15, Clothing: 20, Fuel: 10, Miscellaneous: 15.

During the period 1974–84, the cost of living index rose from 100 to 205.72. Over the same period the percentage rises in prices were: Rent: 60, Clothing: 180, Fuel: 75, Miscellaneous: 165. What was the percentage change in the price of food? **[ICWAI December 1988]**

[HINTS. See worked out Example 24 (2nd Method).]

Group	Weights (w)	Percentage Rise (i)	iw
Food	40	x	$40x$
Rent	15	60	900
Clothing	20	180	3600
Fuel	10	75	750
Miscellaneous	15	165	2475
Total	$100 = \Sigma w$	—	$40x + 7725 = \Sigma iw$

Average percentage rise $= \frac{\Sigma iw}{\Sigma w}$, or, $205.72 - 100 = \frac{40x+7725}{100}$. Hence, $x =$ etc.]

[D]

1. The following shows the consumer price index numbers (base: November 1950 = 100) for December 1953 for a certain class of families in West Bengal, separately for the five broad groups of items. Compute the over-all consumer price index from the given data:

Item Group	Weights of Group	Group Index
Food	58.55	91.4
Clothing	5.37	106.5
Fuel and Light	6.15	102.2
Housing	9.61	100.0
Miscellaneous	20.32	100.3

[C.U. Econ. (Hons.) 1977]

2. (i) During a certain period the cost of living index number goes up from 120 to 210 and the salary of a worker is also raised from Rs. 960 to Rs. 1,575. Does the worker really gain, and if so, by how much in *real terms* ?

[HINTS. Use **Real Wage = (Actual Wage / C.L.I.) × 100** and show that Real Wage decreases from Rs. 800 to Rs. 750.]

(ii) Net monthly income of an employee was Rs. 800 per month in 1980. The Consumer Price Index Number was 160 in 1980. It rises to 200 in 1984.

Calculate the additional dearness allowance to be paid to the employee if he has to be rightly compensated. **[ICWAI June 1986]**

3. Using the following data, show that Laspeyre's price index formula does not satisfy the time reversal test:

Commodity	Base Year		Current Year	
	Price	Quantity	Price	Quantity
A	6	50	10	56
B	2	100	2	120
C	4	60	2	60
D	10	30	12	24
E	8	40	12	36

[ICWAI (Final) January 1971]

4. Calculate the Cost of Living Index Number from the following data:

Items	Price		Weight
	Base Year	Current Year	
Food	30	47	4
Fuel	8	12	1
Clothing	14	18	3
House Rent	22	15	2
Miscellaneous	25	30	1

5. Compute Index Number from the following data by using (i) Laspeyre's Method, (ii) Paasche's Method and (iii) Fisher's Ideal Method:

Commodity	Base Year		Current Year	
	Quantity	Price	Quantity	Price
A	12	10	15	12
B	15	7	20	5
C	24	5	20	9
D	5	16	5	14

6. Calculate Fisher's Quantity Index from the following data and show that it satisfies Time Reversal Test:

Commodity	Base Year		Current Year	
	Price (Rs.)	Value	Price (Rs.)	Value
P	10	200	12	300
Q	8	108	10	220
R	20	160	25	250
S	18	144	20	140
T	35	280	30	300

[B.U. B. Com. 1973]

7. When the cost of tobacco was increased by 50%, a certain hardened smoker, who maintained his former scale of consumption, said that the rise had increased his cost of living by 5%. What percentage of his cost of living was due to buying tobacco before the change in price ?

8. Monthly wages average in different years is as follows:

Year :	1967	1968	1969	1970	1971	1972	1973
Wages (Rs.) :	200	240	350	360	360	380	400
Price Index :	100	150	200	220	230	250	250

Calculate real wages index numbers. How much increase in money wages is required to maintain real wages intact ? **[ICWAI December 1979]**

9. The cost of living index uses the following weights:

Food: 40, Rent: 15, Clothing: 20, Fuel: 10, Miscellaneous: 15.

During the period 1964–74, the cost of living index number rose from 100 to 205.65. Over the same period the percentage rise in prices were: Rent: 60, Clothing: 180, Fuel: 75, Miscellaneous: 165. What was the percentage change in the price of food ?

10. The cost of living index for the working class families for 1983 was 267.22. Using the data, find the weight of the fuel and lighting group:

Groups	Weights	Index Number
Food	46	352
Fuel and Lighting	?	220
Clothing	9	230
House Rent	13	160
Miscellaneous	22	190

11. The following table gives the cost of living index numbers for different commodity groups together with respective weights for 1984 (Base Year = 1961).

Group :	Food	Clothing	Fuel and Light	Rent	Miscellaneous
Group Index :	425	475	300	400	250
Group Weight :	62	4	6	12	16

Obtain the overall cost of living index number. Suppose a person was earning Rs. 600 in 1961, what should be his salary in 1984 if his standard of living in that year is to be the same as in 1961?

[ICWAI December 1985]

12. The total value of retained imports into India in 1960 was Rs. 71.5 million per month. The corresponding total for 1967 was Rs. 87.6 million per month. The index of volume of retained imports in 1967 compared with 1960 (= 100) was 62.0. Calculate the price index for retained imports for 1967 on 1960 as base. **[C.U. B. Com. (Hons.) 1986]**

13. Shift the base period of the following series of index numbers from 1980 to 1987:

Year :	1984	1985	1986	1987	1988	1989	1990
Index Number (Base 1980 = 100) :	125	130	142	150	160	168	180

14. Assuming that an index number is 100 in 1968, it rises 3% in 1969, falls 1% in 1970 and rises 2% in 1971 and 3% in 1972; rise and fall begin with respect to the previous year. Calculate the index for the five years, using 1972 as the base year. **[ICWAI December 1976]**

15. **Splice** the following two series of index numbers with (i) base 1980 and (ii) base 1985:

Year :	1980	1981	1982	1983	1984	1985	1986	1987	1988	1989	1990
Series A :	100	120	135	160	178	200	...	...	...	...	...
Series B :	...	...	...	...	...	100	110	98	115	125	150

Answers

[A]

1. (i) 117, 100, 127, 156, 179; (ii) Composite Index Numbers: 88.33, 85.83, 100, 113.33, 99.67; (iii) 150, 100, 120, 80. **2.** 100, 88.89, 125, 120, 91.67, 136.36. **3.** 100, 104.3, 104.1, 93.1, 103.2, 102. **4.** 110, 176, 246.4, 492.8, 739.2. **5.** (i) 122.3;(ii) 123.4. **6.** 118.77. **7.** (i) 110.95 or 111.0; (ii) 110.85 or 110.9. **8.** 125. **9.** 141.9; 142. **10.** 119.4. **11.** (i) 125.23; (ii) 124.70; (iii) 124.96; (iv) 124.96. **12.** 319. **13.** (i) 141.76; (ii) No, his real wages decrease by Rs. 50. **14.** 170.3; Rs. 2,554.50.

[B]

1. 144.7. **2.** 96. **3.** 106.8. **4.** 114.9. **5.** 124.2. **6.** 124.4. **7.** 250. **8.** 261.36. **9.** 4. **10.** 91.527 or 91.5. **11.** 123.49 or 123.5. **12.** M.E. Index = 49.135 and F.I. Index = 49.134; hence, etc. **13.** 120; 83.33. **14.** 80.63; 70.70; None of the two formulae satisfies Time Reversal Test. **15.** 100, 133.33, 180.7, 229.61, 275.53.

[C]

1. (i) 231.19; (ii) 223.91. **2.** (i) 127.8, 138.04; (ii) 134.55, 147.23. **3.** 110, 105.1, 115. **4.** (i) 81.13; (ii) 80; (iii) 80.56. **5.** 120.65. **6.** 112.88. **7.** $P_{01} = 84.95$ and $Q_{01} = 60.79$. **9.** $w_1 = 7, w_2 = 8$.

[D]

1. 95.51. **2.** (i) No. Real wage decreases by Rs. 50; (ii) Rs. 200. **4.** 128.98. **5.** (i) 118.8; (ii) 112.8; (iii) 115.7. **6.** 103.88. **7.** 10%. **8.** 100, 80, 87.5, 81.8, 78.3, 76, 80 (base year 1967); 0, 60, 50, 80, 100, 120, 100 (in Rs.). **9.** 71. **10.** 10. **11.** 388.5; Rs. 2,331. **12.** 197.6. **13.** 83.33, 86.67, 94.67, 100, 106.67, 112, 120. **14.** 93.5, 96.3, 95.3, 97.2, 100. **15.** (i) 220, 196, 230, 250, 300; (ii) 50, 60, 67.5, 80, 89, 100.

CHAPTER 8

STATISTICAL DECISION THEORY: DECISION MAKING WITHOUT PROBABILITY AND WITH PROBABILITY

8.1. INTRODUCTION

In our daily life, everybody (educated or uneducated) has to make decisions some of which are of routine type and trivial in nature. For example, (i) a man may decide whether to carry an unbrella or not while going to the office, (ii) a student may decide whether to put on a blue or a green shirt while going to college, (iii) a house-wife may decide whether to serve tea or coffee to a guest, etc. These decisions do not involve high thinking or any calculation. But in many situations, we have to make important decisions which involve a lot of reasoning and thinking. For example, decisions whether (i) to accept or not to accept a new job, (ii) to buy or not to buy shares of a particular company, (iii) to launch or not to launch a new product in the market, (iv) to increase or not to increase production of a manufacturing company, etc. are all important decisions which will affect the decision-makers, their family members and other people in the society. Such decisions depend on the personal judgement of the decision-maker. If there is only one course of action, no decision is necessary and we choose the given course of action to solve the problem. But if there are two or more alternative courses of action (or paths), then the decision-maker makes detailed and careful analysis of the various alternative courses of action (or paths) involved in each situation and then decides which one is to be taken.

8.2. ELEMENTS IN DECISION MAKING

There are three elements in decision making:

(i) **Acts,** (ii) **States of Nature,** and (iii) **Decisions**.

The course of action that the decision-maker takes is called an **act** or **strategy**. Decision problems have at least two possible acts available. The results of any action on the part of a decision-maker depend on *certain factors* which are often beyond his or her control. The number of factors influencing the decision problem may be infinite, but usually some relevant set of uncontrollable variables directly affects the decision-maker's act. These factors are known as **states of nature** (or *event* states). The decision-maker is to identify a relevant set of states of nature.

In a decision problem, it is required to measure the degree to which the decision-maker's objective is achieved. In this case, *monetary value* is used to represent achievement (or lack of it) of certain goals. If we can place a monetary value to a consequence (or outcome), then it is called a *payoff* (or *worth*) of the outcome. Thus to each combination of an action and a state of nature, we get a *payoff* or a *conditional value.* In business problems this value is often expressed in terms of *profits* or *costs*, although other payoffs such as *units of satisfaction* or *utility* are sometimes used. If these conditional values (or payoffs) are put in the form of a table, then this table is called a **payoff table** or **payoff matrix**.

ILLUSTRATION 1. *"Narmada Cement Company is evaluating its operations. The Company may expand its current operation or sell its stock to a compreitor. If cement prices decline, then it would be better to sell to their competitor and invest the sale proceeds in a Milk Food Company. If, however, cement prices rise, the company should expand its current stock. If prices remain stable for the next year, it should decide to maintain current level of operations". For this problem list* (i) *the relevant acts* and (ii) *the states of nature.*

(i) The relevant **acts** are

a_1: Expand Operations; a_2: Sell to competitor; a_3: Maintain current level.

(ii) **States of nature** are

S_1: Prices decline; S_2: Prices rise; S_3: Prices remain stable.

ILLUSTRATION 2. *A pig breeder can either produce* 30 *or* 40 *pigs. The total production of his competitors can be either* 4,000 *or* 8,000 *pigs. If they produce* 4,000 *pigs, his profit per pig is* Rs. 55; *if they produce* 8,000 *pigs, his profit per pig is only* Rs. 40. *Construct a pay-off table.*

Here the **acts** are: (i) a_1: Produce 30 pigs; (ii) a_2: Produce 40 pigs, and the **states of nature** are: (i) S_1: Production of competitors is 4,000 pigs; S_2: Production of competitors is 8,000 pigs.

TABLE 8.1 PAYOFF TABLE FOR THE GIVEN INFORMATIONS

States of nature / Act	Production of Competitors	
	4,000 pigs (S_1)	8,000 pigs (S_2)
a_1: Produce 30 pigs	30× Rs. 55 = Rs. 1,650	30× Rs. 40 = Rs. 1,200
a_2: Produce 40 pigs	40× Rs. 55 = Rs. 2,200	40× Rs. 40 = Rs. 1,600

In some *Payoff table, Acts* may be shown in the first row and *States of nature* in the first column.

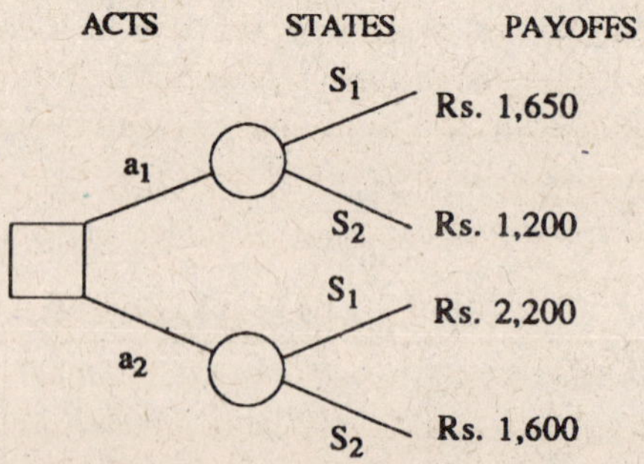

Fig 8.1 Decision tree showing the information of the table 8.1

The information obtained in table 8.1 can be represented by a decision tree in a different way as shown in Fig. 8.1. Since there are two possible acts to choose, the square node has two branches.

Again since these two possible acts can interact with one of two states, each act branch has two state branches. The payoffs corresponding to these possibilities are shown on the right side of the figure. Payoff Rs. 1650 occurs if the decision-maker picks act a_1 (Produce 30 pigs) and state S_1 occurs. Similarly, we can explain for the other three paths through the decision tree.

8.3. DECISION MAKING SITUATIONS

The classification for decision making situations is based upon the knowledge of the decision-maker about the states of nature. There are two types of decision-making situations:

1. **Decision making under certainty;**
2. **Decision making under uncertainty.**

Decision making under certainty is the process of choosing a decision altenative when the state of nature is *known.* In this case there will be only *one state of nature column in the payoff table and the action which yields the best payoff in the column is chosen.*

Decision making under uncertainty is the process of choosing a decision alternative when the states of nature are not known. Most decision making situations involve *decision making under uncertainty* which is relatively difficult. In this case, the decision-maker first selects a criterion and then determines which decision alternative is the best under the chosen criterion.

8.4. DECISION MAKING UNDER UNCERTAINTY WITHOUT PROBABILITY: CHOICE OF CRITERION

In some situations of decision making under uncertainty, the decision-maker prefers to choose a decision criterion which does not require any knowledge of the probabilities of the states of nature. Three of the most popular criteria available are stated below.

(i) **Maximin** (or **Minimax**)

(ii) **Maximax** (or **Minimin**) and

(iii) **Minimax Regret.**

Of the above three criteria the decision-maker can select the most appropriate one according to his or her personal judgement. We shall now discuss the above three criteria for decision making under uncertainty by showing how they can be used to solve decision problems.

Maximin

It is a pessimistic (or conservative) approach to arrive at a decision. In order to pick the *best act* or *strategy* using *maximin,* the decision-maker first finds the minimum payoff for each act and then selects the act which maximizes these minimum values. It is used to maximize the minimum possible profits.

ILLUSTRATION 1. *Consider the following payoff table:*

TABLE 8.2 PAYOFF TABLE

Acts \ States of Nature	S_1	S_2	S_3	S_4
a_1	−2	−3	4	3
a_2	−1	0	6	7
a_3	−3	−4	9	5

From Table 8.2, we see that the minimum payoffs for each act are

Act	Minimum Payoff
a_1	−3
a_2	−1 ⟵
a_3	−4

∴ *Maximum of the minimum payoffs is* −**1** which corresponds to the **act** a_2. Hence the **decision-maker chooses** $\mathbf{a_2}$ **as the best act.**

If Table 8.2 resprsent payoffs of the profit and loss in ten thousand rupees of a firm, then maximin criterion guarantees that the amount of loss will be at most Rs. 10,000.

If in a problem it is required to minimize the maximum possible costs, then the reversed criterion *minimax* is used in which the decision-maker first finds maximum payoff for each act and then selects the act which minimizes these maximum values.

Maximax

It is an optimistic approach to arrive at a decision. In order to pick the *best act or strategy using maximax criterion,* the decision-maker first finds the *maximum payoff* for each act and then selects the act which *maximizes these maximum values.* It concentrates only on an attempt to obtain highest gain possible and ignores possible losses or low returns.

ILLUSTRATION 2. *From the Table* 8.2, *we see that the maximum payoffs for the acts are*

Act	Maximum Payoff
a_1	4
a_2	7
a_3	9 ⟵

∴ Maximum of the maximum payoffs is 9 which corresponds to the act a_3. Hence the **decision-maker selects** $\mathbf{a_3}$ **as the best act.**

For *minimization problems,* the reversed criterion *minimin* is used in which the decision-maker first finds minimum pyaoff for each act and then selects the act which minimizes these minimum values.

ILLUSTRATION 3. (*Decision making by using Decision tree*) *Tree diagram* in Fig. 8.2 respresents the payoffs given in table 8.2. The square node has three branches indicating *three-acts* a_1, a_2 and a_3. Again each act branch has four branches representing the *four states of nature* S_1, S_2, S_3 and S_4. The *payoffs* corresponding to the acts and states of nature are shown on the extreme right side of the decision tree in Fig 8.2.

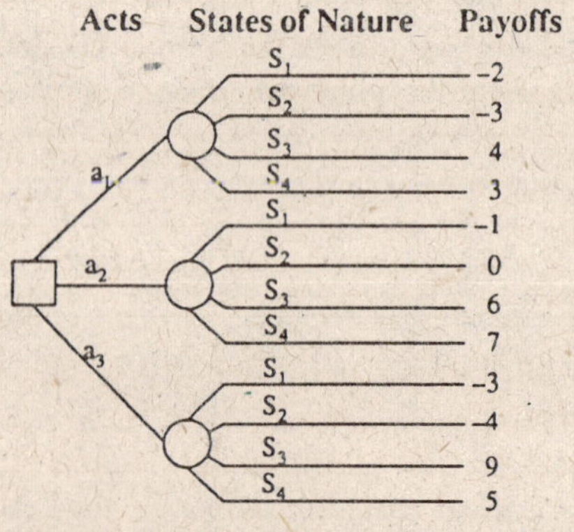

Fig 8.2 Decision tree

(i) From the *tree diagram*, we see that the minimum pay-offs for the acts a_1, a_2, a_3 are $-3, -1, -4$ of which -1 is the *maximum* and -1 corresponds to the act a_2. Hence $\mathbf{a_2}$ *is the* **best act** *according to* **maximin criterion.**

(ii) Again from the *tree diagram*, we see that the maximum payoffs for the acts a_1, a_2, a_3 are 4,7,9 of which 9 is the *maximum* and 9 corresponds to the act a_3. Hence $\mathbf{a_3}$ *is the* **best act** *according to* **maximax criterion.**

Thus *tree diagrams* can be used in decision making under uncertainty withoiut probability. These tree diagrams are called *decision trees.*

Minimax Regret

It is an approach somewhere between maximin and maximax criteria. In this criterion **opportunity loss** or **regret table** is used. To construct the **opportunity loss or regret table** from a payoff table, the payoff of each act under a given state of nature is subtracted from the maximum payoff under the state of nature. Opportunity loss tables will never contain negative values. To apply **minimax regret criterion,** we first construct the opportunity loss or regret table from the given payoff table and find the maximum opportunity loss or regret for each act. Then we select the act which minimizes these maximum opportunity losses or regrets.

ILLUSTRATION 3. *Construct the opportunity loss or regret table and find the best act using minimax regret criterion from the following payoff table:*

Act \ States of Nature	S_1	S_2	S_3	S_4
a_1	0	−1	7	−3
a_2	−5	8	−2	2
a_3	−10	4	15	12

The opportunity loss table for the given payoff table is constructed below:

TABLE 8.3 OPPORTUNITY LOSS TABLE

Act \ States of Nature	S_1	S_2	S_3	S_4
a_1	$0 - 0 = 0$	$8 + 1 = 9$	$15 - 7 = 8$	$12 + 3 = 15$
a_2	$0 + 5 = 5$	$8 - 8 = 0$	$15 + 2 = 17$	$12 - 2 = 10$
a_3	$0 + 10 = 10$	$8 - 4 = 4$	$15 - 15 = 0$	$12 - 12 = 0$

From the table 8.3, we see that the *maximum opportunity loss* or *regret for each act* is

Act	Maximum Regret
a_1	15
a_2	17
a_3	10 ←

The minimum of the maximum regrets is 10 which corresponds to the act a_3. Hence **the best act is** $\mathbf{a_3}$.

EXAMPLE 1. *A pig breeder can either produce* 20 *or* 30 *pigs. The total production of his competitors can be either* 5,000 *or* 10,000 *pigs. If they produce* 5,000 *pigs, his profit per pig is* Rs. 60*; if they produce* 10,000 *pigs his profit per pig is only* Rs. 45. *Construct a payoff table and also state what should the pig breeder decide.* **[CA November 1989]**

SOLUTION. The required payoff table is constructed below:

TABLE 8.4 PAYOFF TABLE FOR THE GIVEN DATA

Act \ State of Nature	Production of Competitors	
	5,000 pigs (S_1) (Profits)	10,000 pigs (S_2) (Profits)
a_1 : Produce 20 pigs	20 × 60 = Rs. 1,200	20 × 45 = Rs. 900
a_2 : Produce 30 pigs	30 × 60 = Rs. 1,800	30 × 45 = Rs. 1,350

If we use *maximin criterion* (assuming the pig breeder to be conservative), then the minimum payoffs for the acts are Rs. 900 and Rs. 1,350 of which Rs. 1350 is maximum. The act "produce 30 pigs" corresponds to Rs. 1350.

Hence **the pig breeder should decide to produce 30 pigs.**

If we use *maximax criterion,* the *maximum payoffs* for the two acts are Rs. 1,200 and Rs. 1,800 of which Rs. 1,800 *is the maximum.* The act "produce 30 pigs" corresponds to Rs. 1,800 and *the decision is the same* in this case.

EXAMPLE 2. *Suppose that a decision-maker faced with three decision alternatives and four states of nature constructs the following profit payoff table:*

Acts \ States of Nature	S_1	S_2	S_3	S_4
a_1	16	10	12	7
a_2	13	12	9	9
a_3	11	14	15	14

Assuming that the decision-maker has no knowledge about the probabilities of occurrence of the four states of nature, find the decisions to be recommended under each of the following criteria:

(i) *Maximin*; (ii) *Maximax*; (iii) *Minimax Regret.*

SOLUTION.

(i) From the given profit payoff table, we see that the minimum payoffs for the acts a_1, a_2, a_3 are respectively 7, 9, 11 of which 11 is maximum. Thus maximum of the minimum payoffs is 11 which corresponds to the act a_3.

Hence using *Maximin Criterion* the *decision-maker recommends* **a_3 as the best act.**

(ii) Under the Maximax criterion, we see that the *maximum payoffs* for the three acts a_1, a_2, a_3 in the given payoff table are respectively 16, 13, 15 of which 16 *is maximum.* Thus maximum of the maximum payoffs is 16 which corresponds to the act a_1.

Hence using *Maximax criterion the decision-maker recommends* **a_1 as the best act.**

(iii) In this case first we have to construct *opportunity loss or regret table* from the given payoff table

TABLE 8.5 OPPORTUNITY LOSS (OR REGRET) TABLE

Acts \ States of Nature	S_1	S_2	S_3	S_4
a_1	16 − 16 = 0	14 − 10 = 4	15 − 12 = 3	14 − 7 = 7
a_2	16 − 13 = 3	14 − 12 = 2	15 − 9 = 6	14 − 9 = 5
a_3	16 − 11 = 5	14 − 14 = 0	15 − 15 = 0	14 − 14 = 0

From the Table 8.5, we see that the *maximum opportunity losses* (or *regrets*) for the three acts a_1, a_2, a_3 are respectively 7, 6, 5 of which 5 *is minimum.* Thus the *minimum of the maximum regrets is* 5 *which corresponds to the act* a_3.

Hence using *Minimax Regret criterion the decision-maker recommends* **a_3 as the best act.**

8.5. DECISION MAKING UNDER UNCERTAINTY WITH PROBABILITY

In many situations of decision making under uncertainty, the decision-maker develops good probability estimates for the states of nature. Two decision criteria involving these probability estimates are used in the selection of an *act* (or *decision alternative*). These two criteria are

(i) **Expected Monetary Value (EMV);**

(ii) **Expected Opportunity Loss (EOL).**

We shall now discuss these two criteria and show how they can be used in decision making under uncertainty.

Expected Monetary Value (EMV)

The Expected Monetary Value (EMV) *for a course of action* (*or decision alternative*) *i and the event* (*or state of nature*) *j is defined by*

$$\mathbf{EMV_i = \sum_j X_{ij} P_j},$$

where X_{ij} is the payoff of action i for the event j and P_j is the probability of occurrence of event j. Clearly $P_j \geq 0$ for all events (*or states of nature*) *j and $\Sigma P_j = P_1 + P_2 + \cdots + P_n = 1$, where n is the number of possible events.*

To apply *EMV* criterion, the decision-maker first finds the expected monetary value for each course of action (or decision alternative) i and then select the alternative (or act) which yields the best expected value.

EXAMPLE 3. *Payoffs of three Acts X, Y, Z and the states of nature of L, M, N are given below:*

Payoff (Rupees)

Acts / States of Nature	X	Y	Z
L	−20	−50	200
M	200	−100	−50
N	400	600	300

The probabilities of the states of nature are 0.3, 0.4 *and* 0.3 *respectively. Calculate the Expected Monetary values for the above data and select the best act.* **[CA May 1991]**

SOLUTION. The expected monetary value (EMV) for an Act i and the event (state of nature) j is given by

$EMV_i = \sum_j X_{ij} P_j$, where X_{ij} = payoff of action i and P_j = Prob. of occurrence of event j.

$\therefore$ EMV for the act $X = -20 \times 0.3 + 200 \times 0.4 + 400 \times 0.3 = -6 + 80 + 120 =$ Rs. 194.

EMV for the act $Y = -50 \times 0.3 + (-100) \times 0.4 + 600 \times 0.3 = -15 - 40 + 180 =$ Rs. 125.

EMV for the act $Z = 200 \times 0.3 + (-50 \times 0.4) + 300 \times 0.3 = 60 - 20 + 90 =$ Rs. 130.

We see that EMV for the act X is Rs. 194 *which is maximum.*

Hence *act X should be selected under EMV criterion.*

EXAMPLE 4. *The payoffs of three acts a_1, a_2, a_3 and states of nature S_1, S_2, S_3 are given below:*

Acts / States of nature	S_1	S_2	S_3
a_1	10	−20	250
a_2	200	50	−30
a_3	−80	150	100

The probabilities of the states of nature are 0.2, 0.5 *and* 0.3 *respectively. Draw* **tree diagrams** *to show the given payoffs and the expected payoffs and then determine the best act according to the EMV criterion.*

SOLUTION. The given payoffs are shown in Fig. 8.3 and the expected payoffs are shown in Fig. 8.4 by decision trees.

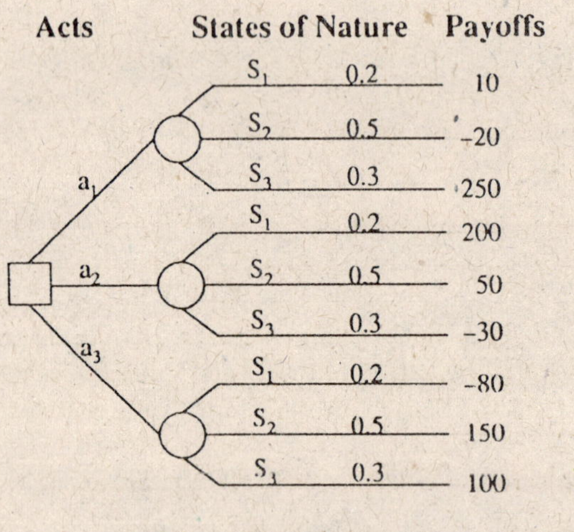

Fig 8.3 Decision tree representing the given payoffs

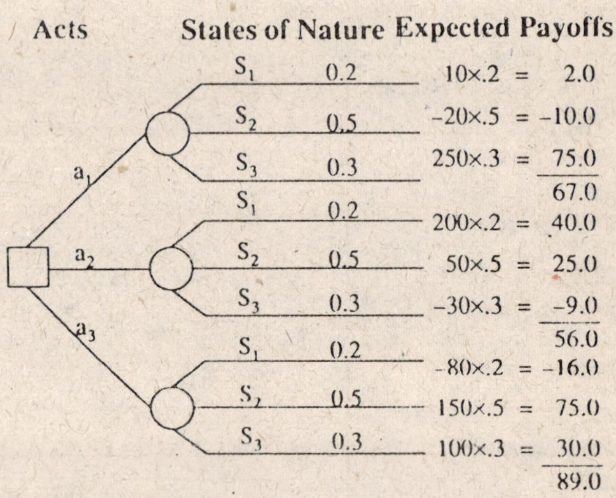

Fig 8.4 Decision tree representing the expected payoffs

From Fig. 8.4, we see that the decision tree represents the expected payoffs and EMV for each act. To find the expected payoff for each state of nature we multiply each payoff by its probability value. Then we compute EMV for each act by adding the expected payoffs of the states of nature for the act. From the *decision tree* in Fig. 8.4, we see that the *maximum EMV is 89.0* which corresponds to the *act* a_3. Hence **the best act according to EMV criterion is a_3**.

EXAMPLE 5. *The conditional pay-offs in rupees for each action-event combination are as under:*

Event	Action			
	1	2	3	4
A	4	−2	7	8
B	0	6	3	5
C	−5	9	2	−3
D	3	1	4	5
E	6	6	3	2

(i) *Which is the best action in accordance with the maximin criterion?*

(ii) *Which is the best action in accordance with EMV criterion, presuming all events have equal probabilities of occurrence?* [CA November 1987]

SOLUTION.

(i) From the given payoff table we see that the *minimum payoffs* for the acts 1, 2, 3 and 4 are respectively $-5, -2, 2$ and -3 of which 2 *is maximum*. Thus the maximum of the minimum payoffs is 2 which corresponds to the act 3.

Hence **the best action in accordance with the maximin criterion is 3.**

(ii) Since all the 5 events have equal probabilities of occurrence, we assign a probability 0.2 to each of the five events A, B, C, D, E. The given payoff table along with assigned probabilities is written below:

TABLE 8.6 PAYOFF TABLE WITH ASSIGNED PROBABILITIES

Event	Probability	Action			
		1	2	3	4
A	0.2	4	−2	7	8
B	0.2	0	6	3	5
C	0.2	−5	9	2	−3
D	0.2	3	1	4	5
E	0.2	6	6	3	2

EMV of the four actions are computed in the following payoff table:

TABLE 8.7 CALCULATIONS FOR EMV OF FOUR ACTIONS

Events	Probability	Expected payoff actions			
	(P_j)	Action 1 $(X_{1j})P_j$	Action 2 $(X_{2j})P_j$	Action 3 $(X_{3j})P_j$	Action 4 $(X_{4j})P_j$
A	0.2	$4 \times 0.2 = 0.8$	$-2 \times 0.2 = -0.4$	$7 \times 0.2 = 1.4$	$8 \times 0.2 = 1.6$
B	0.2	$0 \times 0.2 = 0.0$	$6 \times 0.2 = 1.2$	$3 \times 0.2 = 0.6$	$5 \times 0.2 = 1.0$
C	0.2	$-5 \times 0.2 = -1.0$	$9 \times 0.2 = 1.8$	$2 \times 0.2 = 0.4$	$-3 \times 0.2 = -0.6$
D	0.2	$3 \times 0.2 = 0.6$	$1 \times 0.2 = 0.2$	$4 \times 0.2 = 0.8$	$5 \times 0.2 = 1.0$
E	0.2	$6 \times 0.2 = 1.2$	$6 \times 0.2 = 1.2$	$3 \times 0.2 = 0.6$	$2 \times 0.2 = 0.4$
Total (EMV)		$\Sigma X_{1j}P_j = 1.6$	$\Sigma X_{2j}P_j = 4.0$	$\Sigma X_{3j}P_j = 3.8$	$\Sigma X_{4j}P_j = 3.4$

We see that the *best (highest) EMV is* 4.0 *which corresponds to the action* 2.

Hence **action 2** *is the best action in accordance with the EMV criterion.*

8.5.1. Expected Opportunity Loss (EOL)

We have already defined *opportunity loss* in Minimax Regret criterion (see. Art. 8.4) as the numerical difference between the payoff value of each act under a state of nature and the maximum payoff under the same state of nature.

The Expected Opportunity Loss (EOL) due to an action (or decision alternative) i and the event (or state of nature) j is defined by $EOL_i = \sum_j l_{ij}P_j$, where l_{ij} is the oppotunity loss due to an action i for the event j and P_j is the probability of occurrence of event j.

To apply EOL criterion, we first construct the appropriate opportunity loss table and then compute *the expected opportunity loss* (EOL) for each act. To do so we multiply the opportunity loss for each event (or state) by the corresponding probability for that event and add these values together. Then we select the *best act due to which EOL is minimum.*

EXAMPLE 6. *Calculate expected opportunity loss (EOL) from the following payoff table and hence decide which act is to be selected.*

Events \ Acts	1	2	3	4	Event Probabilities (P_j)
A	50	20	−10	−20	0.2
B	120	50	200	300	0.5
C	200	240	400	350	0.3

SOLUTION. Let us first construct the *opportunity loss table* from the given payoff table.

TABLE 8.8 OPPORTUNITY LOSS (OR REGRET) TABLE

Events \ Acts	Act 1	Act 2	Act 3	Act 4
A	$50 - 50 = 0$	$50 - 20 = 30$	$50 + 10 = 60$	$50 + 20 = 70$
B	$300 - 120 = 180$	$300 - 50 = 250$	$300 - 200 = 100$	$300 - 300 = 0$
C	$400 - 200 = 200$	$400 - 240 = 160$	$400 - 400 = 0$	$400 - 350 = 50$

Expected opportunity loss (EOL) for the four acts are computed in the following table:

TABLE 8.9 EXPECTED OPPORTUNITY LOSS (EOL)

Events	Probability P_j	Act 1 (l_{1j})	Act 2 (l_{2j})	Act 3 (l_{3j})	Act 4 (l_{4j})
A	0.2	$0 \times 0.2 = 0$	$30 \times 0.2 = 6$	$60 \times 0.2 = 12$	$70 \times 0.2 = 14$
B	0.5	$180 \times 0.5 = 90$	$250 \times 0.5 = 125$	$100 \times 0.5 = 50$	$0 \times 0.5 = 0$
C	0.3	$200 \times 0.3 = 60$	$160 \times 0.3 = 48$	$0 \times 0.3 = 0$	$50 \times 0.3 = 15$
Total (EOL)		$\Sigma l_{1j} P_j = 150$	$\Sigma l_{2j} P_j = 179$	$\Sigma l_{3j} P_j = 62$	$\Sigma l_{4j} P_j = 29$

From the above table, we see that the minimum EOL is 29 which corresponds to the act 4.

Hence **act 4 is the best in accordance with the EOL criterion** i.e., **act 4 is to be selected.**

EXAMPLE 7. *A group of students raises money each year by selling souvenirs outside the stadium after a cricket match between Teams A and B. They can buy any of the three different types of souvenirs from a supplier. Their sales are mostly dependent on which team wins the match. A conditional pay-off table is as under:*

	Type of Souvenir		
	I	II	III
Team A wins	Rs.1,200	Rs.800	Rs.300
Team B wins	250	700	1,100

(i) *Construct the opportunity loss table.* (ii) *Which type of souvenir should the students buy if probability of Team A's wining is* 0.6*?* (iii) *Find out the cost of uncertainty.* **[CA May 1987]**

SOLUTION.

(i) The required opportunity loss table is constructed below:

TABLE 8.10 OPPORTUNITY LOSS TABLE

Type of Souvenir / Team Wins	I	II	III
A	1200 – 1200 = 0	1200 – 800 = Rs.400	1200 – 300 = Rs.900
B	1100 – 250 = Rs.850	1100 – 700 = Rs.400	1100 – 1100 = 0

(ii) Since the probability that Team A wins = 0.6;

∴ Probability that Team B wins = 1 – 0.6 = 0.4.

With the probabilities 0.6 and 0.4 for the teams A and B to win, the *expected opportunity loss* are computed in the following table:

TABLE 8.11 EXPECTED OPPORTUNITY LOSS (EOL)

Event	Probability	Type of Souvenior (Action)		
		I	II	III
Team A win	0.6	$0 \times 0.6 = 0$	$400 \times 0.6 =$ Rs.240	$900 \times 0.6 =$ Rs.540
Team B win	0.4	$850 \times 0.4 =$ Rs.340	$400 \times 0.4 =$ Rs.160	$0 \times 0.4 = 0$
Total (EOL)		$\Sigma l_{1j} P_j =$ Rs.340	$\Sigma l_{2j} P_j =$ Rs.400	$\Sigma l_{3j} P_j =$ Rs.540

From the above table, we see that the *minimum EOL is* Rs. 340 *which corresponds to Type I of Souvenir.*

Hence *the students should buy Type I of Sourvenir.*

(iii) If there is certainty for a team to win, then there would be no opportunity loss and *EOL* would be 0. Hence the cost of uncertainty is Rs. 340.

EXAMPLE 8. *Given is the following pay-off matrix:*

State of Nature	Probability	Decision		
		Do not Expand	Expand 200 units	Expand 400 units
		Rs.	Rs.	Rs.
High demand	0.4	2,500	3,500	5,000
Medium demand	0.4	2,500	3,500	2,500
Low demand	0.2	2,500	1,500	1,000

What should be the decision if we use (i) *EMV criterion,* (ii) *the minimax criterion, and* (iii) *the maximax criterion?* **[CA November 1984]**

SOLUTION.

(i) *EMV* of the three decisions (actions) are computed in the following table:

TABLE 8.12 CALCULATIONS OF EMV OF THREE DECISIONS

Event (State of Nature)	Probability (P_j)	Expected Values		
		Do not Expand	Expand 200 units	Expand 400 units
High Demand	0.4	$2{,}500 \times 0.4 = 1{,}000$	$3{,}500 \times 0.4 = 1{,}400$	$5{,}000 \times 0.4 = 2{,}000$
Medium Demand	0.4	$2{,}500 \times 0.4 = 1{,}000$	$3{,}500 \times 0.4 = 1{,}400$	$2{,}500 \times 0.4 = 1{,}000$
Low Demand	0.2	$2{,}500 \times 0.2 = 500$	$1{,}500 \times 0.2 = 300$	$1000 \times 0.2 = 200$
Total (EMV)		$\Sigma X_{1j} P_j =$ Rs. 2,500	$\Sigma X_{2j} P_j =$ Rs. 3,100	$\Sigma X_{3j} P_j =$ Rs. 3,200

From the above table, we see that the highest EMV is Rs. 3,200 which corresponds to the decision "Expand 400 units".

Hence *the required decision should be "Expand* 400 *units"*.

(ii) From the given payoff matrix, we see that the maximum payoffs under the three decisions (acts) "Do not expand", "Expand 200 units" and "Expand 400 units" are respectively Rs. 2,500, Rs. 3,500 and Rs. 5,000 of which Rs. 2,500 is minimum. Also Rs. 2,500 corresponds to the decision "Do not expand".

∴ Under the *minimax criterion, the required decision should be "Do not expand"*.

(iii) Again from the given payoff matrix, we see that the maximum payoffs under the three decisions "Do not expand", "Expand 200 units" and "Expand 400 units" are respectively Rs. 2,500, Rs. 3,500 and Rs. 5,000 of which Rs. 5,000 *is maximum*. This *maximum value* Rs. 5,000 *corresponds to "Expand* 400 *units"*.

Hence under the *maximax criterion, the required decision should be "Expand* 400 *units."*

EXAMPLE 9. *A newspaper distributor assigns probabilities to the demand for a magazine as follows:*

Copies Demanded	Probability
1	0.4
2	0.3
3	0.2
4	0.1

A copy of the magazine sells for Rs. 7 *and costs Rs.* 6. *What can be the maximum possible expected monetary value* (EMV) *if the distributor can return unsold copies for Rs.* 5 *each?*

[CA November, 1986]

SOLUTION. From the given information, we see that *if the demand is for* 1 *copy,* then (i) the distributor makes a profit of (Rs. 7 – Rs. 6) i.e., of Re. 1 if he orders 1 copy, (ii) he makes no profit or suffers no loss if he orders 2 copies, (iii) he suffers a loss of Re. 1 if he orders 3 copies, (iv) he suffers a loss of Rs. 2 if he orders 4 copies. Similarly, *if the demand is for* 2 *copies,* then he makes profits of Re. 1, Rs. 2, Re. 1 and no profit or no loss if he orders for 1 copy, 2 copies, 3 copies and 4 copies respectively, etc.

The payoff table for the possible situations is constructed below:

TABLE 8.13 PAYOFF TABLES FOR THE POSSIBLE SITUATIONS

Copies Demanded	Probability	Acts (Decision to order copies)			
		1	2	3	4
1	0.4	1	0	–1	–2
2	0.3	1	2	1	0
3	0.2	1	2	3	2
4	0.1	1	2	3	4

EMV of the four acts are computed below:

TABLE 8.14 CALCULATIONS OF EMV

Acts (order of copies)	EMV (in rupees)
1	$1 \times 0.4 + 1 \times 0.3 + 1 \times 0.2 + 1 \times 0.1 =$ Re. 1.00
2	$0 \times 0.4 + 2 \times 0.3 + 2 \times 0.2 + 2 \times 0.1 =$ Rs. 1.20
3	$-1 \times 0.4 + 1 \times 0.3 + 3 \times 0.2 + 3 \times 0.1 =$ Re. 0.80
4	$-2 \times 0.4 + 0 \times 0.3 + 2 \times 0.2 + 4 \times 0.1 =$ Re. 0.00

Hence the required maximum EMV is Rs. 1.20

EXAMPLE 10. *Given is the information concerning product A:*

(i) *Unit profit Rs.* 3;

(ii) *Salvage loss per unit Rs.* 2;

(iii) *Demand record over* 300 *days is as under:*

Units demanded :	5	6	7	8	9
Days :	30	60	90	75	45

Find:

(a) *EMV if* 8 *units are ordered and*

(b) *Expected profit presuming certainty of demand.* **[CA November 1990]**

SOLUTION.

(a) If 8 *units are ordered,* profits are Rs. $3 \times 5-$ Rs. 2×3, Rs. $3 \times 6-$ Rs. 2×2, Rs. $3 \times 7-$ Rs. 2×1, Rs. 3×8, Rs. 3×8 i.e., Rs. 9, Rs. 14, Rs. 19, Rs. 24, Rs. 24 when units demanded are 5, 6, 7, 8, 9 respectively.

∴ Payoffs and probabilities when 8 units are ordered in different demand situations are given below:

Demand (Units) :	5	6	7	8	9
Payoff (Rs.) :	9	14	19	24	24
Probability :	(30/300) = 0.1	(60/300) = 0.2	(90/300) = 0.3	(75/300) = 0.25	(45/300) = 0.15

Expected payoff and EMV when 8 units are ordered are computed in the following table:

Table 8.15 CALCULATIONS FOR EXPECTED PAYOFF AND EMV

Demand (units)	Probability	Payoff	Expected payoff (Rs.) = Payoff × Probability
5	0.1	9	9 × 0.1 = 0.90
6	0.2	14	14 × 0.2 = 2.80
7	0.3	19	19 × 0.3 = 5.70
8	0.25	24	24 × 0.25 = 6.00
9	0.15	24	24 × 0.15 = 3.60
Total (EMV)			Rs. 19.00

Hence the required EMV if 8 units are ordered = **Rs. 19.**

(b) Presuming *certainty of demand,* the profits would be Rs. 3×5, Rs. 3×6, Rs. 3×7, Rs. 3×8, Rs. 3×9 i.e., Rs. 15, Rs. 18, Rs. 21, Rs. 24, Rs. 27.

Expected profit presuming *certainty of demand* is given in the following table:

TABLE 8.16 EXPECTED PROFIT PRESUMING CERTAINTY OF DEMAND

Demand (Units)	Probability	Payoff (Rs.)	Expected profit (Rs.)
5	0.1	15	15 × 0.1 = 1.50
6	0.2	18	18 × 0.2 = 3.60
7	0.3	21	21 × 0.3 = 6.30
8	0.25	24	24 × 0.25 = 6.00
9	0.15	27	27 × 0.15 = 4.05
Total			Rs. 21.45

Hence *the required expected profit presuming certainty of demand* = **Rs. 21.45.**

EXAMPLE 11. *A manufacturing company is faced with the problem of choosing four products to manufacture. The potential demand for each product may turn out to be good, satisfactory and poor. The probabilities, estimated for each type of demand, are given below:*

Product	Probabilities of types of demand		
	Good	Satisfactory	Poor
A	0.60	0.20	0.20
B	0.75	0.15	0.10
C	0.60	0.25	0.15
D	0.50	0.20	0.30

The estimated profit or loss under the different states of demand in respect of each product may be taken as:

Product	Rs.	Rs.	Rs.
A	40,000	10,000	1,100
B	40,000	20,000	(–) 7,000
C	50,000	15,000	(–) 8,000
D	40,000	18,000	15,000

Prepare the expected value table and advice the company about the choice of the product to manufacture. **[CA May 1992]**

SOLUTION. We first construct payoff table for the given informations

TABLE 8.17 PAYOFF TABLE

Product (Act) / Type of Demand (Event)	Product A		Product B		Product C		Product D	
	Prob.	Profit (Rs.)	Prob.	Profit (Rs.)	Prob.	Profit (Rs.)	Prob.	Profit (Rs.)
Good	0.60	40,000	0.75	40,000	0.60	50,000	50.0	40,000
Satisfactory	0.20	10,000	0.15	20,000	0.25	15,000	0.20	18,000
Poor	0.20	1,100	0.10	– 7,000	0.15	– 8,000	0.30	15,000

Expected payoff and **EMV of profits** are computed in the following table:

TABLE 8.18 CALCULATIONS OF EXPECTED PAYOFF AND EMV

Product	Expected value and EMV (Rs.)
A	40,000 × 0.60+10,000 × 0.20+1,100 × 0.20 = Rs. 26,220
B	40,000 × 0.75+20,000 × 0.15+(-7,000) × 0.10 = Rs. 32,300
C	50,000 × 0.60+15,000 × 0.25+(-8,000) × 0.15 = Rs. 32,550
D	40,000 × 0.50+18,000 × 0.20+15,000 × 0.30 = Rs. 28,100

We see that the **highest value of EMV is Rs. 32,550** *which corresponds to the product C.* Hence, *by EMV criterion, the company should manufacture the* **product C.**

8.6. EXPECTED VALUE OF PERFECT INFORMATION (EVPI)

Sometimes *EOL* (or *EMV*) criterion is used to determine the value of collecting *additional information* about the probabilities of the states of nature. Most managers would be willing to pay for conducting market research study to evaluate consumer need for their services if the cost of obtaining such information does not exceed its value. Such a study would help to improve the current probabilities of the states of nature.

From a given payoff table, we first find the act which maximizes expected payoff or minimizes the expected opportunity loss. Then, we find the maximum payoff under each state and the corresponding expected payoff. The total of these *expected payoffs gives the expected payoff with perfect information* ($EPPI$).

The *expected value of perfect information* ($EVPI$) is the difference between the expected payoff with perfect information ($EPPI$) and the maximum expected payoff ($\max EP$) with no additional information, i.e., $EVPI = EPPI -$ maximum EP.

ILLUSTRATION. *Consider the following payoff table:*

Acts / States of Nature	a_1	a_2	a_3	Probability
S_1	20	30	55	0.2
S_2	35	50	40	0.5
S_3	10	5	−10	0.3

$$EMV \text{ for } a_1 = 20 \times 0.2 + 35 \times 0.5 + 10 \times 0.3 = 24.5$$
$$EMV \text{ for } a_2 = 30 \times 0.2 + 50 \times 0.5 + 5 \times 0.3 = 32.5$$
$$EMV \text{ for } a_3 = 55 \times 0.2 + 40 \times 0.5 + (-10) \times 0.3 = 28.0$$

$\therefore$ Max. EP = maximum expected payoff (EMV) = 32.5 which corresponds to the act a_2. (Instead of maximum EMV we could find minimum EOL)

The maximum payoffs for the states of nature S_1, S_2, S_3 are respectively 55, 50, 10 and the corresponding probabilities are 0.2, 0.5, 0.3.

$$\therefore \quad EPPI = \text{Expected payoff with perfect information}$$
$$= 55 \times 0.2 + 50 \times 0.5 + 10 \times 0.3 = 39.$$
$$\therefore \quad EVPI = \text{Expected value of perfect information}$$
$$= EPPI - \max EP = 39 - 32.5 = \mathbf{6.5}$$

$EVPI$ *gives an upper limit on the worth of additional information.* In practice, market research study seldom provides perfect information, but $EVPI$ gives us a standard to measure the cost of collecting information.

8.7. BAYESIAN DECISION THEORY

In *decision making under uncertainty with probability* (discussed earlier), we have preliminary or *prior probability estimates* for the states of nature. In this case, we use the decision criterion of maximizing expected payoffs or minimizing opportunity losses. In order to make the best possible decision, we try to collect new information about the states of nature through experiment or tests. When we obtain added sample information about the states of nature, we use it to revise or update the prior probability estimates. These revised probabilities are called *posterior probabilities* and the *revision process is called Bayesian procedure.* The prior probabilities for the states of nature are then replaced by the corresponding *posterior probabilities* in the original payoff table and the whole procedure of decision making under uncertainty with probability discussed earlier is applied. Fig 8.2 illustrates probability revision based on new information

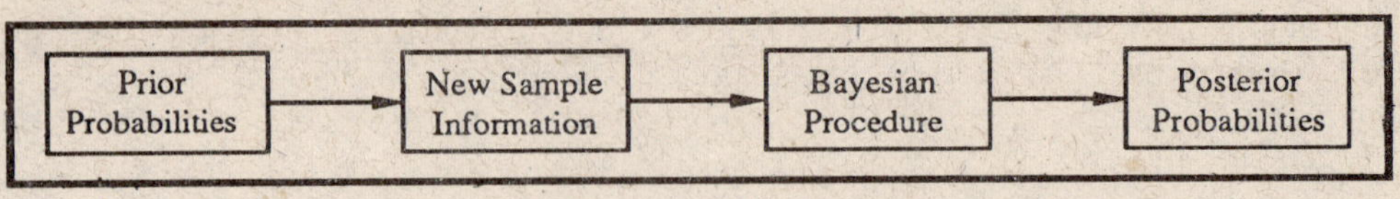

Fig 8.5 Probability revision by Bayesian Process

EXAMPLE 12. *Roy Brothers has a chance to buy* (a_1) *or not to buy* (a_2) 500 *bags of rice from a large stock at a flood damage sale. The decision depends on the number of damaged bags. If less than* 20% *of the bags are damaged* (S_1), *then they face a different payoff than if* 20% *or more are damaged* (S_2). *From past experience they find that there is a* 25% *chance that* S_1 *will occur. Prior to the sale they can examine* 5% *of the whole lot of rice for defective bags. Finding that* 24% *of the bags in the sample to be damaged, they revise their probability estimate for* S_1 *to* 35%. (i) *What are the prior probabilities for the states of nature?* (ii) *What is the new information in this decision? Is this perfect information or sample information?* (iii) *What are the posterior probabilities for the states of nature?*

SOLUTION.

(i)

States of Nature	Prior Probabilities
S_1	0.25
S_2	0.75
Total	1.00

(ii) The new information is that 24% *of a small portion of 500 bags are damaged.* This is a sample information, since it is based on 5% of the whole lot. Perfect information involves examination of each bag.

(iii)

States of Nature	Posterior Probabilities
S_1	0.35
S_2	0.65
Total	1.00

Exercise 8

(Statistical Decision Theory)

Theory

1. What do you mean by the terms "Acts" and "States of nature"? Give an example.
2. Define each of the following terms and give one example for each:
   (i) Maximin; (ii) Maximax; (iii) Minimax Regret.
3. Explain with illustration each of the following criteria:
   (i) Expected Monetary Value (EMV);
   (ii) Expected Opportunity Loss (EOL). **[CA Foundation June 1994]**
4. What are the four elements that decision matrices usually contain? **[CA November 1986]**

[HINTS. (i) Acts, (ii) States of nature or Events, (iii) Probabilities of the events, (iv) Payoff.]

5. "Statistics is a body of methods for making wise decision in the face of uncertainty" - Examine.

[CA November 1990]

6. Write short notes on the following:

(i) Maximin Decision Criterion; [CA May 1990]

(ii) Minimax Regret Criterion; [CA November 1990]

(iii) Expected Value as Decision Criteria. [CA November 1989]

Problems

1. "A Soya Company is evaluating its operations. The Company may expand its current operation or sell to their competitor. If the price of its product decline, then it would be better to sell to their competitor and invest the sale proceeds in Milkfood company. If, however, prices rise, the company should expand its current stock. If prices remain stable for the next year, it should maintain the current level of operations." For this problem list (i) the relevant acts and (ii) the states of nature. Represents the acts and states of nature by a Tree diagram.

[HINTS. See Illustration 1 in Art. 8.2.]

2. A pig breeder can either produce 50 or 60 pigs. The total production of his competitors can be either 4500 or 7500 pigs. If they produce 4500 pigs, his profit per pig is Rs. 50; if they produce 7500 pigs, his profit per pig is only Rs. 40. Construct a pay-off table and represent the payoffs by a decision tree.

[HINTS. See Illustrations 2, 3 in Art. 8.2.]

3 Construct the *opportunity loss or regret table* and find the best act using *minimax regret criterion* from the following pay-off table:

Acts \ States of Nature	S_1	S_2	S_3	S_4
a_1	0	−1	8	−4
a_2	−3	7	−2	5
a_3	−8	5	10	14

[HINTS. See Illustration 4 in Art. 8.4.]

4. A pig breeder can either produce 25 or 40 pigs. The total production of his competitors can be either 3,000 or 6,000 pigs. If they produce 3,000 pigs, his profit per pig is Rs. 40; if they produce 6,000 pigs, his profit per pig is only Rs. 30: (i) Construct a pay-off table and also state what should the pig breeder decide; (ii) Represent the payoffs by a decision and hence find the best act.

[HINTS. See worked out Example 1 and Illustration 3.]

5. Suppose that a decision-maker faced with three decision alternatives and four states of nature constructs the following profit pay-off table:

Acts \ States of Nature	S_1	S_2	S_3	S_4
a_1	18	12	15	8
a_2	15	14	10	11
a_3	13	16	19	15

Assuming that the decision-maker has no knowledge about the probabilities of occurrence of the four states of nature find the decisions to be recommended under each of the following criteria:

(i) Maximin; (ii) Maximax; (iii) Minimax Regret. Represent the given payoffs by a decision tree and hence find the best act according to: (i) Maximum and (ii) Maximax criterion.

[HINTS. See worked out Example 2 and Illustration 3.]

6. Pay-offs of three Acts X, Y, Z and the states of nature L, M, N are given below:

Acts / States of Nature	Payoffs (Rupees)		
	X	Y	Z
L	−10	−30	400
M	300	−80	−50
N	500	700	600

The probabilities of the states of nature are 0.2, 0.5 and 0.3 respectively. (i) Calculate the Expected Monetary values for the above data and select the best act; (ii) Represent the payoffs and expected payoffs by a decision and hence find the best act according to EMV creterion.

[HINTS. See worked out Examples 3 and 4]

7. The conditional pay-offs in rupees for each action-event combination are as under:

Event	Actions			
	1	2	3	4
A	6	−1	9	8
B	0	8	5	6
C	−3	10	4	−2
D	5	3	6	7
E	8	7	5	4

(i) Which is the best action in accordance with the maximin criterion?

(ii) Which is the best action in acordance with EMV criterion, presuming all events have equal probabilities of occurrence?

[HINTS. See worked out Example 5.]

8. Calculate expected opportunity loss (EOL) from the following pay-off table and hence decide which act is to be selected.

Acts / Events	1	2	3	4	Event Probabilities
A	60	40	−5	−10	0.3
B	150	70	250	400	0.6
C	240	300	500	350	0.1

[HINTS. See worked out Example 6.]

9. Pay-offs of the three Acts A, B, C and the states of nature P, Q, R are given below:

Payoff (Rupees)

States of Nature	Acts		
	A	B	C
P	−35	120	−100
Q	250	−350	200
R	550	650	700

The probabilities of the states of nature are 0.5, 0.1 and 0.4 respectively. Tabulate the Expected Monetary Values for the above data and state which one can be chosen as the best act? Represent the expected payoffs by a tree diagram and hence determine the best act.

[HINTS. See worked out Examples 3, 4 and 5.] **[CA November 1988]**

10. You are given the following pay-offs of three acts A_1, A_2 and A_3 and the states of nature S_1, S_2, S_3 :

States of Nature	Three Acts		
	A_1	A_2	A_3
S_1	25	– 10	– 125
S_2	400	440	400
S_3	650	740	750

The probabilities of the states of nature are respectively .1, .7 and .2. (i) Calculate and tabulate the EMV and conclude which of the acts can be chosen as the best; (ii) Represent the expected payoffs by a decision tree. **[CA May 1984]**

11. Marketing staff of a certain industrial organisation has submitted the following pay-off table, giving profits in million rupees, concerning a certain proposal depending upon the rate of technological advance in the next three years:

Decision / Technological Advance	Accept	Reject
Much	2	3
Little	5	2
None	(–) 1	4

The probabilities are 0.2, 0.5 and 0.3 for Much, Little and None technological advance respectively. What decision should be taken? **[CA November 1985]**

12. A group of students raises money each year by selling souvenirs outside the stadium after a cricket match between Teams A and B. They can buy any of the three different types of souvenirs from a supplier. Their sales are mostly dependent on which team wins the match. A conditional pay-off table is as under:

	Type of Souvenir		
	I	II	III
Team A wins	Rs. 1,600	Rs. 1,200	Rs. 700
Team B wins	Rs. 650	Rs. 1,100	Rs. 1,500

(i) Construct the opportunity loss table.

(ii) Which type of sourvenir should the students buy if probability of Team A's winning is 0.7?

(iii) Find out the cost of unvertainty.

[HINTS. See worked out Example 7.]

13. Mr. X quite often flies from town A to town B. He can use the airport bus which costs Rs. 13 but if he takes it, there is a 0.08 chance that he will miss the flight. A hotel limousine costs Rs. 27 with a 0.96 chance of being on time for the flight. For Rs. 50 he can use a taxi which will make 99 of 100 flights. If Mr. X catches the plane on time, he will conclude a business transaction which will produce a profit of Rs. 1,000; otherwise he will lose it. Which mode of transportation should Mr. X use? Answer on the basis of EMV criterion. **[CA May 1990]**

[HINTS.

EMV for using Airport bus = 0.92 × 1000 − 13 = Rs. 907

EMV for using Hotel Limousine = 0.96 × 1000 − 27 = Rs. 933

EMV for using Taxi = 0.99 × 1000 − 50 = Rs. 940.]

14. A management is faced with the problem of choosing one of the three products for manufacturing. The potential demand for each product may turn out to be good, fair or poor. The probabilities of each type of demand were estimated as follows:

Product	Type of Demand		
	Good	Fair	Poor
A	0.75	0.15	0.10
B	0.60	0.30	0.10
C	0.50	0.30	0.20

The estimated profit or loss under the three states of demand in respect of each product may be taken as:

	Rs.	Rs.	Rs.
A	35,000	15,000	5,000
B	50,000	20,000	Loss of 3,000
C	60,000	30,000	20,000

Prepare the expected value table and advice the management about the choice of the product.

[HINTS. See worked out Example 11.] **[CA May 1988]**

Answers

2. Payoffs for the first and second acts are Rs. 2,500, Rs. 2,000 and Rs. 3,000; Rs. 2,400.

3.

Acts \ States of Nature	S_1	S_2	S_3	S_4
a_1	0	8	2	18
a_2	3	0	12	9
a_3	8	2	0	0

a_3 is the best act.

4.

Act \ States of Nature	Production of Competitors	
	3000 pigs	6000 pigs
Produce 25 pigs	1000	750
Produce 40 pigs	1600	1200

The pig breeder decides to produce 40 pigs.

5. (i) a_3; (ii) a_3; (iii) a_3. **6.** EMV for X, Y, Z are respectively Rs. 298, Rs. 164, Rs. 235; X is the best act. **7.** (i) Act 3; (ii) Action 3. **8.** EOL due to acts 1,2,3,4 are respectively 176, 224, 109.5, 36; Act 4. **9.** EMV for the acts A, B, C are respectively Rs. 227.50, Rs. 285, Rs. 250; B is the best act. **10.** EMV for the acts A_1, A_2, A_3 are respectively 412.5, 455, 417.5; A_2 is the best act. **11.** Using EMV criterion, the decision "reject the proposal" should be taken. **12.** The students should buy Type I of Souvenir; Rs. 255. **13.** Mr. X should use Taxi mode of transportation. **14.** EMV for A, B, C are respectively Rs. 29,000, Rs. 35,700, Rs. 43,000; the management should select product C.

Part III

ECONOMIC TECHNIQUES

CHAPTER 0

INTRODUCTION: QUANTITATIVE TECHNIQUES IN ECONOMICS

Experience has shown that each of these three view points, that of statistics, economic theory, and mathematics, is a necessary, but not by itself, a sufficient, condition for a real understanding of the quantitative relations in modern economic life. It is the unification of all these that is powerful. And it is this unification that constitutes econometrics. Ragnar Frisch, 1933

Economics is often described as a social science. It is social because it deals with the behaviour of human beings, in the context of how society makes choices about what output is to be produced, how this output is to be produced and for whom it is to be produced. It is a science inasmuch as it sets out to analyse economic behaviour by means of the scientific method, which is based on developing theories (hypotheses) to help us understand the events we observe.

A theory comprises four elements:

(1) A set of consistent and quantifiable (measurable) definitions.

(2) A set of simplifying assumptions, sometimes known as a model.

(3) A set of logical deductions from the model.

(4) A resulting prediction, which then represents a theory which can be tested against behaviour in the real world.

Mathematical and Statistical Techniques in Economics

Economics makes extensive use of mathematics and statistics. There is now a branch of economics called econometrics which is the application of mathematics and statistics to economic theories. In economics it is sometimes both convenient and judicious to use to the quantitative techniques because

1. The behavioural assumptions, which form the basis of an economic theory can often be formulated more precisely by employing mathematics.

2. Mathematics is a powerful tool for deriving logical implications from the assumptions of economic models.

3. The testing of economic theories against empirical evidence is assisted by mathematical techniques.

In underlying the role of mathematics in economics we must remember that a theory is as good only as the assumptions and data it contains. If these are unsuitable, the theory will be unsuccessful no matter how sophisticated the mathematical and deductive techniques employed.

Econometrics

If we use mathematical and statistical techniques to analyse economic problems then we are said to be entering the arena of econometrics. In this section we will consider some of the most commonly used techniques.

Symbols

We make use of symbols in economics. In so doing we are adopting a kind of shorthand. The symbols are so widely used in economics that once they are learnt, they should help us to speed up our writing on the subject. Typical examples of such symbols are: Y = income; Q = output or quantity; C = cost; π = profit.

Functions

We will often find that the magnitude of one factor is affected by another. For example, the demand for a good is affected by its price. In mathematical terms we could say that demand is a function of price. This can be written as $Q = f(P)$ where Q is the quantity demanded and P is the price.

Often the value of the factor we are considering will be affected by several variables. These we can add up to the function. Thus, for example, $Q = f(P, Y, P_1, \cdots, P_{n-1})$.

This tells us that demand is a function of the price of the commodity (P), consumers' income (Y) and the prices of other commodities ($P_1, P_2, \cdots, P_{n-1}$).

Writing things in this fashion is just a form of shorthand because no values have been ascribed to P, Y, etc. Once we put in value, we obtain one of the following two kinds of functions:

(a) *Linear functions:* This is where, if we plotted the figures as a graph, we would obtain a straight line. For example, consider the function $C = 0.8Y$ where C is total consumer spending and Y is income. This expression simply tells us that consumption is always 0.8 (80%) of income. This would produce a straight line graph.

(b) *Non-linear functions:* Any function which does not give a straight line when plotted as a graph is a non-linear function.

Graphs

The most common method employed for presenting economic data is through *graphs*. The economist makes extensive use of graphs. They are both an illustration and a means of analysis. They are a form of shorthand and a method by which, often complex relationships can be reduced to a few lines on a page. A graph is a method of representing the relation between two or more variables. On the horizontal (or x-) axis of the graph we place the independent variable, and on the vertical (or y-) axis we place the dependent, variable. For example, suppose it is observed in a market that when the price of a commodity (like motor car) rises the quantity offered for sale (or the quantity supplied) also increases. Price and supply are then examples of variables. If we assume that the supply of the good to depend upon its price we can further state that supply is the dependent variable and price the independent variable. Supply is then said to be a function of price.

Equations and Graphs

To illustrate, let us take an example. Suppose the supply of rice rises. When the market price increases from Re. 1 to Rs. 2, the supply of rice in kilos is zero; when the price is Rs. 3, the supply is 10; when the price rises Rs. 4, the supply is 20; and so on. In mathematical terms the relationship between the two variables can be expressed by means of the equation $S = P - 2$ where S is the supply and P is the market price.

In order to plot the graph of this equation we have to ask what the quantity supplied would be if the price were Re. 1, Rs. 2, Rs. 3, and so on. We can present the result as in Table 0.1.

TABLE 0.1 PRICE AND QUANTITY SUPPLIED

Price (Rs.)	Quantity supplied (Kilos)
1	—
2	—
3	10
4	20
5	30
6	40
7	50
8	60
9	70
10	80

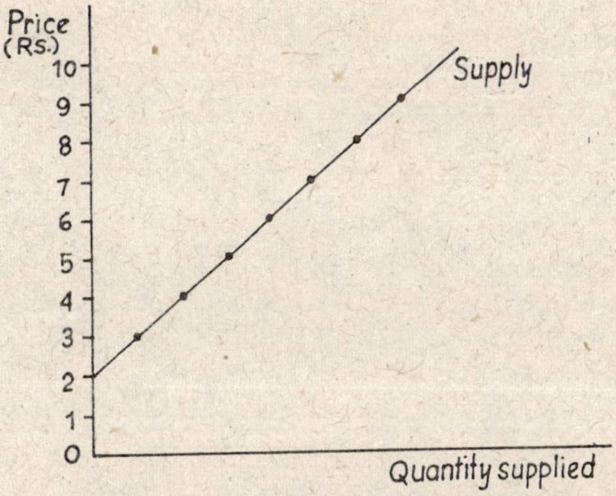

Fig 0.1 A Supply Curve

The data in Table 0.1 can now be plotted as shown in Fig. 0.1. Here we measure the independent variable, price, along the vertical x-axis and the dependent variable, supply, on the horizontal y-axis. The result is called a supply curve even if, as in this example, it traces out a straight line. We can see that the curve we have drawn has a positive gradient, that is, it slopes upwards from left to right. This reflects the fact that when the price of rice rises, the amount supplied also rises. In mathematical terms, supply is said to vary directly with price.

We can use the same procedure to construct a demand curve. Suppose it is observed that buyers' demand for rice, in relation to the market price, is given by the equation $D = 10 - P$ where D is the demand in kilos, and P is the price in rupees. We can use the procedure followed to construct a demand curve. We will observe that the demand curve has a negative gradient, reflecting the fact that the demand and price go in opposite directions—the lower the price, the larger the quantity demanded by buyers. In mathematical terms, demand and price are said to vary inversely with each other. See Table 0.2 and Fig. 0.2.

TABLE 0.2 PRICE AND QUANTITY DEMAND

Price (Rs.)	Quantity Demanded (Kilos)
1	90
2	80
3	70
4	60
5	50
6	40
7	30
8	20
9	10
10	0

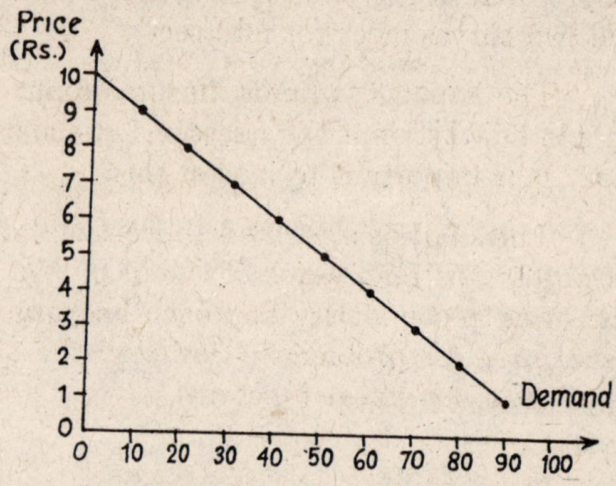

Fig 0.2 A Demand Curve

Problem Solving

Suppose we have drawn two curves, a demand curve, showing the quantity of a product which is demanded and a supply curve, showing the quantity of the same commodity offered for sale at various prices. Also suppose that we ask ourselves the question: at what price will quantity demanded be equal to the quantity supplied? We can answer this question by using the simultaneous equation technique.

Suppose we have the values

$$P = 2Q \text{ (supply)} \tag{1}$$

$$\text{and} \quad P = 10 - Q \text{ (demand)} \tag{2}$$

The price (P) for demand and supply will be the same when

$$20 = 10 - Q \tag{3}$$

If we move all the Qs to one side of the equation and the numbers on to the other, we obtain

$$3Q = 10. \tag{4}$$

Thus,

$$Q = 3\tfrac{1}{3}. \tag{5}$$

To obtain the value for P we now need only insert the value of Q into expression (1) and we obtain

$$P = 2 \times 3\tfrac{1}{3}; \;\; P = 6\tfrac{2}{3}.$$

We can check this result by carrying out a similar exercise with expression (2)

$$P = 10 - 3\tfrac{1}{3}; \;\; P = 6\tfrac{2}{3}.$$

Thus, the quantity is the same for both supply and demand when price = $6\frac{2}{3}$. This can also be checked by putting both the demand and supply curves in the same diagram, as in Fig. 0.3. We see that E is the point where the two curves meet (or intersect).

The student who is unsure about this analysis should now attempt the questions at the end of this section. It is important to master this.

The analysis presented above can also be conducted in purely abstract terms of x and y. We have adopted the price and quantity approach because it is the most usual area for problems. However, the algebra can be applied to any linear functions.

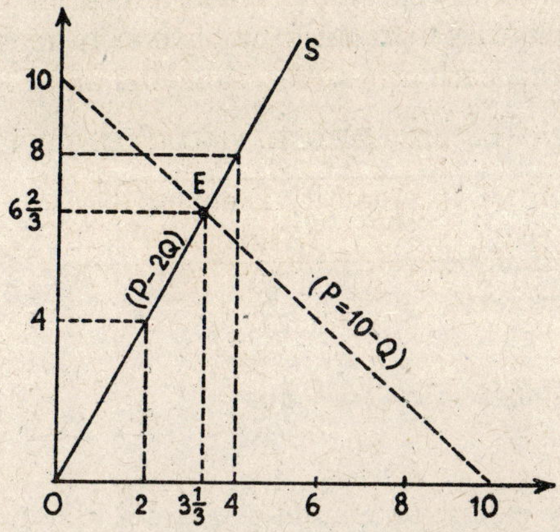

Fig 0.3 Market Price and Quantity

Economic Statistics

Economic statistics provide quantitative measures of economic phenomena in the private and public sectors of the economy. The field is composed of two broad categories:

(1) Collection, classification, and presentation of data; and (2) analysis, interpretation, and projections of future trends.

Macroeconomic Data

Macroeconomic data, or measures of economic activity, are monitored closely in the public and private sectors. Such data are primarily used by the Central Government of India in evaluating and developing fiscal, monetary and wage-price policies for achieving high employment and price stability.

In the private sector, these data are used by companies for analysing prospects for their own products in particular markets and investments in an economy-wide framework. They are also used in labour-management wage negotiations by trade unions and companies.

Regression Analysis

Regression analysis, as we have noted earlier in this book, is a method of estimating functional relationships between (among) two or more variables. Economic theory is concerned with such relations as demand functions, production functions, revenue functions, profit function and the like. Marginal product, marginal revenue, marginal cost, marginal profit and similar concepts are defined as the slops or derivatives of those functions at specified points. When economists first attempted to estimate the demand functions of economic theory market data on prices and consumption of agricultural products regression analysis presented itself as the most logical and appropriate tool.

The most influential of these economists, Henry L. Moore, set out in 1908 to develop 'the statistical complement of pure economics,' and in 1917 he was convinced that multiple regression analysis was both necessary and sufficient for this task:

No matter how complex the functional relations between the variables, it can derive empirical laws which by, successive approximations, will describe the real relations with increasing accuracy.

When the method of multiple correlation [we would now say regression] is thus applied to economic data it invests the findings of deductive economics with the reality and life of fact; it is the statistical complement of Deductive Economics.

In his last book, *Synthetic Economics* (1929), Moore estimated comprehensive sets of demand, supply and production functions by multiple regression techniques. He was the first to bring into focus the range of applications of regression analysis in economics. Another important statistical technique used in business and economics is time series analysis. This technique is used for forecasting purposes.

Computers in Economics

A great deal of economics concerns quantitative analysis. Since economics is data-intensive, the electronic computer plays a very important role in economics today.

Now the computer is a commonplace tool in both teaching and research. It is absolutely necessary in applied econometrics, but it is also widely used by companies for decision-making purposes.

The computer has greatly lightened the burden of data-intensive economics. It enables the investigator to accumulate, use, or tap vast data sources.

Experimentation in econometrics and other quantitative branches of economics has been greatly opened up by the computer. In searching for regularities in economic life, the economist can experiment with many relationships, almost simultaneously, until one is found that satisfies the theoretical and other criteria.

Exercises

1. Construct a graph and on it draw the line which would illustrate the following functions $y = 3x$ and $y = 10 - x$. State the value of x and y where the two lines intersect.

2. Construct a graph to illustrate the following function $y = 4 + \frac{5}{4}$.

3. In the following situations, determine the points at which x and y are equal, i.e., where the graphs would intersect.

(a) $y = 1 + 3x$, $y = 25 - x$ (b) $y = 20 + 5x$, $y = 100 - x$ (c) $y = 10 + x$, $y = 2x - 40$.

SECTION A: DEMAND ANALYSIS, ESTIMATION AND FORECASTING

A demand curve relates the quantity demanded to variations in product price. Moreover, demand and supply curves interact to determine market prices. Thus, market demand is an important building block in microeconomic analysis. Our primary objective in this section is to see how the consumers' choices are influenced by changes in income, changes in prices, and changes in preferences. But our main objective here is the derive an individual consumer's demand curve and then show how the market demand curve is an aggregation of the various individual demand curves [Chapter 1].

Individual choice is the foundation of consumer demand theory. Consequently, a thorough understanding of the determinants of consumer demand for a product or service must be based on a knowledge about how the consumer allocates his income among competing products.

A consumer's choice is determined by both his tastes and the resources available to him. Accordingly economists start by developing a model that describes a consumer's tastes. Subsequently, we introduce the fact that our representative consumer has a limited income. This limits the bundles of commodities that are feasible for him (or her). Given his income, each consumer does the best he can by selecting the most desired bundle among those that are feasible [Chapter 2].

We will also discuss the price elasticity of demand, which is a useful measure of how responsive the quantity demanded is to price changes and the effects of price changes on the revenue that firms receive [Chapter 2].

The demand of a firm's product is of crucial importance to its survival and growth. Many important decisions depend on the firm's having specific knowledge about the determinants of the demand for its product, and this knowledge is obtained by estimating the demand function.

Predictions about the future demand for the firm's product, for example, help the firm make many decisions. This knowledge is particularly useful in guiding the manager's decisions to acquire inputs such as capital equipment and skilled labour which have high acquisition costs. Indian Airlines Corporation, for instance, would be ill-advised to incur the expense of hiring many new engineers just before the beginning of a long slump in the demand for air-travel.

Prediction, however, is not the only reason for understanding the firm's demand. For those firms that are able to affect the price paid for their product, a knowledge of the determinants of demand is essential for choosing a price that will maximise the firm's profit [Chapter 3].

CHAPTER 1

DEMAND ANALYSIS

Demand theory and analysis can be a source of many useful insights for business decision-making. Ultimately, the success or failure of a business depends primarily on its ability to generate revenues by satisfying the demands of consumers. H. C. Petersen and W. C. Lewis

Fundamental Questions
After reading this chapter you will be able to:
1. analyse the purpose of demand analysis;
2. identify the factors influencing the demand for a commodity;
3. examine the properties of demand functions;
4. distinguish among price, income and cross elasticities of demand;
5. assess the importance of time in demand analysis; and
6. have an overall idea of sales forecasting.

PREVIEW

Demand is a key concept in micro-economics, in which it takes the form of aggregate demand. In theory, the demand for any product or service has a function whose specification depends on the purpose of analysis. In general the demand for any commodity is a function of buyers' tastes, their incomes, and the prices of all purchaseable commodities (which may be substitutes or complements). In empirical (statistical) analyses, the particular facts found relevant for a commodity enter into its demand function, which might include, for example, the volumes of advertising.

Much economic analysis focuses on the relation between prices and quantities demanded, the other variables being provisionally held constant. At the various prices that could prevail in a market during some period of time different quantities of a product or service would be bought. Demand, then, is considered a list of prices and quantities, with one quantity for each possible price. Demand is the entire list, or demand schedule, as Alfred Marshall called it. When the schedule is plotted on a diagram, with price on the vertical axis and quantity on the horizontal axis, we arrive at the demand curve.

This curve slopes downward from left to right, signifying that smaller quantities are bought at higher prices and larger quantities at lower prices. The inverse relation between price and quantity is often called the law of demand.

Two foundations: *The law rests on two foundations. One is the theory the consumer. With one exception, the logic of that theory shows that a consumer responds to lower prices by buying more. The other foundation is empirical. Innumerable studies of demand in actual markets have demonstrated the existence of downward-sloping demand curves. And the law has always reflected the universal experience of traders.*

Exceptions to the Law

There are two major exceptions to the law of demand. The best-known exception is the Giffen effect—a consumer buys more, not less, of a commodity at higher prices (when a negative income effect dominates over the substitution effect). Whether the Giffen effect has ever prevailed in real markets is debatable. Another possible exception is the Veblen effect—some commodities are wanted, at least in theory, for their high prices. The higher their prices are the more the use of such commodities as items of conspicuous consumption, and thus the stronger the demand for them.

Changes in Consumer Demand

Changes, i.e., increases or decreases in demand, are changes in the quantities that would be bought at any of the possible prices. Changes in demand are shifts or movements of the entire demand curve. A shift to the right means an increase in demand. It may occur due to any one or a combination of different factors: stronger consumer demand, a rise in consumers' income, a rise in the prices of substitutes, a fall in the prices of complements, and sometimes extra advertising. Opposite changes in these factors cause a decrease in demand, a leftward shift of the curve. The only exception here is observed in case of inferior goods. They are defined as those goods bought in smaller amounts as consumer incomes go up. The law of demand, though, still holds for inferior goods. But increases in consumer incomes, ceteris paribus, cause the downward-sloping demand curves for inferior goods to shift to the right, not to the left.

In an inflationary environment, another influence on changing demands—price expectations—plays an important role. For storable goods, expectations of future prices can be a powerful force on current demand. When they expect future prices to be higher, buyers increase their current demands, thus, tending to make their expectations self-fulfilling.

The demand for durable goods like motor cars, refrigerators, air-conditions, etc. can fluctuate widely over time, as consumers' incomes vary and as producers' profit expectations alter with the business cycle. A durable good has both a stock demand and a flow demand. The stock demand is for the amount that consumers or producers want to hold over a period of years. The flow demand in a given year consists of replacement demand, i.e., for consumers to maintain the stock at some level, and of expansion demand, i.e., for purchases to increases the stock.

If the stock demand increases, the yearly flow demand will increase relatively much more—it will include a positive expansion demand along with the replacement demand. If, on the other hand, the stock demand diminishes, the yearly flow demand will drop relatively far, because the negative expansion demand has to be subtracted from the replacement demand.

Sellers' Demand

From the points of sellers of various goods and services, demand needs another perspective. In markets with many sellers of homogeneous products, the demand for the product of any single seller is infinitely large, that is, the individual seller can sell all of the product at the going price. The seller's own demand curve can be visualised as a horizontal line extending indefinitely to the right. The height of the line is the prevailing price. Such sellers', typically farmers, incur no advertising or promotional expenses. Their business strategies are those of adjusting their outputs to price they cannot individually control. In markets with few sellers, however, demand appears as a line sloping down to the right. But the demand functions of such sellers are critically interdependent, because the most important variable is the prices charged by the other sellers in the same market.

THE MEANING OF DEMAND

In term 'demand' refers to the relationship between the quantity of product, or, service that customers desire, or, are able to purchase during a given period of time under a given set of conditions. The period of time might be an hour, a day, or, a year.

Economists assess 'consumer demand' on the basis of utility, which is the level of satisfaction of consumers and is related to the quantities of goods purchased by the consumers.

For decision making managers focus their attention on market demand. Market demand means aggregate of individual demands, which are determined by (i) the value associated with purchasing and using the goods, or, services and (ii) the ability to purchase it. Consumers are interested in the marginal utility, i.e., satisfaction obtained by purchasing additional units of a given product.

A 'derived demand' represents the demand generated by customers who use the product as an input while producing their own products, e.g., how many packing boxes will be required by a firm manufacturing cast iron fittings will depend on the demand for its product by the customers.

Other examples of derived demand are the following:

(a) The demand for mortgage money, i.e., the quantity of mortgage-credit demanded is derived from the demand for housing.

(b) The demand for air-transportation to major resort areas is derived from the demand for recreation.

(c) The demand for steel, aluminium and plastics is derived from the demands for machine-tools and labour.

(d) The demand for capital equipment, materials, labour and energy, used in manufacture is derived from the aggregate demand for consumption goods and services.

THE BASIS OF DEMAND

Generally, the demand curve for an industry's product slopes downward, showing that consumers prefer to buy more when the price of the product declines. The price of the product, of course, is one determinant of the level of demand. Other factors, which influence the demand for an individual final product, are listed below:

(1) The price of available substitute in the market;

(2) Consumers' disposable incomes;

(3) Consumers' tastes and preferences;

(4) Consumers' expectations of price changes;
(5) The advertising expenditure for the product;
(6) The advertising expenditures for other products, especially substitutes;
(7) The terms of consumer credit;
(8) The rates of interest;
(9) Population—its size and composition;
(10) Legal restrictions;
(11) Public policy;
(12) Quality and life of the product.

The Product's Own Price as a Determinant of Demand

The price of a product generates more demand from consumers when it is low. When a firm builds up huge inventories due to low demand for its products, it allows 'rebates' or offers discounts to generate demand. The rebates lower the effective purchase price of a product and increase the customers' demand (without any negative repercussions of increasing the price of the product once the excess inventory is consumed.)

The effective selling price to consumers cannot be determined by the firm's management alone. Government policy decisions also influence the purchase price of a product. Various sales taxes and excise duties, imposed by governments from time to time, influence the purchase price of a product and affect demand for taxed commodities.

Income as a Determinant of Demand

Economists refer most goods and services as normal goods. The consumption of such goods goes up as the incomes of consumers increase and *vice versa.*

The relationship between the demand for a product and income shows how important the level of G.N.P. (Gross National Product) is as also its distribution. We often use the terms per capita income, personal income, or, disposable personal income in demand analyses, but these measures are all derived from the G.N.P. figures.

Hence changes in G.N.P. give us an idea of changes in the demand for a product.

The income of the buyers is also influenced by public policy. For reducing unemployment and increasing economic growth, public officials often announce tax-cuts. Tax-cuts increase the disposable income of people and thus their demand for consumption goods.

So government decisions affect the aggregate purchasing power of consumers inasmuch as most people consumers pay a certain amount of income and other taxes.

Managers often measure effective demand by collecting data on disposable income.

Tastes and Preferences as Determinants of Demand

Consumers like certain things and dislike others. Even twins born and brought up in an identical environment may have different tastes and preferences. So it is very difficult to form an idea about the factors which influences the tastes and preferences of buyers.[1]

The truth is that the difference in preferences causes difference in consumer demands for goods and services. Let us take an example. In the United States, the consumers liked big and powerful motor cars throughout the 1950s and 1960s. However, in the 1970s, the consumers' suddenly

---

1 Psychologists, sociologists, of course, have different theories and opinions about the formation of consumers preferences.

preferences changed and they liked smaller and less powerful but more fuel-efficient cars. Probably, the change took place due to abnormal and continuous rise in the prices of petrol and diesel. The life-style may be another factor influencing such change in the consumer preference. Consumers now have smaller families and hence, they prefer to have a smaller car. Moreover, parking and driving such cars are easy and convenient.

Such change in the consumer preference is also influenced by peer groups, i.e., the people working with the consuming unit, e.g., classmates, room-mates, neighbours, colleagues and so on.

Advertising is an important factor which strongly influences consumer's tastes and preferences. Advertisement increases product demands by providing information about a product, i.e., the cost, size, use, weight, etc. of the product, to the extent it is available, and so on.

Transformational advertisements emphasise the image of the product or service. They try to enhance the satisfaction of consumers. It is very difficult to measure or quantify the factors responsible for changing the tastes and preferences of consumers.

Other Prices as Determinants of Demand

A consumer decides how much he will buy a product keeping in view the prices charged for other goods and services as well. We have already noted that the price-hike of petrol and diesel has shifted consumer preferences from larger cars to smaller cars in the United States.

Petrol/diesel and cars are complementary goods, i.e., they are used jointly. The higher price of petrol/diesel increased the driving cost and reduced the mileage per litre of gasoline. The consumers, in such a situation, became more interested in fuel efficient cars instead of larger cars.

Thus, we find that if an article B is complimentary to another article A, and if the price of B increases, the demand of A is expected to go down and *vice versa.*

Similarly, if we have two products, X and Y, which are substitutes of each other, we can expect that an increase in the price of X will also increase the demand for Y and *vice versa.* When the prices of cinema tickets increase, the demand for vedeo disks and tapes will also increase.

Thus, we find that complimentary and substitute products influence the demand for consumption goods.

Other Determinants of Demand

Population growth is another factor which increases the demand for all products. Changes in the geographical distribution of the population also affect the demand almost for consumption goods.

Legal restrictions imposed on the free market also restrict demand, e.g., if the raises defines the legal drinking age from 20 to 25 years, the demand for alcoholic beverages will fall considerably. Again, if the driving age of vehicles is increased, the demand for car insurance will decline and *vice versa.*

Public policy also influences the demand of consumers. For example, if the public policy is such that the tuition for private schools is tax-deductible, then the effective cost of private education will be lesser to the users and the demand for private education will increase.

Besides these factors advertising and sales promotion expenditures, interest rate, terms of credit, quality of the product, etc. also exert influence on the demand for consumer goods.

DEMAND AND PRICE

The relation between the price of a commodity and its demand has been a major interest of economists for a long time. A thorough knowledge of this relationship is also of considerable importance to management.

The Law of Demand

The relation between price and demand (i.e., sales) is called in economics the Law of Demand. The law simply states that at a higher price demand is low and *vice versa*, other things (i.e., variables influencing demand) remaining constant.

Demand Schedule, Demand Curve and Demand Function

In economics, the relation between price and quantity (i.e., demand) is shown in the form of a table indicating different prices and the corresponding quantities. Such a table, called a Demand Schedule is presented below:

TABLE 1.1 THE DEMAND SCHEDULE OF A COMMODITY

Price (Rs.)	Quantity Demanded
5	50 units
4	70 units
3	100 units
2	150 units

The law of demand or the price-quantity relationship is normally shown in a graph which is known as the Demand Curve. In fact, the demand curve is a graphical representation of the demand schedule presented in the above table.

From the above demand schedule we draw a graph as shown in Fig. 1.1.

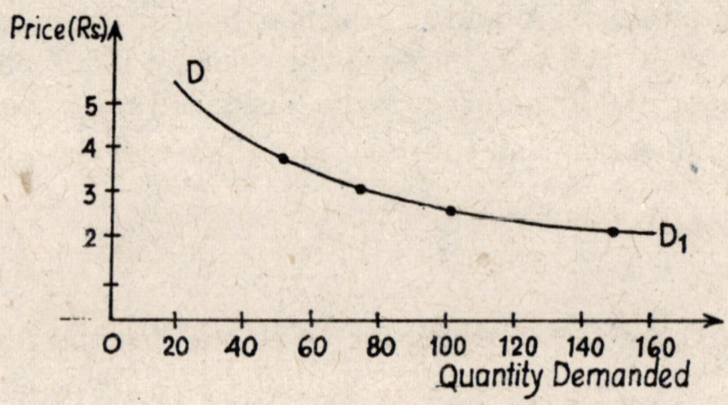

Fig 1.1 An Individual Consumer's Demand Curve

Here DD_1 is the typical demand curve of a commodity. The curve slopes downward from left to right. This means that at higher prices consumers buy less and when the price falls quantity demanded increases. Such a downward slope is called a negative slope.

Generally, the independent variable is shown on the x-axis and the dependent variable on the y-axis. But it is a convention among economists to plot price of the commodity on the y-axis and the quantity demanded of the same on the x-axis.

The demand curve concentrates exclusively on the price-quantity relationship and ignores the relationship between quantity demanded and other variables.

From the demand curve we can the indicate the maximum quantity a consumer will be willing to buy at a particular price. We can also indicate the maximum price the consumer is willing to pay for a particular quantity.

The relation between price and quantity can be expressed algebraically as follows $Q = f(P)$ where Q is the quantity demanded of a commodity and P is its price. This expression is known as the demand function which implies that quantity demanded is a function of price.

INDIVIDUAL DEMAND AND MARKET DEMAND

The quantity demanded of a commodity by an individual consumer at a particular price per period is called individual demand whereas the aggregate quantity demanded by all the consumers is called market demand.

The market demand, i.e., the total commodity demanded can be calculated by adding the quantities demanded by all the consumers. Suppose, there are four consumers *A*, *B*, *C* and *D* buying pens in the market.

We can arrive at the market demand as follows:

TABLE 1.2 MARKET DEMAND FOR PENS

Price per unit (Rs.)	Quantity Demanded by				Total
	A	*B*	*C*	*D*	
12	1	2	0	0	3
10	2	3	1	0	6
8	3	4	1	1	9
6	5	6	1	1	13
4	7	7	2	2	18

The last column shows the total demand for pens, i.e., the market demand at various prices. The market demand curve is just a lateral summation of individual demand curves.

This can be shown graphically as follows:

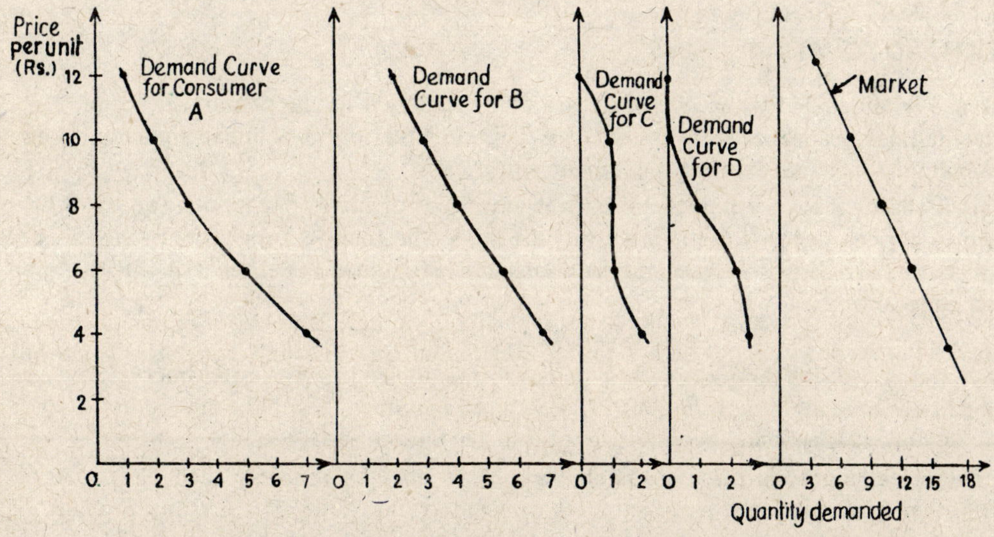

Fig 1.2 The Derivation of the Market Demand Curve

THE MARKET DEMAND FUNCTION

The market demand function of a particular product is a statement which shows the relation between the total quantity demanded and all the factors that influence this quantity. The demand function of a product in general functional form may the expressed as follows:

The quantity of product A demanded $= Q_A = f$ (price of A, consumer incomes, consumer tastes and preferences, prices of related goods, expectations of price changes, advertising expenditures, population growth, legal restrictions, etc.)

The relation between the quantity demanded of a commodity and various demand-determining variables (called demand determinants) must be stated clearly the purpose of managerial decision making.

The demand function of product A can be expressed as follows:

$$Q_A = f(P_A, I, T, P_r, P_C, A, P_G, L)$$

where P_A = price of product A, I = consumers' incomes, T = consumers' tastes and preferences, P_r = prices of related goods; P_C = expectations of price changes, A = advertising expenditures; P_a = population growth and L = legal restrictions.

Application

Let us take the case of salt. The demand of salt arises due to several factors which are listed below:

(1) Salt maintains body temperature. Salt deficiency causes tireness, dehydration or even death.

(2) A pregnant women requires more salt.

(3) Urban dwellers consume more salt.

(4) People engaged in stressful jobs need more salt.

(5) Educated consumers are aware of the health hazards of excess salt consumption. So they consume less salt. Excess use of salt may cause high blood pressure, heart attacks, etc. This is why educated consumers develop tastes for low–salt potato chips, butter, seafish, etc.

THE DEMAND EQUATION

Once it is decided which variables are to be included in the demand function for a particular product, it becomes easier to represent the demand function as a linear equation. Let us consider some demand functions expressed as linear equations.

(i) If the demand for polythene bags in hundreds of boxes per month (Q_b) is a linear function of price in rupees per box (P_b), price oi jute bags, the main competitor, in rupees per box (P_j), average consumer disposable income in thousands of rupees (I), then the linear equation can be written as follows:

$$Q_b = a + bP_b + cP_j + dI$$

where a, b, c and d are the parameters, or constants. If we know the parameters, we can determine the effects of changing any variable in the demand equation. To make the demand equation simple we have ignored advertising expenditure and other factors.

Statistical methods like regression techniques may be applied to find out the values of the coefficients a, b, c and d. For simplicity, let us assume the values of a, b, c and d as $20, -30, 4$ and 8, respectively. Hence the linear equation can be written as follows:

$$Q_b = 20 - 30P_b + 4P_j + 8I. \qquad (1)$$

We can find out the effects of changes of variables in this equation. For example if P_j and I do not change, a one rupee increase in the price of box decreases the quantity demanded by 30 times 100 or 3,000 boxes.

Furthermore, if P_b = Rs. 3, P_j = Rs. 2.5 and I = Rs. 100, the demand equation predicts that Q_b will be:

$$Q_b = 20 - 30 \times 3 + 4 \times 2.5 + 8 \times 100 = 20 - 90 + 10 + 800 = \mathbf{740} \quad \text{or } 74,000 \text{ boxes}$$

So long as the coefficients remain constant with changes in values of the variables, the equation gives useful information about the demand for such bags.

(ii) If the demand for sweet potatoes in 1000 MT per year (Q_p) is a linear function of price of sweet potatoes in rupees per M.T. (P_s), price of white potatoes in rupees per M.T. (P_w), time trend (T); average disposable income of consumers in thousands of rupees (I), two-year moving average of total population in crores (N), then the linear equation can be written as follows:

$$Q_p = a - bP_s + CN + dI + eP_w - fT$$

where a, b, c, d, e and f are the parameters, or constants. The values of the parameters can be found out by regression techniques, or can be assumed to take particular values.

From this equation we find that the demand for sweet potatoes increases with increase of consumer income, since I has a positive coefficient. Again white potatos are substitutes of sweet potatoes, i.e., when the price for white potatoes increases, the demand for sweet potatoes increases. The negative coefficient of time indicates less and less consumer preference for sweet potatoes.

(iii) If the demand for crude oil in thousand barrels per month (Q_C) is a linear function of price of crude oil in rupees per 100 barrels (P_C), price of coal and natural gas in rupees per MT (P_a), per capita disposable income in thousands of rupees (I), the number of motor vehicles per capita (N), then the linear demand equation can be written as follows:

$$Q_c = a - bP_c + cP_a + dI + N$$

where, a, b, c, d and e are the parameters, or constants. The values of parameters can be found by statistical methods or can be assumed to take arbitrary values.

From the equation we find that 1% decrease in the price of gasoline (Pc) would increase its quantity demanded by b%.

(iv) Again, if the demand for automobiles per year (Q_A) is a linear function of the average price of automobiles (P_a), average consumer disposable income (I), population (N), average rate of interest on loans for verticles in per cent (R), and advertising expenditure (A_e), then the linear demand equation can be written as follows:

$$Q_A = aP_a + bI + cN + dR + eA_e$$

where a, b, c, d and e are the parameters, or constants of the demand function. The values of the parameters can be found by statistical methods, or can be assumed to take reasonable values.

Putting a set of assumed parameter values in the equation, we get:

$$Q_A = -1,400P_a + 800I + 0.02N - 1000R + 0.03A_e \tag{2}$$

From the above equation we find that the demand of automobiles falls by 1,400 units for each 1 rupee increase in the average price of the automobile. Here demand increases by 800 units for each 1 rupee increase in the average consumer disposable income. Likewise demand increases by .02 units for each extra individual in the population. We also find that demand decreases by 1000 units for every 1% increase in the interest rates. Again demand increases by .03 units for each 1 rupee expenditure on advertising.

When we multiply the parameters of the equation by the respective values of the variables, and add up the products, we get the estimated demand for automobiles, for a particular year.

In the following table we have presented the estimated demand for automobiles using the hypothetical demand function and assumed values of the variables.

TABLE 1.3 THE ESTIMATED DEMAND FOR AUTOMOBILES

Independent Variables	Parameter	Estimated Value of the Variable for the Particular Year	Estimated Total Demand
Average Price (P_a)	– 1,400	Rs. 10,000	– 140,00,000
Disposable Income (I)	800	Rs. 20,000	160,00,000
Population (N)	.02	200,00,000	4,00,000
Rate of Interest (R)	– 1000	10%	– 100
Advertising Expenses (A_e)	.03	Rs. 100,00,000	3,00,000
		Total Demand	= 26,99,900

INDUSTRY DEMAND VERSUS FIRM DEMAND

Market demand functions can be obtained for an whole industry, or for a firm, though in each case different variables are used. Emphasis should be given on the variables representing competitors' actions in the firm's demand function. For example competitors' prices and expenditures on advertisement should be included in the firm's demand function. The demand for the firm's product varies inversely with its own price and directly with the prices charged by the competing firms. Again, the demand for the firm's products increases with it's own advertising expenditures, but rises, or declines with extra advertising by other firms.

In most cases the demand parameters differ in case of a firm and an industry. Let us consider, for instance, the positive effect of population on the demand for Hindusthan automobiles against automobiles in general. The value of the parameter in Hindusthan automobile demand function will be less than that in the industry demand function. However, if Hidusthan automobiles could capture cent per cent of the market, i.e., if Hindusthan Motors were the industry, we would expect the parameters for the industry and firm demand functions to be identical.

Since in actual practice, industry and firm demand functions are different, different equations are to be used for analysing these two levels of demand. The concept of demand developed here is applicable to both industry and firm demand functions.

THE DEMAND CURVE

The demand function shows the relation between the quantity demanded of a commodity and all variables which influence it. The demand curve is the portion of the demand function which shows the relation between the price of a product and its quantity demanded, treating the effects of all other variables as constant. Often demand curves are drawn on a graph paper, assuming all variables in the demand function, excluding price and quantity of the product demanded, as constants at specified levels. Let us now draw the demand curves of the four demand functions, discussed earlier under the heading **The Demand Equation**, one by one.

(i) Let us create the demand curve for the polythene bags. If in equation (1) we again assume P_j = Rs. 2.5 and I = Rs. 100, then the equation becomes

$$Q_b = 20 - 30P_b + 10 + 800 = 830 - 30P_b.$$

The equation now shows the linear relationship between Q_b and P_b. The graphical representation between Q_b and P_b is shown in Fig. 1.3.

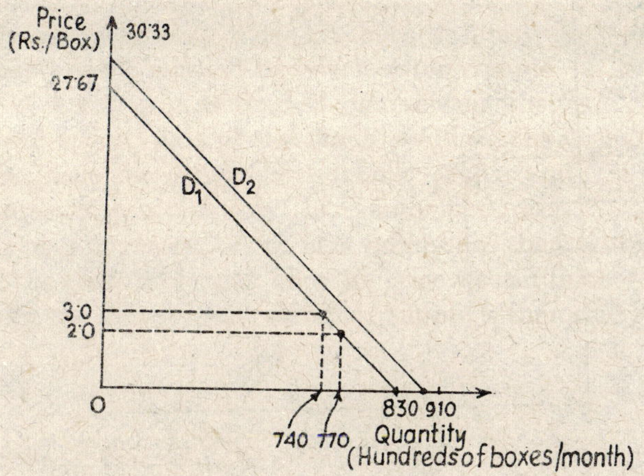

Fig 1.3 The Demand Curve for Polythene Bags

If all other factors influencing demand remain constant, a change in P_b from Rs. 3 to Rs. 2 produces a change in the quantity demanded from 74,000 to 77,000 boxes per month. Any change in P_b results in a movement along the demand curve (D_1) as shown in Fig. 1.3. A change in a demand factor, or variable other than P_b causes the demand curve to shift either to the right, or to the left.

If in equation (1), the value of I changes from Rs. 100 to Rs. 110, the equation becomes

$$Q_b = 20 - 30 \times P_b + 4 \times 2.5 + 8(110) = 20 - 30P_b + 10 + 880 = 910 - 30P_b.$$

The new equation has a price intercept of 30.33 (in place of 27.67) and a quantity demanded intercept of 910 (in place of 830). Hence the new demand curve D_2 lies to the right of the original demand curve D_1. In fact the whole demand curve D_1 has shifted to a new position D_2.

(ii) and (iii) The demand curves of sweet potatoes and crude oil can be drawn on a graph paper in the same way by assuming hypothetical values of parameters and all variables except the quantity demanded and the price of the sweet potatoes and crude oil.

(iv) In the automobile demand function given in equation (2), we find a relation between the prices of automobile and the quantity demanded at various prices by holding income, population, interest rates, advertising expenditures constant.

It we put the values of the variables as shown in Table 1.1, the equation (2) becomes:

$$\begin{aligned} Q_A &= -1400P_a + 800(20,000) + 0.02(200,00,000) - 1,000(.1) + 0.03(100,00,000) \\ &= -1,400P_a + 160,00,000 + 4,00,000 - 100 + 3,00,000 \\ \therefore\ Q_A &= 166,99,900 - 1,400P_a. \end{aligned} \tag{3}$$

The demand curve, given by the equation: $Q_A = 166,99,900 - 1,400P_a$, has a price intercept of 11,928.5 and a quantity demanded intercept of 166,99,900. Any change in P_a results in a movement along the demand curve. The demand curve may be drawn on a graph paper which will take the shape as shown in Fig. 1.4.

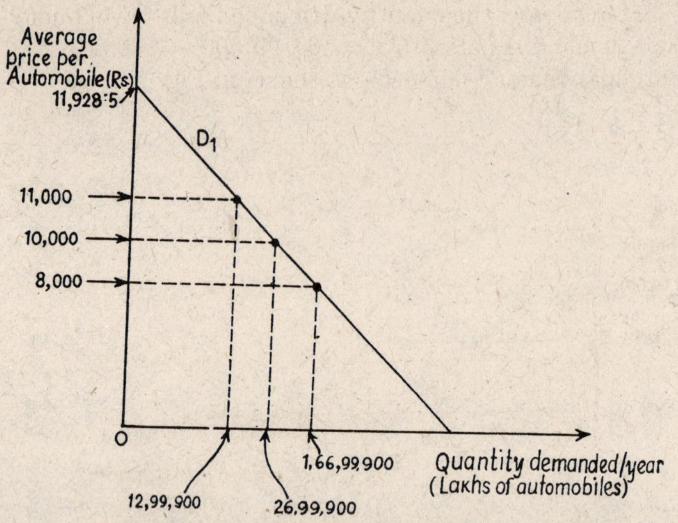

Fig 1.4 A Hypothetical Automobile Demand Curve

From equation(3), we find that decrease in price (P_a) increases the quantity demanded (Q_A) and *vice versa.* The slope coefficient in equation (3), ($-1,400$) means that Re. 1 increase in the average price of automobiles will decrease the quantity demanded by 1400 units and *vice versa.*

Relation between Demand Curve and Demand Function

The relation between the demand curve and the demand function is very significant since it helps the top management to take appropriate decisions. Any change in the average price per automobile (P_a) will change the quantity demanded (Q_A) and the movement can be shown along a given demand curve. For example when P_a changes from Rs. 10,000 to Rs. 11,000 or Rs. 8,000, the corresponding values of Q_A will be 12,99,900 and 54,99,900, respectively.

Suppose the demand equation is

$$Q_A = 166,99,900 - 1,400P_a.$$

When $P_a = 11,000$,

$$Q_A = 166,99,900 - 1,400(11,000) = 166,99,900 - 154,00,000 = 12,99,900.$$

Again, when $P_a = 8,000$,

$$Q_A = 166,99,900 - 1,400(8,000) = 166,99,900 - 112,00,000 = 54,99,900.$$

Thus, we find that when P_a falls from Rs. 12,000 to Rs. 10,000 and then to Rs. 8,000, Q_A increases from 12,99,900 to 26,99,900 and then to 54,99,900. This change in the quantity demanded shows the effect on sales of a change in price, keeping the effects of all other demand-determining factors constant. The changes in quantity demanded take place on a given demand curve and is shown in Fig.1.5 by movements along the same curve.

A shift of demand, i.e., a shift of the demand curve to a new position (either to the right or the left) indicates that there is a change in either one, or more of the non-price variables in the demand function. In the example of automobile demand function we find that the quantity demanded varies inversely with interest rates, i.e., when the interest rate is reduced, the quantity demanded increases. Now, if the rate of interest rises from 10% to 50%, the equation (3) becomes

$$Q_A = 166,99,500 - 1,400P_a.$$

The new demand curve has a price intercept of 11928.2 and quantity demanded intercept of 166,99,500. Thus, at 50% interest rate, the quantity demanded falls by 400 units. If we draw a new demand curve (D_2) for this demand equation $Q_A = 166,99,500 - 1,400P_a$, then this curve will be shifted to the left of the original demand curve D_1 as shown in Fig. 1.5.

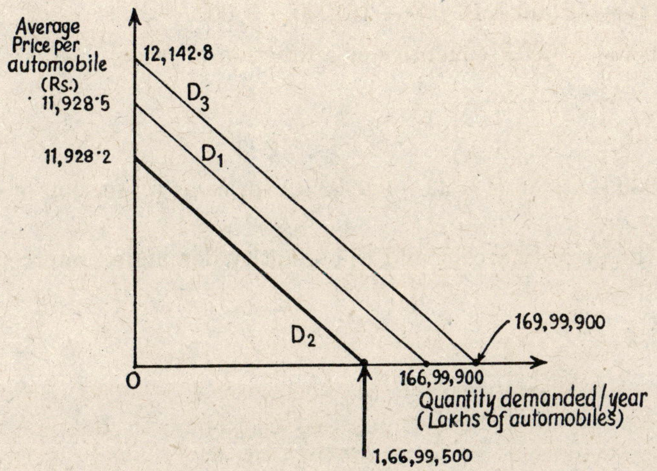

Fig 1.5 Three Hypothetical Automobile Demand Curves

At a price of Rs. 10,000 and at 50% interest, demand for automobiles will be 26,99,500 per year.

Since, the advertising parameter in the demand function in equation (2) is 0.03, the advertising expenditure is directly proportional to the quantity demanded, i.e., when the advertising expenditure increases the quantity demanded also increases and *vice versa.* Thus, if the advertising expenditure is increased from Rs. 100,00,000 to Rs. 200,00,000, then equation (3) becomes $Q_A = 169,99,900 - 1,400P_a$. This demand curve has a price intercept of 12,142.8 and a quantity demanded intercept of 169,99,900. Thus, in this case the demand curve D_1 in Fig. 1.5 will shift to the right to D_3.

The distinction between changes in quantity demanded that show movements along the same demand curve and changes in demand that imply shift of the original demand curve to a new position is very important. If the causes of changes in demand for a company's products cannot be correctly ascertained, it may lead to costly, disastrous managerial decisions. However, demand analysis is not a very easy task since apart from price, demand for a product is related to many other factors like income, interest rates, population, advertising expenditures, quality, consumer preferences, and so on. It is, in fact, one of the most challenging tasks faced by the marketing manager.

EXAMPLE 1. The New Central Book Agency (NCBA) is a book publisher with markets all over India. NCBA books are either directly sold to the public or routed through the agents. Operating experience of previous years suggests the following demand function for NCBA's books:

$$Q = 4,000 - 3,000P + 0.03Pop. + 0.4I + 2.0A,$$

where Q = quantity; P = price (in Rs.); *Pop.* = population, I = disposable income per household (Rs.); and A = advertising expenditure (Rs.).

(i) Obtain the demand curve faced by NCBA in a typical market where P = Rs. 5, *Pop.* = 20,00,000; I = Rs. 40,000 and A = Rs. 8,000. State the demand curve expressing quantity as a function of price and price as a function of quantity.

(ii) Compute the quantity demanded at prices of Rs. 5, 10 and 0, respectively.

(iii) Compute the prices needed to sell 20,000, 25,000 and 35,000 units.

SOLUTION. (i) The demand function for NCBA's books is given as follows:

$$Q = 4,000 - 3,000P + 0.03Pop + 0.4I + 2.0A.$$

When *Pop.* = 20,00,000, I = Rs. 40,000 and A = Rs. 8,000, we have

$$\begin{aligned} Q &= 4,000 + 0.03 \times 20,00,000 + 0.4 \times 40,000 + 2 \times 8,000 - 3,000P \\ &= 4,000 + 60,000 + 16,000 + 16,000 - 3,000P \\ &= 96,000 - 3,000P \text{ (quantity as a function of price)} \qquad (1) \end{aligned}$$

Now,

$$3,000P = 96,000 - Q, \text{ or } P = 32 - 0.00033Q \text{ (price as a function of quantity).} \qquad (2)$$

From (1) we have the price intercept and the quantity demanded intercept as 32 and 96,000, respectively.

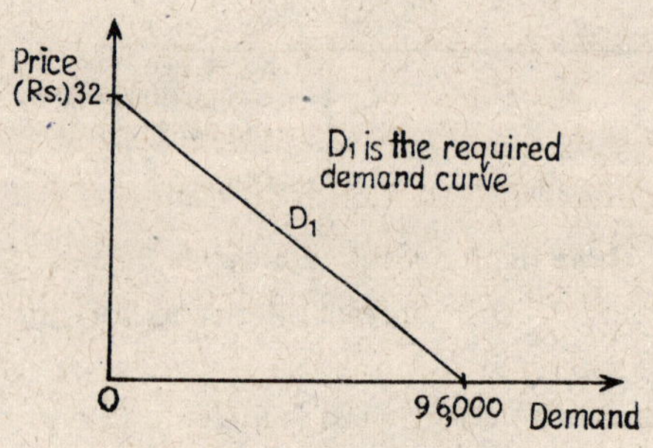

Fig 1.6 The Demand Curve for Books

(ii) We know, $Q = 96,000 - 3,000P$

$$\begin{aligned} \text{When} \quad P &= \text{Rs. } 5, & Q &= 96,000 - 15,000 = 81,000 \\ P &= \text{Rs. } 10, & Q &= 96,000 - 30,000 = 66,000 \\ P &= \text{Rs. } 0, & Q &= 96,000 - 0 = 96,000 \end{aligned}$$

(iii) We know, $P = 32 - 0.00033Q$

$$\begin{aligned} \text{When} \quad Q &= 20,000, & P &= 32 - 0.00033 \times 20,000 = \text{Rs. } 25.4 \\ Q &= 25,000, & P &= 32 - 0.00033 \times 25,000 = \text{Rs. } 23.75 \\ Q &= 35,000, & P &= 32 - 0.00033 \times 35,000 = \text{Rs. } 20.45 \end{aligned}$$

EXAMPLE 2. The demand function of *XY* & Co. is $Q = 200 - 20P + 10I - 4P_1 + 3D$ where P = own price, I = income, P_1 = price of other substitute goods, D = advertising expenditure.

If $Y = 50, P_1 = 3, D = 20, P = 10$, find the current level of demand.

SOLUTION.

$$\begin{aligned} Q &= 200 - 20 \times 10 + 10 \times 50 - 4 \times 3 + 3 \times 20 = 200 - 200 + 500 - 12 + 60 \\ &= 760 - 212 = 548 \text{ units.} \end{aligned}$$

EXAMPLE 3. ABC Co. currently sells 1,000 units of its model R weekly, at Rs. 50 each. Its market research consultant observes that for every additional rupee the company charges, the consumer will buy 20 fewer units per week. Find the demand equation and the revenue function.

SOLUTION. From the problem we find that the demand is 1,000 units less 20 units for each rupee one by which the price (P) is higher than Rs. 50, *i.e.*, x (desired production level) $= 1,000 - 20(p-50)$.

This is the demand equation.

Now, to get the revenue function, we must find out p.

$$x = 1,000 - 20p + 1,000 = 2,000 - 20p$$

$$\text{or} \quad 20p = 2000 - x; \quad P = \frac{2000}{20} - \frac{x}{20} = 100 - \frac{x}{20}$$

$\therefore$ the revenue function is

$$R(x) = xp = x\left(100 - \tfrac{x}{20}\right) = -\frac{\mathbf{x^2}}{\mathbf{20}} + \mathbf{100x}.$$

EXAMPLE 4. The average weekly demand for a pen (Q) in terms of price (P) has been estimated as follows $Q = 100 - 10P$.

(i) (a) How many pens can be sold at a price of Rs. 5 per pen? (b) What will be the sale if the price is decreased to Rs. 2?

(ii) If the firm wants to sell 60 pens per week, what price should it charge?

(iii) What would be the quantity demanded if the sellers of pen were willing to give the pen away?

(iv) What is the maximum price that a consumer will be willing to pay for a pen?

(v) Plot the demand curve.

SOLUTION.

(i) (a) $Q = 100 - 10 \times 5 = 50$

(b) $Q = 100 - 10 \times 2 = 80$

(ii) $60 = 100 - 10P$ or $60 - 100 = -10P$ or $-40 = -10P$ $\therefore$ $P =$ Rs. 4.

(iii) $Q = 100 - 10 \times 0$ (the minimum price of P is zero). $\therefore$ quantity demanded $= 100$.

(iv) The highest price means the minimum quantity, i.e., $Q = 0$.

$\therefore 0 = 100 - 10R$, or $-100 = -10P$, or $P =$ Rs.10.

(v) Here PQ is the demand curve for pens, as shown in Fig. 1.7.

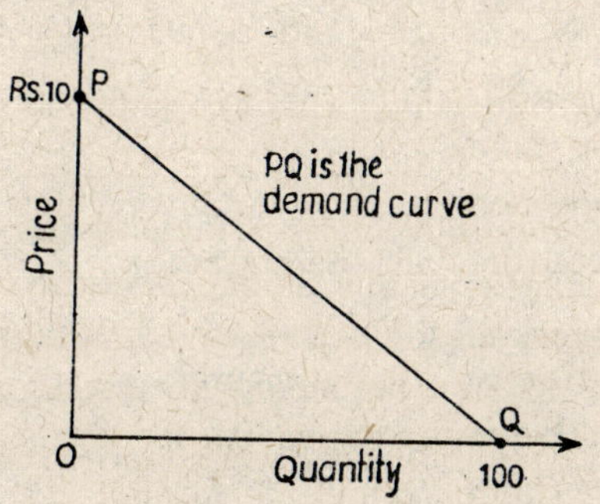

Fig 1.7 The Demand Curve for Pens

EXAMPLE 5. XYZ marketing consultants firm found that stereo-A model has the following demand equation in Calcutta.

$$Q = 8,000 - 100P + .02N + .5I + .4A$$

where Q = quantity per year, P = price in Rs., N = population, I = disposable income per consumer in rupees and A = advertising expenditure in rupees.

(i) Find the demand curve for the firm in a market where $P = 200, N = 20,00,000, I = 40,000$ and $A = 20,000$.

(ii) Compute the quantity demanded at prices of Rs. 200, Rs. 100 and Rs. 5, respectively.

(iii) Compute the price required to sell 50,000 units.

SOLUTION.

(i) $$Q = 8,000 - 100P + .02 \times 20,00,000 + .5 \times 40,000 + .4 \times 20,000$$
$$= 8,000 + 40,000 + 20,000 + 8,000 - 100P = 76,000 - 100P$$

When $Q = 0, P = 760$

When $P = 0, Q = 76,000$

$\therefore$ The demand curve will be the one shown in Fig. 1.8.

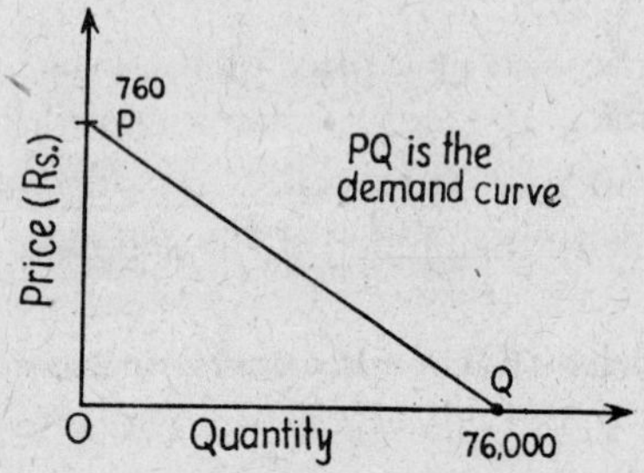

Fig 1.8 The Demand Curve for Stereo-A Model

(ii) Q at price Rs. $200 = 76,000 - 100 \times 200 = 76,000 - 20,000 = 56,000$.

Q at price Rs. $100, = 76,000 - 100 \times 100 = 76,000 - 10,000 = 66,000$.

Q at price Rs. $50, = 76,000 - 100 \times 50 = 76,000 - 5,000 = 71,000$.

(iii) Here $Q = 76,000 - 100P$ or $100P = 76,000 - Q$ or $P = 760 - \frac{Q}{100}$.

When $Q = 50,000$, $P = 760 - \frac{50,000}{100} = 760 - 500 =$ Rs. 260.

EXAMPLE 6. New Bharat Shoes are becoming very popular of late in Calcutta. From the analysis of Bharats various outlets, it was observed that the demand education is:

$$Q = 100 - 200P + 130I + 50T - 300A + 500A$$

where

Q = Number of shoes sold per month

P = Average price of each shoe

I = Average income of each consumer in the market

T = Average temperature

A = Competitors' monthly advertising expenditure

A_1 = Bharat's own monthly advertising expenditure.

For one of the outlets we have the following information:

$$P = 600, \quad I = 20,000, \quad T = 50, \quad A = 15,000, \quad A_1 = 10,000.$$

(i) Find the number of shoes sold per month by this outlet. Also find the relevant demand curve and draw it.

(ii) Find the effect of Rs. 6,000 increase in the competitors' advertising expenditure.

(iii) What would be Bharat's advertising expenditure to counteract this effect?

SOLUTION.

(i) $$Q = 100 - 200 \times 600 + 130 \times 20,000 + 50 \times 50 - 300 \times 15,000 + 500 \times 10,000$$
$$= 100 - 1,20,000 + 26,00,000 + 2,500 - 45,00,000 + 50,00,000 = 29,82,600.$$

Now $Q = 31,02,600 - 200P$

When $Q = 0, P = 15,513$; and when $P = 0, Q = 31,02,600$.

$\therefore$ the demand curve is the one shown in Fig. 1.9.

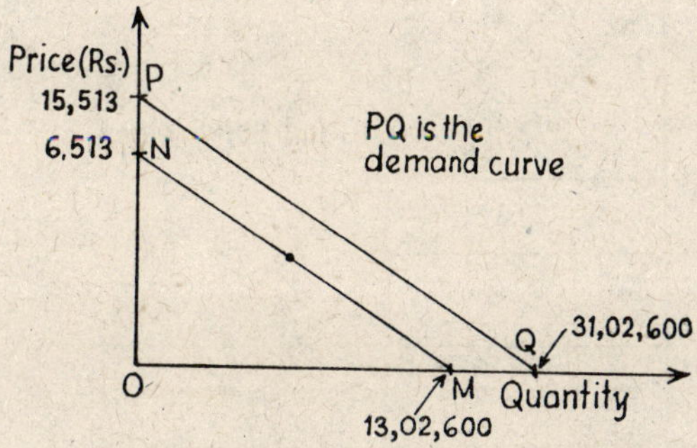

Fig 1.9 The Demand Curve for Shoes

(ii) $$Q = 100 - 200P + 130 \times 20,000 + 50 \times 50 - 300 \times 21,000 + 500 \times 10,000$$
$$= 100 - 200P + 26,00,000 + 2,500 - 63,00,000 + 50,00,000$$
$$= 13,02,600 - 200P.$$

When $P = 0, \quad Q = 13,02,600$

and when $Q = 0, \quad P = 6513.$

Here MN is the new demand curve of the outlet which is shifted to the left of PQ.

(iii) Now,

$$31,02,600 - 200P = 100 + 26,00,000 + 2,500 - 63,00,000 + 500(10,000 + x) - 200P$$
$$\text{or } 31,02,600 = 13,02,600 + 500x, \text{ or } 18,00,000 = 500x, \text{ or } x = 3,600.$$

So Bharat's own advertising expenditure should be increased to Rs. 13,600 to counteract this effect.

EXAMPLE 7. A complete demand function is represented by the following equation:

$$Q_d = -20P + 0.04I + 3P_r + 4T$$

where P is the price of each goods, I is income, P_r is price of a substitute good and T is the taste of the consumers.

(i) Can be function be graphed?

(ii) Draw the demand curve assuming $I = 6000$, $P_r = 25, T = 40$ in the traditional way, i.e., quantity on the x-axis and price on the y-axis.

(iii) What does the typical demand function drawn in (ii) indicate?

(iv) What is the effect on the curve if the price of the goods changes from 4 to 6?

(v) What is the effect on the demand curve if one of the variables, say, income increases to 8,000?

SOLUTION.

(i) Since the demand function has five variables, it cannot be graphed as such. However, in ordinary demand analysis, we assume that all the independent variables excluding price are constant such that the effect of a change in price (P) on the quantity demanded (Q_d) can be found, irrespective of the influence of all other factors or ceteris paribus. Thus, when variables Y, P_r and T are held constant, the demand function can be graphed.

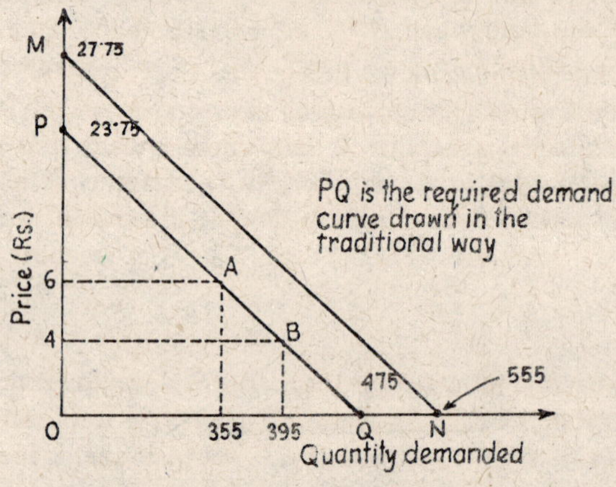

Fig 1.10 A Traditional Demand Curve

(ii) Here PQ is the required demand curve drawn in the traditional way.

$$Q_d = -20P + .04 \times 6,000 + 3 \times 25 + 4 \times 40 = -20P + 240 + 75 + 160 = -20P + 475.$$

When $Q = 0,\ P = 23.75$

When $P = 0,\ Q = 475.$

(iii) The demand curve shown above has been drawn assuming income, the price of a related (substitute) good and taste (i.e., 6000, 25, 40) as constants.

(iv) $Q_d = -20P + 475$

When $P = 4,\ Q_d = -20 \times 4 + 475 = 395$ (point B on the graph).

When $P = 6,\ Q_d = -20 \times 6 + 475 = 355$ (point A on the graph).

(v) $Q_d = -20P + .04 \times 8,000 + 3 \times 25 + 4 \times 40 = -20P + 320 + 75 + 160 = -20P + 555.$

When $Q_d = 0,\ P = \frac{555}{20} = 27.75$

When $P = 0,\ Q_d = 555.$

The effect of the change in income is the shift of the demand curve from PQ to MN, i.e., to the right.

EXAMPLE 8. Mr. Chatterjee, manager of the marketing division of Hindusthan Motors, estimated the following demand function for Ambassador cars,

$$Q = 50,000 - 150P + 3,000N + 60I + 40P_m - 2000P_p + 5A + 30,000P_c$$

where

Q = Quantity demanded per year of Ambassadar cars

P = Price of Ambassadar cars in rupees

N = Population of India in lakhs

I = Disposable Income (per capita) in rupees

P_m = Price of Maruti cars in rupees

P_p = Price of petrol in rupees per litre

A = Advertising expenditure on Ambassador cars in rupees per year

P_c = Credit incentives to buy Ambassador cars, in terms of interest rates below the market rates

(a) Find the change in Q for each unit change in the independent, or explanatory variables;

(b) Find Q if P = Rs. 8,000, N = 400 lakhs; I = Rs. 8,000, P_m = Rs. 6,000, P_p = Rs. 2, A = Rs. 1,00,000 and $P_c = 1$;

(c) State the equation for the demand curve for Ambassador cars, and

(d) Plot the curve.

SOLUTION. (a) Q declines by 150 units for each Re. 1 rise in the price of Ambassador, increases by 3,000 units for each 1 lakh increase in N, increases by 60 units for each Re. 1 increase in I, increases by 40 units for each Re. 1 increase in P_m, declines by 2,000 units for each Re. 1 increase in P_p, increase 5 by units for each Re. 1 increase in A and increases by 30,000 units for each 1 percentage point reduction of the interest rate to borrow money in order to buy Ambassador car (P_c).

(b) $Q = 50,000 - 150 \times 8,000 + 3,000 \times 400 + 60 \times 8,000 + 40 \times 6,000 - 2,000 \times 2$
$+ 5 \times 1,00,000 + 30,000 \times 1$
$= 50,000 - 12,00,000 + 12,00,000 + 4,80,000 + 2,40,000 - 4,000 + 5,00,000 + 30,000$
$= 12,96,000$

(c) $Q = 24,96,000 - 150P$ is the equation for the demand curve for Ambassador cars.

(d) In $Q = 24,96,000 - 150P$, if $Q = 0$, $P = 16,640$; if $P = 0$, $Q = 24,96,000$.

Here PQ is the required demand curve, as shown in Fig. 1.11.

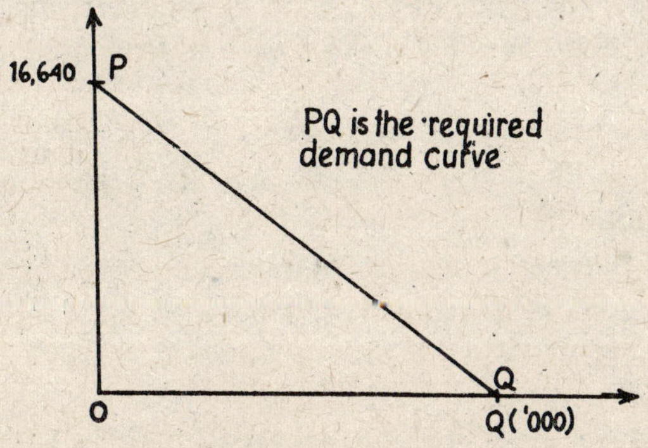

Fig 1.11 The Demand Curve for Ambassador Cars

Summary

Demand analysis refers to finding out and measuring the forces that determine sales. There are various objectives of demand analysis.

Demand analysis serves four managerial purposes:

1. sales forecasting;
2. demand manipulation;
3. appraising salesperson's performance and setting their sales quotas; and
4. watching the trend of the company's competitive position.

Of these the first two are the most important.

Forecasting demand is the most common use of demand studies. Sales forecast is the foundation for planning all phases of the company's operations. In fact, purchasing commitments, production schedules, inventory plans, cash budgets and capital expenditure programmes are all based on the sales forecast. Sales forecasting is passive in nature. It estimates external economic factors and predicts the resulting sales volume the firm can expect if it carries out its present operations successfully.

In practice, sales volumes do differ, depending upon how much money is spent on advertising and sales promotion, what price policy is adopted, what products improvements are made and how accurately sales people and sales effort are matched with potential sales in different territories, and so on. So demand for a firm's product can be manipulated through such measures as adjusting prices, promotion and/or products.

Concepts for Review

1. The Law of Demand,
2. The Demand Function,
3. The Demand Determinants,
4. Individual Demand,
5. Market Demand,
6. Firm Demand,
7. Industry Demand,
8. Derived Demand,
9. Stock Demand,
10. Flow Demand.

Exercises

1. The following demand function has been estimated for a product of X & Y Co.

$$Q = 4 - 5P + .06I + 16P_1 - 10P_2 + 6A$$

where Q = units sold per month, P = price per unit, I = income of consumers, P_1 = price of a substitute goods, P_2 = price of a complementary goods, A = advertising expenditure.

(i) Develop quantity estimating equations for each independent variable, treating all other variables as constants.

The values of the variables are assumed as follows

$$P = \text{Rs. } 1.5,\ P_1 = \text{Rs. } 2,\ P_2 = \text{Rs. } .50,\ I = \text{Rs. } 5{,}000, \text{ and } A = \text{Rs. } 2{,}000.$$

(ii) Plot the demand curve.

2. What is the difference between a demand function and a demand curve?

3. The following function shows the quantity demanded for a company making articles for college and professional teams participating in various games $Q = 4,000 - 150P$ where Q stands for sale of articles and P is the price.

(i) How many articles could be sold at Rs. 10 each?

(ii) What should be the price of the company to sell 1,500 articles?

(iii) At what price the sale of the article would be zero?

(iv) Plot the demand curve.

4. (a) Graph the following demand function

$$Q_d = -5P + .02I - 6P_r + 12T \text{ where } I = 6,000, P_r = 6 \text{ and } T = 5.$$

(b) What do you observe from the price of a related good (P_r)?

(c) Draw the graph in the traditional way, i.e., P on y-axis and Q_d on x-axis.

(d) What is the effect on the graph if taste (T) changes from 5 to 10?

5. What is the difference between direct demand and derived demand? Give some examples of the latter.

6. What are the factors which influence the market demand for a commodity?

CHAPTER 2

THEORETICAL FOUNDATIONS OF DEMAND

Demand for new supplies of durable goods fluctuates more intensely than demand for the current services these durable goods render.

J. M. Clark, 1934

The relative prices of goods arise in principle from the pattern of demand that emerges from the distribution of income.

E. J. Mishan, 1967

Fundamental Questions

1. What is an indifference curve?
2. What is budget line?
3. When does a rational consumer reach the point of maximum welfare?
4. What is Engel Curve?
5. What is the difference between substitution effect and income effect of a change in the price of a commodity?
6. How would you use indifference curves to draw the income consumption curve and price consumption curve?
7. What is price elasticity of demand?
8. Does time exert any influence on price elasticity of demand?
9. What is income elasticity of demand?
10. What is cross elasticity of demand?
11. What is meant by elasticity of derived products?
12. What are different revenue concepts?

PREVIEW

Demand theory or the theory of consumer behaviour is often a very important source of many useful insights for business decision making. Indeed the importance of understanding demand can hardly be overemphasised. In the ultimate analysis, it seems that the success or failure of a business depends primarily on its ability to generate revenues by satisfying the demands of consumers. Firms which are unable to attract a large number of customers or generate sufficient demand for their products are often forced out of the market.

The fundamental objective of demand theory is to identify and analyse the basic determinants of consumer demand. An understanding of the forces behind demand is a powerful tool for managers. Such knowledge provides the background needed to make pricing decisions, forecast sales and formulate marketing strategies.

After discussing individual demand, market demand and the demand faced by the firm, the focus shifts in this chapter to a basic concern of managers—the total revenue earned by the firm. Finally the concept of elasticity is introduced as a tool for measuring the responsiveness of quantity demanded to changes in prices, income and other demand determinants. Four major elasticity measures are discussed price elasticity, income elasticity and cross elasticity as also the elasticity of derived products.

THE THEORY OF CONSUMER BEHAVIOUR

Consumers have various goods and services from to choose from. In practice they purchase some items for consumption but not all. How much of a commodity will be consumed by an individual consumer is determined by factors like the price of the commodity the consumer's income, the price of other (related) commodities, his tastes and preferences and so on.

The tastes and preferences of a consumer depend on factors like education, advertising, experiences of life, social norms, etc. These variables determine the satisfaction achieved from consuming various items. The satisfaction can be represented by a utility function as presented below

$$U = f(X_a, X_b, X_c, \cdots X_n),$$

where X_a, X_b, etc. represent various items of consumption. The function U varies directly with the consumption of an individual (i.e., $\partial U/\partial X_n > 0$ for all n), i.e., more is preferred to less with respect to consumption. Now n i.e., the number of items, is so large that it is very difficult for an individual to state honestly that he would not like to have any more. In fact, an individual is more interested in maximising his satisfaction (U) from consuming different bundles of goods.

Unfortunately an individuals consumption is restricted by his income. Hence an individual faces the problem of allocating his limited income among available items in such a way so as to obtain the maximum possible satisfaction. Thus a consumer's utility function for n items is expressed as

$$U = f(X_a, X_b, X_c, \cdots X_n)$$

Here U is total utility which is a function of various items consumed. He seeks to maximise U subject to the following income (or budget) constraint

$$I = \Sigma P_n X_n = P_a X_a + P_b X_b + P_c X_c \cdots P_n X_n,$$

where I is the consumer's money income and $P_a, P_b, P_c \cdots P_n$ are the prices of purchseable goods.

To determine the utility-maximising consumption bundle, a new function is generated by combining the U-function to be maximised and the income equation (constraint). Such a constrained maximisation problem can be solved by using the Lagrangian Multiplier Technique. If we form a Lagrangian function S by introducing Lagrangian Multiplier λ we can maximise U subject to income constraint by maximising S

$$S = f(X_a, X_b, X_c, \cdots X_n) + \lambda(I - P_aX_a - P_bX_b - P_cX_c, \cdots, -P_nX_n)$$

Partial derivatives of S are taken for each variable and equated to zero to establish the first order condition for maximisation

$$\frac{\partial S}{\partial X_a} = f_a - \lambda P_a = 0$$

$$\frac{\partial S}{\partial X_b} = f_b - \lambda P_b = 0$$

$$\frac{\partial S}{\partial X_c} = f_c - \lambda P_c = 0$$

$$\cdots\cdots\cdots\cdots\cdots\cdots$$

$$\frac{\partial S}{\partial X_n} = f_n - \lambda P_n = 0$$

$$\frac{\partial S}{\partial \lambda} = I - P_aX_a - P_b - X_b - P_cX_c - \cdots - P_nX_n = 0.$$

The above equations can be solved simultaneously to find out the utility-maximising purchase levels for $X_a, X_b, X_c, \cdots X_n$. In order to maximise the constrained utility function for the consumer, the following condition must hold

$$\frac{f_a}{P_a} = \frac{f_b}{P_b} = \frac{f_c}{P_c} = \cdots = \frac{f_n}{P_n}.$$

The terms $f_a, f_b, f_c, \cdots, f_n$ really are the marginal utilities of the items and λ is equal to the marginal utility of income (money). Thus we find that there will be maximum consumer satisfaction when the income is so allocated that marginal utility per rupee spent is equal for all goods. From the last derivative we further find that all the consumers income will be spent.

Let us now consider some specific utility functions for a consumer having income constraint. In order to explain the concept of consumer equilibrium, i.e., assessing the actual bundle of items that will maximise satisfaction we will consider a simple situation where the consumer buys only two-commodities.

PROBLEM 1. If $U = 35 \times +95Y - 0.5X^2 - 0.5y^2$ and $P_x =$ Rs. 3, $P_y =$ Rs. 9 and $I =$ Rs. 60, then find the consumption (in units) of commodities X and Y as also the numerical value of λ.

SOLUTION. Here $S = 35X + 95Y - 0.5X^2 - 0.5Y^2 + \lambda(60 - 3X - 9Y)$

$$\frac{\partial S}{\partial X} = 35 - X - 3\lambda = 0; \quad \frac{\partial S}{\partial Y} = 95 - Y - 9\lambda = 0 \text{ and } \frac{\partial S}{\partial X} = 60 - 3X - 9\lambda = 0.$$

Solving the above three equations simultaneously, we get $X = 5$ units, $Y = 5$ units and $\lambda = 10$.

PROBLEM 2. If $U = XY$ and $P_x = 5$ and $P_y = 10$ and $I = 100$, then find the consumption (in units) of commodities X and Y as also the value of λ.

SOLUTION. Here $S = XY + \lambda(100 - 5X - 10Y)$

$$\therefore \quad \frac{\partial S}{\partial X} = Y - 5\lambda = 0 \quad (1)$$

$$\frac{\partial S}{\partial Y} = X - 10\lambda = 0 \quad (2)$$

$$\frac{\partial S}{\partial \lambda} = 100 - 5X - 10Y = 0 \quad (3)$$

Solving (1) and (2), we have $X = 2Y$.

Putting this in equation (3), we get $Y = 5$ units and $X = 10$ units.

Thus to reach equilibrium the consumer will have to buy 10 units of X and 5 units of Y. This combination exhausts the income of Rs. 100 and at this stage utility is 50 (i.e., $U = XY = 10 \times 5$).

Now $\lambda = \frac{Y}{5} = \frac{X}{10} = 1$.

This value of λ has an economic meaning and can be interpreted in the same way as shadow price in linear programming, i.e., the value of λ denotes the amount of variation in the objective function that would take place if the consumer had Re. 1 more of income. Hence, in this example of utility maximisation with income constraint, λ can be interpreted as the marginal utility of money income.

The result can be shown by solving the maximisation problem with income constraint of Rs. 101 rather than Rs. 100.

Here $S = XY + \lambda(101 - 5X - 10Y)$.

$$\therefore \quad \frac{\partial S}{\partial X} = Y - 5\lambda = 0; \quad \frac{\partial S}{\partial Y} = X - 10\lambda = 0; \quad \frac{\partial S}{\partial \lambda} = 101 - 5X - 10Y = 0.$$

Solving the first two equations we have $X = 2Y$.

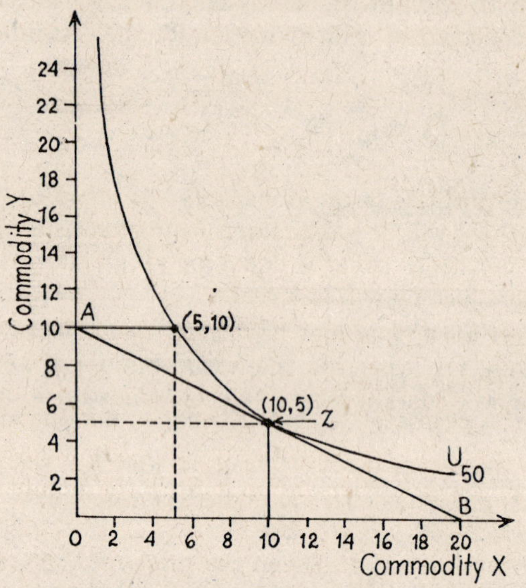

Fig 2.1 Consumer Equilibrium

Putting this value in the third equation, we get, $X = 10.1$ units and $Y = 5.05$ units. Now total utility becomes, $U = 5.05 \times 10.1 = 51.005 \approx 51$, i.e., 1 unit more than when income was Rs. 100 instead of Rs. 101. Hence, the marginal utility of money income is 1 here.

The original situation of example 2 has been shown graphically in Fig. 2.1. The line AB shows the consumers income constraint, i.e., $5X + 10Y = 100$. When this is solved for $Y(Y + 10 - \frac{1}{2}X)$, we find that the gradient is $-\frac{1}{2}$. The curve U_{50} curve shown in Fig. 2.1 indicates different combinations of X and Y for which the utility function has a value of 50.

The curve U_{50} is called an indifference curve since the consumer gets the same degree of satisfaction (50 here) at any point along such a curve. Here N is the point of tangency between the curve U_{50} and line AB called the budget line (or consumption possibility line). The gradiant of U_{50} (or, any indifference curve) is the negative of the ratio of the marginal utility of X and Y respectively $-(\frac{U_X}{U_Y})$ and the gradient of the income constraint is the negative of the ratio of the price of X and to the price of Y, i.e., $-(\frac{P_X}{P_Y})$. Now the gradients of U_{50} and AB are identical at the point of tangency, i.e., N.

Therefore

$$\frac{U_X}{U_Y} = \frac{P_X}{P_Y}, \text{ or, } \frac{U_X}{P_X} = \frac{U_Y}{P_Y}.$$

This is, in fact, the same earlier condition for consumer equilibrium since $U_X = f_X$ and $U_Y = f_Y$.

If, however, the ratio of marginal utility to price is not identical for both the goods (X and Y), the consumer can add to his satisfaction by spending less on the item with a minimum ratio and more on the item with a higher ratio, e.g., if $\frac{U_X}{P_X} = 10$ and $U_Y/P_Y = 5$, the consumer can add to utility by, 10 units if an extra rupee is spent on X and lose 5 units of utility if the same rupee is obtained by reducing the expenditure of Y. Total utility would be added by 5 units as a result of the reallocation of the consumers income. If, however, both the items X and Y are subject to diminishing marginal utility, such reallocation will not improve utility indefinitely. The marginal utilities of X and Y will decrease and increase, respectively as more of X and less of Y are consumed. If the prices to the consumers are constant, the ratios $\frac{U_X}{P_X}$ and $\frac{U_Y}{P_Y}$ will be equal and there will not be any addition to the consumers total utility by further changing the purchase-mix of items X and Y.

Using this model of consumer behaviour, let us obtain a demand function for a consumer. This can be done both mathematically and graphically. Let follow the graphical method. In Fig. 2.2, three income constraints have been drawn for a given income ($I = 1000$), a constant price of $Y(P_Y = 20)$ and three different prices of the item $X[P_{X_1} = 50, P_{X_2} = 25$ and $P_{X_3} = 20]$. The corresponding X intercepts for these income constraints are $20(I/P_{X_1})$, $40(I/P_{X_2})$ and $50(I/P_{X_3})$. These intercepts indicate the maximum amount of item X that a consumer will buy with the given income if no item Y is purchased for each price of item X. From Fig. 2.2 we find that as the price of item X falls, a given income allows a larger maximum consumption of item X.

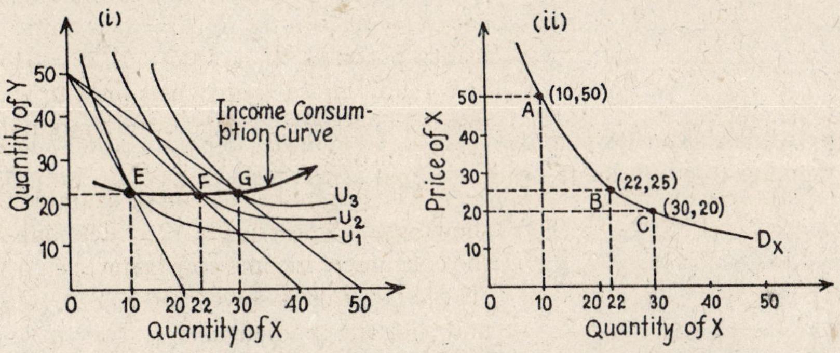

Fig 2.2 The Derivation of a Demand Curve

Alternative consumer equilibria points occur at the points of tangency between the income constraints and the indifference or utility curves U_1, U_2 and U_3. The quantities of item X purchased at different prices are obtained from the x-axis by drawing perpendiculars on it from the points of equilibrium.

The horizontal axis in Fig. 2.2(i) and Fig. 2.2(ii) are identical. When the price of X 50, 10 units of X is consumed. At prices 25 and 20, quantities of X demanded are 22 units and 30 units respectively. These points, i.e., (10, 50), (22, 25) and (30, 20) have been plotted in Fig. 2.2(ii) to derive the demand curve D_X. Since the quantity demanded of X varies inversely with its price the graph follows the Law of Demand.

To obtain the demand curve of the X from the mathematical model of consumer behaviour, we will consider two items X and Y and take I (income) and price of Y as constants. Let us again assume a simple utility function for the consumer of the following type $U = XY$.

Since the consumer will try to maximise utility for each price of item X, the problem becomes one of constrained optimisation. The consumer has to:

Maximise $U = X$

Subject to the budget constraint $I = P_X X + P_Y Y$.

Introducing the Lagrange multiplier technique once again we have

$$S = XY - \lambda(I - P_X X - P_Y Y).$$

Now

$$\frac{\partial S}{\partial X} = Y - \lambda P_X = 0; \quad \frac{\partial S}{\partial Y} = X - \lambda P_Y = 0; \quad \frac{\partial S}{\partial \lambda} = I - P_X X - P_Y Y = 0.$$

Solving the first two equations, we get

$$Y/P_X = \frac{X}{P_Y}, \text{ or, } Y = \left(\frac{P_X}{P_Y}\right)X.$$

Putting this in the third equation, we have

$$I = P_X X + P_Y \left[\frac{P_X}{P_Y}\right] X = 2P_X \cdot X \ \therefore X = \frac{I}{2 \cdot P_X} = \left(\frac{I}{2}\right) \cdot P_X^{-1}.$$

This represents the demand curve for the item X. Since we have shown price on the y-axis, it is better to solve the above equation for P_X. Assuming $I = 50$, we have the following demand equation

$$P_X = \left(\frac{I}{2}\right) X^{-1} = 25X^{-1}.$$

This demand curve follows the law of demand since the quantity demanded of X varies inversely with its price. This demand function has a negative slope as the following equation indicates

$$\frac{dP_X}{dX} = -25X^{-2}.$$

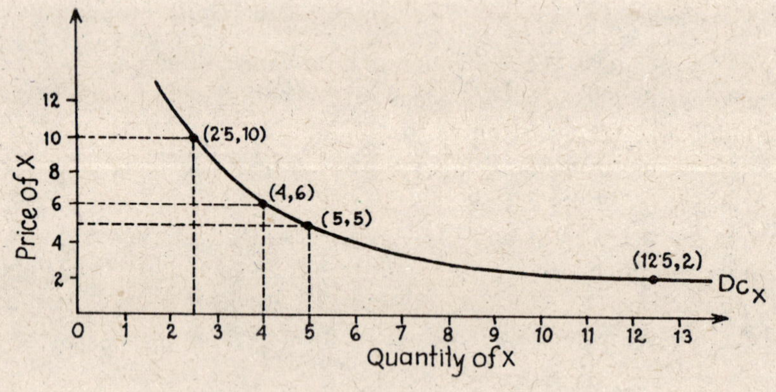

Fig 2.3 A Typical Demand Curve

The curve of the demand equation $P_X = 25X^{-1}$ is shown in Fig. 2.3 below.

Engel Curves

The income consumption curve shown in Fig. 2.2(i) can be used to draw the Engel curve for each item. Engel curves indicate the equilibrium (utility-maximising) quantities of an item which a consumer will be willing to buy at different levels of income, all other things remaining the same.

An Engel curve for item X has been shown in Fig. 2.4. From Fig. 2.4 (i) we find that at an income level of I_1, X_1 units of item X will be the consumer's equilibrium purchase.

Similarly, at income levels of I_2, I_3, I_4, the consumers equilibrium purchases of item X are X_2, X_3 and X_4 units respectively. In Fig. 2.4 (ii), $P(X_1, I_1)$, $Q(X_2, I_2)$, $R(X_3, I_3)$ and $V(X_4, I_4)$ have been plotted. By joining points P, Q, R and V we get the Engel curve which relate purchases of item X to changes in money income.

Two common shapes of Engel curve are shown in Fig. 2.5. Fig. 2.5(i) shows that with the rise of consumers income from very low levels. Initially, his consumption of the item X rises quickly. However, as his income increases further, the consumers purchases rise gradually and disproportionately to the gains in income, i.e., though more of item X is purchased with rise of income, extra purchases become increasingly less sensitive to further gains in income, resulting in the Engel Curve to be steep at higher levels of income. Such types of curves are normally associated with purchases of items like newspapers, salt, bulbs, toothpastes, etc.

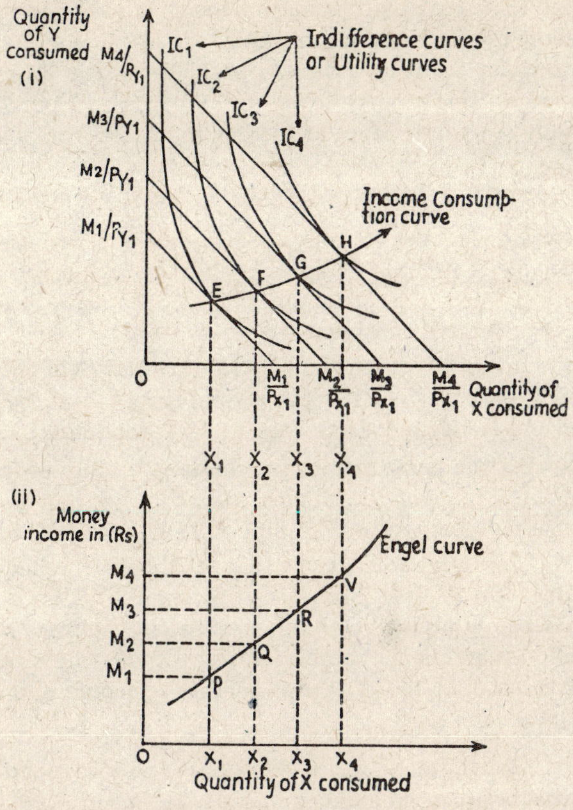

Fig 2.4 An Engel Curve

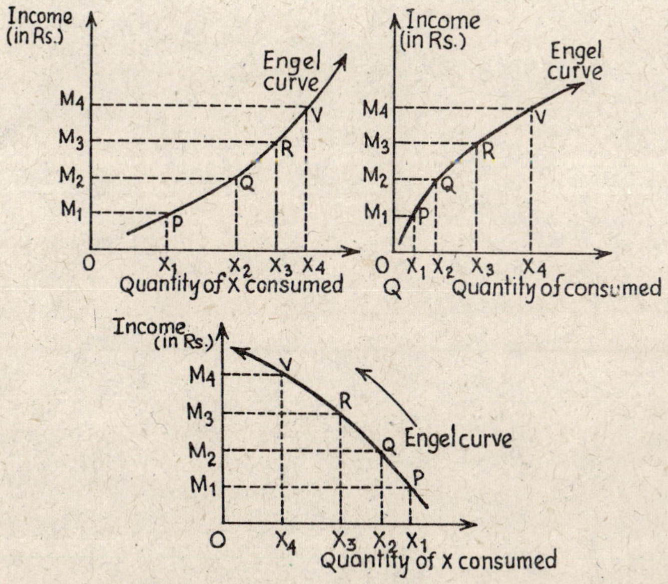

Fig 2.5 Three Engel Curves

For items like restaurant-meals, travel, recreation activities, luxury goods, etc., consumer expenditures increase more quickly than income, as shown in Fig. 2.5(ii). Such increasing trend of sensitivity to income variation results in the Engel curve rising at a decreasing rate. Fig. 2.5(iii) shows an Engel curve for an inferior good X purchases of which fall from X_1 to X_2, X_2 to X_3 and finally X_3 to X_4 units as income increases from I_1 to I_2, I_2 to I_3 and finally from I_1 to I_4.

The Impact of Price Variation Upon Consumer Purchases

Consumers not only react to income variations, but also react to variation in the price purchasable of items. Let up study how the quantity of item X changes when there is a variation of its price assuming other factors like a consumer's income, his tastes and preferences, the price of item Y, etc., remain constant.

In Fig. 2.6(i) the equilibrium purchases of the consumer have been shown as X_1 unit of item X and Y_1 unit of item Y, with given price of X at P_{X1}, price of Y at P_{Y1} and income at I_1. Now if the price of X declines from P_{X1} to P_{X2}, the line of attainable combinations shifts to the right of $\frac{I_1}{P_{X1}}$, allowing the consumer to purchase $\frac{I_1}{P_{X2}}$ units of item X. This new line of attainable combinations will be a tangent to a higher utility curve than the previous one. The equilibrium purchase of the consumer changes to X_2 units of item X and Y_2 units of item Y.

Similarly, when the price of X falls further to P_{X3}, the consumers equilibrium purchase is shifted to an even higher utility curve IC_3 at point C. The line joining the various consumer equilibrium points A, B and C is called the price consumption curve. This curve is the locus of the utility, maximising combinations of items which result from changes in the price of one item when other product prices, the consumer's income and his tastes and preferences, etc. are assumed to remain constant.

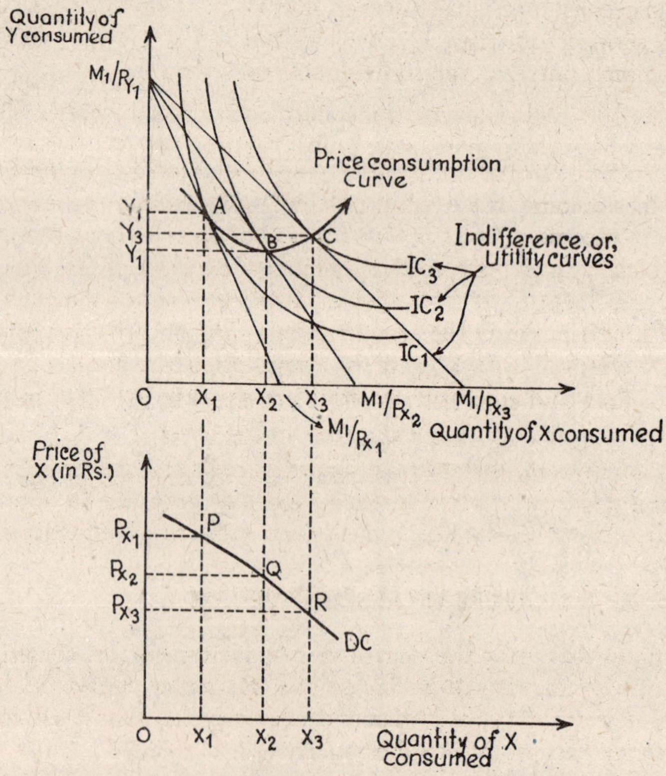

Fig 2.6 Deriving Demand Curve from the PCC

The demand curve of the consumer for item X can be obtained directly from the price consumption curve. The consumers demand curve for X indicates the amounts which the consumer is expected to buy at different prices when other all factors, affecting the purchase of X are taken as constants. From the Fig. 2.6(ii), we find that when the price of X changes from P_{X1} to P_{X2} and finally to P_{X3}, the consumers equilibrium purchase of quantity X changes from X_1 to X_2, and finally from X_2 to X_3.

The consumers demand curve (DD) is obtained by joining the points P, Q and R which indicate that when the price of X falls, the equilibrium purchase of X goes up.

Income and Substitution Effects of a Price Change

With the help of indifference curve analysis, we can separate the substitution effect and income effect of a change in the market price of one of the purchable goods (here item X). This is shown in Fig. 2.7.

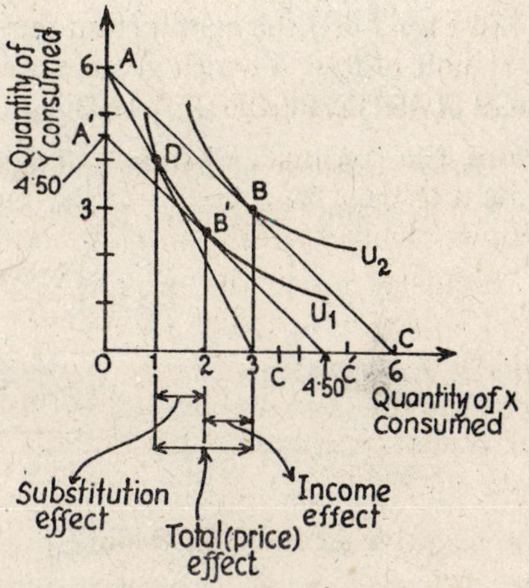

Fig 2.7 The Price Effect

Fig. 2.7 indicates that with I = Rs. 12, P_Y = Rs. 2 and P_X = Rs. 4, the consumer is in equilibrium at point D and he purchases one unit of item X. Again with I = Rs. 12, P_Y = Rs. 2 and P_X = Rs. 2, the consumer is in equilibrium at point B and demands 3 units of item X. The rise in the quantity demanded of X from 1 unit to 3 units indicates the combined result of the substitution and income effects. The substitution effect shows that when the price of X falls, the consumer substitutes X for Y. But the income effect shows that when P_X declines but income (I) and P_Y remain constant, the individuals real income rises and hence, the individual can buy more of item X.

To separate substitution effect from income effect of the price change, we draw a hypothetical income-line AC parallel to income line AC but tangent to the indifference curve U_1 at point B. Here AC involves reduction in income of Rs. 1.5 = AA = CC in order to keep the individual at the same level of real income which he had prior to the change in the price of X. The movement along the same indifference curve U_1 from D to B' is the substitution effect of the change in price, while the shift from B' to B to a new curve is the income effect. The substitution effect and income effect together equal the total effect (2 units of item X) of the price change.

Although income effect and substitution effect are equal in Fig. 2.7, in most cases the substitution effect is found to be much stronger than the income effect.

The reason is that the consumer normally spends only a small proportion of his income on any one item. So even a wide variation in its price does not generate an appreciable income effect. However, the substitution effect can be very large if good substitutes of the item are readily available.

ELASTICITY OF DEMAND: A MEASURE OF RESPONSIVENESS

Elasticity of demand measures the degree of responsiveness (or, sensitivity) of the quantity demanded (or, sales) of a commodity to a change in a particular demand-determining factor. Joel Dean mentioned three important types of demand elasticity for almost all consumer goods—price elasticity, income elasticity and promotional elasticity.

Various goods differ, says Paul Samuelson, in the degree to which the Q bought will response to change in each respective P. Thus sales of rice may go up much less than 1% for each 1% cut in its own price. Hindustan Motors Ambassador car sales may go up by more than 1% for each 1% decrease in the price of cars. Again Calcutta Chemicals Lavender Dew sales may exactly balance the price change.

Price elasticity of demand helps us to distinguish these above mentioned cases. It tells us that the first case is one of the inelastic demand, the second case is of elástic demand and the third one is of unitary elastic demand.

In more general terms, elasticity refers to a percentage relation between two variables, i.e., the percentage change in one variable in relation to a percentage change in another. The coefficient of elasticity (E_d) is given by

$$(E_d) = \frac{\text{Percent change in } X}{\text{Percent change in } Y}.$$

PRICE ELASTICITY OF DEMAND

Price elasticity of demand refers to the percentage change in quantity demanded of a commodity due to 1% change in its own price, *ceteris paribus*. Mathematically, we can state this as

$$E_p = \frac{\text{Percentage change in quantity demanded}}{\text{Percent change in price}}$$

$$= -\frac{\frac{\text{Change in quantity demanded}}{\text{Initial quantity demanded}} \times 100}{\frac{\text{change in price}}{\text{Initial price}} \times 100}.$$

(The negative sign is affixed since price and quantity changes are in reverse direction. When we put a negative sign, we get a positive value of E_p). The definition is in absolute terms, i.e., elasticity is just a number. It is not expressed in terms of rupees, pounds, gallons, etc. Here E_p is called the coefficient of price elasticity which is always a pure number because it is the ratio of two percentage changes. The use of such pure numbers renders easy comparability among different items.

Measurement

The above definition gives us two measures of price elasticity of demand, i.e., arc elasticity and point elasticity.

The formula commonly used in economics for price elasticity is

$$E_p = \frac{\frac{Q_1 - Q_0}{(Q_1 + Q_0)/2} \times 100}{\frac{P_1 - P_0}{(P_1 + P_0)/2} \times 100}$$

where E_p is the coefficient of arc price elasticity, Q_0 if the original quantity demanded, Q_1 is the new quantity demanded, P_0 is original price and P_1 is the new price of the same commodity.

The numerator of E_p, i.e., $\frac{Q_1 - Q_0}{\frac{(Q_1+Q_0)}{2}}$ shows the percentage change in the quantity demanded and the denominator $\frac{P_1 - P_0}{\frac{(P_1+Q_0)}{2}}$ shows the percentage change in the price.

Here the change in each variable is shown relative to the average of its starting and ending values, e.g., if the price of a product increases from Rs. 20 to Rs. 22, resulting in a decline in the quantity demanded from 16 to 14, the formula gives us the following value of E_p

$$E_P = -\frac{\frac{14-16}{(14+16)/2}}{\frac{22-20}{(22+20)/2}} = -\frac{-\frac{2}{15}}{\frac{2}{21}} = -\frac{-2}{15} \times \frac{21}{2} = \frac{7}{5} = 1.4.$$

The reason for using the average of the beginning and ending values in the arc elasticity formula will be clear from the following

E_P (using the initial values)

$$= -\frac{\frac{14-16}{16}}{\frac{22-20}{20}} = -\left(-\frac{2}{16} \times \frac{20}{2}\right) = \frac{5}{4} = 1.25$$

Again if the price declines from Rs. 22 to Rs. 20, resulting in a rise in the quantity demanded from 14 to 16 units, E_p (using the beginning values) will have the following value

$$E_p = -\frac{\frac{16-14}{14}}{\frac{20-22}{22}} = -\left(-\frac{2}{14} \times \frac{22}{2}\right) = \frac{11}{7} = 1.57$$

Hence identical unit changes in price and quantity yield different values of elasticity, depending on whether the price rises or, falls. By using the average of the beginning and ending values we can overcome this ambiguity. The price elasticity coefficient should be the same whether price rises or falls.

Another ambiguity arises in the calculation of elasticity when we consider changes over different ranges of price and quantity, e.g., when the values of price and quantity used in the earlier analysis are part of the hypothetical demand schedule shown in Table 2.1.

TABLE 2.1 A TYPICAL DEMAND SCHEDULE

Price	:	36	34	32	30	28	26	24	22	20	18	16	14	12	10
Quantity	:	0	2	4	6	8	10	12	14	16	18	20	22	24	26

The numbers in Table 2.1 show a linear relationship between quantity demanded and price, with unit variation in price causing unit variation in quantity over the entire range of the schedule. The algebraic expression of this demand equation is $P = 36 - Q$, or, $Q = 36 - P$.

Suppose we want to calculate the arc elasticity for a price variation from Rs. 22 to Rs. 18 rather than between Rs. 22 and Rs. 20. Thus we get

$$E_P = \frac{\frac{14-18}{(14+18)/2}}{\frac{22-18}{(22+18)/2}} = \frac{\frac{-4}{32/2}}{\frac{4}{40/2}} = \frac{-4}{16} \times \frac{20}{4} = \frac{5}{4} = 1.25.$$

Note that the coefficient is separate from the previous calculated value. For a given price, the arc elasticity coefficient varies depending on the difference between the new price and the initial price.

The arc elasticity concept is useful where product prices change significantly in one jump. But it also gives us a rough, or, an approximate measure, since by this measure we are approximating the curvilinear position between the two points on the demand curve by a straight line.

To remove the ambiguity inherent in the arc elasticity formula, economists have introduced the point elasticity concept to compute the coefficient of price elasticity. When price variations are too small, the arc converges to a point and the effective expression of price elasticity is as

$$e_p = -\frac{\frac{dQ}{Q} \times 100}{\frac{dP}{P} \times 100} = -\frac{dQ}{dP} \times \frac{P}{Q}$$

where dP and dQ are infinitesimally small changes in price and quantity demanded.[1]

To find the derivative of Q with respect to P (i.e., $\frac{dQ}{dP}$), we require an algebric expression of the demand equation. The algebric equation of Table 2.7 is $Q = 36 - P$. The derivative of Q with respect to P is -1 and hence, the point elasticity coefficient at Rs. 22 and 14 units is

$$e_p = -(-1) \times \frac{22}{14} = +\frac{11}{7} = +1\frac{4}{7} = +1.6.$$

When the demand equation is linear, there is no need to use calculus for calculating point elasticity. The derivative $\frac{dQ}{dP}$ is identical to the slope of the demand line, $\frac{\Delta Q}{\Delta P}$. Hence the point elasticity of linear demand function can be stated as

$E_p = \frac{\Delta Q}{\Delta P} \times \frac{P}{Q}$ where Δ (delta) indicates an absolute change.

The relationship between arc elasticity and point elasticity can now be established. First, let us take up the variation in price and quantity from some given point P_0 and Q_0

$$e_p = -\frac{\frac{Q_1-Q_0}{Q_0}}{\frac{P_1-P_0}{P_0}} = -\frac{\frac{\Delta Q}{Q_0}}{\frac{\Delta P}{P_0}} = -\frac{\Delta Q}{Q_0} \times \frac{P_0}{\Delta P} = -\frac{\Delta Q}{\Delta P} \times \frac{P_0}{Q_0}.$$

Now let us consider the variation in price and quantity relative to the average, or, mid-point between initial and new values of these variables

$$E_P = -\frac{\frac{Q_1-Q_0}{(Q_0+Q_1)/2}}{\frac{P_1-P_0}{(P_1+P_0)/2}} = -\frac{\Delta Q}{(Q_0+Q_1)} \times \frac{(P_1+P_0)}{\Delta P} = -\frac{\Delta Q}{\Delta P} \times \frac{P_1+P_0}{Q_0+Q_1}.$$

Thus the only difference between point-elasticity and arc-elasticity is that the point elasticity considers $\frac{P_0}{Q_0}$, whereas arc elasticity considers $\frac{P_1+P_0}{Q_0+Q_1}$.

EXAMPLE. Assume that all we know about the demand relationship for a new chocolate supplied by Cadbury is that when the price is Rs. 4.00, quantity demanded is 220,000 units and when the price is Rs. 3.50, quantity demanded is 245,000 units. Since we do not know whether the demand curve is a straight line or not, we could use the arc method to provide an approximation of the elasticity between these two values on the demand curve. The arc method formula in this case is

$$E_p = \frac{Q_1 - Q_o}{P_1 - P_o} \times \frac{\frac{P_1+P_o}{2}}{\frac{Q_1+Q_o}{2}}.$$

If we replace Q_2 with 245,000, Q_o with 220,000, P_1 with 3.5 and P_o with 4, the own-price elasticity of demand becomes

$$E_p = \frac{245,000 - 220,000}{3.5 - 4} \times \frac{\frac{3.5+4}{2}}{\frac{245,000+220,000}{2}} = -50,000 \times \frac{3.75}{232,500} = -0.806.$$

This indicates that a 1% increase in the price of chocolates would result in a 0.806% decrease in the quantity demanded of the same, assuming all other factors remain the same.

---

1 Here P and Q have been used in place of average of two prices and quantities since $\frac{P_0+P_1}{2}$ and $\frac{Q_0+Q_1}{2}$ become P and Q approximately.

Now let us assume instead that the marketing manager of Cadbury actually knew that the equation of the demand curve was $Q = 420 - 50P_o$ where Q is in thousands of units. He could have determined the own-price elasticity when P_o was equal to a specific price as follows.

Assume that P_o equals 4. Then $Q = 420 - 50P_o = 420 - 200 = 220$.

Note that no matter when value is chosen for P_o, Q will always decrease by 50 as P_o increases by one more unit. This is due to the coefficient of -50 in front of the P_o term. The coefficient of the price variable, -50 will thus equal $\Delta Q/\Delta P_o$ and E_p will be as

$$E_p = \frac{\Delta Q}{\Delta P_o} \times \frac{P_o}{Q} = -50 \times \frac{4}{220} = -\frac{200}{220} = -0.909.$$

Since $\Delta Q/\Delta P_o$ will always be -50 along this straight-line demand curve, we could determine the elasticity at each point on the curve by substituting the corresponding values of P_o and Q at each point into this formula in place of 4 and 220 respectively.

For a non-linear demand curve, calculus is to be used for calculating point elasticity. For example, we may now consider the following demand relation.

$Q = 50 - P_o^2$, assuming, $P_0 = 10$ and $Q_0 = 50$. $\therefore \frac{dQ}{dP} = -2P_0$.

e_p (point elasticity) $= -(-2P_0) \times \frac{P_0}{Q_0} = 2P_0 \times \frac{10}{50} = 2 \times 10 \times \frac{1}{5} = 4$.

Economists usually refer to the following categories of price elasticity.

1. Relatively (fairly) Elastic Demand E_p greater than 1 (in absolute terms)

In this case, 1% variation in price results in variation in quantity demanded by more than 1%. The coefficient calculated previously, 1.4, is an example of relatively elastic demand.

2. Relative by Inelastic Demand $0 < E_p < 1$ (in absolute terms)

Here the percentage variation in price is more than the corresponding variation in quantity, e.g., any value of E_p between 0 and 1.

3. Unitary Elasticity of Demand

Here 1% variation in price causes exactly 1% variation in quantity in the opposite direction.

Elasticity at the Midpoint : An Example

Assume that the demand equation is $Q = 150 - 2P$.

The P-intercept term is 75 and the Q-intercept term is 150. The mid-points are 37.5 and 75 for Q. Since $\Delta Q/\Delta P$ remains constant at -2 the own-price elasticity at the mid-point is $-2 \times \frac{37.5}{75} = -1$.

Besides, the above three common categories of elasticity, there are two limiting cases of price elasticity as listed below.

Perfectly (completely) Elastic Demand $E_p \to \infty$ (in absolute terms).

Here only one price is possible at which an unlimited quantity can be sold. In this case the demand curve is a horizontal line.

Perfectly (completely) Inelastic Demand $E_p = 0$.

Here the quantity demanded is constant irrespective of price. So the demand curve is a vertical straight line. Such a demand curve is occasionally found in case of some products within a particular price range.

The Elasticity of Derived Demand

So far we have talked about demand elasticity for the final product, i.e., a product bought for consumption, e.g., soft drinks, consumable goods, clothes, salt, etc. Now we will discuss the demand for materials, machinery and labour which go into the production of final goods. The demand for such items is called derived demand, i.e., these items are demanded not for their own sake, but for making the final product.

According to the British Economist Alfred Marshall, the derived demand curve will be more inelastic,

(1) the more significant is the component in the production process,

(2) the more inelastic is the demand curve for the final good,

(3) the smaller is the fraction of total cost involved in the component, and

(4) the more inelastic is the supply curve of auxiliary factors.

Let us consider, for example, the demand for residential flats (a final good) and the derived demand for masons, electricians plumbers, etc. Here masons, electricians and plumbers are demanded for constructing the flats and not for their own sake.

The elasticity of demand for electricians is low, since even if there is substantial wage-increase for electricians, the contractor has to complete the electrical work. If electrical work involves 10% of the total cost of construction, the 10% wage increase for electricians indicate only 1% increase in the total cost of construction which will not affect the cost of construction and the employment of electricians. Now if the demand for flats is inelastic and the elasticity of supply of auxiliary factors is low, we can predict that the demand elasticity for electricians will also be correspondingly low.

Such conclusions hold much more in the short run rather than in the long run. In the short run, employment of the electricians will not decline very much.

A Real Life Example

So the demand for certain things is derived (indirect) demand. The demand for housing loan is a derived demand. If the market price of houses and flats increases, their demand will fall. This, in its turn, will lead to a fall in demand for housing loan. So a cut in the rate of interest may be necessary to increase the demand for housing loan in a situation where housing demand is falling, due to rise in its price. So the coefficient of such elasticity may be expressed as

$$E_d = \frac{\%\text{ change in the demand for houses}}{\%\text{ change in the rate of interest}}.$$

The coefficient is usually negative. If, for instance, the rate of interest falls by 10% and as a consequence the demand for houses increases by 10%, the value of E_d will be $-\frac{1}{2}$.

Similarly if the price of air conditioners rises the demand for electricity will fall.

Time Impact on Elasticity

Time exerts considerable influence on elasticity. A long run demand curve is normally more elastic than a short-run curve. The short run refers to a time period which does not allow adjustment by consumers to a price change. The demand curve for the short run is almost perfectly inelastic. As time passes, consumers get the scope of responding to price changes by adjusting their consumption levels by switching over to substitutes. Take the case of energy costs. When heating oil prices increased abnormally in 1970s, the consumers immediate response was not great. As time passed, consumers started substituting oil by gas for heating purposes.

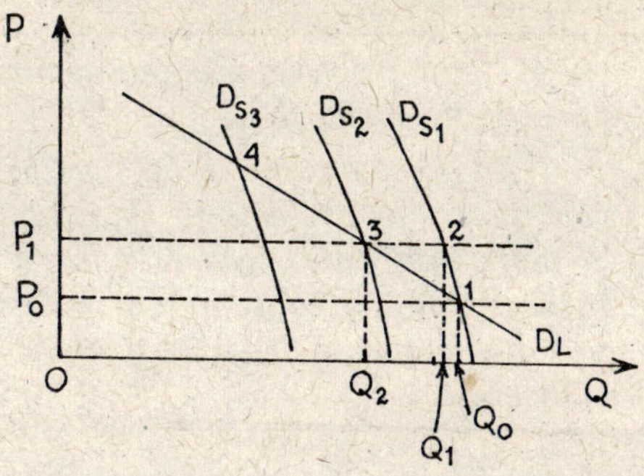

Fig 2.8 Short run vs. Long run Elasticity

We can explain this with the help of short-run and long run demand curves as shown in Fig. 2.8. The short run demand curves (Ds_1, Ds_2, etc.) are inelastic. The original position is at point $1(Q_0, P_0)$. When price increases to P_1, the consumers in the short-run will decrease the quantity demanded by moving to point 2 (i.e., Q_1), which indicates a relatively a small changes in quantity. As time passes, consumers use substitutes and the quantity demanded is indicated by point 2 (Q_1) on the new short-run the demand curve Ds_2 which is a much greater decrease in quantity. In Fig. 2.8 the points 2 and 3 shows the variation in quantity demanded in the long run. For constantly increasing prices, we can generate a series of new short-run demand curves, Ds_1, Ds_2, Ds_3, etc. and join points 1, 3, 4, etc. to get the long-run demand curve.

In the short run, price variation causes very small variation in quantity demanded. With time demand shifts to a new short run curve and a long run demand curve can now be constructed. The long run demand curves are far more elastic than their short run counterparts.

The lengths of long-run and short-run depend on how fast the adjustments can be made by the consumers. In case of heating oil, the long run may be a period of several years.

The Importance of Time

Time influences the quantity demanded in the following ways.

(i) The value of various elasticities may be dependent upon the length of time which passes between the variation in the demand factor and the variation in the quantity demanded, e.g., the rise in the price of gasoline affects its consumption. But this price rise may not affect consumption after two years.

(ii) The waiting time may be a demand factor. For example how long we will have to wait to see a doctor, or to be admitted in a hospital may influence our demand for medical care.

ECONOMIC INSIGHT: TIME IMPACT OF ELASTICITY

Time plays a very important role in demand analysis. One of the important time characteristics of demand relates to the lack of instantaneous response in the market place.

Consumers often react slowly to changes in prices and other demand conditions. To illustrate this delayed or lagged effect, consider the demand for electric power. Suppose an electric supply company raises its rates by 30%. How will this affect the quantity of electricity demanded? In the very short run the effect will be slight. Customers may be more careful to turn off unneeded lights, but total demand which is highly dependent on the appliances owned by domestic users and the equipment operated by industrial and commercial customers, will probably not be much affected. So when tariffs rise the quantity demanded will not fall very much. This means that total revenue will increase substantially. In other words, the short-run demand for electricity is fairly inelastic.

However, in the longer run, the increase in electricity tariff will have more substantial effects. Domestic users will reduce their purchases of air conditioners, electric heating units and other appliances and those appliances that are purchased will be more energy efficient. These actions will reduce the demand for electricity. Similarly, industrial and commercial users will tend to rely on alternative energy sources, will employ less energy-intensive production methods, or will relocate to areas where electricity charges are lower. Thus the ultimate effect of the price increase on demand may be substantial but it will take a number of years for its full impact to be felt.

As a general rule people get better opportunities to respond to price changes in the long run since they are able to obtain more information or feel the price effects much better and as more substitutes become available. There is a similar phenomenon with income changes. It takes time for consumers purchasing habits to respond to changed income levels. For these reasons, long run elasticity tends to be greater than short run elasticity for most commodities and services.

ELASTICITY OF DEMAND AND REVENUE

It is important to note at this stage that there is a close relation between price elasticity of demand and a firm's sales revenue(s). This means that demand elasticity also influences pricing decisions of firms.

It is both interesting and important to note at this stage that a fall in price does not necessarily reduce revenue. Since the demand curve is downward sloping, a fall in price will increase the quantity purchased and hence increase the revenue. We have seen that elasticity is the ratio of percentage variation in quantity to percentage variation in price. If the numerator is large, the quantity effect is strong and if it offsets the opposite price effect total revenue (TR) will increase.

Let us consider a straight line line demand curve where elasticity decreases as we move down and to the right. For such a demand curve total revenue (TR) and arc elasticity at each price interval are computed in Table 2.2.

TABLE 2.2 DEMAND SCHEDULE INDICATING ELASTICITY VALUES AND TR

Price	Quanity	Elasticity	Revenue
36	0	—	0
34	2	35	68
32	4	11	128
30	6	6.2	180
28	8	4.1	224
26	10	3.0	260
24	12	2.3	288
22	14	1.8	308
20	16	1.4	320
18	18	→ 1.1	324
16	20	0.9	320
14	22	0.7	308
12	24	0.6	288
10	26	0.4	260
8	28	0.3	224
6	30	0.2	180
4	32	0.2	128
2	34	0.1	68
0	36	0	0

Fig. 2.9 and Fig. 2.10 show the relationship between elasticity and revenue graphically. As price declines, revenue increases when demand is elastic and decreases when it is inelastic. Total revenue is maximum when elasticity of demand is equal to 1.

Let us introduce some terms in connection with revenue, e.g., Total Revenue (TR); Average Revenue (AR), Incremental Revenue (IR); and Marginal Revenue (MR).

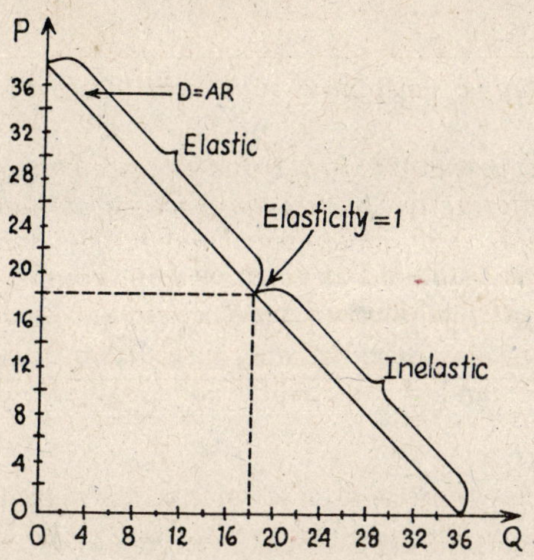

Fig 2.9 The Demand Curve

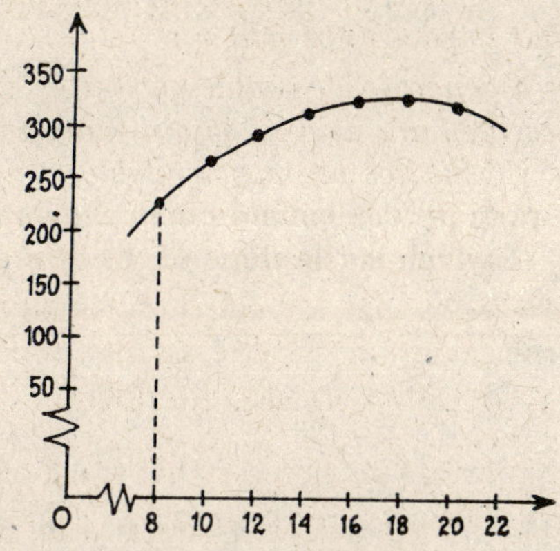

Fig 2.10 The TR Curve

(i) Total Revenue=Total Sales Proceeds=Price × Quantity Demanded (Sold).

(ii) Average Revenue=$\frac{TR}{\text{Sales}}$=Price.

(iii) Incremental Revenue=TR (new)− TR (old)=$R_2 - R_1 = \Delta R$

(iv) Marginal Revenue=$\frac{R_2-R_1}{Q_2-Q_1} = \frac{\Delta R}{\Delta Q}$

Of these MR is very important. MR is the additional revenue earned by a firm selling an additional unit of its product.

Though IR and MR sound much the same, they differ in two important respects.

(i) IR is not necessarily converted into changes in revenue per unit of output change and

(ii) IR is not just restricted to the effects of a change in price, but it can also measure the effect of any kind of managerial decision on the TR.

In Table 2.2 let us introduce the MR column. Table 2.3 shows TR and MR_1.

TABLE 2.3 DEMAND SCHEDULE WITH MR

Price	Quantity	TR	MR	Elasticity
26	10	260	36	3.0
24	12	288	28	2.3
22	14	308	20	1.8
20	16	320	10	1.4
18	18	324	4	1.1
16	20	320	−4	0.9
14	22	308	−12	0.7

Note that MR is positive so long as TR increases and demand is said to be elastic over this range of P and Q. But MR is zero when TR is maximum and this happens when demand is unitary elastic.

Fig. 2.11 shows the relationship between demand curve and MR mathematically and graphically. MR line is twice as steep as the demand curve if it is described as a straight line.

Hence, MR line is drawn bisecting the distance between y-axis and the demand curve. The point where MR line crosses the x-axis, the demand curve is unitary elastic and TR is maximum.

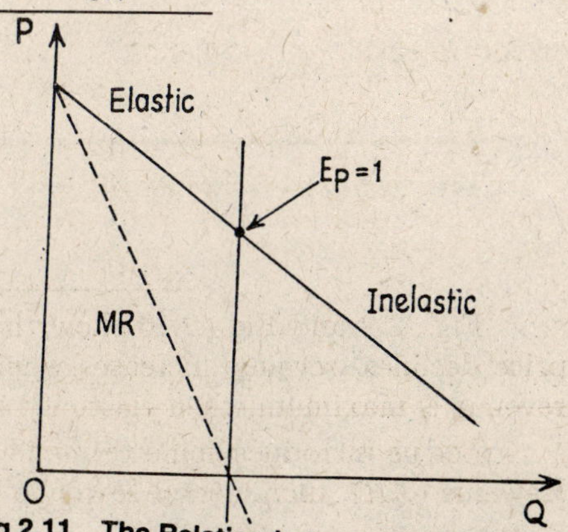

Fig 2.11 The Relation between Elasticity and MR

Mathematical Note

We have presented the formula for point elasticity as

$$e_p = -\frac{dQ}{dP} \times \frac{P}{Q}.$$

The equation for demand curve shown in Table 2.1 is given by $P = 36 - Q$, or, $Q = 36 - P$. Now $\frac{dQ}{dP} = -1$ which is the slope of the straight line demand curve.

We have seen that arc elasticity changes along the demand curve. Point price elasticity also behaves in the same way. Price elasticity of demand at a particular point, say, at $Q = 10$ and $P = 26$ is

$$e_p = -(-1) \times \frac{26}{10} = 2.6.$$

In Table 2.2 the arc elasticity is 3 in the interval between $P = 26$ and $P = 28$ and between $Q = 8$ and $Q = 10$ and 2.3 in the subsequent interval. Point elasticity lies between the two arc elasticities. Again point price elasticity at $Q = 20, P = 16$ will be

$$e_p = -(-1) \times \frac{16}{20} = 0.8$$

which is in the elastic portion of the demand curve.

We have seen that $MR = \frac{dTR}{dQ}$. To make the quantity independent variable, the demand function is reversed, i.e., $P = 36 - Q$.

Now $TR = PQ = (36 - Q)Q = 36Q - Q^2$, $MR = \frac{dTR}{dQ} = 36 - 2Q$.

At $Q = 10, TR = 36 \times 10 - 10 \times 10 = 360 - 100 = 260$ and $MR = 36 - 2 \times 10 = 16$.

We have measured TR at a point instead of over an interval. Hence the result $MR = 16$ is different from the MR in Table 2.3, where discrete differences have been used in the calculation. Again at $Q = 20, MR = 26 - 2 \times 20 = -4$ which is in the area of negative MR.

Total revenue is maximum when $MR = 0 = 36 - 2Q$ or, $36 = 2Q$ or, $Q = 18$.

This again differs from the figure shown in Table 2.3.

The Relationship among Elasticity, Total Revenue and Marginal Revenue

By using calculus one can calculate precisely the relationship between elasticity and marginal revenue. If the demand equation is a straight line, it will have an equation of the following form

$$P = a - bQ \tag{1}$$

or equivalently,

$$Q = \frac{a}{b} - \frac{P}{b}. \tag{2}$$

The standard elasticity formula is

$$\frac{\%\Delta Q}{\%\Delta P} \quad \text{or,} \quad \frac{\Delta Q}{\Delta P} \times \frac{P}{Q}.$$

Since $\Delta Q/\Delta P$ is an approximation for dQ/dP, the elasticity is

$$\frac{dQ}{dP} \times \frac{P}{Q}.$$

The expression dQ/dP equals $-1/b$ which is the coefficient of the P term in the demand equation (2) $Q = a/b - P/b$. By substituting $-1/b$ for dQ/dP, the own-price elasticity of demand we get

$$e_p = \frac{dQ}{dP} \times \frac{P}{Q} = -\frac{1}{b} \times \frac{P}{Q}.$$

The inverse of this expression is

$$\frac{1}{e_p} = -\frac{bQ}{P}. \qquad (3)$$

Since marginal revenue is the change in total revenue resulting from a one-unit change in Q this is the same as the derivative of total revenue with respect to a change in quantity, $d(TR)/dQ$. Total revenue in this case will be

$$PQ = (a - bQ)Q = aQ - bQ^2.$$

The derivative of this expression with respect to Q is

$$MR = \frac{dTR}{dQ} = a - 2bQ$$

which has the same form as the equation for the demand curve, with one exception the slope is twice as large in absolute value. We can rewrite the equation for marginal revenue as

$$MR = a - 2bQ = (a - bQ) - bQ. \qquad (4)$$

Note from equation (1) that $a - bQ$ is the same as P and from equation (3), that $-bQ = P/e_p$. We can substitute these identities into equation (4) to obtain

$$MR = (a - bQ) - bQ = P - \frac{P}{e_p} = P(1 - e_p).$$

Marginal revenue is, therefore equal to $P(1 - 1/e_p)$ since mathematically e_p is always negative.

Determinants

Price elasticity of demand for a commodity is largely determined by the following factors:

(1) the availability of substitutes; (2) the proportion of consumers income spent on the commodity; and (3) the length of time, i.e., the time period under consideration.

Availability (the number and closeness) of substitutes

When there are many good substitutes for a product, elasticity will be high. Again if the product is a good substitute for others, its demand elasticity will be high. The demand elasticity for bread, for example, will be less than that for a particular brand of bread, say, milk bread. If the price of bread increases there will be lesser consumption of bread. If, however, the price of milk bread increases and prices of other varieties of bread remain constant, the demand for milk bread will fall since consumers will quickly switch over to other varieties of bread.

Proportion of income spent on the goods and services

Demand is inelastic for goods and services which account for only a small proportion of consumers' total expenditure. For example, salt is an item on which consumers spend a very small proportion of their incomes. Thus if the price of salt increases by 10 %, its consumption is not affected at all.

Length of Time

Demand is normally more elastic in the long run than in the short run, e.g., long-run elasticity for electricity is much higher than its the short-run elasticity. People living in electrically heated room cannot reduce consumption in the short run but in the long run electricity may be replaced by gas. (This point has already been discussed under the heading **Time Impact of Elasticity**.)

Practical Uses (Applications) of Price Elasticity

The concept of price elasticity can be used for various purposes and to throw light on some real life problems. The following points are of interest to the business manager.

1. Pricing Decision

First of all business people must be aware of the elasticity of demand for their products when they take decisions about the prices of their products. For example, a profit-maximising firm would always operate on the elastic part of its demand curve. If demand is elastic price cut will raise revenue. Even if costs increase at the same time since output is increasing profit will rise. However, even if demand is elastic a price cut does not necessarily raise the total net profit of the firm. The profitability of such an action depends on whether the marginal revenue which is generated by the price reduction exceeds the marginal cost of the added production. A practising manager can use the concept of price elasticity to answer the following **three** questions:

(i) What will be the impact on sales of a 10% increase in price?

(ii) How large a price reduction is necessary to increase sales by 15%?

(iii) Given marginal cost data and information about price elasticity, what is the profit maximising price?

In fact, the availability of price elasticity estimates, along with relevant cost data, is by itself sufficient to allow managers to set a pricing policy consistent with profit maximisation. Since $MR = MC = P\left(1 - \frac{1}{e_p}\right)$, we can prove this point easily and quickly. Suppose MC = Rs. 10 and $e_p = 3$ (1%, 2% price cut leads to 6% increase in sales). Now

$$P = \frac{MC}{\left(1 - \frac{1}{e_p}\right)} = \frac{\text{Rs. } 10}{\left(1 - \frac{1}{3}\right)} = \text{Rs. } 15.$$

2. Energy Crisis

The energy crisis that developed following the oil crisis of 1973 also illustrates the importance of price elasticity. Electric supply corporations were forced to raise tariffs drastically because of rapid increase in fuel costs. The question immediately arose: How much of a fall in quantity demanded and, hence, of a reduction in future capacity would be caused due to oil price hike? In other words, what is the price elasticity of demand for electricity? In view of the long time required to set up power generating plants some rise in the price of electricity was inevitable in the short run. So the above question was of considerable importance to both consumers and generators of electricity.

3. Housing Demand

Interest rates are an important determinant of housing demand. Suppose the interest elasticity of demand for houses is −0.15. This simply means that a 10% rise in the interest rate reduces the demand for houses by 1.5%, *ceteris paribus*. Suppose the Reserve Bank of India is expected to rise the

rate of interest by 20% (from 10% to 12%). In this case one can project a 3% fall ($-0.15 \times 20 = -3$) in housing demand in India.

CROSS-ELASTICITY OF DEMAND

Cross elasticity deals with the effect in percentage terms on the quantity demanded of a particular product due to price variation of related products, i.e., substitutes and complements. When two identical products, say A and B, are sold in the market A may be considered as substitute of B and *vice versa*. Normally chicken and beef, coffee and tea, butter and margarine, jute and plastics, etc. are example of substitutes. Complements are products bread and butter which are consumed simultaneously, e.g., potato chips and fried eggs, computers and floppy disks etc.

Cross elasticity of demand can be defined as a measure of the percentage variation in quantity demanded of a product A due to 1% variation in the price of another product B and is expressed as

$$E_C = \frac{\Delta Q_A/Q_A}{\Delta P_B/P_B} = \frac{\text{\% variation of sales of } A}{\text{\% variation of price of } B} = \frac{dQ_A/Q_A \times 100}{dP_B/P_B \times 100}.$$

If A and B are substitutes, then E_C will be positive but its exact value will depend on the degree of competitiveness. If A and B are complementary items, then E_C will be negative and its numerical value will depend on the degree of complementarity. Finally, if A and B are unrelated goods like butter and shoes, then E_C will be zero, or, very near to it.

Since percentage changes create confusion the following revised formula is often used to calculate arc elasticity

$$E_C = \frac{\{(Q_{1_A} - Q_{0_A})/(Q_{1_A} + Q_{0_A})/2\}}{\{(P_{1_B} - P_{0_B})/(P_{1_B} + P_{0_B})/2\}}.$$

In short, cross elasticity is positive for substitutes and negative for complements.

A knowledge of cross elasticities is useful in defining industry boundaries, especially from the demand point of view, instead of supply or, production point of view. According to Lowes and Sparkes, Goods with high cross elasticities are regarded as being in the same industry.

INCOME ELASTICITY OF DEMAND

The measure of responsiveness of demand (or, sales) to variation of income is called the income elasticity of demand. The general expression of income elasticity is

$$E_I = \frac{\text{\% change in quantity demanded}}{\text{\% change in income}} = \frac{\frac{Q_1 - Q_0}{(Q_1+Q_0)/2} \times 100}{\frac{I_1 - I_0}{(Y_0+Y_1)/2} \times 100}$$

(when income and quantity changes are substantial).

(Subscripts 0 and 1 above refer to old and new situation.)

$$\text{or, } E_I = \frac{\Delta Q}{Q} \times \frac{\Delta I}{I} \times 100, \text{ or, more accurately}$$

$$= \frac{\frac{dQ}{Q} \times 100}{\frac{dI}{I} \times 100}$$

(when changes in income and quantity demanded are infinitesimally small).

Here income means disposable personal income (i.e., total income less taxes).

The income elasticity measure helps us to identify commodities to some extent. Some commodities have low income elasticities, e.g., potatoes, while sale of others increase, or, decrease rapidly with increase, or, decrease in income, e.g., radios, or, T.V. sets.

The coefficient of income elasticity may be either positive or, negative. Products whose $E_I > 1$ are called superior goods. Products whose $E_I > 0$ and < 1, are called normal goods. Products whose $E_I < 0$ are called inferior goods. Consumers demand some products when their income is low but with improvement of income they feel better off and their demand is shifted to superior goods.

In forecasting the impact of changes in general business activity on particular industries, a knowledge of income elasticity may prove to be useful. The forecaster can apply his knowledge of income elasticities, after he has got a forecast of national income, or, disposable personal income, in estimating the changes in purchases of individual commodities. But it suffers from all the problems price-elasticity measure, viz., unreliability of past experience and multiplicity of sales determining factors.

OTHER ELASTICITY MEASURES

Besides the common elasticity measures already discussed, there are other elasticities, e.g., advertising elasticity. It can be defined as the percentage variation in quantity relative to 1% variation in advertising expenses.

Elasticity can be calculated for population size. For example, elasticity of demand for automobile due to increase in population can be measured. Economists use many variables to explain variation in demand and like common elasticities, elasticities of many other variables can also be computed.

A. PROMOTIONAL (OR, ADVERTISING) ELASTICITY OF DEMAND

Advertising has an important role in a competitive, or, semi-competitive market economy. It influences total cost and demand for a product. For measuring advertising elasticity of demand we must have an idea about the following relationship between advertising and sales.

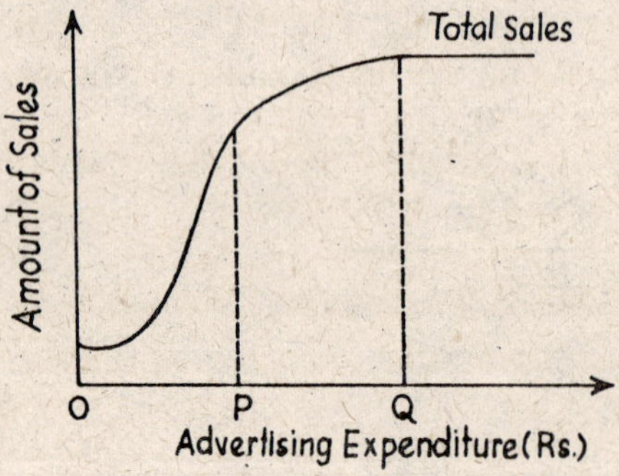

Fig 2.12 Advertising and Sales

(1) For achieving a maximum sales target, no advertisement is required.

(2) Beyond the maximum level of sales, sales can be increased by increasing advertisement and reduced by decreasing advertisement, assuming that other factors like price, quality of goods, etc. affecting sales remain constant.

(3) Initially advertisement expenditure will increase sales more than proportionate to the increase in advertisement expenditure. Beyond this point the sale will increase disproportionately and finally at the saturation point further investment in advertisement will not improve sales. This point is illustrated in Fig 2.12.

Up to the point P, sales increases more than proportionately, between P and Q sales increases disproportionately and beyond Q, sales remain almost constant even with increase in the advertisement expenditure.

The advertising, or, promotional elasticity of demand measures how far the demand for a product will be influenced by advertisement and other promotional activities. Promotional elasticity and price elasticity are not identical especially for luxury goods, such as costly dresses, cosmetics, etc. which are more advertisement elastic than price elastic.

The advertising elasticity of demand is measured by using this formula

$$E_A = \frac{\text{Proportionate change in sales}}{\text{Proportionate change in advertisement expenditure}} = \frac{\frac{Q_2-Q_1}{Q_2+Q_1}}{\frac{A_2-A_1}{A_2+A_1}}$$

where Q and A stand for sales and advertisement respectively.

In a world characterised by product differentiation promotional elasticity plays an important role. It is also known as advertising elasticity of sales. It plays an important role in marketing efforts.

A low advertising elasticity means that a firm will have to spend a huge amount of money to shift demand for its product through advertising. In such cases alternative marketing approaches prove to be more productive.

DETERMINING FACTORS

We have already seen that promotional elasticity of demand varies between products and also between various levels of sales of the same product. It is influenced by various factors some of which are mentioned below.

1. *Prima facie,* promotional elasticity differs for new and old products as well as for products with established, or growing markets.

2. The time-lag in response to advertisement is different for different types of product depending on the media chosen and the general economic environment. This time-lag is maximum for durable goods. The varying nature of time-lag for various products causes the advertising elasticity of demand to be different for various products.

3. The advertising elasticity of demand is influenced by a firms own advertisement as also by the advertising campaign of rival firms. How much additional output a firm will be able to sell by intensifying its advertising campaign depends upon its own media and level of advertisement *vis-a-vis* those of its rivals.

B. SUBSTITUTION ELASTICITY

Substitution elasticity is defined as the degree to which one commodity can be substituted by another owing to a given change in their price ratio and can be expressed as follow

$$E_S = \frac{\text{Proportionate changes in the quantity ratio of commodities } X \text{ and } Y}{\text{Proportionate changes in the price ratios of the commodities } X \text{ and } Y}$$

$$= \frac{\Delta(X/Y)}{(X/Y)} \div \frac{\Delta(P_x/P_y)}{(P_X/P_Y)}$$

where $\frac{X}{Y}$ is the ratio of the quantities of commodities X and Y.

$\Delta\left(\frac{X}{Y}\right)$ is the change in the quantity ratio,

(P_x/P_y) is the price ratio of the commodities X and Y and

$\Delta(P_x/P_y)$ = change the price ratio of the commodities

Suppose mustard oil and Postman (close substitute of mustard oil) are being sold at Rs. 50 and Rs. 60 per kg. respectively. At these prices a customer buys 4 kg. each of mustard oil and Postman. Thus $\left(\frac{X}{Y}\right) = \frac{4}{4} = 1$, while $\left(\frac{P_x}{P_y}\right) = \frac{50}{60} = \frac{5}{6} = 0.83$.

Now suppose the price of Postman increases to Rs. 80 per kg but the price of mustard oil remains constant. At these prices the customer buys 6 kg. of mustard oil and 2 kg. of Postman since Postman has become costlier. Now we get

$$\left(\frac{X}{Y}\right) = \frac{6}{2} = \frac{3}{1} \text{ and } \left(\frac{P_x}{P_y}\right) = \left(\frac{50}{80}\right) = \frac{5}{8} = 0.625.$$

Hence,

$$\Delta\left(\frac{X}{Y}\right) = 3 - 1 = 2 \text{ and } \Delta\left(\frac{P_x}{P_y}\right) = \frac{5}{8} - \frac{5}{6} = \frac{-10}{48} = -\frac{5}{24}$$

$$\therefore \quad E_S = \frac{\frac{2}{1}}{\frac{-5/24}{5/6}} = \frac{2}{-\frac{5}{24} \times \frac{6}{5}} = \frac{2}{-\frac{1}{4}} = -8$$

Types of Substitution Elasticity

(1) Infinite Substitution Elasticity $(E_S = \infty)$

If the two commodities are perfect substitutes of each other, then decline in the price of one commodity may induce the customer to buy only this commodity and abandon the other commodity. But in most real life situations this does not happen.

(2) Zero Substitution Elasticity $(E_S = 0)$

If two commodities, e.g., chairs and tables, etc. cannot be substituted at all and are to be used in fixed proportion for obtaining satisfaction, then E_S in such cases becomes zero.

(3) High and Low Elasticity of Substitution $(0 < E_S < \infty)$

High and low elasticities exist between zero and infinite elasticities described above depending upon the degree to which commodities can be substituted for each other, e.g., E_S between shoes and sandals and woollen and cotton clothes are quite high and low respectively.

C. ELASTICITY OF PRICE EXPECTATIONS

According to J.R. Hicks the demand for a commodity is influenced not only by its current price but also by its expected future price. If the price of a commodity is expected to go up in future, the demand of the commodity increases immediately and this increase in demand depends on the elasticity of price expectations. Consumers price expectations are affected by various factors like socio-economic developments, political changes, previous experiences regarding price changes, etc.

The elasticity of price expectation is defined as the ratio of the percentage change in expected future prices to the percentage change in current prices. It can be expressed as

$$E_{pe} = \frac{\text{Percentage (or relative) change in expected future price}}{\text{Percentage (or relative) change in current price}}$$

$$= \frac{\Delta EP}{EP} \div \frac{\Delta CP}{CP} = \frac{\Delta EP}{\Delta CP} \times \frac{CP}{EP}$$

where EP is the expected price, CP is the current price, ΔEP is the change in the expected price and ΔCP is change in the current price.

The following table shows the elasticities of price expectations of customers in a typical market.

TABLE 2.4 NOMENCLATURE OF ELASTICITY OF PRICE EXPECTATIONS

Elasticity of Price Expectations	Value of the Coefficient (E_{pe})	Consumers' Attitude
High	$E_{pe} > 1$	When consumers expect that the future prices of commodities will rise by a greater percentage than current prices.
Low	$0 < E_{pe} < 1$	When consumers expect that the future prices of commodities will rise by a lesser percentage than current prices.
Unit	$E_{pe} = 1$	When consumers expect that the future prices of commodities will rise by identical percentage as current prices.
Zero	$E_{pe} = 0$	When consumers expect that there will be no effect on future prices even when the current prices of the commodities rise.
Negative	$E_{pe} < 0$	When consumers expect that a rise in the current prices of the commodities will cause a fall in the future prices and *vice-versa*.

Thus from the table we find that the concept of elasticity of price expectations assumes considerable significance in the speculative activities of the business person.

D. MARKET SHARE ELASTICITY

In case of market structures which are neither pure monopolies not purely competitive, demand for a firms product depends on the following factors.

(i) The elasticity of market demand for the entire product. For a perfectly elastic demand for its the product, the firm can sell it only at the indicated price.

(ii) The degree of product differentiation, or, brand loyalty of consumers.

(iii) The factor which determines the elasticity of demand for a firms output is its share of the market. If a firm has huge market share, a fall in its price will need to attract a sizable amount of other firms' customers if the proportionate rise in its demand is to be large. Again a firm having small market share will be able to induce a large proportionate increase in sales by attracting a comparatively less proportion of its rival consumers and

(iv) Elasticity of demand of a firms product depends on its rivals reactions to the price changes.

For undifferentiated products, Needham has suggested the following formula linking the different determinants of demand for a firms product

$$E_f = \frac{(E_m + E_s \times S_r)}{S_f}$$

where E_f is the elasticity of demand of a firms product,

E_m is the elasticity of market

E_s is the elasticity of rivals' supply regarding changes in the firms price,

S_r is the rivals share of market and

S_f is the firm's share of market.

$\therefore \quad E_m = E_f \times S_f - E_s \times S_r$ is the market share elasticity.

From this we find that the elasticity of demand for the firms product is partly influenced by rivals reactions to its own actions. The rivals reactions are usually unknown and are referred to as Conjectural Variation.

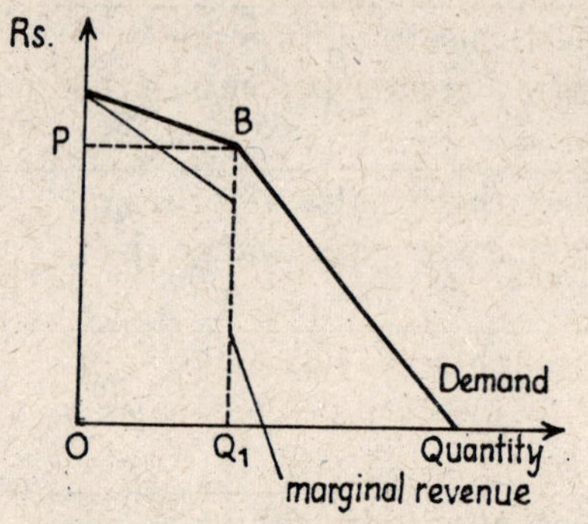

Fig 2.13 A Kinked Demand Curve

The demand curve for a firm with rivals known as the kinked demand curve, is shown in Fig. 2.13.

If a firm is aware that it can sell Q_1 units at price P, then point B is on the firm's demand (average revenue) curve.

It becomes difficult for the firm to evaluate the volume of sales at other prices, as it depends on rivals reactions. However, if the firm thinks that its rivals will not match a rise in its price, but will match any fall in price, then demand will be highly elastic for price increases, but comparatively inelastic for price decreases. This results in the kinked demand curve as shown here.

The demand curve with a link has a dog-leg-shaped marginal revenue curve. If the firm wants to sell output greater than Q_1, it must reduce its price. This will induce rival firms to follow suit and even a slight increase in sales volume would need a comparatively substantial decline in price. For this reason marginal revenue falls dramatically if sales volume increases beyond Q_1. Thus it is quite clear that the firms will be unwilling to decrease prices in such a situation.

Whenever the elasticities of demand differ between customers, they can be charged varying prices for the same commodity. When elasticity of demand in one market is different from another market, the monopolist finds the policy of price discrimination to his advantage see Fig. 2.14.

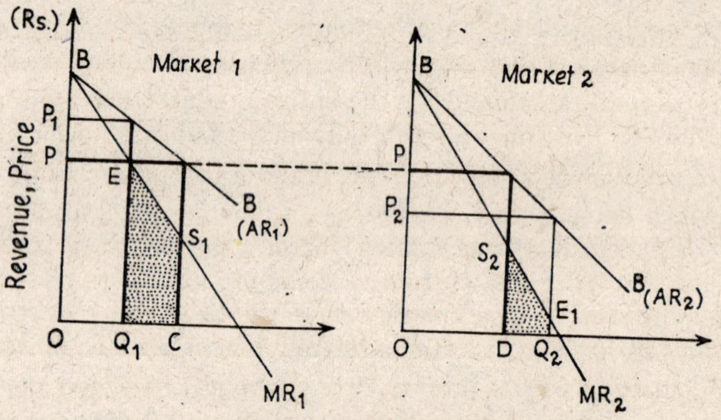

Fig 2.14 Profitable Price Discrimination

Suppose price elasticity of demand is greater in Market 2 than in Market 1. The monopolist increases sales in Market 1 by decreasing sales in Market 2. When the sales in Market 1 rise from $0Q_1$ to $0C$ the monopolist gains Q_1CS_1E. Again by decreasing the same quantity in Market 2, i.e., DQ_2, the monopolist loses $DQ_2E_1S_2$. Since the gain in Market 1 exceeds the loss in Market 2, it is advantageous for the monopolist to transfer a certain amount of sales from the low elasticity market to high elasticity market and charge different prices in the two markets.[1]

---

1 PRICE ELASTICITY OF SUPPLY

Like the price elasticity of demand, the price elasticity of supply measures the percentage variation in quantity supplied due to 1% variation in price, i.e., it measures the responsiveness of quantity supplied by producers to a

PROBLEM 3. If the price of an item is Rs. 25 the quantity demanded is 900 units, but if the price goes up to Rs. 30, then the quantity demanded declines to 600 units only. Compute the price elasticity of demand.

SOLUTION

$$E_p = -\frac{\%\text{ change in quantity demanded}}{\%\text{ change in price}} = -\frac{\frac{Q_1-Q_0}{Q_0}}{\frac{P_1-P_0}{P_0}} = -\frac{\frac{600-900}{900}}{\frac{30-25}{25}} = -\frac{\frac{-300}{900}}{\frac{5}{25}} = \frac{1}{3}\times\frac{5}{1} = \frac{5}{3} = 1.67.$$

PROBLEM 4. Compute price elasticity of demand if $Q_0 = 3000, Q_1 = 4000, P_0 =$ Rs. 25 and $P_1 =$ Rs. 24.

SOLUTION

$$E_p = -\frac{\frac{Q_1-Q_0}{(Q_1+Q_0)/2}\times 100}{\frac{P_1-P_0}{(P_1+P_0)/2}\times 100} = -\frac{(Q_1-Q_0)}{(Q_1+Q_0)}\times\frac{(P_1+P_0)}{(P_1-P_0)} = -\frac{(4000-3000)}{(4000+3000)}\times\frac{(24+25)}{(24-25)} = +\frac{1}{7}\times\frac{49}{1} = 7.$$

PROBLEM 5. Compute price elasticity of demand for different years from the data given below.

Year	% change in quantity	% change in price
1. 1989–90	0	+1.2
2. 1990–91	−2.5	+3.7
3. 1991–92	+4.2	−1.5
4. 1992–93	−7.0	+7.8
5. 1993–94	+4.8	−3.5

SOLUTION

Year	% change in quantity	% change in price	Price elasticity of demand
(1)	(2)	(3)	(4)=[(2)÷(3)]
1989-90	0	+1.2	0
1990-91	−2.5	+3.7	+0.68
1991-92	+4.2	−1.5	+2.80
1992-93	−7.0	+7.8	+0.90
1993-94	+4.8	−3.5	+1.37

PROBLEM 6. When price of an item is Rs. 12 demand for it is 200 units and when the price declines to Rs. 8 the demand rises to Rs. 400 units. Compute Incremental Revenue and Marginal Revenue.

SOLUTION. Incremental revenue $= R_1 - R_o$ where R_1 is total revenue after price variation and R_0 is total revenue before price variation. So $R_1 - R_o$ Rs. $(8 \times 400)-$ Rs. $(12 \times 200) =$ Rs. $(3200 - 2400) =$ Rs. 800.

---

variation in price. The arc coefficient of supply elasticity can be expressed as follows

$$E_s = \frac{\frac{Q_1-Q_0}{(Q_1+Q_0)/2}}{\frac{P_1-P_0}{(P_1+P_0)/2}}.$$

Here E_s is a positive number. The higher the value of the coefficient, the greater will be the degree of responsiveness of the quantity supplied of a commodity to a change in its own in price, *ceteris paribus*.

∴ Incremental revenue = Rs. 800 and marginal revenue = $\frac{R_1-R_0}{Q_1-Q_0} = \frac{800}{400-200}$ = Rs. 4.

PROBLEM 7. Due to an increase in income of a consumer by 5%, his expenditure increases to 10%:

(i) Compute his income elasticity.

When income of a consumer is Rs. 50 his demand for an item is 10 units. When his income rises to Rs. 60, his demand for that item becomes 20 units.

(ii) Compute his income elasticity by the arc method.

SOLUTION.

(i) Income elasticity $= \dfrac{\%\text{ change in demand}}{\%\text{ change in income}} = \dfrac{10}{5} = 2.$

$$\text{(ii) } E_I = \frac{\frac{Q_1-Q_0}{(Q_1+Q_0)/2}}{\frac{M_1-M_0}{(M_1+M_0)/2}} = \frac{(Q_1-Q_0)}{(Q_1+Q_0)} \times \frac{(I_1+I_0)}{(I_1-I_0)}$$

$$\therefore \quad E_I = \frac{20-10)}{(20+10)} \times \frac{(60+50)}{(60-50)} = \frac{10}{30} \times \frac{110}{10} = \frac{11}{3} = 3.67.$$

PROBLEM 8. A and B the two executives of X and Co., submitted the following estimates of sales of product M at different rates.

Price per kg.	(Sales in kg.)	
	A's estimate	B's estimate
18.00	3,000	2,000
16.00	3,200	2,800
14.00	3,600	3,600
12.00	4,000	4,800

Compute the total revenue and the marginal revenue and indicate whether demand is elastic or, inelastic on the basis of each set of estimates.

SOLUTION.

COMPUTATION OF TR AND MR

Price per kg (Rs.)	Sales (kg.)	A's estimate of total revenue (Rs.)	Marginal revenue (Rs.)	Sales (kg.)	B's estimate of total revenue (Rs.)	Marginal revenue (Rs.)
18	3,000	54,000		2,000	36,000	
			−2,800			+8,800
16	3,200	51,200		2,800	44,800	
			−800			+5,600
14	3,600	50,400		3,600	50,400	
			−2,400			+7,200
12	4,000	48,000		4,800	57,600	

Based on A's estimate, the demand is inelastic as in this case. So TR is declining with the fall in price. But based on of B's estimate, the demand is elastic since the TR is rising with fall

in the price. This result can easily be obtained by using the total outlay method has been used for measuring the elasticity of demand.

PROBLEM 9. New Central Book Agency engages an economist to determine the demand for its new mathematics book for the I.C.W.A. course. After months of hard work the economist tells the publishing concern that demand for the book (Q_x) follows the equation stated below

$$Q_x = 1200 - 500P_x + 4I + 50P_c$$

where P_x =price of the book; I = income per capita and P_c = price of a similar book of a competing publisher.

Using the above information the publishers directors want to

(i) assess the effect a price increase would have on total revenue,

(ii) assess how sale of books would change in a period of rising incomes and

(iii) assess the expected impact if competing publishers raise their prices.

Assume the initial values of P_x, I and P_c as Rs. 4, Rs. 1,000 and Rs. 5 respectively.

SOLUTION.

(i) The effect of price increase can be calculated by point price elasticity of demand. Putting the initial values of I and P_c we have $Q_x = 1200 + 4(1000) + 50(5) - 500P_x = 5450 - 500P_x$.
Now $\frac{dQ_x}{dP_x} = -500$. At $P_x = 4$, the quantity demanded is 3,450 books.
$\therefore$ Point price elasticity

$$(E_P) = -\frac{dQ_x}{dP_x} \times \frac{P_x}{\text{Quantity demanded}} = -(-500) \times \frac{4}{3,450} = 0.580.$$

Since demand is inelastic, increasing the price of the books would raise total revenue.

(ii) The income elasticity indicates whether a book is a luxury, or, necessity. We have already seen that the initial quantity demanded at the given price and income variables is 3,450.
Now $\frac{dQ_x}{dI} = I$.
$\therefore$ Income elasticity will be

$$E_I = \frac{dQ_x}{dI} \times \frac{I}{\text{Quantity demanded}} = 4 \times \frac{1,000}{3,450} = 1.16.$$

Since $E_I > 1$, books are luxury goods. Hence as income increases, sales would increase more than proportionately.

(iii) From the demand equation we find $\frac{dQ_x}{dP_c} = 50$. Now if E_c is positive it means that this book and books of competing publishers are considered by customers as substitutes.

$$E_c = \frac{dQ_x}{dP_c} \times \frac{P_c}{\text{Quantity demanded}} = 50 \times \frac{5}{3,450} = 0.073.$$

Thus 1% increase in the price of other books results in 0.073% rise in demand for NCBA's book.

PROBLEM 10. The coefficient of income in a regression of the quantity demanded of an item on price, income and other variables is 12. (a) Compute the income elasticity of demand for this item at income of Rs. 10,000 and sales of 90,000 units; (b) What would be the income elasticity of demand if sales increased from 90,000 to 1,00,000 units and income increased from Rs. 10,000 to Rs. 11,000? What type of item is this?

SOLUTION.

(a) The income elasticity of demand (E_I) can be expressed as follows

$$E_I = \frac{dQ}{dI} \times \frac{I}{Q} = 12 \times \frac{10,000}{90,000} = 1.33$$

(b) For an increase in sales from 90,000 to 1,00,000 units and an increase in the consumers' income from Rs. 10,000 to Rs. 11,000,

$$E_I = \frac{(Q_1 - Q_0)}{(Q_1 + Q_0)} \times \frac{(I_1 + I_0)}{(I_1 - I_0)} = \frac{(1,00,000 - 90,000)}{(1,00,000 + 90,000)} \times \frac{(10,000 + 11,000)}{(11,000 - 10,000)}$$
$$= \frac{10,000}{1,90,000} \times \frac{21,000}{1,000} = \frac{21}{19} = 1.11.$$

As E_I is positive, the item is a normal good and since $E_I > 1$, it is a luxury good, too.

PROBLEM 11. The managers of a steel company estimated the following elasticities for special steel they sell $E_p = -3, E_I = 1$ and $E_{XY} = 1.6$ where X and Y represent steel and aluminium. Next year, the firm intends to increase the price of steel by 5%. The firm further expects that the income will rise by 3% next year and the price of aluminium will decline by 2.5%.

(a) If the sales of the firm this year are 1,000 tons of special steel, how many tons of steel can is it expect to sell in the next year? (b) What will be the percentage change of the price of steel to achieve a sales of 1,000 tons next year?

SOLUTION.

(a) Since $E_P = -3$, if the company increased the price of steel by 5%, its sales would change by $(-3)(5\%) = -15\%$.

With $E_I = 1$, the expected increase in income of 3% itself will result in a $(1)(3\%)=3\%$ increase in the steel sold by the company.

Again since $E_{XY} = 1.6$, a fall in the price of aluminium by 2.5% will result in a $(1.6)(-2.5\%) - -3.75\%$ change in steel sales.

Hence, the net effect of a 5% increase in the steel price by the company, a 3% increase in income and a 2.5% fall in the price of aluminium would result in a net fall in the sale of the company of $-15\% + 3\% - 3.75\% = -15.75\%$.

So the sale of steel by the company in the next year would be $1,000 - (1000)(-15.75\%) = 1000 - 157.5 = 842.5$ tons.

(b) Keeping the steel price constant, the increase in income and fall in the price of aluminium, would result in a 0.75% rise in the steel sales of the company. Hence, to keep sales constant, the company can only increase the steel price so that by itself, it would decrease the demand of steel by 0.75%. Since the price elasticity of demand the steel is -3, the company can increase the steel price by only 0.25%.

PROBLEM 12. Suppose the demand function of a certain commodity is $x = 200 - 5p$, where p is the price (in Rs.) of the commodity per unit and x is the number of units that can be sold per month when the price is Rs. p.

(1) Find the point elasticity of demand as a function of p.

(2) Find the point elasticity of demand when $p = 12$. Interpret your result.

(3) Find the point elasticity of demand when $p = 35$. Interpret your result.

(4) At what price will demand have unitary elasticity?

SOLUTION.

(1) We know that the point elasticity of demand is expressed as $E_P = -\frac{dQ}{dP} \times \frac{P}{Q}$.

Here

$$E_p(x) = -\frac{dx}{dp} \times \frac{p}{x}.$$

Now

$$\frac{dx}{dp} = -5 = -(-5) \times \frac{p}{200 - 5p} = \frac{p}{40 - p}.$$

(2) When $p = 12$,

$$E_p(x) = \frac{12}{40 - 12} = \frac{12}{28} = \frac{3}{7}.$$

This shows that when $p =$ Rs. 12, a small increase in price will induce a relative decrease in demand which is approximately $\frac{3}{7}$ as large as the relative increase in price. Since $\frac{3}{7} < 1$, the demand is inelastic at this price.

(3) When $p = 35$,

$$E_p(x) = \frac{35}{40 - 35} = \frac{35}{5} = 7.$$

Hence, when $p =$ Rs. 35, a small increase in price will induce a relative decrease in demand which is 7 times as large as the relative increase in price. Since $7 > 1$, the demand is elastic at this price.

(4) For unit elasticity $E_p(x)$ should be exactly equal to 1.

$\therefore \frac{p}{40-p} = 1$, or, $p = 40 - p$, or, $2p = 40$; $\therefore \quad p = 20$.

Hence, when the price is Rs. 20, demand has unitary elasticity. At this stage, a small rise in price will induce a relative decrease in demand which is almost equal to the relative rise in price.

PROBLEM 13. Suppose the demand function for a certain item is $p = 5,000 - 5x^2$.

This equation shows us the price which should be charged per unit to sustain a demand of x units.

(1) Find the point elasticity of demand as a function of p.

(2) Find and interpret the elasticity of demand when $p =$ Rs. 25,000.

(3) Find and interpret the elasticity of demand when $p =$ Rs. 3,500.

SOLUTION.

(1) $p = 5000 - 5x^2$, or, $5x^2 = 5000 - P$, or, $x = \sqrt{1000 - \frac{p}{5}}$.

Now

$$E_p(x) = -\frac{dx}{dP} \times \frac{p}{x} = \frac{p}{\sqrt{1000 - \frac{p}{5}}} \times \left(-\frac{1}{{}^{10}\sqrt{1000 - \frac{P}{5}}} \right) = \frac{P}{10\left(1000 - \frac{p}{5}\right)} = \frac{p}{10,000 - 20P}$$

$$\therefore \quad E_p(x) = \frac{P}{2(5,000 - p)}.$$

(2) When $p = 2,500$,

$$E_p(x) = \frac{2,500}{2 \times 2,500} = \frac{1}{2}.$$

Since $\frac{1}{2} < 1$, the demand is inelastic. At this price level, a small rise in price will induce a relative fall in demand which is approximately $\frac{1}{2}$ the relative rise in price.

(3) When $p = 3,500$,

$$E_p(x) = \frac{3,500}{2 \times 1500} = \frac{35}{30} = \frac{7}{6}.$$

Since $\frac{7}{6} > 1$, the demand is elastic. At this price level, a small rise in price will induce a relative fall in demand which is approximately $1\frac{1}{6}$ times the relative rise in price.

PROBLEM 14. XY Company is charging Rs. 90 for its product A. A marketing consultant has assessed that at price p the consumer demand for product A is $x = 1,200 - 5p$. The company is planning to increase its price by a small amount.

How will this increase will affect its revenue? Would you draw the same conclusion if the price were Rs. 150?

SOLUTION. We know

$$E_p(x) = -\frac{dx}{dp} \times \frac{p}{x} = -(-5) \times \frac{p}{1200 - 5p} = \frac{p}{240 - p}.$$

When, $p =$ Rs. 90,

$$E_p(x) = \frac{90}{150} = \frac{3}{5} < 1.$$

Hence, the demand is inelastic at this price level which means that a small rise in price will be associated with a rise in revenue. This means that when price is Rs. 90, it is safe to recommend a price increase.

When $p =$ Rs. 150,

$$E_p(x) = \frac{150}{90} = \frac{5}{3} > 1.$$

Since demand is elastic, a small rise in price will be associated by a fall in revenue. Hence, when the price is Rs. 150, it will be unwise to increase it further. Rather, lowering the price will increase total revenue.

PROBLEM 15. Suppose the function $f(x) = 4x^2 - 3$ at $x = 2$. If x changes from $x = 2$ to $x = 2.06$, then find.

(a) The relative change in x; (b) the absolute change in y; (c) the relative change in y; (d) the average elasticity of f relative to x; and (e) the point elasticity of f at $x = 2$.

SOLUTION.

(a) The relative change in $x = \frac{\Delta x}{x} = \frac{0.06}{2} = 0.03$

(b) The absolute change in

$$y = \Delta y = f(2.06) - f(2) = [4(2.06)^2 - 3] - [4 \times 2^2 - 3] = 13.9744 - 13 = 0.9744.$$

(c) The relative change in $y = \frac{\Delta y}{y} = \frac{0.9744}{13} = 0.0750$

(d) The average elasticity of f relative to $x = \frac{\Delta y/y}{\Delta x/x} = \frac{0.0750}{0.03} = 2.5$

(e) At $x = 2$, the point elasticity is $E_x(y) = \frac{x}{y} \times f(x) = \frac{2}{13} \times 16 = 2.4615$.

The function f is elastic at $x = 2$ since the numerical value of its point elasticity is greater than 1.

PROBLEM 16. The demand function for a certain item is given as $p = \frac{40,000 - x}{20,000}$. Find the marginal revenue, when $x = 10,000$ units and p is in rupees.

SOLUTION. From the given function, p, the revenue function is given as

$$R(x) = \text{Price} \times \text{quantity, i.e.,} \quad x \times p = x\left(\frac{40,000 - x}{20,000}\right) = \frac{40,000x - x^2}{20,000} = 2x - \frac{x^2}{20,000}.$$

In this case MR is $R(x) = 2 - \frac{2}{20,000}x$

When $x = 10,000, R(10,000) = 2 - \frac{2}{20,000} \times 10,000 = 1.0$ or, Re. 1.0 per unit.

Hence, the next unit sold (at a sales level of 10,000) will bring an extra revenue of about Re. 1.0 per unit.

PROBLEM 17. Plot the demand curve, $Q = 100 - 4P$.

Now select the following four points on the curve,

$$A(P = 50, Q - 30), \quad B(P = 40, Q = 60),$$
$$C(P = 30, Q = 90), \quad D(P = 20, Q = 120) \text{ and}$$

find three arc elasticities for the arcs AB, BC and CD.

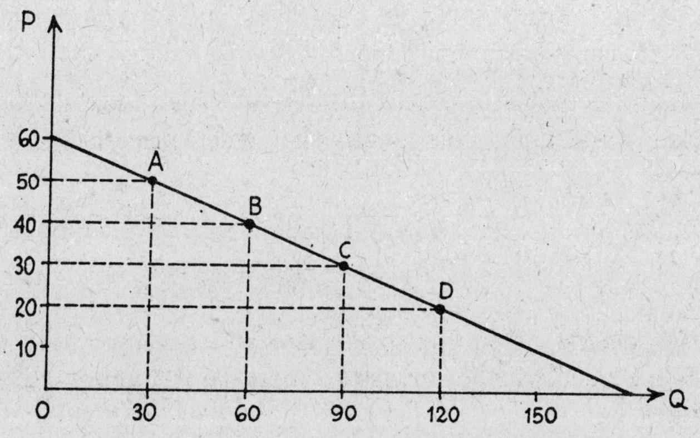

Fig 2.15 A Linear Demand Curve

SOLUTION. $E_p = -\frac{Q_1 - Q_0}{Q_1 + Q_0} \times \frac{P_1 + P_0}{P_1 - P_0}$.

For arc AB, $E_p = -\frac{30}{90} \times \frac{90}{-10} = 3$.

For arc BC, $E_p = \frac{30}{150} \times \frac{70}{-10} = \frac{7}{5} = 1.4$.

For arc CD, $E_p = -\frac{30}{210} \times \frac{50}{-10} = \frac{5}{7} = 0.714$.

PROBLEM 18.

(i) Draw the demand curve, $P = 125 - 5Q$.

(ii) Find the point elasticities at $P = 75, P = 50$ and $P = 25$.

(iii) What is your prediction?

SOLUTION.

(i) $5Q = 125 - P$. $\therefore$ $Q = 25 - .2P$ $\therefore$ $\frac{dQ}{dP} = -.2$

Point price elasticity $E_p = -\frac{dQ}{dP} \times \frac{P}{Q}$.

(ii) $\therefore$ E_p at $A = -(-0.2) \times \frac{75}{10} = 1.5$

E_p at $B = -(-.2) \times \frac{50}{15} = 0.67$

E_p at $C = -(-.2) \times \frac{25}{20} = 0.25$

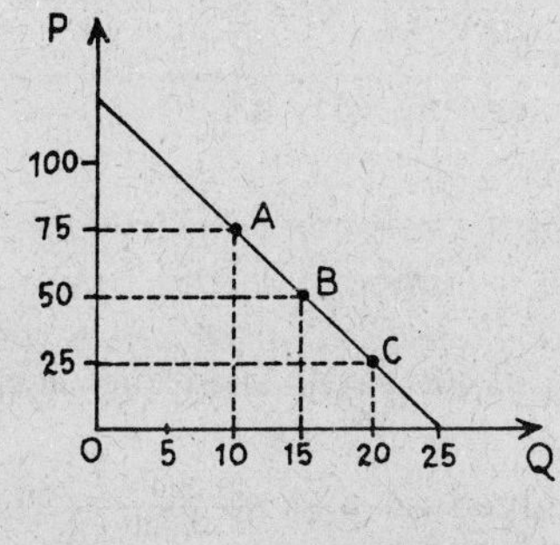

Fig 2.16 Point Price Elasticity

(iii) The curve is elastic at the point A and inelastic at points B and C.

PROBLEM 19. XY Company are the makers of M-60 pump. A linear regression model used to estimate the demand function for M-60 pump gave the following results

$$Q_d = 9,500 - \underset{(1.360)}{2,510P_x} + \underset{(.002)}{.02\ A} + \underset{(3,100)}{9,325P_{op}}$$

where Q_d is the quantity of M-60 pump demanded,
P_x is the price of pump,
A is the companys advertising expenditure in rupees and
P_{op} is the percentage of Indian population.

(i) What is the point price elasticity at a price of Rs. 6 and Rs. 12, when A = Rs. 1,00,000 and $P_{op} = .5$?

(ii) What is the point advertising elasticity at an advertising level of Rs. 2,00,000, if price remains at Rs. 6 and $P_{op} = .5$?

(iii) The standard error for each coefficient is shown in parentheses. If the demand function was estimated by taking 32 observations, can you reject at 95 confidence level the hypothesis that no relationship exists between each of the independent variables and Q_d?

SOLUTION.

(i) $$E_p = -\frac{dQ_d}{dP_x} \times \frac{P_x}{Q_d} \quad \left[\frac{dQ_d}{dP_x} = -2510\right]$$

$$= -(-2510) \times \frac{6}{1102.5} \quad \left[\begin{array}{ll} Q_d & = 9500 - 2510(6) + 0.02(1,00,00) + 9325(.5) \\ & = 1102.5 \end{array}\right]$$

$$= 13.660$$

When P_x = Rs. 12; $Q_d = 9500 - 2510(12) + 0.02(1,00,0000) + 9325(.5) = -13,957.5$.

$\therefore E_p = -(-2510) \times \frac{12}{-13957.5} = -2.158$.

(ii) $$E_A = -\frac{dQ_d}{d_A} \times \frac{A}{Q_d} \quad \left[\frac{dQ_d}{d_A} = 0.02\right]$$

$$= -(0.02) \times \frac{2,00,000}{3,102.5} \quad \left[\begin{array}{ll} Q_d & = 9,500 - 2510(6) + 0.02(2,00,000) + 9325(.5) \\ & = 3102.5 \end{array}\right]$$

$$= -1.2893.$$

(iii) Yes, for A and P_{op}, the t-values are 10 and 3 respectively which are more than 2.0. However, for P_x, the t-value is 1.846. From the t-value table we find that for a t-value with 30 degrees freedom, i.e., $(n - 2, or, 32 - 2)$, the t-value is 2.042 for 95% confidence interval. Thus for P_x the hypothesis that its coefficent is significantly different from zero cannot be rejected.

PROBLEM 20. Das Camera Co. produces automatic camera whose current sale price is Rs. 150. Sales volume per month for the camera is 1,500. Ghosh Photo Co., a competitor, has reduced the price of a similar camera which it produces, from Rs. 120 to Rs. 100. Dass economist has estimated the cross elasticity of demand between the two concerns products at around 0.6, given current price and income levels.

What effect will the action of Ghosh Co have on total revenue generated by Das, if Das Co leaves it current price the same?

SOLUTION.

(i) Let A be Das Camera Co. and B be Ghosh Photo Co.

$\therefore P_{A_0} = \text{Rs. } 150; \quad Q_{A_0} = 1,500; \quad P_{B_0} = \text{Rs. } 120, \quad P_{B_1} = \text{Rs. } 100, \quad E_x = 0.6.$

$$\text{(ii)} \quad E_x = \frac{(Q_{A_1} - Q_{A_0})/(Q_{A_1} + Q_{A_0})}{(P_{B_1} - P_{B_0})/(P_{B_1} + P_{B_0})}$$

$$\text{or,} \quad 0.6 = \frac{(Q_{A_1} - 1500)/(Q_{A_1} + 1500)}{(100 - 120)/(100 + 120)}$$

$$\text{or,} \quad 0.6 = \frac{(Q_{A_1} - 1500)}{(Q_{A_1} + 1500)} \times \frac{220}{-20} = \frac{-11Q_{A_1} + 16500}{Q_{A_1} + 1500}$$

$$\text{or,} \quad 0.6Q_{A_1} + 900 = -11Q_{A_1} + 16,500$$

$$\text{or,} \quad 11.6Q_{A_1} = 15,600 \quad \therefore \quad Q_{A_1} = 1,345$$

(iii) TR for Das Camera Co. falls to about Rs. 2,01,750 per month from Rs. 2,25,000 per month.

PROBLEM 21. (a) What are the equations for TR and MR for a firm whose demand equation is $Q = 2172 - 12P$ where P is price and Q is quantity demanded?

(b) If the firm expects a price increse from Rs. 10 to Rs. 100 will revenue rise, or, fall?

(c) If the firm wants to maximise TR what price should it charge? Find price elasticity at that price.

SOLUTION. (a) $TR = P \times Q$.

Here $Q = 217q - 12P$, or, $12P = 217Q - Q$, or, $P = 181 - 0.0833Q$.

Now $TR = (181 - 0.0833Q)Q = 181Q - 0.0833Q^2$.

Again $MR = \frac{\Delta TR}{dQ} = \frac{dTR}{dQ} 181 - 0.1666Q$.

(b) If $P = 10, Q = 2172 - 120 = 2052$

If $P = 100, Q = 2170 - 1200 = 970 \therefore TR_1 = 10 \times 2052 = 20,520$ and $TR_2 = 100 \times 970 = 97,000$

This means that revenue will rise with the price increase.

(c) To maximise a function take the first derivative and equate it to zero and solve for the TR function to find out where $MR = 0$.

Here $TR = 181Q - 0.0833Q^2$, or, $\frac{dTR}{dQ} = 181 - 0.1666Q = 0$, or, $0.1666Q = 181$. $\therefore Q = 1086$.

Now if $q = 1086$, then $P = 181 - 0.0833Q$, or, $P = 181 - 0.833(1086) = 181 - 90.46 = \text{Rs. } 90.54$.

Therefore the maximum $TR = (90.54)(1086) = 98,326.44$.

The firm can increase price from $P = \text{Rs. } 10$ to $P = \text{Rs. } 90.54$ and make extra revenue. If it raises the price above Rs. 90.54, there will be a fall in the TR.

TR is maximised when $|E_P| = 1$

Now

$$E_P = -\frac{dQ}{dP} \times \frac{P}{Q} \text{ [Here } Q = 2172 - 12P \text{ and } \tfrac{dQ}{dP} = -12]$$

$$= -(-12) \times \frac{90.54}{1086} = 1.$$

PROBLEM 22. A product sells at Rs. p per unit and it is known that the demand, x per month is given by the relation $x = 30 - 4p - p^2$. Determine AR, MR and E_P at $p = 3$. Also verify the relation $E_p = \frac{AR}{AR-MR}$

SOLUTION.

At $p = 3, x = 30 - 4 \times 3 - 3^2 = 9$.

Again

$$\frac{dx}{dp} = -4 - 2p = -(4+2p), \text{ or, } \frac{dp}{dx} = -\frac{1}{(4+2p)}.$$

$$\therefore \left(\frac{dx}{dp}\right)_{p=3} = -(4 + 2 \times 3) = -10 \text{ and } \left(\frac{dp}{dx}\right)_{p=3} = -\frac{1}{10}.$$

Now

$$MR = \frac{dR}{dx} = \frac{dR}{dp} \times \frac{dp}{dx}$$

Here

$$\frac{dR}{dp} = \frac{d}{dp}(30p - 4p^2 - p^3) \; [\because R = p \times x = P(30 - 4p - p^2)] = 30 - 8p - 3p^2$$

and

$$\frac{dR}{dx} = (30 - 8p - 3p^2) \times \frac{dp}{dx} = (30 - 8 \times 3 - 3 \times 3^2) \times \left(\frac{-1}{10}\right) = \frac{21}{10}.$$

Again

$$E_p = -\frac{dx}{dp} \times \frac{p}{x} = -[-(4+2p)] \times \frac{p}{x} = (2+2p) \times \frac{p}{x}$$

$$(E_p)_{p=3} = -(-10) \times \frac{3}{9} = \frac{10}{3}$$

$$\therefore \frac{AR}{AR - MR} = \frac{3}{3 - \frac{21}{10}} = \frac{10}{3} = E_p \quad \text{(since price is identically equal to } AR).$$

PROBLEM 23. From the following market demand schedule (a) find the price elasticity of demand for a movement from A to C and C to A and midway between A and C and (b) repeat this for points E and G.

A TYPICAL MARKET DEMAND SCHEDULE

Point	A	B	C	D	E	F	G
P_y (Rs.)	7	6	5	4	3	2	1
Q_y	600	800	1300	2000	3500	4500	7,500

SOLUTION.

(a) For a movement from A to C

$$E_p = -\left(\frac{700}{-2}\right)\left(\frac{7}{600}\right) = \frac{49}{12} = 4.08$$

For a movement from C to A,

$$E_p = -\left(\frac{-700}{2}\right)\left(\frac{5}{1300}\right) = \frac{35}{26} = 1.35$$

Midway between A and C

$$E_P = -\left(-\frac{700}{2}\right)\left(\frac{12}{1900}\right) = \frac{84}{38} = 2.21$$

(b) For a movement from E to G

$$E_p = -\left(\frac{4000}{-2}\right)\left(\frac{3}{3500}\right) = \frac{120}{70} = 1.71$$

For movement from G to E

$$E_P = -\left(\frac{-4000}{2}\right)\left(\frac{1}{7500}\right) = \frac{20}{75} = 0.27$$

Midway between E and G

$$E_p = -\left(\frac{-4000}{2}\right)\left(\frac{4}{11000}\right) = \frac{8}{11} = 0.73.$$

PROBLEM 24. For the market demand schedule in the above table, (a) Find E_p at points B, and F and (b) state what happens to total expenditure on item y when P_y falls.

SOLUTION.

(a) We can find E_p at points B, F geometrically from Fig. 2.17.

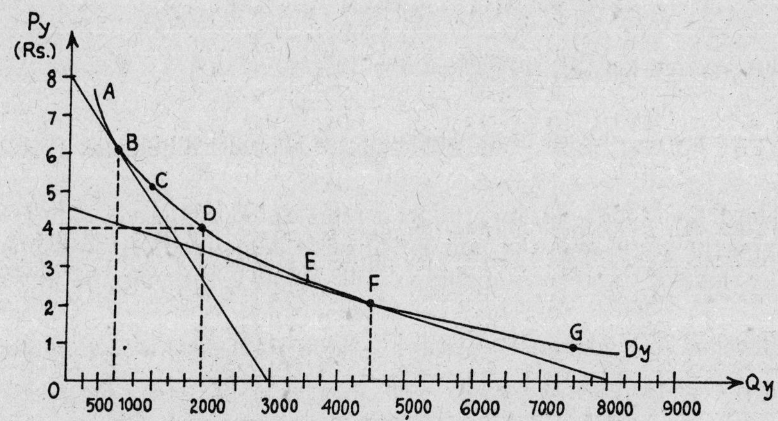

Fig 2.17 A Non-linear Demand Curve

At point $B, E_P = \frac{PQ}{OP} = \frac{3000-800}{800} = \frac{22}{8} = 2.75$

At point $F, E_p = \frac{RN}{OR} = \frac{8{,}300-4{,}500}{4{,}500} = 0.84$

(b)

A MARKET DEMAND SCHEDULE

Point	P_y (Rs.)	Q_y	Total Expenditure (Rs.)	Elasticity
A	7	600	4,200	
B	6	800	4,800	2.75
C	5	1300	6,500	
D	4	2000	8,000	
E	3	3,500	10,500	
F	2	4,500	9,000	0.84
G	1	7,500	7,500	

The fourth column of the above table indicates that as P_y falls, total expenditures on item Y increase as long as $E_p > 1$ and decrease when $E_p < 1$. We find that at we go down along D_y, E_p declines. This is normally the case for curvi-linear demand curve.

PROBLEM 25. Find the optimum commodity purchases for a consumer whose utility function and the budget constraint are $U = x^{1.5}y$ and $3x + 4y = 100$ respectively.

SOLUTION. Construct a new function S as $S = x^{1.5}y + \lambda[100 - 3x - 4y]$.

The first-order condition of maximisation requires that

$$\frac{\partial S}{\partial x} = 1.5x^{0.5}y - 3\lambda = 0 \tag{1}$$

$$\frac{\partial S}{\partial y} = x^{1.5} - 4\lambda = 0 \tag{2}$$

$$\frac{\partial S}{\partial \lambda} = 100 - 3x - 4y = 0. \tag{3}$$

From (1) we get $1.5x^{0.5}y = 3\lambda$

From (2) we get $x^{1.5} = 4\lambda$

$$\therefore \frac{1.5 \cdot x^{0.5} \cdot y}{x^{1.5}} = \frac{3}{4}, \text{ or, } \frac{3}{2} \times \frac{y}{x} = \frac{3}{4}, \text{ or, } y = \frac{x}{2}.$$

Putting this value in equation (3), we have $100 = 3x + 4y = 3x + 4 \times \frac{x}{2} = 5x$.

$$\therefore x = \frac{100}{5} = \mathbf{20} \text{ units; and } y = \frac{1}{2} \times 20 = \mathbf{10} \text{ units.}$$

PROBLEM 26. The demand for a certain product is represented by the equation $P = 36+4x-x^2$ where P is the price per unit and x is the number of units demanded: (i) What is the revenue function? (ii) Find the slope of the revenue function. (iii) What is the marginal revenue (MR) at $x = 2$?

SOLUITON. (i) Revenue R = (demand) (price) = $(x)(36 + 4x - x^2)$, i.e., $R = 36x + 4x^2 - x^3$.

(ii) $R = 36x + 4x^2 - x^3$;

$$\frac{dR}{dx} = 36\frac{d}{dx}(x) + 4\frac{d}{dx}(x^2) - \frac{d}{dx}(x^3) = 36(1x^{1-1}) + 4(2x^{2-1}) - (3x^{3-1})$$
$$= 36 + 8x - 3x^2.$$

The slope of the total revenue function is $(36 + 8x - 3x^2)$, which is marginal revenue.

Here dR/dx represents the change in total revenue R due to a change in quantity (x) and is known as the marginal revenue.

(iii) $MR = \dfrac{dR}{dx} = 36 + 8x - 3x^2$.

Substitute $x = 2$. $MR = 36 + 8(2) - 3(2)^2 = 36 + 16 - 12 = 40$.

The marginal revenue when two units are demanded is Rs. 40.

PROBLEM 27. Given the demand function $Q_d = 650 - 5P - P^2$, where $P = 10$, determine the price elasticity of demand.

SOLUTION. Using the standard elasticty formula

$$E_p = \frac{dQ}{dP}\frac{P}{Q}$$

first take the derivative.

$$\frac{dQ}{dP} = -5 - 2P.$$

Then substitute the given price level ($P = 10$).

$$\frac{dQ}{dP} = -5 - 2(10) = -25.$$

Next, find the level of output (Q) when $P = 10$.

$$Q = 650 - 5(10) - (10)^2 = 500.$$

Substituting these values in the elasticity formula,

$$E_p = -25\left(\frac{10}{500}\right) = -0.5.$$

PROBLEM 28. Find (1) the marginal and (2) the average functions for each of the following total functions. Evaluate them at $Q = 3$ and $Q = 5$.

SOLUTION. (a) $\pi = Q^2 - 13Q + 78$.

(1) $\dfrac{d\pi}{dQ} = 2Q - 13$

At $Q = 3$, $\dfrac{d\pi}{dQ} = 2(3) - 13 = -7$.

At $Q = 5$, $\dfrac{d\pi}{dQ} = 2(5) - 13 = -3$.

(2) $A\,\pi = \dfrac{\pi}{Q} = Q - 13 + \dfrac{78}{Q}$

At $Q = 3$, $A\,\pi = 3 - 13 + \dfrac{78}{3} = 16$.

At $Q = 5$, $A\,\pi = 5 - 13 + \dfrac{78}{5} = 7.6$.

(b) $TR = 12Q - Q^2$

(1) $MR = \dfrac{dTR}{dQ} = 12 - 2Q$

At $Q = 3$, $MR = 12 - 2(3) = 6$.

At $Q = 5$, $MR = 12 - 2(5) = 2$.

(2) $AR = \dfrac{TR}{Q} = 12 - Q$

At $Q = 3$, $AR = 12 - 3 = 9$.

At $Q = 5$, $AR = 12 - 5 = 7$.

PROBLEM 29. P. K. Watch Company currently sells 800 of its Model W monthly at Rs. 75 each. Its mearket research consultant determines that for every additional rupee the company charges, the public will buy 10 fewer watches monthly. Find the demand equation and the revenue function.

SOLUTION. The problem tells us that the demand is 800 units less 10 units for each Re. 1 by which p is greater than Rs. 75; that is, $x = 800 - 10(p - 75)$.

This is the demand equation. To get the revenue function we must first solve for p

$$x = 800 - 10p + 750 = 1550 - 10p$$
$$10p = 1550 - x$$
$$p = 155 - \frac{x}{10}.$$

Therefore the revenue function is

$$R(x) = xp = x\left(155 - \frac{x}{10}\right) = -\frac{x^2}{10} + 155x.$$

PROBLEM 30. Suppose the demand function for a certain product is $x = 200 - 4p$ where p is the price (in rupees) per unit and x is the number of units that can be sold montly when the price is Rs. p.

(a) Find the point elasticity of demand as a function of p.

(b) Find the point elasticity of demand when $p = 10$. Interpret your answer.

(c) Find the point elasticity of demand when $p = 30$. Interpret your answer.

(d) At what price will the demand have unit elasticity?

SOLUTION. (a) From the standard formula used to calculate price elasticity of demand we get

$$E_p = \frac{p}{200 - 4p} \cdot (-4) = \frac{-p}{50 - p}.$$

(b) When $p = 10, E_p = -10/(50 - 10) = -\frac{1}{4}$. This means that when the price is Rs. 10, a slight increase in price will induce a relative decrease in demand that is approximately $\frac{1}{4}$ as large as the relative increase in price.

Since $|E_p| = \frac{1}{4} < 1$, the demand is inelastic at this price level.

(c) When $p = 30, E_p = -30/(50 - 30) = -30/20 = -\frac{3}{2} = -1.5$. Thus when $p = 30$, a slight increase in price will induce a relative decrease in demand that is approximately $1\frac{1}{2}$ times as large as the relative increase in price.

Since $|E_p| = 1.5 > 1$, the demand is elastic at this price level.

(d) To have unit elasticity must have $|E_p| = 1$. That is,

$$\frac{p}{50 - p} = 1; \quad p = 50 - p; \quad 2p = 50; \quad p = 25.$$

Thus when the price is Rs. 25, demand has unit elasticity. At this stage, a slight increase in price will induce a relative decrease in demand that is nearly equal to the relative increase in price.

Suppose the demand function for a certain commodity is given in the form

$$p = 4000 - 5x^2. \tag{1}$$

This equation tell us the price that must be charged per unit to sustain a demand of x units.

(a) Find the point elasticity of demand as a function of p.

(b) Find and interpret the elasticity of demand when $p =$ Rs. 2000.

(c) Find and interpret the elasticity of demand when $p =$ Rs. 3000.

SOLUTION. (a) Solving Equation (1) for x and noting that x is positive, we obtain

$$x = \sqrt{800 - \frac{p}{5}}. \tag{2}$$

Thus

$$E_p = \frac{p}{x}\frac{dx}{dp} = \frac{p}{\sqrt{800 - \frac{p}{5}}}\left(-\frac{1}{10\sqrt{800 - \frac{p}{5}}}\right) = -\frac{p}{8000 - 2p}$$

$$\text{or,} \quad E_p = -\frac{p}{2(4000 - p)}.$$

(b) When $p = 2000$,

$$E_p = \frac{-2000}{2(2000)} = -\frac{1}{2}.$$

So $|E_p| < 1$ and the demand is inelastic. At this stage, a slight increase in price will induce a relative decrease in demand that is approximately $\frac{1}{2}$ the relative increase in price.

(c) When $p = 3000$,

$$E_p = \frac{-3000}{2(1000)} = -\frac{3}{2}.$$

So $|E_p| > 1$ and the demand is elastic. At this stage, a slight increase in price will induce a relative decrease in demand that is approximately $1\frac{1}{2}$ times the relative increase in price.

PROBLEM 31. D. K. Manufacturing Company is currently charging Rs. 80 each for its product x. A marketing consultant has determined that at price Rs. p the consumer demand for x is $x = 1000 - 5p$. The marketing manager is considering raising the price by a small amount. How will that increase its revenue? Would you draw the same conclusion if the current price were Rs. 120?

SOLUTION. We first calculate the elasticity of demand. Thus

$$E_p = \frac{p}{1000 - 5p} \cdot (-5) = \frac{-p}{200 - p}.$$

When $p =$ Rs. 80,

$$|E_p| = \left|\frac{-80}{200 - 80}\right| = \frac{80}{120} = \frac{2}{3} < 1.$$

Thus demand is *inelastic* at this price level. That means that a small increase in price will be accompanied by an increase in revenue. Thus when the price is Rs. 80 it is safe to recommend a price increase.

What if the current price is Rs. 120? At this price level the elasticity of demand is

$$E_p = \frac{-120}{(200 - 120)} = \frac{-120}{80} = \frac{-3}{2}.$$

Since $|E_p| > 1$, demand is elastic; therefore a small increase in price will be accompanied by a decrease in revenue. Thus when the price is Rs. 120, it is uniwise to consider a price increase. In fact, lowering the price will increase the revenue!

PROBLEM 32. An oil producing country is selling 1,000,000 barrels per day at Rs. 10 per barrel. A price increase is contemplated, but it is estimated that each Re. 1.00 per barrel increase in price will result in 20,000 fewer barrels sold per day. How much of an increase, if any, should be made to maximise the daily revenue?

SOLUTION. If we denote the price increase (in rupees) by x then $20,000x$ represents the decrease in the number of barrels sold per day. Thus with a price increase of x rupees per barrel, the number of barrels sold per day will be $1,000,000 - 20,000x$ and the daily revenue $R(x)$ in rupees at the new selling price of $10 + x$ rupees will be

$$R(x) = \begin{pmatrix}\text{number of}\\ \text{barrels sold}\end{pmatrix} \cdot \begin{pmatrix}\text{price per}\\ \text{barrel}\end{pmatrix} = (1,000,000 - 20,000x)(10 + x)$$

$$\text{or,} \quad R(x) = 10,000,000 + 800,000x - 20,000x^2.$$

Since each 1 rupee increase in price reduces the sales by 20,000 barrels and since there are only 1,000,000 barrels currently produced, the maximum possible price increase is $x = 50$ rupees (why?). Thus the problem reduces to maximising $R(x)$ over the interval $[0, 50]$. We begin by find the critical points $R'(x) = 800,000 - 40,000x = 0$. Therefore $x = 20$ is the only critical point. Since $R''(x) = -40,000$ we have $R''(20) = -40,000 < 0$. Therefore $R(x)$ has a relative maximum and an absolute maximum at $x = 20$. Thus the oil producer should raise the price by Rs. 20.00, to Rs. 30.00 per barrel, to maximise its total revenue.

PROBLEM 33. Find the price elasticity of demand for each of the following funcitons at $P = 3$ and $P = 5$.

$$\text{(a) } Q = 75 - 5P; \quad \text{(b) } Q = 42 - 6P; \quad \text{(c) } 8Q + 2P = 56.$$

SOLUTION. (a) $\frac{dQ}{dP} = -5$ and at $P = 3, Q = 75 - 5(3) = 60$. Substituting these values in the elasticity formula $E_p = \frac{dQ}{dP}\frac{P}{Q}$ we get $E_p = -5\left(\frac{3}{60}\right) = -0.25$.

At $P = 5, Q = 75 - 5(5) = 50$. Substituting these values in the elasticity formula, where dQ/dP remains constant at -5, $E_p = -5\left(\frac{5}{50}\right) = -0.5$.

(b) $\frac{dQ}{dP} = -6$. At $P = 3, Q = 42 - 6(3) = 24$. $E_p = -6\left(\frac{1}{24}\right) = -0.75$.

At $P = 5, Q = 42 - 6(5) = 12$. $E_p = -6\left(\frac{5}{12}\right) = -2.5$.

(c) Since $Q = 7 - 0.25P$ $\frac{dQ}{dP} = -0.25$.

At $P = 3, Q = 7 - 0.25(3) = 6.25$. $E_p = -0.25\left(\frac{3}{6.25}\right) = -0.12$.

At $P = 5, Q = 7 - 0.25(5) = 5.75$. $E_p = -0.25\left(\frac{5}{5.75}\right) = -\frac{5}{23} \cong -0.22$.

PROBLEM 34. Find the elasticity of the following functions using marginal and average functions and determine the price level at which the absolute value of the elasticity will be equal to or greater than one $|E_p| \geq 1$.

SOLUTION. (a) $Q = 120 - 4P$ and (b) $Q - 84 - 7P$.

(a) The elasticity formula can be expressed as

$$E_p = \frac{dQ/dP}{Q/P} = \frac{\text{marginal function}}{\text{average function}} \quad \text{or,} \quad E_p = \frac{dQ}{dP}\frac{P}{Q} = \text{marginal function}\left(\frac{1}{\text{average function}}\right).$$

With $Q = 120 - 4P$,

$$\frac{dQ}{d} = -4 = \text{marginal function} \quad \text{and} \quad \frac{Q}{P} = \frac{120 - 4P}{P} = \text{average function}.$$

Substituting in the second formula above and using the reciprocal of the average function,

$$E_p = -4\left(\frac{P}{120 - 4P}\right) = \frac{-P}{30 - P}.$$

For $|E_p| \geq 1$. $P \geq 30 - P; 2P \geq 30; P \geq 15$.

(b) $\frac{dQ}{dP} = -7$; $\frac{Q}{P} = \frac{84-7P}{P}$.

PROBLEM 35. Maximise the following total revenue and total profit functions. Also evaluate the original function at the desired critical value.

SOLUTION. (a) $TR = 32Q - Q^2$, (b) $\pi = -Q^2 + 11Q - 24$, (c) $\pi = -\frac{1}{3}Q^2 + 8Q^2 - 39Q - 50$, and (d) $\pi = -Q^3 + 48Q^2 - 180Q - 800$.

(a) (1) $\frac{dTR}{dQ} = 32 - 2Q = 0$. $Q = 16$.

(2) $\frac{d^2TR}{dQ^2} = \frac{d}{dQ}(32 - 2Q) = -2 < 0$. $Q = 16$ gives a relative maximum.

(3) $TR = 32Q - Q^2 = 32(16) - (16)^2 = 256$.

(b) (1) $\frac{d\pi}{dQ} = -2Q + 11 = 0$. $Q = 5.5$.

(2) $\frac{d^2\pi}{dQ^2} = \frac{d}{dQ}(-2Q + 11) = -2 < 0$. $Q = 5.5$ provides a relative maximum.

(3) $\pi = -Q^2 + 11Q - 24 = -(5.5)^2 + 11(5.5) - 24 = 6.25$.

(c) (1) $\frac{d\pi}{dQ} = -Q^2 + 16Q - 39 = 0$; $(-Q + 13)(Q - 3) = 0$; $Q = 13$; $Q = 3$.

(2) $\frac{d^2\pi}{dQ^2} = \frac{d}{dQ}(-Q^2 + 16Q - 39) = -2Q + 16$.

At $Q = 13, d^2\pi/dQ^2 = -2(13) + 16 = -10 < 0$. At $Q = 3, d^2\pi/dQ^2 = -2(3) + 16 = +10 > 0$.

Thus $Q = 13$ fulfills the second-order requirements for a maximum; $Q = 3$ is rejected because it provides a relative minimum.

(3) $\pi = -\frac{1}{3}Q^2 + 8Q^2 - 39Q - 50 = -\frac{1}{3}(13)^3 + 8(13)^2 - 39(13) - 50 = 62.67$.

(d) (1) $$\frac{d\pi}{dQ} = -3Q^2 + 96Q - 180 = 0$$

$(-3Q + 6)(Q - 30) = 0$

$Q = 2 \quad Q = 30$.

(2) $$\frac{d^2\pi}{dQ^2} = \frac{d}{dQ}(-3Q^2 + 96Q - 180) = -6Q + 96$$

At $Q = 2,\ d^2\pi/dQ^2 = -6(2) + 96 = 84 > 0$

At $Q = 30,\ d^2\pi/dQ^2 = -6(30) + 96 = -84 < 0$

$Q = 30$ provides a relative maximum.

(3) $\pi = -Q^3 + 48Q^2 - 180Q - 800 = -27,000 + 43,200 - 5,400 - 800 = 10,000$.

PROBLEM 36. Prove that total revenue is maximised for a linear demand function, $P = a - bQ$, at the point where $Q = a/2b$.

SOLUTION. $TR = PQ$.

For a typical linear demand function $TR = (a - bQ)Q = aQ - bQ^2$.

For TR to be at a maximum,

(1) $\frac{dTR}{dQ} = MR = a - 2bQ = 0$; $Q = \frac{a}{2b}$.

(2) $\frac{d^2TR}{dQ^2} = \frac{d}{dQ}(a - 2bQ) = -2b < 0$.

At $Q = a/2b$, the function is at a relative maximum. This provides an easy, shortcut method to determine the point of maximum revenue for typical linear demand functions.

PROBLEM 37. Determine the point at which total revenue will be maximised for each of the following linear demand functions. Check the answer to part (a).

SOLUTION. (a) $P = 24 - 3Q$, (b) $P = 50 - 2.5Q$ and (c) $P = 38 - 0.5Q$.

(a) A linear demand function will generate a total revenue function which will be maximised at the level of output (Q) equal to the vertical intercept (a) divided by two times the absolute value of the slope.

$$Q = \frac{a}{2b} = \frac{24}{2(3)} = 4.$$

Checking,

$$P = 24 - 3Q;\ TR = PQ = (24 - 3Q)Q = 24Q - 3Q^2;\ \frac{dTR}{dQ} = 24 - 6Q = 0;\ Q = 4.$$

Testing the second-order conditions, $d^2TR/dQ^2 = -6 < 0$.

(b) TR is maximised at $Q = \frac{a}{2b} = \frac{50}{5} = 10$.

(c) TR is maximised at $Q = \frac{a}{2b} = \frac{38}{1} = 38$.

Summary

1. The theory of consumer behaviour explains the derivation of the demand function. It also provides an understanding of the consumer decision-making process. It also serves as a guide for predicting consumer behaviour under various conditions.

2. Indifference curves are used to provide the theoretical foundations of the theory of consumer demand. The slope of an indifference curve is called the marginal rate of substitution (MRS). It denotes the rate at which an individual is willing to trade two goods (or services). Convex indifference curves depict a decling MRS.

3. The utility-maximising point occurs where the highest indifference curve is tangent to the budget constraint.

4. At the utility-maximising point, the rate at which products are traded in the market is just equal to the rate at which the individual is willing to substitute one good for another.

5. Changes in income are shown by a parallel shift of the budget line. A change in the market price of one of the two purchasable goods causes the budget constraint to rotate.

6. Elasticities measure the responsiveness demand to various factors. Price elasticity is defined as the percentage change in quantity demanded per 1% change in price. Arc price elasticity is used to assess the impact of discrete changes in price. Point price elasticity is appropriate for very small price changes.

7. Demand is elastic where $E_p < 1$ and inelastic for $1 < E_p \leq 0$. Demand is unitary elastic if $E_p = 1$. Demand is more elastic when (1) there are many substitutes for a good or service, (2) a substantial proportion of total income is spent on the product and (3) the time period is long.

8. Marginal revenue is the change in total revenue per 1 unit change in demand. Total revenue is increasing when marginal revenue is positive. Marginal revenue is zero at the point of maximum total revenue and total revenue is declining when marginal revenue is negative. For a linear demand curve, the absolute value of the slope of the marginal revenue curve is twice that of the demand curve.

9. Marginal revenue is positive where demand is elastic, zero for unitary elasticity and negative for inelastic demand.

10. Income elasticity is the percentage change in quantity demanded per 1% charge in income. Inferior goods have negative income elasticities while normal goods are those into positive income elasticities. For necessery goods $0 < E_I < 1$. Luxuries are goods and services with income elasticities greater than 1.

11. Cross elasticity is defined as the percentage change in quantity demanded of one good per 1% change in the price of some other good. Cross elasticities are positive for substitutes (like tea and coffee) and negative for complements (like tea and sugar). Goods with high positive cross elasticities are considered to be in the same industry or market.

12. The demand for a factor is derived demand. There are different determinants of derived demand elasticity.

Concepts for Review

1. Indifference Curve	8. Elasticity of Demand
2. Budget Constraint	9. Price Elasticity
3. Utility Maximisation	10. Income Elasticity
4. Price Effect	11. Cross Elasticity
5. Engel Curve	12. Derived Demand Elasticity
6. Income Effect	13. Total Revenue
7. Substitution Effect	14. Marginal Revenue.

Exercises

1. Consider simple situation in which there are only two goods. An individual has income of Rs. 9,000, the price of rice of Rs. 300 per bag and the price of wheat is Rs. 200 per bag.
   (a) Expressing rice as the dependent variable, write the equation for the budget constraint.
   (b) What is the slope of the budget constraint?
   (c) If the price of wheat increases to Rs. 400 per bag, write the new equation for the budget constraint.

2. Assume that the budget constraint is given by the equation $Q_1 = 1,000 = 5Q_2$, where Q_1 and Q_2 represent quantities of two goods. Normally indifference curves are convex to the origin, but assume in this case that they are linear with a constant slope of −2.
   (a) Graph the budget constraint (with Q_1 on the vertical axis).
   (b) Draw a set of indifference curves and label the utility-maximising point.
   (c) Where would the utility-maximising point have been if the indifference curves had a constant slope of −6?

3. Determine the utility-maximising combinations of X and Y when,

   (i) $TU = 10X + 20Y - 4XY$
   $P_x =$ Rs. 2
   $P_y =$ Rs. 4
   $I =$ Rs. 25

   (ii) $TU = 15X + 20Y - 4X^2 - Y^2$
   $P_x =$ Rs. 3, $P_y =$ Rs. 6, $I =$ Rs. 20.

4. It is known that quantity demanded decreases by 2 units for each Re. 1 increase in price. At a price of Rs. 5, quantity demanded is 10 units.
   (a) What will be the quantity demanded if price is zero?
   (b) Write an equation for total revenue.
   (c) What will be equation for marginal revenue?

5. The demand equation faced by Pieco Electronics for personal computers is given by $P = 10,000 - 4Q$.
   (a) Write the marginal revenue equation.
   (b) At what price and quantity will marginal revenue be zero?
   (c) At what price and quantity will total revenue be maximised?
   (d) If price increased from Rs. 6,000 to Rs. 7,000, what will be the effect on total revenue? What does this imply about price elasticity?

6. Management of Titan watches believes that the price elasticity of demand is −3.0. Currently watches are priced at Rs. 500 and the quantity demanded is 10,000 per year.
   (a) If the price is increased to Rs. 600, how many watches will the company be able to sell each year?
   (b) How much total revenue will change as a result of the price change?

7. The demand equation for a product is given by $Q = \frac{20I}{P}$ where I is income and P is price.
   (a) Write an equation for the point price elasticity. For what values of I and P is demand unitary elastic? Explain.
   (b) Write an equation for the point income elasticity. For what values of I and P is the good a necessity? Explain.

8. The demand for Sampat Mukherjees text *Business and Managerial Economics* is given by $Q = 20,000 - 300P$. The book is initially price at Rs. 175.

(a) Compute the point price elasticity of demand at $P =$ Rs. 175.

(b) If the objective of the publisher is to increase total revenue, should the price be increased or decreased? Explain.

(c) Compute the arc price elasticity for a price decrease from Rs. 175 to Rs. 150.

(d) Compute the arc price elasticity for a price decrease from Rs. 150 to Rs. 140.

9. Write a demand equation for which the price elasticity of demand is zero at all prices.

10. A consultant estimates the price quantity relationship for New Milkfood Icecream to be $P = 50 - 5Q$.

(a) At what output rate is demand unitary elastic?

(b) Over what range of output is demand elastic?

(c) At the current price, 8 units are demanded each period. If the objective is to increase total revenue, should the price be increased or decreased? Explain.

11. The price elasticity of demand for rice is estimated to be -0.4 and the income elasticity is 0.8. At a price of Rs. 4 per kg. and a per capita income of Rs. 20,000, the demand for rice is 50 million tons per year.

(a) Is rice an inferior good, a necessity, or a luxury? Explain.

(b) If per capita income increases to Rs. 20,500, approximately what will be the quantity demanded of rice?

(c) If the price of rice increases to Rs. 4.10 per kg. and per capita income is initially Rs. 20,000, about how much must per capita income change for the quantity demanded to remain at 50 million tons per year?

12. Suppose a firms total revenue from the sale of its product is given by $TR = 120Q - 0.1Q^3$:

(a) Over what range of output is demand elastic?

(b) Initially, the price is set at Rs. 71.60. To maximise total revenue, should the price be increased or decreased? Explain.

13. The demand equation for a product is given by $P = 30 - 0.1Q^2$:

(a) Write an equation for the point elasticity as a function of quantity.

(b) At what price is demand unitary elastic?

14. Suppose that for a function $y = f(x), x$ changes from 26 to 30, y changes from 155 to 165. Find the

(a) the absolute change in x

(b) the absolute change in y

(c) the relative change in x and

(d) the relative change in y.

15. Suppose the demand function for an item is, $x = \frac{400-p^2}{10}$, where x is the number of units which can be sold per week, p is price per unit in Rs.

(a) Find the point elasticity of demand as a function of p.

(b) Find the point elasticity of demand when $p = 10$. Interpret your result.

(c) Find the point elasticity of demand when $p = 25$. Interpret your result.

(d) At what price will the demand have unitary elasticity?

16. What is the E_p if $P_0 =$ Rs. 6, $P_1 =$ Rs. 4, $Q_0 = 20$, $Q_1 = 50$.

Fill in the blanks in the following table:

Nomenclature	Elasticity	Price Change Causes	Revenue Change
Inelastic	$\|E_d\| < 1$	up	—
—	$\|E_d\| < 1$	down	down
—	$\|E_d\| = 1$	—	none
—	$\|E_d\| > 1$	up	—
Elastic	—	—	up

17. Books & Allied Limited published a book on Managerial Economics in June 1994. The price of the book was fixed at Rs. 150. The publisher estimated that there would be a sale of about 500 copies per year. After giving discounts to book-sellers and royalty to the author, the publisher expected to get Rs. 60,000. A retail book-seller was of the opinion that the price of the book was very high. He believed that the publisher could increase the sale of the book substantially, perhaps double or, triple the sales value, if the price of the book was fixed at Rs. 100. However, the publisher believed that sales would be only 50% higher at Rs. 100.

Estimate the elasticity of demand and incremental revenue on the basis of the following assumptions:

(i) a doubling of sales

(ii) a tripling of sales and

(iii) 50% rise in sales.

Also assume that the proportion of the retail price going to the publisher will be identical at different prices.

18. Suppose the demand equation is $x = 10.000 - 50p$ when the selling price is p. Find the revenue function $R(x)$ when production level is x.

19. A company finds that the revenue function for production level x is $R(x) = x^2 + \frac{1}{x+1} - 1$

(a) Find $\bar{R}(x)$, the average revenue per unit. Find $\bar{R}(100)$.

(b) Find the marginal revenue when $x = 100$.

(c) Is the average revenue increasing or decreasing when $x = 50$?

CHAPTER 3

DEMAND ESTIMATION

Statistics are no substitute for judgement. — Henry Clay, 1842

There are three kinds of lies—lies, damned lies and statistics. — Benjamin Disraeli, 1867

Fundamental Questions

1. What is demand estimation?
2. Why is it so important to management?
3. Why does demand estimation require the development of a good set of data, on which to base the analysis?
4. What is identification problem?
5. What is autocorrelation?
6. What is multicollinearity?
7. What is heteroscedasticity?

PREVIEW

The vast majority of business decisions involve some degree of uncertainty. Business managers do not normally know what the outcomes of their choices will be. One way of reducing the uncertainty associated with decision making is to devote resources to demand estimation and forecasting. Demand estimation involves empirically (statistically) determining how factors such as income and prices affect the quantity of a commodity demanded. Forecasting involves predicting future economic conditions and assessing their effect on the operations of the firm.

This chapter focuses on certain basic techniques of demand estimation. In the next chapter we will discuss the most usual methods of demand forecasting.

METHODS OF DEMAND ESTIMATION

In the last two chapters, we assumed arbitrary values of the coefficients of the demand equations. In this chapter we will concentrate on statistically estimating the coefficients of the demand equations. The usual methods of estimating demand equations are the following:

1. Interviews (consumer surveys) and Observational Research;
2. Market Studies;
3. Laboratory Experiments; and
4. Regression Analysis based on Historical Observation.

1. Interviews (Consumer Surveys) and Observational Research

In consumer survey, questions are asked to some potential customers to find out the relation between the demand for a firms products and different variables. For example, changes in price of the commodity, incomes of buyers, the price of related commodities, credit incentives, advertising expenditures, etc. which influence marketing and profit planning activities. Essentially the technique is just to stop shoppers and ask questions about the quantity of the products they would be interested in buying at different prices. Another way is to present questionnaires to selected sample of consumers by trained interviewers. In spite of the potential value of this technique, there are some problems associated with this method. These are the following.

(i) **Sample bias.** Since interviewing all potential customers is much too expensive, the firm interviews a sample of selected customers (buyers) and applies this result to the entire market population. Firms must select a representative sample, otherwise the results of the interviews will be biased. For example, if the interviews are made of the people entering hardware stores, only a specialised segment of population will be considered.

Even if we select people at random, people with higher opportunity cost, i.e., people having high incomes, will not be interested to participate in these studies and the result of the interview is likely to be biased.

(ii) **Validity.** Even if the sample selection is unbiased, many participants are reluctant to give the correct information. For example, poor people have a tendency to overstate their incomes. Moreover, what people say, they do not do it in practice. For instance, even if a customer says that he will spend a certain amount on a product, the actual amount spent may be different since the decision is influenced by price and other variables.

(iii) **Reliability.** A survey method is reliable if repeated applications of the method give identical results. Reliability of a sample depends on the sample size which, in its turn, depends on the complexity of the study. The larger the size of the sample, the more reliable is the result.

(iv) **Cost.** Cost is a major constraint in many surveys. The interview questions must be truly relevant for the concern. Otherwise some effort will be wasted and cost will rise. Once the questions are perperly designed, these are to be tested with a preliminary sample to ensure that the questions are valid and not misleading.

Interviewers must be trained properly and a suitable media for collection of information, e.g., mailings, telephone calls, personal interviews, etc. is to be selected. Moreover, a group of people truly representative of the entire population is to be chosen.

Due to various drawbacks of consumer surveys, many firms are replacing consumer surveys by observational research which refers to collecting information on consumer preferences by simply watching them buying and using the products. Observational research relies on product scanners and does not render consumer serveys useless. In some situations, e.g., introduction of a new product, changing the quality of the existing product, etc. consumer surveys are the only method to obtain appropriate data. Consumer surveys are also very useful for assessing consumer awareness of an advertising campaign by the firm. If in the survey it is found that the consumers are not conversant with the price differences between the firms products and complementary, or substitute products, it indicates that the demand for the firms product is price inelastic.

2. Market Studies

Another technique for getting useful information about the demand for a product is market studies. This technique involves examination of consumer behaviour in actual markets. The firm selects one, or more markets with specific characteristics. Then it changes prices in same markets, advertising and packaging in other markets and other controllable variables appearing in the demand function in still other markets and finally record the different responses of consumers in various markets. For example, a firm can increase the selling price of sliced bread in Gariahat market in relation to that in Lake market and record the sales of bread in both the markets. Alternatively, the firm can make price changes every week or month in one market and record the responses of consumers. By using census, or survey data a firm can find out how demographic characteristics, e.g., income, family size, educational level and ethnic background affect the market demand for a commodity.

Advantages: The advantage of market studies or experiments is that these can be arranged on a bigger scale to ensure the validity of the results. Secondly consumers are not aware that they are the participants of the experiment. So they behave normally.

Drawbacks: Market experiments have, however, certain serious disadvantages. These are the following.

(i) Market studies are expensive.

(ii) In order to minimise cost, the experiment is arranged on very limited scale and over a fairly short period of time and hence the conclusions about the entire market and for a more extended period of time may not be accurate. This approach may not reveal the influences of certain factors which affect only some members of the community and not others belonging to the same community.

(iii) Strike, bad weather, etc. may seriously bias the results of uncontrollable experiments.

(iv) Competetors can make sabotage by changing prices and other controllable demand factors. Moreover, they can collect useful information from the experiments which the firm wants to keep confidential.

(v) A firm is likely lose customers while conducting experiments with higher prices of its products.

Usefulness: In spite of the disadvantages, market-experiments help a firm to fix its best pricing strategy and in testing various product qualities, packaging and assessing packaging and promotional efforts.

Market experiments are specially useful for introducing products where no data are available. They are also useful for verifying the results of statistical techniques applied for estimating demand.

3. Laboratory Experiments or Consumer Clinics

For conducting a laboratory experiment a supermarket environment is set up and consumers are given some fund to spend in the simulated store to assess how they prefer the companys product keeping in view the changes in price of the commodity, product packaging, price of substitute products, displays and other factors influencing demand. The laboratory experiments provide same type of information as that of consumer surveys and has the advantages of lesser cost and greater control of extraneous factors.

Disadvantages: The disadvantages of laboratory experiments are the following:

(i) It is costly and can only be carried out on a small scale.

(ii) Consumers become conscious that they are participating in an experiment and their movements are being watched. This affects their normal behaviour. Consumers may exhibit more price consciousness than is typical in their daily shopping.

(iii) Inferring the market behaviour on the basis of the results of the laboratory experiments may prove to be dangerous.

Laboratory experiments can, however, provide useful information about the firms products if they are supplemented by consumer surveys.

4. Regression Analysis

The statistical method most widely used by economists for estimation of demand is the regression analysis (or the method of least squares). This method helps us to estimate the coefficients of the demand function fairly accurately at relatively low cost. It also enables us to find out the marginal effect of each factor, holding all other factors constant.

If several observations are made relating the quantity demanded of a commodity to various demand-determining factors, we can find out the coefficients of demand equation and the expected results of changing one of the factors. Before we summarise the main features of regression analysis, let us discuss three general conceptual problems which arise at the time of estimating demand by applying regression analysis: (1) selecting the demand factors; (2) the identification problem; and (3) specifying the functional form of the demand equation.

(i) **Selecting the Demand Factors:** The first step in the regression analysis is the selection of variables in the demand function. Product demand, expressed in physical units, is the dependent variable. The independent variables influencing demand include the price of the product, the prices of substitute and complementary products, consumer incomes, advertising expenditures, the size of population and so on. Demand functions for expensive durable goods like building, automobiles, land, etc. however include interest rates and other credit terms. For beverages, air-conditioners, etc. demand functions include weather conditions whereas capital goods like industrial machinery include profitability, output-capacity ratios, wage rates, interest rates, and various other factors.

Obtaining data on the variables: Once the variables are selected, we must get accurate estimates of the variables, i.e., measures of price, output-capacity ratios, incomes of consumers, credit terms, advertising expenditures, consumers expectations regarding quality, etc.

Obtaining such estimates is not very easy. Consumers attitudes towards quality can, however, be assessed by survey (questionnaire and interview) techniques or by market, or laboratory experiments.

(ii) **The Identification Problem:** Regression analysis is not complete unless the right-hand-side, i.e., the independent variables are exogenous. By exogenous variable we mean a variable with a pre-determined value. An endogenous variable is one which depends on the values of the exogenous variables in the equation, e.g., price, quantity demanded, etc.

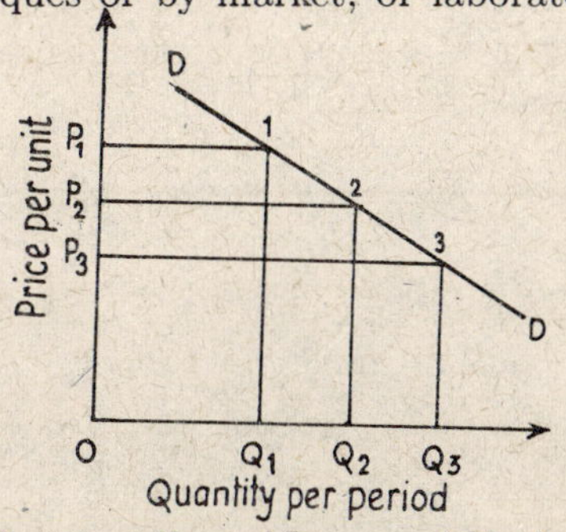

Fig 3.1 A Normal Downward Sloping Demand Curve

If we plot the price charged and quantity purchased at several points in time of a product, say X to derive its demand curve, we obtain a negatively sloped curve DD as shown in Fig. 3.1.

The available data are not sufficient to establish that DD is the demand curve for product X.

We have seen that the demand curve indicates the relation between price charged for a good and quantity demanded, keeping the effects of all other variables in the demand function constant. The line DD in the Fig. 3.2 has been drawn ignoring the effects of all other demand-related variables. Hence DD may or may not be a demand curve. To verify this, the price-quantity data have again been plotted in Fig. 3.2 along with the hypothesised actual supply and demand curves for product X.

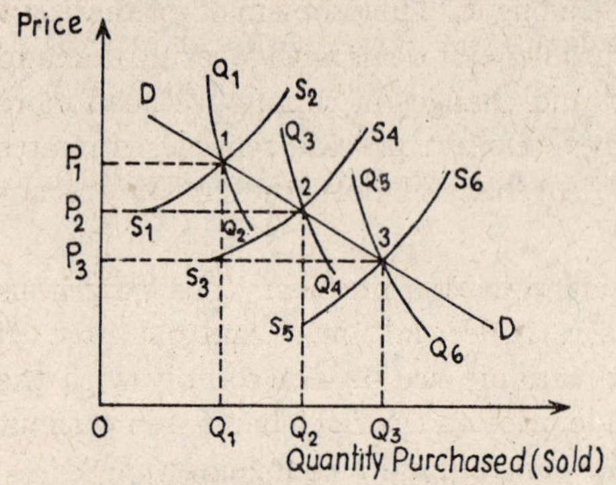

Fig 3.2 Identifying a Demand Curve

Here the data points show nothing more than the simultaneous solution of supply and demand relations at three points in time. The demand curves have negative slopes and the supply curves have positive slopes and the market prices and quantities purchased depend on the intersections of these curves. But the line DD cannot be called a demand curve.

In Fig. 3.2, we find that variables other than price in both supply and demand functions have changed between the data points. For example, the quantity supplied between the observation dates has increased due to the introduction of new techniques of production which have shifted the supply curves from S_1S_2 to S_3S_4 to S_5S_6. Again due to decline in the price of substitute products, or rise in consumers' income, the quantities of X purchased at later periods had increased at given prices which shifted the demand curves from Q_1Q_2 to Q_3Q_4 to Q_5Q_6.

From Fig. 3.2 we find that the supply curve and the demand curve have both shifted with time for which price has declined and quantity purchased has increased. Points 1, 2 and 3 are on different demand curves unlike those Fig. 3.1 and line DD connecting these points, does not trace out the true demand curve for X.

If a firm makes incorrect interpretation of the line DD as the demand curve and assumes that a high price elasticity of demand for its product it will lose money. In this case an increase in quantity demanded from D_1 to D_2 due a decline in price from P_1 to P_2 will lead to a loss since the price cut actually would result in much smaller increase in the quantity demanded. The true demand curve Q_1Q_2 is much less elastic than the line DD. Hence a price cut is not desirable as indicated by the line DD

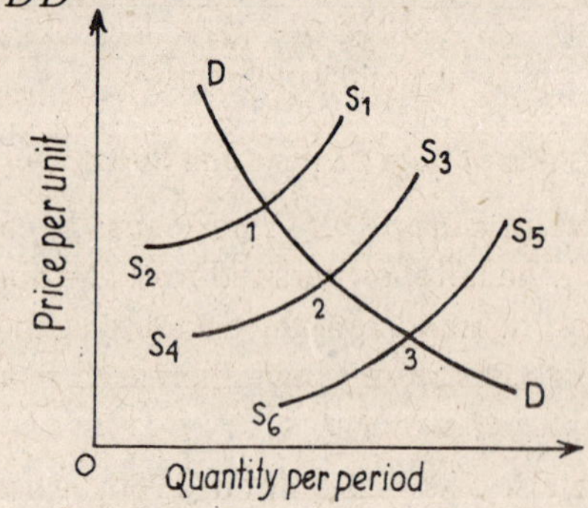

Fig 3.3 Shifts of the Supply Curve Alone

A demand curve can be drawn knowing the interrelation between the demand and supply curves under the following two conditions.

(1) The demand curve has not shifted whereas the supply curve has shifted to a new position.

(2) Alternatively we have enough data to find out how the demand and supply curves have shifted between the observation dates. For example, if the costs of production decline due to introduction of sophisticated machineries and the demand conditions remain stationary, the situation can be described as shown in Fig. 3.3.

The demand curve DD has been assumed to be stable but the supply curve shifts from S_1S_2 to S_3S_4 to S_5S_6. Each price-quantity point is indicated by the intersection of the demand and supply curves. Since non-price demand-determining factors have been assumed as constant, the points 1, 2 and 3 must lie on the same demand curve. Hencé the demand curve DD can be estimated by joining the three points. Such a situation occurs in electronics industry where prices of products like watches, calculators, etc. decline sharply due to rapid technological progress.

Solving the Problem: We find from the above example that the problem of simultaneous relations in demand analysis can be solved if adequate data are available to identify the interrelated functions and distinguish the shifts of a curve, from movements along it. The problem of estimating a function having simultaneous relation is called identification problem. It deals with locating demand and supply curves properly. To distinguish shifts in demand and changes in supply, we need more information than just price-quantity data. Regression analysis cannot provide reliable estimates of the demand function parameters if adequate data regarding shifts of both the curves are not available.

Another Example: Let us take another example of identification problem. The exogenous demand and supply factors fix up the values of endogenous variables, i.e., price and quantity. If we form a demand equation with price as a right-hand-side variable, we do not comply with the condition of regression analysis since. This is so because include price on the right-hand-side without making necessary adjustments in the estimation procedure for controlling its endogeneity.

Ignoring such problems may lead to some implausible statistical results. For example, in spite of 20% fall the value of dollar compared to European currencies, the U.S. tourists in Europe was greater in the summer of 1987 than in the summer in 1986. The fall in dollar value meant that the U.S. tourists could purchase lesser goods and services in European countries. Thus based on this information we conclude that an increase in the cost of travel led to a rise in tourism. Does it mean that the demand curve for tourism has a positive gradient? No.

From earlier discussions we know that changes in non-price demand factors may shift the demand curve to the right, or left, while changes in supply factors shift the supply curve. Such changes could even change the gradient of the demand or of the supply curve. For example, let us assume that the hotel-rooms and other related tourist facilities increase in the short run according to the supply curve S_1S_2 in Fig. 3.4.

In 1986 the demand curve might have looked like S_1S_2 and P_1 and Q_1 would have been the equilibrium price and quantity respectively.

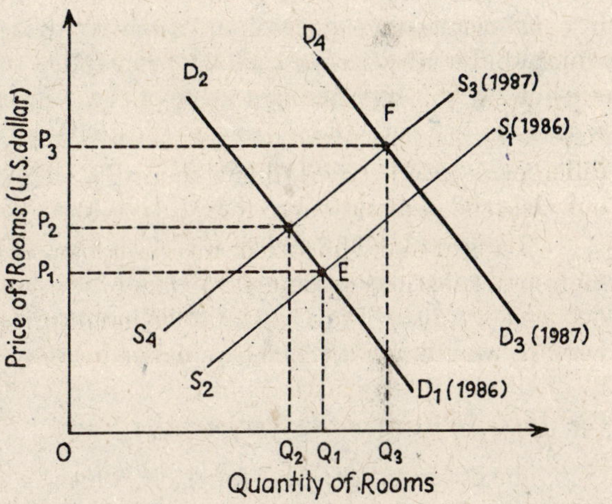

Fig 3.4 Shifts of Both Demand and Supply Curves

The fall in the value of dollar made dollar more expensive in Europe for Americans. It caused the supply curve of foreign hotel services to shift to the left, i.e., the hotel owners reduced the number of hotel rooms that they were willing to supply per dollar. Had demand remained identical in 1987 and 1986 (D_1D_2 in Fig. 3.4), the dollar price of foreign hotel rooms would have increased from P_1 to P_2 and the demand of hotel rooms would have decreased from Q_1 to Q_2.

In 1987 terrorism and other related events declined from those of 1986 levels. In 1986, American tourists were less in European countries compared to previous years due to terrorism which caused shifting the demand curve to the right in 1987 (D_3D_4 in Fig. 3.4).

Since the supply and demand curves both changed in 1987 the new market price and equilibrium output would have been P_3 and Q_3 respectively. By joining E and F in Fig. 3.4 and ignoring the shift of the demand curve, we can come to the wrong conclusion that the demand curve had a positive gradient, i.e., an increase in the equilibrium price was associated with an increase in the equilibrium quantity demanded. This is another example of the identification problem.

(iii) **The Functional Form of Demand Equation:** Once the appropriate variables are specified, we must specify the functional form of the equation which will reflect the exact relationship between the quantity demanded and the demand determinants (i.e., the variables affecting the quantity demanded of a commodity). In this chapter we will confine our discussion to following two functional forms.

(a) The Linear Form, or Model and (b) The Power Function or the Multiplicative Model.

The Linear Form of the Demand Function

The most commonly used linear model is presented below

$$Q = a + bP + cA_d + eI$$

where $Q =$ Quantity of a given product demanded.
$P =$ Price of the product.
$A_d =$ Advertising expenditures.
$I =$ Per capita disposable income of consumers.

Here a, b, c and e are the parameters of the linear demand equation.

Over smaller ranges of the quantity demanded, the demand curves are normally linear. For example, if $b = -2.0$, the quantity demanded of a commodity will fall by 2 units for every one unit rise in its price. By putting a value of the demand factor and the corresponding value of the quantity demanded, we can compute point elasticities. We can estimate the values of the parameters a, b, c and e of the linear equations by applying the least squares regression technique.

Merit: The main merit is of the linear model is that it is easy to work with.

Drawback: The drawback of the linear form is its simplicity. While using the linear form, we assume that the marginal effect of the change in single unit in the demand factor is constant irrespective of the levels of the other demand factors.

To overcome this difficulty we may use power function, or the multiplicative model.

The Power Function or the Multiplicative Model

The standard demand function, which is widely used, is given below

$$Q = a.P^b.P_1^c.I^d.R^e$$

where $Q =$ Quantity demanded of a product.
$P =$ The Price of the product.
$P_1 =$ The Price of the substitute product.
$I =$ Average income of the consumers.
$R =$ Average weekly rainfall in summer.

Here a, b, c, d and e are the parameters or constants.

This is a power function equation since each of the demand factors, or variables is raised to a certain power. Although the parameters can be found out by statistical methods, we can adjust the equation slightly and convert it into a more familiar form.

By taking natural logarithm (to base e) of both sides of the equation, we get the following linear form

$$\log Q = \log a + b \log P + c \log P_1 + d \log I + e \log R.$$

For simplicity we can write this equation as follows by replacing $\log Q, \log a, \log P, \log P_1, \log I$ and $\log R$ by $\log Q^*, a^*, P^*, P_1^*, I^*$ and R^* respectively.

$$Q^* = a^* + bP^* + cP_1^* + dI^* + eR^*.$$

This equation can be solved by applying simple linear regression method. After calculating the value of a we use antilog of a^* and proceed accordingly.

A useful feature of this form is that the above demand function has constant elasticity. Let us consider the price elasticity of demand for the product with this demand function. We know that the point price elasticity can be calculated by taking the partial derivative of the demand function w.r.t. price and then multiplying it by P/Q

$$e_p = \frac{dQ}{dP} \times \frac{P}{Q} \text{ is the point price elasticity.}$$

Now

$$\frac{dQ}{dP} = a.P_1^c.I^d.R^e.b.P^{b-1}$$

$$\therefore \quad e_p = a.P_1^c.I^d.R^e.b.P^{b-1} \times \frac{P}{a.P^b.P_1^c.I^d.R^e} = \frac{b.P^{b-1} \times P}{P^b} = \frac{b.P^b}{P^b} = b.$$

Since the price elasticity of demand is simply equal to b the exponent of price, it is not a function of P/Q and is thus constant. This constant elasticity relation is applicable to any other variable in the above power function.

Constant elasticities give useful information in estimating demand. For example, if the income elasticity of demand for housing is constant, demand of housing increases proportionately with increase in incomes and *vice versa*.

A highly attractive property of the multiplicative form for demand analysis is that it implies a changing absolute effect on demand of changes in different independent variables. Another significant difference is that multiplicative demand functions imply constant demand elasticity whereas on linear demand functions elasticity keeps on changing.

The algebraic form of the demand function—linear, multiplicative, etc. should always be selected at the outset since it specifies the exact relation among variables in the system being studied.

REGRESSION ANALYSIS OF DEMAND

Suppose the management of a firm is interested in knowing the relationship between the firms advertising expenditure and its sales revenue in order to test the hypothesis that increase in the sales can be achieved by increasing advertising expenditure. To introduce regression analsysis data on advertising expenditure and sales revenue for the firm for previous few years are to be collected. A set of such advertising-sales data for the last 10 years for a firm are presented below.

TABLE 3.1 ADVERTISING EXPENDITURE AND SALES REVENUE

(Rs. lakhs)

Year (t)	1	2	3	4	5	6	7	8	9	10
Advertising expenditures (X)	12	8	9	10	12	13	15	16	17	18
Sales Revenue (Y)	48	40	36	44	40	52	60	64	56	50

Here the level of advertising expenditure (X) is the independent, or the explanatory variable and is potted on the x-axis and the sales revenue (Y), being the dependent variable, is plotted on the y-axis. The scatter diagram in Fig. 3.5 shows the spread of the points in the $x - y$ plane.

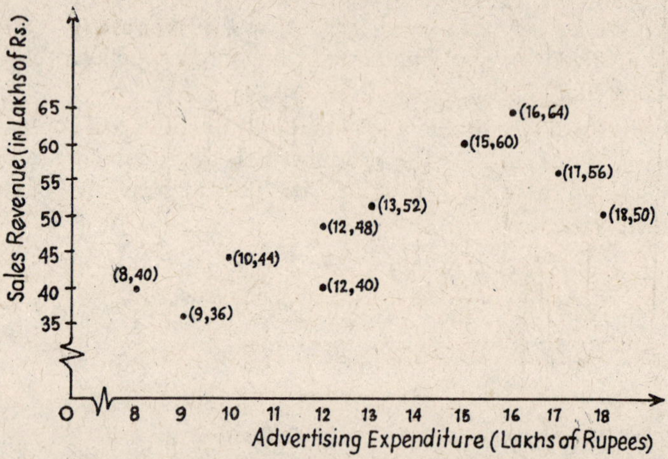

Fig 3.5 An Advertising Expenditure-Sales Revenue Scatter

From the above diagram it is seen that a positive relationship exists between the firms advertising expenditure and its sales revenues, i.e., higher advertising expenditure achieves higher sales revenue and this relationship is almost linear.

The best way to exhibit the linear relationship is to draw a straight line through the points in the $x - y$ plane which best fits them. Then by extending the line on the left we get the vertical intercept which is sales revenue of the firm at zero advertising expenditure. The slope, or gradient of the straight line will give the estimate of the rise in the sales revenue of the firm with every Rs. 1 lakh increase in its advertising expenditure. This relation can be expressed in the form of an equation like the one presented below:

$$Y = a + bX \tag{1}$$

where a is the vertical intercept and b is the gradient, or the slope of the line.

From this line the firm will be able to determine the sales revenue for advertising expenditure anywhere between Rs. 8 lakhs and Rs. 18 lakhs.

The main drawback of the visual fitting of a line is that different people select different lines and get different results. Regression analysis is a statistical technique which helps us to get the line that best fits the data points and everybody gets exactly identical results. The regression line is drawn in such a way that the sum of the squared vertical devations of each point from the regression line is minimum. The regression line drawn by the least squares method is shown in Fig. 3.6.

In Fig. 3.6, Y_1 is the actual/observed sales revenue of Rs. 36 lakhs corresponding to advertising expenditure of Rs. 9 lakhs in the third year and $\hat{Y}_1$ (Y_1 hat) is the sales revenue of the firm estimated from the regression line for the advertising expenditure of Rs. 9 lakhs in the third year. Here e_3 is the difference between Y_1 and $\hat{Y}_1$ in the third year, i.e.,

$$e_3 = Y_1 - \hat{Y}_1 \tag{2}$$

Such errors arise due to (1) omission of several explanatory variables influencing (Y) while forming equation (1); (2) the errors in the measurement of Y; and (3) the random nature of human behaviour.

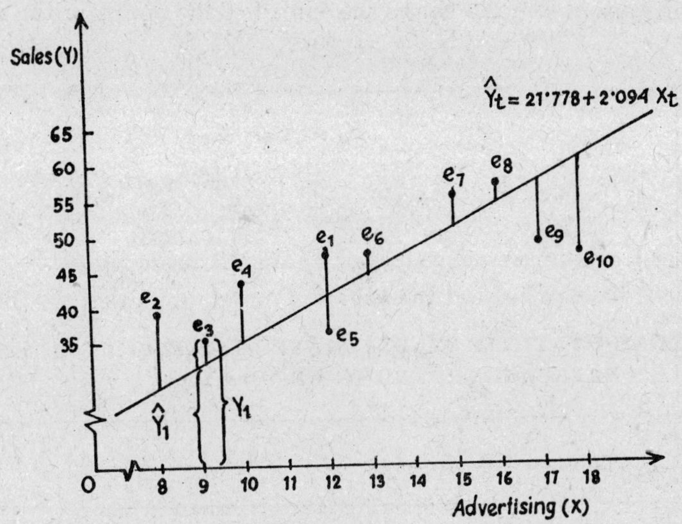

Fig 3.6 Fitting a Regression Line

In Fig. 3.6 we find that there are 10 errors labeled e_1 to e_{10}. The regression line will best fit the data points if the sum of the squares of the 10 different e values is minimum. Let us now find out the values of $\hat{a}$ (vertical intercept) and $\hat{b}$ (the gradient) of the regression line.

A. SIMPLE REGRESSION ANALYSIS

The Least Squares Method

Let us modify the linear equation (1) as stated below to represent the regression line

$$\hat{Y}_t = \hat{a} + \hat{b}X_t \tag{2}$$

where

$\hat{Y}_t$ is the estimate of firms sales revenue in year t-based on the regression line.

X_t is the level of advertising in year t,

$\hat{a}$ and $\hat{b}$ are estimates of parameters a and b, respectively and

e_t is the error from, i.e., difference between Y_t and $\hat{Y}_t$.

$$\therefore \quad e_t = Y_t - \hat{Y}_t = Y_t - \hat{a} - \hat{b}X_t \qquad \text{(from 2)}$$

Now

$$\sum_{t=1}^{n} e_t^2 = \sum_{t=1}^{n}(Y_t - \hat{Y}_t)^2 = \sum_{t=1}^{n}(Y_t - \hat{a} - \hat{b}X_t)^2. \tag{3}$$

The estimated values of a and b, i.e., $\hat{a}$ and $\hat{b}$ can be obtained by taking partial derivative of equation (3) w.r.t. $\hat{a}$ and $\hat{b}$ and setting the two normal equations to zero. The values of $\hat{b}$ and $\hat{a}$ will be as

$$\hat{b} = \frac{\sum_{t=1}^{n}(X_t - \bar{X})(Y_t - \bar{Y})}{\sum_{t=1}^{n}(X_t - \bar{X})^2} \tag{4}$$

$$\text{and} \quad \hat{a} = \bar{Y} - b\bar{X} \tag{5}$$

where $\bar{Y}$ and $\bar{X}$ are the mean, or the average values of Y_t and X_t respectively.

Table 3.2 shows how we have calculated the values of $\hat{a}$ and $\hat{b}$ by using the data of Table 3.1.

TABLE 3.2 COMPUTATIONS TO ESTIMATE REGRESSION LINE FOR SALES/ADVERTISING PROBLEMS

t Year	X_t Advertising	Y_t Sales	$(X_t - \bar{X})$	$(Y_t - \bar{Y})$	$(X_t - \bar{X}) \times (Y_t - \bar{Y})$	$(X_t - \bar{X})^2$
1	12	48	−1	−1	1	1
2	8	40	−5	−9	45	25
3	9	36	−4	−13	52	16
4	10	44	−3	−5	15	9
5	12	40	−1	−9	9	1
6	13	52	0	3	0	0
7	15	60	2	11	22	4
8	16	64	3	15	45	9
9	17	56	4	7	28	16
10	18	50	5	1	5	25
$n = 10$	$\Sigma X_t = 130$ $\bar{X} = 13$	$\Sigma Y_t = 490$ $\bar{Y} = 49$	$\Sigma(X_t - \bar{X}) = 0$	$\Sigma(Y_t - \bar{Y}) = 0$	$\Sigma(X_t - \bar{X})$ $X(\bar{Y}_t - \bar{Y}) = 222$	$\Sigma(X_t - \bar{X})^2$ $= 106$

Hence

$$\hat{b} = \frac{\sum_{t=1}^{10}(X_t - \bar{X})(Y_t - \bar{Y})}{\sum_{t=1}^{10}(X_t - \bar{X})^2} = \frac{222}{106} = 2.094$$

$$\text{and} \quad \hat{a} = \bar{Y} - \hat{b}\bar{X} = 49 - 2.094 \times 13 = 21.778.$$

∴ The equation of the regression line will be the following

$$\hat{Y}_t = \hat{a} + \hat{b}X_t = 21.778 + 2.094X_t.$$

Now if $X_t = 0$, then $\hat{Y}_t$ = Rs. 21.778 lakhs.

When $X_t = 12$, $\hat{Y}_1 = 21.778 + 2.094 \times 12$ = Rs. 46.906 lakhs

When $X_t = 18$, $\hat{Y}_{10} = 21.778 + 2.094 \times 18$ = Rs. 59.47 lakhs.

The regression line shown in Fig. 3.6 must pass through the points $(12, 46.906)$ and $(18, 59.47)$.

The regression equation also helps us to estimate firms sales revenue with advertising expenditure of Rs. 20 lakhs, i.e.,

$$\hat{Y}_t = 21.778 + 2.094 \times 20 = \text{Rs. } 63.66 \text{ lakhs.}$$

Actually, the regression line should be used to estimate firms sales revenues within the range of the advertising expenditures that were considered to estimate the regression line, or expenditures close to this range. The value of $\hat{a}$ is not very reliable since the regression line is to be extended too far to get the vertical intercept. The value of $\hat{b} = \frac{\Delta Y}{\Delta X}$, i.e., the rise in the firms sales revenue for rise in the advertising expenditures by one unit is Rs. 1 lakh.

The regression line is drawn on the basis of the following assumptions.

(i) The dependent variable (Y) is normally distributed;

(ii) Its values in different time periods are unrelated to one another;

(iii) It has mean equal to zero;

(iv) It has constant variance in all time periods and all values of X.

These assumptions have been made to get unbiased estimates of the gradient co-efficient and use the theory of probability to check the reliability of the estimates.

An alternative way of stating the regression equation—by using the least squares method—discussed below.

Let us find the regression equation of Y on X.

Let $(X_1, Y_1), (X_2, Y_2), (X_2, Y_3), \cdots, (X_n, Y_n)$ be the n pairs of the observations and the straight line demand equation to be fitted to the given data be

$$Y = a + bX \tag{1}$$

where a is the vertical intercept and b is the gradient of the line (which is negative).

Using the method of least squares, we obtain the following normal equations

$$\Sigma Y = na + b\Sigma X \tag{2}$$

$$\text{and} \quad \Sigma XY = a\Sigma X + b\Sigma X^2. \tag{3}$$

From (2) we get

$$\frac{\Sigma Y}{n} = \frac{na}{n} + \frac{b\Sigma X}{n} \text{ or } \bar{Y} = a + b\bar{X}. \tag{4}$$

Now by substracting equation (4) from equation (1) we get

$$(Y - \bar{Y}) = b(X - \bar{X}). \tag{5}$$

Again multiplying (2) by and ΣX (3) by n and subtracting we get

$$(\Sigma X)(\Sigma Y) - n\Sigma XY = b(\Sigma X)^2 - nb\Sigma X^2$$

$$\text{or } nb\Sigma X^2 - b(\Sigma X)^2 = n\Sigma XY - \Sigma X\Sigma Y, \text{ or } b = \frac{n\Sigma XY - (\Sigma X)(\Sigma Y)}{n\Sigma X^2 - (\Sigma X)^2}. \tag{6}$$

From (4) $a = \bar{Y} - b\bar{X}$.

Again we can replace b by b^{YX} in (5), since this is a regression equation of Y on X, i.e.,

$$(Y - \bar{Y}) = b_{YX}(X - \bar{X}).$$

Similarly, regression equation of X on Y will be

$$(X - \bar{X}) = b_{XY}(Y - \bar{Y}) \text{ where } b_{XY} = \frac{n\Sigma XY - (\Sigma X)(\Sigma Y)}{n\Sigma Y^2 - (\Sigma Y)^2}. \tag{7}$$

Here the straight line to be best fitted by the method of least squares is $X = a + bY$.

For non-linear demand curves, we may try to fit the following equation

$$Y = a + b_1 X + b_2 X^2. \tag{8}$$

For Fig. 3.7 (a) and (b) we shall recommend the use of equation (1) and equation (8), respectively.

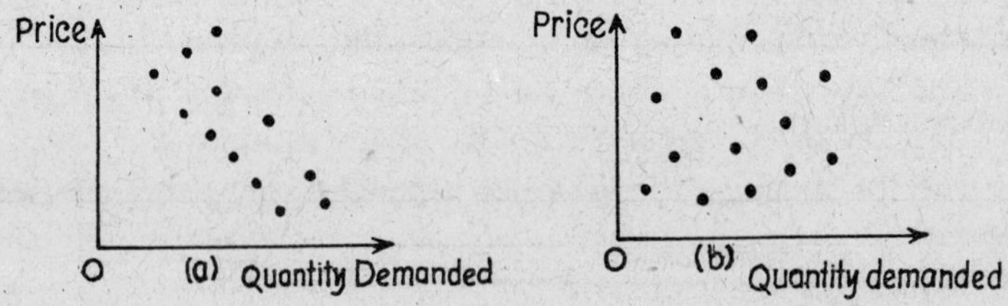

Fig 3.7 Two Price-Quantity Scatter

PROBLEM 1. Using the same figures in Table 3.2 find out the regression equation of Y on X.

SOLUTION. Put $X = X_t - \bar{X}$ and $Y = (Y_t - \bar{Y})$

$$\therefore \quad XY = (X_t - \bar{X})(Y_t - \bar{Y}) = 222 \text{ and } \Sigma X^2 = 106$$
$$\Sigma X = \Sigma(X_t - \bar{X}) = 0, \Sigma Y = \Sigma(Y_t - \bar{Y}) = 0.$$

Now

$$X = X_t - \bar{X} = X_t - 13, \quad \text{or} \quad X + 13 = X_t,$$
$$\text{or} \quad \frac{\Sigma X_t}{n} = \bar{X}_t = \frac{\Sigma X}{n} + 13, \quad \text{or} \quad \bar{X}_t = \frac{0}{10} + 13 = 13.$$

Again

$$Y = Y_t - \bar{Y} = Y_t - 49, \quad \text{or} \quad Y + 49 = Y_t$$
$$\text{or} \quad \frac{\Sigma Y}{n} + 49 = \frac{\Sigma Y_t}{n}, \quad \text{or} \quad \bar{Y}_t = \frac{0}{10} + 49 = 49.$$

Now

$$b_{YX} = \frac{\Sigma XY - \frac{\Sigma X \Sigma Y}{n}}{\Sigma X^2 - \frac{(\Sigma X)^2}{n}} = \frac{222 - \frac{0}{10}}{106 - \frac{0}{10}} = \frac{222}{106} = 2.094.$$

Therefore the regression equation will be the following

$$Y - \bar{Y}_t = b_{YX}(X - \bar{X}_t)$$
$$\text{or} \quad Y - 49 = 2.094(X - 13)$$
$$\text{or} \quad Y - 49 = 2.094X - 27.22$$
$$\text{or} \quad Y = 21.78 + 2.094X.$$

Extension to Multiple Regression

In Table 3.2 we have considered only advertising as a variable. If in addition to advertising the influence of promotion expenditure on sales is also considered, then we have three variables and we call it multiple function or polynomial of three variables, i.e., $Y = a + b_1X_1 + b_2X_2$ can be taken as the linear function of Y in X_1 and X_2 having parameters a, b_1 and b_2. To get these parameters, we solve the following normal equations

$$\Sigma Y = na + b_1\Sigma X_1 + b_2\Sigma X_2 \quad (1)$$

$$\Sigma X_1Y = a\Sigma X_1 + b_1\Sigma X_1^2 + b_2\Sigma X_1X_2 \quad (2)$$

$$\Sigma X_2Y = a\Sigma X_2 + b_1\Sigma X_1X_2 + b_2\Sigma X_2^2 \quad (3)$$

PROBLEM 2. Introducing promotional expenditure in Table 3.2, we have

Y (Sales)	X_1 (Advertising)	X_2 (Promotion Expenses)	X_1Y	X_2Y	X_1X_2	X_1^2	X_2^2
48	12	8	576	384	96	144	64
40	8	7	320	280	56	64	49
36	9	6	324	216	54	81	36
44	10	5	440	220	50	100	25
40	12	8	480	320	96	144	64
52	13	7	676	364	91	169	49
60	15	9	900	540	135	225	81
64	16	10	1024	640	160	256	100
56	17	9	952	504	153	289	81
50	18	11	900	550	198	324	121
490	130	80	6592	4018	1089	1796	670

Now

$$490 = 10a + b_1 130 + b_2 80 \quad (4)$$

$$6592 = 130a + 1796b_1 + 1089b_2 \quad (4)$$

$$4018 = 80a + 1089b_1 + 670b_2 \quad (6)$$

Solving (4), (5) and (6), we get $a = 23.027$; $b_1 = 2.385$ and $b_2 = -0.629$.

Therefore the equation becomes $Y = 23.027 + 2.385X_1 = 0.629X_2$.

Tests of Significance of Parameter Estimates

We estimated $\hat{b}$ from one sample of the firm. If we had taken an entirely different sample, the estimate of $\hat{b}$ would have been different. The more is the dispersion of the estimated values of b the less is the confidence in the single estimated value of b.

To test the hypothesis that b is significant, we are to find out the standard error (deviation) of $b(S_{\hat{b}})$ which is given by the following formula

$$S_{\hat{b}} = \sqrt{\frac{\Sigma(Y_t - \hat{Y}_t)^2}{(n-k)\Sigma(X_t - \bar{X})^2}} = \sqrt{\frac{\Sigma e_t^2}{(n-k)\Sigma(X_t - \bar{X})^2}} \quad (7)$$

where

$Y_t =$ Actual sample observation of the dependent variable in year t.

$X_t =$ Actual sample observations of the independent variable in year t.

$\hat{Y}_t =$ Estimated value of dependent variable from the regression line in year t.

$\bar{X} =$ Mean of the independent variable.

$e =$ Error $= Y_t - \hat{Y}_t$.

$n =$ Number of observations.

$k =$ Number of parameters to be estimated $= 2$ (since the two parameters are $\hat{a}$ and $\hat{b}$)

Here $n - k =$ Degrees of freedom $= 10 - 2 = 8$.

The value of $S_{\hat{b}}$ for an advertising sales example can be computed by putting the values from Table 3.3 which is an extension of Table 3.2, into the equation (6). Table 3.3 is shown below.

TABLE 3.3 CALCULATIONS FOR ESTIMATING THE STANDARD ERROR OF $\hat{b}$

t (Year)	X_t	Y_t	$\hat{Y}_t$	$(Y_t - \hat{Y}_t) = e_t$	$(Y_t - \hat{Y}_t)^2 = e_t^2$	$(X_t - \bar{X})^2$
1	12	48	46.91	1.09	1.1881	1
2	8	40	38.53	1.47	2.1609	25
3	9	36	40.62	−4.62	21.3444	16
4	10	44	42.72	1.28	1.6384	9
5	12	40	46.91	−6.91	47.7481	1
6	13	52	49.00	3.00	9.0000	0
7	15	60	53.19	6.81	46.3761	4
8	16	64	55.28	8.72	76.0384	9
9	17	56	57.38	−1.38	1.9044	16
10	18	50	59.47	−9.47	89.6809	25
$n = 10$	$\Sigma X_t = 130$ $\bar{X} = 13$	$\Sigma Y_t = 490$ $\bar{Y} = 49$			$\Sigma e_t^2 = 297.0797$	$\Sigma(X_t - \bar{X})^2 = 106$

$$\therefore \quad S_{\hat{b}} = \sqrt{\frac{\Sigma e_t^2}{(n-k)\Sigma(X_t - \bar{X})^2}} = \sqrt{\frac{297.0797}{(10-2) \times 106}} = 0.5919.$$

After getting the value of $S_{\hat{b}}$, we can find out the t-statistic, or the t-ratio, i.e., $\frac{\hat{b}}{S_{\hat{b}}}$. The greater the value of t-ratio, the more confident we are that the unknown value of b is $\neq 0$. In our sales-advertising example, the value of t will be

$$t = \frac{\hat{b}}{S_{\hat{b}}} = \frac{2.094}{0.5919} = 3.5378.$$

For carrying out objective, or significance test for $\hat{b}$ we compare the computed t-ratio to t-distributions critical value with $n - k = 10 - 2 = 8$ degrees of freedom. The t-test is normally done at the 5% significance level. The critical value of $t = 2.306$ for the two-tailed t-test as per the table of areas in the tails of the t-distribution.

Since the computed value of t, i.e., $3.5378 > 2.306$ for 5% significance level with 8 degrees of freedom, we ignore the null hypothesis that no relation exists between advertising (X) and sales (Y)

and accept the hypothesis that significant relationship exists between advertising and sales. When we say that statistically significant relationship exists between X and Y at 5% level, we are 95% confident about such relationship, i.e., there is only 1 chance in 20 chances of making a mistake. This is known as the t-test.

Other Aspects of Significance Tests and Confidence Intervals

We can also test the hypothesis that the gradient coefficient is not equal to zero at the 1% level of significance and then we allow only 1 chance in 100 of being wrong. For doing this test we read the critical value of t in 0.01 column against 8 degrees of freedom (henceforth $d.o.f$) from the table of areas in the tails of the t-distribution which is 3.355. Since the computed value of t (i.e., 3.5378) exceeds the critical value of t obtained from the table, we accept the hypothesis that a significant relationship exists between X and Y even at 1% level.

The greater the $d.o.f$, the lesser is the critical t-table values irrespective of the level of significance that we select. Hence at higher $d.o.f.$, there is greater chance of accepting the hypothesis that a statistically significant relationship exists between X and Y.

Significance tests are not done for $\hat{a}$, the vertical intercept, since this has practically no significance. We have tested the hypothesis for $\hat{b}$ only. Since $\hat{b}$ is not equal to zero, it may either be positive or negative for which two-tailed test has been conducted. We can also conduct single-tailed test of $\hat{b}$ either in the right or in the left tail depending on the area where the value of $\hat{b}$ falls in the t-distribution.

We can also find out the confidence intervals of b by using the tabular value of $t = 2.306$ at 5% level of significance with 8 $d.o.f.$, i.e., we can be 95% confident that the actual value of b will be

$$\hat{b} \pm 2.306(S_{\hat{b}}), \text{ or } 2.094 \pm 2.306(0.5919), \text{ or } 2.094 \pm 1.3649, \text{ or } 3.4589 \text{ and } 0.7291.$$

Similarly we are 99% confident that actual value of b will be between

$$2.094 \pm 3.355 \times .5919, \text{ or } 2.094 \pm 1.9858, \text{ or } 4.0798 \text{ and } .1082.$$

Test of Goodness of Fit and Correlation

The overall explanatory power of the entire regression can be tested by computing the coefficient of determination, or R^2. It may now be recalled that R^2 measures the proportion of total variation, or dispersion in the dependent variable about its mean. In our example of advertising and sales, R^2 measures the variation in the firms sales with variation in its advertising expenditure. The greater is the proportion of variation in the firms sales with variation in the advertising expenditure, the nearer the observed data points to the regression line and greater is the value of R^2.

We can find out the value of R^2 by knowing the explained and unexplained variation in the dependable variable (Y). The total variation of Y can be measured by using the following expression.

Total variation in

$$Y = \sum_{t=1}^{n}(Y_t - \bar{Y})^2.$$

Regression analysis shows the total variation in Y has two parts, i.e., the variation in Y explained by independent variable (X) and unexplained variation in Y. The explained variation in Y is expressed as follows.

Explained variation in

$$Y = \sum_{t=1}^{n}(\hat{Y}_t - \bar{Y})^2.$$

Again the unexplained variation in

$$Y = \sum_{t=1}^{n}(Y_t - \hat{Y}_t)^2.$$

Therefore total variation in Y = explained variation + unexplained variation is

$$\Sigma(Y_t - \bar{Y})^2 = \Sigma(\hat{Y}_t - \bar{Y})^2 + \Sigma(Y_t - \hat{Y}_t)^2.$$

Therefore

$$R^2 = \frac{\text{explained variation in } Y}{\text{total variation in } Y} = \frac{\Sigma(\hat{Y}_t - \bar{Y})^2}{\Sigma(Y_t - \bar{Y})^2}.$$

If all the data points lie on the regression line, R^2 will be equal to 1 or 100%. Again if none of the variation in Y can be explained by the variation in X R^2 will be zero. Hence the value of R^2 will lie between 0 and 1.

Let us see how actually we can calculate R^2 for our advertising-sales problem. The calculations are shown in Table 3.4.

TABLE 3.4 CALCULATION OF THE COEFFICIENT OF VARIATION ($\mathbf{R^2}$)

t Year	Y_t	$Y_t - \bar{Y}$	$(Y_t - \bar{Y})^2$	$\hat{Y}_t$	$\hat{Y}_t - \bar{Y}$	$(\hat{Y}_t - \bar{Y})^2$	$(Y_t - \hat{Y}_t)^2$
1	48	−1	1	46.91	−2.09	4.3681	1.1881
2	40	−9	81	38.53	−10.47	109.6209	2.1609
3	36	−13	169	40.62	−8.38	70.2244	21.3444
4	44	−5	25	42.72	−6.28	39.4384	1.6384
5	40	−9	81	46.91	−2.09	4.3681	47.7481
6	52	3	9	49.00	0	0	9.0000
7	60	11	121	53.19	4.19	17.5561	46.3761
8	64	15	225	55.28	6.28	39.4384	76.0384
9	56	7	49	57.38	8.38	70.2244	1.9044
10	50	1	1	59.47	10.47	109.6209	89.6809
$n = 10$	$\Sigma Y_t = 490$ $\bar{Y} = 49$		$\Sigma(Y_t - \bar{Y})^2 = 762$			$\Sigma(\hat{Y}_t - \bar{Y})^2$ $= 464.8597$	Σe_t^2 $= 297.0797$

Therefore the co-efficient of determination for our advertising-sales problem is

$$R^2 = \frac{464.8597}{762} = 0.61.$$

This means that 61% of the total variation of firms sale is due to the variation in the firms advertising expenditure.

The unexplained variation in Y shown in the last column of Table 3.4, is equal to Rs. 297.0797. Hence the sum of explained and unexplained variation in Y is (Rs. 464.8597+ Rs. 297.0797 =) Rs. 761.9394 which is equal to the total variation in Y (= Rs. 762), except for the rounding error.

In simple regression analysis, the $\sqrt{R^2}$ is equal to the absolute value of the coefficient of correlation (r)

$$\therefore \quad r = \sqrt{R^2}, \quad \text{or} \quad r = \sqrt{0.61} = 0.7810.$$

Therefore $r = 0.7810$, in our advertising-sales example. This indicates that X and Y variables vary together 78% of time. The value of (r) ranges between -1 and 1. The sign of r is identical as the sign of the estimated slope coefficient ($\hat{b}$).

Correlation analysis measures only the degree of association or covariation between two variables. The high coefficient of determination between X and Y may be owing to other factors which affect both X and Y and are not included in the regression analysis. For example, expenditures on food and education depend on consumer income rather than on each other.

B. MULTIPLE REGRESSION ANALYSIS

When the dependent variable is a function of several independent, or explanatory variables, we have to rely on multiple regression analysis. Such a regression equation is presented below:

$$Y = a + b_1X_1 + b_2X_2$$

where

$$\begin{aligned} Y &= \text{ Sales revenue, or income of firm (the dependent variable)} \\ X_1 &= \text{ Advertising expenditure of the firm} \\ X_2 &= \text{ Quality control expenditures of the firm.} \end{aligned}$$

Here a, b_1 and b_2 are the parameters to be estimated.

$$\begin{aligned} a &= \text{vertical intercept, i.e., value of } Y \text{ when both } X_1 \text{ and } X_2 \text{ are zero.} \\ b_1 &= \text{change in } Y \text{ (sales) per unit change in } X_1 \text{ (advertisement expenditure),} \\ &= \tfrac{\Delta Y}{\Delta X_1} \text{ when } X_2 \text{ is constant} \\ b_2 &= \text{ change in } Y \text{ per unit change in } X_2 = \tfrac{\Delta Y}{\Delta X_2} \text{ when } X_1 \text{ is constant.} \end{aligned}$$

In our sales-advertising and quality control problem we assume both b_1 and b_2 as positive, i.e., the firm can increase sales by increasing expenditures on both advertising and quality control.

The regression model can be generalised to a number of independent, or explanatory variables (V) as

$$Y = a + b_1X_1 + b_2X_2 + \cdots + b_vX_v.$$

In multiple regression analysis the assumptions made in addition to those made in simple regression analysis are that the number of observations is more than the number of independent variables in regression and there is no perfect linear correlation among the independent variables.

The method of estimating a parameter or co-efficient of a multiple-regression equation is identical to that of a simple regression equation, but as the computations are more complex and time-consuming, they are performed on computers. A computer gives the standard error of the estimates, the co-efficient of multiple determination, the t-statistics and other information to perform statistical tests of the results. Once regression analysis is done, data are fed into the computer and the results are obtained and interpreted.

Correcting Coefficient of Determination $\bar{R}^2$

When each data point falls on the regression line, the value of R^2 becomes 1.0. A regression model with $R^2 = 1.0$ is considered as the ideal forecasting device, but this may not always be true. The coefficient of determination for a regression equation can be made high if a very small sample is selected to estimate the models coefficients. R^2 will be equal to 1, if the number of data observations is identical to the number of estimated coefficients.

To make the regression analysis meaningful, the data sample required to estimate the coefficients of the regression equation must be very large to present the significant characteristics of the exact relation. Actually we require substantial number of degrees of freedom to properly fit a regression model. For example, to find out the vertical intercept, we require at least one observation and to calculate the vertical intercept and the gradient coefficient, we require at least two observations and so on. Since R^2 tends to 1 as degrees of freedom tends to 0, statisticians have developed a formula for correcting R^2 to account for the number of degrees of freedom. The formula is given below.

$$\bar{R}^2 = R^2 - \left(\frac{k-1}{n-k}\right)(1 - R^2)$$

where

$n =$ number of observations or data points, and

$k =$ number of gradient coefficients and intercept.

From the equation we find that adjustment to R^2 is large when n is small relative to k and *vice-versa*. Out confidence in reliability of a regression model will be high when R^2 is high and the number of degrees of freedom is large.

The F-Statistic

This is another useful statistic for measuring the overall explanatory power of a regression equation. It refers to the relation between the explained and unexplained variation of the independent variables. R^2 and $\bar{R}^2$ show whether the proportion of explained variation is high or low whereas the F-statistic shows whether a statistically important proportion of the total variation in the dependent variable has been properly explained. The F-statistic, like $\bar{R}^2$ is also adjusted for the degrees of freedom as

$$F = \frac{\text{Explained variation } /(k-1)}{\text{Unexplained variation } /(n-k)}.$$

Again, the F-statistic can be computed in terms of the co-efficient of determination as

$$F = \frac{R^2/(k-1)}{(1-R^2)/(n-k)}$$

F-statistic will be 0 when the regression equation gives absolutely no explanation of the variation in the dependent variable, i.e., when $R^2 = 0, F$ is also equal to 0.

The F-test is used to find out whether the F-statistic, associated with a particular regression equation, is sufficiently large to enable one reject the hypothesis that the regression model does not show important variation in the dependent variable. The F-statistic for a regression equation is compared with the critical value in the F-distribution table and if it is found to exceed it, the hypothesis of interdependence between the dependent variable and the set of independent variables in the regression is rejected. Thus one can conclude that the regression equation explains important variations in the dependent variables.

Critical values of the F-distribution table are constructed for 10%, 5% and 1% significance levels and if the F-statistic exceeds the F-table values for a regression equation, we can be confident that the model significantly explains 90%, 95%, or even 99% of the variance of the dependent variables. These confidence levels are very popular for the rejection of a hypothesis.

Critical values in the F-distribution is dependent on two degrees of freedom, i.e., one related to the numerator and the other to the denominator. The critical value of F can be written as

$$F_{f_1, f_2}$$

where f_1 and f_2 are the degrees of freedom of numerator $(= k - 1)$ and denominator $(= n - k)$ respectively.

Problems with Regression Analysis

Regression analysis creates three major problems, e.g., (1) multicollinearity, (2) heteroscedasticity and (3) auto correlation (also known as serial correlation).

(i) **Multicollinearity:** Multicollinearity refers to inter-correlation between (among) explanatory variables. It refers to a statistical situation where a number of independent variables are highly correlated so that they all vary together. In such situations it is impossible to disentangle the effect of any one of these independent variables upon the dependent variable in the regression equation. In the example of expenditure on quality control and advertisement, the regression of sales may indicate exaggerated standard errors and low t-values for both co-efficients and may lead one to the conclusion that the gradient co-efficients are statistically inefficient, though R^2 may be very high.

Multicollinearity can be reduced by:

(i) extending the sample size;

(ii) using *a priori* data;

(iii) eliminating highly collinear variables, and

(iv) transforming the functional relationship.

(ii) **Heteroscedasticity:** It refers to a statistical situation where there is a particular pattern in the residuals or error terms after an estimate of a regression equation has been made from sample observations of independent variables and dependent variables. If the estimated regression coefficients are good, unbiased estimates of the true population coefficients of the independent variables, then the residual values should be randomly distributed and have a constant variance. If they are not, then the estimated equation is an inaccurate fit or has missed out other important independent variables which are affecting the dependent variable. Heteroscedastistic error terms occur where the variable of the error term is not constant but grows or declines as the independent variable increases. It occurs in the regression equation when there is violation of the assumption that the variance of the error term is constant. It is very common in cross-section data. For example, the error associated with low-income family expenditures is much less compared to high income family expenditures since low-income families spend more on necessities than on luxuries. They enjoy no discretion in the matter. Hence if family expenditures are considered as an explanatory variable, there may be the problem of heteroscedasticity in the regression analysis.

Due to this problem there may be biased standard errors, incorrect statistical tests and confidence intervals in the estimates of the parameters.

The problem can be solved by using log of the explanatory variable which is causing this problem or by using weighted least squares regression which is obtained by dividing the dependent and all independent variables by the variable which is causing this problem.

The heteroscedastitic disturbances (i.e., errors) are shown in Fig. 3.8.

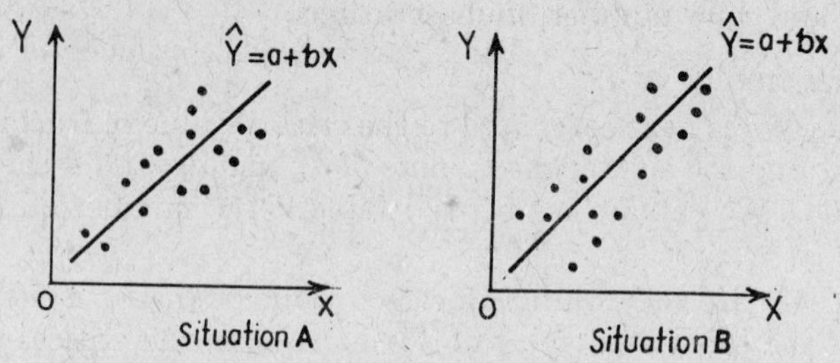

Fig 3.8 Illustrating Heteroscedastic Disturbances

(iii) **Autocorrelation:** When consecutive errors are correlated, we get auto correlation or serial correlation. It refers to a statistical situation where there is a particular pattern in the residuals or error terms after an estimate has been made from sample observations of independent variables and dependent variables. If the estimated regression coefficients are good unbiased estimates of the true population coefficients of the independent variables, then the residual values should be randomly distributed showing no consistent relationship with each other. If they are not, then the estimated regression equation is an inaccurate fit or has missed out other important independent variables which are affecting the dependent variable. Auto correlated error terms occur where a series of error terms are related and they are a frequent problem in time-series analysis, where values of the error terms in consecutive time periods may be correlated. In positive autocorrelation consecutive errors have identical signs [Fig. 3.9(a)] and in negative autocorrelation the consecutive errors change the sign frequently [Fig. 3.9(b)].

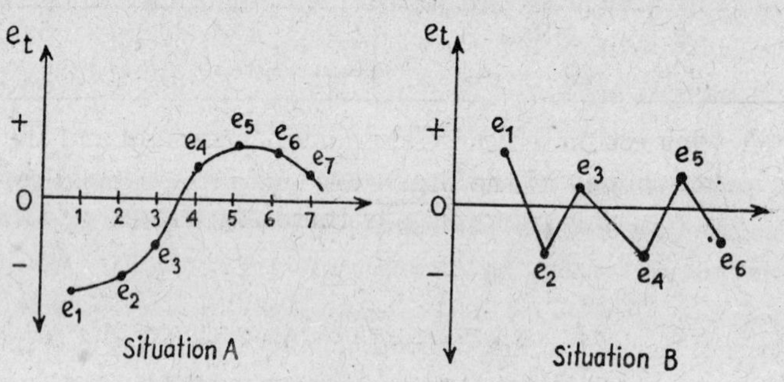

Fig 3.9 Autocorrelated Errors

Autocorrelation is common in time-series data. In economics, positive autocorrelation is very common. Due to autocorrelation t-statistics, $\bar{R}^2$ and F statistic all become unreliable.

The Durbin-Watson Test

It is a statistical test that checks for the presence of a pattern in the residuals or error terms, after an estimated regression equation has been calculated from observations of independent variables and dependent variables. Autocorrelation can be detected by using Durbin-Watson Statistic (d) which can be expressed as

$$d = \frac{\sum_{t=2}^{n}(e_t - e_{t-1})^2}{\sum_{t=1}^{n}(e_t)^2}$$

where e_t = error term in period t;

e_{t-1} = error term in previous time period $t_1 - 1$

and n = number of observations.

The value of d varies from 0 to 4.

The calculated value of d is next compared to the critical value of Durbin-Watson (D-W) tables showing d statistic for 1% and 5% significance points of d_L and d_U and k the number of independent variables in the regression. We cannot use (D-W) table if the number of observations is less than 15.

In the D-W table there are two columns for each value of k', i.e., d_L (the lower value of d) and d_U (upper value of d). If the calculated value of d is more than the critical value of d_U of the table, then there is no autocorrelation at 1% or 5% level of significance. When $d = 2$, there is no auto correlation. If the value of d lies between d_L and d_U the test is inconclusive. Again when $d < d_L$, autocorrelation exists.

To adjust the effect of autocorrelation we are to include time as an additional explanatory variable in the regression. Also by reestimating the regression coefficients for the change in the dependent/independent variables and dropping out the constant term it is possible to greatly reduce autocorrelation.

PROBLEM 3. (a) Estimate the regression equation of a firm's sales revenue (Y) on its quality control expenditure (Q) for the figures given in the following table.

TABLE 3.5 YEARLY EXPENDITURES ON QUALITY CONTROL AND SALES OF THE FIRM (in lakh of rupees)

Year (t)	1	2	3	4	5	6	7	8	9	10
Quality Control (Q)	2	4	3	2	4	5	6	6	7	8
Sales Revenue (Y)	42	40	44	45	50	52	54	55	58	60

(b) Plot a graph showing estimated regression line data points and the errors.

(c) Calculate the sales revenue of the firm when the firms expenditure on quality control is Rs. 3 lakhs per year and Rs. 8 lakhs per year. Is there any reason to think that the results are greatly biased?

SOLUTION.

TABLE 3.6 CALCULATIONS FOR ESTIMATING REGRESSION LINE OF SALES ON QUALITY CONTROL

Year	Y_t	Q_t	$(Y_t - \bar{Y})$	$(Q_t - \bar{Q})$	$(Q_t - \bar{Q})(Y_t - \bar{Y})$	$(Q_t - \bar{Q})^2$
1	42	2	−8	−3	24	9
2	40	4	−10	−1	10	1
3	44	3	−6	−2	12	4
4	45	2	−5	−3	15	9
5	50	4	0	−1	0	1
6	52	6	2	1	2	1
7	54	7	4	2	8	4
8	55	6	5	1	5	1
9	58	7	8	2	16	4
10	60	9	10	4	40	16
$n = 10$	$\Sigma Y_t = 500$ $\therefore\ \bar{Y} = 50$	$\Sigma Q_t = 50$ $\bar{Q} = 50$	$\Sigma(Y_t - \bar{Y}) = 0$	$\Sigma(Q_t - \bar{Q}) = 0$	$\Sigma(Q_t - \bar{Q})(Y_t - \bar{Y}) = 132$	$\Sigma(Q_t - \bar{Q})^2 = 50$

Table 3.6 shows the calculations to be made to arrive at an estimate of a and b.

$$\hat{b} = \frac{\sum_{t=1}^{n}(Q_t - \bar{Q})(Y_t - \bar{Y})}{\sum_{t=1}^{n}(Q_t - \bar{Q})^2} = \frac{132}{50} = \mathbf{2.64}.$$

Again $\hat{a} = \bar{Y} - \hat{b}\bar{Q} = 50 - 2.64 \times 5 = 36.8$.

Therefore the equation of the regression line is $\hat{Y}_t = 36.8 + 2.64Q_t$.

(b) With quality control expenditures of Rs. 2 lakhs in the first observation year, $Y_1 =$ Rs. $36.8 + 2.64(2) =$ Rs. 42.08 lakhs.

Again when $Q_{10} =$ Rs. 9 lakhs, $Y_{10} =$ Rs. $36.8 + 2.64(9) =$ Rs. 60.56 lakhs.

Now plotting (2, 42.08) and (9, 60.56) points and joining the points, we get the required regression line [Fig. 3.10.]

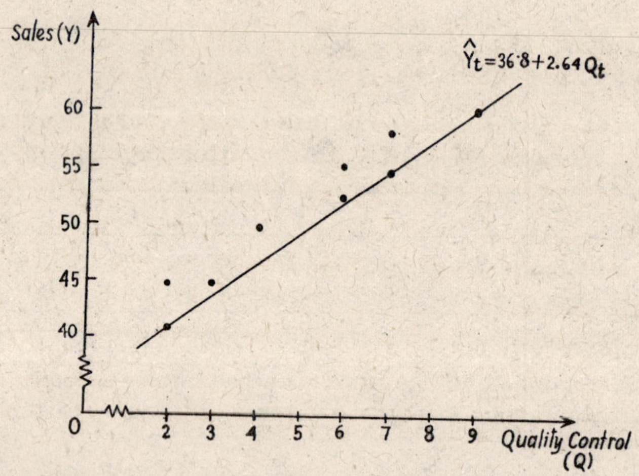

Fig 3.10 A Typical Regression Line

(c) If the firms expenditure on quality control is Rs. 3 lakhs, its estimated sales revenue will be $\hat{Y}_t = 36.8 + 2.64(3) =$ Rs. 44.72 lakhs.

Again when the firms expenditure on quality control is Rs. 8 lakhs, its estimated sales revenue will be $\hat{Y}_t = 36.8 + 2.64(8) =$ Rs. 57.92 lakhs.

The results are biased because, besides quality control expenditures, sales revenue is also influenced by advertising expenditures. Hence the regression line gives biased estimates of a and b parameters and makes a wrong forecast of the firm's sales revenue.

PROBLEM 4. From the following data on income and consumption of a country, fit a linear consumption function.

TABLE 3.7 INCOME-CONSUMPTION RELATION

Year	1988	1989	1990	1991	1992	1993	1994
Income (in billion Rs.)	290	295	300	320	290	300	330
Consumption (in billion Rs.)	240	260	265	270	260	275	280

If income grows at the rate of 5% per annum, what will be the consumption in the year 2000? [Take 1994 income as the base year income.]

Also given $\log 1.05 = 0.0212$, antilog $0.6360 = 4.325$.

SOLUTION. Suppose the linear consumption function is $c = a + by$.

Using the least squares method we can find out a and b.

Suppose the fitted line is $c = a + by$ [where a and b are estimates of a and b respectively]

Now for the second part of the equation we need to forecast income for the year 2000 (y_{2000}, say).

Then
$$y_{2000} = y_{1994}(1 + .05)^{30}, \quad \text{i.e.,} \quad \frac{y_{2000}}{y_{1994}} = (1.05)^{30}$$

$$\text{or} \quad \log\frac{y_{2000}}{y_{1994}} = 30 \log 1.05 = 30 \times 0.0212 = 0.636$$

$$\therefore \quad \frac{y_{2000}}{y_{1974}} = \text{antilog } 0.636 = 4.325$$

$$\therefore \quad y_{2000} = y_{1994} \times 4.325 = 330 \times 4.325 = \text{Rs. } 1427.25$$

Assuming the relationship $c = a + by$ to persist we now get the following result

$$c_{2000} = a + by_{2000} = a + b \times 1427.25. \tag{1}$$

We can calculate the consumption figure for the year 2000 by knowing a and b and putting these values in equation (1).

Note that a and b can be found out by using the method of least squares.

PROBLEM 5. Fit a least squares line for the following data using (a) X as the independent variable and (b) X as the dependent variable.

X	1	2	3	5	7	9	10	12
Y	1	3	4	5	5	7	8	10

SOLUTION. (a) Let the equation of the line is Y be $Y = a + bX$.

The normal equations are

$$\Sigma Y = an + b\Sigma X; \quad \Sigma XY = a\Sigma X + b\Sigma X^2.$$

The detailed calculations are shown in the following table.

TABLE 3.8 CALCULATION OF RELEVANT VALUES OF X AND Y

X	Y	X^2	XY	Y^2
1	1	1	1	1
2	3	4	6	9
3	4	9	12	16
5	5	25	25	25
7	5	49	35	25
9	7	81	63	49
10	8	100	80	64
12	10	144	120	100
$\Sigma X = 49$	$\Sigma Y = 43$	$\Sigma X^2 = 413$	$\Sigma XY = 342$	$\Sigma Y^2 = 289$

Since there are eight pairs of values of X and Y, i.e., $n = 8$ the normal equations can be written as

$$8a + b\ 49 = 43$$
$$49a + b\,413 = 342$$

Solving the above equations we get $b = 0.697$ and $a = 1.106$.

Therefore the least squares line wiil be $Y = 1.106 \pm 0.697X$.

An Alternative Method

We know

$$b = \frac{n\Sigma XY - \Sigma X\Sigma Y}{n\Sigma X^2 - (\Sigma X)^2} = \frac{8(342) - 49 \times 43}{8(413) - (49)^2} = \frac{2736 - 2107}{3304 - 2401} = \frac{629}{903} = 0.697.$$

and

$$a = \frac{\Sigma Y}{n} - b\frac{\Sigma X}{n} = \frac{43}{8} - 0.697 \times \frac{49}{8} = 5.375 - 4.269 = 1.106.$$

Thus the line of least square will be $Y = 1.106 + 0.697X$.

(b) If X and Y are considered as dependent variable and independent variable respectively the equation of the least squares line will be $X = a + bY$ and the normal equations are the following:

$$\Sigma X = an + b\Sigma Y$$
$$\Sigma XY = a\Sigma Y + b\Sigma Y^2,$$

Putting the values from the table we get

$$8a + 43b = 49 \qquad (1)$$
$$43a + 289b = 342 \qquad (2)$$

Solving the equations (1) and (2) we get $b = 1.359$ and $a = -1.180$.

Therefore the least squares line becomes $X = -1.180 + 1.359Y$.

An Alternative Method

We know

$$b = \frac{N\Sigma XY - (\Sigma X)(\Sigma Y)}{N\Sigma Y^2 - (\Sigma Y)^2} = \frac{8(342) - (49)(43)}{8(289) - (43)(43)} = 1.359$$

and $$a = \frac{\Sigma X}{n} - b\frac{\Sigma Y}{n} = \frac{49}{8} - 1.359 \times \frac{43}{8} = -1.180.$$

$\therefore$ the least squares line becomes $X = -1.180 + 1.3589Y$.

PROBLEM 6. (i) Show that the two least squares lines obtained in Example 5 intersect at $(\bar{X}, \bar{Y})$. (ii) Estimate the value of Y when $X = 10$. (iii) Also estimate the value of X when $Y = 4$.

SOLUTION. The equations of the two lines are the following

$$Y = 1.106 + 0.697X \qquad (1)$$
and $$X = -1.180 + 1.359Y \qquad (2)$$

Solving equations (1) and (2), we get $X = 6.1$ and $Y = 5.3$.

Again

$$\bar{X} = \frac{\Sigma X}{n} = \frac{49}{8} = 6.1; \quad \bar{Y} = \frac{\Sigma Y}{n} = \frac{43}{8} = 5.3.$$

$\therefore$ the lines intersect at (6.1 and 5.3), i.e., $(\bar{X}, \bar{Y})$.

(ii) When $X = 10$, $Y = 1.106 + 0.697 \times 10 = 8.076$.

(iii) When $Y = 4$, $X = -1.180 + 1.359 \times 4 = 4.256$.

PROBLEM 7. The following table shows the respective values of advertising (X) and sales (Y) of 10 observations (in Rs. lakhs)

TABLE 3.9 VALUES OF ADVERTISING AND SALES

Values of Advertising (X)	64	62	65	70	66	68	71	61	62	67
Values of Sales (Y)	66	65	68	64	62	63	69	60	62	68

(a) Find the least squares regression line of Y on X.

(b) Find the least squares regression line of X on Y.

Use the following regression lines

$$y = \left(\frac{\Sigma xy}{\Sigma x^2}\right) x \quad \text{and} \quad x = \left(\frac{\Sigma xy}{\Sigma y^2}\right) y$$

where $x = X - \bar{X}$ and $y = Y - \bar{Y}$.

SOLUTION. The detailed calculations are shown in the following table.

TABLE 3.10 CALCULATING X AND Y VALUES

X	Y	$x = X - \bar{x}$	$y = Y - \bar{y}$	x^2	xY	y^2
64	66	−1.6	1.3	2.56	−2.08	1.69
62	65	−3.6	0.3	12.96	−1.08	0.09
65	68	−0.6	3.3	0.36	−1.98	10.89
70	64	+4.4	−0.7	19.36	−3.08	0.49
66	62	+0.4	−2.7	0.16	−1.08	7.29
68	63	+2.4	−1.7	5.76	−4.08	2.89
71	69	+5.4	4.3	29.16	23.22	18.49
61	60	−4.6	−4.7	21.16	21.62	22.09
62	62	−3.6	−2.7	12.96	9.72	7.29
67	68	1.4	3.3	1.96	4.62	10.89
$\Sigma X = 656$ $\bar{X} = 65.6$	$\Sigma y = 647$ $\bar{Y} = 64.7$			$\Sigma x^2 = 106.4$	$\Sigma xy = 45.8$	$\Sigma y^2 = 82.1$

The regression line of Y on X is

$$y = \left(\frac{\Sigma xy}{\Sigma x^2}\right) x = \left(\frac{45.8}{106.4}\right) x = 0.431x, \quad \text{or} \quad Y - 64.7 = 0.431(X - 65.5).$$

Again the regression line of X on Y is

$$x = \left(\frac{\Sigma xy}{\Sigma y^2}\right) y = \left(\frac{45.8}{82.1}\right) y = 0.558y, \quad \text{or} \quad (X - 65.6) = 0.558(Y - 64.7).$$

PROBLEM 8. A pen manufacturing company has seen that the demand for pens depends mainly on the number of educated men. Table 3.11 gives information about the number of pens sold by the company in five cities in India for the year 1994 and the number of educated men staying in these cities.

TABLE 3.11 THE LEVEL OF EDUCATION AND SALES OF PENS

Cities	No. of Educated Men (in 1000)	Sales of Pens (in 100 units)
Delhi	40	25
Bombay	45	20
Calcutta	50	30
Madras	60	35
Bangalore	25	18

The company wants you to fit a linear regression of Y on X by the method of least squares. Estimate the sales for the year 1995 for the city Patna with 50,000 educated men assuming that the same relationship holds for the year 1995.

SOLUTION. The regression equation Y on X is $Y = a + bX$.

Cities	No. of Educated Men (in 1000) (X)	Sales of Pens (in 100) (Y)	(X^2)	(XY)
Delhi	40	25	1,600	1,000
Bombay	45	20	2,025	900
Calcutta	50	30	2,500	1,500
Madras	60	35	3,600	2,100
Bangalore	25	18	625	450
	$\Sigma X = 220$	$\Sigma Y = 128$	$\Sigma X^2 = 10,350$	$\Sigma XY = 5,950$

We know

$$b = \frac{n\Sigma XY - \Sigma X \Sigma Y}{n\Sigma X^2 - (\Sigma X)^2} = \frac{5(5,950) - (220)(128)}{5(10,350) - (220)(220)} = \frac{29,750 - 28,160}{51,750 - 48,400} = \frac{1,590}{3,350} = 0.475$$

and

$$a = \frac{\Sigma Y}{n} - b\frac{\Sigma X}{n} = \frac{128}{5} - 0.475 \times \frac{220}{5} = 25.6 - 20.9 = 4.7.$$

Hence the regression equation becomes $Y = 4.7 + 0.475X$.

Now sales of pens (in numbers) for Patna with 50,000 educated men will be

$$Y = 4.7 + 0.475(50) = 4.7 + 23.75 = 28.45, \text{ i.e., } 2,845.$$

Summary

The data used in demand estimation can be obtained from expert opinion, survey and market experiments. Market experiments have an advantage over surveys because they provide information on actual consumer behaviour. Their limitations include the risk of losing customers, high cost, problems of making consumers aware of changes, and inability to control all factors.

Econometric methods are useful because they provide insights into the relationships between (among) variables. The first step in developing an econometric forecast is to formulate a model based on economic theory. If important variables are omitted from the model, the results may be inaccurate or misleading. In particular, an identification problem may occur if the demand function is not carefully specified.

Econometric techniques may be applied to either time-series or cross-section data. If the equation whose parameters are to be estimated is linear, the coefficients represent the change in the dependent variable resulting from a 1-unit change in the associated independent variables. The coefficients of a multiplicative equation are interpreted as elasticities.

Concepts for Review

1. Identification Problem
2. Auto-correlation
3. Multicollinearity
4. Heterosdasticity
5. Consumer Surveys
6. Observational Research
7. Market Studies
8. Consumer Clinics.

Exercises

1. The management of Milk Food decides to test market a new ice-cream. As the person in charge of the market experiment, what consideration should affect your decisions with respect to:

(a) the number and locations of cities in which the new ice-cream would be test marketed

(b) the duration of the experiment, and

(c) pricing of the product?

2. The following table gives information about price (P) in rupees and quantity sold (Q) in thousand units by 8 firms selected at random from a group of firms.

TABLE 3.12 PRICES AND SALES FIGURES OF EIGHT FIRMS

Price (P)	72	90	72	75	65	82	66	77
Quantity Sold (Y)	75	85	68	69	70	74	68	58

(a) Plot the information graphically.

(b) Find a least squares line fitting the data, considering P as the independent variable.

(c) Find a least squares line fitting the data, considering as the independent variable.

(d) If a firm sets a price of 70, what is his expected sales figure?

(e) If a firm sets a price of 80, what is his expected sales figure?

3. Consider a group of restaurants specialising in fresh lobster dinners. The business has collected data on pricess and the average number of meals served per day for a random sample of 10 restaurants in the group. The data are shown in the following table. Estimate the coefficients of the demand function $Qd = a + bP$ using regression analysis and write the estimated demand equation.

TABLE 3.13 THE DEMAND SCHEDULE FOR MEALS

City	1	2	3	4	5	6	7	8	9	10
Meals per day (Q)	100	80	85	115	125	90	110	100	88	95
Price (P)($Rs.$)	12	15	16	10	9	11	13	13	13	14

4. Describe the used methods of estimating the parameters of a demand equation.

5. Explain the multiplicative model of the demand function.

6. Given the following data on quantities exchnaged and prices, fit a linear demand curve. Interpret the parameters.

Price:	16	10	8	9	5	4	3
Quantity:	70	85	100	115	120	124	130

7. Estimate the parameters of a linear demand curve from the following data. What is the nature of average propensity to consume for the given consumption function?

Consumption demand (000 Rs.)	60	70	75	80	85
Income (000 Rs.)	70	85	94	95	100
Year	1965	1967	1970	1971	1973

8. Hindustan Motors' estimated monthly demand (Q) for its vehicles is given by the equation

$$\log Q = \underset{(1.20)}{1.00} - \underset{(-2.50)}{1.50 \log P} + \underset{(0.02)}{3.00 \log I} \quad R^2 = 0.21$$

where P is price and I is income per capita in thousands. The t-statistic is shown in parentheses and natural logarithms are used to transform the equation.

(a) Rewrite the expression as a multiplicative demand equation.

(b) Based on the equation, is the product an inferior good, a necessity, or a luxury good? How much confidence do you have in your answer?

PROBLEM 9. The quarterly sales of Cycle Corporation of India are as follows:

Period	Sales	Period	Sales
1993: I	100	1994: I	130
1993: II	110	1194: II	135
1993: III	115	1994: III	145
1993: IV	125	1994: IV	150

(a) Plot the sales data and graphically fit a straight line to the points.

(b) Use the data to estimate the coefficients of the equation $S_t = S_\circ + bt$ where S_t are sales in the tth quarter.

(c) Use the same sales data to estimate the coefficients of the equation $S_t = S_\circ(1+g)^t$.

PROBLEM 10. Annual prices and meat consumption per capita in six cities are as follows.

City	Price per kg. (Rs.)	Consumption per capita (kg.)
1	70	55
2	65	60
3	75	50
4	60	70
5	85	45
6	80	48

(a) If a demand equation is to be estimated using these data, would be linear form (i.e., $Q = b + aP$), or the multiplicative form (i.e., $Q = bPa$) to be more appropriate? Explain.

(b) Could the resulting equation be properly interpreted as a demand relation? Explain.

Appendix

THE CASES OF STATISTICAL DEMAND CURVES

The director of marketing research of a firm producing personal computers wants to estimate the market demand curve for such computers. In other words, he wants to estimate the relationship between the price of a personal computer and the quantity of such computers demanded per year in the United States. Based on existing studies, he knows that the demand curve for personal computers has shifted to the right in recent years. That is, when price is held constant, the quantity of such computers demanded in the United States has increased. In addition, he knows that the price of personal computers has fallen in recent years because the cost of producing them has fallen. To estimate the demand curve, he obtains data on the price and quantity of personal computers sold in each of the last 10 years. He calculates the regression of quantity sold on price. When he presents the results to the firms board of directors, one board member says that the resulting regression equation is not a demand curve at all. Is the board member correct? If so what mistake did the marketing research director make?

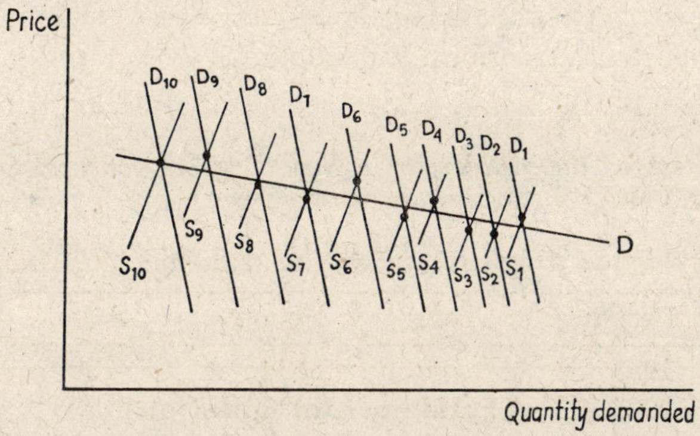

Fig A-1 Another Identification Problem

SOLUTION. The board member is correct. Suppose that in Fig. A-1 the 1994 demand curve was D_1 that the 1993 demand curve was D_2 and so on. And suppose that the supply curve for such computers was S_1 in 1994, S_2 in 1993 and so on. Then the actual combination of price and quantity in each year is shown by each dot in the graph below (if the market is in equilibrium). As we can see, the regression line (shown by DD) is a hybrid that resembles none of the true demand curves. Sophisticated econometric techniques have been developed to deal with this so-called identification problem. But for present purposes, the moral is that a regression equation of this sort is likely to be a poor estimate of a products demand curve.[1]

1 For further discussion of this point, see E. Working, What Do Statistical Demand Curves Show?, in Mansfield *Statistics for Business and Economics: Readings and Cases.*

CHAPTER 4

FORECASTING

The only relevant test of the validity of a hypothesis is comparison of its predictions with experience. Milton Friedman, 1953

I think the greatest error in forecasting is not realizing how important are the probabilities of events other than those everyone is agreeing upon. Paul A. Samuelson, 1974

Fundamental Questions

1. Under what circumstances might the customers understate their true demand for the product? When might they overstate their true demand?
2. What conclusion might the manager draw from the inability of the experts to agree on a projection?
3. What is trend projection?
4. How is input-output analysis useful in forecasting sales in a rapidly changing industry such as electronics?

PREVIEW

The most important business decisions involve some degree of uncertainty. In a vast majority of cases managers do not know exactly what the outcomes of their choices will be. One approach to reducing uncertaintly associated with decision making is to devote resources for demand estimating and forecasting. Forecasting involves predicting future economic conditions and assessing their effect on the operations of the firm.

The basic objective of forecasting is to predict demand. In some cases managers are interested in the total demand for a product. For example, the decision by a firm producing and selling office products to manufacture home computers may be determined by estimates of industry sales growth. In different situations the projection may focus on the firm's probable market share. If a forecast suggests that the sales growth by existing firms will make successful entry unlikely, the company may decide to look for other areas of expansion.

Forecasts may also serve various other purposes. For example, forecasts can provide information on the proper product mix. For an automobile manufacturer such as Hindusthan Motors, managers must determine the optimum number of Ambassador and Contessa classic cars to be produced. In the short run this decision is largely constrained by the firm's existing production facilities for manufacturing each type of car. However, depending on the pattern of demand for different types of cars, managers can build new or modify existing production facilities. But such choices have to be made long before the vehicles are produced and become ready for sale. Accurate demand forecasts can reduce the uncertainty associated with this long gestation period (or lead time). For example, if the price of petrol is expected to rise, the relative demand for fuel-efficient cars is also likely to rise. Conversely, a projection of stable or falling petrol prices might stimulate demand for larger cars.

Forecasting is no doubt a very important management activity. Major decisions in medium and large business enterprises almost always are based on forecasts of same type. In some cases, the forecast may be little more than an intuitive assessment of the future by those involved in the decision. In other circumstances, the forecast may have required thousands of work hours and lakhs of rupees. It may have been generated by the firms own economists, provided by consultants specialising in forecasting, or be based on information provided by governments at different levels.

Forecasting is a statistical technique that has wide applicability in business activities. Forecasting involves making judgement about future events based on an analysis of past events and factors that might affect those events in the future.

The role of forecasting in business is simple. Accurate forecasts of future events can assist managers in making better decisions in the present. For example, forecasting is important for marketing, production, financial and other matters.

The simplest method to forecast is to extrapolate into the future any past data or data based on information from the past. Fitting a trend line is one method to do this and is perhaps the most common quantitative method used by companies. More sophisticated empirical techniques are available and involve what is known as time series analysis. Basically, time series analysis attempts to decompose historical data or the event to be forecast into secular, seasonal, cyclical and irregular components. Once these components are known and assuming that the economic environment in the future is similar to what it has been in the past, accurate projections can be made.

METHODOLOGY

Many economic forecasting techniques are available. Some are basically qualitative and others are quantitative. The most appropriate one for a specific task depends on the following factors.

(i) The cost of preparation of the forecast and the benefit resulting from its use.

(ii) The lead time required before making decisions.

(iii) The time period of the forecast (short-term, or long-term).

(iv) The degree of accuracy required.

(v) The quality and availability of data.

(vi) The degree of complexity of the relationships to be forecasted.

Some techniques are suitable for long-term projections, others need more lead time and are more useful for forecasting into the distant future. The most modern techniques are very expensive.

For selecting the best technique one should consider the benefits of greater accuracy versus the extra cost of achieving this accuracy. In this chapter we will discuss the following forecasting techniques.

(i) Time series decomposition and analysis.

(ii) Forecasts based on smoothing techniques like moving averages.

(iii) Barometric forecasts on the basis of leading indicators.

(iv) Forecasts on the basis of econometric models.

(v) Input-output analysis.

TIME SERIES ANALYSIS

A time series is a set of observations normally taken at equal intervals. Time series data depend on time. Analysis of time series is of special importance to business people, economists and others. It helps us to study the past behaviour of a key variable like demand or sale which helps us to forecast its future variations. Variations in the time series data occur due to such factors as increase in population, consumer tastes and preferences, weather conditions, etc. The purpose of time series analysis is to identify these diverse factors.

A typical time series has the following four components: (i) Secular trend or Trend (T); (ii) Seasonal variation (S); (iii) Cyclical variations or fluctuations (C); (iv) Irregular or random fluctuations (I).

By trend we mean long-term increase, or decrease in a variable. For example, a time series of human population in India exhibits an upward trend, whereas the trend of rare species like Royal Bengal Tiger is downward. The seasonal component represents variations which occur at regular intervals. For example, the demand for electric fans increases in summer and declines in winter. Analysis of time series may locate cyclical patterns, i.e., variables which have high values for certain periods are followed by low values as shown by business cycle movements. Finally, when the variation of a variable does not follow a regular pattern it is called random fluctuations, e.g., changes due to earthquake, flood, war, etc. There are various methods for determining trends, seasonability and cyclical patterns in time series data. But when the random component of a time series is maximum, the forecasts become less accurate.

The variations in the time series data are the result of the joint effect of the above four components. In time series analysis any particular observation is considered to be the product of the effects of these four components. This may be expressed as $Q = T \times S \times C \times I$ where Q may be the quantity of sales (or any other variable to be forecast). It is the result of four components. This model is called the multiplicative model. Some statisticians use the alternative model, viz., the additive model which is expressed as $Q = T + S + C + I$ where Q is the sum of the four components.

Measurement of Trend

There are four methods of finding the trend in a time series: (i) The Graphic, or the Freehand Method; (ii) The Semi-average Method; (iii) The Moving-average Method and (iv) The Method of Least Squares.

The Graphic Method

Table 4.1 is the time-series data of a firm's quarterly sales for the last three years.

TABLE 4.1 TIME-SERIES DATA ON SALES

Period No.	Quarter	Sales (Rs.)
1	1991—I	310
2	1991—II	315
3	1991—III	325
4	1991—IV	350
5	1992—I	356
6	1992—II	362
7	1992—III	374
8	1992—IV	400
9	1993—I	407
10	1993—II	414
11	1993—III	430
12	1993—IV	455

In this method the given data are plotted on a graph paper showing the time-series data (y_t) along y-axis and time (t) on the x-axis. Then a straight line is drawn through these points in such a way as to reflect the trend of the data as perfectly as possible. See Fig. 4.1.

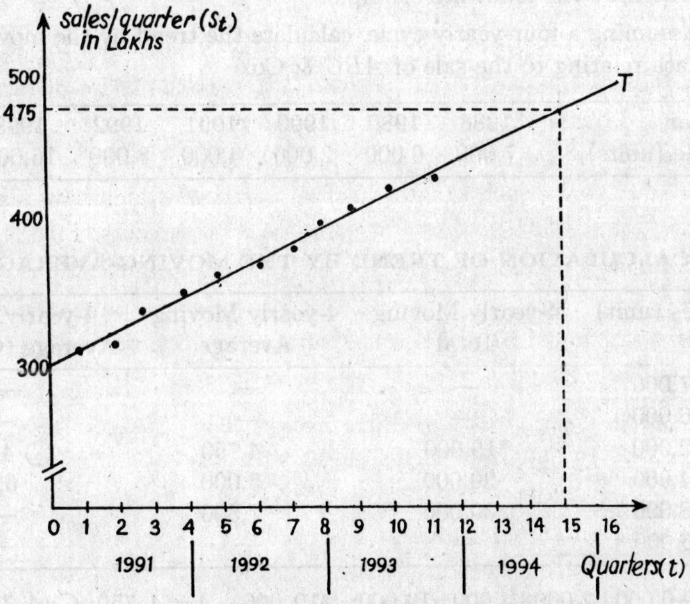

Fig 4.1 Curve Fitting from Time-Series Data

The upward slope of the line T indicates increase in sales over time. By calculating the slope of this trend line, we can find the average rate of increase per quarter which can be used to forecast future sales. Again by extending the line beyond IV quarter of 1993 the sales corresponding to periods 13, 14, 15, etc. can be obtained directly from Fig. 4.1. If sales for 1994, quarter III is to be projected, the data are extrapolated as shown in Fig. 4.1 and the projected sales can be obtained from the graph, e.g., Rs. 475 lakhs.

The graphic method has certain limitations. The accuracy of the forecast by this method depends on the analyst's ability to fit a curve to the given data.

The Semi-average Method

By using this method the given data are divided into two equal parts and average for each part is determined. In the next step, these two averages are plotted on a graph paper against the mid-points of time intervals of the two related parts. These two points are then connected by a straight line which is the trend line and the distances of the line from the x-axis give the trend values. However, this method gives very poor results.

The Moving-Average Method

Under this method for given numbers $Y_1, Y_2, Y_3, Y_4 \cdots$ we can define moving totals of order N as

$$Y_1 + Y_2 + \cdots Y_N, \quad Y_2 + Y_3 + \cdots + Y_{N+1}, \quad Y_3 + Y_4 + \cdots + Y_{N+2}, \cdots$$

$\therefore$ the moving averages of order N are expressed as

$$\frac{Y_1 + Y_2 + \cdots + Y_N}{N}, \quad \frac{Y_2 + Y_3 + \cdots + Y_N + 1}{N} \cdots$$

The method is illustrated by the following example.

PROBLEM 1. Assuming a four-yearly cycle, calculate the trend by the moving average method from the following data relating to the sale of *ABC* & Co.

Year	:	1988	1989	1990	1991	1992	1993
Sale (units)	:	7,000	6,000	2,000	4,000	8,000	16,000

SOLUTION

TABLE 4.2 CALCULATION OF TREND BY THE MOVING-AVERAGE METHOD

Year	Sales (unit)	4-yearly Moving Total	4-yearly Moving Average	4-yearly Moving Average (Centered)
1988	7,000	—	—	—
1989	6,000	—	—	—
1990	2,000	*19,000	√ 4,750	⊙ 4,875
1991	4,000	20,000	5,000	6,250
1992	8,000	30,000	7,500	—
1993	16,000	—	—	—

[NOTE: *7,000+6,000+2,000+4,000=19,000; $\surd 19,000 \div 4 = 4,750$; $\odot(4,750 + 5,000) \div 2$ and so on.]

This method is used to measure trend. It eliminates cyclical, seasonal and irregular fluctuations. When moving averages are badly affected by the extreme values, a weighted moving average with suitable weights is often used. An example of weighted moving average is given below.

PROBLEM 2. Find the trend for the following series using a three-year weighted moving average with weights 1, 2, 1.

Year	:	1	2	3	4	5	6	7
Values	:	2	4	5	7	8	10	13

SOLUTION.

TABLE 4.3 COMPUTATIONS OF 3-YEARLY WEIGHTED MOVING AVERAGE

Year	Values	3-yearly Weighted Moving Total	3-yearly Weighted Moving Average
(1)	(2)	(3)	(4) = (3) ÷ Total Weight, *i.e.*, $(1+2+1)=4$
1	2	—	—
2	4	$2\times1+4\times2+5\times1\quad=15$	3.75
3	5	$4\times1+5\times2+7\times1\quad=21$	5.25
4	7	$5\times1+7\times2+8\times1\quad=27$	6.75
5	8	$7\times1+8\times2+10\times1\;=33$	8.25
6	10	$8\times1+10\times2+13\times1=41$	10.25
7	13	—	

The Method of Least Squares

By this method we can also find the trend. Let us take an example.

PROBLEM 3. Fit a straight line trend by least squares method from the following data and find the trend values. Also forecast the sales value for 1995.

Year:	1990	1991	1992	1993	1994
Sales (in 1000 units):	7	6	2	9	8

SOLUTION.

TABLE 4.4 FITTING A STRAIGHT LINE TREND

Year	Sales (in 1000 units)	Deviation of Year from 1992		
	(Y)	(X)	X^2	XY
1990	7	−2	4	−14
1991	6	−1	1	−6
1992	2	0	0	0
1993	9	1	1	9
1994	8	2	4	16
$n=5$	$\Sigma Y=27$	$\Sigma X=0$	$\Sigma X^2=10$	$\Sigma XY+5$

Let the equation of the line of trend be $Y=a+bX$ where $a=\frac{\Sigma Y}{n}$, $b=\frac{\Sigma XY}{\Sigma X^2}$ and $n=$ number of years under consideration.

[**N.B.** The above expressions are obtained by solving the following normal equations:

$$\Sigma Y = na + b\Sigma X$$

$$\text{and}\quad \Sigma XY = a\Sigma X + b\Sigma X^2]$$

where $\Sigma X = 0$ (mid-point in time taken as the origin)

Here

$$a = \frac{27}{5} = 5.4, \quad b = \frac{5}{10} = 0.5.$$

$\therefore$ the equation for the straight line is $Y = 5.4 + 0.5X$.

TREND VALUES

For 1990	$X = -2,$	$Y = 5.4 + 0.5X - 2$	$= 4.4$
For 1991	$X = -1,$	$Y = 5.4 + 0.5X - 1$	$= 4.9$
For 1992	$X = 0,$	$Y = 5.4 + 0.5X0$	$= 5.4$
For 1993	$X = 1,$	$Y = 5.4 + 0.5X1$	$= 5.9$
For 1994	$X = 2,$	$Y = 5.4 + 0.5X2$	$= 6.4$

So the expected value for 1995, when $X = 3$ is $Y = 5.4 + 0.5X3 = 6.9$. Other trend values can be obtained by adding the values of b to each preceding trend value.

Non-Linear Trend

Second Degree Parabolic Trends

The simplest form of polynomial equation for describing non-linear trend is a parabola with highest power of X variable as 2. Such an equation is presented below

$$Y = a + bX + cX^2$$

where Y = the computed trend value of a given time

X = the assigned number of the given time, e.g., a year

a, b and c are the three unknown constants. The values of a, b and c are obtained by solving the following normal equations

$$\Sigma Y = Na + b\Sigma X + c\Sigma X^2$$

$$\Sigma XY = a\Sigma X + b\Sigma X^2 + c\Sigma X^3$$

$$\Sigma X^2Y = a\Sigma X^2 + b\Sigma X^3 + c\Sigma X^4$$

and where $\Sigma X = 0$ and $\Sigma X^3 = 0$. (Mid-points in time-taken as origin).

The values of a, b and c are

$$a = \frac{\Sigma(Y) - c\Sigma(X^2)}{n}, \quad b = \frac{\Sigma(XY)}{\Sigma(X^2)} \text{ and } c = \frac{n\Sigma(X^2Y) - \Sigma(X^2)\Sigma(Y)}{n\Sigma(X^4) - (\Sigma X^2)^2}.$$

We may now consider the following example.

PROBLEM 4. Using the following sales data for years 1988 to 1994 (7 years) find: (a) the second degree polynomial equation by the least-squares method and (b) trend values for 7 years. (c) Also forecast the sales value for 1995.

Year:	1988	1989	1990	1991	1992	1993	1994
Sales (in Rs. 1000):	8	14	12	13	16	18	22

SOLUTION

TABLE 4.5 CALCULATION OF TREND VALUES OF SALES

Year Original Number	X (unit is 1 year)	Actual Sales (in Rs. 1000) (Y)	XY	X^2	X^2Y	X^4	Trend Sales (in Rs. 1000)
1988	−3	8	−24	9	72	81	9.8
1989	−2	14	−28	4	56	16	10.9
1990	−1	12	−12	1	12	1	
1991	0	13	0	0	0	0	and so on
1992	1	16	16	1	16	1	
1993	2	18	36	4	72	16	
1994	3	22	66	9	198	81	
Total	$\Sigma X = 0$	103	54	28	426	196	

Now

$$c = \frac{7 \times 426 - 28 \times 103}{7 \times 196 - 28 \times 28} = 0.1667 \quad (\text{Here } n = 7)$$

$$a = \frac{103 - 0.1667 \times 28}{7} = 14.05; \text{ and } b = \frac{54}{28} = 1.93$$

(a) The required second degree equation will be $Y = 14.05 + 1.93X + 0.1667X^2$.

(b) The trend values can be obtained as follows:

When $X = 1988 - 1991 = -3$,

$$Y = 14.05 + 1.93 \times (-3) + 0.1667(-3)^2 = 9.8$$

When $X = 1989 - 1991 = -2$,

$$Y = 14.05 + 1.93 \times (-2) + 0.1667(-2)^2 = 10.9 \text{ and so on.}$$

(c) The forecast for 1995 will be as follows:

For $X = 1995 - 1991 = 4$,

$$Y = 14.05 + 1.93 \times 4 + 0.1667 \times 16 = 24.44 \text{ (in Rs. 1000).}$$

Exponential Trend

It is a straight line on a semi-log chart and a curve on an arithmetic chart. The exponential equation used for secular trend is $Y_c = ab^X$, or $\log Y_c = \log a + X \log b$.

If $\Sigma X = 0$, then by applying the method of least squares, we get

$$\log a = \frac{\Sigma \log Y}{n} \quad \text{and} \quad \log b = \frac{\Sigma X \log Y}{\Sigma X^2}$$

where $\log a$ = the mean of the logarithm of Y-values and $\log b$ = the slope of the straight line on a semi-log chart.

The exponential curve is also used to measure the trend. Let us illustrate the method with the aid of the following numerical example.

PROBLEM 4. From the following sales information for years 1984 to 1990, calculate the trend values for the year 1984 and other years. Plot the trend values in (a) semilog chart; and (b) arithmetic chart.

Year:	1984	1985	1986	1987	1988	1989	1990
Sales: (in Rupees 1000)	10	16	13	15	17	14	22

SOLUTION.

TABLE 4.6 CALCULATION OF LOGARITHMIC STRAIGHT LINE (EXPONENTIAL) TREND EQUATION BY THE LEAST-SQUARES METHOD

Year		Sales					
Original Number	X (unit is 1 year)	(in Rs. 1000)					
	(X)	(Y)	$\log Y$	$X \log Y$	X^2	$\log Y_c$	Y_c
1984	−3	10	1.00000	−3.00000	9	1.06318	11.6
1985	−2	16	1.20412	−2.40824	4	1.09989	12.6
1986	−1	13	1.11394	−1.11394	1	1.13660	13.7
1987	0	15	1.17609	0	0	1.17331	14.7
1988	1	17	1.23045	1.23045	1	1.21002	16.2
1989	2	14	1.14613	2.29226	4	1.24673	17.7
1990	3	22	1.34242	4.02726	9	1.28344	19.2
	$\Sigma X = 0$	107	8.21315	1.02779	28	8.21317	105.7

Now

$$\log a = \frac{\Sigma \log Y}{n} = \frac{8.21315}{7} = 1.17331 \text{ and } \log b = \frac{\Sigma X \log Y}{\Sigma X^2} = \frac{1.02779}{28} = .0.03671.$$

The logarithmic equation of the straight line trend is $\log Y_c = 1.17331 + 0.03671X$.

The trend values can be computed from the equation as follows:

Here year (1984-1987)=−3, $\log Y_c = 1.17331 + 0.03671(-3) = 1.06318$

Now antilog (1.06318) = 11.556 ≈ 11.6 = Y_c

Similarly year (1985-1987)=−2,

$$\log Y_c = 1.17331 + 0.03671(-2) = 1.09989$$

$$\therefore \quad Y_c = \text{antilog } (1.09989) = 12.6 \text{ and so on.}$$

Now $\log Y_c$ for each succeeding year after 1984 may also be obtained by adding 0.0367 (i.e., $\log b$) to 1.06318 ($\log Y_c$ for 1984) as follows.

1985	$Y_c = 1.06318 + 0.03671 = 1.09989$	$\therefore \; Y_c = 12.6$
1986	$Y_c = 1.09989 + 0.03671 = 1.13660$	$\therefore \; Y_c = 13.7$
1987	$Y_c = 1.13660 + 0.03671 = 1.17331$	$\therefore \; Y_c = 14.7$
		and so on.

*Antilog 1.09989 = Y_c = 12.6 and so on.

If the values of column (8) of Table 4.6 are plotted on a semilog chart, the result is a straight line but when they are plotted on an arithmetic chart, one gets a non-linear curve.

Now $\log a = 1.17331 \therefore a = 14.904 \approx 14.9$; $\log b = 0.03671 \therefore b = 1.0882 \approx 1.09$.

The exponential equation is $Y_c = 14.9(1.09)^X$ which may be expressed as $Y_c = 14.9(1+0.09)^X$.

Hence the rate of increase for each year is 0.09 or 9%.

If $b = 0.6$, then the rate of decrease =1 – 0.6 = 0.4 or 40%.

THE GOMPERTZ OR S-CURVES

This curve is often used for business and population forecasting. The equation of Gompertz curve is $Y_c = ab^{c^x}, b < 1$

where c is a constant, or, $\log Y_c = \log a + c^X \log b$.

The values of unknowns $\log a, \log b$ and c are computed by using the three subgroup sums of the logarithms of the Y-values in a series and not by the least-squares method. The Gompertz curve is normally fitted by the method of partial totals. The observations are divided into three equal parts covering, say, m years.

If

$$S_1 = \sum_{i=1}^{m} \log Y_i,\quad S_2 = \sum_{i=m+1}^{2m} \log Y_i \text{ and } S_3 = \sum_{i=2m+1}^{3m} \log Y_i$$

then

$$\log a = \frac{1}{m} \times \frac{S_1S_3 - S_2^2}{S_1 - 2S_2 + S_3},\quad \log b = \frac{(S_2 - S_1)(C-1)}{(C^m - 10)^2} \text{ and } c = \left(\frac{S_2 - S_3}{S_1 - S_2}\right)^{1/m}.$$

Let us now consider the following example.

PROBLEM 4. Fit a Gompertz curve to the following data by the method of partial totals.

Year	Production (in 1000 tons) (Y)	$\log Y$	Partial Totals
1985	312	2.49415	
1986	330	2.51851	$S_1 = 7.51781$
1987	320	2.50515	
1988	360	2.55630	
1989	370	2.56820	$S_2 = 7.72656$
1990	400	2.60206	
1990	420	2.62325	
1992	500	2.69897	$S_3 = 8.10037$
1993	600	2.77815	

Now

$$\log a = \frac{1}{m} \times \frac{S_1S_3 - S_2^2}{S_1 - 2S_2 + S_3} \quad \text{(Here } m = 3\text{)}$$

$$= \frac{1}{3} \times \frac{7.51781 \times 8.10037 - (7.72656)^2}{7.51781 - 2 \times 7.72656 + 8.10037} = 2.41794$$

$$\log b = \frac{(S_2 - S_1)(C-1)}{(C^3-1)^2} = \frac{(7.72656 - 7.51781)(1.2145-1)}{(1.79071-1)^2} = 0.07162$$

$$c^3 = \frac{S_2 - S_3}{S_1 - S_2} = \frac{7.72656 - 8.10037}{7.51781 - 7.72656} = 1.79071$$

$$\therefore \quad c = 1.2145.$$

Thus the equation of the Gompertz curve becomes $\log Y_c = 2.41794 + (1.2145)^X \times 0.07162$. The trend value of 1985 (with origin $X = 0$) can be computed as follows:

$$\log Y_c = 2.41794 + (1.2145) \times 0.07162 = 2.48956$$

$$\therefore \quad Y_c = \text{Antilog } 2.48956 = 308.74 \text{ ('000 tons)}.$$

Similarly, trend values for other years can be obtained.

MEASUREMENT OF SEASONAL VARIATION

For this we are to estimate how the time series data change from time to time throughout a year. A set of numbers exhibiting the relative values of a variable from time to time (e.g., month, week, etc.) of a year is called seasonal index of the variable. These indices measure seasonal fluctuations. To measure seasonal fluctuations we often use the following methods: **1.** The Method of Averages; **2.** The Moving Average Method; **3.** The Ratio to Trend Method and **4.** The Link Relative Method

The Method of Averages

This is the simplest method of calculating seasonal fluctuation and is used when trend and cyclical variations have the minimum effect on time series. Let us explain this method with an example.

PROBLEM 7. The tools borrowed (in hundreds) from a tool store on six working days for 4 weeks are given in the following table. Compute the seasonal (daily) index for the series.

TOOLS BORROWED (ON DIFFERENT DAYS)

Week	Mon.	Tues.	Wed.	Thu.	Fri.	Sat.
1	3.5	1.9	4.5	5.0	6.0	5.0
2	2.0	2.0	3.2	4.2	4.5	3.8
3	1.5	4.0	3.5	3.4	2.8	2.5
4	1.8	3.2	2.2	2.1	1.2	3.0

TABLE 4.7 SEASONAL DAILY INDEX CALCULATION

Days	Tools Borrowed in Hundred Weeks 1	2	3	4	Daily Total for 4 weeks	Daily Average for 4 weeks
Mon.	3.5	2.0	1.5	1.8	8.8	2.20
Tues.	1.9	2.0	4.0	3.2	11.1	2.78
Wed.	4.5	3.2	3.5	2.2	13.4	3.35
Thu.	5.0	4.2	3.4	2.1	14.7	3.68
Fri.	6.0	4.5	2.8	1.2	14.5	3.63
Sat.	5.0	3.8	2.5	3.0	14.3	3.58

$$\text{General average} = \frac{2.20 + 2.78 + 3.35 + 3.68 + 3.63 + 3.58}{6} = 3.203.$$

$$\text{Seasonal Index} = \frac{\text{Daily Average}}{\text{General Average}} \times 100 = S \text{ (say)}.$$

$$\therefore S_{\text{Mon.}} = \frac{2.20}{3.203} \times 100 = 68.70; \; S_{\text{Tues.}} = \frac{2.78}{3.203} \times 100 = 86.80.$$

Similarly $S_{\text{Wed.}} = 1.04.59$, $S_{\text{Thu.}} = 114.89$, $S_{\text{Fri.}} = 113.33$ and $S_{\text{Sat.}} = 111.77$.

The Moving Average Method

By using this method the 4-quarter centered moving averages are first calculated, when quarterly data are available, to get the trend. Then the effect of the trend is eliminated by using either the additive, or the multiplicative model.

Moving averages are subtracted from original data in the additive model to eliminate trend and to get the deviations from the trend. Next the seasonal variations are obtained by applying the method of averages to the deviations.

In the multiplicative model the original data are expressed as percentage of the corresponding moving averages. Next we take the average of such percentages for corresponding quarters (months, etc.), by using the method of averages, to get the seasonal indices. This is the essence of Ratio to Moving Average Method. Let us give a few examples to make the method clear.

PROBLEM 8. From the following table find how you would calculate seasonal fluctuations in a time series by using (a) the additive model and (b) the multiplicative model.

Year	Summer (S)	Monsoon(M)	Autumn (A)	Winter (W)
1990	40	71	61	125
1991	42	102	76	182
1992	35	142	95	2357
1993	55	158	115	210
1994	58	205	152	305

SOLUTION.

(a) **THE ADDITIVE MODEL**

(used to calculate short-term variations)

Year	Season	Values	Moving Total in Fours	Season's Moving Average	Moving Average (Centered)	Short term Variations
(1)	(2)	(3)	(4)	(5)	(6)	(7) = (3) − (6)
1990	*S*	40	—	—	—	—
	M	71	—	—	—	—
	A	61	297	74.25	74.5	−13.5
	W	125	299	74.75	78.6	+46.4
1991	*S*	42	330	82.50	84.4	−42.4
	M	102	345	86.25	93.4	+8.6
	A	76	402	100.50	99.6	−23.6
	W	182	395	98.75	103.8	+78.2

Contd.

Contd.

Year	Season	Values	Moving Total in Fours	Season's Moving Average	Moving Average (Centered)	Short term Variations
(1)	(2)	(3)	(4)	(5)	(6)	(7) = (3) − (6)
1992	*S*	35	435	108.75	111.1	−76.1
	M	142	454	113.50	120.1	+21.9
	A	95	507	126.75	129.3	−34.3
	W	235	527	131.75	133.8	+101.2
1993	*S*	55	543	135.75	138.3	−83.3
	M	158	563	140.75	137.6	+20.4
	A	115	538	134.50	134.9	−19.9
	W	210	541	135.25	141.1	+68.9
1994	*S*	58	588	147.00	151.6	−93.6
	M	205	625	156.25	168.1	+36.9
	A	152	720	180.00	—	—
	W	305	—	—	—	—

CALCULATION OF AVERAGE SEASONAL FLUCTUATIONS

Year	Summer	Monsoon	Autumn	Winter
1990	—	—	−13.5	+46.4
1991	−42.4	+8.6	−23.6	+78.2
1992	−76.1	+21.9	−34.3	+101.2
1993	−83.3	+20.4	−19.9	+68.9
1994	−93.6	+36.9	—	—
Total	−295.4	+87.8	−91.3	+294.7
Average	−73.85	+21.95	−22.83	+73.68

$$\text{Grand Average} = \frac{(-73.85) + 21.95 + (-22.83) + 73.68}{4} = -0.26.$$

The seasonal fluctuations are −73.85 − (−0.26), 21.95 − (−0.260, (−22.83) − (−0.26), and (73.68) − (−0.26), i.e., −73.59, 22.21, −22.57 and 73.94 for *S*, *M*, *A* and *W* respectively.

The sum of the seasonal fluctuations is zero.

(b) **THE MULTIPLICATIVE MODEL**

(used to calculate Moving Average and Ratio to Moving Average)

(1)	(2)	(3)	(4)	(5)
Year	Season	Average Value	Moving Average (Centered)	Ratio to Moving Average (Expressed as %)
1990	*S*	40	—	—
	M	71	—	—
	A	61	74.5	81.88
	W	125	78.6	159.03

Contd.

Contd.

(1) Year	(2) Season	(3) Average Value	(4) Moving Average (Centered)	(5) Ratio to Moving Average (Expressed as %)
1991	S	42	84.4	49.76
	M	102	93.4	109.20
	A	76	99.6	76.31
	W	182	103.8	175.34
1992	S	35	111.1	31.50
	M	142	120.1	118.24
	A	95	129.3	73.47
	W	235	133.8	175.64
1993	S	55	138.3	39.77
	M	158	137.6	114.83
	A	115	134.9	85.25
	W	210	141.1	148.83
1994	S	58	151.6	38.26
	M	205	168.1	121.95
	A	152	—	—
	W	305	—	—

Calculation of Seasonal Indices

Year	Summer	Monsoon	Autumn	Winter
1990	—	—	81.88	159.03
1991	49.76	109.20	76.31	175.34
1992	31.50	118.24	73.47	175.64
1993	39.77	114.83	85.25	148.83
1994	38.26	121.95	—	—
Total	159.29	464.22	316.91	658.84
Average	39.82	116.05	79.23	164.71

$$\text{Grand Average} = \frac{39.82 + 116.05 + 79.23 + 164.71}{4} = 99.95.$$

$$\therefore \quad \text{Seasonal Index} = \frac{\text{Average}}{\text{Grand Average}} \times 100.$$

$\therefore$ the seasonal indices for S, M, A and W are, respectively

$$\frac{39.82}{99.95} \times 100, \quad \frac{116.05}{99.95} \times 100, \quad \text{and} \quad \frac{79.23}{99.95} \times 100, \quad \frac{164.71}{99.95} \times 100$$

or, 39.84, 116.11, 79.27, and 164.79.

Here the sum of the seasonal indices is 400.

The Ratio to Trend Method

Here the trend values are first calculated by the method of least squares regression and then the multiplicative model is used. To develop this method we must analyse and break up the original data into their trend and seasonal components. Let us illustrate this method with an example.

PROBLEM 9. The following table shows the quarterly ridership volume (in thousands) for a city mass transit.

TABLE 4.8 RIDERSHIP VOLUME FOR A MASS TRANSIT

Quarter No. (X)	Ridership Volume (Y)	X^2	XY
1	3.2	1	3.2
2	7.5	4	15.0
3	5.6	9	16.8
4	10.2	16	40.8
5	9.8	25	49.0
6	15	36	90.0
7	11.2	49	78.4
8	16	64	128.0
9	15.3	81	137.1
10	20	100	200.0
11	17.8	121	195.8
12	22.0	144	264.0
13	21.2	169	275.6
14	25	196	350.0
$\Sigma X = 105$	$\Sigma Y = 199.8$	$\Sigma X^2 = 1015$	$\Sigma XY = 1844.3$

SOLUTION.

The trend is now found by the least-squares method. Let the regression equation used to forecast the trend be given by the following equation

$$T_c = a + bX$$

where T_c = the trend forecast value of ridership volume Y for period X.

a = the value of y-axis intercept

b = the value of the slope of the demand time

X = the number of time periods

The values of a and b are given the following two equations

$$a = \frac{(\Sigma Y \Sigma X^2) - (\Sigma X \Sigma XY)}{(n\Sigma X^2) - (\Sigma X)^2} \quad \text{and} \quad b = \frac{n\Sigma XY - (\Sigma X \Sigma Y)}{n\Sigma X^2 - (\Sigma X)^2}$$

where n is the number of data periods used in the regression.

Now

$$a = \frac{199.8 \times 1015 - 105 \times 1844.3}{14 \times 1015 - 105 \times 105} = 2.87 \text{ and } b = \frac{14 \times 1844.3 - 105 \times 199.8}{14 \times 1015 - 105 \times 105} = 1.52.$$

$\therefore$ the forecasting equation for the trend in ridership volume is $T_c = 2.87 + 1.52X$.

Now we calculate the four seasonals by the Ratio-to-Trend Method. For each available quarterly data we can measure the seasonality of that quarterly dividing the actual ridership volume by the calculated trend value for that quarter.

At first we calculate the quarterly seasonal factors as follows.

TABLE 4.9 CALCULATION OF QUARTERLY SEASONAL FACTORS

X	Quarter	Y	T	Y/T
1	1	3.2	4.39	0.73
2	2	7.5	*5.91	1.27
3	3	5.6	*7.43	0.75
4	4	10.2	8.95	1.14
5	1	9.8	10.47	0.94
6	2	15	11.99	1.25
7	3	11.2	13.51	0.83
8	4	16	15.03	1.06
9	1	15.3	16.55	0.92
10	2	20	18.07	1.11
11	3	17.8	19.59	0.91
12	4	22	21.11	1.04
13	1	21.2	22.63	0.94
14	2	25	24.15	1.04

$*T_2 = 2.87 + 1.52 \times 2 = 5.91; T_3 = 2.87 + 1.52 \times 3 = 7.43$ and so on.

Next we calculate the seasonal component (S) for quarters 1 to 4 as follows.

QUARTER NUMBERS

Year	1	2	3	4
1	0.73	1.27	0.75	1.14
2	0.94	1.25	0.83	1.06
3	0.92	1.11	0.91	1.04
4	0.94	1.04	–	–
Total	3.53	4.67	2.49	3.24
Average (S)	$S_1 = 0.88$	$S_2 = 1.17$	$S_3 = 0.83$	$S_4 = 1.08$

Now forecasts for the last quarter of the 4th year, i.e., quarter 16 and 1st quarter of the 5th year, i.e., quarter 17 are made as follows.

First trend values in thousands are calculated:

$T_{16} = 2.87 + 1.52 \times 16 = 27.19$; $T_{17} = 2.87 + 1.52 \times 17 = 28.71$.

Next we find the forecast by multiplying the trend values by suitable seasonal factors.

$F_{16} = 27,190 \times 1.08 = 29,365$ and $F_{17} = 28710 \times 0.88 = 25,265$.

Fig. 4.2 shows the quarterly ridership volume and trend line for the mass transit.

The Link Relative Method

Under this method the data of each quarter are expressed as percentages of data for the preceding quarter. Such percentages are called link relatives. From these average link relatives and chain relatives (with respect to the 1st quarter whose chain relative is taken as 100) are calculated.

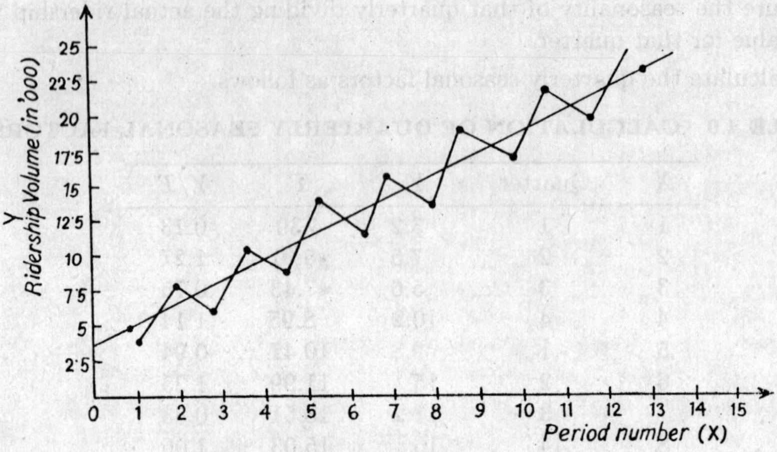

Fig 4.2 A Trend Line for Mass Transit

If $Q_1, Q_2, Q_3, Q_4, C.R.$, and $L.R.$ represent the 1st, 2nd, 3rd, 4th quarters, chain relative, and link relative respectively then

$$C.R._{Q_2} = (\text{Average } L.R._{Q_2} \times C.R._{Q_1}) \div 100$$

$$C.R._{Q_3} = (\text{Average } L.R._{Q_3} \times C.R._{Q_2}) \div 100 \text{ and so on}$$

$$\text{and 2nd } \quad C.R. \text{ for } Q_1 = (\text{Average } L.R_{Q_1} \times C.R._{Q_4}) \div 100$$

The 2nd $C.R.$ for Q_1 may be either more or less than the 1st $C.R.$ 100 for Q_1 depending on increasing or decreasing trend. We can adjust $C.R.$ for this trend.

If d = 2nd $C.R.$ for $Q_1 - 100$, then we deduct $\frac{1}{4}d$, $\frac{3}{4}d$, $\frac{3}{4}d$ and d from $C.R._{Q_2}, C.R._{Q_3}, C.R._{Q_4}$ and the 2nd $C.R._{Q_1}$, respectively to get the adjusted $C.R.$s. The seasonal indices are obtained when these adjusted $C.R.$s are expressed as percentages of their respective $A.M$s.

Now consider the following example.

PROBLEM 10. Find seasonal indices by the method of link relatives from the following data.

Year	Quarterly Output (000 tons) of Coal for 4 Years			
	I	II	III	IV
1991	60	55	50	60
1992	65	60	65	70
1993	70	55	50	45
1994	55	50	55	65

SOLUTION.

TABLE 4.10 CALCULATION OF AVERAGE LINK RELATIVES

Quarter	Link Relatives			
Year	Q_1	Q_2	Q_3	Q_4
1991	—	91.67	90.91	120.00
1992	108.33	92.31	108.33	107.69
1993	100.00	78.57	90.91	90.00
1994	122.22	90.91	110.00	118.18
Total	330.55	353.46	400.15	435.87
Average	110.18	88.37	100.04	108.97

Now

$$C.R._{Q_1} = 100$$
$$C.R._{Q_2} = (88.37 \times 100) \div 100 = 88.37$$
$$C.R._{Q_3} = (100.04 \times 88.37) \div 100 = 88.41$$
$$C.R._{Q_4} = (108.97 \times 88.41) \div 100 = 96.34$$
$$\text{2nd } C.R._{Q_1} = (110.18 \times 96.34) \div 100 = 106.15$$
$$\therefore \quad d = 106.15 - 100 = 6.15$$
$$\therefore \quad \tfrac{1}{4}d = 1.538, \tfrac{2}{4}d = 3.075, \tfrac{3}{4}d = 4.61, \tfrac{4}{4}d = 6.15$$

Now the adjusted chain relatives are, respectively 100, 88.37 − 1.538, 88.41 − 3.075, 96.34 − 4.61, i.e., 100, 86.83, 85.34, 91.73.

Here $A.M.$ of the adjusted chain relatives$=(100 + 86.83 + 85.34 + 91.73) \div 4 = 90.98$

$\therefore$ the required seasonal indices are

$$\frac{100}{90.98} \times 100, \quad \frac{86.83}{90.98} \times 100, \quad \frac{85.34}{90.98} \times 100, \; ; \quad \frac{91.73}{90.98} \times 100$$

i.e., 109.91, 95.44, 93.80, 100.82.

The total of the seasonal indices is 400.

MEASUREMENT OF CYCLICAL FLUCTUATIONS

To measure cyclical fluctuations we first determine trend (T) and seasonal variation (S) and then eliminate them by using the additive, or the multiplicative model. Irregular movement (I) is then eliminated by using suitable moving averages. This leaves only the cyclical fluctuation at the end.

Index Numbers

It is used for comparing price, quantity, or value of a group of articles in different situations. For example, the index number of prices $= \dfrac{\text{Current price}}{\text{Base price}} \times 100$.

There are various methods for calculating index numbers. Let us calculate the cost of living index numbers.

PROBLEM 11. The following are the group index numbers and the group weights of an average working class familys budget. Construct the cost of living index number by assigning the given weights.

Group	Index Number	Weight
Food	352	48
Fuel	220	10
Clothing	230	8
Rent	160	12
Miscellaneous	190	15

SOLUTION

TABLE 4.11 THE CONSTRUCTION OF COST OF LIVING INDEX NUMBER

Group	Index Number	Weight	Index No. × Weight
Food	352	48	168.96
Fuel	220	10	2200
Clothing	230	8	1840
Rent	160	12	1920
Miscellaneous	190	15	2850
Total		93	25706

Therefore, the cost of living index $= \frac{25706}{93} = 276.4$.

Index numbers are used to forecast business activities. The cost of living index helps the employers to adjust dearness allowance of employees. Other indices like wholesale price index number, industrial production index number, business activity index number, stock price index number, retail price index number, etc. help us to forecast and plan future business activities. Index numbers are often termed as barometers in business statistics. Barometers are indicators of present economic situations or future conditions. Index numbers of various business activities may be combined to form a composite business activity index. Such indices will now be discussed in the context of barometric forecasting.

BAROMETRIC FORECASTING

Trend projection is the same as exponential smoothing forecast by using past time-series data when they follow a clear pattern. However, there are time-series whose patterns are not clear and tend to precede (lead) variations in the level of general economic activity, much as variations in the mercury in a barometer precede variations in weather conditions. In such cases a second series of data which is correlated with the time-series under consideration is located from monthly publications like Business Conditions Digest, issued by U. S. Department of Commerce which provides details for more than 300 time series.

By observing the variations in the second series, the variations in the series under consideration can be predicted. For example, suppose the sales of a company do not follow a clear pattern, but are found highly correlated with the number of houses sold. Now if the sale of houses can be predicted, then using this information one can predict the sales of the company.

A time series which is correlated with another time-series is often called an indicator of the second series. It take considerable time and effort to locate a good indicator.

Economic Indicators

When two series of data often increase, or, decrease simultaneously, one series may be considered as a coincident indicator of the other. For example in Fig. 4.3 (a) series A is a coincident indicator of series B since both the series have their peaks and troughs on the same dates. A series which follows, or lags movements in economic activity is called a lagging indicator.

When variations in one series consistantly occur prior to variations in another series, a leading indicator is formed. In Fig. 4.3 (b) series A is a leading indicator of series B since the peaks and troughs of series A consistently occur prior to the peaks and troughs of series B.

Leading indicators are used for purpose of forecasting. Just as a meteorologist predicts weather by seeing changes in barometric pressure, leading indicators help us to forecast changes in general economic activities. The use of leading indicators are generally referred to as barometric forecasting. A few examples of leading indicators are the following.

(i) A rise in building permits precedes building construction and hence it can be used to forecast the rise in housing construction.

(ii) A fall in the contracts for plant and machinery normally precedes a slowdown in general economic activities.

(iii) A rise in stock prices normally precedes an upturn in general business activities, since stock prices indicate higher profits.

In Fig 4.3 (c) the relative positions of leading, coincident and lagging indicators in a typical business cycle have been shown. While leading indicator precede business cycle turning points, i.e., peaks and troughs, coincident indicators coincide with the business cycle and lagging indicators lag the peaks and troughs of the cycle. (See also the chart of p. 127)

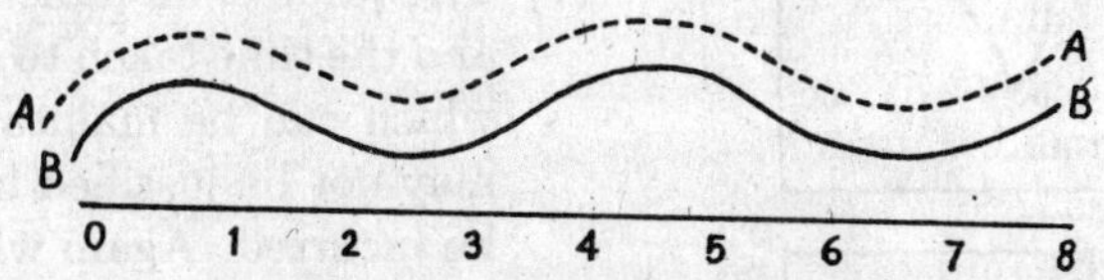

Fig 4.3(a) Coincident Indicator

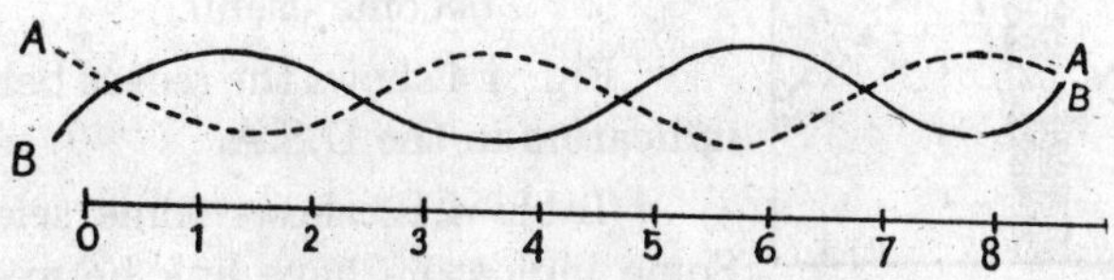

Fig 4.3(b) Leading Indicator

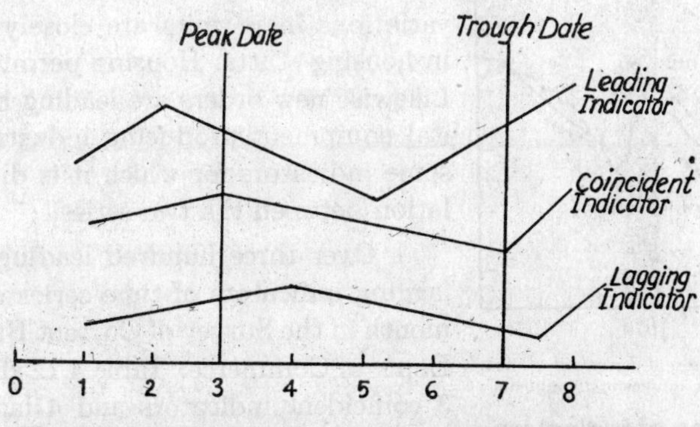

Fig 4.3(c) Three Indicators of a Business Cycle

The value of leading indicator depends on the following factors.

(i) It must be accurate, i.e., its variations should be closely correlated with the variations in the series which is to be predicted.

(ii) There must be adequate lead time, i.e., even if when two series are highly correlated, an indicator will not be of any use when the lead time is very short. For example, since the time required to put idle steel furnaces into operations is considerably long, the series which predicts variations in the demand for steel for a week, say, would be of no use for forecasting purposes in the steel industry.

(iii) Lead time should be relatively constant. If a series leads another by three months at one time and by one year in the next time, the indicator will not serve any useful purpose.

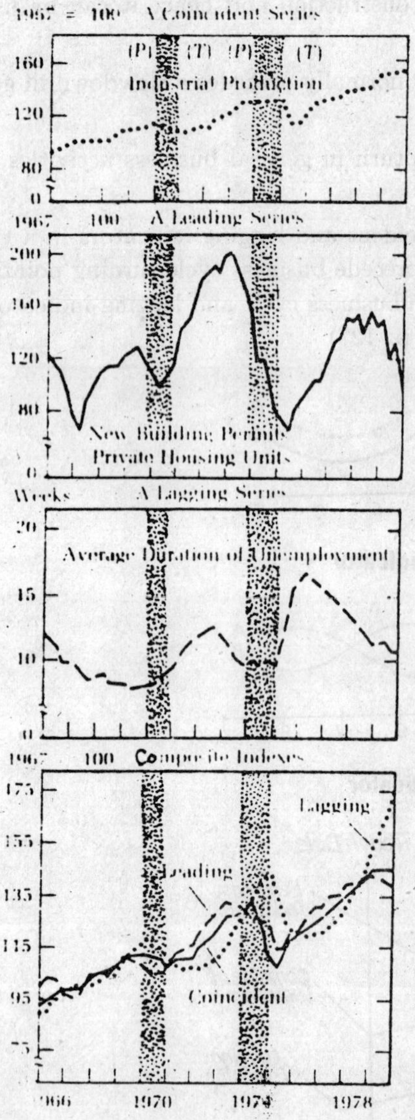

Shaded areas represent periods of cyclical contraction. Data are seasonally adjusted.

Fig. 4.4 Three Types of Indicators

(iv) There must be a logical explanation why one series forecasts another. If an adequate number of time series is studied, correlation can be observed between pairs of series. Unless a relationship exists between two series, the historical pattern is not found quite suitable for forecasting purposes. For example, market rates of interest are a leading indicator of stock prices. Low rates of interest forecast higher share prices. However, the explanation in support of this relationship is not very satisfactory.

(v) The value of an indicator is affected by the cost and the time taken to collect data. A time series which can be maintained only at a high cost, may not be justified by the expense that has to be incurred. Again when there is an inordinate delay prior to availability of data, the effective lead time of the indicator may be too short to become useful.

Fig. 4.4 shows the recent behaviour of some economic indicators in the U.S.A.

Table 4.12 shows some selected leading indicators. Some indicators have link between two series, e.g., new-building permits and private housing starts. When a permit is issued, a new house is likely to be build. Thus variations in permits are closely correlated to variations in housing starts. Housing permits are leading indicators. Likewise new orders are leading indicators of sales in capital equipment producing industries. However, there are some indicators for which it is difficult to establish correlation between the two series.

Over three hundred leading roughly coincident and lagging indicators of time series data are published every month in the Survey of Current Business issued by the U.S. Dept. of Commerce. Table 4.12 shows 7 leading indicators, 3 coincident indicators and 4 lagging indicators. It also shows the lead and lag times of the indicators.

Economic Indicators

Although time series helps us to forecast general economic conditions, no single leading indicator is capable of making a correct forecast. Even when an indicator gives more or less an accurate forecast of the fluctuations of the economic activities, the lead times vary. The problem is that any time series fluctuates at random and does not match with the general pattern of the data.

TABLE 4.12 SOME SELECTED LEADING, COINCIDENT AND LAGGING INDICATORS

LEADING INDICATORS (12 Series)	Mean Lead (−) or Lag (+)
Average workweek of production workers, manufacturing	−7.3
Layoff rate, manufacturing	−8.6
New orders, consumer goods and materials, 1972 dollars	−6.7
Vendor performance, companies receiving slower deliveries	−7.3
Index of net business formation	−7.4
Contracts and orders, plant and equipment, 1972 dollars	−5.5
New building permits, private housing units	−10.9
Changes in inventories on hand and on order, 1972	−5.6
Change in sensitive materials prices	−8.8
Stock prices, 500 common stocks	−7.0
Change in total liquid assets	−8.5
Money supply (M_2), 1972 dollars	−11.8
ROUGHLY COINCIDENT INDICATORS (4 Series)	
Employees on nonagricultural payrolls	−0.3
Personal income, 1972 dollars	−0.6
Industrial production	−1.6
Manufacturing and trade sales, 1972 dollars	−2.3
LAGGING INDICATORS (6 Series)	
Average duration of unemployment	+4.9
Manufacturing and trade inventories, 1972 dollars	+4.0
Labour cost per unit of output, manufacturing	+9.0
Average prime rate charged by banks	+7.1
Commercial and industrial loans outstanding	+3.9
Ratio of consumer installment debt to personal income	+5.6
COMPOSITE INDEXES	
Twelve leading indicators	−8.2
Four roughly coincident indicators	−1.2
Six lagging indicators	+4.8

It is possible to improve the barometric forecasting technique by constructing an appropriate index. Such an index represents a single time series consisting of a number of leading indicators. The idea of uniting the data is to smooth out the random variations in individual series. The combined index gives a more accurate forecast. The common barometric forecasting indices in use are composite indices and diffusion indices.

Composite Indices

It is a weighted average of individual indicators. The weights are assessed depending on the forecasting ability of individual series, i.e., a series which can predict more correctly is given more weights than a less perfect series. The index is expressed in terms of percentage changes from time to time. For example the composite index, commonly used by U.S. Dept. of Commerce, is based on eleven leading indicators.

Every month the U.S. Commerce Dept. publishes the variation in the index. Monthly deviations are not very important, but continuous increases for several months are considered as improvement in general economic conditions. Similarly consecutive fall in the index indicates that the economy is weakening[1].

---

[1] In fact, for macro-economic forecasting we use what is called composite of leading indicators—a set of measurements that provides clues about which way the economy is moving.

Diffusion Indices

Although we have listed only 7 leading indicators in Table 4.12, the U.S. Dept. of Commerce uses 11 such indicators. The 11 leading indicators also help the U.S. Dept. of Commerce to prepare a diffusion index which is a measure of the proportion of each time series that increases from month to month. For example, if 9 of the indicators increased from January to June, the diffusion index for June would be $\frac{9}{11}$ or 81.8%. When the index exceeds 50% for several months consecutively, it can be predicted that economic conditions are improving. When the index moves towards 100%, the improvement touches the maximum level. Similarly if less than 50% of the indicators show an increase, a downturn is indicated.

Though the use of indices improves barometric forecasting, the predictions are not accurate. On several occasions forecasts of the Department of Commerce have not come true. Variation in lead time is another defect. Moreover barometric forecasting gives little indication about the magnitude of the changes in economic activities. It signals only the likely direction of changes in economic activities, i.e., provides only a qualitative forecast. Finally, it is very difficult to locate a leading indicator which will generate accurate forecasts to meet specific requirements.

PROBLEM 12. Three leading indicators for a three-month period are shown below. Construct a composite and a diffusion index from the following data assuming the first month as the base period and attaching equal weights to the three series.

LEADING INDICATORS

Month	I	II	III
1	300	40	100
2	325	35	120
3	380	48	145

SOLUTION. The diffusion index is calculated by observing whether each series increased, or, decreased from month to month. In the second month, series I and III increased but series II decreased. Thus diffusion index for the second month is 66.70 (i.e., $\frac{2}{3}$). In the third month, all the series increased and hence the index for this month is 100% (i.e., $\frac{3}{3}$).

The composite index can be calculated by finding out the percentage changes for each series. In the second month the percentage changes are $\frac{25}{100} \times 100 = 8.33\%$ for series I, $-\frac{5}{40} \times 100 = -12.5\%$ for series II and $\frac{20}{100} \times 100 = 20\%$ for series III. Since the weights of all are equal, the average percentage change in 5.28%. If the value of the composite index for the 1st month is arbitrarily fixed at 100, the index for the second month will be (100+5.28=)105.28.

In the third month, the percentage changes for series I, II and III are $\frac{80}{300} \times 100 = 26.67\%$, $\frac{8}{40} \times 100 = 20\%$ and $\frac{45}{100} \times 100 = 45\%$, respectively. Hence the average percentage change is 30.56%. Thus the index for this month will be (100+30.56=)130.56.

The values of the two indices for the three months are listed in the table below. Both the indices indicate that economic activities would improve in the following months.

Month	Diffusion Index	Composite Index
1	—	100.00
2	66.70	105.28
3	100.00	130.56

CORRELATION

We use the term correlation to show (measure) the degree to which two or more variables are related. It is a statistical measure of determining the degree of association, i.e., tendency of two or more variables to move together. If X and Y are the variables and the movements of X cause movements in Y then X and Y are said to be correlated. If movements of both X and Y are in the same direction, the correlation is positive and when a decrease in X causes an increase in Y and *vice-versa*, the correlation is negative. When changes in X do not affect Y, X and Y are not correlated.

Various methods are available for calculating correlation, e.g., (1) the two-way frequency table; (2) the scatter diagram; (3) the co-variance method, or, the Karl Pearson's method and (4) the Rank method.

The coefficient of correlation (r) is given by the following formula

$$r = \frac{\Sigma dX\, dY - \frac{(\Sigma dX)\times(\Sigma dY)}{n}}{\sqrt{\left[\Sigma(dX)^2 - \frac{(\Sigma dX)^2}{n}\right] \times \left[\Sigma(dY)^2 - \frac{(\Sigma dY)^2}{n}\right]}}$$

The standard error and the probable error of the coefficient are given by

$$\text{S.E. of } r = \frac{1-r^2}{\sqrt{n}} \quad \text{and} \quad \text{P.E. of } r = 0.6745\left(\frac{1-r^2}{\sqrt{n}}\right), \text{ respectively}$$

where n = pairs of observations on variables X and Y.

The Rank coefficient of correlation (R) is given by

$$R = 1 - \frac{6\Sigma D^2}{N(N^2-1)}$$

where D is the difference between the ranks of the two series and N is the number of individuals in each series.

Multiple Correlation and Partial Correlation

Often the values of a variable are influenced by more than one variables. For example, the yield of crop depends on quality of seed, rainfall, soil and weather condition. The study of the combined effect of a group of variables on a single variable is called multiple correlation.

The study of the effect of one variable on another after eliminating the influence of other variables is called partial correlation.

The multiple correlation coefficient is given by

$$R_{1.23} = \sqrt{\frac{r_{12}^2 + r_{13}^2 - 2r_{12}r_{23}r_{13}}{1 - r_{23}^2}}, \quad 0 \le R_{1.23} \le 1$$

where .23 means independent variables which affect 1, i.e., the dependent variable. For example $R_{1.23}$ means that X_1 is associated with variables X_2 and X_3.

PROBLEM 15. In a three-variate multiple correlation analysis the following results have been obtained $X_{12} = 0.6, r_{13} = 0.5, r_{23} = 0.3$.

Find the multiple correlation coefficient $R_{1.23}$.

SOLUTION.

Here

$$R_{1.23} = \sqrt{\frac{(0.6)^2 + (0.5)^2 - 2 \times 0.6 \times 0.5 \times 0.3}{1 - (0.3)^2}} = 0.687.$$

The partial correlation coefficient is given by

$$r_{12.3} = \frac{r_{12} - r_{13} \times r_{23}}{\sqrt{(1 - r_{13}^2)(1 - r_{23}^2)}}, -1 \leq r_{1.23} \leq 1$$

where the subescript 12 denotes partial correlation between X_1 and X_2 and the subscript 3 means X_3 has been kept constant.

PROBLEM 15. If $r_{12} = 0.88, r_{13} = 0.90$ and $r_{23} = 0.91$ find the partial correlation coefficient between X_2 and X_3 when X is constant.

SOLUTION. Here

$$r_{23.1} = \frac{r_{23} - r_{12} \cdot r_{13}}{\sqrt{(1 - r_{12}^2)(-r_{13}^2)}} = \frac{0.91 - 0.88 \times 0.90}{\sqrt{[1 - (0.88)^2][1 - (0.90)^2]}} = -0.5701.$$

REGRESSION ANALYSIS

Regression analysis is used to show the average relationship between the two variables which helps us to predict the most likely value of one variable for a given value of the other variable. We had already discussed the regression method in the previous chapter. We may now illustrate how the technique is used for forecasting.

PROBLEM 13. The following table shows the test scores obtained by salespersons on an intelligence test and their sales every week.

Sales Persons	1	2	3	4	5	6
Test Scores	40	60	50	70	40	50
Sales (Rs. 000)	3	4	2	5	3	6

Calculate the regression line of sales on test scores and forecast the weekly sales volume if a salesperson obtains a score of 60.

Also find the coefficient of determination.

SOLUTION.

Test Score (X)	$dX = (X - 50)$	$(dX)^2$	Sales (Y)	$dY = (Y - 5)$	$(dY)^2$	$(dX) \times (dY)$
40	-10	100	3	-2	4	20
60	$+10$	100	4	-1	1	-10
50	0	0	2	-3	9	0
70	$+20$	400	5	0	0	0
40	-10	100	3	-2	4	20
50	0	0	6	$+1$	1	0
	$\Sigma dX = 10$	$\Sigma(dX)^2 = 700$		$\Sigma dy = -7$	$\Sigma(dY)^2 = 19$	$\Sigma dXdY = 30$

Now

$$\bar{x} = A + \frac{\Sigma dX}{n} = 50 + \frac{10}{6} = 51.67; \quad \bar{y} = B + \frac{\Sigma dY}{n} = 5 + \frac{-7}{6} = 3.83.$$

$\therefore$ for $n = 6$, the coefficient of correlation

$$r = \frac{\Sigma dX\, dY - \frac{(\Sigma dX)\times(\Sigma dY)}{n}}{\sqrt{\left[\Sigma(dX)^2 - \frac{(\Sigma dX)^2}{n}\right] \times \left[\Sigma(dY)^2 - \frac{(\Sigma dY)^2}{n}\right]}}$$

$$= \frac{30 - \frac{10\times -7}{6}}{\sqrt{\left[700 - \frac{100}{6}\right] \times \left[19 - \frac{49}{6}\right]}} = 0.48.$$

Again

$$\sigma X = \sqrt{\frac{\Sigma(dX)^2}{n} - \left(\frac{\Sigma dX}{n}\right)^2} = \sqrt{\frac{700}{6} - \left(\frac{10}{6}\right)^2} = 10.67$$

$$\sigma Y = \sqrt{\frac{\Sigma(dY)^2}{n} - \left(\frac{\Sigma dY}{n}\right)^2} = \sqrt{\frac{19}{6} - \frac{49}{36}} = 1.34$$

$\therefore$ the regression line of sales on score, i.e., Y on X is

$$(Y - \bar{Y}) = r \cdot \frac{\sigma Y}{\sigma X}(X - \bar{X}), \quad \text{or,} \quad Y - 3.83 = 0.48 \times \frac{1.34}{10.67}(X - 51.67).$$

When $X = 60$, $Y = 4.332$.

Similarly the regression of X on Y can be obtained from the following equation

$$(X - \bar{X}) = r \cdot \frac{\sigma X}{\sigma Y}(Y - \bar{Y}).$$

Now the coefficient of determination $(r^2) = (0.48)^2 = 0.2304$.

It means that 23.04% of the variation in sales is explained by test scores. How closely sales and test scores are related can be shown by r^2.

EXPONENTIAL SMOOTHING

Trend projection is really regression analysis in another form on where time acts as the independent variable. Here each observation, i.e., initial and last data are given the same weight.

Exponential smoothing is a technique of time-series forecasting which gives more weight to more current observations. At first we are to select a smoothing constant $\alpha (0 < \alpha < 1)$. When n observations are involved in a time series, the forecast for the subsequent period (i.e., $n+1$) is found as the weighted average of the observed value of the series at period n and the forecasted value for the same period, i.e.,

$$F_{n+1} = \alpha X_n + (1 - \alpha) F_n \tag{1}$$

where F_{n+1} is the forecast value of the subsequent period

X_n is value of the last observation and

F_n is the forecast value of the last period in the time series.

The forecast values of F_n and all previous periods are computed in an identical manner. Specifically

$$F_t = \alpha \cdot X_{t-1} + (1-\alpha)F_{t-1} \tag{2}$$

which is suitable for $t = 2$ to n, but unsuitable for F_1 as X_0 and F_0 are not known. To overcome this problem F_1 is taken as equal to X_1. From (2) we find $F_2 = X_1$.

When α becomes $1.0, (1-\alpha) = 0$ and lower values of α give more weight to observations from previous periods.

A companys sales over the last five weeks are shown in Table 4.16. Assuming $F_2 = F_1 = X_1$ and $\alpha = 0.30$, we have

$$F_3 = 0.30(330) + 0.70(300) = 309.00$$
$$F_4 = 0.30(320) + 0.70(309) = 312.30$$
$$F_5 = 0.30(340) + 0.70(312.30) = 320.61$$

TABLE 4.13 FORECASTS BASED ON EXPONENTIAL SMOOTHING

Week (t)	Sales (Xt)	$\alpha = 0.30$ (Ft)	$\alpha = 0.40$ (Ft)	$\alpha = 0.70$ (Ft)
1	300	300.00	300.00	300.00
2	330	300.00	300.00	300.00
3	320	309.00	312.00	321.00
4	340	312.30	315.20	320.30
5	370	320.61	325.12	334.09
6	—	335.43	343.07	359.23

The forecast values for three different values of α are given in the above table. The table also shows forecast value of sales for week 6. Using $\alpha = .30$, the forecast value for the 6th week is computed as $F_6 = 0.30(370) + 0.70(320.61) = 335.43$. Table 4.16 suggests why this method is called smoothing technique. Consider the forecasts of $\alpha = .30$. Note that the smoothed data show less variation than the original sales data. Also note that as α rises, the variations in F_t increase since the forecasts give more weight to the last observation in the time series.

Selection of a Smoothing Constant

In fact, any value of α can be selected. We know that the coefficients of a regression equation are selected in such away so as to minimise the sum of squared deviations between observed and forecast values. The some principle can also be used for selecting the smoothing constant.

Thus

$$\sum_{t=1}^{n}(X_t - F_t)^2$$

will be minimum for the selected value of α. For the data and values of α shown in Table 4.16, these sums are as follows:

Smoothing Constant	Sum of Squared Deviations
.30	4227.66
.40	3593.25
.70	2578.62

From these results we find that $\alpha = .70$ gives the best forecast using this data. However, there are values of α between .40 and .70 which may give even better results.

Evaluation of the Method

The main advantage of this method is that it gives more weight to the current data and it can update forecasts easily.

The disadvantage is that it cannot make accurate forecasts when there is significant trend in the data.

ECONOMETRIC MODELS

The linear regression method (technique) can also be used, where more than one variable is involved, to explain the behaviour of the dependent variable Y. This is known as multiple regression. For example, besides the number of marriages, the employment rate in the preceding quarter might also indicate the change in housing starts. The modified regression equation will be

$$Y'_{X_1X_2} = a + b_1X_1 + b_2X_2$$

where $Y'_{X_1X_2}$ is the number of housing starts predicted on the basis of new marriages and employment rate; a is the Y-axis intercept, b_1 and b_2 are the slopes of X_1 and X_2. Here X_1 and X_2 are the number of marriages and the employment rate, respectively in the preceding quarter.

Multiple regression models can be solved easily by a computer and are used in causal forecasting. Sometimes the dependent and independent variables used in forecasting models are interdependent. For example, demand may be a function of individual income and *vice-versa*.

Evaluation of the Method

Econometric models take into account these interrelationships while formulating a series of simultaneous regression equations that relate the demand data to all of the interdependent variables.

The main drawbacks of econometric models are the following: **1.** they must be updated with changes in business conditions; **2.** they require highly specialised personnel; **3.** they are both time-consuming and cost-raising (expensive) exercises; and **4.** they require large volume of accurate data.

PROBLEM 16. The demand data for Atlas bicycles of a company for 3 months is given below. Using $\alpha = 0.3$ and a forecast of 700 for the 1st month, calculate the exponentially smoothed forecast values of demand for the months 2 to 4.

Month	Acutal
1	715
2	810
3	660

SOLUTION. The error for the 1st month=Actual – Forecast=(715−700)=15

This is used to adjust the forecast of 700 upward by $0.3 \times 15 = 4.5$.

Hence forecast for the 2nd month =700+0.3(715−700)=**704.5**

The forecast for 3rd month=704.5+0.3(810−704.5)=**736.15**

The forecast for 4th month=736.15+0.3(660−736.15)=**713.31.**

PROBLEM 17. The following are a companys quarterly demand figures for the last 2 years.

Year 1		Year 2	
Quarter	Demand	Quarter	Demand
1	25,209	1	24,390
2	20,402	2	18,064
3	17,677	3	17,175
4	23,681	4	22,860

(a) Calculate 1-year moving average centered at the end of quarters 2.5 through 6.5 respectively to eliminate the seasonality. (Assume that the demand figures are at the center of the time periods they include).

(b) Calculate the linear regression equation for the trend through the five moving averages.

(c) Calculate the average seasonal index (multiplicative) for each quarter of the year.

(d) Forecast the demand for each quarter of year 3.

SOLUTION. The moving average for the first year would be centered between second and third quarters, i.e., at x-coordinate of 2.5. The x-coordinate for the subsequent moving average will be 3.5, and so on.

The four-quarter moving averages and the corresponding X-co-ordinates are listed in the following table.

TABLE 4.14 PROJECTION OF PAST TRENDS

Actual Demand (1)	The Sum of Four Quarters (2)	(3) = [(2) ÷ 4]	x-coordinate
25209			
20402			
17,677			
23,681	86969	21742.25	2.5
24,390	86150	21537.50	3.5
18,064	83812	20953.00	4.5
17,175	83310	20827.50	5.5
22,860	82489	20622.25	6.5

(b) We can find a linear regression equation to show the relationship between the quarter and the trend value of demand.

X	Y	X^2	XY
2.5	21742.25	6.25	54355.63
3.5	21537.50	12.25	75381.25
4.5	20953.00	20.25	94288.50
5.5	20827.50	30.25	114551.25
6.5	20622.25	42.25	134044.62
22.5	105682.50	111.25	472621.25

Now

$$b = \frac{n\Sigma XY - \Sigma X \Sigma Y}{n\Sigma X^2 - (\Sigma X)^2} = \frac{5(472621.25) - (22.5)(105682.5)}{5(111.25) - (22.5)^2} = \frac{-14750}{50} = -295$$

$$a = \frac{\Sigma y - b\Sigma X}{n} = \frac{105682.5 + 295(22.5)}{5} = 22464.$$

(c) The time period when actual demand occurs relate to periods 1, 2, 3, 4, etc. on the time scale. Using the values of X we can find the trend values at each of these times so that we can calculate seasonal indices for a multiplicative model.

Year	Quarter	x-Coordinate	Trend Value	Actual Demand	Actual Trend
1	1	1	22169	25209	1.137
1	2	2	21874	20402	0.933
1	3	3	21579	17,677	0.819
1	4	4	21284	23,681	1.113
2	1	5	20989	24,390	1.162
2	2	6	20694	18,064	0.873
2	3	7	20399	17,175	0.842
2	4	8	20104	22,860	1.347

Now the average indices for the four quarters of the year are:

$$\text{1st quarter} = \frac{1.137 + 1.162}{2} = 1.150; \quad \text{3rd quarter} = \frac{0.819 + 0.842}{2} = 0.831;$$

$$\text{2nd quarter} = \frac{0.933 + 0.873}{2} = 0.903; \quad \text{4th quarter} = \frac{1.113 + 1.137}{2} = 1.125.$$

(d) The forecast for year 3 is obtained by projecting the trend to quarters 9 to 12 and multiplying these by suitable seasonal indices.

Year	Quarter	x-co-ordinate	Trend Value	Seasonal Index	Forecast (Trend×Seasonal Index)
3	1	9	19809	1.150	22780.35
3	2	10	19514	0.903	17621.14
3	3	11	19219	0.831	15970.99
3	4	12	18924	1.125	21289.50

PROBLEM 18. From the following table showing sales of scooters for each season over the period (1989 to 1994), (a) calculate the trend factor; (b) separate out seasonal plus irregular components; (c) identify the seasonal component for each year; (d) and forecast the sales value for winter 1995.

TABLE 4.18 TIME SERIES ANALYSIS OF SALES VOLUME

Year	Time period	t	Actual observation
1989	Spring	1	2419
	Summer	2	2947
	Autum	3	3396
	Winter	4	3500
1990	Spring	5	2742
	Summer	6	3127
	Autum	7	3900
	Winter	8	2439
1991	Spring	9	2686
	Summer	10	3493
	Autum	11	4100
	Winter	12	3920
1992	Spring	13	2690
	Summer	14	3550
	Autum	15	4317
	Winter	16	4035
1993	Spring	17	3100
	Summer	18	3337
	Autum	19	4439
	Winter	20	4242
1994	Spring	21	2900
	Summer	22	3923
	Autum	23	4809
	Winter	24	4570

SOLUTION.

(a) Let us calculate the trend by regression analysis as follows.

TABLE 4.15 FORECASTING THE DEMAND FOR SCOOTERS

X	Y	X^2	XY
1	2419	1	2419
2	2947	4	5894
3	3396	9	10188
4	3500	16	14000
5	2742	25	13710
6	3127	36	18762
7	3900	49	27300
8	2439	64	19512
9	2686	81	24174
10	3493	100	34930
11	4100	121	45100
12	3920	144	47040

Contd.

X	Y	X^2	XY
13	2690	169	34970
14	3550	196	49700
15	4317	225	64755
16	4035	256	64560
17	3100	289	52700
18	3337	324	60066
19	4439	361	84341
20	4242	400	84840
21	2900	441	60900
22	3923	484	86306
23	4809	529	110607
24	4570	576	109680
$\Sigma X = 300$	$\Sigma Y = 84581$	$\Sigma X^2 = 4900$	$\Sigma XY = 1126454$

Here $n = 24$.

Now

$$a = \frac{(\Sigma Y \Sigma X^2) - (\Sigma X \Sigma XY)}{n\Sigma X^2 - (\Sigma X)^2} = \frac{84581 \times 4900 - 300 \times 1126454}{24 \times 4900 - 300 \times 300} = 2772.13$$

$$b = \frac{(n\Sigma XY) - (\Sigma X \Sigma Y)}{n\Sigma X^2 - (\Sigma X)^2} = \frac{24 \times 1126454 - 300 \times 84581}{27600} = 60.17.$$

$\therefore$ **a simple regression of sales volume against time gives $T_t = 2772.13 + 60.17t$ where T_t is the trend value of sales and t is the time period.**

(b) TABLE 4.16 SEPARATING OUT SEASONAL PLUS IRREGULAR COMPONENT

(1) t	(2) Actual observation	(3) Trend values	(4)=(2)− (3) Seasonal plus irregular
1	2419	2832	−413
2	2947	2893	54
3	3396	2953	443
4	3500	3013	487
5	2742	3073	−331
6	3127	3133	−6
7	3900	3193	707
8	2439	3254	−815
9	2686	3314	−628
10	3493	3374	119
11	4100	3434	666
12	3920	3494	426
13	2690	3554	−864
14	3550	3615	−65
15	4317	3675	642

Contd.

Contd.

(1) t	(2) Actual observation	(3) Trend values	(4)=(2)− (3) Seasonal plus irregular
16	4035	3735	300
17	3100	3795	−695
18	3337	3855	−518
19	4439	3915	524
20	4242	3976	266
21	2900	4036	−1136
22	3923	4096	−173
23	4809	4156	653
24	4570	4216	354

(c) TABLE 4.17 IDENTIFICATION OF THE SEASONAL COMPONENT FOR EACH SEASON

(1) Season	(2) Values of Seasonal plus Irregular Components	(3) Average of (2)
Spring	−413	
	−331	
	−628	−678
	−864	
	−695	
	−1136	
Summer	.54	
	−6	
	119	−98
	−65	
	−518	
	−173	
Autum	443	
	707	
	666	606
	642	
	524	
	653	
Winter	487	
	−815	
	426	
	300	170
	266	
	354	

(d) No adjustment for seasonal factors is required since the seasonal values when added is zero.

A forecast for a future period can be obtained by computing trend value for that period and adding the seasonal factor.

$\therefore$ the forecast value of sales for winter 1995 $= 170 + T_t = 2772.13 + 60.17(28) + 170 =$ **4627**.

($\because$ $n = 28$.)

PROBLEM 18. Sen nursing home has estimated its average monthly bed requirements as $N = 600 + 20X$ where N is monthly bed requirement and X is time period (months); January 1994 = 0. Assume: There is no possibility of opening any new nursing home in the area in future.

The following monthly seasonal adjustment factors have been estimated on the basis of the data for the previous five years.

Month	Adjustment factor
January	+ 5%
April	−12%
July	+ 6%
November	− 6%
December	−25%

(a) Forecast Sen's bed demand for: January, April, July, November and December of 1996.

(b) If the following forecast and actual values of demand for bed in June have been recorded, suggest what seasonal adjustment factor should be used to forecast the demand for June?

Year	Forecast	Acutal
1995	1,000	996
1994	800	893
1993	735	797
1992	640	651
1991	503	528
1990	395	460

SOLUTION.

(a)

Month	X	Unadjusted Forecast	Adjustment Factor	Adjusted Forecast
January 1996	24	600+20(24)=1080	+ 5%	1080(1.05)=1134.0
April 1996	27	600+20(27)=1140	−12%	1140(.88) =1003.2
July 1996	30	600+20(30)=1200	+ 6%	1200(1.06)=1272.0
November 1996	34	600+20(34)=1280	− 6%	1280(0.94)=1203.2
December 1996	35	600+20(35)=1300	−25%	1300(0.75)= 975.0

(b)

Year	Forecast	Actual	Actual/Forecast
1995	1000	996	99.6%
1994	800	893	111.6%
1993	735	797	108.4%
1992	640	651	101.7%
1991	503	528	105.0%
1990	395	460	116.5%
			642.8%

Average$=\frac{642.8}{6} = 107.1$, i.e., 107%. So the adjustment factor for June =+7%.

PROBLEM 20. A company producing tractors finds that there is a relation between its sale of tractors and index of farm income. Data collected by the company in connection with farm income and sale of tractors are given below.

Year	Farm Income Index (X)	Sales of Tractors (Y)
1990	100	110
1991	105	120
1992	130	160
1993	140	140
1994	180	200

Fit a regression equation assuming that this relation holds and forecast sale of tractor for the year 1996 when the farm income index is expected to be 250.

SOLUTION.

Year	Farm Income Index (X)	Sale of Tractors (Y)	X^2	XY
1990	100	110	10,000	11,000
1991	105	120	11,025	12,600
1992	130	160	16900	20,800
1993	140	140	19600	19,600
1994	180	200	32400	36,000
$n = 5$	$\Sigma X = 655$	$\Sigma Y = 730$	$\Sigma X^2 = 89925$	$100{,}000 = \Sigma XY$

Let the regression equation of Y on X be $Y = a + bX$.

Now for getting the values of a and b we are to solve the following equations

$$\Sigma Y = na + b\Sigma X \quad \text{and} \quad \Sigma XY = a\Sigma X + b\Sigma X^2$$

$$\text{or,} \quad 730 = 5a + 655b \quad 100,00 = 655a + 89925b$$

$\therefore \quad b = 1.061$ and $a = 7.009$

$\therefore$ the regression equation of Y on X is $Y = 7.009 + 1.061X$.

Now $Y_{1996} = 7.009 + 1.061(250) = 272.26$.

$\therefore$ the expected sale of tractors for 1996 is 272 units.

PROBLEM 21. With the help of the following data project the trend of sales for the next five years.

Year	1989	1990	1991	1992	1993	1994
Sales (Rs. lakhs)	50	60	65	70	75	90

SOLUTION.

Year	Sales (in Rs. lakhs)	Time deviations from the middle of 1991 and 1992 assuming 0.5 = 1		
	(Y)	(X)	X^2	XY
1989	50	−5	25	−250
1990	60	−3	9	−180
1991	65	−1	1	− 65
1992	70	1	1	70
1993	75	3	9	225
1994	90	5	25	450
$n = 6$	$\Sigma Y = 410$	$\Sigma X = 0$	$\Sigma X^2 = 70$	250

Now the regression of Y on X is $Y = a + bX$.

So the values of a and b are found thus

$$a = \frac{\Sigma Y}{n} = \frac{410}{6} = 68.33; \quad b = \frac{\Sigma XY}{\Sigma X^2} = \frac{250}{70} = 3.571.$$

$\therefore \quad Y = 68.33 + 3.571X.$

The forecast value of sales for the next 5 years, i.e., 1995 to 1999 are the following:

$$\begin{aligned}
Y_{1995} &= 68.33 + 3.571(7) = 93.33 \\
Y_{1996} &= 68.33 + 3.571(9) = 100.47 \\
Y_{1997} &= 68.33 + 3.571(11) = 107.61 \\
Y_{1998} &= 68.33 + 3.571(13) = 114.75 \\
Y_{1999} &= 68.33 + 3.571(15) = 121.90
\end{aligned}$$

INPUT-OUTPUT ANALYSIS

Input-output analysis is an attempt to reveal the structural interdependence of the economic system of a country. The input-output model is said to have originated with the inter-industry analysis contained in the famous tableau economique of Francois Quesnay. This was subsequently modified and expanded by the Nobel Laureate economist Wassiley Leontief. This model is now extensively used for national economic planning. The model works on the assumption that for the economy as a whole input is equal to the output, i.e., whatever quantity is produced is fully consumed. In this model each industry produces output to cater to the needs of (i) itself; (ii) other industries and (iii) consumers.

An input-output table shows the use of the output of each industry as inputs by other industries and for final consumption by others. For example, steel-made drills are used to mine coal and the coal, in its turn, is used in the coal fired furnaces to produce steel which again goes into the production of steel-drills. This very fact shows the interdependence of industries.

There are two types of input-output models, i.e., (i) closed type and (ii) open type. In the closed type, total output is consumed by those who are producing them. In this open type a portion of the production is being consumed by the outsiders and the balance is being consumed by those participating in production. Here we will discuss only the open type input-output model. In the open type, labour is considered as a primary input, different from the produced raw materials which enter into the interindustry structure.[1]

Input-Output Tables

Table 4.18 shows the input-output table for a very simple economy consisting of three industries X, Y and Z. The transaction matrix shows how the output of each industry is distributed over all the three sectors/industries of the hypothetical economy and used to meet final demand. It further indicates the value added figure of each industry..

TABLE 4.18 A THREE-SECTOR INPUT-OUTPUT FLOW TABLE

Supplying Industry	X	Y	Z	Final (Outside or Consumers) Demand	Total
	Input (Rs.)	Input (Rs.)	Input (Rs.)	Input (Rs.)	Output (Rs.)
X	40	30	10	30	110
Y	30	20	50	40	140
Z	20	40	30	60	150
Value Added (labour)	20	50	60		130
Total	110	140	150	130	

The rows of Table 4.18 indicate the disposition of the output of industries X, Y and Z. For example, the first row indicates that of the total output of Rs. 110 for industry X, Rs. 80 indicates intermediate sales to firms participating in production (Rs. 40 to firms in industry X, Rs. 30 to firms in industry Y and Rs. 10 to firms in industry Z) and the residue (Rs. 30) goes to consumers to meet final demand.

Again the columns of the table shows the input requirements of individual industries, as well as the value added by them. For example, the first column shows that industry X purchased Rs. 40 of its own output, Rs. 30 from industry Y and Rs. 20 from industry Z while Rs. 20 is the value added (rent, wages, interest, profits, taxes paid, etc.) by industry X. It is to be noted that the total output of each industry (i.e., row-total) equals the total production costs inclusive of value added (i.e., column total).

Direct Requirements Matrix

By dividing the input requirements indicated in each column of Table 4.18 by the column total, we obtain the direct requirements matrix. This is shown in Table 4.19.

1 Since the construction of input-output tables are very expensive and time-consuming, private firms have to rely on such tables periodically prepared by the Bureau of Economic Analysis (BEA) of U.S. Department of Commerce. The input-output table for 1982 is the latest one for the U.S. economy which includes 537 industries and/or commodities.

TABLE 4.19 DIRECT REQUIREMENTS MATRIX

Supplying Industry	Producing Industry X	Y	Z
X	0.364	0.214	0.064
Y	0.272	0.143	0.333
Z	0.182	0.286	0.200

We have obtained the coefficients 0.364, 0.272 and 0.182 in column X by dividing the values of Rs. 40, Rs. 30 and Rs. 20 by the column total of Rs. 110 for industry X in Table 4.19. The coefficients in each column of the table shows the inputs required to produce each rupees of output by each industry. For example, industry X needs inputs of Re. 0.364 from industry X Re. 0.272 from industry Y and Re. 0.182 from industry Z for each rupee of output. Thus for increasing the output of industry X by Rs. 100, additional inputs of Rs. 36.44, Rs. 27.2 and Rs. 18.2 will be required from industries X, Y and Z, respectively. But to increase output by Rs. 27.2 in industry Y additional inputs from industries X, Y and Z will be required. Such extra indirect, or secondary inputs are not considered in the direct requirements matrix.

Total Requirements Matrix

The total (direct and indirect) inputs required to produce on extra rupee of output by each industry can be obtained from the total requirements matrix. Table 4.20 shows the total requirements matrix derived from the Table 4.19.

TABLE 4.20 TOTAL REQUIREMENTS MATRIX

Supplying Industry	Producing Industry X	Y	Z
X	1.97	0.63	0.43
Y	0.93	1.66	0.77
Z	0.78	0.74	1.62

The calculations of Table 4.20 are shown below.

The input-output matrix, or technology matrix B (say) can be expressed as

$$B = \begin{array}{c} \\ X \\ Y \\ Z \end{array} \begin{array}{c} \begin{array}{ccc} X & Y & Z \end{array} \\ \begin{pmatrix} 0.364 & 0.214 & 0.064 \\ 0.272 & 0.143 & 0.333 \\ 0.182 & 0.286 & 0.200 \end{pmatrix} \end{array}$$

The elements of the matrix are called technical, or input coefficients. The sum of each column coefficient is less than 1 which shows that outside (consumers) are also using the product, i.e.,

Total output = internal demand + outside (consumers) demand.

Now internal demand, or consumption $\doteq 0.364X_1 + 0.214X_2 + 0.067X_3$ units of the product of X.

$\therefore$ the input-output balance equation of X

$$= (0.364X_1 + 0.214X_2 + 0.067X_3) + 30 = X_1 \quad (1)$$

Similarly the input-output balance equation for Y

$$= (0.272X_1 + 0.143X_2 + 0.333X_3) + 40 = X_2 \quad (2)$$

and the input-output balance equation for Z

$$= (0.182X_1 + 0.286X_2 + 0.200X_3) + 60 = X_3 \quad (3)$$

Equations (1), (2) and (3) can be expressed as

$$\begin{pmatrix} 0.364 & 0.214 & 0.067 \\ 0.272 & 0.143 & 0.333 \\ 0.182 & 0.286 & 0.200 \end{pmatrix} \begin{bmatrix} X_1 \\ X_2 \\ X_3 \end{bmatrix} + \begin{bmatrix} 30 \\ 40 \\ 60 \end{bmatrix} = \begin{bmatrix} X_1 \\ X_2 \\ X_3 \end{bmatrix} \quad \text{or,} \quad BX + C = X$$

where $X = [X_1, X_2, X_3]$ is the total output for a particular demand, BX = amounts of products X, Y and Z which are needed for internal consumption and C = direct demand of the three products by consumers.

Hence we find that

$$\begin{pmatrix} 0.364 & 0.214 & 0.067 \\ 0.272 & 0.143 & 0.333 \\ 0.182 & 0.286 & 0.200 \end{pmatrix} \begin{bmatrix} 110 \\ 140 \\ 150 \end{bmatrix} = \begin{bmatrix} 80 \\ 100 \\ 90 \end{bmatrix}$$

i.e., $0.364 \times 110 + 0.214 \times 140 + 0.067 \times 150 = 80.05$ and so on.

$\therefore \quad BX$ = Internal demand vector.

The Leontief open type input-output model is a solution of the following equation

$$BX + C = X, \quad \text{or,} \quad X - BX = C \quad \text{or,} \ X(L_3 - B) = C,$$

$$\text{or,} \ X = (L_3 - B)^{-1}XC, \text{where} \quad L_3 = \text{Identity matrix.}$$

Putting $C = [30, 40, 60]$, we can find the value of X. But this will not give the future projected demand. To forecast the future demand, say after 5 years, put $C = [20, 80, 70]$, assuming that the demand vector changes in the next 5 years from $[30, 40, 60]$ to $[20, 80, 70]$.

$$\therefore \quad X = \begin{pmatrix} 0.636* & -0.214 & -0.067 \\ -0.272 & 0.857* & -0.333 \\ -0.182 & -0.286 & *0.800 \end{pmatrix}^{-1} \begin{bmatrix} 20 \\ 80 \\ 70 \end{bmatrix}$$

$[*(1 - .364) = 0.636, (1 - .143) = 0.857, (1 - .2) = 0.800.]$

To solve this, let us put

$$A = \begin{pmatrix} .636 & -0214 & -.067 \\ -.2727 & .857 & -.333 \\ -.182 & -.286 & .800 \end{pmatrix} = \text{Leontief matrix}$$

$$\therefore \quad |A| = \begin{vmatrix} .636 & -.214 & -.067 \\ -.272 & .857 & -.333 \\ -.182 & -.286 & 800 \end{vmatrix}$$

$$= .636[.857 \times .8 - (-.333)(-.286)] - (-.214)[-.272 \times .8 - (-.333)(-.182)]$$
$$(-.0267)[-.272 \times -.286 - .857 \times -.182] = .3.$$

Now

$$A' = \begin{bmatrix} .636 & -.272 & -.182 \\ -.214 & .857 & -.286 \\ -.067 & -.333 & .800 \end{bmatrix}$$

In the next stage we have to obtain the adjugate of A by replacing the elements of A by their co-factors. Adj $.A$ is expressed as

$$\text{Adj}\,.\,A = \begin{bmatrix} .591 & .363 & .128 \\ .279 & .497 & .230 \\ .234 & .221 & .487 \end{bmatrix}$$

First Column: Co-factor of .636 $= [.857 \times .800 - (-.286)(-.333) = 0.591$

Co-factor of $-.214$ $= -[-.272 \times .800 - (-.182)(-.333)] = 0.279$

Co-factor of -0.067 $= [-.272 \times -.286 - (-.182)(.857)] = .234$

Similarly the co-factors of 2nd and 3rd columns can be calculated as shown above.

$$\therefore \quad A^{-1} = \frac{1}{|A|}\,\text{Adj}\,.\,A = \begin{bmatrix} 0.636 & -.214 & -.067 \\ -.272 & .957 & -.333 \\ -.182 & -.2867 & .800 \end{bmatrix}^{-1}$$

$$= \frac{1}{0.3} \times \begin{bmatrix} .591 & 0.190 & .128 \\ .279 & .497 & .230 \\ .234 & .221 & .487 \end{bmatrix} = \begin{bmatrix} 1.97 & 0.63 & 0.43 \\ 0.93 & 1.66 & 0.77 \\ 0.78 & 0.74 & 1.62 \end{bmatrix}$$

$$\therefore \quad X = \begin{bmatrix} 1.97 & 0.63 & 0.43 \\ 0.93 & 1.66 & 0.77 \\ 0.78 & 0.74 & 1.62 \end{bmatrix} \begin{bmatrix} 20 \\ 80 \\ 70 \end{bmatrix}$$

$$\text{or,} \quad X_1 = 1.97 \times 20 + 0.63 \times 80 + 0.43 \times 70 = 119.9$$
$$X_2 = 0.93 \times 20 + 1.66 \times 80 + 0.77 \times 70 = 205.3$$
$$X_3 = 0.78 \times 20 + 0.74 \times 80 + 1.62 \times 70 = 188.2$$

Hence the total output of X, Y and Z which will be required after 5 years to meet the projected demand C is $X_1 = 119.9, X_2 = 205.3$ and $X_3 = 188.2$. Hence in a Leontief open type model of M industries if B is input-output matrix, X is the column vector showing the total output of each related industry and C is the column vector showing the future projected demand for goods, then the output vector X will be $X = (L_M - B)^{-1} \times C$.

The following three important points may be noted this context:

(1) The rank of the matrix $(L_M - B)$ is always M if the sums of the columns of B are less than 1 and all the coefficients of B are positive.

(2) We have assumed that each industry is manufacturing a single product.

(3) If the technological coefficients do not change, $(L_M - B)^{-1}$ will also not change and the equation $X = (L_M - B)^{-1} \times C$ can be used to find new output levels for changed demand vectors.

We find that all the total (direct and indirect) input requirement coefficients in Table 4.20 are greater than the corresponding direct input requirements in Table 4.19. The first column of Table 4.20 indicates that the total inputs required for industry X to produce each rupee of output are Rs. 1.97, Re. 0.93 and Re. 0.78 from industries X, Y and Z respectively. Hence for increasing the output of industry X by Rs. 100, additional inputs of Rs. 197, Rs. 93 and Rs. 78 from industries X, Y and Z respectively will be required.

By multiplying the total requirements matrix by the final demand for each commodity we get the total demand for each commodity as shown in Table 4.18, i.e.,

$$1.97(30) + 0.63(40) + 0.43(60) = 110$$
$$0.93(30) + 1.66(40) + 0.77(60) = 140$$
$$0.78(30) + 0.74(40) + 1.62(60) = 150.$$

We find that the calculation of total requirements matrix is not very easy. In the real commercial world calculation of the total requirements matrix is not required. It is so because official agencies like the Bureau of Economic Analysis of the U.S. Dept. of Commerce publish this matrix with the input-output table at periodic intervals.

Forecasting with Input-Output Tables

Let us now see how the total requirements matrix helps us in forecasting. Suppose econometric forecasts show that the final demand for the output of industry X increases from Rs. 30 to Rs. 100 in one year. Now we may use the information given below:

$$\underset{\text{Total Requirements Matrix}}{\begin{bmatrix} 1.97 & 0.63 & 0.43 \\ 0.93 & 1.66 & 0.77 \\ 0.78 & 0.74 & 1.62 \end{bmatrix}} \quad \underset{\text{Final Demand Vector}}{\begin{bmatrix} 30 \\ 40 \\ 60 \end{bmatrix}} \quad = \quad \underset{\text{Total Demand Vector}}{\begin{bmatrix} 110 \\ 140 \\ 150 \end{bmatrix}}$$

Using the above total requirements matrix, we can forecast the new total output of industries, X, Y and Z respectively as

$$(1.97)(100) + (0.63)(40) + (0.43)(60) = 248$$
$$(0.93)(100) + (1.66)(40) + (0.77)(60) = 206$$
$$(0.78) + (0.74)(40) + (1.62)(60) = 205.$$

These forecasts can again be used to construct a new input-output table indicating the higher input demand of each industry that would arise out of the forecasted increase from Rs. 30 to Rs. 100 in the final demand of the output of industry X. This is shown in Table 4.21. The values of X, Y and Z columns of the Table have been calculated by multiplying the total output of individual industries by the direct requirements coefficients of the industry given in Table 4.19., e.g., the values of column X of Table 4.21 can be obtained by multiplying the direct requirements of 0.364, 0.272 and 0.182 of Table 4.21 by Rs. 248 and so on.

TABLE 4.21 REVISED THREE-SECTOR INPUT-OUTPUT TABLE

Supplying Industries	X	Y	Z	Final Demand	Total
X	90	44	14	100	248
Y	68	30	68	40	206
Z	45	59	41	60	205

Evaluation of the Method

Input-output analysis is used by firms to forecast the requirements of raw materials, labour and capital to meet the forecasted demand for their products. It is also used to forecast environmental impact on development projects and adoption of various disarmament proposals. It helps to forecast employment changes in the different regions of nation arising out of changes in the level of imports and exports, population growth, energy crises, water shortage and a host of other factors.

However, the use of input-output analysis for forecasting has some drawbacks also. The direct and total requirements coefficients have been considered as constant and hence there is no scope for input substitution in production. Similarly commodity substitution in consumption cannot be considered since commodity prices have been assumed to remain fixed. Input-output tables are released with a time lag of many years. Hence the input-output coefficients may become highly biased. Finally, the reliability of the requirements of the industries forecasted by input-output tables depends on the accuracy of the econometric forecasts of the demand for final commodities.

In spite of all these drawbacks, input-output analysis and forecasting are very useful since they consider the inter-relationships among different industries and sectors of the economy in an internally consistent way.

PROBLEM 22. From the following transaction matrix, determine the input-output matrix.

	Users		
Producers	A	B	Projected Demand
A	200	400	100
B	300	800	300

If the projected demand changes to 150 and 450 units, respectively what should be the outputs to meet the changed demand?

SOLUTION. The system is open because there is some outside demand other than internal demand. The input-output matrix can be found out as follows.

	Users			
Producers	A	B	Projected Demand	Total
A	$\frac{200}{700}=\frac{2}{7}$	$\frac{400}{1400}=\frac{2}{7}$	100	700
B	$\frac{300}{700}=\frac{3}{7}$	$\frac{800}{1400}=\frac{4}{7}$	300	1,400

$$\therefore\quad B=\begin{pmatrix}2/7 & 2/7\\ 3/7 & 4/7\end{pmatrix}\quad\text{and}\quad C=\begin{bmatrix}150\\ 450\end{bmatrix}$$

Now

$$X=(L_2-B)^{-1}\times C=\begin{pmatrix}5/7 & -2/7\\ -3/7 & 3/7\end{pmatrix}^{-1}\begin{bmatrix}150\\ 450\end{bmatrix}$$

where L_2 is the identity matrix.

Put

$$A=\begin{pmatrix}5/7 & -2/7\\ -3/7 & 3/7\end{pmatrix}\quad\therefore\ |A|=\begin{vmatrix}5/7 & -2/7\\ -3/7 & 3/7\end{vmatrix}=\frac{9}{49}$$

Now

$$A'=\begin{bmatrix}5/7 & -3/7\\ -2/7 & 3/7\end{bmatrix}\quad\therefore\ \text{Adj. } A=\text{Replaced elements of } A \text{ by the co-factors.}$$

$$\therefore\ \text{Adj}.A=\begin{bmatrix}3/7 & 2/7\\ -3/7 & 5/7\end{bmatrix}.$$

Now

$$A^{-1}=\frac{1}{|A|}\times\text{Adj}.A=\frac{49}{9}\begin{bmatrix}3/7 & 2/7\\ 3/7 & 5/7\end{bmatrix}$$

$$\therefore\quad X=[X_1,X_2]\text{ is the output vector}=\frac{49}{9}\begin{bmatrix}3/7 & 2/7\\ 3/7 & 5/7\end{bmatrix}\quad\begin{bmatrix}150\\ 450\end{bmatrix}=\begin{bmatrix}1050\\ 2100\end{bmatrix}$$

Hence the gross output requirements of A and B are $X_1 = 1050$ units and $X_2 = 2100$ units, repectively.

PROBLEM 23. From the following input-output table, find out the technology matrix and write the balance equations.

	Users		
Producrs	A	B	Demand
A	100	25	150
B	150	175	200

SOLUTION. Total output of $A = (100 + 25 + 150) = 275$ units.

Total output of $B = (150 + 175 + 200) = 525$ units.

The technology matrix may be written as

$$B = \begin{pmatrix} \frac{100}{275} & \frac{25}{525} \\ \frac{150}{275} & \frac{175}{525} \end{pmatrix} = \begin{pmatrix} \frac{4}{11} & \frac{1}{21} \\ \frac{6}{11} & \frac{1}{3} \end{pmatrix}$$

Let X_1 and X_2 be the outputs of A and B respectively.

Here $C = [150, 200]$ and $X = [X_1, X_2]$

$\therefore$ the balance equations are given by

$$BX + C = X \quad \text{or,} \quad \begin{pmatrix} \frac{4}{11} & \frac{1}{21} \\ \frac{6}{11} & \frac{1}{3} \end{pmatrix} \begin{bmatrix} X_1 \\ X_2 \end{bmatrix} + \begin{bmatrix} 150 \\ 200 \end{bmatrix} = \begin{bmatrix} X_1 \\ X_2 \end{bmatrix}$$

$$\text{or,} \quad \frac{4}{11}X_1 + \frac{1}{21}X_2 + 150 = X_1 \quad \text{and} \quad \frac{6}{11}X_1 + \frac{1}{3}X_2 + 200 = X_2$$

$$\text{or,} \quad \frac{7}{11}X_1 = \frac{1}{21}X_2 = 150 \quad \text{and} \quad \frac{6}{11}X_1 + \frac{2}{3}X_2 = 200.$$

PROBLEM 24. If the final consumer requirements are Rs. 80 million of steel, Rs. 20 million of coal and Rs. 55 milion of railway transport, determine from the following matrix the final output goal of each industry.

	Steel	Coal	Railway Transport
Steel	0.2	0.2	0.3
Coal	0.4	0.1	0.3
Railway Transport	0.1	0.3	0.1
Labour	0.3	0.4	0.3

Also estimate the labour requirements for final output of the three industries.

SOLUTION We can form the following equations from the given information:

$$S = 0.2S + 0.2C + 0.3R + 80$$
$$C = 0.4S + 0.1C + 0.3R + 20$$
$$R = 0.1S + 0.3C + 0.1R + 55$$

where S, C and R are gross output levels of steel, coal and railway transport respectively. To find out the final output gools of each industry we need to solve the transposed equation system.

$$(1-0.2)S - 0.2C - 0.3R = 80 \quad (1)$$
$$-0.4S + (1-0.1)C - 0.3R = 20 \quad (2)$$
$$-0.1S - 0.3C + (1-0.1)R = 55 \quad (3)$$

Solving (1), (2) and (3), we get $S = 186.6; C = 149.0$ and $R = 131.5$.

Thus the given system has to turn out Rs. 186.6 million, Rs. 149.0 million and Rs. 131.5 millions of steel, coal and railway services respectively to meet the final demand targets.

Now

$$L = 0.3 \times S + 0.4 \times C + 0.3 \times R = 0.3 \times 186.6 + 0.4 \times 149.0 + 0.3 \times 131.5 = 155.$$

Hence to produce the final outputs of three industries Rs. 155 million worth of labour services are needed.

PROBLEM 25. Given the following information, estimate the gross levels of output of X and Y required to satisfy the given bill of final consumption.

	Technological Matrix		Bills of Final Consumption
	X	Y	
X	0.2	0.4	Rs. 10 million
Y	0.3	0.1	Rs. 2 million
Capital	0.2	0.3	
Labour	0.3	0.2	

Given the amount of capital worth Rs. 2 million and amount of labour equivalent to a wage bill of Rs. 7 million. available at home, determine the amount of capital that has to be imported and the level of employment in rupee terms.

SOLUTION. We form the following equations from the given information

$$X = 0.2X + 0.4Y + 10$$
$$Y = 0.3X + 0.1Y + 2$$

where X and Y are the gross levels of outputs.

$$\text{or,} \quad 0.8X - 0.4Y = 10 \quad (1)$$
$$-0.3X + 0.9Y = 2. \quad (2)$$

Solving (1) and (2), we get $X = 16.35$ and $Y = 7.7$.

Hence the total capital requirement to meet output goods is $0.2X + 0.3Y = (0.2)(16.35) + (0.3)(7.7) =$ Rs. 5.58 million.

∴ capital to be imported (Rs. 5.58– Rs. 2 =) Rs. 3.58 million.

Again total labour requirement is $0.3X + 0.2Y = (0.3)(16.35) + (0.2)(7.7) =$ Rs. 6.44 million.

Thus the level of employment (labour services) = Rs. (7– Rs. 6.44) = Rs. 0.56 million.

PROBLEM 26. Given below is a transaction matrix showing a simple hypothetical input-output relationship (in Rs. million):

Producing sector	Receiving sector X	Y	Z	Final Demand	Total Output
X	10	40	30	120	200
Y	30	20	100	250	400
Z	50	100	20	30	200
Labour	110	240	50		400

Compute the gross output levels of the three sectors when final demand on sector X changes to Rs. 125 million. Assuming an annual averge wage rate equal to 0.001 units of value find the resulting change in total employment.

SOLUTION. From the tranaction matrix we first find out technology matrix as:

	X	Y	Z
X	0.05	0.10	0.15
Y	0.15	0.05	0.50
Z	0.25	0.25	0.10
L	0.55	0.60	0.25

Then denoting gross output levels by X, Y, Z, we construct the following equations

$$X = 0.05X + 0.10Y + 0.15Z + 125$$
$$Y = 0.15X + 0.05Y + 0.50Z + 250$$
$$Z = 0.25X + 0.25Y + 0.10Z + 30$$

$$\text{or,} \quad 0.95X - 0.10Y - 0.15Z = 125 \quad (1)$$
$$-0.15X + 0.95y - 0.50Z = 250 \quad (2)$$
$$-0.25X - 0.25Y - 0.90Z = 20 \quad (3)$$

Solving (1), (2) and (3) we have

$X = 208.85$; $Y = 402.05$ and $Z = 202.2$ (in million Rs.) to produce these outputs total labour required level is given by $L = (208.85)(0.55) + (402.05)(0.60) + (202.2)(.25) = 406.65$.

Thus Rs. 406.65 million worth of labour services will be needed in the changed situation. The resulting increase will thus be of the order of (Rs. 406.65– Rs. 400 =) or Rs. 6.65 million (worth of labour services).

This means that employment opportunities for additional $(\frac{6.65}{0.001})$ or 6650 man-years of labour would be created.

THE HAWKINS–SIMON CONDITIONS

So long we have seen that the gross output vector is positive. The input-output matrix solution may sometimes show negative output levels for some industries. In such cases the system under study is not viable.

The Hawkins-Simon conditions enable us to check whether the data collected is viable or not. There conditions may be stated as: **1.** $|L_M - B| > 0$ and **2.** All diagonal elements of $(L_M - B)$ must be positive.

$\therefore \quad (L_M - B)^{-1} \times C$ will also be positive. For example, let, $B = \begin{pmatrix} 0.8 & 0.4 \\ 0.8 & 0.9 \end{pmatrix}$.

$$\therefore \quad (L_M - B) = \begin{pmatrix} 0.2 & -.4 \\ -0.8 & .1 \end{pmatrix} = 0.2 \times .1 - (-0.4)(-0.8) = -0.30.$$

The system is not viable as this is not satisfying the Hawkins-Simon Conditions.

PROBLEM 27. Find out the input-output coefficients from the following Input-Output Table (figures in thousand Rupees). Interpret the Table and find out the gross outputs of A, B and C to meet the final requirements.

From	To	Intersectional	Final	Total demand		
(Output)	(Input)	Demand	Demand	or, Output		
	A	B	C			
A	4	15	10	29	31	60
B	5	110	30	145	105	250
C	10	40	15	65	135	200
Intersectional Input	19	165	55	239		
Primary Input	41	85	145		271	
Total Input	60	250	200			510

SOLUTION. Here the technology matrix will be

	A	B	C	
A	0.07	0.06	0.05	(i.e., $\frac{10}{200}$)
B	0.08	0.44	0.15	and so on
C	0.17	0.16	0.08	

Interpretation

$$B = \begin{pmatrix} 0.07 & 0.06 & 0.05 \\ 0.08 & 0.44 & 0.15 \\ 0.17 & 0.16 & 0.08 \end{pmatrix}$$

From each unit of A, 0.07, 0.06, 0.05 units are supplied to A, B and C, respectively. Again to produce each unit of A, 0.07, 0.08 and 0.17 units of A, B and C are required. This is the interpretation of the 1st row and the 1st column. Others can be interpreted in the same way.

Determination of Gross Outputs

Let X_1, X_2 and X_3 units be the outputs of A, B and C, respectively.

or, $X = [X_1, X_2, X_3]$ is the output vector and $C = [31, 105, 135]$ is the demand vector.

Now

$$X = (L_3 - B)^{-1} \times C = \begin{pmatrix} 0.93 & -0.06 & -0.05 \\ -0.08 & 0.56 & -0.15 \\ -0.17 & -0.16 & 0.92 \end{pmatrix}^{-1} \begin{bmatrix} 31 \\ 105 \\ 135 \end{bmatrix}$$

$$= A^{-1} \times \begin{bmatrix} 31 \\ 105 \\ 135 \end{bmatrix} = \left[\frac{1}{|A|} \text{Adj}\, A\right] \begin{bmatrix} 31 \\ 105 \\ 135 \end{bmatrix} = \frac{1}{0.4454} \begin{bmatrix} 0.4912 & 0.0632 & 0.0370 \\ 0.0991 & 0.8471 & 0.1435 \\ 0.1080 & 0.1590 & 0.5160 \end{bmatrix} \times \begin{bmatrix} 31 \\ 105 \\ 135 \end{bmatrix}$$

$|A| = 0.4454$ and Adj. A have been calculated as before

$$\therefore \quad X = \begin{bmatrix} 1.1028 & 0.1419 & 0.0831 \\ 0.2225 & 1.9019 & 0.3222 \\ 0.2425 & 0.3570 & 1.1585 \end{bmatrix} \begin{bmatrix} 31 \\ 105 \\ 135 \end{bmatrix}$$

$$\therefore \quad X_1 = 31(1.1028) + 105(0.1419) + 135(0.0831) = 60.3$$

$$X_2 = 31(0.2225) + 105(1.9019) + 135(0.3222) = 250.1$$

$$X_3 = 31(0.2425) + 105(0.3570) + 135(1.1585) = 201.4$$

Hence gross output of A, B and C are 60.3 units, 250.1 units and 201.4 units respectively, i.e., almost near to the given outputs in the input-output table.

Forecasting Demand For New Products

It is very difficult to forecast the demand for new products primarily because no data of past sales are available. So the methods of forecasting demand for new products are quite different from those for well-established products. For products that are new to the economy as well as to the company, an intensive study of the economic and competitive characteristics of the product provides the key to intelligent projections of demand. Forecasting methods need to be tailored to the particular product. However, the following methods may be used for the purpose: (i) Survey of Consumers; (ii) Sample Survey and Test marketing; (iii) Life Cycle Segmentation Analysis and (iv) Bounding Curves Methods.

(i) Consumer Survey

By using this method consumers are individually contacted for knowing their future purchase plans. This can be done either by a complete survey of all consumers, or by selecting some consuming units from the total population, i.e., a sample survey.

(a) The Complete Enumeration Method

Under this method the probable demands of the all consumers for the forecast period are added to get the sales forecast for the forecast period. Though this gives us an unbiased information, it has the following drawbacks: **1.** It is a costly proposition to contact all consumers scattered all over the market. **2.** Consumers may be unwilling to divulge their purchase plans in order to maintain privacy and secrecy. **3.** Consumers may change their purchase plans afterwards.

(ii) The Sample Method

In this case the probable demand of each selected unit is added to get the total demand of the sample units in the forecast period. To get the total market demand the total sample demand is multiplied by the ratio of number of consuming units in the population to the number of consuming units in the sample. If the sample is selected carefully to represent the population, the survey results will be as accurate as that of complete enumeration methods. This method is less costly than the previous method.

Test marketing is used to forecast sales of new products, or determine the potential of existing products in new areas. To start with a test area is selected which is a true representative of the total market. The product is then pushed in this area in the same way as in broad national market. If the product is successful in this area, a forecast can be made that the product will also be successful in the national market. However, this method has the following drawbacks:

1. Firstly, it is both costly and time-consuming in nature.

2. There is need to build up large inventories since only a portion of current output is sold in the test area.

3. The test has to be continued for a long time to study consumers' repurchase cycle. Fig. 4.5 shows how false forecast is made when marketing test is discontinued prematurely.

It is seen that the length of repurchase cycle is longer for durable products and shorter for perishable (consumer) goods.

4. It is not always easy to select a test area representing the total market.

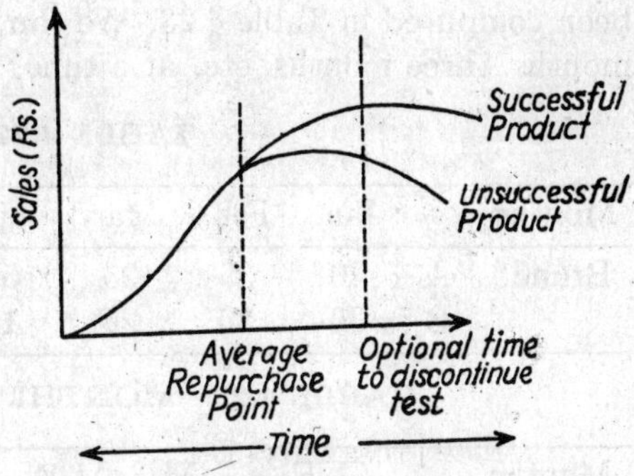

Fig 4.5 Test Marketing

5. Similar products pushed into the test market can be developed simultaneously by competetors.

(iii) Life Cycle Segmentation Analysis

Each product has its own life cycle consisting of introduction, growth, maturity, saturation and decline. Business tactics differ at different stages of the product life cycle. So it is necessary to know at the outset the current stage of the cycle of the product. Again since the total market has also its own segments, timing and tactics differ as per the segment concerned. The sales of a new product in a market segment follow the S-curve as shown in Fig. 4.6.

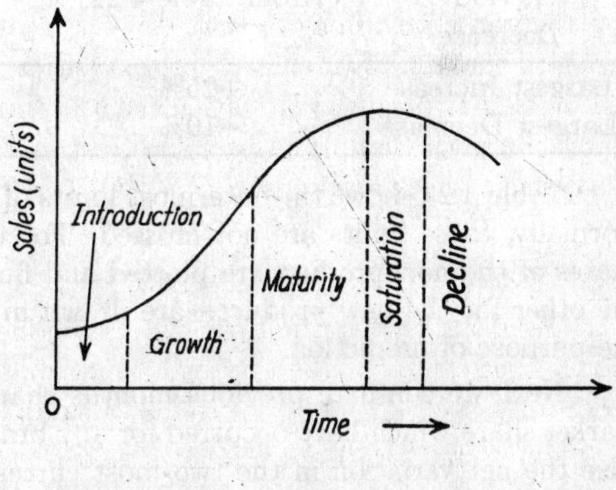

Fig 4.6 The Product Life Cycle.

The five stages of product life cycle are:

(a) **Introduction:** Initially quality has the highest effect. Advertising, price, able-sales-service, etc. have very little effect.

(b) **Growth:** The product is being purchased. This means buyer resistance has been overcome. At this stage quality is less effective than advertising.

(c) **Maturity:** Price insensitive buyers are now buying the product and rivals also enter the market. At this stage price is more important than advertising, quality and service.

(d) **Saturation:** Price is much less important than advertising, quality and packaging at this stage.

(e) **Decline** Price is less important. The use of the new products is found and advertisements are made. Quality and service assume considerable importance.

If we know the total market potential, the potential of each segment, and how fast the current segment is maturing, we can forecast similar diffusion rates of the balance segments. This will enable us to project the aggregate sales figure, i.e., sales figure for the total market.

(iv) Bounding Curves Method

This method is based on market share data. Let us assume that market share data are available for all existing brands of the product for the last few previous months, as given in Table 4.22. Also assume that the new brand is yet to be pushed into the market. Monthly market share changes have been computed in Table 4.23. We can also find changes in market share by considering gaps of two months, three months, etc. at a time.

TABLE 4.22 MARKET SHARE (in percent)

Months		Jan.	Feb.	Mar.	Apr.	May	Jun.	July	Aug.	Sept.	Oct.	Nov.	Dec.
Brand:	A	40	35	25	50	55	50	45	50	40	40	45	45
	B	30	30	25	15	15	10	20	25	30	35	35	35

TABLE 4.23 MONTHLY CHANGE IN MARKET SHARE (in percent)

Months		J–F	F–M	M–A	A–M	M–J	J–J	J–A	A–S	S–O	O–N	N–D
Brand	A	–5	–10	25	5	–5	–5	5	–10	—	5	—
	B	—	–5	–10	—	–5	10	5	5	5	—	—

TABLE 4.24 SUMMARY OF LARGEST CHANGES IN MARKET SHARE

Increase Period Decrease	1 month (from Table 4.22)	2 months	3 months (not shown in Table 4.23)	4 months
Largest Increase	+25%	+30%	25%	+15%
Largest Decrease	–10%	–10%	–20%	–15%

Table 4.23 shows the outermost limits of the variations in market shares of the existing brands. Normally, these limits are not crossed. For using bounding curves month by month the attained shares of the new product are plotted and finally the two curves—one for an existing product and the other for the new product—are drawn in the same diagram for the sake of comparion and for the purpose of prediction.

Next we compare previous months change in market share with all one-month variations in market share which have occurred for any brand in the market in the period before product launch. Also the net variation in the two most current months is compared with that in all previous two-months. If these variations do not violate the bounding curves, the prospect of the new product is neither good nor bad. If the curve showing the market share actually achieved is below the bounding curve most of the time, greater success for the product can be predicted and *vice-versa.* Hence bounding curves form a basis for estimating market penetration of a product.

CRITERIA OF FORECASTING DEMAND FOR NEW PRODUCTS

These are various ways to make guesses about future sales. And economists have developed various forecasting tools to be able to foresee changes in the economy. A good forecast illuminates the economic terrain ahead and helps decision makers adapt their actions to economic conditions. The following are the features of a good demand forecast:

1. Accuracy: It is desirable to have an accurate forecast, but the problem is, how accurate? This question can be answered only in terms of the value of marginal precision compared to its cost.

2. Plausibility: The executives who use the forecasting results must have faith and belief in the method. The implication is that they have to understand how the estimate was made.

3. Durability: The durability of the forecasting power of a demand function depends partly on the reasonableness and simplicity of functions fitted, but primarily on the stability of the underlying relationships measured in the past.

4. Flexibility: The need for flexibility stems directly from the need for durability. Flexibility can be viewed as an alternative to generality.

5. Availability: Immediate availability of data is a pre-requisite. In fact, the non-availability of data and the search for reasonable approximations to relevance in latest data is a constant burden on the forecasters patience.

Under ordinary circumstances the forecasters do a fairly good job of projecting the future value of sales on the basis of current and past trends. At other time, particularly when there are major policy changes forecasting becomes a hazardous exercise. To conclude with Paul Samuelson, experience emphasises that forecasting is as much art as science in our uncertain world. Still, the strength of economic forecasting is that year in and year out, professional forecasters provide more accurate forecasts than do those who use unsystematic or unscientific approaches."

Summary

Data for use in forecasting can be obtained from diverse sources such as expert opinion, surveys and market experiments. Surveys of plans and attitudes by consumers and investors are of tremendous value in forecasting. However, considerable care has to be taken to assure that the responses reflect subsequent consumer choices. Market experiments have an advantage over surveys because they provide information on how consumers actually behave in the market. Their limitations include the risk of losing customers, high cost, problems of making consumers aware of changes and inability to control all demand-determining factors.

Trend projections are made by using time-series data. Basically, the technique involves estimating the coefficients that provide the best fit of data to a specified equation. The two most common equation forms estimate a constant rate of change and a constant percentage rate of change. It is possible to improve forecasts based on trend projection of time-series data by adjusting for seasonal variations.

Econometric models and methods may be applied to either time-series or cross-section data for forecasting purposes. This technique is useful when there is interdependance among several variables in a simultaneous equation system. But it requires the use of modern computers.

There is also the need to evaluate the signs and magnitudes of estimated coefficients in relation to the economic theory on which the model is based. It is also possible to use the t-statistic to test hypothesis about the statistical significance of individual coefficients. However, the overall explanatory power of the model is indicated by the R^2 value.

Input-output analysis has also been used to forecast the direct and indirect impacts of final demand changes in one sector on total demand in other sectors of the economy. The technique is based on data that show patterns of sales and purchases among different sectors. These patterns are summarised in a transactions matrix. The direct requirements matrix is computed by dividing the columns of the transactions matrix by the total sales of each sector. It shows the proportions of total revenues used to make input purchases from various other sectors.

The direct and indirect requirements matrix is the basic tool used for forecasting by using input-output analysis. Each number in a column shows the impact that a Re. 1 change in final demand in one sector would have on total demand in each of the other sectors of the model. By assuming constant employment/total sales ratios, it is also possible to use input-output analysis to estimate sector-by-sector employment impacts.

Concepts for Review

1. **Time Series Analysis**
2. Input Output Analysis
3. Trend Forecasting
4. Gompertz Curve

Exercises

1. The annual sales of as firm are s follows.

Year	1990	1991	1992	1993	1994
Sales	50	60	75	52	70

Find the trend values for each of the five years using the method of least squares. Also forecast the annual sales of 1995 and 1996.

2. Assume that Mr. Reddy has collected the following information about the relationship between annual income of his customers and the number of boxes of jute bags they purchased during the previous months.

Income (in thousands of rupees)	30	32	28	39	20	26	21	41	65
Purchases (in boxes)	2	3	2	4	3	3	2	4	0

(a) Plot this relationship on a graph and draw a straight line which closely fits the points to show the relationship between these variables.

(b) Eliminate the last observation and again draw the line.

(c) What will you do to reconcile the difference in answers (a) and (b)?

3. The sales data over the previous ten years for *XY* & Co. are as follows.

1985: Rs. 2,40,000; 1986: Rs. 2,75,000; 1987: Rs. 3,00,000; 1988: Rs. 3,65,000; 1989: Rs. 4,50,00; 1990: Rs. 5,20,000; 1991: Rs. 6,15,000; 1992: Rs. 6,80,000; 1993: Rs. 7,75,000; 1994: Rs. 8,70,000.

(a) Calculate the compound growth rate for the period of 1985-1994.

(b) Based on the answer (a), forecast sales for both 1995 and 1996.

(c) Also compute the compound growth rate for the period of 1989-1994.

(d) Based on your answer (c), forecast sales for both 1995 and 1996.

(e) What is the reason for the differences in these answers in (b) and (d)? If you make your own projections, what would you forecast? (Drawing a graph will be helpful.)

4. You have the following data for the previous year's sales for Das and Co. (in thousands of rupees)

January: Rs. 490; February: Rs. 510; March: Rs. 510; April: Rs. 505; May: Rs. 525; June: Rs. 560 July: Rs. 600; August: Rs. 615; September: Rs. 570; October: Rs. 560; November: Rs. 520; December: Rs. 490.

(a) Compute a three-month centered moving average.

(b) With the help of (a) forecast sales for February of next year.

(c) If you are asked to forecast February and March sales for next year, will it be proper to forecast them by using the preceding moving averages?

5. Steel Enterprise (SE) manufactures steel-cabinets for office purposes. The economist of the concern has established the following equation of demand for these steel cabinets after considering a large number of previous data $Q = 15,000 + 60B - 80P + 50A$ where Q is the number of cabinets sold per year, B is the index of non-residential construction, P is the average price per cabinet charged by SE and A is the average price per cabinet charged by SE's one close competitor.

The non-residential construction index, SEs average price and the competitors average price are expected to be 150, Rs. 35 and Rs. 30 respectively in the next year.

(a) Forecast sales for the coming year.

(b) What will be the result if a competitor reduces its prices to Rs. 25 and another increases its price to Rs. 35?

(c) What will be the result if SE considers the decrease in price mentioned in (b) and reduces its price to Rs. 32?

(d) If the forecast of the index is wrong and it actually comes to only 130 next year, how will it affect SEs sales?

6. A company wants to expand but before that it wants to study next years level of business. The sales history of the company for previous four years are given below (data are in hundreds of customers served)

Quarter	Year 1991	1992	1993	1994
1	6	9	10	11
2	5	6	8	9
3	77	5	7	10
4	4	7	10	12
Yearly Total	22	27	35	42

(a) Using a simple exponential smoothing model estimate total sales for 1995. Are there any difficulties in using such a model? Explain.

(b) Use a simple linear time trend on yearly totals to forecast sales for 1995. Your model is $Y_s = a + bT$ where Y_s is yearly sales, T is time index, with 1, 2, 3 and 4 for 1991, 1992, 1993, 1994 respectively.

(c) Which model do you think works best and why?

7. (a) From the following time series, find the rate of growth using at least two different techniques. What are the strengths and weaknesses of these techniques?

Period	Time Series Values
1	400
2	500
3	600
4	660
5	720
6	800

(b) A company's sales forecasting team has determined by regression analysis that its sales depend on industry sales and the price of the companys products related to the industry average price $S_t = 30 + .3IS_t + 5.8SD_1 - 4.5SD_2 + 3.5SD_3 - .2RP_t$ where S_t is company sales; IS_t is industry sales and RP_t is the relative price, i.e., the price of the company's product as a percentage of the industry average price.

(All figures are in thousands of units.)

Management is interested in knowing what sales will be in the next year when industry-sales increase to 600 units and the relative price of the company's product is 110%.

Here SD_1, SD_2 and SD_3 are the seasonal dummies for the first, second and third quarters respectively.

8. The demand for newsprint over a 10-year period is given below. The table also shows three time series for the same time period.

		Year									
		1	2	3	4	5	6	7	8	9	10
Quantity of Newsprint		100	115	120	125	130	140	135	140	145	150
Series	*A*	30	25	30	35	30	35	40	45	50	44
Series	*B*	180	200	210	215	220	230	250	225	235	250
Series	*C*	20	20	22	24	25	24	20	25	28	24

(a) Which of the time series is approximately the coincident indicator of newsprint demand?

(b) Which series is a leading indicator of newsprint demand? What is the lead time for the leading indicator?

(c) Confirm whether newsprint demand will increase, decrease, or, remain constant in period 2, based on the leading indicator.

9. The demand data for motor oil of ESSO Co. for 5 years is shown below.

Year	Demand
1	428
2	625
3	700
4	750
5	820

(a) Draw the graph. Should the data for the 1st year be included in calculating a linear regression model to get the trend in annual demand? Explain.

(b) Compute a linear regression equation for annual demand on the basis of data of (a).

(c) Use the equation of (b) to estimate demand for years 6 and 8.

10. The equation describing the sales trend of the Dawson Chemical Company is $S_t = 21.3 + 1.3t$, where S_t is the sales (in millions of dollars per month) of the firm, and t is time measured in months from January 1991. The firms seasonal index of sales is

January	103	May	101	September	121
February	80	June	104	October	101
March	75	July	120	November	75
April	103	August	139	December	78

Construct a monthly sales forecast for the firm for 1997.

11. A copper firms monthly sales have the following trend $C_t = 4.12 + 0.32t$, where C_t is the sales (in millions of dollars per month) of the firm and t is time measured in months from July 1992. The firms seasonal index of sales is

January	81	May	137	September	79
February	98	June	122	October	101
March	102	July	104	November	74
April	76	August	101	December	125

Make a monthly sales forecast for the product of the firm for 1998.

12. Calculate the technical co-efficients from the following table.

Output	Input P	Input Q	Input R	Final Demand	Total Production
P	18	30	45	15	108
Q	27	30	60	3	120
R	54	40	60	26	180

13. From the given technological matrix and final consumer demands, find the gross levels of output of three industries 1, 2 and 3.

	1	2	3	Consumer Demands
1	0.1	0.5	0.4	Rs. 60 million
2	0.2	0.1	0.1	Rs. 40 million
3	0.6	0.2	0.3	Rs. 70 million
Labour	0.3	0.2	0.3	

Also find out the total labour requirement.

14. Given the following technological matrix and the consumers' requirement, determine gross levels of output of the three industries *A*, *B* and *C*.

	A	B	C	Consumers' Requirement (in Rs. million)
A	0.2	0.1	0.3	150
B	0.3	0.4	0.2	115
C	0.2	0.2	0.3	140
L	0.3	0.3	0.2	

15. From the following matrix find the final output goal of each industry assuming that the consumer output targets are Rs. 80 million in steel, Rs. 30 million in coal and Rs. 60 million in rail transport.

	Steel	Coal	Railway Transport
Steel	0.4	0.1	0.2
Coal	0.2	0.2	0.4
Railway Transport	0.2	0.3	0.3
Labour	0.2	0.4	0.2

What would be the labour requirements for final outputs of the three industries ?

16. Given below is a transaction matrix for a simple hypothetical economy.

Sales by	Purchases by X	Purchases by Y	Purchases by Z	Final demand	Total output
X	—	60	40	100	200
Y	40	—	100	260	400
Z	50	100	—	50	200
Labour	110	240	60	—	400
Total input	200	400	200	410	—

Now compute (i) the technical coefficient matrix and (ii) the change in output level of the three sectors if we assume final demand level of the sector X only to change from 100 to 120.

Appendix A

HAZARDS AND PROBLEMS IN REGRESSION AND CORRELATION

There are a number of pitfalls in regression and correlation analyses that should be emphasised. First, it is by no means true that a high coefficient of determination (or correlation coefficient) between two variables means that one variable causes the other variable to vary. For example, if one regresses the size of a persons left foot on the size of his (or her) right foot, this regression is bound to fit very well, since the size of a persons left foot is closely correlated with the size of his (or her) right foot. But this does not mean that the size of a persons right foot causes a persons left foot to be as large or small as it is. Two variables can be highly correlated without causation being implied.

Second, even if an observed correlation is due to a causal relationship, the direction of causation may be the reverse of that implied by the regression. For example, suppose that we regress a firm's profits being the dependent variable and its R and D expenditures being the independent variable. If the correlation between these two variables turns out to be high, does this imply that high R and D expenditures produce high profits? Obviously not. The line of causation could run the other way— high profits could result in high R and D expenditures. Thus in interpreting the results of regression and correlation studies, it is important to ask oneself whether the line of causation assumed in the studies is correct.

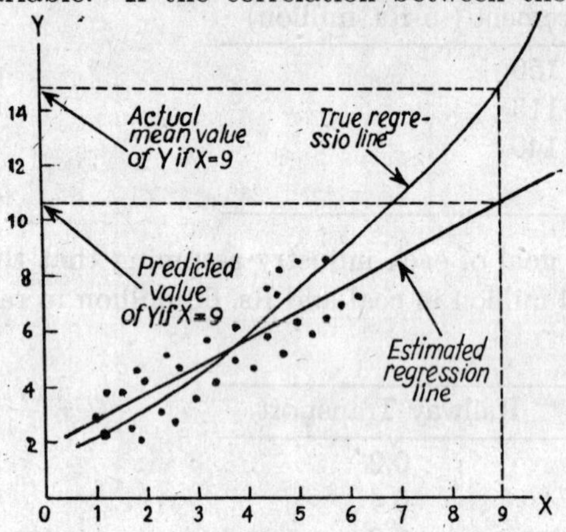

Fig A-1 Two Regression Lines

Third, regressions are sometimes used to forecast values of the dependent variable corresponding to values of the independent variable lying beyond the sample range. For example, in Fig. A-1, the scatter diagram shows that the data for the independent variable range from about 1 to 7. But the regression may be used to forecast the dependent variable when the independent variable assumes a value of 9 which is outside the sample range. This procedure, known as *extrapolation*, is dangerous because the available data provide no evidence that the true regression is linear beyond the range of sample data. For example, the true regression may be shown in Fig. A-1, in which case a forecast based on the estimated regression may be very poor.

Fourth, it is important to recognise that a regression based on past data may not be a good predictor, due to shifts in the regression line. For example, suppose that a textile mill experiences considerable increases over time in wage rates and m erials prices. If so the regression line relating cost to output is likely to underestimate future costs. On the other hand, suppose that while input prices remain constant, the textile mill experiences considerable productivity growth due to new technology. If this happens, the regression line relating cost to output is likely to shift downward and to the right. Predictions based on historical data are likely to overestimate future costs in a situation of this sort.

Finally, when carrying out a regression, it is important to try to make sure that the assumptions underlying the linear regression model are met. Statisticians often plot the regression line on the scatter diagram and look for evidence of departures from the assumptions. For example, the scatter diagram may indicate that the relationship between the variables is curvilinear, not linear. If this is so, logarithmic regression techniques or multiple regression may be more appropriate rather than the simple linear regression techniques. There are a considerable number of tests that can be carried out to determine whether the assumptions underlying the use of regression techniques are met.

Appendix B

ECONOMETRIC MODELS AS FORECASTING TECHNIQUES

In recent years, statisticians and economists have tended to base their forecasts less on simple trend extrapolation and more on multiple-regression techniques and multi-equation models. As economics entered the age of statistics and computers, business forecasting has made great progress. Due largely to the pioneering work of Holland's Nobel Laureate Jan Tinbergen, today we have dozens of econometric models. Lawrence Klein of the Wharton School has built a number of forecasting systems over the last three decades. Commercial consulting firms such as Data Resources Inc. (DRI) have developed models that are widely used by modern business firms for forecasting purposes. The emphasis has shifted toward the construction and estimation of an equation or system of equations that will show the effects of various independent variables on the variable or variables one wants to forecast. For example, we may want to estimate the quantity of onions that will be supplied by Indian producers next year. Based on elementary economic theory, one would expect this quantity to depend on this year's price of onions and this year's level of production costs. To make such a forecast, modern statisticians and economists would be likely to estimate an equation relating these independent variables to the quantity of onions supplied; then they would use this equation to make the forecast.

To illustrate this, lets consider the study by D. B. Suits and S. Koizumi which determined that the quantity of onions supplied in year t (designated as Y_t) was related in the following way to the price of onions in year $t-1$ (designated as P_{t-1}) and the level of costs of producing onions in year $t-1$ (designated as C_{t-1})

$$\log Y_t = 0.134 + 0.0123(t - 1924) + 0.324 \log P_{t-1} - 0.512 \log C_{t-1}.$$

Given the known price of onions this year and the known level of this years production costs, this equation may be used to forecast the quantity of onions that will be supplied next year. If we insert the relevant values of $P, C,$ and t into the right-hand side of this equation, the resulting value of Y is the desired forecast.

To forecast many economic variables (such as national output) statisticians often use multi-equation models. One of these is the Wharton Econometric Model. The forecasts produced by the Wharton Model and other large ones like it are followed closely by major business firms and government agencies. Indeed, some firms and agencies have constructed their own multi-equation models. Of course, this does not mean that these large models have an unblemished forecasting record. On the contrary, they, like all other forecasting techniques, are quite fallible.

Both the single-equation model used to forecast the quantity of onions supplied and the Wharton Model, with its hundreds of equations, are examples of econometric models. It is important here to know the definition of an econometric model.

Econometric Model: An econometric model is a system of equations (or a single equation) estimated from past data that is used to forecast economic and business variables.

The use of econometric models has been made possible due to the use of modern computers. How are computer models constructed? Generally, modelers start with an analytical framework containing demand equations. Using the regression analysis or other techniques of modern econometrics each equation is fitted to the data to obtain its parameter estimates. Of course at each stage modelers use their own experience and judgment to assess whether the results are accurate and acceptable.

Finally, the whole model is put together and run as a system of equations. Once the external variables, (e.g., population, age composition of people, tax rates, availability of consumer credit, etc.) are specified the system of equations projects important economic variables into the future.

The essence of any econometric model is that it blends economic theory with statistical techniques. Of late, econometric models have come to play a very important role in business and economic forecasting.

The Wharton Econometric Model

One of the most widely used econometric models is the Wharton Model. Composed of hundreds of equations, this model has been in operation for over 20 years. In addition to being used to forecast national output, it attempts to forecast the composition of national output, the price level, unemployment and other major variables pertaining to the national economy. With the help of modern computer technology, the coefficients of the many equations in this model can be estimated and revised from time to time.

Due to the model's large size it is not feasible to list all its equations. But it is possible to describe the nature of some of the more important equations, thus providing some feel for the structure of the model. First, there are equations to explain the level of personal consumption expenditures, one equation pertaining to autos, one to nonautomotive durables, one to nondurables and one to services. In each of these equations, the level of expenditure is dependent on disposable income and prices, among other things. This is in keeping with basic economic theory.

Second, there are equations which are used to explain the levels of investment, one equation pertaining to business purchases of plant and equipment, one pertaining to construction of houses and apartments and one pertaining to changes in inventories. In the case of expenditures on plant and equipment, the relevant equation makes these expenditures dependent on changes in output or the extent of capacity utilisation as well as on the cost of capital. In the case of residential investment, the tightness of monetary markets is an important explanatory variable in the relevant equation.

Third, there are equations to explain output and employment. These variables are determined in the model primarily by the level of aggregate demand which depends on consumption expenditure, investment, imports and exports and government expenditures. Government expenditures are an exogenous variable in the model. Equations are included to explain imports and exports, these variables being functions of things like the prices of imported goods relative to domestic goods and the competitiveness of U.S. export prices relative to world prices. To estimate employment, production functions are estimated. Given the estimates of output, these production functions can be used to forecast employment. Unemployment can also be forecasted, based on information concerning the size of the labour force.

Fourth, these are equations to explain wages, prices and interest rates. The wage equations make the rate of increase of wages depend on the rate of unemployment and the rate of increase of prices. The price level is determined by the extent of capacity utilisation, among other things. A number of equations relate to the monetary sector of the economy. These equations attempt to explain interest rates, the money supply and other financial variables.

Every three months the Wharton Model is used to produce forecast of gross domestic product, the price level, the unemployment rate and other such variables for the next two years. During the 1960s its forecasting performance was particularly impressive; the average error of its forecasts of gross domestic product during the period 1959 to 1967 was only about 53 billion (less than $\frac{1}{2}$ of 1 percent). During the mid-1970s, its forecasting performance was less impressive, due in part to political events such as the behaviour of the OPEC oil producers (Obviously, such events are difficult to predict and incorporate into such a model.). Nonetheless, this and other multi-equation models have an influence on both government policy and business decision making in the U.S.A. and other industrially advanced countries.

Appendix C

THE ROLE OF FORECASTING IN BUSINESS DECISION-MAKING

Forecasting is undoubtedly important in various planning and decision-making situations. In recent years increased emphasis has been placed on improving decision making in business and government. A key aspect of decision making is the ability to predict the circumstances surrounding individual decision situations. However, due to the diversity of requirements in planning and decision-making situations no single forecasting method or narrow set of methods can meet the needs of all types of situations.

Because the general management function is central to the successful operation of the firm, forecasts that can be used as the basis for decision-making at this level are perhaps the most critical. Especially helpful here are forecasts of economic factors that can serve as a common background for all of the planning and decision-making that go on in the various managerial functions.

Six major factors appear to be important in describing forecasting methods. These reflect their inherent capabilities and adaptability.

1. *Time Horizon*: Two aspects of the time horizon relate to individual forecasting methods. First is the span of time in the future for which different forecasting methods are best suited. Generally speaking, qualitative methods of forecasting are used more for longer term forecasts, whereas quantitative methods are used more with intermediate and shorter term situations. The second important aspect of the time horizon is the number of periods for which a forecast is desired. Some techniques are appropriate for forecasting only one or two periods in advance; others can be used for several periods.

2. *Pattern of Data*: Underlying the majority of forecasting methods is an assumption as to the type of pattern(s) found in the data to be forecast. Because different forecasting methods vary in their ability to predict different types of patterns, it is important to match the presumed pattern(s) in the data with the appropriate technique.

3. *Cost*: Generally three direct elements of cost are involved in the application of a forecasting procedure. There are also opportunity costs in terms of other techniques that might have been applied. The variation in costs obviously affects the attractiveness of different methods for different situations.

4. *Accuracy*: Closely related to the level of detail required in a forecast is the needed accuracy. For some decision situations, plus or minus 10% may be sufficient; in others, a variation of as little as 5% could spell disaster.

5. *Intuitive Appeal, Simplicity and Ease of Application*: Managers will not base decisions for which they are responsible on forecasts they do not understand or in which they have no confidence. Thus, the forecasting technique must fit with the manager who will use the forecast.

6. *Availability of Computer Facilities*: It is seldom possible to apply a given quantitative forecasting method unless appropriate computer programmes exist. Such programmes must be easy to use, well documented, and free of major "bugs", so that managers can apply them and understand and interpret their results.

At least four key areas need to be considered by management as it assesses alternative forecasting methods for a specific situation. First is the item to be forecast. This requires studying the characteristics of the situation, paying particular attention to whether one is trying to predict the continuance of a historical pattern, the continuance of a basic relationship, or a turning point. Second if a manager can use a more straightforward and less expensive forecasting method (as opposed to a more sophisticated and expensive one) and still achieve the required level of accuracy. he or she generally should do so.

A third consideration is the amount of information available. Since different methods (particularly quantitative methods) are based on historical data, the manager must consider the quantity of data at hand, the appropriateness of the data, and what it would cost to gather additional data. Often it is most effective to start with a simple forecasting method that does not require many data, and then, as the manager builds experience and gathers more data, increasingly sophisticated methods can be used.

Fourth, the manager must consider the time allowed for preparing the forecast. Urgency and the amount of time allowed for data gathering therefore are factors in the selection of a forecasting method.

In selecting a forecasting method, it is wiser to apply a straightforward. simple approach initially and to upgrade gradually to more sophisticated methods if this proves beneficial and necessary.

Forecasting is not a substitute for management judgement in decision making: it is simply an aid to that process. Forecasting is not a substitute for prophecy that can eliminate future uncertainty. Instead, it is a systematic way of facing the future that can enhance and often improve unaided human judgement.

Finally, is beneficial to use more than one forecasting method and then combine their predictions. In fact, one method may be used as a cross-check against another. This has proved to be an extremely effective way of increasing forecasting accuracy and decreasing the variance in errors. Thus, when in doubt managers should combine (that is, average) multiple forecasts that come from a variety of independent sources.

SECTION B

In this section, the focus moves from the consumer side of the market to the production, or supply, side. All firms engage in the production of some good or service. In the production process various inputs are transformed into some form of output. The theory of production has been empirically tested in the context of manufacturing units by using various types of production functions and a few interesting results have been obtained [Chapter 5].

From the theory of production economists have developed certain decision rules for determining the quantity of various inputs to use in producing a firm's output under different circumstances. The theory of production also serves as a basis upon which a firm's cost curves can be constructed. Such curves can also be derived and tested by using both accounting and engineering data. Empirical analysis of cost serves a very useful practical purpose, viz., cost analysis and cost control at the plant (firm) level.

Empirical evidence reported in this section [Chapter 5] suggests that most industries are characterised by some initial range of output in which there are increasing returns to scale. However, in some cases, the economies of scale are exhausted at a relatively low level of production.

The theory of production leads us to a discussion of two other important topics, viz., factor demand (i.e., the quantity of various inputs to use in producing a firm's output under different circumstances) and pricing of joint products. The optimum purchase of inputs is made by equating marginal revenue product of a resource and its cost (or market price), called marginal resource cost [Chapter 6].

Many firms produce multiple products (i.e., jointly produced products). These are considered as a package consisting of two or more separate products. Not only do many firms produce more than one product, many also produce in multiple production facilities. This adds another dimension to managerial decision making: how should production facilities be allocated among plants? [This question is answered in Chapter 7].

Break-even analysis is frequently used in economic analysis, applying the various short-run cost concepts. The simple break-even format can be extended to determine the sales volume necessary to obtain any specified level of profit or to determine which of several price-quantity combinations will yield maximum expected profit under uncertain conditions [Chapter 8].

CHAPTER 5

EMPIRICAL PRODUCTION AND COST ANALYSES

Mass production is the focusing upon a manufacturing process of the principles of power, accurary, economy, system, continuity and speed and the normal result is a productive organisation that delivers in quantities a useful commodity of standard material, worksmanship and design at minimum cost.

Henry Ford, 1926

Fundamental Questions
1. What is the objective of empirical analysis of production and cost functions?
2. What we are steps involved in estimating production and cost functions?
3. When estimating a production function, what problems are to be faced in measuring output and inputs?
4. What key assumptions must be made in using data from actual company operations to estimate a long-run cost function?
5. What are the advantages and disadvantages of the cross-section and time-series approaches to estimating cost functions?

PREVIEW

The principles of production and cost theory developed in traditional economics (economic theory), provide an important conceptual framework for analysing managerial problems. However, managerial decisions regarding price and output in the short run and fixed asset investment in the long run require quantitative estimates of the parameters of the production and cost functions.

In any activity that is concerned, to derive the greatest benefit from the available resources, some assessment of cost will be essential. This is so because the term cost implies a measurement of the value of the resources, broadly defined, that are sacrificed as a consequence of any profit-seeking activity.

In everyday business usage of the term 'cost' implies just a money measurement of some item or items of expense, though more broadly, a cost might arise whenever the level of the company's performance, measured in some way, is reduced, even if no cost in a formal sense is entered in the company's book of accounts. However, the cost accountant has available to him a number of established procedures whereby the various elements of cost can be classified and measured. Costing techniques as such can always give precise figures, but what they cannot always do is provide figures that are both precise and relevant. The treatment that the economist gives to cost is no doubt more flexible and is concerned more with underlying cause and effect relationships.

There are three broad purposes for which cost information is required.

1. *Decision-making: the expected effects on profits of any possible action by the decision-maker will be an important if not decisive factor in that decision. In this, estimates of the cost effects of the decision are of obvious relevance.*

2. *Forecasting future cost levels: here some event or process of change is anticipated (such as rising raw material or energy prices) which will affect the company's cost levels in some degree. The company must plan its response to these changes.*

3. *Control system by setting target cost levels for various sections of the company, or perhaps for individual products, the company has a basis for monitoring and evaluating subsequent performance. One systematic way of using cost data for this purpose is standard costing.*

The following four steps are involved in any estimation of production and cost functions.

1. *Using the principles of cost and production theory to specify the appropriate functional form, that is, the specific relationship among the relevant economic variables.*
2. *Collecting the appropriate data.*
3. *Estimating the function using the data.*
4. *Evaluating and interpreting the results.*

Each step involves problems and special considerations. For example, there are a number of functional forms that can be used to describe a production process. The question faced by the analysit is: which of these is best suited to the problem being studied? Moreover, it is very difficult to collect data on inputs and cost. And the fact remains that the process of specifying and estimating production and cost fuctions require skill that can be acquired only after considerable training and experience.

PRODUCTION

Production means conversion of inputs or resources into outputs of goods and services. Inputs mean the resources which are used in the production of goods and services. Fixed inputs are those which cannot be changed readily during the time period under consideration. Fixed inputs can, however, be changed with huge expenses, e.g., replacement of company's plant and special machinary, etc. Variable inputs can be changed easily, e.g., unskilled labour, raw materials, etc. A period, during which at least one input remains fixed is called short run whereas, a period, during which all inputs can be changed, is called the long run. The duration of the two periods does not depend on any calander time (like a month or a year) but varies from firm to firm and industry to industry.

The relation between different inputs used in the production process and the level of output is expressed by the production function. The production function only indicates the maximum output which can be obtained by combining any, or all, inputs. It does not indicate the least-cost combination of factors such as labour and capital for achieving a given level of output, or the level of output which maximises profit.

THE PRODUCTION FUNCTION

The economics of production management takes as its starting point the study of the entire group of possible factor combinations that could be used to produce a certain output, with a given state of technology. This type of analysis is carried on through the production function.

A production function is an expression of the dependent or functional relationship that exists between the inputs (factors) of a production process and the output (product) that results. Hence it is sometimes known as the input-output relation.

Of the various types of production function, the Cobb-Douglas function is the most celebrated because it has certain important properties which are useful for managerial decision-making as also for economic analysis.

The study of production function is useful not for its own sake but because it answers certain questions faced by management. It enables management to know beforehand the most profitable decisions concerning the employment of resources and the scheduling of output. It is also useful in deriving a firm's cost function. For once the physical relationship between a firm's productive input services and its output are known, i.e., its production function, the firm's cost function can be derived from it, if the market prices of inputs (like rent, wage and interest rate) are known.

The production process consists of collecting various inputs at the production site and combining them in a way which yields the required finished product. For example, a farmer producing potatoes combines soil, manure, seeds, water, labour, insecticides, capital equipment, etc. to grow potatoes. Of these inputs soil and capital are relatively fixed in supply whereas other inputs may be changed with a change in the level (rate) of output (or the volume of production).

The relationship between various inputs used in the production process and the level of output is shown by the production function. Production functions only indicate efficient levels of output, i.e., the output related to each combination of inputs and the maximum output possible with that set of inputs and existing technology. When the technology of a production process changes, production functions change as well.

Production with One Variable Input

The production function may be shown in a tabular, graphic, or, algebraic form and may have one, two, or, more variable inputs. Let us now start with the tabular and graphic forms of a function which shows the production of screw in a small engineering plant.

Let Q be the quantity of screws produced and L be the number of labourers per eight-hour shift. Table 5.1 indicates the level of output which result from various labour inputs.

TABLE 5.1 A PRODUCTION FUNCTION FOR SCREWS [Q = f(L)]

Labour (L)	Output (Q)	Labour (L)	Output (Q)
1	5	6	90
2	21	7	98
3	36	8	96
4	56	9	81
5	75	10	50

Here we assume that in the short run the labour input is combined with other fixed inputs. And technology is assumed to remain constant. The relationship shown in Table 5.1 between labour input and output is shown in the form of a graph in Fig. 5.1.

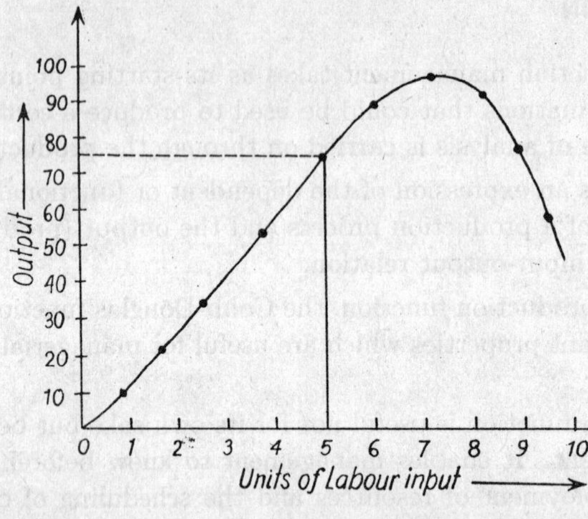

Fig 5.1 A Typical Short-run Production Function

The production function passes through the origin, showing that output is zero when labour input is zero. Some labour will be required to produce even one unit of output.

The information given in the production schedule in Table 5.1 and the graphic production function in Fig. 5.1 can be expressed by the following algebraic function $Q = f(L)$; in this case $Q = 5.5L^2 - 0.5L^3$.

From this expression we find that when the number of labourers is zero, output is also zero. For any positive value of labour input, the corresponding output can be obtained from the production function. For example if 5 labourers are engaged for a given 8-hour shift, Table 5.1 shows that 75 screws can be produced. Again in Fig 5.1, if we move horizontally 5 units from the origin and then proceed vertically upwards, we will reach that point of the curve at 75 units of output. We can also estimate output by using we following mathematical relation $Q = 5.5(5)^2 - 0.5(5)^3 = 75$.

Suppose one is interested to know how many screws can be produced if 5 workmen are engaged for full 8 hour shift and 1 worker is engaged for only $\frac{1}{2}$ shift, i.e., what level of output will be achieved when $L = 5.5$. The tabular production function is not helpful here since the table does not contain this information.

We can find the output level as the mid-point between $L = 5$ and $L = 6$ ($Q = 83.2$) assuming that the production function is linear between 5 and 6 units of labour. But this assumption is not always true. The production function is nearly linear between 5 and 6 in this case and the estimate 83,2 units of output for 5.5 units of labour input is not wrong. Similarly, from Fig 5.1, we can estimate the level of output against 5.5 units of labour only approximately, i.e., one can read the output as 84 units while others may read some other value.

However, the most appropriate method for obtaining the output corresponding to 4.5 units of labour input is to use the above the algebraic form of production function. By doing this we get $Q = 5.5(5.5)^2 - 0.5(5.5)^3 = 83.2$.

The algebraic function gives the same value irrespective of who uses the production function (or how many people use it.) Hence it is an appropriate method of quantifying how output changes are related to input changes.

Cost Minimisation

Here the firm seeks to minimise its cost of producing a given level of output. To find the least cost combination of factors for fixed level of output we combine Fig. 5.2 and Fig. 5.3 in Fig 5.4. Suppose, the producer wants to produce six units of output. He could do so using the combination represented by points A, B or C in Fig 5.4. For example, the cost would be Rs. 48 at C, Rs. 36 at B and Rs. 24 at A. The cheapest method is at A, where the isoquant for output of six ($Q = 6$) is tangent to an isocost line ($C =$ Rs. 24). In Fig. 5.4 the firm tries to find out the least expensive factor combination along its isoquant. It looks for that factor combination that is on the lowest of the isocost lines. Where the isoquant touches (but does not cross) the lowest isocost line is the least cost position. The tangency point shows that optimisation in production is reached when factor prices and marginal products are proportional, with equalised marginal product per rupee. The minimum-cost methods of isoquants and isocost lines are at points D and E. This may be called equilibrium factor combination for maximising output subject to cost constraint, i.e., subject to fixed factor prices and fixed outlet (on resources).

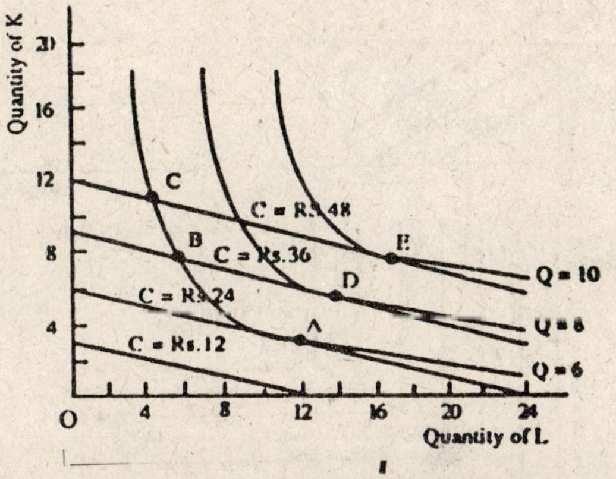

Fig 5.4 Optimisation in Production

We may now speak a few words about the slopes of isoquant and isocost lines. The slope of an isoquant gives the Marginal Rate of Technical Substitution ($MRTS$) defined as the increase in the quantity of one factor that is required to replace a unit decrease in another factor, when output is held constant along any isoquant. It is also known as the desired rate of factor substitution, i.e., the rate at which the producer wants to substitute one factor by the other.

$MRTS$ is, in fact, the ratio of the marginal products of the factors. To see this, consider an example. Assume that output is such that the MP_L and the MP_K are both equal to 2, (units of output), i.e., $MP_K = MP_L$. If the firm is to maintain the same level of output while reducing capital by one unit, it needs to replace one unit of capital by one unit of labour. If at another point on the same isoquant, the $MP_L = 2$, while the $MP_K = 1$, the firm needs to replace a unit of capital with only half unit of labour[1].

An isocost line shows the alternative quantities of two factors viz., capital and labour that can be purchased or hired with a fixed sum of money. Its slope is given by the ratio of the prices of the two factors. It is known as the actual rate of factor substitution, the rate at which the firm can substitute labour by capital in the market place. Thus, in Fig. 5.4, given the prices of labour and capital at Re.1 and Rs. 4 per unit, respectively, the slope of $C =$ Rs. 12 is determined by drawing the line joining points $3K + 0L$ (which represents outlay of Rs. 12 entirely on capital) and $12L + 0K$ (Rs. 12 spent entirely on labour). All the isocost lines in the diagram have the same slope because the relative prices of labour and capital are the same. If labour were relatively more expensive, the isocost lines would be steeper in Fig. 5.4.

[1] Isoquants have two important characteristics: they slope downwards and are convex to the origin. The downward slope indicates that both factors have positive marginal products. For example, if the quantity of labour is reduced, holding the quantity of capital constant, output falls. Convexity relates the marginal rate of substitution (the ratio MP_L/MP_K) at different points on an isoquant. If units of one factor are reduced one at a time, the quantities of the other factor needed as replacements increase continually, if we assume that diminishing returns apply to each factor.

The conclusion here is that cost minimisation occurs when an isoquant is just tangent to (but does not cross) an isocost line. When this happens the ratio of the prices of factors is the same as the ratio of their marginal products. Symbolically $MP_L/MP_K = P_L/P_K$.

Perfect Substitures and Complements

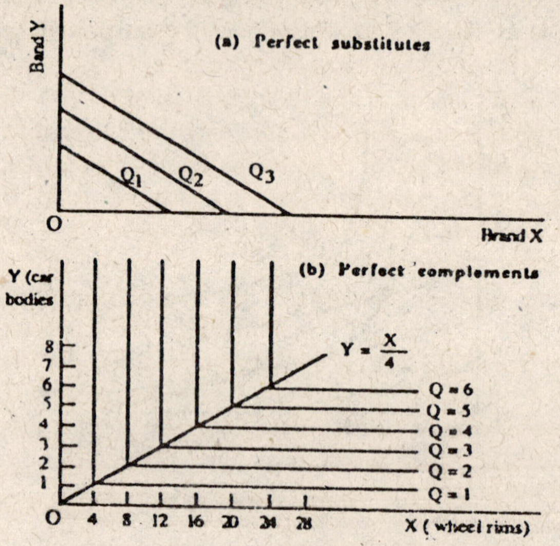

Fig 5.5 **Exceptional Isoquants**

Not all isoquants look like those in Figs. 5.5(a) and 5.5(b). If they are straight lines, the slope is the same at all X, Y combinations are the two goods are perfect substitutes. Fig 5.5 shows some straight-line isoquants. For example, a transportation company might consider two brands of gasoline, X and Y, to be perfect substitutes, as long as they have the same octane ratings.

Fig. 5.5(b) shows some perfect complements, e.g., in this case, wheel rims and car bodies. Two goods are perfect complements if a firm uses the inputs in the same proportion regardless of the output level.

For example, most automobiles require four wheel rims and one car body to give the best performance. The addition of fewer than four wheel rims will make the marginal product of an additional car body equal to zero. The isoquants will be L-shaped, with the kink in the isoquant occurring where the proportion of wheel rims to car bodies is 4 to 1.

The Leontief, or Fixed-Proportions, Production Function

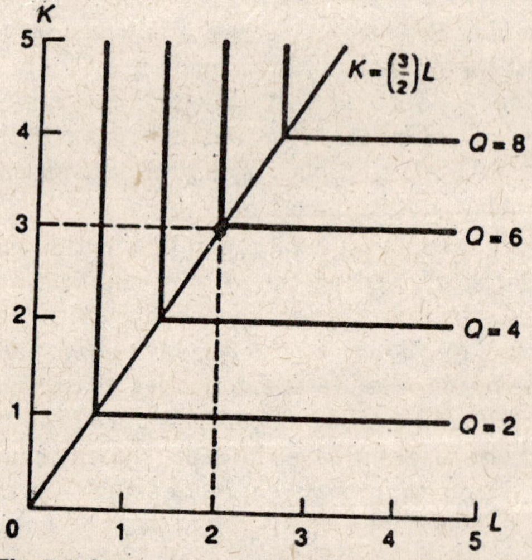

Fig 5.6 Isoquant map for the Leontief Production Function Q = min (2K, 3L)

The simplest among all production functions that are widely used is the Leontief, named after the Nobel laureate Wassily Leontief who devised it. For the two-input case, it is given by

$$Q = \min(aK, bL). \qquad (1)$$

This simply means that Q is equal to either aK or bL, whichever of the two is smaller. Suppose, for example, that $a = 2, b = 3, K = 4$ and $L = 3$. Then $Q = \min(2\times4, 3\times3) = \min(8,9) = 8$. The isoquant map for $Q = \min(2K, 3L)$ is shown in Fig. 5.6.

To see why the Leontief is also called the fixed-proportions production function, note first in Fig. 5.6 that if we start with 3 units of K and 2 units of L, we get 6 units of output. If we then add more L—so that we have, say, 3 units of L instead of 2—we still get only $Q = \min(2\times3, 3\times3) = \min(6,9) = 6$ units of output. By the same token, adding more K when we are at $K = 3$ and $L = 2$ will not lead to any additional output. In the Leontief case, K and L are used most effectively when $aK = bK$—in our example, when $2K = 3L$. In Fig. 5.6, the locus of points for which $2K = 3L$ is shown as the ray $K = \left(\frac{3}{3}\right) L$. It is along this ray that the cusps of all the right-angled isoquants of the Leontief production function will be.[1]

Returns to Scale

We often wonder whether a company is too small to operate efficiently. By carefully determining the nature of isoquants, we can answer this question. We can use the information about the production process to determine the impact on its output rate of a proportional increase in both of the inputs.

The effect that the proportionate increase in all inputs has on output is a question of returns to scale. A firm changes its scale when it increases all of its inputs in fixed proportion. Average output per unit of inputs can do one of three things, increase, decrease, or stay the same. For example, if by doubling inputs, the firm doubles its output rate, it experiences constant return to scale. If output were to more than double as inputs doubled, there would be increasing returns to scale. If output were to less than double, there would be decreasing returns to scale.

A simple relationship exists between a production function's returns to scale and the spacing of its isoquants. Consider the isoquant map in Fig. 5.7. As we move outward into the isoquant map along the ray throught the origin (R) each input grows by exactly the sampe proportion. The particular production function whose isoquant map is shown in the diagram exhibits increasing returns to scale in the region from A to C. For example, when we move from A to B, both inputs double while output goes up by a factor of 3; likewise, when we move from B to C, both inputs grow by 50 percent while output increases by 100 percent. In the region from C to F, this same production function exhibits constant returns to scale. For example, when we move from D to E, both inputs grow by 25% and output also grows exactly by 25%. Finally, Fig. 5.7 exhibits decreasing returns when we move from F to G. In this case both inputs increase by 16.7% while output grows by only 11.1%.

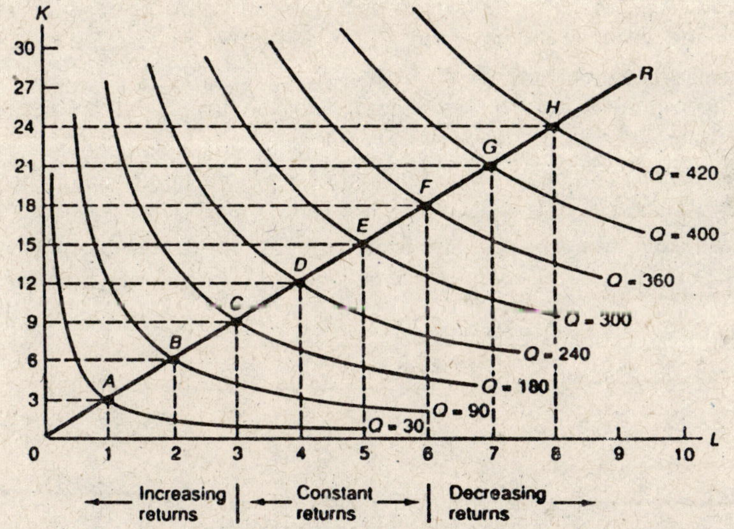

Fig 5.7 Returns to Scale shown on the Isoquant Map

---

[1] In the case of perfect complements, consumption indifference curves have the same right-angled shape as the isoquants for the Leontief production function. This means that the MRS is infinite on the vertical arm of the indifference curve, zero on the horizontal arm, and undefined at the cusp. For exactly the same reasons, the MRTS in the Leontief case will be infinite on the vertical arm of the isoquant, zero on the horizontal and undefined at the cusp.

So a production function need not exhibit the same degree of returns to scale over the entire range of output. Instead it is normally observed that there are increasing returns to scale at low levels of output, followed by constant returns to scale at intermediate levels of output, followed finally by decreasing returns to scale at high levels of output.

The airline industry is a real life example of an industry with increasing returns to scale. It is anybody's guess having a large number of flights helps an airline fill each flight by feeding passengers from its incoming flights to its outgoing flights. Local airport activities also exhibit increasing returns to scale. Ticket counter space, ticket agents, reservations equipment, baggage handling equipment, ground crews and passenger boarding facilities are all resources that are utilised more efficiently at high activity levels than at low activity levels. (The ticket counters, gates and agents of a carrier with only a few flights a day will stand idle much of the time.) Moreover due to the law of large numbers, maintenance operations, flight crew scheduling and other inventory-related activities are all accomplished more efficiently on a large scale than on a small scale. Increasing returns to scale in commercial air transport constitute the underlying explanation for why the industry has been moving much faster than other industries in recent years.

FUNCTIONAL FORMS

Economists use various functional forms of the production function. Perhaps the multiplicative form presented below is widely used $Q = AK^{\alpha}L^{\beta}$.

The reason is easy to find out. The properties of such a function represent many production processes in the real commercial world. Here Q, K and L are the quantities of output, capital and labour, respectively. A is a positive constant (i.e., the scale factor) and α and β are the exponents of the function. This multiplicative form is often referred to as the Cobb-Douglas production function.

A more general form of the Cobb-Douglas type of function with n variable factors of production is given as $Q = AX_1^{\alpha_1}X_2^{\alpha_2}X_3^{\alpha_3}\cdots X_n^{\alpha_n}$ where each X_i is an input factor and each α_i is a positive constant $[0 < \alpha_i < 1]$ indicating elasticity of output for that input, i.e., if X_1 increases by 1%, output will increase by α_i%.

Table 5.2 has been prepared on the basis of a Cobb-Douglas production function with parameters $A = 10$, $\alpha = 0.5$ and $\beta = 0.5$ i.e., $Q = 10K^{0.5}L^{0.5}$.

The table indicates the maximum rate of outputs for various input combinations, i.e., if $K = 4$ and $L = 3$, then $Q = 35$, or if $K = 5$ and $L = 5$, then $Q = 50$ and so on.

The table shows three important relationships, i.e., (1) there are many ways of producing a particular rate of output. For example, 35 units of output can be achieved with either of the following input combinations.

Combination	K	L
(a)	6	2
(b)	4	3
(c)	3	4
(d)	2	6

This means that the factors of production are substitutable. The firm can use either a capital -intensive production process (a), or a labour-intensive process (d), or an optimum combination of resources such as (b), or (c). The whole concept of production is based on the law of substitution. The law simply states that the usage of one factor is always at the expense of the other. The law is important since it allows managers to select a suitable mix of capital and labour depending on the relative prices of the two inputs.

(2) Table 5.2 also indicates that if the rates of inputs are doubled, the output rates also double. For example, when $K = 3$ and $L = 1, Q = 17$ and when $K = 6$ and $L = 2$, $Q = 35$. This is referred to as returns to scale.

(3) When output changes by changing any one of the inputs, the change in the output rates is referred to as the returns to a factor. From Table 5.2 we find that if the amount of labour (L) input is increased, for a given stock of capital (K) then output (Q) increases but the successive increments become smaller. For example, if the rate of capital input is held constant at 3 and labour is increased from $L = 1$ to $L = 6$, the successive increases in output are 8, 5, 5, 4 and 3. This relationship holds virtually for all production processes and forms the basis of the law of diminishing marginal returns. Diminishing marginal productivity is also observed when capital is increased, keeping labour fixed.

In Table 5.2 changes in output have been shown for discrete changes in the inputs only. When $K = 5.25$, or $L = 2.28$ i.e., capital, or, labour change continuously, a production function traces a smooth, continuous surface as shown in Fig 5.8.

In this three-dimensional diagram, capital, labour and output are shown in K, L and Q (vertical) axes. Q axis is perpendicular to K and L plane. The rate of output for a particular capital-labour combination can be obtained by locating the point (M, say) and drawing a perpendicular line till it touches the production surface (N, say). Here MN is the rate of output relating to input combination K' and L'. A point on the production surface includes the maximum possible output that can be produced from the input combinations related to that point.

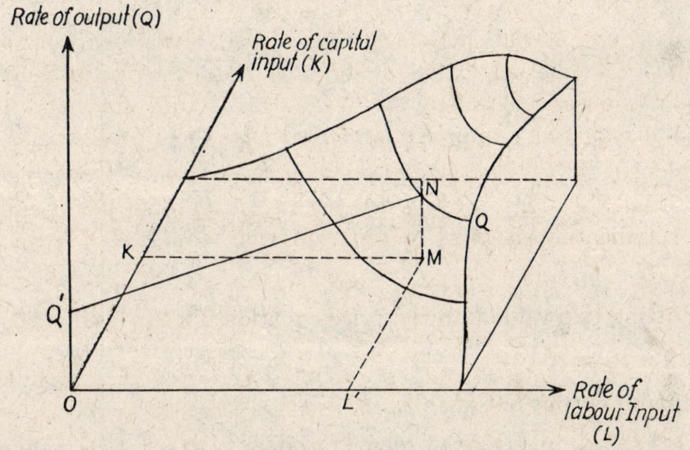

Fig 5.8 The Production Surface

PROBLEM 1. Find the marginal physical product of the different inputs or factors of production for each of the following production functions (Q):

SOLUTION.

(a) $Q = 6x^2 + 3xy + 2y^2$

$$MP_x = \frac{\partial Q}{\partial x} = 12x + 3y$$

$$MP_y = \frac{\partial Q}{\partial y} = 3x + 4y$$

(b) $Q = 0.5K^2 - 2KL + L^2$

$$MP_K = K - 2L$$

$$MP_L = 2L - 2K$$

(c) $Q = 20 + 8x + 3x^2 - 0.25x^3 + 5y + 2y^2 - 0.5y^3$

$$MP_x = 8 + 6x - 0.75x^2$$

$$MP_y = 5 + 4y - 1.5y^2$$

(d) $Q = x^2 + 2xy + 3y^2 + 1.5yz + 0.2z^2$

$$MP_x = 2x + 2y$$

$$MP_y = 2x + 6y + 1.5z$$

$$MP_z = 1.5y + 0.4z$$

PROBLEM 2. Given the production function $Q = L^{\frac{1}{2}}K^{\frac{1}{2}}$ and prices per unit of K and L Rs. 2 and Rs. 4, respectively and total cost of Rs. 80, determine the maximum output subject to the cost constraint.

SOLUTION. Our price line is $2K + 4L = 80$.

The problem is to

$$\text{maximise} \quad Q = L^{\frac{1}{2}}K^{\frac{1}{2}}$$
$$\text{subject to} \quad 2K + 4L = 80.$$

Thus we form a Lagrangian expression (the maximand)

$$V = L^{\frac{1}{2}}K^{\frac{1}{2}} + \lambda[80 - 2K - 4L].$$

Setting partial derivatives of V with respect to K, L and λ equal to zero we get

$$\frac{\partial V}{\partial K} = \frac{1}{2}L^{\frac{1}{2}}K^{-\frac{1}{2}} - 2\lambda = 0; \quad \frac{\partial V}{\partial L} = \frac{1}{2}L^{-\frac{1}{2}}K^{\frac{1}{2}} - 4\lambda = 0; \quad \frac{\partial V}{\partial \lambda} = 80 - 2K - 4L = 0.$$

From the first two, we get

$$\frac{1}{2}L^{-\frac{1}{2}}K^{\frac{1}{2}} = 4\lambda \quad \text{and} \quad \frac{1}{2}K^{-\frac{1}{2}}L^{\frac{1}{2}} = 2\lambda$$
$$\therefore \quad \frac{\frac{1}{2}L^{-\frac{1}{2}}K^{\frac{1}{2}}}{\frac{1}{2}K^{-\frac{1}{2}}L^{\frac{1}{2}}} = \frac{4\lambda}{2\lambda} = 2, \quad \text{or,} \quad \frac{K}{L} = 2.$$

$\therefore$ $K = 2L$. Putting this value into the price-equation $2 \times 2L + 4L = 80$, we get, $L = 10$. Therefore $K = 2 \times 10 = 20$.

Hence the maximum output obtainable,

i.e., $Q_{\max} = K^{\frac{1}{2}}L^{\frac{1}{2}} = (20)^{\frac{1}{2}}(10)^{\frac{1}{2}} = (200)^{\frac{1}{2}} = 20\sqrt{2} = 10 \times 1.4 = 14$ units (approx.)

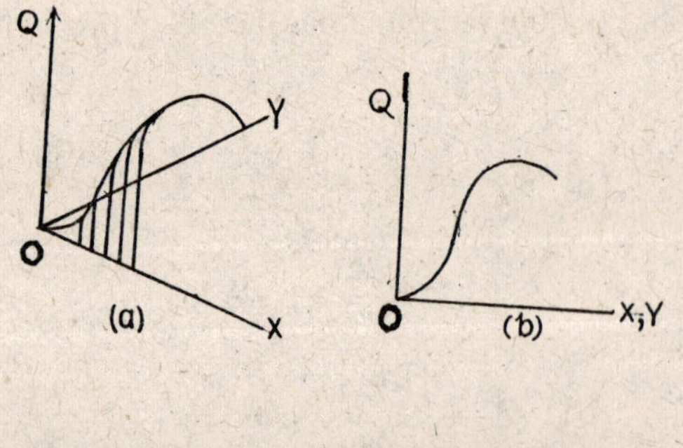

Fig 5.9 The Case of Variable Returns

POWER FUNCTIONS

From the theoretical point of view, the most common form of a production function is presented as

$$Q = a + bXY + cX^2Y + dXY^2 - eX^3Y - fXY^3. \tag{1}$$

This form can be diagrametically represented as in Fig. 5.9.

Fig. 5.10 shows that the returns to scale are first increasing and then decreasing. It also shows that the marginal product of input X is first, increasing and then decreasing.

From a number input-output observations, either over time for an individual firm, or at a point in time for several firms in an indusfry, the parameters of the production function can be estimated by using the regression technique. Often the observations do not show enough dispersion to capture the whole range of increasing and decreasing returns. In such cases simpler functional forms are used to estimate the parameters.

A power function like (1) allows marginal productivity of a particular input to depend upon all inputs used in production, a condition which is often satisfied in a number of actual production processes. Power functions help us to find returns to scale.

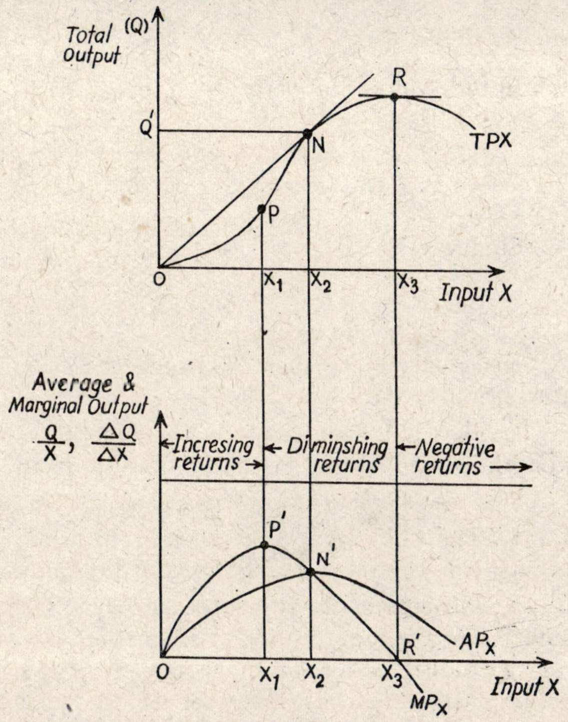

Fig 5.10 Returns to Scale and Return to a Factor

ESTIMATING THE PRODUCTION FUNCTION

In order to take decisions regarding short-run output and long-run production planning managers need additional information about production and cost behaviour within the firm. For this they need quantitative estimates of the parameters of the production function.

The Cobb-Douglas Production Function

To estimate a production function, first we are to select a functional form which clearly represents the relationship among the relavant economic variables. Although various production functions are available, as noted above, the Cobb-Douglas production function is most celebrated of all. It has already been presented in the following functional form $Q = A \cdot K^{\alpha} \cdot L^{\beta}$, where A, α and β are the parameters. The quantitative relationship between the output value (Q) and the inputs values (K, L) can be found out by putting the values of the parameters in the production function.

PROPERTIES. The Cobb-Douglas production function has some interesting mathematical properties which make them very useful for managerial decision-making. The important properties are the following:

1. The marginal product of capital and labour depends only on the quantities of capital and labour used in the production process. The equation for the marginal product of capital is given by

$$MP_K = \frac{\Delta Q}{\Delta L} = \alpha A \cdot K^{\alpha-1} \cdot L^{\beta} = \alpha \times \frac{Q}{K} \quad [\because \quad Q = A \cdot K^{\alpha} \cdot L^{\beta}].$$

Similarly, the equation for the marginal product of labour is given by

$$MP_L = \frac{\Delta Q}{\Delta L} = \beta \cdot A \cdot K^{\alpha} \cdot L^{\beta-1} = \beta \times \frac{Q}{L} \quad [\because \quad Q = A \cdot K^{\alpha} \cdot L^{\beta}].$$

It is to be noted here that MP_K and MP_L both are positive but constantly diminishing.

2. Secondly α and β the exponents of K and L respectively, show the output elasticities of labour (E_L) and capital (E_K).

For $Q = A.K^{\alpha}.L^{\beta}$, the percentage rise in Q for 1% rise in L will be

$$\frac{\%\Delta Q}{\%\Delta L} = \frac{\frac{\Delta Q}{Q}}{\frac{\Delta L}{L}} = \frac{\Delta Q}{\Delta L} \times \frac{L}{Q}.$$

In terms of partial derivatives, we can write

$$E_L = \frac{\partial Q}{\partial L} \times \frac{L}{Q} = \left(\beta \times \frac{Q}{L}\right) \times \frac{L}{Q} = \beta.$$

Similarly,

$$E_K = \frac{\partial Q}{\partial K} \times \frac{K}{Q} = \left(\alpha \times \frac{Q}{K}\right) \times \frac{K}{Q} = \alpha.$$

Hence if $\beta = 0.5$ then 1% rise in the amount of labour used (keeping capital constant) will raise output by 0.5%.

3. The Cobb-Douglas production function can be estimated by regressing the natural lagarithm of output on the natural logarithm of capital and labour inputs, i.e., $\ln Q = \ln A + \alpha \ln K + \beta \ln L$.

The result of such a regression exercise has been shown in Problem 3.

4. The Cobb-Douglas production function can be extended easily to more than two inputs outputs, e.g., capital and labour, natural resources, non-production labour, etc.

5. The sum of the two exponents (α and β) shows returns to scale. It may be noted in this context that the term returns to scale refers to the change in output which occurs when the entire scale of production of the firm changes. Strictly speaking, this happens when there is an increase in the size of the firms, i.e., when there is a proportionate increase in all inputs. Recall that returns to scale are to be classified into the following three categories.

(i) *Increasing Returns to Scale:* When all the inputs are increased by a certain amount, output increases exactly by the same amount.

(ii) *Constant Returns to Scale:* When all the inputs are increased by a certain amount, output increases exactly by the same amount.

(iii) *Decreasing Returns to Scale:* When all the inputs are increased by a certain amount, output increases by a smaller amount.

In the Cobb-Douglas case the returns to scale can be predicted as follows.

(i) When $(\alpha + \beta) = 1$ the production function exhibits constant returns to scale;

(ii) when $(\alpha + \beta) > 1$ it exhibits increasing returns to scale; and

(iii) when $(\alpha + \beta) < 1$ it exhibits decreasing returns to scale.

This property may now be explained and illustrated.

Let us take the Cobb-Douglas function, i.e., $Q_1 = A \cdot K^{\alpha} \cdot L^{\beta}$ and multiply each input by the factor a. So we get $Q_2 = A \cdot (aK)^{\alpha} \cdot (aL)^{\beta}$.

$$Q_2 = A \cdot a^{\alpha} \cdot K^{\alpha} \cdot a^{\beta} \cdot L^{\beta} = A \cdot K^{\alpha} \cdot L^{\beta} \cdot a^{(\alpha+\beta)} = Q_1 \cdot a^{(\alpha+\beta)}.$$

In fact, the Cobb-Douglas production function enables us to can determine the extent of scale economies directly from the equation of the production function. For example, assume that the production function is as follows $Q = 10X^{0.4}Y^{0.6}$.

By the definition of scale economies we must increase both X and Y in the same proportion and observe whether output increases in the same proportion. Assume that we multiply both X and Y by a constant, a. For example, let a equal 2. We will use the constant, a , to show the generality of the result.

Assume that we start with X_1 and Y_1 units of the inputs. These inputs produce Q_1 units of the output, that is, $Q_1 = 10X_1^{0.4}Y_1^{0.6}$.

Now multiply the inputs by the constant, a, so that X_2 equals aX_1 and Y_2 equals $a\ Y_1$. We now have $Q_1 = 10X_2^{0.4}Y_2^{0.6}$.

Substitute for both X_2 and Y_2.

$$Q_2 = 10(aX_1)^{0.4}(aY_1)^{0.6} = 10a^{0.4}X_1^{0.4}a^{0.6}Y_1^{0.6} = 10a^{(0.4+0.6)}X_1^{0.4}Y_1^{0.6} = a^{1.0}(10X_1^{0.4}Y_1^{0.6}) = aQ_1.$$

Since Q_2 equals $a\ Q_1$ this production function exhibits constant returns to scale. By multiplying the inputs by a, we increase output in the same proportion. This result depends critically on the exponents, of the inputs in the production function. In this case the two exponents, 0.4 and 0.6, added up to 1.

In Table 5.2, at $K = 2$ and $L = 3, Q_1 = 25$. If K and L are doubled, i.e., at $K = 4$ and $L = 6$, $Q_1 = 49$, i.e., output is also doubled, i.e., $49/25 \approx 2.0$, or, output has increased by a factor 2.0. Hence the production function exhibits increasing returns to scale in this range of values..

Let us consider the algebraic form of the production function $Q = 10.K^{0.5}.L^{0.5}$.

Let Q_2 be the new output when K and L are replaced by $2K$ and $2L$, respectively.

$$\therefore \quad Q' = 10.(2K)^{0.5}.(2L)^{0.5} = (2^{0.5}.2^{0.5}).10.K^{0.5}.L^{0.5} = 2.Q.$$

Thus when both the inputs are doubled, output is also doubled.

So long we have been discussing what is called homogeneous production function[1]. For non-homogeneous production functions, we should consider each case separately to find out the nature of the returns to scale. Let us consider the following production function

$$Q = f(K, L) = 5K + 4L - 0.1KL.$$

When $K = 5, L = 10, Q_1 = 5 \times 5 + 4 \times 10 - 0.1 \times 5 \times 10 = 60$.

If we double the values of inputs K and L, i.e., $K = 10, L = 20$, we get the new output as follows: $Q_2 = 5 \times 10 + 4 \times 20 - 0.1 \times 10 \times 20 = 110$.

Now $\frac{Q_2}{Q_1} = \frac{110}{60} = 1.83$. Hence output increases by only 83% when both the inputs are doubled. Hence thus production function shows decreasing returns to scale in this range of values.

6. The Cobb-Douglas production function has an additional property. It is a homothetic production function. A homothetic production function has a straight line expansion path, i.e., changes in the level of output will have no effect on relative input usage (the ratio of labour to capital usage in the two-input case).

---

[1] A function is said to be homogeneous of degree n if the multiplication of all of the independent variables by the same constant, say, λ results in the multiplication of the dependent variable by λ^n. Thus the function $Y{=}X^2{+}Z^2$ is homogeneous of degree 2 since $(\lambda X)^2{+}(\lambda Z)^2{=}\lambda^2(X^2{+}Z^2){=}\lambda^2 Y$. A function which is homogeneous of degree 1 is said to be linearly homogeneous, or to display linear homogeneity. A production function which is homogeneous of degree 1 displays constant returns to scale since a, say, doubling of all inputs will lead to doubling of output.

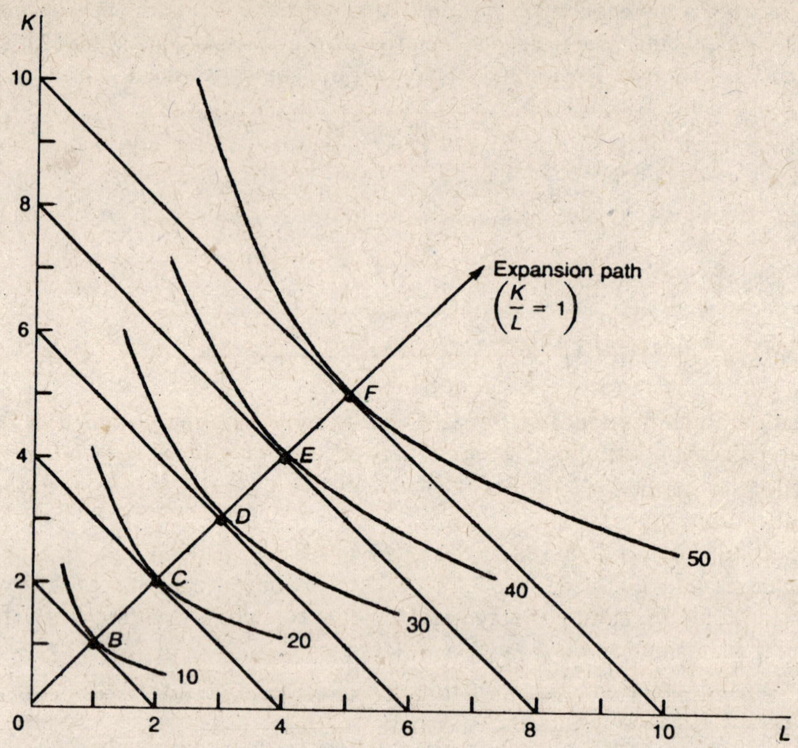

Fig 5.11 The Expansion Path for the Cobb-Douglas Function

We can also define the isoquants for this Cobb-Douglas production function. For this we have to express the production function in different form:

$$Q = 10L^{0.5}K^{0.5} = 10\sqrt{L}\sqrt{K} = 10\sqrt{LK} \tag{1}$$

For example, the isoquant for $50Q$ can be defined by substituting 50 for Q in equation (1). By then substituting various quantities of labour into the resulting equation, we get the corresponding quantities of capital required to produce the $50Q$. That is,

$$50 = 10\sqrt{LK};\ 5 = \sqrt{LK};\ 25 = LK;\ 25/L = K. \tag{2}$$

Thus, if $L = 10, K = 2.5$; if $L = 5, K = 5$; if $L = 2.5, K = 10$, and so on. Other isoquants can be similarly derived. Isoquants are parallel along any ray from the origin and are equally spaced to reflect constant returns to scale. If, in addition, the wage rate (w) equals the interest on capital (r), the slope of the isocost lines is $w/r = -1$. and the expansion path is a straight line through the origin with $K/L = 1$. This is shown in Fig. 5.11.

For such a production function the elasticity of factor substituion is equal to one[1].

PROBLEM 3. The following table shows a production function of screws with two variable inputs.

---

[1] For a proof of this property see S. Mukherjee and D. Mukherjee: *Elementary Economic Analysis* (2nd edn., NCBA, 1995)

TABLE 5.3 OUTPUT OF SCREWS AS A FUNCTION OF BOTH LABOUR AND CAPITAL INPUTS

6	25	35	42	49	55	60
5	22	32	39	45	50	55
4	20	28	35	40	45	49
3	17	25	30	35	39	42
2	14	20	25	28	32	35
1	10	14	17	20	22	25
	1	2	3	4	5	6

Labour Input (L)

(i) Estimate the parameters (A, α and β) of a Cobb-Douglas production function by applying the least squares regression method.

(ii) Use the estimated parameters to find: (a) the returns to scale as also; (b) the equations for the marginal product of capital and labour

(iii) Compute the marginal products of labour and capital for the input combination

$$\{K = 15, L = 20\}.$$

SOLUTION. (i) First, transform the Cobb-Douglas production function $Q = A.K^{\alpha}.L^{\beta}$ by taking the logarithm of each term, i.e., $\ln Q = \ln A + \alpha \ln K + \beta \ln L$.

The least squares regression method gives the following estimates[1] of the parameters:

$$\ln Q = 2.30 + 0.5 \ \ln K + 0.5 \ \ln L$$
$$\text{or,} \quad Q = e^{2.30} \times K^{0.5} \times L^{0.5} = 2.718^{2.30} \times K^{0.5} \times L^{0.5} = 10.K^{0.5}.L^{0.5}.$$

The estimated parameters are $\alpha = 0.5, \beta = 0.5$ and $A = 10$. Hence the estimated production function will be $Q = 10.K^{0.5}.L^{0.5}$.

(ii) (a) The returns to scale are constant because $\alpha + \beta = 0.5 + 0.5 = 1$.

(b) The marginal product functions for labour and capital are given below

$$MP_L = \beta.A.K^{\alpha}.L^{\beta-1} = 0.5 \times 10 \times K^{0.5} \times L^{-0.5}$$
$$\text{and} \quad MP_K = \alpha.A.K^{\alpha-1}.L^{\beta} = 0.5 \times 10 \times K^{-0.5} \times L^{0.5}.$$

(iii) Putting the estimated values of A, α and β and $K = 15$ and $L = 20$, we get the following marginal products

$$MP_L = 0.5 \times 10 \times (15)^{0.5} \times (20)^{-0.5} = 0.5 \times 10 \times \left(\frac{15}{20}\right)^{0.5} = 5 \times 0.866 = 4.330.$$
$$MP_K = 0.5 \times 10 \times (15)^{-0.5} \times (20)^{0.5} = 5 \times \left(\frac{20}{15}\right)^{0.5} = 5 \times 1.155 = 5.774.$$

The significance of $MP_L = 4.330$ is that one-unit variation in labour, keeping capital constant at 15, will result in 4.330-unit variation in output.

---

[1] Applying a standard multiple regression computer programme, similar results can also be obtained.

Again the significance of $MP_K = 5.774$ is that one-unit variation in capital, keeping labour constant at 20, will result in 5.774-unit variation in output.

Problems of Estimation

The Cobb-Douglas production function can be estimated either from information on a single firm, or, a group of firms at the same point of time.

However, while doing this the researchers may face the following difficulties:[1]

1. When a firm manufactures various products output may have to be measured in monetary terms and not in physical units. This will need deflating the value of output by the price indices of different years by using time series data.

2. The amount of capital actually consumed in producing the output should only be considered.

3. In time-series analysis, the time trend is included to show the effect of technological change over time whereas in cross-section analysis, we must ensure that the same technology is being adopted by all firms at a fixed point of time.

Economic Insight/Empirical Estimation of the Cobb-Douglas Production Function

One method of estimating the paramaters of the Cobb-Douglas production function (i.e., A, α and β) applies statistical (i.e., regression) analysis to time series data on the inputs used and the output produced. For example, the researcher may collect data on the number of automobiles produced by an automaker in each year from 1950 to 1994 and on the quantity of labour and capital used in each year to produce the automobiles. The data are usually transformed into natural logarithms (indicated by the symbol ln*) and the regression analysis is conducted on the transformed data. The form of the estimated Cobb-Douglas production function is then* $\ln Q = \ln A + \alpha \ln L + \beta \ln K$.

The researcher thus obtains an estimate of the value of $\ln A, \alpha$, *and* β. *Of primary interest to the researcher is the value of* α *and* β.

Another method of estimating the value of A, α, *and* β *is by regression analysis using cross-section data. In this case, the researcher collects data for a given year (or other time unit) for each of many producers or firms in a particular industry on the quantity of labour and capital used and the output produced. That is, instead of collecting data for one firm over many years (time series), the researcher now collects data for a given year for many firms in the same industry (cross section). As in the previous case, the researcher usually first transforms the data into natural logarithms and then estimates the above equation by regression analysis to obtain the values of parameters* A, α, *and* β. *Once again the researcher is primarily interested in the value of* α *and* β. *Table A-1 (in the Appendix–A to this chapter) presents the values of* α *and* β *estimated for various U.S. manufacturing industries for the year 1957.*

Input-output relationships can also be obtained from engineering studies. All of these methods (i.e., regression analysis using time series or cross-section data and engineering studies) face difficulties. One of these is that we must assume that the best production techniques are used by all firms at all times. Due to a lack of information or wrong decisions, this may not be the case. Another difficulty arises in the measurement of the capital input, since machinery and equipment are of different types, ages (vintage) and productivities. A further

[1] For further details see Sampat Mukherjee: *Business and Managerial Economics* (NCBA 1995).

shortcoming of engineering studies is that they typically cover only some production activities of the firm. Despite these and other problems, numerous studes have been conducted over the years using these different approaches. They have provided very useful information on production for the entire economy and for various industries.[1]

Evaluating the Cobb-Douglas Production Function for Diminishing Marginal Product

To statistically test whether the Cobb-Douglas production function is characterised by diminishing marginal productivity, we have to first investigate the nature of marginal and average product functions of the two inputs used in the production process.

Recall that $Q = A \cdot K^{\alpha} \cdot L^{\beta}$.

Here the marginal product of labour is expressed as

$$MP_L = \frac{\partial Q}{\partial L} - \beta \cdot A \cdot K^{\alpha} \cdot L^{\beta-1}$$

Now the slope of $MP_L = \frac{\partial MP_L}{\partial L} = (\beta-1)(\beta)A \cdot K^{\alpha} \cdot L^{\beta-2}$. Since $0 < \beta < 1$, the slope of MP_L is always negative which means that MP_L is positive but diminishing. Hence there is diminishing marginal product of labour for the whole range of output.

Again the marginal product of capital

$$MP_K = \frac{\partial Q}{\partial K} = \alpha \cdot A \cdot K^{\alpha-1} \cdot L^{\beta}$$

Now the slope of

$$MP_K = \frac{d\,MP_K}{dK} = (\alpha)(\alpha-1) \cdot A \cdot K^{\alpha-2} \cdot L^{\beta}.$$

Since $0 < \alpha < 1$, the Cobb-Douglas production function also shows diminishing marginal product for capital. If we extend the function to include more inputs, we will observe that the same result is applicable, i.e., we can prove the hypothesis of diminishing marginal physical product of a factor.

In a Cobb-Douglas production function the average product (AP) is greater than the marginal product (MP) and diminishes over the entire range of production.

$$MP_L = \beta \cdot \frac{Q}{L} = \beta \times AP_L \qquad \left[\because \quad AP_L = \frac{Q}{L}\right]$$

$$\text{and} \quad MP_K = \alpha \cdot \frac{Q}{K} = \alpha \times AP_K \qquad \left[\because \quad AP_K = \frac{Q}{K}\right]$$

Now

$$AP_L = \frac{Q}{L} = \frac{A \cdot K^{\alpha} \cdot L^{\beta}}{L} = A \cdot K^{\alpha} \cdot L^{\beta-1} \quad \therefore MP_L = \beta \cdot A \cdot K^{\alpha} \cdot L^{\beta-1}.$$

Since $0 < \beta < 1, MP_L < AP_L$.

The relationship that $MP_K = \alpha \times AP_K$ can be shown in the same way.

1 D. Salvatore: ***Microeconomics*** (McGraw-Hill, 2nd edn., 1994)

Let us consider the MP and AP for the Cobb-Douglas production function given in Table 5.3, i.e., $Q = 10 \cdot K^{0.5} \cdot L^{0.5}$.

The MP_L can be found as follows

$$\frac{dQ}{dL} = 10(0.5) \cdot K^{0.5} \cdot L^{-0.5} \quad \therefore \quad MP_L = 5 \cdot K^{0.5} \cdot L^{-0.5}.$$

To find out whether MP_L is declining, we are to find its slope, i.e.,

$$\frac{dMP_L}{dL} = 5 \times -0.5 \cdot K^{0.5} \cdot L^{-1.5} = -2.5 \cdot K^{0.5} \cdot L^{-1.5}.$$

Since the slope of MP_L is negative, we can conclude that the marginal product of labour is also declining.

Now AP_L = Average Product of Labour $= \frac{Q}{L} = \frac{10 \cdot K^{0.5} \cdot L^{0.5}}{L} = 10 \cdot K^{0.5} \cdot L^{-0.5}$.

$\therefore$ the slope of $AP_L = \frac{dAP_L}{dL} = (-0.5)(10) \cdot K^{0.5} \cdot L^{-1.5} = -5 \cdot K^{0.5} \cdot L^{-1.5}$.

Since the slope of AP_L is negative, it declines throughout. The MP and AP for this Cobb-Douglas production function are shown in Table 5.4 for both 3 and 6 units of of capital.

TABLE 5.4 MP AND AP FOR COBB-DOUGLAS PRODUCTION FUNCTION ($Q = 10.K^{0.5}.L^{0.5}$)

	For K=3		For K=6	
L	MP	AP	MP	AP
1	8.5	17.0	12.5	25.0
2	6.3	12.5	8.6	17.5
3	5.0	10.0	7.0	14.0
4	4.4	8.8	6.2	12.3
5	3.9	7.8	5.5	11.0
6	3.5	7.0	5.0	10.0

[N.B. $\frac{MP}{AP} = \beta = 0.5$].

From Table 5.4, we find that $MP < AP$ and both MP and AP diminish throughout. We also find that the AP and MP for $K = 6$ are greater than AP and MP for $K = 3$.

So the implication is clear. If managers provide workers with adequate complementary resource (capital), labour productivity will improve.

COST ANALYSIS AND ESTIMATION

The Cost Function

Cost-output relations are expressed through the cost functions which depends on the production function and market supply-fuction of inputs[1]. There are two types of cost functions—(1) short run (2) long run. The cost function can be represented symbolically as $C = f(Q, T, P_f, K)$ where C, Q, T, P_f and K stand for total cost, quantity produced, technology, factor price and capital

[1] Cost function is a mathematical expression that depicts the general relationship between the costs of factor inputs and the cost of output in a firm. In order to determine the cost of producing a particular output it is necessary to know not only the required quantities of the various inputs but also their prices. The cost function can be derived from the production function by adding the information about factor prices.

respectively. Since all determinants of costs, except Q, are constant in the short run the short run cost function can be expressed as $C = f(Q)$.

Short-Run Cost Analysis

Short-run costs refer to the costs which vary with changes in output, the size of the firm remaining constant. The basic cost concepts which are used in the analysing cost behaviour are total cost (TC) average cost (AC) and marginal cost (MC). TC refers to the total actual cost which is incurred to produce a given quantity of output. The short-run TC consists of total fixed cost (TFC) and total variable cost (TVC). Hence $TC = TFC + TVC$. Note that TFC remains fixed in the short-run up to a certain level of output (called capacity output) whereas TVC varies with changes in the level (rate) of output.

The average total cost (ATC, or, AC), average fixed cost (AFC), and average variable cost (AVC), for a given quantity of output Q can be determined as follows

$$AC, \text{ or, } ATC = \frac{TC}{Q} = AFC + AVC = \frac{FC + VC}{Q}$$

$$AVC = \frac{TVC}{Q}; \; AFC = \frac{TFC}{Q}$$

Since $TC = TFC + TVC$, $AC = AFC + AVC$.

Marginal cost (MC) refers to the ratio of the change in TC to the change in total output, i.e.,

$$MC = \frac{\Delta TC}{\Delta Q}$$

Now $\Delta TC = \Delta TFC + \Delta TVC$.

In the short run $\Delta TFC = 0$.

Therefore $\Delta TC = \Delta TVC$.

In other words, $MC = TVC$ in the short run.

The short run cost-output relationship is shown in Table 5.5 and Fig. 5.12. Table 5.5(a) shows the relation between output and total variable cost. The equation of the total variable cost in this case will be of the following form $TVC = 20Q - 2.2Q^2 + 0.12Q^3$.

TABLE 5.5(a) TOTAL VARIABLE COST (TVC) AS A FUNCTION OF OUTPUT (Q)

Q	TVC	Q	TVC	Q	TVC
1	17.92	6	66.72	11	113.52
2	32.16	7	73.36	12	130.56
3	43.44	8	80.64	13	151.84
4	52.48	9	89.28	14	178.08
5	60.00	10	100.00	15	210.00

We find that TVC increases at a decreasing rate up to $Q = 8$ and after that TVC increases at an increasing rate.

In the short-run the (TC) total cost of production consists of TVC and TFC, i.e., $TC = TVC + TFC$.

If $TFC = 20$, we can express TC, as $TC = 20 + 20Q - 2.2Q^2 + 0.12Q^3$.

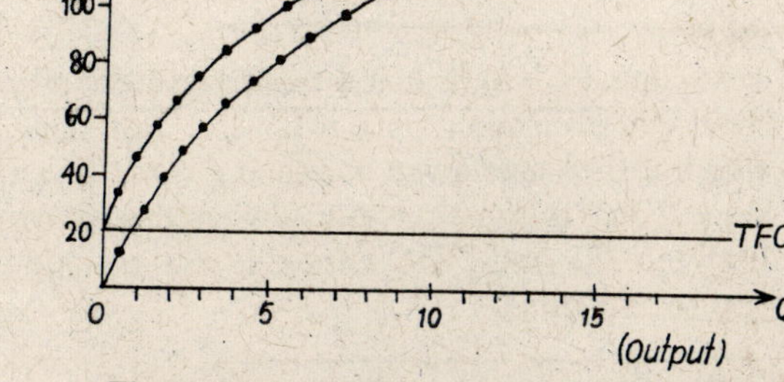

Fig 5.12(a) Short-run Total Cost Curves

TABLE 5.5(b) COST AS A FUNCTION OF OUTPUT[1]

Q	TFC	TVC	TC	AFC	AVC	AC	MC
0	20	—	20	—	—	—	—
1	20	17.92	37.92	20.00	17.92	37.92	17.92
2	20	32.16	52.16	10.00	16.08	26.08	14.24
3	20	43.44	63.44	6.67	14.48	21.15	11.28
4	20	52.48	72.48	5.00	13.12	18.12	9.04
5	20	60.00	80.00	4.00	12.00	16.00	7.52
6	20	66.72	86.72	3.33	11.12	14.45	6.72
7	20	73.36	93.36	2.86	10.48	13.34	6.64
8	20	80.64	100.64	2.50	10.08	12.58	7.28
9	20	89.28	109.28	2.22	9.92	12.14	8.64
10	20	100.00	120.00	2.00	10.00	12.00	10.72
11	20	113.52	133.52	1.82	10.32	12.14	13.52
12	20	130.56	150.56	1.67	10.88	12.55	17.04
13	20	151.84	171.84	1.54	11.68	13.22	21.28
14	20	178.08	198.08	1.43	12.72	14.15	26.24
15	20	210.00	230.00	1.33	14.00	15.33	31.92

Table 5.5 (b) is the short-run cost schedule of a typical firm. It gives complete information on different types and components of a firm's costs. From Table 5.5 (b), we notice the following.

1. TFC is not increasing with increase in output (Q).

2. With increase in Q, TVC increases at a decreasing rate till $Q = 8$ units and then increases at a rapid rate.

3. With increase in output, TC first increases at a decreasing rate and then increases at an increasing rate.

4. Since TFC is a constant AFC continues to fall with an increase in output (i.e., the volume or rate of production)

5. With increase in Q, AVC decreases till the rate of increase in TVC declines beyond which it increases.

6. Up to $Q = 7, MC$ decreases continuously. Beyond that output level it continues to increases.

Graphic Presentation

Fig. 5.12 (a) shows the relationship between TC, TVC and TFC and output. The TFC curve is a horizontal line, since it remains fixed throughout the entire range of output. But the TVC curve shows that it increases at first at a decreasing rate and then at an increasing rate as total output increases. The rate of increase can be found from the gradient of the TVC curve. The pattern of change in TVC can be derived from the law of increasing and diminishing returns to the variable inputs.

The TC curve has a positive intercept on y-axis since a fixed cost (Rs. 20) is incurred in the short run even when output is zero. Note that TC increases at a decreasing rate up to $Q = 8$ beyond which it increases at an increasing rate. The TC curve shows the same pattern of behaviour as TVC since TFC is constant and always lies above TVC by the amount of TFC. The vertical distance between TC and TVC curves is exactly equal to the TFC and constant at all the levels of output (up to capacity).

[1] In Table 5.5 (b) $AFC = \frac{20}{Q}$

Fig 5.12 (b) makes the laws of production more clear. According to the law of diminishing returns, when more units of a variable input are added to other inputs, the returns from the marginal units of the variable inputs at first increase and then decrease. This is also true for costs, i.e., when more units of variable inputs are added to other fixed inputs, the marginal cost decreases at first and then increases. Hence both the laws give the same information. But there is a difference. While the former is expressed through the production function and refers to marginal productivity of the variable input, the latter is expressed through the cost function and has relevance to cost behaviour.

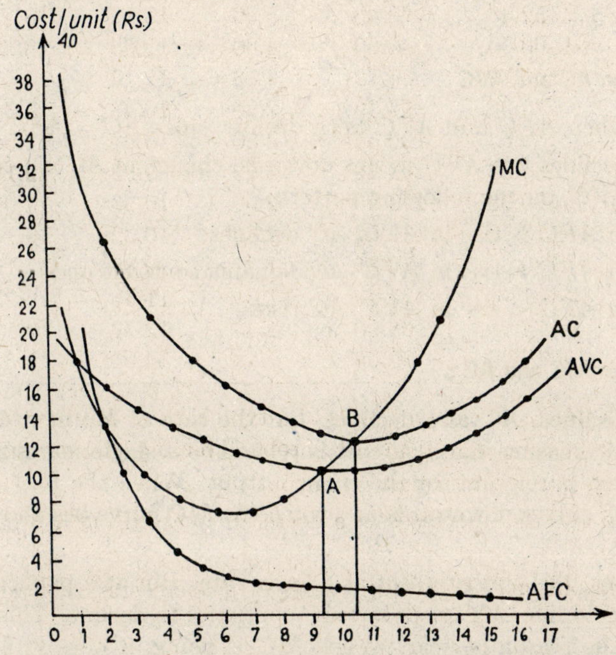

Fig 5.12 (b) Short-run Average and Marginal Cost Curves

Fig. 5.12 (b) can be interpreted using laws of returns in terms of cost of production. We find from Fig. 5.12 (b) that at the initial stage of production, AFC and AVC are both decreasing. Here AVC is declining due to increasing return to the variable factors. For the same reason $AC(= AFC + AVC)$ is also declining. But after a certain level of output, say 8 units, AVC starts increasing due to faster increase in TVC but AFC continues to decline. Accordingly, the rate of decline in AC decreases. AC is minimum when output is approximately 9 units. Beyond this point, AC continues to rise indicating that the law of diminishing returns comes into operation. The MC curve shows the patterns of change in TVC and TC curves as output changes. The downward trend in MC indicates increase in the marginal product of the variable factor(s).

EXAMPLE 4. Calculate average cost from total cost in the following two cases at the different levels of output $Q = 3$ and $Q = 5$.

1. $TC = 3Q^3 + 7Q + 12$

(1) $MC = \dfrac{dTC}{dQ} = 6Q + 7$

At $Q = 3,\ MC = 6(3) + 7 = 25$

At $Q = 5,\ MC = 6(5) + 7 = 37.$

(2) $AC = \dfrac{TC}{Q} = 3Q + 7 + \dfrac{12}{Q}$

At $Q = 3,\ AC = 3(3) + 7 + \dfrac{12}{3} = 20$

At $Q = 5,\ AC = 3(5) + 7 \times \dfrac{12}{5} = 24.4$

2. $TC = 35 + 5Q - 2Q^2 + 2Q^3$.

(1) $MC = \dfrac{dTC}{dQ} = 5 - 4Q + 6Q^2$

At $Q = 3$, $MC = 5 - 4(3) + 6(3)^2 = 47$.

At $Q = 5$, $MC = 5 - 4(5) + 6(5)^2 = 135$.

(2) $AC = \dfrac{TC}{Q} = \dfrac{35}{Q} + 5 - 2Q + 2Q^2$

At $Q = 3$, $AC = \dfrac{35}{3} + 5 - 2(3) + 2(3)^2 = 28.67$.

At $Q = 5$, $AC = \dfrac{35}{5} + 5 - 2(5) + 2(5)^2 = 52$.

The Relationship between AC and AVC

1. AC declines when AFC and AVC both decline, since $AC = AFC + AVC$.

2. When AFC declines but AVC moves upwards, change in AC depends on the magnitude of change in AFC and AVC, on the following pattern:

(i) when fall in $AFC >$ rise in AVC, AC declines,

(ii) when fall in $AFC =$ rise in AVC, AC remains constant and

(iii) when fall in $AFC <$ rise in AVC, AC rises.

The Relationship between MC and AC

1. When MC declines, AC also declines, but the rate of fall in MC is higher than that of AC since in MC the decreasing marginal cost is related to a single marginal unit while in AC, the decreasing marginal cost is relevant for the entire output. When the MC curve lies below the AC curve, it pushes the AC curves downwards and when the MC curve lies above the AC curve, it pulls the AC upwards.

2. When MC rises, AC also rises but at a lower rate. But at a particular range of output this relationship does not hold, i.e., MC rises but AC continues to decline. This range of output is from 6 units to 10 units. The reason is clear. When MC is rising, it does so at a relatively lower rate which is not adequate to pull AC upwards.

3. The MC curve intersects the AC curve at its minimum point. The argument is that when MC declines it pulls AC downwards and *vice versa*. When AC is at its minimum, it is neither pulled downward nor pushed upward by MC, i.e., $MC = AC$, when AC is at its minimum.

4. At point A and point B, AVC and AC attain their respective minimum values.

Optimum Output and Cost Curves

The optimum level of output is one which is produced at a minimum average cost with available technology. The minimum level of AC can be obtained from the point of intersection between AC and MC curves. Recall that where $AC = MC$, AC is at its minimum.

Any level of production above, or, below this level leaves some scope of adjusting AC either by reducing, or, increasing output as required. Cost curves are thus useful in finding the optimum level of output which is not necessarily the maximum profit output.

Short-run Average and Marginal Costs

Average cost (AC) of producing a product is the total cost (TC) divided by units of output (Q), i.e.,

$$AC = \frac{TC}{Q} = \frac{FC + VC}{Q} = AFC + AVC.$$

Marginal cost (MC) is another important cost concept particularly useful in economic analysis. It is the rate of change in total cost divided by changes in output and is represented by the first derivative of TC with respect to Q as follows $MC = \frac{dTC}{dQ}$.

U-shape of Cost Curves

MC, AVC and AC are often referred to as U-shaped cost functions. Consider the following example. For a given TC function, how can you find the equations for MC, AVC and AC and the range of output over which each is decreasing, or increasing? Find out the level of output at which average cost is minimum.

To answer this question let us start with the following equation of the total cost curve $TC = 20 + 20Q - 2.2Q^2 + 0.12Q^3$.

The corresponding marginal and average cost equations are presented below.

Marginal Cost (MC)

$$MC = \frac{dTC}{dQ} = 20 - 4.4Q + 0.36Q^2; \quad \frac{dMC}{dQ} = -4.4 + 0.72Q = 0.$$

$\therefore$ the critical value is at $Q = \frac{4.4}{0.72} = 6.11$.

Now $\frac{d^2MC}{dQ^2} = 0.72 > 0$.

Hence at $Q = 6.11$, MC is minimum, i.e., $MC = 20 - 4.4 \times 6.11 + .36(6.11)(6.11) = 6.55$. MC will be a decreasing function up to $Q = 6.11$ and beyond this level of output it is an increasing function.

Average Variable Cost (AVC)

$$VC = 20Q - 2.2Q^2 + 0.12Q^3 \;\therefore\; AVC = \frac{VC}{Q} = 20 - 2.2Q + 0.12Q^2.$$

Now $\frac{dAVC}{dQ} = -2.2 + 0.24Q = 0$ or, the critical value is at $Q = \frac{2.2}{0.24} = 9.17$.

Now $\frac{d^2AVC}{dQ^2} = 0.24 > 0$.

Hence AVC is minimum at $Q = 9.17$, at which point $AVC = 20 - 2.2 \times 9.17 + 0.12 \times 9.17 \times 9.17 = 9.92$. So AVC is a decreasing function up to output less then 9.17 and beyond this it will increase.

Average Cost (AC)

$$AC = \frac{TC}{Q} = \frac{20}{Q} + 20 - 2.2Q + 0.12Q^2, \quad \text{or,} \quad \frac{dAC}{dQ} = (-1)\frac{20}{Q^2} - 2.2 + 0.24Q = 0.$$

The critical value is at $Q = 10$.

Now $\frac{d^2AC}{dQ^2} = \frac{40}{Q^3} + 0.24 > 0$.

Hence AC is minimum at $Q = 10$, when $AC = 12$. This means that AC declines up to 10 units of output and rises thereafter.

[**N.B.** (1) For negative slope of $MC(\frac{dMC}{dQ} < 0), TC$ and VC will be increasing at a decreasing rate.

(2) For positive slope of $MC(\frac{dMC}{dQ} > 0), TC$ and VC will be increasing at an increasing rate.]

For our function, we have

$$MC = 20 - 4.4Q + 0.36Q^2; \quad AC = \frac{20}{Q} + 20 - 2.2Q + 0.12Q^2; \quad AVC = 20 - 2.2Q + 0.12Q^2.$$

We know that AC is minimum when $Q = 10$ and AVC is minimum at $Q = 9.17$.
When $Q = 10$, we have

$$MC = 20 - 4.4 \times 10 + 0.36 \times 10 \times 10 = 12$$
$$AC = \frac{20}{10} + 20 - 2.2 \times 10 + 0.12 \times 10 \times 10 = 12$$

and when $Q = 9.17$, we have

$$MC = 20 - 4.4 \times 9.17 + 0.36 \times 9.17 \times 9.17 = 9.92$$
$$AVC = 20 - 2.2 \times 9.17 + 0.12 \times 9.17 \times 9.17 = 10.07.$$

The short-run cost functions and interrelationships among them, discussed above, are typical of a wide variety of manufacturing industries.

PROBLEM 5. Find the marginal cost functions for each of the following average cost functions.
(a) $AC = 1.5Q + 4 + \frac{46}{Q}$.

SOLUTION. Given the average cost function, the marginal cost function is determined by first finding the total cost function and then taking its derivative, as follows

$$TC = AC(Q) = \left(1.5Q + 4 + \frac{46}{Q}\right)Q = 1.5Q^2 + 4Q + 46; \quad MC = \frac{dTC}{dQ} = 3Q + 4.$$

(b) $AC = \frac{160}{Q} + 5 - 3Q + 2Q^2$

$$TC = \left(\frac{160}{Q} + 5 - 3Q + 2Q^2\right)Q = 160 + 5Q - 3Q^2 + 2Q^3; \quad MC = \frac{dTC}{dQ} = 5 - 6Q + 6Q^2.$$

(c) $AC - \frac{18}{Q} - 0.1 - 0.5Q = 0$

$$AC = \frac{18}{Q} + 0.1 + 0.5Q; \quad TC = \left(\frac{18}{Q} + 0.1 + 0.5Q\right)Q = 18 + 0.1Q + 0.5Q^2; \quad MC = \frac{dTC}{dQ} = 0.1 + Q.$$

PROBLEM 6. Minimise the following cost functions.

SOLUTION. (a) $AC = 200 - 24Q + Q^2$

(1) $\frac{dAC}{dQ} = 2Q - 24 = 0$; $Q = 12$;

(2) $\frac{d^2AC}{dQ^2} = \frac{d}{dQ}(2Q - 24) = 2 > 0$; $Q = 12$ gives a relative minimum;

(3) $AC = 200 - 24(12) + (12)^2 = 56$.

(b) $TC = \frac{1}{3}Q^3 - 4.5Q^2 + 14Q + 22$

(1) $MC = Q^2 - 9Q + 14 = 0$; $(Q - 7)(Q - 2) = 0$; $Q = 7 \quad Q = 2$;

(2) $\frac{d^2TC}{dQ^2} = \frac{d}{dQ}(Q^2 - 9Q + 14) = 2Q - 9$.

At $Q = 7$, $d^2TC/dQ^2 = 2(7) - 9 = 5 > 0$.

At $Q = 2$, $d^2TC/dQ^2 = 2(2) - 9 = -5 < 0$.

$Q = 7$ gives a relative minimum.

(3) $TC = \frac{1}{3}(7)^3 - 4.5(7)^2 + 14(7) + 22 = 13.83$.

(c) $TC = \frac{1}{3}Q^3 - 8.5Q^2 + 60Q + 27$.

(1) $MC = Q^2 - 17Q + 60 = 0$; $(Q - 5)(Q - 12) = 0$; $Q = 5 \quad Q = 12$;

(2) $\frac{d^2TC}{dQ^2} = \frac{d}{dQ}(Q^2 - 17Q + 60) = 2Q - 17$

At $Q = 5$, $d^2TC/dQ^2 = 2(5) - 17 = -7 < 0$.

At $Q = 12$, $d^2TC/dQ^2 = 2(12) - 17 = +7 > 0$.

$Q = 12$ gives a relative minimum.

(3) $TC = \frac{1}{3}(12)^3 - 8.5(12)^2 + 60(12) + 27 = 99$

PROBLEM 7. Find the marginal cost of a firm's different products when the total cost function is $c = 3x^2 + 7x + 1.5xy + 6y + 2y^2$. (b) Determine the marginal cost of x when $x = 5, , \bar{y} = 3$.

SOLUTION. (a) $MC_x = 6x + 7 + 1.5y$; $MC_y = 1.5x + 6 + 4y$.

(b) The marginal cost of x when $x = 5$ and y is held constant at 3, is $MC_x = 6(5) + 7 + 1.5(3) = 41.5$.

LONG RUN COST ANALYSIS

We have seen that in the short run at least one input remains fixed but in the long run all the inputs become variable. The reason is that the supply of all the inputs in the long run become elastic. In the long run the firm can expand the scale of its production. In the long run the cost-output relationship is between total costs and the total output whereas in the short run the relationship is between total output and total variable costs since fixed costs remain constant.

A long run is just a continuation of a series of short-run production decisions, i.e., a long-run curve combines a series of short-run curves. Let us now draw the long-run cost curves and find their relationship with output.

Long-run Total and Average Cost Curves

Suppose a firm with only one plant size has its short-run total cost curve STC_1 and average cost curve SAC_1. If the firm adds two more plants to its size, one after the other, two short run cost curves STC_2 and STC_3 are added to STC_1 and the corresponding short run average cost curves are SAC_2 and SAC_3. Thus the firm has a number of short run average cost curves, each with a minimum point indicating the minimum average cost. For example, with one plant C_1Q_1 is the minimum SAC_1, with two plants SAC declines to C_2Q_2 due to economies of scale, and SAC move up to C_3Q_3 with three plants. The long-run average cost curve (LAC) can be drawn by connecting the minimum points of STC_1, STC_2 and STC_3. The LAC curve is often called the envelope curve, or the planning curve.

Let us now study the relationship between LTC and output and LAC and output. The long run cost-output relationship has similarity with the short run cost-output relation. With increase in output, the LTC at first increases at a decreasing rate and then at a rapid rate. Due to this, LAC declines initially and then gradually moves up.

This relation refers to the law of returns to scale which states that if a firm increases all inputs at a time, total output rises initially more than proportionately and thereafter less than proportionately, i.e., when the scale of the firm expands, per unit cost at first declines, but ultimately rises. The decrease in per unit cost is due to internal and external economies. Similarly the increase in cost is attributed to the internal and external diseconomies.

Long-Run Marginal Cost-Curve (LMC)

The LMC is derived from the short-run marginal cost curves (SMC) which is shown in Fig. 5.13. For deriving LMC the points of tangency between SAC and LAC, i.e., points A, B and C are considered. In any long run production planning these points fix up the output levels at various levels of production. For example, if parpendiculars are drawn from points A, B and C on the horizontal axis, the output levels will be OQ_1, OQ_2 and OQ_3, respectively. The parpendicular AQ_1 cuts SMC_1 at point M which means that LMC is MQ_1 at output OQ_1. When output rises to OQ_2, marginal cost will be BQ_2. Again if parpendicular CQ_3 is extended upwards, it cuts SMC_3 at N. This means that NQ_3 is the LMC at output OQ_3. If we draw a line through the points M, B and N, it shows the behaviour of marginal cost in the long run. This line is called the long run marginal cost curve (LMC).

From Fig. 5.13, the following important points may be noted. $LMC = SMC$ for the output at which the related SAC is tangent to LAC and $LAC = SAC$ at the point of tangency.

$SAC > LAC$ for all other levels of output. Again for all outputs related to $LAC = SAC$, the $LMC = SMC$. LMC is either higher, or, lower than the SMC for all other levels of output. LMC cuts LAC when LAC is at its minimum point B. There is only one short-run plant size whose minimum SAC coincides with the minimum LAC. The point is B where $SAC_2 = SMC_2 = LAC = LMC$. With the given technology, Point B represents the optimum scale of the firm in the long run.

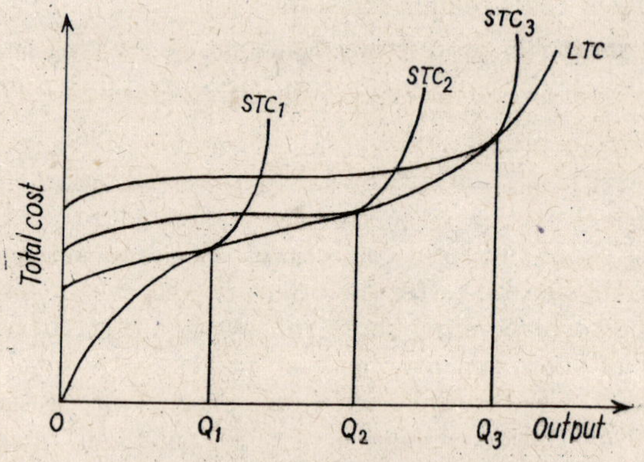

Fig 5.13 (a) Derivation of Long-run Total Cost Curve

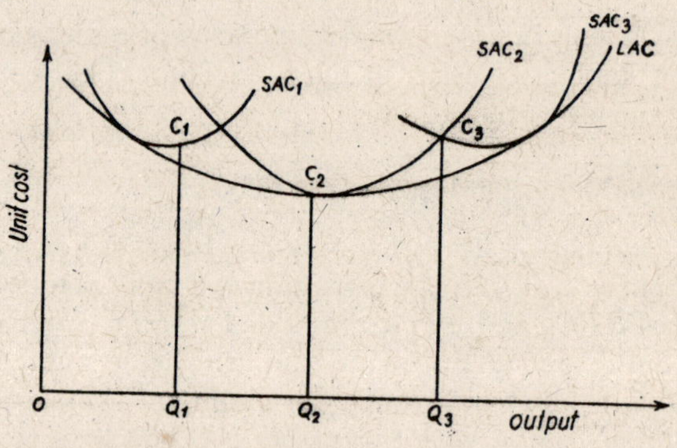

Fig 5.13 (b) Derivation of Long-run Average Cost Curve

Optimum Size and the Long-run Cost Curves

The short-run cost curve can guide how a firm takes the decision on the optimum utilisation of a plant, or, it helps us to determine the least cost output level for a given size of plant. Long-run cost curves, however, are used to show how a firm takes decision on the optimum size of the firm. By optimum size, we refer to that scale of a plant which utilises the resources most efficiently. With a given state of technology, there is a unique size of plant which minimises cost per unit and the associated output is called the optimum output. This unique size of the firm can be determined by LAC and LMC. In Fig. 5.14, the unique size has two plants which produce OQ_2 units of a product with minimum long-run average cost (LAC) of BQ_2. The downward trend in LAC shows that the firm is of non-optimal size until output touches the level of OQ_2. Again expansion of production capacity beyond OQ_2 results in an increase in SMC and LAC. Thus with a given technology a firm attempting to minimise its average cost over a period must select a scale of production which minimises its LAC at a point where $SAC = SMC = LAC = LMC$. This point indicates the most efficient utilisation of resources.

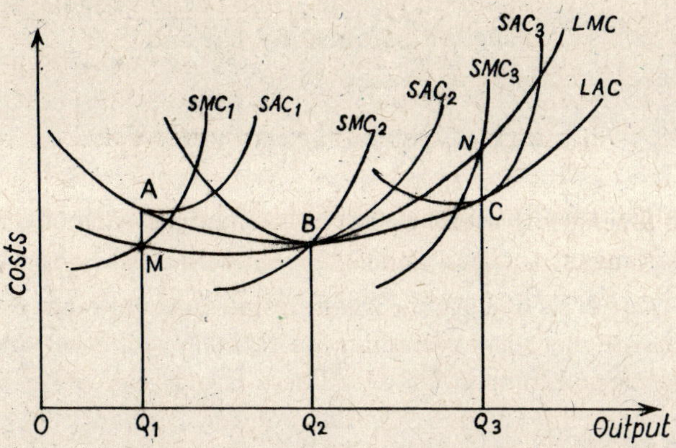

Fig 5.13 Short-run and Long-run Average and Marginal Costs

COST ESTIMATION

Estimation of cost curves is of considerable practical significance to the production manager. A knowledge of the short-run cost curves helps him to take decide on short-run price and output, whereas a knowledge of the long-run cost curve helps him to predict the requirement of long-term production capacity and determine the optimum size of the plant.

There are various methods for empirically estimating the parameters of a firm's cost functions. However, for scientifically studying the relationship between cost and output the statistical method is most widely used. The basic technique is the regression analysis with time-series, or, cross-section data which we have discussed in previous chapters.

J. Johnston and A. Walters have suggested some important points in statistical cost analysis. The cost and output data must be properly matched. For example, wages paid in a given week must be matched with the output of that particular week. Cost data are normally collected and recorded by accountants for their own use. Hence they become inadequate for the purpose of economic analysis. Accountants generally use historic cost for the valuation of assets and inventories. The use of straightline depreciation introduces a linearity bias in the estimated cost function. Where more than one product is manufactured it may not be possible to segregate costs in a meaningful way.

Using Engineering Relationships to Determine Cost Functions

The second method of determining cost functions does not use regression analysis. This approach relies on engineering data on the relation between inputs and output and then uses the prices of inputs to estimate costs. This method is based on the empirical proposition that the shape of any cost function is dependent on the prices of inputs and the production function.

Let us assume that the technology of production is such that output (Q), can be expressed as a function of inputs X_1 and X_2 as shown below

$$Q = AX_1^{\alpha}X_2^{\beta} \tag{1}$$

where A is a constant. Assuming constant factor prices the variable cost (VC) may be expressed as

$$VC = P_1X_1 + P_2X_2 \tag{2}$$

where P_1 and P_2 are two factor prices of the X_1 and X_2 respectively. If the firm wants to minimise cost for a given level of output, we can obtain an expression of the variable cost from our knowledge of factor prices P_1 and P_2 as also production parameters A, α and B.

The relavant Lagrangian function can be stated as

$$L = P_1X_1 + P_2X_2 + \lambda(AX_1^\alpha X_2^\beta - Q) \tag{3}$$

For minimizing L we will take the partial derivatives and set each of them equal to zero.

$$\therefore \frac{\partial L}{\partial X_1} = P_1 + \alpha\lambda A X_1^{\alpha-1}X_2^\beta = 0; \ \frac{\partial L}{\partial X_2} = P_2 + \beta\lambda A X_1^\alpha X_2^{\beta-1} = 0; \ \frac{\partial L}{\partial \lambda} = AX_1^\alpha X_2^\beta - Q = 0.$$

Now

$$\frac{P_1}{P_2} = \frac{\alpha\lambda A X_1^{\alpha-1}X_2^\beta}{\beta\lambda A X_1^\alpha X_2^{\beta-1}} \quad \text{or,} \quad \frac{\beta\lambda A X_1^\alpha X_2^{\beta-1}}{P_2} = \frac{\alpha\lambda A X_1^{\alpha-1}X_2^\beta}{P_1} \tag{4}$$

$$\text{or,} \quad \frac{X_1^\alpha}{X_1^{\alpha-1}} = \frac{\alpha\cdot \lambda\cdot A\cdot X_2^\beta}{\beta\cdot \lambda\cdot A\cdot X_2^{\beta-1}} \times \frac{P_2}{P_1} \quad \text{or,} \quad X_1^{\alpha-\alpha+1} = \frac{\alpha}{\beta}\cdot X_2^{\beta-\beta+1} \times \frac{P_2}{P_1}$$

$$\text{or,} \quad X_1 = \frac{\alpha}{\beta}\cdot X_2 \cdot \frac{P_2}{P_1}. \tag{5}$$

Putting (5) into (1), we have

$$Q = AX_1^\alpha X_2^\beta = A\left(\frac{\alpha}{\beta} \times \frac{P_2}{P_1}\right)^\alpha .X_2^{\alpha+\beta}. \tag{6}$$

Now

$$X_2^{\alpha+\beta} = \frac{Q}{A(\frac{\alpha}{\beta} \times \frac{P_2}{P_1})^\alpha} \ \therefore X_2 = Q^{\frac{1}{\alpha+\beta}} \times \left[A\left(\frac{\alpha}{\beta} \times \frac{P_2}{P_1}\right)^\alpha\right]^{-\frac{1}{\alpha+\beta}} = Q^{\frac{1}{\alpha+\beta}} \times C \tag{7}$$

where

$$C = \left[A\left(\frac{\alpha}{\beta} \times \frac{P_2}{P_1}\right)^\alpha\right]^{-\frac{1}{\alpha+\beta}}$$

Now putting (5) in (2), we get

$$VC = P_1\left[\frac{\alpha}{\beta}.X_2.\frac{P_2}{P_1}\right] + P_2X_2\left[P_1\left(\frac{\alpha}{\beta}\cdot\frac{P_2}{P_1}\right) + P_2\right]X_2 = DX_2 \tag{8}$$

where

$$D = \left[P_1\left(\frac{\alpha}{\beta}\cdot\frac{P_2}{P_1}\right) + P_2\right] \quad \therefore \quad VC = D.C.Q^{\frac{1}{\alpha+\beta}} = k.Q^{\frac{1}{\alpha+\beta}} \tag{9}$$

where $k = D.C.$

Here k is a constant comprising the factor prices and the parameters of the production function.

The variables can be estimated if we have information about factor prices and production parameters. Other cost functions can be presented if we have knowledge of variable cost functions.

When $(\alpha + \beta) = 1$, the variable cost function is linear and average cost and marginal cost are both equal to k. When $(\alpha+\beta) > 1$, average and marginal costs are both decreasing (variable cost rising at a decreasing rate). When $(\alpha + \beta) < 1$, average and marginal costs are rising (variable cost rising at an increasing rate). Note that total cost = variable cost since in the long run all inputs are variable.

Let us take three examples to show how variable cost function can be obtained from Cobb-Douglas production functions and input prices. Here the only difference is in the degree of homogeneity of the production functions.

Using equation (1), i.e., $Q = AX_1^{\alpha}X_2^{\beta}$, let us keep A constant at 10 and use different values for α and β. Moreover, we assume that the price per unit for input X_1, i.e., $P_1 = 10$ and the price per unit for input X_2 i.e., $P_2 = 20$ for all the three examples. In equation (9), putting the values of D and C we have

$$VC = \left[A\left(\frac{\alpha}{\beta}.\frac{P_2}{P_1}\right)^{\alpha}\right]^{-\frac{1}{\alpha+\beta}}\left[P_1\left(\frac{\alpha}{\beta}.\frac{P_2}{P_1}\right) + P_2\right]Q^{\frac{1}{\alpha+\beta}}.$$

EXAMPLE 1. Assume $\alpha = \beta = 0.5$ so that the production function is homogeneous of degree 1 and shows constant returns to scale. With the given values of A, P_1 and P_2, the VC can be computed as follows

$$VC = \left[10\left(\frac{0.5}{0.5} \times \frac{20}{10}\right)^{.5}\right]^{-\frac{1}{.5+.5}}\left[10\left(\frac{.5}{.5}.\frac{20}{10}\right) + 20\right]Q^{\frac{1}{.5+.5}}$$

$$= [10 \times (2)^{.5}]^{-1}[40]Q = \frac{40}{14.14}Q = 2.83Q.$$

We find that the variable cost function is linear. So the returns to scale are constant.

EXAMPLE 2. Assume $\alpha = .3$ and $\beta = .4$ and use the same values of A_1, P_1 and P_2. As $\alpha + \beta = .7$, the production function is homogeneous of degree 0.7 and has diminishing returns to scale. We can compute variable cost as follows

$$VC = \left[10\left(\frac{.3}{.4} \times \frac{20}{10}\right)^{.3}\right]^{-\frac{1}{.7}}\left[10\left(\frac{.3}{.4} \times \frac{20}{10}\right) + 20\right]Q^{\frac{1}{.7}} = [10 \times (1.5)^{.3}]^{-\frac{1}{.7}}[35]Q^{\frac{1}{.7}}$$

$$= \frac{35Q^{1.43}}{(11.29)^{1.43}} = \frac{35}{32.02}Q^{1.43} = 1.093Q^{1.43}.$$

The variable cost function is non-linear and rises at an increasing rate. It then shows decreasing returns to scale.

EXAMPLE 3. Assume $\alpha = .7$ and $\beta = .6$ and values of A, P_1, P_2 as constant. Since $(\alpha+\beta) = 1.3$, then production function is homogeneous of degree 1.3 and exhibits increasing returns to scale.

The variable cost function becomes

$$VC = \left[10\left(\frac{.7}{.6} \times \frac{20}{10}\right)^{.7}\right]^{-\frac{1}{1.3}}\left[10\left(\frac{.7}{.6} \times \frac{20}{10}\right) + 20\right]Q^{\frac{1}{1.3}}$$

$$= [10 \times 2.33^{.7}]^{-0.769}[10 \times 2.33 + 20]Q^{0.769}$$

$$= \frac{43.3}{(18.08)^{.769}}Q^{.769} = \frac{43.3}{9.26}.Q^{.769} = 4.68\,Q^{.769}.$$

This variable cost function rises at a decreasing rate and hence exhibits increasing returns to scale.

This approach to estimating the cost function of a firm depends on the knowledge of the current production processes which is not always available. In the petroleum industry, for instance, different production processes are well defined and linear and according to Griffin the process analysis can be applied to generate cost functions for that industry to establish the microeconomic theory relating to U-shaped average cost.

SHORT-RUN COST ESTIMATION

The parameters of short-run cost function can be estimated by using regression method which is based on both time-series and cross-section data. For decision making purposes the total variable cost function rather than the total cost function is estimated. Since fixed costs remain constant at all levels of output, they not affect business decisions. So the marginal cost function has to be used for estimation purposes.

For estimating short-run cost functions with regression analysis, two main difficulties arise, viz., (1) collection and modification of data; and (2) stating the functional form of the regression equation.

Data

We must know what is relevant cost and match it to the change in short-run output. Time series data collected at different points in time are considered as best for short-run cost estimation. Besides variable costs the factors mentioned below are also to considered while estimating short-run cost functions. This is so because they exert considerable influence on total costs.

(i) **Historical Costs:** Since we cannot get data on future costs until we actually incur them, we are to rely on historical, or accounting data as a first approximation. These data require some modifications before they can be be used for estimation purposes.

(ii) **Opportunity Costs:** Historical or accounting data do not consider opportunity cost which is very important for short-run decisions. Hence unadjusted accounting data are inappropriate.

(iii) **Cost-Output Matching:** In the short-run cost analysis, only variable costs are to be considered. But at times it becomes difficult to identify partly variable costs. For example, only economic depreciation of capital equipment or its actual usage is to be included in the short-run cost estimation. However, accounting depreciation is function of time rather than usage of capital and is called capital consumption. Accounting data combine both user cost of capital and capital consumption over time in depreciation. It is very difficult to distinguish user costs from obsolescence, or, time-related costs.

Similarly, semi-variable costs, i.e., costs which remain fixed up to a certain level of output and vary only when this level is exceeded also create a problem in cost-output matching. This problem must be sorted out for accurate estimation of short-run cost functions.

(iv) **Timing of Costs:** Data used for cost estimation should be adjusted for leads and lags between cost reporting and output production. Maintenance expenses, for example, may be too high for the current period due to excessive production in the previous period. In a period of high production, a firm's existing equipment is fully utilised and only the minimum essential essential maintenance is carried out. Hence maintenance cost is very low in a period of high production and high in the subsequent period. While estimating cost it is necessary to make proper adjustment of maintenance expenditure over time.

(v) **Inflation:** The prices of inputs, e.g., costs of labour, raw materials, etc. increase over time due to inflation. If output also increases and it is not adjusted for price increases, one may think that the average cost has gone up with the rise in output. To overcome this problem, one must use a measure of the change in the price of each of the inputs. For example inflation-adjusted wage rate may be used as a measure of the cost of labour.

(vi) **Period of Observation:** Short-run cost curves are based on a certain amount of fixed inputs and an unchanged technology. For accurate estimation of short-run cost function, we must use data for a period of time during which the product remains unchanged and there is the same fixed cost and technology. The difficulty is that a large number of observations are required to estimate the cost function over a range of output, while still remaining within the short period when both technology and costs of fixed factors remain the same. The real rate of interest [1] may be used as a cost of capital.

(vii) **Functional Form:** In any statistical estimation the selection of a proper functional form of the equation to be estimated becomes a genuine problem. In demand estimation we consider linear and power functions because of simplicity and the likelihood that the true relationship is represented by the functional forms over short ranges of the independent variables.

The functional form must represent the theoretical relationship between dependent and independent variables. Since we have already discussed the theoretical relationship between total variable cost and output, we will now deal with the linear functional form as also quadratic and cubic forms.

LINEAR SHORT-RUN COST FUNCTIONS

For many production systems, the linear form shown below accurately fits the cost-output data

$$TC = a + bQ + \sum_{i=1}^{n} C_i X_i$$

where

TC is total cost (i.e., total variable cost during an observation period),

Q is output of that period,

X_i are the independent variables which the analyst wants to include in his estimation and

a, b and c_i are the coefficients of the model as obtained by the least squares regression technique.

Total variable cost is zero when output is zero. The independent variables to be considered include items like wage rates, input quality, production lot size, fuel and material costs, weather, changes in product design, etc.

Here a is the intercept coefficient, i.e., it just represents the intercept of the estimated cost curve with the vertical axis and not the firm's fixed costs. This intercept occurs when the firm's output is zero. Again estimates of b are important since b represents the best measure of marginal cost for the whole see of the data.

Fig. 5.15 shows the total cost (TC) curve with a linear approximation to the curve superimposed. In the output range Q_1 and Q_2 the true relationship is a linear one. When fitted to the data, we get a straight line as in Fig 5.14.

---

[1] The real rate of interest is the nominal rate ± change in the general price level per annum. If the nominal rate of inflation is 12% and the annual rate of inflation is 9%, the real rate of interest is only 3%.

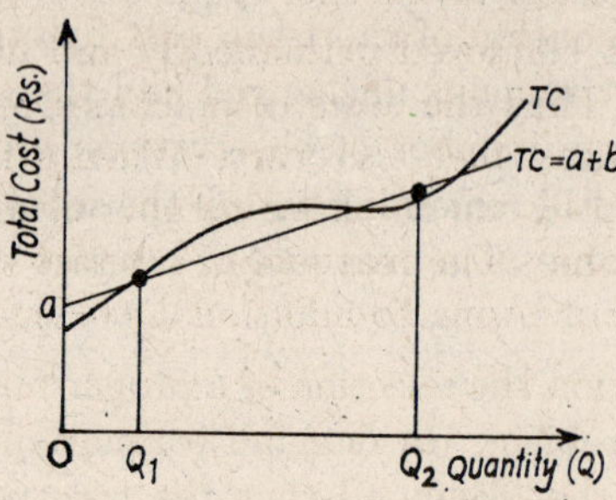

Fig 5.15 A Typical Short-run TC Curve

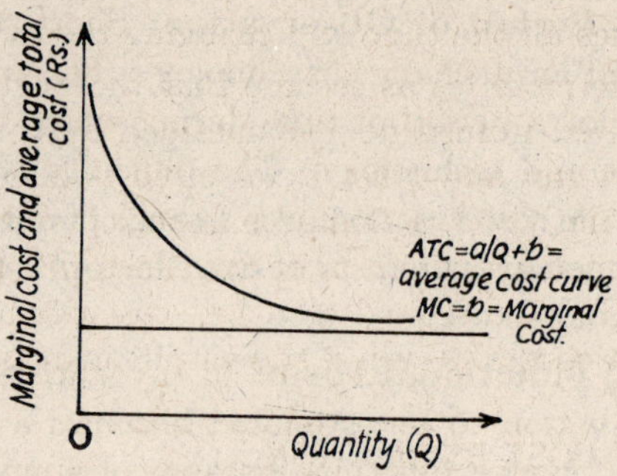

Fig. 5.16 ATC and MC for TC = a + bQ

Fig. 5.16 indicates ATC and MC curves which match with the equation $TC = a + bQ$.

Now $ATC = \frac{TC}{Q} = \frac{a}{Q} + b$ and $MC = b$.

When Q increases, $\frac{a}{Q}$ decreases and finally, is zero. Therefore ATC becomes equal to b.

QUADRATIC AND CUBIC COST FUNCTIONS

The following quadratic and cubic cost functions are widely used in empirical cost studies:

(a) $TC = a + bQ + cQ^2$ (quadratic form).

Now $ATC = \frac{TC}{Q} = \frac{a}{Q} + b + cQ$ and $MC = b + 2cQ$.

Fig. 5.17 shows both ATC and MC for the above linear TC equation.

(b) $TC = a + bQ - cQ^2 + dQ^3$ (cubic form).

$\therefore ATC = \frac{TC}{Q} = \frac{a}{Q} + b - cQ + dQ^2$ and $MC = b - 2cQ + 3dQ^2$.

Fig. 5.18 shows the ATC and MC for TC (cubic form).

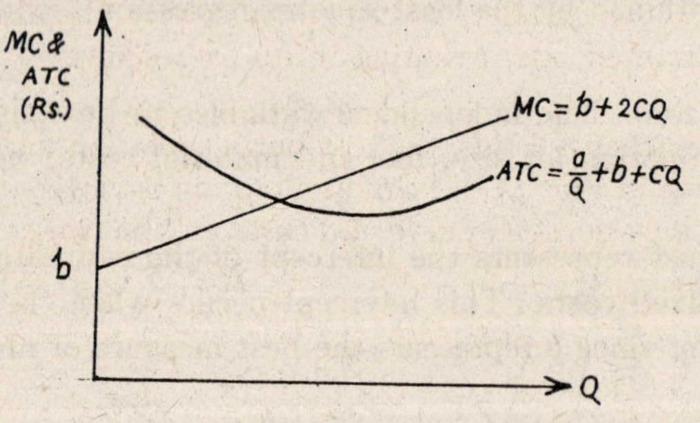

Fig 5.17 MC and ATC for TC=a+bQ+cQ^2

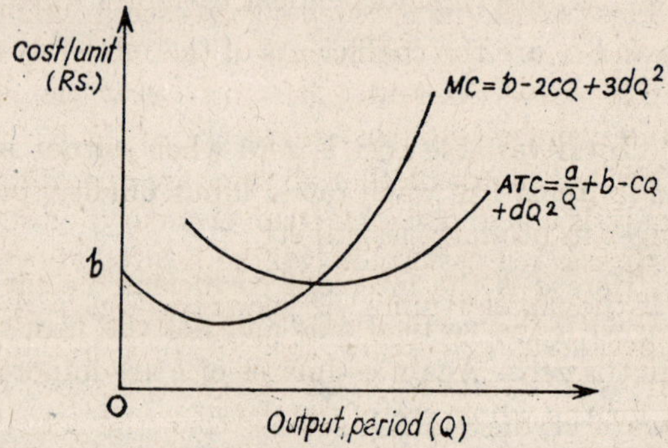

Fig 5.18 MC and ATC for TC=a+bQ–cQ^2+dQ^3

Empirically Estimated Short-run Cost Functions

Other empirical studies have shown that short-run MC remains constant over output levels under observation and the average cost functions tend to be linear.

Although inputs like land or machines remain fixed in the short run, the use of these inputs may be variable. For example, we can engage two workers for each machine instead of running all the machines all the time and changing the number of workers in the short run.

Furthermore let us assume that the workers are not employed permanently and hired as and when required from a pool maintained by contractors. Thus the costs of machines remain fixed in the short run and other items of costs like workers wages, fuel, etc. vary. When a firm's order position is not good, a limited number of workers is hired to run the fixed number of machines. If more workmen are hired, more machines will be used in the same proportion, say, two workers per machine. Hence marginal cost, i.e., cost per unit of output owing to additional workmen and fuel will remain constant even if the output increases.

LONG-RUN COST ESTIMATION

Though the estimation of long-run cost curves is similar to that of short-run cost curves, it is much more complicated. In the long run all costs are variable. The real problem arises due to changes in technology. We have to collect adequate information over a range of output for estimation of the cost function. If a firm replaces its old machinary with new one over the long run, production technology will be changed. To overcome this problem we have to use either a data set with observations of constant technology, or, adopt some measure for controlling the variations in technology in the estimation equation.

Owing to the difficulties faced in using time-series data to estimate long-run cost functions and controlling changes in technology, researchers use cross-section data, i.e., observations from different production units, or, firms at the same point in time, using the same technology. The cross-section regression equations have total cost (TC) as the dependent variable and output as an independent variable. To account for the variations in factor which affect various firms in various ways, other independent variables like firms' wage rates, fuel costs, etc., are to be added. Wages at different regions vary due to changes in the cost of living. Moreover, the problem of inflation does not arise since the data relate to the same point in time.

Another difficulty which may arise in using cross-section data is that different accounting procedures are adopted by different firms. The depreciation schedules and the cost reports on machinery for different firms may vary. Hence estimation of cost function by using data from different firms may be misleading if such problems are not properly tackled.

This techniques is based on the assumption that all firms are running efficiently and located on their respective long-run average total cost curves. If the firms are running inefficiently, the average total cost curve takes its place just below the estimated one, resulting in an overestimate of the long-run average total cost curve.

If the assumption that all firms are operating efficiently holds, the cost-output relation found in the analysis traces out a long-run cost curve as shown in Fig. 51.9. f this assumption is violated, the least squares regression line will be located above the true LAC curve and costs will be overstated.

If the smaller units, as shown in Fig. 5.19, are functioning well to the right of their optimal output, the estimated LAC curve will show a downward gradient much steeper than the actual LAC curve and this will mislead one to overestimate economies of scale in the industry. Likewise scale economies may be underestimated owing to bias in selection which may result if small and high-cost firms cannot compete successfully, go bankrupt and thus fail to become eligible for cost-study.

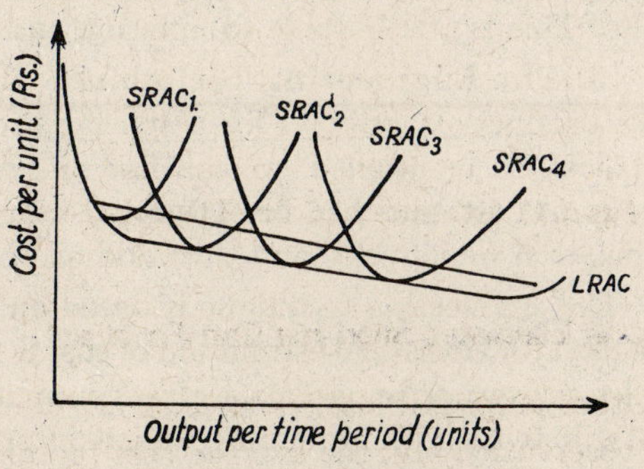

Fig 5.19 Estimating Long Run AC Curves with Cross-Section Data

Most of the empirically estimated long-run cost functions show sharply increasing returns to scale at minimum output levels, but the magnitude of these scale economies falls as output goes up and finally becomes constant, i.e., the long-run average cost curve declines at a decreasing rate as output increases and finally becomes horizontal. Very few studies have shown decreasing returns to scale and upturn in the average cost curve at high levels of output. These results caused researchers to think that long run average cost curves are generally *L*-shaped and not *U*-shaped as assumed in micro-economic theory.

Alternative Estimation Procedures

Two other procedures for estimation of cost functions are available for situations where adequate data for statistical cost estimation cannot be collected. These procedures are: (i) the survivor technique and (ii) the engineering technique.

(i) **The Survivor Technique:** In 1958 Prof. George Stigler of the University of Chicago formulated a technique for measuring economies of scale when detailed cost-data for firms were not available. He stated that efficient firms with low average costs prosper and survive over time. He suggested classification of firms in size-categories and calculated the share of the industry captured by each size class. Stigler noticed that in the steel industry, the share of the market captured by the smallest and largest firms was steadily declining, with a steady share spread across a broad range of class-sizes inbetween.

This approach is limited by the definition of the market. This is so because if the market is wide enough, large and small firms can co-exist. For example, in India's textile industry the handloom sector and the mill sector exist side by side.

The problem related to technology may become prominent here also. Variations in the share of the market by class-size may cause changes in technology and product diversification within an industry rather than a change in scale over time. Since highly aggregated industries are selected for studies, the significance of the results obtained is questionable.

Drawbacks: The survivor technique has the following drawbacks.

(1) It assumes that survival is directly related to minimisation of the long-run average costs. It further assumes the firms examined are running in a highly competitive market structure. If markets are protected by various regulations regarding entry even smaller firms, running inefficiently, can survive for extended periods.

(2) Strategically located firms can survive due to low transport costs in spite of operational inefficiencies.

(3) Inefficient smaller firms in many industries survive by emphasising personalised service, or customised production. Moreover, successful product differentiation helps smaller firms not only to survive but also to improve their performance and compete with their large rivals.

(4) Owing to the very long-run nature of analysis, this technique is likely to have distorted results. This is attributable to inflation and changes in technology.

(ii) **The Engineering Technique:** This technique is based on the physical relations expressed in the production function for a specific product, or firm. From the knowledge of the production technology to be applied, we can find the optimal input combination for producing a certain output. Total cost can then be estimated by multiplying the quantity of each input in the least-cost combination by its price and then adding them.

The engineering technique is based on currently available technology and unlike cost observations used for statistical estimation of cost is not contaminated by extraneous factors. This technique couples current price quotations from suppliers with the estimates of required quantities of different inputs. It is used in oil refining, chemical production, nuclear power generation, etc.

Drawback: The main drawback of this technique is t... pilot plant operations are often applied to full-scale commercial productio... ts become abnormally high and often exceed the estimated costs. However, if ... y applied, it may become a useful alternative to statistical cost estimation.

Summary

Business decision-making at the top level often requires a quantitative e... para-meters of production and cost functions. It is possible to estimate these function... levels of aggregation, including plant, firm, industry and economy-wide levels. It is also ... use time-series data to estimate production or cost functions for a particular plant. In... ne may draw cross-section data from a number of production facilities and use these to ... a production or cost function for the average or typical plant.

Quantitative estimates of the parameters of a production function allow determination ... marginal product of each input, production elasticities and economies of scale. For a Cobb-Dou... production function, returns to scale are constant, increasing, or, decreasing, depending on wheth... the sum of the estimated exponents is equal to 1, greater than 1, or less than 1 respectively.

The estimation of cost functions also involves various data collection problems. Furthermore, the period of study must be long enough to generate enough observations to estimate the functions.

Concepts for Review

1. Production Surface
2. Isoquant
3. Cost Function
4. Cobb-Douglas Production Function
5. Survivor Technique
6. Engineering Technique
7. Quadratic Cost Function
8. Cubic Cost Functions
9. Cross-section Data
10. Time-series Data.

Exercises

1. Use the production function $Q = 10K^{.5}L^{.5}$ to complete the following table

Quantity of Capital Input (K)				
4				40
3		24.5		
2	14.1			
.1			17.3	
	1	2	3	4

Quantity of Labour Input (L)

(a) State whether returns to scale are increasing, decreasing, or, constant.

(b) Suppose the wage rate is Rs. 20, the price of capital is also Rs. 20 per unit and the current production of the firm is 24.5 units per period, using 3 units of capital and 2 units of labour. State whether this is an efficient resource combination.

What will be a more efficient combination?

2. For each of the undernoted production functions, find whether returns to scale are decreasing, constant, or, increasing (i) $Q = 10K^{.6}L^{.5}$; (ii) $Q = \frac{K}{L}$; (iii) $Q = 50 + 2K + 5L$.

3. The total and marginal cost functions for ABC Co. are as follows

$$TC = 100 + 5Q - .05Q^2 + .002Q^3$$
$$MC = 10 - .06Q + .005Q^2.$$

the company is of the opinion that the knowledge of these equations is not n making. You have been advised to do the following:

e level of fixed cost, if any, and obtain the equations for average total cost, average ble cost and average fixed cost.

d the rate of output which results in minimum average variable cost.

fixed costs increase to 300, what output rate will result in lowest average variable costs?

competitive firm whose product sells for Rs. 12 maximises profit at the point where product of raw materials equals 6 when the price of raw materials equals Rs. 3. State the statement is true, or, false. Explain your answer.

. Suppose 2 metres of cloth and 8 buttons are needed to complete one shirt. Buttons cost .15 each and cloth sells at Rs. 3.00 per metre. What is the marginal cost of a shirt assuming no other inputs are required?

6. The economics department of a natural gas drilling company has estimated the long-run total cost function for natural gas distribution as $TC = 250Q - 0.005Q^3$ where TC = Total cost and Q = millions of cubic feet (MCF) of natural gas per day.

(i) Write an equation for the long-run average cost of distributing natural gas and plot this on a graph in the range $15 \leq Q \leq 200$.

(ii) At present the company does not distribute natural gas but only produces it. X & Co., the only distributor of gas, carries 150 MCF per day approximately. The manager of the Natural Gas Co. estimates that the market will grow from 150 to 200 MCF per day and thinks that it might capture 50% of the increase in the size of the market. Y & Co. can deliver 250 MCF per day. Will the natural gas co. be able to compete against Y & Co. in the distribution of gas? Explain, (Assume that Y & Co. has the same total cost function as that of the natural gas co.).

Appendix A

Output Elasticity of Labour and Capital in U.S. Manufacturing

Table A-1 reports the estimated output elasticities of labour (α) and capital (β) for various U.S. manufacturing industries in 1957. A value of $\alpha = 0.90$ for furniture means that a 1% increase in the quantity of labour used (holding K constant) results in a 0.90% increase in the quantity produced of furniture. A value of $\beta = 0.21$ means that a 1% increase in K (holding L constant) increases Q by 0.21%. Increasing both L and K by 1% increases Q by 0.90 + 0.21 = 1.11%. This means that the production of furniture is subject to increasing returns to scale.

Table A-1 ESTIMATED OUTPUT ELASTICITY OF LABOUR (α) AND CAPITAL (β) IN U.S. MANUFACTURING

Industry	α	β	$\alpha + \beta$
Furniture	0.90	0.21	1.11
Chemicals	0.89	0.20	1.09
Printing	0.62	0.46	1.08
Food, beverages	0.51	0.56	1.07
Rubber, plastics	0.58	0.48	1.06

Contd.

Contd.

Industry	α	β	$\alpha+\beta$
Instruments	0.84	0.20	1.04
Lumber	0.65	0.39	1.04
Apparel	0.91	0.13	1.04
Leather	0.96	0.08	1.04
Electrical machinery	0.66	0.37	1.03
Nonelectrical machinery	0.62	0.40	1.02
Transport equipment	0.79	0.23	1.02
Textiles	0.88	0.12	1.00
Paper pulp	0.56	0.42	0.98
Primary metals	0.59	0.37	0.96
Petroleum	0.64	0.31	0.95

Source: J. Moroney, Cobb-Douglas Production Functions and Returns to Scale in U.S. Manufacturing Industry, Western Economic Journal, December 1967.

The values of α and β reported in Table A-1 were estimated by regression analysis using cross-section data for many firms in each industry for the year 1957. The value of α ranges from 0.51 for food and beverages to 0.96 for leather. This is the output elasticity of production and nonproduction workers combined. The value of β ranges from 0.08 for leather to 0.56 for food and beverages. Note that most industries exhibit close-to-constant returns to scale (i.e., the value of $\alpha+\beta$ is close to 1).

Appendix B

The CES Production Function

The constant elasticity of substitution (CES) production function is similar to the Cobb-Douglas function. However, empirical investigation of it was prompted by the observation that the share of wages in national income was not fixed but variable as the wage rate varied.

So the CES production function, tested by Arrow, Chenery, Minhas and Solow also constraints the value σ to be constant, in the sense that it does not change with changes in relative prices or factor inputs. Its value is determined by underlying technology and may change with technical progress. But in any event it is not necessarily equal to one.

The function is $Q = \gamma\{\delta K^{-\rho} + (1-\delta)L^{-\rho}\}^{-\nu/\rho}$.

In the original study the function was supposed to be homogeneous of degree one. But Brown and de Cani derived the function independently. This permits any degree of returns to scale. Here γ is the *scale parameter*. A shift in γ is an example of neutral technical change. The degree to which technology is capital intensive is indicated by δ. When the production function is embedded in a particular economic model δ can be interpreted as the *distribution parameter*. The substitution parameter ρ is equal to $(1-\sigma)/\sigma$. Rewriting the production function as

$$Q^{-\rho/\nu} = \gamma^{-\rho/\nu}\{\delta K^{-\rho} + (1-\delta)L^{-\rho}\}$$

and differentiating w.r.t. K and L we have

$$-\frac{\rho}{\nu}Q^{-1-\rho/\nu}\frac{\partial Q}{\partial K} = -\rho\gamma^{-\rho/\nu}\delta K^{-\rho-1}$$

$$\text{and} \quad -\frac{\rho}{\nu}Q^{-1-\rho/\nu}\frac{\partial Q}{\partial L} = -\rho\gamma^{-\rho/\nu}\delta L^{-\rho-1}$$

Therefore the marginal products of capital and labour are

$$\frac{\partial Q}{\partial K} = \nu\delta\gamma^{-\rho/\nu}\frac{Q^{1+\rho/\nu}}{K^{1+\rho}}, \quad \frac{\partial Q}{\partial L} = \nu(1-\delta)\gamma^{-\rho/\nu}\frac{Q^{1+\rho/\nu}}{L^{1+\rho}}$$

and the marginal rate of substitution is given by

$$R = \frac{\partial Q}{\partial L}\bigg/\frac{\partial Q}{\partial K} = \frac{1-\delta}{\delta}\left(\frac{K}{L}\right)^{1+\rho}$$

Taking logarithms in this relation we get

$$\log R = \log\frac{1-\delta}{\delta} + (1+\rho)\log\frac{K}{L}.$$

So the elasticity of substitution is equal to

$$\sigma = \frac{d\log(K/L)}{d\log R} = \frac{\text{logarithm of change in capital labour ratio}}{\text{logarithm of change in the } MRS} = \frac{1}{1+\rho}.$$

The CES function reduces to the Cobb-Douglas as $\sigma \to 1$, i.e., as $\rho \to 0$.

A major problem with the CES production function is that unlike the Cobb-Douglas, we cannot transform it into a linear-in-parameters form by taking logarithms.

Appendix C

STATISTICAL COST FUNCTIONS: A CASE STUDY

One of the classic studies carried out in industrial economics used precisely these techniques to estimate the relationship between cost and output for a hosiery mill. This study,[1] carried out by Joel Dean of the Columbia University Graduate School of Business, obtained the following regression line $\hat{Y} = 2936 + 1.998X$ where $\hat{Y}$ is the computed monthly cost of production in dollars and X is the monthly output of the mill in dozens of pairs of stockings. The scatter diagram and the above regression line are shown in Fig. C-1. The standard error of estimate was \$6,110. The correlation coefficient was .973.

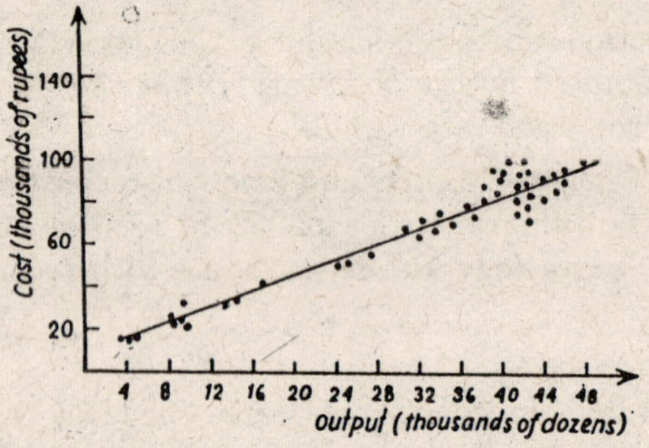

Fig C-1 A Regression Line

This study is famous for several reasons, one being that it provided some early evidence concerning the shape of firm's cost functions. In particular, the study suggested that within the relevant range marginal cost (that is, the extra cost of an extra unit of output) did not vary with the output level of the firm. However, this may have been due in considerable part to the limited range of the observations. In other words, if data were obtained concerning much higher output levels than those shown in Fig. C-1, it is likely that costs could not longer conform to the linear relationship, due to capacity constraints. Since Dean's pioneer study, a large number of similar investigations have been made for other firms in a variety of industries. The results, based on the types of regression and correlation techniques described in this chapter, have proved valuable both to the firms themselves and to economists and government agencies.

---

[1] Dean, Statistical Cost Functions of a Hosiery Mill, reprinted in part in Mansfield, Statistics for Business and Economics, Readings and Cases.

CHAPTER 6

FACTOR DEMAND

The basic purpose of a theory of demand for labour is to determine how much labour employers will want to employ at different wages rates. Albert Rees

Demand for new supplies of durable goods fluctuates more intensely than demand for the current services these durable goods render. J. M. Clark, 1934

Fundamental Questions
1. What determines the mix of labour and capital used by the firm to produce output?
2. Why is the term derived demand used to describe the demand for factors of production?
3. What is the marginal revenue product of an input? How is related to the demand curve for a factor of production of a firm under perfect competition?
4. Why is the input supply curve faced by a firm under perfect competition horizontal and why is it upward sloping for a monopsonist?

PREVIEW

People earn their incomes by seling factors of production to business firms. The profit-seeking firm uses these resources to produce the goods and services demanded by consumers. What is of considerable importance to both the individual and the firm is the price of a unit of the resource. Input prices are also of critical importance to the firm because they are a critical factor in determining the amount and mix of resources employed. In the chapter the focus is on the determination of those input prices and how firms decide how much of an input to employ.

There is, in fact, no difference between the pricing of a commodity and that of a factor. In a free market, where there is no government intervention or trade union pressure, the price of a factor is determined by the impersonal market forces, i.e., by the forces of demand and supply. However, a firm's demand for a factor is an indirect (or derived) demand. Firms demand land, labour and capital not because they have values as such, but because those resources can be used to produce goods and services that have value to consumers. Thus the demand for factors is dependent on the demand for the goods and services those factors are used to produce; hence the use of the term derived demand.

FACTOR DEMAND

A profit-maximising firm seeks to produce its optimal level of output at the minimum cost in a given market structure. To achieve this the manager must decide how much of each input to use in the production process and what price to pay for these inputs.

There are three stages of production. In stage I, the average product of labour, i.e., total output ÷ number of units of labour reaches its maximum. In stage II, both marginal and average product decline, but both are positive. In stage III the marginal product of labour is negative. Generally the range of production is restricted to stage II. No manager would knowingly employ any input whose marginal product is negative. To be more specific, no manager would hire a labourer if the cost of hiring, i.e., wages and other benefits exceeds the revenue it would get by selling the extra output attributable to that labourer.

Special Features

There are four special features of demand for productive factors as stated below.

1. The demand for a factor is derived demand, i.e., derived from the demand of the commodity which the factor helps to produce. A factor is required to produce something which is in demand. It is not demanded for its own sake.

2. The demand for a factor means joint demand. Only one factor cannot produce a commodity or a service. For example, a machine without labour, material, tools, etc., a workman without tools, drawings; a land without a tiller, cannot give the required output. Hence different factors must be used jointly to produce anything at all.

3. The technology and the direction of its change affect the demand for a factor input and affect the marginal productivity of that input.

4. The demand for inputs is also affected by their relative prices. When inputs are substitutable among themselves, their relative prices help to select the technology to be used by the firm. This, in its turn, determines the demand for inputs. A costlier input has lesser demand.

The demand of a productive factor is dependent on its marginal product. So long an extra unit of a factor contributes more to the firm than it receives from the firm, it is worth using the extra unit of the factor. Let us now define a few terms in this context.

(a) Marginal Product, or Marginal Physical Product (MPP)

The addition to the total output made by employing an extra unit of a factor is known as the marginal physical product of that factor. For example, when the employment of the 10th worker leads to an increase in the output of a commodity, say, X from 500 units to 550 units, the MP of 10th worker is 50 units of output. Since marginal product is measured in physical terms, it is often called marginal physical product (MPP).

(b) Marginal Revenue Product (MRP)

It is the additional revenue the firm makes by selling the output contributed by one additional worker (i.e., the last worker) is sold. Thus it is a rupee measure of the additional output attributable to the effort of the additional worker. Note that MRP can be computed by multiplying MPP by the marginal revenue (MR). For example, if the 50 units of additional output of, say, trouser (in the previous example) contributed by 10th unit of labour, are sold in the market at rupees 150 per unit, then MRP labour = Rs. 150 × 50 = Rs. 7,500. Symbolically it can be written as:[1]

$$MRP_{\text{labour}} = MPP_{\text{labour}} \times MR_{\text{trousers}}.$$

(c) Value of Marginal Product (VMP)

It measures the addition to revenue due to one unit increase in the quantity of the productive factor. The difference between MRP and VMP lies in the methods of measurement. Here VMP is determined by multiplying MPP by price (rather than by MR) of the commodity which the factor helps to produce. Hence $VMP_{\text{labour}} = MPP_{\text{labour}} \times \text{Price}_{\text{trousers}}$.

(d) Marginal Resource Cost (MRC)

It is the additional cost to the firm of employing one additional unit of labour. MRC consists of the wage rate and other costs to the firm of employing the additional worker.

The difference between MRC and MC is that MRC refers to the variation of costs due to one unit variation in output.

The Behaviour of MRP and MRC

So long as $MRP > MRC$ it is profitable to continue employing more labour. The optimum number of units of any variable resource to be used is determined by the relation $MRP = MRC$.

If $MRP < MRC$, production should be stopped and the fewer units of labour is to be employed.

The Behaviour of MRP and VMP

The relationship between the units of variable factor (say labour L) with their MRP and VMP are shown in Table 6.1.

---

1 These results can be easily shown mathematically. Let the production function be

$$q=f(V_1,V_2,\cdots,V_m)$$

where q is output and the V_i are the quantities of the variable inputs used.

Suppose the firm is a monopolist (whose $MR<p$). So we can write the demand function as

$$p=h|q|=h[f(V_1,V_2,\cdots,V_m)]$$

where $h'<0$. Let w_i be the price of input V_i. Profit is, therefore

$$\pi=h[f(V_1,V_1,\cdots,V_m)]f(V_1,V_2,\cdots,V_m)-\sum_{i=1}^{m} w_i V_i.$$

Profit maximisation requires

$$\left(\frac{dP}{dq}q+p\right)f_1=w_1$$

$$\vdots \qquad \vdots \qquad \vdots$$

$$\left(\frac{dP}{dq}q+p\right)f_m=w_m.$$

Since total revenue is $h(q)\times q$, marginal revenue is $\frac{dP}{dq}q+p$. Therefore profit maximisation requires that for each input, V_i,$\left(\frac{dP}{dq}q+p\right)f_i=w_i$. Since f_i is the marginal product of the i-th input, $MR\times MPP_i=MRP_i=w_i=$ input price.

TABLE 6.1 THE MPP AND THE VMP OF THE VARIABLE FACTOR

Units of Variable Factor (L)	Total output of Commodity B, (units) (Q_B)	MPP_L or MP_L	$MRP_L =$ ($MPP_L \times MR_B$)	MR_B	VMP $= (MPP_L \times P_B)$ and ($P_B = MR_B$)	MRC_L ($P_L = 200$)
1	20	20	400	20	400	200
2	37	17	340	20	340	200
3	52	15	300	20	300	200
4	67	10	200	20	200	200
5	67	5	100	20	100	200
6	67	0	0	20	0	200

From Col. (3) we find that MPP_L gradually decreases. This is due to the fact that other factors which are required along with L to produce B are adequate for two units only. Hence any further addition of L does not get the support from other factors which remain fixed. Thus the contribution to output of each extra unit of L becomes smaller than the contribution of the previous unit. Assume that the market for the commodity is perfectly competiture which means that the firm can sell its entire outout at a given price (say, P_B = Rs. 20). Col (4), i.e., MRP_L also shows the same behaviour as MP_L, i.e., it gradually falls.

If the selling price of the output of a firm remains constant even when the commodity market is perfectly competitive, the price of the commodity becomes equal to its marginal revenue, i.e., MRP equals VMP. In an imperfectly competitive market, i.e., when the sale can be increased by reducing the price of the product, $MR <$ the price of the commodity. Thus $VMP > MRP$ in an imperfectly competitive market, i.e., VMP overstates the revenue addition made by one extra unit of the variable factor employed in such a situation.

The MRP curve, or demand curve for a factor is actually the firm's demand curve for the variable factor.. The maximum price a profit-seeking entrepreneur will be ready to pay for employing one extra unit of the variable factor is the likely contribution to be made to the firm's revenue by the last unit of the factor. The firm's demand curve can be obtained by plotting Col. (4) again Col. (1) of Table 6.1. This is shown in Fig. 6.1.

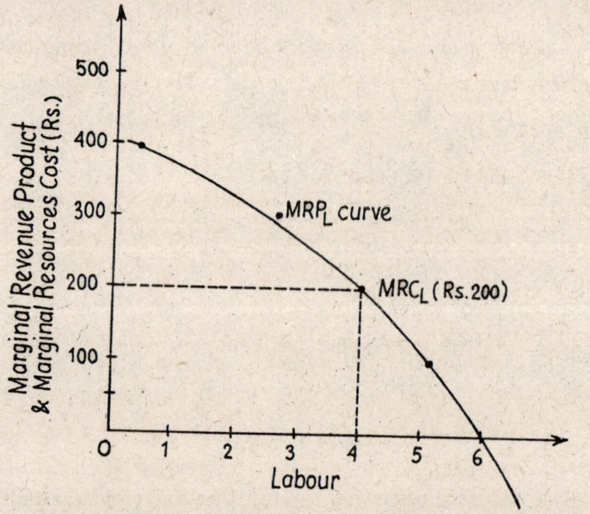

Fig 6.1 Determination of Optimum Purchase of Labour by a Firm

Fig 6.1 shows that the optimum level of employment is 4 units of labour where $MRP_L = MRC_L =$ Rs. 200. So long as $MRP_L > MRC_L$, the firm gets the benefit of hiring additional units of labour and production increases. When $MRP_L < MRC_L$ production should be cut back and fewer units of labour are to be employed.

INPUT DEMAND BY A COMPETITIVE INDUSTRY

A competitive firm can change its level of usage of an input if price of the input changes and hence can change output without affecting fewer the price of the commodity produced. But if all firms respond to the price changes of an input simultaneously by changing the level of usage of the input, the price of the product of the industry changes. As input demand for each firm is derived by holding commodity price constant, input demanded by all firms change when they change their output levels simultaneously, i.e., at the same time.

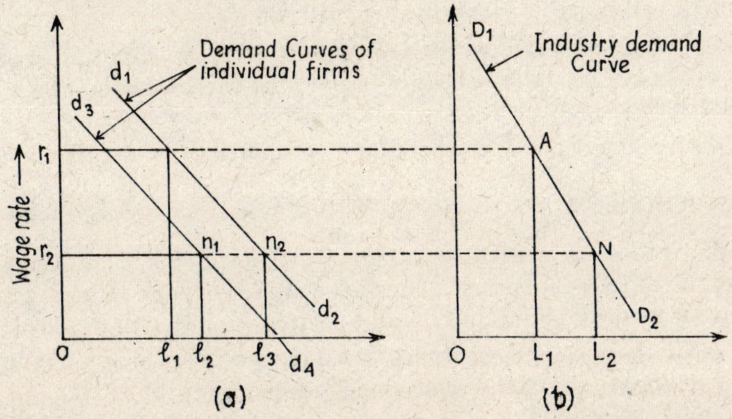

Fig 6.2 Derivation of the Industry Demand for a Variable Factor

Fig. 6.2 (a) shows a typical firm using only labour as a variable input. Let d_1d_2 be the firm's demand curve for labour at the current market price of the commodity produced. If r_1 is the wage rate, the firm uses l_1 units of labour. Total labour employed by all the firms in the industry (L_1) is shown in Fig. 6.2 (b). Hence A is a point on the industry demand curve for labour, D_1D_2.

Now if the price of labour falls from r_1 to r_2 and all other things remain equal, a firm would employ l_3 units of labour and the position is shifted to n_2 on d_1d_2 curve. Since other things are not equal and all firms increase their inputs, total output increases, i.e., the market supply curve for the commodity is shifted to the right due to the fall in the price of the input. The market price of the commodity falls, MR falls and a firm's $MRP(= VMP)$ curve shifts to the left and the individual firm's demand for labour also falls.

The fall in the individual firm's demand for labour due to fall in commodity price is shown in Fig. 6.2 (a) as a leftward shift of the demand curve for labour from d_1d_2 to d_3d_4. At the wage rate r_2, n_1 is the equilibrium point, with l_2 units of labour. Total labour employed by all the firms of the industry is shown as L_2 units in Fig. 6.2 (b). Several other points like A and N can be generated by changing the market price of the input, i.e., the wage rate. The industry demand curve for labour (the variable input) D_1D_2 can be obtained by joining these points. The curve is negatively sloped but steeper than that of a firm.

The supply curve of input in the market is positively sloped. Since additional labour must be obtained from other occupations, high prices are to be paid for such additional inputs. Hence the wage rate the firms intend to pay for a particular input is fixed by the supply and the demand for the input in the market.

Thus the wage rate is determined by the supply of and demand for the labour. Any factor which increases (decreases) the demand for labour (or any other input) must increase (decrease) the price that firms must pay for such input.

OUTPUT EFFECT AND INPUT SUBSTITUTION EFFECT

The quantity of an input required in an industry is a function of its own price, the state of technology and the demand for the end product. An input demand curve relates to a single homogeneous input and shows the input quantities required at various prices. An input demand curve has downward slope for the following reasons:

(1) An increase in the price of an input results in increase in the firm's marginal cost and shifts the supply curve of its product to the left. Moreover, product price increase leads to a fall the output of the industry. Again lesser inputs are used to produce a smaller output. This decrease in usage of input due to a rise in its price is called the OUTPUT EFFECT.

(2) If it is possible to change or vary the proportions of inputs, input price increases may cause firms to substitute expensive inputs by cheaper ones. This change in the usage of inputs is called the input SUBSTITUTION EFFECT.

We may now discuss input demand where input proportions remain fixed.

FIXED INPUT PROPORTIONS

Some production processes need fixed input proportions. For example, six buttoms and 1 metre of cloth are required to manufacture a finished good like a shirt. Hence with 60 buttoms and 15 metres of cloth, 10 shirts can be produced and 5 metres of cloth will be surplus.

Ditch digging is another example. Suppose in 1 hour a worker can dig a hole with one crowbar and this is the point at the corner of the right angled isoquant.

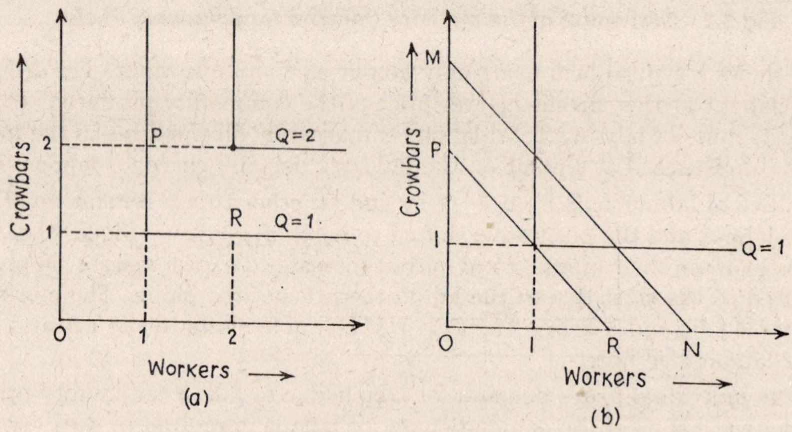

Fig 6.3 Right-angled Isoquants in a Fixed Proportions Production Function

Fig. 6.3 (b) shows minimisation of operating costs in a fixed proportions production function at the corner of an isoquant.

By giving two crowbars to one worker or by giving one crowbar to two workmen, the digging of hole will not be more than one per hour. Hence there is no chance of substituting one input by another. See Fig. 6.3(a).

From Fig (6.3) (b) we find that the cost of digging one hole is minimum at the corner of the isoquant, irrespective of input prices. This point is on the isocost line PR as also on the line MN.

The cost of each hole (MC) equals the cost of hiring a worker for 1 hour (w) plus the cost of hiring a crowbar for one hour (P_K), i.e., $MC = w + P_K$.

The supply curve of each competitive firm is horizontal at $(w + P_K)$ and the industry supply curve at $(w + P_K)$ is also horizontal since this is the summation of the individual firms' supply curves.

Now the cost of each hole will be Rs. 10 if wages per hour and the rental for hiring crowbar bar per hour are Rs. 8 and Rs. 2 respectively. At these input prices, the supply curve (S_0) of the hole digging industry is horizontal. See Fig. 6.4.

Point L shows the equilibrium of the competitive hole digging industry. From Fig. 6.4 we find that 12,000 holes are dug at a cost of Rs. 10 by using 12,000 hours of labour and 12,000 crowbar hours.

The demand for an input depends on the output of the industry, i.e., lesser the output lesser is the demand for an input and *vice versa.* Hence the demand for an input is derived from the demand for the output of the industry.

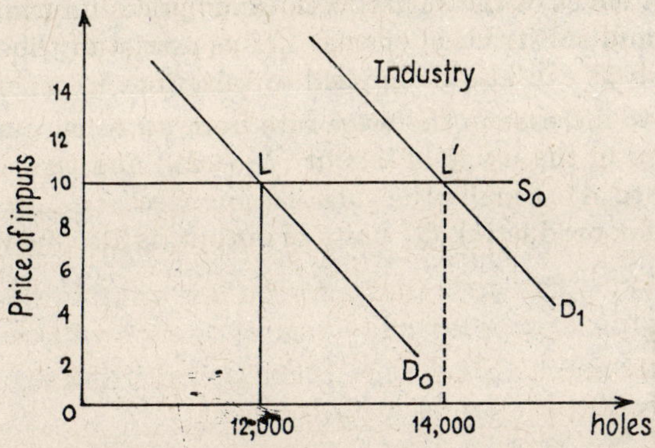

Fig 6.4 Shift of Factor Demand Curve

The shift of the industry demand curve for the input affects both output and input usage. For example in Fig. 6.4, if the demand curve moves to D_1 the new equilibrium will be at L' where 14,000 holes are to be dug at a cost of Rs. 10 per hole. The larger output is achieved by using more inputs, i.e., 14,000 hours of labour and 14,000 crowbar hours.

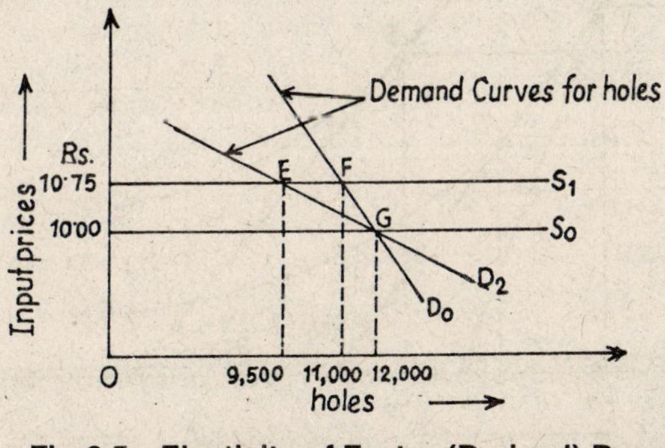

Fig 6.5 Elasticity of Factor (Derived) Demand

Fig 6.5 shows that output falls from 12,000 to 11,000 when the industry supply curve moves from S_0 to S_1. Under a more elastic demand curve D_2 the fall in output due to shift of the supply curve from S_0 to S_1 is much greater, i.e., from 12,000 to 9,500.

Input prices do affect input usage. In Fig. 6.5, D_0 is the demand curve for holes dug. The supply curve S_0 shows that at a unit cost of Rs. 10, 1200 holes are dug. When the wage rate rises from Rs. 8 to Rs. 8.75, but the crowbar hiring charges remain constant at Rs. 2, the marginal cost (MC) of firm increases from Rs. 10 to Rs. 10.75. With the new industry supply curve S_1 only 11,000 holes are supplied, and lesser inputs are required, i.e., 11,000 hours of labour and 11,000 crowbar hours. This reduction of inputs owing to the decline in output and rise in input prices is the output effect, discussed earlier.

The magnitude of the output effect depends on the elasticity of the demand curve for the output of the whole industry.

In Fig. 6.5 the elasticity of D_2 is greater than D_0. When the supply curve moves from S_0 to S_1 there is greater reduction of output under D_2 than under D_0, i.e., the output effect becomes stronger when the industry faces a more elastic demand for its product.

VARIABLE INPUT PROPORTIONS

Firms prefer to substitute variable inputs when the input prices change provided their isoquants are not right-angled. The net effect of the variation in input prices on the usage of inputs depends on the interaction of output and substitution effects. Let us now study the effects of an increase in the wage rate. The same analysis can also be applied to variations in other input prices.

Fig 6.6 shows that due to increase in the wage rate from w_0 to w_1 output declines from Q_0 to Q_1. The consequent reduction in the usage of labour $(L_1 - L_0)$ and that of capital $(K_1 - K_0)$ are shown in this figure (point B to A). Finally the substitution effect, i.e., use of less labour $(L_2 - L_1)$ and more capital $(K_2 - K_1)$ for producting Q_1 units of output, is also shown in the figure (point A to C).

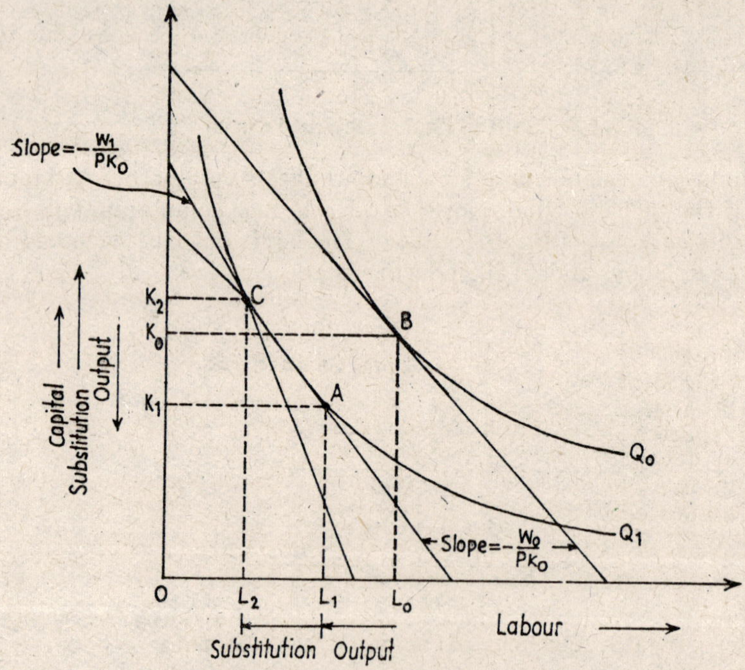

Fig 6.6 Output Effect and Input Substitution Effect

We have noted earlier that a rise in the wage rate causes a fall in industry output. This may happen either due to a fall in the number of firms in the industry, or by a reduction of average output of existing firms. Fig. 6.6 shows that at input prices w_0 and PK_0 a firm produces Q_0 units of output with L_0 labour and K_0 capital (point B). Suppose with rise of wage rate to w_1 the firm's output declines to Q_1. Now only Q_1 units are produced by the firm at the old input prices, with L_1 both labour and K_1 capital (point A). The reduction of output results in the reduction of labour $(L_1 - L_0)$ and capital $(K_1 - K_0)$ inputs. This is the output effect.

At increased price of labour, Q_1 units of output are obtained with L_2 labour and K_2 capital. Due to substitution effect, less labour $(L_2 - L_1)$ and more capital $(K_2 - K_1)$ are needed to produce Q_1 units of output (point C).

The substitution and output effects conjointly reduce labour usage. The output effect is more pronounced when the demand for the industry's product is fairly elastic. The substitution effect is more prominent where it is easy to substitute between inputs. Both substitution and output effects account for the downward slope of the demand curve for labour.

A rise in the wage rate causes output to fall. As a result the usage of capital will also fall. But if output remains unchanged (or even falls) the usage of capital may increase if the firm substitutes labour by capital. In Fig 6.6 the substitution effect is more pronounced than the output effect and the firm uses more capital and less labour when the wage rate rises. In some other industries the converse is true.

THE FIRM'S MRP RULE

We have already seen that $MRP_K = MPP_K \times MR$ or $MRP_K = MR \times MP_K$ and $MRP_L = MR \times MP_L$.

By combining MRP_K and MRP_L are arrive at two other rules of profit maximisation.

(1) $\frac{MR \times MP_L}{MR \times MP_L} = \frac{MRP_L}{MRP_K} = \frac{MP_L}{MP_K}$

This condition is satisfied when the isoquant is a tangent to an isocost line and this is the condition of cost minimisation.

(2) $MR = \frac{MRP_K}{MP_K} = \frac{MRP_L}{MP_L}$

We know from the definition of $MP_L = \frac{1}{MP_L} = \frac{\Delta L}{\Delta Q}$, i.e., increase in labour input required to increase output by one unit. Hence $MR.MP_L$ $\left(\frac{1}{MP_L}\right)$, i.e., MR is the expenditure on L which is required to increase the output by one unit with increased L only. A similar explanation can be given for K. The profit-maximising condition is once again $MR = MC$.

We may now see how a manager selects the optimal level of use of a variable factor of production—labour.

Suppose from the data for the period 1992 II–94 IV the manager of X Co. estimated a production function of the form $Q - AL^{\beta}$.

More specifically, the manager used the 10 quarterly observations to estimate $\log Q = \log A + \beta \log L$ where output (Q) was expressed in thousand units and labour usage (L) was in thousand hours. Using the estimated coefficients from the computer printout, the estimated production function was $\log Q = 1.004 + 0.6 \log L$.

This equation has an R^2 of 0.9210 and an F value of 93,266. The appropriate t-tests were performed to determine that the estimate of β was significantly greater than zero and less than one.

Rewriting the estimated production function in its exponential form, the empirical production function was $Q = (2.73)L^{0.6}$.

From this estimated production function, the marginal product function for labour was $MP_L = (0.6)(2.73)L^{0.6-1.0} = (1.638)L^{-0.4}$.

Using the price and wage forecasts and the estimated marginal product function the profit-maximisation condition $(P \times MP_L = w)$ can be expressed as $(20) \times (1.638L^{-0.4}) = 16$ or $L^{-0.4} = 0.4884$.

Taking logarithms of both sides of the proceding equation $-0.4 \log L = -0.717$; so $\log L = 1.792$ and it follows that (using natural logs) $L = 6.0$. That is, the profit-maximising level of labour usage in the first quarter of 1995 is 6,000 hours. (This is the equivalent of 12 full-time employees.)

Summary

Prices of productive factors (inputs) are determined by the interaction of supply and demand. The demand for inputs is derived from the demand for the output that those inputs are used to produce. The marginal revenue product function, computed by multiplying marginal revenue and marginal physical product, is the firm's input demand function.

Determining input prices in important because these prices are used in deciding on the optimal mix of labour, capital and other resources to be employed by the firm. The approach to input price determination depends on the structure of both the input and output markets. A perfect competitor in an input market faces constant price of inputs. Thus the only decision made by the firm is the quantity of the input to be employed. A monopsonist has enough power in the input market and, thus faces an upward-sloping input supply curve. The input price and quantity employed by the monopsonist is determined by the intersection of the input demand curve with the firm's marginal factor cost curve.

There is a unique correspondence between output and input decisions. A decision to produce a given rate of output implies a decision to hire certain rates of capital and labour input and *vice versa*. The condition for a profit-maximising output rate (i.e., marginal cost equals marginal revenue) is equivalent to the condition for a profit-maximising input usage (i.e., marginal revenue product equals input price).

A monopolist who purchases a variable productive resource or input in a perfectly competitive input market (the price of the input is given to the firm) will employ that amount of the input for which marginal revenue product equals the price of the input. Consequently, the marginal revenue product curve, within the relevant range, is the monopolist's demand curve for the variable input when only one variable input is employed. Marginal revenue product declines for two reasons: (1) the marginal product of the input declines as more units of the variable input are added and (2) to sell the additional output, the monopoly must lower the price of its output.

Concepts for Review

1. Marginal Physical Product
2. Marginal Revenue Product
3. Value of Marginal Product
4. Derived Demand
5. Marginal Resource Cost
6. Output Effect
7. Fixed Input Proportions
8. Variable Input Proportions.

Exercises

1. To find the optimising level of usage of a single variable input, what condition must be satisfied for a firm in a perfectly competitive market? In order that the level of usage indicated by the preceding condition actually be optimal, what must be the relation between average product and marginal product?

2. Suppose a firm operating in a perfectly competitive market has only one variable input—labour. The manager of the firm estimated a short-run production function for the firm of the form $Q = AL^{\beta}$. The resulting estimated function was $\log Q = 1.176 + 0.7 \log L$ where Q was measured in 1,000 units and L was measured in 1,000 hours of labour input.

(a) Using the estimates obtained, rewrite the production function in the form $Q = AL^{\beta}$.

(b) What is the marginal product of labour function? The manager has forecasted the price of the firm's output to be Rs. 10 per unit and the price of labour (the wage rate) to be Rs. 14 per hour.

(c) What is the firm's value of the marginal product function?

(d) What is the indicated optimal level of usage of labour?

(e) Ensure that this level of usage is indeed optimal (i.e., compare AP_L and MP_L at this level of usage of labour).

3. Using your results in Problem 2,

(a) How much output will this firm produce?

(b) What is the firm's total revenue?

(c) What is the firm's total variable cost?

If total fixed cost of the firm is Rs. 50,000.

(d) How much profit (loss) will the firm make?

(e) If the firm has decided to shut down, how much profit (loss) would it have made?

4. A monopsonist's demand curve for labour is given by $w = 12 - 2L$, where w is the hourly wage rate and L is the number of person-hours hired.

(a) If the monopsonist's supply or average resource cost curve (ARC) curve is given by $w = 2L$, which gives rise to a marginal factor cost curve of $MRC = 4L$, how many units of labour will he employ and what wage will he pay?

(b) How would your answers to part (a) be different if the monopsonist were confronted with a minimum wage bill requiring him to pay at least Rs. 7 per hour..

(c) How would your answers to parts (a) and (b) be different if the employer in question were not a monopsonist but a perfect competitor in the market for labour?

5. A firm produces output according to the production function $Q = K^{1/2}L^{1/2}$. If it sells its output in a perfectly competitive market at a price of 10 and if K is fixed at 4 units, what is this firm's short-run demand curve for labour?

6. Using the data of problem 1 (Ch. 5) answer the following questions:

(a) If $K = 2$ and output sells for Rs. 4 per unit, find the total, average and marginal product functions and the marginal revenue product function for labour in the following table.

L	TP_L	AP_L	MP_L	MRP_L
0	—	—	—	—
1	—	—	—	—
2	—	—	—	—
3	—	—	—	—
4	—	—	—	—

(b) Using the data from (a), find how much labour will be employed if the wage rate is Rs. 20 per unit.

(c) If the rate of labour input is kept constant at 3 and the price of output is Rs. 4 per unit, find the total, average and the marginal product functions for capital and the marginal revenue product of capital in the following table.

K	TP_K	AP_K	MP_K	MRP_K
0	—	—	—	—
1	—	—	—	—
2	—	—	—	—
3	—	—	—	—
4	—	—	—	—

(d) Use data from (c) to find the units of capital to be employed when the price of capital is Rs. 20 per unit.

CHAPTER 7

JOINT PRODUCT AND MULTI-PRODUCT FIRMS

When firms produce many products, managers must consider the interrelationships among those products.
H.C. Petersen and W.C. Lewis, 1993

Fundamental Questions

1. Should goods produced in fixed proportions be regarded as a product package in developing production and pricing strategies?
2. Should a sheep-ranching operator consider lamb and wool as a product package?
3. How should common costs be allocated among different products?

PREVIEW

Of the various decisions made by a manager, setting the price of the product seems to be the most important. However, economic theory involves simplification of reality. A large corporation might produce several hundred products that are sold in many different markets. Sometimes the price set for one of these products can affect the demand for the other products sold by the firm. For example, the price Sony fixed for movie cameras affect the quality of coloured films demanded which fit these camaras and vice versa. Similarly output decisions relating to one product may affect the manufacturing or marketing costs of other products. A manufacturer of household products (consumer non-durables) may be able to promote a new brand of soap more efficiently than a firm in an unrelated market.

JOINT AND MULTIPLE PRODUCT FIRMS

The success of a firm largely depends on its pricing policy and strategy. The effect of pricing decision is reflected in short-run profits. The price of a commodity can affect future profits. When a firm has control over price, the rule is to produce till marginal revenue = marginal cost and charge the price shown by the demand curve for that quantity. A large company producing hundreds of products sells them at different markets and the price, fixed for one of these products, may affect the demand for another product. Again production decisions of one product may affect the production, or marketing costs of other products.

So we may now discuss how firm producing multiple products take decision regarding allocation of costs among different products and pricing the products.

PRICING OF MULTIPLE PRODUCTS

A firm may produce and sell hundreds of products. Some of these products are unrelated, i.e., the demand for a product is unlikely to be affected by the price of another product. Again production cost of one product may be independent of that of another. However, demand and production of other brands produced by the firm may be interrelated. In such cases the price of one affects the demand for the other. If pricing decisions are made on the basis of costs, prices will depend on the allocation of costs among the products. When a firm produces more than one product, the manager(s) should take the interrelationships among these products into consideration.

Products with Inter Dependent Demands

Multiple products are either substitutes, or complements. For substitute products, an increase in price for one product tends to increase the demand for another product. The magnitude of the increase depends on the availability of substitutes from other vendors. For complements, an increase in price tends to decrease the demand for the other product. The sale of power-windows, stereo-systems, automatic locks, etc. by an automobile dealer depends on the number of cars sold by him. If the price of the car is increased, the sale of cars will fall and the demand for these spares will also fall.

For taking accurate pricing decisions, demand interrelationships are to be considered. Instead of fixing the price of each product separately, the impact of each price on the demand for other products manufactured by the firm should be taken into consideration. The manager must fix up the prices of different product in such a way that the total profit of the firm, rather the profit of each individual product is maximised.

When demands are interrelated, managers should consider the marginal revenue equations of all the products. Suppose a firm produces two items A and B and the sale of A has an impact on the demand of B and *vice versa*. This can be mathematically expressed as

$$MR_A = \frac{dTR_A}{dQ_A} + \frac{dTR_B}{dQ_A} \tag{1}$$

$$\text{and} \quad MR_B = \frac{dTR_B}{dQ_B} + \frac{dTR_A}{dQ_B} \tag{2}$$

Equation (1) shows the MR related with variations in the quantity of A can be separated into two parts. The first part $\frac{dTR_A}{dQ_A}$ indicates the variation in revenues for product A arising out of a one-unit rise in sales of product A and the second part $\frac{dTR_B}{dQ_A}$ shows the demand interdependency.

It shows the variation in revenue from the sale of product B arising out of a one-unit rise in sales of product A. Equation (2) can be explained in the same way in terms of a one-unit increase in sales of product B.

The signs of $\frac{dTR_B}{dQ_A}$ and $\frac{dTR_A}{dQ_B}$ depend on the nature of the relationship between A and B. When A and B are complements, both the terms become positive and increasing sales of A increases sales of B also. Again if A and B are substitutes, both the terms will be negative, since additional sales of A decrease sales of B.

For taking optimal pricing and output decisions in such situations, the firm must take demand interdependencies into consideration. Let us assume that A and B are complements. For finding out the profit-maximising rate of output for A if the effect of sales of A on the demand for B is not taken into consideration, output of A will increase till $\frac{dTR_A}{dQ_A}$ equals the marginal cost of producing A. But from equation (1) we find that $\frac{dTR_A}{dQ_A}$ understates the actual incremental revenue obtained by selling an extra units of A. Also revenue is affected by $\frac{dTR_B}{dQ_A}$, whose sign is positive when A and B are complements. So profit maximisation needs greater rate of output for A when demand interdependency is taken into consideration. Output of A will increase until $\frac{dTR_A}{dQ_A} + \frac{dTR_B}{dQ_A} = MC_A$ where MC_A is the extra cost needed by the firm in manufacturing on extra unit of A. Similarly, for substitutes, it can be shown that ignoring the demand interdependency will cause production of too many units.

JOINT PRODUCTS

When goods are jointly produced in fixed proportions, one type of production interdependency exists, e.g., mutton and hides. Each goat gives a certain amount of meat and hide and the slaughter-house cannot change the proportions of the two products.

When goods are manufactured in fixed proportions, they should be considered as a product package. Since both the goods in the package are to be manufactured simultaneously, there is no conceptual basis for allocation of total production costs between the two goods. These costs have significance only in terms of the product package. This important point is explained in the Fig. 7.1.

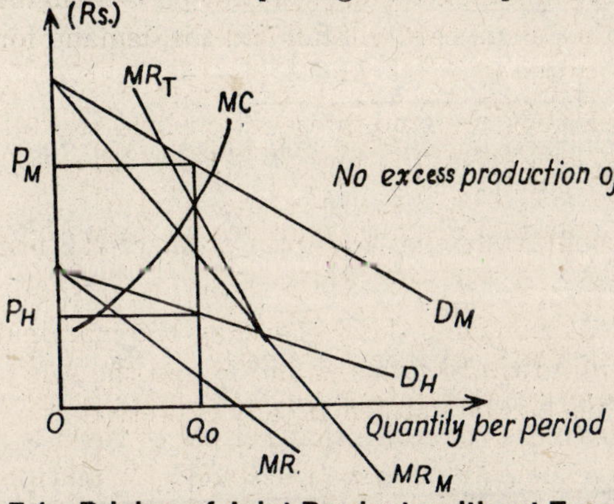

Fig 7.1 Pricing of Joint Products without Excess Production

Here D_M and D_H are the demand curves for mutton and hide respectively. The demand for mutton (M) and hide (H) are different though they are being produced simultaneously. However, the marginal cost curve (MC) is the same for both M and H. The common marginal cost (MC) curve indicates the extra cost of producing one unit more of the product package.

When goods are manufactured jointly, pricing decisions should take this interdependency into consideration. Fig. 7.2 shows how profit-maximising prices and quantities are obtained. Here MR_M

and MR_H are the marginal revenue curves for mutton and hides. When an extra animal is processed both mutton and hide are available for sale. Thus the marginal revenue received by selling one unit of the product package is equal to the sum of the marginal revenues which is represented by the MR_T line. This line can be found by adding MR_H and MR_M for each rate of output. In Fig. 7.1, it is the vertical sum of the marginal revenue curves of products M and H.

The profit-maximising rate of output ($Q_\circ$) is found by the intersection of MR_T and MC. The profit-maximising prices, P_H and P_M are located from the demand curves for goods H and M at the output rate, $Q_\circ$. We find from Fig. 7.1 that both MR_H and MR_M are positive at $Q_\circ$.

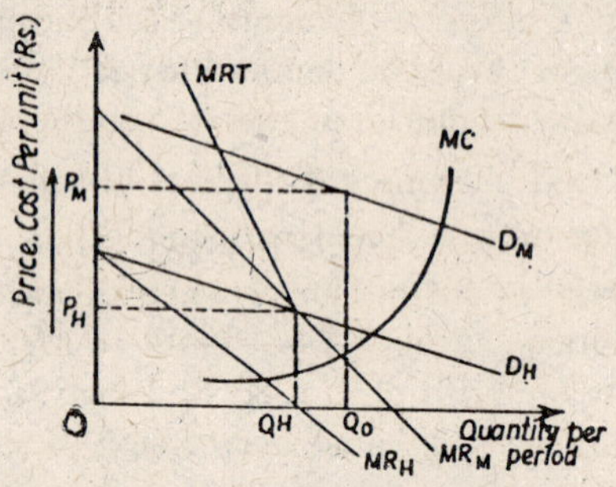

Fig 7.2 Pricing of Joint Products with Excess Production of Hides

From Fig. 7.2, we find that MR_H is negative at the profit-maximising quantity, i.e., sale of an additional hide decreases the revenues obtained from that product. Hence $Q_\circ$ cannot be considered as the optimal rate of output for hides in this case. A firm is not advised to produce the output rate at which marginal revenue is negative. But since the products are jointly produced, some problems may arise, i.e., stopping production of hides would mean reduction in the supply of mutton for which marginal revenue is positive.

From Fig. 7.2, we find that the profit-maximising choice for mutton is to sell Q_H at a price of P_H. Though the production of hides will be continued, sales should be restricted to the point where marginal revenue is negative. Hence Q_H should only be sold at price P_H. Unless disposal, or storage costs are very high, the excess hides should be withheld from the market to achieve overall profit maximisation.

PROBLEM 1. A trader sells hides and mutton which are jointly produced in fixed proportion. The marginal cost equation for mutton-hide-product-package is $MC = 30 + 6Q$.

The demand and marginal revenue equations for products mutton and hides are given below.

Mutton	Hides
$P = 65 - 1Q$	$P = 85 - 2Q$
$MR = 65 - 2Q$	$MR = 85 - 4Q$

Find out the prices to be charged for mutton and hides. Also find how many units of the product package should be manufactured.

SOLUTION. Adding the two marginal revenue equations we have $MR_T = 150 - 6Q$.

The optimal quantity is found by equating MR_T and MC and solving for the value of Q. Therefore $150 - 6Q = 30 + 6Q$ or $12Q = 150 - 30 = 120$ $\therefore$ $Q = 10$.

Putting $Q = 10$ in the two demand equations, we get $P =$ Rs. 55 for mutton and Rs. 65 for hides. Before accepting that these prices maximise profits, the marginal revenue at this output rate must be calculated for mutton and hides to ensure that neither of them is negative. Again putting $Q = 10$ into the two marginal revenue equations we get Rs. 45 for mutton and hides. Since both marginal revenues are positive, the two prices maximise profits. If marginal revenue of any of the products, mutton and hides, is negative, the quantity sold of that product should be restricted to the point where marginal revenue just equals to zero.[1]

PROBLEM 2. Suppose Z & Co. produces X and Y that are substitutes in consumption. The demand functions of the two products were forecasted to be $Q_X = 80 - 8P_X + 6P_Y$ and

[1] For joint products produced in variable proportions see S. Mukherjee's: Business and Managerial Economics (NCBA, Calcutta, 1995)

(iii) The multiproduct firm producing subject to fixed-proportions production process will produce equal amounts of all products.

(iv) Customers with higher demand prices value a product more than those with lower demand prices.

5. Provide some examples of products that are complements in production. Can you provide any examples of products that have been produced and destroyed in a joint production process?

6. Can you think of examples of firms that produce products that are both related in consumption and substitutes in production? In general, how would this additional complication affect the profit-maximisation condition?

7. Look again at the division of BCCL that produces two products that are substitutes in production. Suppose that the forecasted demand function was changed to $Q_X = 76 - \frac{1}{2}P_X$

(a) How will an eight-hour production day be allocated between the production of the two products?

(b) What will be the daily outputs?

(c) What prices will be charged?

8. Suppose that the plant supervisor of BCCL changes the estimate of the incremental (marginal) cost for usage of the plant to $MC = 150 = 3H$

(a) What is the optimal level of usage for the plant (hours per day)?

(b) How will this level of usage be allocated between the production of the two products?

(c) What will be the daily outputs?

(d) What prices will be charged?

9. A firm traps rabbits for their fur and feet. Each rabbit gives one pelt and two feet (only the rear feet are taken to make good-luck charms). The demand for pelts is expressed as $P_P = 3 - .002Q_P$ and the demand for feet is expressed by $P_f = 2.5 - .002Q_f$.

The marginal cot for trapping and processing per rabbit is Re. 1.

(i) What are the profit-maximising prices and quantities of pelts and feet?

(ii) If the demand for feet is $P_f = 2 - .002Q_f$, what are the profit-maximising prices and output rates?

CHAPTER 8

RISK, UNCERTAINTY AND DECISION-MAKING

··· all true profit is linked with uncertainty or imperfect information. ··· Once the implicit returns are subtracted, what remains is pure profit which is the reward for undertaking investments with uncertain returns.

Paul A. Samuelson

Fundamental Questions
1. What is the difference between risk and uncertainty?
2. What role does risk play in production planning?
3. How can a business firm plan for profit under conditions of risk and uncertainty?

PREVIEW

Perhaps the most certain thing about modern businessman is that all important business decisions are taken under uncertain conditions. This is why business firms seek to eliminate uncertainty by collecting as much information as possible about the decision variables. For example, before introducing new products, managers undertake consumer surveys, assess product line of their competitors and closely check estimated product costs. These actions are to taken to collect as much information as possible. On the basis of information acquired business decisions will be made. Yet the are few sure things in the world of management. Many business failures have occurred despite management having taken all possible steps to ensure success. It is not even possible to predict consumer behaviour or changes in production technology with complete accuracy. Every decision carries with it the possibility that something will go wrong and that instead of earning large profits as expected, losses are incurred. Despite the various techniques developed in recent years, learning to make decisions where there is risk and uncertainty is the essence of modern management.

We are the two terms risk and uncertainty interchangeably in our day-to-day conversation. However, the two are different. Risk is said to be exist when the outcomes associated with a decision and the possibilities of those outcomes occurring are known or can be estimated by using probability calculations. In contrast, a manager faces uncertainty when the possible outcomes are known but the probabilities of those outcomes are unknown.

Suppose a firm is considering the production of an altogether new product. Since consumers have had no experience with the product, there is no way to estimate the potential demand for it. The marketing manager may instruct his subordinates to carry out various market surveys in an attempt to estimate how many people might buy the product but it is doubtful that much confidence can be placed in such efforts. There may simply be no way to provide anything but some rough guesses about demand. This is an example of uncertainty. Such uncertainty makes production and profit planning a difficult and extremely complicated exercise.

UNCERTAINTY IN PRODUCTION FUNCTION

An important dimension often ignored in the theory of the firm is the role of randomness. However, some new models of production have been developed in recent years to take account of these elements.

A production function depicts the technological relationships between inputs and outputs in physical terms. It specifies the maximum quantity of an item that can be produced per unit of time with available inputs and technology. A production function may be represented by a table, graph, algebraic equation or mathematical model. A real life production function is highly complex and uncertain. It has too many inputs, e.g., land, labour, capital, raw material, time, space, etc. However, for the sake of convenience and simplicity economists consider only two variables, viz. capital and labour, in the production function. They assume that except capital and labour, all other inputs remain constant in the short run.

Suppose the algebraic form of production function of a coal-mine employing two inputs, i.e., capital (K) and labour (L) is expressed as $Q = f(K, L)$, where Q = quantity of coal produced per unit of time, K = capital, and L = labour.

The production function implies that Q is the maximum quantity of coal which can be produced, with fixed capital (K) and fixed labour (L). To increase coal production, more K and L will be required. In the short run, some factors of production remain fixed. In the long run all factors, however, are variable. Thus the firm can increase production of coal by increasing labour, holding capital constant. In the long run production can be increased by employing more of both capital and labour. Thus the short-run production function is expressed as $Q = f(L)$.

But in the long run, the production function can be expressed as $Q = f(K, L)$.

Assumptions Any discussion of theoretical production function is based on the following assumptions:

1. Perfect divisibility of both factor inputs and output.
2. Constant technology.
3. Limited substitution of one factor by another.
4. Inelastic (or fixed) supply of certain factors of production in the short run.

If these assumptions are changed, the production function becomes uncertain.

Two statistical production functions are (1) the Cobb-Douglas production function; and (2) the Constant Elasticity of Substitution (CES) production function, discussed in Chapter 5. Since both the functions have certain major limitations there is tremendous uncertainty in production function.

Limitations of the Cobb-Douglas Production Function

The Cobb Douglas production function helps us to compare manufacturing industries, both demestically and internationally. It captures the essential non-linearities of production process. Its main advantage is the simplification of computations by being converted into a linear form. However, critics have pointed out the following drawbacks and uncertainties of the function:

1. It includes only labour and capital input and ignores other significant inputs like raw material, etc. used in the production process.

2. It assumes constant returns to scale. But this assumption is highly uncertain. Factors of production like entrepreneurship cannot be increased in the desired proportion. Even if we can increase all factors in the same proportion it is not possible to ensure constant returns to scale in the long run.

3. The measurement of capital becomes a problem. Labour can be measured in terms of labour services per hour, whereas it is difficult to measure capital services per hour, since depreciation over time has to be considered.

4. Since raw material is not included in input, the output side shows the value added figure for each industry. When we assume constant returns to scale, we assume that there is a fixed relation between raw material and output which is not always true.

5. It assumes that the perfect competition exists in the factor market. But if we try attempt to make the analysis more realistic, we find α and β do not represent factor shares.

Limitations of the CES Production Function

1. The economies of scale have two main sources:

(a) Expansion in the scale of operation with available technology.

(b) Technological change with the given scale of operation.

The scale parameter cannot differentiate between these two sources.

2. Secondly, the function has K as capital intensity parameter which is not dimensionless.

3. When the factor inputs increase, it is difficult to use the production function.

4. The function specifies elasticity of substitution which is invariant to changes in factor proportions. This is a unrealistic assumption.

Limitations of Leontief-type Production Function

Let us now take the fixed coefficient type of production function which does not permit capital-labour subsitution. There is no guarantee that the producer would get, when he hired an extra worker, the labour services he expected? The worker might fall sick. There may be a strike in the factory. Or the labourer might turn out to be much more efficient than expected by the entrepreneur. So there are various sources of uncertainty. The producer can only think of a distribution of labour services and another of capital services, which he would get as a consequence of hiring fixed resources. By doing this he will find that the expected-output isoquants are smoothed out and he will be back in a neoclassical world with rounded corners to his isoquants. Such a smooth neoclassical function would relate inputs purchased to expected output.

PROFIT PLANNING UNDER RISK AND UNCERTAINTY

So long we discussed parameters like prices, variable costs, quantities of output, etc. which were known with certainty. Economic models under uncertainty in most cases assume that the decision makers are risk-averse. Risk-averse decision makers normally are interested in higher expected returns from higher-risk investments. Hence a knowledge of the degree of riskiness of an investment project is very significant and thus of considerable practical relevance to a decision maker.

Short-run Decisions under Uncertainty

For a risk-averse firm, the optimum output level is lower than the output level at which marginal revenue (MR) = marginal cost (MC). Cost-volume-profit analysis (CVP) is an important tool which the management uses to decide matters like (1) the sales volume needed to attain a given level of profit, (2) the most profitable combination of products to produce and sell and so on. The traditional CVP analysis does not make any adjustments for risk and uncertainty. This explains why its usefulness is so limited. No doubt the CVP analysis helps us to determine the break-even volume of each product. But it does not distinguish among the relative desirability of the products since it cannot predict the Expected Sales Volume of each product. If the sales estimates are uncertain, the decision process can, however, be improved by adjusting for the relative risk associated with the marketing of each product.

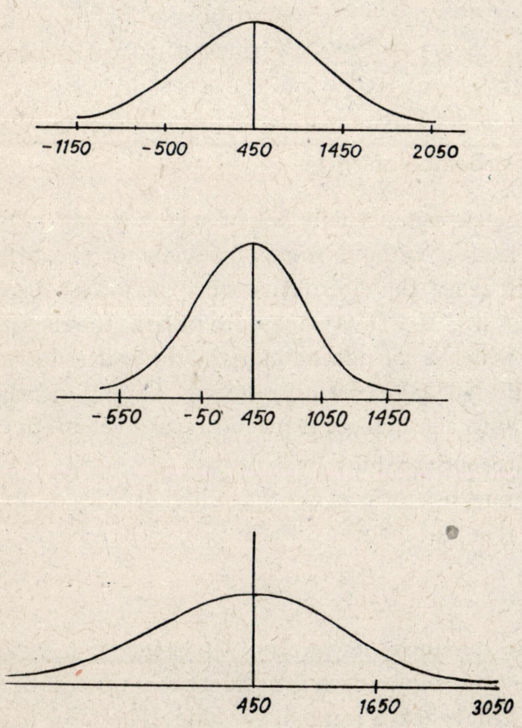

Fig 8.1 The Probability Distribution of Profit Variables

According to Jaedicke and Robichek information on uncertainty can be used to compare different pricing policies, or different products. Suppose that the expected profit for a particular product is Rs. 4,50,000, given expected output = 5000 units, price = Rs. 3,000, variable cost = Rs. 1,750 and fixed cost = Rs. 5,800,000, respectively. Based on the probability distributions of these random variables, calculated standard deviation (S.D.) σ^2 for this expected profit is Rs. 681,500. Two other products promise identical expected profit of Rs. 4,50,000, with σ^2 = Rs. 500,000 and σ^2 = 1,253,000 respectively. Assuming that the random profit variables are normally distributed, we can display them as in Fig. 8.1.

The price expected to prevail on a particular day is indicated in Fig. 8.2 by the height of the bell-shaped curve. The average or expected price $\bar{P}$ is close to the highest point of the curve and is thus the most likely price. However, too high or two low prices are possible but unlikely.

Let us consider the following discrete probability distribution of prices.

Price (Rs.)	:	5	4	6	7	8	9
Probability	:	.09	0.20	.18	.19	.24	0.10

Although, we cannot forecast the actual price for tomorrow, we can compute the expected price by multiplying each possible price by the probability of its occurrence and then adding up the results.

Fig. 8.2 shows that for random demand, the actual price is subject to a probability distribution. The price becomes equal to the mean price of $\bar{P}$ on an average. Profit will be uncertain, as price is a random variable.

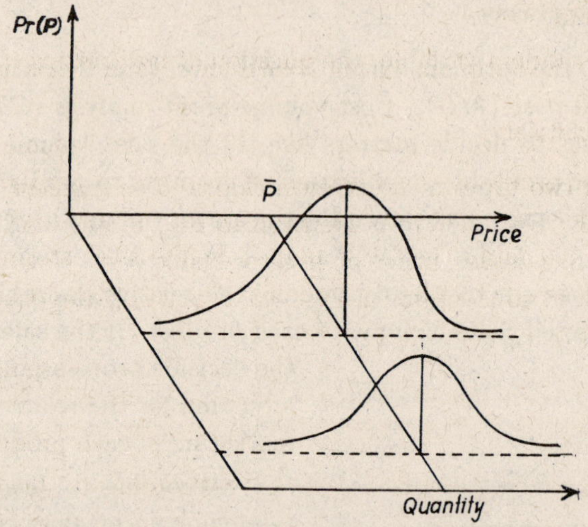

Fig 8.2 The Probability Distribution of Prices

Jaedicke and Robichke do not suggest how managers will actually act in such a situation but have admitted that the best alternative cannot be chosen without some statement of the firm's attitude toward risk. A risk-averse decision maker will select the alternative with the lowest degree of risk if all the alternatives have identical expected return. If S.D. is a measure of risk, the decision maker will select the product with S.D. = Rs. 5,00,000 which is the minimum of the three alternatives, given that each has an expected return or profit of Rs. 450,000. For alternatives, having identical S.D., a risk-averse decision maker will select the one with the highest expected return (or profit).

However, the selection becomes difficult when alternatives differ by expected returns and standard deviations. Generally, alternatives with higher expected returns also have higher S.Ds and the decision maker achieve make some trade-off between risk and return.

Profit Maximisation and Uncertainty[1]

Under conditions of certainty, a firm's aim is to maximise its profits. Uncertainty, however, upsets this aim. Suppose, the horizontal demand line of a competitive firm fluctuates up and down in a random manner. The price of the product of the firm is also a random variable. The price likely to prevail can be calculated from the above table which shows a probability distribution of prices.

Here $\bar{P} = 5 \times .09 + 4 \times .20 + 6 \times .18 + 7 \times .19 + 8 \times 24 + 9 \times .1 =$ Rs. 6.48.

Hence the average (or expected) price is Rs. 6.48.

---

[1] For an excellent discussion of this topic see Kenny and Blair: *Microeconomics with Business Applications* (John Wiley & Sons, 1986)

Random Profit

Now the random price for the firm's output is available. Before knowing the actual price the customers are ready to pay for the commodity, the manager must fix up the quantity of output. This is a common real life problem. Farmers, producers of new fashion items and new products, often face such a situation. When the product under consideration is perishable the manager is supposed to sell the entire output as quickly as he can. As profit is given by (price × quantity – cost of production of the quantity), profit becomes a function of the random price. This means that profit itself becomes a random.

When profit itself is a random variable, the question of maximizing it does not arise.

Break-Even Analysis under Uncertainty

In Fig. 8.3 we present two types of break-even charts. The gradient of the line indicates the contribution margin per unit. Fig. 8.3 (b) is identical to Fig. 8.3(a) with the only difference that the profit line originates from a higher price, or lesser variable cost. Now whether the higher price in Fig. 8.3(b) is more preferred to the price in Fig. 8.3(a) is a decision question.

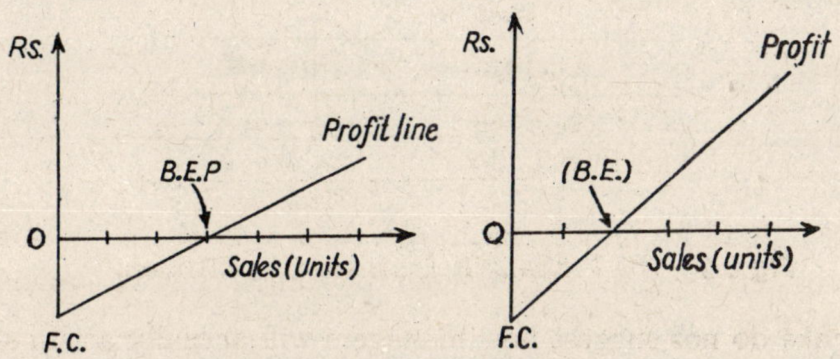

Fig 8.3 Two Break-Even Charts

The break-even point (BEP) is lower in Fig. 8.3(b) due to higher average contribution margin. This, however, does not ensure the likely occurrence of different possible profits due to the implementation of different pricing policies. The shifting of the B.E.P. cannot be treated as the criterion for taking the decision.

To make the decision-making process more meaningful, at first we are to establish the probability function for a given price policy indicating the likelihood of selling various amounts of a product. In Fig. 8.4 such a distribution has been superimposed on a break-even chart.

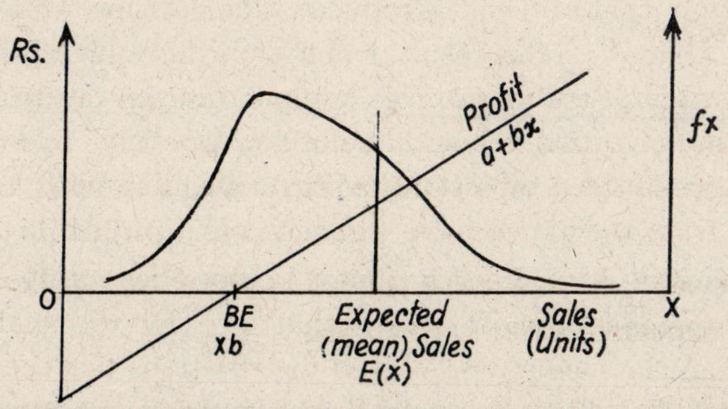

Fig 8.4 Probability Function for a Given Price Policy

The vertical axes on the left hand and right hand sides represent prices and the probability of sales at different prices, respectively. We assume that the distribution is continuous and unimodal but not normal, or symmetrical.

The probability density function of demand indicates the relative possibility of individual level of sales. The curve covers a total area equal to 1 and the area over any sales interval equals the probability that sales will lie in the particular interval. Such a curve can be drawn on the basis of historical data and can be suitably modified afterwards to match with the existing situation.

If the decision maker wants to produce, the profit (Y) for a given price policy becomes $Y = a + bx$ and the expected profit can be obtained by $E(Y) = a + bE(X)$ where $a \leq 0$ and measures the negative of the fixed costs. For 'Do Not Produce' decision, the return is zero in all cases. Hence a decision maker is to calculate the expected profit for the decision 'Produce' and commence production if the expected profits exceed zero. He takes the decision on the basis of expected profits. Here we have assumed that fixed costs refer to the opportunity costs of using the production facilities in the best possible way.

When the pay-off functions for actions are all linear, the decision can be taken on the basis of the expected sales value, e.g., expected demand. Suppose that the pay-offs for two separate decisions involving linear pay-offs are as follows.

	Action	Pay-off
(1)	Produce	$a_1 + b_1X$
(2)	Don't Produce	$a_2 + b_2X$

where X represents sales. Here we impose two restrictions $b_1 > b_2$ and $a_1 < a_2$ to ensure that the two lines intersect and the actual value of X does not depend on the two actions. Then the difference in sales levels, X_b can be found as follows

$$a_1 + b_1X_b = a_2 + b_2X_b \therefore a_2 - a_1 = X_b(b_1 - b_2); \therefore X_b = \frac{a_2 - a_1}{b_1 - b_2} \qquad (1)$$

Now Produce is better than Don't Produce if its expected value is higher

$$E(a_1 + b_1X) > E(a_2 + b_2X) \text{ or } a_1 + b_1E(X) > a_2 + b_2E(X) \text{ or } b_1E(X) - b_2E(X) > a_2 - a_1.$$

Hence Produce is a better decision if $E(X) > \dfrac{a_2 - a_1}{b_1 - b_2} = X_b$ (2)

Equation (2) shows that if the expectation exceeds the indifference level, the expected pay-off from 'Produce' is greater than that of 'Don't Produce'. The decision 'Don't Produce' is better if the expected value of X is less than X_b. This result depends on the value of the expectation only and is independent of the shape of the distribution. For example, the pay-offs from the decision to produce are denoted by the equation of action (1) with a positive gradient, whereas the pay-offs from the decision 'Don't Produce' are denoted by a straight line coinciding with the horizontal axis and the gradient of zero.

The mean, or the expected level of sales cannot be obtained easily. The modal value of sales is most desirable and the median value of sales is that level for which the odds are equal. Mean sales tend to be greater than the median for skewed distributions like the one shown in Fig. 8.4. If median sales are higher than the indifference level, the decision Produce is better since the mean exceeds the median. When median sales are $\leq$ the indifference level, it becomes difficult to make the best decision. Moderately skewed distribution shows that the median lies about $\frac{2}{3}$ of the distance from the mode toward the mean. The mean for a moderately skewed distribution can be obtained by using the following standard formula $E(X)$ = Mode + $\frac{3}{2}$ (median − mode).

For symmetrical probability distributions, the mean, median and mode are the same and the decision process becomes fairly simple.

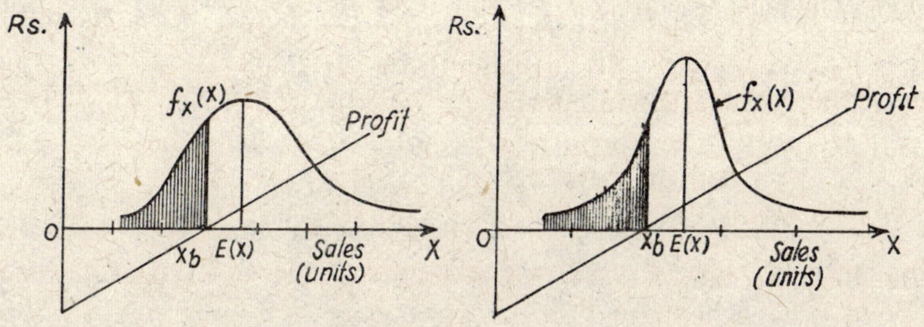

Fig 8.5 B.E. Charts for Two Separate Prices for the Same product and Separate Demand Distributions

Considering the two prices whose profit functions have been shown in Fig. 8.3, a decision can be taken by examining the expected profits, since both the pay-off functions are linear. Different probability distributions are applicable to each price-decision since the amount sold is influenced by price. The distributions, shown in Fig. 8.5(a), indicate that at a lower price, the sales level is likely to increase and the distributions have different means and variances. Since the expected sales are more than the indifference, or the break-even level in both (a) and (b), a selection is to be made between the two prices on the basis of expected profits. Hence a solution is possible by evaluating the following expression for both prices and selecting the price which gives higher expected profit.

$$\int_0^{\infty} (a + bX) f_X(X) dX.$$

Also the following expression, i.e., equation (3), can be used $Y = a + bX \therefore E(Y) = a + bE(X)$.

At the break-even point $Y = 0$ since $a = -bX_b$.

Now $E(Y) = -bX_b + bE(X)$.

$$\text{Here the expected profit is} \quad = E(Y) = b[E(X) - X_b] \qquad (3)$$

where b is the gradient of the profit function, i.e., contribution margin per unit. $E(X)$ is expected sales; and X_b is the break-even sales volume in units.

From equation (3) we see that the expected profit, related to any price, is obtained by multiplying the contribution margin and the amount by which expected sales exceed the break-even sales volume.

PROBLEM 1. Suppose the contribution margin per unit is Rs. 3 and Rs. 3.5 for product A and product B, respectively, fixed costs are Rs. 1 lakh and expected sales are 50,000 units and 40,000 units for A and B, respectively. Find the break-even sales levels (X_b) for A and B. Also find the expected profits for (a) and (b) and comment.

SOLUTION. For product A we get $E(Y) = b[E(X) - Xb]$.

Now

$$\begin{aligned} E(Y) &= \text{Expected sales} \times \text{contribution margin} - \text{Fixed Cost} \\ &= 50,000 \times \text{Rs. } 3 - \text{Rs. } 1,00,000 \\ &= \text{Rs. } (1,50,000 - 1,00,000) = \text{Rs. } 50,000. \end{aligned}$$

$$\therefore \text{Rs. } 50,000 = 3[50,000 - X_b] \text{ or } 3X_b = 1,00,000 \therefore \quad X_b = \text{Rs. } 33,333.$$

For product B we get the following result:

$$\begin{aligned} E(Y) &= 40,000 \times \text{Rs. } 3.5 - \text{Rs. } 1,00,000 \\ &= \text{Rs. } (1,40,000 - 1,00,000) = \text{Rs. } 40,000 \end{aligned}$$

$$\therefore \quad \text{Rs. } 40,000 = 3.5[40,000 - X_b] \text{ or } 3.5X_b = 1,00,000 \therefore X_b = \text{Rs. } 28571.$$

If $X_b > E(X)$, equation (3) generates negative outcome, i.e., $E(Y)$ represents expected loss here.

In most practical situations there are various uncertainties associated with probable costs of production, likely performance of employees, possible economic life of machines and equipment, etc.

The concept of probability distribution can be introduced to measure the risk related to each possible price. The shaded areas in Fig. 8.5 (a) and (b) indicate the probability of failure to achieve the break-even level of sales.

PROBLEM 2. The area of the shaded portion can be obtained from the table of the normal probability distribution function.

Assuming $\sigma(X) = 10,000$ and using the table of normal probability distribution (function) we have,

$$P(X < X_b) = P\left[\frac{X - E(X)}{\sigma(X)} < \frac{X_b - E(X)}{\sigma(X)}\right].$$

For product A

$$= P\left[Z < \frac{33,333 - 50,000}{10,000}\right] = P[Z < -1.6667] = 0.04746cr$$

For product B

$$P(X < X_b) = P\left[Z < \frac{28571 - 40,000}{10,000}\right] = P[Z < -1.1429] = 0.12714.$$

The selection between the alternatives can be made on the basis of on these probabilities when expectations are uncertain due to inadequate information.

The type of uncertainty we have introduced in this chapter is one that is continually faced by decision makers. Managers do not know with certainty what the future will hold, e.g., precisely where the demand function will be located in some future period. Obviously the manager could try to collect information in order to reduce this uncertainty. But, since information gathering is costly, one can never expect the manager to eliminate all uncertainty, indeed, the rational manager will collect additional information only so long as the marginal benefit from the information (the gain in profit to the firm from reduced uncertainty) exceeds the marginal cost of collecting additional information.

Since the elimination of uncertainty is not an optimal (or even feasible) choice for the firm, the manager is forced to make decisions facing uncertainty. How the decision is made depends on a number of factors, including the manner in which the manager is compensated. (For example, one might try to guess how the manager would approach the decision if the manager was paid a given salary with a bonus based on the profits and then compare this with the case in which the manager is notified that he or she will be fired if the firm suffers a loss.)

Nonetheless, a strategy for decision making under uncertainty that has received a great deal of attention is one referred to as "Minimax." In essence, this strategy might be characterised as "making the best out of the worst possible outcome."

Summary

1. Uncertainty refers to a situation in which a decision maker does not have information about the outcomes of an action. Unlike with risk, with uncertainty no estimates can be made about the probabilities associated with alternative strategies.

2. A decision maker faces uncertainty when there are several outcomes associated with a decision and the probabilities of those outcomes are known. The greater the variation in those outcomes, the greater the risk.

3. The set of outcomes and their associated probabilities comprise a probability distribution. If the probabilities of these outcomes are not known, the decision maker faces uncertainty.

Concepts for Review

1. Probability Distribution of Price
2. Random Profit
3. Expected Profit
4. Minimax.

Exercises

1. A firm produces two products X and Y. Demands are independent and marginal costs are nil. The products are sold to two customers at the same price.

(i) For the following reservation prices, can profits increase by bundling? What will be the maximum profit?

	Product X	Product Y
Customer I	Rs. 40	Rs. 30
Customer II	Rs. 50	Rs. 40

(ii) For the reservation prices given here what will be the profit-maximising pricing strategy. Explain.

What will be the maximum profit?

	Product X	Product Y
Customer I	40	Rs. 50
Customer II	50	Rs. 50

2. The figure given below shows the combination of a traditional break-even analysis and uncertainty concerning demand. The figure further shows that the probability distribution of sales is skewed to the right. The letter E indicates median sales.

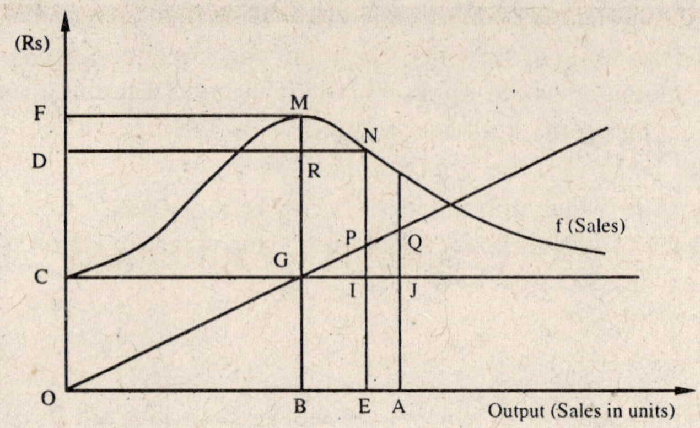

Using the letters shown on the graph,

(i) Can you obtain an expression for the unit price? If yes, carry out the exercise.

(ii) Write the expression for the unit contribution margin in the graph.

(iii) Find the break-even output level.

(iv) State the probability that the firm will fail to make a profit.

(v) Which line segment approximately indicates the best expected profit/loss?

3. From the given break-even chart where cost is shown on the left ordinate and the probability density function (p.d.f.) of sales on the right, find:

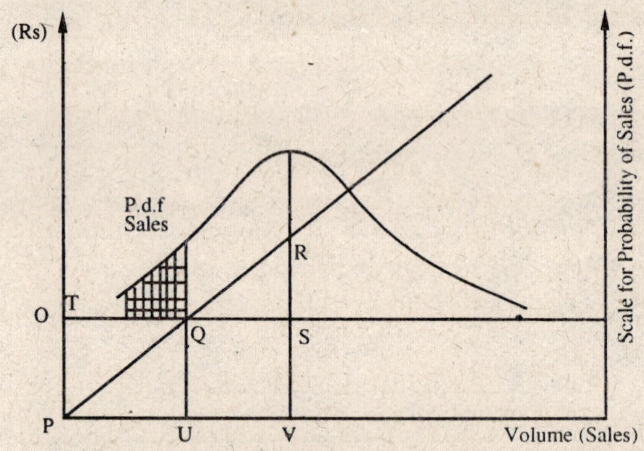

(i) What does the gradient of the line PQ indicate?

(ii) What is the break-even volume of output?

(iii) What does the shaded area represent?

(iv) Write an expression for expected profit which is independent of the form of p.d.f. assuming that V equals the expected sales.

APPENDIX (Economic Techniques)

Self-Test Questions and Additional Problems

1. True or false: If you know the slope of the budget constraint (for two goods), you know the prices of the two goods. Explain.

2. Originally P_y is Rs. 120 and P_r is Rs. 80. True or false: If P_y increases by Rs. 18 and P_r increases by Rs. 12, the new budget line will be shifted inward and parallel to the old budget line. Explain.

3. Which of the following statements are correct?

(a) the substitution effect always leads more of a good to be bought at lower prices;

(b) the income effect always leads more to be bought at lower prices;

(c) inferior goods have upward-sloping demand curves;

(d) indifference analysis involves ordinal, rather than cardinal measurement.

4. Draw indifference map for beer and a cigarette for consumers with the following preferences: (a) likes both beer and cigarettes; (b) gets no enjoyment (or discomfort) from cigarettes, likes beer; (c) the opposite of (b); (d) is made ill by both beer and cigarettes.

5. Boris budgets Rs. 9 per week for his morning coffee with milk. He likes it only if it is prepared with 4 parts coffee and 1 part milk. Coffee costs Re. 1 per cup, and milk costs Re. 0.50 per cup. How much coffee and how much milk will Boris buy per week? How will your answers change if the price of coffee rises to Rs. 3.25 per cup? Show your answers graphically.

6. Explain in your own words how the slope of an indifference curve provides information about how much a consumer likes one good relative to another.

7. Explain why a consumer will often buy one bundle of goods even though he prefers another.

8. True or false. The downward slope of indifference curves is a consequence of the diminishing marginal rate of substitution.

9. Ram spends all his Rs. 100 weekly income on two goods, X and Y. His utility function is given by $U(X, Y) = XY$. If $P_x = 4$ and $P_y = 10$, how much of each good should he buy?

10. Same as Problem 9, except now Ram's utility function is given by $U(X, Y) = X^{\frac{1}{2}}Y^{\frac{1}{2}}$.

Note the relationship between your answers in Problems 9 and 10. What accounts for this relationship?

11. Given that an individual consumer's demand curve is $P = 200 - 4Q$:

(a) Find the quantity this consumer would purchase at a price of Rs. 20.

(b) Suppose that the price increased to Rs. 60. How much would the consumer now purchase? Would this represent a change in demand or a change in quantity demanded? Why?

(c) What is the arc price elasticity of demand between these observations? What does this imply about how the price increase would affect the total amount of money the consumer would spend on this product? Explain. Verify your answer by calculating total expenditures at both prices.

12. Calculate all of the meaningful arc elasticities of demand (price, income, and cross price) based on the following observations. Consider only contiguous points in evaluating potential elasticities.

Observation	Quantity	Price	Income	Other Price
A	10	100	3000	14
B	20	90	3000	14
C	30	80	4000	12
D	40	80	5000	12
E	50	70	6000	10
F	60	70	6000	8
G	70	60	7000	6
H	80	50	7000	6

For each of the elasticities you calculate, explain in one or two sentences what your result means.

13. (i) Which of the following goods is likely to have inelastic demand with respect to price?

(a) table salt; (b) domestic gas; (c) small family cars; (d) daily newspapers.

(ii) Which of the following goods is likely to have a negative income elasticity of demand?

(a) bus travel; (b) cheap margarine; (c) expensive margarine; (d) petrol; (e) car accessories; (f) daily newspapers.

14. If the demand curve for a product is a straight line, cutting both axes, which of the following statements are correct?

(a) there is a price above which none of the product will be purchased;

(b) an infinite amount of the product could be given away;

(c) elasticity of demand is lower as price is higher;

(d) a rise in price above the mid-point of the curve will increase revenue;

(e) elasticity of demand is zero at the point where the curve crosses the horizontal axis.

15. In an oligopolistic industry, does elasticity of demand for an individual firm's product rise or fall with:

(a) increasing market share for the firm;

(b) decreasing market elasticity of demand;

(c) increasing rivals' cross-elasticity of supply with respect to changes in the firm's price.

16. Which of the following statements are correct?

(a) petrol and tyres have positive cross-elasticities of demand;

(b) when demand is own-price elastic, marginal revenue is negative;

(c) the demand for food is less elastic than the demand for rice;

(d) the Engel curve for bread is vertical for most of its range;

(e) the price sensitivity of buyers is positively related to the importance of the product in their total purchases.

17. True or false: For a budget spent entirely on two goods, an increase in the price of one will necessarily decrease the consumption of both, unless at least one of the goods is inferior. Explain.

18. Larry demands strawberries according to the schedule $P = 4 - (\frac{Q}{2})$, where P is the price of strawberries (Rs. per kg.) and Q is the quantity (per week). Assuming that the income effect is negligible, how much will he be hurt if the price of strawberries goes from Rs. 100 per kg. to Rs. 200 per kg.?

19. Joy spends all his income on two goods, X and Y. The prices he paid and the quantities be consumed last year are as follows: $P_x = 15$; $X = 20$; $P_y = 25$; and $Y = 30$. If the prices next year are $P_x = 6$ and $P_y = 30$, and Joy's income is Rs. 1020, will he be better or worse off than he was in the previous year? (Assume that his tastes remain unchanged.)

20. To get the market demand curve for a product, why do we add individual demand curves horizontally rather than vertically?

21. Summarise the relationship between price elasticity, changes in price, and changes in total expenditure.

22. Why don't we measure the responsiveness of demand to price changes by the slope of the demand curve instead of using the more complicated expression for elasticity?

23. For a straight line demand curve, what is the price elasticity at the revenue-maximising point?

24. How can changes in the distribution of income across consumers affect the market demand for a product?

25. The monthly market demand curve for calculators among engineering students is given by $P = 100 - Q$, where P is the price per calculator in rupees and Q is the number of calculators purchased per month. If the price is Rs. 30, how much revenue will calculator makers get each month? Find the price-elasticity of demand for calculators. What should calculator makers do to increase revenue?

26. What price will maximise total expenditure along the demand curve $P = 27 - Q^2$?

27. An ice-cream vendor faces a daily demand curve of $Q = 1800 - 15\ P$, where P is the price of an ice-cream in paise and Q is the number of ice-creams purchased each day.

(a) If the vendor has been selling 300 ice-creams each day, how much revenue has he been collecting?

(b) What is the price elasticity of demand for ice-creams?

(c) The vendor decides that he wants to generate more revenue. Should he raise or lower the price of his ice-creams?

(d) At what price would he achieve maximum total revenue?

28. Rank the absolute values of the price elasticities of demand at points A, B, C, D, and E on the three demand curves below.

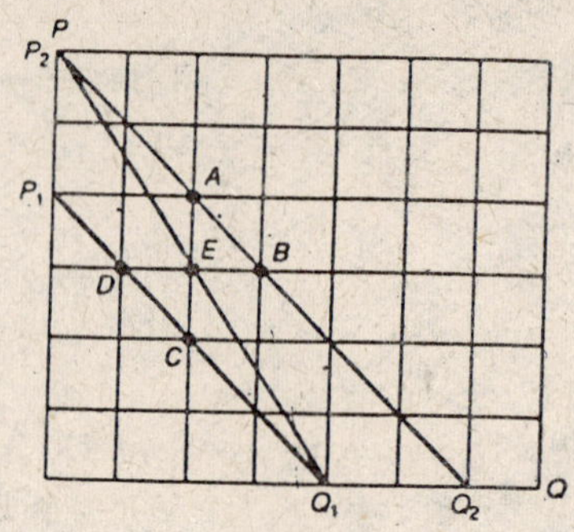

Fig A-1 Comparing Demand Curves

29. Draw the Engel curves for the following goods: food, winter vacations, cashews, K-mart brand T-shirts (Rs. 500 per shirt).

30. Is the cross-price elasticity of demand positive or negative for the following pairs of items?

(a) Tennis racquets and tennis balls; (b) Peanut butter and jelly; (c) Hot dogs and hamburgers.

31. In 1993, X cost Rs. 3 and 400 units were sold. That same year, a related good Y cost Rs. 10 and 200 units were sold. In 1994, X still cost Rs. 3, but only 300 units were sold, while Y rose in price to Rs. 12 and only 150 units were sold. Other things the same, and assuming that the demand for X is a linear function of the price of Y, what was the cross-price elasticity of demand for X with respect to Y in 1993?

32. Demand schedules A, B, and C are the aggregate demands for three types of consumers in a market. There are 10 consumers of type A, 5 of type B, and 12 of type C. Derive and graph the market demand for the entire group of consumers.

A		B		C	
Price (Rs.)	Quantity demanded	Price (Rs.)	Quantity demanded	Price (Rs.)	Quantity demanded
10	2	10	0	10	1
8	6	8	4	8	2
6	10	6	8	6	3
4	12	4	10	4	4
2	13	2	12	2	5

33. "I earn Rs. 90 a day and spend it all on beer, no matter what the price of beer is." What is this person's elasticity of demand for beer?

34. A company sells mineral water in dry area of Rajasthan; its costs are virtually zero. The marketing manager knows that its demand function is $Q = 25 - \frac{3}{2}P$. Presently it charges a price of Rs. 2. The company wishes to increase its profits. Do you recommend a price change? If so what price would you suggest?

35. The following data relate the percentage change in the purchase of automobiles to percentage changes in income and the price of automobiles. (The numbers in the body of the table give the percentage change in auto purchases.)

		Percentage change in income				
		−10	−5	0	+5	+10
Percentage change in price	+10	−20	−15	−10	−5	0
	+5	−15	−10	−5	0	+5
	0	−10	−5	0	+5	+10
	−5	−5	0	+5	+10	+15
	−10	0	+5	+10	+15	+20

(a) What is the own-price elasticity of demand for automobiles?

(b) What is the income elasticity of demand for automobiles?

(c) One automaker reduces the price of one of its models from Rs. 10,000 to Rs. 9,000. Sales of this car increase 10 percent. But at the same time incomes increase by 5 percent. What does this indicate about the own-price elasticity of demand for this particular car?

36. Recall from our definitions that own-price, income, and cross-price elasticities must be calculated holding all other variables constant. Using data from the following table, calculate, where possible, the own-price, income, and cross-price elasticity. Use the averaging method.

Quantity	Price Rs.	Price of a related good Rs.	Per capita income Rs.
10,000	20	30	3,000
12,000	20	30	2,000
12,000	20	40	3,000
10,000	30	40	3,000

Is demand elastic or inelastic? Is the related good a complement or a substitute? Is the good inferior or normal?

37. Use the definition of own-price elasticity to answer the following questions:

(a) You know that the own-price elasticity of demand is 1.5. Price rises by 10 percent. How will quantity demanded change?

(b) Suppose elasticity is still 1.5 but the quantity supplied to the market falls by 10 percent. What will happen to price?

38. What is impact of time on elasticity?

Ans. Time has an important effect on people's responses to changes in prices. Let us consider the oil price increases of the 1970s. One response of a consumer confronted with a higher price of petrol is simply to drive less. But many auto trips are part of a larger pattern and cannot be abandoned, or even altered, very quickly. A person cannot simply stop going to work, for example. He can cut down his daily journey by joining a car pool or by purchasing a house closer to his work place. He can also curtail his petrol consumption by selling his car and buying one that gets better mileage. But all these actions take time, and as a result the demand for petrol will be much more elastic in the long run than in the short run.

The short and long-run effects of a supply shift in the market for petrol are contrasted in Fig. A–2. The initial equilibrium at A is disturbed by a supply reduction from S to S'. In the short run, the effect is for price to rise to P_{SR} = Rs. 1.40 per litre and for quantity to fall to Q_{SR} = 5 million litres per day. The long-run demand curve is more elastic than the short-run demand curve. When consumers have more time to adjust, therefore, price effects tend to moderate while quantity effects tend to become more pronounced. Thus the new long-run equilibrium in Fig. A–2 occurs at a price of P_{LR} = Rs. 1.20 per litre and a quantity of Q_{LR} = 4 million litres per day.

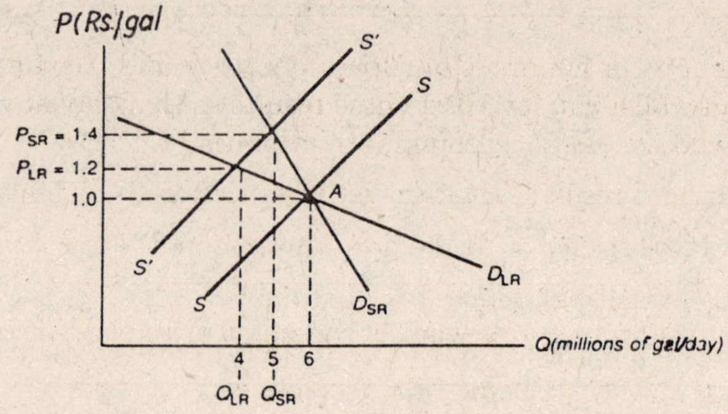

Fig A–2 Price Elasticity is Greater in the Long Run than in the Short Run

39. Which of the following goods would you expect to have very low price and income elasticities of demand?

(a) table salt; (b) brandy; (c) golf club membership; (d) designer clothing; (e) telephone calls.

40. Of the goods listed in 39 above, which would you expect to have very high income elasticities of demand?

41. Cite the three major problems with consumer interviews or surveys and provide an example of each.

42. Following are four sets of demand and supply functions. For each set, determine if the demand and supply functions are identified and explain why or why not.

(a) $D: Q = \alpha + \beta P$; $S: Q = a + bP$

(b) $D: Q = \alpha + \beta P + \gamma Y$; $S: Q = a + bP$

(c) $D: Q = \alpha + \beta P$; $S: Q = a + bP + cT$

(d) $D: Q = \alpha + \beta P + \gamma Y$; $S: Q = a + bP + cT + dP_F$

43. Using the following demand schedule, show the relation amoung marginal revenue, price, and own-price elasticity.

Price Rs.	Quantity demanded
20	1,000
15	1,400
10	1,800

44. The following regression results were obtained in a study of demand for a local bakery:

Variable	Coefficient	Standard Error	t-Ratio
Constant	12.42	2.43	5.11
Price	0.83	0.27	3.07
Income	0.04	0.02	2.00
Advertising	1.91	0.86	2.22

Adjusted R^2 = .875; SE of the estimate = 4.89; F-ratio = 8.42; n = 34.

(a) The dependent variable is sales (S) in thousands of units per week. Write the regression equation:

$S =$ ______________________________

(b) Given that advertising is in hundreds of rupees per week and income is in average weekly earnings, write a paragraph in which you interpret these results as though you were explaining them to the owner of the bakery, who has no background in economics.

(c) What level of sales would result if the firm set the price at Rs. 7.50 while income was Rs. 580 and advertising was Rs. 1200?

$S =$ ______________________________

(d) For the conditions given in part (c), what is the point price elasticity of demand?

$e_p =$ ______________________________

What is the point income elasticity of demand?

$e_I =$ ______________________________

What is the point advertising elasticity of demand?

$e_A =$ ______________________________

(e) If income is constant at Rs. 580 and advertising stays at Rs. 1200, what is the equation for the relationship between sales and price?

$Q = f(P) =$ ______________________________

(f) Find the algebraic expressions for total revenue (TR) and marginal revenue (MR) as functions of sales (Q) :

$TR = f(Q) =$ ______________________________

$MR = f(Q) =$ ______________________________

Plot the marginal revenue function, along with the demand function, on the graph above.

(g) What level of sales will maximise the bakery's total revenue? At what price would that level of sales result?

45. A firm has the following demand curve $P = 1000Q^{-2}$

(a) What is the equation for total revenue?

$TR =$ ______________________________

(b) What is the equation for marginal revenue?

$MR =$ ______________________________

(c) What is the equation for average revenue?

$AR =$ ______________________________

(d) What is point price elasticity of demand at a price of Rs. 1,000? Is demand inelastic, elastic, or unitarily elastic at $P = 1000$?

$e_p =$ ______________________________

Demand: = ______________________________

46. Which of the following best describes a leading indicator?

(a) a variable in which changes follow changes in a variable we are trying to forecast;

(b) a variable which changes in advance of a variable we are trying to forecast.

(c) a variable which changes at the same time as one we are trying to forecast.

47. The list below shows a number of goods and a number of forecasting techniques. Which technique is best suited to which good?

1. An industrial product with a limited potential market.
2. A consumer good which has been on sale for many years.
3. A new product whose full-scale launch will be very expensive.
4. A technically very complex new product, to be sold in a very wide market.

(a) Time-series analysis; (b) Regression analysis; (c) Market testing; (d) Survey of buyer intentions.

48. In which of the following situations will there be no identification problem?

(a) if it is known that neither supply nor demand curves has shifted;

(b) if it is known that both supply and demand-curves have shifted;

(c) if it is known that only the supply curve has shifted;

(d) if it is known that only the demand curve has shifted.

49. Contrast and compare qualitative and statistical forecasting methods.

50. A linear trend equation for sales of the form $Q_t = \alpha + \beta t$ was estimated for the period 1980-94 (i.e., $t = 80, 81, \cdots, 94$). The results of the regression are as follows:

DEPENDENT VARIABLE:QT		F-RATIO:13.1792
OBSERVATIONS:15		R-SQUARE:0.8786
VARIABLE	PARAMETER ESTIMATE	STANDARD ERROR
INTERCEPT	73.7146	10.1315
T	3.7621	1.0363

(a) Test the estimated coefficients for statistical significance at a 95 percent confidence level. Does this estimation indicate a significant trend?

(b) Perform an F–test for significance of the equation at a 95 percent confidence level.

(c) Using this equation, forecast sales in 1995 and 2000.

(d) Comment on the precision of these two forecasts.

51. These supply and demand functions were specified for commodity X :

Demand : $Q_{X,t} = a + bP_{X,t} + cY_t + dP_{R,t}$

Supply : $Q_{X,t} = e + fP_{X,t} + gP_{F,t}$

Using quarterly data for the period 1988 I through 1994 IV, these functions were estimated. The resulting parameter estimates are presented in the following estimated equations.

Demand : $Q_{X,t} = 50 - 30P_{X,t} + 0.10Y_t - 20P_{R,t}$

Supply : $Q_{X,t} = -40 + 20P_{X,t} - 10P_{F,t}$

Predicted values for the exogenous variables (Y, P_R, and P_F) for the first quarter of 1995 were obtained from a macroeconomic forecasting model. These predicted values are:

Income (Y) = 10,000.

The price of the commodity related in consumption (P_R) = 20.

The price of factor inputs (P_F) = 6.

(a) Are the signs of the estimated coefficients as would be predicted theoretically? Explain.

(b) Predict the price of commodity X in 1995 III.

(b) Predict the sales of commodity X in 1995 III.

52. Describe the major shortcomings of time-series models.

53. Suppose that you have an estimate of the demand function $Q_{X,t} = a + bP_{X,t} + cY_t + dP_{R,t}$. Obviously you could use historical trend to forecast the values for all of the right-hand side variables and thereby obtain a prediction for sales. What is the major shortcoming of such an approach?

54. Suppose that you were given the following data representing 14 observations of a firm's sales, the price charged for the product, and a measure of income:

Price	Sales	Income	Price	Sales	Income
5.00	20	2620	6.01	18	3868
5.20	16	2733	5.92	21	4016
5.30	16	2898	5.90	26	4152
5.48	14	3056	5.85	30	4336
5.60	16	3271	5.80	26	4477
5.80	19	3479	5.85	27	4619
6.03	17	3736	5.80	29	4764

(a) Estimate the linear equation for the demand curve using just price (P) and sales (Q), with $Q = f(P) : Q =$ — —; $\bar{R}^2 =$ — —; t-ratio for $P =$ — —.

(b) Interpret this regression equation, including a statement of what the t-ratio and $\bar{R}^2$ tell you. Does the relationship you have estimated between P and Q make sense, given what you know about the law of demand? Explain.

(c) Now estimate sales (Q) as a function of both price (P) and income (M) in a multiple linear regression:

$Q =$ ______________________________

Variable	Coefficient	Standard Error	t-Ratio
P	______	______	______
M	______	______	______
$\bar{R}^2 =$			

Which model is better, this one or the one estimated in part (a)? Explain why.

55. The following table shows the business expenditure on new plant and equipment:

Years	Expenditures (in crores of rupees)
1990	75
1991	76
1992	81
1993	84
1994	86

Project the business expenditure on new plant end equipment for the year 1995.

Solution. We know, $y = a + bx; \Sigma y = na + b\Sigma x; \Sigma xy = a\Sigma y + b\Sigma x^2$.

Taking 1992 as origin and unit $x = 1$ year we get:

Years	Expenses	x	x^2	xy
1990	75	−2	4	−150
1991	76	−1	1	−76
→ 1992	81	0	0	0
1993	84	1	1	84
1994	86	2	4	172
	402	0	10	30

$\Sigma y = na + b\Sigma x$ or $402 = 5a + 05a = 402; a =$ **80.4**.

$\Sigma xy = a\Sigma x + b\Sigma x^2$ or $30 = 0 + 10b$ or $y = \frac{30}{10} =$ **3**. $\therefore$ $y =$ **80.4 + 3x**.

In 1990, x will be 3, so the expenses will be Rs. $80.4 + 3 \times 3 =$ **Rs. 89.4 crores.**

56. The annual sales of a company are as follows:

Years	1990	1991	1992	1993	1994
Sales (in 1000)	45	56	78	46	75

Find out the trend values far each of the five years and also estimate the annual sales for the year 1995.

We know, $y = a + bx$ and $\Sigma y = na + b\Sigma x; \Sigma xy = a\Sigma y + b\Sigma x^2$.

Taking 1992 as origin and unit = 1 year = x we get:

	y	x	xy	x^2	Trend Value
1990	45	−2	−90	4	50
1991	56	−1	−56	1	55
1992	78	0	0	0	60
1993	46	1	46	1	65
1994	75	2	150	4	70
	300	0	50	10	

$\Sigma y = na + b\Sigma x$ or $300 = 5a + 0$ or $5a = 300$ or $a = \frac{300}{5} = 60$;

$\Sigma xy = a\Sigma x + b\Sigma x^2$; or $50 = \Sigma + 10b$ or $10b = 50$ or $b = \frac{50}{10} = 5$. $\therefore$ $y =$ **60 + 5x**.

57. Graph the short-run total product curves for each of the following production functions il K is fixed at $K_o = 4$.

(a) $Q = F(K, L) = 2K + 3L$. (b) $Q = F(K, L) = K^2L^2$.

58. Do the two production functions obey the law of diminishing returns?

59. Suppose the marginal product of labour is currently equal to its average product. If you were one of ten new workers the firm was about to hire, would you prefer to be paid the value of your average product or the value of your marginal product? Would it be in the interests of an employer to pay you the value of your average product?

60. *True or false:* If the marginal product is decreasing, then the average product must also be decreasing. Explain.

61. Suppose capital is fixed at 4 units in the production function $Q = KL$. Draw the total, marginal, and average product curves for the labour input.

62. Distinguish between diminishing returns to a variable input and decreasing returns to scale.

Ans. *It is important to bear in mind that decreasing returns to scale have nothing whatsoever to do with the law of diminishing returns.* Decreasing returns to scale refer to what happens when all inputs are varied by some proportion. The law of diminishing returns, by contrast, refers to the case in which one input varies while all others are held fixed. As an empirical generalisation, it applies with equal force to production functions having increasing, constant, or decreasing returns to scale.

A production function for which proportional changes in all inputs lead to a more than proportional change in output is said to exhibit **increasing returns to scale.** Thus, for example, if we double all inputs in a production function with increasing returns to scale, we get more than twice as much output as before. Such production functions generally give rise to conditions in which a small number of firms supply most of the relevant market.

The technical property of the production function used to describe the relationship between scale and efficiency is called *returns to scale.* The term tells us what happens to output when all inputs are increased by exactly the same proportion. Because returns to scale refer to a situation in which all inputs are variable, *the concept of returns to scale is an inherently long-run concept.*

A production function for which a proportional change in all inputs causes output to change by the same proportion is said to exhibit **constant returns to scale.** In such cases, doubling all inputs results in an exact doubling of output. In industries in which production takes place under constant returns to scale, large size is neither an advantage nor a disadvantage.

Finally, a production function for which a proportional change in all inputs causes a less than proportional change in output is said to exhibit **decreasing returns to scale.** Here large size is a handicap, and we do not expect to see large firms in an industry in which production takes place with decreasing returns to scale. It may be noted that the constant and decreasing returns cases often enable many sellers to coexist within the same narrowly defined markets.

63. Can you suggest a mathematical definition of returns to scale?

Ans. Mathematically, to increase all inputs in the same proportion means simply to multiply all inputs by the same number $c > 1$. By way of illustation, consider the production function $Q = F(K, L) = 2KL$. For this particular function, when we multiply each input by c we get

$$F(cK, cL) = 2(cK)(cL) = c^2 2KL = c^2 F(K, L). \tag{1}$$

The result of multiplying each input by c in this production function is thus to multiply the original output level by c^2. Output thus grows more than in proportion to input growth in this case [proportional output would have been $cF(K, L)$], so this production function has increasing returns to scale. Thus, for example, if $c = 2$ (a doubling of each input), we get $F(2K, 2L) = 2(2K)(2L) = 4(2KL)$, a quadrupling of output.

Drawing on these obserations, the definitions of our three cases may be summarised as follows:

$$\text{Increasing returns:} \quad F(cK, cL) > cF(K, L); \tag{2}$$

$$\text{Constant returns:} \quad F(cK, cL) = cF(K, L); \tag{3}$$

and

$$\text{Decreasing returns:} \quad F(cK, cL) < cF(K, L). \tag{4}$$

The following two exercises will help to test your ability to apply these definitions to specific examples.

64. Does the production function $Q = \sqrt{K}\sqrt{L}$ have increasing, constant, or decreasing returns to scale?

65. Does the production function $Q = K^{\frac{1}{3}}L^{\frac{1}{3}}$ have increasing, constant, or decreasing returns to scale?

In the case of the Cobb-Douglas production function, $Q = AK^{\alpha}L^{\beta}$. Equations (1)—(4) imply a simple relationship between the parameters α and β and the degree of returns to scale. Specifically, if $\alpha + \beta > 1$, there are increasing returns to scale; $\alpha + \beta = 1$ means constant returns to scale; and $\alpha + \beta < 1$ means decreasing returns to scale. To illustrate for the constant returns case, suppose $Q = F(K, L) = AK^{\alpha}L^{\beta}$, with $\alpha + \beta = 1$. Then we have

$$F(cK, cL) = A(cK)^{\alpha}(cL)^{\beta}, \tag{5}$$

which reduces to

$$c^{(\alpha+\beta)}AK^{\alpha}L^{\beta} = cAK^{\alpha}L^{\beta} = cF(K, L), \tag{6}$$

which, by Equation (5), is the defining characteristic of constant returns to scale.

66. Identify the regions of increasing, constant, and decreasing returns to scale on the isoquant map below.

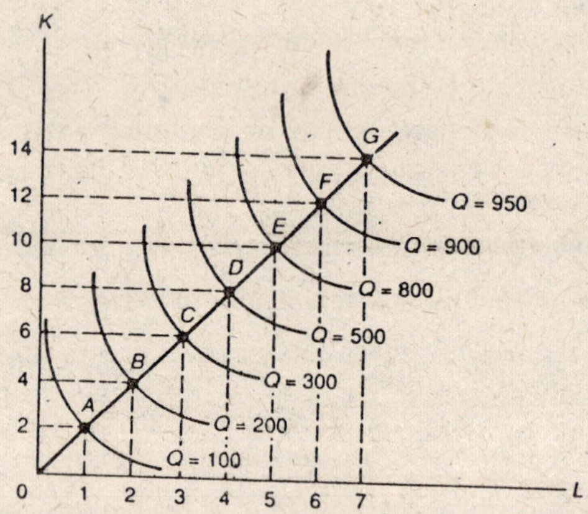

Fig A-3 Identifying Returns to scale from the Expansion Path

67. Do the following production functions have increasing, decreasing, or constant returns to scale? Which ones fail to satisfy the law of diminishing returns?

(a) $Q = 4K^{\frac{1}{2}}L^{\frac{1}{2}}$; (b) $Q = aK^2 + bL^2$; (c) $Q = \min(aK, bL)$; (d) $Q = 4K + 2L$; (e) $Q = K^{0.5}L^{0.6}$; (f) $K_1^{0.3}K_2^{0.3}L^{0.3}$.

68. What is the marginal product of labour in the production function $Q = 2K^{\frac{1}{3}}L^{\frac{1}{3}}$ if K is fixed at 27?

69. Which of the following statements are correct?

(a) an isoquant shows economies of scale;

(b) an isoquant shows the different techniques which can be used to produce a fixed quantity of a product;

(c) a technology may be described as 'labour-intensive' or 'capital-intensive';

(d) a given set of plant and equipment may exhibit economies of scale;

(e) if a large firm is experiencing higher costs per unit than a small firm, this means that there are diseconomies of scale.

70. If a firm has selected the cost-minimising technique of production, which of the following conditions must hold?

(a) the isocost line is a tangent to the isoquant;

(b) the extra output per extra rupee spent on labour must equal the extra output per extra rupee spent on capital;

(c) the ratio of the factor prices must equal the ratio of the marginal products of the factors;

(d) a higher level of spending cannot lead to a higher level of output;

(e) the same output cannot be produced with less labour or less capital.

71. Which of the following factors leads the short-run cost curve to rise beyond a certain level of output?

(a) diseconomies of scale; (b) diseconomies of capacity utilisation; (c) the principle of diminishing returns; (d) reduced availability of inputs; (e) higher input prices.

72. Consider the linear production function $Q = \alpha K + \beta L$. Examine the marginal rate of technical substitution and explain why this functional form does not adhere to the theoretical properties of a production function.

73. We estimated a Cobb-Douglas production function $Q = AK^{\alpha}L^{\beta}$. Following is the resulting computer output

```
DEPENDENT VARIABLE: LOGQ                    P-RATIO:

OBSERVATIONS: 30                            R-SQUARE:

                             PARAMETER     STANDARD
VARIABLE                      ESTIMATE       ERROR
INTEREST                       -3.0          0.50
LOGK                            0.60         0.15
LOGL                            0.55         0.20

            VARIANCE-COVARIANCE MATRIX FOR
               ESTIMATED COEFFICIENTS

                             INTERCEPT      LOGK      LOGL
INTERCEPT                       0.25       -0.03      0.10
LOGK                           -0.03        0.023    -0.02
LOGL                            0.10       - 0.02     0.04
```

The values for output and input usage (all the thousand units) for the firm under consideration are $Q = 100.0; K = 150.0; L = 1.0$.

(a) Determine if these estimates indicate:

(1) Positive marginal products.

(2) Diminishing marginal products.

(b) Calculate the marginal products for capital and labour. (Use the values provided for Q, K, and L.)

(c) Suppose capital usage increases by 10 percent. By what percentage would output be expected to increase? What would be expected to happen to output if labour usage increased by 5 percent?

(d) Determine whether these estimates indicate increasing, constant, or decreasing returns to scale. (Make sure you test for statistical significance.)

74. Use the estimates presented in Queston 73 and let the values of the input prices for the firm under consideration be $r = 0.5; w = 50.0$. Determine whether or not the firm is using the optimal combination of capital and labour.

75. (a) Given the following cost data, use regression analysis to estimate the corresponding cubic total cost function:

Quantity	10	20	30	40	50	60	70	80	90	100
Total cost	485	705	790	825	850	935	1100	1500	2200	3100

(b) Given the total cost function estimated above, derive algebraic equations for average cost, marginal cost, and average variable cost.

(c) Plot the data given above along with the curve for the total cost function you estimated. Does your cost equation provide a good fit to the data? What is the R^2 value for your cost function?

(d) Show average cost and marginal cost in tabular form and plot the data points. Also plot the equations for average cost and marginal cost derived in part (b). Do these equations correspond reasonably well to the scatter diagram of data points for marginal and average cost?

76. Suppose the following Cobb-Douglas production function was estimated for Bell Canada $V = .56L^{.705}K^{.405}D^{.01}$. The t-ratios were 4.9, 6.8, and 9.5 for the variables L, K, and D, respectively. The coefficient of determination was .998, and the Durbin-Watson statistic was 1.78. V is the value added (in thousands of dollars), L is labour-hours (in millions,) K is net capital stock (in thousands of dollars), and D is a proxy for technological change (measured as the percentage of station-to-station toll calls dialed by the customer). All data are on a yearly basis, and values in parentheses under each variable are the t-ratios.

(a) Is this production homogeneous and, if so, to what degree?

(b) Does this production function exhibit increasing, constant, or decreasing returns to scale? Why?

(c) Suppose that $K = 2500, L = 60$, and $D = 52$. What would be your estimate of value added for Bell Canada?

(d) For the same values of K, L, and D used in part (c), determine the marginal productivity of labour and capital.

(e) Is this function characterised by diminishing marginal productivity for labour and for capital? Prove that you are correct.

(f) Given the value calculated in part (c) and assuming a constant state of technology (i.e., D is fixed at 52), derive the equation for the isoquant. Using this equation, plot the isoquant with labour on the horizontal axis and capital on the vertical axis (use odd values of labour from 45-65). Does this isoquant have the expected shape? Explain.

(g) Show what happens to that isoquant if technology improves such that $D = 60$. Plot the new isoquant along with the original. Is the relationship between the two as you expected? Explain.

77. Compare and constrast short-run and long-run cost estimation with respect to: (a) Objectives; (b) Type of data employed.

78. Describe the data problems involved in cost estimation using: (a) Time-series data; (b) Cross-section data.

79. Suppose that an average variable cost function of the form $AVC = a + bQ + cQ^2$ has been estimated. The computer output obtained from this regression is as follows:

(a) Determine if the estimated coefficients are as required to yield a U-shaped average variable cost curve.

(b) What is the marginal cost function associated with this average variable cost function?

DEPENDENT VARIABLE: AVC		P-RATIO:214.16
OBSERVATIONS: 30		R-SQUARE: 0.9407
	PARAMETER	STANDARD
VARIABLE	ESTIMATE	ERROR
INTERCEPT	40.0	10.0
Q	-4.0	1.0
Q^2	0.2	0.04

(c) What is average variable cost at $Q = 10$? What is marginal cost at $Q = 10$?

(d) At what output level would average variable cost be at a minimum?

(e) What is the minimum average variable cost?

80. Consider the cost function $TC = \alpha Q^{\beta} w^{\gamma} r^{\delta}$. What condition is necessary in order that doubling input prices will double the total cost of producing a given level of output? Explain.

81. Following are the results of an estimation of the cost function $(TC/r) = \alpha Q^{\beta}(w/r)^{\gamma}$

DEPENDENT VAR: LOG (TC/R)		P-RATIO:265.690
OBSERVATIONS: 35		R-SQUARE: 0.9432
	PARAMETER	STANDARD
VARIABLE	ESTIMATE	ERROR
INTERCEPT	-0.5	0.4
LOGQ	1.6	0.2
LOG(W/R)	0.7	0.3

What do these estimates indicate with respect to economies or diseconomies of scale?

82. Why should a person in charge of hiring productive inputs care more about marginal products than about average products?

83. Find the marginal physical product of the different inputs or factors of production for each of the following production functions.

(a) $Q = 6x^2 + 3xy + 2y^2$

$$MPP_x = \frac{\partial Q}{\partial x} = 12x + 3y$$

$$MPP_y = \frac{\partial Q}{\partial y} = 3x + 4y$$

(b) $Q = 0.5k^2 - 2KL + L^2$

$$MPP_K = K - 2L$$

$$MPP_L = 2L - 2K$$

(c) $Q = 20 + 8x + 3x^2 - 0.25x^3 + 5y + 2y^2 - 0.5y^3$

$$MPP_x = 8 + 6x - 0.75x^2$$

$$MPP_y = 5 + 4y - 1.5y^2$$

(d) $Q = x^2 + 2xy + 3y^2 + 1.5yz + 0.2z^2$

$$MPP_x = 2x + 2y$$
$$MPP_y = 2x + 6y + 1.5z$$
$$MPP_z = 1.5y + 0.4z$$

(a) Assume $\bar{y} = 4$ in Problem 83(a) and find the MPP_x for $x = 5$ and $x = 8$. (b) If the marginal revenue at $\bar{x} = 5, \bar{y} = 4$ is Rs. 3, compute the marginal revenue product for the fifth unit of x.

(a)
$$MPP_x = 12x + 3y$$
$$\text{At } x = 5,\ \ \bar{y} = 4, MPP_x = 12(5) + 3(4) = 72.$$
$$\text{At } x = 8,\ \ \bar{y} = 4, MPP_x = 12(8) + 3(4) = 108.$$

(b)
$$MRP_x = MPP_x(MR)$$
$$\text{At } \bar{x} = 5,\ \ \bar{y} = 4, MRP_x = (72)(3) = 216.$$

GLOSSARY

A

ALTERNATIVE HYPOTHESIS: In regression analysis, the hypothesis that stands in contrast to the null hypothesis. It generally states that the true (but unknown) population coefficient assumes some value other than zero.

ARC ELASTICITY OF DEMAND: The price elasticity of demand between two points on the demand curve; it uses the average price and the average quantity in calculating the percentage change in price and quantity.

ARC ELASTICITY OF SUPPLY: The price elasticity of supply between two points on the supply curve; it uses the average price and the average quantity in calculating the percentage change in price and quantity.

AVERAGE FIXED COST (AFC): Total fixed costs divided by output.

AVERAGE PRODUCT (AP): The total product divided by the quantity of the variable factor used.

AVERAGE REVENUE (AR): Total revenue divided by the quantity sold.

AVERAGE TOTAL COST (ATC): Total costs, divided by output. Also equals $AFC + AVC$.

AVERAGE VARIABLE COST (AVC): Total variable costs divided by output.

B

BAROMETRIC FORECASTING: The prediction of turning points in one economic time series through the use of observations on other time series called barometers or indicators. Economic time series are of three general categories: leading indicators, roughly coincident indicators and lagging indicators.

BREAK-EVEN POINT: The point where total revenues equal total costs and profits are zero.

BUDGET CONSTRAINT: The limitation on the amount of goods that a consumer can purchase imposed by his or her limited income and the prices of the goods.

BUDGET LINE: A line showing the various combinations of two goods that a consumer can purchase by spending all income at the given prices of the two goods.

C

CARDINAL UTILITY: The ability to actually provide an index of utility from consuming various amounts of a good or baskets of goods.

CAUSAL (EXPLANATORY) FORECASTING: A quantitative forecasting method that attempts to search out functional relationships between independent variables and the dependent variable.

CHANGE IN THE QUANTITY DEMANDED: The result of a change in the price of a good or service, graphically represented by a movement along a particular demand curve.

CHANGE IN DEMAND: The result of a change in one or more of the non-price determinants of demand, graphically represented by a shift of the demand curve to a new position (rightward for an increase in demand and leftward for a decrease in demand).

COBB-DOUGLAS PRODUCTION FUNCTION: The relationship between inputs and output expressed by $Q = AK^{\alpha}L^{\beta}$, where Q is output, K is capital, L is labour and A, α and β are positive parameters estimated from the data.

COEFFICIENT OF DETERMINATION (R^2): A measure indicating the percentage of the variation in the dependent variable accounted for by variations in some designated independent variable. Its value ranges from 0 to 1. Zero indicates that variations in the independent variable account for none of the variation in the dependent variable. One indicates that 100% of the variation in the dependent variable can be accounted for by the variations in the independent variable. In multiple regression analysis, this measure is referred to as the *multiple coefficient of determination.*

COEFFICIENT OF ELASTICITY: The percentage change in one variable divided by the percentage change in the other variable.

COEFFICIENTS OF THE REGRESSION EQUATION: Also referred to as *parameters*, the values that indicate the quantitative impact on the dependent variable of a unit change in an independent variable. The main objective of regression analysis is to estimate the values of these coefficients from a sample of data. For this the method of ordinary least squares is often employed.

COEFFICIENT OF VARIATION: The ratio of the standard deviation and the expected value (mean).

COINCIDENT INDICATORS: Indicators that change at the same time as the time series being studied.

COMPLEMENTARY INPUTS: Inputs related to one another in such a way that an increase in the employment of one input raises the marginal product of the other input.

COMPLEMENTS: Two commodities are complements if an increase in the price of one of them leads to less of the other being purchased.

COMPOUND GROWTH RATE PROJECTION: Forecasting by projecting the average growth rate of the past into the future.

CONSTANT RETURNS TO SCALE: Output changes in the same proportion as factor inputs.

CONSTRAINED UTILITY MAXIMISATION: The process by which the consumer reaches the highest level of satisfaction given his or her income and the prices of goods. This occurs at the tangency of an indifference curve with the budget line.

CONSUMER EQUILIBRIUM: Constrained utility maximisation.

CONSUMER SURVEY: The attempt to obtain data about demand directly by asking consumers about their purchasing habits through such means as face-to-face interviews, focus groups, telephone surveys, and mailed questionaries.

CROSS-ELASTICITY OF DEMAND (E_c): The percentage change in the quantity purchased of a commodity divided by the percentage change in the price of another commodity.

CROSS-SECTIONAL DATA: Data on a particular set of variables for a given point in time for a cross section of indivisual entities (e.g., persons, households, cities, states, countries).

D

DECREASING RETURNS TO SCALE: Output changes by a smaller proportion than inputs.

DEGREES OF FREEDOM: An adjustment factor that is required in conducting the t-test. This number is found by subtracting the number of independent variables plus 1 from the number of observations in the sample; that is, d.f. $= n - (k + 1) = n - k - 1$.

DELPHI METHOD: A form of expert opinion forecasting that uses a series of written questions and answers to obtain a consensus forecast, most commonly employed in forecasting technological trends.

DEMAND: Quantities of a good or service that people are ready to buy at various prices, other factors besides the price held constant. Demand can be expressed as a numerical schedule, as a demand curve or a graph, or as an algebraic equation.

DERIVED DEMAND: The demand for an input that arises from the demand for the final commodities that the input is used in producing. It represents the demand coming from customers who use the product as an input in the production of their own products.

E

ECONOMICS: A field of study that deals with the allocation of scarce resources among alternative uses to satisfy human wants.

ECONOMETRIC FORECASTING METHOD: A quantitative, causal method that utilises a number of independent variables to explain the dependent variable to be forecast. Econometric forecasting employs both single and multiple-equation models.

ECONOMETRICS: The application of statistical methods to the estimation of economic models.

ECONOMIC INDICATORS: A barometric method of forecasting in which economic data are formed into indexes to reflect the state of the economy. Indexes of leading, coincident and lagging indicators are used to forecast changes in economic activity.

ECONOMIES OF SCALE: Reductions in cost which arise from the utilisation of larger sets of plant and equipment.

ENDOGENOUS VARIABLE: A variable that depends on the values of the exogenous variables in the equation. Unlike the exogenous variables, its value is not predetermined by factors excluded from the equation.

ENGEL CURVE: It shows the amount of a good that a consumer would purchase at various income levels.

ENGEL'S LAW: The proportion of total expenditures on food declines as family incomes rise.

ENGINEERING COST ESTIMATING: A method of estimating long-run costs. Professional facilities calculate optimal combinations of inputs needed to produce given quantities of output. Monetary values are then assigned to calculate cost figures.

ESTIMATION OF LONG-RUN COST FUNCTIONS: Analysis that assumes that all factors, especially capital, are variable. Cross-sectional regression analysis is customarily employed in the estimation.

ESTIMATION OF SHORT-RUN COST FUNCTIONS: An analysis in which certain factors are assumed to be fixed during the period analysed. Time series regression analysis is customarily employed in estimation.

EXOGENOUS VARIABLE: A variable having a predetermined value. In other words, the variable's value is not determined by the values of the dependent variable or the other independent variables in the equation.

EXPECTED VALUE: The sum of all the probability-weighted outcomes possible due to a decision.

EXPONENTIAL SMOOTHING: A smoothing method of forecasting that assigns greater importance to more recent data than to those in the more distant past.

EXTERNAL DISECONOMY: An upward shift in all firms' per-unit cost curves, resulting from an increase in input prices as the industry expands.

EXTERNAL ECONOMY: A downward shift in all firms' per-unit cost curves resulting from a decline in input prices as the industry expands.

F

F-STATISTIC: The F-statistic tests whether a significant proportion of the total variation in the dependent variable is due to the variation in the independent variables.

F-TEST: A test for the statistical significance of the R^2 value. If this test is passed, a researcher can be quite confident that all the estimated coefficients of a regression model together are not zero for the population under study.

FIRM: An organisation that combines and organises resources for the purpose of producing goods and services for sale at a profit.

FIXED INPUTS: The resources that cannot be varied or can be varied only with excessive cost during the time period under consideration.

FORECASTING: Predicting future value of a variable on the basis of current and past trends.

Functional form of total cost: Economic analysis considers three basic functional forms of total cost: cubic, quadratic, and linear. In economic analysis the reliance is almost entirely on the cubic function. But break-even analysis generally uses the linear form.

G

Giffen good: An inferior good for which the positive substitution effect is smaller than the negative income effect, so that less of the good is purchased when its price falls.

H

Homogeneous of degree 1: In production, it refers to constant returns to scale.

I

Identification problem: A problem concerning the proper location of the demand and supply curves. The difficulty sometimes encountered in estimating the market demand or supply curve of a commodity from quantity-price observations.

Income effect: The increase in the quantity purchased of a good resulting only from the increase in real income that accompanies a price decline.

Income elasticity of demand (E_I): The percentage change in the quantity purchased of a commodity over a specific period of time divided by the percentage change in consumer's income.

Income-consumption curve: The locus of consumer equilibrium points resulting when only the consumer's income varies.

Indifference curve: The curve showing alternative combinations of two commodities that give the consumer equal satisfaction and among which the consumer is indifferent.

Indifference map: The entire set of indifference curves reflecting the consumer's tastes and preferences.

Individual's demand curve: It shows the quantity that the individual would purchase of the good per unit of time at various alternative prices of the good, while keeping everything else constant.

Inferior good: A good of which a consumer purchases less with an increase income.

Input-output analysis: The empirical study of the interdependence among the various sectors and industries in the economy; it usually assumes fixed input proportions in production.

Inputs: The resources or factors of production used to produce goods and services.

Intermediate good: The output of a firm or industry that is used as input by another firm or industry producing final commodities.

J

Jury of executive opinion: A forecast generated by experts (e.g., corporate executives) in meetings. A similar method is to ask the opinion of sales representatives who are exposed to the market on a daily basis.

L

Lagging indicators: Indicators which confirm that a change has really occurred.

Law of demand: The inverse price-quantity relationship illustrated by the negative slope of the demand curve.

Law of diminishing marginal utility: Each additional unit of a good eventually gives less and less extra utility.

Law of diminishing returns: After a point, the marginal product of the variable input declines.

Leading indicators: Indicators that provide advance warning of change.

Least-cost input combination: The condition where the marginal product per rupee spent on each input is the same. Graphically, it is the point where an isoquant is tangent to an isocost line.

Long-run: The time period when all inputs can be varied. A time period in which new sellers may enter a market or sellers already in market may leave.

Long-run average cost (LAC): The minimum per unit cost of producing any level of output when the firm can build any desired scale of plant. It equals long-run total cost divided by output.

Long-run marginal cost (LMC): The change in long-run total costs per unit change in output; the slope of the LTC curve.

LONG-RUN TOTAL COST (LTC): The minimum total costs of producing various levels of output when the firm can build any desired scale of plant.

LUXURY: A commodity with income elasticity of demand greater than 1.

M

MARGINAL COST: The change in the total cost, or extra cost, that result from an economic action.

MARGINAL PRODUCT (MP): The change in total product per-unit change in the variable input used.

MARGINAL PRODUCTIVITY THEORY: The theory according to which each input is paid a price equal to its marginal productivity.

MARGINAL RATE OF TECHNICAL SUBSTITUTION ($MRTS$): Given two inputs K and L, the $MRTS$ of K and L represents the reduction in L relative to the amount of K that a firm must add to replace L to maintain the same amount of output. Mathematically speaking, it is represented by the slope of some given isoquant or $\Delta K/\Delta L (\delta K/\delta L$ for continuous isoquent).

MARGINAL RESOURCE COST (MRC): The extra cost of hiring an additional unit of the input.

MARGINAL REVENUE (MR): The change in total revenue per-unit change in the quantity sold.

MARGINAL REVENUE PRODUCT (MRP): The marginal physical product of the input (MPP) multiplied by the marginal revenue of the commodity (MR).

MARGINAL UTILITY (MU): The extra utility received from consuming one additional unit of the good.

MINIMUM EFFICIENT SCALE (MES): The minimum scale of production at which all known scale economies have been achieved.

MOVING METHOD AVERAGE: A smoothing technique that compensates for seasonal fluctuations.

MULTICOLLINEARITY: Inter-correlation between (among) explanatory variables.

MULTIPLE REGRESSION: A statistical technique that allows the economist to disentangle the independent effect of the various determinants of demand, so as to identify from the data the average market demand curve for the commodity.

N

NAIVE FORECASTING: Quantitative forecasting that projects past data without explaining the reasons for future trends.

NECESSITY: A commodity with income elasticity of demand between 0 and 1.

NON-PRICE DETERMINANTS OF DEMAND: (1) Tastes and preferences; (2) income, (3) prices of related products (i.e., substitutes or complements), (4) future expectations; (5) number of buyers.

NORMAL GOOD: A good of which the consumer purchases more with an increase in income.

NULL HYPOTEHSIS: In regression analysis, the hypothesis used in testing for the statistical significance of the estimated regression coefficient. It states that the true (but unknown) regression coefficients for the population are zero.

O

OPINION POLLS: A forecasting method in which sample populations are surveyed to determine consumption trends.

ONE-TAIL TEST: This refers to the nature of the alternative hypothesis in the t-test. If the alternative hypothesis states that the population coefficient is positive, then the upper tail of the t-distribution is used. If the alternative hypothesis states that the population coefficient is negative, then the lower tail is used. In either case, only one tail is used.

ORDINARY LEAST SQUARES (OLS): In simple regression analysis, a method designed to fit a line through a scatter of points indicating values of a dependent variable and an independent variable in such a way that the sum of the squard deviations of the points from the line is minimized.

ORDINAL UTILITY: The rankings of the utility received by an individual from consuming various amounts of a good or various baskets of goods.

OUTPUT ELASTICITY OF CAPITAL: The percentage increase in output resulting from a 1% increase in the quantity of capital used. For the Cobb-Douglas production function, this is given by the exponent of K.

OUTPUT ELASTICITY OF LABOUR: The percentage increase in output resulting from a 1% increase in the quantity of labour used. For the Cobb-Douglas production function, this is given by the exponent of L.

P

PLANNING HORIZON: The time period when the firm can build any desired scale of plant; the long run.

POINT ELASTICITY OF DEMAND: The price elasticity of demand at a specific point on the demand curve.

POWER FUNCTION: A mathematical function of the form $Y = x^n$, where the index n is a fixed number and X takes positive values continuously.

PRICE ELASTICITY OF DEMAND: [illegible] percentage change in the quantity demanded of a commodity during a specific period of time divided by the percentage change in its price.

PRICE-CONSUMPTION CURVE: The locus of consumer equilibrium points resulting when only the price of a good varies.

PROBABILITY DISTRIBUTION: A complete list of both the possible outcomes and the probabilities of their occurrence.

PROBABILITY: The chance, or odds that an event will take place.

PRODUCTION FUNCTION: The unique relationship between inputs and output represented by a table, graph, or equation showing the maximum output of a commodity that can be produced per period of time with each set of inputs.

PRODUCTION: The transformation of resources or inputs into outputs of goods and services.

Q

QUALITATIVE FORECASTING: Forecasting based on the judgment of individuals or groups.

QUANTITATIVE FORECASTING: Forecasting that examines historical data for projecting future trends.

R

REGRESSION ANALYSIS: A statistical technique for finding the best relationship between a dependent variable (such as sales) and selected independent variables (such as price, advertising expenditures, population size, etc.). If one independent variable is used this technique is referred to as simple regression. If more than one independent variable is used, it is called multiple regression.

RETURNS TO SCALE: The relationship between the unit cost of output and the scale at which the output is produced.

RISK: The possibility of a gain or loss from an action when the decision maker knows the probabilities of all possible outcomes.

RULE OF TWO: A general rule of thumb employed by economists in conducting the t-test. Essentially, it states that any t-ratio of 2 or more indicates that the estimated coefficient is statistically significant at the .05 level.

S

SHORT-RUN: The time period when at least one input is fixed.

SHUTDOWN POINT: The output level at which price equals average variable cost and losses equal total fixed costs, whether the firm produces or not. Also, the lowest point on the AVC curve at which $MC = AVC$.

STAGE I OF PRODUCTION: The range of increasing average product.

STAGE II OF PRODUCTION: The range from maximum average product to zero marginal product.

STAGE III OF PRODUCTION: The range over which marginal product is negative.

STANDARD ERROR OF THE COEFFICIENT: A measure of the confidence that we have in the estimated value of the coefficients. The standard error approximates the range of probability of likely values for the coefficient.

STANDARD ERROR OF THE ESTIMATE (SEE): A measure of the deviation of the estimated value of the dependent variable, given the values of the independent variables. In forecasting, the standard error of the estimate is used to develop an interval that contains the true value of the dependent variable, subject to a designated degree of confidence.

SUBSTITUTES: Two commodities are substitutes if an increase in the price of one of them leads to more of the other being purchased.

SUBSTITUTION EFFECT: The increase in the quantity demanded of a good when its price falls, resulting only from the relative price decline and independent of the change in a real income.

SURVIVORSHIP TECHNIQUE: A method for estimating long-run cost curves. The proportion of total industry output by firms of different sizes is observed over a period of time. That segment of the industry that gains in proportion of industry output over time is deemed most efficient (convert-cost).

T

T-TABLE: A numerical table indicating the different values of the *t*-ratio and the frequency of their occurrence in a *t*-distribution whose mean value is zero.

T-TEST: A test for the statistical significance of the estimated regression coefficients. If a coefficient passes the test, then a researcher can be quite confident that the value of the true population coefficient is not zero.

TECHNICAL COEFFICIENTS: Coefficients in input-output analysis that indicate the rupee value of each input required to produce one rupee's worth of output in each industry or sector; also called production or input coefficients.

TECHNOLOGY: The state of the art or techniques available to combine resources or inputs to produce goods and services.

TIME SERIES DATA: Data for a particular set of variables that track their values over a particular period of time at regular intervals (e.g. monthly, quarterly, annually).

TIME-SERIES ANALYSIS: A term applied to a number of different forecasting methods.

TIME-SERIES FORECASTING: A method of forecasting from past data by using least squares statistical methods. A time-series analysis usually examines trends, cyclical fluctuations, seasonal fluctuations and irregular movements.

TOTAL COST (TC): TFC plus TVC.

TOTAL FIXED COSTS (TFC): The total obligations of the firm per time period for all fixed inputs.

TOTAL PRODUCT (TP): Total output.

TOTAL REVENUE (TR): The price of the commodity times the quantity sold of the commodity.

TOTAL UTILITY (TU): The aggregate amount of satisfaction received from consuming various amounts of a good or baskets of goods.

TOTAL VARIABLE COSTS (TVC): The total obligations of the firm per time period for all the variable inputs the firm uses.

TREND PROJECTION: A form of naive forecasting that projects trends from past data. Trend projections usually employ compound growth rates, visual time series, or least squares time-series methods.

T-STATISTIC: A measure of the confidence that we have in the estimated value of the coefficients in a regression equation. Can be used even for small sample sizes. It is the ratio of the difference between the estimated value and a bench-mark value and the standard error of the estimated coefficient.

TWO-TAIL TEST: A *t*-test in which the alternative hypothesis states that the population coefficient may be either positive or negative (i.e., it is not zero); that is, either the upper or the lower tail of the *t*-distribution may be used.

U

UNCERTAINTY: The state in which decision makers do not know the possible outcomes of their actions and do not know the probabilities attached to a set of known possible outcomes.

UTIL: The arbitrary unit of measure of utility.

UTILITY: The ability of a good to satisfy a want. It is a measure of the well-being or level of satisfaction of consumers, and depends on the quantities of goods bought by the consumers.

V

VALUE OF THE MARGINAL PRODUCT (VMP): The marginal (physical) product of the input (MP) multiplied by the commodity price (P).

VARIABLE INPUTS: The resource that can be varied easily and on short notice during the time period under consideration.

APPENDIX

LOGARITHMS

	0	1	2	3	4	5	6	7	8	9	1	2	3	4	5	6	7	8	9
10	0000	0043	0086	0128	0170						5	9	13	17	21	26	30	34	38
						0212	0253	0294	0334	0374	4	8	12	16	20	24	28	32	36
11	0414	0453	0492	0531	0569						4	8	12	16	20	23	27	31	35
						0607	0645	0682	0719	0755	4	7	11	15	18	22	26	29	33
12	0792	0828	0864	0899	0934						3	7	11	14	18	21	25	28	32
						0969	1004	1038	1072	1106	3	7	10	14	17	20	24	27	31
13	1139	1173	1206	1239	1271						3	6	10	13	16	19	23	26	29
						1303	1335	1367	1399	1430	3	6	10	13	16	19	22	25	29
14	1461	1492	1523	1553	1584						3	6	9	12	15	19	22	25	28
						1614	1644	1673	1703	1732	3	6	9	12	14	17	20	23	26
15	1761	1790	1818	1847	1875						3	6	9	11	14	17	20	23	26
						1903	1931	1959	1987	2014	3	6	8	11	14	17	19	22	25
16	2041	2068	2095	2122	2148						3	6	8	11	14	16	19	22	24
						2175	2201	2227	2253	2279	3	5	8	10	13	16	18	21	23
17	2304	2330	2355	2380	2405						3	5	8	10	13	15	18	20	23
						2430	2455	2480	2504	2529	3	5	8	10	12	15	17	20	22
18	2553	2577	2601	2625	2648						2	5	7	9	12	14	17	19	21
						2672	2695	2718	2742	2765	2	4	7	9	11	14	16	18	21
19	2788	2810	2833	2856	2878						2	4	7	9	11	13	16	18	20
						2900	2923	2945	2967	2989	2	4	6	8	11	13	15	17	19
20	3010	3032	3054	3075	3096	3118	3139	3160	3181	3201	2	4	6	8	11	13	15	17	19
21	3222	3243	3263	3284	3304	3324	3345	3365	3385	3404	2	4	6	8	10	12	14	16	18
22	3424	3444	3464	3483	3502	3522	3541	3560	3579	3598	2	4	6	8	10	12	14	15	17
23	3617	3636	3655	3674	3692	3711	3729	3747	3766	3784	2	4	6	7	9	11	13	15	17
24	3802	3820	3838	3856	3874	3892	3909	3927	3945	3962	2	4	5	7	9	11	12	14	16
25	3979	3997	4014	4031	4048	4065	4082	4099	4116	4133	2	3	5	7	9	10	12	14	15
26	4150	4165	4183	4200	4216	4232	4249	4265	4281	4298	2	3	5	7	8	10	11	13	15
27	4314	4330	4346	4362	4378	4393	4409	4425	4440	4456	2	3	5	6	8	9	11	13	14
28	4472	4487	4502	4518	4533	4548	4564	4579	4594	4609	2	3	5	6	8	9	11	12	14
29	4624	4639	4654	4669	4683	4698	4713	4728	4742	4757	1	3	4	6	7	9	10	12	13
30	4771	4786	4800	4814	4829	4843	4857	4871	4886	4900	1	3	4	6	7	9	10	11	13
31	4914	4928	4942	4955	4969	4983	4997	5011	5024	5038	1	3	4	6	7	8	10	11	12
32	5051	5065	5079	5092	5105	5119	5132	5145	5159	5172	1	3	4	5	7	8	9	11	12
33	5185	5198	5211	5224	5237	5250	5263	5276	5289	5302	1	3	4	5	6	8	9	10	12
34	5315	5328	5340	5353	5366	5378	5391	5403	5416	5428	1	3	4	5	6	8	9	10	11
35	5441	5453	5465	5478	5490	5502	5514	5527	5539	5551	1	2	4	5	6	7	9	10	11
36	5563	5575	5587	5599	5611	5623	5635	5647	5658	5670	1	2	4	5	6	7	8	10	11
37	5682	5694	5705	5717	5729	5740	5752	5763	5775	5786	1	2	3	5	6	7	8	9	10
38	5798	5809	5821	5832	5843	5855	5866	5877	5888	5899	1	2	3	5	6	7	8	9	10
39	5911	5922	5933	5944	5955	5966	5977	5988	5999	6010	1	2	3	4	5	7	8	9	10
40	6021	6031	6042	6053	6064	6075	6085	6096	6107	6117	1	2	3	4	5	6	8	9	10
41	6128	6138	6149	6160	6170	6180	6191	6201	6212	6222	1	2	3	4	5	6	7	8	9
42	6232	6243	6253	6263	6274	6284	6294	6304	6314	6325	1	2	3	4	5	6	7	8	9
43	6335	6345	6355	6365	6375	6385	6395	6405	6415	6425	1	2	3	4	5	6	7	8	9
44	6435	6444	6454	6464	6474	6484	6493	6503	6513	6522	1	2	3	4	5	6	7	8	9
45	6532	6542	6551	6561	6571	6580	6590	6599	6609	6618	1	2	3	4	5	6	7	8	9
46	6628	6637	6646	6656	6665	6675	6684	6693	6702	6712	1	2	3	4	5	6	7	7	8
47	6721	6730	6739	6749	6758	6767	6776	6785	6794	6803	1	2	3	4	5	5	6	7	8
48	6812	6821	6830	6839	6848	6857	6866	6875	6884	6893	1	2	3	4	4	5	6	7	8
49	6902	6911	6920	6928	6937	6946	6955	6964	6972	6981	1	2	3	4	4	5	6	7	8

	0	1	2	3	4	5	6	7	8	9	1	2	3	4	5	6	7	8	9
50	6990	6998	7007	7016	7024	7033	7042	7050	7059	7067	1	2	3	3	4	5	6	7	8
51	7076	7084	7093	7101	7110	7118	7126	7135	7143	7152	1	2	3	3	4	5	6	7	8
52	7160	7168	7177	7185	7193	7202	7210	7218	7226	7235	1	2	2	3	4	5	6	7	7
53	7243	7251	7259	7267	7275	7284	7292	7300	7308	7316	1	2	2	3	4	5	6	6	7
54	7324	7332	7340	7348	7356	7364	7372	7380	7388	7396	1	2	2	3	4	5	6	6	7
55	7404	7412	7419	7427	7435	7443	7451	7459	7466	7474	1	2	2	3	4	5	5	6	7
56	7482	7490	7497	7505	7513	7520	7528	7536	7543	7551	1	2	2	3	4	5	5	6	7
57	7559	7566	7574	7582	7589	7597	7604	7612	7619	7627	1	2	2	3	4	5	5	6	7
58	7634	7642	7649	7657	7664	7672	7679	7686	7694	7701	1	1	2	3	4	4	5	6	7
59	7709	7716	7733	7731	7738	7745	7752	7760	7767	7774	1	1	2	3	4	4	5	6	7
60	7782	7789	7796	7803	7810	7818	7825	7832	7839	7846	1	1	2	3	4	4	5	6	6
61	7853	7860	7868	7875	7882	7889	7896	7903	7910	7917	1	1	2	3	4	4	5	6	6
62	7924	7931	7938	7945	7952	7959	7966	7973	7980	7987	1	1	2	3	3	4	5	6	6
63	7993	8000	8007	8014	8021	8028	8035	8041	8048	8055	1	1	2	3	3	4	5	5	6
64	8062	8069	8075	8082	8089	8096	8102	8109	8116	8122	1	1	2	3	3	4	5	5	6
65	8129	8136	8142	8149	8156	8162	8169	8176	8182	8189	1	1	2	3	3	4	5	5	6
66	8195	8202	8209	8215	8222	8228	8235	8241	8248	8254	1	1	2	3	3	4	5	5	6
67	8261	8267	8274	8280	8287	8293	8299	8306	8312	8319	1	1	2	3	3	4	5	5	6
68	8325	8331	8338	8344	8351	8357	8363	8370	8376	8382	1	1	2	3	3	4	4	5	6
69	8388	8395	8401	8407	8414	8420	8426	8432	8439	8445	1	1	2	2	3	4	4	5	6
70	8451	8457	8463	8470	8476	8482	8488	8494	8500	8506	1	1	2	2	3	4	4	5	6
71	8513	8519	8525	8531	8537	8543	8549	8555	8561	8567	1	1	2	2	3	4	4	5	5
72	8573	8579	8585	8591	8597	8603	8609	8615	8621	8627	1	1	2	2	3	4	4	5	5
73	8633	8639	8645	8651	8657	8663	8669	8675	8681	8686	1	1	2	2	3	4	4	5	5
74	8692	8698	8704	8710	8716	8722	8727	8733	8739	8745	1	1	2	2	3	4	4	5	5
75	8751	8756	8762	8768	8774	8779	8785	8791	8797	8802	1	1	2	2	3	3	4	5	5
76	8808	8814	8820	8825	8831	8837	8842	8848	8854	8859	1	1	2	2	3	3	4	5	5
77	8865	8871	8876	8882	8887	8893	8899	8904	8910	8915	1	1	2	2	3	3	4	4	5
78	8921	8927	8932	8938	8943	8949	8954	8960	8965	8971	1	1	2	2	3	3	4	4	5
79	8976	8982	8987	8993	8998	9004	9009	9015	9020	9025	1	1	2	2	3	3	4	4	5
80	9031	9036	9042	9047	9053	9058	9063	9069	9074	9079	1	1	2	2	3	3	4	4	5
81	9085	9090	9096	9101	9106	9112	9117	9122	9128	9133	1	1	2	2	3	3	4	4	5
82	9138	9143	9149	9154	9159	9165	9170	9175	9180	9196	1	1	2	2	3	3	4	4	5
83	9191	9196	9201	9206	9212	9217	9222	9227	9232	9238	1	1	2	2	3	3	4	4	5
84	9243	9248	9253	9258	9263	9269	9274	9279	9284	9289	1	1	2	2	3	3	4	4	5
85	9294	9299	9304	9309	9315	9320	9325	9330	9335	9340	1	1	2	2	3	3	4	4	5
86	9345	9350	9355	9360	9365	9370	9375	9380	9385	9390	1	1	2	2	3	3	4	4	5
87	9395	9400	9405	9410	9415	9420	9425	9430	9435	9440	0	1	1	2	2	3	3	4	4
88	9445	9450	9455	9460	9465	9469	9474	9479	9484	9489	0	1	1	2	2	3	3	4	4
89	9494	9499	9504	9509	9513	9518	9523	9528	9533	9538	0	1	1	2	2	3	3	4	4
90	9542	9547	9552	9557	9562	9566	9571	9576	9581	9586	0	1	1	2	2	3	3	4	4
91	9590	9595	9600	9605	9609	9614	9619	9624	9628	9633	0	1	1	2	2	3	3	4	4
92	9638	9643	9647	9652	9657	9661	9666	9671	9675	9680	0	1	1	2	2	3	3	4	4
93	9685	9689	9694	9699	9703	9708	9713	9717	9722	9727	0	1	1	2	2	3	3	4	4
94	9731	9736	9741	9745	9750	9754	9759	9763	9768	9773	0	1	1	2	2	3	3	4	4
95	9777	9782	9786	9791	9795	9800	9805	9809	9814	9818	0	1	1	2	2	3	3	4	4
96	9823	9827	9832	9836	9841	9845	9850	9854	9859	9863	0	1	1	2	2	3	3	4	4
97	9868	9872	9877	9881	9886	9890	9894	9899	9903	9908	0	1	1	2	2	3	3	4	4
98	9912	9917	9921	9926	9930	9934	9939	9943	9948	9952	0	1	1	2	2	3	3	4	4
99	9956	9961	9965	9969	9974	9978	9983	9987	9991	9996	0	1	1	2	2	3	3	3	4

ANTILOGARITHMS

	0	1	2	3	4	5	6	7	8	9	1	2	3	4	5	6	7	8	9
.00	1000	1002	1005	1007	1009	1012	1014	1016	1019	1021	0	0	1	1	1	1	2	2	2
.01	1023	1026	1028	1030	1033	1035	1038	1040	1042	1045	0	0	1	1	1	1	2	2	2
.02	1047	1050	1052	1054	1057	1059	1062	1064	1067	1069	0	0	1	1	1	1	2	2	2
.03	1072	1074	1076	1079	1081	1084	1086	1089	1091	1094	0	0	1	1	1	1	2	2	2
.04	1096	1099	1102	1104	1107	1109	1112	1114	1117	1119	0	1	1	1	1	2	2	2	2
.05	1122	1125	1127	1130	1132	1135	1138	1140	1143	1146	0	1	1	1	1	2	2	2	2
.06	1148	1151	1153	1156	1159	1161	1164	1167	1169	1172	0	1	1	1	1	2	2	2	2
.07	1175	1178	1180	1183	1186	1189	1191	1194	1197	1199	0	1	1	1	1	2	2	2	2
.08	1202	1205	1208	1211	1213	1216	1219	1222	1225	1227	0	1	1	1	1	2	2	2	3
.09	1230	1233	1236	1239	1242	1245	1247	1250	1253	1256	0	1	1	1	1	2	2	2	3
.10	1259	1262	1265	1268	1271	1274	1276	1279	1282	1285	0	1	1	1	1	2	2	2	3
.11	1288	1291	1294	1297	1300	1303	1306	1309	1312	1315	0	1	1	1	2	2	2	2	3
.12	1318	1321	1324	1327	1330	1334	1337	1340	1343	1346	0	1	1	1	2	2	2	2	3
.13	1349	1352	1355	1358	1361	1365	1368	1371	1374	1377	0	1	1	1	2	2	2	3	3
.14	1380	1384	1387	1390	1393	1396	1400	1403	1406	1409	0	1	1	1	2	2	2	3	3
.15	1413	1416	1419	1422	1426	1429	1432	1435	1439	1442	0	1	1	1	2	2	2	3	3
.16	1445	1449	1452	1455	1459	1462	1466	1469	1472	1476	0	1	1	1	2	2	2	3	3
.17	1479	1483	1486	1489	1493	1496	1500	1503	1507	1510	0	1	1	1	2	2	2	3	3
.18	1514	1517	1521	1524	1528	1531	1535	1538	1542	1545	0	1	1	1	2	2	2	3	3
.19	1549	1552	1556	1560	1563	1567	1570	1574	1578	1581	0	1	1	1	2	2	3	3	3
.20	1585	1589	1592	1596	1600	1603	1607	1611	1614	1618	0	1	1	1	2	2	3	3	3
.21	1622	1626	1629	1633	1637	1641	1644	1648	1652	1656	0	1	1	2	2	2	3	3	3
.22	1660	1663	1667	1671	1675	1679	1683	1687	1690	1694	0	1	1	2	2	2	3	3	3
.23	1698	1702	1706	1710	1714	1718	1722	1726	1730	1734	0	1	1	2	2	2	3	3	4
.24	1738	1742	1746	1750	1754	1758	1762	1766	1770	1774	0	1	1	2	2	2	3	3	4
.25	1778	1782	1786	1791	1795	1799	1803	1807	1811	1816	0	1	1	2	2	2	3	3	4
.26	1820	1824	1828	1832	1837	1841	1845	1849	1854	1858	0	1	1	2	2	3	3	3	4
.27	1862	1866	1871	1875	1879	1884	1888	1892	1897	1901	0	1	1	2	2	3	3	3	4
.28	1905	1910	1914	1919	1923	1928	1932	1936	1941	1945	0	1	1	2	2	3	3	4	4
.29	1950	1954	1959	1963	1968	1972	1977	1982	1986	1991	0	1	1	2	2	3	3	4	4
.30	1995	2000	2004	2009	2014	2018	2023	2028	2032	2037	0	1	1	2	2	3	3	4	4
.31	2042	2046	2051	2056	2061	2065	2070	2075	2080	2084	0	1	1	2	2	3	3	4	4
.32	2089	2094	2099	2104	2109	2113	2118	2123	2128	2133	0	1	1	2	2	3	3	4	4
.33	2138	2143	2148	2153	2158	2163	2168	2173	2178	2183	0	1	1	2	2	3	3	4	4
.34	2188	2193	2198	2203	2208	2213	2218	2223	2228	2234	1	1	2	2	3	3	4	4	5
.35	2239	2244	2249	2254	2259	2265	2270	2275	2280	2286	1	1	2	2	3	3	4	4	5
.36	2291	2296	2301	2307	2312	2317	2323	2328	2333	2339	1	1	2	2	3	3	4	4	5
.37	2344	2350	2355	2360	2366	2371	2377	2382	2388	2393	1	1	2	2	3	3	4	4	5
.38	2399	2404	2410	2415	2421	2427	2432	2438	2443	2449	1	1	2	2	3	3	4	4	5
.39	2455	2460	2466	2472	2477	2483	2489	2495	2500	2506	1	1	2	2	3	3	4	5	5
.40	2512	2518	2523	2529	2535	2541	2547	2553	2559	2564	1	1	2	2	3	4	4	5	5
.41	2570	2576	2582	2588	2594	2600	2606	2612	2618	2624	1	1	2	2	3	4	4	5	5
.42	2630	2636	2642	2649	2655	2661	2667	2673	2679	2685	1	1	2	2	3	4	4	5	6
.43	2692	2698	2704	2710	2716	2723	2729	2735	2742	2748	1	1	2	3	3	4	4	5	6
.44	2754	2761	2767	2773	2780	2786	2793	2799	2805	2812	1	1	2	3	3	4	4	5	6
.45	2818	2825	2831	2838	2844	2851	2858	2864	2871	2877	1	1	2	3	3	4	5	5	6
.46	2884	2891	2897	2904	2911	2917	2924	2931	2938	2944	1	1	2	3	3	4	5	5	6
.47	2951	2958	2965	2972	2979	2985	2992	2999	3006	3013	1	1	2	3	3	4	5	5	6
.48	3020	3027	3034	3041	3048	3055	3062	3069	3076	3083	1	1	2	3	4	4	5	6	6
.49	3090	3097	3105	3112	3119	3126	3133	3141	3148	3155	1	1	2	3	4	4	5	6	6

ANTILOGARITHMS

	0	1	2	3	4	5	6	7	8	9	1	2	3	4	5	6	7	8	9
.50	3162	3170	3177	3184	3192	3199	3206	3214	3221	3228	1	1	2	3	4	4	5	6	7
.51	3236	3243	3251	3258	3266	3273	3281	3289	3296	3304	1	2	2	3	4	5	5	6	7
.52	3311	3319	3327	3334	3342	3350	3357	3365	3373	3381	1	2	2	3	4	5	5	6	7
.53	3388	3396	3404	3412	3420	3428	3436	3443	3451	3459	1	2	2	3	4	5	6	6	7
.54	3467	3475	3483	3491	3499	3508	3516	3524	3532	3540	1	2	2	3	4	5	6	6	7
.55	3548	3556	3565	3573	3581	3589	3597	3606	3614	3622	1	2	2	3	4	5	6	7	7
.56	3631	3639	3648	3656	3664	3673	3681	3690	3698	3707	1	2	3	3	4	5	6	7	8
.57	3715	3724	3733	3741	3750	3758	3767	3776	3784	3793	1	2	3	3	4	5	6	7	8
.58	3802	3811	3819	3828	3837	3846	3855	3864	3873	3882	1	2	3	4	4	5	6	7	8
.59	3890	3899	3908	3917	3926	3936	3945	3954	3963	3972	1	2	3	4	5	5	6	7	8
.60	3981	3990	3999	4009	4018	4027	4036	4046	4055	4064	1	2	3	4	5	6	6	7	8
.61	4074	4083	4093	4102	4111	4121	4130	4140	4150	4159	1	2	3	4	5	6	7	8	9
.62	4169	4178	4188	4198	4207	4217	4227	4236	4246	4256	1	2	3	4	5	6	7	8	9
.63	4266	4276	4285	4295	4305	4315	4325	4335	4345	4355	1	2	3	4	5	6	7	8	9
.64	4365	4375	4385	4395	4406	4416	4426	4436	4446	4457	1	2	3	4	5	6	7	8	9
.65	4467	4477	4487	4498	4508	4519	4529	4539	4550	4560	1	2	3	4	5	6	7	8	9
.66	4571	4581	4592	4603	4613	4624	4634	4645	4656	4667	1	2	3	4	5	6	7	9	10
.67	4677	4688	4699	4710	4721	4732	4742	4753	4764	4775	1	2	3	4	5	7	8	9	10
.68	4786	4797	4808	4819	4831	4842	4853	4864	4875	4887	1	2	3	4	6	7	8	9	10
.69	4898	4909	4920	4932	4943	4955	4966	4977	4989	5000	1	2	3	5	6	7	8	9	10
.70	5012	5023	5035	5047	5058	5070	5082	5093	5105	5117	1	2	4	5	6	7	8	9	11
.71	5129	5140	5152	5164	5176	5188	5200	5212	5224	5236	1	2	4	5	6	7	8	10	11
.72	5248	5260	5272	5284	5297	5309	5321	5333	5346	5358	1	2	4	5	6	7	8	10	11
.73	5370	5383	5395	5408	5420	5433	5445	5458	5470	5483	1	3	4	5	6	8	9	10	11
.74	5495	5508	5521	5534	5546	5559	5572	5585	5598	5610	1	3	4	5	6	8	9	10	12
.75	5623	5636	5649	5662	5675	5689	5702	5715	5728	5741	1	3	4	5	7	8	9	10	12
.76	5754	5768	5781	5794	5808	5821	5834	5848	5861	5875	1	3	4	5	7	8	9	11	12
.77	5888	5902	5916	5929	5943	5957	5970	5984	5998	6012	1	3	4	5	7	8	10	11	12
.78	6026	6039	6053	6067	6081	6095	6109	6124	6138	6152	1	3	4	6	7	8	10	11	12
.79	6166	6180	6194	6209	6223	6237	6252	6266	6281	6295	1	3	4	6	7	9	10	11	13
.80	6310	6324	6339	6353	6368	6383	6397	6412	6427	6442	1	3	4	6	7	9	10	12	13
.81	6457	6471	6486	6501	6516	6531	6546	6561	6577	6592	2	3	5	6	8	9	11	12	14
.82	6607	6622	6637	6653	6668	6683	6699	6714	6730	6745	2	3	5	6	8	9	11	12	14
.83	6761	6776	6792	6808	6823	6839	6855	6871	6887	6902	2	3	5	6	8	9	11	13	14
.84	6918	6934	6950	6966	6982	6998	7015	7031	7047	7063	2	3	5	6	8	10	11	13	15
.85	7079	7096	7112	7129	7145	7161	7178	7194	7211	7228	2	3	5	7	8	10	12	13	15
.86	7244	7261	7278	7295	7311	7328	7345	7362	7379	7396	2	3	5	7	8	10	12	13	15
.87	7413	7430	7447	7464	7482	7499	7516	7534	7551	7568	2	3	5	7	9	10	12	14	16
.88	7586	7603	7621	7638	7656	7674	7691	7709	7727	7745	2	4	5	7	9	11	12	14	16
.89	7762	7780	7798	7816	7834	7852	7870	7889	7907	7925	2	4	5	7	9	11	13	14	16
.90	7943	7962	7980	7998	8017	8035	8054	8072	8091	8110	2	4	6	7	9	11	13	15	17
.91	8128	8147	8166	8185	8204	8222	8241	8260	8279	8299	2	4	6	8	9	11	13	15	17
.92	8318	8337	8356	8375	8395	8414	8433	8453	8472	8492	2	4	6	8	10	12	14	15	17
.93	8511	8531	8551	8570	8590	8610	8630	8650	8670	8690	2	4	6	8	10	12	14	16	18
.94	8710	8730	8750	8770	8790	8810	8831	8851	8872	8892	2	4	6	8	10	12	14	16	18
.95	8913	8933	8954	8974	8995	9016	9036	9057	9078	9099	2	4	6	8	10	12	15	17	19
.96	9120	9141	9162	9183	9204	9226	9247	9268	9290	9311	2	4	6	8	11	13	15	17	19
.97	9333	9354	9376	9397	9419	9441	9462	9484	9506	9528	2	4	7	9	11	13	15	17	20
.98	9550	9572	9594	9616	9638	9661	9683	9705	9727	9750	2	4	7	9	11	13	16	18	20
.99	9772	9795	9817	9840	9863	9886	9908	9931	9954	9977	2	5	7	9	11	14	16	18	20

LOGARITHMS

	0	1	2	3	4	5	6	7	8	9	Mean Differences 1	2	3	4	5	6	7	8	9
10	00000	00432	00860	01284	01703						42	85	127	170	212	254	297	339	381
						02119	02531	02938	03342	03743	40	81	121	162	202	242	283	323	364
11	04139	04532	04922	05308	05690						37	77	116	154	193	232	270	309	348
						06070	06446	06819	07188	07555	37	74	111	148	185	222	259	296	333
12	07918	08279	08636	08991	09342						36	71	106	142	177	213	248	284	319
						09691	10037	10380	10721	11059	34	68	102	136	170	204	238	272	307
13	11394	11727	12057	12385	12710						33	66	98	131	164	197	229	262	295
						13033	13354	13672	13988	14301	32	63	95	126	158	190	221	253	284
14	14613	14922	15229	15534	15836						30	61	91	122	152	183	213	244	274
						16137	16435	16732	17026	17319	29	59	88	118	147	177	206	236	265
15	17609	17898	18184	18469	18752						28	57	85	114	142	171	199	228	256
						19033	19312	19590	19866	20140	28	55	83	110	138	165	193	221	248
16	20412	20683	30951	21219	21484						27	53	80	107	134	160	187	214	240
						21748	22011	22272	22531	22789	26	52	78	104	130	156	182	208	233
17	23045	23300	23553	23805	24055						26	50	76	101	126	151	176	201	227
						24304	24551	24797	25042	25285	25	49	73	98	122	147	171	196	220
18	25527	25768	26007	26245	26482						24	48	71	95	119	143	167	190	214
						26717	26951	27184	27416	27646	23	46	69	93	116	139	162	185	208
19	27875	28103	28330	28556	28780						23	45	68	90	113	135	158	180	203
						29003	29226	29447	29667	29885	22	44	66	88	110	132	154	176	198
20	30103	30320	30535	30750	30963	31175	31387	31597	31806	32015	21	43	64	85	106	127	148	170	190
21	32222	32428	32634	32838	33041	33244	33445	33646	33846	34044	20	41	61	81	101	121	141	162	182
22	34242	34439	34635	34830	35025	35218	35411	35603	35793	35984	20	39	58	77	97	116	135	154	174
23	36173	36361	36549	36736	36922	37107	37291	37475	37658	37840	19	37	56	74	93	111	130	148	167
24	38021	38202	38382	38561	38739	38917	39094	39270	39445	39620	18	35	53	71	89	106	124	142	159
25	39794	39967	40140	40312	40483	40654	40824	40993	41162	41330	17	34	51	68	85	102	119	136	153
26	41497	41664	41830	41996	42160	42325	42488	42651	42813	42975	16	33	49	66	82	98	115	131	148
27	43136	43297	43457	43616	43775	43933	44091	44248	44404	44560	16	32	47	63	79	95	111	126	142
28	44716	44871	45025	45179	45332	45484	45637	45788	45939	46090	15	30	46	61	76	91	107	122	137
29	46240	46389	46538	46687	46835	46982	47129	47276	47422	47567	15	29	44	59	74	88	103	118	132
30	47712	47857	48001	48144	48287	48430	48572	48714	48855	48996	14	29	43	57	72	86	100	114	129
31	49136	49276	49415	49554	49693	49831	49969	50106	50243	50379	14	28	41	55	69	83	97	110	124
32	50515	50650	50786	50920	51054	51188	51322	51455	51587	51720	13	27	40	54	67	80	94	107	121
33	51851	51983	52114	52244	52375	52504	52634	52763	52892	53020	13	26	39	52	65	78	91	104	117
34	53148	53275	53403	53529	53656	53782	53908	54033	54158	54283	13	25	38	50	63	76	88	101	113
35	54407	54531	54654	54777	54900	55023	55145	55267	55388	55509	12	24	37	49	61	73	85	98	110
36	55630	55751	55871	55991	56110	56229	56348	56467	56585	56703	12	24	36	48	60	71	83	95	107
37	56820	56937	57054	57171	57287	57403	57519	57634	57749	57864	12	23	35	46	58	70	81	93	104
38	57978	58092	58206	58320	58433	58546	58659	58771	58883	58995	11	23	34	45	57	68	79	90	102
39	59106	59218	59329	59439	59550	59660	59770	59879	59988	60097	11	22	33	44	55	66	77	88	99
40	60206	60314	60423	60531	60638	60746	60853	60959	61066	61172	11	21	32	43	54	64	75	86	97
41	61278	61384	61490	61595	61700	61805	61909	62014	62118	62221	10	21	31	42	53	63	74	84	95
42	62325	62428	62531	62634	62737	62839	62941	63043	63144	63246	10	20	31	41	51	61	71	82	92
43	63347	63448	63548	63649	63749	63849	63949	64048	64147	64246	10	20	30	40	50	60	70	80	90
44	64345	64444	64542	64640	64738	64836	64933	65031	65128	65225	10	20	29	39	49	59	68	78	88
45	65321	65418	65514	65610	65706	65801	65896	65992	66087	66181	10	19	29	38	48	57	67	76	86
46	66276	66370	66464	66558	66652	66745	66839	66932	67025	67117	9	19	28	37	47	56	65	74	84
47	67210	67302	67394	67486	67578	67669	67761	67852	67943	68034	9	18	27	36	46	55	64	73	82
48	68124	68215	68305	68395	68485	68574	68664	68753	68842	68931	9	18	27	36	45	53	63	72	81
49	69020	69108	69197	69285	69373	69461	69548	69636	69723	69810	9	18	26	35	44	53	62	70	79

	0	1	2	3	4	5	6	7	8	9	Mean Differences								
											1	2	3	4	5	6	7	8	9
50	69897	69984	70070	70157	70243	70329	70415	70501	70585	70672	9	17	26	34	43	52	60	69	77
51	70757	70842	70927	71012	71096	71181	71265	71349	71433	71517	8	17	25	34	42	50	59	67	76
52	71600	71684	71767	71850	71933	72016	72099	77281	72263	72346	8	17	25	33	42	50	58	66	75
53	72428	72509	72591	72673	72754	72835	72916	72997	73078	73159	8	16	24	32	41	49	57	65	73
54	73239	73320	73400	73480	73560	73640	73719	73799	73878	73957	8	16	24	32	40	48	56	64	72
55	74036	74115	74194	74273	74351	74429	74507	74586	74663	74741	8	16	23	31	39	47	55	63	70
56	74819	74896	74974	75051	75128	75205	75282	75358	75435	75511	8	15	23	31	39	46	54	62	69
57	75587	75664	75740	75815	75891	75967	76042	76118	76193	76268	8	15	23	30	38	45	53	60	68
58	76343	76418	76492	76567	76641	76716	76790	76864	76938	77012	7	15	22	30	37	44	52	59	67
59	77085	77159	77232	77305	77379	77452	77525	77597	77670	77743	7	15	22	29	37	44	51	58	66
60	77815	77887	77960	78032	78104	78176	78247	78319	78390	78462	7	14	22	29	36	43	50	58	65
61	78533	78604	78675	78746	78817	78888	78958	79029	79099	79169	7	14	21	28	36	43	50	57	64
62	79239	79309	79379	79449	79518	79588	79657	79727	79796	79865	7	14	21	28	35	41	48	55	62
63	79934	80003	80072	80140	80209	80277	80346	80414	80482	80550	7	14	20	27	34	41	48	54	61
64	80618	80686	80754	80821	80889	80956	81023	81090	81158	81224	7	13	20	27	34	40	47	54	60
65	81291	81358	81425	81491	81558	81624	81690	81757	81823	81889	7	13	20	26	33	40	46	53	59
66	81954	82020	82086	82151	82217	82282	82347	82413	82478	82543	7	13	20	26	33	39	46	52	59
67	82607	82672	82737	82802	82866	82930	82995	83059	83123	83187	6	13	19	26	32	38	45	51	58
68	83251	83315	83378	83442	83506	83569	83632	83696	83759	83822	6	13	19	25	32	38	44	50	57
69	83885	83948	84011	84073	84136	84198	84261	84323	84386	84448	6	12	19	25	31	37	43	50	56
70	84510	84572	84634	84696	84757	84819	84880	84942	85003	85065	6	12	19	25	31	37	43	50	56
71	85126	85187	85248	85309	85370	85431	85491	85552	85612	85673	6	12	18	24	31	37	43	49	55
72	85733	85794	85854	85914	85974	86034	86094	86153	86213	86273	6	12	18	24	30	36	42	48	54
73	86332	86392	86451	86510	86570	86629	86688	86747	86806	86864	6	12	18	24	30	35	41	47	53
74	86923	86982	87040	87099	87157	87216	87274	87332	87390	87448	6	12	17	23	29	35	41	46	52
75	87506	87564	87622	87679	87737	87795	87852	87910	87967	88024	6	12	17	23	29	35	41	46	52
76	88081	88138	88195	88252	88309	88366	88423	88480	88536	88593	6	11	17	23	29	34	40	46	51
77	88649	88705	88762	88818	88874	88930	88986	89042	89098	89154	6	11	17	22	28	34	39	45	50
78	89209	89265	89321	89376	89432	89487	89542	89597	89653	89708	6	11	17	22	28	33	39	44	50
79	89763	89818	89873	89927	89982	90037	90091	90146	90200	90255	6	11	17	22	28	33	39	44	50
80	90309	90363	90417	90472	90526	90580	90634	90687	90741	90795	5	11	16	22	27	32	38	43	49
81	90848	90902	90956	91009	91062	91116	91169	91222	91275	91328	5	11	16	21	27	32	37	42	48
82	91381	91434	91487	91540	91593	91645	91698	91751	91803	91855	5	11	16	21	27	32	37	42	48
83	91908	91960	92012	92064	92117	92169	92221	92273	92324	92376	5	10	16	21	26	31	36	42	47
84	92428	92480	92531	92583	92634	92686	92737	92788	92840	92891	5	10	15	20	26	31	36	41	46
85	92942	92993	93044	93095	93146	93197	93247	93298	93349	93399	5	10	15	20	26	31	36	41	46
86	93450	93500	93551	93601	93651	93702	93752	93802	93852	93902	5	10	15	20	25	30	35	40	45
87	93952	94002	94052	94101	94151	94201	94250	94300	94349	94399	5	10	15	20	25	30	35	40	45
88	94448	94498	94547	94596	94645	94694	94743	94792	94841	94890	5	10	15	20	25	29	34	39	44
89	94939	94988	95036	95085	95134	95182	95231	95279	95328	95376	5	10	15	19	24	29	34	39	44
90	95424	95472	95521	95569	95617	95665	95713	95761	95809	95856	5	10	14	19	24	29	34	38	43
91	95904	95952	95999	96047	96095	96142	96190	96237	96284	96332	5	9	14	19	24	28	33	38	42
92	96379	96426	96473	96520	96567	96614	96661	96708	96755	96802	5	9	14	19	24	28	33	38	42
93	96848	96895	96942	96988	97035	97081	97128	97174	97220	97267	5	9	14	18	23	28	32	38	42
94	97313	97359	97405	97451	97497	97543	97589	97635	97681	97727	5	9	14	18	23	28	32	37	42
95	97772	97818	97864	97909	97955	98000	98046	98091	98137	98182	5	9	14	18	23	27	32	36	41
96	98227	98272	98318	98363	98408	98453	98498	98543	98588	98632	5	9	14	18	23	27	32	36	41
97	98677	98722	98767	98811	98856	98900	98945	98989	99034	99078	4	9	13	18	22	27	31	36	40
98	99123	99167	99211	99255	99300	99344	99388	99432	99476	99520	4	9	13	18	22	26	31	35	40
99	99564	99607	99651	99695	99739	99782	99826	99870	99913	99957	4	9	13	17	22	26	31	35	39

ANTILOGARITHMS

	0	1	2	3	4	5	6	7	8	9	Mean Differences 1	2	3	4	5	6	7	8	9
.00	10000	10023	10046	10069	10093	10116	10139	10162	10186	10209	2	5	7	9	12	14	16	19	21
.01	10233	10257	10280	10304	10328	10351	10375	10399	10423	10447	2	5	7	10	12	14	17	19	21
.02	10471	10495	10520	10544	10568	10593	10617	10641	10666	10691	2	5	7	10	12	15	17	20	22
.03	10715	10740	10765	10789	10814	10839	10864	10889	10914	10940	3	5	8	10	13	15	18	20	23
.04	10965	10990	11015	11041	11066	11092	11117	11143	11169	11194	3	5	8	10	13	15	18	20	23
.05	11220	11246	11272	11298	11324	11359	11376	11402	11429	11455	3	5	8	11	13	16	18	21	24
.06	11482	11508	11535	11561	11588	11614	11641	11668	11695	11722	3	5	8	11	13	16	19	21	24
.07	11749	11776	11803	11830	11858	11885	11912	11940	11967	11995	3	5	8	11	14	16	19	22	25
.08	12023	12050	12078	12106	12134	12162	12190	12218	12246	12274	3	6	8	11	14	17	20	22	25
.09	12303	12331	12359	12388	12417	12445	12474	12503	12531	12560	3	6	9	11	14	17	20	23	26
.10	12589	12618	12647	12677	12706	12735	12764	12794	12823	12853	3	6	9	12	15	18	21	24	26
.11	12882	12912	12942	12972	13002	13032	13062	13092	13122	13152	3	6	9	12	15	18	21	24	27
.12	13183	13213	13243	13274	13305	13335	13366	13397	13428	13459	3	6	9	12	15	18	21	25	28
.13	13490	13521	13552	13583	13614	13646	13677	13709	13740	13772	3	6	9	13	16	19	22	25	28
.14	13804	13836	13868	13900	13932	13964	13996	14028	14060	14093	3	6	10	13	16	19	22	26	29
.15	14125	14158	14191	14223	14256	14289	14322	14355	14388	14421	3	7	10	13	16	20	23	26	30
.16	14454	14488	14521	14555	14588	14622	14655	14689	14723	14757	3	7	10	13	17	20	24	27	30
.17	14791	14825	14859	14894	14928	14962	14997	15031	15066	15101	3	7	10	14	17	21	24	28	31
.18	15136	15171	15205	15241	15276	15311	15346	15382	15417	15453	4	7	11	14	18	21	25	28	32
.19	15488	15524	15560	15596	15631	15668	15704	15740	15776	15812	4	7	11	14	18	22	25	29	32
.20	15849	15885	15922	15959	15996	16032	16069	16106	16144	16181	4	7	11	15	18	22	26	30	33
.21	16218	16255	16293	16331	16368	16406	16444	16482	16520	16558	4	8	11	15	19	23	26	30	34
.22	16596	16634	16672	16711	16749	16788	16827	16866	16904	16943	4	8	12	15	19	23	27	31	35
.23	16982	17022	17061	17100	17140	17179	17219	17258	17298	17338	4	8	12	16	20	24	28	32	36
.24	17378	17418	17458	17498	17539	17579	17620	17660	17701	17742	4	8	12	16	20	24	28	32	36
.25	17783	17824	17865	17906	17947	17989	18030	18072	18113	18155	4	8	12	17	21	25	29	33	37
.26	18197	18239	18281	18323	18365	18408	18450	18493	18535	18578	4	8	13	17	21	25	30	34	38
.27	18621	18664	18707	18750	18793	18836	18880	18923	18967	19011	4	9	13	17	22	26	30	35	39
.28	19055	19099	19143	19187	19231	19275	19320	19364	19409	19454	4	9	13	18	22	26	31	35	40
.29	19498	19543	19588	19634	19679	19724	19770	19815	19861	19907	5	9	14	18	23	27	32	36	41
.30	19953	19999	20045	20091	20137	20184	20230	20277	20324	20370	5	9	14	19	23	28	32	37	42
.31	20417	20464	20512	20559	20606	20654	20701	20749	20797	20845	5	10	14	19	24	29	33	38	43
.32	20893	20941	20989	21038	21086	21135	21184	21232	21281	21330	5	10	15	19	24	29	34	39	44
.33	21380	21429	21478	21528	21577	21627	21677	21727	21777	21827	5	10	15	20	25	30	35	40	45
.34	21878	21928	21979	22029	22080	22131	22182	22233	22284	22336	5	10	15	20	25	31	36	41	46
.35	22387	22439	22491	22542	22594	22646	22699	22751	22803	22856	5	10	16	21	26	31	37	42	47
.36	22999	22961	23014	23067	23121	23174	23227	23281	23336	23388	5	11	16	21	27	32	37	43	48
.37	23442	23496	23550	23605	23659	23714	23768	23823	23878	23933	5	11	16	22	27	33	38	44	49
.38	23988	24044	24099	24155	24210	24266	24322	24378	24434	24491	6	11	17	22	28	34	39	45	50
.39	24547	24604	24660	24717	24774	24831	24889	24946	25003	25061	6	11	17	23	29	34	40	46	51
.40	25119	25177	25236	25293	25351	25410	25468	25527	25586	25645	6	12	18	23	29	35	41	47	53
.41	25704	25763	25823	25882	25942	26002	26062	26122	26182	26242	6	12	18	24	30	36	42	48	54
.42	26303	26363	26424	26485	26546	26607	26669	26730	26792	26853	6	12	18	24	31	37	43	49	55
.43	26915	26977	27040	27102	27164	27227	27290	27353	27416	27479	6	13	19	25	31	38	44	50	56
.44	27542	27606	27669	27733	27797	27861	27925	27990	28054	28119	6	13	19	26	32	39	45	51	58
.45	28184	28249	28314	28379	28445	28510	28576	28642	28708	28774	7	13	20	26	33	39	46	52	59
.46	28840	28907	28973	29040	29107	29174	29242	29309	29376	29444	7	13	20	27	34	40	47	54	60
.47	29512	29580	29648	29717	29785	29854	29923	29992	30061	30130	7	14	21	28	34	41	48	55	62
.48	30200	30269	30339	30409	30479	30549	30620	30690	30761	30832	7	14	21	28	35	42	49	56	63
.49	30903	30974	31046	31117	31189	31261	31333	31405	31477	31550	7	14	22	29	36	43	50	58	65

	0	1	2	3	4	5	6	7	8	9	Mean Differences								
											1	2	3	4	5	6	7	8	9
.50	31623	31696	31769	31842	31916	31989	32063	32137	32211	32285	7	15	22	29	37	44	52	59	66
.51	32359	32434	32509	32584	32659	32735	32809	32885	32961	33037	8	15	23	30	38	45	53	60	68
.52	33113	33189	33266	33343	33420	33497	33574	33651	33729	33806	8	15	23	31	39	46	54	62	69
.53	33884	33963	34041	34119	34198	34277	34356	34435	34514	34594	8	16	24	32	40	47	55	63	71
.54	34674	34754	34834	34914	34995	35075	35156	35237	35318	35400	8	16	24	32	40	48	56	65	73
.55	35481	35563	35645	35727	35810	35892	35975	36058	36141	36224	8	16	25	33	41	50	58	66	74
.56	36308	36392	36475	36559	36644	36728	36813	36898	36983	37068	8	17	25	34	42	51	59	68	76
.57	37154	37239	37325	37411	37497	37584	37670	37757	37844	37931	9	17	26	35	43	52	61	69	78
.58	38019	38107	38194	38282	38371	38459	38548	38637	38726	38815	9	18	27	35	44	53	62	71	80
.59	38905	38994	39084	39174	39264	39355	39446	39537	39628	39719	9	18	27	36	45	54	63	72	82
.60	39811	39902	39994	40087	40179	40272	40365	40458	40551	40644	9	19	28	37	46	56	65	74	83
.61	40738	40832	40926	41020	41115	41210	41305	41400	41495	41591	9	19	28	38	47	57	66	76	85
.62	41687	41783	41879	41976	42073	42170	42267	42364	42462	42560	10	19	29	39	49	58	68	78	87
.63	42658	42756	42855	42954	43053	43152	43251	43351	43451	43551	10	20	30	40	50	60	70	80	89
.64	43652	43752	43853	43954	44055	44157	44259	44361	44463	44566	10	20	30	41	51	61	71	81	91
.65	44668	44771	44875	44978	45082	45186	45290	45394	45499	45604	10	21	31	42	52	62	73	83	94
.66	45709	45814	45920	46026	46132	46238	46345	46452	46559	46666	11	21	32	43	53	64	75	85	96
.67	46774	46881	46989	47098	47206	47315	47424	47534	47643	47753	11	22	33	44	54	65	76	87	98
.68	47863	47973	48084	48195	48306	48417	48529	48641	48753	48865	11	22	33	45	56	67	78	89	100
.69	48978	49091	49204	49317	49431	49545	49659	49774	49888	50003	11	23	34	46	57	68	80	91	103
.70	50119	50234	50350	50466	50582	50699	50816	50933	51050	51168	12	23	35	47	58	70	82	93	105
.71	51286	51404	51523	51642	51761	51880	52000	52119	52240	52360	12	24	36	48	60	72	84	96	108
.72	52481	52602	52723	52845	52966	53088	53211	53333	53456	53580	12	24	37	49	61	73	85	98	110
.73	53703	53827	53951	54075	54200	54325	54450	54576	54702	54828	13	25	38	50	63	75	88	100	113
.74	54954	55081	55208	55336	55463	55590	55719	55847	55976	56105	13	26	38	51	64	77	90	102	115
.75	56234	56364	56494	56624	56754	56885	57016	57148	57280	57412	13	26	39	52	66	79	92	105	118
.76	57544	57677	57810	57943	58076	58210	58345	58479	58614	58749	13	27	40	54	67	80	94	107	121
.77	58884	59020	59156	59293	59429	59566	59704	59841	59979	60117	14	27	41	55	69	82	96	110	123
.78	60256	60395	60534	60674	60814	60954	61094	61235	61376	61518	14	28	42	56	70	84	98	112	126
.79	61659	61802	61944	62087	62230	62373	62517	62661	62806	62951	14	29	43	58	72	86	101	115	130
.80	63096	63241	63387	63533	63680	63826	63973	64121	64269	64417	15	29	44	59	74	88	103	118	132
.81	64565	64714	64863	65013	65163	65313	65464	65615	65766	65917	15	30	45	60	75	90	105	120	135
.82	66069	66222	66374	66527	66681	66834	66988	67143	67298	67453	15	31	46	62	77	92	108	123	139
.83	67608	67764	67920	68077	68234	68391	68549	68707	68865	69024	16	32	47	63	79	95	110	126	142
.84	69183	69343	69503	69663	69823	69984	70146	70307	70469	70632	16	32	48	64	81	97	113	129	145
.85	70795	70958	71121	71285	71450	71614	71779	71945	72111	72277	17	33	50	66	83	99	116	132	149
.86	72444	72611	72778	72946	73114	73282	73451	73621	73790	73961	17	34	51	68	85	101	118	135	152
.87	74131	74302	74473	74645	74817	74989	75162	75336	75509	75683	17	35	52	69	87	104	121	138	156
.88	75858	76033	76208	76384	76560	76736	76913	77090	77268	77446	18	35	53	71	89	107	125	142	159
.89	77625	77804	77983	78163	78343	78524	78705	78886	79068	79250	18	36	54	72	91	109	127	145	163
.90	79433	79616	79799	79983	80168	80353	80538	80724	80910	81096	19	37	56	74	93	111	130	148	167
.91	81283	81470	81658	81846	82035	82224	82414	82604	82794	82985	19	38	57	76	95	113	132	151	170
.92	83176	83368	83560	83753	83946	84140	84333	84528	84723	84918	19	39	58	78	97	116	136	155	175
.93	85114	85310	85507	85704	85901	86099	86298	86497	86696	86896	20	40	60	79	99	119	139	158	178
.94	87096	87297	87498	87700	87902	88105	88308	88512	88716	88920	20	41	61	81	102	122	142	162	183
.95	89125	89331	89536	89743	89950	90157	90365	90573	90782	90991	21	42	62	83	104	125	146	166	187
.96	91201	91411	91622	91833	92045	92257	92470	92683	92897	93111	21	42	64	85	106	127	149	170	191
.97	93325	93541	93756	93972	94189	94406	94624	94842	95060	95280	22	43	65	87	109	130	152	174	195
.98	95499	95719	95940	96161	96383	96605	96828	97051	97275	97499	22	44	67	89	111	133	155	178	200
.99	97724	97949	98175	98401	98628	98855	99083	99312	99541	99770	23	46	68	91	114	137	160	182	205

TABLE 1 AREAS UNDER THE STANDARD NORMAL CURVE $y = \frac{1}{\sqrt{2\pi}} e^{\frac{-z^2}{2}} (z > 0)$

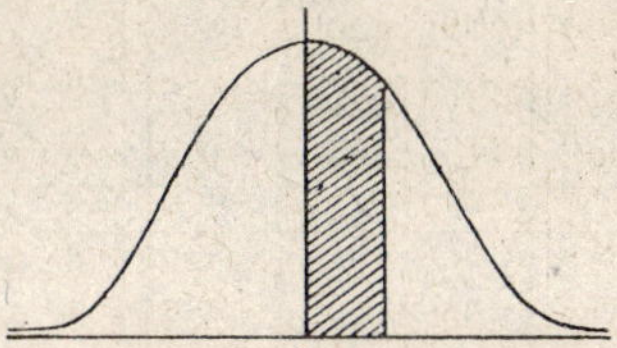

(Area Under the Standard Normal Curve from 0 to z)

z	0	1	2	3	4	5	6	7	8	9
0.0	.0000	.0040	.0080	.0120	.0160	.0199	.0239	.0279	.0319	.0359
0.1	.0398	.0438	.0478	.0517	.0557	.0596	.0636	.0675	.0714	.0754
0.2	.0793	.0832	.0871	.0910	.0948	.0987	.1026	.1064	.1103	.1141
0.3	.1179	.1217	.1255	.1293	.1331	.1368	.1406	.1443	.1480	.1517
0.4	.1554	.1591	.1628	.1664	.1700	.1736	.1772	.1808	.1844	.1879
0.5	.1915	.1950	.1985	.2019	.2054	.2088	.2123	.2157	.2190	.2224
0.6	.2258	.2291	.2324	.2357	.2389	.2422	.2454	.2486	.2518	.2549
0.7	.2580	.2612	.2642	.2673	.2704	.2734	.2764	.2794	.2823	.2852
0.8	.2881	.2910	.2939	.2967	.2996	.3023	.3051	.3078	.3106	.3133
0.9	.3159	.3186	.3212	.3238	.3264	.3289	.3315	.3340	.3365	.3389
1.0	.3413	.3438	.3461	.3485	.3508	.3531	.3554	.3577	.3599	.3621
1.1	.3643	.3665	.3686	.3708	.3729	.3749	.3770	.3790	.3810	.3830
1.2	.3849	.3869	.3888	.3907	.3925	.3944	.3962	.3980	.3997	.4015
1.3	.4032	.4049	.4066	.4082	.4099	.4115	.4131	.4147	.4162	.4177
1.4	.4192	.4207	.4222	.4236	.4251	.4265	.4279	.4292	.4306	.4319
1.5	.4332	.4345	.4357	.4370	.4382	.4394	.4406	.4418	.4429	.4441
1.6	.4452	.4463	.4474	.4484	.4495	.4505	.4515	.4525	.4535	.4545
1.7	.4554	.4564	.4573	.4582	.4591	.4599	.4608	.4616	.4625	.4633
1.8	.4641	.4649	.4656	.4664	.4671	.4678	.4686	.4693	.4699	.4706
1.9	.4713	.4719	.4726	.4732	.4738	.4744	.4750	.4756	.4761	.4767
2.0	.4772	.4778	.4783	.4788	.4793	.4798	.4803	.4808	.4812	.4817
2.1	.4821	.4826	.4830	.4834	.4838	.4842	.4846	.4850	.4854	.4857
2.2	.4861	.4864	.4868	.4871	.4875	.4878	.4881	.4884	.4887	.4890
2.3	.4893	.4896	.4898	.4901	.4904	4906	.4909	.4911	4913	.4916
2.4	.4918	.4920	.4922	.4925	.4927	.4929	.4931	.4932	.4934	.4936
2.5	.4938	.4940	.4941	.4943	.4945	.4946	.4948	.4949	.4951	.4952
2.6	.4953	.4955	4956	.4957	.4959	.4960	.4961	.4962	.4963	.4964
2.7	.4965	.4966	.4967	.4968	.4969	.4970	.4971	.4972	.4973	.4974
2.8	.4974	.4975	.4976	.4977	.4977	.4978	.4979	.4979	.4980	.4981
2.9	.4981	.4982	.4982	.4983	.4984	.4984	.4985	.4985	.4986	.4986
3.0	.4987	.4987	.4987	.4988	.4988	.4989	.4989	.4989	.4990	.4490
3.1	.4990	.4991	.4991	.4991	.4992	.4992	.4992	.4992	.4993	.4993
3.2	.4993	.4993	.4994	.4994	.4994	4994	.4994	.4995	.4995	.4995
3.3	.4995	.4995	.4995	.4996	.4996	.4996	.4996	.4996	.4996	.4997
3.4	4997	.4997	.4997	.4997	.4997	.4997	.4997	.4997	.4997	.4998
3.5	.4998	.4998	.4998	.4998	.4998	.4998	.4998	.4998	.4998	.4998
3.6	.4998	.4998	.4999	.4999	.4999	.4999	.4999	.4999	.4999	.4999
3.7	.4999	.4999	.4999	.4999	.4999	.4999	.4999	.4999	.4999	.4999
3.8	.4999	.4999	.4999	.4999	.4999	.4999	.4999	.4999	.4999	.4999
3.9	.5000	.5000	.5000	.5000	.5000	.5000	.5000	.5000	.5000	.5000

TABLE 2 VALUES OF e^{-m}

m	e^{-m}	m	e^{-m}	m	e^{-m}
0.0	1.0000	1.5	0.2231	3.0	0.0498
0.1	0.9048	1.6	.2019	3.2	.0408
0.2	.8187	1.7	.1827	3.4	.0334
0.3	.7408	1.8	.1653	3.6	.0273
0.4	.6703	1.9	.1497	3.8	.0224
0.5	.6065	2.0	.1353	4.0	.0183
0.6	.5488	2.1	.1225	4.2	.0150
0.7	.4966	2.2	.1108	4.4	.0123
0.8	.4493	2.3	.1003	4.6	.0100
0.9	.4066	2.4	.0907	4.8	.00823
1.0	.3679	2.5	.0821	5.0	.00674
1.1	.3329	2.6	.0743	5.5	.00409
1.2	.3012	2.7	.0672	6.0	.00248
1.3	.2725	2.8	.0608	6.5	.00150
1.4	.2466	2.9	.0550	7.0	.00091

TABLE 3 RANDOM NUMBERS

51772	74640	42331	29044	46621	62898	93582	04186	19640	87056
24033	23491	83587	06568	21960	21387	76105	10863	97453	90581
45939	60173	52078	25424	11645	55870	56974	37428	93507	94271
30586	02133	75797	45406	31041	86707	12973	17169	88116	42187
03585	79353	81938	82322	96799	85659	36081	50884	14070	74950
64937	03355	95863	20790	65304	55189	00745	65253	11822	15804
15630	64759	51135	98527	62586	41889	25439	88036	24034	67283
09448	56301	57683	30277	94623	85418	68829	06652	41982	49159
21631	91157	77331	60710	52290	16835	48653	71590	16159	14676
91097	17480	29414	06829	87843	28195	27279	47152	35683	47280
50532	25496	95652	42457	73547	76552	50020	24819	52984	76168
07136	40876	79971	54195	25708	51817	36732	72484	94923	75936
27989	64728	10744	08396	56242	90985	28868	99431	50995	20507
85184	73949	36601	46253	00477	25234	09908	36574	72139	70185
54398	21154	97810	36764	32869	11785	55261	59009	38714	38723
65544	34371	09591	07839	58892	92843	72828	91341	84821	63886
08263	65952	85762	64236	39238	18776	84303	99247	46149	03229
39817	67906	48236	16057	81812	15815	63700	85915	19219	45943
62257	04077	79443	95203	02479	30763	92486	54083	23631	05825
53298	90276	62545	21944	16530	03878	07516	95715	02526	33537

TABLE 4 SIGNIFICANT VALUES OF t-DISTRIBUTION

Values of t for given probabilities P i.e., Table Values of t

Here P = Prob. $(t > t_\alpha)$ or Prob. $(t < -t_\alpha)$.

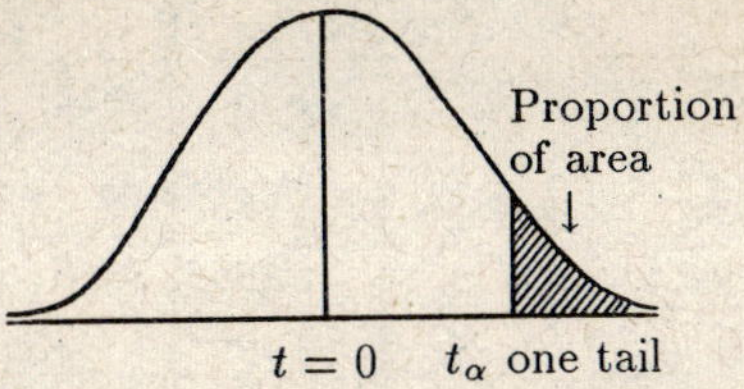

d.f.(ν) \ Prob.(P)	.10	.05	.025	.01	.005
1	3.078	6.314	12.706	31.821	63.657
2	1.886	2.920	4.303	6.965	9.925
3	1.638	2.353	3.182	4.541	5.841
4	1.533	2.132	2.776	3.747	4.604
5	1.476	2.015	2.571	3.365	4.032
6	1.440	1.943	2.447	3.143	3.707
7	1.415	1.895	2.365	2.998	3.499
8	1.397	1.860	2.306	2.896	3.355
9	1.383	1.833	2.262	2.821	3.250
10	1.372	1.812	2.228	2.764	3.169
11	1.363	1.796	2.201	2.718	3.106
12	1.356	1.782	2.179	2.681	3.055
13	1.350	1.771	2.160	2.650	3.012
14	1.345	1.761	2.145	2.624	2.977
15	1.341	1.753	2.131	2.602	2.947
16	1.337	1.746	2.120	2.583	2.921
17	1.333	1.740	2.110	2.567	2.898
18	1.330	1.734	2.101	2.552	2.878
19	1.328	1.729	2.093	2.539	2.861
20	1.325	1.725	2.086	2.528	2.845
21	1.323	1.721	2.080	2.518	2.831
22	1.321	1.717	2.074	2.508	2.819
23	1.319	1.714	2.069	2.500	2.807
24	1.318	1.711	2.064	2.492	2.797
25	1.316	1.708	2.060	2.485	2.787
26	1.315	1.706	2.056	2.479	2.779
27	1.314	1.703	2.052	2.473	2.771
28	1.313	1.701	2.048	2.467	2.763
29	1.311	1.699	2.045	2.462	2.756
30	1.310	1.697	2.042	2.457	2.750
40	1.303	1.684	2.021	2.423	2.704
60	1.296	1671	2.000	2.390	2.660
120	1.289	1.658	1.980	2.358	2.617
∞	1.282	1.645	1.960	2.326	2.576

NOTE. The above table gives the values of t for one-tail test (either left-tail or right-tail test). If we have to find the value of t for a two-tail test at α level, we take the value of $\alpha/2$ for α. For example, the value of t at 5% level with 9 d.f. is $t_{.025} = 2.262$ and the value of t at 1% level with 11. d.f. is $t_{.005} = 3.106$.

TABLE 5 SIGNIFICANT VALUES OF χ^2

Values of χ^2 for given probabilities P, i.e., Table Values of χ^2

Here $P = \text{Prob. } (\chi^2 > \chi^2_\alpha)$.

Prob.(P) / d.f.	Probability (Proportion of Area)								
	0.990	0.950	0.900	0.500	0.100	0.050	0.025	0.010	0.005
1	0.00016	0.00393	0.0158	0.455	2.71	3.84	5.02	6.63	7.88
2	0.0201	0.103	0.211	1.386	4.61	5.99	7.38	9.21	10.60
3	0.115	0.352	0.584	2.366	6.25	7.81	9.35	11.34	12.84
4	0.297	0.711	1.064	3.357	7.78	9.49	11.14	13.28	14.86
5	0.554	1.145	1.61	4.251	9.24	11.07	12.83	15.09	16.75
6	0.872	1.64	2.20	5.35	10.64	12.59	14.45	16.81	18.55
7	1.24	2.17	2.83	6.35	12.02	14.07	16.01	18.48	20.28
8	1.65	2.73	3.49	7.34	13.36	15.51	17.53	20.09	21.96
9	2.09	3.33	4.17	8.34	14.68	16.92	19.02	21.67	23.59
10	2.56	3.94	4.87	9.34	15.99	18.31	20.48	23.21	25.19
11	3.05	4.57	5.58	10.34	17.28	19.68	21.92	24.73	26.76
12	3.57	5.23	6.30	11.34	18.55	21.03	23.34	26.22	28.30
13	4.11	5.89	7.04	12.34	19.81	22.36	24.74	27.69	29.82
14	4.66	6.57	7.79	13.34	21.06	23.68	26.12	29.14	31.32
15	5.23	7.26	8.55	14.34	22.31	25.00	27.49	30.58	32.80
16	5.81	7.96	9.31	15.34	23.54	26.30	28.85	32.00	34.27
17	6.41	8.67	10.09	16.34	24.77	27.59	30.19	33.41	35.72
18	7.01	9.39	10.86	17.34	25.99	28.87	31.53	34.81	37.16
19	7.63	10.12	11.65	18.34	27.20	30.14	32.85	36.19	38.58
20	8.26	10.85	12.44	19.34	28.41	31.41	34.17	37.57	40.00
21	8.90	11.59	13.24	20.34	29.62	32.67	35.48	38.93	41.40
22	9.54	12.34	14.04	21.34	30.81	33.92	36.78	40.29	42.80
23	10.20	13.09	14.85	22.34	32.01	35.17	38.08	41.64	44.18
24	10.86	13.85	15.66	23.34	33.20	36.42	39.36	42.98	45.56
25	11.52	14.61	16.47	24.34	34.38	37.65	40.65	44.31	46.93
26	12.20	15.38	17.29	25.34	35.56	38.89	41.92	45.64	48.29
27	12.83	16.15	18.11	26.34	36.74	40.11	43.19	46.96	49.64
28	13.56	16.93	18.94	27.34	37.92	41.34	44.46	48.28	50.99
29	14.26	17.71	19.77	28.34	39.09	42.56	45.72	49.59	52.34
30	14.95	18.49	20.60	29.34	40.26	43.77	46.98	50.89	53.67
40	22.16	26.51	29.05	39.34	51.81	55.76	59.34	63.69	66.77
50	29.71	34.76	37.69	49.33	63.17	67.50	71.42	76.15	79.49
60	37.43	43.19	46.46	59.33	74.40	79.08	83.30	88.38	91.95
70	45.44	51.74	55.33	69.33	85.53	90.53	95.02	100.4	104.2
80	53.54	60.39	64.28	79.33	98.58	101.9	106.6	112.3	116.3
90	61.75	69.13	73.29	89.33	107.6	113.1	118.1	124.1	128.3
100	70.06	77.93	82.36	99.33	118.5	124.3	129.6	135.8	140.2

TABLE 6 SIGNIFICANT VALUES OF F at 5% LEVEL

Degrees of freedom ($d.f.$) for numerator

	1	2	3	4	5	6	7	8	9	10	12	15	20	24	30	40	60	120	∞
1	161	200	216	225	230	234	237	239	241	242	244	246	248	249	250	251	252	253	254
2	18.5	19.0	19.2	19.2	19.3	19.3	19.4	19.4	19.4	19.4	19.4	19.4	19.4	19.5	19.5	19.5	19.5	19.5	19.5
3	10.1	9.55	9.28	9.12	9.01	8.94	8.89	8.85	8.81	8.79	8.74	8.70	8.66	8.64	8.62	8.59	8.57	8.55	8.53
4	7.71	6.94	6.59	6.39	6.26	6.16	6.09	6.04	6.00	5.96	5.91	5.86	5.80	5.77	5.75	5.72	5.69	5.66	5.63
5	6.61	5.79	5.41	5.19	5.05	4.95	4.88	4.82	4.77	4.74	4.68	4.62	4.56	4.53	4.50	4.46	4.43	4.40	4.37
6	5.99	5.14	4.76	4.53	4.39	4.28	4.21	4.15	4.10	4.06	4.00	3.94	3.87	3.84	3.81	3.77	3.74	3.70	3.67
7	5.59	4.74	4.35	4.12	3.97	3.87	3.79	3.73	3.68	3.64	3.57	3.51	3.44	3.41	3.38	3.34	3.30	3.27	3.23
8	5.32	4.46	4.07	3.84	3.69	3.58	3.50	3.44	3.39	3.35	3.28	3.22	3.15	3.12	3.08	3.04	3.01	2.97	2.93
9	5.12	4.26	3.86	3.63	3.48	3.37	3.29	3.23	3.18	3.14	3.07	3.01	2.94	2.90	2.86	2.83	2.79	2.75	2.71
10	4.96	4.10	3.71	3.48	3.33	3.22	3.14	3.07	3.02	2.98	2.91	2.85	2.77	2.74	2.70	2.66	2.62	2.58	2.54
11	4.84	3.98	3.59	3.36	3.20	3.09	3.01	2.95	2.90	2.85	2.79	2.72	2.65	2.61	2.57	2.53	2.49	2.45	2.40
12	4.75	3.89	3.49	3.26	3.11	3.00	2.91	2.85	2.80	2.75	2.69	2.62	2.54	2.51	2.47	2.43	2.38	2.34	2.30
13	4.67	3.81	3.41	3.18	3.03	2.92	2.83	2.77	2.71	2.67	2.60	2.53	2.46	2.42	2.38	2.34	2.30	2.25	2.21
14	4.60	3.74	3.34	3.11	2.96	2.85	2.76	2.70	2.65	2.60	2.53	2.46	2.39	2.35	2.31	2.27	2.22	2.18	2.13
15	4.54	3.68	3.29	3.06	2.90	2.79	2.71	2.64	2.59	2.54	2.48	2.40	2.33	2.29	2.25	2.20	2.16	2.11	2.07
16	4.49	3.63	3.24	3.01	2.85	2.74	2.66	2.59	2.54	2.49	2.42	2.35	2.28	2.24	2.19	2.15	2.11	2.06	2.01
17	4.45	3.59	3.20	2.96	2.81	2.70	2.61	2.55	2.49	2.45	2.38	2.31	2.23	2.19	2.15	2.10	2.06	2.01	2.96
18	4.41	3.55	3.16	2.93	2.77	2.66	2.58	2.51	2.46	2.41	2.34	2.27	2.19	2.15	2.11	2.06	2.02	1.97	1.92
19	4.38	3.52	3.13	2.90	2.74	2.63	2.54	2.48	2.42	2.38	2.31	2.23	2.16	2.11	2.07	2.03	1.98	1.93	1.88
20	4.35	3.49	3.10	2.87	2.71	2.60	2.51	2.45	2.39	2.35	2.28	2.20	2.12	2.08	2.04	1.99	1.95	1.90	1.84
21	4.32	3.47	3.07	2.84	2.68	2.57	2.49	2.42	2.37	2.32	2.25	2.18	2.10	2.05	2.01	1.96	1.92	1.87	1.81
22	4.30	3.44	3.05	2.82	2.66	2.55	2.46	2.40	2.34	2.30	2.23	2.15	2.07	2.03	1.98	1.94	1.89	1.84	1.78
23	4.28	3.42	3.03	2.80	2.64	2.53	2.44	2.37	2.32	2.27	2.20	2.13	2.05	2.01	1.96	1.91	1.86	1.81	1.76
24	4.26	3.40	3.01	2.78	2.62	2.51	2.42	2.36	2.30	2.25	2.18	2.11	2.03	1.98	1.94	1.89	1.84	1.79	1.73
25	4.24	3.39	2.99	2.76	2.60	2.49	2.40	2.34	2.28	2.24	2.16	2.09	2.01	1.96	1.92	1.87	1.82	1.77	1.71
30	4.17	3.32	2.92	2.69	2.53	2.42	2.33	2.27	2.21	2.16	2.09	2.01	1.93	1.89	1.84	1.79	1.74	1.68	1.62
40	4.08	3.23	2.84	2.61	2.45	2.34	2.25	2.18	2.12	2.08	2.00	1.92	1.84	1.79	1.74	1.69	1.64	1.58	1.51
60	4.00	3.15	2.76	2.53	2.37	2.25	2.17	2.10	2.04	1.99	1.92	1.84	1.75	1.70	165	1.59	1.53	.147	1.39
120	3.92	3.07	2.68	2.45	2.29	2.18	2.09	2.02	1.96	1.91	1.83	1.75	1.66	1.61	1.55	1.50	1.43	1.35	1.25
∞	3.84	3.00	2.60	2.37	2.21	2.10	2.01	1.94	1.88	1.83	1.75	1.67	1.57	1.52	1.46	1.39	1.32	1.20	1.00

Degrees of freedom (d.f.) for denominator

TABLE 6 (Contd.) SIGNIFICANT VALUES OF F at 1% LEVEL

Degrees of freedom (*d.f.*) for numerator

	1	2	3	4	5	6	7	8	9	10	12	15	20	24	30	40	60	120	∞
1	4,052	5,000	5,403	5,625	5,764	5,859	5,928	5,982	6,023	6,056	6,106	6,157	6,209	6,235	6,261	6,287	6,313	6,339	6,366
2	98.5	99.0	99.2	99.2	99.3	99.3	99.4	99.4	99.4	99.4	99.4	99.4	99.4	99.5	99.5	99.5	99.5	99.5	99.5
3	34.1	30.8	29.5	28.7	28.2	27.9	27.7	27.5	27.3	27.2	27.1	26.9	26.7	26.6	26.5	26.4	26.3	26.2	26.1
4	21.2	18.0	16.7	16.0	15.5	15.2	15.0	14.8	14.7	14.5	14.4	14.2	14.0	13.9	13.8	13.7	13.7	13.6	13.5
5	16.3	13.3	12.1	11.4	11.0	10.7	10.5	10.3	10.2	10.1	9.89	9.72	9.55	9.47	9.38	9.29	9.20	9.11	9.02
6	13.7	10.9	9.78	9.15	8.75	8.47	8.26	8.10	7.98	7.87	7.72	7.56	7.40	7.31	7.23	7.14	7.06	6.97	6.88
7	12.2	9.55	8.45	7.85	7.46	7.19	6.99	6.84	6.72	6.62	6.47	6.31	6.16	6.07	5.99	5.91	5.82	5.74	5.65
8	11.3	8.65	7.59	7.01	6.63	6.37	6.18	6.03	5.91	5.81	5.67	5.52	5.36	5.28	5.20	5.12	5.03	4.95	4.86
9	10.6	8.02	6.99	6.42	6.06	5.80	5.61	5.47	5.35	5.26	5.11	4.96	4.81	4.73	4.65	4.57	4.48	4.40	4.31
10	10.0	7.56	6.55	5.99	5.64	5.39	5.20	5.06	4.94	4.85	4.71	4.56	4.41	4.33	4.25	4.17	4.08	4.00	3.91
11	9.65	7.21	6.22	5.67	5.32	5.07	5.89	4.74	4.63	4.54	4.40	4.25	4.10	4.02	3.94	3.86	3.78	3.69	3.60
12	9.33	6.93	5.95	5.41	5.06	4.82	4.64	4.50	4.39	4.30	4.16	4.01	3.86	3.78	3.70	3.62	3.54	3.45	3.36
13	9.07	6.70	5.74	5.21	4.86	4.62	4.44	4.30	4.19	4.10	3.96	3.82	3.66	3.59	3.51	3.43	3.34	3.25	3.17
14	8.86	6.51	5.56	5.04	4.70	4.46	4.28	4.14	4.03	3.94	3.80	3.66	3.51	3.43	3.35	3.27	3.18	3.09	3.00
15	8.68	6.36	5.42	4.89	4.56	4.32	4.14	4.00	3.89	3.80	3.67	3.52	3.37	3.29	3.21	3.13	3.05	2.96	2.87
16	8.53	6.23	5.29	4.77	4.44	4.20	4.03	3.89	3.78	3.69	3.55	3.41	3.26	3.18	3.10	3.02	2.93	2.84	2.75
17	8.40	6.11	5.19	4.67	4.34	4.10	3.93	3.79	3.68	3.59	3.46	3.31	3.16	3.08	3.00	2.92	2.83	2.75	2.65
18	8.29	6.01	5.09	4.58	4.25	4.01	3.84	3.71	3.60	3.51	3.37	3.23	3.08	3.00	2.92	2.84	2.75	2.66	2.57
19	8.19	5.93	5.01	4.50	4.17	3.94	3.77	3.63	3.52	3.43	3.30	3.15	3.00	2.92	2.84	2.76	2.67	2.58	2.49
20	8.10	5.85	4.94	4.43	4.10	3.87	3.70	3.56	3.46	3.37	3.23	3.09	2.94	2.86	2.78	2.69	2.61	2.52	2.42
21	8.02	5.78	4.87	4.37	4.04	3.81	3.64	3.51	3.40	3.31	3.17	3.03	2.88	2.80	2.72	2.64	2.55	2.46	2.36
22	7.95	5.72	4.82	4.31	3.99	3.76	3.59	3.45	3.35	3.26	3.12	2.98	2.83	2.75	2.67	2.58	2.50	2.40	2.31
23	7.88	5.66	4.76	4.26	3.94	3.71	3.54	3.41	3.30	3.21	3.07	2.93	2.78	2.70	2.62	2.54	2.45	2.35	2.26
24	7.82	5.61	4.72	4.22	3.90	3.67	3.50	3.36	3.26	3.17	3.03	3.89	2.74	2.66	2.58	2.49	2.40	2.31	2.21
25	7.77	5.57	4.68	4.18	3.86	3.63	3.46	3.32	3.22	3.13	2.99	2.85	2.70	2.62	2.53	2.45	2.36	2.27	2.17
30	7.56	5.39	4.51	4.02	3.70	3.47	3.30	3.17	3.07	2.98	2.84	2.70	2.55	2.47	2.39	2.30	2.21	2.11	2.01
40	7.31	5.18	4.31	3.83	3.51	3.29	3.12	2.99	2.89	2.80	2.66	2.52	2.37	2.29	2.20	2.11	2.02	1.92	1.80
60	7.08	4.98	4.13	3.65	3.34	3.12	2.95	2.82	2.72	2.63	2.50	2.35	2.20	2.12	2.03	1.94	1.84	1.73	1.60
120	6.85	4.79	3.95	3.48	3.17	2.96	2.79	2.66	2.56	2.47	2.34	2.19	2.03	1.95	1.86	1.76	1.66	1.53	1.38
∞	6.63	4.61	3.78	3.32	3.02	2.80	2.64	2.51	2.41	2.32	2.18	2.04	1.88	1.79	1.70	1.59	1.47	1.32	1.00

Degrees of freedom (d.f.) for denominator

INDEX

Part I: Mathematical Techniques

Part II: Statistical Techniques

Part III: Economic Techniques

59

I.C.W.A.I (Inter)

December 1994

Quantitative Methods **Full Marks : 100**

Answer Question No. 1 *which is compulsory and* any two *from each of Section* 1 *and* 2, *and* any one *from Section* 3

1. (a) If $A = \begin{bmatrix} 1 & 2 & 3 \\ 2 & 4 & 6 \\ 3 & 6 & 9 \end{bmatrix}$ and $B = \begin{bmatrix} -1 & -2 & -4 \\ -1 & -2 & -4 \\ 1 & 2 & 4 \end{bmatrix}$, find AB.

[**Hints.** See worked out Ex. 15 on page 46] $\left[\textbf{Ans.} \begin{bmatrix} 0 & 0 & 0 \\ 0 & 0 & 0 \\ 0 & 0 & 0 \end{bmatrix}\right]$

(b) Find the following limit: $\lim_{x\to 0} \left(\frac{a^x - 1}{x}\right)$. [**Ans.** $\log_e a$]

[**Hints.** $a^x = 1 + x\log_e a + \frac{x^2}{\underline{|2}}(\log_e a)^2 + \cdots$. Put this series for a^x and evaluate the limit. See also page 167 (Calculus)]

(c) The following table gives all samples of same size, drawn from a population according to criteria for testing the null hypothesis H_o.

	H_o true	H_o false	Total
Reject H_o	5	145	150
Accept H_o	90	10	100
Total	95	155	250

Find (i) level of significance; (ii) Power of the test; (iii) critical region.

[**Ans.** (i) 0.02; (ii) 0.96; (iii) region of 150 samples.]

[**Hints.** (i) Level of significance = (No. of samples of same size indicating rejection of H_o when H_o is true.) : (Total no. of samples) = 5: 250. (ii) Power of the test = 1− Prob. of Type II error $= 1 - \frac{10}{250}$ = etc. (iii) Critical region = No. of samples indicating rejection of H_o when H_o is true or false = 150. See also art 4.6.2.]

(d) A pair of dice is tossed together. What is the probability that the sum of points on the two dice is (i) 6? (ii) more than 8?

[**Hints.** See worked out Ex. 5 on page 18.] [**Ans.** (i) 5/36; (ii) 5/18]

(e) Total cost function of a manufacturing firm is given by $C = 2x^3 - x^2 + 3x + 5$ and the marginal revenue $= 8 - 3x$ where x = output. Determine the most profitable output of the firm.

[**Ans.** 5/6]

[**Solution.** Total Profit = Total Revenue − Total Cost

$$\text{or,} \quad P = R - C \tag{1}$$

where P = Total Profit, R = Total Revenue and C = Total Cost.

By differentiating (1), we get

$$\frac{dP}{dx} = \frac{dR}{dx} - \frac{dC}{dx} \qquad \left[\begin{array}{l} \text{where } \frac{dR}{dx} = \text{Marginal Revenue} \\ \qquad\quad = 8 - 3x \text{ (given)} \end{array}\right]$$

Profit will be maximum where $\frac{dP}{dx} = 0$ and $\frac{d^2P}{dx^2} < 0$

$$\therefore \quad \frac{dR}{dx} - \frac{dC}{dx} = 0$$

or, $(8-3x) - \frac{d}{dx}(2x^3 - x^2 + 3x + 5) = 0$

or, $(8-3x) - (6x^2 - 2x + 3) = 0$

or, $-6x^2 - x + 5 = 0$

or, $6x^2 + x - 5 = 0$

or, $(6x-5)(x+1) = 0$

$\therefore \quad x = -1, \frac{5}{6}.$

Since output (i.e., x) cannot be negative, $x = \frac{5}{6}$.

Now

$$\frac{d^2P}{dx^2} = \frac{d}{dx}[(8-3x) - (6x^2 - 2x + 3)]$$
$$= -3 - 12x + 2 = -1 - 12x$$
$$= -1 - 12 \times \frac{5}{6} = -1$$

Thus, $\frac{d^2P}{dx^2} < 0$; $\therefore$ Profit will be maximum where output $(x) = \frac{5}{6}$.]

Section 1

2. (a) Solve the following simultaneous equations by using inverse matrix:

$$2x - 3y + z = 4$$
$$x - y + z = 6$$
$$3x + 4y - z = 19.$$

[**Hints.** See worked out Ex. 6 on page 92.] [**Ans.** $x = 4, y = 3, z = 5$]

(b) Draw the graph of the function: $y = x|x|, -\infty \leq x \leq \infty$.

[**Hints.** $|x| = x$, if $x > 0$, $= 0$ if $x = 0$, $= -x$ if $x < 0$. $\therefore$ $y = x^2$ if $x > 0$, $= 0$ if $x = 0$, $= -x^2$ if $x < 0$.]

(c) Prove that $\begin{vmatrix} 1 & x & x^2 \\ 1 & y & y^2 \\ 1 & z & z^2 \end{vmatrix} = (x-y)(y-z)(z-x)$.

[**Hints.** See worked out Ex. 14 on page 69.]

3. (a) Find the extreme value of the function: $f(x, y) = x^2 - y^2 + xy + 5x$ subject to $x + y + 3 = 0$.

[**Ans.** Max. value $= -5$]

[**Hints.** If $z = f(x, y)$, then $z = x^2 - (x+3)^2 + x(-x-3) + 5x \cdots\cdots (1)$

[Since $x + y + 3 = 0$; $\therefore$ $y = -x - 3$ and $y^2 = (x+3)^2$]

$\therefore$ $\frac{dz}{dx} = -2x - 4$ and $\frac{d^2z}{dx^2} = -2$. For extreme value of z, we must have $\frac{dz}{dx} = 0$ and $\frac{d^2z}{dx^2} < 0$, etc.]

(b) If $f(x, y) = x^2 - 3xy + y^2$, then prove that $\frac{\partial f}{\partial x} - \frac{\partial f}{\partial y} = (x - y)\left(\frac{\partial^2 f}{\partial x^2} - \frac{\partial^2 f}{\partial x \partial y}\right)$.

[**Hints.** See worked out Ex. 3 on page 207.]

(c) Evaluate $\int \frac{1-x}{\sqrt{1+x}} dx$. [**Ans.** $4\sqrt{1+x} - \frac{2}{3}(1+x)^{3/2} + C$]

[**Hints.** Put $1+x = z^2$; then $dx = 2zdz$ and $-x = 1 - z^2$]

4. (a) Solve the following linear programming problem by using simplex method:

$$\begin{aligned} \text{Maximize} \quad & z = 4x + 2y, \\ \text{subject to} \quad & x + 2y \le 15, \\ & 2x - y \le 5, \\ & x, \ y \ge 0. \end{aligned}$$

[**Ans.** 30]

[**Hints.** See worked out Ex. 1 on page 322.]

(b) For the function $f(x) = x + \frac{1}{x}$, show that its minimum value is greater than its maximum value.

[**Hints.** If $f(x) = x + \frac{1}{x}$, then $f'(x) = 1 - \frac{1}{x^2}$ and $f''(x) = \frac{2}{x^3}$. For extreme values of $f(x)$, we must have $f'(x) = 0$, or, $1 - \frac{1}{x^2} = 0$, or, $x = \pm 1$. At $x = 1$, $f''(1) = 2 > 0$ and at $x = -1$. $f''(-1) = -2 < 0$, etc.]

(c) Find the area bounded by the curve $xy = 2$, the x-axis and the ordinates at $x = 2$ and $x = 10$.

[**Hints.** Reqd. area $= \int_a^b y\, dx = \int_2^{10} \frac{2}{x} dx =$ etc.] [**Ans.** $2 \log_e 5$ sq. units]

Section 2

5. (a) From the past experience a stock broker finds that 70% of the telephone calls he receives during the business hours, are orders and the remaining are for other business. What is the probability that out of first 8 telephone calls during a day: (i) exactly 5 calls are order calls? (ii) at least 6 are order calls?

[**Hints.** See worked out Ex. 9 on page 64.] [**Ans.** (i) 0.254; (ii) 0.3516]

(b) Number of items produced by 3 machines A, B and C are 300, 200 and 500 respectively. Draw a proportional stratified sample of size 20 using the following random numbers starting from first row:

41206	53802	76310	94283	11245
12638	91165	19152	11143	12583
39276	05284	00135	28105	90312
11390	02487	03001	89001	66530

[**Hints.** The no. of items produced by A, B, C are in the proportion $300 : 200 : 500 = 3 : 2 : 5$. $\therefore$ The sizes of the samples to be drawn from A, B and C are respectively $\frac{3}{10} \times 20$, $\frac{2}{10} \times 20$, $\frac{5}{10} \times 20$ i.e., 6, 4, 10. As number of items produced by each of A, B, C consists of 3 digits, we select 3 consecutive digits from the given random numbers starting from the first and proceeding in a row. Thus sample of size 6 from A consists of random numbers of 3 digits less than 300 and is given by 065, 380, 276, 124, 211, 143, 125. [$\because$ other numbers are greater than 300]. Similarly, a sample of size 4 from machine B consists of numbers 001, 113, 016, 041 (omitting numbers less than 200 and coming back to the first row), and a sample of size 10, from machine C consists of numbers 206, 027, 094, 283, 112, 451, 263, 165, 191, 114.]

(c) A random sample of 100 patients suffering from a certain disease, was given a syrum treatment. It was observed that 75 patients were relieved of the disease. Find 95% confidence limits for the percentage of patients cured. [**Ans.** 66.5 and 83.5]

[**Hints.** See II on page 838. Here $p = 0.75, q = 1 - 0.75 = 0.25$, S.E. of $p = \sqrt{\frac{pq}{n}}$].

6. (a) A municipal corporation puts 10,000 light bulbs on the streets in a city. If lives of bulbs follow a normal distribution with a mean of 60 days and a standard deviation of 20 days, how many bulbs will have to be replaced after (i) 20 days? (ii) 35 days? (iii) 75 days?

[Given: $z = 0.75 \quad 1.25 \quad 2.00$

Area $= 0.2734 \quad 0.3944 \quad 0.4772$]

[**Hints.** See worked out Ex. 7 on page 513.] [**Ans.** (i) 228; (ii) 1056]

(b) Suppose that there is a chance for a newly constructed flyover to collapse whether the design is faulty or not. The chance that the design is faulty is 5%. The chance that the flyover collapses if the design is faulty is 95%, otherwise it is 30%. A flyover collapsed. What is the probability that it collapsed because of faulty design?

[**Hints.** Use Bayes' theorem.] [**Ans.** $\frac{1}{7}$]

(c) The following table gives daily demand (x) for hot plates in 200 days:

$x =$	0	1	2	3	4	5
No. of days $=$	28	32	36	46	38	20

Determine the demand on each of 10 days by simulating for 10 days. Use random numbers in Q. 5(b). [**Ans.** $2, 1, 3, 2, 0, 4, 2, 0, 2, 4$]

7. (a) The two regression lines are given by $3x + 2y = 6$, and $7x + 5y = 12$.

(i) Estimate y when $x = 10$.

(ii) Calculate the correlation coefficient value between x and y.

(iii) What percentage of total variation remains unexplained by the regression equation of y on x? [**Ans.** (i) -11.6; (ii) -0.966; (iii) $6\frac{2}{3}\%$]

(b) A certain drug administered to 10 patients showed the additional hours of sleep: -1.0, 0.5, 2.7, -0.6, 1.2, 1.8, 1.6, 3.5, 0.2, -1.7. Can it be concluded that the drug does produce additional hours of sleep?

[Given: $t_{.025} = 2.262 \quad 2.228$

d.f. $= 9 \quad 10$]

[**Hints.** See worked out Ex. 7 on page 154.] [**Ans.** No.]

(c) A Bombay film director claims that his films are liked equally by males and females. An opinion survey of a random sample of 1000 film-goers revealed the following results:

	Liked	Disliked
Males	402	193
Females	245	160

Is the film director's claim supported by the data?

[Given: $\chi^2_{.05} = 3.8 \quad 5.99 \quad 7.81$

d.f. $= 1 \quad 2 \quad 3$]

[**Hints.** See worked out Ex. 12 on page 161.] [**Ans.** No, since $\chi^2 = 5.27 > 3.8$]

Section 3

8. (a) Demand functions for two commodities are $x_1 = p_1^{-0.8} p_2^{1.2}$ $x_2 = p_1^{0.2}\ p_2^{-1.6}$ where p_1, p_2 and x_1, x_2 are prices and quantities demanded of the two commodities.

Examine whether the commodities are complementary or competitive. [**Ans.** Competitive]

[**Solution.** Commodities are competitive when

$$\frac{dX_1}{dP_2} > 0 \quad \text{and} \quad \frac{dX_2}{dP_1} > 0.$$

Now,

$$\frac{dX_1}{dP_2} = P_1^{-0.8} \cdot 1.2 \cdot P_2^{0.2} > 0$$

$$\frac{dX_2}{dP_1} = 0.2 \cdot P_1^{-0.8} \cdot P_2^{-1.6} > 0.$$

$\therefore$ The commodities are competitive.]

(b) The following data refer to sales, in thousands of rupees (x), of a certain product during five years:

Year	:	1988	1989	1990	1991	1992
x	:	605	715	830	790	835

Assuming the present trend continues, in which year will you expect 1989 sales to be doubled?

[**Ans.** 12.6 years after 1989]

[**Solution.** Let t = year–1990, $5y$ = (Sale in Rs. 1000)–700

t	$y = \frac{x-700}{5}$	t_y	t^2
(1988–1990) = –2	$\frac{605-700}{5} = -19$	38	4
(1989–1990) = –1	$\frac{715-700}{5} = 3$	–3	1
and so on 0	and so on 26	0	0
1	18	18	1
2	27	54	4
$\Sigma t = 0$	$\Sigma y = 55$	$\Sigma t_y = 107$	$\Sigma t^2 = 10$

Now, Regression equation of y on t is given by $y = a + bt$ where

$$\Sigma y = 5a + b\Sigma t \qquad [\because n = 5]$$

$$\Sigma t_y = a\Sigma t + b\Sigma t^2$$

$\therefore 55 = 5a + b \times 0 = 5a.$ $\quad \therefore a = 11.$

Again, $107 = 11 \times 0 + b \times 10$ $\quad \therefore b = \frac{107}{10}.$

$\therefore$ The Regression equation is $y = 11 + \frac{107}{10}t = 11 + 10.7t.$

Now, Double the sale of the year 1989 = 2 × 715 = 1430

$$\therefore \quad y = \frac{1430-700}{5} = 146$$

$$\therefore \quad t = \frac{y-a}{b} = \frac{146-11}{10.7} = 12.6 \approx 13 \text{ (approx.)}.$$

$\therefore$ In (1990 + 13) = 2003 year the 1989 sales will be doubled if the present trend continues.]

(c) The following table gives the index numbers for different groups together with their respective weights for 1990 (base year = 1985):

Group	Group Index No.	Group Weight
Food	130	60
Clothing	280	5
Lighting and fuel	190	7
Rent	300	9
Miscellaneous	200	19

(i) Find out the overall cost of living index number for the year 1990.

(ii) Suppose a person was earning Rs. 1,500 per month in 1985, what should be his salary in 1990, if his standard of living in that year to be the same as in 1985?

[**Hints.** See worked out Ex. 16 on page 260 and Ex. 15 on page 259.][**Ans.** (i) 170; (ii) Rs. 2,554.50]

9. (a) The demand curve for a commodity is given by $x = 20 - 2p - p^2$ where p and x are the price and the quantity in demand, respectively.

Find the elasticity of demand for $p = 2.5$. For which demand the elasticity will be unity?

[**Ans.** 2.12; 12]

[**Solution.** Elasticity of demand $= E = -\frac{p}{x} \cdot \frac{dx}{dp}$.

The Demand curve is $x = 20 - 2p - p^2$

$$\therefore \quad \frac{dx}{dp} = -2 - 2p.$$

When $p = 2.5$,

$$\frac{dx}{dp} = -2 - 2 \times 2.5 = -7$$

and

$$x = 20 - 2 \times 2.5 - (2.5)^2$$

$$= 20 - 5 - \frac{25}{4} = 15 - \frac{25}{4}$$

$$= \frac{35}{4} = 8.75$$

$$\therefore \quad E = -\frac{2.5}{8.75} \times (-7) = 1.999 \approx 2 \text{ Approx.}$$

Again,

$$E = \frac{p}{20 - 2p - p^2} \cdot \{-2(HP)\}$$

$$= \frac{2p(1+p)}{20 - 2p - p^2} = 1 \text{ (given)}$$

$\therefore \quad 2p + 2p^2 - 20 + 2p + p^2 = 0$

or, $\quad 3p^2 + 4p - 20 = 0$

or, $\quad 3p^2 + 10p - 6p - 20 = 0$

or, $\quad p(3p + 10) - 2(3p + 10) = 0$

or, $\quad (3p + 10)(p - 2) = 0 \; \therefore p = \frac{10}{3}$, or, 2

Since p cannot be negative, $\quad \therefore p = 2$.

At $p = 2$, $x = 20 - 2p - p^2$

$= 20 - 2 \times 2 - 4 = 12$.]

(b) The sales of readymade garments of a particular brand, of a departmental store rise from Rs. 25,000 in January to Rs. 30,000 in February, the seasonal indices for these months being 105 and 135 respectively. While the sales manager of the store was satisfied with Rs. 5000 increase the owner of the store expressed his dissatisfaction. Who is right? Justify your answer.

[**Ans.** Owner of the store]

[**Solution.** Since the seasonal index of February is $\frac{135}{105} = 1.286$ times that of January, the sales in February should have been $1.286 \times 25,000 =$ Rs. 32,150, instead of Rs. 30,000. The owner is right since the actual sales in February were Rs. 2,150 less than the target.]

(c) Find Laspeyre's and Fisher's price index numbers for the following data for the year 1990 with base year 1986:

Commodity	1986		1990	
	Price Rs./Kg.	Quantity Kg.	Price Rs./Kg.	Quantity Kg.
Wheat	4.0	20	5.5	20
Sugar	5.0	10	7.0	9
Edible oil	10.5	5	14.5	4
Vegetables	4.5	4	8.0	4

[**Hints.** See worked out Ex. 6 on page 247 and Ex. 9 on page 249.] [**Ans.** 141.9; 142]

I.C.W.A.I (Inter)

June 1995

Quantitative Methods **Full Marks : 100**

Answer Question No. 1 *which is compulsory and other* five *questions taking* two *from Section I,* two *from Section II and* one *from Section III.*

1. (a) If $A = \begin{bmatrix} 1 & -1 \\ 0 & 2 \end{bmatrix}$ and $B = \begin{bmatrix} 1 & 0 \\ 1 & 2 \end{bmatrix}$, write down the matrices $(A+B)(A-B)$ and $(A^2 - B^2)$, and determine whether they are equal.

[**Ans.** $(A+B)(A-B) = \begin{bmatrix} 1 & -2 \\ -4 & -1 \end{bmatrix}$, $A^2 - B^2 = \begin{bmatrix} 0 & -3 \\ -3 & 0 \end{bmatrix}$, not equal]

[**Hints.** See worked out Ex. 18 on page 48. Find $A+B, A-B, A^2, B^2$ and $(A+B)(A-B)$ and then verify the result.]

(b) Sketch the curve $y = |x|, -2 \leq x \leq 2$.

(i) From the graph state whether y is continuous at $x = 0$. [**Ans.** Continuous]

(ii) Test whether $\frac{dy}{dx}$ exists at $x = 0$. [**Ans.** Does not Exist]

[**Hints.** See worked out Ex. 3 on page 125 and Ex. 12 on page 150.]

(c) India's imports from 1982-83 to 1986-87 are as given below:

Year	:	1982-83	1983-84	1984-85	1985-86	1986-87
Imports (crores of Rs.)	:	142.9	158.3	171.3	197.7	200.8

Fit a linear trend by the method of least squares and compare the trend values with the observed values. [**Ans.** $Y = 174.2 + 18.52x$ trend values are 143.16, 158.68, 174.2, 189.72, 205.24]

[**Solution.** To fit a linear trend $y = a + bx$ by the method of least squares we are to solve the following equations:

$$\Sigma y = na + b\Sigma x \tag{1}$$

$$\Sigma xy = a\Sigma x + b\Sigma x^2 \tag{2}$$

to get the values of a and b.

Put $x =$ year 1984–85

$y =$ Imports in crores of Rupees, $n = 5$, then we have,

Year	x	y	xy	x^2
1982–83	−2	142.9	−285.8	4
1983–84	−1	158.3	−158.3	1
1984–85	0	171.3	0	0
1985–86	1	197.7	197.7	1
1986–87	2	200.8	401.6	4
	$\Sigma x = 0$	$\Sigma y = 871$	$\Sigma xy = 155.2$	$\Sigma x^2 = 10$

Putting the values in (1) and (2), we get

$$871 = 5 \times a + b \times 0 = 5a \quad \therefore\ a = 174.2$$

$$\text{and} \quad 155.2 = a \times 0 + b \times 10 \quad \therefore\ b = 15.52.$$

$\therefore$ The regression equation of y on x is

$$y = 174.2 + 15.52x. \qquad (3)$$

Putting the different value of x in Eq.(3), we get the trend values of y as follows:

x	=	−2	−1	0	1	2
y	=	143.16	158.68	174.2	189.72	205.24

Comparing with the given import values, we find that in the last two years the variation is very large.]

(d) A group of 200 persons was classified according to age and sex as given below:

Age in years	Male	Female	Total
Below 30	60	50	110
30 and above	80	10	90
Total	140	60	200

(i) What is the probability that a randomly chosen person from this group is a male below 30 years of age? **[Ans.** 0.30]

(ii) What is the probability that a person is below 30 years of age given that he is a male?
[**Hints.** See worked out Ex. 3 on page 22.] **[Ans.** 0.43]

(e) Rankings of 10 trainees at the beginning (x) and at the end (y) of a certain course are given below:

Trainees	=	A	B	C	D	E	F	G	H	I	J
x	=	1	6	3	9	5	2	7	10	8	4
y	=	6	8	3	7	2	1	5	9	4	10

Calculate Spearman's rank Correlation Coefficient. **[Ans.** 0.394]

[**Hints.** See worked out Ex. 9 on page 209.]

Section I

2. (a) Find $\lim_{x\to 0} \dfrac{\sqrt{2+x^2}-\sqrt{2-x^2}}{x^2}$ [**Ans.** $\frac{1}{\sqrt{2}}$]

[**Hints.** See worked out Ex. 6 on page 147.]

(b) Prove that

$$\begin{vmatrix} a+b+2c & a & b \\ c & b+c+2a & b \\ c & a & c+a+2b \end{vmatrix} = 2(a+b+c)^3.$$

[**Hints.** See worked out Ex. 12 on page 68.]

(c) Solve the following simultaneous equations by using inverse matrix:

$$\begin{aligned} 4x - 3y + \ z &= 1 \\ x + 4y - 2z &= 10 \\ 2x - 2y + 3z &= 4 \end{aligned}$$

[**Hints.** See worked out Ex. 6 on page 92.] [**Ans.** $x = 2, y = 3, z = 2$]

3. (a) Evaluate: $\displaystyle\int_0^\infty x^2 c^{-2x} dx$ [**Ans.** $\frac{1}{4}$]

[**Note.** Improper Integral is not included in the syllabus.]

(b) If $u = \frac{xy}{x+y}$, prove that

$$x^2 \frac{\partial^2 u}{\partial x^2} + 2xy \frac{\partial^2 u}{\partial x \partial y} + y^2 \frac{\partial^2 u}{\partial y^2} = 0.$$

[**Hints.** See worked out Ex. 3, 4, 11 on page 208, 213. $\frac{\partial u}{\partial x} = \frac{y^2}{(x+y)^2}$, $\frac{\partial^2 u}{\partial x^2} = -\frac{2y^2}{(x+y)^3}$, etc.]

(c) Determine the extreme values of

$$f(x, y) = 4x + 2y - x^2 + xy - y^2$$

[**Ans.** $f(\frac{10}{3}, \frac{8}{3}) = \frac{28}{3}$. (maximum value)]

[**Hints.** Necessary conditions for $f(x, y)$ to have an extreme value are $f_x = 0$, $f_y = 0$ which give $4 - 2x + y = 0 \cdots\cdots (1)$ and $2 + x - 2y = 0 \cdots\cdots (2)$. Solving (1) and (2), $x = \frac{10}{3}$ and $y = \frac{8}{3}$. Now $f_{xx} = -2$ and $f_{yy} = -2$ and $f_{xy} = 1$. At $(\frac{10}{3}, \frac{8}{3})$, $f_{xx} = -2$ and $f_{xx} \cdot f_{yy} - (f_{xy})^2 = 4 - 1 = 3 > 0$. i.e., $f_{xx} \cdot f_{yy} - (f_{xy})^2 > 0$ and $f_{xx} < 0$.

Hence $f(x, y)$ is maximum at $(\frac{10}{3}, \frac{8}{3})$ and the maximum value is $f(\frac{10}{3}, \frac{8}{3}) = \frac{28}{3}$. See art. 9.5.]

4. (a) Draw a rough sketch of the curve $3y = (2x + 1)(x - 2)$ and find the area bounded by the curve and the axis of x.

[**Hints.** $y = 0$ gives $x = -\frac{1}{2}, 2$. Required area $= \int_{-\frac{1}{2}}^{2} y\, dx =$ etc.] [**Ans.** $\frac{125}{72}$ sq. units]

(b) Solve the following LPP by using simplex method:

$$\begin{aligned} &\text{Maximize} \quad Z = 8x + 6y \\ &\text{subject to} \quad 4x + 2y \le 60 \\ &\qquad\qquad\quad 2x + 4y \le 48,\ x, y \ge 0. \end{aligned}$$

[**Hints.** See worked out Ex. 1, 2 on page 322.] [**Ans.** $Z_{\max.} = 132; x = 12, y = 6$]

(c) A monopolist has a demand curve

$$x = 106 - 2p$$

and average cost curve A.C. $= 5 + \frac{x}{50}$ where p is the price per unit output and x is the number of units of output. If the total revenue is $R = xp$, determine the most profitable output and the maximum profit. [**Ans.** Output $= 46\frac{2}{13}$ units, profit $= 1107\frac{9}{13}$]

[**Solution.** We know that Total Cost is equal to Averge Cost × No. of units.

$$\therefore \quad \text{Total Cost} = x\left(5 + \frac{x}{50}\right) = 5x + \frac{1}{50}\cdot x^2$$

Now, Profit = Total Revenue − Total Cost.

$$\therefore \quad \text{Profit function } Y \text{ (say)} \quad = R - 5x - \frac{1}{50}\cdot x^2 = xp - 5x - \frac{1}{50}\cdot x^2.$$

Now, $x = 106 - 2p$ or, $p = \frac{106-x}{x} = 53 - \frac{x}{2}$

$$\text{or,} \quad Y = x\left(53 - \frac{x}{2}\right) - 5x - \frac{1}{50}x^2$$

$$= 48x - \frac{26}{50}x^2 = 48x - \frac{13}{25}x^2$$

For maximization of profit $\frac{dy}{dx} = 0$ and $\frac{d^2y}{dx^2} < 0$.

Now, $$\frac{dy}{dx} = 48 - \frac{13}{25}\cdot 2x = 0$$

$$\text{or,} \quad x = \frac{48 \times 25}{26} = \frac{600}{13} \text{ units.}$$

Again, $$\frac{d^2y}{dx^2} = -\frac{26}{25} < 0.$$

$\therefore$ The most profitable output is $\frac{600}{13}$ units and the maximum profit will be

$$= 48 \times \frac{600}{13} - \frac{13}{25} \times \left(\frac{600}{13}\right)^2 = \frac{600}{13}\left(48 - \frac{13}{25} \times \frac{600}{13}\right) = 1107.69.]$$

Section II

5. (a) Ratio of probability of 3 successes in 5 independent trials to the probability of 2 successes in 5 independent trials is $\frac{1}{4}$. What is the probability of 4 successes in 6 independent trials? [**Ans.** $\frac{48}{3125}$; $p = \frac{1}{5}$, $q = \frac{4}{5}$]

(b) The distribution of monthly incomes of 500 workers may be assumed to be normal with mean of Rs. 2,000 and a standard deviation of Rs. 200. Estimate the number of workers with incomes (i) exceeding Rs. 2,300 p.m.; (ii) between Rs. 1,800 and Rs. 2,300 p.m. What is the lowest income of the 25% workers in the highest income group?

[Given	$Z = 0.67$	1.00	1.50
	Area = 0.25	0.3413	0.4332]

[**Ans.** 33.4 or 33; 387.25 or 387; Rs. 2,134 per month]

(c) An oil exploration firm finds that 5% of the test wells it drills, yield a deposit of natural gas. If the firm drills 6 wells, what is the probability that (i) exactly 2 wells; (ii) at least one well yield gas? [**Ans.** (i) 0.0305; (ii) 0.2649]

6. (a) The standard deviation of the tube life for a particular brand of ultraviolet tube is 500 hours, and the operating life of the tubes is normally distributed. The manufacturer claims that average tube life is at least 9000 hours. Test the claim at 5% level of significance, given that a random sample of 15 tubes gave a mean operating life of 8800 hours. [**Ans.** $Z = -1.55$, accept $H_\circ$]

(b) A company surveyed employees to see whether they preferred a large increase in retirement benefits or a smaller increase in salary. From a group of 1000 male employees, 850 supported the retirement benefits. Of 500 female employees, 400 supported the retirement benefits. Test the null hypothesis that the proportions of men and women supporting retirement benefits are equal.

[Given $\chi^2_{0.05}$ = 3.80 5.99 7.81
d.f. = 1 2 3]

[**Ans.** Reject $H_\circ$ since $\chi^2 = 6$]

(c) Due to turnover and absentecism at an assembly plant, 20% of the items are assembled by inexperienced employees. Management has determined that customers return 12% of the items assembled by inexperienced employees, whereas only 3% of the items assembled by experienced employees are returned. What is the probability that an item was assembled by an inexperienced employee, given that the item was returned? [**Ans.** 0.5]

7. (a) A courier service advertises that its average delivery time is less than 6 hours for local deliveries. A random sample of 10 for the amount of time this courier takes to deliver packages to an addressee across town produced the following times (rounded to the nearest hour):

7, 3, 4, 6, 10, 5, 6, 4, 3, 8.

Is this evidence sufficient to support the courier claim at 5% level of significance?

[Given $t_{.025}$ = 2.262 2.228
d.f. = 9 10]

[**Ans.** Reject $H_\circ$, since $t = 0.56$]

(b) There is 40% chance that a patient admitted to the hospital, is suffering from cancer. A doctor has to decide whether a serious operation should be performed or not. If the patient is suffering from cancer and the serious operation is performed, the chance that he will recover, is 70%, otherwise it is 35%. On the other hand, if the patient is not suffering from cancer and the serious operation is performed, the chance that he will recover is 20%, otherwise it is 100%. Assume that recovery and death are the only possible results. Construct an appropriate decision tree. What decision should the doctor take? [**Ans.** The doctor should not operate]

Section III

8. (a) For the following two demand functions for two commodities, examine whether the commodities are complementary or competitive:

$$x_1 = \frac{4}{p_1^2 p_2} \quad \text{and} \quad x_2 = \frac{16}{p_1 p_2^2}$$

where x_1 and x_2 are quantities of demand for the two commodities respectively, p_1 and p_2 being their unit prices. [**Ans.** Complementary]

[**Solution.** From the given demand functions, we have

$$\frac{dx_1}{dp_2} = \frac{d}{dp_2}\left(\frac{4}{p_1^2}\cdot p_2^{-1}\right) = \frac{4}{p_1^2} \times -1 \times p_2^{-2}$$

$$= -\frac{4}{p_1^2 \cdot p_2^2} < 0$$

Again, $$\frac{dx_2}{dp_1} = \frac{d}{dp_1}\left(\frac{16}{p_2^2}\cdot p_1^{-1}\right) = -\frac{16}{p_2^2}\cdot p_1^{-2}$$

$$= -\frac{16}{p_2^2 \cdot p_1^2} < 0.$$

Since both $\frac{dx_1}{dp_2}$ and $\frac{dx_2}{dp_1}$ are less than zero, a fall in either p_1 or p_2 will increase both x_1 and x_2.

∴ The commodities are complementary.]

(b) Given below is a transition matrix showing input-output analysis:

(Unit: million Rs.)

Producing Sector	Receiving Sector A	B	C	Final Demand	Total Output
A	20	100	50	30	200
B	100	20	30	250	400
C	30	40	10	120	200
Labour	50	240	110		400

Construct the technology matrix and explain how to compute the gross output levels of all the sectors if the final demand of sector C changes to Rs. 125 million.

[**Solution.** Total output corresponding to input A

$$= 20 + 100 + 50 + 30 = 200.$$

Hence, input coefficients for output A are,

$$\frac{20}{200}, \frac{100}{200}, \frac{30}{200}, \frac{50}{200}, \text{ i.e., } 0.1, 0.5, 0.15, 0.25$$

Similarly, input coefficients for output B are

$$\frac{100}{400}, \frac{20}{400}, \frac{40}{400}, \frac{240}{400}, \text{ i.e., } 0.25, 0.05, 0.1, 0.6.$$

Again, input coefficients for output C are

$$\frac{50}{200}, \frac{30}{200}, \frac{10}{200}, \frac{110}{200}, \text{ i.e., } 0.25, 0.15, 0.05, 0.55$$

∴ Technology, matrix will be as following:

	A	B	C
A	0.1	0.25	0.25
B	0.5	0.05	0.15
C	0.15	0.1	0.05
Labour	0.25	0.6	0.55

Now, output equations will be as follows:

$$A = 0.1A + 0.25B + 0.25C + 30$$

$$\text{or,} \quad 0.9A - 0.25B - 0.25C = 30 \qquad (1)$$

Similarly,

$$-0.5A + 0.95B - 0.15C = 250 \qquad (2)$$

$$-0.15A - 0.1B + 0.95C = 125 \qquad (3)$$

[since the final demand of sector C has changed from 120 to 125 million]

Solving (1), (2) and (3), we get $A = 202.20, B = 402.08$ and $C = 205.83$

$\therefore$ Requirement of Labour $= 0.25 \times 202.2 + 0.6 \times 402.08 + 0.55 \times 205.83 = 405.01.$]

(c) Given $r_{12} = 0.5, r_{23} = 0.7$ and $r_{31} = 0.5$. Calculate $r_{23.1}$ and $R_{1(23)}$

[**Ans.** $r_{23.1} = 0.6$; $R_{1(23)} = 0.5423$]

9. (a) Show that the elasticity of demand with respect to price, for the demand function $x = 3p^{-2}$ is constant, p and x being the price and quantity in demand respectively.

[**Ans.** Elasticity of demand=2.]

[**Solution.** We know that elasticity of demand

$$= -\frac{p}{x} \times \frac{dx}{dp}$$

$$= -\frac{p}{3p^{-2}}\left[\frac{d}{dp}(3p^{-2})\right]$$

$$= -\frac{p}{3p^{-2}} \times -2 \times 3 \times p^{-3} = \frac{2p \times p^2}{p^3} = 2 \text{ (Const.)}]$$

(b) What is a trend in a time series? The following table gives the annual sales (in Rs. 1,000) of a commodity:

Year	Sales	Year	Sales
1980	710	1986	644
1981	705	1987	783
1982	680	1988	781
1983	687	1989	805
1984	757	1990	872
1985	629		

Determine the trend by calculating the 5-yearly moving averages.

[**Ans.** 707.8, 691.6, 679.4, 700, 718.8, 728.4, 777]

(c) The seasonal indices of the sale of garments of a particular type in a store are given below:

Quarter	:	I	II	III	IV
Seasonal Index	:	98	89	83	130

If the total sales in the first quarter of a year be worth Rs. 10,000, find how much worth of garments of this type should be kept in stock to meet the demand in each of the remaining quarters.

[**Ans.** Sales: 1st Qr.=Rs. 10,000; 2nd Qr.=Rs. 9082; 3rd Qr.=Rs. 8469; 4th Qr.=Rs. 13,265.]

I.C.W.A.I (Inter)

December 1995

Quantitative Methods **Full Marks : 100**

Answer Question No. 1 *which is compulsory. Attempt any two questions from each of Section* I *and* II *and any one question from Section* III

1. (a) If $A = \begin{bmatrix} 2 & 1 \\ 1 & 2 \end{bmatrix}$ and $B = \begin{bmatrix} 1 & -2 \\ -1 & 2 \end{bmatrix}$, examine whether the following statements are true or not:

(i) $AB = BA$; (ii) $B^2 = (-A)^2$; (iii) $(A - B)^2 = A^2 - 2AB + B^2$.

[**Ans.** (i) Not true; (ii) Not true; (iii) Not true.]

[**Hints.** See worked out Ex. 5, 10, 11.]

(b) If $f(x) = \frac{1-x}{1+x}$, show that $f\left(\frac{1-x}{1+x}\right) = x$.

[**Hints.** $f(u) = \frac{1-u}{1+u} = \frac{1-\frac{1-x}{1+x}}{1+\frac{1-x}{1+x}} = \frac{2x}{2} = x$, where $u = \frac{1-x}{1+x}$.]

(c) If A, B and C are mutually exclusive and exhaustive events, and $P(A) = \frac{1}{2}P(B)$ and $P(B) = \frac{2}{3}P(C)$, find $P(A), P(B)$ and $P(C)$. [**Ans.** $\frac{1}{6}, \frac{1}{3}, \frac{1}{2}$.]

[**Hints.** $1 = P(A \cup B \cup C) = P(A) + P(B) + P(C) = 2P(B) + P(B) + \frac{3}{2}P(B)$.]

(d) A manufacturer must buy coil springs which will stand at least a 15 kg. load. Supplier A guarantees that his springs stand an average load of 20.5 kg. with a S.D. of 2.1 kg. Supplier B guarantees that his springs stand on an average load of 18.2 kg. with a S.D. of 1.1 kg. All distributions are assumed to be normal. On the basis of the guarantees, which springs seem preferable to the manufacturer? [**Ans.** Supplier B's spring.]

[**Hints.** Apply Normal distribution; find z-values for $x = 20.5, 18.2$.]

(e) The following table gives daily demand for hot plates in 100 days:

Demand	:	0	1	2	3	4	5	Total
Frequency	:	14	16	18	23	19	10	100

Draw a random sample of size 10, using the following random numbers:

2379	1482	0652	3009	1984
6132	7065	9310	8053	4192

Section I

2. (a) Solve the following equations by using inverse matrix:

$$2x + y + z = 1$$
$$x - 2y - 3z = 1$$
$$3x + 2y + 4z = 5$$

[**Ans.** $x = 1, y = -3, z = 2$.]

[**Hints.** See worked out Ex. 6 on page 92.]

(b) Plot the graph of the function $y = \dfrac{x-1}{x}$.

(c) Find the co-ordinates of the points on the curve $y = \dfrac{x}{4-x}$ for which $\dfrac{dy}{dx} = 1$.

3. (a) A closed rectangular container has a capacity of 243 cubic metres. If the length of the container is twice its width, obtain the dimensions of the container of least surface area.

[**Ans.** 9 cm., $\frac{9}{2}$ cm., 6 cm.]

(b) Evaluate: $\displaystyle\int_2^3 \frac{6x^2+1}{\sqrt{2x^3+x-2}}dx.$ [**Ans.** $2(\sqrt{55}-4)$.]

[**Hints.** Put $2x^3+x-2=z^2$.]

(c) Find the area above x-axis and bounded by

$y=4x-x^2-3,\ x=1$ and $x=3.$ [**Ans.** $\frac{4}{3}$ sq. units]

[**Hints.** See worked out Ex. 3 in page 285.]

4. (a) If $u=\dfrac{x^3+y^3}{x+y}$, prove that $x\dfrac{\partial u}{\partial x}+y\dfrac{\partial u}{\partial y}=2u.$

[**Hints.** See worked out Ex. 7, 8 in page 211.]

(b) Find the extreme values of the function $f(x,y)=x^2-y^2+xy+5x$ subject to $x-2y=0$.

[**Ans.** -5.]

[**Hints.** See Q. 3(a) set in December, 1994.]

(c) Solve the following LPP by simplex method:

Minimise $z=4x+2y$ subject to $3x+y\le 27,\ x+y=21,\ x+2y\ge 30,\ x,y\ge 0.$

[**Ans.** $Z_{\text{min}}=48$ at $x=3, y=18$.]

Section II

5. (a) A cosmetic company is considering the introduction of a new brand. The company estimates that it will be possible for them to sell 50,000 to 1,00,000 pieces in a given period according to the following probability distribution:

No. of pieces sold (in '000)	=	50	60	70	80	90	100
Probability	=	0.13	0.20	0.35	0.25	0.05	0.02

If the company launches the product, it will incur a fixed cost of Rs. 50,000. However, each piece sold would fetch them a profit of Re. 1.00.

Should the company introduce the brand?

[**Solution.**

No. of pieces (in '000)	x (say) :	50	60	70	80	90	100
Probability	P (say) :	0.13	0.20	0.35	0.25	0.05	0.02

$\therefore\ E(x)=$ Expected number of pieces sold $=\Sigma px.$

$=[50\times .13+60\times .20+70\times 0.35+80\times 0.25+90\times 0.05+100\times 0.02]$

$=[6.5+12+24.5+20+4.5+2]=69.5$ (in '000)

$\therefore$ Gross Profit $=69.5\times 1000\times 1.00$ = Rs. 69,500

Less: Fixed Cost = Rs. 50,000

Net Profit Rs. 19,500

$\therefore$ The company should introduce the brand since the expected net profit is Rs. 19,500.]

(b) Life of a machine part is assumed to follow the following probability distribution:

$$f(x)=\frac{1}{100}e^{-x/100}.\ 0\le x<\infty, x=\text{life in hours.}$$

Find the probability that a part chosen at random will last for more than 1200 hours.

[**Ans.** e^{-12}.]

[**Hints.** $P(x > 1200) = \int_{1200}^{\infty} f(x)dx$ = etc. since the probability function indicates that x is a continuous random variable.]

(c) The production manager of a company maintains that the flow time, in days (y), depends on the number of operations (x) to be performed. The following data give the necessary information:

x =	2	2	3	4	4	5	6	6	7	7
y =	8	13	14	11	20	10	22	26	22	25

Plot a scatter diagram. Calculate the value of the Karl Pearson's Product Moment Correlation Coefficient.

[**Ans.** 0.78.]

[**Hints.** See worked out Ex. 2, 6 in Page 204.]

6. (a) Three machines A, B and C produce 50%, 30% and 20% respectively of the total number of items of a factory. The percentages of defective output of these machines are 3%, 4% and 5% respectively. An item from day's production of the factory is selected at random and it is found to be defective. What is the probability that the item was produced by machine A? [**Ans.** $\frac{15}{37}$.]

[**Hints.** Apply Baye's theorem.]

(b) A variety store manager wishes to know the demand of a particular type of item for 7 days. Assuming that the daily demand (number of items) follows a Poisson distribution with mean 5, generate demand for 7 days by Monte Carlo Simulation method using the following random numbers:

41206	53802	76310	12698	91165	19152
39276	05284	00135	11990	02487	03001

Given, $e^{-5} = 0.0067$.

[**Hints.** Use Poisson distribution to find probability and cum. probability and random intervals.]

(c) A certain oil corporation conducts a seismic test on land to assess the possibility of extraction of oil from the land. From the past 200 records, the following test results and oil yields were obtained:

Test results	Oil yield frequencies		
	High	Medium	Law
Good	44	22	13
Fair	15	19	26
Bad	5	8	47.

Can we say, at 1% significance level, that oil yields and test results are associated?

[**Hints.** Apply χ^2-test.]

[**Ans.** Yes.]

7. (a) A manufacturing company has to select one of the two products A or B for manufacturing. Product A requires investment of Rs. 20,000 and product B, Rs. 40,000. Market research survey shows high, medium and low demands with corresponding probabilities and returns from sales, in Rs. thousand, for the two products, in the following table:

Market Demand	Probability		Return from sales	
	A	B	A	B
High	0.4	0.3	50	80
Medium	0.3	0.5	30	60
Low	0.3	0.2	10	50

Construct an appropriate Decision Tree. What decision the company should take?

[**Ans.** The company select product B.]

(b) Wire cable is manufactured by two processes. Laboratory tests were performed by putting samples of cables under tension and recording the load required (coded units) to break the cable, giving the following data;

Process 1:	9	4	10	7	9	10	
Process 2:	14	9	13	12	13	8	10

Can we say that the two processes have the same effect on the mean breaking strength, at 5% level of significance? [**Ans.** No.]

[**Hints.** Apply t-test.]

(c) Marks in management accounting, follow a normal distribution with mean 55 and a standard deviation of 8 when a random sample of 64 students in an examination was taken. Construct 95% confidence limits for the true mean marks. [**Ans.** 53.04, 56.96]

[**Hints.** S.E. of $\bar{x} = \sigma/\sqrt{n} = 8/8 = 1$; confidence limits an $\bar{x} \pm 1.96$ (S.E. of $\bar{x}$) = etc.]

Section III

8. (a) To knew the effect of a certain fertiliser and rainfall on yield of a certain crop, experiment observations were collected as given below:

x_1 = yield, in kg./acre

x_2 = fertiliser used, in kg./acre

x_3 = rainfall, in cms.

x_1 =	40	50	50	70	65	65	80
x_2 =	10	20	30	40	50	60	70
x_3 =	10	20	10	30	20	20	30

(i) Estimate the yield, if fertiliser used is 30.5 kg./acre and rainfall is 15 cms.

(ii) Calculate the partial correlation coefficient $r_{12,3}$ and the multiple correlation coefficient $R_{1(23)}$.

(b) Determine the trend for the following data by

(i) moving average of length 4, and

(ii) the least square method.

Year	Quarter No.			
	I	II	III	IV
1991	210	191	216	200
1992	218	197	230	211
1993	246	215	235	225

9. (a) The following data refer to the per capita yearly consumption (d) of butter, in kg., and the price, in Rs. per kg.(p) from 1970 to 1978:

Year	=	1970	1971	1972	1973	1974	1975	1976	1977	1978
d	=	13.46	15.65	17.62	18.44	18.75	18.80	18.95	19.10	19.25
P	=	1.70	1.68	1.52	1.49	1.47	1.42	1.37	1.35	1.32

Fit a demand curve $d = k\,p^{-\alpha}$ to the above data and obtain the price elasticity of demand.

[**Solution.** Taking logarithm of the demand curve $d = K \cdot p^{-\alpha}$, we get

$$\log d = \log K - \alpha \log p$$

$$\text{or,} \quad y = a + bt \qquad \text{(Linear form)} \qquad (1)$$

where, $y = \log d, a = \log k, b = -\alpha$ and $t = \log p$.

Year	$y = \log d$	$t = \log p$	t^2	yt
1970	*1.1290	0.2304	0.0531	0.2601
1971	*1.1945	0.2253	0.0508	0.2691
1972	1.2460	0.1818	0.0331	0.2265
1973	1.2657	0.1732	0.0300	0.2192
1974	1.2729	0.1673	0.0280	0.2130
1975	1.2742	0.1523	0.0232	0.1941
1976	1.2776	0.1367	0.0187	0.1747
1977	1.2810	0.1303	0.0170	0.1669
1978	1.2844	0.1206	0.0146	0.1549
	$\Sigma y = 11.2253$	$\Sigma t = 1.5179$	$\Sigma t^2 = 0.2685$	$\Sigma yt = 1.8785$

[* $\log 13.46 = 1.1296$; * $\log 15.65 = 1.1945$ and so on. $\log 1.70 = 0.2304$; $\log 1.68 = 0.2253$ and so on.]

Now, Regression equation of y on t is given by $y = a + bt$, where

$$\Sigma y = na + b\Sigma t \qquad (2)$$

$$\text{and} \quad \Sigma yt = a\Sigma t + b\Sigma t^2 \qquad (3)$$

Putting the respective values, we get

$$11.2253 = 9a + b \times 1.5179 \qquad (4)$$

$$1.8785 = a \times 1.5179 + b \times 0.2685 \qquad (5)$$

Solving (4) and (5), we get

$$a = 1.4457 \quad \text{and} \quad b = -1.1769$$

Now, $a = 1.4457 = \log K$

$$\therefore K = \text{Anti log } 1.4457 = 27.90 \approx 28.$$

$$\text{and } \alpha = -b = 1.1769 \approx 1.2$$

$$\therefore d = K \cdot p^{-\alpha} = 28p^{-1.2}$$

Now, Price elasticity $= |e_p| = \left| \dfrac{\frac{d}{dp}(K \cdot p^{-\infty})}{\frac{K \cdot p^{-\infty}}{p}} \right| = \left| \dfrac{K \cdot -\alpha \cdot P^{-\alpha-1}}{K \cdot p^{-\alpha-1}} \right|$

$= |-\infty| = 1.2]$

(b) The following table gives the cost of living index-numbers for different groups with their respective weights for the year 1990 (base year: 1975):

Group	Cost of living index	Weight
Food	430	60
Clothing	480	5
Lighting and fuel	320	7
Rent	390	10
Misc.	300	18

(i) Calculate the overall cost of living index number.

[**Solution.**

Group	Cost of Living Index (I)	Weight (W)	IW
Food	430	60	25,800
Clothing	480	5	2,400
Lighting & fuel	320	7	2,240
Rent	390	10	3,900
Misc	300	18	5,400
Total		$\Sigma W = 100$	$\Sigma IW = 39,740$

$\therefore$ Overall Cost of living index number $= \frac{\Sigma IW}{\Sigma W} = 397.4 = I$.]

(ii) Suppose, a person was earning Rs. 700/- p.m. in 1975. What should be his salary in 1990, if his standard of living in 1990 to be the same as in 1975?

[**Solution.** A person who was drawing Rs. 100 in 1975 should draw Rs. 397.4 in 1990 to maintain the same standard of living since $I_1 = 397.4$.

$\therefore$ A person who was earning Rs. 700 p.m. in 1975 should draw Rs. $700 \times \frac{397.4}{100}$ = Rs. 2,781.8 p.m. in 1990.]

June 1996

Attempt 6 Questions. Question No. 1 and No. 2 are compulsory, and any 4 questions out of the remaining 6 questions

Graph papers and log tables will be provided on request.

1. (*a*) Using inverse matrix, solve the following simultaneous equations:

$$3x + 5y = 21$$
$$\text{and } 4x + y = 11.$$

[**Ans.** $x = 2, y = 3$]

[**Hints.** See worked out Ex. 5 on page 91]

(*b*) Find the minimum value of $f(x,y) = x^2 + y^2$ subject to $x + y = 10$. [**Ans.** 50]

[**Hints.** See Q. 3(a) set in December, 1994]

(*c*) Find the area bounded by the curve $y = x^2$ and the straight line $y = 2x$.

[**Ans.** $\frac{4}{3}$ sq. units]

[**Hints.** See worked out Ex. 4 on page 286; here required area

$$= \int_0^2 (y_1 - y_2)dx = \int_0^2 (2x - x^2)dx = \text{etc.}]$$

(*d*) Solve the following linear programming problem by the simplex method:

Maximize $Z = 3x + 5y$
subject to $x + y \leq 10, \quad 2x - 3y \leq 12, x, y \geq 0.$

[**Ans.** 50]

[**Hints.** See worked out Ex. 1 on page 322]

2. (*a*) The probability known is 0.99 that a 30-year old man will survive one year more. An insurance company offers to sell such a man a Rs. 10,000 one-year term life insurance policy at a premium of Rs. 110. What is the insurance company's expected gain?

[**Ans.** Rs. 10]

[**Hints.** If Rs. x be the Insurance Co's gain, then prob. distribution of x is given by

x	110	$-10000 + 110$	Total
p	.99	.01	1

$\therefore E(x) = \sum p_i x_i = 110 \times .99 + (-9890) \times 0.01$

$= 108.9 - 98.9 = \text{Rs.}\mathbf{10}.$]

(*b*) In a certain area, 8 per cent of the families have their monthly income above Rs. 6,400 and 31 per cent have below Rs. 4,500. Assuming normality for the income distribution, find the percentage of families with monthly income below Rs. 5,000. [**Ans.** 50%]

[**Hints.** See worked out Ex. 31 on page 82 (Statistics)]

(*c*) For certain data, the following regression equations were obtained:

$$4x - 5y + 33 = 0$$
$$20x - 9y - 107 = 0$$

Estimate y when $x = 20$ and x when $y = 20$. [**Ans.** 22.6; 14.35]

[**Hints.** See worked out Ex. 21 on page 221]

(*d*) A shopkeeper has the facility to store a large number of perishable items. He buys them at a rate of Rs. 3 per item and sells at the rate of Rs. 5 per item. If an item is not sold at the end of the day, then there is a loss of Rs. 3 per item. The daily demand of the item has the following probability distribution:

Number of items sold	=	4	5	6
Probability	=	0.2	0.5	0.3

How many items should he store so that his daily expected profit is maximum? Use decision tree approach. [**Ans.** 5 items; Expected daily max profit is Rs. 9]

3. (*a*) Without expanding the determinant, show that

$$\begin{vmatrix} a & b & c \\ a & a+b & a+b+c \\ a & 2a+b & 3a+2b+c \end{vmatrix} = a^3$$

[**Hints.** See worked out Ex. 8 on page 66]

(*b*) A random sample of 400 oil tins lebelled '5 kg. net weight' gave an average net weight of 4.985 kg. with a standard deviation of 0.215 kg. Determine 99 per cent confidence limits for the true mean weight of the tins. [**Ans.** (4.957, 5.013) kg.]

(*c*) Demand for a certain item for the last 5 weeks was as given below:

Week No.	:	1	2	3	4	5
No. of items demanded	:	21	22	24	25	23

Assuming demand function to be linear, estimate the demand for the item in 7th week by using least square method.

[**Ans.** 25.8, Linear demand trend equation being $Y = 23 + 0.7X$]

4. (*a*) Ten students were given tests in English amd Mathematics. Their marks are given below:

Student No.	:	1	2	3	4	5	6	7	8	9	10
Marks in English	:	78	40	50	55	52	49	60	54	59	58
Marks in Mathematics	:	70	60	60	75	69	55	70	65	65	61

Determine Spearman's rank correlation coefficient. [**Ans.** 0.71]

[**Hints.** See worked out Ex. 10 on page 210]

(*b*) Integrate *any two* of the following:

(i) $\int \frac{dx}{x^2+6x+8}$; (ii) $\int x^2 \log x dx$; (iii) $\int_a^{\infty} \frac{dx}{x\sqrt{x^2-a^2}}$.

[**Ans.** (i) $\frac{1}{2}\log\left|\frac{x+2}{x+4}\right| + c$; (ii) $\frac{x^3}{3}\left(\log x - \frac{1}{3}\right) + c$; (iii) $\frac{\pi}{2a}$]

[**Hints.** (i) See worked out Ex. 2 on page 254; (ii) See worked out Ex. 13 on page 249; (iii) Put $x^2 - a^2 = z^2$]

(*c*) Prove that

$$MR = p\left(1 - \frac{1}{e}\right)$$

where MR is the marginal revenue, p is the average price and e is the elasticity of demand.

[**Hints.** If x be the demand when the average price is p, then $R = px$ and $e = -\frac{p}{x}\cdot\frac{dx}{dp}$, or, $\frac{1}{e} = -\frac{x}{p}\cdot\frac{dp}{dx}$. $\therefore MR = \frac{dR}{dx} = p + x\frac{dp}{dx} = p\left(1 + \frac{x}{p}\cdot\frac{dp}{dx}\right) = p\left(1 - \frac{1}{e}\right)$.]

5. (*a*) Draw the graph of the function $y = x|x|$, where x is real.

[**Hints.** $y = x \cdot x = x^2$ if $x \geq 0$ and $y = x(-x) = -x^2$ if $x < 0$. Now draw the graph] (*b*) Calculate mean and variance of a Poisson distribution of a variable x, if $P(x = 4) = P(x = 5)$. [**Ans.** Mean = 5, variance = 5]

[**Hints.** See worked out Ex. 18 on page 71 (Statistics)]

(*c*) A demand function of an item is $p = \frac{8}{x+1} - 2$ and supply function is $p = \frac{x+3}{2}$. Determine the equilibrium price and the consumer's surplus. [**Ans.** 2 units; 1.59 units.]

[**Hints.** For equilibrium price,

$$\frac{8}{x+1} - 2 = \frac{x+3}{2} \Rightarrow x = 1. \quad \therefore p = \frac{8}{2} - 2 = 2, \text{ i.e., } x_0 = 1, p_0 = 2.$$

$$\text{CS} = \left|\int_0^{x_0} p\,dx - p_0x_0\right| = \left|\int_0^1 \left(\frac{8}{x+1} - 2\right) dx - 2 \times 1\right| = \left|[8\log(x+1) - 2x]_0^1 - 2\right| = \text{etc.}]$$

6. (*a*) Find the volume of the solid obtained by revolving the ellipse, $\frac{x^2}{a^2} + \frac{y^2}{b^2} = 1$, about the x-axis. [**Ans.** $\frac{4}{3}\pi ab^2$ cu. units]

[**Hints.** See hints given in Q. 4 on page 291]

(*b*) A new drug manufactuer wants to market a new drug only if he could be quite sure that the mean temperature of a healthy person taking the drug could not rise above 98.6 F; otherwise, he will withhold the drug. The drug is administered to a random sample of 17 healthy persons. The mean temperature was found to be 98.4 F, with a standard deviation of 0.6 F. Assuming that the distribution of the temperature is normal and $\alpha = 0.01$, what should the manufacturer do?

[**Ans.** The manufacturer should market the new drug]

[**Hints.** Apply t-test]

(*c*) Find Fisher's and Marshall-Edgeworth index numbers for the following data:

Commodities	1989		1990	
	Price, Rs.	Qty., Kg.	Price, Rs.	Qty., Kg.
A	20	8	40	9
B	50	10	60	10
C	40	15	60	12
D	10	15	15	15

[**Ans.** 145.23; 145.22]

[**Hints.** See worked out Ex. 9 on page 249]

7. (*a*) The total cost C, and the total revenue R of a firm are given by

$$C(x) = x^3 + 60x^2 + 8x \text{ and } R(x) = 3x^3 - 3x^2 + 656x$$

where x is the output. Determine the output for which the firm gets the maximum profit. Also obtain the maximum profit. [**Ans.** 9; 2187]

[**Hints.** $\pi(x) = R(x) - C(x) = 2x^3 - 63x^2 + 648x$. Now find x when $\pi(x)$ is maximum and then the maximum value of $\pi(x)$]

(*b*) A correlation coefficient between marks in two successive tests for 12 candidates gave a value of 0.65. Can it be regarded as significant at 1% level? State the assumptions involved.

[**Ans.** No. The null hypothesis H_0 is that the correlation cofficient is not significant, against the alternative hypothesis indicating that the correlation coefficient is significant] (*c*) The demand functions for two commodities are:

$x_1 = p_1^{-1.7}p_2^{0.8}$, and $x_2 = p_1^{0.5}p_2^{-0.2}$, where p_1, p_2 and x_1, x_2 are prices and quantities demanded of the two commodities.

Determine whether the commodities are complementary or competitive.

[**Ans.** Competitive]

[**Hints.** See solution of Q. 8(a) set in December, 1994]

8. (*a*) If $A = \begin{pmatrix} 3 & 5 \\ 2 & a \end{pmatrix}$, $B = \begin{pmatrix} 4 & b \\ 2 & 9 \end{pmatrix}$, and $C = \begin{pmatrix} 26 & a \\ 14 & 45 \end{pmatrix}$, find a and b when $2A + 5B = C$.

[**Ans.** $a = 0$, $b = -2$]

(*b*) 1200 children were classified according to intelligence and clothes they wore. The following table gives the necessary information:

	Clothing			
Intelligence	Poorly clad	Well clad	Very well clad	Total
Dull	72	90	78	240
Intelligent	184	305	111	600
Very intelligent	144	105	111	360
Total	400	500	300	1,200

Test whether intelligence is associated with clothing at 1 per cent level of significance.

[**Ans.** Yes, intelligence is associated with clothing]

[**Hints.** Apply χ^2-test: See worked out Ex. 14 on page 163 (Statistics)]

(*c*) Total correlation coefficients between the three variables x_1, x_2 and x_3 are as given below:

$$r_{12} = 0.2, \quad r_{23} = 0.1, \quad r_{13} = 0.3$$

Find the multiple correlation coefficient between x_1 and (x_2, x_3); and partial correlation coefficient between x_1 and x_2 given x_3. [**Ans.** 0.35; 0.18]

Statistical Table Values

$p(-1.96 < z < 1.96) = 0.95$; $p(-2.58 < z < 2.58) = 0.99$

$t_{0.01}$ with 16 d.f. $= 2.58$; $t_{0.01}$ with 15 d.f. $= 2.60$

$\chi^2_{.01}$ with 4 d.f. $= 13.28$; $\chi^2_{.01}$ with 6 d.f. $= 16.81$

$t_{.01}$ with 10 d.f. $= 3.17$

[**Hints.** See pages 131, 132 (Economic Techniques).]

December 1996

Section A (Mathematical Techniques: 40 marks)

Answer *Question No.* 1 (Compulsory–10 marks) and *two other questions* from this section (15 × 2 = 30 marks)

1. Attempt *any two* of the following:

(*a*) Show that $A = \begin{bmatrix} 1 & 2 & 2 \\ 2 & 1 & 1 \\ 2 & 2 & 2 \end{bmatrix}$ satisfies $A^2 - 4A - 5I = Q$, where Q denotes the zero matrix. Hence find the inverse of A.

(b) If $y = C_1 e^{kx} + C_2 e^{-kx}$, show that $y_2 = k^2 y$.

(c) Show that $\int_b^a \frac{\log v}{v} dv = \frac{1}{2}\log(ab)\log\left(\frac{a}{b}\right)$.

[**Hints.** (a) See worked Ex. 12 on page 45. (b) See worked out Ex. 1 on page 188. (c) See worked out Ex. 11 on page 272]

2. (a) Given that $\vec{a} = 2i + 3j + 6k$, $\vec{b} = 3i - 6j + 2k$ and $\vec{c} = 6i + 2j - 3k$, show that $\vec{a} \times \vec{b} = 7\vec{c}$. Also find a unit vector perpendicular to each of the vectors $\vec{a}$ and $\vec{b}$. [**Ans.** $\frac{6}{7}i + \frac{2}{7}j - \frac{3}{7}k$]

[**Hints.** See worked out Ex. 13, 14 on pages 16, 17]

(b) Express the square of $\begin{vmatrix} x_1 & y_1 & 0 \\ x_2 & y_2 & 0 \\ x_3 & y_3 & 0 \end{vmatrix}$ as a third order determinant without any zero element. What is its value? [**Ans.** 0]

[**Hints.** See worked out Ex. 2 on page 76]

(c) A factory producing bags has three types of workers: Skilled (Grade-I), skilled (Grade-II) and semi-skilled. Average number of bags produced per day by the skilled (Grade I), skilled (Grade II) and semi-skilled are 8, 6 and 4 respectively, the average daily production being 108 bags. One day due to local strike only half of the skilled (Grade II) and semi-skilled and one-fourth of skilled (Grade I) workers attained the factory and only 46 bags were produced. Find the number of workers of each type, the total number of workers in the factory being 20 only. [**Ans.** 4, 6, 10]

[**Hints.** If x, y, z be the no. of skilled (Grade I), skilled (Grade II) and semi-skilled workers respectively, then $x + y + z = 20 \quad \cdots$ (1), $8x + 6y + 4z = 108 \quad \cdots$ (2) and $8 \times \frac{1}{4}x + 6 \times \frac{1}{2}y + 4 \times \frac{1}{2}z = 46$, or, $2x + 3y + 2z = 46 \quad \cdots$ (3). Now solve for x, y, z.]

3. (a) Evaluate $\lim\limits_{h \to 0} \dfrac{\sqrt{x+h} - \sqrt{x}}{h}$.

[**Hints.** See worked out Ex. 9 on page 148] [**Ans.** $\frac{1}{2\sqrt{x}}, x > 0$]

(b) Draw the graph of $f(x)$ and show that $f(x)$ is continuous at $x = 0$ and $x = 1$ where

$$\left.\begin{aligned} f(x) &= -x \quad \text{for } x \leq 0 \\ &= x \quad \text{for } 0 < x < 1 \\ &= 2 - x \text{ for } x \geq 1. \end{aligned}\right\}$$

[**Hints.** See worked out Ex. 13 on page 150].

(c) An open cylindrical can has an area of surface equal to 200 cm^2. Find the maximum volume. [**Ans.** $\frac{2000\sqrt{2}}{3\sqrt{3\pi}}$ cu. cm.]

[**Hints.** If r be the radius of the circular base and h the height of the can, then $\pi r^2 + 2\pi rh = 200$ and $V = \pi r^2 h = \pi r^2 \left(\frac{200 - \pi r^2}{2\pi r}\right) = 100r - \frac{1}{2}\pi r^3$. Now find the max. value of V]

4. (a) If $f'(x) = \frac{e^{3x} + e^{5x}}{e^x + e^{-x}}$ and $f(0) = \frac{1}{4}$, find $f(x)$. [**Ans.** $\frac{1}{4}e^{4x}$]

[**Hints.** Integrating, $f(x) = \int \frac{e^{3x}+e^{5x}}{e^x+e^{-x}} dx + c = \int e^{4x} \frac{(e^{-x}+e^x)}{(e^x+e^{-x})} dx + C =$ etc.]

(b) Find the area of the region bounded by the curves $y^2 = 6x$ and $x^2 = 6y$.

[**Hints.** See worked Ex. 5 on page 287] [**Ans.** 12 sq. units]

(*c*) Solve the following LPP graphically or by simplex method:
Maximize $Z = 5x_1 + 7x_2$ subject to $2x_1 + 3x_2 \leq 13$, $3x_1 + 2x_2 \leq 12$, $x_1, x_2 \geq 0$.

[**Ans.** $x_1 = 2$, $x_2 = 3$; 31]

[**Hints.** See worked out Ex. 3 on page 306 or Ex.3 on page 326]

Section II (Statistical Techniques: 40 marks)

5. Attempt *any two* of the following:

(*a*) Of 500 employees, 280 participate in company's profit sharing plan (P), 400 have Major Medical Insurance Coverage (M) and 200 employees participate in both programmes. (i) What is the probability that a randomly selected employee will be a participant in at least one of the two programmes? (ii) Determine the probability that an employee will be a participant in the plan (P), given that he has insurance coverage (M).

[**Ans.** (i) $\frac{24}{25}$; (ii) $\frac{1}{2}$]

[**Hints.** $P(P) = \frac{280}{500} = \frac{28}{50}$, $P(M) = \frac{400}{500} = \frac{4}{5}$, $P(P \cap M) = \frac{200}{500} = \frac{2}{5}$. Now find $P(P \cup M)$ and $P(P/M)$. See worked out Ex. 1, 2 on page 21 (Statistical Technique)]

(*b*) If the two regression lines are $x + 2y = 5$ and $2x + 3y = 8$, and $\text{var}(x) = 12$, find $\bar{x}, \bar{y}, r$ and $\text{var}(y)$. [**Ans.** $\bar{x} = 1, \bar{y} = 2$; $r = -\frac{\sqrt{3}}{2}$, $\text{var}(y) = 4$]

[**Hints.** See worked out Ex. 20, 21 on pages 220, 221]

(*c*) X is a normal variate such that $P(X < 61) = 0.44$ and $P(X > 80) = 0.04$, find its mean and s.d. Also find $P(X > 65)$.

[Given: $\int_0^t \frac{1}{\sqrt{2\pi}} e^{-\frac{u^2}{2}} du = 0.06, 0.10, 0.46$ according as $t = 0.15, 0.25$]

[**Hints.** See worked out Ex. 30, 31 on page 82 (Statistical Technique). Here area between $x = 61$ to $x = m$ is $0.5 - 0.44 = 0.06$ and for $z_1 = \frac{61-m}{\sigma}$, $z_1 = -0.15$; $\therefore$ $\frac{61-m}{\sigma} = -0.15 \cdots (1)$. Similarly, $\frac{80-m}{\sigma} = 1.75 \cdots (2)$. Now solve (1) and (2)]

6. (*a*) Suppose there is a chance for a newly constructed building to collapse whether the design is faulty or not. The chance that the design is faulty is 10%. The chance that the building collapses is 95% if the design is faulty and otherwise it is 45%. It is seen that the building collapsed. What is the probability that it is due to faulty design?

[**Ans.** $\frac{19}{100}$ or, 0.19]

[**Hints.** Let A be the event that the design is faulty and B the event that the building collapsed. Then $P(A) = \frac{10}{100} = \frac{1}{10}$, $P(A^c) = 1 - P(A) = \frac{9}{10}$, $P(B/A) = \frac{95}{100} = \frac{19}{20}$, $P(B/A^c) = \frac{9}{20}$.

We have to find $P(A/B)$. By Bayes' Theorem

$$P(A/B) = \frac{P(A) \cdot P(B/A)}{P(A) \cdot P(B/A) + P(A^c)P(B/A^c)} = \frac{\frac{1}{10} \times \frac{19}{20}}{\frac{1}{10} \times \frac{19}{20} + \frac{9}{10} \times \frac{9}{20}} = \frac{19}{19+81} = \frac{19}{100}$$]

(*b*) A random variable X is binomially distributed with mean 4 and standard deviation $\sqrt{2.4}$. Find the probability that more than half the trials are successes.

[**Ans.** $n = 10$; 0.166]

[**Hints.** See worked out Ex. 6 to find $n = 10$, $p = 0.4$, $q = 0.6$. Required Probability $= f(6) + f(7) + f(8) + f(9) + f(10) = \text{etc.} = {}^{10}C_6 \times p^6 q^4 + {}^{10}C_7 p^7 q^3 + {}^{10}C_8 p^8 q^2 + {}^{10}C_9 p^9 \cdot q^1 + {}^{10}C_{10} p^{10} = \text{etc.}$]

(c) It is observed that 80% of television viewers watch "*Aap ki Adalat*" programme. What is the probability that at least 80% of the viewers in a random sample of five watch this programme? **[Ans.** 0.73728]

[Hints. Use Binomial distribution. Here $n = 5$, $p = \frac{80}{100} = 0.8$, $q = 1 - 0.8 = 0.2$.
$f(x) = {}^nC_x p^x q^{n-x} = {}^5C_x (0.8)^x \cdot (0.2)^{5-x}$. Now 80% of 5 = 4.
The required probability $= f(4) + f(5) = {}^5C_4(0.8)^4(0.2)^1 + {}^5C_5(0.8)^5(0.2)^0$; etc.]

7. (a) A simple random sample of size 2 is drawn with replacement from a population of 4 values 50, 60, 64, 70. Find the sampling distribution of the sample mean ($\bar{x}$) and verify that $E(\bar{x})$ = population mean and $V(\bar{x}) = \frac{1}{2}$ the population variance.

[Ans.

$\bar{x}_i$	50	55	57	60	62	64	65	67	79	Total
p_i	$\frac{1}{16}$	$\frac{2}{16}$	$\frac{2}{16}$	$\frac{3}{16}$	$\frac{2}{16}$	$\frac{1}{16}$	$\frac{2}{16}$	$\frac{2}{16}$	$\frac{1}{16}$	1

$E(\bar{x}) = 61$]

[Hints. See worked out Ex. 5 on page 114 (Statistics)]

(b) In a mass compaign signatures were collected on 200 sheets. Each sheet was provided with space for 30 signatures, but the signatories put their signatures at random, so that the number of signatures per sheet was not definite. Of these sheets a random sample of 25 sheets was drawn and the numbers of signatures per sheet were recorded as below:

No. of signatures	10	16	17	18	19	20	22	23	28	29	30
No. of sheets	1	1	1	2	1	4	3	5	2	1	4

Estimate the total number of signatures and calculate 95% confidence limits. [You are given: $P(z > 1.96) = 0.025$ where z is $N(0, 1)$ variate] **[Ans.** 4512; 2489.3, 6534.7]

[Hints. $\bar{x}$ = average no. of signature per sheet $= \frac{\sum fx}{\sum f} = \frac{564}{25}$.
$\therefore$ Estimate of the total no. of signatures $= \frac{564}{25} \times 200 = 4512$.
Find σ for 200 sheets and then the confidence limits]

(c) The eye-sight of 1000 randomly selected people from a town were tested:

	Poor Eye-sight	Good Eye-sight
Male :	200	350
Female :	200	250

Can we conclude at 5% level of significance that sex has no bearing on the quality of eye-sight? [Given: Value of χ^2 at 5% level = 3.84, 5.99, 7.81, 9.49 for d.f. 1, 2, 3 and 4] **[Ans.** No, quality of eye-sight depend on sex]

[Hints. Use χ^2-test. See worked out Ex. 12 on page 161 (Statistics)]

8. (a) Chemical Products Ltd. produces a compound which must be sold within the month it is produced, if the normal price of Rs. 100 per drum is to be obtained. Anything unsold in that month is sold in a different market for Rs. 20 per drum. The variable cost is Rs. 55 per drum. During the last five years monthly demand was recorded and showed the following frequencies.

Monthly demand (No. of drums)	:	2000	300	6000
Frequency	:	24	12	24

(i) Prepare an appropriate pay-off table; (ii) Advise the production menagement on the number of drums that should be produced next month.

[**Ans.** 6000 drums should be produced next month]

[**Hints.** See worked out Ex. 9, 10 on page 296-297 (Statistics)]

(*b*) Pay-offs of three acts A, B and C, and the states of nature X, Y and Z are given below:

Pay-off (in Rs.)

State of nature \ Acts	A	B	C
X	−20	−50	200
Y	200	−100	−50
Z	400	600	300

The probabilities of the states of nature are 0.3, 0.4 and 0.3. Calculate the expected monetary value (EMV) for the above data and select the best act. Also find the expected value of perfect information (EVPI).

[**Ans.** Rs. 194, Rs. 125, Rs. 130; Best act is A; Rs. 126]

[**Hints.** See Illustration given on page 299 (Statistics)]

(*c*) The means of two large samples of sizes 1000 and 2000 are 67.5 and 68 respectively. Test the equality of means of the two populations each with s.d. 2.5.

[**Ans.** The two means are not equal]

[**Hints.** See worked out Ex. 9 on page 136 (Statistics)]

Section III (Economic Techniques : 20 Marks)

9. Answer *any four parts*:

(*a*) The following table gives the *cost of living index numbers* for different groups with their respective weights for the year 1992 (base year : 1982):

Groups	Cost of living index	Weight
Food	525	40
Clothing	325	16
Light & Fuel	240	15
Rent	180	20
Others	200	9

Calculate the *over all Cost of Living Index Number.*

Mr. Bose got a salary of Rs. 550 in 1982. Determine how much he should have to receive as salary in 1992 to maintain his same standard of living as in 1982.

[**Ans.** 352; Rs. 1,936]

[**Hints.** Similar to Q. 9(b) set in December 1995; see solution of the question]

(*b*) Show that elasticity of demand $= \frac{AR}{AR-MR}$, where AR and MR are, respectively average and marginal revenue at any output. Verify this for linear demand law $p = a + bx$.

[**Hints.** Elasticity of Demand $= e = -\frac{p}{x} \cdot \frac{dx}{dp}$. Since $MR = AR\left(1 - \frac{1}{e}\right)$; $e = \frac{AR}{AR-MR}$. See Q.4, June 1996]

(c) The following table gives the annual sales (in '000 Rs.) of a commodity:

Year	:	1980	1981	1982	1983	1984	1985
Sales	:	75	68	70	78	80	88.

Obtain the trend by (i) Semi-average method; (ii) Fitting a straight line using least squares method.

[**Ans.** $Y = 76.5 + 1.557X$ with the origin at the mid point of 1982 and 1983 and unit of X as $\frac{1}{2}$ year]

[**Hints.** (i) Draw a straight line joining the two points. (1981, 71) and (1984, 82).

(ii) Let the straight line trend by the least squares method with the origin at the mid point of 1982 and 1983 be $Y = a + bX \cdots (1)$

Then the normal equations are $a = \frac{\sum Y}{N}$ and $b = \frac{\sum XY}{\sum X^2}$.

Here $N = 6$, $a = \frac{459}{6} = 76.5$ and $b = \frac{109}{70} = 1.557$. [Using totals of the table-values]

$\therefore$ **Y = 76.5 + 1.557X**

Year	Y	X	X^2	XY
1980	75	−5	25	−375
1981	68	−3	9	−204
1982	70	−1	1	− 70
1983	78	1	1	78
1984	80	3	9	240
1985	88	5	25	440
Total	$459 = \Sigma Y$	0	$70 = \Sigma X^2$	$109 = \Sigma XY$

]

(d) Deseasonalise the following sales data and interpret them

Quarter	Sales ('000 Rs.)	Seasonal Index
1st	23.7	78
2nd	25.2	124
3rd	21.4	50
4th	65.4	148

(e) For a trivariate distribution the following correlation coefficients were obtained: $r_{12} = 0.77$, $r_{13} = 0.72$ and $r_{23} = 0.52$.

Find the partial correlation coefficient $r_{12.3}$ and multiple correlation coefficient $R_{1.23}$.

[**Ans.** 0.667; 0.856]

[**Hints.** See worked out Problem No. 15 on page 131, 132 (Economic Techniques)]

(f) Write short notes on any one of the following:

(i) Input-output analysis; (ii) Construction of Index numbers.

June 1997

Section A (Mathematical Techniques: 40 marks)

Answer *Question No.* 1 (Compulsory–10 marks) and *two other questions* from this section ($15 \times 2 = 30$ marks)

1. Attempt *any two* of the following: [$5 \times 2 = 10$]

(a) Reduce the following system of equations to matrix form and solve: $x + 2y + z = 4$, $x - y + z = 5$, $2x + 3y - z = 1$. [**Ans.** $x = \frac{20}{9}$, $y = -\frac{1}{3}$, $z = \frac{22}{9}$]

[**Hints.** See worked out Ex. 6 on page 92]

(*b*) Show that $\int_0^1 \frac{dt}{\sqrt{1+t}-\sqrt{t}} = \frac{4\sqrt{2}}{3}$.

[**Hints.** See worked out Ex. 10 on page 247. Here Integral $= \left[\frac{2}{3}(t+1)^{3/2} + \frac{2}{3}t^{3/2}\right]_0^1 =$ etc.]

(*c*) Find two positive numbers whose sum is 16 and the sum of whose squares is minimum.

[**Ans.** 8, 8]

[**Hints.** See worked out Ex. 19 on page 229.
Here $x + y = 16$, or, $y = 16 - x$ and $A = x^2 + y^2 = x^2 + (16-x)^2$
i.e., $A = 2x^2 - 32x + 256$; $\therefore\ \frac{dA}{dx} = 4x - 32$ and $\frac{d^2A}{dx^2} = 4$, etc.]

2. (*a*) Draw the graph of $f(x)$ defined by $f(x) = \frac{|x-1|}{x-1}$, if $x \neq 1$ and $f(x) = 0$, if $x = 1$ and discuss its continuity at $x = 1$.

[**Ans.** $f(x)$ is not continuous at $x = 1$]

[**Hints.** $f(x) = |x-1| = x-1$ if $x > 1$, $f(x) = |x-1| = -(x-1) = 1-x$ if $x < 1$ and $f(1) = 0$. Now draw the graph of $f(x)$ and from the graph discuss continuity at $x = 1$]

(*b*) If $\vec{u} = 2i + j - k$ and $\vec{v} = i + j + 3k$, show that $\vec{u}$ is perpendicular to $\vec{v}$. Also find the value of $|\vec{u} + \vec{v}|$.

[**Ans.** $\sqrt{17}$]

[**Hints.** See worked out Ex. 8 on page 13]

(*c*) Solve the following L.P.P. graphically or otherwise:
Maximize $z = 7x + 5y$ subject to $x + 2y \leq 6$, $4x + 3y \leq 12$, $x, y \geq 0$.

[**Ans.** Max. $z = 21$ at $(3, 0)$]

[**Hints.** See worked out Ex. 4 on page 306 and Ex. 6 on page 308]

3. (*a*) Show that $\begin{vmatrix} 1+a & 1 & 1 \\ 1 & 1+b & 1 \\ 1 & 1 & 1+c \end{vmatrix} = abc\left(1 + \frac{1}{a} + \frac{1}{b} + \frac{1}{c}\right)$ without expanding it.

[**Hints.**

$$\text{L.H.S.} = abc\begin{vmatrix} \frac{1}{a}+1 & \frac{1}{b} & \frac{1}{c} \\ \frac{1}{a} & \frac{1}{b}+1 & \frac{1}{c} \\ \frac{1}{a} & \frac{1}{b} & \frac{1}{c}+1 \end{vmatrix} = abc\begin{vmatrix} 1+\frac{1}{a}+\frac{1}{b}+\frac{1}{c} & \frac{1}{b} & \frac{1}{c} \\ 1+\frac{1}{a}+\frac{1}{b}+\frac{1}{c} & \frac{1}{b}+1 & \frac{1}{c} \\ 1+\frac{1}{a}+\frac{1}{b}+\frac{1}{c} & \frac{1}{b} & \frac{1}{c}+1 \end{vmatrix}$$

$$= abc\left(1+\frac{1}{a}+\frac{1}{b}+\frac{1}{c}\right)\begin{vmatrix} 1 & \frac{1}{b} & \frac{1}{c} \\ 1 & \frac{1}{b}+1 & \frac{1}{c} \\ 1 & \frac{1}{b} & \frac{1}{c}+1 \end{vmatrix} = abc\left(1+\frac{1}{a}+\frac{1}{b}+\frac{1}{c}\right)\begin{vmatrix} 1 & \frac{1}{b} & \frac{1}{c} \\ 0 & 1 & 0 \\ 0 & 0 & 1 \end{vmatrix}$$

$$= abc\left(1+\frac{1}{a}+\frac{1}{b}+\frac{1}{c}\right)\begin{vmatrix} 1 & 0 \\ & 1 \end{vmatrix} = abc\left(1+\frac{1}{a}+\frac{1}{b}+\frac{1}{c}\right)$$]

(*b*) If $A = \begin{pmatrix} 1 & -1 \\ 2 & -1 \end{pmatrix}$, $B = \begin{pmatrix} 1 & [illegible] \\ y & [illegible] \end{pmatrix}$ [illegible]d $(A+B)^2 = A^2 + B^2$, find x and y.

[**Hints.** See worked out Ex. 18 on page, 48]

(*c*) Find the area cut off from the parabola $y^2 = 12x$ by its latus rectum.

[**Ans.** 24 sq. units]

[**Hints.** Required area $= 2\int_0^a y\,dx = 2\int_0^3 \sqrt{12x}\,dx =$ etc.]

4. (*a*) If $f'(a)$ exists, show that $\lim\limits_{x \to a} \frac{xf(a)-af(x)}{x-a} = f(a) - af'(a)$.

[**Hints.** L.H.S. $= \lim\limits_{x \to a} \left[\frac{(x-a)f(a)+af(a)-af(x)}{x-a}\right] = \lim\limits_{x \to a} \left[f(a) - \frac{a\{f(x)-f(a)\}}{x-a}\right]$]

(*b*) If $x^3y^4 = (x+y)^7$, show that $y = x\frac{dy}{dx}$.

[**Hints.** See worked out Ex. 16 on page 179]

(*c*) If $u = x^2y + y^2x$, find the value of $\left(x\frac{\partial u}{\partial x} + y\frac{\partial u}{\partial y}\right)$ when $x = y = 1$. [**Ans.** 6]

[**Hints.** $\frac{\partial u}{\partial x} = 2xy + y^2$ and $\frac{\partial u}{\partial y} = x^2 + 2yx$, etc.]

Section II (Statistical Techniques : 40 marks)

Answer *Question No.* 5 (Compulsory–10 marks) and *two other questions* from this section (15 × 2 = 30 marks)

5. Attempt *any two* of the following: [5 × 2 = 10]

(*a*) If $P(A) = \frac{1}{4}$, $P(B) = \frac{2}{5}$ and $P(A \cup B) = \frac{1}{2}$, find (i) $P(A \cap B^c)$, (ii) $P(A^c \cup B^c)$, where A and B are two non-mutually exclusive events connected with a random experiment E. [**Ans.** (i) $\frac{1}{10}$; (ii) $\frac{17}{20}$.]

[**Hints.** See worked out Ex. 4 on page 18]

(*b*) If X be a Poisson variate such that $P(X = 2) = 9P(X = 4) + 90P(X = 6)$, find the mean and s.d. of X. [**Ans.** Mean = 1; S.D. = 1]

[**Hints.** See worked out Ex. 19 on page 72]

(*c*) Rank correlation coefficient between the marks in Mathematics and Statistics obtained by a group of students is $\frac{2}{3}$ and the sum of the squares of the differences in rank is 55. Find the number of students in the group. [**Ans.** 10]

[**Hints.** See worked out Ex. 11 on page 211 (Statistical Techniques)]

6. (*a*) For a binomial variate X with mean = 4 and variance = 3, find $P(X$ = a non-zero value). [**Ans.** $1 - \left(\frac{3}{4}\right)^{16}$]

[**Hints.** See workd out Ex. 6 on page 63 (Statistical Technique)
$f(x) = {}^{16}C_x \left(\frac{1}{4}\right)^x \cdot \left(\frac{3}{4}\right)^{16-x}$; $\therefore$ $f(0) = {}^{16}C_0 \left(\frac{1}{4}\right)^0 \cdot \left(\frac{3}{4}\right)^{16} = \left(\frac{3}{4}\right)^{16}$]

(*b*) If X be a normal variate with mean 3 and variance 16, find the value of t such that $P(3 \le X \le t) = 0.4772$. [Given $P(Z \le 2) = 0.9772$, where Z is $N(0,1)$ variate.] [**Ans.** $t = 11$]

[**Hints.** $Z = \frac{x-m}{\sigma} = \frac{3-3}{4} = 0$ if $X = 3$, $Z = \frac{t-3}{4}$ if $X = t$. Now $P(Z \le 2) = 0.9772 \Rightarrow P(0 \le Z \le 2) = 0.9772 - 0.5 = 0.4772$, etc.]

(*c*) The p.d.f of a continuous random variate X is given by

$$f(x) = kx^2(1-x);\ 0 < x < 1$$
$$= 0, \quad \text{elsewhere.}$$

Find the constant $k, E(X)$ and var (X). [**Ans.** $k = 12; E(X) = \frac{3}{5}$; var $(X) = \frac{1}{25}$]

[**Hints.** $\int_0^1 f(x)dx = 1 \Rightarrow k = 12$. $\therefore$ $f(x) = 12x^2(1-x)$, $0 < x < 1$.
Now see worked out Ex. 23 on page 74 (Statistical Techniques)]

7. (*a*) There are two identical urns containing respectively 3 red and 4 white balls, and 7 red and 3 while balls. An urn is chosen at random and a ball is drawn from it. If the ball is white, what is the probability that it is drawn from the first urn? [**Ans.** $\frac{40}{61}$]

[**Hints.** See worked out Ex. 1 on page 27 (Statistical Techniques)] (*b*) From the following results obtain the two regression equations and estimate x when $y = 600$:

$$\bar{x} = 26.7, \quad \bar{y} = 508, \quad \sigma_x = 4.6, \quad \sigma_y = 36.8, \quad r_{xy} = 0.52.$$

[**Ans.** $y = 4.16x + 397.328$, $x = 0.065y - 6.346$; 32.654]

[**Hints.** See worked out Ex. 18 on page 219 (Statistical Techniques)]

(*c*) 20, 25, 19, 17, 14 constitute a random sample from a population. Estimate the mean and s.d. of the population. Also find the estimate of the S.E. of sample mean.

[**Ans.** Mean = 19, s.d. = 4.062; S.E. = 2.24]

[**Hints.** See worked out Ex. 6 on page 114 (Statistical Technique)]

8. (*a*) In order to test whether a coin is perfect, it is tossed 5 times. The null hypothesis of perfectness is rejected if and only if more than 4 heads is obtained. Obtain the (i) critical region, (ii) probability of type I error, and (iii) the probability of type II error when the corresponding probability of getting a head is 0.2.

[**Ans.** Critical region is the "occurrence of 5 heads"; (ii) $\frac{1}{32}$ or 0.03125, (iii) $1 - (0.2)^5$ or, 0.99968]

[**Hints.** Let $H_0 : p = \frac{1}{2}$. Then $H_1 : p \neq \frac{1}{2}$. Accept H_0 when $x = 0, 1, 2, 3, 4$ and reject H_0 when $x = 5$ in $f(x) = {}^5C_x \left(\frac{1}{2}\right)^x \left(\frac{1}{2}\right)^{5-x}$]

(*b*) A random sample of size 20 yields a mean of 40 and variance of 25. Test the hypothesis that the population s.d. is 8. [Given $\chi^2_{0.05} = 28.87$ for 18 d.f.; $= 30.14$ for 19 d.f.; $= 31.41$ for 20 d.f.]

[**Ans.** H_0 is accepted i.e., $\sigma = 8$]

[**Hints.** See worked out Ex. 15 on page 164 (Statistical Techniques)]
Here $n = 20$, $\bar{x} = 40$, $s^2 = 25$, $\sigma_0 = 8$]

(*c*) Suppose that a decision-maker faced with three decision alternatives and four states of nature. Given the following profit pay-off table:

Acts \ States of Nature	S_1	S_2	S_3	S_4
a_1	16	10	12	7
a_2	13	12	9	9
a_3	11	14	15	14

Assuming that he has no knowledge of the probabilities of occurrence of the states of nature, find the decisions to be recommended under each of the following criteria: (i) Maximin, (ii) Maximax, (iii) Minimax Regret.

[**Ans.** (i) Act a_3 is recommended; (ii) Act a_1 is selected; (iii) Act a_3 is recommended]

[**Hints.** See worked out Ex. 2 on page 290 (Statistical Techniques)]

Section III (Economic Techniques : 20 Marks)

9. Attempt *any four* parts of the following: $5 \times 4 = 20$

(*a*) The marginal cost function when output is x units is given by $MC = x^2 - 2x + 5$. Find the total cost function C and average cost function AC, if the fixed cost is 30. Also show that the slope of the average cost curve is $\frac{MC - AC}{x}$.

[**Ans.** $\frac{1}{3}x^3 - x^2 + 5x + 30$; $\frac{1}{3}x^2 - x + 5 + \frac{30}{x}$]

[**Hints.** If C be the total cost of x units, then $\frac{dC}{dX} = MC = x^2 - 2x + 5$, or, $dC = (x^2 - 2x + 5)dx$. Integrating, $C = \frac{1}{3}x^3 - x^2 + 5x + k$. Here k = fixed cost = 30]

61

(*b*) The demand function is $x = 100 + 4p + 10p^2$, where x the quantity is demanded of the commodity at price p. Compute: (i) the marginal quantity demanded, (ii) the average quantity demand, and (iii) elasticity of demand. Hence show that the quantity demanded at a price $p = 4$ is elastic.

[**Ans.** (i) $4 + 20p$; (ii) $\frac{100}{p} + 4 + 10p$; (iii) $\frac{dx}{dp} \cdot \frac{p}{x} = 84\left(\frac{4}{176}\right) = 1.2$ (pp.) at $p = 4$.]

(*c*) **Find the 5-year weighted moving averages with weights 1, 2, 2, 2, 1 respectively for measuring trend of the following time series:**

Year	1974	1975	1976	1977	1978	1979	1980	1981	1982
Sales (Rs. '00000)	2	6	1	5	3	7	2	6	4

[**Ans.** –, –, 3.625, 3.875, 4.125, 4.375, 4.625, –, –]

[**Hints.** The following Table gives the moving averages for measuring trend:

Year	Sales (Rs. '00000)	5-years weighted moving total	5 year weighted moving average
1974	2	....	....
1975	6	....	....
1976	1	$2\times1+6\times2+1\times2+5\times2+3\times1=29$	$29\div8=3.625$
1977	5	$6\times1+1\times2+5\times2+3\times2+7\times1=31$	$31\div8=3.875$
1978	3	$1\times1+5\times2+3\times2+7\times2+2\times1=33$	$33\div8=4.125$
1979	7	$5\times1+3\times2+7\times2+2\times2+6\times1=35$	$35\div8=4.375$
1980	2	$3\times1+7\times2+2\times2+6\times2+4\times1=37$	$37\div8=4.625$
1981	6	....	....
1982	4	....	....

(*d*) **The price relatives and weights of a set of commodities are given in the following table:**

Commodity	C_1	C_2	C_3	C_4
Price relative	120	127	125	119
Weight	$2w_1$	w_2	w_1	w_2+3

If the index for the set is 122 and the sum of the weights is 40, find w_1 and w_2.

[**Ans.** $w_1 = 7$, $w_2 = 8$]

[**Hints.** See hints of Q.9 on page 281 (Statistical Techniques)]

(*e*) **Given the following transaction table, find the gross output to meet the final demand of 80 units of industry and 40 units of agriculture:**

Producing sector \ Purchasing sector	Industry	Agriculture	Current demand	Total output
Industry	30	40	60	130
Agriculture	20	10	40	70

[**Ans.** $x_1 = 160$; $x_2 = \frac{980}{13}$]

(*f*) **Write short notes on *any one* of the following:**

(i) Least squares theory, (ii) Cost of living index, (iii) Multiple correlation.

December 1997

Section A (Mathematical Techniques: 40 Marks)

Answer *Question No.* 1 (Compulsory–10 marks) and *two other questions* from this section ($15 \times 2 = 30$ marks)

1. Attempt *any two* of the following: [$5 \times 2 = 10$]

(*a*) If $A = \begin{bmatrix} 1 & a & -2 \\ 2 & 2 & 4 \\ 0 & 0 & 2 \end{bmatrix}$, find a for which $A^2 + 2I_3 = 3A$, where I_3 is the unit matrix of order 3. Hence (and not otherwise) find A^{-1}. [**Ans.** $a = 0$; $A^{-1} = \begin{bmatrix} 1 & 0 & 1 \\ -1 & \frac{1}{2} & -2 \\ 0 & 0 & \frac{1}{2} \end{bmatrix}$.]

[**Hints.** See worked out Ex. 7 on page 96]

(*b*) Show that $\begin{vmatrix} a-b-c & 2a & 2a \\ 2b & b-c-a & 2b \\ 2c & 2c & c-a-b \end{vmatrix} = (a+b+c)^3$. Hence find the value of x from $\begin{vmatrix} 3-x & 2x & 2x \\ 2x-2 & 1-x & 2x-2 \\ 2x-4 & 2x-4 & -1-x \end{vmatrix} = 0.$ [**Ans.** $x = 1$]

[**Hints.** See worked out Ex. 12 on page 68; put $a = x$, $b = x-1$ $c = x-2$]

(*c*) If $f(x) = \frac{x-1}{x+1}$, show that (i) $f\left\{f\left(\frac{1}{x}\right)\right\} = -x$ and (ii) $f\left[f\left\{\frac{1}{f(x)}\right\}\right] = -f(x)$ for $x \neq 1, 0, -1$.

[**Hints.** $f\left(\frac{1}{x}\right) = \frac{\frac{1}{x}-1}{\frac{1}{x}+1} = \frac{1-x}{1+x}$ where $x \neq 0, -1$; $f\left\{f\left(\frac{1}{x}\right)\right\} = \frac{\frac{1-x}{1+x}-1}{\frac{1-x}{1+x}+1} =$ etc.

$\frac{1}{f(x)} = \frac{x+1}{x-1}$; $\therefore f\left\{\frac{1}{f(x)}\right\} = \frac{\frac{x+1}{x-1}-1}{\frac{x+1}{x-1}+1} = \frac{\frac{2}{x-1}}{\frac{2x}{x-1}} = \frac{1}{x}$, etc]

(*d*) A firm assumes a cost function $C(x) = x \quad {}_{10} + 200\Big]$, where x is the monthly output in thousand of units. Its revenue function is given by $R(x) = \frac{1}{2}(2200 - 3x)x$. Find (i) the firm's total cost, marginal cost, total revenue and the marginal revenue if the firm decides to produce 10,000 units per month; (ii) the output per month to make the marginal profit equal to zero and find the profit at this level of output.

[**Ans.** (i) 2100; 230; 10850; 1070; (ii) 50 units; 28750]

[**Hints.** $MC(x) = \frac{3x^2}{10} + 200$; $TR(x) = R(x) = \frac{1}{2}(2200 - 3x)x$; $MR(x) = 1100 - 3x$; $\pi(x) = R(x) - C(x)$; marginal profit $= \frac{d\pi}{dx}$]

2. (*a*) Show that the vectors $2i - j + k$, $i - 2j - 4k$ and $5i - j - k$ form the sides of a right-angled triangle, where i, j and k are the unit vectors perpendicular to each other.

(*b*) Assume that for a closed economy $E = C + I + G$, where E is the total expenditure on consumption goods, I is expenditure on investment goods and G is government spending. For equilibrium, we must have $E = Y$ where Y is total income received. For a certain economy, it is given that $C = 15 + 0.9Y$, $I = 20 + 0.05Y$ and $G = 25$. Find the equilibrium values of Y, C and I. How will these change if there is no government spending?

[**Hints.** $Y = C + I + G$; put the values of C, I, G and solve for Y.]

(*c*) Show that $\lim_{x \to 0} \frac{a^x - b^x}{x} = \log \frac{a}{b}$.

[**Hints.** See hints of Q. 20(i) on page 156. Here $a^x - b^x = (a^x - 1) - (b^x - 1)$]

3. (*a*) Solve by Cramer's Rule: $3x + y - z = 1$, $-2x + 3y + z = 6$, $3x - y - 4z = 3$.

[**Ans.** $x = -1$, $y = 2$, $z = -2$]

[**Hints.** See worked out Ex. 7 on page 81]

(*b*) If $y = x^3 \cdot 5^{x^3}$, find $\frac{dy}{dx}$ and $\frac{d^2y}{dx^2}$.

[**Ans.** $3x^3 \cdot 5^{x^3}\left(\frac{1}{x} + x^2 \log 5\right)$; $3x^3 5^{x^3}\left\{\frac{2}{x^2} + 3x^4(\log 5)^2 + 8x \log 5\right\}$]

(*c*) A company is planning to market a new model of a doll. Rather than setting the selling price of the doll based only on production cost estimates management polls the retailers of the doll to see how many dolls they would buy for various period. From the survey it is determined that the unit demand function (the relationship between the amount x each retailer would buy and the price he would pay) is $x = 30,000 - 1,500p$. The fixed costs of the production of the dolls are found to be Rs. 28,000 and cost of material and labour to produce each doll is estimated to be Rs. 8 per unit. What price should the company charge retailers in order to obtain a maximum profit?

[**Hints.** If $C(x)$ be the total cost of x dolls and $R(x)$ be the total revenue, then $C(x) = 2800 + 8x = 2800 + 8(30000 - 1500p)$ and $R(x) = px = p(30000 - 1500p)$, $P(x) =$ total profit $= R(x) - C(x) = 30000p - 1500p^2 - 268000 + 12000p$. Now find $\frac{dP}{dp}$ and $\frac{d^2P}{dp^2}$ and obtain the maximum profit]

4. (*a*) Evaluate: $\int \frac{e^x + e^{-x}}{e^x - e^{-x}} dx$.

[**Ans.** $\log(e^x - e^{-x}) + C$]

(*b*) Verify that a saddle point exists for the function $z = 18x^2 - 6y^2 - 36x - 48y$.

[**Hints.** $\frac{\partial z}{\partial x} = 36x - 36$, $\frac{\partial z}{\partial y} = -12y - 48$, $\frac{\partial^2 z}{\partial x^2} = 36$, $\frac{\partial^2 z}{\partial y^2} = -12$. $\frac{\partial z}{\partial x} = 0 \Rightarrow x = 1$ and $\frac{\partial z}{\partial y} = 0 \Rightarrow y = -4$. $\frac{\partial^2 z}{\partial x \partial y} = 0$. $\therefore$ $\frac{\partial^2 z}{\partial x^2}\frac{\partial^2 z}{\partial y^2} - \left(\frac{\partial^2 z}{\partial x \partial y}\right)^2 = 36(-12) - 0^2 = -432 < 0$.

Hence *the function has a saddle point at* $x = 1$, $y = -4$]

(*c*) A company produces two types of container K and L. Each product has resource requirements and profit contribution as follows:

Resource	K	L	Total resource available
Material (Kg/unit) :	1	2	10 Kg.
Labour (hr/unit) :	6	6	36 hr.
Profit :	4	5	

In addition, because of demand, a maximum of 4 units of container K will be produced. By graphical method obtain producetion plan that maximizes the profit.

[**Ans.** Max. profit = 28 when $x = 2$, $y = 4$]

[**Hints.** Let x be the no. of containers of type K and y, the no. of containers of type L. Then we have to maximise profit $z = 4x + 5y$ subject to the conditions $x + 2y \leq 10$, $6x + 6y \leq 36$, $x \leq 4$, $x, y \geq 0$. Now see worked out Ex. 8 on page 310 and Ex. 11 on page 313]

Section II (Statistical Techniques : 40 marks)

Answer *Question No.* 5 (compulsory–10 marks) and *two other questions* from this section ($15 \times 2 = 30$ marks)

5. Attempt *any two* of the following:

(*a*) If $P(A) = \frac{3}{4}$, $P(B) = \frac{1}{2}$, $P(A - B) = \frac{3}{8}$, find the probabilities that (i) exactly one of A and B occurs, (ii) none of them occurs. Also examine whether the events A and B are independent or not.

[**Ans.** (i) $\frac{1}{2}$; (ii) $\frac{1}{8}$; A and B are independent events]

[**Hints.** $P(A \cap B) + P(A - B) = P(A)$, or, $P(A \cap B) = P(A) - P(A - B) = \frac{3}{8}$. Again, $P(B) = P(B - A) + P(B \cap A) = \frac{1}{8}$; $P(A - B) + P(B - A) = \frac{1}{2}$]

(*b*) The marks scored by five students in a test of statistics carrying 100 marks are 50, 60, 50, 60 and 40. If a simple random sample of size 4 is drawn *without replacement*, draw up the sampling distribution of sample mean. Hence find the standard error of the sample mean.

[**Ans.**

$\bar{x}$:	50	52.5	55	Total
Prob. :	$\frac{2}{5}$	$\frac{2}{5}$	$\frac{1}{5}$	1

; $\sqrt{3.5}$ or, 1.87]

[**Hints.** See worked out Ex. 6 (6th part) on page 116 (Statistical Technique)]

(*c*) The data in the following table relates the weekly maintenance cost (in Rs.) to the age (in months) of ten machines of similar type in a manufacturing company. Find the least squares regression line of maintenance cost on age and use this to predict the maintenance cost for a machine of this type which is 40 months old.

Machine :	1	2	3	4	5	6	7	8	9	10
Age (x) :	5	10	15	20	30	30	30	50	50	60
Cost (y) :	190	240	250	300	310	335	300	300	350	395

[**Ans.** $y = 2.8033x + 212.901$; Rs. 325]

[**Hints.** See worked out Ex. 19 on page 219 (Statistical Technique)]

(*d*) A person wants to invest in one of three alternative instalment plans : stock, bonds or a saving account. It is assumed that the person wishes to invest in all of the funds in one plan. The conditional pay offs of the investment are based on three potential economic conditions : accelerated, normal or slow growth. The pay-off matrix is given below:

Alternative	Economic conditions		
Investment	Accelerated Growth Rs.	Normal Growth Rs.	Slow Growth Rs.
Stocks	10,000	6,500	−4,000
Bonds	8,000	6,000	1,000
Svings	5,000	5,000	5,000

Determine the best investment plan using each of the following criteria:
(i) Laplace, (ii) Maximin, (iii) Maximax, (iv) Hurwich with coefficient of optimism $\alpha - 0.6$ [**Ans.** (i) Bonds or savings; (ii) Savings; (iii) Stock; (iv) Bonds]

[**Hints.** See worked out Ex. 2 on page 290 (Statistical Technique):
(i) For Laplace criterion, find average stocks, average bonds and average savings and note that *average bonds* or *average savings* is better than average stocks]

6. (*a*) An unbiased coin is tossed 5 times independently and let X denote the number of tails obtained. Find the probability distribution of X, $P(X < 2)$ and variance of X.

[**Ans.**

x	0	1	2	3	4	5	Total
p	$\frac{1}{32}$	$\frac{5}{32}$	$\frac{10}{32}$	$\frac{10}{32}$	$\frac{5}{32}$	$\frac{1}{32}$	1

; $\frac{3}{16}$, $\frac{5}{4}$]

(*b*) In a summer, a truck driver gets on an average one puncture in 1000 km. Find the probability that he will have (i) no puncture, (ii) at most one puncture in a journey of 3000 km. [**Ans.** (i) e^{-3}; (ii) $4e^{-3}$]

[**Hints.** Here $p = \frac{1}{1000}$, $n = 3000$; $\therefore\ m = np = 3$; $f(x) = \frac{e^{-3}.3^x}{x!}$, $x = 0, 1, 2, \cdots$]

(*c*) A sample of 100 dry battery cells tested to find the length of life produced, has mean 12 hours and standard deviation 3 hours. Assuming the data to be normally distributed, what percentage of battery cells are expected to have life (i) more than

15 hours, (ii) less than 6 hours and (iii) between 6 hours and 15 hours? It is given that $\frac{1}{\sqrt{2\pi}} \int_0^x e^{-\frac{1}{2}t^2} dt = 0.34, 0.48$ according as $x = 1, 2$ respectively.

[**Ans.** (i) 16%; (ii) 2%; (iii) 82%]

[**Hints.** See worked Ex. 28 on page 80 (Statistical Techniques)]

7. (*a*) Define statistic, parameter, critical region, level of significance, power of a test.

(*b*) In a partially destroyed laboratory-record of an analysis of correlation data, the following results only are obtained:
Regression equations are $8x - 10y = 64$ and $40x - 18y = 320$. What are (i) the mean values of x and y, and (ii) the coefficient of correlation between x and y?

[**Ans.** $\bar{x} = 8, \bar{y} = 0, r_{xy} = 0.6$]

[**Hints.** See worked out Ex. 21 on page 221 (Statistical Techniques)]

(*c*) A random variable X has probability density function

$$\left.\begin{aligned} f(x) &= k \text{ for } -3 < x < 3 \\ &= 0 \text{ otherwise} \end{aligned}\right\}, \text{ where } k \text{ is a constant.}$$

Find the value of k, expectation of X and $P(|X| < 2|X > 1)$. [**Ans.** $k = \frac{1}{6}$; $E(x) = 0$; $\frac{1}{2}$]

[**Hints.** See the hints of Q 10 on page 94.

Here $P(|X| < 2/X > 1) = \frac{P(|X|<2 \cap X>1)}{P(X>1)} = \frac{P(1<X<2)}{P(X>1)} = \frac{\int_1^2 k dx}{\int_1^3 k dx} = \frac{1}{2}$]

8. (*a*) The following table shows the means and standard deviations of the cost (in Rs.) per square-foot of floor area randomly selected 6 schools and 5 nursinghomes from two independent normal populations with different means μ_1 and μ_2 but with equal variances (unknown):

Building type	mean	s.d.
Schools	287	21
Nursing-homes	352	18

Find a 95% confidence interval of $\mu_1 - \mu_2$ when it is given that $P(t_n > a) = 0.025$, where t_n follows t-distribution with n degrees of freedom and $a = 2.26, 2.23, 2.20$ according as $n = 9$, 10 and 11.

[**Ans.** 35.204, 94.796]

[**Hints.** $(\bar{x}_2 - \bar{x}_1) \pm t_\alpha \cdot s\sqrt{\frac{1}{n_1} + \frac{1}{n_2}}$ i.e., $(352 - 287) \pm t_{0.025} \cdot s\sqrt{\frac{1}{6} + \frac{1}{5}}$ where $s^2 = \frac{n_1 s_1^2 + n_2 s_2^2}{n_1 + n_2 - 2} = \frac{6 \times (21)^2 + 5 \times (18)^2}{6+5-2} = 474$, etc]

(*b*) A survey of 240 families with 4 children each revealed the following distribution:

No. of boys	:	4	3	2	1	0
No. of families	:	10	55	105	58	12.

Is the result consistent with the hypothesis that male and female births are equally probable? Given that $P(\chi^2 > a)$ and where χ^2 follows the chi-square distribution with n degrees of freedom and $a = 7.81, 9.49, 11.07$ according as $n = 3, 3, 5$.

[**Ans.** Yes, male and female births are equally probable.]

[**Hints.** See worked out Ex. 10 on page 158 (Statistical Techniques)]

(*c*) A newspaper agent's experience shows that the daily demand X of newspapers in his area has the following probability distribution:

Daily demand (x)	:	300	400	500	600	700
Probability (p)	:	0.1	0.3	0.4	0.1	0.1.

He sells the newspapers for Rs. 2.00 each while he buys each at Re. 1. Unsold copies are traded as scrap and each such copy fetches 10 paise. Assuming that he stocks the newspapers in multiple of 100 only, how many should he stock so that his expected profit is maximum? **[Ans.** Stock is 500]

[Hints. See worked out Ex. 11 on page 298 (Statistical Techniques)].

Here *profit* on each sold newspaper = Rs. 2– Re. 1 = Re. 1 and *loss* on each unsold newspaper = Rs. (1 – 0.10) = Rs. 0.90.

Stock, demand and corresponding profit are given below.

Stock \ Demand (Profit)	300	400	500	600	700
	Profit (Rs.)				
300	300	300	300	300	300
400	300 – 90	400	400	400	400
500	300 – 180	400 – 90	500	500	500
600	300 – 270	400 – 180	500 – 90	600	600
700	300 – 360	400 – 270	500 – 180	600 – 90	700

Now construct table showing expected pay-off and EMV.]

Section III (Economic Techniques : 20 Marks)

9. Attempt *any four* of the following questions: $5 \times 4 = 20$

(*a*) Fit a straight line trend by the method of least squares from the following figures of production of sponge iron in a factory and estimate the production in 1991:

Year	:	1985	1986	1987	1988	1989	1990
Production (in lakh tons)	:	15	18	16	18	20	19.

[Ans. $Y = \frac{53}{3} + \frac{2}{5}X$; 20.467 lakh tons]

[Hints. See hints of **Q. 9(c)** (ii) set in the year December 1996. In 1991, $X = 7$.]

(*b*) Calculate price index number of the year 1996 with 1986 as base year from the following data using: (i) Laspeyre's, (ii) Paasche's and (iii) Fisher's Formulae:

Commodity	Unit	1986		1996	
		Price (Rs.)	Value (Rs.)	Quantity consumed	Value (Rs.)
A	Kg.	10	1500	160	1760
B	Kg	12	1080	100	1300
C	Metre	15	900	60	960
D	Packets	9	450	40	480

[Ans. (i) 111.45; (ii) 110.84; (iii) 111.14]

[Hints. See worked out Ex. 15 on page 257.]

(c) From heights (x_1) in inches, weights (x_2) in kg. and ages (x_3) in years of a group of students the following means, variances and correlation coefficients were obtained:

$$\bar{x}_1 = 40, \quad \bar{x}_2 = 50, \quad \bar{x}_3 = 20$$
$$s_1 = 3, \quad s_2 = 4, \quad s_3 = 2$$
$$r_{12} = 0.4, \quad r_{23} = 0.5, \quad r_{13} = 0.25$$

where $\bar{x}_1$ = man of x_1, s_1^2 = var (x) and r_{ij} = correlation between x_i and x_j for $i, j = 1, 2, 3$. Find the multiple regression equation of x_3 on x_1 and x_2 and estimate the value of x_3 when $x_1 = 43$ inches and $x_2 = 54$ kg.

[Ans. $x_3 - 20 = 0.04(x_1 - 40) + 0.24(x_2 - 50)$; 21.08 years.]

[Hints. The multiple regression equation of x_3 on x_1 and x_2 is $x_3 - \bar{x}_3 = b_{31.2}(x_1 - \bar{x}_1) + b_{32.1}(x_2 - \bar{x}_2)$, where $b_{31.2} = \left(\frac{r_{31} - r_{23} \cdot r_{12}}{1 - r_{12}^2}\right) \cdot \frac{s_3}{s_1}$ and $b_{32.1} = \left(\frac{r_{32} - r_{13} \cdot r_{12}}{1 - r_{12}^2}\right) \cdot \frac{s_3}{s_2}$, s_1, s_2, s_3 being S.D. of x_1, x_2, x_3 respectively]

(d) Define price elasticity of demand. Find the price elasticity for the demand function $Q = \frac{5P}{(1-3P)^2}$ at the price $P = 20$. **[Ans.** 13.03]

[Hints. Price elasticity of demand $(e_p) = -\frac{P}{Q} \cdot \frac{dQ}{dP} = -\frac{P}{Q}\left\{\frac{(1-3P)^2 . 5 - 5P \cdot 2 \cdot (1-3P) \cdot (-3)}{(1-3P)^4}\right\} = -\frac{P}{Q} \times \frac{5(1+3P)}{(1-3P)^3} = -\frac{(1-3P)^2}{5} \times \frac{5(1+3P)}{(1-3P)^3}$. Now calculate the numerical value of e_p by putting $P = 20$.]

(e) The demand function for a particular brand of pocket calculater is stated below: $P = 75 - 0.3Q - 0.05Q^2$. Find the consumer's surplus at a quantity of 15 calculaters.

[Ans. 146.25]

[Hints. CS $= \int_0^{x_0} p\,dx - p_0 x_0$, where $x_0 = 15 = Q_0$, $p = P$, $x = Q$; At $Q = x_0 = 15$, $p_0 = 75 - 0.3 \times 15 + 0.05 \times 15^2$]

(f) Write short note on any one of the following:

(i) Spearman's rank correlation coefficient; (ii) Leontief's input output model.

June 1998

Section I (Mathematical Techniques : 40 marks)

Answer *Question No. 1* (Compulsory–10 marks) and *two other questions* from this section ($15 \times 2 = 30$ marks).

1. Attempt *any two* of the following:

(a) If $A = \begin{bmatrix} 2 & 0 & -1 \\ 2 & 4 & -1 \\ 1 & -8 & -3 \end{bmatrix}$, show that $A(\text{Adj. } A) = |A|I_3$, where Adj. A is the adjoint matrix of A and I_3 is the unit matrix of order 3.

[**Hints.** See worked out Ex. 1 in the Art. 4.1]

(b) The marginal cost of a product having output of q units is $90 - 12q + 0.3q^2$. Find the total and average cost function of the firm when its fixed cost is Rs. 200.

[**Ans.** $C(q) = 90q - 6q^2 + 0.1q^3 + 200$; $AC = 90 - 6q + 0.1q^2 + \frac{200}{q}$.]

[**Hints.** If $C(q)$ be the total cost of q units, then $\frac{dC}{dq} = 90 - 12q + 0.3q^2$.
Integrating, $C = 90q - 6q^2 + 0.1q^3 + k$ when k is a constant $\cdots$(1). Given $C = 200$ when $q = 0$.
$\therefore\ k = 200, C = 90q - 6q^2 + 0.1q^3 + 200$ and average cost $= \frac{C}{q} = 90 - 6q + 0.1q^2 + \frac{200}{q}$.]

(c) Find the extreme value of $x^3 - 6x^2 + 9x - 8$.

[**Hints.** See worked out Ex. 6 in Art. 9.3.]

(d) Find $f(x+1)$ when $f(x+3) = 2x^2 - 3x - 1$. [**Ans.** $2x^2 - 11x + 13$.]

[**Hints.** $f(x+3) = 2x^2 - 3x - 1$. Replacing x by $(x-2)$, $f(x-2+3) = 2(x-2)^2 - 3(x-2) - 1$.]

2. (a) Prove that $|f(c) - f(-c)| = 2$ when $f(x) = \frac{|x|}{x}$ and $c(\neq 0)$ is a real number.

[**Hints.** $f(x) = \frac{x}{x} = 1$ if $x > 0; = \frac{-x}{x} = -1$ if $x < 0$. $\therefore\ f(c) = 1$ and $f(-c) = \frac{c}{-c} = -1$ if $c > 0; = -1$ and 1 if $c < 0$. $\therefore$ If $c > 0, f(c) - f(-c) = 1 - (-1) = 2$ and if $c < 0, f(c) - f(-c) = -1 - 1 = -2$, etc.]

(b) Draw the graph of $f(x)$ defined by $f(x) = [x], -1 \leq x \leq 2$, where $[x]$ is the greatest integer contained in x, and discuss about the limit of $f(x)$ as $x \to 1$.

[**Hints.** See worked out Ex. 5 on page 127. Here $f(x) = -1$ for $-1 \leq x < 0; = 0$ for $0 \leq x < 1$; $= 1$ for $1 \leq x < 2; = 2$ for $x = 2$.]

(c) Find a unit vector perpendicular to each of the vectors $2i - j + 2k$ and $i + 2j + 2k$.

[**Hints.** See worked out Ex. 14 on page 17.] [**Ans.** $\frac{1}{\sqrt{65}}(-6i - 2j + 5k)$.]

3. (a) If $\begin{vmatrix} p & b & c \\ a & q & c \\ a & b & r \end{vmatrix} = 0$, then evaluate $\frac{p}{p-a} + \frac{q}{q-b} + \frac{r}{r-c}$, where $p - a \neq 0$, $q - b \neq 0$, $r - c \neq 0$.

[**Hints.** From the given condition, after simplification, $r(p-a)(q-b) + b(p-a)(r-c) + a(q-b)(r-c) = 0$. Dividing by $(p-a)(q-b)(r-c)$, $\frac{r}{r-c} + \frac{b}{q-b} + \frac{a}{p-a} = 0$,
or, $\frac{r}{r-c} + \left(\frac{b}{q-b} + 1\right) + \frac{a}{p-a} + 1 = 0 + 1 + 1$, etc.]

(b) Integrate: $\displaystyle\int \frac{e^{x-1} + x^{e-1}}{e^x + x^e} dx$. [**Ans.** $\frac{1}{e}\log(e^x + x^e) + c$.]

[**Hints.** $I = \displaystyle\int \frac{\frac{1}{e}(e^x + e \cdot x^{e-1})}{e^x + x^e} dx$. Put $e^x + x^e = z$.]

(c) If $y = \log(x + \sqrt{a^2 + x^2})$, prove that $(a^2 + x^2)\frac{d^2y}{dx^2} + x\frac{dy}{dx} = 0$.

[**Hints.** See worked out Ex. 3 on page 189.]

4. (a) Find the area bounded by the curve $y = 2x - x^2$ and the straight line $y = -x$.

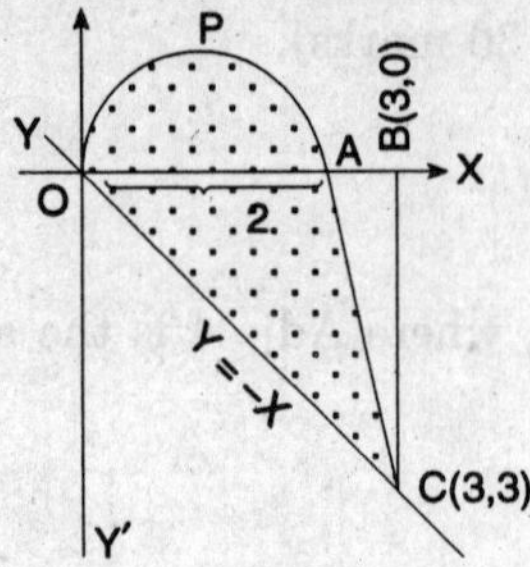

[**Ans.** 4.5 sq. units.]

[**Hints.** Solving $y = 2x - x^2$ and $y = -x$, we get $x = 0, 3$. The curve cuts x-axis at $O(0, 0)$ and $A(2, 0)$ and the line at $C(3, 3)$. The required area = Area OPA + (Area of $\triangle OCB$ − Area ACB)

$$= \int_0^2 y_1\,dx + \left(\frac{1}{2}\cdot 2\cdot 3 - \int_2^3 y_1\,dx\right), \text{ where } y_1 = 2x - x^2$$

$$= \int_0^2 (2x - x^2)dx + 4.5 - \int_2^3 (2x - x^2)dx = \text{etc.}]$$

(b) Solve the following L.P.P. by simplex method:

Maximize $Z = 2x_1 + 3x_2$

subject to $7x_1 + 4x_2 \le 28, 7x_1 + 12x_2 \le 52$ and $x_1, x_2 \ge 0$.

[**Hints.** See worked out Ex. 3 on page 306. Also see page 326.] [**Ans.** $13\frac{4}{7}$.]

Section II (Statistical Techniques)

Answer *Question No. 5* (Compulsory–10 marks) and *two other questions* from this section ($15 \times 2 = 30$ marks).

5. Attempt *any two* of the following:

(a) If $P(A) = \frac{1}{3}, P(B) = \frac{3}{4}$ and $P(A \cup B) = \frac{11}{12}$, find (i) $P(A/B)$, (ii) P (exactly one of A and B occurs), (iii) whether B is independent of A.

[**Ans.** (i) $\frac{2}{9}$; (ii) $\frac{3}{4}$; (iii) Not independent.]

[**Hints.** (i) See worked out Ex. 1 on page 21; (ii) $P(A \cap B^c) + P(A^c \cap B) = P(A) - P(A \cap B) + P(B) - P(A \cap B)$; (iii) Show that $P(A \cap B) \ne P(A)\cdot P(B)$.]

(b) Let X be a normal random variable with $\sigma^2 = 9$. Using a sample of size 10 with mean $\bar{x}$, to test the hypothesis $\mu = 24$ against the alternative $\mu > 24$ at 5% level of significance, obtain the critical region. Also obtain power of the test when $\mu = 25$. Given $\phi(1.645) = 0.95$ and $\phi(0.59) = 0.7224$ where $\phi(x) = \frac{1}{\sqrt{2\pi}}\int_{-\infty}^{x} e^{-\frac{1}{2}t^2}\,dt$.

[**Hints.** See worked out Ex. 3 on page 132. Here $H_0 : \mu = 24$ and $H_1 : \mu > 24$.]

(c) From the following data calculate Spearman's rank correlation coefficient where $X$and Y are the marks in Mathematics and Statistics of a student:

X :	48	33	40	9	16	16	65	24	16	57
Y :	13	13	24	6	15	4	20	9	13	19

[**Hints.** See worked out Ex. 10 on page 210. Here $N = 10; t = 3, 3; \Sigma D^2 = 50$.] [**Ans.** 0.67.]

(d) In random samples of 600 and 1000 men from two cities 400 and 600 men are found to be smokers. Do the data indicate that the populations are significantly different in the percentage of smoking at 5% level of significance after calculation of standard error of difference between proportion of smokers in the samples from two cities? [Given $P(Z > 1.96) = 0.025$ when Z follows $N(0, 1)$]. [**Ans.** Yes.]

[**Hints.** See worked out Ex. 13 on page 138. Here $n_1 = 600$, $n_2 = 1000$, $p_1 = \frac{2}{3}$, $p_2 = \frac{3}{5}$, $p = \frac{n_1p_1 + n_2p_2}{n_1 + n_2} = \frac{5}{8}, q = 1 - p = \frac{3}{8}$, S.E. of $(p_1 - p_2) = \frac{1}{40}$ and $z = 2.67 > 1.96$ at 5% level.]

6. (a) A box of 100 gaskets contains 10 gaskets with type A defects, 5 gaskets with type B defects and 2 gaskets with both types of defects. Find the probabilities that (i) a gasket to be drawn has a type B defect under the condition that it has a type A defect, and (ii) a gasket to be drawn has no type B defect under the condition that it has no type A defect. **[Ans.** (i) $\frac{1}{5}$; (ii) $\frac{29}{30}$.]

[Hints. If A denote A defect and B denote B defect, then $P(A) = \frac{10}{100} = \frac{1}{10}$, $P(B) = \frac{1}{20}$, $P(A \cap B) = \frac{1}{50}$. (i) $P(B/A) = \frac{P(A\cap B)}{P(A)}$ and (ii) $P(B^c/A^c) = \frac{P(A^c \cap B^c)}{P(A^c)}$, etc.]

(b) A box contains 4 right handed and 6 left handed screws. Two screws are drawn at random without replacement. Let X be the number of left handed screws drawn. Find (i) the probability distribution of X, and (ii) expectation of X.

[Ans.

x	0	1	2	Total
P	$\frac{2}{15}$	$\frac{8}{15}$	$\frac{5}{15}$	1

; $\frac{6}{5}$.]

[Hints. $P(x=0) = \frac{^4C_2}{^{10}C_2}$, $P(x=1) = \frac{^4C_1 \times {}^6C_1}{^{10}C_1}$, $P(x=2) = \frac{^6C_2}{^{10}C_2}$.]

(c) A manufacturer of cotter pins knows that 2% of his product is defective. If he sells cotter pins in boxes of 200 and guarantees that not more than 5 pins will be defective, what is the probability that a box will fail to meet the guaranteed quality? [Given $e^{-4} = 0.0183$] **[Ans.** 0.216.]

[Hints. See worked out Ex. 15 on page 70. Here $x = 5, 6, 7, \cdots$ and required probability $= 1 - \{f(0) + f(1) + f(2) + f(3) + f(4) + f(5)\}$.]

7. (a) If the distribution of marks received in an examination is normal, 44% of candidates got marks below 61%, 4% of candidates got marks above 80, find the percentage of candidates received above 65 marks. [Given $\frac{1}{\sqrt{2\pi}} \int_{-\infty}^{x} e^{-\frac{1}{2}t^2} dt = 0.06, 0.10, 0.46$ according as $x = 0.15, 0.25, 1.75$.] **[Ans.** 40%.]

[Hints. See worked out Ex. 31 on page 82. Find m and σ. Here $m = 62.5, \sigma = 10$. Standardised value of $65 = \frac{65-62.5}{10} = 0.25$. Now find $P(x > 65) = P(z > 0.25)$.]

(b) What is a scatter diagram? Draw the scatter diagram when (i) $r = +1$, (ii) $r = -1$ and (iii) $r = 0$.

[Hints. See Art. 6.3.1.]

(c) For a set of 10 pairs of values of x and y, the regression line of x on y is $x - 2y + 12 = 0$, mean and standard deviation of y being 8 and 2 respectively. Later it is known that a pair $(x = 3, y = 8)$ was wrongly recorded and the correct pair detected is $(x = 8, y = 3)$. Find the correct regression line of x on y. **[Ans.** $x = y - 3$.]

[Hints. If $\bar{x}, \bar{y}$ be the mean of x and y respectively, there $\bar{y} = 8$ and $\bar{x} - 2\bar{y} + 12 = 0 \Rightarrow \bar{x} = 4$, $b_{xy} = 2 \Rightarrow \frac{\text{cov}(x,y)}{\sigma_y^2} = 2$, or, $\text{cov}(x, y) = 2 \times 4 = 8$, or, $\frac{\Sigma xy}{10} - \bar{x} \cdot \bar{y} = 8$, or, $\Sigma xy = 400$. Again $\sigma_y^2 = 4 \Rightarrow \frac{\Sigma y^2}{10} - \bar{y}^2 = 4$, or, $\Sigma y^2 = 680$. Now correct $\bar{x} = \frac{4\times10-3+8}{10} = \frac{9}{2}$, correct $\bar{y} = \frac{8\times10-8+3}{10} = \frac{15}{2}$, correct $\Sigma y^2 = 680 - 8^2 + 3^2 = 625$, correct $\text{cov}(x, y) = \frac{400}{10} - \frac{9}{2} \times \frac{15}{2} = \frac{25}{4}$, correct $b_{xy} = 1$. $\therefore$ Correct regression line of x on y is $x - \bar{x} = b_{xy}(y - \bar{y})$, or, $x - \frac{9}{2} = 1 \cdot \left(y - \frac{15}{2}\right)$.]

8. (a) Out of sample of 120 persons in a village, 76 were administered a new drug for preventing influenza and out of them 24 persons were attacked by influenza. Out of those who were not administered the new drug, 12 persons were not affected by influenza. Prepare a 2 × 2 contingency table showing the actual and expected frequencies and test to find out whether the new drug is effective or not. [At 5% level of significance for 1 degree of freedom the value of chi-square is 3.84.]

[Hints. See worked out Ex. 12, 13 on page 161.] **[Ans.** The new drug is effective.]

(b) A population consists of 5 units and the values of a characteristic for these units are 2, 4, 3, 6, 7. Take all possible samples each of size 3 from this population and verify that the mean of sample means is exactly equal to the population mean, the sampling being done without replacement.

[**Hints.** See worked out Ex. 5, 6 on page 114.]

(c) A company is trying to manufacture a new type of toy. The company is attempting to decide whether to bring out a full, partial or minimal product line. The company has three levels of product acceptance and has estimated their probability of occurrence. Management will make the decision on the basis of maximizing the expected profit from the first year of production. The relevant data are shown in the following table where first year profits in thousand rupees are given:

State of nature		Good	Fair	Poor
Product line	Probability	0.2	0.4	0.4
Full		90	60	−15
Partial		80	65	−10
Minimal		60	50	0

(i) What is the optimum product line and its expected profit?

(ii) What is the optimum value of expected opportunity loss and the optimum course of action?

[**Ans.** (i) Partial product line; Rs. 38 thousand;
(ii) Minimum EOL is Rs. 6,000; partial product line.]

[**Hints.** See worked out Ex. 3 on page 291 and Ex. 6 on page 294.]

December 1998

Section I (Mathematical Techniques : 40 marks)

Answer *Question No. 1* (Compulsory–10 marks) and *any two other questions* from this section ($15 \times 2 = 30$ marks).

1. Attempt *any two* of the following:

(a) Given $A = \begin{pmatrix} 3 & 1 \\ 0 & 2 \end{pmatrix}$, show that $A^3 + A^2 - 24A + 36I = 0$, and hence (not otherwise) find A^{-1}.

(b) Solve the following system of simultaneous equations by Cramer's Rule:

$$2x + 3y + 3z = 22, \quad x - y + z = 4, \quad 4x + 2y - z = 9.$$

[**Hints.** See worked out Ex. 7 on page 81.]

(c) If $y = x + \sqrt{x^2 + a^2}$, show that $\frac{d^2y}{dx^2} = \frac{1}{2\sqrt{2a}}$ at $x = a$.

[**Hints.** $\frac{dy}{dx} = 1 + \frac{1}{2}(x^2 + a^2)^{\frac{1}{2}-1} \times (2x + 0) = 1 + \frac{x}{\sqrt{x^2+a^2}}$ and $\frac{d^2y}{dx^2} = 0 + \frac{d}{dx}\left(\frac{x}{\sqrt{x^2+a^2}}\right)$.]

(d) A quadratic function $f(x)$ attains its minimum value -2 at $x = -1$ and $f(0) = 0$. Find the function explicitly. [**Ans.** $f(x) = 2x^2 + 4x$.]

[**Hints.** Let $f(x) = ax^2 + bx + c$. Then $f(0) = 0 \Rightarrow c = 0$; $f'(x) = 2ax + b$, $f''(x) = 2a$. Since $f(x)$ is minimum at $x = -1$, $\therefore f'(-1) = 0 \Rightarrow -2a + b = 0$. Again $f(-1) =$ minimum value $= -2 \Rightarrow a - b = -2$. Now solve for a and b.]

(e) Given the function $f(x) = \frac{1}{2}(a^x + a^{-x}), a > 0$; show that

(i) $f(x+y) + f(x-y) = 2f(x)f(y)$;

(ii) $f(x+y) \times f(x-y) = \frac{1}{2}[f(2x) + f(2y)]$.

[**Hints.**

$$\begin{aligned}\text{(i) L.H.S.} &= \frac{1}{2}[a^{x+y} + a^{-(x+y)}] + \frac{1}{2}[a^{x-y} + a^{-(x-y)}]\\ &= \frac{1}{2}[a^x \cdot a^y + a^{-x} \cdot a^{-y} + a^x \cdot a^{-y} + a^{-x} \cdot a^y] = \frac{1}{2}[a^x(a^y + a^{-y}) + a^{-x}(a^y + a^{-y})]\\ &= \frac{1}{2}(a^x + a^{-x})(a^y + a^{-y}) = 2 \cdot f(x) \cdot f(y).]\end{aligned}$$

2. (a) If two matrices A and B of order $4 \times p$ and $5 \times q$ respectively conform to multiplication to form $C = A \cdot B$ of order $r \times 6$, find the values of p, q and r. [**Ans.** $p = 5, q = 6, r = 4$.]

[**Hints.** Since product AB is possible; $p = 5$ and order of AB is $4 \times q$;
$\therefore r \times 6 = 4 \times q$; $\therefore r = 4$ and $q = 6$.]

(b) If $a \neq b \neq c$, solve for x from $\begin{vmatrix} a+x & b+x & c+x \\ b+x & c+x & a+x \\ c+x & a+x & b+x \end{vmatrix} = 0$. [**Ans.** $x = -\frac{1}{3}(a+b+c)$.]

[**Hints.** Add 2nd and 3rd columns to the 1st and take $(3x + a + b + c)$ common.]

(c) Show that the points whose position vectors are $i - 2j + 3k$, $2i - 3j + 4k$ and $-2i + j$ are collinear.

[**Hints.** See hints of Q. 9 on page 25.]

3. (a) Show that $f(x) = 3x^2 - x + 2$ is continuous at $x = 1$.

[**Hints.** Use definition: $\lim_{x \to 1} f(x) = f(1)$.]

(b) Draw a sketch graph of the function $f(x)$ as defined below and ascertain from the graph if the function is continuous at $x = 0$ and $x = 2$,

$$f(x) = x^2, x < 0; = x, 0 \leq x < 2; = 2x - 1, x \geq 2.$$

[**Ans.** Continuous at $x = 0$, but not continuous at $x = 2$.]

[**Hints.** See worked out Ex. 8 on page 129 and Ex. 10 on page 130.]

(c) Integrate: $\int e^x x^3 dx$. [**Ans.** $e^x(x^3 - 3x^2 + 6x - 6) + c$.]

[**Hints.** See worked out Ex. 12 on page 248.]

4. (a) Differentiate: 10^{10^x} w.r.t. 'x'. [**Ans.** $10^{10^x} \cdot 10^x \cdot (\log_e 10)^2$.]

[**Hints.** $y = 10^{10^x} = e^{10^x \log_e 10}$; $\therefore \frac{dy}{dx} = e^{10^x \log_e 10} \times 10^x \cdot \log_e 10 \cdot \log_e 10$.]

(b) Shade the region in a graph bounded by the parabola $y^2 + 1 = x$, the straight line $2x - y = 2$ and the ordinate $x = 2$ in the first quadrant and use integration to find its area. [**Ans.** $\frac{31}{48}$ sq. units.]

[**Hints.** Solving $y^2 + 1 = x$ and $2x - y = 2$ for x, we get $x = 1, \frac{5}{4}$. Draw a figure. Required area $= \int_1^{\frac{5}{4}} y_1 dx + \int_{\frac{5}{4}}^{2} y_2 dx$ where $y_1 = 2x - 2$ and $y_2 = \sqrt{x-1}$.]

(c) Given the restrictions: $x, y \leq 0, 3x + 4y \leq 32, 4x - 3y \leq 1$, draw the feasible region and maximize the function $2x + 3y$. [**Ans.** 24 at $(0, 8)$.]

[**Hints.** See worked out Ex. 6 on page 308 and Ex. 8 on page 310.]

Section II (Statistical Techniques : 40 marks)

Answer *Question No. 5* (Compulsory–10 marks) and *two other questions* from this section ($15 \times 2 = 30$ marks).

5. Attempt *any two* of the following:

(a) A committee of 4 persons is to be appointed from 3 officers of the production department, 3 officers of the sales department and 2 officers of the purchase department and 1 cost accountant. Find the probability of forming a committee in the following manner:

(i) There must be one from each category;

(ii) It should have at least one from the purchase department. **[Ans.** (i) $\frac{1}{7}$; (ii) $\frac{13}{18}$.]

[**Hints.** 4 persons can be selected out of $(3+3+2+1)$ in ${}^9C_4$ ways $= \frac{9 \cdot 8 \cdot 7 \cdot 6}{4 \cdot 3 \cdot 2 \cdot 1} = 126$ ways and

(i) 1 person from each category can be selected in ${}^3C_1 \times {}^3C_1 \times {}^2C_1 \times {}^1C_1$, i.e., 18 ways. Prob. $= \frac{18}{126}$.

(ii) No. of favourable cases $= {}^2C_1 \times {}^7C_3 + {}^2C_2 \times {}^7C_2 = 70 + 21 = 91$.]

(b) If $P(A) = 0.4, P(B) = 0.7$ and P (at least one of A and B) $= 0.8$, find P (only one of A and B). **[Ans.** 0.5.]

[**Hints.** Required probability $= P(A \cap B^c) + P(A^c \cap B) = P(A) - P(A \cap B) + P(B) - P(A \cap B)$. Now $P(A \cup B) = P(A) + P(B) - P(A \cap B) \Rightarrow 0.8 = 0.4 + 0.7 - P(A \cap B)$, or, $P(A \cap B) = 0.3$.]

(c) Two variables have the regression lines $3x + 2y = 26$ and $6x + y = 31$. Find the mean values, the correlation coefficient between x and y and the ratio of variances of the variables. **[Ans.** $\bar{x} = 4, \bar{y} = 7, r_{xy} = -\frac{1}{2}; 1 : 9$.]

[**Hints.** See worked out Ex. 20, 21 on pages 220, 221. Here $b_{yx} = r\frac{\sigma_y}{\sigma_x}$ and $b_{xy} = r \cdot \frac{\sigma_x}{\sigma_y}$; $\therefore \frac{b_{xy}}{b_{yx}} = \frac{\sigma_x^2}{\sigma_y^2}$. Also $b_{yx} = -\frac{3}{2}$ and $b_{xy} = -\frac{1}{6}$.]

(d) From a simple random sample without replacement of size 8, which are 46, 08, 38, 24, 35, 29, 36, 40 drawn from the marks obtained by a class of 18 students in monthly test in mathematics out of the marks 50, estimate the total marks of the students in the whole class and the standard error of your estimate. **[Ans.** 576; 55.84.]

[**Hints.** Find $\bar{x}$ (sample mean) and $18 \times \bar{x}$.]

6. (a) Examine the validity of the statement, "the standard deviation of a binomial variate with mean 8 is 3". **[Ans.** The statement is not valid.]

[**Hints.** See worked out Ex. 6 on page 63.]

(b) Air Corporation having had just 2 aircrashes during its first fifty years of existence wants to make the next decade "aircrash free". Assuming that the same trend will continue, what is the probability of the corporation meeting the target?

[Ans. $e^{-0.4}$, or, 0.67.]

(c) In a bolt factory machines A, B and C manufacture respectively 20%, 30% and 50% of the total of their output. Of them 5, 4 and 2 per cent respectively are defective bolts. One bolt is drawn at random from the products and is found to be defective. What is the probability that it was manufactured by machine B?

[**Hints.** See worked out Ex. 2 on page 28.] **[Ans.** $\frac{3}{8}$.]

7. (a) Point out the inconsistency in the statements.

(i) the regression of y on x is $2y + 3x = 4$ and correlation coefficient between x and y is 0.8;

(ii) the correlation coefficient of $3x$ and $-2y$ is the same as the correlation coefficient of x and y.

[**Ans.** (i) Here $r_{xy} = 0.8$ and $b_{xy} = -\frac{3}{2}$ are opposite sign which is not possible. (ii) If $u = 3x$, $v = -2y$, then $r_{uv} = -r_{xy}$, i.e., the statement is inconsistent.]

(b) The result of an investigation by an expert on a fire accident in a skycroper are summarised below:

(i) Prob. (there could have been short circuit) = 0.8

(ii) Prob. (LPG cylinder explosion) = 0.2

(iii) Chance of fire accident is 30%, given a short circuit and 95% given on LPG explosion.

Based on these, what do you think is the most probable cause of fire? Statistically justify your answer. [**Ans.** Short circuit is the most probable cause of fire.]

[**Hints.** If S denote the event of short circuit, L the event of LPG explosion and F the event of fire, then $P(S) = 0.8, P(L) = 0.2, P(F/S) = \frac{30}{100} = 0.3, P(F/L) = 0.95$. Now $P(F) = P(F \cap S) + P(F \cap L) = P(S) \cdot P(F/S) + P(L)P(F/L) = 0.8 \times 0.3 + 0.2 \times 0.95 = 0.43$, and $P(S/F) = \frac{P(S \cap F)}{P(F)} = \frac{P(S) \times P(F/S)}{P(F)} = \frac{0.8 \times 0.3}{0.43} = \frac{24}{43}$ and $P(L/F) = \frac{P(L \cap F)}{P(F)} = \frac{P(L) \times P(F/L)}{P(F)} = \frac{0.2 \times 0.95}{0.43} = \frac{19}{43}$. $\therefore P(S/F) > P(L/F)$. This shows that S, i.e., *short-circuit is the most probable cause of fire.*]

(c) A normal variable has mean 165 and standard deviation 7. If the probability that the variable exceeds a particular value is one in one-thousand, find that value. [$\int_{-3.1}^{3.1} \phi(t)dt = 0.998$ where $\phi(t)$ is the standard normal probability density function.]

[**Ans.** 186.7.]

[**Hints.** If k be the particular value, then $P(x > k) = \frac{1}{1000}$, where $z = \frac{x-165}{7}$, or, $P\left(z > \frac{k-165}{7}\right) = 0.001 \quad \cdots (1)$. Given $P(-3.1 < z < 3.1) = 0.998$; $\therefore 2P(z > 3.1) = 1 - 0.998 = 0.002 \quad \therefore P(z > 3.1) = 0.001 \quad \cdots (2)$. (1) and (2) $\Rightarrow \frac{k-165}{7} = 3.1$, etc.]

8. (a) Write down the degrees of freedom for the chi-square statistic for the following: (i) a (3×4) contingency table; (ii) a test to see if the borrowings from a library on a particular day is higher than in other days given the number of books borrowed on each of six working days. [**Ans.** (i) 6; (ii) 5.]

[**Hints.** (i) d.f. $= (3-1) \cdot (4-1) = 6$ and (ii) d.f. $= 6 - 1 = 5$.]

(b) In 120 throws of a die face marked one turned up 10 times, faces marked two or three 38 times, faces marked four or five 48 times and face marked six remaining number of times. From the given information would you conclude that the die is perfect? [Given the upper 5% point of chi-square distribution with 3, 4 and 6 degrees of freedom are 7.815, 9.488 and 12.592 respectively.] [**Ans.** Yes, the die is perfect.]

[**Hints.** See worked out Ex. 8 on page 157 (Statistical Techniques).]

(c) A florist stocks a highly perishable flower. A dozen of flowers costs Rs. 3.00 and sells for Rs. 10.00. Any flower not sold the day are worthless. Demand in dozen of flowers is as follows:

Demand in doz.	0	1	2	3	4
Probability	0.1	0.2	0.4	0.2	0.1

Assuming that failure to satisfy any one customer's request will result in future lost profit amounting to Rs. 5.00, in addition to the lost profit on the immediate sale, how many flowers should the florist stock to expect maximum profit? [**Ans.** 3 dozen.]

[**Hints.** If s denote stock in dozen and d the demand in dozen, then profit P is given by

$$P = 10d - 3s, \text{ if } s \geq d$$
$$\text{and } P = (10-3)s - 5(d-z) \text{ if } s < d$$
$$\text{i.e., } P = 12s - 5d, \text{ if } s < d$$

Now construct a pay off table for $s = 0, 1, 2, 3, 4$ and $d = 0, 1, 2, 3, 4$ and then calculate the expected profits in rupees for $s = 0, 1, 2, 3, 4$.

Pay-Off Table

Stock(s) \ Demand (d)	0	1	2	3	4
0	0	−5	−10	−15	−20
1	− 3	7	2	− 3	− 8
2	− 6	4	14	9	4
3	− 9	1	11	21	16
4	−12	−2	8	18	28
Probability	0.1	0.2	0.4	0.2	0.1

Stock	Expected Profits (in Rs.)	EMV
0	$0 \times 0.1 + (-5 \times 0.2) + (-10 \times 0.4) + (-15 \times 0.2) + (-20 \times 0.1)$	= −10
1	$-3 \times 0.1 + 7 \times 0.2 + 2 \times 0.4 + (-3) \times 0.2 + (-8 \times 0.1)$	= 0.5
2	$-6 \times 0.1 + 4 \times 0.2 + 14 \times 0.4 + 9 \times 0.2 + 4 \times 0.1$	= 8
3	$-9 \times 0.1 + 1 \times 0.2 + 11 \times 0.4 + 21 \times 0.2 + 16 \times 0.1$	= 9.5 ←
4	$-12 \times 0.1 + (-2 \times 0.2) + 8 \times 0.4 + 18 \times 0.2 + 28 \times 0.1$	= 8.]

June 1999

Section I (Mathematical Techniques : 40 marks)

Answer *Question No. 1* (Compulsory–10 marks) and *two other questions* from this section ($15 \times 2 = 30$ marks).

1. Attempt *any five* of the following:

(a) Are the vectors $\begin{pmatrix} 3 \\ 2 \end{pmatrix}$ and $(3 \quad 2)$ equal? [**Ans.** No.]

[**Hints.** No, since column vector $\begin{pmatrix} 3 \\ 2 \end{pmatrix}$ cannot be equal to the row vector $(3 \quad 2)$.]

(b) If $A = \begin{pmatrix} 1 & -1 \\ 2 & 3 \end{pmatrix}$, obtain a matrix B such that $AB = BA = I_2$. [**Ans.** $\begin{pmatrix} 3 & -1 \\ -2 & 1 \end{pmatrix}$.]

[**Hints.** Since $AB = BA = I_2$, B is the inverse of A. $\therefore$ $B = A^{-1} = \frac{1}{|A|} \text{adj } A = \frac{1}{5} \begin{pmatrix} 3 & 1 \\ -2 & 1 \end{pmatrix}$.]

(c) If $y = f(x) = \frac{1-x}{1+x}$, find $f(y)$. [**Ans.** x.]

[**Hints.** See hints given in Q. 1(b) set in December 1995.]

(d) Examine the validity of the following statement:
If for two matrices A and B, $AB = BA$, then both matrices must be square.

[**Ans.** Both matrices are square matrices.]

[**Hints.** If the order of the two matrices A and B be $m \times n$ and $p \times q$ respectively, then $n = p$ and $q = m$, since AB and BA are both defined. Again $AB = BA \Rightarrow n = q$ and $p = m$. $\therefore$ $m = n$ and $p = q$.]

(e) Evaluate: $\begin{vmatrix} 2 & 3 \\ 1 & 4 \end{vmatrix} \times \begin{vmatrix} 2 & 4 \\ 3 & 1 \end{vmatrix}$. [**Ans.** $\begin{vmatrix} 16 & 9 \\ 18 & 7 \end{vmatrix}$.]

[**Hints.** $\begin{vmatrix} 2 & 3 \\ 1 & 4 \end{vmatrix} \times \begin{vmatrix} 2 & 4 \\ 3 & 1 \end{vmatrix} = \begin{vmatrix} 2\times2+3\times4 & 2\times3+3\times1 \\ 1\times2+4\times4 & 1\times3+4\times1 \end{vmatrix} = \begin{vmatrix} 16 & 9 \\ 18 & 7 \end{vmatrix}$.]

(f) If $A(1,2,0)$ and $B(3,2,-1)$ be points, find the unit vector along $\overrightarrow{AB}$.

[**Ans.** $\frac{1}{\sqrt{5}}(2i - k)$.]

[**Hints.** Referred to O as origin, $\overrightarrow{OA} = i + 2j$, $\overrightarrow{OB} = 3i + 2j - k$ and $\overrightarrow{AB} = \overrightarrow{OB} - \overrightarrow{OA}$.]

(g) Find $\lim_{x \to 3}(x+4)(x-1)$. [**Ans.** 14.]

[**Hints.** $\lim_{x \to 3}(x+4)(x-1) = \lim_{h \to 0}(3+h+4)(3+h-1)$, where $x = 3 + h$ and as $x \to 3, h \to 0$.]

(h) If $y = x^{\frac{1}{x}}$, find $\frac{dy}{dx}$. [**Ans.** $x^{\frac{1}{x}-2} \cdot (1 - \log x)$.]

[**Hints.** $\log y = \frac{1}{x}\log x$; $\therefore$ $\frac{1}{y}\cdot\frac{dy}{dx} = \frac{1}{x^2} - \frac{1}{x^2}\log x = \frac{1}{x^2}(1 - \log x)$.]

(i) What is the function whose derivative is $\frac{1}{2\sqrt{x}}$? [**Ans.** $\sqrt{x} + c$.]

[**Hints.** $\frac{dy}{dx} = \frac{1}{2\sqrt{x}}$. Integrating w.r.t. '$x$', $y = \frac{1}{2}\int x^{-\frac{1}{2}}dx + c$.]

(j) The total cost C of output x is given by $c = \frac{2}{3}x + 10$; find the marginal cost when output is 4 units. [**Ans.** $MC = \frac{dC}{dx} = \frac{2}{3}$.]

2. (a) Obtain a quadratic function $f(x)$ such that $f(0) = 5, f(-1) = 10$ and $f(1) = 4$.

[**Ans.** $f(x) = 2x^2 - 3x + 5$.]

[**Hints.** Let $f(x) = ax^2 + bx + c$. Then $f(0) = c$, $f(-1) = a - b + c$, $f(1) = a + b + c$. $\therefore$ $c = 5$, $a - b + c = 10$, $a + b + c = 4 \Rightarrow a - b = 5$ and $a + b = -1$; $\therefore$ $a = 2$ and $b = -3$.]

(b) If $y = \sqrt{1 - x^2}$, show that $(1 - x^2)y_2 - xy_1 = \frac{x}{y_1}$.

[**Hints.** $y_1 = \frac{dy}{dx} = \frac{1}{2}(1 - x^2)^{-\frac{1}{2}} \times -2x = -\frac{x}{\sqrt{1-x^2}}$, or, $y_1^2(1 - x^2) = x^2$ $\cdots$(1). Differentiating both sides of (1), $2y_1y_2(1 - x^2) + y_1^2\cdot(-2x) = 2x$, etc.]

(c) Show that $i + 2j + k, i + j - 3k$ and $7i - 4j + k$ are mutually orthogonal.

[**Hints.** See worked out Ex. 11 on page 14.]

3. (a) Integrate $\int\left(\frac{2x^2 - 12x + 60}{2x^2 - 14x + 30}\right)dx$.

[**Ans.** $x + \frac{1}{2}\log|x^2 - 7x + 15| + \frac{37}{\sqrt{11}}\tan^{-1}\left(\frac{2x-7}{\sqrt{11}}\right) + c$.]

[**Hints.**

$$I = \int\frac{x^2 - 6x + 30}{x^2 - 7x + 15}dx = \int\left(1 + \frac{x + 15}{x^2 - 7x + 15}\right)dx = x + \frac{1}{2}\int\frac{(2x - 7) + 37}{x^2 - 7x + 15}dx + c$$

$$= x + \frac{1}{2}\log|x^2 - 7x + 15| + \frac{37}{2}\int\frac{dx}{(x - \frac{7}{2})^2 + (\frac{\sqrt{11}}{2})^2} + c.]$$

[This question is not included in the syllabus as trigonometry is not included.]

62

(b) The cost of an industrial component is made up of 2 parts — a fixed cost of Rs. 500 and a variable cost of Rs. 10 per unit produced. The market price of the component is determined by the demand function $p = 25 - \sqrt{x}$ where p represents the price (Rs.) per unit at a demand x. Find the production level at which prodit is maximum.

[**Ans.** Profit is max. at production level of 100 units.]

[**Hints.** $C(x)$ = Total cost of production of x units = $500 + 10x$ and $R(x)$ = Total revenue for x units = $px = 25x - x\sqrt{x} = 25x - x^{\frac{3}{2}}$. Now see worked out Ex. 12 on page 224.]

(c) Set up the initial simplex table for the following linear programming problem : Maximize $z = 5x_1 + 6x_2$ subject to $x_1 + x_2 < 100, 2x_1 + 3x_2 = 170, 3x_1 + 5x_2 \geq 430$. (The table must also have net evaluations.)

[**Hints.** See worked out Ex. 6 on page 332 and Ex. 7 on page 333.]

4. (a) If $A = \begin{pmatrix} 1 & 1 \\ a & 2 \end{pmatrix}, B = \begin{pmatrix} 1 & 0 \\ 0 & 1 \end{pmatrix}$ and $C = \begin{pmatrix} 6 & 1 \\ 3 & 3 \end{pmatrix}$, find the values of a and b for which $A + B = BC$.

[**Ans.** $a = 3$ and $b = 2$.]

(b) Find the inverse of the matrix $\begin{pmatrix} 2 & 3 \\ 5 & -4 \end{pmatrix}$ and hence solve the system of equations: $2x + 3y = 12, 5x - 4y = 7$.

[**Ans.** $x = 3, y = 2$.]

[**Hints.** See worked out Ex. 3 on page 94.]

(c) Show that the rectangle of area 36 sq. cm. whose perimeter is the least is a square.

[**Hints.** See worked out Ex. 19 on page 229. Here $A = 36$.]

Section II (Statistical Methods : 40 marks)

Answer *Question No. 5* (Compulsory–10 marks) and *two other questions* from this section ($15 \times 2 = 30$ marks).

5. Attempt *any five* of the following:
Choose the correct alternative, stating proper reason.

(a) If the mean and variance of a binomial distribution with parameters (n, p) are 40 and 30 respectively, then parameters are
(i) $(40, 0.75)$, (ii) $(30, 0.25)$, (iii) $160, 0.25)$, (iv) $(120, 0.5)$.

(b) A binomial variable on 100 trials has 6 as it standard deviation. This statement is (i) valid, (ii) invalid (iii) cannot say.

(c) For two equally likely, exhaustive and independent events A and B, $P(AB)$ is
(i) 0, (ii) 0.25, (iii) 0.50, (iv) 1.

(d) The regression of y on x is $y + 2x - 8 = 0$ and that of x on y is $4x + y = 2$, then r_{xy} is (i) 1, (ii) $\frac{1}{\sqrt{2}}$, (iii) -1, (iv) $-\frac{1}{\sqrt{2}}$.

(e) If the probability of male birth is 0.5, then the probability that in a family of 4 children there will be at least 1 boy is
(i) $\frac{4}{16}$, (ii) $\frac{14}{16}$, (iii) $\frac{11}{16}$, (iv) $\frac{15}{16}$.

(f) If the mean of 9 observations drawn from a normal population with mean μ and s.d. 3 is 1.96, then 90% confidence limits for μ is (given $Z_{0.05} = 1.65$)
(i) $(0, 3.92)$, (ii) $(0.31, 3.61)$, (iii) $(1.41, 2.51)$, (iv) $(1.30, 3.25)$.

(g) A machine is set to produce nails with a mean length of 1 inch. Nails that are too long or too short do not meet the customer's specifications and must be rejected. Suppose in a random sample of nine nails, the mean length is 1.05 inches. To test whether the sample indicates that machine is producing nails of the desired average length the null (H_0) and alternative (H_1) hypotheses can be written as

(i) $H_0 : \mu = \bar{x}; H_1 : \mu \neq \bar{x}$, (ii) $H_0 : \mu = 1; H_1 : \mu \neq 1$,
(iii) $H_0 : \mu = 1.05; H_1 : \mu \neq 1.05$, (iv) $H_0 : \mu = \bar{x}; H_1$: not so.

(h) For a random variable X, the probability mass function is

$$\begin{aligned} f(x) &= kx, \text{ for } x = 1, 2, 3, \cdots n \\ &= 0, \text{ otherwise.} \end{aligned}$$

The expectation of X is (i) $\frac{2}{n(n+1)}$, (ii) $\frac{n(n+1)(2n+1)}{6}$, (iii) $\frac{(2n+1)}{3}$, (iv) none of these.

[**Ans.** (a) (iii) i.e., (160, 0.25); (b) (ii) i.e., invalid; (c) (ii) i.e., 0.25; (d) (iv) i.e., $-\frac{1}{\sqrt{2}}$; (e) (iv) i.e. $\frac{15}{16}$; (f) (ii) i.e., 0.31, 3.61; (g) (ii) i.e., $H_0 : \mu = 1; H_1 : \mu \neq 1$; (h) (iii) i.e., $\frac{2n+1}{3}$.]

[**Hints.** (a) $np = 40$ and $npq = 30$; $\therefore\ q = \frac{3}{4}, p = \frac{1}{4}$ and $n = 40 \times 4 = 160$. (b) $36 = npq = \frac{n}{4}\{4pq\} = \frac{n}{4}\{(p+q)^2 - (p-q)^2\} = \frac{n}{4}\{1-(p-q)^2\} \leq \frac{n}{4}$, i.e., ≤ 25 which is absurd. (d) See worked out Ex. 20 on page 220. (e) P (no boy, i.e., all girls) $= \frac{1}{2} \times \frac{1}{2} \times \frac{1}{2} \times \frac{1}{2} = \frac{1}{16}$; $\therefore$ P (at least 1 boy) $= 1 - \frac{1}{16} = \frac{15}{16}$. (f) 90% confidence limits for μ are $\bar{x} \pm 1.65 \cdot \frac{\sigma}{\sqrt{x}} = 1.96 \pm 1.65 \times \frac{3}{\sqrt{9}} = 0.31, 3.61$. (h) $\Sigma f(x) = 1$ gives $\Sigma kx = 1$, or, $k = \frac{1}{\Sigma x} = \frac{2}{n(n+1)}$ and $E(x) = \Sigma p_i x_i = \Sigma k x_i \cdot x_i$.]

6. (a) (i) If $P(A) = \frac{1}{2}, P(B) = \frac{1}{3}, P(AB) = \frac{1}{12}$, find the probability that at least one of A and B occur. [**Ans.** $\frac{3}{4}$.]

(ii) State the Bayes' theorem.

[**Hints.** See Art. 1.7.]

(b) Find the probability that in 5 tossings a perfect coin turns up head at least 3 times in succession. [**Ans.** $\frac{1}{4}$.]

[**Hints.** A perfect coin turns up head at least *3 times in succession* if (i) there is no tails or (ii) only one tail in 1st or 2nd, or 4th or 5th tossing, or, (iii) two tails in 1st and 2nd or 1st and 5th or 4th and 5th tossings. $\therefore$ No. of favourable cases $= 1 + 4 + 3 = 8$. Prob. $= \frac{8}{2^5} = \frac{1}{4}$.]

(c) A guest house has two rooms which it hires out by the day. The number of demands for a room one day follows Poisson distribution with mean 1.5. Calculate the probability that (i) all rooms are vacant on a particular day, and (ii) some demand is refused on that day. (Given $e^{-1.5} = 0.233$) [**Ans.** (i) 0.233; (ii) 0.1916.]

[**Hints.** $f(x) = \frac{e^{-1.5} \cdot (1.5)^x}{x!}$, where (i) $x = 0$, (ii) $x > 2$. Find $f(0)$ and $f(x > 2)$.]

7. (a) If X be a normal variable with mean 10 and variance $\frac{1}{4}$, find the mode and hence show that modal ordinate is $\sqrt{\frac{2}{\pi}}$. [**Ans.** 10.]

[**Hints.** $f(x) = \frac{1}{\sigma\sqrt{2\pi}} e^{-\frac{(x-m)^2}{2\sigma^2}} = \frac{2}{\sqrt{2\pi}} e^{-\frac{(x-10)^2}{\frac{1}{2}}} = \frac{2}{\pi} \cdot e^{-2(x-10)^2}$, $f'(x) = \sqrt{\frac{2}{\pi}} \cdot e^{-2(x-10)^2} \times -4(x-10)$ and $f''(x) = \sqrt{\frac{2}{\pi}} \left[e^{-2(x-10)^2} \times 16(x-10)^2 - 4e^{-2(x-10)^2}\right]$

For mode, $f(x)$ is maximum; $\therefore$ $f'(x) = 0$, or, $x - 10 = 0$, or, $x = 10$. At $x = 10, f''(10) = -4 < 0$. Hence mode $= 10$ and $f(10) = \sqrt{\frac{2}{\pi}}$.

Otherwise: For a *normal distribution* (symmetrical about the mean), Mean = Median = Mode. Hence Mode = 10 and ordinate = $f(10)$.]

(b) The following is an excerpt from the correlation-regression study of variables x and y. Obtain the correlation coefficient between x and y and the estimate of y when $x = 8$:

$$n = 5, \Sigma x = 15, \Sigma y = 40, \Sigma x^2 = 55, \Sigma y^2 = 420, \Sigma xy = 150.$$

[**Ans.** 0.95; 23.]

[**Hints.** $r_{xy} = \dfrac{\Sigma xy - \frac{(\Sigma x)(\Sigma y)}{n}}{\sqrt{\Sigma x^2 - \frac{(\Sigma x)^2}{n}} \times \sqrt{\Sigma y^2 - \frac{(\Sigma y)^2}{n}}} = \dfrac{150 - \frac{1}{5} \times 15 \times 40}{\sqrt{55-45} \times \sqrt{420-320}} = \dfrac{30}{\sqrt{10 \times 10}} =$ etc. Regression equation of y on x is $y - \bar{y} = b_{xy}(x - \bar{x})$, or, $y - 8 = \frac{30}{10}(x-3) = 3(x-3)$. If $x = 8, y = 8+3(8-3) = 23$.]

(c) From a group of 10 students with score in Statistics as 50, 80, 85, 40, 60, 70, 45, 55, 75 and 65, obtain a simple random sample of size 5 without replacement and estimate the population mean from the sample:

[Random numbers: 4062 9228 6347 1043 5824 1560 6507 2405 3832 2993 6489 7404]

8. (a) To test effectiveness of vaccination to people in a ward to prevent attack from malaria, the following table of number of people were obtained:

	Attacked	Not attacked
Vaccinated	80	220
Not vaccinated	120	580

Does vaccination prevent attack from malaria?

(You may use the following value $\chi^2_{0.05,1} = 3.84, \chi^2_{0.05,2} = 5.99, \chi^2_{0.05,3} = 7.81$)

[**Hints.** See worked out Ex. 12, 13 on page 162.] [**Ans.** Yes.]

(b) An educational entrepreneur is planning to run a complete course. He has narrowed down his options to two courses: CUR and FUT CUR is based on the existing software packages whereas FUT is based on new packages which are expected to storm the software market in the near future. In consultation with software specialists he has arrived at the following estimates:

(i) Probability of getting a return of Rs. 5 crores is 0.6 for FUT and 0.2 with CUR;

(ii) FUT's return could be as low as Rs. 40 lakhs with a probability 0.4 and the corresponding probability for CUR is 0.8;

(iii) FUT will cost him Rs. 1 crore and CUR only Rs. 30 lakhs. Using EMV obtain the optimum strategy. [**Ans.** Optimum strategy is to go for FUT.]

[**Hints.** See worked out Ex. 3. Here EMV for FUT = $5 \times 0.6 + .40 \times 0.4 - 1$ = Rs. 2.16 crores and EMV for CUR = $5 \times 0.2 + .40 \times 0.8 - .30$ = Rs. 1.02 crores and EMV for FUT > EMV for CUR.]